The Victoria History of the Counties of England

EDITED BY WILLIAM PAGE, F.S.A.

A HISTORY OF SOMERSET

VOLUME II

THE
VICTORIA HISTORY
OF THE COUNTIES
OF ENGLAND
SOMERSET

PUBLISHED FOR

THE UNIVERSITY OF LONDON
INSTITUTE OF HISTORICAL RESEARCH

REPRINTED FROM THE ORIGINAL EDITION OF 1911

BY

DAWSONS OF PALL MALL
LONDON
1969

Issued by
Archibald Constable and Company Limited
in 1911

Reprinted for the University of London
Institute of Historical Research
by
Dawsons of Pall Mall
16 Pall Mall, London, S.W. 1
1969
SBN: 7129 0376 3

Reprinted by Stephen Austin and Sons Ltd., Caxton Hill, Hertford

INSCRIBED
TO THE MEMORY OF
HER LATE MAJESTY
QUEEN VICTORIA
WHO GRACIOUSLY GAVE
THE TITLE TO AND
ACCEPTED THE
DEDICATION OF
THIS HISTORY

Glastonbury

THE
VICTORIA HISTORY
OF
SOMERSET

EDITED BY

WILLIAM PAGE, F.S.A.

VOLUME TWO

PUBLISHED FOR
THE UNIVERSITY OF LONDON
INSTITUTE OF HISTORICAL RESEARCH
REPRINTED BY
DAWSONS OF PALL MALL
LONDON

CONTENTS OF VOLUME TWO

CONTENTS OF VOLUME TWO

CONTENTS OF VOLUME TWO

LIST OF ILLUSTRATIONS AND MAPS

LIST OF ILLUSTRATIONS AND MAPS

EDITORIAL NOTE

IN the compilation of this volume the Editor is especially indebted to Rev. E. H. Bates Harbin, M.A., and to Sir Henry Maxwell-Lyte, K.C.B., M.A., F.S.A., etc., for advice and assistance, and for reading the proofs. The Editor has also to acknowledge the help of Mr. A. F. Somerville, and Mr. Nichol Reid regarding the article on Agriculture, of Mr. J. McMurtrie, F.G.S., for his great assistance on the history of mining in the county, and of Mr. John Coles, jun., Mr. T. Sturge Cotterell, Mr. J. H. Davis, Mr. J. Fortt, Mrs. Gifford, Mr. L. B. Lee, Mr. J. MacMillan, Mr. R. F. Martyr, Rev. C. Powell, B.A., Mr. Frederick Shum, F.S.A., Messrs. Southcombe & Sons, Rev. Prebendary Street, M.A., Mr. H. B. Walters, M.A., F.S.A., the *Western Gazette* Company, Yeovil, Mr. James Wheatley, and the late Mr. G. F. Luttrell for information regarding other sections of the article on Industries, of Dom H. Norbert Birt for information as to the history of Downside School, and of Miss Clay for help on the history of the Hospitals of the county.

The Editor regrets that owing to unforeseen circumstances the publication of this volume has been delayed for some time since the work was completed.

ECCLESIASTICAL HISTORY

DISTINCT historical evidence for English Christianity in Somerset is not earlier than the first decade of the 8th century. No English traditions go back to times earlier than those of Bishop Aldhelm and Ine king of the West Saxons. When the true story of the origin of a monastery or the builder of a church was lost, tradition [1] claimed this great king as the founder. To English minds all church work in the west seemed to begin in his time or to have St. Aldhelm as its author.

Yet there are traditions and evidence, if not strictly historical yet too important to be neglected, of Christian work anterior to the time of St. Aldhelm. They are not English traditions, but traditions preserved and cherished by others, while the English kept a firm hold on their own stories. In process of time these became mingled with English traditions, and in still later times were expanded, so that as we contemplate to-day the whole story, partly traditional and partly historical, care has to be taken to trace up the distinct streams to their fountain-head.

On the north-west side of Somerset, as well as on its eastern border between Bath and Wells, there are certain church dedications which are very rare, and seem to be anterior to the times of English Christianity, and are suggestive of Roman or Celtic Christianity. Saints are recorded whose cult was strange to English devotion and for whose presence we have to account. At Wellow on the east, with its Roman remains, we meet with St. Julian,[2] which seems to point to the martyr of the Diocletian persecution. At Stratton-on-the-Fosse we have St. Vigor. Only one other church in England,[3] that at Fulbourn in Cambridgeshire, claims St. Vigor as its patron saint. Both places are on or close to Roman roads, and the choice of the saint seems to point to that connexion between the insular and the continental Christianity which was severed by the English invasion.

On the western side these traces are more numerous. At Tickenham we have Sts. Cyriacus and Julitta, and at Chelvey and at Brean we have St. Bridget. Congresbury possibly derives its name from St. Congar, and Badgworth is dedicated to his honour.

Of these St. Bridget, as an ancient dedication, is only found in the west, and in that part of England which did not become England until after the

---

[1] Wharton, *Angl. Sacra,* i, 553 ; *Muchelney Cartul.* (Somers. Rec. Soc.), 4.
[2] Arnold Foster, *Studies of Church Dedications,* i, 165.   [3] Ibid. 468.

II   I   I

Angles had become Christians. The same can be said of Sts. Cyriacus and Julitta and St. Congar. Of St. Julian it is no longer possible to decide, since the first Bishop of Le Mans had that name, and as a dedication his name may have been brought to England with Henry II, who was born at Le Mans. The evidence will be found to fit in with what is known of the conques. of that which is now called Somerset by the Saxons. These invaders came as heathen and entered the county from the north,[4] after the victory gained by Ceawlin at the battle of Dyrham. The first advance was certainly the march of heathen Saxons. They destroyed all traces of Christianity which may have existed. No memories of Christian churches of the earlier times cling to Bath and Cirencester. Nothing is to be found in North Somerset as far as the Axe.

Then about 635 Cynegils,[5] the Saxon king, was baptized by Birinus, the missionary bishop from Rome, with Oswald his son-in-law as his sponsor. Seventeen years later, in 652,[6] Cenwealh won the battle of Bradford, and in 658[7] he advanced south as far as Yeovil and the Parrett. Finally in 710[8] Ine conquered Geraint of Domnonia and built a castle at Taunton, and extended the south-west border of Wessex as far as the highlands of Devonshire.

The traces, therefore, of earlier Christianity, if they are traces, are not to be found in that part of Somerset which was conquered while the Saxons were heathens. The dedications which seem to suggest it are only in the districts won by the Saxons after 635. If the evidence is not strictly historical, yet there is much to be said in favour of it. Dedications such as these and in such localities seem to point to the continuous survival of Christianity. The English priest seems to have taken up the service and ministered to the conquered people in the very churches they had built.

In Glastonbury, also, the county had an undoubted relic of British Christianity.[9] The origin of the monastery is unknown, nor can we tell how Inisvytryn, the 'perpetual choir' of the Celtic Church, came to be known as Glastonbury. Early Welsh traditions, as recorded in the Triads, regarded Glastonbury as one of the three perpetual choirs of Britain where the services of God ceased not day nor night [10]—'the three chief perpetual choirs of the Isle of Britain : the choir of Llan Iltud Vawr in Glamorganshire, the choir of Ambrosius in Ambresbury, and the choir of Glastonbury. In each of these three choirs there were 2,400 saints, that is there were a hundred for every hour of the day and night in rotation, perpetuating the praise of God without rest or intermission.'

The Saxons did not enter Glastonbury until after their monarch had been baptized. The site is, as far as we know, unique, for on it was a Christian sanctuary that was never desecrated, that was British and became English, and if there was a temporary cessation of worship there was at least no throwing down by the heathen of an altar which British Christianity had erected.

It is, however, difficult to say when and why a monastery was erected in Glastonbury. William of Malmesbury's 'History of the Antiquities of Glastonbury' is only partially historical. He went to Glastonbury at the

[4] Guest, *Orig. Celt.* ii, 242 ; Angl.-Sax. Chron. *sub anno.*   [5] Angl.-Sax. Chron. *sub anno* ; Bede. *Hist. Eccl.* iii, 7.
[6] Angl.-Sax. Chron. *sub anno.*   [7] Ibid.   [8] Ibid.
[9] Cf. Freeman, *Presidential Address,* 1880 (Somers. Arch. Soc.).   [10] Probert, *Triad,* 84.

invitation of the monks, and wrote down [11] for them what they wanted him to write. He had already written his 'Deeds [12] of the Kings of England' and his 'Deeds of the Bishops,' and he shows us that nothing definite was then generally known of the origin of Glastonbury. The extracts from the Arthurian Legends and the legend of Joseph of Arimathea are interpolations of the original MSS. of his history of the Antiquities of Glastonbury. He gives us a list [13] of abbots, and the first three are certainly British—Worgret, Lodemund, and Bregoret. Then the English names begin, quite regardless of the fact of the conquest that had intervened. He quotes as from a charter of 601 [14] the grant of the land of Glastonbury to Worgret and the monastery. The Domnonian king has been identified as Gwrgan Varvtrwch, [15] possibly the founder of the monastery. Malmesbury has no earlier documents to show us. It was probably to one of these abbots that some British king gave the estate of Brent Knoll, the *mons Ranarum*, regranted [16] to the monks by Ine and a possession of this monastery until the Dissolution in 1539. There are two other traditions which seem to give us evidence of this earlier Christianity even as it lingered, the faith of the Welsh, in the midst of many signs of religious fervour of the victorious Saxons. The wandering of the Irish Christians had certainly begun in the early years of the 7th century. When Ine, at the end of that century, had established his power in Somerset, Celtic and Irish Christians still made pilgrimages to shrines that were hallowed by ancient memories. The policy of Ine made it possible for them, though the country was still unsettled and travelling was certainly attended with danger. In 689, [17] so William of Malmesbury tells us, a certain Indractus, the son of an Irish king, having been to Rome, decided as he was returning home to visit the sanctuary of Inisvytryn. At Huish on the moors, i.e. Huish Episcopi, or as some say, near Sharpham, [18] he was attacked and murdered by the servants of one of the nobles of King Ine's court. When Ine heard of it he was much grieved at the action of his followers, and took care to commemorate the martyrdom in order to show his innocence of the murder. The other tradition, which bears some truth on the face of it, points to Congresbury as a place where a Christian bishop lived before the time of St. Athelm. If St. Congar was a real person and gave his name to Congresbury he must have been a Celtic saint, but the survival of his name in the dedication of the church in Badgworth, which place-name is entirely English, seems to suggest a date subsequent to the time of St. Aldhelm and King Ine, when the Celtic Christians, though in subjection, could revere their own saints. The fusion of the two races was becoming more and more an accomplished fact. In the history of the Bishops of Bath and Wells which is known as that of the Canon of Wells, [19] as also in the shorter narrative known as the 'Historiola de primordiis episcopatus Somersetensis,' [20] an attempt is made to connect the English bishopric at Wells with a Celtic bishop who is said to have lived at Congresbury. His name is given as Daniel, and he is said to

---

[11] *Mem. of St. Dunstan* (Rolls Ser.), Introd. p. xxxv.

[12] Cf. Pref. to Will. Malmes. *Gesta Pontif.* (Rolls Ser.). The Gesta Reg. was written in 1120; Gesta Pontif. 1125, and Antiq. Glaston. 1129.

[13] Will. Malmes. *De Antiq. Glaston.*

[14] Ibid. 'De terra Inisvytryn.'

[15] Guest, *Orig. Celt.* ii, 270.

[16] Will. Malmes. *De Antiq. Glaston.* 'De Brente.'

[17] Ibid. 'De Indracto.'

[18] Ibid.

[19] Wharton, *Angl. Sacr.* i, 553.

[20] *Eccl. Doc.* (Camden Soc.).

have celebrated the marriage of King Ine with Adelburga, whom the 'Historiola' describes as a Northumbrian princess.[21] Both documents relate that Ine granted Tyderton,[22] which is identified as Wells, to their bishop, and then pass on to the statement that it was Daniel of Congresbury who transferred the see from Congresbury to Wells. The traditions at Wells certainly claim Ine as the founder of the church, and it is not at all unlikely that at Congresbury was some organization for church work which may have been originally Celtic. The legend, however, that links the two places together is a mere invention, and the names of the successors of Daniel in the supposed eighth-century bishopric of Wells are all borrowed from the list of the successors of Athelm in the tenth and eleventh centuries. Obviously as the English organization grew, that which was at Congresbury and was not English would slowly pass away.

The history of the English Church in Somerset from its origin to the time of the great changes brought about by the Norman Conquest falls naturally into two parts. The earlier period includes that which happened before Somerset had a bishopric of its own. The later period begins with the Wells episcopate in 909, and takes us on to the transference in 1088 by John de Villula of the bishop's seat from St. Andrew's Church in Wells to the monastic church of Sts. Peter and Paul at Bath. The earlier period is obscure, and chiefly centred in the labours of Bishop Aldhelm and the benefactions of King Ine.

As the conquest of Western Britain went on, so a nominally Christian nation entered upon the lands of a nation that had been Christian for two or three centuries. The battles of Dyrham, 577, Bradford, 652, and at the Pens in 658 had placed all Somerset north of the Parrett in the hands of the West Saxons. Cenwealh, who had succeeded Cynegils in 643, and his West Saxon subjects were definitely Christian. We do not, however, know as yet anything of Christian work in Somerset. On the eastern border of the county there are certain place-names, Kilmersdon, Kilmington, and Chilcompton which offer us traces of Christian work, and seem to point to Celtic missions. The Christianity of the west must have been left to the zeal of the priests of the defeated British.

But the work certainly began with Aldhelm, and he is the apostle of Somerset. He was of noble birth,[23] and is said to have been a nephew of Ine. In 661[24] he probably retired from the world to live, for some eight years, with the hermit Maidulf in the forest of Braden, and to learn from him the principles of the Christian faith. In 675, when Maidulf was dead, Aldhelm returned to this place, which was then becoming known as Malmesbury.[25]

Aldhelm seems at once to have undertaken active missionary work on the border land of the forests of Braden and Selwood, and traces of his labour exist on the east of Somerset and down the Stour valley. At Bradford[26]-on-Avon

---

[21] When in 705 Ine appointed two bishops for Wessex, and assigned them seats at Winchester and Sherborne, the bishop who was sent to Winchester was named Daniel ; Angl.-Sax. Chron. *sub anno* 703.

[22] The origin of this name is not known. It is called by Wharton 'Tideston' and Godwin's *De Praesulibus* calls it 'Tydington,' and quotes a charter of the Confessor. Camden calls it 'Theorodunum.'

[23] Will. Malmes. *Gest. Pontif.* vi, 1. 'Vita Aldhelmi'.

[24] He had been attached to the monastery forty-four years when he became bishop in 705. Cf. Leland, *Coll.* iii, 266.

[25] Bede, *Hist. Eccl.* v, 18.   [26] Will. Malmes. *Gest. Pontif.* v, § 198.

he built a church in honour of St. Lawrence, and there and at Frome, where he built a church in honour of St. John the Baptist, he is said to have founded monasteries. Then later, and probably after 688, when Ine had become king of the West Saxons, he built a church at Bruton and induced Ine[27] to found another. His church he dedicated in honour of St. Peter, and that which King Ine built in honour of St. Mary. On Aldhelm's return, in 690,[28] from his pilgrimage to Rome, he brought with him a small marble altar slab, which he gave to King Ine, and the king had it placed in St. Mary's Church at Bruton. The affairs of his kingdom seem to have kept Ine very much in the eastern borders, and the bishops of the West Saxons, Wine (662), Leutherius (670–5), and Haeddi (676–703) were naturally drawn away from Dorchester, and were becoming localized at Winchester. It is obvious, therefore, that they could do little for the western parts of Wessex, the parts that were beyond the forest. Another bishop was wanted who should work in the west, and when Ine had peace he seems to have recognized this need. Haeddi, Bishop of Winchester, or rather of the West Saxons, died in 703, and in 704 Ine appointed two bishops in his place, Daniel for Winchester and Aldhelm for the new see of Sherborne, and Brihtwald Archbishop of Canterbury in 705 hallowed them. Thus began for Somerset not only a territorial in place of a missionary episcopate, but also that organic connexion with Canterbury which has developed but has not changed in subsequent centuries. Rome had at first sent forth Birinus, but now the mission in Wessex was being organized on national lines. With Aldhelm began a national episcopate, and the Chronicle recording his death[29] localizes him as the bishop on the west of the great barrier forest.

It is not, however, easy to trace the work of Aldhelm in Somerset.[30] His life, written in 1125 by William of Malmesbury, gives us what was known of him in the first half of the 12th century, and is our chief authority. To his influence is certainly due the refounding of Glastonbury by King Ine.[31]

It was in the east of Somerset, going from Malmesbury through Frome and Bruton to Sherborne, that Aldhelm laboured. We have no positive evidence, however, of his founding more than the two churches at Frome and Bruton. His biographer, William of Malmesbury, knew of no other. His episcopate was very short, barely five years ; and he died at Doulting, on the western border of the forest, 25 May 709.

We cannot, nevertheless, imagine that his work was confined to this narrow border district between the uplands of Wiltshire and those valleys of Somerset that run westward towards the sea. The interest he showed in the re-establishment of the monastic life at Glastonbury proves that he had at times penetrated further into Somerset, and tradition claims him and his great patron King Ine as the founders of the church of St. Andrew in Wells, and probably, for the conditions are exactly the same, and the foundations are

---

[27] Will. Malmes. *Gest. Pontif.* v, §222. [28] Ibid. [29] Angl.-Sax. Chron. *sub anno*, 709.

[30] Ethelweard calls Aldhelm's diocese—provincia quae vulgo Sealuudscire dicitur, *anno* 709.

[31] 'Ejus monitu Glastoniense monasterium ut dixi in Gestis Regum a novo fecit ;' Will. Malmes. op. cit. v, §209. The passage in *Gesta Regum* runs, 'indicio sunt monasteria regiis sumptibus nobiliter excitata praecipue Glastingense in quo beati martyris Indracti et sociorum ejus corpora de loco martyrii translata jussit inferri.' The Parker MS. of the Chronicle under the year 688 records of Ine, 'and he getimbrade þæt menster æt Glæstingabyrig.' This is an addition, and cannot belong to this date, but is rather a note of the deeds of Ine during his reign, which began then ; Plummer, *Two Saxon Chrons.* i, 40.

certainly very ancient, of the churches dedicated in honour of St. Andrew at Cheddar and at Banwell.

Anterior, however, to this work of Aldhelm, a church had been erected in Bath in 676 by Osric, nephew of Wulfhere of Mercia. Bath was not at this time part of Wessex, but had become included in the kingdom of Mercia, and it so remained[32] from about 645 to 950. Whatever work was done there would not have been done by the bishops at Sherborne. Mediaeval traditions cling to great names, and Kings Ine, Alfred, Edward, and Edgar were claimed as founders or benefactors, and charters were forthcoming which can no longer be accepted as genuine. There is, however, some reason for accepting the statement that Ine was interested in the foundation at Muchelney in 725,[33] if not of a monastery yet of a church which afterwards became monastic. A charter of Muchelney,[34] granted by King Cynewulf in 762 and conferring on the monastery lands on the banks of the Yeo, is certainly based on some genuine charter about that time. In the history of the monastic foundations of Somerset Muchelney comes second in the order of erection, and is not very much later than Glastonbury. Then comes the monastery of Athelney,[35] which claims Alfred as its founder, and is said to have been established about 888 to commemorate Alfred's trials and his victory over the Danes in 878. Asser in his life of Alfred[36] tells us that he placed John the Old-Saxon there as the first abbot, and his statement[37] that Alfred gave him the 'monastery' of Banwell proves the existence of the church there, whatever meaning may be attached to the word 'monastery.'

When King Ine turned to the western side of Wessex he not only established the bishopric at Sherborne, but in 709[38] built a castle at Taunton to protect his border, and may probably have founded a church there. Taunton was certainly a royal estate, and in 904 Edward the son of Alfred gave this estate to Denewulf, Bishop of Winchester.[39]

It is not easy to decide what is meant by the word 'monasterium' or its English equivalent 'minster.' We have seen the term applied to Banwell; and in the charter by which King Cnut gave it and Cheddar to Duduc, Bishop of Wells,[40] both foundations at Banwell and at Cheddar are called minsters. There are other place-names which introduce the term, and evidently show how early the church had possession of these sites, e.g. Ilminster, Pitminster, and Bedminster; and in a charter of Edred in 953 East Pennard is described as 'Pengearth Mynster.'[41] It is probable that this term indicates the permanent settlement at these places of a priest, as compared with other places where a missionary priest would go at stated times.

King Edward had hardly given Taunton to the bishopric of Winchester when he was called upon to fill up several vacancies in the diocese of Wessex and to increase the number in order the more effectually to organize the church in his kingdom.[42] The Danish wars had been destructive of much of the

---

[32] Taylor, 'Bath, Mercian and West Saxon' in *Glouc. Arch. Soc. Proc.* xxiii, 29.
[33] *Muchelney Cartul.* (Somers. Rec. Soc.), 35. [34] Ibid. 47.
[35] *Athelney Cartul.* (Somers. Rec. Soc.), 127, &c.; also *Somers. Arch. Soc. Proc.* xliii (2), 94
[36] *Mon. Hist. Brit.* 493. [37] Ibid 488.
[38] Angl.-Sax. Chron. *sub anno*; cf. Plummer, *Two Saxon Chrons.* i, 42.
[39] Kemble, *Cod. Dipl.* v, 157.
[40] *Cal. Wells D. and C. MSS.* (Hist. MSS. Com.), i, 431. [41] Birch, *Cart. Sax.* iii, 63.
[42] Cf. Stubbs, *Epis. Succession* under year 909.

early organization of the church, and King Alfred had done all he could, but yet not enough to remedy the evil. His great difficulty was to find competent men for the posts that were vacant. Pope Formosus (A.D. 891–6) seems to have written to the English bishops deploring the state of the English Church and calling upon them to take immediate steps to remedy it. Then, shortly after, Pope Sergius IV also wrote, and in 909 Archbishop Plegmund, with the consent of King Edward, consecrated seven bishops who were not only to fill up the vacancies caused by death but also to occupy three new sees in the kingdom of Wessex. The old western diocese, with the bishop's seat at Sherborne, now became the four sees of Ramsbury, Wells, Sherborne, and Crediton. Ethelweard [43] was consecrated to Sherborne, rendered vacant by Asser's death, and Athelm, a monk of Glastonbury, became the first Bishop of Wells. [44] The church of Wells, founded by Ine and Aldhelm, had received, from Cynewulf in 766, an increase of endowment of eleven hides of land. [45] The charter is perhaps doubtful, but the fact cannot be questioned. In his story of the foundation of the bishopric William of Malmesbury describes [46] the site—'tertius episcopatus West Saxonum fuit apud Wellas, villam in Sumersetensi pago pro copia fonticulorum ibi ebullantium ita dictam.'

The diocese of Wells began then with a Benedictine monk as its first bishop. As to the constitution of the church and the cathedral clergy nothing is known, but the church was probably served by secular canons. The see was in its infancy. It was an age of great reform, and a reform that often exchanged in cathedral churches secular canons for Benedictine monks. There is no evidence, however, that Benedictine monks were ever established in Wells.

During the 10th century the list of bishops offers us for the most part only names. Three of the bishops, Athelm, Wulfhelm, and Lyfing, were translated to Canterbury, and Brihthelm (956–73) is said to have granted to Glastonbury, where he had been a monk, certain rights, over the churches possessed and served by the monks, which would otherwise have been exercised by the bishop. Dunstan, one of the great reformers of the Benedictine Order in England, became Abbot of Glastonbury about 940 when Wulfhelm was Bishop of Wells. In 973 Dunstan, [47] as Archbishop of Canterbury, officiated at the second coronation of King Edgar at Bath, and this may mean that Bath had by that time become West Saxon territory. The church there was a royal chapel and belonged to a house of Benedictine monks. [47a] In 1033 [48] Duduc, the Old-Saxon, was consecrated Bishop of Wells. In his extremity Alfred had brought in foreigners to fill up the vacancies and to encourage learning. Asser the Celtic bishop he placed at Sherborne, John from Old Saxony he made the first Abbot of Athelney, and Grimbald [49] of St. Bertin, Flanders, he made abbot of the New Minster of Winchester. Fifty years afterwards Dunstan was much influenced

---

[43] Flor. Wigorn. *Chron.* (Engl. Hist. Soc.), 914.

[44] The story is, however, complicated by a doubtful letter, 'Audito nefandos,' said to have been sent to England by Pope Formosus, and the reader must refer for details to the references given in the notes ; cf. also an important paper in *Somers Arch. Proc.* for 1898, p. 149.

[45] Kemble, *Cod. Dipl.* i, 141. 'Ad augmentum monasterii quod situm est juxta fontem magnum quem vocitant Wielea.'

[46] Will. Malmes. *Gest. Pontif.* ii, 193.   [47] Plummer, *Two Saxon Chrons. anno* 973.

[47a] *Bath Cartul.* (Somers. Rec. Soc.), Introd.

[48] June 11.   [49] Angl.-Sax. Chron. *anno* 903, note recording his death.

in his reforms for the English Church by what he had seen and learnt during his exile and stay at Blandinium [50] and Ghent. The appointment, therefore, of Duduc to the see of Wells, which was due to King Cnut, was only one more step in the effort to strengthen the English Church by giving it some learned bishops from abroad. Duduc was certainly in favour with Cnut, and received from him as a personal grant the estates of Banwell [51] and Congresbury. Giso, Duduc's successor, has written [52] a short account of his predecessor, and of his own efforts for the endowment of the see. He says that his predecessor had given over to the bishopric, on his appointment, all his private fortune, and at his death left valuable ornaments, books, and vestments for the Church. Giso had intended also to add Banwell and Congresbury to the see, but Earl Harold had seized them as an escheat. Giso seems to have tried to induce Harold to give them up, and even went so far as to threaten him with excommunication, but he did not venture on this, nor did he appeal to King Edward. Giso was himself also a stranger, a native of Hasbania, and the town of S. Trond, near Liège. He had been a chaplain to the Confessor, [53] and had been sent on an embassy [54] to Rome, where he was consecrated by Pope Nicholas II on 15 April 1060. In his early days he had probably seen at Metz how the cathedral clergy lived as a community under the rules drawn up for them by a previous bishop, [55] St. Chrodegang, in 760. When he [56] came to Wells he found the church small, and the four or five canons of the cathedral church living in the town. He determined, therefore, to follow the example of his contemporary and neighbour, Bishop Leofric of Crediton, [57] who a few years before had imposed this rule of St. Chrodegang on his clergy at Crediton. To the south of the cathedral church of Wells he built a cloister, refectory, and common dormitory, and apparently a dwelling for himself. Then he increased the number of canons to ten and appointed one of their number, Isaac by name, as provost over them, and imposed upon them this rule of St. Chrodegang. [58] He did not turn out the secular canons and introduce monks, but while preserving their status as members of the household and canons of his church, he laid on them a stricter private life, enjoining them to obey and follow out the rules of the Bishop of Metz.

Giso was certainly a great benefactor to the church of Wells, and he was active in obtaining gifts with which to increase its endowment. From King Edward he obtained the estates of Chew [59] and Wedmore, [60] and from Queen Edith lands at Mudgley [61] and Mark. From Alured [62] he purchased the estate of Litton, and from Adzor [63] in 1070 that of Combe St. Nicholas, and from others he got the estates of Kilmersdon, Wormister, and Yatton. [64] Later he is said to have obtained from William the Conqueror the estate of Banwell, which Earl Harold had seized. His caution and interest is shown in his obtaining from King Edward, first of all a confirmation to him of all

[50] *Vita Dunstani* (Rolls Ser.), 59.   [51] Cf. *Hist. Wellen.* (Camden Soc.), 15.
[52] In *Hist. Wellen.* above.   [53] Kemble, *Cod. Dipl.* no. 835. Gisan minan preste.
[54] Canon Wellen. in *Angl. Sacr.* i, 559 ; Freeman, *Norm. Conq.* ii, 456.
[55] Cf. W. Schmitz, *S. Chrodegangi Regula Canonicorum* (Hanover, 1889).
[56] *Angl. Sacr.* i, 559.   [57] Will. Malmes. *Gest. Pontif* (Rolls Ser.), 201.   [58] *Angl. Sacr.* i, 550.
[59] Kemble, *Cod. Dipl.* no. 836 ; *Cal. Wells D. and C. MSS.* (Hist. MSS. Com.), i, 16.
[60] Kemble, *Cod. Dipl.* no. 837.   [61] *Cal. Wells D. and C. MSS.* (Hist. MSS. Com.), i, 16.   [62] Ibid. i, 12.
[63] Ibid. 434. We seem in this charter to have the names of most of the cathedral clergy of the time.
[64] Cf. Eyton, *Somers. Dom.* i, 80 ; *Cal. Wells D. and C. MSS.* (Hist. MSS. Com.), i, 429, 439.

the property of the see which Duduc [65] had held, and then, after he had been established in the see, a confirmation [66] with specification of all these estates. The charter is dated 2 May 1065, and the next year he seems to have obtained a charter of confirmation from King Harold. [67]

The episcopate of Giso, which lasted for twenty-eight years, carries us over the troubles of the Norman Conquest. When he died, in 1088, the Great Survey had been made and changes were imminent, if indeed they had not already begun. His life closes the Early English period, as that of his successor, John de Villula, begins that of the Norman. It would be well then to examine, before we enter the new era, the position of the Church in Somerset. The details of the Survey [68] have already been given us in the earlier volume, and it is needless to repeat them here. It was not the purpose of the Survey Inquisition to give us full information concerning the Church, and therefore the statements made in Domesday cannot be said to be complete. There were certainly other churches in addition to those mentioned. There may have been in the county churches, without endowment, served by clergy from the monasteries or from Wells. Perhaps in some places a priest was one of the household of the large local landowner, and so neither he nor the manor chapel he served would be mentioned.

Certainly there were churches in Wells (not only the cathedral church, but also the parish church of St. Cuthbert), Bath, Glastonbury, Muchelney, and Athelney. Taunton, the great fief of the Bishops of Winchester, must also have had a church, though none is recorded in Domesday, and also the four royal boroughs of Axbridge, Ilchester, Langport, and Milborne Port, though only St. Andrew's, Ilchester, and a church at Milborne Port are specified. Churches are actually mentioned at Chewton Mendip, Yatton, Kilmersdon, Milverton, Cannington, St. John the Baptist's Frome, St. Mary's 'Warverdinestoc,' i.e. Stogumber, Horsey Pignes, i.e. Bridgwater, Congresbury, Long Ashton, North Curry, St. Mary's North Petherton, Curry Rivel, Carhampton. The following clergy are also entered, and we may assume that in most cases there were churches on their lands, i.e. Liuric at Ilminster, Raimar at Huish in Brent, Brismar near Wincanton, Aluric at Kingston Seymour, Rainbold at Road, Ralf at Thorn Coffin, Sanson the chaplain at Combe (Temple), Alviet at South Petherton, Spiritus at Lamyatt, Godwin at East Brent. Priests are mentioned also as holding land at King's Brompton, Charlton Adam, Kingsbury, South Cadbury, and Beaminster; a monk held Woodwick in Freshford of the abbot of Bath; two men, Brithuin and Livinc, held Drayton of the abbot of Muchelney, and were probably priests; Ulgar the monk held Downhead from the Abbot of Glastonbury; a priest is mentioned with two Englishmen as holding lands at Evercreech, and there was also a priest at Keynsham. Two nuns held land at Huntscott in Wootton Courtney, and may have had a church to worship in, and so perhaps had Edith the nun, but where she held her lands is not recorded. Turstin, who held Abbots Leigh, and Godwin, who held Ridgehill in Winford, were both *clerici*, but it cannot be said that they actually resided on their land. The churches at Bruton,

---

[65] *Cal. Wells D. and C. MSS.* (Hist. MSS. Com.), i, 12 ; Kemble, *Cod. Dipl.* no. 835.

[66] Ibid. no. 816, and for the other copy with names of witnesses cf. *Cal. Wells D. and C. MSS.* i, 428–9.

[67] Ibid. 12 ; Kemble, *Cod. Dipl.* no. 976.   [68] *V.C.H. Somers.* i, 383, 434.

Banwell, and Cheddar [69] we know of from other sources, but no record of them appears in the Domesday.

The 'terra Gisonis' of the Survey amounted to 280 hides, of which fifty was demesne in Wells and the neighbourhood. The canons of Wells held 14 hides as Giso's tenants, and 8½ hides at Litton, and 4 at Wanstrow for their support and the needs of the cathedral church. In addition to the large Wells estate with the outlying estates of Binegar, Dinder, Wookey, Priddy, and Westbury, the estates of the Church comprised the manors of Evercreech with Chesterblade, Chew Magna, Dundry, Kingsbury Episcopi, Chard and Tatworth, Huish Episcopi, Combe St. Nicholas, part of Winsham, Wiveliscombe, Fitzhead, Wellington, West Buckland, Bishops Lydeard, Banwell, Puxton, Churchill, Compton Bishop, Wedmore with Theale and Blackford, Mark, Biddisham, Wanstrow, and part of Yatton. The only diocesan officer who is mentioned is Benthelinus the archdeacon, who held the church of Yatton. Isaac the provost of St. Andrew's Wells we have already referred to. When Giso bought Combe from Adzor the deed of sale was witnessed by several clergy, and probably they were those of his household, possibly the then canons of Wells, i.e. Sæxi, Kyppincg, and Brihtmaer, priests, Godric and Valdere, deacons, and Sumorlæte, a sub-deacon.

The ecclesiastical history of Somerset for the period from the Norman Conquest to the Reformation changes in the reign of Henry VIII does not offer us any natural divisions. The development of forms of worship and the increase of organization continued through all the political crises of the time, though much of the earlier enthusiasm had passed away. We can, however, make use of the series of bishops' registers to help us in this earlier period of our story. It begins in the first decade of the 14th century, and from that time we have with one considerable break a continuous official record of the affairs of the diocese. That earlier registers existed is quite certain. A small fragment of Bishop Giffard's register (1265–7) was found at York at the end of his register as Archbishop of York, and this has been published by the Somerset Record Society, but our first complete register is that of Bishop John de Drokensford, 1309–29.[69a]

The first portion of this earlier period practically ends with the great assessment of Church property made at the end of the 13th century, known as the *Taxatio* of Pope Nicholas IV, and we get this interesting result, that for the three periods of the history of the diocese from the appointment of Bishop Athelm to the Reformation we have at their close three great Surveys of the endowments of the Church. The Early English period closes with the great Domesday Survey of 1086. The Norman period ends with the *Taxatio* of 1291, and the pre-Reformation period comes to an end with the *Valor Ecclesiasticus* of Henry VIII in 1535.

The successor of Bishop Giso brings before us the period which saw the Norman changes in the Church of England. John de Villula, a priest of Tours, and by profession a doctor of medicine, was consecrated Bishop of Wells [70] at Canterbury by Archbishop Lanfranc in July 1088. He is said to have amassed considerable wealth as a physician, and his appointment was not free from suspicion of simony. The statement [n] made by the dean and

---

[69] *Cal. Wells D. and C. MSS.* i, 431.
[70] Stubbs, *Epis. Succession,* 23.

[69a] Edited by Bishop Hobhouse (Somers. Rec. Soc.).
[n] *Cal. Wells D. and C. MSS.* i, 115, 116.

canons of Wells in the 13th century as to his free election by the canons is clearly a statement made for the furtherance of their contest with the monks of Bath.[72] The death of Giso in 1088 had been preceded only by a few months by the death of Ælfsige, abbot of the Benedictine monastery at Bath. In 1075 the Council of London,[73] under the guidance of Archbishop Lanfranc, had ordered the transference as soon as practicable of all episcopal sees from villages and small towns to the cities. The time had clearly now come, therefore, to obey this order, and Bishop John of Tours at his accession obtained from William Rufus, 27 January 1090,[74] the grant of the abbey of St. Peter, Bath, and all the possessions of the abbey in augmentation of the bishopric of Wells, and in order that he might establish there his episcopal seat. The charter is very definite, for the bishop is practically granted all the estates of the abbey, and as he meant to live at Bath the convent ceased to have that liberty which it had formerly enjoyed. The bishop was henceforth to be its titular abbot, and its affairs, as far as he would allow them, were to be managed by a prior under him.[75] The change was made with the consent and 'contrivance' of Archbishop Lanfranc, and therefore the complaints of the canons of Wells and the bias of William of Malmesbury,[76] who naturally sympathized with the monks of Bath in this loss of their independence, must not be taken too literally. The city of Bath had lately been ravaged by Robert of Mowbray,[77] one of the leaders of the rebellion against William Rufus, and the church and convent was in a most dilapidated condition. Bishop John therefore bought the city and its mint from the king[78] for five hundred pounds of silver, and this may have suggested the charge of simony. This grant was made to him by the king with the consent of his brother Henry, who when king confirmed this sale, 8 August 1111,[79] and John had the precaution to get it yet further confirmed by Robert[79a] as Duke of Normandy in 1103.

Wells thus ceased to be a cathedral church. The bishop ceased to be called of 'Wells,' and was now definitely 'of Bath.' Nor did the injury which Bishop John inflicted on Wells end here. He pulled down the quasi-conventual buildings which Bishop Giso had erected, and drove forth the canons, 'coegit' the Wells Chronicler says,[80] to find as before lodging for themselves in the town. Then to the south of the church he built for himself a palace or manor house as if to show that the canons were no longer members of his household. He left behind him, however, his brother Hildebert as provost and steward of the property of the canons of the collegiate church of Wells, and Hildebert seems to have exerted some authority over his fellow canons. He took the demesne of St. Andrew to farm, and paid a yearly sum of 60s. each to the ten canons, a transaction which may not at first have been unfair. When he died, however, his son John, who was Archdeacon of Wells, entered into possession as by inheritance, regarding the estates as those of his father, and subject only to a fixed rent-charge of 60s. to each of the ten canons of Wells.[81] In 1123 Godfrey, a German (*Teutonicus nativus*) and a chaplain

[72] Hunt, *Bath Cartul.* (Somers. Rec. Soc. vii), p. xlii.
[73] Will. Malmes. *Gesta Pontif.* 66, 67 ; cf. also Freeman, *Norman Conq.* iv, 415.
[74] *Cal. Wells D. and C. MSS.* i, 12.   [75] Ibid.   [76] Will. Malmes. *Gesta Pontif.* 194–5.
[77] Flor. Wigorn. *Chron.* an. 1088 ; Hunt, *Bath*, p. xliii.
[78] Will. Malmes. speaks of his having bought the city from Henry I, op. cit. (Rolls Ser.), 194.
[79] *Cal. Wells D. and C. MSS.* i, 13.   This was clearly not the first confirmation.   [79a] Ibid.
[80] Wharton, *Angl. Sacr.* i, 560.   [81] Ibid.

of Adela of Louvain, second wife of Henry I, was appointed bishop in succession to John of Tours and was consecrated [82] on 26 August in that year in St. Paul's, London, by William de Corbeuil, Archbishop of Canterbury. He endeavoured to get back for the church of Wells this estate alienated by Hildebert the former provost, but John the archdeacon had in the meantime died leaving his estate to his brother Reginald the precentor, and the difficulty of recovery had increased through lapse of time. The story, therefore, is somewhat protracted. Reginald the precentor was bought out through Bishop Robert of Lewes (1136–66) by the grant of a life tenure of the estate of Combe St. Nicholas.[83] His nephews, however, resisted this arrangement and clung to the estates of Winsham, Wanstrow, Mudgley, Mark, and Biddisham, and not till the later years of his episcopate was Bishop Robert able to purchase from them for the sum of 70 marks their doubtful and certainly unrighteous claim.

Another question arose in reference to this transference of the see from Wells to Bath. The canons of Wells were like to lose their claim to the election of the bishop. This idea of a free election by the clergy of the diocese, or of the cathedral church as representative of the diocese, of the man who was to be their bishop, though indefinite and often ignored either by the king, or the pope, or both in collusion, yet was a very real claim. The canons of Wells said that they had elected John de Villula of Tours, and that he had afterwards left them for Bath.[84] His successor Godfrey the German, Queen Adela's chaplain, was probably accepted by the monks of Bath rather than elected. We have no evidence, and the canons of Wells do not say, as they certainly would have said if they had done so, that they had been consulted or recognized as the legal electors of the bishop. In the spring of 1136 Robert, a Cluniac monk from Lewes and greatly in favour with Henry of Blois, Bishop of Winchester, Abbot of Glastonbury, and brother of King Stephen, was appointed to succeed Bishop Godfrey. In a charter of Stephen [85] addressed to the convent of Bath he grants the see and all its rights and privileges &c. to Robert—'canonica prius electione precedente et communi vestro consilio, vota et favore prosequente.' Clearly there had been the form of an election at Bath, and the silence of Stephen concerning the canons of Wells seems conclusive against them. It was time, therefore, for them to move in the matter. If they lost their ancient right of joining in the election of the bishop they would cease to be canons of the cathedral church, and up to this moment, though the bishops had lived in Bath and called themselves Bishops of Bath only, yet the ancient cathedral church of St. Andrew had not irrevocably descended into the lower rank of a collegiate church. In Bishop Robert the canons of Wells found a true friend. He gave them a constitution for their church, he greatly increased the number of canons, and his help alone enabled them to establish their claim as electors. The canons as usual had appealed to Rome, and Pope Hadrian IV [86] took them under his protection in 1157, and again in 1176 [87] Pope Alexander III confirmed the new constitution and dignitaries which Bishop Robert had made, and also the arrangements he had laid down concerning the procedure for the election of his successor. The monks won so far as that the title of the bishop was

---

[82] Stubbs, *Epis. Succession*, 27.　　　[83] *Cal. Wells D. and C. MSS*. i, 39.　　　[84] Ibid. 116.
[85] *Bath Cartul.* (Somers. Rec. Soc.), vii, 57.　　[86] *Cal. Wells D. and C. MSS*. i, 533.　　[87] Ibid. 534.

to be 'of Bath' and not 'of Wells,' and Bath was recognized as the bishop's seat, but Pope Alexander endorsed Robert's constitution :

1. That both churches, the church of Wells and the conventual church at Bath, were to be the seats of the bishop.

2. That both canons and monks were to join in electing him.

3. That the Prior of Bath (though Wells afterwards claimed that it was the Dean of Wells) should announce the election to the Archbishop of Canterbury, and

4. That the bishop was to be enthroned in Wells as well as in Bath, but first of all in Bath.

On the death of Bishop Robert the see was vacant for eight years, and in 1174 Henry II nominated Reginald Fitz Jocelin, and apparently both chapters gladly accepted him. On the translation of Bishop Reginald to Canterbury he was succeeded in 1192 by Bishop Savaric. Richard I was in the Holy Land, and Walter Archbishop of Rouen [88] and the king's justiciar gave the formal consent of King Richard without waiting for any action by the canons of Wells. In 1205 Bishop Savaric died. He had added to the dispute between Bath and Wells a third dispute with the monks of Glastonbury, for having obtained the abbotship of Glastonbury he styled himself Bishop of Bath and Glastonbury. The story of this quarrel, however, we will record presently. In the room of Savaric Jocelin Trotman, a canon and native of Wells, was chosen by the joint and general approval of both monks [89] and canons, and at his consecration only the monks of Glastonbury protested, and that because of the action of Savaric, which would make his successor their abbot. The canons of Wells, however, had been reorganized and the charters of Popes Hadrian IV and Alexander III were bearing fruit. The next election brought the quarrel to an end. Bishop Jocelin died at Wells on 19 November 1242. The canons of Wells thereupon invited the monks of Bath to join with them in the election of a successor. But the monks, ignoring the bull of Alexander III, obtained from Henry III licence to elect, and in the following January chose as bishop Roger the precentor of Salisbury. Henry III had wished them, however, to elect as bishop Peter Chaceporc, the Treasurer, and on their refusal he gave licence to the canons of Wells to proceed to an election. The chapter at Wells appealed to Rome against the action of the monks, and the case was brought before Pope Innocent IV. [90] Innocent recognized the irregularities in the election of Roger, and condemned the monks, but at the same time he confirmed the election 3 February 1244, [91] and on 11 September 1244 Roger was consecrated in the abbey church of Reading [92] by William de Ralegh Bishop of Winchester, the see of Canterbury being vacant. Then on 3 January 1245, in a letter dated at Lyons, Innocent IV settled the terms which were to cover future elections. Canons and monks were jointly to take part in the election, the meeting for the election was to take place alternately in the chapter-houses at Wells and at Bath, the installation was to be in both cathedral churches, and first in that church where the election had taken place, and his title was to be 'Episcopus Bathoniensis et Wellensis.' So the quarrel came to an end, and Roger became

[88] Ric. Devizes, *De rebus gestis Ric. I* (Rolls Ser.), 421.
[89] Cf. Wells Chap. Reg. Chart. 45–6 with signature of Bath monks to election.
[90] *Cal. Wells D. and C. MSS.* i, 119, 127, 129.
[91] *Cal. of Papal Letters,* i, 205–6.
[92] Matt. Paris, *Chron. Maj.* (Rolls Ser.), iii, 285.

the first Bishop of Bath and Wells.[93] The canons had won. For close on a hundred and fifty years they had striven to preserve their ancient rights, and through their efforts Wells was now again definitely established as a cathedral church. Subsequent elections were generally peaceful, and Innocent's arrangement lasted until, in 1539, the church at Bath ceased by the suppression of the monastery, to rise again in 1573 as the parish church of the city.

Bishop Robert of Lewes was not only the protector of the rights of the church of Wells, but was also the reformer and reorganizer of its constitution. During the 10th and 11th centuries there had been a revival of the Benedictine order, with its natural evolution in new and stricter forms of monastic life, and this led to the stricter ordering of the life of the secular clergy. Among the changes which the Norman bishops introduced into England was a thorough reform of the English monasteries. The Archbishop of York and the Bishops of Sarum, Lincoln and Wells in the middle of the 12th century began to reform also the constitutions of their cathedral churches. The pattern,[94] as far as it can be traced, was that of Bayeux. The principle of the reform seems to have been that there should be not only corporate responsibility, but also individual responsibility. The canons were to administer a common fund, and also have separate estates for their private incomes. Bishop Robert therefore apparently in the first year of his episcopate began to plan for the division of certain portions of the corporate funds of Wells among the several canons. His draft[95] scheme belongs to the year 1136, and when he died there were twenty-four prebends for so many canons. The principle of which this reform was evidence demanded yet other changes consequent on the increase of the number of the canons. There must be order, and so some one must be placed in a position of authority. Thus among the first of Bishop Robert's creations was the office of the dean, who was to be a canon and have the duty of ruling and keeping order in the church and in the chapter. Bishop Robert created also the office of precentor, a canon who should have the duty of arranging for all the complex services of the church the music that should be sung, and the ordering of those who should sing it. As the church also increased in wealth there was the more need for a treasurer who should have the care of all the vestments, altar vessels, relics, and valuables that belonged to St. Andrew. So Bishop Robert created the office of treasurer, and probably also that of the sub-dean, to act in the absence of the dean in such matters as were urgent. Bishop Robert's plan of reform was not at once carried out.[96] The lawsuits with the descendants of Bishop John's provost made it impossible. But the plan was laid down, and his successor, Bishop Reginald Fitz Jocelin, continued to work on the same lines. The details of the division of the estate belong rather to the history of the cathedral church. There was a common fund for the support of the church and those who were actually ministering in it. There were the particular estates, or portions of estates, for the individual canons; the manor of Combe St. Nicholas, for instance, became very soon the endowment for fifteen canons, and there were also

[93] *Cal. Wells D. and C. MSS.* i, 306; Charter given at Chew, 13 Aug. 1246.
[94] Bradshaw, *Black Bk. of Linc.* 76, 101, 106; Chevalier, *Coutumier de Bayeux,* 284.
[95] *Cal. Wells D. and C. MSS.* i, 33. Carta de ordinatione prebendarum et institutione communae.
[96] Church, *Early Hist. of Ch. of Wells,* 18.

additional estates for the dignitaries of the church. Among these we must mention two whose position was at first rather diocesan than connected with the church of the bishop. The bishop's personal officer—his eye and administrator in the diocese—the archdeacon, was often absent from Wells, and especially of late, when the bishop lived at Bath. But he was so much a member of his household that he would not be excluded from his cathedral church. So the Archdeacon of Wells, as the successor of the more personal attendant of earlier days, was made one of the dignitaries of the church of Wells as well as being always a canon. Another officer, the chancellor, was at first more attached to the bishop than to his church. He had care [97] of the younger clergy, instructing and preparing them for holy orders, and as he would possess knowledge not only of theology, but also of canon law, his services would be valuable in the church. The chancellor was also made, certainly by the time of Bishop Reginald [98] if not by Bishop Robert, one of the dignitaries of the church. The archdeacon and the chancellor were not as the dean, precentor, and treasurer; their offices were not created by Bishop Robert. As officers of the bishop they existed before and apart from the cathedral church, and as members of his household they were naturally canons of his church. Bishop Robert or Bishop Reginald increased their endowments, and made them also dignitaries of his church. The special office [99] assigned to the chancellor in the church was the care of the books, documents, and charters, to be the keeper of the corporate seal, and to act as the official secretary of the chapter. It does not appear that the archdeacon had duties other than those which were diocesan. So by the end of the episcopate of Bishop Reginald the reformed constitution of the church of Wells was an accomplished fact. The canons immediately responsible for the service and welfare of the church, the *quinque personae*, the dean, precentor, archdeacon, chancellor, and treasurer, were always supposed to reside, they had special houses within the cathedral inclosure, while in addition other canons came and resided as houses were found for them. But the whole enlarged chapter, the fifty canons of Bishop Jocelin's time, seldom or never came all together, and there were not houses for more than a small portion of them.

We have already seen how the Norman bishops in many dioceses changed their seats from the churches of retired villages to those in the larger cities. Another change was that of the position of the archdeacons and the consequent increase of their number. The archdeacon was at first a personal officer. The compact,[100] however, between William the Conqueror and Archbishop Lanfranc could not but alter this. When church litigation was separated from secular, and the sheriff was no longer to take cognizance of ecclesiastical cases, church officers would have to be created to preside over ecclesiastical courts. The bishop and his court were naturally supreme, but the diocese was too large for a single court, and, moreover, the bishop's court would be naturally a court of appeal. So the archdeacon was made a territorial officer, and instead of the one personal attendant there are found in the early days of the 12th century three archdeacons—of Wells, of Bath, and of Taunton—the diocese being divided into three spheres of

---

[97] Reynolds, *Wells Cath.* 45 ; Statuta Eccl. Wellen, Lambeth MSS. 729.
[98] *Cal. Wells D. and C. MSS.* i, 26.   [99] Cf. Church, op. cit. 16.
[100] Stubbs, *Select Chart.* 85 ; Edict of William I to the Sheriffs of Essex and Herts.

responsibility for them.   In the year 1106 [101] Walkerius appears as Archdeacon of Wells, Gisbert as Archdeacon of Bath, and Robert as Archdeacon of Taunton.[102] Bishop Jocelin in 1241 made the Archdeacon of Taunton a canon of Wells by adding to his office the prebend of Milverton.[103]

In the earliest register extant, the fragment of the register of Bishop Giffard,[104] we find reference to the three archdeaconries, and also to the jurisdictions of the Dean of Wells and the Abbot of Glastonbury. The process of exemption from the jurisdiction of the bishop of the diocese had been growing for many years. Bishop Brihthelm [105] is said at the request of Abbot Dunstan to have granted a certain exemption to Glastonbury in reference to the churches which it possessed within the ancient 'xii hides.' In the time of Bishop Giso the abbey of Glastonbury [106] had constituted itself the protector of the two smaller abbeys of Muchelney and Athelney, and they had agreed on account of the small number of monks in the two monasteries to choose their abbot when a vacancy occurred from among the monks of Glastonbury. It was in the later years of his episcopate that Bishop Giso decided to visit these two small monasteries. His citation, however, was ignored, for the Abbot of Glastonbury denied the right of the bishop to visit these convents. So Bishop Giso appealed to the Council of the English Church that sat at Gloucester in 1085 and to Archbishop Lanfranc. The answer he received was that he must go to Glastonbury and cite the abbots of the two monasteries to meet him there. Then Thurstin, the Norman abbot of Glastonbury, refused him permission to hold a meeting in the chapter-house at Glastonbury without his sanction. So Giso was only able to obtain answers to his visitation questions concerning Muchelney and Athelney through the Abbot of Glastonbury, their self-constituted protector.

It was obviously a great hindrance to the organization of the Church in Somerset that certain ecclesiastical corporations in it should assert their independence, and as the abbots of these houses refused to obey, it was necessary for the bishop to try some other course. Bishop Reginald therefore (1174–91), whose influence was greater than that of many of his predecessors, approached these monasteries in another way. The monks of Glastonbury had always claimed certain privileges for the 'xii hides' and the churches therein, asserting their immunity from archidiaconal and episcopal visitation. Bishop Reginald therefore decided to create a special archdeaconry for the Glastonbury churches, for whom the abbey was to supply the endowment and the abbot to choose the officer.   Robert of Winchester [107] was abbot at that time (1171–8), and seems to have yielded somewhat readily to Bishop Reginald's proposal. The church of Pilton was to be the endowment, and was given over to the cathedral church of Wells to found the prebend, on condition that the Abbot of Glastonbury, as the archdeacon of the Glastonbury churches, was to be the new canon. So a new canonry was created in the cathedral, and the Abbot of Glastonbury became *ipso facto* a member of the chapter, and therefore a priest of the obedience of the Bishop of Bath. When the monks of Glastonbury realized what had happened they soon com-

[101] Le Neve, *Fasti*, i, 161.
[103] *Cal. Wells D. and C. MSS.* i, 469.
[105] Wharton, *Angl. Sacr.* i, 556.
[107] *Cal. Wells D. and C. MSS.* i, 24, 26.
[102] No definite ordination of the archdeaconries is known.
[104] Somers. Rec. Soc. *Publ.* vol. xiii.
[106] Will. Malmes. *Antiq. Glaston.* (ed. Gale), 331.

pelled their abbot to retire from such a position, and in the controversy that followed not only lost the church of Pilton, which was assigned to the precentor as his prebend, but had to compensate the Archdeacon of Wells for the permanent withdrawal of the Glastonbury churches from his jurisdiction by handing over to him the church of South Brent.[108]

The failure of Bishop Reginald to bring the abbey of Glastonbury into subjection did not restrain his successor, Bishop Savaric.[109] He was a near kinsman of the Emperor Henry IV, and when King Richard on his return from the Crusades fell into the emperor's hands, Savaric induced the emperor to lay down as one of the conditions for the king's release that Bishop Reginald should be promoted to Canterbury, and that he should be made Bishop of Bath and Abbot of Glastonbury. Henry de Soliaco had been made abbot in 1189, and in 1192 the necessary vacancy was created by the promotion of Abbot Henry to the bishopric of Worcester. Savaric had secured the consent of Pope Celestine III to this union ; great secrecy was, however, observed, and in November 1193 the abbot was summoned to London, and Savaric, then bishop, summoned Henry, the Prior of Glastonbury, to come to him at Bath. The prior and two other monks came, and Savaric asked them where their abbot was. They replied that he had gone to London. Then Savaric said, 'You are released from him ; I am your abbot.' Soon after he sent and took possession of the great monastery he had desired. Of course his action was deeply resented by the monks, and they appealed to the pope and to the king, and continued a very bitter struggle with Savaric. But all through his episcopate he remained Bishop of Bath and Abbot of Glastonbury,[110] and left such a position to his successor Jocelin. The monks persevered, and burdened themselves with an enormous debt, but did not get rid of the Bishop of Bath as their abbot until the peace of 17 May 1219.[111] Bishop Jocelin was not unwilling to surrender the position, but the monks had to pay heavily for their freedom. As compensation for the loss in surrendering the post of abbot, the bishops were given the manors [112] of Winscombe, Pucklechurch, Blackford, and Cranmore, and while the bishop gave up the title of Bishop of Glastonbury he kept [113] the very important position of patron of the abbey. Not till 1275 did the abbey get rid of this bishop as patron, when Edward I,[114] wishing to bring the controversy to an end, compensated the bishop by a rent-charge on the manor of Congresbury [115] and city of Bath, and compelled the abbey to reimburse him by the payment of 1,000 marks.

We must return, however, to Savaric, abbot-bishop of Bath and Glastonbury. His influence now was very great, and he determined to strengthen it yet more to the advantage of Wells and at the expense of the other Benedictine monasteries. In 1200 he prevailed with Benedict II,[116] Abbot of Athelney, to endow a canonry at Wells with the church of Long Sutton, so that the abbot holding this canonry should become a member of his

[108] *Cal. Wells D. and C. MSS.* 26 ; Adam de Domerham, *Hist.* i, 235.
[109] Cf. the story as told by John of Glastonbury, *Chron.* (ed. Hearne), i, 180, &c.
[110] Cf. *Cal. of Papal Letters*, i, 22. [111] Ibid. 67.
[112] *Cal. Wells D. and C. MSS.* i, 311, 355.
[113] Ibid. 309, Inspeximus, 2 Aug. 1242, of charter of Hen. III.
[114] Ibid. 111–12, 167, 168. [115] Adam de Domerham, *Hist.* i, 267.
[116] *Cal. Wells D. and C. MSS.* i, 57.

chapter at Wells. Then in 1201 he prevailed with Richard of Muchelney [117] to do the same, and give for that purpose the church of Ilminster. A third canonry he got from the monastery of Cleeve, where the monks by arrangement with the Abbot of Bec gave the church of Old Cleeve,[118] and the alien Abbot of Bec became a canon of Wells through his deputy the Abbot of Cleeve.

Thus in his strong masterly way Savaric endeavoured to obviate the evils of exempt jurisdiction, and to strengthen the power of the bishop of the diocese. As Bishop of Bath and Glastonbury, abbot of both these monasteries, and with the Abbots of Muchelney, Athelney, and Cleeve members of his chapter at Wells, he had almost solved the difficulty. The movement was, however, too strong for him. The monasteries in their efforts for independence received encouragement from Rome. The abbotship of Glastonbury for the bishop lasted for twenty years only. The Abbots of Muchelney and Athelney were absentee canons, and looked to Glastonbury for direction, and the great Abbot of Bec never came to the bishop's councils. A hundred years afterwards even the chapter at Wells claimed, as granted to them by Savaric,[119] the privilege of exemption from episcopal visitation for the churches of their endowment, and in 1321,[120] after a prolonged controversy between Dean Godley and Bishop Drokensford, the claim was allowed. From that time till 1836 the prebendal churches were peculiars of the canons who held those prebends, and the churches of the common fund were visited by the dean, or, in his absence, by the sub-dean.

In the life of St. Wulfric [121] we get a glimpse, and it is about the only glimpse we have, of the ordinary religious life of the country places in Somerset in the 12th century. This saint was born in the parish of Compton Martin and brought up there, the child of honest but humble parents. Ordained to the priesthood he went back to act as parish priest of his native village. At the Conquest the English owner Euroacro had been dispossessed and Serlo de Burceio had become the tenant in chief, and Wulfric seems to have gained the friendship of the Norman overlord. A casual incident in reference to the new coinage of Henry I awoke in him serious religious views, and retiring from Compton Martin he took up his abode in a cell attached to the prebendal church of Haslebury Plucknett. There he seems to have lived in friendly intercourse with Osbern, an Englishman and parson of the church, and by austerity and holiness of life gained an influence over the people of the neighbourhood. The River Parrett runs to the west of the church, and tradition tells that a man whose evil life had at last created alarm in him was crossing the stream on his way to consult the saint when the devil stopped him, and only the intercession of Wulfric, who sent a man with holy water, enabled the penitent to escape from the influence of the devil. St. Wulfric is said [122] to have been visited by Bishop Robert of Lewes, and in 1154, when the hermit lay dying, the bishop was present and closed his eyes. Osbern the priest buried him in his cell, but afterwards his body was removed and laid under the altar of the church.

[117] *Cal. Wells D. and C.* MSS. i, 48.
[118] Ibid. 489. The question was complicated by a claim of Wells to this Church.
[119] In 1203 ; ibid. 30.   [120] Ibid. 535. Cf. Reynolds, *Wells Cath.* App. G. 131.
[121] Bolland, *Acta Sanct.* 20 Feb. iii, 231 ; Matt. Paris, *Chron. Maj.* (Rolls Ser.), ii, 205 ; Gervase of Cant. *Chron.* (Rolls Ser.), i, 130.   [122] Leland, *Coll.* i, fol. 645.

ECCLESIASTICAL HISTORY

We must now tell somewhat briefly the story of the church in Wells.[123] The earliest building, whether built by King Ine or not, was probably erected over or by the side of the stream that ran westward from the springs of St. Andrew.[124] When the church was raised to cathedral rank it was probably rebuilt on an enlarged scale, and when Giso added his conventual buildings, in which his canons were to live, we hear nothing of any alteration to the church. Bishop John de Villula employed himself in rebuilding the monastic church at Bath, and Bishop Robert of Lewes (1136–66)[125] showed his interest in Wells, not merely in his reform and enlargement of the chapter, but also in rebuilding the church. He found the church ruinous, and likely every day to fall to the ground ; he pulled down a great part of it and repaired it.[126] This church was consecrated in 1148. Then after an interval of eight years, during which the see was vacant, in 1174 Bishop Reginald began the work anew on a yet grander scale, but left his church unfinished, and Bishop Savaric was too much occupied with his controversy with Glastonbury to have any leisure for such a task. It was Bishop Jocelin (1206–42) who completed in a lighter and later style the scheme which Reginald had conceived. In 1220[127] he set to work on the west façade, and then joined it on to the end of Reginald's nave. The church was dedicated on 23 October 1239,[128] though it is uncertain how far by that date the work was completed.[129]

During the second half of the 13th century three bishops call for notice because of the part they took in English politics, and also of their relations with the dean and chapter of Wells. William Button was jointly chosen by the convent of Bath and the chapter of Wells[130] on 24 February 1248, and was consecrated at Lyons 14 June. He spent much of his time in Rome, and from Pope Innocent IV[131] obtained letters to Henry III testifying of his zeal for the king's cause. The peace of 1219 between the monks of Glastonbury and the Bishop of Bath and Wells had ended with the reluctant acquiescence on the part of the monks in Bishop Jocelin's claim to the patronage of the abbey. This had made the bishop tenant in chief to all the possessions of the monastery, and compelled the abbey to approach the king only through the bishop. Henry III was unwilling to accept this,[132] and Prince Edward probably encouraged him. Innocent IV, however, requested the king to sanction this arrangement, and the claim created a coolness between the latter and Bishop Button. The chapter of Wells[133] also was alarmed by the claim of the bishop in 1249 to the revenues of all vacant benefices in the diocese, and after much controversy granted them to him for his life on his renunciation of any right to them. The chapter was strongly Royalist, and was governed by one of the ablest of the mediaeval deans, Edward de la Knoll, while Bishop Button had slowly drifted to the side of the National party, and in 1253 joined the other bishops in demanding, in his place in Parliament, that the king should recognize the

---

[123] Church, *Hist. of Ch. of Wells*, deals thoroughly with the work of Bishops Robert, Reginald, and Jocelin.
[124] *Somers. Arch. Soc. Proc.* (new ser.), xx, 19.   [125] *Angl. Sacr.* i, 561.
[126] Godwin, *Lives of the Bishops* (Engl. ed.), 1601 ; also *Historiola de Primordiis Epis. Somers.* 25.
[127] Cf. Close Roll, 7 Aug. 1220.   [128] *Cal. Wells D. and C. MSS.* i, 359.
[129] The subsequent structural history of the church will be fully dealt with in the account of the cathedral under 'Topography.'
[130] *Cal. Wells D. and C. MSS.* i, 72.   [131] *Cal. of Papal Letters,* i, 196, 249.
[132] *Cal. Wells D. and C. MSS.* i, 309.   [133] Ibid. 5.

Church's claim for freedom of election of the bishops, and in excommunicating those who transgressed the charter. Bishop Button died in May 1264,[134] and on 22 May the chapter of Wells and the convent of Bath, under the instigation of Dean Edward de la Knoll, elected Walter Giffard, a canon of Wells, as their bishop, without waiting for the usual formalities. Giffard was certainly on the side of the king, and having received the temporalities on 1 September 1264 passed over to Paris and was consecrated there 4 January 1265 by the Bishop of Hereford.[135] This action of his gave great offence to the National party, and his pledge to the Archbishop of Canterbury that he would not take up arms against the king only increased it. The barons are said to have ravaged some of his manors, while he is recorded as having excommunicated in 1265 Simon de Montfort and his party. In October 1266 he took part in drawing up the Dictum of Kenilworth. He had, however, then ceased to be bishop, for on 15 October he was provided by Clement IV with the archbishopric of York,[136] rendered vacant by the death of Archbishop Godfrey de Ludham.

Giffard was succeeded by the second William Button, whose saintly character was recognized in England, but whose quiet life calls for no comment. He died in November 1274, and was succeeded in January 1275 by Robert Burnell, who with Giffard and Roger Mortimer had been guardians of the kingdom during the interval between the death of King Henry and the return of Edward I from the Holy Land. Burnell was already a canon of Wells and Archdeacon of York, and in 1274 had been made Chancellor of England. The trusted friend and adviser of Edward I, he succeeded in bringing about a final arrangement between the Crown, the monks of Glastonbury, and himself as bishop in reference to the patronage of the abbey. He surrendered the lordship of the temporalities and the patronage and obtained for[137] the see in 1275 the manors of Pucklechurch, Winscombe, Blackford, and Cranmore. He procured also for the see the churches of Yeovilton, Burnham, Stanton Drew, and Closworth, and built the great banqueting hall and chapel at his palace at Wells. When Archbishop Kilwardby was raised to the cardinalate, Burnell, through the influence of King Edward, was postulated in January 1279 Archbishop of Canterbury, and the king was greatly annoyed when Nicholas III refused him and chose John Peckham.[138]

In 1289 Bishop Robert took the cross and proposed to set out for the Holy Land with a fitting body of soldiers, obtaining from the pope a grant[139] for three years of the first year's revenues of all dignities and benefices falling vacant in the diocese. He was very much taken up with the affairs of state and by his work as Chancellor, and was consequently seldom in his diocese. He died at Berwick on Tweed 25 October 1292 when with the king in his Scottish war.

The Jews, who were expelled from England in 1290,[140] do not seem to have settled much in Somerset, though in 1284 the Prior of Montacute[141] got into trouble on a charge of clipping the coin of the realm and of

[134] *Cal. Wells D. and C. MSS.* i, 101–3.   [135] Stubbs, *Epis. Succession,* 44.
[136] T. Stubbs, *Acta Archiep. Ebor.* p. 1726, in Twysden's *X Scriptores.*
[137] *Cal. Wells D. and C. MSS.* i, 111–12 ; Adam de Domerham, *Hist.* i, 26.
[138] *Cal. of Papal Letters,* i, 456.   [139] Ibid. 510.
[140] *Cal. Close,* 1288–96, pp. 95–6.   [141] *Cal. Pat.* 1281–92, p. 147.

receiving the goods of the Jews. The people of Chard [142] in their charter of municipal independence were expressly forbidden to mortgage their goods to the Jews. Leo de Warwick [143] seems to have been sometimes in Wells, and Abraham fil' Jude de Parisiis and Jacob fil' Samuel de Oxon were much in the county, and had money transactions with Somerset families. Ralph Lovel [144] had mortgaged his lands at Cary to Vives the son of Aaron, and paid 60 marks to King John to recover them.

The 13th century, which for the Church in Somerset was so full of crises, struggles, and developments, ended, as we have said, with the important assessment of ecclesiastical benefices known as the Taxatio of Pope Nicholas IV.[145] In 1253 Pope Innocent IV had given Henry III for three years the first-fruits and tenths of all ecclesiastical benefices in England, and in 1288 Nicholas IV gave to Edward I the tenths of all such benefices for six years in order to defray the expenses of an expedition to the Holy Land. This grant empowered King Edward to make a thorough assessment of the wealth of the Church. It was begun in 1288 and, for the province of Canterbury, was finished in 1291. It was the basis of all estimates of Church Subsidies to the State until the Valor of Henry VIII in 1534–5, and was therefore of great importance. It brings before us the diocese of Bath and Wells with its deaneries,[146] its impropriations, and all the various ways by which the maintenance of ecclesiastical corporations was effected by means of the funds of the parochial churches. The spiritualities are entered separately from the temporalities, and for the whole diocese the spiritualities were reckoned as worth £4,219 12s. 7½d. and the temporalities £2,395 5s. 5d.

The Alien Priories entered as possessed of benefices or ecclesiastical property in the diocese are: Montacute, £163 11s. 1d.; Bermondsey, £29 18s. 11d.; the Benedictine Priory of Goldcliff in Monmouthshire, £30 10s. 6d.; the Prior of Hayling, acting as proctor for the Abbot of Jumièges, £28 17s. 4d.; the Prior of St. Michael de Periculo Maris, £26 13s. 4d.; the Prior of Wilmington in Sussex, acting as proctor for the Abbey of Grestain (i.e. Fatouville Grestain near Honfleur), £22 3s. 4d. The Abbot of Bec in Normandy received £26 13s. 4d. as prebendary of Cleeve in the cathedral church of Wells, and the value of the *temporalia* and *spiritualia* of the Prior of Stogursey came to £34 19s. 6d., amounting in all to £363 6s. 9d. The only portionary church entered on the assessment is that of Crewkerne with distinct endowments for three vicars.

The *Taxatio* throws valuable light on the ordination of vicarages, which formed so great a feature of English church life during the 13th century. Towards the end of the 12th century attention was called to the way in which absentee rectors, both secular and monastic, appropriated almost the whole revenues of their churches, leaving the parochial duties to be discharged by a vicar chosen for cheapness rather than fitness, and liable to dismissal at any moment. The Councils of 1170 and 1200 laid down the rule that vicars were to be perpetual, and to have a fixed and sufficient endowment. The

---

[142] *Cal. Pat.* 1281–92, p. 216.   [143] Cf. Roberts' edition of *Fine and Oblate R.* i, 197–236.
[144] *Oblate R.* i, 198.
[145] The inquest of knights' fees made in 1284, known as ' Kirkby's Quest,' though imperfect for Somerset (*Feud. Aids*, iv, 272–98), demonstrates the position of the church as a great local landowner.
[146] See App. on the ecclesiastical divisions of the county.

number of appropriations, with the accompanying ordination of vicarages, was remarkably small in Somerset, only forty-two vicarages being recorded in the *Taxatio* out of 276 livings.[147]   Of these only eight were worth more than 10 marks, but at the same time no vicarages had so low a value as some of the rectories, of which Brean was only worth £2, Cricket St. Thomas £2 10s., Withiel £3 6s. 8d., and four others £4 each.   On the other hand, the rectory of North Curry was worth £36 13s. 4d., Bedminster £46 13s. 4d., Petherton £53 6s. 8d., and Taunton £60.

The process of appropriation continued during the 14th century, and we find vicarages ordained[148] for Wembdon (1304), Burnham (1309), Bathampton, Stockland, Bathwick, Corston, and Twerton (1317), High Littleton and St. Mary at Stalls, Bath (1322), Berrow and Yatton (1327), Woolavington and West Harptree (1336), Mudford (1340), Pilton (1342), Hinton (1344), Meare (1351), and East Coker (1385).   In many cases the endowments of the vicarage proved too small, and a re-ordination was made by the bishop, e.g. at Northover in 1337[149] and at Berrow in 1338.[149a]

We have now the help of the two registers of Bishop Drokensford and Bishop Ralph of Shrewsbury[150] for the important period from 1309 to the years immediately succeeding that of the Great Pestilence.

The first decade of this century brings before us a strange and somewhat tragic event, namely, the suppression of the order of the Knights Templars. The movement against this order was forced upon England by pressure from without.   Edward II was influenced by the repeated requests of Philip of France and Pope Clement V, and on 8 January 1308 he ordered the apprehension of all the Templars in England, Scotland, and Ireland. The papal inquisitors who came over to England in 1309 to see that this work of suppression was effectively carried on were the Abbot of Lagny and Canon Sicarde-de-la-Larvaur of Narbonne.   One of the first Templars to be examined was William Raven of Templecombe,[151] who was placed on his trial 21 October 1309.   The provincial councils of the English Church in 1311 seem to have found a difficulty in condemning men on the charges that were laid against them of apostasy and immorality, and therefore did little to promote the suppression.   It was in April 1312 that the order was suppressed by papal decree, and this mandate was obediently carried out in England.   Since 1311 the Templars had been sent as prisoners to neighbouring monasteries, and Bishop Drokensford in his Register[152] records in September 1315 payment for the board of four Templars, namely, William de Warwick in Glastonbury, William de Grandcombe in Muchelney, Richard Engayne at Taunton, and Richard de Colingham at Montacute.   The allowance made for

---

[147] In Frome Deanery (27 benefices) : Frome, Marston, Wellow, Chewton, Norton ; in Cary Deanery (34) : Doulting, Evercreech, and Shepton Mallet ; in Marston (23) : Yeovil, Milborne, Charlton, and Queen Camel ; in Axbridge (21) ; Congresbury and Weare ; in Ilchester (24) : Martock, Montacute, and Somerton ; in Pawlett (7) : Puriton ; in Glastonbury jurisdiction (7) : Shapwick and Middlezoy ; in Bridgwater (15) : Bridgwater and N. Petherton ; in Dunster (25) : Carhampton, St. Decuman, and Winsford ; in Taunton (24) : Taunton, Pitminster, Wellington, North Curry, and Milverton ; in Crewkerne (19) : S. Petherton ; in Bath (11) : Bathford ; in Redcliffe (26) : Keynsham and Bedminster ; and in the Deanery of Wells (13) : St. Cuthbert Wells, Pilton, Sutton, Wiveliscombe, Henstridge, Huish, Cheddar, and Westbury.
[148] See *Reg. of Drokensford* and *Reg. of R. of Shrewsbury* (Somers. Rec. Soc.).
[149] *Reg. of R. of Shrewsbury* (Somers. Rec. Soc.), no. 1295, 1676.   [149a] Ibid. no. 1676.
[150] Printed by the Somers. Rec. Soc. vol. i, ix, and x.
[151] Wilkins, *Concilia, sub annis* 1309 and 1311.
[152] Somers. Rec. Soc. *Publ.* i, 98.

the three was 4*d.* a day, and payment was claimed from the Crown of £18 8*s.* for their keep for 276 days.

The rivalry between France and England during the 14th century, intensified by the claim of Edward III to the French crown, had made it necessary to inquire as to the number of Frenchmen holding English benefices, and generally as to all foreigners enjoying the endowments of the English Church. In 1324, when Charles V of France was threatening an invasion of England, Bishop Drokensford was ordered to remove all secular priests who were foreigners and who held benefices near the sea-coast (with the exception of the Flemings) to places further inland, and to allow them out of their benefices a competent sum for their maintenance. The first return of foreigners was found to be seven. George Fromund, vicar of Stogursey,[153] Reginald or Roger Fromund, rector of Holcombe, and Oliver, rector of the free chapel at South Petherton (these three were resident) ; while Phillip de Sapcot, rector of Merriott, the Abbot of Bec, prebendary of Cleeve, Peter de Grennyngcourt, Bursal prebendary, and Gerald de Tyllet, rector of Bedminster, are returned as non-resident.

About thirty years later, in 1351, Bishop Ralph of Shrewsbury made the following return :—[154]

Non-resident foreigners :—Raymund Peregrine, prebendary of Henstridge, Isnard Gasquy, prebendary of Wiveliscombe, the Abbot of Bec, prebendary of Cleeve, the Abbot of Grasse, rector of Norton-sub-Hamdon, and the Abbot of St. Michael's de Periculo Maris, rector of Martock, the Abbot of Jumièges, rector of Chewton Mendip, and the Prior of Goldcliff, holding the churches of Puriton and Woolavington ; resident foreigners : the Prior of Montacute holding the rectory of Montacute, William de Monte, vicar of Woolavington, the Prior of Stogursey holding the vicarage of Stogursey, Guido de Gellano Monte, rector of Chilton, and Bernard Brocaz, prebendary of St. Decuman.

The registers of the two bishops we have already mentioned give us most valuable information concerning the monasteries in the diocese and their moral and general condition.[155]

Bishop Drokensford [156] attempted in 1311 to visit the two great Benedictine monasteries of Bath and Glastonbury, but was met by what he truthfully called a conspiracy of silence. They could not refuse him admission, but they did not give him information. At Glastonbury he seems only to have been able to make himself assured that the vicars of the abbey churches were really in priests' orders. He excommunicated formally those who withheld the truth, absolved any who were prepared to give him information from the illicit oaths of secrecy by which they appeared to have been bound. In 1323 Bath [157] seems to have changed its manner towards him, and accepted his visitation, but Glastonbury remained obdurate.

In 1331 Glastonbury [158] was visited by Archbishop Mepeham, and something very like an attack on the followers of the archbishop was made there. In the autumn of this year Bishop Ralph was called upon to inquire into

---

[153] Adam de Domerham, *Hist.* (ed. Hearne), i, 208.
[154] *Wells Epis. Reg. R. of Shrewsbury* (Somers. Rec. Soc. x), 404, 673.
[155] For details see accounts of the different houses below.
[156] *Reg. of Drokensford* (Somers. Rec. Soc.), 135. [157] Ibid. 217.
[158] *Reg. of R. of Shrewsbury* (Somers. Rec. Soc. ix), 77.

these disturbances, and he seems again [159] to have met with a conspiracy of silence such as that of which his predecessor, Drokensford, had to complain.

A far more serious attack on the bishop and his servants was made at Yeovil in December 1349, when certain 'sons of Belial' attacked the church during the bishop's visitation, wounded many of his attendants, thereby polluting the cemetery, and keeping them shut up in the church till nightfall. During part of the next day also they besieged the bishop in the rectory until certain 'devout sons of the Church' effected his rescue.[160] As a result some sixty persons were ordered to do public penance.[161] Other cases of disrespect shown to the persons of ministers of the Church are recorded. A man who had laid violent hands upon a clerk at Newton St. Loe in 1336 was ordered to do public penance every Friday for seven years,[162] and sentence of excommunication was passed on the assailants of the rector of Exbourne,[163] the vicar of Pitminster,[164] and Nicholas Lange of Burnham, clerk.[165] A century later, about 1470, the vicar of Meare returning from hearing confession was assaulted by a parishioner, who set at him 'an horryble grate dogge called a lymer'; which would have murdered him had he not fortunately 'smote the said dogge with the Chyrche dore key under his eye.'[165a]

In 1348 Bishop Ralph held another visitation at Glastonbury, when the monks proved more amenable, and certain things were discovered to be amiss, but they were for the most part of slight moment, and the general state of the abbey appears to have been satisfactory.[166]

In 1361 he was called upon to inquire into a curious case of a breach of promise of marriage,[167] where Henry Brikebet had escaped from Christiana Courtney by becoming a monk at Glastonbury.

During Bishop Ralph's time Bath was visited in 1333,[168] and later on in 1346, owing to some correspondence with the Bishop of Worcester, Bishop Ralph was called upon to investigate a terrible case of immorality on the part of John de Iford, the prior. We are not told the penalty that was inflicted on the prior, but he does not seem to have been removed, and was acting as prior at the time of the Great Pestilence.

Muchelney was visited in 1315, 1328, and in 1330; there the monastery seems to have suffered from a relaxation of rules which allowed strangers, and women, and even 'impudent girls'[169] to come into the cloister garth, and also the life of the monks was influenced by the manners of those who held corrodies in the monastery. Bishop Ralph was responsible for one of these, for in 1332 he got the monastery[170] to accept William le Irissch, a small squire, as a corrodist, whose secular habits were destructive of monastic austerity. The man seems to have invited the monks to gather in his private chamber not only for his meals, but also for his amusements. The bishop was shocked at the laxity which abounded in the refectory; the vessels were too costly and magnificent, and in the dormitories he found some of the monks in possession of fine and costly beds, with 'tabernacles' over them. The church was in need of repair, and generally the endowments of the convent were wastefully administered.

[159] *Reg. of R. of Shrewsbury* (Somers. Rec. Soc. ix), 71–9.   [160] Ibid. 596–7.
[161] Ibid. 602–3.   [162] Ibid. 264.   [163] Ibid. 313.   [164] Ibid. 737.
[165] Ibid.   [165a] *Somers. and Dorset N. and Q. ix*, 302.
[166] *Reg. of R. of Shrewsbury* (Somers. Rec. Soc.), x, 605.   [167] Ibid. 755.
[168] Ibid. 535.   [169] Ibid. ix, 194.   [170] Ibid. 27.

At Keynsham, Stavordale, and Bruton wastefulness and a general relaxation of rules were discovered. At Keynsham, in 1353,[171] after the Great Pestilence, the bishop seems to have endeavoured to organize the house on a better principle, directing them to keep better accounts, and to provide a chest for the preservation of the title deeds and charters of the abbey.

At Taunton a serious case was discovered in 1353,[172] and the offending canon, Robert Cundyt, was sent for stricter custody to the Prior and Convent of St. Germans, Cornwall. Of the four houses of nuns, Whitehall in Ilchester and Cannington seem to have troubled both these bishops very much. At Ilchester there were grave reports of certain of the sisters, who seem to have been in the habit of walking in the streets of Ilchester at night, and entertaining in their houses suspected persons.[173] At Cannington matters were worse.[174] The rules of the house were not kept, and at least one sister had fallen beyond doubt; but here the whole tone of the house seems to have been influenced for harm by the presence of corrodists and paying guests. At Barrow Gurney[175] there seems to have been general incompetence as to the management of the estates, and an obstinate rivalry among the ladies of the house, which caused elections and resignations of various prioresses, and showed clearly a want of humility and religious fervour.

At Stogursey[176] there was great mismanagement of the property of the priory, and Bishop Ralph was involved in a lawsuit with Godfrey the prior.

In the autumn of 1348 the diocese was devastated by the great plague, which raged through the winter and the early summer of the next year. The summer of 1348 had been very wet, and the scarcity which the inclement weather created prepared a suitable soil for the progress of the plague. It seems to have entered the diocese from the south-east, through Dorset, from Weymouth, and on the north from the ports of Bridgwater and Bristol. Our first notice of it is in the registers of Bishop Ralph, where, from Evercreech, where he was staying on 17 August, he issued prayers[177] for general use in the diocese. Processions and offices at the stations were to take place every day of the week, in all collegiate, conventual, and parochial churches. The bishop[178] retired to his manor-house at Wiveliscombe, and directed the affairs of the diocese as best he could from that retreat.

On 10 January 1349[179] he issued a mandate concerning confession for those who had been seized with sickness, and were *in articulo mortis*. In the absence of a priest they might confess to a layman, and, if necessary, to a woman; but if they recovered they were to make the same confession over again to a priest. Clergy in deacons' orders were permitted to administer the holy eucharist. The average number of institutions to vacant benefices had been from eight to ten a month. In December 1348 they rose to 32; in January 1349 to 47; standing in February at 43, and in March at 36.[180]

[171] *Reg. of R. of Shrewsbury* (Somers. Rec. Soc. x), 708.
[172] Ibid. 726.　　　　[173] *Reg. of Drokensford* (Somers. Rec. Soc.), i, 228–45.
[174] *Reg. of R. of Shrewsbury* (Somers. Rec. Soc. ix), 240.
[175] Ibid. ix, 370; x, 557.　　　[176] Ibid. ix, 174.
[177] 'Omnipotens Deus de cujus trono procedunt tonitrua,' &c. *Reg. of R. of Shrewsbury* (Somers. Rec. Soc. x), 555.　　　[178] Ibid. 558.
[179] Ibid. 571; Wilkins, *Conc.* ii, 735–6, 745.
[180] *Reg. of R. of Shrewsbury* (Somers. Rec. Soc.), seriatim.

At Hardington, on the east of the diocese, Nicholas Crass was appointed vicar 1 January;[181] Stephen de Chitterne was appointed 17 January, and William de Bradelegh on 15 March 1349. At Yeovil a similar case is offered.[182] Hugh de Risingdone was appointed 18 December 1348; John de Whiteknyt 1 January 1349; and William Boter 29 January 1349. These are only two instances among many that could be adduced to show the great mortality among the parish clergy. Great confusion naturally prevailed, and in the uncertainty as to whether a benefice were vacant by death, or had only been deserted through fear, the bishop felt himself compelled to insert a saving clause for his own protection, if, in error, he had instituted a man to a benefice that was not really vacant. The plague raged at Evercreech in November 1348, and devastated Castle Cary and Ansford in December.[183] In Bristol, Clevedon, Weston super Mare and Bridgwater the mortality amounted to 50 per cent. Grass grew high in the streets of Bristol,[184] for there were not people to trample it down. Both the monasteries of Athelney and Muchelney lost their abbots. At Muchelney John de Cudeworth succeeded John de Somerton in the first week of May,[185] and Thomas de Overton succeeded John de Cudeworth on 22 May 1349. The monks of Glastonbury fell from eighty to forty, and at Bath[186] to half their previous number.

Bath and its neighbourhood suffered equally with Bristol. The parishes of Bathford, Batheaston, Bathampton, Weston Bath, Twerton, Babington, Cloford, Holcombe, and Stanton Drew all lost their vicars in January.[187] At Doulting there were two appointments in that month. At Batheaston the man appointed in January died in February. A crisis such as this naturally engendered labour troubles. The royal edict, issued by Edward III on 18 June 1349, *Quia magna pars populi*, is duly copied in the register of Bishop Ralph.[188] In August 1350 the bishop[189] writes to the rectors of Hutton and Axbridge and the clergy of the deanery of Axbridge, urging upon them to cause all labourers dwelling in their parishes to be admonished that they observe the royal edict.

As with the labourers, so with those in Holy Orders,[190] and the mandate of Archbishop Simon Mepeham, which denounced those priests who, surviving the plague, strove to better their position through the greater demand for spiritual persons, was cordially received by Bishop Ralph, and, as far as was possible, published in his diocese.

The careful management of its endowments and the simple life that the clergy led enabled the Church to recover from the trouble more easily than the great landowners of the country. It was on that account the object of much envy, and, as we shall see, the victim of many attacks and of much slander. The Statute of Labourers laid down conditions under which labourers might be paid higher wages than those generally offered. In 1354,[191] and again in 1356,[192] we find the Carthusians of Witham petitioning under the statute for permission to pay wages above the sum

[181] *Reg. of R. of Shrewsbury*, x, 564, 575, 584.
[182] Ibid. x, 558, 564, 576.
[183] Hen. de Knighton, *Chron.* iv, 2699.
[184] Seyer, *Mem. of Bristol*, ii, 143.
[185] *Cal. Pat.* 1348–50, p. 293 ; *Reg. of R. of Shrewsbury* (Somers. Rec. Soc. x), 567.
[186] Hunt, *Bath Cart.* (Somers. Rec. Soc. vii), 73 ; P.R.O. Clerical Subs. (Somers.), bdle. 4, no. 2.
[187] Cf. Weaver, *Somers. Incumbents*, under the parish.
[188] *Reg. of R. of Shrewsbury* (Somers. Rec. Soc. x), 593.
[189] Ibid. 640.
[190] Ibid. 639.
[191] Pat. 28 Edw. III, pt. i, m. 20.
[192] Pat. 36 Edw. III, pt. ii, m. 7.

Robert Burnell (1275–1292).

Ralph of Shrewsbury (1329–1363).

John Barnet (1363–1366).

John Harewell (1366–1386).

Dean and Chapter of Wells :
Seal ad Causas.
13th Century.

Chapter of Bath : Second Seal.

Chapter of Bath : First Seal.
10th Century.

SOMERSET EPISCOPAL AND DEAN AND CHAPTER SEALS.

which they had originally given. After the death of Bishop Ralph of Shrewsbury, we lose for a time the help of the bishops' registers. We have no registers for Bishops Barnet (1363–6), Harewell (1366–86), Skirlaw (1386–8), and Erghum (1388–1400), and little is known, except from the general history of England, of the diocese of Bath and Wells during that period. Labour troubles were experienced in the diocese, as they were elsewhere in England. In Bristol and Bridgwater they caused special anxiety, and the semi-religious and semi-political movement known as that of the Lollards was certainly to be found in Somerset. Bristol seems to have afforded refuge to many who propagated those principles of social and religious change for which John Wycliffe was made responsible.[193]

In 1408 Bishop Bubwith[194] wrote to the Dean of Redcliffe, bidding him allow none but graduates and holders of licences to preach on the doctrines of the Church, and, indeed, as early as 1401 Archbishop Arundel had commissioned Canon Melton of Salisbury to inquire concerning heretical preaching in Bristol. William Taillour, a priest, was tried in 1420 and 1421[195] on the charge of having preached heresy in Bristol, and in 1422[196] Henry Webb of Batheaston was brought before the archbishop, at the instance of the Bishop of Worcester, on a charge of having performed priestly functions without being ordained. He confessed his crime, submitted, and was sentenced to be flogged in Bath and two other places. William Emayn,[197] of Bristol, who had been imprisoned two years for heresy, and had been summoned before the Bishop of Lincoln five times, was brought before the Bishop of Bath and Wells, Bishop Stafford, in the chapter-house at Wells on 10 March 1428, in the presence of the Dean of Wells and the Abbot of Glastonbury and others. He remained in custody after his first examination for fourteen days, in the bishop's prison, locally known as 'the stochouse,' and, on his second appearance before the bishop, abjured his errors.

Again, in 1441, John Jurdan[198] of Bristol was brought to trial at Wells before Bishop Stafford's proctor, and in the chapter-house abjured. In 1449[199] John Young of Bristol, chaplain of St. Cross at Winchester, was arrested by order of Bishop Beckington, and committed to the charge of the Abbot of Muchelney.[200] When brought a second time before the bishop sitting in his manor-house at Chew, he abjured. Five years later, in 1454,[201] Thomas Northorne (or Nordon), a chaplain of Bishop Beckington, was arrested on a strong suspicion of heresy. He appeared before the bishop in the chapel of the palace at Wells on 5 November ; certain questions had been put to him seven days before, when he was confined in the 'stochouse.' These he now answered satisfactorily and abjured.

In 1457[202] Walter Combes of Bristol, a layman attached to the hospital of St. Katherine, Bristol, appeared before Bishop Beckington in his manor-house at Banwell, and afterwards at Wells, and on 29 April satisfied the

[193] Cf. *V.C.H. Glouc.* ii, 21–3.
[194] Wells Epis. Reg. Bubwith, *sub anno.*
[195] Wilkins, *Conc.* iii, 407–12 ; Gregory, *Chron.* 149.
[196] Wilkins, *Conc.* iii, 404.
[197] Wells Epis. Reg. Stafford, fol. 152 d.
[198] Ibid. fol. 179.
[199] Wells Epis. Reg. Beckington, fol. 94.
[200] The fact that these cases of heresy were dealt with by the Bishop of Bath and Wells shows that the men must have resided on the southern side of the Avon, that is to say, in the Somerset part of Bristol.
[201] Wells Epis. Reg. Beckington, fol. 187 d.
[202] Ibid. fol. 212.

bishop of his orthodoxy. Thomas Cold (or Baker)[203] and Agnes his wife of Norton St. Philip were accused before the Chancellor of Wells on 18 January 1459 in the Lady chapel of the cathedral. Both these abjured, and it is satisfactory to know that no execution of the Lollards for heresy took place in the county of Somerset.

On the death of Archbishop Chicheley in 1443 Bishop John Stafford of Bath and Wells was promoted to Canterbury, and as his successor at Wells the Crown appointed one of the most influential men of the age. Thomas Beckington was born in the village of that name near Frome in Somerset. After having been for eleven years[204] fellow of New College, Oxford, he entered, in 1420, the service of Humphrey, Duke of Gloucester. Three years afterwards he was appointed Dean of the Court of Arches, and in 1439[205] became Canon of Wells, after he had held the high office of Prolocutor of the Lower House of Convocation of the Province of Canterbury from 1433 to 1438. In 1432 he had been employed by Henry VI in the embassy sent to France, and again he was one of the ambassadors sent to Calais in 1439. For the next four years Beckington was continually in attendance at court, and in 1442 was one of the ambassadors sent to negotiate with John IV at the court at Armagnac for the marriage of one of his daughters with Henry himself. Beckington returned to England in February 1443, and though the object of his journey for which he was sent was not obtained, the embassy probably averted for a time the loss of Guienne to England. On 13 October 1443 he was consecrated, in the old chapel at Eton, Bishop of Bath and Wells by the Bishops of Lincoln, Salisbury, and Llandaff. His great political influence naturally enabled him to grapple successfully with much in his diocese that called for reform. At Glastonbury, notwithstanding the opposition of the Abbot Nicholas Frome, he insisted on holding a visitation, and at Keynsham, as Bishop Ralph of Shrewsbury had found a century before, he saw much for very grave reproof. Many serious crimes were reported concerning the Austin Canons there, and some of them were suspected of homicide. In Wells he is still remembered for his munificence, and his strange rebus, a flaming beacon in a tun or barrel, which is to be seen in many parts of the cathedral precincts, records his performances as a builder. He is said to have spent 6,000 marks in building and repairs, and the market-place of Wells, with the three gate towers leading from the cathedral green and the palace to the town, the western walk of the cloisters, and the connecting passage between the cathedral church and the vicar's close over the chained gateway, testify to his love and generosity towards his cathedral city. He found the vicars of the canons in great need of discipline, and, after a careful inquiry in 1450, issued a series of new ordinances which are still for the most part the rules by which the College of Vicars Choral is governed to-day.

On 18 June 1452, on account of old age, he was exempted from further attendance in Parliament, and he died at Wells on 14 January 1465. His tomb is under one of the arches of the south choir aisle, and the magnificent canopy for the chantry altar which ran out northwards into the sanctuary is now to be seen on the eastern wall of the chapel of St. Calixtus.

---

[203] Wells Epis. Reg. Beckington, fol. 299.
[205] Cf. *Corres. of Bekynton* (Rolls Ser.), i, Introd.
[204] Wharton, *Angl. Sacr.* i, 573.

ECCLESIASTICAL HISTORY

Bishop Beckington was succeeded by Robert Stillington,[206] an unflinching Yorkist. He belonged to Nether Acaster, Yorkshire, and in 1445 had been made canon of Wells, and in 1447 treasurer of the cathedral church. He held in succession the archdeaconries of Taunton (1450) and Wells (1465). His patron, Edward IV, had made him, in 1461, Keeper of the Privy Seal, and in 1467 he became Chancellor of England. This office he resigned in 1470, when Henry VI was restored to the throne, but we find him Chancellor again in 1472, and he seems to have continued in office until 27 July 1475. In the Escheator Rolls of the Dean and Chapter[207] for the years 1469–70 there is an entry of an oblation of 10s. offered by King Edward IV, of 5s. given by the Duke of Clarence, of 5s. given by the Duchess of Clarence, and of 5d. given by the Earl of Warwick. These oblations are said to have been made in the Dean's Chapel. This is probably evidence[208] of the reconciliation of King Edward IV with the Duke of Clarence and the Earl of Warwick, for certainly on 11 April 1470 Edward IV was in Wells. Edward seems to have been on his way west to arrest the Duke of Clarence and the Earl of Warwick, and it would appear as if he had overtaken them here, an explanation had followed, and they had once more become reconciled.

On the death of Edward IV Bishop Stillington adhered to the party of Richard, Duke of Gloucester,[209] and was at Richard's side when, at Westminster, he declared himself King of England.[210]

The very night after the battle of Bosworth Field, 23 August, Henry VII issued a warrant from Leicester[211] for the arrest of the bishop, and on 27 August 1485 we find him a prisoner in York Castle.[212] Soon after this he purchased his freedom, but becoming implicated in the rising of Lambert Simnel after the battle of Stoke in 1487, he was again arrested and imprisoned at Windsor, and there he remained, with occasional permission to go to his manor of Dogmersfield,[213] till his death in 1491.[214] On 15 May of that year the dean and chapter gave permission to Thomas Cornish,[215] who seems to have acted for some years as his suffragan bishop, to make arrangements for Stillington's burial.

During his episcopate[216] Bishop Stillington was active in building in the cathedral precincts. He pulled down the old Lady chapel in the east cloister of the church, and rebuilt it on a much larger and more magnificent scale, designing it to be his mortuary chapel. It is doubtful whether he actually finished the work, and it is more probable that it was finished by his successor, Bishop Fox. The building did not exist for long. Under the Chantry Act of 1547, its endowments were taken over by the Crown, and in 1552[217] it was given to Sir John Gates on condition that he pulled it down and carried away the material.

It was in the autumn of 1497 that Perkin Warbeck landed at Whitesand Bay, and about a year later Henry VII issued a commission to Thomas Sherborn, Archdeacon of Taunton, and Sir Amias Paulet and others to deal

---

[206] Wharton, *Angl. Sacr.* i, 574. Cf. a careful précis of his life in *Somers. Arch. Proc.* xl (2), 1.
[207] *Hist. MSS. Com. Rep.* x, App. iii, 284. [208] Cf. *Archaeologia*, lxi, no. 243, p. 155.
[209] Sloane MSS. 3479. Cf. Camd. Soc. (1854), p. xxi; Grants of Edw. V.
[210] Drake, *Eboracum*, 123. [211] Cf. Gardiner, *Letters of Ric. III. and Hen. VII*, ii, 368.
[212] Pat. 1 Hen. VII, no. 22. [213] Wells Cath. Chart. no. 717.
[214] Godwin, *De Praesulibus*, 438. [215] Reynolds, *Wells Cath.* Appendix M, 181; Lib. Rub. fol. 34 d.
[216] Cf. Escheator R. *Hist. MSS. Com. Rep.* x, App. iii, 284.
[217] Wells Cath. Chart. no. 773; Chap. Rec. Bk. E, fol. 65.

with those in Somerset who had been guilty of contempt in favouring and assisting a certain rebel, Michael Joseph, who had led the insurgents in the spring of 1497, and a certain impostor, Peter Warbeck, a Fleming born.[218] The result of this commission was that John George, Abbot of St. Saviour's, Athelney, was fined £66 13s. 4d.; Henry, Abbot of St. Mary of Cleeve, £40; William Wyke, Abbot of St. Peter, St. Paul, and St. Andrew, Muchelney, £60; the deanery of Taunton had to pay £441 6s. 8d.; the hundred of Taunton Deane, £250; the deanery of Bridgwater, £66; the hundred of North Petherton, £505; the hundred of Glastonbury, £428; the hundred of Kingsbury, £426; and the borough of Wells £321. In addition to these, many of the parochial clergy also suffered. The vicar of North Petherton and the vicar of Ashill were fined 24s. each; the chaplain of Curry Load £4; the chaplain of Thurlbear £10, and the rector of Goathurst £10.

On 6 August 1500 the king issued another commission for the same object, and the vicar of Shapwick, the rector of Norton sub Hamdon, the rector of Chiselborough, the vicar of Lyng, and the vicar of Wellington, were fined 20s.

On the death of Bishop Oliver King in 1504, an Italian bishop, Hadrian de Castello, was appointed by papal provision as his successor. Innocent VIII[219] had sent him to Scotland on an embassy, and when passing through London he had commended himself to Archbishop Morton, and by him was introduced to the king as one likely to expedite all his business at the Papal Curia. In 1503[220] he was appointed to Hereford, but Wells becoming vacant in the next year, he was, on 9 August 1504, transferred there, and enthroned by proxy on 20 October 1504, Polidore Vergil, the papal sub-collector in England, acting on his behalf. He was, however, only bishop in name, for during the whole of his episcopacy he never visited the diocese, and his history belongs to the darker side of the history of the papacy. It is probable that he was responsible for the appointment by Henry VII of Polidore Vergil as Archdeacon of Wells in January 1506, a man of European fame, famous both as a scholar and an historian.

On 19 January 1506 Bishop Hadrian, whose continual absence from England was becoming scandalous, gained the indulgence of Henry VII by the surrender to him of all his patronage in the diocese. In 1514 he was removed[221] from his office as collector of Peter's Pence and of all other payments due to the papacy, at the request of Henry VIII, and in 1517, having intercepted some correspondence between him and his agent, Polidore Vergil, the Archdeacon of Wells, Henry banished him from England. The next year events in Italy brought about his downfall. He was suspected of being implicated in a plot to poison Pope Leo X,[222] and on that account was deprived of his cardinalate and all his benefices, and on 6 July declared excommunicate.

The vacant bishopric was then conferred[223] *in commendam* on Thomas Wolsey, who held the see as *episcopus commendatorius* from 30 July 1518 to 22 February 1522, on the authority of a papal bull.

During the 14th and 15th centuries the absence of the bishops from their diocese on affairs of state made it necessary that other bishops should be

---

[218] *Letters of Ric. III and Hen. VII* (Rolls Ser.), Appendix B, xvii, 335.
[219] Cf. Wharton, *Angl. Sacr.* i, 576.
[220] Cant. Archiepis. Reg. Warham.
[221] Rymer, *Foedera*, xiii, 467.
[222] Ibid. 607.
[223] *Cal. Venet. Papers*, 1509–19, no. 954.

called in to perform those episcopal acts which the diocese needed. At first we find that they made use of bishops in the neighbouring diocese, and on several occasions Bishop Drokensford made use of the Bishops of Sarum and Llandaff. He also used John MacCanoll, Bishop of Cork, when himself engaged in Parliament.[224]

Bishop Ralph of Shrewsbury, his successor, made systematic use of other bishops, John de Langebrugge, *episcopus Budensis*, acting as suffragan from 1354 to 1361, and afterwards Thomas *episcopus Chrysopolis*.

In 1401 John Greenlaw, *episcopus Soltanensis in Media*, was consecrated as Suffragan of Wells, and he acted as such from December 1401 to 1408. In 1436 John Bloxwych, *episcopus Olensis*, was appointed Suffragan of Bath, and did work in the diocese during the six years 1437 to 1443. In 1458 we find William Westkarre, Bishop of Sidon, an Austin Canon, acting as suffragan ; in 1459 another Austin Canon, John, *episcopus Tinensis*, was appointed, and acted as suffragan for twenty years. He was followed in 1480 by another *episcopus Tinensis*, Thomas Cornish, who laboured in the diocese until 1513. In that year we find on 30 September Thomas Wolf, Bishop of Lacedaemon, engaged as suffragan, and soon after, probably in 1519, William Gilbert, Abbot of Bruton, was consecrated as Bishop of Mayo in Ireland. In 1534 the Suffragan Bishops Act was passed, and Taunton and Bridgwater were specified as the titles of assistant bishops, and on 7 April 1538 William Finch was consecrated as Bishop of Taunton, the only man who has hitherto held that title.[224a]

On Wolsey's appointment to the see of Durham in 1523, the bishopric of Bath and Wells was filled by John Clerk.[225] He had been a monk of Bury St. Edmunds and Professor of Theology in the University of Cambridge, and Henry VIII had made use of him as an ambassador, sending him to present Henry's book against Martin Luther to the pope, and afterwards on the very unpleasant embassy to explain to the Duke of Cleves why his sister, Queen Anne, had been divorced by his master. His episcopate, however, brings us down to the great religious change known popularly as the Reformation. In 1534 Parliament had passed an Act abolishing the authority of the pope, and in November granted to Henry VIII the first-fruits and tenths of the temporalities and spiritualities of all ecclesiastical dignitaries and benefices. This naturally called for an inquiry as to the endowments of the Church of England, and on 30 January 1535 a commission was appointed to arrange for this new survey of church lands, rentals, and the annual income of the clergy. The commissioners were Sir William Stourton and Sir Hugh Powlett, William Portman, esq., and Roger Kynsey, auditor. The bishopric of Bath and Wells was returned as worth £1,939 7s. 9¼d., against which payment was charged to the extent of £95 13s. 4d., the net value being £1,843 14s. 5¼d. The deanery was assessed at £295 13s. 1½d., and the common fund of the Cathedral Church of Wells amounted to £729 3s. 4d. This did not include the income of the separate prebends of the canons and dignitaries, nor were included in it the rents of the College of Vicars Choral or of the new College of Annuellars and Chantry Priests and Chaplains.

As we have said before, this survey of Church endowments, which is known as the *Valor Ecclesiasticus*, brings to an end the mediaeval history of

---

[224] *Reg. of Drokensford* (Somers. Rec. Soc.), i, 43, 45.
[225] Wharton, *Angl. Sacr.* i, 577 ; Wood, *Athen. Oxon.* ii, 752.

[224a] Stubb's, *Epis. Succession*, App. v.

the Church in Somerset. With the pope's authority rejected and a new record of Church property drawn up, the question would soon be asked whether there should not be a readjustment of the national wealth of the kingdom, and that brings us to the story of the Reformation changes, the Dissolution of the Monasteries, and a very large confiscation by legal process of the property of the Church of England.

Early in January 1535 Thomas Cromwell received a commission for a general visitation of the monasteries and churches of England, and in order that his path might be made the easier to deal with ecclesiastical bodies he was created Vicar-general. For some reason the visitation did not begin until June of that year, but so eager were Cromwell's agents to begin their work that the House of Austin Canons at Bruton was visited twice that year, first of all by Dr. Richard Layton without any written instructions, and afterwards by Dr. Thomas Legh in more orderly manner. In February 1536 the Long Parliament accepted the king's word as to the correctness of the statement concerning the monasteries made to them in the book known as the Compendium Compertorum.[226] The bias against the monastic orders was very strong. It is doubtful, however, whether even a small portion of the statements made against these houses was true. No opportunity for examination or inquiry was allowed, and most of the statements concerning them disappeared as soon as the object was accomplished. That year Parliament granted to the Crown all monasteries whose income was less than £200 a year. Henry, however, granted to some houses a licence of exemption from suppression, and the next year it was hoped for some months that on account of its isolated position and the fact that it was the only refuge for the poor in that district, the Cistercian monastery at Cleeve might be spared.

Meanwhile the condition of the larger monasteries became more desperate, for the royal commissioners for the visitation had imposed regulations upon the abbots, priors and monks which made the life of the house almost impossible. They forbade the abbot or the prior to leave the precincts of the monastery without permission from the Vicar-general. Times had changed since the houses had been founded : the life of a monk as it had been regulated in the 8th and 10th centuries was very much altered, and to insist upon conditions which had become antiquated and impossible even several centuries before, while it might appear strictly according to law, was nevertheless only another way of bringing about the inevitable dissolution of the house.

In 1536 therefore the small houses [227] of the Austin Canons in Somerset fell, viz. Barlynch, Burtle and Worspring, also in September the two Benedictine nunneries of Barrow Gurney and Cannington, and in 1537 the Cistercian abbey of Cleeve.

Parliament had also in this year granted to the Crown the goods and revenues and lands of all monasteries that should be surrendered into the king's hand or should otherwise come into his hand through the attainder of the abbot, and the Court of Augmentations was this year established to receive and manage the lands and goods that were already being surrendered.

It was, however, early in 1539 that the larger proportion of the Somerset houses was suppressed.[228] In January Muchelney, Keynsham, Bath

[226] Cott. MS. Cleop. E, iv, 147.   [227] Section on the Religious Houses.
[228] Rymer, *Foedera*, xiv, 629, 636.

and its cell at Dunster were surrendered. February saw the fall of Athelney, Buckland Sororum, Taunton, and its annexed priory at Stavordale.[229] Witham, Montacute, and Hinton ceased in March,[230] and on 1 April[231] the Austin Canons at Bruton were suppressed.

Glastonbury alone remained, the last as it was the earliest monument of monasticism in the county. For six months the visitors exercised their ingenuity and persuasiveness in vain. The house was well ordered and the monks were blameless, and when it fell on 14 November it was from no fault of the abbot or his monks. Richard Whiting was condemned on evidence which nothing but the most debased ingenuity could explain as in any way treasonable, and with his attainder and execution this house passed by the usual legal process into the hands of the king.

The next year Parliament gave to Henry the goods of the Knights Hospitallers of St. John of Jerusalem, and so in 1540 the commandery at Templecombe passed away.

The Dissolution of the Monasteries may have been justified on political and economic grounds, but the appetite of the king and his court, whetted by the share they had in the property taken from the monks was unlikely to end with it. Attached to the cathedral churches of the old foundation and to many of the parish churches were small chapels built for the purpose of commemorating the departed, and chaplaincies and altars and lights were endowed that in these chapels masses might perpetually be sung for the repose of the souls of the men and women thus commemorated. Hitherto these endowments had escaped. Reform, however, was now attacking the old religious opinions of the country, and chantry chapels would only be justified by mediaeval doctrines. In November 1545 an Act was passed to prevent the alienation of the endowments of the chantries and to carry out a survey of the property belonging to them, and a commission was issued for this purpose.[232] There had been a considerable alienation during the year subsequent to the suppression of the monasteries and, as will be shown from the survey, many chantries had almost ceased, while their endowments had passed perhaps into unauthorized hands. The reports of the commissioners only tell us of what had belonged to each chapel and that it still existed or that it had vanished. Much of the endowments of chantries in parish churches vanished with the suppression of the neighbouring monasteries, disappearing with their general fund. In November 1547, the previous Act having become void by the death of Henry, another Act of Parliament handed over to the Crown, as the cause of much false teaching, the endowments of all chantries, chapels, and colleges that had been founded for such reasons. At the time it was stated that the lands so acquired should be restored to the locality for the maintenance of necessary schools, and this accounts for the several entries, in the reports concerning Wells, Bridgwater, Bruton, Crewkerne, and Taunton, of schools or of the wish of the inhabitants to have schools. A royal commission of inquiry was issued 13 February 1548,[233] and the commissioners for the survey in Somerset were Thomas Speke, Hugh Powlett, John Rogers, John Seyntlow, Thomas Dyer, knights, and William Moryce, George Lyne, Robert Kelway, Robert Metcalfe, esquires.

---

[229] Rymer, *Foedera*, xiv, 632, 634, 635. [230] Ibid. 614, 638. [231] Ibid. 614.
[232] Pat. 37 Hen. VIII, pt. x, m. (1) 36 d. [233] Pat. 2 Edw. VI, pt. vii, m. 32 (13) d.

The inquiry was of two kinds. First, a list had to be drawn up of chantries, free chapels, colleges, obits, anniversaries, and trentals; and, secondly, an explicit statement was drafted of the endowments possessed by their foundations, their actual value, the regularity of the payments, and the names of those men who were at the time enjoying these emoluments as chaplains or chantry priests.

The free chapels had an uncertain origin. In many cases, as the rights of the churches of the parishes where they were situated had limited their sphere of utility, they had at last come to be merely places where masses for the dead without any eucharistic oblations could be celebrated. In Somerset these chapels were,[234] St. John's South Petherton, St. James Curry Mallet, St. Michael of Burrow in the parish of Lyng, Idstoke in Cannington, Sherston in North Petherton, Forde in Bawdrip, Ayleston Sutton in Over Weare, Hydall in Clevedon, Norton Hauteville, Claverham in Yatton, St. Catherine's Chapel and Knowle Chapel in Bedminster, St. Catherine's Frome Selwood, the Holy Trinity Chapel of Whitehall in the town of Ilchester, the Chapel of the Holy Ghost Charlton Adam, St. Nicholas Chapel Stoke-sub-Hamdon, Foddington Chapel, Babcary, South Cheriton Chapel Horsington, Yeovilton Chapel Yeovilton, and East Horrington Chapel Wells.

Others, probably like that of St. Thomas of Henton in the parish of Wookey,[235] escaped the notice of the commissioners and were illegally destroyed. This later was pulled down in 1550 by a parishioner who was compelled on the order of a royal commission in 1562 to disburse his plunder.

There were in all 250 such chantry chapels and mortuary endowments for obits and lights, and the sum total of their revenues amounted to £933 yearly. Many of these chantry chapels are found still existing in our parish churches, being thrown into the space given for the accommodation of the parishioners. The largest probably was that built by Bishop Stillington in the churchyard east of the cloisters of the cathedral church of Wells, and as it stood alone, and was no longer needed, it was pulled down in 1552.[236] Of the altar plate belonging to the chantries the returns from thirty-three chantries declare that there was none. One hundred and eighteen are returned as possessing chalices,[237] of which the heaviest was one at Croscombe, weighing 26 oz., a proof of the wealth and devotion of the clothmakers of this village, and the lightest, a chalice at North Curry, which only weighed 5 oz. The bell metal weighed 3,647 lb., and was sold in 1549 for £128 10s. to Laurence Hide. Of the chaplains who ministered at these altars[238] eighty-seven received pensions varying from £6 13s. 4d. to £1 4s., with careful provisos for the reduction of the pension should any of them receive a benefice. But many of the returns record that there were no priests attached to them,[239] while at Badgworth and Wedmore bequests were made for chaplains as late as 1547, and by the time of the survey the priests had only received three-quarters of their first year's stipend.

It is evident, however, that the need for the chapels no longer existed. At Yatton[240] the people wished to buy the materials of the old chapel to make a

---

[234] Green, *Somers. Chant.* (Somers. Rec. Soc. ii), *seriatim*.
[235] Cf. Wookey Parish MSS. in Holmes, *Hist. of Wookey*, 77.
[236] *Hist. MSS. Com. Rep.* x, App. iii, 238. [237] R.O. Exch. K.R. Ch. Gds. bdle. 8, no. 236.
[238] Green, *Somers. Chant.* (Somers. Rec. Soc. ii). [239] Ibid. 71, 79. [240] Ibid. 88.

sluice to protect them against the force of the sea, and at Milverton[241] the inhabitants desired the lead of the chapel to make water-pipes with. St. Michael's Chapel[242] at Congresbury was used as a storehouse for lime, and lumber was stored in the chapel at Wiveliscombe, while rents had been withheld for several years at Wraxall, Ashbrittle, North Cadbury, Long Load, Pawlett, and Wiveliscombe. Ayleston Sutton and Foddington Chapels had already fallen down ; at Winford[243] the parishioners had purchased the chapel there, and three years before the survey the chapel had been seized at East Pennard[244] and the priest expelled ; while at Charlton Adam[245] the chapel had not been used for nearly thirty years, though the priest received his stipend duly. At St. John's Hospital, Bath,[246] the commissioners met with their only case of contumacy. The master would not appear, nor was any information offered as to the foundation. Clearly the master did not consider the hospital as coming within the terms of the inquiry.

It is perhaps advisable to mention here as we leave the mediæval Church the remarkable absence of ancient plate in a county where ancient churches of great beauty abound. There is a pre-Reformation chalice and paten at Nettlecombe, a paten at Pilton, and a chalice at Chewton Mendip. This scarcity is doubtless due to the very strong action taken by the Dean and Chapter of Wells,[247] which on 19 November 1572 decreed that in the cathedral church and the churches of their jurisdiction the ancient chalices should be melted down, and out of the metal so obtained fitting communion cups with covers should be made. There are about 225 parish churches with communion cups of the time of Queen Elizabeth, and about half of them have chalices with this date marked on them.

The Royal Injunction for the entry of all baptisms, marriages, and burials was issued in 1538, and about thirty-three parishes have registers going back to the reign of Henry VIII, and another 100 parishes have registers which go back to the early years of the reign of Queen Elizabeth, though in some cases these registers are not original, but copies made in the reign of James I of entries which had been written on loose sheets.

The cathedral churches of mediæval England which were also monastic chapels naturally fell to the Crown at the suppression of the monasteries. In 1539 the cathedral church of Bath was thus suppressed, and in 1542–3, the Dean and Chapter of Wells was made by Act of Parliament the sole chapter for the election of the Bishop of Bath and Wells, and in 1573 the church of Sts. Peter and Paul became the parish church of Bath. The cathedral church of St. Andrew of Wells had always been served by secular canons, and so was not touched in 1539, though in 1548 it suffered from the indiscriminate plunder of the chantry chapels[248] within the building. But as early as 1535 the process of plunder had begun. The new vicar-general had to be propitiated, and not only do we find the bishop and the chapter offering worthy gifts to him,[249] but the deanery itself was given to Cromwell, and the office was soon afterwards made one in the royal patronage.

On 23 September 1537 the chapter[250] petitioned the bishop for a licence

---

[241] Green, *Somers. Chant.* (Somers. Rec. Soc. ii), 38.   [242] Ibid. 75.   [243] Ibid. 86.
[244] Ibid. 124.   [245] Ibid. 112.   [246] Ibid. 148.   [247] *Hist. MSS. Com. Rep.* x, App. iii, 241.
[248] Cf. Green, *Somers. Chant.* 160, 340 and *seriatim*.
[249] An annuity of £20 was assigned to him in December 1535 ; Chapter Rec. Bk. D. fol. 9 d.
[250] Ibid. fol. 21.

to elect a dean in the place of Richard Woolman, deceased, and on 1 October they received a letter from the king thanking the canons for electing as their dean the Lord Privy Seal.[251]

To our trustie and wellbelovyd the president and chapitre of our Cathedral Church of Wellys.

Trustie and wellbelovyd we grete you well. And for asmoche as upon significacion by our letters made unto you of our determynacion for the preferment of our right trustie and wellbelovyd counsaillour the lorde pryvye seale to the rome of the deane in that our cathedrall churche of Wells as we understonde with a right honest and a lovinge sorte ye have been contentyd therein to gratifie us. And soo have proceeded thereunto so farre as with thobservacion of your laudable ceremonyes in that behalf accustomyd ye have elected chosen and enstalled our sayd counsaillour in the saide deanery. To thyntent ye shulde knowe yᵗ we doo accept and take your proceeding in the same in moste thankfull parte we thought yt convenyent for us not onely by these our letters to geve unto you therefore our expresse and condyne thanks. But also to advertyse you yᵗ in all your reasonable pursuites we shall soo further declare our good favour and affection towards you and every of youe as ye shall have cause to thinke your confyrmyty therein well employed. Geven under our sygnett at Asher the fryste day of October.

The Deanery of Wells was especially exempted in the Bill of Attainder of Thomas Cromwell, and on 2 November 1540 the sub-dean[252] and chapter petitioned the bishop for a licence to elect a dean in place of Thomas Cromwell, Earl of Essex, deceased. The licence was granted, and on 8 February 1541 we find the new dean, Fitzwilliam, and the chapter[253] petitioning the king for a licence to elect a bishop in place of John Clerk, deceased, and choosing William Knight, Fellow of New College, Oxford. So far the procedure had been on the lines of earlier times, and it would seem as if the deanery had not been jeopardized by the attainder of Cromwell.

In 1547 Fitzwilliam, the dean, was induced to resign,[254] and the dean's house and its endowments were granted to Edward, Duke of Somerset. Now it was re-created as a royal donative,[255] and the plunder of the Church began. The office of dean was endowed with the estates of the archdeaconry of Wells, the prebend of Curry, and the endowments of the provostship and succentorship of the church, and the house of Thomas Dakin, Chancellor of the Church, was assigned for the use of the new dean.[256] On 7 January 1548 John Goodman was appointed to this new office by letters patent. Bishop Knight died on 29 September 1547, and since the Act of Parliament had granted to the Crown (4 November 1547) the right to appoint bishops by letters patent, on 3 February 1548 William Barlow, Bishop of St. David's,[257] was transferred to Wells. He was a tool in the hands of the Duke of Somerset, and the story of his surrender of the estates of the bishopric shows how completely he was under the influence of the court.

On 12 July 1548, for 'great sums of money paid beforehand,'[258] which Bishop Barlow does not seem to have ever received, he gave over to the Duke of Somerset by licence of Edward VI the manors of Banwell, Wells,

---

[251] Chapter Rec. Bk. D. fol. 22. [252] Ibid. fol. 53.

[253] Ibid. fol. 55 and fols. 57 and 58.

[254] Dean Fitzwilliam, in his surrender of the deanery to Edward VI on 15 Mar. 1547 gave up all that office and dignity of the deanery, and ' my Manors of Mark, Modesley, Wedmore, and More, and my hundred of Bempston, and the Rectories of Mark and Wedmore and my Prebendary of Biddisham, and the advowsons of Mark and Wedmore to the king and his heirs.' In the Act of Parliament of the same year, re-creating the deanery, reference is made to this surrender, and it is coupled with the surrender of the archdeaconry made by Polidore Vergil to Henry VIII on 20 Dec. 1546; Wells Cath. MSS. Archer's Note Bk. ; Chapter Rec. Bk. E. fol. 18.

[255] Chapter Rec. Bk. E. fol. 18.   [256] Ibid.   [257] Ibid.   [258] Ibid. fol. 21.

Chew, Blackford, Cranmore, Evercreech, the borough of Wellington, the hundreds of Wells Forum, Winterstoke, and Chew, also the bishop's palaces at Wells, Banwell, and Evercreech. This transaction was confirmed by the Dean and Chapter on 10 January 1549. Then on 4 February 1549 [259] he sold the manor of Wookey to the same duke for ever, and that was confirmed on 17 January 1549 by the Dean and Chapter. It is possible that some of these estates were transferred to the duke with a view of their being re-transferred to Bishop Barlow. Certainly the episcopal manor of Wookey having been sold to the duke was transferred back again to Bishop Barlow and his heirs, with permission to sell it, and on 10 December 1550 [260] the duke gave him £400 and the dean's house for his residence.

The next year, 1 March 1550,[261] the manors of Congresbury and Yatton were sold to the king by Bishop Barlow, and on 10 December 1550 he handed over to the Duke of Somerset the estates of Wells, Westbury, the hundreds of Wells and Wells Forum and Westbury Park.

John Goodman had hitherto acted in obedience to the orders of the court. He seems, however, to have been in favour of the unreformed Church, and was unpopular in the chapter. In order to increase the endowments of the deanery he had obtained the prebend of Wiveliscombe, and this was regarded as the surrender of the deanery, it being impossible for a member of the chapter to hold two prebendal stalls. The king's mandate for the installation of his successor, Dr. William Turner, is dated 24 March 1551.[262] The next month, 10 April, the king gave Dean Turner dispensation from residence, and he was sent on a roaming commission to preach the Reformation all over England. This commission naturally took Dr. Turner away from Wells, and gave strength to Dean Goodman's claim to be the legal dean of the cathedral. In 1552 Goodman sued Dean Turner in the Court of Chancery, claiming his rights as dean and the emoluments of the office, and the next year he was confirmed in his office as dean by Queen Mary,[263] still holding the stall of Wiveliscombe, apparently in compensation for the deanery estates which had been granted away.

One of the first acts of Queen Mary was to give back the palace to the bishop, and the deanery to the dean, but Dean Goodman does not appear to have occupied the house of Chancellor Dakyns ; he lived in a house granted him by Bishop Bourne.

Queen Mary's accession in July 1553 was followed by the restoration of the service of the Mass, and of the old form of public worship. Bishop Barlow, as a married man, was deposed, and Gilbert Bourne, a chaplain of Bishop Bonner, and a zealous Romanist,[264] was on 1 April 1554 consecrated at St. Saviour's Southwark Bishop of Bath and Wells by the Bishops of London, Durham, and Winchester. That year saw a great expulsion from their benefices of the parochial clergy.[265] In addition to the bishop and Dr. Turner, who had now to flee to the Continent, Archdeacon Cretyng was

---

[259] Chapter Rec. Bk. E. fol. 21.   [260] Ibid. fol. 44.   [261] Ibid. fol. 34 d.
[262] Ibid. fol. 48.   [263] Ibid. fol. 70.
[264] On 13 Aug. 1553 Dr. Bourne, then one of the canons of St. Paul's, preaching before Queen Mary against the late Reformation, spoke so strongly against Edward VI and in commendation of Bishop Bonner, whom the queen had just released from the Tower, that an uproar was created among the audience, stones and even a dagger being thrown at him as he was in the pulpit. Neal, *Hist. of the Puritans*, i, 59 ; cf. Rymer, *Foedera*, xv, 384.   [265] See App. I.

deprived of the archdeaconry of Bath, and Canon Williams of the prebendal stall of Bedminster, situated in the diocese of Bath and Wells, but attached to the cathedral church of Salisbury. Of the parochial clergy eighty-six were deprived, and others, in favour of the old services, put in their place. Though Bishop Bourne was an active partisan in the trial of heretics, and in the weeding out from his diocese of all clergy who were in any way favourable to the reformed religion, no burning for heresy is known to have taken place in Somerset during his episcopate. Two clerks, John More and Richard Brereton, and a layman, Richard Lush, were condemned for heresy and handed over to the sheriff, but there is no evidence that they suffered the extreme penalty.

The instructions which Bishop Bourne issued to the vicar-general in accordance with the royal injunction would allow us to infer that a large percentage of the deprivations [266] that took place during the first year of his episcopate were due to the fact that so many of the beneficed clergy had contracted marriage, 'upon show of feigned and pretended matrimony,' against the canon law of the Church. The great obstacle, however, to a return to the old state of religion was Pope Paul IV's demand for the restoration of the monasteries. A petition was sent up to the queen about 1557 [267] by four Glastonbury monks—John Phagan, John Neott, William Adelnold, and William Kentwyn—who were then living in the revived monastery at Westminster, for the restoration of Glastonbury Abbey ; but Edward, Duke of Somerset, upon whom it had been bestowed in the reign of Edward VI, had placed there a colony of Walloon weavers, and to accommodate them the work of demolition had already begun. The Walloons had been sent back in 1553, but the funds for restoration were not forthcoming. The lands had all been granted or sold to others, and an attempt to confiscate them would have endangered the Crown. So monasticism was not revived in Somerset, and the same autumn the queen died.

On the accession of Queen Elizabeth, 17 November 1558, a return was made in a somewhat cautious manner to those forms of worship which were embodied in the Prayer Book of 1552.

There were two parties in England, the active Romanists, who desired the state of things that had prevailed in Queen Mary's time, and the extreme reformers who were not even satisfied with the most advanced of the reforms of Edward VI. Between these two parties Queen Elizabeth had to steer carefully. The Act of Uniformity of 1559 made the forms of worship which prevailed in her sister's reign illegal, and the declaration of the Royal Supremacy added a further difficulty for those who would have been content to accept things as they were or had been allowed a modified form of the earlier Roman offices. In Somerset her accession was followed by a series of deprivations consisting of twelve dignitaries and at least eighteen parish priests. [268]

As early as February 1559, Bishop Bourne, who was known as a favourer of the old religion, was removed from the presidency of Wales, and during the session of Parliament in that spring he put in no appearance. In

---

[266] Strype, *Mem.* v, 352. [267] Cf. Weldon, *Engl. Benedictine Congreg.* p. xix.

[268] Gee, *Eliz. Clergy*, 271–2. These deprivations are prior to the end of 1564 ; of later deprivations some were probably due to Puritan nonconformity.

the autumn he returned to Somerset, and four justices of the peace were immediately ordered to tender to him the oath of allegiance and the declaration of the royal supremacy. The latter he refused to accept, and after some hesitation, probably due to the fact that he was now an old man and that the Ecclesiastical Commission hoped that by leniency he would come round, he was formally deprived of the bishopric, and on 18 June 1560 was sent to the Tower. There he remained a prisoner till 1561, when, on account of the plague, he was enlarged and committed to the charge of Dr. Bullingham, Bishop of Lincoln. In 1562 he was sent to his friend, Dean Carewe, of Exeter, and on 10 September 1569 he died at Silverton, near Exeter. On 11 January 1560 a licence to elect a bishop to the vacant see was granted to the dean and chapter by Queen Elizabeth.[269]

Dean William Turner seems to have returned from the Continent in 1559, and to have brought a suit [270] before the Ecclesiastical Commissioners for the restitution to himself of the office of Dean of Wells. The ground of his appeal was the irregularity of the proceedings by which he had been turned out. The Commission decided in his favour, and on 18 June 1560 an order was issued by the queen for his restoration, and John Goodman was formally deprived.[271] His protest against the decision is dated 19 June 1560,[272] and in December 1562 he died.

The chapter had already, without waiting for a decision as to the claims of the two deans, in accordance with the Congé d'élire and Letter Missive, elected [273] as bishop, in place of Gilbert Bourne deprived, Gilbert Berkeley, a native of Norfolk, who had been an Austin canon. The election is dated 29 January 1560,[274] and he was consecrated 24 March of the same year.

Archbishop Parker's visitation of the southern province began in 1559, but owing to the stress of business he was unable personally to conduct it, and on 8 August 1560 he issued a commission to the new Bishop of Bath and Wells, Dr. Berkeley, concerning whose devotion to the new religion he was assured, to visit the diocese of Bath and Wells, as his commissary. The deprivations to which we have referred already resulted from these visitations.

The religious difficulties therefore of this reign fell under two heads, those caused by the suppression of the Romanists and those caused by the extreme Puritans. There were, however, not a few strong Romans in the diocese, not merely among the ranks of the clergy, but also of the laity.

In 1562 Sir Edward Waldegrave of Chewton Mendip, one of the principal recusants of the diocese, was, with his wife, sent to prison on the charge of secreting mass priests in his house, and having mass celebrated secretly there.[275] Berkeley is said to have been lethargic in the administration of the diocese, especially in the later years of his life. In Wells he encountered much opposition from his neighbour, Dean William Turner, who, as a strenuous Puritan, had so small a respect for the office of bishop that he used openly to rail against the episcopate.

---

[269] *Hist. MSS. Com. Rep.* x, App. iii, 240. [270] Ibid. 233.
[271] Ibid. 233, 271.   [272] Ibid. 240.   [273] Ibid.
[274] Rymer, *Foedera*, xv, 572.   [275] *Cal. S.P. Dom.* 1547–80, pp. 560, 565.

In 1564 Berkeley wrote to the Lord Treasurer as follows :— [276]

> I am much encumbred with Mr. Doctor Turner, deane of Wells, for his indiscrete behaviour in the pulpitt, where he meddleth with all matters and unsemelie speaketh of all estates more than is standinge with discression. I have advertised him by wrytynges and have admonished secretlie by his own frendes ; notwithstandinge he persisteth still in his follie ; he contemneth utterlie all bishoppes, and calleth them white coates, tippett gentlemen, with other wordes of reproach more unsemelie, and asketh who gave them authoritie more over me than I over them, eyther to forbidd me preachinge or to deprive me, unless they have it from their holy father the pope.[277]

The deanery seems to have been sequestrated for nonconformity as the result of this appeal, but the punishment at any rate did not extend beyond 1568, the year of his death, in which year the chapter had already complained to the Lord Treasurer of the dean's non-residence.

In 1565 John Bridgwater [278] had been appointed rector of Porlock in place of Robert Brock, deprived for recusancy, and in 1573 he was himself deprived [279] for the same reason and fled to Douai, taking with him not only several students from Oxford, but as his personal attendant one of the vicars choral of the cathedral church of Wells. Bridgwater was for a time prebendary of Compton Bishop,[280] and in 1572 had been made a canon residentiary of Wells. On 24 October 1577 Berkeley wrote to the Council that he had not been able to make out a list of the recusants yet, and he hoped someone would be joined to him in the work. In November,[281] however, he sent a certificate of seven recusants, the most important of whom were Lord Stourton and Mr. Tinte. Berkeley acted on the cautious advice given by Archbishop Parker in the first year of his episcopate, and it is more than doubtful whether this list was in any way a complete roll of those who are known to have been in favour of the old religion. Robert Parsons, a native of Nether Stowey, was a very active Romish priest, and seems to have moved a good deal in the diocese. He fled in 1574 to Douai.

Bishop Berkeley died in 1581, and his successor seems to have found a good many more recusants in the diocese. In 1584 Dr. Thomas Godwin, Dean of Canterbury, was made Bishop of Bath and Wells,[282] the bishopric having been vacant for three years. He was a much more vigorous administrator, and in 1586 returned two justices of the county, Sir John Sydenham and John Lancaster, as unfit for their office, because they were slack in discovering recusants. In 1587 John Hambley, a priest, was executed at Chard, and two others, Bryant and Hart, who suffered with him, were certainly natives of Somerset.

The Recusant Rolls, which began in 1591, give us information as to the names of the recusants living in Somerset who were fined as such under the Act against Popish Recusants of 1593. Up to then the punishments inflicted were often an increased local burden and share of a subsidy or loan. These Rolls continue down to the first year of William and Mary.

---

[276] Lansdowne MSS. 8, no. 3.

[277] Tradition says that Turner trained his dog to help him to show his contempt for the episcopal dress. Once, when the bishop dined with him, the dean, during the dinner exclaimed, 'The Bishop sweats,' and the dog immediately jumped up, pulled off the bishop's square cap, and carried it to his master.

[278] Wells Epis. Reg. Berkeley, fol. 18.

[279] Ibid. fol. 39.

[280] Cal. S.P. Dom. 1547–80, p. 560.

[281] Ibid. 565.

[282] Cant. Archiepis. Reg. Whitgift, fol. 15, 18.

In the first Roll [283] we find Edmund Marvyn of Ashbrittle, John Straker of St. Decuman's, Thomas Griffiths of Ashbrittle, and Stanley, Margaret, and Humphry Prater of Nunney, Richard and Grace Prater, George Champness of Bath, John Lewick of Bath, Alice Saffe of Ilminster, Jane Kemis wife of John Kemis of Cucklington, Stephen Morrys of Queen Camel, and Henry Morrys, also of that parish.

In 1604 [284] recusancy had not been stamped out from Wells. The Bishop of Llandaff complained in that year to the dean and chapter of a certain William Moore, a priest vicar of the cathedral, who had taken Mrs. Mary Turner, a widow and a recusant, from Wells, and had been married in his diocese by a fugitive priest, Walter Powell, hiding somewhere near Raglan. Walter Powell is described as a 'common mass monger,' a man who had been ordained to the priesthood in the days of Queen Mary. In 1625 a considerable list existed of people in Wells who were cited for non-attendance at divine service, and were suspected of being recusants. Among them we find William Beamont and his wife Maria, his servant George Clerke, and Maria and Alice Clerke. These are said to have been living in the Liberty ; also William Evans, gentleman, his wife and daughter, James Morton, sen., and many others.

The deprivation of the clergy who had remained faithful to the old religion created a difficulty in filling up the livings in Somerset. A return made in 1562 by Berkeley [285] of the number of churches and annexed chapels gave for the archdeaconry of Wells 180 churches and 15 chapels ; in the archdeaconry of Bath 58 churches and 15 chapels ; in the archdeaconry of Taunton 147 churches and 37 chapels ; in the jurisdiction of Glastonbury 10 churches and 7 chapels. This does not of course include the peculiars and the prebendal churches.

He tells us that in the archdeaconry of Wells 51 of these parishes, in the archdeaconry of Bath 17, in the archdeaconry of Taunton 36, and in the jurisdiction of Glastonbury 1, were served by curates.

The age of pluralists had not ceased with the Reformation ; indeed there were fourteen churches in Wells archdeaconry, nineteen in Taunton, and two in Bath which were served by curates only, and this statement, perhaps, points to the fact that the livings themselves were held by men not in holy orders.

The injunctions and the articles of the visitation of 1559, ordered by the queen and carried out by the archbishop or his commissaries, laid stress on the importance of sermons. The people needed instruction, and preachers were required who would explain the doctrines and practices of the Church of England. In the cathedral church this seems at first to have been carried out, a sermon being preached every Sunday morning by the dean or one of the canons, and it is said that in the afternoon the cathedral clergy were wont to go to St. Cuthbert's Church, where the vicar preached, and to return to the cathedral at four o'clock for the evening service. In the charter granted in November 1591 to the dean and chapter this duty of preaching was definitely enforced, and in July 1592 the dean and chapter

[283] Recusant R. Exch. L.T.R. (Pipe R. Ser.), 34 Eliz. 1591. For a summary of these rolls from 1597 to 1605 see *Somers. and Dorset N. and Q.* v, 112-16.
[284] Chapter Act Bk. F, fol. 178.   [285] Lansdowne MSS. 6, no. 80.

made an ordinance regulating this matter of sermons. They also ordered that every canon resident preaching in his own course or for any other dignitary should always be habited in a surplice and hood.

Bishop Still (1593-1608) and Bishop Montagu (1608–16) were vigorous administrators of the diocese. In 1607 Bishop Still came to the assistance of the dean and chapter,[286] and called for the interference of the archbishop to enforce the chapter order on the prebendaries of Wells, who neglected the service of the cathedral church, allowed, as he said, the fabric to fall to ruin, and failed to reside as well as to preach the word of God sincerely and faithfully. Bishop Montagu, his successor, prosecuted Edmund Peacham, rector of Hinton St. George, and deprived him of his benefice, 19 December 1618, for libelling the bishop's consistory court. The following year, being obdurate, Peacham was committed to the Tower.

In the latter years of Queen Elizabeth's reign and the early decades of the 17th century Puritanism had been steadily growing in the diocese. In 1592 we find a reference to the foundation of lectureships in parish churches, a popular method by which the founders, being Puritans, could secure an afternoon lecture in the parish church from a man of whose opinions they thoroughly approved. At Bridgwater the aldermen of the town had instituted a lectureship in the parish church, and in 1592 the Rev. Cadwallader Hughes was lecturer. The next year he became vicar.

In 1605 we find the well-known Puritan, John Devenish, holding this office. To obviate the dangerous tendency of this movement Charles I issued instructions in 1629, and Bishop Piers endeavoured to compel the lecturers to conform by making them read the prayers of the Church before they preached, further enforcing the order to wear surplices and a hood, and to preach in a gown and not in a cloak. He also tried to compel the parish priest to catechize on Sunday afternoon instead of giving his church over to the lectureship. At Wrington the rector, Samuel Crooke, was a very strong Puritan, and his earnest preaching resulted in a great moral improvement not only in his parish but also in the immediate neighbourhood. Bishop Piers stopped him from giving a Tuesday evening lecture, and in 1636 [287] at Bridgwater he suppressed the lectures which the vicar, John Devenish, was wont to give on market days, saying that he saw no such need of preaching now as was in the apostles' days. Devenish he suspended, and Humphrey Blake, the churchwarden, he put to penance for neglecting to present his vicar as a delinquent. Afterwards, when he absolved him on his promise to give the lecture no more, he said : ' Go thy way, sin no more, lest a worse thing befall thee.'

Bishop Piers,[288] an earnest supporter of the vigorous policy of Archbishop Laud, who had himself been Bishop of Bath and Wells from 1626 to 1628, also put down all afternoon sermons on Sunday, and suspended Mr. Cornish of Dunkerton for preaching a funeral sermon in the evening, and Mr. Tobias Barrett, rector of Barwick, was also suspended for introducing in his public catechizing questions and answers other than those in the Prayer Book, and prefacing his catechizing with a long prayer.

---

[286] *Hist. MSS. Com. Rep.* x, App. iii, 204 ; 1 April 1607.
[287] Neal, *Hist. of the Puritans*, i, 587 ; Prynne, *Canterburies Doome*, 377.　　　　[288] Ibid.

At Batcombe, the churchwardens had painted their church walls with the words of Isaiah lviii, 13 and 14: 'If thou turn away thy foot from the Sabbath' &c., and Piers sent his chaplain to wash over the inscription, saying that a Jewish piece of scripture was not to be allowed in a Christian church.[289]

We find also considerable resistance made by the Puritans of the county to the *Book of Sports* issued by James I in 1617.

The Star Chamber Proceedings [290] in 1592 give us an interesting account of the parish wakes or church ales as they occurred at Skilgate. It is said that invitations were sent out to sixteen or seventeen parishes in the neighbourhood, and these invitations were read at the time of public service. The contingent of holiday-makers from other parishes arrived at Skilgate while service was proceeding, whereupon the congregation noisily broke up, the church bells were rung, 'dyvers bagpipes blowne out,' and all departed to join the drinking bout. A similar preference for unholy enjoyments is noted at Chew in 1536, when Mr. Claxton, the bishop's chaplain, excused himself for omitting to pray for the king and queen on the ground that the congregation consisted of gross and rude people disposed to gaming and pastime, and not to tarry long in church, and it being Shrovetide he merely exhorted them to pray for those quick and dead for whom they were accustomed to pray.[291]

In 1615 two cases of manslaughter [292] were heard by the justices, the result of the riotous conduct that was not always absent from these gatherings. The justices of the county, as at Bridgwater on 10 September 1596, had condemned the lawlessness and inebriety which at times prevailed there. In 1627 the judges of assize had ordered, at the request of the county authorities, that the proclamation of the county justices against tippling should be yearly published by all ministers in the parish church.

On 19 March 1632 Lord Chief Justice Richardson and Baron Denham inquired officially as to the observance of the order which they had given in the winter assize, prohibiting church ales and parish revels, and calling upon the county justices to treat wandering minstrels and men leading bears as rogues under the statute; and finding that some had not published the order, punished them for their breach of it.

Sir Robert Phelips complained to Archbishop Laud immediately after the spring assize, and the archbishop was indignant at the chief justice's ordering any proclamation to be made by the clergy in the parish churches.[293] He brought the matter before Charles I, and the king called upon Chief Justice Richardson to revoke the order in the coming Lent assize (1633).

On 2 May 1633 Charles wrote to Sir Robert Phelips and to Dr. Godwin, the bishop, demanding accurate information of the charge issued by the judge of assize concerning the suppression of these feasts, adding that the people, after evening service on Sunday, may use decent and sober recreation, but that all excesses at such feasts were to be repressed.

In November of that year the king ordered the Archbishop of Canterbury and others to call before them the lord chief justice, Sir Robert Phelips, and others, and to report the result to the king. Richardson did not at first

---

[289] Stated in Bastwick, Burton, and Prynne's *Petition* to Charles complaining of Bishop Piers.
[290] Cf. Star Chamb. Proc. 34 Eliz. 1592, quoted in *Somers. Arch. Proc.* xxiv (2), 60.
[291] *L. and P. Hen. VIII,* x, 625.
[292] Cf. Prynne, *Cant. Doome,* 153; Neal, *Hist. of Pur.* i, 558.
[293] Cf. *Hist. MSS. Com. Rep.* iii, App. 286; Prynne, *Cant. Doome,* 142, 143, 251; Heylin, *Laud,* 242-3.

obey the order of the king, and when, on the present action of Charles, he formally revoked his previous order at the summer assize, he showed clearly that he was acting under compulsion. Richardson, when he appeared before the Council, was severely reprimanded by the Bishop of London, and it is said that he came out weeping and complaining that he had been almost choked with a pair of lawn sleeves.

Meanwhile the king ordered from Bishop Piers a report as to what generally prevailed at these sports. Piers[294] sent out questions of inquiry to seventy-two clergy of his diocese, and summed up their answers very much in favour of the wakes.[295] He said that at such times the attendance at church was better than usual. King Charles, however, did not wait for the report of Piers, but republished his father's Declaration of Sports, and this was his answer to the Precisians who had desired a more correct observance of Sunday.

Two clergy, Humphrey Chambers, vicar of Claverton, and William Thomas, rector of Ubley, were punished in 1633[296] for refusing to read the Declaration of Sports. Chambers was imprisoned and suspended for two years, and Thomas for three years, and on 28 July 1635 the latter was deprived of his benefice, but restored in 1638 on a strong petition from his friends to Archbishop Laud. This action, however, did not suppress entirely the Puritans among the clergy of the diocese. Bishop Piers censured Robert Lutley, rector of Beer Crocombe, for preaching twice on the parish revel-day, because he said it was a hindrance to the revel, and an utterance against the church ale provided.

Thomas Budd, vicar of Montacute, was bold enough to preach from Joel ii on the day of the Montacute Wake, on a text which the bishop described as scandalous to a revel.

In 1634 we find Bishop Piers[297] active in carrying out the royal injunction for the removal of the holy table from the body of the church to its eastern end, and for inclosing it with a railing to protect it from profanation. This order was obeyed in about one hundred and fifty churches. At Beckington,[298] near Frome, the churchwardens refused to obey Bishop Piers, and were excommunicated by him. The whole of the parish supported them, as well as the lord of the manor, and provided means for an appeal to the Court of Arches. They appealed, however, in vain, and they could get no answer from the king, and in 1637, being excommunicated persons, they were imprisoned, and only released on the condition that they publicly acknowledged at Beckington and two other churches of the diocese that they had grievously offended the Divine Majesty of Almighty God. In obedience to this order, on Sunday 26 June 1637, they made this declaration in the churches of Beckington, Frome, and Bath.[299]

As early as 1593 the chapter had ordered[300] that the communion table was to be placed in the east end of the cathedral church, and railed in. In 1635 we find they removed,[301] under order from the archbishop, all seats from

[294] Laud, *Works*, iv, 133.   [295] *Hist. MSS. Com. Rep.* iii, App. 286.
[296] Calamy, *Nonconf. Mem.* iii, 213.   [297] Rushworth, *Hist. Coll.* ii, 193.
[298] Prynne, *Cant. Doome*, 94 ; High Commission Act Bk. 25 Nov. 1635 ; 11 Feb. 1636 ; Rushworth, *Coll.* ii (2), 300 ; Walker, *Sufferings of the Clergy*, i, 52.
[299] Prynne, *Cant. Doome*, 97.   [300] Chap. Act Bk. H. fol. 88.   [301] Ibid. fol. 171.

the nave, and in the autumn of that year discussed the question of what ornaments they were to introduce.[302]

On 9 June 1632[303] the Secretary of State wrote to the dean and chapter as follows :—

> Sir, His Majesty is informed that the Communion Table in your Church is not furnished with such decent ornaments as are requisite, and as in other Cathedral Churches are supplied. He therefore commands me to let you know that he expecteth from you a speedy redress on that behalf that he will not have cause to charge you with the neglect of your duty which he will not forbear to do if he do not receive a better account of your care herein.
>
> Wherefore not doubting,
>
> I remain,
> Your loving friend,
> JOHN COKE.

In 1644 the Chapter Minutes end with the following statement, which shows that the canons realized the seriousness of the crisis :—

> Ordered by consent of the persons here present that if it shall here happen that the Corporation of the Dean and Chapter[304] be dissolved by Act of Parliament or any other lawful means that every Canon that had paid his portion or their executors shall receive it back out of the debts due to the Dean and Chapter or their successors.

In 1642, at the outbreak of the Civil War, the real feelings of the people were at last revealed. The noblemen and chief county families were on the side of the king, but undoubtedly many of the small landed gentry and those who had made money in the cloth trade were not only on the side of Parliament, but seem also to have been very dissatisfied with the Church of England and her services. In August of that year,[305] the Marquis of Hertford, after having taken counsel with the leading people of the county at the assizes at Bath, chose Wells as the centre of the king's party in the county. He had no sooner done so than the leaders of the opposite party, under Sir John Horner and Mr. Alexander Popham, assembled near Shepton Mallet, and when the marquis found he was not strong enough to hold Wells he retired by way of Street and Somerton to Sherborne, and the cathedral city was entered by the victorious Parliamentary party. For a year the county was in the hands of the Parliamentary party, and in religion under the regulation of the Assembly of Divines for the reformation of the Church.

A volume in the Chapter Library, Ludolphus *de vitâ Christi*, has two or three notes on the margin which give us an insight into what was taking place in the city. As early as the month of April 1642, we have the following note :—

> Mr. Richard Allen, (Alline), junr. clerk, being instituted to the Parsonage of Batcombe, which was lately belonging to our Mr. Richard Barnard, a great Precisian, coming for an induction with a brother of his being likewise a Clergyman, and another stranger, a layman, being a Londoner, there being a very fair crucifix at the upper end of the south end of the Cathedral Church of St. Andrew in Wells behind the Choir. This Londoner most maliciously threw a stone at it and broke it, the said Mr. Allen standing at the lower end of the aisle and beholding it and watching that no one came the while.

This Mr. Richard Allen was the son of the Puritan rector of Ditcheat, and succeeded Prebendary Barnard as rector of Batcombe in 1642.

---

[302] Chap. Act Bk. H. fol. 176.　　[303] Ibid. 1621–35, fol. 122.　　[304] Ibid. fol. 96.
[305] Cf. John Ashe's 'A perfect relatione,' 1642 ; *Lords' Journ.* v, 278.

The register of the adjoining parish of Bruton shows how in this year parish was set against parish in the political struggle into which the villagers entered but which they imperfectly understood. Bruton belonged to the Royalist house of Berkeley, and in that year the town seems to have been attacked by the Parliamentarians of Batcombe. In the Church Register we find the following note commemorating the defeat of the enemy.

> All praise and thanks to God still give
> For our deliverance Matthias Eve (23 Feb.)
> By his great power we put to flight
> Our foes, the raging Batcombites.

Bishop Piers had been too zealous an advocate of the policy of Archbishop Laud to escape the notice of the Puritans, and was the subject of an inquiry in the House of Commons in reference to the imprisonment of the churchwardens of Beckington.

In December 1640 the Commoners desired the House of Lords to take security for Bishop Piers' forthcoming to answer diverse heinous crimes attending the corruption and subversion of religion in the diocese of Bath and Wells.[306] This was the result of the petition of the churchwardens and parishioners of Beckington, in reference to his action about the position of the communion table. He retired the next year to a private estate at Cuddesdon, but joining afterwards in the remonstrances of the bishops against the action of the Commons in voting the abolition of their order, he was arrested and committed to the Tower. Afterwards he was deprived and allowed to go back to Cuddesdon, where he remained in obscurity until the Restoration in 1660. He died at Walthamstow in Essex in 1670.[307]

To the Assembly of Divines for the Reformation of the Church, Crooke of Wrington and Conant of Limington were chosen as the representatives of Somerset. The Assembly, however, did not meet till June 1643, and Crooke never sat on it, for the victorious Royalist party in that year put a temporary end to the Puritan movement for reform in Somerset.

The ordinance of 1 April 1643, which had announced the sequestration of the bishops' lands, appointed committees and sequestrators for each county, and all who openly espoused the king's cause were denounced as delinquents and malignants whose possessions were to be taken over for the benefit of the Parliamentary party. Among the MSS. at Coker Court is an account of Mr. Edward Curl,[308] one of the sequestrators for the hundred of Catsash, which deals with portions of the years 1645–7. The wives and children of delinquents were to receive one-fifth of the yearly income of the estate for their maintenance, and the sequestrators were allowed one shilling in the pound for every sum sent up to the Treasury. Curl's narrative gives us a very vivid picture of the times, and allows us to see what grounds were assigned for the dismissal of the loyal clergy in Somerset.

The Rev. William Haskett, rector of Maperton, was deprived for railing against the Parliament in his sermons, and stirring up the people to go against the Parliament forces, and for being of a scandalous life. The Rev. Guy

---

[306] Walker, *Sufferings of the Clergy*, ii, 70. [307] Cf. Cassan, *Lives of the Bishops of Bath and Wells*, 68.
[308] Cf. *Somers. Arch. Proc.* iv (ii), 60 ; xvi (ii), 13.

Clinton, rector of Alford, was deprived for reading the Book of Common Prayer, and being very insufficient in his ministry and scandalous in his life, and his son, who had been very active since the tumult at Bruton, was conceived to be maintained in arms by him against the Parliament forces. Mr. Wilkinson, rector of Weston Bampfylde, was ejected as a pluralist, since he held Weston and Bradford together. The Standing Committee gave Weston to Mr. Buck, the curate. The Rev. Hugh Collins, rector of Compton Pauncefoot, was ejected because : 1st, he was a lewd and scandalous minister ; 2nd, that within the last four years a base child had been laid to his charge, and it was found to be his own ; 3rd, that he had been to Oxford and carried intelligence to the king ; and 4th, that he had made a bonfire on top of a high hill for joy of the overthrow of the Parliament forces at Edgehill.

Papists were equally the object of the inquiries of these committees, and Curl's list shows us how inquisitorial they were towards the lay recusants.

Parliament, however, soon grew jealous of the committees appointed by the Westminster Assembly, and purposely left the Comital Presbyteries incomplete, and none were created until 1648, when the county of Somerset was made a province.

The book in the Chapter Library which we have already referred to has two more notes in the margin which show us what was going on under the Parliament soldiers at Wells in the spring of 1643 :—

> On Saturday, 7 April, 1643 [the Parliamentary Troopers] broke down diverse pictures and crucifixes in the Church and our Lady Chapel. Likewise they did plunder the Bishop's Palace and broke all such monuments and pictures as they espied, either of religion, antiquity, or the Kings of England, and made havoc or sold for little or nothing the household stuff. One of the Captains had a note given him of diverse of the town and of their estate who had thought to adhere to the King.
>
> On Wednesday, 10 May, being Ascension, Mr. Alexander Popham's soldiers, he being a Colonel for the Parliament, after dinner rushed into the Church, broke down the windows, organs, fonts, seats in the Choir, and the Bishop's seat, besides many other villainies.

On the return of the Royalist soldiers in the summer of 1643, commissioners were sent out to enforce submission and re-establish church order. Crooke of Wrington naturally occupied their attention. It is said that he was affronted by rude ruffians and bloody-minded soldiers, who tyrannized over him in his own house, not permitting him to enjoy himself and his God in his private study. Even there would they pursue him with drawn swords, vowing his instant death for not complying with their bloody-minded engagements. Under such conditions Crooke[309] was compelled to subscribe to a declaration of eight articles asserting that all resistance to the king was unlawful, and that he had ever been opposed to the defacing of churches and images, and the condemning of the Book of Common Prayer, and he pledged himself to preach a sermon both at Wells and at Wrington, upholding this view. His neighbour, Mr. Thomas of Ubley, was less easy to move, and until the reconquest of Somerset by the Parliamentarians in 1646, he was suspended from the performance of his duties as rector.

Dean Walter Raleigh[310] was rector of Street and Walton and vicar of Chedzoy, and became dean in 1641. During the year of the Parliamentarian

---

[309] *Mercurius Aulicus,* 27 Sept. 1643.   [310] Walker, *Sufferings of the Clergy,* ii, 71.

ascendancy he seems to have been with the king, and afterwards to have gone to his vicarage at Chedzoy. In 1645, on the approach of the Parliamentary forces, under General Fairfax, Dean Raleigh withdrew from Chedzoy to Bridgwater, and his rectory at Chedzoy was made the head quarters of the Parliamentary general. When Bridgwater fell, the dean[311] was seized and placed on a horse with his legs tied beneath its belly, and so he was led prisoner to his own house. The benefice, however, was desired by a strong upholder of Presbyterianism, Henry Jeanes, vicar of Kingston, and so Raleigh was led off to Ilchester gaol. From there he was taken to the bishop's manor-house at Banwell, and ultimately to the deanery at Wells, which for a time was turned into a gaol for loyalists. His custodian was a shoemaker of the city, of the name of Barrett, who held the office of constable of the town.

In September 1646 Barrett saw the dean writing a letter to his wife, and demanded to see it. Raleigh, however, refused to show the letter until Barrett produced his authority for making such a demand. Thereupon Barrett struck him several times with his sword. After suffering for some days from these wounds, Raleigh died on 10 October. He was buried by one of the priest vicars, Standish, who, because he had read the Church service over the body of the dean, was punished by imprisonment for the rest of his life. Barrett himself was left unpunished.

The following members of the chapter at Wells[312] were also deprived, and for a time imprisoned :—

Robert Creighton, canon residentiary and treasurer. He escaped ultimately and went into exile to France. In 1660 he returned, became dean, and in 1670 bishop, dying in 1673.

William Piers, a son of the bishop, who was canon residentiary, and Archdeacon of Taunton, was deprived, and in his distress acted as a day-labourer and sold cheeses in Ilminster market, and finally was imprisoned in Ilchester gaol. He lived to be restored to his benefice.

James Dugdale, canon residentiary and rector of Shepton Beauchamp and Evercreech, was nearly killed by the Parliamentary soldiers, being rescued by the women of the place, who threw stones at the soldiers, and stopped them in their brutality.

Richard Busby, canon residentiary and head master of Westminster School, and in 1660 treasurer of the cathedral ; William Watts, Archdeacon of Wells ; Hugh Robinson, Thomas Walker, Paul Goodwin, Roger Wood, Christopher Prior, John Morley, Thomas Holt, prebendaries, and four parochial clergy ; Samuel Payne, vicar of Woolavington ; Samuel Peryam, vicar of Minehead ; Richard Powell, rector of Spaxton ; and George Collier are also mentioned.

There were in all about 110 clergy ejected, and the grand Committee for inquiry concerning scandalous ministers filled up the vacancies by appointing men of their own views.

In 1647 the following scheme was proposed by William Prynne,[313] and embodied in a petition to Parliament as 'a means for the present settling in the County of Somerset of the Presbyteral Government.'

---

[311] Walker, *Sufferings of the Clergy*, ii, 71.   [312] Ibid. 71–6.
[313] W. Prynne, 'The County of Somerset divided for settling of Presbyteral Government, 1647.'

The petition ran :—

> We desire that Somerset may be made one entire province, and divided into nine distinct classes. We have, with the advice of Godly Ministers, and others, subscribers, considered how the County of Somerset may most conveniently be divided into districts, classes, presbyteries, and what ministers and others are fit to be of each classis; which decision and nomination of persons is here accordingly certified and presented to the honourable Houses of Parliament,

and the petition is signed by :—John Horner, Roger Gorges, William Prynne, Henry Fenley, William Thomas, and George Newton.

The nine divisions or classes were named after their head towns, and were Bath, Wrington, Wells, Bruton, Ilchester, Ilminster, Taunton, Bridgwater, and Dunster. These were, however, ultimately grouped together—Bath and Wrington, which comprised the archdeaconry of Bath, being united under twelve ministers and thirty-two elders. Wells was united with Bruton, Ilchester was joined to Ilminster; while Taunton, Bridgwater, and Dunster were made one large group.

In the Bath and Wrington group, there were 137 districts, of which all were parishes, except Thrubwell, Wriggleton, Wolley, Widcombe near East Harptree, Felton, Coldhinton, and Bishport; and among the leading ministers appear the names of Samuel Crooke of Wrington, William Thomas of Ubley, Thomas Codington of Keynsham, and Anthony Parker of Blagdon.

In the Wells and Bruton union there were 110 districts, and amongst the ministers appears the name of Samuel Oliver, and among the thirty-two elders are the names of Richard Hippisley of Wookey, Joseph Galhampton of Wells, Thomas Salmon of Wells, and Stephen Hasket.

The opposition to the Church of England, which passed such censure on all the bishops, and especially on all which Archbishop Laud had done, was Presbyterian, and the Assembly of Divines for the reformation of the Church consisted solely of Presbyterian Nonconformists. It was an organized nonconformity, opposed to any but properly trained ministers, who alone were to be allowed to perform divine service in the churches. In Somerset the action of the Assembly at first was checked by the Royalist successes in 1643, and in the autumn of that year, owing to the action of a Voluntary Association of the country people of Somerset to enforce in religious matters the orders of the Church of England, there was very little militant nonconformity.[314]

The next year Colonel Blake seized Taunton for the Parliamentary party. It was the stronghold in the county of the Puritans, and the Royalists naturally were bent on its recapture. It was defended by Colonel Blake, and besieged by Sir John Berkeley. Mr. Thomas Wellman, vicar of Luppitt, who had fled into Taunton to escape the cruelties of the Royalist soldiers, was preaching in St. James's Church[315] on Sunday, 11 May, on Malachi, iii, 6 : 'I am the Lord, I change not.' The inhabitants were anxiously waiting news of the approach of Lord Fairfax and the Parliamentary forces. During the sermon some people ran into the church, crying

---

[314] The Association for the Enforcement of Conformity was, however, often guilty of great cruelty. In 1644 Sir Francis Dodington, a Royalist, meeting a minister on the road near Taunton, asked him, 'Who art thou for, priest ?' 'For God and His Gospel,' replied the minister. Whereupon Sir Francis immediately shot him dead. Whitelocke, *Mem.* 96.   [315] Whitelocke, *Mem.*

out, 'Deliverance, deliverance,' and on Monday, Colonel Weldon with the advance guard of Fairfax's army entered Taunton.

In a sermon [316] licensed and printed by order of Parliament this year, the preacher called upon his congregation to give thanks unto God for what He had done on behalf of their cause, and based this appeal in the language of the psalmist :—

> He remembered us at Naseby, for His mercy endureth for ever.
> He remembered us in Pembrokeshire, for His mercy endureth for ever.
> He remembered us at Taunton, for His mercy endureth for ever.

By 1646 Somerset was again in the hands of the Parliamentary party, and remained so till the Restoration. It was in that year that Mr. Thomas Gauler [317] suffered so much at their hands on account of his churchmanship. Refusing to sign the Solemn League and Covenant he was imprisoned at Ilchester, his goods were seized, and it was only after some time, the parishioners having urgently petitioned on his behalf, that he gained his release. The next year, the county being at peace and entirely in the hands of the Nonconformists, we have the plan for Presbyterian government in classes to which we have referred above. But already the country in its religious views had gone beyond the opinions of the Presbyterian divines that formed the first assembly five years ago. The Independents were rapidly rising in power and other sectaries were appearing, so that the Presbyterians were no longer able to enforce strict adherence to the plans for Church government which they had formed. In 1648 an address was sent up to Parliament signed by seventy-one Somerset ministers called 'the Testimony to the Truth of Jesus Christ, and to our Solemn League and Covenant.' They said that they desired a Church government and an organized ministry. They strongly condemned the toleration that was spreading so rapidly. Among the foremost to advocate this view were Mr. Crooke [318] of Wrington, and the two Allens of Batcombe and Ditcheat. Mr. Thomas of Ubley lamented that he found men everywhere beginning to disdain a duly called minister, 'under pretence of being more perfect saints.' It is from this time that we have the rise of the Independent party, and political influences were at work to give it ever-increasing assistance. The Presbyterian clergy were now being suspected of doubtful adherence to the government, and were called upon to take an engagement that they would be faithful to the Commonwealth. At Taunton so opposed were the clergy to the proposals made by the Independents in Parliament that they refused to observe the appointed fast day in 1648.

Meanwhile another body of Nonconformists had been steadily growing in power. The Baptists had formed a congregation as early as 1630 and were wont to meet in the neighbourhood of Taunton, and had their first place of worship at Hatch, and in 1646 in St. Mary Street, Taunton. They were perhaps as distasteful to the Presbyterians as ever the bishops and clergy of the English Church had been. A Baptist minister [319] named John Sims preached this year in Middlezoy Church; the congregation, being largely Presbyterians, afterwards seized him on a charge of preaching without a licence.

---

[316] Walker, *Sufferings of the Clergy*, i, 18. [317] Nalson, *Coll.* i, 738, 776.
[318] Cf. Green's notice of Crooke, *Bath Antiq. Soc.* iii, 1877, pp. 1–10.
[319] Neal, *Hist. of the Puritans*, iii, 365 ; Crosby, *Hist. of the Baptists*, i, 232.

At Taunton there was considerable persecution of the Baptists by the Presbyterians, but the next year they were supported by the Protector himself, who compelled the local magistrates to grant the Shire Hall at Chard for the use of a congregation of Baptists in that town.

In 1653 the Baptist congregations began to organize themselves into an association for the county under George Collier.

From 1648 to 1654 no provision was made for supplying the churches with duly qualified ministers. The Baptists and the Independents had accepted livings, but always refused to regard themselves as parish ministers or bound to administer all the ordinances of religion to the residents of that parish. At last, in 1654, was formed the Board of Triers, a committee of laymen and ministers whose duty it was to examine the fitness of those who were acting as ministers in the parishes, and also to supply vacancies as from time to time they occurred.

Joseph Alleine was appointed to assist Mr. Newton at St. Mary's, Taunton. He was a most hard-working and earnest Puritan minister, preaching [320] always once on Sunday and on every Tuesday evening, and very often in the neighbourhood; he is said to have preached more than a dozen sermons a week.

In 1656 we find a further advance of the Baptists. The congregations at Bridgwater, Taunton, Hatch, Chard, Montacute, Wincanton, Wells, Wedmore, Stoke, and Somerton, drew up a confession of faith, a definite step towards a test for full membership.

There had also arisen another sect, the Quakers or Society of Friends, which appears first in 1647, and was constantly being persecuted. In 1658 [321] they drew up a petition to the Lord Protector and to the Council against the persecutions to which they had been so cruelly subjected. Their first chapel in Taunton was not erected until 1693.

Meanwhile the religious feeling in the county steadily decreased in face of the diversity of religious opinions and the multiplication of religious societies. These congregations or associations of congregations, which were called the gathered churches, only admitted to their union those who were full members of their body, and membership involved a careful examination and a formal admission. The consequence was that the communicants diminished in a painful manner. Mr. John Humphry, the intruded vicar of Frome, who was a Royalist and a Presbyterian, wrote strongly against refusing to admit those who desired it, to come to the Holy Communion. From the pulpit he is said to have prophesied the return of the Royalists. When, however, they came, he was expelled from his benefice. At the same time, as an instance of individual earnestness it is interesting to record the missionary enterprise of four Somerset men who in 1650 sold their property and embarked for Palestine, believing they had a call from God to preach the Gospel in Galilee.[321a]

The final abolition of the order of bishops in 1646 and the dissolution of the cathedral chapters gave the Parliamentary party large estates and many houses, and these were placed in the hands of trustees known as the trustees of Church lands. In the autumn of 1647 Parliament ordered that these lands were to

---

[320] Cf. Calamy, *Nonconf. Mem.* iii, 207. [321] *Cal. S.P. Dom. Interreg.* 1658, p. 480.
[321a] *Somers. and Dorset N. and Q.* i, 58, quoting Wakeman, *The Church and the Puritans,* 173.

be sold, and the adventurers for the confiscated land in Ireland were asked to double their loan and take the full amount out in Church lands in England.

Dr. Cornelius Burgess, who is said to have been a native of Batcombe, became vicar of Watford in 1613.[322] In 1640 he sided with the Parliamentarians, and in 1642 was evening lecturer at St. Paul's Cathedral. He had lent to the government two sums of £300 and £700, and now increased his loan, and stated that he had lent to the government £3,900. In accordance with the arrangements made by the government, Burgess took out his debts in bishops' lands in Wells. He purchased the palace and the deanery, and soon after came into collision with the corporation of the city.

On 28 November 1647[323] we find the corporation arranging with one of their members, who was then in London, to buy the royalties of the dissolved bishopric of Wells and also of the deanery, desiring to get complete hold of the three Courts of Record that were held in Wells, and the income arising from the four fairs in the town, at Binegar and at Priddy.

When Burgess came to Wells he is said to have stripped the lead off the roof of the palace, and to have left nothing but the bare walls remaining. The deanery he chose as the house he intended to live in, and made certain additions to it, using the material he had taken from the palace. He was appointed preacher in the greater church in Wells, i.e. the cathedral church, but was very unpopular; the people of Wells did not value him highly as a preacher, and annoyed him by walking about in the nave during the time of his sermon. At the Restoration Canon Creighton was appointed to the vacant deanery. He was not, however, prepared to live in the dean's[324] house at first, and let it to a Mr. Giles Hunt on a lease for three years. Dr. Burgess still claimed the house, and ejected Mr. Hunt by main force. Burgess appears in the statement of his case, for he resisted Dean Creighton's authority in the court, to have asserted that the deanery had ceased to be Church property since the surrender of Dean Fitzwilliam in 1547. The details of the trial are not known, but Burgess lost his claim.

It was natural, after the restoration of Charles II, and when uniformity was attempted by the use of the revised Book of Common Prayer, that there should be again a disturbance of the clergy in the parishes in Somerset. There were still living some clergy who had been illegally expelled in 1642 and 1647, and these claimed the restoration of their benefices and compensation for their losses.

Among those holding office there were many good men who had been duly placed in charge of parishes, and who were conscientiously opposed to episcopacy and the English Order for Public Worship, and soon after 24 August 1662 we find the following Puritan ministers ejected, and in some cases imprisoned :—[325]

George Newton and Joseph Alleine of Taunton, John Norman of Bridgwater, Richard Allen of Batcombe, Samuel Cradock of North Cadbury, Richard Fairclough of Mells, Henry James of Chedzoy, Cornelius Burgess of Wells, William Thomas of Ubley, Mr. Long and

---

[322] Cf. Calamy, *Nonconf. Mem.* iii, 217.
[323] Cf. Chyle, 'Hist. of Cathedral,' quoted in Reynolds, *Wells Cath.* p. cxlii.
[324] Cf. *Hist. MSS. Com. Rep.* x, App. iii, 271.   [325] Calamy, *Nonconf. Mem.* iii, 166–226.

William Green of Bath, Thomas Creese of Combe Hay, John Arthur of Beckington, Mr. Alslot of Clutton, Harry Albin of West Camel, Mr. Thompson of Lullington, Mr. Parker of Stapleton, William Hopkins of Milborne, George Day of Wiveliscombe, Mr. Robinson of Porlock, William Alsop of Ilminster, George Pierce of North Curry, John Sacheverell of Wincanton, George Bindon of Wilton, Harry Butler of Yeovil, Timothy Butt of Ruishton, Emanuel Hertford of Upton Noble, James Stevenson of Martock, John Humfrey of Frome.

Mr. Samuel Winney of Glastonbury retired to Bristol, and Mr. Matthew Warren of Downhead[326] became the minister of a large congregation of Dissenters at Taunton. Many of these undoubtedly suffered great hardships both from the fact of their ejectment and because of the lawlessness of many who had come back to power, but there does not appear to have been anything done to them equal in cruelty to the Act of 1655 in preventing their gaining by other means an honest living or forbidding the charitable to take them into their houses.

The time between the passing of the Act and 24 August, when it was enforced, was one of great uncertainty as to how many of the ministers would conform.

Crooke of Wrington had passed away on 25 December 1649; his neighbour, William Thomas of Ubley,[327] was strongly urged to obey and accept the Book of Common Prayer. He found a difficulty in deciding as to whether he ought to give up that charge and parish where he had laboured so long and so faithfully. Bishop Piers was anxious to retain him, but on 21 August he made his decision. He had no wish to despise the Book of Common Prayer; 'I bless God,' he wrote; 'it is so good, but yet it might be better'; and he was allowed to preach on Sunday 24 August. From that day he ceased his ministration, becoming 'a hearer elsewhere.' He lived on amicable terms with his successor, James Whiteing, and died in 1667. Some of the clergy, such as John Norman of Bridgwater, and Joseph Allen or Alleine,[328] assistant to Mr. George Newton of Taunton, were imprisoned in Ilchester Gaol for unlicensed preaching, and it is certain that many suffered from the delight shown by the county justices in carrying out the vindictive laws of the Parliament of 1661.[329]

It was some time before the clergy and churchwardens were able thoroughly to furnish the churches that had been laid so bare during the Puritan domination. As late as October 1664, at the visitation of Stoke St. Gregory, the churchwardens had to confess that they had no white linen cloth for the holy table or surplice for the vicar. In one way certainly the Church benefited by the example set by the Puritans during the Commonwealth; there was an increased attention paid to preaching. In the cathedral church, since the Restoration, there have always been two sermons on Sunday.

Bishop Piers,[330] though he was restored to his bishopric, does not seem to have been very active. He was an old man, and had married a second

---

[326] Calamy, *Nonconf. Mem.* iii, 194.   [327] Ibid. 215.   [328] Neal, *Hist. of the Puritans*, iii, 164.

[329] The following ministers, who were deprived in 1662, afterwards conformed :—James Strong of Ilminster, John More of Aller, John Chetwind of Wells, Charles Dartz of Montacute, Dr. Martin of Yeovil, Mr. Tomkins of Crewkerne, and Mr. Oak of Ilchester ; Calamy, *Nonconf. Mem.* iii, 226.

[330] Cf. Cassan, *Lives of the Bishops of Bath and Wells*, 67.

time, and spent most of his time in his private house at Walthamstow in Essex, where he died in 1670, aged ninety-four.

On 15 March 1672 Charles II, whose leanings towards Roman Catholicism had been steadily growing, ventured to draw up a Declaration of Indulgence, and it was issued by order of the Council the same day.[331] He hoped to secure the loyalty of the Nonconformists in order that he might obtain some relaxation of the laws against the Papists. The Nonconformists certainly took advantage of it, and how strong was the influence of Nonconformity in Somerset during the earlier years of the reign of Charles II is shown by the fact that 82 licences were applied for, a number only exceeded by London and Devon, each of which had 105, Yorkshire coming next with 80, and no other county exceeding 55. Of these, 54 were for Presbyterian meetings, only 6 for Congregational or Independents (a number exceeded by eighteen counties), and 22 for Baptists, for which denomination Somerset ranks second only to Kent with 24.[332] At Curry Rivel, Shepton Mallet, and St. Mary Stoke were Nonconformist congregations whose sects are not defined.

In 1684 Bishop Peter Mews, a strong Royalist, was promoted from Bath and Wells to Winchester, and, as his successor, Charles II chose the saintly Thomas Ken, Fellow of Winchester College. Ken, though not born in the county, belonged to the family of Ken Court, near Clevedon. He was consecrated 25 January 1685, at Lambeth, by Archbishop Sancroft. At the time when he was chaplain to the Princess of Orange he boldly spoke out against the treatment by the prince of his wife, and at Winchester he was equally bold in refusing his house as a place in which the king might lodge his mistress, Eleanor Gwynne. Charles II, though he did not follow his advice, recognized his saintliness and admired his character. He was the last English clergyman to minister to him on his deathbed, urging him to repentance with a force which struck with wonder those who stood by.

The first year of his episcopate in Wells was troubled by the rebellion of James, Duke of Monmouth. There were many Puritans still existing in Taunton and Bridgwater and in the country villages of Somerset, and the welcome shown to Monmouth by the dissenting ministers and the people in the south-west of the county must naturally have caused anxiety to all who were on the king's side. On 4 May the duke was expected in Wells. He was proclaimed king at Taunton on 20 June. Then he marched to Bridgwater and Glastonbury, and on 23 June he was in Wells.[333] Here he was a second time proclaimed king. He hoped to seize Bristol, and moved forward towards Pensford and Keynsham; but when he found that Bath and Bristol were alike impossible, he retired through Norton St. Philip back to Wells, and his rebel force, disappointed of their hopes of sacking Bristol, showed their anger and hatred to the Church by spoiling the cathedral, which they

---

[331] *Cal. S.P. Dom.* 1671–2, pp. 203–4.   [332] Ibid. 1672–3, Pref. p. lv.

[333] In a letter from A. Paschall of Bridgwater to Robert Nelson, 14 Aug. 1686, Ken's work and the troubles of the times are thus described: 'Our good bishop in his visitation took up his lodging with me for two nights, which I took extremely kindly. He takes immense pains, and with great success, among the people. A clergyman called upon me this week and said on Sunday July 5, 1685, a man came from a parish about fifteen miles from him and spake to the people in the churchyard after they came out of church, and bade them go and help the Duke of Monmouth, who had got the king's army in a pound at Weston (Zoyland) and needed help lest they should get away. I mention it as an instance of the great diligence of the party.' Add. MSS. 30277.

did, no doubt, the more readily because the dean and chapter[334] had lent £100 to the Duke of Somerset, Lord Lieutenant, for the defence of the county. Soldiers were stabled in the nave, and tore the lead off the roof, and melted it into bullets; they pulled down the corner statues in the west front, and shot at those statues which were out of their reach. The mutilated statue of our Lord on the top still bears the marks of their bullets. Some were inclined to desecrate the altar, but Ford, Lord Grey of Wark, Lieut.-General to the duke, and Sir Gervase Gerome defended it with drawn swords.[335] On 1 July, the usual day for the chapter meeting, the chancellor, Thomas Holt, made the following entry in the Chapter Minute Book[336]:—

> The Civil War still grows. This Cathedral Church has suffered very grievously from the rebel fanatics, who have this very morning laid hands upon the furniture thereof, have almost utterly destroyed the organ, and turned the sacred building into a stable for horses. The chapter meeting is therefore adjourned to the 29th July, before which it is hoped that the nefarious rebels will be utterly put down.

An additional note was added afterwards :—

> Nor was the President of the Chapter deceived in his expectation, for that happy day the 6th July, put an end to the rebels at Weston Zoyland in this county. 'Deus, Deus nobis haec otia fecit.'

In the autumn[337] we find the following payments made in reference to the destruction wrought by the rebels :—

Mrs. Creighton was paid £20, being the money which was extorted from her by General Sam Story, the duke's commissary, under a threat that he would sack not only the cathedral church, but also the canons' houses. £4 was paid for a new silver verge to replace the one stolen by the rebels, and £10 was given to James Wilbe, sacrist, for his good services in having hid, and so preserved, the ornaments and plate of the church from the rebels.

After the battle of Sedgemoor, on 6 July, Bishop Ken did all he could to protect the prisoners from the cruelty of General Lord Feversham and Judge Jeffreys. In addition to the fugitives that were butchered on their way from Westonzoyland back to Bridgwater, at Taunton 134 were condemned to death, and at Wells 95.[338] Out of 320 who were put to death as the result of Judge Jeffreys' campaign in the west, 233 suffered in Somerset. The maids of Taunton[339] who had welcomed the duke and presented him with a banner and a Bible, did not escape the vengeance of the Government. Some of those involved were allowed to buy their pardon, but 800 from the west were sent as slaves to the West Indies. Bishop Ken's efforts on behalf of

---

[334] *Hist. MSS. Com. Rep.* x, App. iii, 264.

[335] *Lond. Gaz.* Thursday 2 July to Monday 6 July 1685. Whitehall, 4 July : 'The rebels marched from Shepton Mallet to Wells, where they robbed and defaced the Cathedral Church, drinking their villainous healths at the altar, plundered the town, ravished the women, and committed all manner of outrages.' Oldmixon, *Hist. of Engl.* 703 : 'The duke's soldiers, thinking some of the Cathedral men at Wells a little too impertinent, were somewhat free with their appurtenances, which I think was all the damage done by them.' *Historisch Genootschap Gevestigd de Utrecht, Werken,* 1863–6 (no. 2), 119 : 'Met een Expressen gisteren int'r Campement tot Bath is tijding, dat men aldaeradvys hadde dat de rebellen waren getrocken binnen de Stad Wells ; dat sij deselve hadden geplonderd ende het lood van de Kathedral kerke afgenomen om de kogels te gieten. Dat den Lord Gray dewelke Lt.-Generael van Monmouth is, met den bloote degen in de hand den Altaer hadde berschermd tegens de insulten en baldadigheden van semmigen onder haer en dat de rebellen daerna naer Glastonbury waren gemarcheerd.'

[336] *Hist. MSS. Com. Rep.* x, App. iii, 264.

[337] Ibid.

[338] Cf. *Somers. Arch. Proc.* xxxviii (2), 312.

[339] Cf. Toulmin, *Hist. of Taunton.*

these poor sufferers were the more conspicuous in that the majority of them were opposed to him as a bishop, and to the Church of England and its service. They would again have abolished the bishops as they had again mutilated the cathedral church. Years afterwards, when, in 1696, deprived of his see as a nonjuror, he was summoned before the Privy Council to justify his offence in collecting money for the relief of his destitute brethren who had been unable to take the oath of allegiance to William and Mary, he is said to have replied [340] :—

> My lords, In King James' time there were about 1,000 or more imprisoned in my diocese who were engaged in the rebellion of the Duke of Monmouth, and many of them were such that I had reason to believe to be ill men, and void of all religion, and yet for all that I thought it my duty to relieve them. It is well known to the Diocese that I visited them night and day, and I thank God I supplied them with necessaries myself as far as I could, and encouraged others to do the same, and yet King James never found the least fault with me.

Among those who were executed was John Hickes, a dissenting minister at Wells. A letter is extant from George Hickes, Dean of Worcester, the brother of the sufferer, which he wrote to Bishop Ken, asking his good offices on behalf of his unfortunate brother. The bishop did not get the letter till after the execution. He was away at Taunton, doing what he could to mitigate the cruelty of Judge Jeffreys. John Hickes was tried at Wells, and executed on 6 October at Glastonbury. In reply to his letter, Bishop Ken told his brother that he had already done all that he desired him to do, and ministered to the sick man in his last moments. His zeal on behalf of his poor, uneducated people in the diocese is shown in the two little books which he wrote, *The Practice of Divine Love* and the *Directions for Prayer*, which he compiled for their spiritual welfare.

He often went in the summer time to some great parish where he would preach twice, confirm and catechize. For the clergy he did what he could to furnish them with a stock of necessary books for the use of children, and encouraged the formation of parochial libraries within his diocese. His interest in the young caused him to set up many schools in all the great towns in his diocese for poor children to be taught to read and to say their Catechism. At Wells he much deplored the condition of the poor, and was very earnest in contriving proper experiments of relief; he is said to have advocated the erection of a model workhouse, not exactly one after the pattern of the present time, but an industrial institution where the poor might be supplied with work, and, by the sale of their productions, obtain an honest and fair livelihood.

Bath demanded his most serious attention. It was the head of English watering places ' without a rival,' and the resort of many wealthy invalids. Many also in good health flocked there from all parts of England in search of amusement. He issued, on their behalf, ' prayers for the use of all persons who come to the baths for cure.' The times were very critical for the English Church, the open adherence of James II to the Roman faith demanded from the bishop great caution as well as boldness of speech.

Queen Mary had been since the spring of 1687 taking the waters at Bath, and the king himself meditated a royal tour in the West of England that summer.

[340] Cf. Hawkins, *Life of Ken*, 48.

On Ascension Day Bishop Ken [341] preached in the abbey church at Bath, and his sermon was attacked by an Irish Jesuit. In August James himself went there, accompanied by his chaplain Huddleston. The Roman Catholics around him persuaded him to touch for the king's evil in the abbey church, and all the unusual ceremonies connected with the service caused great disturbance among the inhabitants. The next Sunday Bishop Ken preached in the abbey, explaining that the occasion was one of charity, and that what the king had done was not to be held to create a precedent. His eloquence greatly impressed and delighted the congregation, and confounded Huddleston and his royal bigot. [342]

The Dissenters of Taunton and the dissenting teachers in the county and the Presbyterians of Bath sent addresses to James thanking him for his Declaration of Indulgence, and the Roman Catholics and Nonconformists in Bath were so strong that it does not appear that Bishop Ken was able effectually to oppose them.

From Bath the king had purposed to go to Wells, but in September he gave up the plan, and his action made it clear that a serious crisis was drawing on.

On 17 February 1688 Bishop Ken wrote a pastoral letter to the diocese, calling on his clergy to imitate the example of St. Cyprian, to deprecate public judgement and to mourn for public provocation. The same year, on Friday, 8 June, the Archbishop, Sancroft, and the six bishops, of whom Ken was one, were summoned before the king in Privy Council because of their refusal to publish the Declaration of Indulgence, and because of the petition which they had sent up to James. Their imprisonment, trial, and acquittal belong to the general history of England. That autumn Bishop Ken seems to have spent most of the time with his friend George Hooper, vicar of Lambeth.

The month of November saw the arrival of William Prince of Orange and his wife Princess Mary, and the flight of James. The invading army passing through Somerset is said to have come to Wells, and Bishop Ken, on 24 November, wrote to the archbishop to explain why he had left the diocese in this juncture. A friend of the Princess Mary, he had lived with her as her chaplain in the early days of her marriage, and was anxious that he should not be suspected of any disloyalty to James. Therefore, as the Dutch had 'seized houses within 10 miles of Wells,' he retired to Wiltshire, probably to Poulshot, near Devizes, where his nephew, Isaac Walton, was rector. On hearing that the king had gone back from Andover to London, he said that he only waited till the Dutch had passed his diocese, when he resolved to return thither again, as being his proper station.

On 12 February 1689 Ken sat for the last time in the House of Lords. The next day the majority of the peers took the oath of allegiance to William and Mary. On 5 March the oath was tendered to and refused by

---

[341] Warner, *Bath*, 257.

[342] The poet laureate thus describes the action of the bishop during these years :—

> When to the Bath her royal highness came
> Kenn made the Abbey Church resound his fame ;
> Floods of grave eloquence did from him fall,
> Kenn in the pulpit thundered like St. Paul.
> Poem by Joseph Perkins, Latin Laureate, 1711.

Archbishop Sancroft, and Bishops Ken, Lake, Turner, Frampton, Lloyd, White, Thomas, and Cartwright. In April an Act was passed requiring public functionaries (ecclesiastical and lay) to take the oath on pain of dismissal. Suspension would follow on refusal, and if they persisted, six months later deprivation.

Ken's desire for peace brought suspicion upon him from some of his fellow nonjuring bishops. They were afraid that under the influence of George Hooper, vicar of Lambeth, who had taken the oath, he might be induced to change his mind, but Ken remained and waited for the time when he should be driven from Wells. In February 1690 Ken was still unmolested at Wells, and he remained here all that year. In the autumn of 1690 we find him drinking the waters at the king's bath at Bath. In April 1691 he was formally deprived.

In a pamphlet entitled *A Modest Enquiry into the Causes of the Present Disturbances*, he was singled out among the nonjuring bishops as one who was active in plotting for the invasion of England by the King of France and for bringing back James II. The pamphlet was written by a dissenting minister, and probably by one living in Somerset. Archbishop Sancroft and four of the nonjuring bishops, including Bishop Ken, drew up a vindication denying the charges made against them, and repudiating any intercourse or correspondence with the French government. The *Modest Enquiry* was extensively circulated, but the vindication was refused a licence for publication.

His successor, or as Ken called him his 'supplanter,' Dr. Kidder, Dean of Peterborough,[343] was consecrated on 30 August 1691. Bishop Ken delivered his formal protest in the cathedral church of Wells, publicly asserted his canonical right, saying that he regarded himself as the canonical bishop of the diocese, and that he was ready to perform his pastoral duties. From the cathedral he went to the market square in Wells and made the same declaration. Then he retired to Longleat, where his friend, Viscount Weymouth, who had formerly been a college companion, received him as a welcome guest, and there he remained for the rest of his life. With Ken there were two members of the chapter,[344] Walter Hart, prebendary of Ashill, and vicar of St. Mary's Taunton, and Samuel Thomas, vicar of Chard and prebendary of Compton Bishop, who refused to take the oath of allegiance, and among the parochial clergy nine certainly were deprived of their benefices on this account :—James Crossman, vicar of Banwell ; Matthew Bryant, rector of Limington ; Joseph Franklyn, rector of Locking ; Richard King, rector of Marston Bigot ; Robert Crouch, vicar of South Stoke ; Samuel Thomas, vicar of Chard ; Thomas New, vicar of Staplegrove ; Walter Hart, vicar of St. Mary's, Taunton, and Christopher Brown, vicar of Priston. Three or four others seem not to have waited for deprivation, but to have retired in 1691. The vicar of Chard, Samuel Thomas, was the son of William Thomas of Ubley, deprived for nonconformity in 1662. He was a friend of George Bull of Wells, who had gone to Ubley as a pupil of Thomas's father, the vicar. The difference of opinion between the father and the son was such that his father is said to have remarked that the son, Samuel Thomas, would corrupt Mr. Bull, and it is probable that the future Bishop of St. David's

[343] Congé d'élire, 11 June 1691 ; *Cal. S.P. Dom.* 1690–1, p. 409.   [344] Ibid. 389.

owed much of his staunch churchmanship to the example shown him by the son of the Puritan vicar of Ubley.

Bishop Ken took very little part in the councils of the nonjurors. He was anxious for peace, and desired to heal the schism whenever and as soon as ever it was possible. He died at Longleat on 19 March 1711, and is buried in the churchyard of St. John the Baptist, Frome.

Bishop Kidder [345] was extremely unpopular in Somerset. All through his episcopate he seems to have had a more or less continuous quarrel with the Wells Chapter ; an uncertain churchman, having accepted the see somewhat against his own judgement, and having often repented doing so, he seems to have calmed his conscience by little acts of stern rectitude, which failed to bring him any approval. His conduct in ordaining Mr. Mallarhé, who had been a Nonconformist and was probably a French Huguenot, without requiring a specific recantation of his former opinions, brought much displeasure upon him. He was killed with his wife in the terrible storm of the autumn of 1703, when a chimney in the palace was blown down and fell on him as he lay asleep in his bed.

The sufferings of the religious Society of Friends, known as the Quakers, during the reigns of Charles II and James II, were brought about partly because they would insist on preaching without a licence, and because, though ready to declare their allegiance, they would not swear to it, and partly because they had conscientious objections to the payment of tithes. When [346] in 1666 John Sage of Chewton Mendip, a passive resister to the demand for tithes, was sent to Ilchester Gaol, he found thus lodged in the old convent of Whitehall thirty-three companions all imprisoned for the same cause. One of the foremost of the Quakers was Jasper Batt, who for some years had escaped the efforts of the authorities. Bishop Mews spoke of him as 'the greatest seducer in the West, and the most seditious person in the County.' He was captured in 1679 at Stoke-sub-Hamdon. At the quarter sessions Sir Edward Phelips endeavoured to reason with him, but as he refused to swear allegiance he, too, was committed to Ilchester.

On 30 March 1686 the Quakers imprisoned at Ilchester ventured to petition the Chief Justice Herbert and Judge Wright when they went to Wells for the assize. They assured them of their loyalty, of the harmless character of their lives, and they pleaded for leniency in the punishments inflicted on them. The petitioners were sixteen in number, of whom two, Marmaduke Coat and William Liddon, had been in gaol fifteen years, John Parsons and John Chappel ten, Thomas Powell nine, John Whiting and John Allen nearly seven, Thomas Martin five ; Stephen Holder, Richard Grabham, Rufus Coram, more than four ; John Hipsley, Jasper Batt, Thomas Comb, and Edmund Chappel more than two ; and Vincent Boldy one year.

Whiting, in his Memorials, tells an interesting story of the visit of John Penn to Wells on 14 September 1694. They had been holding a meeting at Wrington, and Whiting went on to Wells to seek the bishop and ask permission to hold another in the city. Bishop Kidder asked him why they desired a place for meeting, and he replied that it was for the purpose of declaring the truth. So Bishop Kidder gave them permission to use the

[345] Cf. MS. Autobiography in Chapter Library, Wells.
[346] Cf. *Memoirs of the Suffering of John Whiting and many others called Quakers*, seriatim.

Market House, a building erected on pillars in the centre of the Market Place. The clerk of the market seems at first to have agreed to this assembly, but some of the envious party having been drinking Colonel Berkeley's election ale, talked over the clerk, and so at the end he refused to give up the room. They had, however, put up at the Crown Inn, and as there was a large room on the first story overlooking the Market Place, and the landlord was willing to permit it, they summoned all who would to assemble there. The bishop in the meantime had given them the necessary licence, and so the people retired from the Market Place, where Penn seems already to have begun to preach, and gathered in the upper room of the Crown Inn. During the meeting the constable and other officers came with a warrant from Matthew Baron, the mayor, to arrest William Penn, and only retired after they had been assured that the meeting was in order, and had been sanctioned by the lord bishop.

The death of Bishop Kidder made it possible for Queen Anne to invite Bishop Ken to assume again his post as Bishop of Bath and Wells, but on hearing that the queen had approached his friend, George Hooper, who like himself had ministered to the Princess of Orange in Holland, and was then Dean of Canterbury, Ken refused to take up the work of the diocese, and so George Hooper, with Ken's full consent, succeeded. His work in the diocese (1704–27) was such as Ken would have approved. He was beloved and esteemed[347] by the good and wise. His clergy were his family, his spiritual sons, and to them he was all gentleness. He encouraged them to reveal their wants, and, when necessary, his patronage and purse raised the distressed laborious and orthodox pastor to ease and competence.

Hooper's successors in the 18th century—Dr. John Wynne, bishop from 1727–43 ; Dr. Edward Willes, 1743–73 ; and Dr. Charles Moss, 1774–1802 —were not men of note.

Willes's chief claim for promotion was the fact that he held the office of decipherer to the king, and he is said to have recommended himself to the ministry of the day by certain evidence he gave concerning some handwriting, which in his trial was asserted to be that of Dr. Atterbury.[348] Lord Chesterfield is said to have given the advice to Edward Willes to 'patrisare,' i.e. 'do as your father did before you.' Willes left no literary remains, and was buried at Westminster Abbey. His successor, Charles Moss (1774–1802) is credited with having repaired a widows' almshouse in Wells, and with having amassed, chiefly from the revenues of the Church, a fortune of £140,000.

The religious history of the 18th century in Somerset is almost confined to the story of the rise of the Methodist body, its influence on the Church, and its efforts, with those of the Church people who were in partial sympathy with it, for education.

The repeal of the Schism Act and the Occasional Conformity Act in 1718 took away many of the disabilities under which the Nonconformists had been suffering, and they were thus able the more easily to show their zeal and win converts to their views.

In 1737 the Rev. George Whitefield had created a sensation in Bath—preaching in the abbey and other places to crowds attracted by his enthusiasm and eloquent style. His extravagances, however, soon offended the clergy of

[347] Cassan, *Lives of Bishops of Bath and Wells*, ii, 172. [348] Quoted in Cassan, *Life*, ii, 169.

the diocese, and with the exception of the vicar of Publow, who gave him the use of his church in 1739, nearly every church was closed to him.

At Bridgwater he was welcomed by the vicar of the parish, but the people furiously attacked him, and brought the fire-engine to pump upon him as he preached. In 1739 he made his first impression upon the miners at Kingswood, near Bristol, and having won their confidence, established there, by means of their offerings, the first charity school for the education of their children. It was in this year that Whitefield summoned to his assistance the Rev. John Wesley, who had lately returned from Georgia.

In his diary [349] on 30 April 1739 Wesley remarks the sensation he felt at preaching for the first time in unconsecrated ground : 'I could scarce reconcile myself at first to this strange way of preaching in the fields, of which he (Whitefield) set me an example on Sunday, having been all my life till very lately very tenacious of every point relating to decency and order that I should have thought the saving of souls almost a sin if it had not been done in a church.' In the spring or summer of that year Wesley preached many times in Bath. On 22 May he records of his audience that there were 'several fine, gay things among them.'

On 5 June it is evident that an opposition was being formed for the purpose of stopping the excitement which his preaching, following that of Whitefield, was creating. 'There was great expectation at Bath of what a noted man was to do to me there, and I was much entreated not to preach, because no one knew what might happen. When their champion appeared he asked me by what authority I did these things.' He said they were seditious meetings, and I said they were not. He replied, 'I say they are, and besides your preaching frightens people out of their wits.' 'Sir, did you ever hear me preach ?' I asked. 'No.' 'How then can you judge of what you never heard ?' 'Sir, by common report.' 'Common report is not enough. Give me leave, Sir, to ask is not your name Nash ?' 'My name is Nash.' 'Sir, I dare not judge of you by common report.'

The next month public opinion was influencing people against him. Richard Merchant had allowed him to preach on his ground, and now he said that he was obliged to refuse him permission. 'I have already, by letting you be here, merited the displeasure of my neighbours.'

From that year till September 1790 we find numerous instances recorded in his diary of his preaching in Bath. The fashionable world there seems to have weighed upon his mind, 'Hath God left Himself without witness ?' he writes in 1741, 'did He never raise up such as might be shining lights even in the midst of this sinful generation?' At times he records that there were noisy people making a disturbance, and again at times that some of the rich and great were present, and several of the gentry desired to speak at the meeting of the Society.

In 1764 he records that he allowed a woman to pray at his meeting, and he comments on her efforts as being ' odd and unconnected, made up of disjointed fragments, and yet like a flame of fire.' In 1765 he records preaching in Lady Huntingdon's chapel in Bath, and again in 1766, the year in which Horace Walpole heard him preach and was struck with his great power.

[349] *Extracts from Wesley's Diary*, 4 vols. 1903 (Wesleyan Conference Office).

In 1767 he seems more hopeful of his work at Bath. 'I know not where I have seen a more serious and more deeply attentive congregation ; is it possible, can the Gospel have place where Satan's throne is ?' In 1758 he encouraged his fellow Methodists to build a chapel in Bath.

On his last visit in September 1790, he records that he 'has dropped that vile custom of preaching three times a day by the same preacher to the same congregation ; enough to wear out both the body and mind of the speaker as well as hearers.'

At Taunton he preached at the Cross in 1743. A man had placed himself near in order to make some disturbance. The audience, however, were very angry with him. The next month the mayor-elect, a tradesman of the town, made so much noise that his gathering was broken up, but many followed him to the large room in his inn. In 1775 he records preaching in the great Presbyterian meeting-house to a brilliant congregation, and in 1785 he says 'there was a solemn awe sat upon the whole congregation, and God spoke to their hearts.'

At Frome he preached for the first time in 1753, describing the place as dry, barren, and uncomfortable. In 1767 he preached in a meadow there, where a multitude of all denominations attended, and he thought that God was at length giving a more general call to this town. The next year he was again, on visiting the town, struck with the variety of religious opinions of the people. He describes his congregation as a mixture of men of all opinions : Anabaptists, Quakers, Presbyterians, Arians, Antinomians, Moravians, and what not.

During the opposition shown towards his earlier visits to Frome two women were imprisoned for making a disturbance and another was fined £20 for allowing her house to be used for meetings, and as she was unable to pay, her goods were seized, and on another occasion the mob broke into the preaching-place and burnt the benches. His last visit there was in 1789.

At Bridgwater he appeared in 1746. 'The great vulgar endeavoured to stir up the small,' but apparently the people of the town were afraid of making a disturbance, the Grand Jury the week before his arrival having found a true bill against the rioters who had assaulted Mary Lockyer's house. He visited the town at regular intervals, and his last record is in 1769. At Wincanton he was welcomed in 1762, and seems to have greatly impressed the people at first, but in 1769 he records that the people there 'had just as much feeling as the benches on which they sat,' and the next year he describes it as ' one of the dullest places in all the county.'

At Ditcheat he invariably got a welcome ; there was no opposer in the town, but rich and poor all acknowledged the work of God.

At Shipham in 1782 (just seven years before Hannah More and her sister began their great educational work there) he writes :—

'I was surprised to see such a congregation at so short a warning, and their deep and serious attention seems to be a presage that some of them will profit by what they hear.'

At Chew Magna he was welcomed by the people, but the church was closed against him, and in 1784 he preached in the Methodist preaching-house there. At Midsomer Norton he appeared in 1767, and was invariably welcomed, and in 1789 he says, ' I never saw the church so full before.'

At Wells he preached in a private garden in 1739, and was fairly well received. In 1780, however, there seems to have been an attempt to stop him, as in September he records :—' The weather being so intensely hot we could not well bear the room, I preached on the shady side of the market-place. As I was concluding a sergeant of militia brought a drum, but he was a little too late. I pronounced the blessing, and quietly walked away.'

A strange incident happened to him at Mells in 1785. 'Just as I began to preach a wasp, though unprovoked, stung me upon the lip. I was afraid it would swell, so as to hinder me speaking, but it did not. I spoke distinctly nearly two hours in all, and was no worse for it.'

At Shepton Mallet in 1746 there was considerable opposition. A few drunken people made a disturbance, ' screaming out a psalm as soon as I began to preach, but our singing quickly swallowed up theirs.' In 1748 a hired mob attacked him with stones and dirt ; but in 1764 only one man seems to have opposed him. He preached constantly there till 1771, and seems to have lived down the opposition that he met with at first.

At Pensford in 1742 they brought a bull, and baited it and tried to drive it against him. Yeovil he visited in 1751, and Minehead on two occasions (in 1744 and 1745) as he was crossing from Devonshire to Wales by the packet-boat.

It cannot be said that the opposition was on the part of the Church. In many places he seems to have been welcomed at first, and the clergy probably stood aloof from him because they regarded his methods as unlicensed and against the usual Church order.

In 1776, at Shepton Mallet, though the Methodists had now become established as a religious body, the rector cheerfully granted the use of the church, and in 1785 Wesley records how that the curate, Mr. Sims, ' read prayers for me, and read them admirably well, and the church was filled with a numerous congregation.' At Chew Magna in 1784 he was told that the church was at his disposal, but when he arrived there they said that they had changed their mind.

His desire to keep in touch with the Church of England is shown in the controversy he had at Bath in 1779. Mr. Smith, a clergyman from the north of Ireland, seems to have been staying at Bath with his wife for her health, and Wesley had asked him to preach in the Methodist Chapel every Sunday evening. He had no sooner gone, however, than Mr. McNab, one of the Methodist preachers, vehemently opposed this offer, speaking all manner of evil against Mr. Smith, and apparently the Methodist Society at Bath was on the side of Mr. McNab. The breach that Wesley had created, for he did not give way, was not healed for more than two years afterwards.

Among the clergy of the diocese who sympathized with him was the curate of South Petherton, Dr. Thomas Coke, who was curate there in 1775. Wesley records of him that on visiting Kingston on one occasion when he had been preaching at Taunton in 1776 he met in the parsonage-house there Dr. Coke, who came 20 miles on purpose to see him. 'I had much conversation with him, and a union then began which I trust shall never end.'

The next year he records (in 1777) that Dr. Coke having been dismissed from his curacy, ' had determined to cast in his lot with us.' Dr. Coke had been preaching at South Petherton vigorous revival sermons to overflow congregations, and it was a great disappointment to the parishioners when, on one Sunday, after they had gathered together at the parish church to hear him, the vicar informed them that Dr. Coke would be allowed to preach no more in the church. However, in 1782, he revisited his old parish and was allowed to preach in the church, where a large number (computed at upwards of 1,000 souls) listened eagerly to what he said. On this occasion he was saluted by a joyful, not an ironical, peal from the old church tower. ' We rung him out,' said the inhabitants, ' and now we will ring him in.'

For the last two centuries schools had been increasing in number in the county, and during the 18th century some fifty schools had been founded for the education of the children of the poor.

Miss Hannah More[350] and her sister did admirable work in the Mendip district from 1789 to 1828, starting schools at Cheddar, Nailsea, Shipham, and Wedmore, and doing much to promote Sunday schools after the manner of those at Gloucester carried on by Mr. Robert Raikes.

The opposition at first was caused by a misunderstanding ; the movement was suspected of Methodism, and near Bridgwater one of the local gentry,[351] ' who is very rough and very brutal,' gave her to understand that religion was the most unsettling thing in the world for the poor ; ' it made them lazy and useless.' At Cheddar the benefice was held by one ' who has something to do, but I cannot here find out what, in the University of Oxford, where he resides. The curate lives at Wells twelve miles distant.' At Axbridge the vicar ' is intoxicated about six times a week, and very frequently is prevented from preaching by two black eyes honestly caused by fighting.' The efforts of Miss Hannah More at Blagdon were nearly ruined by clerical jealousy. The Rev. Thomas Bere, the curate there, had considerable local influence from the fact that he was one of the county magistrates. His rector was non-resident, and he was apparently all-powerful. He declared he would set up an evening service in the church in order to ruin the class, and he tried to arouse the farmers to present the school at the next visitation of the bishop as a harmful influence which disseminated French principles. He accused the master of immorality, and he succeeded in reducing the number of the scholars from more than two hundred to something between twenty and thirty. Bishop Beadon, however (1802–24), who succeeded a somewhat easy-going predecessor, Bishop Moss, thoroughly approved of the work, and did all he could to support her, and though Bere was able to close the school in 1800 it was opened again in 1802. In 1801 Miss Hannah More[352] appealed to Bishop Beadon, professing her loyalty to the Church and to the Establishment, and in reply he said :—[353] ' So far from desiring that your remaining schools should be abolished I heartily wish them success, and you may assure yourself they will have my protection and every encouragement I can give them.'

During the last century there has been a steady increase in the number of churches, which has almost kept pace with the increase of the population. This important work has been greatly promoted by the Diocesan Church Building Society, started by Bishop Law in 1836. This movement has provided more than £40,000 towards this object, and the Curates' Fund, founded in 1838,

[350] Cf. *Memoirs of H. More,* 1838.
[352] Ibid. 275.
[351] Cf. Miss H. More's letter to Mr. Wilberforce, ibid. 183.
[353] Ibid. 289.

and the Bath and Wells Diocesan Society for the education of poor children in the principles of the Established Church, which was founded in 1812 and restarted in 1838, have largely helped in meeting the needs of the Church of England in the county of Somerset. The yearly meetings of a Diocesan Conference, begun in 1870 by Bishop Hervey, have also largely contributed to promote the welfare of the Church and the cause of religion in the diocese.

APPENDIX I

LIST OF DEPRIVATIONS ON THE RETURN OF THE ROMAN PARTY TO POWER, 1554-7 [354]

Date	Name	Parish	Folio of Epis. Reg. Bourne
—	Bishop : Barlow, William	Bath and Wells	—
—	Dean : Turner, William	Wells	—
—	Archdeacon : Cretyng, Walter	Bath	—
October 1554	Prebendary : Williams, Henry	Bedminster	15
May 1554	Woodroff, William	Ashbrittle	4
June ,,	Wattes, Richard	Beer Crocombe	6
,, ,,	Trebyll, Thomas	Brompton Ralph	5
,, ,,	Webb, John	Buckland St. Mary	6
September 1554	Webster, Christopher	Burnham	13
May 1554	Tryvet, John	Butleigh	3
June ,,	Tybott, William	Camely	6
,, ,,	Stote, William	Camerton	6
,, ,,	Clausie, John	Chaffcombe	5
July ,,	Hoskyns, John	Charlcomb	9
May ,,	Mason, Nicholas	Chedzoy	3
October 1554	Stakelyns, Ralph	Chelvey	15
September 1554	Dogyon, George	Chew Magna	13
October ,,	Wickham, James	Chew Stoke	15
June 1554	Guy, John	Chewton Mendip	6
May 1555	Haydon, Edward	Clapton	18
June 1554	Nicols, John	Closworth	5
November 1554	Broke, Edward	Compton Dando	16
June 1556	Kynsey, Thomas	Compton Martin	5
May 1554	Welshe, John	Curry Mallet	4
September 1554	Webbe, John	Eastham	13
July 1554	Scott, William	Fivehead	8
,, ,,	Langford, John	Freshford	8
,, ,,	Tytherley, John	Hatch Beauchamp	9
,, ,,	Austwayte, Richard	Holton	9
September 1554	Webbe, Thomas	Hutton	12
June 1554	Lock, Thomas	Ilminster	5
March 1555	Sydenham, Hugo	Ilton	21
August 1554	Paslow, John	Isle Abbots	9
May 1554	Lyons, Stephen	Isle Brewers	4
August 1554	Harwyke, Ambrose	Keinton Mandeville	11

[354] Dixon in his *Church History* gives also as ejected in April and May, 1554 :—Chancellor, Taylor *alias* Cardmaker ; and five prebendaries, Robert Keamys of White Lackington, John Faber of Timberscombe, William Wrytheosley of Litton, George Carew of Barton, Thomas Trewbodye of Combe.

LIST OF DEPRIVATIONS (*continued*)

Date	Name	Parish	Folio of Epis. Reg. Bourne
June 1554	Dawks, Thomas	Kewstoke	5
May 1555	Hatch, Christopher	Keynsham	18
October 1554	Rodberd, William	Kingsbury	15
September 1554	Laws, Ralph	Kingweston	12
November 1556	Eire, Robert	Langridge	30
„ 1554	Marshal, Thomas	Litton	16
June 1556	Andrew, John	Lyng	20
July 1554	Jenyson, William	Marksbury	9
„ „	Worthy, Reginald	Marston Bigot	9
June „	Harres, Adam	Martock	6
October 1554	Fox, Thomas	Middlezoy	15
August „	Magge, Thomas	Midsomer Norton	11
July 1554	Smyth, Richard	North Barrow	8
June „	Pyers, William	North Cheriton	6
November 1554	Austyn, Richard	North Curry	16
August 1554	Rose, John	North Petherton	12
May „	Genyng, Thomas	Norton Fitzwarren	3
August „	Hodgson, William	Norton Malreward	11
June 1554	Hartly, Ralph	Norton-sub-Hamdon	5
March 1554	Marlex, John	Nynehead	17
June 1554	Herre, William	Oare	5
May „	Dun, Humfrey	Pawlett	4
July „	Fisepool, John	Podimore Milton	8
April 1556	Sandeford, Nicholas	Portbury	23
September 1554	Pollard, John	Portishead	13
„ „	Coles, John	Priston	13
July 1554	Reynolds, James	Pylle	8
May 1555	Slatter, Reginald	Rowberrow	18
May 1554	Brown, Alexander	St. Decumans	4
August 1554	Parker, Thomas	Saltford	12
February 1554	Rawe, Thomas	Shepton Beauchamp	17
May 1554	Rodberd, William	Somerton	4
August 1554	Jurye, Thomas	Spaxton	10
July „	Loketon, Edward	Stogumber	7
November 1556	Goldwyn, William	Stogursey	30
June 1554	Clegge, William	Stoke Trister	6
September 1554	Morgan, Thomas	Stratton-on-the-Fosse	13
October 1554	Cresse, John	Sutton Montis	15
June 1554	Whitchurch, Thomas	Tellisford	6
August 1554	Ling, Richard	Thorn Coffin	11
July 1554	Walter, Owen	Tickenham	9
June „	Crosse, John	Tolland	6
August 1554	Lane, Peter	Weare	11
„ „	Smyth, John	Wedmore	12
March 1554	Mason, Nicholas	Wembdon	17
May 1554	Smyth, John	West Camel	—
August 1554	Hopkins, Simon	West Coker	12
March „	Blonde, Ralph	West Dowlish	17
July „	Moore, John	West Monkton	7
October „	Cresse, John	Weston Bampfylde	15
August 1554	Smyth, John	Weston in Gordano	11
July 1554	Came, John	Winscombe	7
March 1554	Green, Christopher	Winsham	17
September 1554	Netheway, Richard	Wraxall	13
May 1554	Dey, Thomas	Yeovilton	2

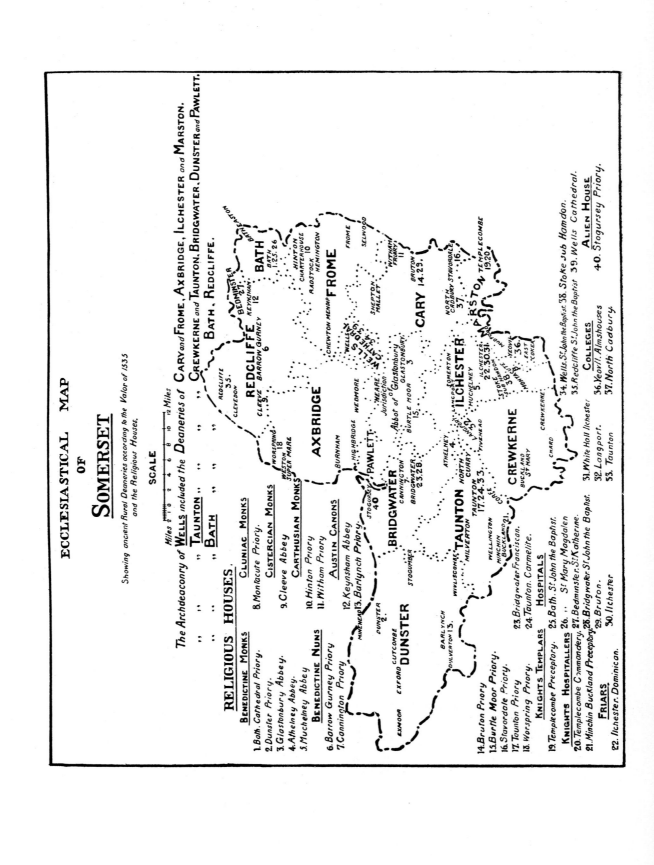

NOTES

Address Your postcode may not be quoted in full. This is only a temporary measure because the correct full postcode was not given. Please supply your full postcode when you next have occasion to send in the Registration Document so that it can be included in your vehicle record.

The county has been omitted from most addresses by arrangement with the Post Office. This should not affect delivery because of the special arrangements by which the Driver and Vehicle Licensing Centre presents mail to the Post Office.

Vehicle Details Only the details appropriate to your type of vehicle will be shown. In particular, seating capacity and unladen weight will often not need to appear. For vehicle registration purposes the vehicle type and colour are described in the manufacturer's basic terms only and may not match his full description.

VIN is short for Vehicle Identification Number. This is a unique identifier currently being introduced by manufacturers which is expected to replace the chassis number of most vehicles.

Please query what is given only if it is clearly wrong.

Number of Former Keepers If the vehicle was registered before 1 October 1974 or was not new when first registered, the number of former keepers is counted only from the date on which the centralised record was set up. The vehicle keeper may obtain any available details of previous registered keepers free of charge on request from DVLC, Swansea, SA99 1AN.

10.000 M 56-2579-32B 5/82 MP

1. The Registration Document for your vehicle is enclosed.

2. Please check the details shown on the document. If they are correct keep it in a safe place. If there is any mistake or if you have any query not covered by the notes overleaf return the document to DVLC, Swansea, SA99 1AR with a letter saying what is wrong.

NOTE: Taxation Class

A new taxation class structure was announced in the 1982 budget which affects most vehicle keepers . Goods vehicles weighing over 1525 kg unladen are now taxed according to gross weight and axle configuration and fall into one of the HGV taxation classes. Goods vehicles whose unladen weight does not exceed 1525 kg are now taxed at the same rate as private vehicles and both categories now fall into a new taxation class called Private/Light Goods (PLG). This change is included on the enclosed Registration Document. Vehicle licence discs and Registration Documents issued before the change do **NOT** need amendment.

3. If you change your name and/or address, or vehicle particulars, or scrap or export the vehicle please comply with the instructions on the reverse of the document. If you sell or transfer the vehicle complete the 'Notification of Sale or Transfer' slip as instructed on the document. Give the top part to the new keeper so that he can use it to notify acquisition.

APPENDIX II

ECCLESIASTICAL DIVISIONS OF THE COUNTY

Few English dioceses have preserved their ancient boundaries so completely as that of the Wells bishopric. Bounded on the north by the River Avon, and on the far west by the highlands of Exmoor, the diocese and the county of Somerset have been almost conterminous. In 1540 the diocese of Bristol was created, the church of the Austin Canons at Bristol being named (4 June) the cathedral church. It consisted of the county of Bristol and the county of Dorset, and in the county of Bristol the parishes of Bedminster and Redcliffe, hitherto in the diocese of Wells. Then, in 1836, when the dioceses of Bristol and Gloucester were united, Bedminster and Redcliffe were given back to Wells, but in an Order of Council, 19 July 1837, it was decided that on the demise of the then bishop, George Henry Law, Bedminster and Redcliffe were again to be added to the diocese of Bristol, and this took effect in 1845. At the present time the parish of Brislington, which is wholly in the diocese of Bath and Wells, finds half of its area incorporated in the boundaries of the city of Bristol. The boundaries of Somerset and of the diocese of Wells on its eastern side have slightly changed. In 909 the city of Bath was on Mercian territory, and, therefore, was not included in the new West Saxon diocese, and there is evidence of an eastern boundary of the county farther west than the present; but from the earliest days the Forest of Selwood seems to have formed the acknowledged, as it certainly was the natural, boundary on that side.

The division of the diocese into the three archdeaconries of Bath, Wells, and Taunton has been already dealt with, but the date at which these were subdivided into rural deaneries is not known. By the end of the 13th century, however, these divisions were fully established, and in the *Taxatio* of 1291 the archdeaconry of Bath contained the deaneries of Bath and Redcliffe; the archdeaconry of Wells the deaneries of Frome, Cary, Marston, Axbridge, Ilchester, and so much of Pawlett as was not in the jurisdiction of the Abbot of Glastonbury; the archdeaconry of Taunton comprised the deaneries of Bridgwater, Dunster, Taunton, and Crewkerne. It would seem that in this diocese the office of rural dean was held by the incumbents of the benefices within the deanery in regular rotation, and not by a special grant from the bishop. Thus in the ordination of the vicarage of Keynsham in 1404, it was stipulated that the vicar should serve as rural dean 'in his turn.'[355] The exact order of rotation in Bridgwater deanery between 1607 and 1632 has been preserved, and shows that each incumbent held office in turn for one year.[356] This list is also evidence for the continuation of the office during the first half of the 17th century; it, however, subsequently fell into disuse, and appears to have been revived by Bishop Law in 1842, and by his successor, Lord Auckland, who divided some of the larger deaneries and increased their number. The present occupant of the see has slightly reduced the number of rural deans, and there are now twenty-six deaneries in the three archdeaconries.

As late as 1810 the jurisdiction of the bishop was largely hampered by the existence of 'peculiars,' parishes that were subject to some special jurisdiction of the patrons, of the dean and chapter, or of the Crown.

The following were peculiars of the dean and chapter :—Cheddar, Lovington, South Barrow, Combe St. Nicholas, Winsham, Long Sutton, Bishop's Lydeard, North Curry.

The peculiars of the dean were :—Aller, Biddisham, Mark, Wedmore, Westbury, Broomfield, Nether Stowey, Dinder, Evercreech, Carhampton, Binegar, Chilcompton.

The Archdeacon of Wells :—Pitney, Huish Episcopi.

The Archdeacon of Taunton :—Bathealton, Milverton, and Thorne St. Margaret.

The Dean and Chapter of Bristol :—Banwell, Churchill.

The patron :—Barrow Gurney, Publow.

The rector :—West Lydford.

Royal peculiar :—Ilminster.

Wm. Beckford, esq. :—Witham Friary.

All the prebendal churches were peculiars of the prebendaries holding those stalls.

[355] *Somers. Rec. Soc.* xiii, 46. [356] *Somers. and Dorset N. and Q.* vi, 45–6.

THE RELIGIOUS HOUSES OF SOMERSET

INTRODUCTION

THE houses for Benedictine monks in Somerset were all, with the exception of Dunster, which was a cell of Bath, of great antiquity and importance. Glastonbury claims a longer continuous monastic occupation than any other site in England; and the abbeys of Bath, Athelney and Muchelney were all founded before the Norman Conquest.

The Benedictine nuns had establishments at Barrow Gurney and Cannington. The Cluniacs were settled at Montacute and the Cistercians at Cleeve.

At Witham was founded the first English house of the austere order of Carthusians, who had also a second monastery in the county at Hinton.

The less strictly monastic order of Austin Canons had seven houses in Somerset, of which Bruton, Keynsham, and Taunton were the most important, the others being at Barlynch, Burtle Moor, Stavordale and Worspring. There was also a short-lived priory of this rule at Buckland in Durston. It is possible that the sisters of the Hospital of White Hall, Ilchester, belonged to this order, but in the absence of definite evidence their house is here treated as a hospital.

The military order of the Knights Templars had a preceptory at Templecombe, which passed on the dissolution of the Templars to the Hospitallers, who had also a commandery or preceptory at Buckland. Attached to this latter was the only house in England for women belonging to the order of the hospital.

The Dominican Friars settled at Ilchester, the Franciscans at Bridgwater, and the Carmelites made an abortive attempt to establish themselves in Taunton.

Of hospitals the most important were those at Bath, Bedminster, Bridgwater, Wells and White Hall, Ilchester. Others, apparently unendowed lazar houses, existed at Langport, Ilchester, Taunton and probably elsewhere, while at Yeovil almshouses were founded in 1476 for twelve paupers under a warden with two assistant officers in connexion with a chantry.[1] There was also a hospital of St. John the Baptist at Glastonbury closely connected with the abbey, and other monasteries may have maintained similar establishments.

The chief collegiate church in the county was the cathedral of Wells,

---

[1] Inq. a.q.d. 17 Edw. IV, no. 61.

connected with which were the college of vicars choral and the college of chantry priests called New Hall. There were colleges also at Stoke-under-Hamdon, or Stoke-sub-Hambdon, and North Cadbury, while at Puckington there was a semi-collegiate chantry founded by Gilbert de Knovill in 1301, consisting of four chaplains, of whom the chief was called the archpresbyter.[2]

The only alien house which was not made denizen in Somerset was the priory of Stogursey, a cell of the Norman abbey of Lonlay.

Examples of the solitary orders of hermits and anchorites, if not so frequent as in some counties, are not uncommon. Hermits are mentioned at Winscombe[3] and Glastonbury[4] in 1335, and an anchoress at Twerton about the same date.[5] In 1328 a case occurs of a man apparently passing from the less rigid order of hermits to the strictly secluded position of an anchorite, becoming 'inclusus' in the hermitage of Worth in Aller parish.[6] A century later, in 1420, a Franciscan friar received papal licence to retire to a cell or hermitage near the Hospitallers' house of Buckland.[7]

BENEDICTINE HOUSES

1. THE CATHEDRAL PRIORY OF BATH

Our first English notice of Bath is the statement in the charter, which certainly does not come down to us in its original form, how Osric[8] the under-king of the Hwiccas in the kingdom of Mercia gave to Bertana the abbess[9] one hundred manentes of land adjacent to the city of Bath for the erection there of a monastery of holy virgins. The charter is dated 6 November 676. An Osric who was a follower and perhaps nephew of Ethelred King of Mercia founded the monastery at Gloucester[10] in 681 and this may be the same as the founder of the nunnery at Bath.

Another charter[11] concerning Bath records the gift by Æthelmod with the consent of King Ethelred of Mercia of some land on the River Cherwell to the venerable abbess Bernguidis and to Folcburga. The charter is attested by Archbishop Theodore who died in 690, and is probably of the year 681. Folcburga was doubtless the under abbess or prioress.

The nuns appear no more. In 758 Cynewulf King of the West Saxons[12] with the consent of Offa King of Mercia granted five manentes of land at North Stoke to the monks and to

their monastic church of St. Peter. It has been supposed that the monastery which Osric founded was a double monastery for monks and nuns, but there is no evidence for the supposition.

This new foundation of monks was made dependent on Hæthored, Bishop of Worcester; but he seems to have offended Offa King of Mercia, who claimed that the grant made by Æthelbald of Mercia to Hæthored, or his predecessor, of the land at Bath was not in perpetuity but only for a life, either that of Æthelbald or of the predecessor of Hæthored. So at the Synod of Brentford[13] in 781, Hæthored gave back to Offa all that 'celebrated monastery' at Bath, and south of the river the land he had bought from Cynewulf King of the West Saxons.

So Bath becomes part of the royal demesne of Offa and we hear no more of the monastery for two hundred years. William of Malmesbury[14] in the 12th century says that Offa founded the monastery there, and Leland[15] records the tradition that he founded there a college of secular priests. Offa may have rebuilt the church and reconstituted the body of clergy which served in it.

The gifts from the West Saxon monarchs begin with Æthelstan (925-40)[16] who bestowed upon St. Peter the Apostle and the 'venerable family' which is located æt Bathum lands at Cold Ashton and Priston. Edmund (940-94)[17] gave Tidenham, Bathford, Corston, Bathamp-

[2] *Cal. Pat.* 1301-7, p. 3. Presentations of these archpresbyters occur in the Epis. Regs. of Bishops Drokensford and R. of Shrewsbury, *passim.*

[3] *Somers. Rec. Soc. Publ.* ix, no. 279.

[4] Ibid. no. 934.   [5] Ibid. no. 1132.

[6] Ibid. i, p. 284.

[7] *Cal. Papal Letters,* vii, 182.

[8] Bede, *Eccl. Hist.* iv, cap. 23.

[9] Kemble, *Codex Dipl.* no. xii.

[10] Dugdale, *Monasticon* i, 541; *Gloucester Chartulary* (Rolls Ser.), i, p. lxxi.

[11] Birch, *Cart. Sax.* i, no. 57.   [12] Ibid. no. 327.

[13] Kemble, *Codex Dipl.* no. clxiii; Haddan and Stubbs, *Church Councils,* iii, 438.

[14] Will. of Malmesbury, *Gest. Pontif.*(Rolls Ser.),194.

[15] Leland, *Coll.* (ed. 1774), i, 84.

[16] Hunt, *Two Chartularies of Bath* (Somers. Rec. Soc. vii), 8.

[17] Ibid. 153.

ton and lands at Weston, and Edwy (955–9) gave again Corston and Bathampton. The exact tenure of these lands is somewhat obscure. Some of the lands granted by Edmund seem to have reverted to the Crown, for Edwy is said to have given Corston to one of the ladies of his court, Ælfswyda; and part of Bathampton to one of his faithful attendants Hehelm, and again he grants 'meo sacerdoti Wulfgar' lands at Tidenham and Bathford.[18]

Under Edgar (944–75) took place the great monastic reform of Archbishops Dunstan[19] of Canterbury and Oswald of York, and Bath may have been affected. Now we hear for the first time of the head of the clergy as an abbot and Abbot Æscwig[20] may have been appointed as the head of a new family of priests organized on stricter monastic principles. Here on Whitsunday 11 May 973, Archbishops Dunstan and Oswald took part in the solemn crowning of King Edgar. The anonymous life of St. Oswald[21] gives us minute details of the service in the church, but does not mention a monastery or an abbot.

About the year 980 Ælpheah, generally known as St. Elphege,[22] came to Bath from the monastery of Deerhurst, dissatisfied with the laxity and worldliness which prevailed there. At first he lived in a cell apart from the other religious as a hermit rather than as a monk. But soon his fame for sanctity was noised abroad and many flocked to consult and to live near him. Certainly this seems to be the beginning of a monastery. Though he did not forsake his cell he seems to have had the administration of the funds which the endowments of St. Peter's Church provided and he appointed a provost to arrange for the maintenance of those who had gathered round him.[23] After a time many fell away, wandering in the town and giving themselves up to drunken habits.

St. Elphege could not have been in Bath for many years. In 983 he was appointed Bishop of Winchester, and in 1012 Archbishop of Canterbury, in which year he also fell a martyr to the Danes.[24]

During the reign of Æthelred (979–1016) a certain Wulfaru[25] bequeathed 'into Badum to sancte Petres mynstre' certain mass robes, two gilt crosses and sixty gold marks and to Abbot

Ælfere, whose name we only meet with on this occasion, land at Freshford. To our confusion also we find in the first half of the 11th century two abbots at the same time, whatever their functions may have been. Wulfwold was abbot in 1061 when Edward the Confessor gave him— 'meo abbati'—a phrase which seems to indicate a special relationship to the king—land at Ashwick with right to bequeath it to whom he would.[26] On his death[27] he gave it and an estate at Evesty to St. Peter's minster. While Wulfwold was abbot we meet with Ælfig, also described as abbot,[28] and Ælfig is succeeded by Sewold, Wulfwold being still alive, and then Ælfsige succeeds Sewold and in 1084 Wulfwold and Ælfsige are mentioned together.[29] Then Wulfwold died and Ælfsige ruled alone until 1087, when his death opened the way for the union of the monastery with the bishopric of Wells. In the Domesday[30] record of the lands of the church of Bath Wulfwold and Sewold are both mentioned as abbots in 1066, Wulfwold being entered as abbot T.R.E. in reference to Evesty in Wellow, and Sewold, also as abbot T.R.E., in reference to Corston.

The post which Wulfwold held in Bath and which he vacated by his death soon after 1084 was not filled up and in 1087 his colleague Abbot Ælfsige also died.[31] The church of Bath was thus bereft of both its abbots when William Rufus succeeded to the throne of England. Early in the summer of 1088 the bishopric of Wells[32] also became vacant through the death of Bishop Giso.

In 1088 William Rufus conferred the bishopric on John de Villula, a native of Tours[33] and a rich and skilled physician, and he was consecrated by Archbishop Lanfranc in July of the same year. Immediately afterwards and with the help of Archbishop Lanfranc[34] the king made Bishop John a grant of the abbey of Bath and all its endowments in augmentation of the income of his bishopric. At the time perhaps the gift was of little value, for in the summer of 1088 Bath had been burnt by Robert de Mowbray,[35] and Bishop John received a ruined church and devastated estates. The gift, however, facilitated the transfer of the bishopric from Wells to Bath, and this was made forthwith under sanction apparently of the king and the archbishop.[36]

---

[18] Hunt, *Two Chartularies of Bath* (Somers. Rec. Soc. vii), 15, 21, 22.
[19] Cf. *Memorials of St. Dunstan* (ed. Stubbs, Rolls Ser.), p. cvi.
[20] Hunt, op. cit. 30; Kemble, *Codex Dipl.* no. dlxvi.
[21] Raine, *Lives of the Archbishops of York* (Rolls Ser.), i, 436–9.
[22] Osbern's 'Vit. Elphegi' *Angl. Sac.* ii, 123.
[23] Ibid—'delegato qui eis victualia ferret idoneo praeposito.' [24] *Angl. Sac.* ii, 141.
[25] Hunt, *Two Chartul.* 32.

[26] Hunt, *Two Chartul.* 34.
[27] Ibid. 35. [28] Ibid. 19. [29] Ibid. 37.
[30] *V.C.H. Somers.* i, 460.
[31] Flor. Wigorn, *Chron.* (Engl. Hist. Soc.) ii, 19.
[32] *Angl. Sac.* i, 559.
[33] Will. of Malmesbury, *Gesta Pontif.* (Rolls Ser.), 195.
[34] *Cal. Wells D. and C. MSS.* (Hist. MSS. Com.) I, 13; Dugdale, *Mon.* ii, 266.
[35] *Chron. Anglo-Petrib,* anno 1088; Flor. Wigorn, *Chron.* same year.
[36] Bishop John's Charter, *Mon.* ii, 268.

Neither the canons of Wells nor the monks of Bath were consulted, though the change affected both very seriously.

In addition to this grant of the church and its endowments the bishop obtained by purchase or by a bribe a grant of the city of Bath [37] so that the city of Bath should be as the vill of Wells his own property as bishop of the see. There were thus three grants made to John de Villula. There was the gift of the church of Bath [38] and its endowments made in 1088. Then followed immediately the licence to transfer the bishopric from Wells [39] to Bath and assume the title of Bishop of Bath instead of that of Bishop of Wells, and lastly in 1091 there was the transaction which ended in his obtaining possession of the city of Bath.[40] This grant Bishop John was careful to have confirmed by Henry I[41] in 1101, for which he paid the sum of five hundred pounds of silver.

Thus the church of Bath was raised to the rank of a cathedral church and the monks attached to it were brought into close relationship to their abbot bishop.[42] William of Malmesbury has little to say of Bishop John de Villula to his credit.[43] He was accused of having confiscated the monastic endowments and clung to them even on the approach of death. Certainly he met with opposition and he acted in a somewhat high-handed manner. The monks resented what seemed like a confiscation and he did not consult them in the management of their endowments as perhaps their abbots had. He saw in them the enemies of reform and he counted them as ignorant and of barbarous habits. As opportunities occurred he sent away English monks and filled their places with his Norman friends.

It was a time of great reform and magnificent building schemes, and in Bath the bishop seems to have been busy in both directions. The small family of monks under his fostering direction developed into a well-organized monastery with the new officers, called obedientiaries. The ignorance which had prevailed gave place to literary activity, and it has been claimed as under his abbotship that the scholar Adelard or Æthelhard of Bath acquired the knowledge that made him famous.[44] When the monastery was reorganized there in 1106 Bishop John began to place in the hands of the monks the estates which

he had managed for them. He obtained also for them an estate of five hides at Weston which King Edmund had given the church and which had been lost, and he also procured for them the manors[45] of Claverton, Dogmersfield, Batheaston, Warleigh and Arnwood (Hernewuda on the Sea). The enumeration of these estates is somewhat perplexing. During the next fifty years some disappear and are not recovered and to trace their fate seems beyond our province.

Like most contemporary bishops, John de Villula had great building schemes, and for this purpose he devoted the revenues he derived from the city as well as those he could save from the endowments of the church.[46] On a scale much larger than the earlier churches he set about rebuilding the abbey church [47] and had completed it as far as the lower vaultings before his death. His influence seems to have brought to the monks the assistance of two great Norman barons of Somerset. William de Moion [48] gave them the church at Dunster and all that belonged to it, and Walter de Douai [49] gave the church of Bampton in Devonshire and half a hide of land. The bishop also built for himself something more than an abbot's lodging. [50] It was outside the monastery and was known as the Bishop's Bower, and Leland [51] said that when he visited the place one great tower still remained amid the rapidly increasing ruins.

It was impossible with the care of all the diocese on his shoulders that he could supervise the internal affairs of the monastery, and he gave the monks as their especial ruler a prior, about whom we only know that he was a Norman and that his name was John.[52]

On 29 December 1122 [53] John de Villula died and was buried in his cathedral church before the altar of the Blessed Virgin Mary.

Bishop John's organization of the monastery at Bath, giving the monks a prior and surrendering to them in 1106 the estates which their church had possessed before the Conquest, placed them in a state of comparative independence. They had certainly more power and they must now be consulted by the bishop. Their church was his cathedral church, he indeed was their abbot and their prior was appointed by himself, but the prior and the monks formed a chapter which as years went on became more and more independent.

John de Villula was succeeded [54] by Godfrey, Queen Adelais' chaplain, whom the king nomi-

[37] Roger of Wendover, *Flor. Hist.* (Engl. Hist. Soc.) ii, 42.

[38] *Cal. Wells D. and C. MSS.* (Hist. MSS. Com.) I, 12.

[39] Ibid. i, 13.   [40] Ibid. 12.

[41] Dugdale, *Mon.* ii, 268.

[42] Will. of Malmesbury, *Gesta Pontif.* (Rolls Ser.), 196.

[43] Ibid. 195; *Angl. Sac.* i, 560; *Historiola Episcopatus* (Camden Soc. 1840), 21.

[44] Cf. Hunt, *Two Bath Chartularies* (Somers. Rec. Soc. vii), p. xlv.

[45] Cf. Hunt, *Two Bath Chartularies* (Somers. Rec. Soc. vii), p. 53.

[46] Ibid. p. 153.   [47] *Angl. Sac.* i, 561.

[48] Hunt, op. cit. 38.   [49] Ibid. 39.

[50] Ibid. 139.

[51] Leland, *Itin.* (ed. Hearne), ii, 61.

[52] Hunt, op. cit. 156.

[53] *Historiola Episcopatus* (Camd. Soc.), 22.

[54] *Angl. Sac.* i, 560, note.

nated as Bishop of Bath at the Easter Council 1123. He was consecrated at St. Paul's on 26 August 1123.[55]

Bishop Godfrey's successor was Robert of Lewes, the first appointment made by King Stephen, in 1136, and of him we are told [56] 'Canonica prius electione precedente,' a statement which seems to show that the monks of Bath were formally consulted by the Crown.

On 29 July 1137 the church of Bath was burned,[57] and soon after in the struggle between the party of King Stephen and the empress, Bishop Robert, who was an adherent of King Stephen, had the misfortune to be captured by the Bristol garrison.[58] A short time before, the bishop's following at Bath had captured Geoffrey Talbot, one of the supporters of the empress, and the exchange of Talbot for the bishop so enraged King Stephen that he meditated depriving Bishop Robert of the temporalities of his see.

The bishop was as great a builder in Bath as he was an organizer in Wells, and he erected in Bath [59] a chapter-house, cloister, dormitory, refectory and infirmary and other conventual buildings for his monks. He certainly did not meditate a return to Wells or a raising of the canons of Wells into an equal position with the monks of Bath as the members of his diocesan chapter. In 1157[60] he obtained from Pope Hadrian IV a formal recognition that Bath was the seat of the bishopric and that his title was Bishop of Bath and a confirmation of his possessions as bishop of the diocese. In 1166 Bishop Robert [61] died and the see was vacant for seven years.

In 1173 the monks of Bath at the instigation of Henry II[62] elected as their abbot and bishop Reginald Fitz Jocelin.

Though Bishop Reginald in his endowments of the church of Wells seemed to be preparing the way for its recognition as jointly with Bath the cathedral church of the diocese, yet he did not regard it as such. In 1180 appealing for the Whitsuntide offerings to the faithful of the diocese for the repair of the church of Bath, he called it the cathedral and mother church of the whole diocese,[63] and he endowed it with many relics and ornaments and books,

and the body of St. Euphemia and two precious copes and he acquired also for the monastery a precious alb of cloth of gold and the amice and mitre of St. Peter of Tarentaise.

In the autumn of 1191 Bishop Reginald [64] was elected to the see of Canterbury, rendered vacant by the death of Archbishop Baldwin.[65] His appointment had been materially advanced by Savaric Archdeacon of Northampton, by race a Burgundian and a kinsman of the Emperor Henry VI.

In November 1191, Reginald left Bath on his way to Canterbury, and Walter the prior accompanied him on his journey. At Dogmersfield, Reginald was taken seriously ill and perceiving that his end was drawing near, he clothed himself in the dress of a Benedictine monk, exclaiming to his faithful prior,[66] 'It is not the will of God that I should be Archbishop, neither is it my will, but God wills that I should be a monk and such is my will also.' He died on 26 December, 1191. It is said that during his last illness Reginald procured from the prior a promise to nominate Savaric for the see of Bath, and after his death Prior Walter seems to have had no difficulty in inducing his fellow monks to elect Savaric as their bishop.

Savaric designed to make himself in every way bishop of the diocese; for this purpose it was necessary for him to gain authority over all the Benedictine monasteries in Somerset. He was Abbot of Bath and so could influence the monks there. Within a year he surrendered to the Crown the city of Bath and received in exchange the abbacy of Glastonbury [67] and the right to call himself Bishop of Bath and Glastonbury. Then he induced the Abbots of Athelney and Muchelney [68] to become canons of the church of Wells and members of his chapter there. Thus while Savaric had recognized at first the monks of Bath as the members of his cathedral chapter, his action towards the church of Wells tends to show that he did not ignore its ancient claims.

On his death on 8 August 1205,[69] the arrangements for the election of a successor which had been foreshadowed by Bishop Robert were loyally adhered to.[70] The prior, the sub-prior,

[55] *Angl. Sac.* i, 560.
[56] *Cal. Wells D. and C. MSS.* (Hist. MSS. Com.), i, 13; *Som. Rec. Soc. Publ.* vii, 57.
[57] *Cont. F. Wigorn. Chron.* (Engl. Hist. Soc.) ii, 98.
[58] Ibid. 108; *Gest. Stephani* (Engl. Hist. Soc.), 38–43.
[59] *Historiola Episcopatus* (Camd. Soc.), 24.
[60] *Cal. Wells D. and C. MSS.* i, 533; Hunt, *Two Chartul. Bath* (Somers Rec. Soc. vii), 68.
[61] *Angl. Sac.* i, 561.
[62] R. de Devizes, *De Rebus Gestis Ric. I* (Rolls Ser.), i, 391.
[63] Hunt, *Two Chartul. Bath* (Somers. Rec. Soc. vii), 154.

[64] Gervase of Canterbury, *Opera* (Rolls Ser.), i, 511.
[65] *Epist. Cant.* (Rolls Ser.), ccclxxxi, 2.
[66] Ric. Devizes, op. cit. (Engl. Hist. Soc.), 45.
[67] Adam de Domerham, *Hist. Glaston.* (ed. Hearne), 356–7.
[68] *Cal. Wells D. and C. MSS.* (Hist. MSS. Com.), i, 57, 282; *Muchelney Cartulary* (Somers Rec. Soc. xiv), 51.
[69] Cf. Wells Charter cciii; *Cal. Wells D. and C. MSS.* (Hist. MSS. Com.), i, 63; Hunt, *Two Chartul. of Bath* (Somers. Rec. Soc. vii), pp. li, lii.
[70] For details of the struggle between the monks of Bath and the canons of Wells over the right to elect the bishop, see above, pp. 12–20.

and two monks, were chosen to represent the convent of Bath, and the dean, precentor, subdean and Canon Ralph de Lechlade the chapter of Wells, and the unanimous choice of the delegates fell on Jocelin Trotman of Wells. This election by compromise was then formally ratified by both chapters and each ratification was signed by the full body of the canons of Wells and the monks of Bath. The Bath notification[71] gives us the names of all the monks of the abbey at the time. The convent of Bath then consisted of forty-one monks.

The life as of a community connected with and yet distinct from the household of the bishop began when Bishop John de Villula gave them about 1106[72] their first prior, by name John. This act of the bishop probably shows the completion of their organization as a Benedictine priory with the usual monastic officers or obedientiaries. The convent would have thus a complete organization and could act through its various officers as a compact household.

The papal confirmation of Pope Adrian IV, which at some time between 1156 and 1159[73] the bishop obtained for them and which secured for them all their possessions and privileges, completed the process which gave them an independent existence. Certainly the 12th century was for Bath the period of its greatest development and probably of its greatest influence. Bishop Reginald (1174–91) was as friendly as Bishop Robert had been and gave them also a prior, Walter,[74] a man of remarkable piety, who had been sub-prior of the Benedictine monastery of Hyde and was noted for his learning. After a time Prior Walter grew dissatisfied with his life at Bath and retired to the seclusion of Witham, intending apparently to adopt the Carthusian habit. It chanced however that while at Witham a monk of the abbey of Hyde[75] arrived and seeing Prior Walter, and recognizing him as his former obedientiary, accosted him somewhat enigmatically—' pater, quod facis est kere, quod tractas kirewiwere.'[76] The remark, whatever its exact meaning, went home to Prior Walter, and he returned to Bath[77] and resumed the work to which Bishop Reginald had appointed him and which he had rashly forsaken.

Bishop Savaric, 1192–1205, like his predecessors was a kind friend to the monks, and when collections were made from the churches and monasteries of England for the payment of King Richard's ransom[78] he paid the demand made on the monks out of the revenue of the see.

It was in 1204 during the episcopate of Bishop Savaric that the priory of Bath became possessed of lands in Ireland.[79] The brethren of the Hospital of St. John at Waterford surrendered their house and estates in Ireland to the monks of Bath, in order that they might become affiliated to them as a priory belonging to a great English monastery. There were four brethren and three sisters to be maintained and they were known as the brethren and sisters of St. Leonard. Their Irish property at Waterford and other places in Ireland was of no real advantage to the monks. The rents barely supported the brethren of the hospital. The estates demanded considerable attention and the presence from time to time either of the prior or his proctors, and a hundred years later we are not surprised to find that the monks tried to rid themselves of it.

From 1208 to 1213 Bishop Jocelin of Bath and Glastonbury was abroad in exile[80] and during that period the priory suffered heavily from the vengeance of King John,[81] who was himself in Bath 13–14 May 1209, 17 October 1212, and 13 March 1213. The prior and monks were forced by the king's servants to make a free grant in 1213 to the king of all that he had taken forcibly from them for the maintenance of his court, and the monks found themselves in such straits for their own sustenance that they had to borrow from Canon Ralph de Lechlade of Wells for the purpose of buying corn for the monastery.

In 1241 in obedience to the summons of Cardinal Otho,[82] the papal legate, the priory sent a representative to the Council summoned by Pope Gregory IX to assemble at Rome, but apparently the Bath delegate suffered the same fate as his English colleagues who were captured by Pisan and Sicilian sailors acting under orders from the Emperor Frederick II.[83]

It was only to be expected that the vast expenditure that had been incurred by the monks of Bath in their contest for precedence with the canons of Wells should greatly impoverish them. The gift by Matilda de Champflour[84] of the

[71] Wells D. and C. Charters, no. 45, 46.

[72] Hunt, *Two Bath Chartul.* (Somers. Rec. Soc. vii), 49.   [73] Ibid. 68.

[74] 'Ann. de Winton' in *Annales Monastici* (Rolls Ser.), ii, 68.

[75] Ibid.

[76] Kitchener, *Obedientiares of S. Swithun* (Hants. Rec. Soc.), 30. The exact meaning is obscure ; probably it involves a colloquialism, and may be rendered ' what you are making is potage, what you are doing is pottering.'

[77] Cf. Ric. of Devizes, op. cit. (Engl. Hist. Soc.), 26.

[78] Cf. Hunt, *Two Bath Cartularies* (Somers. Rec. Soc. vii), 155.

[79] *Cal. Doc. Ireland*, 1171–1251, no. 219, 220.

[80] Matt. Paris, *Hist. Angl.* (Rolls Ser.), ii, 116.

[81] Hardy's Itin. of King John, in Introd. *Cal. Rot. Pat.* (Rec. Com.).

[82] Hunt, *Two Bath Chartul.* (Somers. Rec. Soc. vii), pt. ii, 40.

[83] Cf. Matt. Paris, op. cit., *sub anno.*

[84] *Somers. Rec. Soc. Publ.* vii, pt. ii, 1, 124.

advowson of Batheaston and by Bishop Roger of Bath and Wells of the fines coming to him from the manor of South Stoke [85] were at this time extremely welcome and we find that soon after Bishop William Button I [86] granted them an indulgence for the furtherance of their effort to complete and beautify their chapel of the blessed Virgin Mary.

This bishop also in May 1261 [87] granted to the monks permission to elect their own prior, and in that year they chose on 26 November Walter de Anno the cellarer of the priory, in succession to Thomas de Scolton who had died on 23 June of that year.

During the Civil War 1264–6 Walter the prior, in the name of the monks, had to seek for absolution from the papal legate Cardinal Ottoboni [88] from the excommunication which had fallen on them owing to the assistance they had given to the barons against the king. When in 1197 Bishop Savaric obtained for himself the abbotship of Glastonbury he surrendered to the Crown his right over the city of Bath, but when Robert Burnell, Chancellor of England, became Bishop of Bath and Wells in 1275, Edward I at once began negotiations with him for the surrender of this patronship of Glastonbury, [89] and in exchange Burnell received a regrant of the city of Bath which Bishop Savaric had surrendered, charged however with a rent-charge on the barton at Bath. [90]

Edward I looked well after the property of the Crown. He visited Bath on two occasions, [91] on 15 September 1276 and on 23 January 1285. Immediately after and probably because of what had been seen on the first visit there was an inquisition *ad quod damnum*, [92] when the jury at Bath presented the prior as unlawfully acting as patron of the church of Walcot and as having pulled down a building on the wall of the city and taken the materials into the monastery, and though bound to keep in repair the king's bath and lodgings, as having allowed them to fall into a ruinous condition. [93]

In June 1295 the position of the prior was recognized by the State in the writ [94] that was sent to him to attend the Great Council at Westminster in the following August, and from this time the prior took his place in Parliament and in the deliberations of the nation.

In 1301 Robert de Clopcote succeeded Thomas de Winton as prior. He seems to have been both an ambitious man and a bad financier and soon strong discontent prevailed in the monastery on account of the way he was administering the funds of the house. On 22 February 1311 Bishop Drokensford attempted to stop the reckless extravagance of the prior and sent a commission [95] of his officials to inquire into it. He was met however by a conspiracy of silence so that he felt compelled to pronounce excommunication against all who withheld the truth.

In 1321 Bishop Drokensford [96] wrote to the prior to say that he had heard of the scandalous waste of the revenues and the stinting of the monks' diet, and urged him to be a more careful steward of the priory; and on 5 November 1321, [97] he appointed a commission of two canons of Wells and one other to hold an inquiry concerning the evil reports against the Prior of Bath. In 1323 the sub-prior and convent, who apparently had been authorized by their abbot bishop to write directly to him, informed him that the new ordinance concerning the kitchen, which was probably the result of their commission, was working smoothly and they asked him to confirm it. [98] The prior himself seems to have submitted in part, as he wrote in November 1321, [99] promising to consult the bishop on certain points, and on 6 July 1323 [100] he wrote thanking the bishop for postponing the visitation and asking for it in the following August.

The ambition of the prior is shown in his desire to obtain the right to wear the pontifical insignia. On 25 October 1321 [101] Pope John XXII wrote to Edmund Earl of Kent that he should not take it amiss that he is unable to grant to the Prior of Bath the right to wear the pontifical insignia.

On the death of Prior Clopcote, 26 February 1332, [102] the convent proceeded at once to elect Robert de Sutton, on 7 March 1332, as prior, but the election appears to have been irregular, for the resignation of Clopcote or a promise to that effect had been forwarded to the pope and the pope's acceptance of it had not arrived in Bath when he died. The pope [103] therefore claimed to appoint to the priorship and Thomas Crist was chosen by him, and on 24 September 1332 Bishop Ralph of Shrewsbury confirmed Crist in his appointment as prior. [104] To compensate Sutton he was made Prior of Dunster and that distant property became a dependent

[85] *Somers. Rec. Soc. Publ.* vii, pt. ii, 155.
[86] Ibid. 40.   [87] Ibid. 57.   [88] Ibid. 59.
[89] Cf. Adam of Domerham, *Hist. Glaston.* (ed. Hearne), 559.
[90] *Somers Rec. Soc. Publ.* vii, 116.
[91] Cf. H. Gough's *Itin. Edw. I*, i, 63, 163.
[92] Cf. Hundred Rolls no. 123 and 132; King, *Records of Bath*, 15.
[93] The west gate with royal lodgings above was taken down 1776. Collinson, *Hist. and Antiq. of Somerset*, i, 32.
[94] *Parliamentary Writs* (Rec. Com.), i, 28.

[95] *Bishop Drokensford's Reg.* (Somers. Rec. Soc. i), 153.
[96] Ibid. 193.   [97] Ibid. 195.   [98] Ibid. 217.
[99] Ibid. 196.   [100] Ibid. 217.
[101] *Cal. Papal Letters*, ii, 447.
[102] Hunt, *Two Bath Chartul.* 134.   [103] Ibid. 135.
[104] R. of Shrewsbury's *Reg.* (Somers. Rec. Soc. ix), 121.

priory rather than an isolated cell. He was granted also a pension of £20 and permission to have with him at Dunster such friends as he desired. If any of them should prove troublesome Sutton had only to complain and the offender would be summoned to Bath ' et alius magis quietus et maturus loco sui subrogetur.'

During the priorship of Robert de Clopcote, the priory suffered not only from his wastefulness but from the estates in Ireland, i.e. the three small dependent priories at Waterford, Cork and Youghal. In 1306 Clopcote himself went over there to inquire into the cause of the poverty and to put an end to the mismanagement. Bishop Drokensford also had hoped that Hugh de Dover, who had done well as sacristan at Bath, would prove there an able warden. But Dover disappointed him and proved as inefficient there as Clopcote was at Bath, and when Archbishop Mepeham heard of the appointment of Sutton he wrote in March 1332[105] to bid him recall Hugh de Dover, the incompetent Irish warden.

Thomas Crist filled the office of prior for eight years only.[106] The disorders in the monastery seem to have been greater than he could cope with, and in August 1340[107] he retired on an ample pension consisting of a life interest in the manor and church of North Stoke, a chaplain, a squire and a groom to attend him, sufficient meat and drink for them all and a supply of wood for his fire.

His successor John de Iford or Ford does not seem to have checked the steady increase of the monastic debt and was in every way unworthy of the high post to which he had been elected. To pay off old debts the convent became involved in a bond for £1,300[108] with some Lucca merchants. He provided for friends and relations in England and Ireland at the expense of the priory. In 1346 Bishop Ralph of Shrewsbury had his attention called also to his immoral character.[109] The priory held the manor of Hameswell in Gloucestershire within the diocese of Worcester, and on 7 August 1346 Bishop Wulstan of Worcester wrote from Henbury near Bristol, to inform the Bishop of Bath and Wells that he had found at Hameswell one Agnes Cubbel who was living there as the prior's mistress. The bishop seems to have discovered something of the scandal before he received this letter, but we know nothing of the punishment that was inflicted on the unworthy prior. He was certainly not removed from his office, for he died as prior in 1359.

His term of office extended through the period when England was visited in 1348 and 1349 by the Great Pestilence. We know nothing of the details of the havoc in Bath. The pestilence reached there probably viâ Bristol as well as viâ Bruton and Frome and the convent never recovered the loss it then sustained. The average number of monks during the 12th and 13th centuries seems to have been about forty.[110]

As late as 1344[111] thirty monks joined the prior in a power of attorney executed on October 5 and this list did not include those who were at Dunster or those who were looking after the Irish priories, and there may have been some sick monks at Bath who did not sign. After the plague the priory never seems to have had more than half this number. In a Clerical Subsidy of 1377[112] there were only sixteen monks and that number was never greatly exceeded till the dissolution of the priory in 1539.

On 1 December, 1352,[113] Andrew Brooke was proposed by the Crown for John le Harpour's lodging and the convent replied that they could not receive him since the substance of the monastery was exhausted. The Great Pestilence had emptied many chambers but had also greatly reduced the income of the house. This was one of numerous examples of corrodies which were merely pensions for old servants, or relatives of monks, but there were others which carried rooms and accommodation for servants. In 1296[114] Richard de Wedmore was granted a corrody and lodging in the chamber called Cork and stabling for two horses. About the same time Roger de Depeford[115] was taken into the monastery. In 1328 John de Bathon,[116] a physician, was granted a chamber within the gate of the priory and a corrody and he was appointed physician to the monastery. A similar condition was attached to the corrody granted John Wulfrich.[117] He was to serve the priory all his life as plumber and glazier. In 1336,[118] John de Combe was granted, by a formal deed witnessed by three witnesses, which looks as if he had bought this refuge of his old age, a corrody of 20s. a year, one furred robe or suit of an esquire, and a chamber for himself and his grooms; and the same year Sir Tristram de Hanvyll[119] was granted another next the chamber which John de Combe expected to occupy within the court of the prior. In December 1349 Sir John Garrard,[120] chaplain, was granted a corrody and living and the chamber

---

[105] *Somers Rec. Soc. Publ.* vii, 135, 137.

[106] Ibid. 105.

[107] *R. of Shrewsbury's Reg.* (Somers. Rec. Soc. ix), 371.

[108] *Two Bath Chartul.* (Somers. Rec. Soc. vii), 171.

[109] *R. of Shrewsbury's Reg.* (Somers. Rec. Soc. x), 535.

[110] Cf. Original Documents no. 40, D. and C. Wells, and *Arch.* 1890, no. 52.

[111] *Somers. Rec. Soc. Publ.* vii, 73.

[112] P.R.O. Clerical Subsidy, bdle. 4, no. 2.

[113] *Somers. Rec. Soc. Publ.* vii, 181.

[114] *Two Bath Chartularies* (Somers. Rec. Soc. vii), pt. ii, 121.

[115] Ibid. 94. [116] Ibid. 121. [117] Ibid. 164.

[118] Ibid. 140. [119] Ibid. 146. [120] Ibid. 180.

which Peter de Derby had. This probably was the ordinary provision for a priest necessary from the small number of priests among the monks, a provision common enough at the present time in our colleges at Oxford and Cambridge. When the convent received in December 1299 Brother Eugenius,[121] formerly an abbot in Germany, at the request of Margaret Queen of England, they did not grant him a corrody but enrolled him among the monks of the convent.

In 1352[122] we find Prior Ford involved with Robert Gyene, to whom the convent had granted some years before a lease of their manor of Olveston and at a later date that of the advowson of the church. Robert Gyene was a Bristol merchant and had lent the convent £100, and when afterwards he was outlawed and his property became forfeit to the Crown the prior of Bath took him into the priory. The Crown claimed also to appoint to the church of Olveston, and in 1352 brought an action against the prior in that he and Gyene and others had assembled in a chamber of the priory and had bound themselves to uphold each other's claims against the Crown. Prior John de Ford was arrested, but was acquitted, and the advowson of Olveston ultimately came back to the priory.

The date of Ford's death cannot be definitely fixed, but it may have been in 1359, for on 31 July of that year we find the sub-prior acting where certainly the prior would have acted had there been one at the time.[123]

He was succeeded in the priorship by John Berewyck, and he by John Dunster, and the latter in 1412 by John Tellesford. In 1423 under John Tellesford there were four novices admitted as monks by Bishop Bubwith.[124]

In 1412[125] a dispute arose between the city authorities and the monks concerning the ringing of the church bells. It had been customary for the bells of the priory to begin and end the day. In 1408 the mayor and corporation of the city broke through this custom and caused the bells of the parish churches to be rung earlier and later than those of the monastery. The quarrel thus begun resulted four years afterwards in litigation and it did not end until 1421 when the king gave judgement in favour of the monks.

From 1425 to 1447 William Southbroke was prior. From the action of Bishop Stafford[126] it is evident that the discipline of the monastery deteriorated under him. On 24 June 1445,

Bishop Beckington[127] wrote to reprove the prior for allowing a monk Robert Veyse to live a secular life alone at the church of Stokeney and a life of adultery also. He had not been recalled by the prior, though it was against all rules of monasticism for a monk to live alone. So notorious was the man's evil life that Bishop Beckington obtained a royal writ to have him arrested as an apostate and had him sent under custody to the prior for punishment and imprisonment, and for a perpetual diet of bread and water. So careless however was the prior that on 27 December the bishop had to write to say that he heard Veyse was again at large and had gone back to live at Stokeney his old life of sin.

There had never been any great object of pilgrimage in Bath, though there is not wanting evidence that the monks were trying to create it. The canons of Wells had endeavoured to encourage pilgrimages to the tomb of William de Marchia, and the growing legend of St. Joseph of Arimathea and his tomb at Glastonbury was attracting greater numbers to that sanctuary. When under Bishop Robert of Lewes the monastic church at Bath was completed and rededicated there seems to have been an attempt to stamp with peculiar sanctity a cross erected in some unspecified part of the church. Archbishop Theobald of Canterbury and the Bishops of Llandaff and Clonmacnoise,[128] as well as the bishop of the diocese, all granted indulgences to those who should go and worship and make their offerings at it. In the 15th century there appears to have been another object of special veneration, some representation of the Trinity, probably the reredos of the altar of that dedication, and the efforts to promote this veneration in accordance with the spirit of the times created an opposition. A certain Agnes, wife of Thomas Cold or Baker of Norton St. Philip,[129] had openly denounced it and said it 'was waste time to offer to the Trinity at Bath.' For this she was brought up before the bishop's consistory court, and on 18 January 1459 before the Chancellor of Wells in the Lady Chapel at Wells she publicly confessed her crime and abjured her errors.

On the death of William Southbroke in 1447 the monks were unable to agree as to a successor and they appealed to Bishop Beckington, who chose for their prior Thomas Lacock, then the Prior of Dunster.[130]

Twice during his episcopate Bishop Beckington held a visitation of the priory, in 1449 and in 1454.[131]

---

[121] *Two Bath Chartularies* (Somers. Rec. Soc. vii), pt. ii, p. 90.
[122] *Somers. Rec. Soc. Publ.* vii, 181–7.
[123] Ibid. 181.
[124] Bath Epis. Reg. Bubwith. Folios at end on various elections.
[125] Warner, *Bath*, App. no. 41 and 51.
[126] Cf. Bath Epis. Reg. Stafford.

[127] Cf. Bath Epis. Reg. Beckington, fol. 31, 32, 33 and 46.
[128] Hunt, *Two Bath Chartul.* (Somers. Rec. Soc. vii), 2.
[129] Bath Epis. Reg. Beckington, fol. 299.
[130] Cf. ibid. folio unnumbered.
[131] Ibid. fol. 91, 92 and 187.

In 1476 Bishop Stillington gave notice of a visitation, and in 1499 Bishop Oliver King [132] held another visitation just before the death of Prior Cantlow.

On the death of Cantlow the convent proceeded to an election of a successor before they had obtained the bishop's licence. Bishop King therefore quashed the election and then himself postulated the nominee of the convent, William Birde. [133] Bishop King in his visitation censured the lax discipline in the priory. There was feasting out of the refectory, [134] idleness prevailed among the monks, and women were very often and at unseemly times allowed within the precincts of the monastery. The church too had been neglected by the former prior Cantlow and was grievously dilapidated. The bishop therefore enjoined on the monks that they should eat their meals only in the appointed places, and meat was not to be allowed except to those who were physically weak. [135] One of the monks was to set out for the others their appointed portions of food, and their clothes were to be of coarse and inexpensive material. Lastly each monk was to produce an inventory of the things he was using himself and what was superfluous was to be sent back into the common store.

The bishop found that the yearly revenue of the priory was about £480, and having allowed sufficient for the support of the prior and his sixteen monks he set aside about £300 a year for the repair or rather, since it seems to have been in a hopelessly ruinous condition, for the rebuilding of the monastic church. William Birde therefore pulled down the earlier church, which had been begun by Bishop John of Tours and completed by Bishop Roger, and on the site of the original nave began the building of the present church.

He died however on 22 May 1525 and left the work to his successor. In the instrument which [136] records the election of his successor the names of twenty-two monks are entered, a larger number than at any other period since the visitation of the Great Pestilence in 1349. The choice of the monks fell on William Holleway or Gybbs, who held the office of pittancer.

It was in the summer of 1535 that Dr. Richard Layton came to Bath to discover material for that Black Book of the Monasteries which Cromwell hoped would procure their dissolution. On 7 August [137] he wrote to the Vicar-General a letter, for the statements in which there seems to have been no authority but his desire to stand well with the man who employed him.

Hit may please yo[r] goodnes to understande that we have visited Bathe wheras we found the prior a right vertuose man and I suppose no better of his cote a man simple and not of the gretesteste wit, his monkes worse then I have any fownde yet both in bugerie and adulterie sum one of them haveyng x women sum viii and the reste so fewer. The house well repared but foure hundreth powndes in dett. . . the prior of Bathe hath sent unto yowe for a tokyn a leisse of Yrisshe Laners brede in a selle of hys in Yrelonde, no hardier hawkes can be as he saythe.

Layton had been in the monastic library to look out ancient literature which would help on his cause and continues in his letter [138]—' Ye shalle receve a bowke of o[r] lades miracles well able to mache the canterberie tailles. Such a bowke of dremes as ye never sawe wich I fownde in the librarie.'

The visitors acted in every case as if the dissolution of the monastery was decided on. They took steps to prevent any alienation of monastic property and they left behind an injunction forbidding the prior and his monks to leave the precincts of the monastery. So Prior Holleway wrote on 24 September [139] of the same year to Cromwell to protest against this restraint and to ask permission to leave the monastery to defend an action brought at that time by some woman in the king's court—' I hartlie desire yo[r] honorable maistershipp to know by yo[r] lres or other insinuacion whethre I may sit yn suche commyssions,' and then follows as a bribe—' I have send yo[r] maistershipp hereyn an old Boke Opera Anselmi whiche one William Tildysleye after scrutinye made here in my libarye willed me to send unto youe by the kynge ys grace and commawndment.'

In 1537, [140] the convent endeavoured to gain the goodwill of Cromwell by granting him an annuity of £5, and the prior wrote to thank him for his protection against some secret and hostile efforts against him.

One year was to go by before the end came. It was a year during which the prior and convent seem to have done more than they were justified in doing in order that they might win for themselves friends among the noble families of the neighbourhood. Prior Holleway's Register [141] gives us details of this action which could be pardoned only because the dissolution of the house was regarded as inevitable. Next presentations to benefices, corrodies, leases of estates, tenements and cottages, the register is filled with a painful succession of surrenders of

[132] Bath Epis. Reg. King, fol. 62.
[133] Ibid. fol. 38.
[134] Cf. Dugdale, *Mon.* ii, 270.
[135] In 1457 the prior on account of his ill-health was allowed to eat meat in Advent. Bath Epis. Reg. Beckington, fol. 219.
[136] Bath Epis. Reg. Clark, fol. 81.
[137] Cromwell Correspondence (P.R.O.) xx

[138] Cromwell Correspondence (P.R.O.) xx.
[139] *L. and P. Hen.* VIII, ix, 426.
[140] Ibid. xii, 360.
[141] Cf. Harl. MS. 3970; and Mr. Hunt's notice of contents in *Somers. Rec. Soc. Publ.* vii, introd. p. 63.

property which they knew would soon be absorbed by the Crown.

On 27 January 1539 [142] Drs. Tregonwell and Petre came to Bath to receive the surrender of the priory. For four years the monks had been under restraint and the prior had been confined to the house. Resistance would only bring trouble upon them, for they knew how unscrupulous were the men with whom they had to deal. And so they surrendered, and the noble foundation well-nigh a thousand years of age was blotted out from the history of this most ancient city. The deed of surrender was signed by the prior, sub-prior, Prior of Dunster and eighteen monks.

The prior William Holleway received a pension [143] of £80 a year and a house in Stall Street; the sub-prior a pension of £9, and the next three received pensions of £8 each, and all the others pensions varying from £6 13s. 4d. to £4 13s. 4d.

In 1553 all the monks are mentioned in Cardinal Pole's pension list, [144] except the prior, Thomas and Nicholas Bathe, John Edgar and John Humylyte.

William Clement had become vicar of St. Mary de Stalls at Bath and perhaps Thomas Powell rector of Tellesford. The fate of Prior Holleway [145] was very sad. In a poem of 1 January 1557 called 'The Breviary of Natural Philosophy,' Thomas Charnock the alchemist refers to the great learning of the last prior, stating how he used the bath of Bath in the place of fire in his chemical experiments.

He had our Stores, our Medicine, our Elixir and all
Which when the Abbie was suppresst he hid in a
    wall.

Finding his deposit stolen he seems to have lost his reason and becoming also blind he wandered about the country led by a boy.

The monastic church after the surrender of the priory was offered by the Crown to the citizens of Bath for the sum of 500 marks, and when they refused to pay that price the lead was stripped from the roof and melted and sold. Eight bells in one tower were sold to Francis Edwards and three bells elsewhere to Richard Morian. [146] The materials of the dormitory were bought by Robert Cocks, those of the fratry by Sir Walter Denys, and the cloisters by Henry Bewchyn, while Ralph Hopton purchased in a lump the superfluous buildings. The glass and iron were sold for £30, and the great church which Prior Holleway had spent all the time of his priorship in completing was allowed for some years to go into ruin. [147]

Leland [148] visited the monastery probably about 1540 before the work of demolition had begun. His description of what he saw is not only interesting but of value.

This John (i.e. John of Tours) pullid down the old church of S. Peter at Bath and erected a new and much fairer one and was buried in the middle of the Presbyteri thereof whos image I saw lying there an 9 yere sins at the which tyme al the Chirch that he made lay to waste and was onrofid and wedes grew about this John of Tours sepulchre.

I saw at the same tyme a great marble tumbe ther of a bisshope of Bath out of which they sayid that oyle did distill : and likely : for his body was enbaumid plentifully. There were other divers bisshops buried ther. Oliver King bisshop of Bath began of late dayes a right goodly new chirch at the west part of the olde church of S. Peter and finished a great peace of it. The residue of it was sins made by the priors of Bath : and especially by Gibbes the last prior ther, that spent a great summe of mony on that Fabrike.

Oliver King let almost al the old chirch of S. Peter's in Bath to go ruins. The walles yet stande.

The estates in Somerset reckoned as belonging to the church of Bath in 1086 [149] consisted of over 80 hides of land. The manors and lands were situated in Priston, Stanton Prior, Wilmington in Priston, Weston, Bathford, Monkton Combe, Charlcombe, Lyncombe, Batheaston, Bathampton, Woodwick in Freshford, Corston, Evesty and Ashwick. In addition to these, there were estates at Tidenham, Cold Ashton and Olveston in Gloucestershire comprising about 40 hides. Much of this was of the gifts of English kings and the donors are all mentioned in the chartularies already published. [150] Bishop John also obtained from William II the temporal lordship of the borough of Bath and this was confirmed to him by Henry I in 1101, [151] and the details of this lordship, which was probably purchased and not freely granted, are given in the confirmation. The estates of the monastery were then all in the bishop's hand by grant of the Crown, but in 1106 [152] when he had organized the convent he gave back the estates and appointed a prior to rule the monastery in his absence. Some of the estates he did not restore because in the troubles during the reign of Rufus they were lost, as the manor of Tidenham, [153] which was overrun by the Welsh and afterwards got into the hands of

---

[142] Close, 30 Hen. VIII, pt. v, no. 34.

[143] Aug. Off. Misc. 245, fol. 109.

[144] Exchequer K. R. Misc. Bks. vol. 32, fol. lxxix.

[145] Cf. Warner, *Bath*, and Hunt, Introd. to *Two Bath Chartularies* (Somers. Rec. Soc. vii), 60.

[146] Mins. Accts. Exchequer and Aug. 30–31 Hen. VIII, no. 224.

[147] *Dep. Keeper's Rep.* ix, Appendix ii.

[148] Leland, *Itin.* (ed. Hearne) ii, 61.

[149] See *V.C.H. Somers.* i, 458.

[150] *Somers. Rec. Soc. Publ.* vii.

[151] Cf. *Somers. Rec. Soc. Publ.* vii, pt. i, 43 ; Will. of Malmesbury, *Gesta Pontif.* (Rolls Ser.) 194.

[152] Cf. *Two Bath Chartularies* (Somers. Rec. Soc. vii), pt. i, 53.

[153] Ibid. pt. i, 5 and note.

the Earl of Pembroke, and as the manor of Dogmersfield,[154] which was seized by Ralph Flambard.

The priory also gained greatly from the fact that it had become the cathedral church of the diocese. William de Mohun gave the church of Dunster [155] and all that pertained to it. This in later times was formed into a dependent priory with its own succession of priors. Walter de Douai gave them the church of Bampton [156] in Devonshire, half the tithes of Castle Cary and the church of Brigge or Bridgwater. Bishop John had obtained from Henry I the manor of Dogmersfield [157] and Bishop Godfrey obtained from King Stephen its restitution and also got back the manor of Monkton Combe. In 1153 the monks purchased from Alexander de Alno the manor of Camely,[158] and between 1156 and 1159 Bishop Robert procured for them from Pope Adrian IV a confirmation of their possessions,[159] privileges and diocesan status. In 1180 Bishop Reginald [160] gave them the Hospital of St. John in Bath which he had built and endowed. This was for the benefit of the sick poor that thus they might take the Bath waters and go through a treatment.

He also gave them permission to appropriate the church of Bathford [161] for the maintenance of the fabric of the monastic church, and assigned the Whitsuntide offerings of the diocese to the rebuilding of it.

Bishop Savaric (1192–1202) did not forget Bath in his ambition to secure Glastonbury. He gave them the rectories of Chew [162] and of Weston and confirmed the gift of Fulco de Alneto of the church of Compton Dando. In memory of his many benefactions a hundred poor people were fed annually by the monastery on the anniversary of his death.

It was during his episcopate, 1204, that the brethren of the hospital of St. John at Waterford in Ireland [163] surrendered their house and lands to become affiliated to Bath.[164] This was the beginning of that list of estates and churches in Ireland which the priory possessed and of which afterwards in the time of Edward III they would have been glad to be rid.[165] In addition to certain lands there were the advowsons and rectories of Rathmoylan, Kilkee, Kilcop, Balycohyn and Ballytruckle. Soon after there came to the monastery in a similar way a small priory at Cork,[166] and about 1333 another at Youghal.

The rents of these foundations seem barely to have supported the brethren for which they were established and in 1333 [167] an attempt was made to exchange the lands in the counties of Waterford and Cork for other lands in England or to lease them to any person in the king's fealty.

In the middle of the 13th century when the priory was exhausted with its long contest with Wells, Matilda de Champflour [168] made some exchanges of pasture land with them greatly to the advantage of the monks, and sold them the advowson of Batheaston, giving back a considerable portion of the price. Sir Alexander de Alneto and Sir Hubert Husee were also benefactors towards whom the convent showed their gratitude by their prayers.[169]

In 1275 Bishop Burnell (1275–92) exchanged with the Crown the patronship of Glastonbury for the city of Bath which Bishop Savaric had surrendered.[170] The farm of the royal barton for which a fixed charge of £20 was due yearly to the Crown was generally profitable.

This bishop also gave the monks £10 to build two fishponds, and the advowson of the church of St. James in Bath.[171] The dispute about Bampton Church [172] and the church of Uffculme which was attached to it did not end until 1295 when the right of the priory was at last acknowledged.

In the *Taxatio Ecclesiastica* [173] in 1291 the *temporalia* of the priory are valued at £71 11s. 11d. and the *spiritualia* at £11 7s. 8d. The *temporalia* are recorded as issuing from lands at Weston, North Stoke, Bathford, Lyncombe, Monkton Combe and Combe Down, Compton Dando, Corston, Priston, Stanton Prior, Newton St. Loe and Ashwick in the diocese of Bath and Wells, the manor of Melford in the diocese of Winchester, the manors of Hameswell and Olveston in Gloucestershire and in the diocese of Worcester and Stapleford in the diocese of Salisbury. The *spiritualia* in the diocese of Worcester were portions due to the prior from the churches of Olveston, Hawkesbury and Cold Ashton; in the diocese of Bath and Wells pensions from Camely and Radstock Churches, pittances for the monks from Cannington, allowances for the cook and the almoner from Kelston Church and for the almoner and sacrist from Batheaston and for the firmarius from Walcot Church. The prior had also a pension from Bathwick and the convent certain pittances from St. Mary de Stalls. There were also pay-

[154] Cf. *Two Bath Chartularies* (Somers. Rec. Soc. vii), pt. i, 54.
[155] Ibid. 38.   [156] Ibid. 39.   [157] Ibid. 54.
[158] Ibid. 63.   [159] Ibid. 68.
[160] Dugdale, *Mon.* ii, 257.
[161] *Two Bath Chartul.* pt. i, 154.
[162] Ibid. 155.   [163] Ibid. pt. ii, 49 and note.
[164] Cf. Warner, *Bath*, App. xl.
[165] Archdall, *Mon. Hibern.* 700.
[166] *Somers. Rec. Soc. Publ.* vii, 141.

[167] *Cal. Pat.* 1330–4, p. 403.
[168] *Two Bath Chartul.* pt. i, 1; pt. ii, 36.
[169] Ibid. pt. ii, 25–50.
[170] Warner, *Bath*, App. 37; Adam de Domerham, *Hist. Glaston.* (ed. Hearne) ii, 551.
[171] *Two Bath Chartul.* pt. ii, 156.
[172] Ibid. 88.
[173] *Pope Nich. Tax.* (Rec. Com.) 186–97, 199, etc.

ments due to the monks for pittances from Englishcombe, Newton St. Loe and Corston.

In 1302 the convent, which had already the grant of a fair in Bath, obtained a licence to hold two fairs on their manor of Lyncombe on the festival of the Invention of the Cross (3 May) and on the feast of St. Lawrence (10 August).

In 1308 they obtained licence to appropriate Batheaston Church [174] and Bishop Drokensford enriched the church with many costly eucharistic vestments. Bishop Ralph Shrewsbury,[175] who is described as a citizen of Bath and afterwards a professed monk, gave them a precious reliquary, built for them two great towers at a cost of one hundred marks and completed the principal tower of the church.

In 1535 [176] the net revenues of the foundation were estimated as worth £617 2s. 3d. a year, Bath being the second in the value of its endowments of the monasteries of Somerset.

ABBESSES OF BATH

Bertana, 676 [177]
Bernguidis, 681 [178]

ABBOTS

Æscwig [179]
Ælfhere [180]
Wulfwold, 1061–84 [181]
Ælfwig [182]
Sewold, 1066 [183]
Ælfsige, died 1087 [184]
John de Villula, Bishop of Wells, 1088 [185]

PRIORS

John, occurs 1122 [186]
Benedict, occurs 1151 [187]
Peter, occurs 1157 [188]
Hugh, 1174–c. 1180 [189]
Gilbert, appointed 1180 [190]
Walter, occurs 1191, died 1198 [191]

Robert, appointed 1198 [192]
Thomas, 1223–61 [193]
Walter de Anno, appointed 1261, occurs 1263 [194]
Walter de Dune, occurs 1266,[195] 1283 [196]
Thomas de Winton, occurs 1290 [197]
Robert de Clopcote, 1301–32 [198]
Thomas Crist, 1332 [199]
John de Iford, *alias* Ford, appointed 1340, died 1359 [200]
John de Berewyk, 1359–77 [201]
John Dunster, died 1412 [202]
John Tellesford, 1412–24 [203]
William Southbroke, 1425–47 [204]
Thomas Lacock, appointed 1447 [205]
John, occurs 1468 [206]
John Dunster, occurs 1481, 1482 [207]
Peter, occurs 1482 [208]
Richard, occurs 1476 [209]
John Cantlow or Cauntlowe, occurs 1493,[210] died 1499 [211]
William Birde, 1499–1525 [212]
Willam Holleway or Gybes, 1525–39 [213]

The first seal of the Chapter of Bath [214] is believed to belong to the period of the refounding of the Abbey in the 10th century. It is circular, $2\frac{1}{4}$ in. in diameter, with a conventional representation of the house with three towers, pointed roofs and pinnacles, and this legend :—

+ SIGILLUM SC'I PETRI BADONIS ECCLESIE.

---

[174] *Cal. Pat.* 1307–13, p. 149 ; *Two Bath Chartul.* pt. ii, 159.
[175] Ibid. 159.
[176] Cf. *Valor Eccl.* (Rec. Com.) i, 174.
[177] Hunt, *Two Chartul. of Bath* (Somers. Rec. Soc. vii), 6.
[178] Ibid. 7 ; and Kemble *Codex Dipl.* no. xiii.
[179] *Two Bath Chartul.* 30 ; Kemble, op. cit. no. lxvi.
[180] *Two Bath Chartul.* 32 ; Kemble, op. cit. no. dcxciv.
[181] *Two Bath Chartul.* 34 ; Kemble, op. cit. no. dccccxi.
[182] *Two Bath Chartul.* 19 ; Birch, *Cart. Sax.* iii, no. 929.
[183] Cf. *V.C.H. Somers.* i, 460.
[184] Hunt, *Two Bath Chartul.* 3.
[185] See above.
[186] Hunt, *Two Bath Chartul.* 54.
[187] Ibid. 65.
[188] *Hist. Mon. Glouc.* (Rolls Ser.) ii, 106.
[189] Hunt. *Two Bath Chartul.* pt. ii, 4.
[190] Ibid.
[191] *Ann. de Winton* (Rolls Ser.) ii, 68.

[192] Hunt, op. cit. pt. ii, 5 ; Adam of Domerham, *Hist. Glaston.* (ed. Hearne) ii, 478 ; *Somers. Feet of Fines* (Somers. Rec. Soc. xi), 29.
[193] Called Thomas de Scolton, *Cal. Close,* 1333–7, p. 201.
[194] *Somers. Feet of F.* (Somers. Rec. Soc. xi) 208.
[195] *Somers. Rec. Soc. Publ.* vii, pt. ii, 59.
[196] *Cal. Pat.* 1281–92, p. 77.
[197] *Cal. Pat.* 1281–92, p. 348.
[198] Hunt, *Two Bath Chartul.* 112, 134.
[199] Cf. *Cal. Papal Letters* ii, 357.
[200] Ibid. ii, 368.
[201] Clerical Subsidy Roll, bdle. 4, no. 2.
[202] MSS. List of Elections at end of Bishop Bubwith's Reg.
[203] *Cal. Pat.* 1422–9, p. 265.
[204] Ibid. p. 452.
[205] Unnumbered folio at end of Bishop Beckington's Reg.
[206] *Cal. Pat.* 1467–77, p. 65 ; Hunt, *Two Bath Chartul.* pt. ii, 187.
[207] *Cal. Pat.* 1476–85, pp. 278, 301.
[208] Ibid. p. 571.
[209] *Angl. Sac.* i, 587 ; date given in Tewkesbury annals seems wrong. Perhaps he succeeded Prior Peter.
[210] *Cal. Wells D. and C. MSS.* (Hist. MSS. Com.) i, 482.
[211] Bath Epis. Reg. King, fol. 38.
[212] Ibid. fol. 39.
[213] Bath Epis. Reg. Clerk, fol. 81 ; *Hist. MSS. Com. Rep.* x. App. iii, 225.
[214] *Cat. of Seals B.M.* 1437. Harl. Chart. 75 A. 30.

A counterseal of Prior Thomas [215] (c. 1226) is vesica-shaped, 1¾ in. by 1 in., shewing St. Paul holding sword and book. The legend is:—

✠ SIGILL' THOME PRIORIS BATHONIE R.P.T.G.

The second seal,[216] which seems to belong to the latter part of the 13th century, is a very large vesica, 4¼ in. by 2¼ in., with the figures of St. Peter and St. Paul under a triple canopy holding between them the abbey church. Below are three monks adoring the Saints. The legend is:—

SIGILLUM CAPITULI BATHONIENSIS ECCLESIE

2. THE PRIORY OF DUNSTER

William de Mohun and Adeliza his wife gave in 1090 to John de Villula, just appointed Bishop of Bath, and to his new cathedral church of St. Peter at Bath [217] the church of St. George of Dunster with various lands and tithes.

The donor, William de Mohun, who was sheriff in 1086, expressly states in his deed of gift that he had conferred this church on the monks of the cathedral church that they might build and edify it (ædificent et exaltent).

This gift was confirmed to the monks by Archbishop Theobald (1139–61), and the archbishop states[218] in his charter that there had been a previous confirmation by Archbishop Anselm and King William Rufus. There is also among the Bath charters another confirmation[219] by a William de Mohun, probably the fourth, which gives the boundaries of the monastic estate at Alcombe.

The church and property was so far from Bath that they could not be managed and served from the mother priory, and there must have been from the earliest times a cell formed there. The Bath records[220] show very clearly that the revenues of Dunster were administered at Bath, leases of lands were made out in the name of the priors of the mother convent,[221] and though we read of the prior's garden and his vineyard, yet the cell had no separate existence with its own prior and family of monks until the 14th century. In 1282[222] there was a dispute concerning the tithes of Shurton in the parish of Stogursey which had been given to the priory of Dunster but which were claimed by the monks of Stogursey. The Prior of Dunster is mentioned in the process, but he takes no part in the litigation. The Prior of Bath is the plaintiff, and the Prior of Stogursey the defendant, and judgement was

given in favour of the monks of Bath as owners of the priory of Dunster.

In the *Taxatio*[223] of Pope Nicholas IV, 1291, the priory is valued as enjoying an income from lands and rents of £5 13s. 3d., and from churches and ecclesiastical dues of £13 7s. 4d. The *spiritualia* came from the churches of Dunster and Carhampton, and pensions due to the prior from the churches of Stogumber, Cutcombe and Luxborough. The *temporalia* were derived from lands etc. at Doverhay, Timberscombe, Wynard, Kyrington, Wylaler, Cowbridge, Cutcombe, Kenwardston and Lollokesworth.

The appointment of Robert de Sutton [224] as prior of Dunster in 1332, of which the announcement was made by the Prior of Bath to Ralph of Shrewsbury, Bishop of Bath and Wells, marks probably the beginning of the existence of Dunster as a distinct priory, dependent on Bath but able to a certain extent to manage its own affairs. Robert de Sutton had been elected by the monks of Bath as their prior in succession to Robert de Clopcote, who died March 1332. It would seem that Clopcote had forwarded something like a deed of resignation to the pope when he unexpectedly died in Bath.[225] Whatever had actually occurred Pope John XXII claimed the right to appoint the new prior and appointed Thomas Crist. Provision had therefore to be made for Robert de Sutton, who had been so hurriedly elected prior and so unexpectedly removed from office. So he was appointed by Crist as Prior of Dunster. He was allowed an income of £20 and to have such companions (socios) as he chose. If any of those sent him at Dunster should prove himself troublesome or should not be pleasing to the prior he was to be recalled, and another sent from Bath in his place. When Prior Sutton became old and infirm he might return at any time to Bath. Such terms as these were of course only personal, and would not apply to future priors.

The priory began now a new and distinct existence. It was to consist of a prior and four monks, and a charter in the Bath Chartulary [226] points to this change as largely due to Sir John de Mohun and Ada his wife, whose assistance made the change possible, and who certainly befriended the cell. A fragment of the tomb of Sir John,[227] it is conjectured, is still to be seen in the monastic portion of the church. A grandson of this John de Mohun, of the same name, in 1342[228] remitted to the prior and monks some

[215] *Cat. of Seals B.M.* 1439. Add. Chart. 19067.

[216] Ibid. 1441. Add. Chart. 5478.

[217] *Two Bath Chartularies* (Somers. Rec. Soc. vii), pt. i, 38.   [218] Ibid. 61.

[219] Ibid. pt. ii, 170; Maxwell-Lyte, *Hist. of Dunster*, 385.

[220] *Somers. Pleas* (Somers. Rec. Soc. xi), 202.

[221] *Two Bath Chartul.* pt. ii, 55.   [222] Ibid. 169.

[223] *Pope Nich. Tax* (Rec. Com.) 198, 205.

[224] *Ralph of Shrewsbury's Reg.* (Somers. Rec. Soc. ix) 121.

[225] Cf. *Two Bath Chartul.* Introd.

[226] *Two Bath Chartul.* (Somers. Rec. Soc. vii) 132.

[227] Cf. Hancock, *Dunster Church,* 51.

[228] Dunster Castle MSS.; Maxwell-Lyte, *Hist. of Dunster*, 392.

of the rent due by them for burgages at Dunster.

The priory was not certainly free from interferences or burdens which the mother house might wish to lay upon it. In 1345,[229] the Prior of Bath, borrowing for his priory, pledged the Prior of Dunster for £32 of silver. Simon de Wynton was [230] granted by the Prior of Bath a corrody and lodging 'in his house at Dunster' so long as he should live. In 1330[231] Sir John de Chueberri, chaplain, received a corrody out of the funds of the house at Dunster, and in 1357[232] John Osebern received a similar corrody.

Two records of corrodies or grants seem to refer to the building of the priory. In 1345[233] John the Prior of Bath granted to Adam de Cheddar, Prior of Dunster and chamberlain of the church of Bath, in consideration of his sumptuous buildings which he had made, and other many and notable good works that he had done, an annual rent of 50s., payable out of the priory of Dunster and soon after Adam de Barry of Dunster[234] obtained a corrody and 'the lower chamber next the great gate.'

During the 15th century the priory did not lack friends. In 1417,[235] Canon Richard Bruton of Wells left 26s. 8d. to the Prior and convent of Dunster. In 1392 [236] Peter de Bratton gave some lands in Sparkhay to the priory.

In the Valor of 1535[237] the priory is valued at £37 4s. 8d.

Leland,[238] in his Notes of Perambulations (c. 1540) says, 'the late priory of Blake Monkes stoode yn the rootes of the north west side of the Castelle and was a celle to Bathe.

'The hole chirche of the late priory servith now for the paroche chirch. Afore tymes the monkes had the Est parte closid up for their use.'

The priory was not called upon to surrender but was included in the surrender of the priory of Bath on 27 January 1539, and in that deed the signature of Richard Griffith, Prior of Dunster, is third on the list.

PRIORS OF DUNSTER [239]

Martin, 1274 [240]
Richard, 1301 [241]
Walter, 1308 [242]

Robert de Sutton, 23 October 1332 [243]
Adam de Cheddar, 1337 [244]
William Tover, 1355
John Hervey, 1376 [245]
William Bristow, 1411 and 1417 [246]
John Buryton, 1423
John Henton, 25 July 1425 [247]
William Cary, 1437
Thomas Laycock, 1447 [248]
Richard, 1449 [249]
William Hampton, 1463
William Bristowe, 1470
John Abyndon, 1489 [250]
Thomas Brown, 1498 [251]
Richard Pester, 1504 [252]
Thomas Bath, 1525 [253]
Richard Griffiths, 1539 [254]

3. THE ABBEY OF GLASTONBURY

Round few places in England has so much legend grown up as round the abbey of Glastonbury. The origin of this monastic settlement, which seems almost alone to have carried the traditions of the British church in unbroken sequence down to Saxon times, is lost in obscurity nor have we space here to discuss the many legends concerning it. Two British names are ascribed to Glastonbury, 'Ynyswytrin' and 'The Isle of Avalon,' [255] and under the former name it is referred to as one of the three 'perpetual choirs,' where the service of God was carried on unceasingly day and night.[256] The other two 'perpetual choirs' were Llan Iltud Vawr and Ambresbury, of which the latter appears to have been destroyed about 554 A.D.;[257] the settlement at Glastonbury may therefore be assigned to an earlier date than the middle of the 6th century. There is therefore little reason to doubt the tradition that Brent Knoll was given to the

[229] *Two Bath Chartul.* (Somers. Rec. Soc. vii) 175.
[230] Ibid. 93.   [231] Ibid. 133.
[232] Ibid. 181.   [233] Ibid. 175.
[234] Dunster Castle MSS.
[235] *Somers. Med. Wills* (Somers. Rec. Soc. xvi), 95.
[236] *Cal. Pat.* 1391–6, p. 70.
[237] *Valor Eccl.* (Rec. Com.), i, 220.
[238] *Itin.* (ed. Hearne) ii, 100.
[239] Cf. Hancock, *Dunster*, 65 ; Maxwell-Lyte, *Hist. of Dunster.*
[240] Wells Cath. Wills 57.
[241] *Two Bath Chartul.* (Somers. Rec. Soc. vii) 112.
[242] Ibid. 109.

[243] *R. of Shrewsbury's Reg.* (Somers. Rec. Soc. ix) 121.
[244] *Two Bath Chartul.* 147.
[245] Dunster Castle MSS.
[246] Ibid.
[247] Bath Epis. Reg. Stafford.
[248] Ibid. Beckington, folio unnumbered.
[249] Dunster Castle MSS.
[250] Bath Epis. Reg. Fox, fol. 25.
[251] Ibid. King, fol. 45.
[252] Will of T. Upcot (P. C. C. 9 Holgrave).
[253] Dunster Castle MSS.
[254] Bath Deed of Surrender.
[255] It is said that both Glast and Avallac are names of Celtic deities of the lower world (Rhys, *Arthurian Legend*, 328). Possibly this site was the place of the departed, 'the Island of the Blest,' in pagan times and was selected by the Christian missionaries for its sacred traditions.
[256] Probert, *Welsh Triads*, 84.
[257] Plummer, *Two Sax. Chron.* i, 16.

monks by King Arthur,[258] the victorious successor of Ambrosius, and the historic personage on whom were afterwards fathered the exploits of his legendary namesake. There appears, indeed, little doubt that this King Arthur and his queen were buried at Glastonbury, where their remains were afterwards found, as will be related below. The tradition that would carry the foundation of this monastery back to apostolic times, attributing it to St. Joseph of Arimathea and his companions, sent by St. Philip from Gaul, appears to be a comparatively late accretion, while the famous and beautiful legend of the Holy Grail is an exotic of still later date, coming, with much of the Arthurian legend, from France not earlier than the end of the 12th century.[259]

It is possible that in the legend of St. Collen[260] we have the elements of truth regarding the origin of Glastonbury. The saint is said to have settled during the 5th or 6th century at the foot of Glastonbury Tor, on the summit of which he met and conquered Gwyn ap Nûd, Prince of the Lower World, consecrating the site by building a chapel in honour of St. Michael. That this 'Isle of Avalon' should have been a sacred spot in Celtic times and should therefore have been selected as the settling place of one or more of the early Christian hermit missionaries, whose disciples gradually formed themselves into a semi-monastic establishment, is quite within the bounds of possibility.

Among the documents which the Glastonbury monks showed to William of Malmesbury was a charter which was then almost illegible from age and of which the characters were archaic and difficult to read. The charter was dated 601,[261] and was a grant by a king of Damnonia at the request of Abbot Worgret of the isle of Yneswytrin to the monastery there. The king's name was illegible, but he has been identified with Gwrgan Varvtrwch who in his earlier days had been a lieutenant of Arthur,[262] the victor in 520 of the battle of 'Mons Badonicus,' and who perhaps succeeded him in his rule over Damnonia and Cornwall. Malmesbury then tells us of two other Celtic abbots, Lodemund and Bregoret, and states that Bregoret was succeeded by Berthwald. Now Berthwald is clearly the Beorwald

who was abbot about 705, and the three Celtic abbots were probably those who ruled at Glastonbury during the first half of the 7th century. It is moreover clear that to Malmesbury and the Glastonbury monks this charter was the one item of a documentary character which they possessed and which belonged to Celtic times. It was a link which seemed to suggest a continuous life for the monastery from the days of its Celtic foundation to the days of its vigorous existence as an English house of Benedictine monks. And however impossible this may seem when we contemplate the ruthless shock of the heathen Saxon invasion history supports the belief.[263] For it has already been pointed out[264] that the Saxons probably did not obtain possession of this district until after the battle of Bradford in 652, by which date they were Christians or at least were men who would not destroy a Christian sanctuary. King Ine is said to have taken and buried at Glastonbury the body of St. Indractus,[265] an Irish pilgrim making his way across England from Gaul to Ireland, who had fallen a victim to the lawless violence of some of King Ine's courtiers. He had turned aside to visit Glastonbury, and this he would hardly have done had Glastonbury lain desolate and deserted, but it is possible that it had already been refounded by Ine.

The earliest historical notice of the monastery of Glastonbury comes to us from the life of St. Boniface, written by his disciple St. Willibald towards the middle of the 8th century. It refers to the mission of St. Boniface to Ghent and the sanction given by Ine King of the West Saxons. Among those who brought St. Boniface[266] to King Ine the name occurs of Beorwald, who guided and ruled the monastery which in 'the language of the ancients is called Glæstingaburg.' The incident referred to here took place in the first decade of the 8th century, and therefore it is more than probable, as will appear shortly, that Beorwald was the first of the long subsequent list of English abbots.

Our next reference comes from one of the versions of the Old English Chronicle, and belongs to the early years of the 10th century.[267] In a note made by the original scribe in the Parker MSS. A. we read of Ine ' and he getimbrade þæt menster æt Glæstingaburg.' Our fullest information, however, is derived from William of Malmesbury. In his *Gesta Regum* he tells us under the reign of King Ine[268] that the monastery of Glastonbury, where was buried the body of

[258] Will. of Malmesbury, *Antiq. of Glastonbury.* Written about 1130 under the direct inspiration of the monks of Glastonbury, this contains much of importance mingled with much merely traditional and some instances of ' that huge system of monastic lying, in which Glastonbury had a bad pre-eminence'(Plummer, note to Bede's *Op. Hist.* ii, 167); it has been printed by Gale, *Quindecim Scriptores* (1691) and Hearne, Adam de Domerham, *Hist. Glaston.* (1727).

[259] Nutt, *Studies on the Legend of the Holy Grail,* 100.

[260] Rhys, *Arthurian Legend,* 338.

[261] Cf. Gale, *XV Scriptores,* 308.

[262] Guest, *Origines Celticæ* ii, 270.

[263] Earle and Plummer, *Two Sax. Chron.* i, 18.

[264] See above, ' Eccl. Hist.' p. 2.

[265] Cf. Will. Malmesbury, *Gesta Regum* (Rolls Ser.) 35, and also his ' Passio Indracti ' which was worked up into Capgrave's *Life.*

[266] Jaffé, *Monum Moguntina* (1866), 439.

[267] Earle & Plummer, *Two Sax. Chron.* i, 40.

[268] *Gesta Regum* (Rolls Ser.), i, 35.

St. Indractus, was nobly restored at the cost of the monarch. Five years later in 1125 appeared the 'History of the Deeds of the English Bishops,' and under the life of St. Aldhelm,[269] Malmesbury tells us that on the advice of St. Aldhelm King Ine founded anew the monastery of Glaston.

It is evident therefore that King Ine was definitely recognized as the founder of the English monastery at Glastonbury, and that Ine's restoration belongs to the period when St. Aldhelm had most time to consider the needs of Somerset and the West. It is probable therefore that Ine's refoundation took place when St. Aldhelm was Bishop of Sherborne (705–9), and that Beorwald began his work as abbot in the first decade of the 8th century.[270] Certainly he was abbot here between 705 and 712, and the murder of Indractus had probably occurred not very many years before.

Glastonbury therefore as an English monastery was founded by King Ine, and Beorwald was its first abbot. It seems at once to have entered into possession of the isle of Glastonbury, and Ine confirmed to the monks the estate of Brent, the 'Mons Ranarum'[271] which there is no reason to doubt had been given to them originally by King Arthur. In addition the monastery was soon endowed with lands at Sowy, Pilton, Doulting, Pennard, Polden, Leigh-on-Mendip, Meare, Beckery, Godney and Nyland.

We have one glimpse of the unrecorded quiet life of the place at the very beginning of its existence as an English monastery. Forthere was the successor of St. Aldhelm as Bishop of Sherborne and died in 737,[272] and Berhtwald or Brihtwald was his contemporary as Archbishop of Canterbury 693–731. How it had come to pass we can only conjecture, but Beorwald the first English abbot of Glastonbury had a Kentish slave girl in his household whom he refused to give up though the archbishop had apparently written already on her behalf. So Brihtwald wrote to Forthere, the bishop who had the oversight of Glastonbury, and begged him to urge Beorwald to allow his slave girl to be redeemed. The girl's uncle Eoppa carried the letter, and was prepared to pay the price of thirty solidi so that Beorwald should not lose by the surrender. The kinsman's name is English, and it seems as if in the incident we get a reminiscence of the days when King Ine harried Kent on account of the murder of Mul.

Our next glimpse of the convent comes to us in the life of St. Dunstan, and what we learn from it seems to suggest that Glastonbury had been ravaged by the Danish invaders and was only nominally a monastery when Dunstan as abbot restored to it new life and good discipline.

Dunstan was born near or at Glastonbury, and was in some way connected with the family of King Athelstan. His education[273] was undertaken by some Irish pilgrims who had settled down at Glastonbury near the supposed burial-place of St. Patrick the younger. As a youth he was delicate and imaginative,[274] and a story is recorded how that in the delirium of some fever he escaped and climbed up to the roof of the monastic church and was found inside asleep and convalescent. The condition of the abbey was to him a matter of constant thought and regret, and he dreamed of larger buildings and many reforms. Dunstan is said to have become a monk under the influences[275] of Bishop Elfheah of Winchester, and through his friendship with the lady Æthelfleda, who had a house at Glastonbury, he became intimate with King Edmund[276] who probably in 946 made him Abbot of Glastonbury. His general work as a reformer and his subsequent advancement to the see of Worcester do not concern the history of Glastonbury. But his later work was certainly begun when he was Abbot of Glastonbury. He restored the Benedictine monastic system and is said to have built and strengthened a boundary wall round the monastic buildings to cut off the more effectually the conventual life from the gaze of the world. His biographer, the Saxon priest 'B,' says that there were two churches at Glastonbury, one the earlier, dedicated to the honour of the Virgin Mary, and the other a stone oratory attached to it and dedicated in honour of St. Peter. There seems however to be some confusion. When Ine renewed the life of the abbey he seems to have built to the east of the old church a larger one dedicated to the honour of St. Peter and St. Paul. There were also two more oratories, one of St. Mary, said to have been erected by St. David, and another to the north-east erected[277] by the fictitious British pilgrims from the north. What is clear is that the old church was the westernmost and Ine's church was easternmost, and William of Malmesbury[278] regarded Ine's church as the latest. If we imagine Glastonbury as Iona, Bangor or Clonmacnoise, it consisted of a series of bee-hive cells surrounded by an earthen rampart, the churches being larger and oblong, while the cells were circular and much smaller. Dunstan's reforms were probably in stone, and it seems probable also that he rebuilt on a larger scale the church of King Ine and inclosed in his new building the two small oratories which were to the west of it.

The work of St. Dunstan while Abbot of Glastonbury (946–57), was continued by King Edgar,

[269] *Gesta Pontif.* (Rolls Ser.) 352.
[270] Cf. Jaffé, *Monum. Moguntina,* 48.
[271] Cf. Gale, op. cit. 367 and 369.
[272] Jaffé, *Monum. Moguntina* (1866), 48.

[273] *Memorials of St. Dunstan* (Rolls Ser.), 10.
[274] Ibid. 55.   [275] Ibid. 13.   [276] Ibid. 56.
[277] Will. of Malmesbury, *Antiq. of Glaston.* (Gale's ed.) cap 14, p. 299.
[278] Ibid. cap 41, p. 310.

whose memory was held dear by the monks.[279] He repaired and rebuilt the churches and cherished and raised up the monks. Dunstan as archbishop frequently visited the monastery and continued to direct the reforms, laying aside the pomp of a bishop and living as a brother among his brethren. To Dunstan and King Edgar were due an organ for the church,[280] a precious pall and a belfry with bells near the refectory.

For the high altar Edgar[281] gave a precious cross of silver gilt, of which a story was often told in later times.[282] After the fire, from which it had been rescued, it was placed close by the holy water stoup near the entrance of the church. As the monks went in and out they never failed to bow in reverence towards it. There was, however, a monk Ailsi who passed by it on his way to the altar without obeying the rule of the house in this bow. After a time, however, struck by compunction he paused as he passed, and this time he bowed his head. But to his horror he heard a voice from the cross exclaim 'Now too late, Ailsi, now too late, Ailsi,' and the shock was too much for him. He immediately expired.

Under Dunstan Glastonbury was not only re-created as a Benedictine house, but came under the patronage of the English kings. Edred made the sanctuary his treasury, and the increase of its endowments during the 10th century shows how popular it had become. In his life of Dunstan William of Malmesbury says that which probably is literally true[283] that Dunstan enlarged Glastonbury with monks and new buildings and additional estates. Three English monarchs were buried here in this century:[284] Edmund I in 946, Edgar in 975 and Edmund Ironside in November 1016. The first Edmund[285] died and was buried before the reforms of St. Dunstan could have been carried out, and the church which the abbot built was doubtless erected over his tomb.

One more reference to Glastonbury comes to us before the Norman Conquest. Cnut had returned from Rome full of schemes for reform,[286] and in 1032 he came with Archbishop Æthelnoth of Canterbury to pray at the tomb of Edmund. And ere he left the abbey he gave to the shrine a costly pall and confirmed to the monks all the privileges and immunities from taxation which they had already begun to claim.

William of Malmesbury has however no word of praise for the last two English abbots. He couples Ægelnoth (1053–78) with his predecessor Ægelward II as men who had squandered the estates of the monastery as well as some of its internal treasures. The rule of both, he says,[287] was harmful to the church, and from that time the affairs of Glastonbury went from bad to worse. It is certain that King William laid a heavy hand on the estates of the monastery— 'quamplures ex suis commilitionibus ex Glastoniæ feudavit possessionibus.'[288] Malmesbury does not tell us of the losses but only the fact that afterwards the Conqueror relented somewhat towards this old English monastery, and gave back the estates of Podimore, Milton, Fullbrook, Berrow, Burrington, Lympsham, Blackford and Wootton.[289] The information comes to us however from the Domesday Survey of 1086.[290] Ægelnoth's evil deed was the grant of seven hides of land at Batcombe to his mother Ælfilla. Brompton Ralph had gone since the Conquest to William de Mohun or Moion the sheriff, Wheathill to Serlo de Burceio, and Kingston to Robert of Mortain. Maurice, Bishop of London was in possession of the church of St. Andrew at Ilchester,[291] and the king held Lodreford in Butleigh and Stone in East Pennard, estates that had T.R.E. belonged to the abbey. Limington had been bought by the father of Roger de Courcelle, and Camerton had been exchanged with the sheriff for Tintinhull.

The Survey[292] shows the manors of Glastonbury practically forming one huge estate in the centre of the county, stretching from Mells in the north-east to the right bank of the Parrett in the south-west. It comprised an eighth of the whole land of the county and amounted to 442 hides, and a tenth of the population of Somerset was reckoned as belonging to it.

Little is known of the Conqueror's first march into Somerset, but his action towards Abbot Ægelnoth shows how anxious he was to remove any chance of resistance in the county.[293] When he returned to Normandy in 1067 he took Ægelnoth with him, and thus he remained in exile until 1078 when at the Council of London he was formally deposed from his abbotship.[294]

He was succeeded by Thurstin, a monk of Caen, and though Malmesbury[295] writes as if he was not appointed until 1082, it seems certain from the events of 1083, which demanded time for the progress made in the new buildings, that Thurstin must at any rate have acted as abbot

[279] John of Glastonbury, *Chron.* (ed. Hearne) 131.
[280] Ibid.
[281] Ibid. i, 139.
[282] Ibid. 140.
[283] *Mem. of St. Dunstan* (Rolls Ser.), 301.
[284] Earle & Plummer, op. cit. i, 112.
[285] Ibid. 153.
[286] Cf. Gale, *XV Scriptores* (1691), 323.

[287] Will. of Malmes. in Gale's *XV Scriptores*, 324.
[288] Ibid. 330.   [289] Ibid.
[290] See *V.C.H. Somers.* i, 465.
[291] Ibid. 470.   [292] Cf. ibid. 460.
[293] Earle & Plummer, *Two Sax. Chron.* i, 200.
[294] App. Chron. Winton. 'Octavo anno concilium Londoniæ. . . Ailnodum . . . deposuit.' Cf. also Gervasius in Twysden, *Decem Scriptores*, col 1654.
[295] Op. cit. 330.

soon after the deposition of his predecessor. He seems also to have carried on his predecessor's policy for promoting the independence of his Order.[296]

He was a great builder, and seems to have set to work to rebuild the church which St. Dunstan[297] had erected in place of the three oratories east of the old chapel of St. Mary. He desired also to introduce into the monastery the improvements in ecclesiastical music which William Abbot of Fécamp had promoted. To this the monks seem to have greatly objected, and there was something very like rebellion in the abbey.[298] So Thurstin endeavoured to coerce them by calling in the aid of some Norman soldiers, the followers probably of the sheriff of the county, William de Mohun. The monks fled for refuge to the church and strove to barricade themselves within. Their efforts however were futile, the soldiers made their way in upon them as they fled for refuge round the altar, and that they might the better spy them out the soldiers mounted to the upper floor of the new church which was then being built, and thence shot their arrows at the cowering monks. One was pierced with a spear, one killed with an arrow even as he clung to the altar, and fourteen others were seriously injured.

Of course, such a catastrophe could not be kept secret, and when William the Conqueror[299] heard of it he ordered Thurstin to be sent back to his former monastery at Caen, and the ringleaders of the disobedient monks he distributed among the monasteries of England.

It is not very clear when Thurstin's exile began. It was probably early in 1084 if not in the autumn of 1083. Malmesbury[300] tells us also as a tradition that when William Rufus in 1087 succeeded his father, Thurstin, with the aid of his parents and after payment of a fine of £500, was allowed to return. He lived on crushed and wretched until 1101.

Malmesbury however weighs his character and metes out praise to him, bidding us remember not his rash indiscretion but his zeal and good work for the abbey itself. It was during his exile that the Survey[301] was made which resulted in the Domesday Record, and it is clear that Thurstin had been a good steward of the endowments. The property was enhanced in value under his abbotship.

Thurstin was succeeded in 1101[302] by Herlewin, another monk of Caen, whom Henry I appointed as abbot. At first he seems to have been regarded by the monks as parsimonious, but afterwards, when he had realized the greatness of the endowments, he came to be considered as extravagant. The church which Thurstin had begun seemed to him to be too small, so he pulled it down and built a new one. He enlarged also the chambers of the monks, and is said to have received without the payment of any bonus any priests who desired to adopt the vocation of a monk. He was certainly a great benefactor to the monastery, for he managed to get back many estates which were in danger of being permanently alienated from the abbey, being held only on the tenure of military service,[303] Cranmore, Lympsham, Middlezoy and Pucklechurch being especially mentioned. Herlewin was followed by Seffrid, a monk of Seez,[304] who held office only for six years and in 1126 became Bishop of Chichester, and then in Henry of Blois Glastonbury obtained as its abbot one of the most influential ecclesiastics of the age. A grandson of Henry I[305] he was the brother of Theobald, Count of Blois, and became in 1129 Bishop of Winchester, which office he held while still retaining until 1171 the abbotship of Glastonbury. It was during his period of office that William of Malmesbury[306] was invited to undertake the history of the Antiquities of Glastonbury, and when his work was accomplished he dedicated his book to the enlightened and influential abbot and bishop. Malmesbury closes his narrative with a very brief note of praise for the learning of his patron and his great dislike of flattery. The history of Malmesbury was continued by Adam of Domerham, a Glastonbury monk. He gives us Abbot Henry's[307] own memoir of his deeds, the impression formed by his first visit to the monastery, his struggle to regain estates that were passing away, and his efforts to improve the monastic buildings. He says that he found the monastery in a serious state owing to the action of some of his predecessors. The buildings were ruinous, the monks in need of the necessaries of life, and the church deprived of many estates that belonged to it. There was a certain soldier,[308] Odo by name, who had married a near relation of Abbot Seffrid. This man had been made butler to the abbey and had been endowed with three manors. When called upon to produce his title deeds Odo displayed others that were forged and had been altered for his advantage. His crime however was discovered, and Odo confessed and Abbot Henry allowed him for life a

---

[296] See above, 'Ecclesiastical History,' for the combination of Muchelney, Athelney and Glastonbury under Thurstin's lead against Bishop Giso.

[297] Cf. Gale, *XV Scriptores*, 333.

[298] Cf. John of Glastonbury, *Chron.* (ed. Hearne) i, 158.

[299] Ibid.; Gale, op. cit. 332.

[300] Gale, op. cit. 332.

[301] Cf. *V.C.H. Somers.* i, 460.

[302] Gale, op. cit. 332–3.

[303] Gale, op. cit. 333.   [304] Ibid. 334.

[305] Adam of Domerham, *Hist. Glaston.* (ed. Hearne) i, 304.

[306] Cf. Will. of Malmesbury's Dedication of his history to Henry of Blois.

[307] Adam of Domerham, *Hist. Glaston.* i, 305.

[308] Ibid.

small rent-charge on the manor of Ashbury in Berkshire, and on his early death continued it to his son Roger for his life also.

In his memoir he mentions how he recovered the whole, or portions, of the manors of Mells,[309] Brent Marsh, Moorlinch, Uffculme, Syston, Camerton, Ashcott, Andersea and Damerham, and he assigned the church of Pucklechurch to the office of the sacrist of the old church, the chapel of St. Mary which was called 'ealde churiche.' Henry however was remembered [310] for his important work in rebuilding the monastic chambers. He erected a certain regal palace which was called the castle and in addition he built the bell tower, chapter-house, cloister, lavatory, refectory, dormitory, infirmary with its chapel, a remarkably fine entrance gate-house of squared stones, a great brewing house and stables for many horses.

His influence availed to procure a papal privilegium from Pope Innocent II in 1136 [311] confirming to the abbey the estates that had been given, and among them the manor of Uffculme which had lately been recovered. Another privilegium from Pope Lucius II in 1144[312] recapitulates the estates that had been recovered, and again confirms the monks in their possessions, and a bull of Alexander III in 1168[313] reiterates this papal confirmation, so that no further loss should be incurred through the lawlessness or dishonesty of powerful neighbours. Henry of Blois died in 1171[314] and was succeeded in the abbotship by Robert, prior of Winchester, a man whom Adam of Domerham classes with Henry of Blois, as a pair of bright stars which had illumined with their splendour the abbey of Glastonbury. Robert comes before us in reference to another attempt made by the bishop of the diocese to subject the monks to episcopal supervision. Bishop Reginald of Bath (1174–91), took an active part in the restoration of the church of Wells to cathedral rank. The churches of the Glastonbury Twelve Hides, i.e. of the territory that formed the original endowment of the abbey, had claimed exemption from archidiaconal inspection because of the privileges which the monks asserted had been granted to the abbey by King Ine. The Twelve Hides had certainly been omitted in the great Survey[315] of 1086 as never having paid geld, being, no doubt, exempt for some peculiar sanctity belonging to them. Bishop Reginald however induced Abbot Robert to place these churches, St. John's Glastonbury, Meare, Street, Butleigh, Shapwick, Moorlinch and Middlezoy under a special officer,

the abbot's archdeacon,[316] and to compensate the Archdeacon of Wells in the surrender of his claim to them the church of South Brent was assigned by the monastery for the augmentation of his income.

In addition Bishop Reginald[317] induced Abbot Robert to give the church of Pilton to form the prebend of a canon's stall in St. Andrew's church at Wells and to accept the office of a canon of Wells for himself and his successors so that the Abbots of Glastonbury should become *ex officio* canons of Wells and so members of the bishop's chapter and his sworn subordinates. The monks when they realized what had occurred refused to consent to this arrangement, and the monastery was compelled to surrender the church of Pilton for the permanent increase of the endowment of Wells in order to cancel this arrangement. Abbot Robert died on 29 April 1184[318] and the abbey was placed by Henry II in the custody of Peter de March, a Cluniac monk and brother to the Bishop of Albenga, a man whose influence at the time was very great at Rome. Peter endeavoured to insinuate himself into the esteem of the monks in order that he might be elected abbot, but for some reason, and probably chiefly because he was a Cluniac, they met his advances with scorn. He shut up the abbot's lodging known as the castle and on the monks objecting to this irregularity he is said to have compassed the death of several of them.

On 25 May 1184,[319] however, a calamity occurred which put an end to Peter's stewardship, and the monks' resentment. All the monastic buildings, except the bell tower which Abbot Henry of Blois had erected, together with the great church of Abbot Herlewin and the old chapel of the Virgin Mary on the west of it, were burnt to the ground. All the treasures, relics, books and ornaments of the church perished, and what seemed a yet greater loss, the tombs of the many saints and great heroes who had been buried there were reduced to ashes. One chamber with its oratory alone escaped, probably because it was apart from the domestic buildings of the monks, and thither the terrified monks fled for refuge. The story of the calamity as told by Adam de Domerham ends in a spirit of resignation and confidence. There was a silver lining to the cloud. Peter de March[320] died in the following spring. As this catastrophe had taken place when the affairs of the monastery were in the king's hands, Henry II felt a certain responsibility and set over the convent his

[309] Adam of Domerham, *Hist. Glaston.* i, 306–7.
[310] Ibid. 309. [311] Ibid. 320.
[312] Ibid. 322. [313] Ibid. 325.
[314] Ibid. 331.
[315] *V.C.H. Somers.* i, 460 ; cf. Eyton, *Somerset Domesday*, ii, 10.

[316] Cf. *Cal. Wells D. and C. MSS.* (Hist. MSS. Com.) i, 26 ; Adam of Domerham, *Hist. Glaston.* ii, 345.
[317] *Cal. Wells D. and C. MSS.* loc. cit.
[318] Adam of Domerham, *Hist. Glaston.* i, 332.
[319] Ibid. 333. [320] Ibid. 334.

chamberlain Ralph Fitz Stephen.[321] He increased the allowance for the maintenance of each monk and began at once with squared stones and much ornament to rebuild the ancient chapel of St. Mary. He then restored all the monastic offices and zealously and generously set about the erection of the great church to the east.

As far as possible [322] the cost of these new buildings was defrayed by the endowments of the abbey, and what was still wanting Henry II gave out of the revenues of the Crown. Ralph Fitz Stephen had planned out a good portion of the great church when the death of Henry II on 6 July 1189 brought the work of restoration to a temporary end. Richard I had no interest in the effort and was engaged in the Crusades. One church, however, had been completed. The work of rebuilding the old church of our Lady at the west had been carried on with remarkable activity, and whether or not it was actually completed, this beautiful specimen of late Norman architectureon, the site of the old historic chapel to which so many legends had already begun to cling, was consecrated by Bishop Reginald of Bath on St. Barnabas Day, 11 June 1186.[323] An addition to the chapter in which Adam de Domerham gives us this information is evidently an afterthought to safeguard the assertion of the monks that they were still in possession of the relics and remains of those ancient heroes of the past of whose tombs they were so proud. He says that the remains of Edmund Ironside and of St. Dunstan were found,[324] and this statement is perhaps true concerning the former but certainly not of the latter.

The death of Henry II in 1189 was soon followed by the appointment of Henry de Sully Prior of Bermondsey as Abbot of Glastonbury. His abbotship is memorable for the grant in 1191[325] by Pope Celestine III to the Abbots of Glastonbury for the time being of the right to wear the mitre, ring and other ornaments of the episcopal order and also for the part which he took in bringing about a long and bitter quarrel between the monks and the bishop of the diocese.

It has been already related how in 1192 when Savaric succeeded to the bishopric of Bath he contrived also to obtain the abbacy of Glastonbury. The wearisome tale of appeals and counter appeals to Rome need not here be repeated. The election of William Pica as abbot in 1198 [326] came to nothing, and with the succession of King John in 1199 Savaric's position became unassailable. He was enthroned as abbot on Whit-

sunday 1199,[327] when a form of submission was signed by the three priors, precentor, succentor, chamberlain, almoner and forty-two other monks.

In June 1200 the former election of William Pica [328] was quashed, and Innocent issued a bull definitely uniting the see of Bath with the abbey of Glastonbury; and in that same summer Pica[329] and some of his companions unexpectedly died at Rome, the monks at Glastonbury being convinced that they were poisoned. Savaric seemed to have completely succeeded. The pope gave him a mandate to enforce the obedience of the monks and issued an ordinance[330] which should regulate the duties of the obedientiaries and the manner of their appointment.

The details of this ordinance formed the basis of all future discussions for a settlement of the controversy. The commission appointed by Innocent III assembled at St. Albans on 8 September 1202 and the result of their deliberations was confirmed on 23 September. By this the revenues of the abbey were divided on an estimate of sixty monks. The bishop, as abbot, was to have ten manors and the patronage of the churches on those manors, with the abbot's house in the precincts at Glastonbury and the house at Meare. The manors proposed to be assigned to him were those of Pucklechurch, Winscombe, Badbury in Wilts, Ashbury, Buckland, Lyme, Blackford, East Brent, Berrow and Cranmore.

In the late autumn of 1205 Savaric died, and Jocelin of Wells was consecrated Bishop of Bath and Glastonbury on 12 May 1206. Already in November 1205 [331] King John had written to Pope Innocent and to some of the cardinals and had recommended a restoration of the conditions that prevailed under Bishop Reginald, and very soon after letters were directed towards the same end to Pope Innocent[332] from the earls and barons of England, and the canons and monks[333] of Bath, Wells, Cerne, Muchelney, Sarum, Abbotsbury and Norwich. Nor was Jocelin averse to some terms of agreement.

In March 1207[334] the pope wrote to the monks that they were at perfect liberty to present their claims, but in 1208 the papal interdict had fallen on England, and not until 1213 could the controversy be taken up again. In January 1215 Jocelin received from King John the patronship of the abbey.[335] It was the first step towards a separation, for if he was not to be abbot yet he would have an opportunity of making

[321] Adam of Domerham, *Hist. Glaston.* i, 335.
[322] Ibid.
[323] John of Glastonbury, *Chron.* (ed. Hearne) i, 180.
[324] Op. cit. 336.
[325] Adam de Domerham, *Hist. Glaston.* (ed. Hearne) ii, 344.   [326] Ibid. 376.

[327] Adam de Domerham, *Hist. Glaston.* (ed. Hearne) ii, 382.   [328] Ibid. 396–8.
[329] Ibid. 399.   [330] Ibid. 410–13.
[331] A. de Domerham, *Hist. Glaston.* ii, 425.
[332] Ibid. 428.   [333] Ibid. 429.
[334] Ibid. 437 ; *Cal. Papal Letters*, i, 25.
[335] A. de Domerham, *Hist. Glaston.* ii, 447.

his influence felt when the time came to elect one. Meanwhile the monks drew up a series of criticisms or charges against Bishop Jocelin as their abbot,[336] to most of which Jocelin formally replied.

Matters dragged on for several years, but at last Honorius III commissioned Pandulf the Bishop of Norwich and Richard le Poor Bishop of Sarum to adjudicate.[337] Pandulf instructed Simon Abbot of Reading to act for him and during the autumn of 1218 these two commissioners sat at Shaftesbury and worked out the terms of the final peace.

On 13 February 1219[338] William Vigor and Michael de Ambresbury, monks of Glastonbury, set out for Rome carrying with them the final decision of the commissioners, and in May 1219[339] Honorius III formally confirmed the agreement. Then to show that he intended it to be final, he renewed the privileges, granted by Celestine III in 1191[340] to Henry de Sully, to the new abbot to wear the mitre and ring and other insignia of the episcopal order.

The peace of Shaftesbury[341] dissolved at once the union between the abbey and the bishop of the diocese. He ceased to be the Abbot of Glastonbury. His right of visitation in the monastery was however definitely recognized and this was a distinct advance on the position of Bishop Giso. The see was to be permanently endowed with the manors of Winscombe, Pucklechurch, Blackford and Cranmore and the advowsons of the churches of Ashbury, Camerton, Christian Malford, Kington and Buckland. The other manors and patronage which Jocelin as abbot had enjoyed he was to hand back to the monastery, and he was to confirm the pensions which had already been attached to the churches of which he was now to have the absolute patronage.

The monks had gained their end but certainly paid dearly for it. They proceeded at once to elect an abbot, and after a period of twenty-six years at last they had in Brother William an abbot from among their own community,[342] and on 12 June 1219[343] he was solemnly blessed as abbot by Bishop Jocelin.

Abbot William died on 18 September 1223 and Bishop Jocelin as patron seems to have put pressure upon them to elect Robert the Prior of Bath. The monks could not agree and they delegated their rights[344] to David the Abbot of St. Augustine's, Bristol, Giles Prior of

the Carthusian house at Witham and William de Bardenay Archdeacon of Wells, but seem to have expressed a desire not to have Prior Robert. Bishop Jocelin however was behind the delegates as he had been behind the monks, and when these three seemed to hesitate Jocelin provided Robert as the Abbot of Glastonbury.

The work of Abbot Robert was certainly hindered by his unpopularity. The monks did not wish for him and only most unwillingly obeyed him. It was not therefore a time for any great building scheme. He added various pittances to improve the food of the monks[345] and he increased the allowance made to the sacrist of the chapel of St. Mary. This was now the only place of worship for the monks. The debt of the monastery called for serious effort, and Abbot Robert was already too old to undertake it, and in 1234 retired[346] from office and returned to Bath. The grateful monks made him an allowance for life of £60 a year.

Then the new life of the monastery began.[347] Michael de Ambresbury who, with his colleague and future abbot William, had gone in 1219 to Rome carrying the consent of the monks to the Peace of Shaftesbury, was the unanimous choice of the monks, and on St. Mark's day, 25 April 1234 Bishop Jocelin in London solemnly blessed him as abbot.

He began his work cautiously. There were the manors to recover if possible from the patron.[348] There was the large debt on the monastery to wipe out. With the latter he was most successful. With the former he availed nothing. Certain offices in the monastery seem to have become almost hereditary. One William possessed the office of gate porter and another Walter had enjoyed the office[349] of steward. Both these men he bought out and directed the profits of their office to the general interests of the abbey. Work was going on in the great church, and, if Leland's[350] remark that Ambresbury was buried in the north transept does not refer to some later translation, it is clear that at least the north transept was far enough advanced in 1253 to allow of his burial there. Towards the end of his tenure of the abbotship Bishop Button, who had been consecrated Bishop of Bath and Wells in 1248, firmly enforced his rights as patron[351] and the prospect of another controversy created the desire for retirement. At the end of 1252 he gave up[352] the post he had held so well and was allowed as his private

[336] A. de Domerham, *Hist. Glaston.* ii, 457.
[337] Ibid. 471.   [338] Ibid. 467.
[339] Ibid. 469; *Cal Papal Letters*, i, 67.
[340] A. de Domerham, op. cit. ii, 474; *Cal. Papal Letters*, i, 68.
[341] A. de Domerham, op. cit. ii, 469.
[342] Cf. John of Glastonbury, *Chron.* i, 209.
[343] Adam of Domerham, *Hist. Glaston.* ii, 475.
[344] Ibid. 478; John of Glastonbury, *Chron.* i, 211.

[345] Cf. A. de Domerham, op. cit. ii, 502. [346] Ibid.
[347] John of Glastonbury, *Chron.* i, 213; A. de Domerham, *Hist. Glaston.* ii, 503.
[348] John of Glastonbury, *Chron.* i, 214.
[349] A. de Domerham, op. cit. ii, 505; John of Glastonbury, op. cit. i, 216.
[350] Leland, *Itin.* iii, 116.
[351] A. de Domerham, op. cit. ii, 518.
[352] Ibid. 523; John of Glastonbury, op. cit. 224.

apartments within the abbey a chamber which Thomas the prior had built, with the hall and chapel attached and the cellar under both, the garden adjacent to it and the manor house at Meare as a place of retirement. His successor Roger de Ford [353] was elected after scrutiny in which he was almost defeated by a brother monk Robert de Petherton, and was confirmed as abbot by Bishop Button at Wells on 9 March 1253. For six months Michael de Ambresbury enjoyed his rest, dying at Michaelmas next after his resignation.

Bishop Button in 1253 levied scutage on all the tenants of the abbey and as its overlord answered to the king for the abbot and all his dependants. Abbot Roger strenuously resisted this and his action was approved by the Crown. Soon after, however, when the cost of this litigation [354] was added to the debt of the monastery, Roger became intensely unpopular to the monks. The great majority of them desired to depose him and for that purpose in 1255 invited the bishop to hold a visitation. He had already [355] visited the monastery in that year and to come again, as Roger pleaded, was decidedly irregular. After service and sermon in the monastic chapel Bishop Button took his seat in the chapter-house and having heard the complaints of the monks formally deposed Roger de Ford from being abbot. Roger thereupon went out and bade his servants arm themselves and drive out the officials of the bishop, and while he collected his papers and valuables out of his private chamber the bishop dined with the monks in the refectory. Roger immediately after appealed to the king and left the abbey. The next day the monks requested licence to elect and chose Robert de Petherton as abbot. Then came the servants of the justiciar [356] and by royal authority reinstated Roger, and though the bishop excommunicated him the archbishop supported the king in his action. Then both parties appealed to Rome and after nearly five years, in 1259, the pope ordered Roger to be reinstated and provision to be made for Robert de Petherton from the manors of Christian Malford and Kington.

As soon as the monks had heard of Roger's death at Bromley on 2 October 1261 they elected as his successor Robert of Petherton his former rival.

The appeals of Abbot Roger and his monks had increased the debt of the monastery and Robert's first work was to try and pay this off. His controversy with the bishop Walter Giffard [357]

concerning the patronship ended in 1266 in a compromise. [358] The bishops do not seem to have given up [359] all their claim to the manors and advowsons which in 1202 had been assigned to Bishop Savaric. Bishop Giffard however and Abbot Petherton agreed that in future the bishop should have the manors of Pucklechurch, Winscombe, Blackford and Cranmore and the advowsons of Ashbury in Berkshire, Christian Malford and Kington in Wiltshire and Buckland in Dorsetshire and one knight's fee in Camerton and should give up all claims to the manors of Ashbury, Badbury, Kington, Christian Malford, Buckland and Meare.

On 31 March 1274 Abbot Petherton [360] died, and immediately the monastery was seized by the bailiffs of the bishop and soon after by the escheator of the Crown. [361] It was a definite issue between the Crown and the bishop and the monastery could stand aside and wait the issue.

Robert of Petherton had soon after the accession of Edward I in 1272 informed King Edward of the opinion [362] of the abbey on the question of the patronship, and just before his death the monks had received a royal mandate forbidding them in case of a vacancy of the abbotship to receive a licence to elect from any one but the king. When therefore rumour had reached Wells that Abbot Petherton was dead [363] the seneschal and the bailiff of the bishop and the Dean of Wells came over to make inquiries. The king however issued his *congé d'élire* and John de Taunton was elected abbot. The bishop naturally appealed and the archbishop quashed the election but provided John de Taunton to that post. Meanwhile on 23 August 1274 [364] Edward I decided that he was the patron and that Bishop Button was not. Button died in the autumn of that year and was succeeded in 1275 by Robert Burnell, a great lawyer and statesman and a personal friend of the king. In May 1275 [365] the conflicting claims were finally settled, the claims of the bishop first of all to certain manors of the abbey endowment, and secondly the matter of the patronship. He received for himself and the see the manors of Pucklechurch, Blackford, Winscombe and Cranmore and the advowsons of Christian Malford and Kington in Wiltshire, Ashbury in Berkshire and Buckland in Dorset. Then to compensate the bishop for his surrender of the patronship the Crown granted to him a yearly payment of £53 out of the revenues

[353] John of Glastonbury, op. cit. i, 225.
[354] Ibid. 228.
[355] Ibid. 229; *Cal. Wells D. and C. MSS.* (Hist. MSS. Com.) i, 139.
[356] John of Glastonbury, op. cit. i, 230.
[357] Adam de Domerham, op. cit. ii, 536; John of Glastonbury, op. cit. i, 234.

[358] Adam of Domerham, op. cit. ii, 540.
[359] *Cal. Wells D. and C. MSS.* (Hist. MSS. Com.) i, 311.
[360] John of Glastonbury, op. cit. i, 241.
[361] *Cal. Close,* 1272–9, p. 74.
[362] John of Glastonbury, op. cit. i, 240.
[363] Ibid. 241.   [364] Ibid. 243.
[365] *Cal. Close,* 1272–9, p. 245.

Glastonbury Abbey (*Obverse*)
14th Century.

Glastonbury Abbey (*Reverse*)
14th Century.

Glastonbury Abbey (*Obverse*)
13th Century.

Glastonbury Abbey (*Reverse*)
13th Century

SOMERSET MONASTIC SEALS. PLATE I.

of the royal barton at Bath and the royal manor of Congresbury. Finally to compensate himself for this arrangement with the bishop Edward levied on the monks a fine of 1,000 marks.[366]

In 1278 Edward and Queen Eleanor kept Easter at Glastonbury.[367] They arrived on Thursday in Holy Week and were followed the next day by Archbishop Kilwardby. On Easter Monday [368] the king proposed to hold an assize, but this seemed to be an infraction of the rights of the monastery, so the assize was held at Street and the privilege of the abbey was respected. That week the remains of King Arthur and his queen were exposed to view for the benefit of the royal party and were afterwards solemnly placed in wooden chests and deposited in the presbytery behind the high altar. Abbot Taunton was a great builder and it is not improbable that this disinterment of the remains of King Arthur was connected with the work on the great church. His zeal for letters is shown by his large benefaction of books and by the library which he compiled for the monastery. He built the court at Middlezoy, lodgings for the abbot at Ashbury, Domerham, Buckland, and Westonzoyland, a new entrance gate for the monastery and several granges on the abbey lands.[369] His gifts to the monastic church seem to show that several altars were already being used and that the great church was in steady progress. In the autumn of 1290,[370] though ill himself, he attended the funeral of Queen Eleanor the mother of Edward I at Amesbury and died at Damerham on Michaelmas day 1291. His successor John of Kent received the royal assent to his election 22 October 1291.[371]

Abbot Kent's gifts to the monastery were chiefly ornaments and vestments for Divine service and seem to tell of yet further advance in the building. He was buried in the north choir aisle, a fact which shows how great had been the progress in the erection of the church. His successor Geoffrey Fromond's abbotship marks an epoch in the annals of the monastery. The church was so far advanced that it was now dedicated.[372] We know nothing of the details nor can we tell the actual date. He was abbot from 1303 to 1322, and during that time the dedication took place. No mention is made of the event in the register of Bishop Drokensford, the earliest extant of the registers of the bishops of the see, and so we may limit

the date as being between 1303 and 1309 when Bishop Drokensford began his episcopate. Fromond was succeeded by Walter de Taunton whose two months' term of office was distinguished by the building of the great choir screen and rood-loft or pulpit with a great rood above it.[373]

Adam de Sodbury was elected abbot on 5 February 1323 [374] and solemnly blessed as such on 6 March. To him was due the vaulting of the nave of the church and its adornment with splendid pictures.[375] He gave also a great statue of the Virgin Mary and enriched her altar with a large tabernacle.[376] He also caused to be constructed for the church a large clock enriched with processions and various scenes and an organ of great size and he gave eleven bells to the monastery, of which six were placed in the church tower and five in the bell tower, a statement which suggests somewhere in the monastery a detached campanile. On St. Thomas' day 1331 Abbot Sodbury welcomed at Glastonbury King Edward III and his consort Queen Philippa, and the royal party after a stay of three days went on to Wells and there kept Christmas.

The register of Bishop Drokensford gives us evidence of the bishop's authority and the monks' dislike of it. In Lent 1311 he had issued notice of his intention to visit Glastonbury[377] and did visit the seven churches of the abbot's jurisdiction. In all cases the abbot replied to his queries and nothing of importance occurred. In the abbey itself however he was met by a conspiracy of silence which baffled his efforts, and he announced that owing to the illicit oaths of secrecy[378] made to defeat correction the truth could not be detected and he warned them that all such devices were unlawful. He annulled and recalled all such oaths and pronounced excommunication on all who joined in them. Yet for all that his visitation was barren of results.

There had been for some time a considerable controversy between the abbey and the Dean and canons of Wells concerning the boundaries of their estates on the moors, and Prior Breynton had proved a firm defender of the rights of the monastery. In 1334 [379] therefore on the death of Sodbury he was elected by the monks as abbot. His work and his gifts, which latter, as coming out of his revenues as abbot, prove the increasing wealth of the foundation, were on a very considerable scale. He began the private chapel for the abbot and left marble and glass for its completion. To the abbot's

[366] John of Glastonbury, op. cit. i, 245.
[367] Adam de Domerham, op. cit. ii, 587.
[368] John of Glastonbury, op. cit. i, 247.
[369] Ibid. 574.
[370] Adam of Domerham, op. cit. (ed. Hearne) ii, 596.
[371] Cal. Pat. 1281–92, p. 448.
[372] John of Glastonbury, op. cit. i, 255.

[373] John of Glastonbury, op. cit. i, 260. [374] Ibid. 263.
[375] Leland, Itin. iii, 102.
[376] John of Glastonbury, op. cit. i, 263.
[377] Drokensford's Reg. (Somers. Rec. Soc. i, 159).
[378] Ibid. 153.
[379] John of Glastonbury, op. cit. i, 269.

camera he attached another long chamber and changed a noxious hollow into a fish pond which he inclosed with a wall for the private use of the abbot. At Oxford [380] he built four honest chambers for the use of Glastonbury monks studying at the University and he gave them also 20s. wherewith they might purchase a processional cross.

Breynton was succeeded by Walter de Monyngton [381] who was confirmed as abbot by Bishop Ralph of Shrewsbury on 7 November 1342. He is said to have admitted sixty-four monks into the abbey and their names are written down in a copy of his *Secretum* now in the Bodleian Library at Oxford.

In 1342 [382] the inner life of the abbey was disturbed by a conflict between a monk, Thomas Everard, and one of the monastic chaplains. Everard had drawn blood and so had incurred excommunication. He was not aware however of the consequence of his action and continued to minister as if under no such sentence. So when he learnt his condition he appealed to Avignon, and from the Papal Curia Bishop Ralph of Shrewsbury received instruction to inquire, and in February 1343 the monk was absolved. In 1345 [383] Glastonbury was called upon to receive a monk of Eynsham, John de Noux, who had taken too leading a part in a struggle between rival candidates for the abbacy of Eynsham to allow of his remaining in the same monastery.

In March 1349 [384] Bishop Ralph again visited the monastery and on this occasion he admonished Walter de Monyngton to be more approachable to the monks and to allow them better food. The charities of the monastery he ordered to be fully maintained, and for the services in the chapel of the Virgin Mary the full number of chaplains were to be employed.

In 1363 [385] the see of Wells was vacant through the death of Bishop Ralph and the canons of Wells elected Monyngton as their bishop. The monks of Bath however would not accept it, and the canons of Wells, to mark their disapproval of the monks, pronounced excommunication against them, and Archbishop Simon Langham had to be called in to absolve them. During Monyngton's term of office Glastonbury and the rest of Somerset was visited 1348–9 by the Great Pestilence. We have no record of the mortality, but the number of novices accepted by the abbot suggests that it had been considerable. In the earlier part of the century there had been some eighty or more monks at Glastonbury and we know from the list prepared for the clerical subsidy of 1377 [386] that there were then only forty-five. Certainly here monasticism never recovered the blow which the pestilence inflicted on it.

In 1375 [387] John Chinnock was elected abbot of Glastonbury, and he held office for the long period of forty-five years. The story of his abbotship is told somewhat briefly by John of Glastonbury and it is certain that much happened in the monastery which was never recorded. It may have been a case of a contested election when the defeated candidate bore ill-will to his successful rival. On 20 June 1380 [388] order was issued by the Crown for the arrest and delivery to the Abbot and convent of Glastonbury of Thomas Coffeyn a monk of Glastonbury who had absented himself from his convent without leave and intended to cross the sea to the king's prejudice. On 19 September 1381 [389] an order was issued to arrest Thomas Coffeyn as an apostate monk, and on 20 September 1381 his letters of protection were formally revoked.

The abbot appears to have been inefficient or perhaps incapacitated by ill-health. In 1385 Bishop John Harewell of Bath and Wells visited the abbey and confirmed an arrangement made by the convent for some appropriations of the churches of the Twelve Hides and other estates of the monastery to the support of the monks and also defined once more the arrangement by which these churches should be visited by an archdeacon appointed by the abbot. [390]

Soon after the abbey was visited by William Courtenay Archbishop of Canterbury, [391] and these appropriations were again confirmed.

It does not seem however as if the object of both these visitations was merely the confirmation of these pensions and appropriations. The convent seems to have been passing through some internal crisis.

In 1386 [392] the abbot was excused further attendance at Parliament on account of his age. Again on 28 January 1387 [393] the arrest of Thomas Coffeyn was ordered by the Crown because he had brought to England various papal bulls annulling the election of the present abbot.

---

[380] John of Glastonbury, op. cit. i, 270.
[381] Ibid. 272.
[382] *R. of Shrewsbury's Reg.* (Somers. Rec. Soc. x) 459.
[383] *Cal. Papal Letters*, iii, 189.
[384] *R. of Shrewsbury's Reg.* (Somers. Rec. Soc. x) 605–6.
[385] Cf. *Cal. Wells D. and C. MSS.* (Hist. MSS. Com.) i, 266.

[386] Cf. Gasquet, *The Great Pestilence*, 85; Cler. Subs. bdle. 4, no. 2.
[387] *Cal. Wells D. and C. MSS.* (Hist. MSS. Com.) i, 275.
[388] *Cal. Pat.* 1377–81, p. 517.
[389] Ibid. 1381–5, pp. 43, 79.
[390] Cf. *Cal. Wells D. and C. MSS.* (Hist. MSS. Com.) i, 296.
[391] *Cal. Papal Letters*, v, 370.
[392] *Cal. Pat.* 1385–9, p. 202.   [393] Ibid. p. 316.

On 29 June 1389 [394] the temporalities of the monastery were in the king's hands. The abbot seems to have resigned and yet there is no record of it. In 1395 [395] however he is again described in the Crown documents as Abbot of Glastonbury, and in 1397 obtained a papal indult as an old man expecting his demise to choose his own confessor. [396]

Then on 17 July 1398 [397] the Dean of Wells and others were ordered to see to the transfer to Glastonbury of Thomas Lemyngton a monk of Winchester who desired to enter the monastery on account of its "stricter regular life."

In 1397 [398] John Tabeler, a monk of Glastonbury, was promoted to the office of a papal chaplain, and on 5 January 1399 [399] Richard Houndsworth, another monk, being aged and weak, and desiring to remain in the abbey, obtained a papal licence to hold the office of chamberlain for his life and not be forcibly removed from it.

In 1400 [400] John Chinnock and the monastery obtained from Henry IV the confirmation of several charters and privileges, so that it is clear that Abbot Chinnock was still nominally the head of the monastery. In 1407 however during the vacancy before the consecration of Bishop Bubwith Archbishop Arundel was called in to visit the monastery. [401] He found that the discipline was very defective, for the abbot was too old and feeble to carry out his duties. Yet he lived on to 1420.

Then, living on for three years in the abbotship of Nicholas Frome, we find Thomas Coffeyn Prior of Glastonbury preparing for his approaching end and gaining a papal indult [402] to choose his own confessor.

Nicholas Frome was elected abbot in 1420. In 1424 he obtained a papal indult [403] which sanctioned the promotion to Holy Orders of forty monks of the house, a step which would leave very few lay monks remaining in the abbey. He is said to have completed the chapter-house and to have built the misericord house, the great camera of the abbot, the camera of the bishop, and to have erected an embattled wall [404] He died on 24 April 1456 and was succeeded first of all by Walter More, who only lived for seventeen weeks, and then by John Selwood, the unanimous choice of the monks. [405]

In 1472 Bishop Stillington issued a commission to John, Bishop of Rochester, to visit Glastonbury, in consequence of the neglect of the abbot. [406]

In 1489 Innocent VIII in a bull directed to Archbishop Morton of Canterbury [407] drew attention to the censures that were being cast on the lives of the clergy and the moral and spiritual condition of the monasteries. The archbishop was on that account given special legatine authority to visit and if necessary to correct the monasteries of England. In 1490 he came to Glastonbury and made a searching inquiry into everything. He found that on the whole the lives of the monks were without blame. Abbot Selwood was found faithful to the great responsibilities of his important office.

Once more before the dissolution of the monastery we find the bishop of the diocese exerting his authority. On the death of Abbot Selwood [408] the monks obtained licence from Henry VII to elect an abbot and their choice fell on John Wasyn. They had not however notified their action to Bishop Fox, nor had they asked his consent to proceed to an election. He therefore with the consent of the Crown quashed the election and nominated on 12 November 1493 Richard Beere or Bere, and on 20 January 1494 Beere was enthroned at Glastonbury.

The chroniclers of Glastonbury, William of Malmesbury and his continuators, testify to the pride of the monks in the memory of St. Dunstan, and it is clear that they believed that they possessed considerable relics if not the remains of his body.

In the early years of the 16th century a controversy broke out between the prior and monks of Christchurch, Canterbury, and the abbot and monks [409] of Glastonbury concerning the relics of St. Dunstan. Both convents claimed to be in possession of them and a scrutiny was made by order of Archbishop Warham on 22 April 1508, which, while it placed the question in a clearer light, did not bring the monks of Glastonbury to acknowledge their mistake. William of Malmesbury [410] relates that in the year 1012 Edmund Ironside came to Glastonbury and told the monks how that Canterbury had been consumed by fire and that the church had been destroyed by the Danes. The monks were much grieved at this news, for they remembered how that their former abbot St. Dunstan, as archbishop, had been buried there. So they obtained the sanction of King Edmund and sent forth Abbot Beohtred and four monks to Canterbury and the place they found to be all desolate and forsaken. They soon however

[394] *Cal. Pat.* 1388–92, p. 74.
[395] Ibid. 1393–6, p. 547.
[396] *Cal. Papal Letters*, v, 50.
[397] Ibid. 154.
[398] Ibid. 212.   [399] Ibid. 202.
[400] *Cal. Pat.* 1399–1401, p. 228.
[401] Cf. Entry in unnumbered folio at end of Bishop Beckington's Register.
[402] *Cal. Papal Letters*, v, 302.
[403] Ibid. vii, 372.
[404] John of Glastonbury, op. cit. i, 278.
[405] Wells Epis. Reg. Beckington's folio at end.

[406] Wells Epis. Reg. Stillington, folio 8.
[407] Wilkins, *Concilia*, iii, 632.
[408] *Fox's Reg.* (Batten's ed.) 170–4.
[409] *Angl. Sacra*, ii, 227.
[410] Will. of Malmesbury, *Antiq. Glaston.* (ed. Hearne) i, 31.

discovered the grave of St. Dunstan, and having opened it they recognized the remains from a ring on one of the fingers. These remains they took up and carried to Glastonbury and with joy placed them carefully in a new tomb. In 1120 [411] Eadmer of Canterbury wrote to the monks of Glastonbury to know by what authority they claimed to have the bones of St. Dunstan. He said that as a boy he had distinct recollections of being present at the opening of St. Dunstan's grave by order of Archbishop Lanfranc and he remembered that he saw the body of the saint within the tomb. He wondered also why up to 1066 the monks of Glastonbury had made a pilgrimage to Canterbury to pray at the tomb of St. Dunstan and why when Abbot Ægelnoth the deprived abbot of Glastonbury was received at Canterbury he for years kept silent and never revealed that the bones of St. Dunstan were not there but at Glastonbury.

Glastonbury nevertheless clung to the assertion that St. Dunstan's bones were buried in their church, and when Abbot Beere had made a new shrine and placed the relics of their great abbot in their new home the prior of Canterbury and Archbishop Warham felt bound to protest and make a fresh inquiry into the matter. At Canterbury Prior Goldston found the bones, and on opening the inner leaden coffin they discovered a tablet with the inscription—'hic requiescit sanctus Dunstanus archiepiscopus.' Then Archbishop Warham [412] wrote to Abbot Beere, but he was too unwell to go to Canterbury to see for himself, and the monks would not be convinced. So the controversy slumbered on until in 1539 the Dissolution closed it.

Abbot Beere was also a great builder. He erected the church of St. Benignus [413] to the west of the abbey for the use of the poor who were attracted by the alms of the monastery, and at Northwood and Sharpham close by he built two sumptuous houses for the abbot. The abbot's lodgings in the abbey were also enlarged by a new wing called the king's lodging in the gallery, and in London new accommodation was provided for himself and the monks who had to go there. New buildings were erected for the secular priests who served in the chapels of the great church and for the chaplains known as clerks of our Lady. In the church itself he vaulted the space under the central tower and because the piers of the tower were showing signs of collapse he inserted on the north and south transept sides St. Andrew's arches such as already existed in Wells. The eastern part of the church was also in danger, and Leland tells us that Abbot Beere ' archid on bothe sides the Est Parte of the Chirch that began to cast owt.' In the north transept he

made the chapel known as our Lady de Loretta in memory of his embassy to Italy, and to the east of the choir [414] he began and Abbot Whyting finished the chapel known as the Edgar Chapel. He founded also the almshouse for poor women to the north-west of the monastery and gave them a chapel for their private use. He founded also a chapel of the Holy Sepulchre on the south side of the nave. He died 20 January 1524 and was buried in the nave.

On the death of Beere the convent, which consisted of forty-seven monks,[415] deliberated 11–16 February 1525, and were unable to come to a decision and finally asked Cardinal Wolsey to nominate an abbot for them. Wolsey chose Richard Whyting, and since the monks accepted him he was solemnly blessed as abbot on 8 March 1525 by William Gilbert, Abbot of Bruton and bishop suffragan to John Clerk the Bishop of Bath and Wells. Richard Whyting was the son of a Glastonbury tenant at Wrington, and was brought up at the monastic school at Glastonbury with a view to his becoming a monk and a priest. He took his degree of M.A. at Cambridge 1483 and was ordained priest 1501. Whyting must have been nearly sixty years of age when he was appointed to rule this great religious foundation, and all his wisdom and caution were needed for the dark future before him.

On 3 November 1534 the Act of Supremacy was passed and attached to it was another act which declared it to be high treason to deny this royal claim. On 19 September [416] Whyting had subscribed to this act. The document is signed also by fifty-one monks, but many of the signatures are by the same hand and some have clearly been added. The general visitation of the monastic houses began in September 1535, but it is certain that Dr. Layton was active in Somerset some two or three months before that date. On 25 August 1535 he arrived at Glastonbury and after a careful examination he seems to have recognized that the task before him to discover immorality or general wrongdoing was a difficult one. He wrote to Cromwell immediately to say that there was nothing notable at Glastonbury [417]—'the brethren be so strait kept that they cannot offend : but fain they would if they might, as they confess, and so the fault is not with them.' Abbot Whyting now clearly saw that evil times were coming. On 26 August 1535 he sent as a present to Cromwell a deed of gift of the advowson of West Monkton [418] 'which of trewthe is the firste that hathe been

---

[411] *Angl. Sacra,* ii, 222.   [412] Ibid. 229–33.
[413] Cf. Leland *ut supra.*

[414] *Somers. Arch. Soc. Proc.* liv (2), 107 ; lv, 104.
[415] Cooper, *Athen. Cantab.* 71 ; Cf. Adam of Domerham, op. cit. (ed. Hearne) i, p. xcvii.
[416] Whyting's Reg. B.M. Add. MSS. 17451; cf. *Deputy Keeper's Rep.* vii, 287.
[117] Wright, *Suppression of the Monasteries,* 59.
[418] *L. and P. Hen. VIII,* ix, 188.

graunted oute of this monasterye as farre as I can finde knowledge.'

On 9 September he sent [419] also to Cromwell the grant of the corrody under the convent seal which Sir Thomas More had enjoyed and £5 of arrears due to Sir Thomas More and £5 due from the corrody up to Michaelmas next.

Dr. Layton had meanwhile laid down certain injunctions which restricted the movements of the abbot. He desired as much as possible to keep the monks apart from the abbot, and on 26 October [420] Whyting wrote to Cromwell begging some relaxation of these orders, as subversive of the discipline of the abbey. He had already induced his friend Sir John Fitzjames [421] on 2 September to write on his behalf. It does not however appear that they were ever removed.

Yet Dr. Layton had been so much impressed with the character of Whyting that he wrote to the king in his praise and had consequently brought down on himself the displeasure of Cromwell. He wrote from Reading on 16 September [422] a humble letter of apology, promising to be more circumspect next time and acknowledging that now he perceived that the abbot [423] neither then nor now knew God or his prince or any other part of a good Christian man's religion.

On 28 March 1537 the abbot wrote to Cromwell regretting he could not give Mr. Maurice Berkeley [424] the mastership of the game on his parks at Northwood and Sharpham, for already at Cromwell's request he had given the reversion of it to Mr. John Wadham.

On 28 October however he wrote again to Cromwell and offered him the park at Northwood for Maurice Berkeley, and on 26 January 1538 he offered Cromwell the game in his park at Sturminster Newton, and the advowson of Nettleton in Wiltshire, regretting at the same time that he could not give him Batcombe since Dr. Tregonwell had already got it for a friend. [425]

The Act of April 1539 had given into the king's hands such monasteries as should voluntarily be surrendered or should be forfeit through attainder of treason. Whyting had not been to Convocation this year, having excused himself by reason of age and ill-health.

After March 1539 Glastonbury was the only monastery left standing in Somerset. The commissioners had found Whyting such that they could not hope to force him into a surrender and had evidently reported so to Cromwell, for he decided to proceed against him in Somerset.

During the summer various agents of Cromwell had been to Glastonbury, and already in anticipation of the end they had begun to collect and forward to Cromwell many of the valuables of the monasteries. On 2 May Pollard, Tregonwell and Petre [426] sent up to the Treasury from the west of England 493 ounces of gold, 16,000 ounces of gilt plate, and 28,700 ounces of parcel gilt and silver plate. On Friday 19 September 1539 Layton, Pollard and Moyle arrived at Glastonbury, and as they were not expected they learnt that Whyting was at his lodging at Sharpham about two miles off. They went therefore to Sharpham to question him, bidding him ' to call to his remembrance that which he had forgotten and so declare the truth.' His answers they took down in writing and made him append his signature to their manuscript, and with this document Whyting was sent up to the Tower of London to be examined if necessary by Cromwell himself.

Then began the wholesale spoliation of the monastery. The servants of the abbot were discharged and a search was made for valuables. £300 in cash was soon found, and they wrote to Cromwell immediately after to say, ' we have found a fair chalice of gold and divers other parcels of plate which the abbot had hid secretly from all such commissioners as have been there in time past whereby we think he ought to make his hand by this untruth to his King's Majesty.'

Again on 28 September they wrote to Cromwell that they had found money and plate hidden in secret places in the monastery, preparatory to being sent out of the country. They had also found in the abbot's library a book containing arguments against the divorce of Queen Katherine, and a life of Thomas Becket, Archbishop of Canterbury, and now they include in that which they are determined to prove to be treason two monks who were the treasurers of the church.

Again on 2 October they wrote to say that they had come to know of ' divers and sundry treasons committed ' by the abbot, of which the certainty ' shall appear unto your lordship in a book herein inclosed with the accusers' names put to the same which we think to be very high and rank treasons.' This document however no longer exists and was probably destroyed at the time. Meanwhile Pollard sent up 24 October [427] another harvest of valuables from Glastonbury, 71 ounces of gold with precious stones, 7,214 ounces of gilt plate and 6,387 ounces of silver. He described them as the possessions of attainted persons.

What was happening in London with Whyting is not very clear. He had been subjected to examination and apparently had not com-

[419] L. and P. Hen. VIII, ix, 313.   [420] Ibid. 685.
[421] Cott. MSS. Cleopatra, E. iv.
[422] Cromwell, Correspondence, xx, 14.
[423] Ellis, Original Letters (3rd Series), iii, 247.
[424] Cromwell, Correspondence, xii, 46.
[425] Ibid. 49.
[426] Monastic Treasures (Abbotsford Club), 24.
[427] Ibid. 38.

mitted himself. Cromwell in his 'Remembrances' [428] says—'Item. Certain persons to be sent to the Tower for the further examination of the abbot of Glaston.' And again—'Item Councillors to give evidence against the abbot of Glaston, Richard Pollard, Lewis Forstell and Thomas Moyle. Item. To see that the evidence is well sorted and the indictments well drawn against the said abbot and his accomplices. Item. The abbot of Glaston to be tryed at Glaston and also executed there with his complycys.'

So he was condemned, on evidence which was never made public, on a charge of treason in that he and two monks in charge of the treasury at Glastonbury had feloniously concealed from the king some of the treasures of the abbey. Then in Wells preparation was being made for the reception of the condemned, and while in London it seems to have been given out that they were being sent for trial to Somerset, in Somerset itself it was known that they came as already condemned. John Lord Russell had already been busy collecting a jury which should accept without any scruples the evidence that was sent to them. Among the jurymen were John Sydenham, Thomas Horner and Nicholas Fitzjames and 'my brother Paulet' for whom was destined the surveyorship of the monastic estates. Whyting and his fellow monks John Thorne and Roger James reached Wells on Friday November 14. The inquiry had already begun, and Pollard, who managed the case, had brought together various tenants and dependants on whom he could rely to say just what was needed. But there was no real trial at Wells. The jury accepted what had been done elsewhere, and on Saturday 15 November Whyting and his companions were delivered over to Pollard for execution. From Wells they were carried to Glastonbury and hanged on the summit of St. Michael's Tor, and as usual afterwards Whyting's head was cut off and stuck on the gateway of the abbey and his body, divided into four parts, was distributed to Bridgwater, Ilchester, Wells and Bath.

That same autumn Cromwell [429] notes the value of that which had come into the king's hands—the plate of Glastonbury 11,000 ounces and over, besides golden, the furniture of the house at Glastonbury, in ready money from Glastonbury £1,100 and over, the rich copes from Glastonbury, the whole year's revenues from Glastonbury, the sums due to Glastonbury £2,000 and above.

The *Valor Ecclesiasticus* which had been drawn up in 1535 gives us a clear idea of the enormous influence and wealth of this monastery. It is returned as worth £3,301 7s. 4d.

The manors which it possessed will be found stated in the list of the endowments ; £140 16s. 8d. was to be distributed yearly in alms to the poor on the foundation, as the monks had induced themselves to believe, of King Arthur and King Lucius, the first Christian kings of Britain, and Kings Kenwalch, Kentwine, Edgar, Æthelwulf, Æthelbald, Æthelred, Henry VII, and other kings as well as Queen Guinevere and other princes.

Twenty-five names of Glastonbury monks appear in Cardinal Pole's pension list of 1553. [430]

On 21 November 1556 [431] four survivors of the monastery who had found a refuge at Westminster petitioned the queen for a restoration of the abbey of Glastonbury. They asked for no endowment and offered to pay rent for the lands they needed if only they might have a grant of the site and buildings. Queen Mary was certainly in favour of the project—it would be a great honour to the memory of Joseph of Arimathea who lay there—but similar applications from the monks of other monasteries created a delay and the queen died before any real step could be taken. The monks' names were John Phagan, John Nott, William Adelwold and William Kentwyne. [432] Of these all but Nott had signed the Act of Supremacy.

That the effort to bring about the restoration of the abbey in Queen Mary's reign was regarded as serious is shown by the will of Sir Thomas Shackell, priest, rector of Hinton St. George, made 17 July 1557, where he leaves 40s. ' to the edefyenge of the Abbye of Glastonbury yf it be not payed in my lyfetyme.'

The learning of the monastery must chiefly be tested by the zeal the monks displayed for the creation of a library and for the transcription of books. No great theologian or historian can be claimed as entirely its own by Glastonbury, though Abbot Dunstan was among the first scholars of his age and Abbot Beere was a friend of the New Learning. Of course at first, if any record is made, it would be of books for the service of the church, and perhaps the earliest notice is that of the *Evangelistarium* given by King Ine [433] which was richly ornamented and lettered in gold. William of Malmesbury, [434] when writing of the many gifts made by King Edmund to the monastery, refers to the books he gave. Soon after it is recorded, that Abbot Brihtwold or Brihtwin, first Bishop of Wilton, gave two *Evangelistaria* to the abbey, [435] and this concludes our knowledge of the books of the old English monastery. Under the Normans however we begin a series of records which tell

[428] Cromwell's Remembrances, Cott. MSS. Titus B. i, fol. 41.

[429] Cotton MSS. Titus B. i, fol. 446.

[430] Exchequer R. Misc. Bks. vol. 32.

[431] Harleian MSS. 3881, fol. 38b.

[432] *Dep. Keeper's Rep.* vii, App. ii.

[433] John of Glastonbury, *Chron.* i, 95.

[434] *Gesta Pontif.* (Rolls Ser.) 196.

[435] John of Glastonbury, *Chron.* i, 151.

of literary activity and intelligence. Henry de Blois was abbot from 1125 to 1171 [436] and gave more than forty books ' *librario*,' to the monastic collection, and these included both Service Books and books of other kinds.

Henry de Blois encouraged also the transcription, of books, and Adam de Domerham [437] gives us the list of books copied in the monastery during his tenure of office. The superintendence of the work was confided to the prior, and Priors Martin and William were in office when Henry was abbot. Under Martin's care there was copied, besides a complete Bible and numerous theological works, Pliny's Natural History, Lives of the Caesars, the *Gesta Anglorum*, *Gesta Britonum*, *Gesta Franconum*, a book of the abbots of Clairvaux, a book on physiognomy and geology, and the work of Peter Alfonsius in one volume, and a volume on Rhetoric, and Quintilian, show that the more secular aspects of learning were not neglected.

In the second volume of Hearne's edition of John of Glastonbury's *Chronicle* [438] he inserts a list of books the property of the monks of Glastonbury in the year 1247. The list is remarkably long and occupies twenty pages. It is taken from a MS. in the library of Trinity College, Cambridge, and reveals to us the wealth of the library. The studies of the monks were certainly of a very general kind, and while theological works of course predominate, there are many books on Monasticism, of general Church History, on medicine and language, and Aristotle and Plato are represented by the Timœus and the Logic. They had also two copies of Virgil and a portion of Cicero. The same MS. [439] gives us a list of books, eight in number, given by Richard de Culmton, and through William Brito, the precentor of Glastonbury, the library of the monastery was enriched by the legacy or gift of more than twenty books of Geoffrey of Bath and Brother Laurence.

A little later in the century further additions were made through the zeal of Abbot John of Taunton. After his death the books which he had purchased or caused to be transcribed were brought into the chapter house [440] and formally entered into the library register. They were twenty-five in number.

The 14th century however witnessed an equal zeal on the part of the abbots for the promotion of learning and a similar flow of books to the great collection the monks already had. In 1322 [441] William of Taunton left his books to the monastery, and in 1333 [442] Abbot Adam de Sodbury enriched the abbey in a similar way.

Abbot John de Breynton's benefactions were of another kind. [443] He built a lodging for Glastonbury monks at Oxford that so those who were studious in his household might the better increase their knowledge of laws and theology. For the 15th century we have little or no information, but the condition of the abbey at the end proves the diligence and learning of its abbots. Richard Beere was one of the foremost scholars of England, the friend of Erasmus, a Greek scholar whom Erasmus consulted in his Greek Testament and on other critical work.

When John Leland visited [444] Glastonbury in his antiquarian commission about 1538, he mentions with admiration the library in which he tells us there were more than 400 books. His list however is very small and gives us no clue to the value of the spoils. There are two or three Glastonbury MSS. now in the British Museum and some in the library of Trinity College, Cambridge.

William of Malmesbury [445] towards the end of his Antiquities tells us of seven Glastonbury monks who had risen to be Archbishops of Canterbury. The first however cannot be accepted since he was archbishop before the restoration of Glastonbury by King Ine. He has clearly been confused with Beorwald the first English abbot. The others were Athelm 914, St. Dunstan 960, Ethelgar 988, Sigeric or Siric 990, Æphege, 1005 and Æthelnoth 1020. He gives us also a list of Glastonbury monks who had risen to be bishops, and both lists testify to the learning and character to which the monastery attained.

At the time of the Conquest the monks suffered the loss of some of their estates, but these were afterwards recovered and even William the Conqueror made reparation for what he had robbed them of. The possessions of the abbey amounted to the huge extent of 818 hides. The ' twelve hides ' consisting of the site, precincts and immediate demesne of the abbey was regarded as an ungeldable and unhidated liberty of which the islands of Meare, Panborough, and Edgarley formed part. As far as these estates lay in Somerset the details of the endowment will be found in the account of the Survey. [446]

The monastery also owned large estates in other counties and since these are not recorded under the Somerset Survey it is necessary at least to mention their names and their extent.

In Wiltshire the property of the abbey was returned as amounting to 258 hides which consisted of the manors etc. of Damerham, Hanindone, Longbridge and Monkton Deverill, Christian Malford, Badbury in Chisledon, Mil-

[436] John of Glastonbury, *Chron.* i, 168.
[437] A. de Domerham, *Hist. Glaston.* ii, 317.
[438] *Op. cit.* ii, 423. [439] Ibid. 443.
[440] John of Glastonbury, *Chron.* i, 251.
[441] Ibid. 262. [442] Ibid. 265.

[443] John of Glastonbury, *Chron.* i, 271.
[444] Leland, *Coll.* iv, 153.
[445] *Op. cit.* (ed. Hearne) i, 92.
[446] *V.C.H. Somerset*, i, 460.

denhall, Winterbourne Monkton and Winterbourne in Idmiston, Nettleton, Grittleton, Kington Langley, Idmiston and Steeple Langford. In Dorset there were fifty-eight hides at Sturminster Newton, Buckland Newton and Buckland Abbas, Woodyates, Pentridge and Lyme.

In Berkshire there was the manor of Ashbury of forty hides, and in Gloucestershire, Pucklechurch of twenty hides.

Soon after the expedition of Henry II to Ireland in 1171, the monastery became possessed of some Irish estates out of which they formed a distinct but dependent priory. Philip of Worcester [447] the Constable of Ireland gave the monks the vill and church of Kilcummin near Killarney and a hundred carucates of land and built there for them a college or priory in honour of St. Philip and St. James and also of St. Armin. A certain monk James was chosen and sent there as the first prior.

About the same time William de Burgh gave to Richard, a monk of Glastonbury, the vill of Ardimur, with the church and many adjacent hamlets and their chapels. He endowed this project with further mills and fisheries for the purpose of building a house or priory in honour of God and the Virgin Mary. The priory came to be known as Ocunild and Richard was sent out as its first prior.

It is probable that these gifts were not of great value. We soon lose sight of them and the priories were doubtless destroyed in the many internecine wars that occurred there.

The total revenues therefore of the abbey at the end of the 13th century [448] amounted to the large sum of £1,406 1s. 8d., of which over £1,355 was derived from the temporalities, the largest item being £515 8s. 8d. for the 'Twelve Hides.'

Four years before the monastery was dissolved we have the estimate of its revenues from the Valor Ecclesiasticus [449] of 1535. They are returned as worth £3,311 7s. 4d. yearly, which sum is nearly equal to that of the yearly revenues of all the other conventual houses in Somerset.

On the attainder of Abbot Whyting and the surrender of the abbey to the Crown in 1539 these possessions were again assessed on a survey made by Richard Pollard and Thomas Moyle.[450] This assessment raises the value of the rental to £4,085 6s. 8d. and gives us a good deal of information concerning the woods, fisheries and swanneries which was not recorded in the earlier survey.

[447] John of Glastonbury, *Chron.* (ed. Hearne) i, 171, 172.
[448] *Pope Nich. Tax.* (Rec. Com.) *passim*.
[449] Cf. *Valor Eccl.* (Rec. Com.) i, 142–7.
[450] Cf. Hearne, *Langtoft's Chron.* (Bagster's Reprint 1810) ii, 343.

ABBOTS OF GLASTONBURY [451]

A	B
Worgret, occurs 601	
Lademund	
Bregoret	
Beorthwald	
Hemgisel	Haemgils
Beorwald [452]	Wealstod
Aldeorth	Coemgils
Atfrith	Beorhtwald
Kemgisel	Cealdun
Guba	Muca
Ticca, 754	Wicca
Cuma	Bosa
Walthun, 762 [453]	Stitheard
Tumbert	Herefrith
Beadulf	Humbeorht
Muca	Andhun
Guthlac	Guthlac
Ealmund	Cuthred [454]
Herefryth	Ecgwulf
Striwerd, *alias* Stithherd, 991 [455]	
Ealthun, 992 [456]	
Ælfric, 927 ?	Ælfric
Dunstan, 946–957	Dunstan
Ælfward *alias* Ægelward, 962	Ælfweard 975
Sigegar, 973	Sigegar,—975
Beorhtred, 1000	
Brichtwin, 1017 [457]	
Ægelward II, 1027–53 [458]	
Ægelnoth, 1053–78	
Thurstin, 1078–1100	
Herlewin, 1101–20	
Seffrid Pelochin, 1120–26	
Henry of Blois, 1126–71	
Robert of Winchester, 1171–78	
[Vacancy, 1178–89]	
Henry de Soliaco, 1189–92	
Savaric, Bishop of Bath, 1192–1205	
Jocelin, Bishop of Bath, 1206–18	
William, 1219–23	
Robert of Bath, 1223–34	
Michael of Ambresbury, 1235–52	

[451] There are two lists of the early abbots of Glastonbury; that given by William of Malmesbury (Adam of Domerham, *Hist. Glaston.* i, 103) and one of apparently the 10th century (Cotton MS. Tiberius B. 5). Some names are common to both, but the order is different and neither can be regarded as reliable. Malmesbury's list is here marked A and the Cottonian list B.
[452] Cf. Jaffé, *Monum. Moguntina*, 48. Flourished c. 720.
[453] Adam of Domerham, *Hist. Glaston.* i, 64.
[454] Cf. Goldast, *Script. Rerum Aleman.* ii (2), 153.
[455] Adam of Domerham, op. cit. i, 71.
[456] Cf. Stubbs, *Mem. of St. Dunstan* (Rolls Ser.), p. lxxx.
[457] Adam of Domerham, op. cit. 87.
[458] Ibid. 89. For references to the subsequent abbots see body of the article.

Roger of Ford, 1252–61
Robert of Petherton, 1261–74
John of Taunton, 1274–91
John of Kent, 1291–1303
Geoffrey de Fromond, 1303–22
Walter of Taunton, 1322–23
Adam of Sudbury, 1323–34
John of Breynton, 1334–42
Walter of Monington, 1342–75
John Chinnock, 1375–1420
Nicholas Frome, 1420–55
Walter More, 1456
John Selwood, 1456–92
Richard Beere, 1493–1524
Richard Whyting, 1525–39

Seal[459]: 13th century; circular, 3½ in. in diameter. Obverse: In the centre, under a carved canopy, the Blessed Virgin with the Child on her left arm and a branch of the Holy Thorn in her right hand; on the plinth below ✴ S. MARIA. On either side in smaller niches St. Catherine and St. Margaret with their names below. In base, three carved arches, with a church under the centre arch and a bird under each of the others.

TESTIS ✴ ADEST ✿ ISTI ✴ SCRIPTO ✿ GENETRIX ✴ PIA ✿ XPI ✴ GLASTONIE

Reverse: Three niches, in which St. Dunstan between St. Patrick and St. Benignus with names below. In base three carved niches: in the centre St. Dunstan taking the Devil by the nose with a pair of pincers; on the right three fishes; the subject on the left is uncertain.

CONFIRMANT〰 HAS 〰 RES 〰 INSCRIPTI〰 PONTIFICES 〰 TRES

4. THE ABBEY OF ATHELNEY

The island of Athelney is on the north side of Stanmoor, and on the north bank of the River Tone, being about 4 miles south-west of Bridgwater. It consists of two low hills divided by a shallow depression, containing 24 acres in extent, of which the eastern and slightly higher hill where was the monastery of our Blessed Saviour, St. Peter, St. Paul, and St. Athelwine, comprises 11½ acres. It is still often in winter-time an island to which people have to go by boats.

It was to this place that Alfred retreated in the autumn of 877, and in the spring of 878 he built here a fortress called Ethelingaeigge.[460]

Asser,[461] whose account is vivid and valuable, having visited the place as chaplain to Alfred himself, describes it as a small island in the midst of an impassable morass, and says that Alfred, while he often thought of the needs of his soul, among other good deeds ordered that two monasteries should be built, of which the one for monks

was at Athelney. In this monastery he collected monks from every quarter, and placed over them, as their first abbot,[462] John, an Old-Saxon priest and monk, and certain other priests and deacons from beyond the sea, of whom, finding that he had not as large a number as he wanted, he procured as many as possible from the same race in Gaul, and among them Asser tells us he had seen a young lad who was born a pagan, who had been educated in the monastery and was by no means the least in advancement of the monks there.

It has been questioned[463] whether Alfred really founded the monastery—or whether he did not enlarge a hermitage or monastery already in existence. The dedication of St. Egelwine or Athelwine, the brother of King Kenewalch, suggests a greater antiquity, and the charter which Alfred granted to the monastery suggests that he rather enlarged than founded the house.

Asser, however, who is our best authority, speaks of the monastery as recently founded by Alfred. He tells us that the monks who were gathered at first under Abbot John were not all men devoted to the service of God, and some of them resisted the discipline which the abbot would impose upon them.

On one occasion[464] a priest and a deacon of Gallic birth, having laid their plans, hid at night in the chapel waiting for the abbot to come alone in the early morning for his prayers, and intending then and there to slay him before the altar and carry his dead body and lay it before a house of ill fame. When the abbot, John, appeared that night they attacked him, but his efforts to resist them and his shouting roused the brother monks, and though the men wounded their abbot, he was rescued, and his assailants were ultimately caught and imprisoned.

William of Malmesbury,[465] writing in the first half of the 12th century, tells us of a church which was there built, which seems to have been erected on piles and to have had apsidal chapels attached. He says the monks there in his time were few in number and poor, but they were consoled in their poverty by their love of a quiet solitude.

The early history of the abbey is very obscure. There was a cartulary in existence in the first half of the 18th century, of which a transcript[466] of the earlier portion was made by Dr. Harbin in 1735, and this is now in the Phillipps library at Cheltenham. The original however has disappeared, and it seems as if probably the second

459 *Cat. of Seals B.M.* 3189, lxxi, 61, 62.
460 Ingulf, *Script. post Bedam*, 869.
461 Asser, 'Vit. Ælfred,' *Mon. Hist. Brit.* i, 493.
462 Will. Malmesbury, *Gesta Reg. Angl.* (Rolls. Ser.) i, 130.
463 Reyner, *De. Antiq. Benedict. in Angl.* ii, Sec. 6, p. 132.
464 Asser, De 'Rebus Gest. Ælf,' *Mon. Hist. Brit.* i, 494.
465 Will. Malmesbury, *Gesta Pontif.* (Rolls Ser.) 199.
466 Cf. *Somers. Rec. Soc. Publ.* xiv, Introd.

portion contained the story of the abbey rather than copies of its charters.

Collinson quotes the names of one or two Saxon abbots, which seems to suggest that he had actually seen the vanished manuscript. The Harbin transcript has been published by the Somerset Record Society, and it gives us a considerable group of early charters. A charter of King Alfred granting the manor of Sutton to the monastery is given in this cartulary in which he describes the place as ' the Island of Nobles.'[467]

At the time of the Conquest, we find the abbey allied, together with Muchelney, to the great monastery at Glastonbury, so that the three foundations were acting together to resist Bishop Giso, who attempted to assert his visitorial authority as bishop of the diocese over Muchelney and Athelney but was compelled to do so through the medium of the Abbot of Glastonbury.

In 1160 [468] we find the abbey providing for the conduct of its legal affairs by assigning to Robert de Beauchamp their lands in Frogmore, on condition of his representing them at the county assize and going to the pleas and business of their church whenever he should be called.

Soon after a considerable change took place in the position of the abbot.[469] Bishop Savaric, as we have shown in our general historical sketch, persuaded Abbot Benedict II of Athelney to give the church of Long Sutton to found a prebend in the cathedral church of Wells; the Abbot of Athelney for the time being was to be *ex-officio* prebend of Sutton, with the stall next to the sub-dean.[470] It was also decided that he should not be bound to reside in Wells, but must provide a vicar with four marks a year stall wages.

In 1249 the then abbot realized the loss of freedom which ensued from his holding the prebendal stall at Wells.

On the morrow of St. George, 24 April, 1249,[471] he was summoned to a chapter meeting at Wells, and sent as his proctor one of the monks of his abbey. The chapter refused to accept the proxy because the monk was not a canon, and they condemned the abbot for a breach of the customary rules and laws of the chapter, because he had also made complaint before one of the lords of assize concerning some fishery dispute the abbey had with the dean and chapter about their estate at North Curry, without first making application to the chapter itself.

There are two other entries in the chapter manuscripts which are not easy of explanation, as they involved loss of estate to the abbey itself. During the episcopate of Bishop Jocelin [472] Abbot Benedict gave him the advowson of Ilton to form a prebend in Wells. The gift could not have been popular with the convent, for we find them soon after quarrelling with John, Chancellor of Wells, who held that prebendal stall. Benedict's successor, Abbot Roger,[473] gave also to Bishop Jocelin the tithes of Pitney and Wearne in the parish of Huish to support the endowments of that prebendal church.

In the 14th century we have a good deal of evidence concerning the extent to which monastic houses were burdened by royal pensioners.

In 1304 Gilbert de Ragun went to the monastery with a royal letter, bidding them receive him as a pensioner, and they appealed against this, claiming exemption because already they had two of the aged servants of the king, John de Hanele and Nicholas Freyn, living there and provided with board and lodging at the expense of the abbey.

On 6 September 1325,[474] John de Blebury also arrived with a similar request from Edward II. On 17 November 1327 [475] William de Rainton, the king's yeoman, came demanding such maintenance as Philip de Redynges had received in the late king's time.

On 8 September 1341,[476] Edward la Chamberleyn, clerk, came with a royal request which was based on the fact of the creation of a new abbot and the king's claim to a corrody on each such occasion.

In 1342 (15 December),[477] the abbey was called upon to receive Henry de Acum, ' Spygurnel,' to house, to provide, and to maintain him by reason of his previous good conduct to the king himself, and six years after, 5 March 1348,[478] as Henry de Acum was dead, Walter de Stodley, yeoman of the king's kitchen, was to receive such maintenance as Henry de Acum was wont to receive there, and there was a complaint added that Henry de Acum did not receive, through his own modesty and humility, all that was due to him.

In 1314 Bishop Drokensford's [479] register introduces us to a disciplinary case. He received a letter from John Dalderby, Bishop of Lincoln, asking him to place William de Walton, a monk of Peterborough, in Athelney Abbey, or some other Benedictine house at the cost of his own abbey. He was sent away on account of his wickedness and disobedience to his abbot. The bishop asks that he may be placed in a separate cell and suggests fetters for his better keeping.

[467] Cf. *Somers. Rec. Soc. Publ.* xiv, 127.
[468] *Somers. Rec. Soc. Publ.* xiv, 152.
[469] *Cal. Wells D. and C. MSS.* (Hist. MSS. Com.) i, 57.
[470] *Angl. Sacra,* i, 563 ; *Cal. Wells D. and C. MSS.* (Hist. MSS. Com.) i, 57.
[471] *Cal. Wells D. and C. MSS.* (Hist. MSS. Com.) i, 86–7.

[472] *Cal. Wells D. and C. MSS.* (Hist. MSS. Com.) i, 43.   [473] Ibid. 47.
[474] *Cal. Close,* 1323–7, p. 503.
[475] Ibid. 1327–30, p. 235.
[476] Ibid. 1341–3, p. 272.
[477] Ibid. 666.   [478] Ibid. 1346–9, p. 497.
[479] *Somers. Rec. Soc. Publ.* i, 8.

On 13 June 1319, Bishop Drokensford wrote to the Bishop of Lincoln to say that Walton had twice escaped from his fetters, and that as he caused a great scandal to Athelney, he must go back to his own abbey.

In 1321 [480] Bishop Drokensford issued a pastoral letter to his officials, the archdeacons, the rural deans and the rectors in the diocese, concerning the ruinous state of the conventual church of Athelney. There were no funds, he said, to repair it, and he begged them to allow the monks to plead their cause in the churches on holy days after the Gospel, and he would assure contributors *vere contritos* of 30 days' indulgence *ab injunctis penitentiis*.

On 22 October 1322 [481] the bishop appointed Roger de Stalbridge, the rector of Aller, and two monks as a commission to visit and inspect and report on all the buildings belonging to Athelney Abbey.

In 1349 the abbey seems to have been devastated by the plague. On 15 September Abbot Richard de Gothurst fell a victim; [482] on 23 September John Stoure was appointed but died on 22 October on his way to the king, and Robert de Hache [483] succeeded him.

In January 1401 [484] there is a strange entry of a licence to Robert Wynchestre, a monk of Athelney, to whom Pope Boniface IX grants for life a room formerly assigned to him by the abbot and still in his possession, and the right to dispose, without requiring licence of the abbot and convent or others, of the goods acquired in the monastery from his offices or salary, or acquired without the same. This recognition of private property seems to be a direct annulling of the Benedictine rule.

In 1462 [485] Abbot Robert Hill was granted a licence to have divine service celebrated in his oratory; this suggests that some sort of rebuilding of the church was taking place at that time.

On 17 August 1499 [486] the Feast of the Dedication was changed from 20 December to 30 August, and it is probable that this coincides with some extensive repairs, if not the entire rebuilding of the conventual church, the new dedication day being the day when the church was once more capable of being used for public worship. The buildings, however, do not seem to have been completely restored, for in 1503 [487] Bishop King issued a commission to inquire into their state.

In the Valor of Henry VIII the house is said to be in debt to the king to the extent of £33 6s. 8d. which was possibly some outstanding portion of the fine of 100 marks levied on Abbot John George [488] and the convent in 1498 because of the assistance he gave to the insurgents under Perkin Warbeck in 1497.

On 17 September 1534 [489] the convent subscribed the Act of Supremacy and the Succession Act. The deed was signed by Robert Hamblyn, the newly elected abbot, Richard Welles, the prior, and eleven other monks.

On 4 November 1535 [490] Robert Hamblyn, the abbot, wrote to Cromwell to inform him of the visit of Dr. Tregonwell and to express his joy that the house had been found ' yn metely good order.' The visitor had however enjoined him to remain in the monastery, and Hamblyn desired from Cromwell permission to go abroad on the necessary business of the abbey, and to take a chaplain with him.

On 10 April 1536 [491] he wrote again to Cromwell, lamenting the debts of the house, and requesting Cromwell to devise some means that every man may the sooner be paid. ' Yff Y cowlde have a frynd that wolde lene me iiii. or v hundret poundes without ony prophete or lucoure, Y wolde gladly bynde me and my howse for the repayment of a hundret poundes yerely untyll the full some be payde.' To this letter he adds a schedule or book of the debts. He owed the Abbot of Dunkeswell £80, and the Abbot of Tavistock £40, and it is evident that he had borrowed recklessly when he became abbot. The Prior of Taunton and the Prior of St. John's Bridgwater had also lent money. Various sums also are due to Ilton, North Curry, and Thurloxton Churches, and the prebendal vicar at Wells was in arrear of his stipend for two years. The sum total of debts is reckoned at £869 12s. 7d.

On 2 November 1538 [492] John Dycensen, rector of Holford, went to Athelney apparently to sound the abbot about resignation. He wrote afterwards to Cromwell, giving a report of the abbot's words. To him and to the convent he had held out hope that neither religion nor the poor would suffer by the surrender of the house, for the Lord Chancellor Audley would probably settle down there. The abbot held out however for something more than a bribe of 100 marks, though the monks ' ware all glade to be advysed by my Lorde and to yelde thare howse and landes ynto ye kynges handes.'

On 20 February 1539 [493] John Tregonwell, William Petre, and John Smyth, the royal commissioners, wrote to Cromwell and told him that with as much expedition as possible they had taken the surrender of the abbey. It

480 *Somers. Rec. Soc. Publ.* i, 189.
481 Ibid. 207.
482 Add. MSS. B.M. 6165.
483 *Cal. Pat.* 1348–50, p. 410.
484 *Cal. Papal Letters*, v, 357.
485 Wells Epis. Reg. Beckington, fol. 244.
486 Ibid. King, fol. 99.   487 Ibid. fol. 110.

488 B.M. Rol. Reg. 14 B. vii.
489 *Dep. Keeper's Rep.* viii.
490 *L. and P. Hen. VIII*, ix, 763.
491 Harl. MSS. no. 604.
492 Cotton MSS. Cleop. E. iv.
493 Cromwell Correspondence (P.R.O.) xiv, 70.

had indeed been surrendered on 8 February,[494] and the deed was signed by Robert Hamblyn, the abbot, Richard Wells, the prior, John Athelwyne, Henry Ambros, Robert Edgar, John Laurens, and Thomas Genynges. The abbot was awarded a pension of £50 a year, and on 24 February the prebend of Sutton was confirmed to him by Letters Patent. In Cardinal Pole's pension List of 1556,[495] pensions were still paid to Robert Hamblyn, Robert Edgar, Henry Poynings, and Thomas Genynges.

After the surrender[496] the materials of the buildings were valued at £80. The site of the abbey had been leased to Lord Audley, but on 17 August 1544[497] it was sold to John Clayton, gentleman, for £182 15s. and in April[498] of the following year he obtained a licence to sell it to John Tynbere.

The charter of Alfred of the manor of Sutton[499] exists with a careful statement of the boundaries of the manor. In 1007 King Ethelred[500] granted Ham to the small monastery (*monasteriolum*) of Athelney and to Alfric, the abbot. A charter of King Cnut,[501] witnessed by Earls Leofric and Godwin and Stigand, the priest, grants the manor of Sevenhampton (Seavington) to Athelney, and belongs to the period 1020–5.

An abstract of the Domesday Survey is entered in the cartulary, describing the possessions as in Long Sutton, Ilton, Sevenhampton, Hamp, Lyng and Montacute, and records the encroachment of the Count of Mortain in Ashill, of Roger de Curcelle in Sutton, and of Ralph de Limesey in Bossington. The manor of Purse Caundle[502] in Dorset came to them just before the Survey by an exchange with the Count of Mortain. The abbey had previously received the manor of 'Biscopestone' on which the earl desired to build his castle of Montacute,[503] and he exchanged his manor of Purse Caundle for this manor.

In 1267 Henry III[504] granted the abbey a weekly market on Mondays in their manor of Lyng, and a yearly fair on the eve, day and morrow of St. James the Apostle, in their manor of Sutton.

Roger de Mandeville[505] had given 'Andresia,' with fishery rights on the Parrett to the abbey and convent of Athelney, at the request of Herduin, the venerable hermit, and these rights being somewhat indefinite were constantly

causing quarrels between the abbey and the dean and chapter of Wells who held the adjacent manor of North Curry.

In the *Taxatio* of 1291 the abbey is recorded as enjoying pensions in Bawdrip and Selworthy churches, and in possession of the manors of Sutton Abbots, Hurcot, and lands in North Curry, Combe Florey, and 'Hyda,' Hamp, Lyng, 'Hoggestle,' Clavelshay in North Petherton and Bossington.

On the election of Robert de Hacche,[506] a monk of Athelney, to be prior in 1349, the property consisted of Sutton, Lyng, Ilton and Hurcot in the county of Somerset, and Purse Caundle in the county of Dorset. These are returned as worth £25 6s. 5d.

In the *Valor*[507] of Henry VIII, 1535, the endowments of the house are returned as worth £209 a year.

ABBOTS OF ATHELNEY

John, the 'Old Saxon,' temp. Alfred[508]
Seignus, occurs 937[509]
Alfric, occurs 1007[510]
Alfward[511]
Simon
Athelward
Athelwin, occurs 1020–5[512]
Ralph Maledoctus, occurs 1125[513]
Simon, occurs 1135[514]
Benedict I, occurs 1159[515]
Roger I, 1174–92[516]
Benedict II, 1198–1227[517]
Roger II, elected 1227[518]
Robert, elected 1245[519]; occurs 1263[520]
Osmund de Reigny[521]
Richard de Derham, occurs 1267[521]
Andrew de Sancto Fonte, 1280[523]–1300[524]
Osmund de Sowi, 1300[525]–25[526]

---

[494] Lansdowne MSS. 97, fol. 3.
[495] Aug. Off. Misc. Bks. vol. 233, fol. 105.
[496] P. R. O. Exchequer Bks. no. 224, 1539–40.
[497] Orig. R. 36 Hen. VIII, vol. 100, fol. 3.
[498] Ibid. vol. 60, fol. 6.
[499] *Somers. Rec. Soc. Publ.* xiv, 126.
[500] Ibid. 146.   [501] Ibid. 141.   [502] Ibid. 182.
[503] Cf. Account of Cluniac Priory at Montacute.
[504] Chart R. 52 Hen. III, m. 11, no. 147.
[505] Ibid. no. 78.

[506] *Cal. Pat.* 1348–50, pp. 410, 419.
[507] *Valor Eccl.* (Rec. Com.) i, 206.
[508] See above.
[509] *Somers. Rec. Soc. Publ.* xiv, charter 98.
[510] Ibid. charter 64.
[511] Collinson gives this and the two following names, but does not mention his authority. He may have copied them from the now lost cartulary or chronicle of the abbey.
[512] *Somers. Rec. Soc. Publ.* xiv, charter 57.
[513] Ibid. charter 26.
[514] *Two Bath Cartularies* (Somers. Rec. Soc.), i, 61.
[515] *Som. Rec. Soc. Publ.* xiv, 116.
[516] Ibid.
[517] He died 1227, cf. charter 60; and *Cal. Pat.* 1225–32, p. 123.
[518] *Somers. Rec. Soc. Publ.* xiv, charter 202; *Cal. Pat.* loc. cit.
[519] *Cal. Pat.* 1232–47, p. 458.
[520] *Somers. Rec. Soc. Publ.* xiv, charters 24 and 78.
[521] Temp. Hen. III, charter 241.   [522] Charter 106.
[523] *Cal. Pat.* 1272–81, p. 368.
[524] Ibid. 1292–1301, p. 503.
[525] Ibid. pp. 510, 513.   [526] Ibid. 1324–7, p. 86.

Robert de Ile, 1325 [527]–41 [528]
Richard de Gothurst or Cotehurst, 1341–9 [529]
John Stoure, 23 September–22 October, 1349 [530]
Robert de Hache, elected 1349 [531]
John Hewish, 1390 [532]
John Brygge, 1399 [533]
John Petherton, 1424 [534]
Robert Hylle, 1458 [535]
John George, 1485 [536]
John Wellington, 1503 [537]
Richard Wraxall [538]
John Herte, 1518 [539]
Thomas Sutton, 1527 [540]
John Maior, 1531 [541]
Robert Hamlyn or Hamblyn, 1533–9 [541]

The earliest extant seal [542] of the Benedictine Abbey of St. Saviour, St. Peter, St. Paul and St. Athelwine of Athelney is a vesica of the 11th century, 2 in. by 1½ in., with a design of the abbey church. Of the legend there remains only—

✠ SIGILLUM SCI SA . . . . . HELING . . . E.

The second seal [544] is circular, 2½ in. in diameter, and is 15th-century work. It shews the three principal patrons of the house in canopied niches. In the middle is Our Lord, blessing with His right hand and holding in His left an orb from which rises a long cross and flag. On the left is St. Peter, habited as pope, and on the right is St. Paul with sword and book. On either side of the niches are shields—that to the left charged with a horn between three crowns, that to the right has three crowns set palewise quartered with a cross formy throughout. The legend is—

SIGILLUM COMUNE ABBATIS ET CONUENTUS DE ATHELNEY.

The seal of Abbot Benedict [545] (1159) is a vesica 2⅜ in. by 1½ in., and shews the abbot standing and holding his staff and a book.

[527] Cal. Pat. 1324–7, pp. 88, 109; Drokensford's Reg. (Somers. Rec. Soc.) i, 243.
[528] Cal. Pat. 1340–3, p. 253.   [529] Ibid. p. 278.
[530] Died of the Plague, see above.
[531] Cal. Pat. 1348–50, pp. 410, 419; R. of Shrewsbury's Reg. (Somers. Rec. Soc. x).
[532] Charters 20, 140, 165, Somers. Rec. Soc. Publ. xiv; Cal. Pat. 1388–92, pp. 312, 318.
[533] Pat. 23 Ric. II, m 7; Cal. Wells D. and C. MSS. (Hist. MSS. Com.) i, 303.
[534] Cal. Pat. 1422–9, p. 262.
[535] Wells Epis. Reg. Stillington, unnumbered folios at end.   [536] Ibid.
[537] Confirmed July 27. Installed as prebendary 2 August 1503. Cf. Wells Epis. Reg. King, fol. 140.
[538] né Bele, confirmed as abbot 7 Jan. 1517. Cf. Wells Epis. Reg. Hadrian, fol. 102.
[539] Athelney Cart. (Somers. Rec. Soc. xiv) 117.
[540] Ibid.
[541] Ibid.
[542] See above.
[543] Cat. of Seals B.M., 2570, lxxi, 44.
[544] Ibid. 2571, lxxi, 46.   [545] Ibid. 2572, lxxi, 45.

5. THE ABBEY OF MUCHELNEY

The founder of Muchelney Abbey is said to have been Athelstan, King of England, and one tradition says that he founded it in expiation of his complicity in the murder of the Atheling Edwin in 933, and another that it was founded as a thank-offering for his great victory at Brunanburgh in 937. A still earlier origin however has been claimed for the abbey. [546]

Ine, King of Wessex, lived at the time when the extension of the Church was very rapid, and the munificence of kings and nobles very great, and afterwards when the monks were desirous to regard their foundation as earlier than that of Athelstan, it was not strange that they should have cherished the tradition that the original founder was not Athelstan but Ine himself; nor is there any great reason for supposing that he was not.

The charters of King Ine copied in the cartulary, though forgeries, may contain true history. Moreover, among the charters is a genuine one by Kynewulf, in 762, giving certain land between the Isle and the Earn to the monastery of Muchelney, and this alone proves that Athelstan was not the original founder, though he may have been the restorer of the abbey.

During the 9th and early part of the 10th century this district suffered much from the Danes, and the church life that had begun in the reign of Ine and had been fostered by the generosity of Kynewulf may have ceased; and thus, while we claim Athelstan as being the refounder, there is no historical argument against the tradition that the monastery was founded by the earlier monarch, Ine.

If the charter of Ine is a forgery as it stands in the cartulary, so also is the charter of King Athelstan, which describes him as the founder.

The original gift of Muchelney, with its adjacent islands of Thorney and Middleney, no longer exists.

In the cartulary there are copies of seven charters said to be granted by English kings to Muchelney before the Conquest. Two of Ine, of which the first is in its present shape clearly a forgery (dated 725), granting to Frody, the abbot at 'Mycleneya', 20 mancuses of land, and the other, which is rather a record than a charter, is dated 693, in which Ine is recorded to have granted 37 cassates of land on the banks of the Isle to this said Frody.

[546] A cartulary of the abbey at Savernake Park, the property of the Marquess of Aylesbury, seems to have gone with the abbey itself to the Protector Somerset and found its way to Savernake, and so it remained in the Seymour family when that property came to the Earls of Aylesbury, and when the site of Muchelney passed to the Long family, the cartulary seems to have been overlooked. It has been printed by the Somerset Record Society, vol. xiv.

The one genuine charter is that of Kynewulf who in 762 granted eight cassates of land between the Isle and the Earn. Then comes the so-called charter of King Athelstan, granting half the manor of Curry Rivel to the monastery.

Then there are two transcripts of charters, of Edgar, one dated 964 granting to 'Miclani' and the brethren there the right to elect their own abbot, and in 966 ten cassates of land at Isle. The last of this group of early royal charters is a confirmation by King Ethelred in 995 of the possessions of the abbey at Ilminster, West Camel and all other lands that they possess.

In the Domesday Survey[547] the abbey is said to hold Chipstable, Ilminster, Isle Abbots, Cathanger in Fivehead, Drayton, Camel (West) and the three islands of Muchelney, Middleney, and Thorney.

In 1239[548] the rectory of Chipstable was granted by Bishop Jocelin for the endowment of the abbey, but how the monastery obtained the advowson we do not know.

In the *Taxatio*[549] of 1291 the temporalities were valued at £44.

In the Valor[550] of Henry VIII the revenues of the abbey were valued at a net value of £447 4s. 11d.

Muchelney never was a large foundation. In 995[551] King Ethelred speaks of it as a little monastery, *monasteriolum*, and our first item of information comes to us through William of Malmesbury's history of Glastonbury Abbey.[552] There we find Muchelney and Athelney seeking protection under the more powerful monastery of Glastonbury.[553]

Bishop Giso's manor of Huish joined the land of the abbey of Muchelney, and in a dispute between him and the abbey, Bishop Giso referred the matter to Lanfranc. The Archbishop of Canterbury therefore took occasion to summon the Abbot of Muchelney to appear before a general council of the English Church,[554] and the abbot replied that he would answer by command of the Abbot of Glastonbury in the chapter-house of Glastonbury and nowhere else, and he based his answer on the royal privileges which the abbey had received from Kings Ine, Kentwin and Edward. We know nothing of the authority for this assertion, but it is said that the bishop did appeal in the chapter-house of Glastonbury and lost his case, and it seems probable that the action of the abbots of the two smaller houses was due to some arrangement made by the ambitious Abbot Thurstin of Glastonbury.

In 1201[555] Abbot Richard was induced to give the church of Ilminster to the cathedral church of Wells. Bishop Savaric of Bath was then also Abbot of Glastonbury, and so the Abbot of Muchelney could not save himself as his predecessor had done more than a century earlier. Bishop Savaric created a prebend out of the church of Ilminster, and made the Abbot of Muchelney for the time being prebendary and a member of the chapter of the cathedral church of Wells, and thus while Muchelney did not benefit by the change, the bishop was henceforth able to claim the obedience of the abbot, because the abbot was a member of his chapter at Wells.

Bishop Savaric[556] seems to have given to the abbey on account of its poverty certain small tithes and dues arising out of the church of Somerton.

In 1315[557] Bishop Drokensford appointed William de Dillington and Richard de Forde commissaries with final powers of correction to visit the abbey of Muchelney, but the result of this visit is not recorded.

In the same year[558] there is a receipt in the bishop's register from the Abbot of Muchelney for the keep of a Knight Templar from Templecombe who had been maintained at Muchelney for 276 days.

In 1329[559] we find Bishop Ralph of Shrewsbury commissioning Canon Walter de Hull, the rector of Shepton Beauchamp, to go to Muchelney and absolve Henry de Eastcammel, monk.

In 1332[560] the bishop writes to the abbot asking him to grant a corrody or pension to William le Iressch, a small squire, who seems to have been an attendant on the bishop, and who was now too old to perform his customary duties. This request must be considered with evidence shown us in the Close Rolls, where we find that for the last 50 years at least the Crown had been forcing on the abbey the maintenance of its aged servants.

In 1309[561] Richard le Devenish was sent there to be maintained in the abbey for the rest of his life. In 1325[562] John le Foullere, who had long served the king and his father, was sent to occupy the place vacated by the death of Richard le Devenish. In 1328[563] John de Trentham, the king's harper, was sent because Foullere was dead. In the next year[564] however he was removed to Bath. In 1342[565] Thomas Prest of Twickenham was sent to occupy the place which his father Thomas Prest (now dead) had enjoyed, and the elder Prest himself had succeeded to

[547] *V.C.H. Somers.* i, 468, 469.
[548] *Somers. Rec. Soc. Publ.* xiv, charters 13 and 15.
[549] *Pope Nich. Tax.* (Rec. Com.) 203, 204.
[550] *Valor Eccl.* (Rec. Com.), i, 193.
[551] *Somers. Rec. Soc. Publ.* xiv, 44.
[552] Will. of Malmesbury, *Antiq. Glaston.* (ed. Gale) 331.   [553] See above, 'Eccl. Hist.' p. 16.
[554] Probably Synod of Gloucester, 1085.

[555] *Cal. Wells D. and C. MSS.* (Hist. MSS. Com.) i, 48.
[556] Ibid. 57.
[557] *Somers. Rec. Soc. Publ.* i, 93.   [558] Ibid. 98.
[559] Ibid. ix, 26.   [560] Ibid. 127.
[561] *Cal. Close*, 1307–13, p. 232.
[562] Ibid. 1323–7, p. 508.
[563] Ibid. 1327–30, p. 365–6.
[564] Ibid. p. 567.   [565] Ibid. 1341–3, p. 475.

the corrody granted by Edward I to Peter le Messayer.

In a monastery that was never large the presence of men like these must have been detrimental to the authority of the abbot, and also to the observance of the rule of St. Benedict by the monks themselves.

In 1335[566] Bishop Ralph of Shrewsbury wrote to the abbot concerning the *comperta* of a recent visitation of his. He says he found the monks living in luxury and enjoying private privileges which were quite unauthorized. They were not content with the simple cubicles in the dormitory but had made themselves larger beds in the form of tabernacles, which were too ornate and richly covered. They were in the habit of leaving the convent without permission and rode on horseback through the country, and some were wont to take their meals in private and not as they should, in common with the others in the refectory. Secular men, women and girls were allowed in the cloister area. In the refectory the utensils were far too costly and good for the simple life that should be lived there. All this was to be corrected by the festival of St. Michael. He forbade the monks to leave the precincts of the abbey unless they had obtained the abbot's permission, and if the abbot was absent, they must obtain the licence of the prior, and this licence was only to be granted for very good reasons.

The church of the monastery the bishop had found in a state of bad repair, and he ordered that it was to be restored and made good by that time on pain of a penalty of 100s. which the abbey would have to pay to the poor. The letter is dated from Banwell, 10 July 1335.

The visitation to which the bishop here refers probably took place in the previous year. The abbey had just lost its head, John de Henton, who had been abbot for thirty years, and so prolonged a term of office suggests that the abbot was of great age when he died, and this circumstance would account for a weakened discipline.

His successor, John de Somerton, was a man of great mark, and much valued by Bishop Ralph. Hearne says ' he was of great name in his monastery and also elsewhere.' His efforts at reform clearly had raised an opposition on the part of the monks who had been accustomed to the easy rule of his predecessor, Abbot Henton, and in 1338 [567] the bishop interfered with reference to John de Worthy, a monk there, who, on account of his disobedience, was ordered to be kept in prison in a separate chamber and to have a limited and prescribed dietary. On feast days as well as on other days he was bound to say one psalter a day. The next year,[568] hearing that

there was some sympathy shown to this monk by his fellow-monks and even by the abbot, he writes to forbid the abbot and convent entering into conversation with him.

Another decade and we find the monastery visited by the Great Pestilence. John de Codeworth, who had been appointed in 1347, died in May 1349, and Thomas de Overton succeeded, and was admitted on 16 June 1349. The new abbot, like his predecessor, Somerton, had to receive a royal clerk, and to maintain him until such time as the monastery could provide him with a competent benefice.

In 1334 John de Feriby had received this benefit on the ' new creation ' of Abbot Somerton, and now William de Okebourne profited by the new creation of Abbot Overton.[569] Unable however to find a benefice for him they had to keep him until 1352 when he went to Cirencester.[570] During his abbotship Overton granted a corrody to Ralph Drake,[571] the cantor, whose duty it was to sing at high mass, and to teach four boys, and one monk to play the organ.

The intimate relationship [572] between Abbot Somerton and Bishop Ralph of Shrewsbury is shown by the perpetual chantry which was founded in the chapel of St. Martin in the church of Wells by the convent of Muchelney for the soul of their late abbot, and it is an instance of the close interconnexion between these religious foundations in mediaeval times that, in return, Bishop Ralph of Shrewsbury founded a chantry in the chapel of the hospital of St. John in Wells on behalf of himself and Abbot Somerton, on condition that the prior and brethren of the hospital should pay a chaplain 6 marks a year to celebrate at the altar of St. Martin in the cathedral church.

It is interesting to note also that in 1433 [573] the abbot and convent established a chantry on behalf of Bishop Nicholas Bubwith, late Bishop of Bath and Wells, because he had gone to their aid when they were burdened with debt and had given them certain valuable vestments.

During the 15th century we know very little of the history of the monastery. Early in the century there seems to have been a rebuilding of the monastic church, and probably of the greater part of the monastic buildings.[574]

In the middle of that century, there were thirteen monks present at the election of Thomas Pipe in 1463, and in 1489 fifteen monks took part in the election of William Wyke as abbot. At

---

[566] *Somers. Rec. Soc. Publ.* ix, 194.
[567] Ibid. 342.
[568] Ibid. 347.

[569] *Cal. Close* 1349–54, p. 85.
[570] Ibid. p. 507.
[571] 16 June 1349; *Cal. Pat.* 1348–50, p. 306.
[572] *Somers. Rec. Soc. Publ.* x, 633; *Cal. Wells D. and C. MSS.* (Hist. MSS. Com.) i, 257.
[573] *Cal. Wells D. and C. MSS.* (Hist. MSS. Com.) i, 458.
[574] These were excavated in 1873 by the Rev. S. O. Baker. *Proc. Somers. Arch. Soc.* xix (2).

the time of the Dissolution there seem to have been eight monks in addition to the abbot and prior. The election of the last abbot reveals the disgraceful pressure that was put upon the monastery by the ministers of the Crown, and the extraordinary dishonesty that existed among them. John Shirborne was induced to resign on 28 August 1532,[575] and on 11 June Henry Thornton wrote to Cromwell that he had received his and the king's letters to the abbot and convent, and that as soon as the resignation actually took place he would proceed to carry out the directions given therein. Inde or Yve was the ablest monk of the abbey, but he was young, and it was questionable whether he was of canonical age. He was certainly the ablest in wit and learning of the monastery. 'There are many among his elders who would fain be abbot, and make friends in these parts as Sir Nicholas Wadham and others, and so by the obstinacy of two or three simple monks of the king's foundation little regard shall be had to the king's letter.[576] If they are wilful cleave the more to the poor monk you have begun withal.'

A few days later[577] Thornton wrote another letter to Cromwell, and he adds 'no creature living shall know what shall be done between you and me touching Muchelney. I hope that my Lord Chief Justice will say something for my truth. I marvel where the fond monks have comfort; they are so full of cracks. If Dan Ine obtain it, as I trust he shall, he will prove a good husband to the monastery.'

Then again on 12 July[578] he writes :—

Four of the monks are put in comfort to be abbot, and all their efforts are set against dan Thomas Ine ; so that the bishop, if he can, will make a monk of another place abbot there, perhaps from Glastonbury. Divers Canons residing in the Cathedral Church of Wells say that Ine shall never 'rejoise' that room ; but I do not fear them as I remember your promise. It is necessary that the King's letter should be speedily sent to the Bishop of Bath, with another from you before the doctor comes into these parts. Rather than I should fail I had liever be where I shall be a thousand years hence.

On 13 August[579] he writes again :—

The time of Mr. Dr. Lee is being at Muchelney he that is vicarie of the same parish is godfather to dan Thomas Ine. Much labor hath been made by various monks of the house, especially by dan John Michell, who would fain be abbot, and has so laboured with the vicar that he now affirms that Ine is only 23 years old. The contrary can be proved by many in the parish of Ilminster, among them by Thomas Caslyn, his god-father, who are ready to be examined, who will state that at Christmas last he was 24 years old.

Then on 16 August[580] another letter was sent by Thornton : 'As touching dan Thomas Ine, monk of Muchelney, unless that your master cleeve according to my lowly and meek suit before this made unto you in his favour, he shall have so much wrong in such a matter as ever poor religious man had. He is 25 years old, which can be proved by a hundred besides the fourteen names I sent you. If Ine fails my credit will fail also.'

On 19 August 1532[581] the licence was issued by the Crown for the election of an abbot in the place of John Shirborne. Then shortly afterwards came out the ground for Thornton's anxiety. He died that autumn, and it appears that Serjeant Thornton had promised to Cromwell a fee of £40 in the event of Ynde or Ine being elected, but he had obtained £100 from Ine to procure his election.[582] Ine had paid the money to Thornton, and had to pay again to Cromwell, and so the revenues of the abbey[583] were pledged to provide the illegal bribe.

Cromwell had applied to Dr. Lee to obtain this, and Ine seeing that he had lost his £100 could only promise to pay again the £40 to Cromwell 'besechyng you for a tyme to take hytt yn good worthe.'

On 2 July 1534[584] Thomas Ynde, with Robert Coscob, prior, John Montacute, and eight others, subscribed to the king's supremacy.

On 3 January 1538[585] the monastery was visited by Thomas Legh :— 'When I found the abbot negligent and of doubtful character ; and ten brethren which all war ignorant and unlernyd and in manor no servauntes maynteynyd or hospitalite kept and after examynation withe theym had they all subscrybid to the instrument of their submyssion and surrender and sealyd the same withe their common seale and delivered the same as their acte to me to thuse and pleasure of our soverayne lord the kyng, etc.'

The surrender was made in the presence of Sir Thomas Speke, John Sidenham, William Wittcombe, Nicholas Seger, John Southwood, John Crosse, Thomas Philippes, and Robert Warmington,[586] who seem to have sat as a commission of inquiry for two days previously and had arranged for the surrender before Legh arrived. The deed of surrender is no longer in existence, but in Cardinal Pole's pension list[587] George Moore and John Plumber are entered as in receipt of pen-

[575] L. and P. Hen. VIII, v, g. 1370 (11).
[576] Ibid. 1088. [577] Ibid. 1089.
[578] Ibid. 1167. [579] Ibid. 1225.
[580] L. and P. Hen. VIII, v, g. 1229, 1230.
[581] Ibid. 1270 (7).
[582] Thornton was serjeant in the Court of the King's Bench, and had obtained a lease of the house of the Buckland Sisters. Cf. Somers. Arch. Soc. Proc. x (2), 42.
[583] Cf. Ellis, Orig. Letters (3rd ser.) ii, 334.
[584] Cf. Dep. Keeper's Rep. viii.
[585] L. and P. Hen. VIII, xiii (i), 27, 42.
[586] Cf. Crom. Corres. (P.R.O.) xxii.
[587] Exch. K. R. Misc. Bks. vol. 32, fol. 30.

sions of £3 a year. The abbey and its site [588] were granted to the Earl of Hertford in the spring of that year.

ABBOTS OF MUCHELNEY

Frody, 693 [589]
Edwald, 762 [590]
Alfwold, 964 [591]
Leofric, 995 [592]
Liward, temp. Edward the Confessor [593]
Eadulf, temp. William II [594]
Alan, occurs 1159 [595]
Hugh, occurs 1175 [596]
Richard, occurs 1198 [597]
Richard, elected 1235 [598]
Walter de Cerne, occurs 1237-8 [599]
John de Barnville, occurs 1251 [600]
William de Gyvele, 1274 [601]
Ralph de Muchelney, 1294 [602]
John de Henton, 1305 [603]
John de Somerton, 1334-47 [604]
John de Codeworth, elected 1347,[605] died May 1349 [606]
Thomas de Overton, elected May 1349 [607]
William de Shepton, December 1 1371,[608] cf. October 30 1394
Nicholas Strotton, 27 February 1397 [609]

John Bruton [610]
John Cherde, 1433 [611]
Thomas Pipe, 1463 [612]
William Crokethorne, 1465 [613]
John Bracey or Bracy, 1470-89 [614]
William Wyke, 1489-1504 [615]
Thomas Broke, 21 January 1505 [616]
John Shirborne, 1522-32 [617]
Thomas Inde, Ynde or Yve, 1532-8 [618]

The 14th-century seal of the Benedictine Abbey of St. Peter and St. Paul at Muchelney [619] is circular, 2¾ in. in diameter. It shows two niches with St. Peter, habited as pope in the left, and St. Paul with his sword and book in the right. Outside these in smaller niches are two angels holding shields. That to the left has the arms of the abbey which were (Argent) St. Peter's keys crossed with St. Paul's sword (gules) ; the shield to the right is charged with a saltire. Very little remains of the legend.

The seal of an unknown abbot of the 14th century [620] is a tiny vesica, ⅞ in. by ¾ in., with a figure of St. Paul holding his sword and the model of a church, and the abbot kneeling before him.

Of this seal also the legend is much broken.

HOUSES OF BENEDICTINE NUNS

6. THE PRIORY OF BARROW GURNEY

The founder of the Priory of Barrow Gurney, also called Minchin Barrow, is not known, but appears to have been a Gurney, and one connected with the family of Fitzhardinge lords of Berkeley. In 1283 the Berkeley family were certainly patrons of the priory.[1]

The foundation was dedicated to the honour of the Blessed Virgin Mary, and St. Edward, king and martyr, and had clearly been established before 1212, when Hugh de Wells, Bishop of Lincoln, made his will, and left 10 marks to the nuns of Barrow.[2] Some time before its dissolution it seems as if the additional dedication in honour of the Holy Trinity had been made.

[588] Pat. 29 Hen. VIII, pt. ii.
[589] *Somers. Rec. Soc.* xiv, Charter 5.
[590] Ibid. Charter 6.   [591] Ibid. Charter 3.
[592] Ibid. Charter 4.
[593] Domesday Survey of Ilminster, *Exon. Domesday* (Rec. Com.), 174.   [594] Ibid. Charter 126.
[595] *Cal. Wells D. and C. MSS.* (Hist. MSS. Com.) i, 27.
[596] Witnesses a charter of Bishop Reginald, *Somers. Rec. Soc. Publ.* viii, 192.
[597] Witnesses a Bath Abbey Charter, *Somers. Rec. Soc. Publ.* vii, 18.   [598] Pat. 19 Hen. III, m. 9.
[599] Feet of F. 22 Hen. III, *Somers. Rec. Soc. Publ.* vi, 105.
[600] Pat. 36 Hen. III, *Somers. Pleas* (Somers. Rec. Soc. xi), 434.
[601] *Cal. Pat.* 1272-81, p. 58 ; *Cal. Wells D. and C. MSS.* (Hist. MSS. Com.) i, 282.
[602] *Cal. Pat.* 1292-1301, p. 78.
[603] Ibid. 1301-7, pp. 310, 315 ; cf. *Cal. Pat.* Ibid. p. 231 ; *Somers. Rec. Soc. Publ.* ix, 300.
[604] *Cal. Pat.* 1330-4, p. 567 ; *Somers. Rec. Soc. Publ.* x, 630.
[605] *Cal. Pat.* 1345-9, pp. 375, 403.
[606] Ibid. 1348-50, p. 293.
[607] Ibid. p. 295, *Somers. Rec. Soc. Publ.* x, 611.
[608] *Cal. Papal Letters*, iv, 490.
[609] Ibid. v, 154.

[610] *Cal. Wells D. and C. MSS.* (Hist. MSS. Com.), i, 458.
[611] *Cal. Pat.* 1461-7, p. 285.
[612] Ibid. p. 457.
[613] Ibid. pp. 457, 478.
[614] Ibid. 1467-77, p. 266. Cf. Wells Epis. Reg. King, fol. 24 ; Stillington, folios at end.
[615] Wells Epis. Reg. Hadrian, fol. 1.
[616] Summoned to Convocation 26 Jan. 1506 and 24 June 1514. Installed as preb. of Ilminster 6 Feb. 1505. Wells Epis. Reg. Hadrian, fol. 10.
[617] *Somers. Rec. Soc. Publ.* xiv. 23.
[618] See above.
[619] *Cat. of Seals B.M.* 3666, lxxi, 69.
[620] Ibid. 3667. Harl. Chart. 57 G. 18.
[1] Esch. R. 53 Hen. III, fol. 23.
[2] This is borne out by the appearance of ' Bearwe ' in the ' Mappa Mundi ' usually ascribed to about 1200 : Gervase of Cant. *Op. Hist.* (Rolls Ser.) ii, 422.

Previous to the *Taxatio*[3] of 1291, the house obtained a pension on the church of Twerton, near Bath, the advowson of which church belonged to the Prioress and convent of Kington.

Richard de Acton, in 1362,[4] gave land and houses in Wells and Barrow Gurney to provide a chaplain to pray for the soul of Guy de Brian,[5] and seven years later he and others gave 72 acres of arable and 7 acres of meadow in Barrow Gurney to provide a lamp to burn in the priory church of the Blessed Mary of Barrow. Next year, 1370,[6] John Blanket of Bristol gave property in Bristol and the suburbs to provide bread and wine for the high altar.

In the Valor of 1535[7] the property of the house was assessed as worth £29 6s. 8½d. on which there were charges of £5 12s. 4¾d., leaving a clear value of £23 14s. 3¾d.

The nuns of the house seem all to have been drawn from good families, but were not therefore exempt from jealousies and worldly interests.

On 26 June 1315 the bishop[8] wrote to the prioress enjoining obedience, on pain of excommunication, to the regulations he was going to lay down and to the custodian he was going to appoint over the possessions of the house. She should for the future cease to interest herself with worldly and secular matters, should above all things apply herself to the worship of God and obediently and carefully attend to the government of her sisters. The prioress and the other nuns should eat and sleep together unless hindered by ill-health or other just cause. She should not concede to any one of her nuns permission to go into or beyond the vill, except for great and lawful cause, and then they should go in pairs and in their nuns' habits, and should not wander to places where their leave did not extend, nor voluntarily absent themselves beyond the time of their leave. Silence, too, was to be observed as their rule demanded, and the prioress should not carry herself harshly towards her nuns, but should live in charity, love, and unanimity.

In the next month (July) the bishop writes to William de Sutton,[9] asking him to take over the administration of the priory, the prioress being evidently incompetent. What happened as the result of this we do not know, but on 4 October 1316 the bishop wrote to the Dean of Wells and Canon Penkridge, asking them to examine the election process of Joan de Gurney, elected prioress, and if they were satisfied with the procedure to induct her into the office.[10]

In July 1317 we find that the bishop blessed four nuns of the house of Barrow, who had just made their profession before him in his chapel at Banwell, namely, Joan de Gurney, Agnes de Saut Marais, Milburga de Durnford, and Basilia de Sutton.[11] It then appeared that Dame Joan had been elected prioress before she was professed, and as this was uncanonical the election was void, but on 26 October 1317, as she was now a professed nun, Bishop Drokensford collated her on his own authority as Prioress of Barrow.[12] Dame Joan, however, though of noble birth, seems to have been incompetent and quite unfitted for her post. The nunnery was mismanaged, and the prioress given to wandering, and Bishop Drokensford appointed the rectors of Chew and Harptree to inquire and take measures on 6 September 1323.[13] The arrangements made by these two commissioners seem to have been of little avail, for on 18 January 1325 he issued a commission to his official to visit the priory and to remove the prioress.[14] On 3 May 1325 Joan de Gurney resigned, and on 4 June the bishop bade his official examine into the election of Agnes de St. Cruce.[15] There were clearly however difficulties in the way, for on 4 October 1325 he again issued a commission to three canons to examine into the election of Agnes de St. Cruce as prioress, and if it was regular to confirm her in her office.[16]

The prioress who had been removed was closely related to the patron of the priory, and possibly difficulties had been placed in the way of obtaining from the patron his licence for the election.

The next year (9 February 1326), the bishop wrote to the nuns bidding them obey their new prioress.

On entering into his diocese, Bishop Ralph of Shrewsbury, according to the prevailing custom, claimed the right to nominate a member of the house, and sent word to the prioress that the convent should receive Elizabeth daughter of Sir Hamon Fitz Richard.[17]

On 28 March 1398[18] Pope Boniface IX wrote to the Prior of Bath to inquire into the facts concerning Isabella Poleyns and Joan Bozum, Benedictine nuns of Barrow in the diocese of Wells. On their own authority and without seeking licence, with no intention of apostatizing, but on account of penury of victuals, they had transferred themselves to another monastery of the same order in the diocese of Llandaff, and now they desired to return and be restored, each of them, to her old room over the parlour.

On 2 September 1410 Bishop Bubwith, at the request of Margery Fitz Nichol, prioress, who, on account of extreme old age and infirmity desired to be relieved of the government of the

[3] *Pope Nich. Tax.* (Rec. Com.) 199.
[4] Harl. MSS. 4120, fol. 178.
[5] Inq. p. m. 44 Edw. III, no. 46, Appendix xi.
[6] Pat. 44 Edw. III, pt. ii, no. 3.
[7] *Valor Eccl.* (Rec. Com.) i, 183.
[8] *Drokensford's Reg.* (Somers. Rec. Soc. i) 92.
[9] Ibid. 93.   [10] Ibid. 115.

[11] *Drokensford's Reg.* (Somers. Rec. Soc. i) 167.
[12] Ibid. 115.   [13] Ibid. 221.   [14] Ibid. 238.
[15] Ibid. 246.   [16] Ibid. 248.
[17] *R. of Shrewsbury's Reg.* (Somers. Rec. Soc. ix) 38.
[18] *Cal. Papal Letters*, v, 162.

house, issued a commission of inquiry.[19] About a year and a half afterwards, it seems that the late prioress regarded her application to be allowed to resign as if it also had relieved her of her duties and her vows as a sister. For, on 14 April 1412, Bishop Bubwith sent instructions to her [20] to submit herself to the regular observance of her order, and not to allow old age to excuse her attendance at the services of the chapel. She must punctually attend the services, both of the night and the day, when she could conveniently be present, and any neglect on her part to do so would endanger her soul's welfare, and be a manifest violation of the rule of the Order to which she was pledged.

On 20 May 1432 Bishop Stafford wrote to Joan Stabler, one of the nuns of Barrow, telling her that since from lapse of time the nomination to the vacant post of prioress had fallen to him, he therefore appointed her to that office.[21]

On 3 February 1463 [22] Bishop Beckington issued a commission to John Erl, rector of Backwell, to receive the profession of two nuns of Barrow, Sibyl Prest and Isabella Bacwell.

The later history of the priory is unknown, and nothing remains to be recorded beyond the fact that in August 1535 the prioress, Isabella Cogan, resigned on a pension of £4, which was continued to her in 1537 by the Court of Augmentations.[23]

The house was dissolved on 19 September 1536. No list exists of the sisters who were dispersed, but a pension was granted to the prioress, Katharine Bowle or Bulle, of £5 yearly.

PRIORESSES OF BARROW GURNEY

Alice, occurs 1300 [24]

Joan de Gurney, elected 1316, resigned 1325 [25]

Agnes de Sancta Cruce, elected 1325, died 1328 [26]

Basilia de Sutton, elected 1328 [27]

Juliana de Groundy, elected 1340 [28]

Agnes Balun, elected 1348 [29]

Joan Panes, occurs 1377, 1388 [30]

Margery Fitz Nichol, resigned 1410 [31]

Joan Stabler, appointed 30 May 1432 [32]

Agnes Leveregge, 1463 [33]

Isabel Cogan, occurs 1502, resigned 1534 [34]

Katharine Bowle or Bull, 1535-7 [35]

7. THE PRIORY OF CANNINGTON

Cannington is a village about 3 miles north-west of Bridgwater, on the road to Nether Stowey and Holford. The priory, founded about 1138 by Robert de Courci, an adherent of the Empress Matilda, was situated 'hard adnexid to the est of the parish church.' [36]

The endowment began with the grant of the manor and the advowson of the church at Cannington.

Hugh de Wells, Archdeacon of Wells, and afterwards Bishop of Lincoln (1209-35), left in his will (1212) 5 marks to the nuns of Cannington.[37]

In the *Taxatio* of 1291 Cannington, on account of its poverty, escaped assessment.

In 1333 [38] Robert Fitz Pain obtained licence to alienate to the prioress and nuns 80 acres of land at Cannington and Rodway, to maintain a chaplain to pray for his soul, and in 1354,[39] John de Chidiok and Robert de Sambourn obtained similar permission to give to the convent a rent-charge, and the advowson of the church of Witheridge in Devonshire, and this was confirmed in 1380.[40]

In 1382 [41] the rector of Spaxton, Robert Crosse, was the intermediary for a grant to the nuns of 120 acres of land in Pawlett.

In the Valor [42] of 1535 the house is declared in possession of the church and manor of Cannington, the church and lands in Witheridge, the free chapel of Puddletown St. Mary, Dorset, and lands and tenements at Stowey, Skilgate, Bridport and Bradford, Fiddington, Blackdown, Bristol and Godley. The value of the property was declared at £39 15s. 8d., of which 75s. had to be distributed in alms under Robert de Courci's bequest.

The nuns were drawn largely from the local county families,[43] and the house was used, as

[19] Bath Epis. Reg. Bubwith, fol. 40b.
[20] Ibid. fol. 57.
[21] Ibid. Stafford, fol. 75b.
[22] Ibid. Beckington, fol. 287.
[23] Aug. Off. Misc. Bks. vol. 92.
[24] Assize R. 1318, m. 20.
[25] *Somers. Rec. Soc. Publ.* i, 115.
[26] Ibid. 246, 248.   [27] Ibid. 294.
[28] Ibid. ix, 370.   [29] Ibid. x, 557.
[30] Harl. MSS. 4120, fol. 305; occurs as 'late prioress' in 1402.
[31] Wells Epis Reg. Bubwith fol. 40 in dorso.
[32] Ibid. Stafford fol. 75 in dorso.

[33] Collinson, *Hist. and Antiq. of Somers.* ii, 311. The bishops' registers are silent concerning her, and Collinson gives no authority. But cf. Wells Epis. Reg. Beckington, fol. 282.
[34] Wells Epis. Reg. King, fol. 139.
[35] Aug. Off. Misc. Bks. vol. 92 (Orders and Decrees, vol. ii), fol. 3.
[36] Leland, *Itin.* ii, 98.
[37] Cal. *Wells D. and C. MSS.* (Hist. MSS. Com.) i, 432.
[38] *Cal. Pat.* 1330-4, p. 394.
[39] Ibid. 1350-4, p. 541.
[40] Ibid. 1377-81, p. 447.
[41] Inq. p. m. 5 Ric. II, no. 81.
[42] *Valor Eccl.* (Rec. Com.) i, 209, 210.
[43] At Combe Florey there is an incised slab of 13th-century work, with an inscription to the memory of Dame Maud de Merriete, a nun of Cannington. The Merrietes were of Hestercombe.

most houses of this size and kind were, as a place of retirement for the ladies of the county, either for the festivals of the church that they might observe them the better, or for their convenience and safety at times when their husbands and brothers were away.

Nominally the permission of the bishop had to be obtained before these houses could receive as paying guests the ladies who desired to retire there, but the ease with which these licences seem to have been granted is noticeable. The danger to the sisters from receiving these ladies was obvious. They were not bound by the rules which the sisters had to observe; they were not under any vows; they had been trained in the world; and they brought worldly ideas and all the pride of their position into these simple houses of sisters. Moreover those who were called upon to attend them, and the state in which they lived in the vacant rooms of the nunneries, must all have influenced detrimentally the good discipline of the house.

In the spring of 1313[44] we find Bishop Drokensford granting to Dyonisia Peverel permission to stay (*perhendinandum*) at her own cost with the nuns of Cannington. Then the next year[45] the wife and sisters of John Fychet were allowed to spend their Christmas there, and a similar licence was granted to Isabel Barayl in 1315.[46] His successor, Bishop Ralph, in June 1336[47] granted such a permission to Isabel Fychet, and in the same autumn he allowed[48] Joan Wason and Maud Poer to stay there for Christmas and till the following Easter with their two maids. In 1354[49] Ralph issued a licence to Isolda, the wife of John Byccombe, to spend some time in the house.

In September 1311[50] some disturbance had taken place in the churchyard, for Bishop Drokensford issued a commission to his suffragan, John, Bishop of Cork, to reconcile the cemetery of the poor nuns of Cannington, polluted by effusion of blood.

On 4 May 1317[51] for some reason which is not stated, Emma de Bytelscomb, the prioress, resigned her office, and Matilda de Morton[52] appeared before Bishop Drokensford at Wiveliscombe, together with two sisters, Agnes de Newmarket and Sibyl de Horsy, who desired confirmation of Matilda's election as prioress in succession to Emma. On inquiry the election seems to have been found irregular; the sanction of the patron appears not to have been obtained, and at his request the house was granted permission to carry out the new election on 10 May.

On 31 May the commission appointed by the bishop to inquire into the details of the proce-

dure of the election of Matilda de Morton demanded from the sisters whether any objections were made to the elected one, and Joan de Bratton, one of the sisters, objected on the ground of irregularity. The commission sat again on 9 June, when, in addition to the four mentioned, seven other sisters gave their evidence, and on 18 June the election of Matilda, which had been provisionally confirmed by the bishop, was quashed by the commissioners, and she was found to be unfit and irregularly chosen. In her place Joan de Bere was substituted. On 12 July Joan seems to have been induced to resign; Matilda and Joan renounced any intention of appeal against the bishop's decision, and on 15 August[53] the bishop, being satisfied that the house would accept his judgement, formally collated to the prioress-ship Matilda de Morton.

In 1328[54] rumours seem to have reached Bishop Drokensford, and he appointed Canon Walter de Hulle to go to Cannington to inquire. It was said that some of the nuns were in the habit of walking about at night and wandering, without permission, from the precincts of the convent. The result of this inquiry is not recorded, but in 1351 Bishop Ralph issued a commission to John de Sydenhale and Nicholas de Pontesbury to inquire and correct things they might find amiss at Cannington. Here a painful exposure resulted from their inquiries.[55]

The prioress, Avice de Raigners, was found to have taken a bribe of £20 each from four whom she had admitted as nuns, and to have sold several corrodies, that is to say rights to nominate a pensioner to live in the house. This lay as a burden on the estates of the priory which were already insufficient for the support of the nuns, and brought in ladies with no vocation for a religious life to live with those who were professed. Two nuns, Matilda Pulham and Alice Northlode, the lady whom the bishop himself had forced on the house in 1333,[56] were found guilty of nightly conferences with the two chaplains, Richard Sompnour and Hugh Wyllinge, in the nave of the church of the said monastery. Matilda also had used threats and had acted in an indecent manner towards the servants of the house. Worse was to be feared from their conduct. Matilda was ordered to sit at the bottom of the choir, and at the bottom in the refectory, and Alice was to take the seat next above her, and they were on no account for a whole year to be allowed to go beyond the cloister of the house. Joan Trimelet who, to the grave confusion of their religious profession and scandal of the house, had given birth to a child, was ordered a year's penance. The sub-prioress was suspended for neglect of her duty, and for absence

44 *Somers. Rec. Soc. Publ.* i, 165.   45 Ibid. 81.
46 Ibid. 83.   47 Ibid. ix, 278.   48 Ibid. 277.
49 Ibid. x, 744.   50 Ibid. i, 43.
51 Ibid. 126.   52 Ibid. 6.

53 *Somers. Rec. Soc. Publ.* i, 167.
54 Ibid. 289.   55 Ibid. ix, 284.
56 The bishop had the right of appointing a nun to the priory on his election to the see.

from the morning offices in the chapel, and two other nuns were joined in commission with her to carry out the duties of that post.

The charge against the prioress of having sold corrodies without a licence took a definite form in 1370 as the result of an inquest, in 1368, on the death of Roger Montfort, who died an outlaw and whose sole possessions consisted of a life interest in a corrody at Cannington Priory.

Some slight evidence of the terror caused by the Great Pestilence is perhaps shown in the licences sought and obtained from the pope [57] by ' Avis de Reigneres ' the prioress in January 1349, and by Joan Trimelet June 1349, to choose any confessor they could find at the hour of their death.

Little is known of the later history of the priory. In 1504 Cecilia de Verney was elected and the mandate for her induction was issued by Archbishop Warham [58] during the vacancy of the see owing to Bishop Hadrian de Castello's appointment not having been as yet confirmed.

In 1534 the house appears to have accepted the Act of Supremacy and the Succession Act, and on 23 September 1536 was dissolved.

On 20 November 1536 [59] the prioress, Cecilia de Verney, received a pension of 10 marks. In 1556 none of the sisters are mentioned in Cardinal Pole's list, but Thomas Hache, the steward of the house, was still in receipt of a pension. [60]

PRIORESSES OF CANNINGTON

Emma de Bytelescumb, resigned 1317 [61]
Joan de Bere, elected and deposed, [62] 1317
Matilda de Morton, collated 1317 [63]
Willelma de Blachyngdon, elected 1334, died 1336 [64]
Joan de Bere, re-elected 1336, died 1343 [65]
Avice de Reigners, elected 1343 [66]
Joan, occurs 1412 [67]
Joan de Chedeldon, died 1440 [68]
Joan Gofyse, elected 1440 [69]
Eleanor [70]
Cecilia de Verney, elected 1504, surrendered 1536 [71]

HOUSE OF CLUNIAC MONKS

8. THE PRIORY OF MONTACUTE

Tofig, the great Danish standard-bearer of King Cnut, had large estates in Essex and in Somerset. On the hill-top of his land at Lutgaresbury in Somerset there was found about the year 1035 [1] a wonder-working crucifix safely concealed under a large slab of stone, and this was regarded by Tofig as so precious that he determined to build a church for its preservation on his estate in Essex, and to endow two priests to act as guardians of it. This was the origin of the church of Waltham, which ultimately developed into an abbey of Austin Canons. The finding of this relic at Lutgaresbury made the site precious to the minds of churchmen, and Tofig handed it over to the church and so it became known as Bishopston. [2] Before 1066 we find it had been given to the Abbot and convent of Athelney. [3] The site however was a hill site, naturally suited for fortification, and William the Conqueror gave it to his half-brother Count Robert of Mortain, who built a castle there.

The English monks at Athelney prudently surrendered the place and received as an exchange the count's estate at Purse Caundle, in Dorset. [4]

Towards the end of the 11th century William the son of this Count Robert of Mortain, gave the church at Montacute and his castle and burgh and market and the manor of ' Biscopestune ' with its hundred and mill to the abbey of Cluny. The first charter in the *Montacute Cartulary* [5] belongs to the period between 1091 and 1104. The deed must be earlier than 1104, when William of Mortain was banished by Henry I.

We know little of the history of the earlier priors. The first who comes into special notice was Durand, prior at the end of the 12th century. [6] He was accused by Bishop Savaric (1192–1205) of maladministration, and suspended (1207–17), and though afterwards restored, was eventually expelled. [7]

In 1261 the Prior of Montacute was appointed visitor of the Order in England, [8] and next year it was reported that the service of God was well

---

[57] *Cal. Papal Letters*, iii, 288, 326.
[58] Cant. Archiepis. Reg. Warham, fol. 201.
[1] Cf. *De Invent. Crucis* (ed. Stubbs), 1–10.
[2] Cf. *Somers. Rec. Soc. Publ.* xiv, 182.
[3] *V. C. H. Somers.* i, 483.
[4] Ibid,

[59] Misc. Vols. Aug. Off. 244, no. 110, App. 10.
[60] Card. Pole Pension List, fol. xxix, App. no. ix.
[61] *Somers. Rec. Soc. Publ.* i, 126.
[62] Ibid. 130–67.   [63] Ibid. 6.
[64] Ibid. ix, 284.   [65] Ibid. 286.
[66] Ibid. x, 486.
[67] Mem. in Scace, 1 Hen. v, m. 13.
[68] Wells Epis. Reg. Stafford, fol. 145.
[69] Ibid.   [70] Ibid. King, fol. 52.
[71] Cant. Archiepis. Reg. Warham, fol. 201.
[5] Printed by *Somers. Rec. Soc.* vol. viii.
[6] *Rot. Lit. Pat.* (Rec. Com.) 78.
[7] Annals of Lewes in *Monasticon* v, 163
[8] Duckett, *Visitations of Cluni*, 222,

performed here, that there were twenty-five monks and that the house owed 300 marks.[9] In 1275 the debt had been reduced to 190 marks, but the buildings were in bad repair. The maintenance of a lamp burning before the Sacrament was neglected, as was the reading of the lesson during meals; moreover the monks ate meat in the houses of laymen and did not wear the footgear ordered by their rules when riding.[10] By 1279 the debt had risen to 260 marks, but the buildings had been repaired and there were now twenty-eight monks of honourable life. 'A clerk called Solomon of Rochester,' the well known justice of that name, was said to have 'violently despoiled' the prior during the last two years, and it is apparently in connexion with this that the visitor continues, 'the fame of the prior has been somewhat, nay rather very much, blackened and incurably injured and I believe unjustly. The prior seems to have been somewhat careless so far as externals are concerned, whatever he may have been in truth, now by the grace of God he both is and appears an excellent, faithful, humble, discreet, obedient and devout person.'[11] The blackening of the prior's character seems to be explained when we find that in 1279 Prior Guy de Mereant[12] was accused of clipping coins and fined 60 marks. The injustice of the charge seems rather doubtful, as he was again charged with the same offence, and with uttering counterfeit money and receiving goods of the Jews in 1284, and fined 200 marks.[13] This seems to have resulted in Prior Guy's removal, for the office of prior was evidently vacant in 1285, when the sub-prior was appointed visitor of the order. During the last years of the 13th century the priory seems to have been in good reputation, as the Prior of Montacute was made visitor on six occasions between 1288 and 1300.[14]

Prior John Cheverer, or Caprarius, in 1317,[15] was accused with Stephen, the late prior, Philip the chamberlain, the sub-prior, and two of the brethren of sending corn, victuals, and arms to the Scots who were then at war with Edward II. An order was sent out for his arrest, but this was afterwards withdrawn. In 1325[16] he had licence from the pope for a year's non-residence, and he shortly afterwards resigned.

Though the priory had powerful friends, it must be remembered the Cluniac order was never popular in England because it was regarded as a foreign order, not too loyal to the English people. All the brethren were aliens, owing service and making payment to an abbot who was a subject of the French king.

Among the Petitions to the Crown in 1330[17] is one called *Supplicatio Cluniacensium*, which condemns this dependency on Cluny as the cause of the great reduction of monks at Montacute, and protests against the large sums of money derived from English estates which were sent to support subjects of the French king.[18] It is moreover stated that there were only twenty professed monks in the English priories, because by the law of the order a monk could only be professed at the mother abbey of Cluny, and some monks it was stated had been in their priories forty years without being professed.

In 1326 the Abbot of Cluny appointed Guichard de Jou as prior.[19] The pope however claimed the right to appoint and nominated a Benedictine monk, Robert Busse of Tavistock,[20] but neither the convent at Montacute nor the abbey of Cluny would recognize him. The pope then appointed Peter de Mortemart and summoned Guichard to Avignon. Guichard went to Avignon in October 1328,[21] and eventually appealed to King Edward for help, and in February 1331 Edward III declared him to be rightly the Prior of Montacute.[22]

The next year the pope appointed Guichard Prior of Lenton, and Philip de Chintraico Prior of Montacute.[23] The story, however, is somewhat complicated, for soon after, John de Henton, a monk of Sherborne,[24] charged Guichard, as prior, with betraying the secrets of the realm, communicating with the Abbot of Cluny, and taking in at Montacute certain aliens, namely, the priors of Carswell and of Barnstaple without licence from the Crown. The matter was ultimately referred to Thomas de Marleberge and Ralph de Middelneye, who in 1339 acquitted Guichard and declared John de Henton's charges false.[25]

Montacute as an alien priory under the Acts of Edward II and Edward III naturally came into the king's hands, and the prior and convent had to pay rent to the Crown equal to the amount which they would have transmitted to Cluny.[26] In 1339 Edward III granted the advowson and custody of the priory of Montacute to William, Earl of Salisbury, Marshal of England,[27] and

[9] Duckett, *Rec. of Cluni*, ii, 123.
[10] Ibid. 126.   [11] Ibid. 133.
[12] *Cal. Pat.* 1272–81, p. 318.
[13] Ibid. 1281–92, p. 147.
[14] Duckett, *Visitations of Cluni*, 235. Ibid. 239, 242, 249, 252, 256, 263.
[15] *Cal. Close* 1313–18, p. 395.
[16] *Cal. Papal Letters*, ii, 216, 248, 249.

[17] Anct. Pet. (P.R.O.) 4 Edw. III.
[18] Montacute Priory was supposed to send 12 marks yearly to the mother abbey. Duckett, *Rec. of Cluni*, i, 184.
[19] *Cal. Pat.* 1324–7 p. 274.
[20] *Cal. Papal Letters*, ii, 257, 277 and 278.
[21] *Cal. Close* 1327–30, p. 415.
[22] Rymer, *Foedera*, ii, 807.
[23] *Cal. Papal Letters*, ii, 346, 347.
[24] *R. of Shrewsbury's Reg.* (Somers. Rec. Soc. ix) 368.
[25] Anct. Pet. (P.R.O.) no. 10,488.
[26] *Montacute Cartul.* (Somers. Rec. Soc. viii) 211.
[27] Rymer, *Foedera*, viii, 104.

the priory had to pay to Earl William the rent which it had for a short time paid to the Crown. To this grant to Earl William was also added the custody of the four dependent cells of Montacute, viz. of Carswell in Devonshire, Holme in Dorset, St. Karroc in the parish of St. Veep in Cornwall, and Malpas in Monmouthshire.[28]

In 1362 Francis de Baugiaco, who had been appointed prior of Prittlewell in Essex in the previous year, applied to the pope [29] for the priorship of Montacute, and in 1371 agreed to pay £120 a year to the Crown on condition of his being recognized as prior, but afterwards he was expelled from the priory on the ground of his French sympathies, and he was succeeded by Nicholas Hornyk de Montibus, a Friar Minor, who in 1399 tried to get his predecessor arrested for treason.[30]

Henry IV seems to have given back the priory of Montacute to Francis, who appears again as prior in January 1403.[31] The close relationship between the monks and the papal court is shown by the fact that in 1393 Thomas Samme of Montacute, and in 1398, Francis, a monk of Montacute, were made papal chaplains.[32] Francis died in January 1404 and was succeeded by William Cryche.[33] Up to this time it will be noticed that all the priors had been foreigners or had foreign names, and they were appointed by the Abbot of Cluny, or occasionally by the pope.

In 1407, under this new prior, Montacute renounced allegiance to Cluny, became denizen and ceased to be an alien priory, recognizing as the head of the Order in England the Prior of Lewes, who now began to be looked upon by the English Cluniacs as holding the authority over them which formerly had been exercised by the Abbot of Cluny,[34] and from that time to the Dissolution Montacute was regarded as an English monastic house. The priory had to pay for this recognition of their English citizenship the sum of 300 marks.[35] In the reign of Henry V the convent was given permission to elect its own prior, and was released from all dependence on the Abbot of Cluny.

In 1458 the monks gave the right of election of the prior to the Bishop of Winchester and the Earl of Winchester, and received from them Robert Newton, a Benedictine monk from Glastonbury.[36]

Thomas Chard, who became prior in 1514, was already a bishop *in partibus*, having been consecrated Bishop of Selymbria in Thrace in 1506, and was also warden of the College of St. Mary Ottery.[37] He resigned in 1532, and in lieu of a pension, took the office of Prior of Carswell, a cell dependent on Montacute.[38] He must not be confounded with Thomas Chard, an almost contemporary abbot of the Cistercian monastery of Ford.[39]

Robert Shirborne, the last abbot, who seems to have gone under the three names of Whitlocke, Shirborne, or Gibbs, had agreed to pay £100 to Henry for his recognition as prior.[40]

On 10 March 1538–9 the priory was visited by Hugh Pollard, under a commission issued by Cromwell in the name of Henry VIII. He went there to try and bring about his surrender, but the following letter from him and Petre to Cromwell shows that the prior was not inclined to yield [41] :—

Or most bownden duetyes remembryd it may please yor lordeshipp to bee advertised that this day wee resortyd to the priorie of montigue for the execution of the Kinges highnes commission ther, wher after long (? communication) wt the prior and as many persuasions for the setting forthe of the King graces pleasure in this behalf as wee cowd devise wee fownd the prior in lyke obstinacy as wee hadd befor fownd thabbott of Bruton. And by so moche as by his awnswars we might conjecture ther hadd byn some pryvey conference between them in this mater, before our commyng he hadd leassyd allmost all his demeynes to dyvers persones.

We may infer from the fact that Pollard in his letter brings no charges against the prior or the monks that the monastery was in good order. All he seems to have to complain about was the unwillingness of the priory to surrender to the king. However, it was visited again on 20 March 1539, and surrendered to Dr. Petre, and pensions were awarded to sixteen monks, while the prior received a pension of £80, and a dwelling-house at East Chinnock.[42]

The priors of the cell at Malpas, John Clerke, and of the cell at Holme in Dorset, John Walles, were also included in the list. The pension list amounted to £186 a year.

In Cardinal Pole's pension list,[43] 24 February 1556, twelve of the monks were still alive, including the prior Whitelock or Sherborne. The parishioners of Montacute purchased for their own use five of the bells of the conventual church and paid £8 18s. 8d. for them.[44]

[28] *Parl. R.; Cal. Pat.* iii, 409 ; 1399–1401, p. 453.
[29] *Cal. Papal Pet.* i, 393.
[30] Cf. *Somers. Rec. Soc. Publ.* viii, 218, and Anct. Petitions (P.R.O.) no. 6,219, 9,917.
[31] *Acts of P.C.* i, 192.
[32] *Cal. Papal Letters,* iv, 286 and 302.
[33] *Cal. Pat.* 1401–5, p. 335.
[34] *Parl. R.* iv, 27.
[35] *Cal. Pat.* 1405–8, p. 337.
[36] Pat. 37 Hen. VI, pt. i, m. 14.

[37] Oliver's *Mon. Exon.* p. 261.
[38] *L. and P. Hen. VIII,* vi, 504 ; *Valor Eccl.* (Rec. Com.) 196.
[39] *Proc. Somers. Arch. Soc.* xlii, 67.
[40] *L. and P. Hen. VIII,* v, 1213 ; vi, 1613.
[41] Ibid. xiv. (1) 491.
[42] Bodl. Lib. Rawlinson MSS. B. 419 ; Aug. Off. Bks. vol. 245, fol. 72.
[43] Exch. R. Misc. Bks. vol. 32, fol. xxix.
[44] Mins. Accts. Exch. 30–31 Hen. VIII, no. 224.

The incident recorded in the following remarks of Leland,[45] who visited Montacute between 1540 and 1542, does not appear in the Cartulary. It preserves however an interesting tradition of the priory.

This Counte of Moreton began a Priory of Black Monkes, a 3 or 4 in number under the rootes of Montegue Hille, enduing it with 3 faire lordeshippes, Montegue and Titenhul joining to it. The 3rd was Criche a 10 miles from Montegue W. S. W. The Counte of Moreton toke part with Robert Curthose agayn king Henry the first and after was token put in prisone and his landes attainted; at the which time the 3 lordeshippes given to Montegue priory were taken away and then were the monkes compellid to beg for a certain season. At the last king Henry the firste had pyte on them and offered them their own landes again and more so that they would leave that place and go to Lamporte, wher at that time he entendid to have a notable monasterie. But the monkes entredid him that they might kepe theyr old house: and upon that he restorid them their lordshippes, translating his minde of building an abbay from Lamporte to Readyng.

Then cam one Reginaldus Cancellarius, so namid by likelyhood of his office, a man of great fame about king Henry the first, and he felle to Relligion and was prior of Montegue and enlarged it with buildings and possessions.

The Montacute Cartulary begins with the foundation charter of William son of Count Robert of Mortain. First comes the gift of the founder himself, the church at Montacute and the castle, burgh, market, mill, manor and hundred of 'Biscopestune,' the manor, church, hundred, mill and fair at Tintinhull, the manor and church of (East) Chinnock. To this is added the churches of Nynehead, Yarlington, Brympton, Odcombe, Closworth and Mudford, in Somerset, of Elerky in the parish of Veryan, Altarnun, Sennen and St. Cadoc in Cornwall, of Gussage All Saints in Dorset and Monkleigh and Frizenham in Devonshire. This was increased also by the manors of Creech and Closworth and lands at Ham, Widcombe in Montacute, Adbeer in Trent parish and Dene Woldesham in Devonshire, and the whole or portions of the tithes of Child Okeford, Purse Caundle, the three Cernels in the parish of Charminster, Toller, Loders, Thorpe, Hooke and Durweston in Dorset, and of Chiselborough, Cloford, Norton Fitzwarren, Marston Magna, Hascombe, Bickenhall, Chilthorne Domer, Carnicott or Carlingcott (Cridelincot) and Poyntington in Somerset.

There are three charters of confirmation by Henry I given in the cartulary. There is also a charter of confirmation by King Stephen and five charters of Henry II of which four are recorded in the Inspeximus of Henry IV (12 Feb. 1400).[46]

These gifts of churches and tithes are confirmed to the monks by charters of Bishop Robert (1135-66), Bishop Reginald (1174-80) and Bishop Jocelin dated 29 September 1239.

In the *Taxatio* of 1291 [47] these endowments are recapitulated, the *temporalia* and *spiritualia* of the priory being valued at £163 11s. 1d., and we find in addition to those already recorded pensions out of the endowments of the churches at Camerton and Yeovil and in the temporalities, additional lands and tenements at Yeovil, Preston, Ilchester, Wadeford and Stringston in Somerset, and at Wyke, Gillingham and Melbury in Dorset.

To this we find from the Valor of 1535 [48] further increments of endowment at Cadbury, Gillingham, Leverleigh, Erlestoke, Wylye and Monkholme and among the *spiritualia*, the rectories, or pensions out of them, of the churches of Chilthorne Vagge, Ermington, Holme, East Holme, Carswell, Carrock or St. Cadoc, Malpas, St. Neots and Launceston.

The net income of the house was valued at £456 14s. 3d., and they were bound to distribute in alms for the soul of William Count of Mortain their founder, and for the soul of King John and for Richard de Chilthorne the sum of £23 8s. 7d.

Holme in Dorset near Abbotsbury, Carswell in Devonshire near Exeter, Carrock, St. Cadoc, or as it is called in the pension list St. Cyrus in Cornwall near East Looe (in the parish of St. Veep), and Malpas in Monmouthshire were cells of the priory having their own priors and forwarded all excess of income to the mother priory.

PRIORS OF MONTACUTE

R., occurs 1120 [49]
E., occurs 1136 [50]
Durand [51]
Arnold [52]
Reginald (?) [53]
William, occurs 1159 [54]
Thomas, occurs 1169,[55] resigned 1775
Guy, occurs 1179 [56]
Oliver, occurs 1186 [57]
Jocelyn, occurs 1187 [58]

[47] *Pope Nich. Tax.* (Rec. Com.).
[48] *Valor Eccl.* (Rec. Com.) i, 195.
[49] *Mont. Cart.* (Somers. Rec. Soc. viii) charter 47
[50] Ibid. charter 48.
[51] Ibid. charters 141 and 142.
[52] Ibid. charter 155.
[53] Leland, *Itin.* ii, 92.
[54] *Mont. Cart.* charter 130; *Cal. Wells D. and C. MSS.* (Hist. MSS. Com.) i, 27.
[55] *Cal. Doc. France*, 320; *Ann. Mon.* (Rolls Ser.) ii; he became Abbot of Hyde that year.
[56] *Mont. Cart.* charter 38.
[57] *Ancient Charters* (Pipe Roll Soc.), 78, 79.
[58] *Mont. Cart.* charter 58.

[45] Leland, *Itin.* ii, 92.
[46] *Cal. Pat.* 1399-1401, p. 196.

Durand, 1192–1205 [59]
Mark, occurs 1237, 1245 [60]
Roger, occurs 1260 [61]
Hugh de Noyen, 17 September 1260 [62]
Gibert de Bexolio, 30 January 1266 [63]
Guy de Mercant, occurs 1269 [64]
Peter Gandemer, occurs 1290 [65]
John de Bello Ramo, appointed 1292 [66]
Geoffrey de Dosa, appointed 1293 [67]
Stephen Raulun, 1297–1316 [68]
John Cheverer or Caprarius, appointed 1316 [69]
Guichard de Jou, appointed 1326 [70]
John de Porta I, died 1345 [71]
John de Porta II, appointed 1345 [72]
Gerald de Roche, occurs 1362 [73]
Francis de Baugiaco, 1371 [74]
Nicholas Hornyk de Montibus [75]
Francis de Baugiaco, restored 1399, died 1404 [76]
William Cryche, appointed 1404 [77]

John Bennet, occurs 1449 [78]
Robert Montague, appointed 1452 [79]
Robert Newton, 1458, resigned 1462 [80]
Robert Criche, appointed 1462,[81] died 1467 [82]
John Dove, appointed 1467 [83]
John Walter or Water, appointed 1483 [84]
Thomas Chard, appointed July 1514,[85] resigned July 1532 [86]
Robert Shirborne, Whitlocke or Gibbes, appointed 1532, [87] surrendered 1539

The 14th-century seal of the Cluniac Priory of St. Peter and St. Paul at Montacute [88] is a vesica, $2\frac{3}{8}$ in. by $1\frac{5}{8}$ in., with figures of Our Lady crowned and seated with the Child on her left knee, between St. Peter and St. Paul standing with their emblems. Beyond them are the sun and moon. Below, under an arch, is the Prior in prayer. Of the legend there only remains—

s' . . . . . MONTIS ACVTI.

HOUSE OF CISTERCIAN MONKS

9. THE ABBEY OF CLEEVE [1]

The monastery was founded by William de Roumara, third Earl of Lincoln, who had a grant of the Crown estate of Cleeve in Somerset, and gave first of all the church of Cleeve to Bishop Reginald of Bath for the endowment of the church of Wells, and afterwards all his lands at Cleeve, with the liberties and customs he enjoyed from them, to God, St. Mary, and to the monks of St. Laurence of Revesby, a Cistercian abbey in Lincolnshire, founded by his grandfather, to the end that Hugh, the abbot of Revesby, might found at Cleeve an abbey of the Cistercian order. The foundation charter is witnessed by Bishop Reginald (1174–91), and in the confirmation of this gift Hugh Bishop of Lincoln (1186–1202) appears as one of the witnesses. The date of the foundation thus falls between the years 1186 and 1191

The buildings of the Cistercian Abbey [2] seem to have been begun by 1198. A new church was rising, the monastic church as distinct from the parochial prebendal church, and so the distinction arose that the parochial church was called the church of Old Cleeve, a term which is found as early as 1387. [3]

It was difficult however for a distant monastery like that at Bec, of which the abbot held the prebend of Cleeve, to look after the *temporalia* of the parish church, and in order to relieve them from such responsibility the Benedictine monastery of Bec [4] let out on a perpetual lease the church of Cleeve to the Cistercians for an annual rent of 40 marks, and this arrangement was confirmed by Archbishop Hubert (1193–1207). Thus the two monasteries were linked

[59] *Cal. Wells D. and C. MSS.* (Hist. MSS. Com.) i, 57.
[60] Cott. MSS. Tib. A. 10, charters 102, 187.
[61] *Mont. Cart.* charter 152.
[62] Pat. 44 Hen. III, m. 3.
[63] Pat. 50 Hen. III, m. 32.
[64] *Mont. Cart.* charter 95 ; *Abbrev. Rot. Orig.* (Rec. Com.) i, 33.
[65] *Cal. Pat.* 1281–92, p. 348.   [66] Ibid p. 493.
[67] Ibid. 1292–1301, p. 33.
[68] Ibid. 1292–1301, p. 288, occurs as 'late prior' in Feb. 1317.
[69] Ibid. 1313–17, p. 553.
[70] Ibid. 1324–7, p. 274.
[71] *Cal. Papal Pet.* i, 42 ; *Cal. Papal Letters*, iii, 15.
[72] *Cal. Papal Pet.* i, 90.
[73] *Mont. Cart.* charters 200, 204 ; *R. of Shrewsbury's Reg.* (Somers. Rec. Soc. x) 778.
[74] *Cal. Papal Pet.* i, 393 ; *Somers. Rec. Soc. Publ.* viii, 218 ; *Mont. Cart.* (Somers. Rec. Soc.) charter 217.
[75] Cf. P.R.O. Anct. Pet. no. 6,219, 9,917 and 12,495.
[76] *Cal. Pat.* 1401–5, p. 335.   [77] Ibid.
[1] The place name appears in the documents as Clyve, Clive, Cleve, Cliffe and Clyffe and in Latin as Clyva or Cliva.

[78] Cf. Willis, note in the *Monasticon*.
[79] Wells Epis. Reg. Beckington in *Monasticon*, v, 164.
[80] *Cat. Pat.* 1461–7 p. 137.   [81] Ibid. p. 107.
[82] Ibid. 1467–77, p. 14.   [83] Ibid. p. 15.
[84] Ibid. 1476–85, p. 349.
[85] Pat. 6 Hen. VIII, pt. ii, m. 25.
[86] Pat. 24 Hen. VIII, pt. ii, m. 17.
[87] Ibid.
[88] *Cat. of Seals B.M.* 3660, lxxi, 68.
[2] Cotton MSS. Faustina, B. viii, fol. 36.
[3] *Cat. Pat.* 1385–9, p. 370.
[4] Ibid.; *Cal. D. and C. Wells MSS.* (Hist. MSS. Com.) i, 489.

together in their common interest in the pre-bendal church of Old Cleeve; and in the 14th century the convent of Cleeve [5] was called upon as lessee to answer for the alien abbot, the lessor.

The internal history of the abbey is extremely meagre, as the order claimed exemption from the ordinary visitation of the bishops. The convent started with Ralph the first abbot and his twelve companions who had left their house at Revesby [6] to found in Somerset the only monastery of their order in that county. It was not a large house and was never rich. Holding the two churches of Cleeve and East Camel, the monks had to make provision for the maintenance of the vicars there, and in 1320 [7] Bishop Drokensford confirmed the ordination of the vicarage of Cleeve. Though the monastery of Bec is mentioned, the Norman abbey had no responsibility, for the convent at Cleeve had the farm of the church.

The church of East Camel had been given to the monks by Hubert de Burgh,[8] and the gift had been confirmed by King John as early as 1202. A vicarage had been ordained there in 1282, but on account of poverty the abbey had obtained licence to let out the church to farm, and the lessee had apparently appropriated all that he could, regardless of the rights of the vicar. Bishop Drokensford came to the rescue of the latter in 1317, and in 1348 Bishop Ralph of Shrewsbury,[9] on his institution of John Moone as vicar, records carefully the details of the endowment.

The monastic church was certainly built as early as 1232, for in that year Henry III [10] made a grant of oaks from the park of Newton for the choir stalls.

In the grant made to the monks by Reginald de Mohun, 1204–13,[11] they are described as 'monachi Vallis Floridæ quæ vulgo dicitur Clyva.'

Gilbert de Woolavington, rector of Huntspill, in 1297 agreed with Henry, Abbot of Cleeve, so that the monastery bound itself to provide for two secular priests to serve in the new chapel at Woolavington, and offered the church of East Camel as a pledge; and in return Gilbert de Woolavington endowed the abbey with means for the support of two extra monks, for cowls for fifteen monks and for certain pittances.[12] In 1400 this foundation comes before us through a papal confirmation.[13] The prior of the hospital of St. John at Bridgwater was connected with the foundation, as there were three secular priests serving in the chapel at Woolavington, the third being maintained by the hospital, whose agreement with Gilbert de Woolavington is dated 1285, twelve years earlier than that with the abbey of Cleeve. This confirmation states that the number of monks in 1297 was twenty-six, and this benefaction provides for two more.

In January 1339 Pope Benedict XII [14] wrote to the Dean of Wells and others to carry out the papal regulations touching apostates, in reference to Bartholomew Ace, a Cistercian monk of Cleeve, who had left the order and now desired to return to it. In 1390 William Oliver,[15] a monk of Cleeve, was raised to the rank of a papal chaplain, and in 1424 [16] the abbot John Stone received the same distinction.

On 23 August 1455 Bishop Beckington [17] issued a commission to James, Bishop of Bangor, to dedicate the chapel of the B. V. Mary near Old Cleeve, which David the abbot had rebuilt and enlarged. This chapel in the record of the confirmation of the vicarage of Old Cleeve in 1320 [18] was called the Chapel of St. Mary juxta Mare, and the monks were to receive the oblations made at it. In 1398 [19] we find Bishop Stafford of Exeter granting an indulgence for its repair, since it had been greatly damaged by the sea, and in 1400 [20] the pope granted an indulgence to those who should give for its maintenance and repair. In 1466 [21] the monastery received from the Crown the right to hold a weekly market on Wednesdays and yearly fairs on the festival of St. James the Apostle and of the Exaltation of the Holy Cross, to recoup the monks the heavy expenses they had been put to in the repair of the chapel. Owing to the continuous rain a serious landslip had occurred in the adjoining hill, and this had fallen on the chapel which had been built on the sea shore in the manor of Cleeve, and in which miracles had been wrought. The chapel with the adjoining buildings had been crushed to the ground, except the altar of the chapel and the image of the Virgin, which had been miraculously preserved uninjured. The new chapel was not on the site of the older one, but in another place and was afterwards a place of pilgrimage, being coupled in the will of Richard Player,[22] vicar of Kingston, with St. Joseph's chapel at Glastonbury, and to the time of the Dissolution was a source of considerable profit to the monks. In 1536 [23] it possessed four bells, and the next year

[5] Somers. Rec. Soc. Publ. x, 404.
[6] Cotton MSS. Tib. E. viii, fol. 208.
[7] Somers. Rec. Soc. Publ. i, 185.
[8] Cleeve Register, chart. 3.
[9] Somers. Rec. Soc. Publ. x, 720.
[10] Cal. Close, 1231–4, p. 77.
[11] Cleeve Register, no. 687.
[12] Somers. Rec. Soc. Publ. ix, 358.
[13] Cal. Papal Letters, v, 280.

[14] Cal. Papal Letters, ii, 545. [15] Ibid. iv, 274.
[16] Ibid. v, 20.
[17] Wells Epis. Reg. Beckington, fol. 208.
[18] Somers. Rec. Soc. Publ. i, 186.
[19] Reg. Edm. Stafford Bp. of Exeter, 62.
[20] Cal. Papal Letters, v, 400.
[21] Cal. Pat. 1461–7, p. 527.
[22] Weaver, Wells Wills, 98.
[23] P.R.O. Exch. Aug. Off. Accts. 27–8 Hen. VIII, 169, m. 2.

Anthony Bustard, gentleman, offered to give £20 a year rent for the chapel, together with all oblations and profits. In 1542[24] it was granted to Robert Earl of Sussex and Mary his wife.

The later years of the existence of the monastery were years of great financial embarrassment. The last two abbots had been extravagant, and leases and grants seem to have been made for the sake of gaining the support of the laity in the neighbourhood. Notwithstanding its poverty the cloisters of the monastery were being rebuilt in 1534,[25] for in that year Sir Hugh Roper, vicar of Stogumber, left in his will £60 for 'the newe bewylding of the clawsta of the abbey of Clif.' The house was visited preparatory to its dissolution in the autumn of 1535 by Dr. John Tregonwell under orders from Cromwell, and on leaving the monastery for Cornwall he gave injunctions to Abbot Dovell not to depart from his convent. So Dovell wrote on 8 November 1535[26] to Cromwell to say how Tregonwell 'hathe by ynjunction commanded me and all my convent to kyype withyn the precyncts of our monasterie the whiche yff I shulde not sometymes see for the provysyon of my pour house being of small landes I canot be abyll to mayntayne my seyd house nor observe or kype hospitalyte . . . and also I have lycens and commandment of my lord of Bath to preche at certayne places withyn the Dyocese yff yor goodness wyll so suffer me.'

In 1536[27] Tregonwell wrote himself to Cromwell to let him have at a convenient rent, whereby he may have some help towards his living and feeding of his wife and children, one of certain underwritten monasteries in Somerset, specifying Bridgwater and Cleeve.

In 1537[28] the monastery had not yet been dissolved when Sir Thomas Arundell, the king's receiver, wrote to Cromwell — 'riding downward to Cornwall and passing the monastery of Clyffe, hearing such lamentation for the dissolution thereof, and a bruit in the country that the king at your lordship's suit had pardoned it, I sent to Mr. Chancellor of the Augmentations to know whether to dissolve it as I had his letters for the dissolution of the residue of Somerset and it seemed to be omitted by oversight, he being very busy. I beg in behalf of the honest gentlemen of that quarter that the house may stand. In it are seventeen priests of honest life who keep hospitality.' The house however fell that spring, and the abbot William Dovell received a pension of 40 marks,[29] and John Webbe, the 'sub-prior,' received an annuity of £4 3s. 10d., and thirteen monks received as a present (*pro regardo suo*) 26s. 8d. Among these was John Hooper, who was probably the same as John Hooper, Bishop of Gloucester, burnt as a heretic at Gloucester in 1555.

In 1543 we find £8 paid to John Webbe,[30] 'sometyme religious,' for his year's pension. In February 1556[31] the abbot's name still appears in Cardinal Pole's pension list in receipt of his 40 marks yearly.

On 30 January 1538[32] Robert, Earl of Sussex, was granted the reserved rent and the site of the abbey which was then held on a lease of 21 years by Anthony Busterd and the same of the chapel and ground of St. Mary of Cleeve.

The abbey of Cleeve was not a wealthy abbey. In the Valor of 1535[33] it is entered as only worth £155 9s. 5d. The original grant consisted of the lands, liberties and customs which William de Roumara possessed at Cleeve. These included the hamlets of Lindon, Bilbrook, Washford, Hungerford, Golsencott, Roadwater, Leigh and Binham. Then by arrangement with the abbey of Bec the monks became the perpetual lessees of the rectory and advowson of Old Cleeve. This was confirmed by Bishop Savaric, and therefore belongs to the period 1192–1205. About the same time Hubert de Burgh, Earl of Kent, gave to the abbey the church of East Camel and land in Rougham in Norfolk, and a small freehold in Cleeve and his manor of Poughill near Bude, and Treglaston in Cornwall near Otterham.[34] Immediately afterwards Reginald de Mohun gave the monks his land at Shortmansford and Slaworth. To this Henry III added his manor of Braunton[35] near Barnstaple in Devonshire, the monks at first taking it to farm at a yearly rent of £22.

In the *Taxatio* of 1291[36] the *temporalia* are declared as consisting of the manors of Braunton, Treglast and Poughill in the diocese of Exeter, and the manor of Binham in the parish of Cleeve in the diocese of Bath and Wells.

In 1535 the Valor[37] records the possessions of the abbey as consisting of the manors of Old Cleeve, Treborough, Brown in Treborough and Sandell, and manorial rights in Luxborough and Clatworthy, and rents from lands at East Oaktrowe and West Oaktrowe, Smallcombe, Northcombe, Dunster, Marsh, Carymore Mede, Watchet, Bagborough, Blackford and West Anstey, Walworthy, Bristol and Taunton, and in the counties of Devon and Cornwall the manors of Braunton Abbots, Poughill and Treglaston.

---

[24] *L. and P. Hen. VIII*, xvii, g. 220 (84).
[25] Weaver, *Wells Wills*, 153.
[26] *L. and P. Hen. VIII*, ix, 790.
[27] Ibid. 796.   [28] Ibid. xii, 4.
[29] Exch. Aug. Off. Mins. Accts. 27–8 Hen. VIII, 169, m. 2.
[30] Aug. Off. Misc. Bks. No. 248.
[31] Card. Pole's Pension Book, P. R. O.
[32] *L. and P. Hen. VIII*, xiii (1), g. 190 (42).
[33] *Valor Eccl.* (Rec. Com.) i, 218.
[34] Cleeve Charters in *Monasticon*, **v**.
[35] *Hund. R. Devon* (ed. 3), i, 65.
[36] *Pope Nich. Tax.* (Rec. Com.) 152b, 153b, 205b.
[37] *Valor Eccl.* (Rec. Com.) i, 217, 218.

The *spiritualia* consisted of the lease of the rectory of Old Cleeve, out of which 40 marks had to be paid to the canon holding that prebend in the cathedral church of Wells, the rectory of East or Queen Camel and the rectory of the Island of Lundy, valued this year as worth 10s. annually.

Out of the endowments of ·the abbey the monks were bound to distribute £25 a year in alms to the poor.

ABBOTS OF CLEEVE

Ralph, first abbot, occurs 1198 [38]
Hugh [39]
William, occurs 1219 [40]
John, occurs 1237 [41]
Symon, occurs 1253 [42]
John, occurs 1255 [43]
Henry, occurs 1297 [44]
Richard le Bret, elected 1315 [45]
Robert de Clyve, elected 1321 [46]
Michael, occurs 1342 [47]
James, occurs 1344 [48]; 1367 [49]

John, occurs 1400 [50]
John Mason, occurs 1407 [51]
John Plympton, occurs 1416 [52]
Leonard Lythenerstoke, occurs 1416 [53]
William Seylake, elected 1419 [54]
John Stone, elected 1421 [55]
David Juyner or Joyner, elected 1435 [56]
Humphrey, occurs 1486 [57]
Henry, occurs 1494 [58]
John Paynter, 1506 [59]
William Dovell, elected 1507, [60] surrendered 1537

The vesica-shaped seal, 1¾ in. by 1¼ in., of David Juyner, Abbot of the Cistercian house of St. Mary at Cleeve [61] (c. 1435), has a figure of Our Lady crowned and seated on a throne, holding the Child on her right knee. Below under an arch the abbot with his staff kneels in prayer. To the left of him is a shield of England with a label. To his right are the arms of the abbey, seven lozenges. The legend is :—

S' DAVID JUYNER ABBATIS DE CLEYUA.

HOUSES OF CARTHUSIAN MONKS

10. THE PRIORY OF HINTON

The foundation of the Charterhouse at Hinton was due to the devotion of Ela, Countess of Salisbury, and to her desire to fulfil her husband's wish. William Longespée [1] was supposed to have been the son of the fair Rosamund. He was certainly the natural son of Henry II, and in 1198 married Ela d'Evreux, daughter and heiress of Patrick, first Earl of Salisbury. On 7 March 1226 [2] Earl William died and was buried in the new cathedral church at Salisbury, which he had helped to build. During his lifetime he appears to have contemplated the foundation of a house of Carthusian monks at Hatherop in Gloucestershire, and had not only located there some monks,

but had formally conveyed to them a small estate in Chelwood, and also made them an allowance of wood from the forest of Braden. When he died he did not forget them, but bequeathed certain jewels and cattle for their enrichment. Within a short time however the monks appealed to the widowed countess for further help since, as they stated, their endowment was insufficient for their maintenance.

The manors of Hinton and Norton had been granted by the Conqueror to Edward of Salis-

[38] Charter xi, Cleeve Reg.; Dugdale, *Mon.* v, 734.
[39] *Somers. Arch. Proc.* lii, pt. ii, 38.
[40] *Feet of F.* (Somers. Rec. Soc. vi) 1228, p. 35.
[41] *Cal. Pat.* 1232–47, p. 191.
[42] *Somers. Rec. Soc. Publ.* vi, 157; xi, 306.
[43] *Cal. Pat.* 1317–21, p. 581.
[44] *Cal. Papal Letters*, v, 279; *Somers. Rec. Soc.* ix, 356.
[45] *Somers. Rec. Soc.* i, 85, 97.
[46] Ibid. 193.
[47] *Cal. Close*, 1341–3, p. 469.
[48] Ibid. 1343–6, p. 458.
[49] Nettlecombe Charters 41 Edw. III.
[1] *Dict. Nat. Biog.*
[2] Roger of Wendover, *Flor. Hist.* (Engl. Hist. Soc.) iv, 105 and 107.

[50] *Cal. Pat.* 1399–1401, p. 413.
[51] Nettlecombe Charters.
[52] Nettlecombe Charters; Memoranda Easter 4 Hen. V. Rec.
[53] Rowe, *Cist. Mon. of Devon*, 155.
[54] Confirmed 28 Sept. 'ad instanciam Nicholai Abbatis Mon. Be. Marie de Newham Ord. Cist. Exon. Dioc.' Wells. Epis. Reg. Bubwith. In one of the windows of Dunster Church is an ancient quarry inscribed 'W. Donesterre abbas de Cliva' (Maxwell-Lyte, *Hist. of Dunster*). This abbot may perhaps be identified with William Seylake.
[55] Profession received by Richard 'Episcopus Katensis.'
[56] Exeter Epis Reg. Stafford, 1466; *Cal. Pat* 1461–7, p. 527.
[57] Dunster Castle MSS. bdle 13, no. i. [58] Ibid.
[59] Summoned to Convocation 26 Jan. 1507. *Star Chamb. Proc.* Hen. VII, vol. i, p. 4, no. 77. Cf. Wells Epis. Reg. Hadrian, unnumbered folio at end.
[60] Surrendered 1537.
[61] *Cat. of Seals B.M.* 2960, xlvii, 473.

bury,[3] the sheriff of Wilts, and had descended to Countess Ela through her father; and in May 1232 she responded to the petition of the monks by conferring these manors upon them. The Laycock Register [4] says that on the same day in May she founded the house of Austin Nuns at Laycock in Wiltshire and the Carthusian House at Hinton. There are no early charters, and we are dependent on the register [5] of Bishop Ralph of Shrewsbury for a copy of the foundation charter. It mentions Hatherop and Braden, and the manors of Hinton and Norton and the advowson of the church there. The deed is witnessed by Hubert de Burgh, and therefore it cannot be later than 1232, nor can it be earlier than 1229 when Robert Bingham, another of the witnesses, became Bishop of Salisbury.

Beyond the record of the increase of endowments and the lawsuits that were necessary at times to maintain their right to them, we know nothing of the early history of the monastery.[6] In the early days of the settlement of the monks at Hinton Bishop Jocelin, in 1262, had to arrange a dispute between the vicar of Hinton and the monks concerning the small tithes of the parish and the title to three acres of land.[7] The rectory and the advowson, though stated in the charter as granted to the monks, were in the hands of the bishop, and in 1342 [8] Bishop Ralph of Shrewsbury conveyed the advowson and rectory of Hinton, said to belong to the see, to the Prior and convent of Hinton, and three years later [9] he also conveyed to them through Walter de Rodeney the advowson of Norton.

The documents copied into Bishop Ralph's register,[10] in addition to the foundation charter, include a confirmation by Bishop Jocelin in 1230, and a papal confirmation by Innocent IV in 1245, and papal charters of protection and confirmation of privileges from Clement IV in 1265 and 1266, John XXII in 1318 and Innocent IV in 1345.

In 1371 at a general chapter of the order held in London, John Luscombe or Luscote the prior was allowed to resign that he might be made 'rector' of the new Carthusian foundation at Smithfield, London.[11] In 1444 the priory shared in the grants made by Henry VI out of the property and revenues accruing to the Crown from the sequestration of the alien priories, and its yearly income was increased by a grant of 50 marks.[12]

Towards the end of the 15th century one of the monks of Hinton became famous as an ecstatic visionary. Brother Stephen, 'the admirable Stephen,' professed a devotion for St. Mary Magdalene. In Durandus' Chronicle of the Carthusian Order,[13] a work which preserves to us many anecdotes concerning the lives of prominent Carthusians, we are told that Stephen in a religious ecstasy seemed to be transported to the top of a mountain. Before him stretched a garden full of lovely flowers, and while he prepared to go forth and explore it he saw advancing towards him a lady of extreme beauty, from whose head the hair hung like golden glory, and from whose face streamed forth rays of sunlight. As he drew near the lady accosted him—'God keep thee, my lover, Stephen.' Then he threw himself at her feet, but recognizing his saintly patroness he took courage to speak to her.

The conversation, which is of the erotic style common to the age, goes on to say that he told his patroness that the wish of his heart was to be taken back into favour as was Stephen after his many sins. This Stephen was known as Stephen of Flanders, whose pardon through the intercession of the Magdalene was an incident often quoted in monastic religious works of the time. The conversation ends with his promise of his heart, and a pledge from him that he would inwardly rejoice at the Magdalene's blessedness and privileges.

Stephen of Hinton [14] died at Hinton at the very end of the 15th century.

As early as 1508 Edward, the third Duke of Buckingham, who was often wont to stay at his manor house of Thornbury in Gloucestershire, appears to have had some interest in Hinton, and on 9 May [15] of that year he paid a fee for a servant of the Prior of Hinton named Hoxton. The interest grew out of the duke's connexion with Nicholas Hopkins, a monk of the priory and vicar of the conventual church. Nicholas Hopkins was the duke's spiritual director,[16] and seems to have had a great influence over him, while on the other hand the duke seems to have had recourse to him for advice and to have placed great trust in his instructions. We find Hopkins writing to the duke [17] early in the century, to ask his help and interest on behalf of a poor child of fourteen years, an inmate of the priory, and begging him to provide for the boy's education until he should reach his twentieth year. The

---

[3] *V.C.H. Somers.* i, 518.
[4] Cotton MSS. Vitellius A. viii.
[5] *R. of Shrewsbury's Reg.* (Somers. Rec. Soc. x) 482-9.
[6] Charter Rolls, 24 Hen. III, m. 1.
[7] *R. of Shrewsbury's Reg.* (Somers. Rec. Soc. ix) 280.
[8] *Cal. Pat.* 1340-3, p. 413.
[9] Ibid. 1343-5, p. 569.
[10] *Somers. Rec. Soc. Publ.* x, 482-9.
[11] Doreau, *Hen. VIII, et les martyrs de la Chartreuse*; Dugdale, *Mon.* vi, 9.

[12] Pat. 24 Hen. VI, pt. i, m. 32.
[13] Book v, cap vi.
[14] Add. MSS. 17092, 17085.
[15] *L. and P. Hen. VIII,* iii (I), 1285.
[16] Ibid.   [17] Ibid. 1277.

duke did so, and the boy Francis [18] was brought up at Oxford by the prior of St. John of Jerusalem, and as late as 1521 items of expenditure on his behalf appear in the duke's account book.

Meanwhile Hopkins had discerned the duke's most secret ambitions, and knowing his relationship to Henry VIII, is said to have predicted for him the succession to the throne. Hopkins had acquired some fame as one who uttered cryptic prophecies, and people were wont to resort to him for advice. When therefore in 1521 the duke [19] was summoned to London, his arrival was preceded by that of Nicholas Hopkins, whose favoured relationship to the duke had won for him the envy and enmity of Knyvet, the duke's surveyor, and Delacourt, the duke's chaplain. The fate of the duke was sealed. He had roused the jealous suspicion of Henry VIII and the resentment of Wolsey. Hopkins was sent to the Tower, and a careful search was ordered at Hinton for any papers of Hopkins' or concerning the duke which would provide evidence at the trial. The prior however and his fellow monks [20] were anxious that they should not be incriminated with their vicar, and wrote to the Lord Chamberlain (the Earl of Worcester) assuring him of the innocence of the monks and their readiness to do all in their power to search for papers. They hoped that their proctor who had gone up with him might be allowed to come home again, and that Hopkins might be sent to some other house of Carthusians, there to be punished for his offences. This letter was not only signed by the prior Henry, but in witness of the truth of his statement he caused all his fellow monks, eight in number, to sign it also, i.e. Hew Lakoq, Thomas Wellys, Robert Frey, Anton Ynglych, Thomas Flatcher, Wyllyam Stokes, Nicholas Lycchefeld and John Hartwell. The trial of the Duke of Buckingham is no part of the history of Hinton. Shakespeare, however, in the play of *Henry VIII*, refers twice to Hopkins—

ACT i, SCENE 2.

Surveyor. 'He was brought to this
By a vain prophecy of Nicholas Hopkins.'
King. 'What was that Hopkins?'
Surveyor. 'Sir, a Chartreux friar,
His confessor, who fed him every minute
With words of sovereignty.'

And again ACT ii, SCENE I.

'. . . . that devil-monk
Hopkins, that made this mischief.'

The correspondence between the duke and Hopkins was stated to have gone on since 1512, and John Delacourt, the duke's chaplain, seems to have been his messenger in this intimacy.[21] Buckingham was executed on 17 May 1521 mainly on the evidence of his alleged conversations with Hopkins.[22]

Hopkins seems to have been kept in confinement and is said to have died soon after, broken hearted on account of the fate of his great and generous confidant.

The successor to Prior Henry in 1523 was John Batmanson,[23] a man of some note. In 1509 [24] he was sent as one of an embassy to Scotland to take the oath of James IV in confirmation of the treaty between England and Scotland and he was also one of the commissioners of the Scotch marches. In 1519 he entered the lists against Erasmus and wrote at the instigation of Dr. Lee, the Archbishop of York, against Erasmus' New Testament which he had published that year at Basel. In May 1520 Erasmus [25] wrote to Bishop Fox of Winchester protesting against Dr. Lee's bitterness, and said ' he has suborned a Carthusian of London John Batmanson by name, I think, a young man as appears by his writings altogether ignorant, but vain glorious to madness.' Afterwards Batmanson wrote a book against certain writings of Martin Luther, a work which has not come down to us but which was probably directed against Luther's *De Captivitate Babylonica* which appeared in 1521. His retirement to Hinton from 1523 to 1529 seems to have been a period of great literary activity, for during this time he is said to have written [26] *On the Song of Songs, On the Proverbs of Solomon, On the Words of the Gospel Missus est Angelus, On the Identity of the Magdalen in the Gospels, On the Child Jesus amidst the Doctors in Jerusalem,* and *On Contempt of the World.*

While Prior of Hinton Batmanson was appointed assistant visitor of the English province of Carthusians, and in 1529 he was called to London to become prior of the house at Smithfield,[27] where he died 16 November 1531.

While Batmanson was at Hinton another Carthusian there, Thomas Spencer, was engaged in writing a commentary on the Epistle of St. Paul to the Galatians and ' A trialogus between Thomas Bilney, Hugh Latimer and William Repps.' Spencer spent some years in study at Oxford, but he seems to have done his writing at Hinton and to have died there in 1529.[28]

Batmanson was succeeded as prior by Edmund Horde, another Carthusian whose influence

---

[18] *L. and P. Hen. VIII*, iii (i), 1285.
[19] Ibid. iii (i), 1204.   [20] Ibid. 1276.

[21] *L. and P. Hen. VIII*, iii (i), g. 1484 (2).
[22] Cotton MSS. App. xlviii, fol. 109.
[23] Cf. *Dict. Nat. Biog.* 'He was born in the bishopric of Dorom in Shorborne house': Exch. Dep. by Com. 19 Eliz. Hil. 3.
[24] *L. and P. Hen. VIII*, i, 467, 488, 548, 714.
[25] Epist. Erasm. Lib. xii.
[26] Cf. Cotton MSS. Nero A. iii, fol. 139.
[27] Pits, *Relat. Hist. de rebus Anglicis.*
[28] Wood, *Athen. Oxon.* (ed. Bliss) i, 54.

during the few troublous years that preceded the Dissolution was very considerable. He was recognized as of some importance by the Government, but Cromwell seems to have distrusted him. The Act of Supremacy and the stand made by the English monarch against the encroachments of the papal curia do not seem to have been a serious offence to him, but there is evidence of his unwillingness to accept the statements which would have made Anne Boleyn rightful queen of England. When called upon in 1534 to acknowledge this succession he seems to have brought his monks round to accept it,— but only in such a way as saved him from punishment while it left him under suspicion. On 1 September 1534 [29] he felt it necessary to write directly to the king to assure him of his loyalty. He said he had received instructions 'by master Layton of your grace's pleasure concerning the subscrybyng and sealyng of a certeyn profession in wrytyng which I have sent unto your grace wyth as trew and feythfull hart and mynd as any yowr grace's subject lyvying,' and he also would have the king believe that 'durying my lyfe I woll sett forth fortifie and defend agaynst almen according to my bounden duetie,' the truth which the Act of Supremacy and Succession declared.

At Smithfield the monks were not so easily brought to submission, and some of them openly desired to consult 'the prior of Hinton, [30] Dr. Hourde,' and in July 1535 Dr. Lee, the Archbishop of York, recommended Cromwell to employ Horde—'a prior of their religion whom all the religious esteem for virtue and learning. They will give him more credence and rather apply their conscience to his judgment than to any other although of greater learning, especially if some other good father be joined with him.' The order of the vicar-general that the clergy should preach the doctrine of the Royal Supremacy was a serious obstacle in the way of Horde's obedience, and not till Cromwell had sent Sir Walter Hungerford to argue with him did he yield, writing immediately afterwards to Cromwell to commend himself to him and to say [31]—'if there in me be any qualities or hability to do you service I wolde be glad to do yt to the uttermoste of my little power soo fer forth as should beseeme a poore Religious preste to do.'

Probably it was at this time that Andrew Boorde, Carthusian of Smithfield, wrote to Cromwell [32] asking him to be a good friend to Dr. Horde, the Prior of Hinton, and wrote also to Horde [33] requesting his prayers and saying that if the prior at London would allow he would go and see him oftener.

Cromwell however distrusted the prior and did not employ him, though in July 1536 he received a letter from one of his agents then at Mountgrace which assured him—'if a commission was issued to Dr. Horde, [34] one of their religion, and one joined with him, there would be no stop and all of that Order in the north part will be inclinable.'

Meanwhile the dissolution of the monastery was drawing near. Hinton had escaped the confiscation of 1536 since the endowments which it had enjoyed were valued at a net £248 a year; but the monks were no longer suffered to manage their own estates. Sir Walter Hungerford was placed as steward of all their lands and already an application [35] had been received in 1537 by the Crown from Sir Henry Longe, who had been sheriff of Wiltshire 1536-7, for the chance of taking the estates on a fee-farm rent.

In January 1539 [36] Tregonwell and Petre arrived at Hinton, having already forced the Abbot and canons of Keynsham to yield up their house to the king, and they found Prior Horde less easy to move. His answers in effect were—'that if the kinges majestie wold take his howse so it procedyd nott of his voluntary surrender he was contentyd to obey but otherwise he said his conscience wold nott suffer hym wyllingly to give over the same.' The visitors therefore seeing him in this frame of mind left him alone and waited till the morrow, but then they found him 'of the same mynd he was yesternight or rather more styff in the same.' So they attacked the monks and found only three who were prepared to surrender. The others clung to their prior and showed no signs of yielding, and as if to increase the trouble of the hour one Nicholas Balland began to defy them saying that the Bishop of Rome was 'the vicar of Christ and that he is and ought to be taken for supreme hedd of the churche.'

It was vain then for the prior to protest that Balland should not be taken seriously and that—'he hathe byn in tymes past and yett many tymes is lunatick.' Action such as that and incautious words like those that had fallen from his lips could be construed in a serious manner. The commissioners had been balked and could do no more, and they deferred any further attempt to accomplish the surrender until they had heard from Cromwell as to the best course to be taken.

When it was known in London that the Hinton Carthusians had resisted the commissioners the prior's brother Alan Horde, an advocate, wrote to him expressing astonishment at his temerity and doubtless warning him also of his

---

[29] *L. and P. Hen. VIII*, vii, 1127.
[30] Ibid. viii, 778, 1011 ; ix, 49.
[31] Ibid. viii, 402.   [32] Ibid. 901.
[33] Ibid. vii, 730.

[34] *L. and P. Hen. VIII*, xi, 73.
[35] Ibid. (2) App. 4.
[36] Ibid. xiv (1), 145.

danger.[37] To this the prior replied in words which show how serious he recognized the situation to be. He seems baffled by the amazing wickedness which should suggest so dishonest a course[38]—'brother I marvelle gretly that ye thynk soo; but rather that ye wolde have thought us lyghte and hastye in gevyn upe that thynge which is not ours to geve but dedicate to Allmyghte God for service to be done to hys honoure contynnuallye with other many good dedds of charytye which daylye be done in thys howse to our Christen neybors.'

On March 31 Tregonwell came again to Hinton, and now the prior and sixteen monks signed the deed of surrender.

Three months afterwards, on 4 June [39] Nicholas Balland was brought by John Clerke, a Somerset weaver and Roger Prygan, a Wiltshire fuller, before Sir Walter Hungerford on a charge that as they were drinking in a tavern Balland had come in and denounced the king's supremacy and upheld the authority of the pope. Balland was kept in confinement by Sir Walter Hungerford until he should hear from Cromwell. Possibly his prior was able again to shield him from the anger of the vicar-general, for he received his £6 13s. 4d. pension [40] with the other fifteen and the six lay brothers and was still in receipt of it in 1556 when Cardinal Pole's list was drawn up; when Queen Mary came to the throne he joined Prior Maurice Chauncy in the new Charterhouse at Sheen, and on her death left England and died at Bruges in 1578.

Edmund Horde, the prior, received the very large annuity of £44 and a cash gift of £11.

In Cardinal Pole's list [41] the names of Bowman, Balland, Hellier, Savage, Frye, Nelling and Bagecross appear and also that of the lay brother Howe.

A Fletcher was among the Carthusians who rallied round Prior Chauncy at Sheen. He may have been the Thomas Fletcher who signed the surrender at Hinton and was certainly dead in 1556. In 1571 Sir Francis Englefield [42] was dining with Prior Chauncy and his monks at Bruges and he told them that his tenants at Sheen had written to him to say that for nine nights together they had heard the monks whom Chauncy had buried at Sheen chanting the night offices and mysterious lights had been seen in the church. So interested were they, they wrote, that they brought ladders to look in through the windows, but then all light and sound vanished. Yet they were positive that among the voices they had distinctly heard the voice of Father Fletcher.

Immediately after the surrender Dr. Tregonwell sold part of the monastic buildings to Sir Walter Hungerford, and he complained afterwards how that when he was away in London Sir Thomas Arundell, who had been sent to survey the property, had sold and despoiled and quite carried away a great part of the church and other superfluous buildings which he, Sir Walter, had bought.[43] He hoped therefore that Cromwell would compel Arundell to recompense him for the damage that was done. He also complained that the back door of the prior's cell had been removed and the documents of the house had been abstracted and he knew not where they were.[44]

Henry III confirmed the grant of Hinton and Norton to the Carthusians in 1228 [45] and on 7 June 1239 granted them the same privileges as those enjoyed by their brethren at Witham, and this was repeated on 7 September 1240.[46]

The growth of the endowment belongs almost entirely to the 13th and 14th centuries.

In 1255 the prior obtained the grant of a yearly fair at Norton on the vigil, feast and morrow of the festival of St. Philip and St. James, and at Hinton for the feast of the Decollation of St. John the Baptist.[47] This was strongly opposed by the Prior and monks of Bath, who in 1273 complained that they lost 100s. yearly by reason of the fairs.[48] It was however confirmed by Edward I in 1293 and by Edward III in 1345 and extended in 1351 [49] to five days.

In 1259 [50] the monks gained from Henry III the right of free warren over their lands at Hinton and Norton, and in 1279 the prior proved his right on a grant from the foundress Countess Ela to inflict capital punishment in the two manors.

In 1275 [51] Henry, Earl of Lincoln, granted one knight's fee at Hinton to the prior in return for the prayers of the monastery, and so in 1300 [52] we find the prior and convent called upon to pay his assessment for the expenses of the Scotch war and the muster of the English army at Carlisle. This land was probably the hamlet of Midford.[53]

In the *Taxatio* of 1291 the temporalities of the priory are given as: Chewton £4 10s., Norton £12, Hinton £24 15s.

---

[37] Cotton MSS. Cleop. E. iv, fol. 270.
[38] Ellis, *Orig. Letters* (ser. 2) ii, 130.
[39] *L. and P. Hen. VIII*, xiv (1), 1154.
[40] Aug. Off. Misc. Books, no. 233, fol. 242.
[41] Exch. Q. R. Misc. Books, vol. 32, fol. xxix.
[42] Cf. Dom. Hendriks, *The London Charterhouse*.

[43] *L. and P. Hen. VIII*, xiv (1), 1154.
[44] 'Mr. Ayleworth carried away the evidences of the whole priory to Wells.' Exch. Dep. by Com. Hil. 19 Eliz. 3.
[45] *Cal. Charter R.* 1226-57, p. 77.
[46] Ibid. 254; cf. *Mon.* vi, 5.
[47] *Cal. Charter R.* 443; 1257-1300, ii, 320.
[48] Ibid. 1257-1300, p. 432.
[49] Charter R. 25 Edward III, no. 10.
[50] *Cal. Chart R.* 1257-1300, p. 23.
[51] Feet of F. 3 Edw. I, *Somers. Rec. Soc. Publ.* vi, 237.
[52] *Parl. Writs.* i, 533.   [53] *Feudal Aids*, iv, 323.

In 1310 [54] and again in 1345 [55] the monks were exempted from taxation.

In 1322 [56] they secured from John Sobbury and Roger de Compton 35 acres for the endowment of a chaplain to perform service daily in the conventual church, and in 1407 [57] John Wykyng and Isabell Tanner founded a light in this church of the monks.

In 1363 [58] Edward III granted them a binn of wine in the port of Bristol to strengthen them the better to pray for his good estate.

At late as 1529 [59] the Longleat property which had belonged to the Augustinian priory of St. Radegund was given to Hinton by Lorenzo Campeggio the papal legate and cardinal Bishop of Salisbury.

In 1535 the possessions of the monks as recorded in the *Valor Ecclesiasticus* [60] amounted in yearly value to £262 13s., and out of this gross sum £13 12s. 10d. had to be deducted for pensions and eleemosynary grants for which the monks were only the agents and trustees.

The income was derived from the manors of Hinton and Norton as well as from rents at Midford, The Friary, Iford in Freshford, Woodwick, Lutecombe's mill, Peglinch near Wellow, White Ox Mead and Eckweek, 'Hopper,' 'Lemerslond,' Oldford, 'Greneworth' and Whitnell in the parish of Binegar, Westwood, 'Rewleigh' or Rawleigh near Farleigh, Longleat, Lullington and Beckington.

PRIORS OF HINTON

Robert, occurs 1246–9 [61]
Peter, occurs 1272–5 [62]
John Luscote, resigned 1378 [63]
Adam, occurs 1391 [64]
Thomas Wyne, appointed 1403 [65]
William Whitby, occurs 1421 [66]
Thomas, occurs 1431 [67]
Richard, occurs 1442 [68]
William Marchall, occurs 1449 [69]
William Hatherles, occurs 1465, 1476 [70]

Edmund Storan or Storer, occurs 1477 [71]
John Iver, occurs 1478–9 [72]
Thomas Torburigenaci, occurs 1482 [73]
John Taylor, 1513–21 [74]
Henry Corsley, 1521–23 [75]
John Batmanson, 1523–29 [76]
Edmund Horde, 1529–39 [77]

11. THE PRIORY OF WITHAM

In England there were nine Carthusian houses: two in Somerset at Witham and Hinton, Kingston upon Hull and Mountgrace in Yorkshire, Coventry in Warwickshire, Sheen in Surrey, Beauvale in Nottinghamshire, Epworth in Lincolnshire and the Charterhouse in London, and of these nine the earliest foundation was that of Witham.

The rash words which Henry II let fall in his anger at the obstinacy of Archbishop Thomas of Canterbury made him an accomplice in the murder, and the horror which that deed aroused had to be satisfied by an adequate penance on the part of the murderers and all their accomplices. In 1172 [78] Henry II agreed to perform as a penance a three years' crusade either in the Holy Land or in Spain against the Moors. In 1175 he had not found time to accomplish this, and the punishment was commuted for the foundation of three religious houses, which he reluctantly and in a very niggard spirit performed. [79] In England he changed the college of secular canons at Waltham into a house of Canons Regular of the Order of St. Augustine, at Ambresbury he turned out some nuns and replaced them with nuns from the convent at Fontevrault, and at Witham he decided to found a house of Carthusians, as representative of the most austere of the monastic orders. The Carthusian annals [80] represent him as founding two such houses, one at Witham and the other at Liget in Touraine, in expiation of his crime, but the English chroniclers are silent on this point.

When in 1142 William de Moion the earl founded the house of Austin Canons at Bruton he endowed it with the manor of Brueham and very early in their existence the canons of that house erected a chapel in that part which was called Little Witham. In the second half of

[54] *Cal. Rot. Pat.* (ed. 2) i, 207.
[55] Charter Rolls, 1 Hen. V, pt. i, no. 13 which confirms it.
[56] *Cal. Pat.* 1321–4, p. 233.
[57] Ibid. 1405–8, p. 370.
[58] Pat. 37 Edw. III, pt. ii, m. 25.
[59] Rymer, *Foedera*, xiv, 297.
[60] *Valor Eccl.* (Rec. Com.) i, 156.
[61] *Feet of F.* (Somers. Rec. Soc. vi) 130 (1247).
[62] Ibid. 234.
[63] In that year he became Prior of the London Charterhouse. *Monasticon*, vi, 9.
[64] *Cal. Pat.* 1388–92, p. 441.
[65] *Bowett's Reg.* (Somers. Rec. Soc. xii) 44.
[66] Exch. K. R. Accts. bdle. 81, no. 10.
[67] Ibid. bdle. 81, no. 13.
[68] Pat. 21 Hen. VI, pt. ii, m. 36.
[69] Exch. K. R. Accts. bdle. 81, no. 20.
[70] Ibid. bdle. 82, no. 10, 13.

[71] Hendriks, *London Charterhouse.*
[72] Exch. K. R. Accts. bdle. 82, no. 16.
[73] Add MSS. 17092.
[74] 'Alias John Chamberlayn, so called that he was born in Chamberlayne Streete in Wells.' Exch. Dep. by Com. Hil. 19 Eliz. 3.
[75] *L. and P. Hen. VIII*, iii (1), 1276. A native of Frome. Exch. Dep. by Com. Hil. 19 Eliz. 3
[76] Rymer, *Foed.* xiv, 297.
[77] See above.
[78] Cf. *Mat. Life Thomas Becket* (Rolls Ser.) vii, 517.
[79] Girald. Cambr. *Opera* (Rolls Ser.), viii, 170.
[80] Le Couteulx, *Ann.* ii, 325.

the 12th century[81] Witham seems to have passed partly into the hands of the Malet family and partly, as we have said, to the canons of Bruton. Before therefore a new house could be founded here the present owners had to be considered. The interest of the Malet family was bought out by a grant of land in the hundred of North Curry and the canons of Bruton received the advowson of South Petherton and its dependent chapels at Seavington and Barrington. Moreover, the king proclaimed in the boroughs and vills of Somerset, Dorset and Wiltshire that if anyone claimed land within the limits of the precincts of the new monastery they should come forward within two years of the date of foundation and should receive a fair exchange.[82]

It was probably in 1179[83] that at the request of Henry II a few Carthusian monks, how many we do not know, left their home near Grenoble to found in England the first house of their order. Norbert[84] came as the leader of the band and the first prior of the new house and with him Aynard and one Gerard of Nevers. But no preparations had been made for them, the villein tenants did not welcome them, for they were foreigners, nor did they agree, except after compensation, to be removed from their houses and lands. For the monks themselves no shelter had been provided. So very soon Prior Norbert gave up in despair and returned to Carthusia, regarding it as impossible to establish a house there unless they had more support than the king seemed disposed to give. In succession to him another, whose name is not given, was sent forth, and he died soon after from exposure and the severity of the climate. Then it was that Henry II took up the matter with some earnestness. He was arranging a marriage for his son John with Agnes the daughter of Humbert III Count of Maurienne and he asked the latter's advice concerning the difficulties at Witham. Count Humbert mentioned Hugh of Avalon, already the foremost of the monks of Carthusia, as the man most likely to succeed, though he warned Henry how he was valued, and how difficult it would be to get him to leave his monastery and come to England. Henry nevertheless persevered and sent Reginald, Bishop of Bath, and others on the errand to the monastery to ask definitely for Hugh of Avalon. At first the prior was unwilling to part with him,[85] for he was procurator of the house and much valued, and Hugh on his part regarding himself as unfit to undertake the task, definitely refused his consent ; but the Bishop of Grenoble, John de

Sassenage, had been won over, probably by Bishop Reginald, and at his entreaty the prior gave way and Hugh of Avalon started for England. On his arrival, which seems to have been in 1180, he found that nothing had been done at Witham and all practically had to be begun towards the new foundation. He stipulated that the tillers of the soil, the poor villein tenants, should receive no loss in being compelled to change their abode, and he endeavoured to persuade the king to indemnify them for the houses they had built, which now had to be pulled down. Certainly he seems to have set about the work in earnest, obtaining only after constant pressure on Henry II the necessary means. He is said to have built houses for the monks and the lay brethren, and the metrical life of St. Hugh records that he built the walls of the chapel and vaulted it in stone. The existing church at Witham is generally regarded as the church of the *Conversi* or lay brethren. The walls seem older than the time of Hugh, and apparently had buttresses attached to them for the purpose of strengthening them to carry the weight of the stone roof.

Meanwhile the king grew weary of the importunities of St. Hugh, and though several messengers were sent from Witham only vague and evasive promises of assistance were received. Then the prior himself went to see the king and took with him his brother monks Gerard and Aynard. Gerard was impatient and used very forcible language, and threatened to leave the country, but St. Hugh told the king he did not despair of him and ultimately he obtained from him all that was necessary. The monks bewailed also that they were in want of a copy of the Holy Scriptures[86] and the prior told the king of their need. Henry asked him why he did not make his monks copy one or hire a writer to do it. Hugh replied that he had no parchment. To this the king replied by asking how much money he wanted for that, and when he heard that a mark of silver would go a long way he bade an attendant give to one of St. Hugh's monks ten marks and he promised the prior a complete copy of the Old and New Testament as soon as he could meet with one. Soon after King Henry heard that the monks of St. Swithun's monastery at Winchester had just completed a very fine copy which they intended for their refectory, and having put all the pressure he could upon the prior, succeeded in obtaining it as a gift. Thereupon he sent the book to Witham and there was great joy among St. Hugh's monks at so valuable a gift.[87] Then after a time there came a monk from St. Swithun's and he recognized the volume and told them how the king had forced them to give up their treasure.[88] So St. Hugh sent the volume back and it remained to the time of the Dissolution one of the most treasured

[81] *Cal. Wells D. and C. MSS.* (Hist. MSS. Com.) i, 353.
[82] Assize R. 762, m. 29.
[83] *Pipe R. 26 Hen. II* (Pipe R. Soc.), 106 ; *Somers. & Dors. N. and Q.* vi, 170.
[84] Le Couteulx, *Annales*, ii, 325.
[85] *Mag. Vit. Hugonis* (Rolls. Ser.), 61 ; Girald Cambr. *Opera* vii, 92.
[86] *Mag. Vit. Hugonis* (Rolls Ser.), 92.
[87] Ibid.   [88] Ibid. 102.

possessions of the monastery of St. Swithun at Winchester.

At the Council of Eynsham in May 1186 Henry II nominated Hugh the Prior of Witham to the bishopric of Lincoln. The canons who announced this promotion were sent back by Hugh to inquire whether it was the real wish of the chapter or only their acceptance of the king's pleasure. His reception of them had greatly impressed them, and in a free election the objection that he was a foreigner and ill acquainted with the English language was set aside and he was again elected. Strong letters were then sent to the Prior of Carthusia in whose obedience the Prior of Witham of course was, and as he gave permission, St. Hugh was consecrated by Archbishop Baldwin at Westminster on 21 September 1186, and enthroned at Lincoln on 29 September. As a bishop he still observed the severities of the Carthusian monk, and was wont to return twice a year to this lonely house at Witham and live with his brethren once more the simple austere life of a Carthusian. His immediate successor was Bovo, and a later successor Prior Albert admitted into the order Adam Scotus, the Præmonstrant, Abbot of Dryburgh, one of the most learned churchmen of the age in England and the writer of many theological books.[89] He is said to have spent the last twenty years of his life here and was a source of comfort and help to St. Hugh during his yearly retreat at Witham.

Another visitor who stayed for a short time but did not take the vows as a Carthusian was the Benedictine monk Walter Prior of Bath (1191–8), and formerly sub-prior of Hyde [90] near Winchester. At Bath he had done good work, but he was dissatisfied with himself and yearned for the spiritual peace hoped for from monastic austerity. When at Witham he was visited by a monk of Hyde who rebuked him for deserting his post, and Prior Walter returned to Bath to carry on the good work interrupted by his flight.

Another recruit at Witham was Robert Fitz Henry the Prior of St. Swithun, who spent the last fifteen years of his life there.

At first certainly the monastery was an experiment. It attracted men, but time only would show whether they could adopt the rigid rules of the order. Hence from time to time we read of desertions, and St. Hugh, when prior, took a very definite line in reference to those who turned away. Among the early recruits were Andrew a monk of Muchelney and Alexander of Lewes.[91] Soon they began to rebel, and Andrew was wont to reproach the prior for his harshness, and Alexander did so in no moderate terms. So both retired, or according to the language of the

biographer became apostates and left the priory. Andrew went back to the Benedictines at Muchelney. Alexander after a time repented and sought readmission, but was refused, and so he joined the Cluniacs in his native town. Other desertions are referred to, but the names are not given. In 1339,[92] however, we find a lay brother John Russell forsook them and in penitence sought readmission and obtained a papal recommendation to help him, and in 1341 [93] we read of William de Standish, a fully professed monk who had gone off *ad limina Apostolorum* without permission from his superior, and so was guilty of apostasy. In September of that year the pope sent him back with an order for his case and penitence to be considered, and his readmission obtained.

From the very first the order received the protection and good will of the bishops of the diocese. Reginald gave them a charter to this effect, and this charter was confirmed by Bishop William de Button and in 1254 [94] by Innocent IV.

The annals of the priory are very scant and little is known except the receipt of gifts for the endowment, of which an account will follow.

Though there are no details of the mortality at Witham caused by the Great Pestilence in 1349, the convent felt the loss of the *Conversi* or Lay Brethren, for they petitioned on two occasions, 16 January 1354 and 20 October 1363,[95] for licence to bring labourers from other parts to supply the needs of the priory and to pay their men more than the wages sanctioned by statute.

In 1441 a charter of confirmation of Henry VI [96] declared the house at Witham to be the first house and mother of the order in England.

In 1443 [97] Bishop Beckington of Bath and Wells gave the monks permission to build a dormitory for the convenience of the guests and lay brethren who should visit them, and on 20 May 1458,[98] at the petition of the prior he granted licence for the placing of a baptismal font in the chapel of the Blessed Virgin Mary, being the chapel of the lay brethren.

About the year 1531 [99] Richard Peers, the Prior of Witham, wrote to the prior of the London Charterhouse concerning a monk William Bakster who had been sent from London to Witham for correction : ' owre geste danne William Bakster desyreth you to have an answer of his letter late sent unto you ; he is vere busy desyning to come home to you agayne. God knawyth if he wold stabyll himselff he myghte lyve with us in grete

---

[89] Cf. Migne *Patrolog. Lat.* vol. cxcviii.

[90] Cf. Kitchin, *Obed. Rolls of St. Swithun* (Hants Rec. Soc. 1892), 30.

[91] *Mag. Vit. Hugonis* (Rolls Ser.) 87.

[92] *Cal. Papal Letters*, ii, 549.

[93] Ibid. 552.   [94] Ibid. 308.

[95] Pat. 28 Edw. III, pt. i, m. 20 ; 36 Edw. III, pt. ii, m. 7.

[96] *Cal. Pat.* 1436–41, p. 490.

[97] W. Worcestre, *Itin.* (ed. Nasmith).

[98] Wells Epis. Reg. Beckington, fol. 233.

[99] *L. and P. Hen. VIII*, viii, 611 (*B*).

reste and quietness and I am sure non of our cloyster gyveth hym contrary cause.'

Peers or Perys ceased to be prior in 1532, but apparently stayed on at Witham, for an important letter was addressed by him in 1534 from Witham.

There was a rumour that the liberties of the Carthusian house at Beauvale were questioned, and Peers thought fit to state what liberties had been enjoyed at Witham [100] where for thirty years he had acted as prior. He claimed them as the gift of the founder Henry II which had been confirmed to the priory by Henry III. First, he said, we have been accustomed to have within all our bounds sanctuary to all manner of persons for murder and felony and to tarry at their pleasure and in case at any time the said felons have been taken out our bounds by violence they have been afterward restored unto us again and the parties that so violently have taken them have made satisfaction for so doing . . . all the king's deer that have come within our bounds we have hunted and killed and licensed gentlemen our neighbours being our friends and lovers to hunt and kill at our liberty . . . no sheriff, bailiff or constable, but only our own bailiff at all intermeddles or executes any manner of thing within our said bounds.

To what extent there was a general inquiry or attack on the liberties of the Carthusians we are not informed, but in 1532 the Abbot of Glastonbury, whose land adjoined on the west that of the priory of Witham, had been asserting some claim or other and Prior John Huse, the successor of Peers, wrote to Cromwell to secure the protection of Henry VIII against any attempt to infringe the privileges granted in the past to the priory. He hopes to 'obtain the king's letters patent for my lord of Glastonbury that he doo not enquiet us any mor herafter.' [101] Huse did not stay for long as prior at Witham in succession to Peers, for almost as soon as he had obtained restitution of the temporalities he seems to have gone off to London to join Prior Stafford in the Charterhouse there.

His successor Henry Man has the distinction of being with St. Hugh the only Carthusian appointed to an English bishopric. In 1546 he was appointed Bishop of Sodor and Man. [102] In his early life he seems to have been an earnest enthusiastic man and a great admirer of Elizabeth Barton the Maid of Kent. Soon after we find him the faithful servant of Cromwell, and as proctor of the house at Sheen he seems to have made the way easy for the acceptance by the monks there of the Act of Submission and Succession to the throne.

Meanwhile, and probably during the vacancy after Huse had gone and before the appointment of Man, Edward Lord Stourton as a royal commissioner went to Witham to administer to the monks the oath for the Supremacy and Succession Act. He wrote to Cromwell [103] that he found the 'prior is gone in pylegremage and this xiii dayes hath byn from home and vij of hys monkes will not take no othe untyll they see the sayde priore comythe home.' Since however we hear no more of this it is probable that Lord Stourton went again when Man had arrived and met with no obstinacy among the monks. It was probably in this year 1534 [104] that Peter Watt, a Carthusian of Witham, told Lord Stourton that the Prior of Hinton had come to Witham and related how he had dreamed that he saw as it were a stage royal and all the nobles of England stood on it, and they with one consent drew up on to the stage the queen's grace that now is (as he thought) by a line. Whereupon he put forth his hand to aid the same and then suddenly came again into his remembrance and sore repented his folly that he had so much done in prejudice to the law of God and holy church.

Lord Stourton could do nothing else at the time than send the monk to London, but the fate of the Prior of Hinton belongs to the narrative of that house.

At the end of August 1535 Dr. Layton visited Witham under the Act for a general visitation of the monasteries, and he wrote to Cromwell on 24 August [105] evidently not anticipating any difficulty in the future—'Witham the Charterhouse has professed and done all things as I shall declare unto you at large to-morrow.' The Prior Man was the 'assuryd bedesmen and servant of Cromwell,' [106] and it seems as if Layton had hoped the monastery would be classed with the smaller houses whose fate was already decided and whose dissolution took place six months later on.

Man however was too useful an agent for Cromwell to be left at Witham, and in 1536 John Michell was appointed to succeed Henry Man. There must have been certainly an interval when the priory was again without its prior, for Man and Michell were both sent for to argue with Maurice Chauncy and John Fox, Carthusian monks in London, and were further commissioned to act as visitors of their order in England. [107] The monks as a body petitioned [108] the vicar-general 24 September, through Layton, to give them some relief 'for the grete payments that we have payede and must paye for the whiche we have solde plate off owre Churche stoke off catell a grete parte, sale of woode to the moste that I can and also borrowyd and browghte our house in dette for the same.'

[100] L. and P. Hen. VIII, vii, 1269.
[101] Ibid. v, 920.
[102] Lond. Epis. Reg. Bonner.
[103] L. and P. Hen. VIII, vii, 834.
[104] Ibid. vi, 510.   [105] Ibid. ix, 42, 168.
[106] Ibid. vii, 622.
[107] Cotton MSS. Cleopatra E. iv. fol. 247.
[108] L. and P. Hen. VIII, xi, App. 16.

Similar letters for time to arrange for a reduction of the charges were written to Cromwell and Dr. Layton on 11 October.[109] Cromwell had desired the lease of a farm belonging to the monks and was endeavouring to procure it through the commissioner, and the monks were unwilling to make any grant while the prior was absent, but on 17 October Layton wrote to Cromwell from Harrow as if he had secured the farm for his master and was anxious that all he had done and said should not be known to his master.[110] He begs him not to listen to a ' brabullyng felowe one basyng ' who seems to have been defrauded of his right in it.

The last year of the existence of the priory there seems to have been some difference between the prior John Michell and the proctor Tristram Hyckemans, for Walter Lord Hungerford, who had been appointed under the Act for the restraint of the sale of monastic lands steward of Witham, was called in and on 10 September 1538 wrote[111] to Cromwell recommending the removal of the proctor as no good husband for the said house. The house is undone if he remain in office.

On 15 March 1539[112] John Tregonwell and William Petre, the commissioners to take the surrender of the greater houses, came to Witham, and in the presence of Petre the prior and twelve monks signed a surrender.[113] All of the monks received pensions[114] and some of them also obtained gifts of money, and the prior the pension of £33 a year and a cash payment of £8 6s. 8d. In Cardinal Pole's Pension List[115] the prior John Mychell was still in receipt of his large pension, and two monks, John Cliffe and John Swymestowe, were alive and drawing their pensions in 1556.

In the reign of Queen Mary[116] Thurstan Hyckmans, another of the Witham brethren, joined Prior Chauncy in the revived monastery at Sheen, but in 1559 retired with him to Bruges and died there 6 December 1575.

The foundation deed of Henry II, which we have shown reason for assigning to the year 1179, carefully defines the boundaries of the estate which the king granted to the monks.[117] To help them in their building Henry gave largely though somewhat reluctantly during his life, but in his will he left 2,000 marks to the order of Carthusians[118] and a part of this would certainly come to Witham.

In 1229[119] Henry III confirmed to them the charter of his grandfather reaffirming all their rights, privileges and exemptions.

In 1250[120] the lands of the priory were exempt from forest dues, and the royal forester was forbidden to enter the seclusion of the ' desert,' and this afterwards included the grange and its lands on Mendip near Cheddar.

In 1293[121] Edward I confirmed the Inspeximus and Confirmation of Henry III in 1264, and in 1295 the house was exempted from aids, tallages and customs levied by the Crown.

In the *Taxatio*[122] of 1291 the *temporalia* of the Prior of the Charterhouse of Witham in Selwood were valued at £30 a year.

In 1310[123] the monks were relieved from all taxation of their *temporalia* and *spiritualia*, and in 1318[124] the priory was exempted from all papal levies.

That same year 1318[125] a livery was granted by Prior Walter to John the Fisher and Edith his wife for their lives. John was to work at his craft as a fisherman and a plumber or on any other honest work whatever to which he might be appointed by the prior.

In 1377[126] the monks gained a charter of confirmation which cited a charter of 1282 granting to the priory the right to dig any lead found on their estates.

The second half of the 14th century brought to the monks many benefactions of lands, houses and rents. In 1362[127] Robert Cheddar of Bristol gave them 10s. rent-charge and four houses in Bristol, and in 1376[128] the monks acquired by purchase from the same Robert and a William Cheddar fourteen houses, and four shops in Bristol as part of an endowment for a chaplain at Charterhouse on Mendip, and in 1379[129] Isabel Tannere of Wells gave three houses and six acres of land at Wookey, and Robert Neel of Maiden Bradley gave two houses.

The possession of this new class of property of course compelled the prior or the procurator of the monastery to be often absent from his place and explains how the house in process of time and regardless of the example set by St. Bruno came into touch with the outside world.

In 1413[130] they received the largest benefaction that had been made to them since the foundation of the priory in the gift by Henry V

---

[109] *L. and P. Hen. VIII*, xii (2), 882, 883.
[110] Ibid. xii (2), 934.
[111] Ibid. xiii (2), Appendix no. 39.
[112] Ibid. xiv. (1), 524.
[113] Aug. Off. Deeds of Surrender, no. 270.
[114] Aug. Off. Misc. Bks. vol. 245, fol. 91.
[115] Exch. K. R. Misc. Bks. vol. 32, fol. 30.
[116] Cf. Gasquet, *Engl. Mon.* ii, 487.
[117] Dugdale, *Mon.* vi, 1.
[118] Gervase of Cant. *Op. Hist.* (Rolls Ser.) i , 299.

[119] Pat. 14 Hen. III, pt. i, m. 9.
[120] Pat. 34 Hen. III, m. 1.
[121] *Cal. Pat.* 1292–1301, p. 54.
[122] *Pope Nich. Tax.* (Rec. Com.) 203b.
[123] Cal. Pat. 1307–13, p. 207.
[124] Ibid. 1317–21, p. 192.
[125] P. R. O. Aug. Off. papers.
[126] Charter R. 1 Ric. II.
[127] Pat. 36 Edw. III, pt. ii, m. 19 (2 November).
[128] Ibid. 50 Edw. III, pt. ii, m. 2. (6 October).
[129] Ibid. 10 Hen. IV, pt. i, m. 9 (1 February).
[130] Ibid. 1 Hen. V, pt. i, m. 20.

out of the lands of the Alien Priories, which had reverted to the Crown, the manors of Warmington in Warwickshire, Spettisbury in Dorset and Aston in Berkshire with all the revenues, woods, vicarages, chapels and chantries belonging to the same. These estates had formerly belonged to the Benedictine monastery of Préaux in Normandy.

Henry VI in the Act of Resumption in 1455 exempted Witham from all harm and loss and in 1461[131] Edward IV confirmed all charters, privileges and possessions.

On 3 December 1461[132] Edward IV granted a tun of wine yearly in the port of Bristol for the sustenance of their bodies, weakened by their vigils and fasts, that they may pray for the good estate of the king.

In the *Valor Ecclesiasticus*[133] of 1535 the possessions of Witham were valued at £215 15s. yearly and consisted of

Temporalia :

The manors of Aston, Warmington and Spettisbury and rents at Fonthill Gifford, Marston, Clink, Bradley, Bristol, Newbury, Wookey and Yarley, Chilthorne Vagg, Morland, Witham and 'Hidon,' Billerica, West Barn, Quarr, Monksham, East and West Poundhays, Hollymead, 'Newhichyns,' Hicks's Park and Drowfe.

Spiritualia :

Witham Friary and pensions from the churches of Aston, Warmington, Spettisbury, Newbury and Willey.

PRIORS OF WITHAM

Norbert, c. 1178[134]
A prior who died at Witham
Hugh of Avalon, c. 1180–86[135]
Bovo, appointed 1186[136]
Hamo, occurs 1190[137]
Albert, 1191[138]

Robert, occurs 1200[139]
Giles, occurs 1226[140]
John, occurs 1242[141]
William, occurs 1279[142]
John, occurs 1279[143]
Walter, occurs 1318[144]
John de Evercriche, 1387[145]
Nicholas de la Felde, 1402[146]
William Fitzwilliam, occurs 1415[147]
John Cobham, occurs 1421[148]
Richard Vyell, occurs 1449[149]
John Porter or Perter, occurs 1458[150]
John, occurs 1476[151]
Richard Peers or Perys, appointed 1500[152]
John Huse, appointed 1532[153]
Henry Man, appointed 1534[154]
John Mychell, appointed 1536[155]

There are two seals of this Carthusian house. The earlier is of the 13th century,[156] a vesica. $1\frac{7}{8}$ in. by $1\frac{1}{8}$ in., and has the unusual design of the Holy Rood with Our Lady and St. John. The legend is :—

S DOMUS BEATE MARIE DE WITTEHAM.

The later seal[157] is 15th-century work, a vesica, $2\frac{1}{8}$ in. by $1\frac{3}{8}$ in. It also has the Rood with Our Lady and St. John. Below is a bishop in prayer, a figure thought to represent Prior Hugh, afterwards Bishop of Lincoln, 1186–1200, and canonized as St. Hugh. The legend is :—

S COE DOMUS BE MARIE DE WITHAM ORDINIS CARTHUS.

---

[139] *Mag. Vita Hugonis* (Rolls Ser.), Pref. p. i ; St. Hugh's Life dedicated to him.
[140] *Cal. Pat.* 1225–32, pp. 79, 292.
[141] Ibid. 1232–47, p. 326.
[142] Assize R. 8. Edw. I, m. 5, 14, I.
[143] Ibid.
[144] Annual livery granted by him ; Madox, *Formulare Anglicanum.*
[145] Collinson, *Somerset,* ii, 234.
[146] Ibid.
[147] Exch. K. R. Accts. bdle. 81, no. 10.
[148] Ibid.
[149] Ibid. bdle. 81, no. 20.
[150] Ibid. bdle. 82, no. 10 ; and Wells Epis. Reg. Beckington, fol. 233.
[151] Exch. K. R. Accts. bdle. 82, no. 15.
[152] *L. and P. Hen. VIII,* vii, 1269.
[153] Ibid. vi, 299 (ix) cf.
[154] Ibid. vi, 835.
[155] Aug. Off. Deed of Surrender, no. 270.
[156] *Cat. of Seals B.M.* 4349, lxxi, 76.
[157] Ibid. 4351, lxxi, 77.

[131] *Cal. Pat.* 1461–7, p. 156.
[132] Ibid. p. 157.
[133] *Valor Eccl.* (Rec. Com.) i, 157.
[134] For the first two priors cf. *Magna Vita Hugonis* (Rolls Ser.) 53 ; for name of first Le Couteulx, *Annales,* ii, 325.
[135] *Mag. Vita Hugonis* (Rolls Ser.) ; Girald Cambr. *Opera* (Rolls Ser.), vii.
[136] *Mag. Vita Hugonis* (Rolls Ser.), 60.
[137] *Bruton Cart.* (Somers. Rec. Soc. viii), 32.
[138] Cotton MSS. Vespasian D. ix.

HOUSES OF AUGUSTINIAN CANONS

12. THE ABBEY OF KEYNSHAM

William Earl of Gloucester founded at Keynsham, on the south side of the River Avon, a house of Austin Canons soon after 1166, the year in which his son Robert died, and traditionally at his son's dying request. At its foundation the canons seem to have adopted the then popular monastic discipline of St. Victor, so that the head of this house is always called the abbot, and the house known as the house of the Canons of the Order of St. Austin and St. Victor.

The whole of the manor and hundred of Keynsham was conferred on these canons, together with the church[1] of St. Mary and St. Peter and St. Paul, and its dependent chapels of Brislington, Charlton, Felton (or Whitchurch), Publow and Pensford. All however of these chapels may not be coeval with the date of the foundation.

The first summary of endowments is that of the *Taxatio* of 1291,[2] when the *spiritualia* consisted of the churches of Keynsham, and its dependent chapels, Backwell, Burford (in Oxfordshire) and a portion of the church of St. Lawrence, Bristol.

The chief authority for its foundation is an *inspeximus* of 1318 of Edward II[3] who confirmed a charter of confirmation granted by the hereditary patron, Gilbert de Clare, 1291–1314, tenth Earl of Hertford, and ninth Earl of Gloucester, On 13 March 1336 Edward III[4] confirmed this *inspeximus* and confirmation of his father.

On 26 October 1276[5] the claim of the Abbot of Keynsham to fell trees in his wood at Fillwood within the royal chase of Kingswood without view of the forester was allowed in an order to the Constable of Bristol Castle, and in 1280[6] the abbot was given licence to inclose a pasture called 'Wynterleye' with a wall and make of it a rabbit warren.

On 15 July 1310[7] the advowson of the church at High Littleton was given to the abbey by Gilbert Aumery, and Bishop Drokensford sanctioned its appropriation by the abbey in 1322, but the royal licence is dated 1328.[8]

In 1386[9] owing to the inclosure made in the parish of Eltham by Edward III, which impoverished the church there, the Abbot and convent of Keynsham, to which that church was appropriated, obtained licence to acquire lands up to a rental of 10 marks yearly, and on May 1387[10] definite sanction was given for the purchase of land in Bitton, West Hanham in the parish of Bitton, Upton (Gloucestershire) and Littleton (Somerset).

On 21 July 1395[11] Pope Boniface IX granted permission to the abbot and convent on the death or resignation of the perpetual vicar of Keynsham to appropriate the vicarage, and to serve the church through one of the canons, or by a secular priest removable at pleasure. The vicarage was valued at 40 marks, and the convent at 250 marks. Apparently the appropriation was never brought into effect, as in 1404 there was an elaborate reordination of the vicarage by agreement between Abbot Thomas and John Jenyns the vicar.[12]

On 15 June 1423,[13] the abbot received licence to provide a proctor to look after the estates of the convent in Ireland. The proctor, after paying all dues for the sustenance of the war against the Irish rebels, was to forward all rents and profits from the lands in Ireland to the abbot and convent at Keynsham.

On 29 November 1461[14] Edward IV confirmed a charter of the first year of Edward II (1307), granting a weekly market at Keynsham on Tuesdays, and a yearly fair on the festival of the Assumption ; and in 1463[15] he confirmed also a charter of 1265 granting a weekly market at Marshfield on Tuesdays, and a yearly fair on the festival of St. Oswald (5 August).

The Valor of 1535[16] gives the endowments of the abbey as worth £419 10s. 4¼d.

The *spiritualia* consisted of the churches of Brislington, Publow, Newton St. Loe, Cloford, High Littleton, and a pension out of the church of Norton Maireward, the church of West Harptree, a pension out of the church of St. Mary le port, and the church of 'Warborowse' (St. Werburgh) in Bristol, and the church of Burford in Oxfordshire. The gross total income came to £450 13s. 6d., out of which there had to be paid dues, pensions, etc., £30 13s. 1¾d., leaving the clear yearly value of £419 10s. 4¼d.

In 1242[17] it seems as if the efficiency of the monastery was generally recognized, for the canons of St. Augustine, Bristol, elected as their abbot the chamberlain of Keynsham.

---

[1] Rymer, *Foedera* xiv, 629.
[2] *Pope Nich. Tax.* (Rec. Com.) 199, 200.
[3] *Cal. Pat.* 1317–21, p. 68 ; *Mon.* vi, 452, 453.
[4] *Cal. Pat.* 1334–8, p. 227.
[5] *Cal. Close,* 1272–9, p. 314.
[6] *Cal. Pat.* 1272–81, p. 371.
[7] Ibid. 1307–13, p. 268 ; *Somers Rec. Soc. Publ.* i, 178.
[8] *Cal. Pat.* 1327–30, p. 397.
[9] Ibid. 1385–9, p. 187.

[10] *Cal. Pat.* 1385–9, p. 300.
[11] *Cal. Papal Letters,* iv, 524.
[12] *Somers. Rec. Soc. Publ.* xiii, 46.
[13] *Cal. Pat.* 1422–9, p. 104.
[14] Ibid. 1461–7, p. 59.   [15] Ibid. p. 307.
[16] *Val. Eccl.* (Rec. Com.) i, 181.
[17] *Cal. Pat.* 1232–47, p. 299.

In 1276[18] Edward I stayed here on 17 and 18 September on his way from Bath to Bristol.

On 25 October 1277[19] in an action brought by Simon de Whyte of Bristol, Robert the Abbot of Keynsham is said to be too infirm to appear before the justices in eyre, and his depositions are ordered to be recorded before the local justices. Five of his fellow-canons are mentioned by name.

In September 1300[20] Edward I called upon the house to receive an old and faithful servant, Gilbert le Braconer, and find him for life necessaries according to the requirements of his estate.

Bishop Drokensford made provision in January 1309 for the ordination of two of the canons of Keynsham, and in April 1310[21] sanctioned three more who were then acolytes to receive two steps further in Holy Orders.

In 1314[22] reference is made to the new Lady chapel at Keynsham, and Sir John Bitton in his will left large bequests to it, and £20 for his funeral, expressing his desire to be buried there.

In 1315[23] the bishop ordered the house at Keynsham to receive from Taunton a canon, Andrew de Sowy, who had been found guilty of immorality. He was assigned to Keynsham for penance, and the abbot and canons were desired to treat him wisely according to his contrition. The cost of his keep was to be defrayed by a payment from Taunton.

In 1322[24] the bishop approved the appropriation of the church of High Littleton to Keynsham, because of the losses which the abbey had sustained in the floods, rain, and murrain in its lands in Ireland and Wales, and in its loss of the tithes of Chewstoke.

In November 1336[25] Sir Walter de Rodney gave West Harptree Church for the support of the abbey. The Irish estates of the convent seem at this time to have been a source of constant anxiety and of very little profit, and their lands in Wales had been injured by floods, on which account the bishop and the king allowed the grant.[26] Proper provision at the same time was to be made for a vicar.

On 1 September 1333[27] Bishop Ralph of Shrewsbury visited the house, and from Blackford he wrote soon after to the abbot to say that he considered the canons were insufficiently clothed.

On 14 February 1350[28] the bishop drew the attention of the abbot and canons to the neglect they displayed in reference to their keeping of the abbey gates. They were not shut at the fixed hours of the day. The ornaments of the church and the treasures of the house could easily be stolen, so carelessly were they guarded. At the hour of refection the lay folk were allowed to enter the refectory instead of being rigidly excluded. There were too many servants for the work, and the bishop laid down certain rules for the order and the work of the kitchen, the cellars, and the infirmary, the cook being ordered to send in a more regular account of expenditure to the abbot. The canons were not to keep dogs, particularly sporting dogs, and when they went forth to work they were not to eat and drink abroad, but wait till they returned to the monastery.

The lands and tenements of the monastery were not to be let out in perpetual copyhold. The nightly devotions were to be said more regularly, and with due intervals, and greater devotion. John de Wamberge, chamberlain of the monastery, was at once to be removed from his office, and a fit canon to be chosen in his place. In his visitation the bishop had already removed him, but had allowed him to continue for the time.

In January 1353[29] the bishop again wrote in reference to what he had seen amiss at Keynsham 'during his late visitation.' Since the year of the pestilence, there had been a general neglect on the part of the abbot and other obedientiaries, and of the *conversi* who had the management of the tannery, the smithy, the barton and the vineyards, to draw up and present to the convent, as they should do, a proper account of receipts and expenditure.

Again the keepers of the outer doors were neglectful of their duty, and laymen and women were allowed to enter the monastery at unlawful hours. The canons did not observe at the proper times the rule of silence, and by the ensuing Easter the bishop commands all those in authority in the house to produce accounts of their administration.

The charities for the poor which were bequeathed by Gilbert, late Earl of Gloucester,[30] seem to have been, during the interval of the Great Pestilence, altogether lost.

Not one-third of the convent seems to have been in the habit of assembling in the refectory at the hours of meals, and two-thirds of the convent had their meals at other times and in other places. The chamberlain did not pay his debt to the convent, the bread was inferior in quality, and there was an irregular distinction made between the food given to the old and that given to the young. The canons were not to associate with those enjoying corrodies in the house, nor to play games with them. John Tankard, Robert Grindere and John Twynere,

18 Gough, *Itin. Edw. I*, i, 63.
19 *Cal. Pat.* 1272–81, p. 245.
20 *Cal. Close*, 1296–1302, p. 406.
21 *Somers. Rec. Soc. Publ.* i, 14, 32.
22 Ibid. 71.   23 Ibid. 90, 103.
24 Ibid. 178, 211.   25 Ibid. ix, 298.
26 *Cal. Pat.* 1334–8, pp. 270, 387.
27 *Somers. Rec. Soc. Publ.* ix, 153, 154.
28 Ibid. x, 603–5.

29 *Somers. Rec. Soc. Publ.* x, 708.
30 *Cal. Pat.* 1334–8, p. 227

shepherds to the convent, were accused of stealing bread in large quantities, and selling some of it outside. Edmund, the chamberlain's servant, was very inefficient and the convent suffered from it. John Golynge was to be removed from being the servant in the infirmary, and the chantry of John Seymour was to be kept up. The deeds and charters of the abbey were to be kept in a chest secured by three keys, one to be held by the abbot, another by the sub-prior, and the third by the canon, John Wamberge.

A hundred years afterwards the same lack of discipline compelled Bishop Beckington to look into the affairs of the abbey. In 1451 he ordered a commission of inquiry which was followed almost immediately by a mandate to the abbey to obey and to cause to be obeyed the bishop's injunctions.[31] The abbot Walter Bekynsfield was aged and incapable. In 1455 another commission was issued to compel action on the *Comperta* of the previous inquiry and the abbot offering resistance was compelled to resign. In his place Thomas Tyler was elected, and in 1456 Bekynsfield was granted a pension.[32] Another canon, John Ledbury, probably a leader of resistance to the bishop's orders, was sent in 1458 to Worspring for discipline, and the abbey of Keynsham received in exchange John Blake, a canon of Worspring.[33] Matters were settling down, but in 1458, and again in 1459 commissions of inquiry were issued as to the obedience of the canons.[34]

During the 15th century the canons received some benefit from legacies by way of payment for masses for the souls of the dead.

In 1448[35] Henry Warleigh of Keynsham desired to be buried in the conventual church of the Blessed Mary of Keynsham, and left 3s. 4d. to every canon regular to pray for his soul. His executor was Richard Whitewade, vicar of the parish church of St. John the Baptist, Keynsham. These two dedications show that there were two distinct churches in Keynsham, one the parish church of St. John the Baptist, and the other the conventual church of St. Mary, and not as at Bruton two distinct churches under one roof.

In 1489[36] John Chaunceler, leaving certain benefactions to the canons, desired to be buried in the conventual church of the Blessed Virgin Mary. In 1493 again John Daysshell desired to be buried in the conventual church.

In 1495[37] so great a person as Jasper, Duke of Bedford, Earl of Pembroke, and uncle to Henry VII desired to be buried in the monastery of our Lady at Keynsham, and in his will he hoped

he should be laid in a place convenient, where ' I will that my tomb be honourably made after the state that it has pleased God to call me to.' His monument was to cost 100 marks, and his lands were to be burdened for the payment of four priests to sing perpetually in the said church for his soul and for the souls of others, his relations and friends.

In 1501[38] John Sturrage of Keynsham bequeathed to the church of the Holy Trinity of Keynsham a whole piece of cloth. This refers to the parish church, and indicates that the parish church had a double dedication in honour of the Holy Trinity and St. John the Baptist.

In 1534[39] John Staunton, the last abbot, with William Herne, the prior, John Given, the sub-prior, John Arnold, and twelve other canons subscribed to the Act of Supremacy.

Richard Layton visited the house in August 1535[40] and on 23 January 1539[41] the abbot and ten monks surrendered the abbey to the king through the visitors, Tregonwell and Petre.

The conventual church was not left standing very long. Within two years of the surrender of the house, £12 was paid to Richard Walker for melting the lead on the church,[42] the cloister, and the steeple at Keynsham. Francis Edwards bought the seven bells of the monastery, and various useless buildings attached to it.[43]

Among the canons who were pensioned, John Fowler was granted £5 6s. 8d. out of his £6 13s. 4d. on condition that he acted as parish priest of the church of St. Margaret at Charlton, and a similar reduction was made in the pension of Canon Thomas Parker, should he, in after years, be promoted to any benefice.[44]

Robert Smart, one of the canons, was given an annuity of £6 which was certainly paid him as late as 1541.[45]

In Cardinal Pole's pension list, 1553,[46] nine canons received pensions, and eight others received annuities, among whom appear Canon Smart and Canon Parker.

ABBOTS OF KEYNSHAM

William, occurs 1175,[47] 1205[48]

George de Eston[49]

---

[38] *Somers. Rec. Soc. Publ.* xix, 27.
[39] *Dep. Keeper's Rep.* viii.
[40] *L. and P. Hen. VIII*, ix, 42.
[41] Rymer, *Foedera* xiv, 629.
[42] Gasquet, *Hen. VIII and the Monasteries*, ii, 426.
[43] Min. Accts. Exch. and Aug. 30-31, Hen. VIII, no. 224.
[44] P.R.O. Aug. Off. Misc. Bks. vol. 233, fol. 117.
[45] Ibid. fol. 120.
[46] P.R.O. Exch. K. R. Misc. Bks. 32, fol. 30.
[47] Tanner, *Notitia*, p. xlvi. *Ann. Monas.* (Rolls Ser.) i, 57.
[48] *Feet of F.* (Somers Rec. Soc. vi) 23.
[49] Collinson gives this name but not his authority.

[31] Wells Epis. Reg. Beckington, fol. 92, 149.
[32] Ibid. fol. 200, 207.   [33] Ibid. fol. 227.
[34] Ibid. fol. 229, 244.
[35] *Somers. Rec. Soc. Publ.* xvi, 161.
[36] Ibid. 282.   [37] Ibid. 327.

Richard, occurs 1225 [50] and 1230
John, occurs 1233 [51]
Peter, occurs 1253,[52] 1259 [53]
Gilbert, 1274 [54]
Robert, occurs 1272,[55] 1277 [56]
Adam, 1308 [57]
Nicholas de Taunton, occurs 1308,[58] 1343 [59]
John Bradford, elected 1348 [60]
William Peschon, 1377 [61]
Thomas, occurs 1396 [62] 1427
Walter Bekynsfield, occurs 1438, 1455 [63]
Thomas or John Tyler, elected 1456 [64]
John Gybruyn, 1486 [65]
John Graunt, elected 1496 [66]
Philip Keynsham, 1499,[67] died 1505
William Rolfe, elected 1506, occurs [68] 1514
John Staunton or Sturton, 1528–1539 [69]

The first seal of the Austin Canons' House of St. Mary at Keynsham [70] is 13th-century work, and shows Our Lady seated, with a bridge or arcade below. The legend is lost. The counter-seal, also much damaged, has a representation of the Annunciation. Below is a canon in prayer.

The second seal [71] is late 14th-century work. It is a vesica, $2\frac{3}{4}$ in. by $1\frac{5}{8}$ in., with Our Lady, crowned and standing in a niche, holding the Child on her right arm and a sceptre in her left hand. On either side are smaller niches with figures of St. Peter and St. Paul. Below is a shield of the arms attributed to the founder. (Gules), six clarions (or). The legend is :—SIGILLUM COMMUNE MONASTERII SANCTE MARIE DE KEYNESHAM.

The seal of Abbot Adam [72] (c. 1269) is a vesica, about 2 in. by $1\frac{1}{4}$ in., with a figure of the abbot holding book and crozier. The legend is much defaced.

[50] *Feet of F.* (Somers. Rec. Soc. vi) 48.
[51] *Cal. Close*, 1231–4, p. 265. *Cal. Pat.* 1232–47, p. 24.
[52] *Somers. Pleas* (Somers. Rec. Soc. xi), 414.
[53] *Feet of F.* (Somers. Rec. Soc. vi), 160 182.
[54] Collinson gives this name but no authority.
[55] *Feet of F.* (Somers. Rec. Soc. vi) 234.
[56] *Cal. Pat.* 1272–81, p. 245.
[57] *Cat. of Seals in B.M.* i, 599.
[58] *Cal. Pat.* 1307–13, 140.
[59] Ibid. 1343–5, p. 26.
[60] *R. of Shrewsbury's Reg.* (Somers. Rec. Soc. ix), 581.
[61] Clerical Subsidy, bdle. 4, no. 2.
[62] *Cal. Pat.* 1422–9, p. 373 ; *Bowett's Reg.* (Somers. Rec. Soc. xiii) 46.
[63] Tanner, loc. cit.
[64] Wells Epis. Reg. Beckington, unnumbered folios at end. Inq. p.m. 1–2, Hen. vol. 889, no. 9.
[65] Cant. Epis. Reg. Morton, fol. 137.
[66] Wells Epis. Reg. King, fol. 6.
[67] Ibid. fol. 139.
[68] Ibid. Hadrian, unnumbered folios at end.
[69] Aug. Off. Misc. Bks. 233, fol. 120.
[70] *Cat. of Seals B.M.* 3345 ; Add. Chart. 15205.
[71] Ibid. 3346, lxxi, 66.
[72] Ibid. 3347 ; Add. Chart. 15205.

13. THE PRIORY OF BARLYNCH

The priory of St. Nicholas was in the parish of Brompton Regis, which in the 12th century had come into the possession of William de Say. From him it passed, through his daughter Matilda, into the hands of the Ferrers family. It claims William de Say as its founder, and his daughter Matilda endowed it with the advowson of the church of Brompton Regis. The authority for its origin is to be found in a confirmation by Henry III in 1256, which is recited in a confirmation of the priory endowment by Edward III in 1339.[73] Our earliest notice is to be found in the acts of Bishop Reginald (1174–91) creating the prebends of Holcombe, White Lackington, Timberscombe, in the cathedral church of Wells.[74] These gifts are witnessed among others by Walter, Prior of 'Berliz' or Barlynch.

In 1236 the priory benefited to the extent of 3 marks under the will of Hugh of Wells, Bishop of Lincoln.[75]

About 1260 [76] Isolda, Abbess of Godstow, conveyed to the canons as of the benefaction of Canon Lolinton some land at Morebath, and John Comyn increased the grant. Robert Brunell sold them the manor of Morebath, and Reginald de Moion gave them the manor and church of 'Marinaley' or 'Marrynaleigh' (Mariansleigh) in Devonshire, and Warin de Bassingborn gave them the advowson of Morebath.

In 1268 [77] Robert the prior and his brother canons engaged to pay to the dean and chapter 100s. yearly towards the stipend of a chaplain to pray for the soul of Canon Hugh de Rumenal. The executors of Canon Hugh had provided 200 marks for the canons, and with that they had procured the advowson of Winsford and 100s. a year in rents.

In 1273 [78] Robert the prior bound himself and the canons to pay 26 marks yearly to the communar in return for 520 marks advanced by the bishop, the dean and chapter and the executor of John de Bruton to the priory, with which they had purchased the manor of Morebath. This was again confirmed in 1277.

In 1276 [79] the priory's right to exercise manorial rights in the manor of 'Bromland' was contested by Matthew de Beril and his wife, Elizabeth ; the prior claimed that his predecessor had enjoyed these rights, but he yielded to Matthew, only reserving the patronage of the parish church.

Soon after we find the dean and chapter of Wells allocating the 25 marks yearly paid by the Prior and canons of Barlynch towards

[73] Chart. R. 13 Edw. III, m. 3, no. 7.
[74] *Cal. Wells D. and C. MSS.* (Hist. MSS. Com.) i, 19.
[75] Ibid. 431.
[76] Ibid. i, 148.
[77] Ibid. 106.   [78] Ibid. 110.
[79] *Abbrev. Plac.* (Rec. Com.) 188 b.

the payment of a priest and the equipment of a chantry for John de Button, William, his brother, and William, his nephew, the two latter being the two bishops of that name.[80]

In the *Taxatio* of 1291[81] the prior is said to own the lands and rents at Morebath and 'Marmelegh' in Devonshire, a pension of 40s. a year out of the vicarage of Brompton, and 10s. rent from Winsford and from the parish of Stogumber.

In 1329[82] Hugh, the prior, pleaded age and illness as a reason for resigning his office, and desired Bishop Drokensford speedily to grant a licence to the convent to elect a successor lest the goods of the impoverished house should be wasted.

In 1381[83] licence was given to John Waskham[84] to alienate the glebe of Bradford, and give it and the advowson of Bradford Church to the prior and convent of Barlynch. This was again confirmed in the following year.[85]

In 1478[86] William Hampney, the prior, and the convent of Barlynch received a grant of two yearly fairs at Bury, a hamlet of Brompton, a mile south of Barlynch, where formerly the Besils had a court-house on the eastern side of the Exe, together with a court of pie powder and all issues.

In 1532[87] James Hadley of Withycombe in his will left 20s. to the Prior and convent of Barlynch, and also a bequest to his brother, Sir William, at Barlynch.

In 1535[88] the Valor gives the endowment of the monastery as worth £98 14s. 8d.

The following letter[89] from Dr. Tregonwell to Cromwell was written after he had visited the priory, while on his way into Devonshire. He had authority to accept the surrender of the smaller monasteries, and it is possible that his choice of the sub-prior to take the place of the prior may have been designed for the purpose of furthering surrender from a man more easy to move than John Norman.

My moaste bounden dewtye to youre masterchype premysed, Pleasithe the same to be aduertysede, that at this my beyng at Barlyche in Somersetschere (a house of chanons of thordre of Seynt Augustyne) I percue that the prior of that howse wilbe and ys contentyde to resygne his rome and offyce of prior-schipe of the same, soo that his supprior namede Syr John Barwyke may suceyde hym yn that rome. The same Barwyke ys (of trowthe) moaste apt and meate for that rome of any wᵗ yn that monasterye, bothe of dyscreacyon and also of undrestondyng. And althoghe hit hathe pleasede you to geve me authorytye by youre commysson to receue resygnacyons and to dyrecte and ordre electyons of all Abbottes and priors beyng wᵗ yn the lymettes of youre sayde commyssyon, yet wᵗowte youre speciall pleasure to me knowen I wyll attempte nothing concernyng the same. Besechyng youre mastreschipe that hit maye stande wᵗ youre pleasure to sygnyfye unto me (by youre wretyng) yo commawndemente co cernyng the same howse off Barlyche. The landys therof ys cᵘ yerly, the howse ys yn dette lxᵘ, and yn some rewen and dekey. This daye I ryde to Barnastaple and soo yn to thother partyes of Devonschere. As knowithe oure lorde godde whoo preserue your mastreschipe. from Barlyche the IX daye of Novembre.

The ordynarye wolde have electyde the sayde Barwyke to be prior yff my comyng hether hadd not byn, for the howse ys not of the kynges fowndacyon. Mr. phetyplace of beselles lyghe ys ther founder I have showyde the partyes that all this matter lyeth yn yoʳ mastreschipes hond and therfor y have advised them to make sewet to you for thopteynyng of ther purpose.

Yoʳ moast bownden
JOHN TREGONWELL.

No signature to the Act of Supremacy or Deed of Surrender is any longer extant, and it is uncertain when the priory was dissolved.

In July 1537[90] John Berwick, the prior, seems to have been assigned a pension of 20 marks, but in Cardinal Pole's pension list (1553)[91] an annuity of 60s. is entered as due to Edmund Gregory, and nothing is said about Berwick, who probably in the meantime died.

A priory in so remote and thinly populated a district and so slenderly endowed could never have supported any considerable number of canons. The largest number recorded was nine, who in 1524 united to request Dr. Thomas Bennet, commissary of Cardinal Wolsey, to nominate a prior for them, at the time when John Norman was chosen.

In 1456 there were seven canons, but in 1492, when Robert Wynde ceased to be prior, there were only three canons. Nothing is known of the ordinary life of the house, and no visitation returns are extant. Thomas Thornbury in 1461 was suspended for neglect in keeping the house in proper repair, and in 1492 Robert Wynde is spoken of in the election of his successor as deprived and at the same time as having made a free resignation, both statements probably being correct, the deprivation preceding the formal resignation. In place of Robert Wynde the three canons who were present united to elect Thomas Birde, a canon of Taunton, as

80 *Cal. Wells D. and C. MSS.* (Hist. MSS. Com.) i. 23.
81 *Pope Nich. Tax.* (Rec. Com.).
82 *Somers. Rec. Soc. Publ.* i, 77.
83 *Cal. Pat.* 1377–81, p. 599.
84 The name is variously given as Radyngton, Waskham and Walsham.
85 *Cal. Pat.* 1381–5, pp. 53, 167.
86 Ibid. 1476–85, p. 93.
87 *Somers Rec. Soc. Publ.* xxi, 13.
88 *Valor Eccl.* (Rec. Com.) i, 219.
89 *L. and P. Hen. VIII*, ix, 795.
90 Misc. Bks. 244, fol. 109.
91 Exch. Misc. Bks. 32, fol. 90.

their prior.[92] Robert Williamson, a notary apostolic, was called in to preach the sermon, and John Brodrybbe, rector of Skilgate, and John Edyngton, vicar of Dulverton, were the formal witnesses. The selection of Thomas Birde required the consent of the Prior of Taunton, and on this being given he succeeded Wynde in the management of the affairs of the house. Thirty-two years afterwards, as an old man, he resigned the office of prior, and received a pension of £6 13s. 4d. and food allowance, and the best chamber in the priory after that of the priors.

In the pension list [93] of the canons of Taunton a Thomas Matthewe appears, and it is possible that this may have been the Thomas Matthewe of Barlynch who took part in the election of Birde.

Priors of Barlynch

Walter, temp. Bishop Reginald (1174–91) [94]
John, occurs 1243 [95]
Robert, occurs 1263, 1277 [96]
Umfray, occurs 1288 [97]
Hugh Price, resigned 1321 [98]
Humphrey de Umbiri, resigned 1347 [99]
Symon Pile, elected 1347 [100]
William Wroxhale, occurs 1387 [101]
John de Taunton, occurs 1390 [102]
Robert, 1390
John Porter, died 1430 [103]
Thomas Bury, elected 1430 [104]
Thomas Thornbury, elected 1457 [105]
William Hampne, 1478 [106]
John Chester, died 1488 [107]
Robert Wynde, elected 1488 [108]
Thomas Birde, elected 1492 [109]
John Norman, appointed 1524 [110]
John Berwick or Barwyke, last prior, appointed 1535 [111]

[92] Fox's Reg. (ed. Batten) 160.
[93] Aug. Off. Misc. Bks. no 245, fol. 144.
[94] Cal. Wells D. and C. MSS. (Hist. MSS. Com.) i, 19, 38, 45.
[95] Feet of F. (Somers. Rec. Soc. vi) 120.
[96] Cal. Wells D. and C. MSS. (Hist. MSS. Com.) i, 106, 110, 148.
[97] Collinson, Somers. iii, 503.
[98] Drokensford's Reg. (Somers. Rec. Soc. i) 177.
[99] Somers. Rec. Soc. Publ. x, 540.
[100] Ibid.
[101] Cal. Wells D. and C. MSS. (Hist. MSS. Com.) i, 397.
[102] Chan. Inq. p.m. 14 Ric. II.
[103] Wells Epis. Reg. Stafford, Harl. MS. 6966, fol. 119.
[104] Ibid. fol. 56, 119.
[105] Ibid. Beckington, unnumbered folio at end.
[106] Cal. Pat. 1476–85, p. 93.
[107] Harl. MSS. 6966, fol. 144.
[108] Wells Epis. Reg. Stillington, unnumbered folio at end.
[109] Fox's Reg. (ed. Batten) 160–9.
[110] See above.   [111] See above.

14. THE PRIORY OF BRUTON

The House of Austin Canons at Bruton was founded in 1142 by William de Moion Earl of Somerset. He endowed it with the manor of Bruton and the rectory of St. Mary and St. Aldhelm's Church,[112] which William, the chaplain, surrendered for that purpose. Earl William enriched the house also [113] with the churches of Moion, Pierreville, Regouefe, Lyon-sur-Mêr, on his Norman property in the dioceses of Coutances and Bayeux, and also with estates at Cresserons, Secqueville, and Messons and gave the canons the right to elect their own prior.[114] Bishop Robert of Bath (1136–66) confirmed this benefaction, and the impropriation [115] to the house of the tithes of Bruton, and of its dependent churches at Pitcombe, Redlynch, Wyke, Witham, and Brewham. He also gave the rectories of Westbury, Priddy, and Banwell to the priory.[116] Alexander de Cantelu soon after gave the Hundred of Bruton, with the market and the land of La Combe.[117] He also gave the land at Bruton[118] which Alfric, son of Godman, held, and the land which Seric held. Henry Careville and Robert Fitz Geoffrey gave the rectory of Luxborough,[119] near Dunster, and William and Richard de Montague gave the church of Shepton Montague,[120] while William de Lovell sanctioned the gift by William de Clevedon of the church of Milton Clevedon.[121]

In 1175[122] Henry II, who had decided to found a house of Carthusians at Witham, gave to the priory at Bruton the church of South Petherton, with its dependent chapelries of Seavington St. Michael, Barrington, Chillington and Lopen in exchange for the prior's rights as patron and rector of Witham. William le Dennis gave the church of St. Lawrence, Creech Hill; Walter de Asselegh the church of Swell;[123] John FitzHamon the church and manor of Charlton Adam,[124] and William de Moion, the third of that name, gave the churches of Minehead and Cutcombe.[125] The Bishop of Coutances confirmed the endowment of a prebendal stall at Coutances out of lands in the manor of Moion, to be held by the Prior of Bruton for the time being.[126]

In 1260 [127] however the Priory of Bruton exchanged its lands in Normandy with the Abbey of Troarn, near Caen, for lands possessed by that Norman abbey at Runcton in Sussex, and Horsley and Whitminster in Gloucestershire, and the Prior of Bruton gave up then his prebendal stall at Coutances.

In the Taxatio of 1291 Bruton appears to have

[112] Bruton Cartulary (Somers. Rec. Soc. viii), 1.
[113] Ibid. 105.   [114] Ibid. 2, charter 7.
[115] Ibid. 12.   [116] Ibid. 29, 32.
[117] Ibid. 3.   [118] Ibid. 3.   [119] Ibid. 11.
[120] Ibid. 26.   [121] Ibid. 27.   [122] Ibid. 34.
[123] Ibid. 40.   [124] Ibid. 41.   [125] Ibid. 54.
[126] Ibid. 112.   [127] Bruton Cart. 76.

Bruton Abbey,
13th Century.

Chapel of Our Lady, at Milverton,
13th Century.

Athelney Abbey,
15th Century.

Priory of Witham,
13th Century.

Hospital of St. John Baptist, Wells,
13th Century.

SOMERSET MONASTIC SEALS. PLATE II.

been possessed of *temporalia* £47 2s. 4d. from Bruton, Batcary, Charlton Adam, Chedzoy, Horsington, Brewham and Horsley, Runcton, South Stoke, Pulborough Graffham, and Mundham, and *spiritualia* £45 6s. 8d. from Bruton, Banwell, Chilthorne, Shepton Montague and Milton Clevedon.

Owing to the increased charges for hospitality,[128] due to the numerous travellers on the road from Mere in Wiltshire to Ilchester, in Somerset, the priory seems to have been burdened with debts, and in 1301 William of March, Bishop of Bath and Wells, confirmed the gift to the canons of Bruton of the church of Chilthorne Domer to enable it the better to continue the hospitality it had shown.

On 11 April 1533 [129] the convent received a licence for two annual fairs held on the eve and day of St. George, and on the eve and day of the Nativity of St. Mary ' with a court of pie-powder at the said fairs before the steward of the said abbot and convent with the same tolls and customs as at Bartholomew fair.'

In the Valor of 1535 [130] we find the priory valued at £480 17s. 2d. per year, on which there were pensions and yearly payments amounting to £41 10s. 6d., leaving a clear yearly income of £439 6s. 8d.

When the house of Austin Canons was founded in the 12th century it seems as if the ancient church had been, while structurally one, yet formally divided into two—the church of the canons and the church of the parishioners, the latter being the north aisle of the present building. The church had lost its earliest dedication and was now only known as the church of St. Mary and St. Aldhelm ; once only do we hear of the church of St. Peter and St. Paul when in 1319 [131] Sir William de Montague dying at Bordeaux bequeathed in his will his body to be buried in the church of St. Peter and St. Paul, Bruton.

In 1311 [132] Bishop Drokensford issued a commission to the Bishop of Cork, acting as his suffragan, to reconcile the cemetery of the parish church, which is described as ' within the inclosure of the priory of Bruton,' and which had been defiled by bloodshed.

The bishops would always look to houses of this kind as places where they could send men who seemed to them called to the sacred ministry. Thus in 1315 [133] Bishop Drokensford recommends to the prior and convent of Bruton Matthew Alewy to be received and trained for the priesthood. He is described as a soldier ' Domino idoneus.' From time to time men who were received into this house would, after training, be ready for holy orders, and in 1314 [134] we find the Prior of Bruton obtaining from Bishop Drokensford a licence for Roger de Wyk, one of his household, to obtain ordination from any Catholic bishop. At times trouble would naturally arise, and men, for their welfare and for the good order of their house, would have to be transferred from priory to priory. In November 1317 [135] Bishop Drokensford called upon the Prior and convent of Bruton to receive Thomas le Taverner, a convicted canon of Worspring, to be kept at the cost of the priory of Worspring until he was penitent. He is said to have been rebellious against rules, and he was to be confined in the priory *in carcerali conditione*,[136] rules being laid down for his fasting, his devotion, his silence, and his scourging.

Bishop Ralph of Shrewsbury[137] seems to have had a special regard for Canon Richard de Dunster, one of the canons of Bruton, and at least twice in his register a licence is recorded as having been issued to him to act as a public confessor in the diocese of Bath and Wells.

The 15th century was one of trouble and disorder in the priory. John Schoyle was elected prior in 1419.[138] He seems to have been singularly unfit for his office, and in 1423 was accused of serious offences, some of which had been certainly proved, and of others the report had reached the bishop's ears. In 1428 Bishop Stafford [139] seems to have found it necessary to take steps to deprive Schoyle of his office, and in 1429, as his presence at Bruton was not for the good of the house, he was sent to live at the house of Austin Canons at Poughley in the parish of Chaddleworth in Berkshire.

Richard of Glastonbury was elected on 8 August 1429, in succession to John Schoyle deposed. He seems however to have been too much influenced by his predecessor, so that Bishop Stafford, in 1430, and Bishop Beckington in 1444 had to issue a commission of inquiry concerning grave charges of immorality brought against the prior and the house generally.[140]

Prior Richard died in 1448,[141] and was succeeded by John Henton, a man of a very different type. He was a reforming prior, and Bishop Beckington,[142] to assist him in his efforts, issued a series of injunctions on 14 April 1452.

The canons were not to sleep in the same bed or away from the convent without permission. They were to eschew oaths *per Humanitatem*

---

128 *Cal. Wells. D. and C. MSS.* (Hist. MSS. Com.) i, 164, 165.
129 *L. and P. Hen. VIII.* vi, g. 417 (18).
130 *Valor Eccl.* (Rec. Com.) i, 149.
131 *Somers. Rec. Soc. Publ.* i, 143.
132 Ibid. 45.   133 Ibid. 93.
134 *Somers. Rec. Soc. Publ.* i, 69.
135 Ibid. 173.   136 Ibid. 171.
137 Ibid. ix, 430 ; x, 524.
138 Min. Accts. bdle. 971, no. 24.
139 Wells Epis. Reg. Stafford, fol. 203.
140 Ibid.
141 Cf. *Somers. Rec. Soc. Publ.* viii, p. xxxv.
142 Wells Epis. Reg. Beckington, fol. 44, 47, 149.

seu per Membra Christi and were not to play at dice. The younger ones were to be taught by the seniors in the rudiments of classical learning. The senior canons were not to attract the juniors to themselves, and the rules of their order in the dormitory were to be observed. The juniors were to show all reverence to the seniors. Women were not to enter the convent. The canons were to keep the secrets of the house, they were not to hunt, but were to eschew ' perevagationes in diversis ecclesiis et capellis prioratus,' i.e. going out for services at the dependent churches of the priory and so neglecting their canonical duties at home. Canons who had private chambers were not to allow *confabulationes et potationes* in them. After compline all were to betake themselves to the dormitory without further conversation. The infirmary was to be rebuilt and the beer was to be improved and the convent bread was to be of unmixed grain and pure leaven. Letters addressed to the canons were if necessary to be opened by the sub-prior. The *coquinarius* and cellarer were not to attend the markets dressed as mere laymen. The prior was to take care to collect the dues of the convent.

In June of the same year a slight change was made in these injunctions to allow canons appointed for that purpose to serve in the parish church of Bruton and the two dependent chapels of Wyke and Redlynch. The other churches were to be served by secular priests.

In 1455[143] the prior, John Henton, petitioned the pope for absolution from the possible crime of simony. He stated that he had discovered, seven years after he had become prior, that his father had paid money to two noblemen of those parts to further his election, and he was afraid of impeachment for simony.

Pope Calixtus III in December 1455[144] absolved him and confirmed him in the priorship, and forbad the convent to grant any more corrodies under pain of excommunication.

Henton belonged to a wealthy family in Bruton. His father, John, had founded a chantry at the altar of St. Aldhelm, in the conventual church of Bruton, and the confirmation of this endowment was granted by Bishop Beckington on 1 July 1459.[145]

In 1494 John Henton was succeeded as prior by William Gilbert. Like his predecessor he was of a good family that had long settled at Corton Denham, and was related to the family of Fitz James, of great influence at Bruton in the early decades of the 16th century. He took his degree of Doctor of Divinity at Oxford[146] on 8 February 1507, and three years afterwards

went to Rome. His object in going appears in the next year, 1511, when, on 21 June [147] he received the royal licence to assume the style of abbot, so that for the last twenty-eight years of its existence Bruton ceased to be a priory, and had an abbot and not a prior as its head.

Soon after we find him consecrated Bishop of Mayo in Ireland and acting as suffragan to the Bishops of Bath and Wells from 1519 to 1526, namely during Cardinal Wolsey's episcopate and that of Bishop Clerk, and in that capacity, on 28 March 1525 he blessed Richard Whiting, the new abbot of Glastonbury.[148]

In 1519 he also received as abbot to hold for the house of Bruton an endowment which Richard Fitz James, Bishop of London, and his nephew, John Fitz James of Redlynch near Bruton, afterwards Chief Justice of the King's Bench, and Dr. Edmondes, a native of Bruton, had given for the endowment of a free school at Bruton,[149] where boys and young men might be trained for regular canons, the abbot agreeing that he and the house ' should take into their religion and prefer to the same part of such able scholars in virtue and cunning as shall from time to time be brought up in the same school.' What happened afterwards is unknown, but in 1532 something more than a coolness had arisen between the now Chief Justice Fitz James and the Abbot of Bruton.

On 9 September 1532 the Chief Justice wrote to Cromwell in reference to a successor to Abbot Gilbert :—[150]

The Abbey of Brewton is within a mile of my house. The abbot is sick and old, and upon his death or resignation the monks desire to have one that I dislike. The abbot has been to me an unkind neighbour, and I would gladly have a better one. The house is not of the King's foundation but of Sir Andrew Lutterells (the Luttrells succeeded the Mohuns as patrons) and he and his ancestors have given the monks licence for election. But still the King's letter and your policy can do much in the matter. . . . . I shall be glad to know what applications have been made to you in the matter.

Cromwell replies to this letter on 24 September [151] :—

Has received his letter and has accordingly moved the King touching the election of the Abbot of Bruton. . . . As he understands that both you and Lord Lisle sue for the advancement of the same person to be abbot there, he has directed his letters for that purpose. But if you see cause to stay the election for the trial of his title, his Grace is therewith right well contented, so that his Highness may be remembered somewhat, like as your Lordship wrote unto me in your last

---

[143] Wells Epis. Reg. Beckington, folios at the end unnumbered.
[144] Ibid. fol. 240.
[145] Cf. *Somers. Rec. Soc. Publ.* viii, p. xl.
[146] Boase, *Reg. Univ. Oxon.* i, 45.

[147] *L. and P. Hen. VIII*, i, 1819.
[148] Cf. Gasquet, *Last Abbot of Glastonbury*, 38.
[149] Cf. *Somers. and Dors. Notes and Queries*, iii, xxii, 272.
[150] *L. and P. Hen. VIII*, v, 1304.
[151] Ibid. 1340.

which he only remitteth to your wisdom and discretion. He would as fain that ye were well neighboured as ye would yourself: 'will always be ready to do his Lordship's service in this and other things.'

Gilbert seems to have died at the end of May or the beginning of June, for on 14 July of that year[152] a licence was granted for the restitution of the temporalities on the election of John Ely as abbot, and his oath is ordered to be taken by Sir John Fitz James for divers manors belonging to the said monastery.

Lord Stourton wrote a letter on 16 September 1533[153] to Cromwell, complaining of the abbot's withholding from a certain John White an annuity of £10, which had been granted to him by Abbot Gilbert. White seems to have been a servant or bailiff of the house and Lord Stourton begs Cromwell's interference on his behalf. On 7 October 1533[154] Lady Lisle, the wife of another of those who had wished for Ely's election, writes to Cromwell against the abbot for his action towards John Legat who had killed a man in self-defence. On 28 January 1534[155] Abbot Ely wrote to Lady Lisle, appealing to her not to accept the statements that were made against him, and explaining his conduct, and assuring her of his prayers and his regard. The servant, White, seems to have been busy in slandering the abbot.

On 10 August 1534 John Ely and seventeen canons signed the acknowledgement of the royal supremacy.

On 7 December of the same year[156] Cromwell seems to have received a complaint from John Downer of Mundham in Sussex against Abbot Ely who had objected to his action as a tenant of the abbey on the Runcton estate. On this occasion Thomas, Lord La Warr, wrote in the abbot's defence.

The next year, 7 August 1535,[157] Layton, one of the commissioners for visiting the monasteries, writes to Cromwell referring to Bruton and assures him that in a few days there is every chance of obtaining this surrender.

On 24 August[158] he again writes to Cromwell:—

'I sende yowe also oure Lades gyrdell of Bruton, rede silke, wiche is a solemne reliqui sent to women travelyng wiche shall not miscarie in partu.'

Meanwhile Dr. Legh claimed to have received the king's commission to visit Bruton, and on the same day wrote[159] to Cromwell protesting against Layton's interference, telling him that instead of commanding the abbot to confine himself within the precincts of the house, he had allowed him a considerable discretion.

Abbot Ely was naturally somewhat annoyed at receiving two commissioners with two authorities to visit on the same day, and Legh complains that the abbot little regarded the authority committed to him, and gave him sharp and quick answers, saying that if he wished to visit afresh the house, it would be the undoing of all abbots and monasteries. He also showed himself very haughty, and obstinate. Then on 23 September[160] Legh sends his formal report of his visitation of the house.[161] He says that he has forbidden the abbot to go out of his house without licence.

On 16 October[162] John ap Rice, another commissioner, complaining to Cromwell of Legh's haughty conduct towards the heads, says :—
'he handleth the fathers where he cometh very roughely, and many tymes for small causes as thabbote Brueton, for not meting of hym at the doore where he had no warnyng of his comyng. . . . The man is young and of intolerable elation of mind but he is too insolent and pompalique, and on his visitations he refuses many times his reward, though it be competent, because they offer him so little, and maketh them to send after him such rewards as may please him.'

What follows reveals a conspiracy against the abbot in the monastery itself. White's slanders seem to have continued, and on 12 June 1536[163] we find Richard Halford, one of the canons, in the Fleet prison, and there examined by Thomas Bedill as to what he had said and what he had heard the Abbot of Bruton say. He seems to have obtained a licence from the Archbishop of Canterbury to go out of the abbey and be abroad in a secular clerk's habit, but the importance of his examination has reference to the action of Abbot Ely. He was asked of what crimes he suspected him, and whether he (Richard Halford) together with John Harold and Richard Harte, and the man, White, had conspired together to bring about the abbot's death, and why ? White certainly seems to have handed over to Lord Stourton an accusation against the abbot, and Halford, while he acknowledged that there had been some conversation about them, acquitted the abbot of ever speaking unfitting words against the queen's grace. We do not know what was the result of these accusations. The abbot certainly, though unpopular, seems to have deserved well of the house. He was also a good friend to the town. Leland tells us[164] :—

'Ther is in the Market Place of the Town a new Crosse of 6 Arches and a piller yn the midle, for Market folkes to stande yn, begon and brought up to fornix by Ely laste abbate of Brutun.'

[152] L. and P. Hen. VIII, vi, 9, 429 (38).
[153] Ibid. 1132.   [154] Ibid. 1235.
[155] Ibid. vii, 120, 723.   [156] Ibid. 1513.
[157] Crom. Corres. (P.R.O.) xx.
[158] Cotton MSS. Cleop. E. iv.
[159] L. and P. Hen. VIII. ix, 167.

[160] This may be a mistake for August.
[161] L. and P. Hen. VIII, ix, 159.
[162] Ibid. 622.   [163] Ibid. x, 1126.
[164] Leland, Itin. ii, 74.

On 1 April 1539 [165] Dr. John Tregonwell received the surrender of the house, signed by Ely, the abbot, Bogye, the prior, and thirteen canons.

Ely was however suspected, and we find him a prisoner in the Tower in November 1539.[166]

Ely received the unusually large pension of £80 a year, and fifteen others the following pensions :—[167]

Richard Bogye, prior, £7 ; Richard Bisshopp, sub-prior, £6 ; Richard Herte, B.D., chamberer, £6 ; John Gyles, fermerer, £5 6s. 8d. ; Thomas Eton, cellarer, £5 6s. 8d. ; John Dunster, B.D., chaunter, £6 ; Robert Welles, 'stuard,' £5 6s. 8d. ; William Burges, fraterer, £5 6s. 8d. ; William Wylton, LL.B., chaplain, £6 ; Rich. Stacye, £5 6s. 8d. ; John Harrold, scholar in Oxon., £5 6s. 8d. ; Hugh Backwell, scholar in Oxon., £6 ; John Spicer, £5 6s. 8d. ; John Castelyne, £5 6s. 8d. ; Rich. Alvorde, £5 6s. 8d.

Halford does not appear in the list of those who signed the Deed of Surrender, but his name comes at the end of the pension list. He had probably in the meantime been released from prison.

The house was certainly a house of scholars, five at least were graduates of the University of Oxford, two were Bachelors of Divinity (Harte and Dunster) and Wilton was an M.A. ; Ely and Bishop were B.A.'s.[168]

Three weeks after the surrender, on 21 April,[169] Sir Thomas Arundel wrote to Cromwell, acknowledging the receipt of his letter. He had placed in possession of the surrendered house John Drew of Bristol, on the authority of the Chancellor of the Court of Augmentations. He now dispossessed Drew, and, under the orders of Cromwell, placed in charge of the parsonages Master Maurice Berkeley.

In Cardinal Pole's pension list, 1556, the abbot's name still appears, together with ten canons. His pension however is now only £13 6s. 8d.[170] This perhaps may be accounted for by his appointment on 12 August 1541, on the presentation of the Dean and chapter of Wells to the vicarage of Pucklechurch[171] in the county of Gloucester and diocese of Worcester.

PRIORS OF BRUTON [172]

Gilbert, occurs 1144 [173]
William, occurs 1159 [174]
Robert, occurs 1184 [175]

Philip, occurs 1188 [176]
Gilbert, occurs 1194, 1209 [177]
Ralph, [178]
Richard, occurs 1222 [179]
Stephen de Kari, occurs 1235, removed 1255 [180]
William de Sancto Edwardo, *alias* de Sheftysbury, elected 1255 [181]
Thomas de Deverell, 1267
Stephen de Carevyll, 1270
John de Grindenham, 1274
Richard de la Grave, 1301, died 1309
Walter de Leghe, died 1334
Robert Coker, 1335
Richard Cokkynge, 1361
John Corsham or Cossam, 1396
John Schoyle, 1418
Richard of Glastonbury, 1429
John Henton, 1448

ABBOTS OF BRUTON

William Gilbert, 1495
John Ely, 1532–39

The 13th-century seal of Bruton Priory [182] is a large vesica, 3⅛ in. by 2⅛ in., showing Our Lady crowned and seated on a throne, holding the Child on her left knee. On either side of the throne is a monk's head. Above these are the sun and moon, and below, under an arch, are half-length figures of the abbot and three monks in prayer. The legend is :—

SIGILLUM ECCLESIE BEATE MARIE BRIUTONIE.

There are two seals of Prior Stephen, both of the 13th century.

The first [183] is a vesica, 1⅜ in. by ⅞ in., showing a half-length of Our Lady with the Child on her left knee. Below, under an arch, is the prior, half length, in prayer. The legend is :—

✠ SIGILL' STEPH'I PRIORIS D' BRIWTONE.

The second seal [184] is a larger vesica, 1¾ in. by 1⅛ in., with Our Lady crowned and seated on a throne and holding the Child on her left knee. In the canopy above the throne is a hand holding a crozier, and to left and right of the throne are the sun and moon. Below, under an arch, is the prior, half length, in prayer. The legend is :—

. . . . STEPHANI PRIORIS BRIWTONIE.

[165] *Hist MSS. Com. Rep.* viii, App. ii, 7, 51.
[166] Cotton MSS. Titus, B. i, 129.
[167] Aug. Off. Misc. Bks. 245, p. 33.
[168] Boase, *Reg. Univ. Oxon.* i, 80, 82, 143, 148, 156.
[169] *L. and P. Hen. VIII*, xiv (1), 824.
[170] Exch. K. R. Misc. Bks. vol. 32, xxix.
[171] Wigorn Epis. Reg.
[172] *Somers. Rec. Soc. Publ.* viii, Introd.   [173] Ibid. 2.
[174] *Cal. Wells D. and C. MSS.* (Hist. MSS. Com.) i, 27 ; *Cal. of Doc. France,* 176.
[175] *Cal. Wells D. and C. MSS.* (Hist. MSS. Com.) i, 56.

[176] *Cal. Wells D. and C. MSS.* i, 53.
[177] Ibid. 57 ; *Somers. Rec. Soc. Publ.* viii, 60 ; *Cal. of Doc. France,* 181.
[178] *Somers. Rec. Soc. Publ.* viii, 18.
[179] *Feet of F.* (Somers. Rec. Soc. vi) 45.
[180] *Somers Rec. Soc. Publ.* viii, 65. ; Chan. Inq. Misc. File 9 (18).
[181] William de Mohun the fourth granted to the canons of Bruton the right of choosing their own prior, upon condition that they should present the person so chosen to him or his heirs, whether in England or Normandy (Maxwell - Lyte, *Hist. of Dunster,* 13). Hence there are at Dunster Castle documents giving the succession of priors and abbots from 1255 to 1532, and from these the accompanying list has been supplied by Sir H. Maxwell-Lyte.
[182] *Cat. of Seals B.M.* 2743, lxxi, 57.
[183] Ibid. 2744, lxxi, 58.   [184] Ibid. 2745, lxxi. 59.

15. THE PRIORY OF BURTLE MOOR

Some time in the second half of the 13th century, a hermit built himself a lodging on the moor, part of the possessions of the Abbey of Glastonbury held by Godfrey de Edington. It was situated on what was known as 'Sprawlesmede,' and the hermitage is referred to as the priory of the Holy Trinity, the Blessed Virgin Mary and St. Stephen of Burtle, Burcle, or Sprawlesmede. This settlement was formally endowed by William de Edington, son of Godfrey de Edington, and the grant was confirmed by Robert, the son of William.

In the 'Secretum Abbatis'[185] of Abbot Walter de Monyngton in the Bodleian Library, the private register and charters concerning the Abbey of Glastonbury, made by order of that abbot (1341–72), there is a series of six charters concerning the foundation of this priory, copies of which are in the *Monasticon*. The first is a confirmation by Archbishop Boniface (1245–73), concerning the patronage of the priory of Sprawlesmede. It recites the letter which William son of Godfrey, in his own and in his son's name, wrote to Bishop William Button (1267–75) declaring his intention to found a priory as a memorial of himself and his wife Alice, and giving, for that purpose, to Brother Walter, the hermit, that house which he had in Sprawlesmede, with 10 acres of land which the predecessor of that Walter had marked off with a ditch. The priory was to enjoy an eleventh part of the profits of his mills at Edington and was to consist of the said Walter and his successors with two brethren who were to worship God in the chapel of the Holy Trinity, the Blessed Virgin Mary, and St. Stephen in Sprawlesmede. He added also half a virgate of land in his manor of Edington, namely, 5 acres, and the cottage which Hugh Buterestake held, and 5 acres then held by William de Pedewell, with Walter Sperling's cottage and croft, and 5 acres of demesne. Then follow two documents dated, however, 14 Edward I (1285), transferring through Antony de Bradeneye the endowment of the priory to John of Kent, Abbot of Glastonbury (1291–1303),[186] and to his successors and the convent at Glastonbury.

The next charter[187] is a statement that the priory, of which Stephen is the prior, though in the parish of Moorlinch, is subject to none but the Abbot and convent of Glastonbury. This charter is dated 20 January 1270.

The above seems to prove that Walter succeeded to the hermitage made by Stephen, and as Stephen was prior in 1270 Walter belongs to the time of Abbot John de Taunton or Abbot John de Kent. On 23 September 1312[188] Bishop Drokensford quashed an election of Nicholas Drake, canon of this Augustinian priory as prior, because, on scrutiny, he had found that the election which was dated in May had really taken place in September, and so the collation had lapsed to himself as bishop. He thereupon, in his own right, appointed Nicholas Drake as prior.

On 25 November 1343[189] Bishop Ralph of Shrewsbury wrote to Robert de Cadecote, since the appointment had devolved on the bishop, appointing him as prior of Burtle, and again in February 1349,[190] Robert de Baltesborow being dead (most likely of the plague), Bishop Ralph confirmed the election as prior of William de Fulbrok, a canon of Burtle.

The Valor in 1535[191] reports the priory as worth £6 5s. 2d., and Stephen Stowell is mentioned as prior.

PRIORS OF BURTLE

Stephen, occurs 1276[192]
Walter, c. 1275[193]
Nicholas Drake, appointed 1312[194]
Robert de Cadecote, appointed 1343[195]
Robert de Baltesborow, died 1349[196]
William de Fulbroke, elected 1349[197]
Thomas Hornblouton, elected 1409[198]
John Romney, elected 1420[199]
Thomas Bone, 1463[200]
John Faireman, 1467[201]
John Bennett[202]
Thomas Vele, 1488[203]
William Badcock, 1499[204]
Stephen Stowell, 1516 occurs 1535[205]

16. THE PRIORY OF STAVORDALE

Stavordale lies about 3 miles north-east of Wincanton, and about the same distance south-east of Bruton. It is a secluded dale running into the western slopes of the uplands of Selwood. The origin of the house is not very clear, and it is difficult to understand the reason for the foundation of a house of Austin Canons within 3 miles of the house of the same order at Bruton.

---

[185] See under Glastonbury Abbey, Bodl. Lib. Oxon. Charter 34.
[186] Secretum Abbatis, Charters 35 and 36.
[187] Ibid. Charter 37.

[188] *Somers. Rec. Soc. Publ.* i, 54.
[189] Ibid. x, 479.   [190] Ibid. 603.
[191] *Valor Eccl.* (Rec. Com.) i, 148.
[192] See above.   [193] See above.
[194] *Somers. Rec. Soc. Publ.* i, 54.
[195] Ibid. x, 479.   [196] Ibid. 603.   [197] Ibid.
[198] Wells Epis. Reg. Bubwith, fol. 4.
[199] Ibid. fol. at end.
[200] Ibid. Beckington, fol. 296.
[201] Ibid. Stillington, fol. 28.
[202] Ibid. fol. 149.   [203] Ibid.
[204] Ibid. King, fol. 67.
[205] Ibid. Wolsey, fol. 13 ; *Valor Eccl.* (Rec. Com.) i, 148.

The earliest notice of the priory occurs in 1243,[206] when Roger Tyrel gave to it lands at Shalford, near Charlton Musgrove, and was received, with his wife Sarah, into the spiritual fellowship of the priory. In the same year the prior defended his right to lands at Clayhanger,[207] and proved that they were a gift from Christina Cleyhenger six weeks before her death.

In 1263 [208] we find the canons purchasing Cuddlesome (Churchelesham) by means of a gift of 40 marks from John de Axebridge, the sub-dean of the cathedral church of Wells, and, in return, the sub-dean received an annuity of 30s. and, after his death, the canons were to continue the payment to the Dean and chapter of Wells for masses at the altar of St. Mary Magdalene in the cathedral church.

In 1287 [209] we find the prior claiming the advowson of Buckhorn Weston in Dorset. In 1298[210] the prior is entered as having encroached upon lands at Eastrip.

In 1345 [211] Robert de Mandeville of Coker granted to the priory a rent-charge of 6s. 8d. on his land at Buckhorn Weston, for the support of a chaplain to say mass in the chapel of St. Andrew at Marsh, near Wincanton, and to keep a taper burning before the altar of St. Mary in the priory.

In 1350[212] Richard Lovel, the last of the house of the lords of Castle Cary, obtained licence to give lands at Priestley, in the parish of Doulting, to endow a chaplain in the priory church to say daily mass for the founder.

In March 1374 [213] Bishop John Harewell of Bath and Wells confirmed an earlier appropriation of the rectory of Wincanton; the duty of a resident vicar was laid upon the canons, and mass was to be said at the altar of St. James under the bell tower among others for members of the Stourton family.

In 1442 John de Stourton left three parts of the manor of Thorne Coffin with the advowson of the church there for the endowments.

The endowments prove the existence of the priory, but give us no hint as to its origin. Undoubtedly it was due to the generosity of the Lovel family, and it is probable that it was founded by Henry, Lord Lovel, who died about 1199.

In 1322 [214] Bishop Drokensford issued a commission for the visitation of the priory to inquire into the complaints as to Prior Eton's neglect of its possessions. He was accused of being wasteful of the goods of the priory, and the result of the inquiry was that he resigned. In 1361[215] Richard St. Maur, son and heir of Nicholas St. Maur and Muriel, his wife, was declared patron of the priory, and in 1400[216] he was buried ' in the new chapel of the priory.' At this time the canons are said to have been eight in number. The reconstruction of the conventual buildings and of this church seems to have been due not to Alicia, the wife of Lord Zouch and great-granddaughter of Richard Lovel, but to John Stourton, uncle of the first Lord Stourton. He left in his will, 1439,[217] provision that the church and the cloister at Stavordale should be completed in all things and the windows glazed, and that his and his wife's body should be buried in the middle of the choir of the said church. The rebuilding was completed in 1443, when it was consecrated by the suffragan of Bishop Stafford,[218] whose commission was ' to dedicate the nave and the conventual church of Stavordale with the choir and chancel which John de Stourton, while yet alive, had caused to be rebuilt at his own cost, and to concede to him the right of sepulture in the said church.'

The priory however was always hampered by its poverty, and in 1452 Bishop Beckington granted permission, as Bishop Bowett had done in 1403,[219] for one of the canons to gather alms throughout the diocese on behalf of his house. Certainly in the 15th century the number of canons seems to have been reduced as much as possible, and it would appear as if the Zouch family had begun to look upon the place as one they could make their own private house.

In 1526 the will[220] was proved of John, Lord Zouch, who, as a Yorkist fighting against Henry VII, had lost all his property after the battle of Bosworth Field. He appears in the latter years of his life to have settled at Stavordale, and he speaks in his will of his title, interest, lodging and other ground within the priory of Stavordale. He directs that his body should be buried within the priory in the chapel of the chantry of Jesus there, founded by himself, and he seems to have endowed this chantry with land at Pitcombe and Cole.

In 1524, after the canons had had the benefit of Richard Crie, a canon of Bruton, as their prior, they elected in his place William Grendon, canon of Taunton, and so great was the poverty of the house that Grendon was able to induce the remaining canons to apply for the union of

[206] *Feet of F.* (Somers. Rec. Soc. vi) 114.
[207] *Somers. Rec. Soc. Publ.* xi, 433, 701.
[208] *Cal. Wells D. and C. MSS.* (Hist. MSS. Com.) i, 152.
[209] J. Batten, *Notes on S. Somerset,* 124-5.
[210] *Somers. Arch. Proc.* xxxvii (ii), 80.
[211] *Cal. Pat.* 1345-8, p. 11.
[212] Inq. a.q.d. 24 Edw. III, no. 10.
[213] *Cal. Wells D. and C. MSS.* (Hist. MSS. Com.) i, 394.
[214] *Drokensford's Reg.* (Somers. Rec. Soc. i) 204, 205.

[215] *R. of Shrewsbury's Reg.* (Somers. Rec. Soc. x) 764.
[216] *Somers. Rec. Soc. Publ.* xix, 309.
[217] Ibid. xvi, 143.
[218] Wells Epis. Reg. Stafford, –anno 1443.
[219] *Somers. Rec. Soc. Publ.* xiii, 41.
[220] Ibid. xix, 241.

the house with the priory of Taunton. This took place in 1533 [221] and six years afterwards the house fell with the dissolution of the priory at Taunton on 12 February 1539. Had the house remained independent it would naturally on account of its poverty have fallen in 1536.

In that same year, Richard, the son of John, Lord Zouch, wrote the following letter to Cromwell,[222] but he was unable to undo what had been accomplished two years before, and the Zouches did not get hold of Stavordale as their private residence :—

Sure plesyt yor goode masterchipe to underston yᵗ wer I dwelle ys a pore pryery, A fundacion off my nawynsetres wyche ys my lord my fatheres ynerytens ande myne and be the reson off a lowyde pryor wᵗ was ther whyche was a schanon off Tawnton a for browytt hytt to be a sell unto Tawnton. Ande now his hytt dystryde and ther ys but to chanons wyche be off no goode luyng ande yt ys gret petty the pore howyse scholde be so yll yntretyde werfor yff ytt may plese yoʳ goode masterchype to be so goode master to me to gett me the pore howse wyche ys callyde Staverdell I wer bownde to pray for yoʳ masterchyp. And also I schal bere you my harty seruys nexte the kynge ys gras and be at yoʳ commayndment be the gras off Gode he ever presserue yoʳ goode masterchype yoʳ howyne pore seruantt ande bedman Rycharde Zouche.

We find however in 1548 [223] confirmation of this action of the Zouch family in the certificate concerning the chantry in the conventual chapel which is described as ' the chapel of the chantry being situate within the said Lord Zouch's house at Stavordale.'

PRIORS OF STAVORDALE

Walter, occurs 1249 [224]

Robert, occurs 1254, 1263 [225]

Robert de Cherleton, died 1310 [226]

Walter de Eton, elected 1310 [227]

William de Nymefield or Nymsfield, on resignation of previous prior [228]

Henry de Nymefield, elected 1333 [229]

John Bodman, died 1361 [230]

John de Wincanton, elected 1361 [231]

Robert [232]

Oliver [233]

John Penne, 1418 [234]

William Poyntington, elected 1440,[235] occurs 1468 [236]

John Selke or Sylk, 1468, died 1520 [237]

Andrew Grey, elected 1501 [238]

John Legge, 1508, resigned 1513 [239]

Richard Creed or Crie elected 1513 [240]

William Grendon, elected 1524 [241]

The 13th-century seal of the house of Austin Canons at Stavordale [242] is a vesica, 2⅛ in. by 1⅜ in., with a full-length figure of St. James the greater, the patron saint, standing on a corbel, having in his right hand his pilgrim's staff and in his left a book. At his side hangs a wallet upon which is his emblem of a scallop shell. The legend is :—SIGILL' ECCLESIE SCI IACOBI DE STAVERDALE.

17. THE PRIORY OF TAUNTON

The connexion of the Bishops of Winchester with the manor of Taunton most probably dates back to the days of the undivided bishopric of Wessex. In 904 we have a charter of King Edward, which proves that a settlement of clergy then existed here. He grants [243] to Bishop Denewulf of Winchester for the perpetual freedom and protection of the monastery which is called Taunton, that it shall be for ever exempt from royal and comital dues. There are also three charters of King Athelstan, 938, and King Edgar, 978, which recognize this endowment, and make additions to it for the benefit of the clergy there.[244]

In 1086 [245] we find from the Domesday Survey two priests holding a portion of this estate. The house of Austin Canons absorbed the endowment of these priests, and occupied their place. Its foundation was due to William Giffard, Bishop of Winchester, about the year 1115, but its early history is very obscure. About 1180, when the house of Austin Canons at Buckland in Durston was dissolved and the land granted to the Hospitallers,[246] the two canons who lived there were transferred to the priory at Taunton. We are indebted however to an inquisition of the king's escheator [247] of 6 January 1317 for the formal proof of the foundation. The evidence then given went not merely to

---

[221] Pat. 24 Hen. VIII, pt. ii, m. 31 (5).

[222] Cotton MSS. Cleop. E. iv, G. x, 390.

[223] Cf. *Chantry Returns* 1548 (Somers. Rec. Soc. ii), 127, 128.

[224] Feet of F. 33 Hen. III, no. 28.

[225] Ibid. 38 Hen. III, no. 142.

[226] *Drokensford's Reg.* (Somers. Rec. Soc. i) 30.

[227] Ibid.

[228] *Somers. Rec. Soc. Publ.* i, 205.

[229] Ibid. ix, 148.   [230] Ibid. x, 764.   [231] Ibid.

[232] *Cat. Anct. D.*, C. 3694.

[233] Cf. will of Ela, Lady St. Maur, *Somers. Rec. Soc. Publ.* xix, 310.

[234] Wells Epis. Reg. Bubwith, fol. 150.

[235] Wells Epis. Reg. Beckington, fol. 312.

[236] Ibid. fol. 142.

[237] Ibid. King, fol. 139.

[238] Ibid.   [239] Ibid.

[240] Ibid. Hadrian, unnumbered folio at end.

[241] Canon of Taunton

[242] *Cat. of Seals B.M.* 4085, lxxi, 70.

[243] Kemble, *Codex Dipl.* mlxxxii, iv.

[244] Ibid. ccclxxviii, dxcviii and dc.

[245] *V.C.H. Somers.* i, 442.

[246] See below.

[247] Inq. a.q.d. 10 Edw. II, no. 172.

claim William Giffard as the founder, but to assert a date for the foundation before the time of King Edmund Ironside, i.e. 1016. This latter statement of course is impossible, but it probably points to the fact that the college or monastery of resident priests which existed before the Conquest and had been endowed by the English kings was continued in the later foundation of the Bishop of Winchester. The extent of the endowment is therefore to be judged from the evidence of the later documents. Prior Stephen[248] made certain arrangements with Bishop Reginald, 1174, in reference to the bishop's claim on the churches that formed the early endowment of the priory. He granted that all the churches and chapels belonging to the priory were to be answerable to the bishop and his officials, but he reserved as being, with the house itself, free from these claims the churches of St. James, Taunton, St. Margaret's 'infirmorum,' Wilton, and St. Peter de Castello. Ash Priors and Withiel were to be answerable as mother churches, and the canons who served those churches were to obey as other clerks in the diocese would.

On 1 October 1334[249] Edward III confirmed by an *inspeximus* the charters and grants of the priory, which by that time numbered 130 charters. Of these the earliest is that of Henry II who granted the house a charter of confirmation which gives us a list of the gifts which the priory had received up to that time. It is witnessed by Richard de Beaumes, Bishop of London, who died in 1161. The gift of the founder is said to have consisted of all the churches of Taunton with their dependent chapels, of Kingston Church and its chapel, and of the churches of Lydeard St. Lawrence, Angersleigh, and Bishop's Hull. To these Henry de Blois, Bishop of Winchester (1129–74), added the church of Pitminster, and its chapels. Robert Arundel gave two hides at Ash, and a church at Ash, which then became known as Ash Priors. William Fitz Otho gave the church and land at Willand, in Devonshire, William de Moion land at Lydeard St. Lawrence, and Richard de Turberville the church of Dulverton, and land at 'Gelialand' in the parish of Tolland. Then, by a charter of 17 July 1204, King John gave to the priory the pastures of King's Hull in the Quantocks.

In 1249 we find[250] the archdeacon of Taunton holding his visitation in the church of St. Mary Magdalene, and as the confirmation charter of Henry II refers to the church of St. Peter and St. Paul, we have here our first evidence of the existence of the two churches, the priory church

and the parish church. This was also the case at Keynsham, where there were two distinct churches, whereas at Bruton the two churches were structurally one, the parishioners having the use of the north aisle.

In 1278[251] Bishop Bronscombe of Exeter authorized the canons of Taunton to collect within this diocese alms for the rebuilding of the conventual church.

Bishop Drokensford[252] in April 1314 duly confirmed by *inspeximus* the ordination by Bishop Walter Hasleshaw on 5 November 1308 of the vicarage of the church of St. Mary Magdalene, and recognized it as a parish church, Simon de Lym being the first vicar. To him was assigned as his stipend a weekly supply of bread and ale from the convent, 15s. a year, and food for his horse; he was to receive freely all legacies made to him in the parish, but to serve at his own cost by himself or his curate the churches of St. Mary Magdalene and of Trull, and of the Castle, and St. George at Wilton, and to find a priest to reside constantly at Trull. On the other hand the prior was to provide a secular priest for the chapels or parish churches of Stoke St. Mary and Ruishton, and another secular priest for the churches of Staplegrove, and St. James, Taunton; also a further secular priest for the church at Bishop's Hull. At St. James and at Ruishton, on Sundays and holy days, the prior might, if his help should be required, send, with the permission of the bishop of the diocese, some well reputed of his brethren to help the priest at mass.

In 1327 the conventual church was not completed, for Bishop Stratford of Winchester[253] issued a licence to some of the canons to beg for alms in his diocese for the completion of the church, and notified his sanction to the archdeacons of Winchester and Surrey.

Again, in 1335, Ralph of Shrewsbury,[254] Bishop of Bath and Wells, allowed the canons to collect alms in his diocese for a period of two years for the completion of the new work of the fabric of the conventual church of the Apostles St. Peter and St. Paul, and he further, in 1337, granted an indulgence to all those who contributed to the completion of the conventual church.

In the *Taxatio* of 1291[255] we find the prior in possession of the churches of Taunton (seven in number) and of Pitminster, Nynehead, Kingston, Combe Florey, West Monkton, Thurlbear, Lydeard St. Lawrence, Ash Priors, and the advowsons of Angersleigh, Runnington, Thurloxton, Willand and Clannaborough.

[248] Cf. *Cal. Wells D. and C. MSS.* (Hist. MSS. Com.) i, 38.

[249] Chart. R. 8 Edw. III. xii, m. 5, 6.

[250] Cf. *Somerset Pleas* (Somers. Rec. Soc. xi), 387; *Abbrev. Plac.* (Rec. Com.) 121a.

[251] Hingeston Randolph, *Bronscombe's Reg.* (Exeter Epis. Reg.) 265.

[252] *Somers. Rec. Soc. Publ.* i, 69.

[253] *John de Stratford's Reg.* (Hants Rec. Soc.) 29.

[254] *Somers. Rec. Soc. Publ.* ix, 263, 302.

[255] *Pope Nich. Tax.* (Rec. Com.).

In 1340 [256] they obtained from Nicholas de Beleville an interest in the manor of Dulverton, amounting to one-third, to which, however, was attached a payment of 10 marks to the Prior and convent of Bisham, and 5 marks for the chapel of Donyatt. The Valor of 1535 [257] give us the value of the lands, tenements, and rents of the priory as £286 8s. 10d.

The priory never seems to have consisted of more than twenty-six canons at a time. That number was recorded in 1339, [258] at the time of the election of Robert de Messingham as prior. At later times, in 1377 [259] and in 1476, [260] fifteen canons are recorded. At the time of the dissolution [261] there were twelve canons, all of whom received pensions. In 1315 we find that the priory had received Richard Engayne, [262] a Knight Templar, as a prisoner on the dissolution of his order, for whose maintenance the Crown was paying.

In 1332 [263] the conventual church was polluted by bloodshed, and Bishop Ralph issued a commission to Roger, the prior, to purify it. On 19 March 1342 [264] Bishop Ralph sanctioned a morning mass for St. Mary Magdalene's Church. This seems to indicate the completion of the new conventual church, and the distinct separation of the worship of the townsfolk from that of the canons.

In 1351 [265] a letter written by Bishop Ralph to the vicar of St. Mary Magdalene seems to point to inappreciation on the part of the parishioners of West Monkton of the ministry of one of the canons acting as rector in their church. They were flocking to the church of St. Mary Magdalene, and the vicar was ordered to refuse them admission to his church.

In 1345 Canon John de Payton [266] was pardoned for a rape on the wife of Hugh de Holdon and for robbing him of his goods, and in 1353 [267] Bishop Ralph had to interfere on account of the evil conduct of one of the canons, Robert Cundyt. In his late visitation of the house, the bishop had discovered that he, as one of the obedientiaries, had been disobedient to the prior, wasteful of the goods of the priory, and guilty of immorality. His rebellious conduct

made his removal necessary for the good order of the house, and he was transferred, under the instructions of the bishop, for stricter custody into the hands of the prior and convent of St. German's, Cornwall.

In 1377, [268] again we find Bishop Harewell holding a commission of inquiry into the affairs of the convent. Walter Grateley the prior and fifteen canons were present, and the commission had to inquire into certain controversies and discords that had arisen, and disobediences which had been shown towards Walter the prior whose age, weakness of body, and great simplicity seem to have made him unable to maintain good discipline. Grateley, as the result of this inquiry, was induced to resign, and the next year John de Kyngesbury was elected prior in his place.

Prior Kyngesbury in 1382 [269] had to bring an action against the abbey of Glastonbury in reference to the Bathpool Mills on the River Tone, a short distance below the priory. These mills had been rebuilt in 1364, and commanded more than ever the flow of the water of the river. The priory complained that boats and fish were obstructed in their course up and down between Taunton and Bridgwater, and the abbey was compelled to make arrangements that would satisfy them.

The celebrated William of Wykeham, Bishop of Winchester, did not forget the priory [270] in his will, leaving them in 1403 100 marks as a gift that they might pray for his soul. On 1 March 1415 [271] Thomas Ulfcome the prior received a papal indult for a portable altar.

In 1452 Bishop Beckington, on the report of a visitation commission, ordered the sub-prior to improve the supply of bread and cheese for the canons. [272] Another commission of inquiry was issued in 1459. [273]

In 1499 the Prior of Taunton, in a bull granted by Pope Alexander VI, gained the privilege [274] of using the ring, the pastoral staff, and other pontifical ornaments, except the episcopal mitre, and of pronouncing solemn benediction after mass, vespers and compline ; also of admitting to minor orders the canons and choristers of the said monastery.

In 1524 one of the canons of Taunton, William Grendon, was elected Prior of Stavordale, a small house of Austin Canons near Wincanton. [275] Stavordale was never rich, its finances had been

[256] Cal. Pat. 1338–40, p. 479 ; 1334–8, p. 422.
[257] Valor Eccl. (Rec. Com.) i, 170.
[258] R. of Shrewsbury's Reg. (Somers. Rec. Soc. ix) 350.
[259] Wykeham's Reg. (Hants Rec. Soc.) ii, 291.
[260] Winton Epis. Reg. Waynflete, ii, fol. 37–9.
[261] Aug. Off. Misc. Bks. 245, fol. 145.
[262] Drokensford's Reg. (Somers. Rec. Soc. i) 98.
[263] R. of Shrewsbury's Reg. (Somers. Rec. Soc. ix) 88.
[264] Ibid. (Somers. Rec. Soc. x) 444.
[265] R. of Shrewsbury's Reg. (Somers. Rec. Soc. x) 673.
[266] Cal. Pat. 1343–5, p. 561.
[267] Cf. R. of Shrewsbury's Reg. (Somers. Rec. Soc. x) 726.

[268] Cf. Kirkby, Wykeham's Reg. (Hants. Rec. Soc.) ii, 291.
[269] Cal. Pat. 1381–5, p. 511.
[270] Moberly, Life of W. of Wykeham, 345.
[271] Cal. Papal Letters, vi, 364.
[272] Wells Epis. Reg. Beckington, fol. 135.
[273] Ibid. fol. 244.
[274] Lambeth MSS. no. 643, 13 ; Wells Epis. Reg. King, fol. 56.
[275] See above.

badly managed, and external help was needed. Grendon had not been prior for many years before he induced his fellow canons to desire a union of their house with that at Taunton, and on 9 April 1533 [276] Henry VIII sanctioned this union and placed the cell of Stavordale and six canons under the authority of William Yorke, Prior of Taunton. The next year saw a change of priors. William Wyllyams (or Andrewes) had succeeded William Yorke, and on 15 September 1534 the prior and fourteen canons subscribed to the act of the King's Supremacy. On 12 February 1539 the prior and canons surrendered their house and all its possessions into the hands of the royal commissioner, John Tregonwell. The deed is signed by William Wyllyams, the prior, and William Gregory, the sub-prior, and ten canons. [277] The same day somewhat substantial pensions were assigned. The prior received £60 a year; the sub-prior £10; William Dale was allowed £5 6s. 8d. which was to be deducted from his stipend of £8 8s. as vicar of St. James. Similar pensions of £5 6s. 8d. were allowed to William Baylye, Nicholas Beram, John Heywarde, Thomas Matthewe, William Parson, John Warren, William Brinsmede, William Culronde and John Cockeram. The pension list for the first half-year is signed by Thomas Cromwell, and the three commissioners John Tregonwell, William Petre, and John Smith.

In Cardinal Pole's pension list of 1553 [278] we find the same list of names, with the exception of Thomas Matthewe and William Culronde.

During the years 1540 and 1542 Leland, [279] the antiquary, passed through Taunton, and, as was his wont, inspected the library. He mentions among the books three which seem to him rare, namely *Chronicon Ivonis*, *Philaretus de Pulsibus* and *Theophilus de Urinis*.

PRIORS OF TAUNTON

Stephen, occurs 1159 . . . 1189 [280]
Robert, occurs 1197 [281]
John, occurs 1204 [282]
John, occurs 1313 [283]
Stephen de Pycoteston, died 1325 [284]
Ralph de Culmstok, elected 1326, [285] resigned 1339 [286]

Robert de Messingham, elected 1339, died 1346 [287]
Thomas Cok or le Coke, elected 1346, occurs 1353 [288]
Thomas de Pederton, died 1362 [289]
Walter de Grateley, elected 1362, [290] resigned 1377 [291]
John de Kyngesbury, elected 1378, died 1391 [292]
Walter Coke, elected 1391, died 1408 [293]
Robert Newton, elected 1408, died 1413 [294]
Thomas de Ufculme, elected 1413, occurs 1429 [295]
Thomas Benet, occurs 1438 [296]
Richard Glene or Gleve, occurs 1449, died 1476 [297]
John Asshe or Ayshent, elected 1476 [298]
John Prous or Prowse, elected 1492, [299] resigned 1514, [300] died 1519
Nicholas Peper, elected 1514, died 1523 [301]
William Yorke, nominated 1523 [302]
William Wyllyams or Andrewes, 1533–9 [303]

The 13th-century seal of the Austin Canons' Priory of St. Peter and St. Paul at Taunton [304] is a vesica, $2\frac{3}{4}$ in. by $1\frac{5}{8}$ in. It shows two niches, with St. Peter in the right, holding his keys and the model of a church, and in the left St. Paul with his sword. The legend is :—

+ s. SCORV APOSTOLOR PETRI ET PAVLI TANTONIESI S E[CCLESIE].

18. THE PRIORY OF WORSPRING

About 4 miles north of Weston-super-Mare are the remains of the priory of Worspring, a name which since Collinson's time has been wrongly changed to Woodspring.

This priory was of the double order of St. Augustine and St. Victor, and was dedicated to the honour of the Holy Trinity, St. Mary

[276] Pat. 24 Hen. VIII, pt. ii, m. 31 (5).
[277] Aug. Off. Misc. Bks. 245, fol. 144.
[278] Exch. Misc. Bks. xxxii, 29.
[279] Leland, *Coll.* iii, 153.
[280] *Cal. Wells D. and C. MSS.* (Hist. MSS. Com.) i, 27, 493.
[281] *Somers Arch. Proc.* ix, 8.   [282] Ibid. 57.
[283] Pleads old age and obtains sanction from Bishop Drokensford for coadjutors *in spiritualibus et in temporalibus. Drokensford's Reg.* (Somers. Rec. Soc. i) 158.
[284] *John de Stratford's Reg.* (Hants Rec. Soc.) 136.
[285] *Drokensford's Reg.* (Somers. Rec. Soc. i) 276.
[286] *R. of Shrewsbury's Reg.* (Somers. Rec. Soc. ix) 88.

[287] *R. of Shrewsbury's Reg.* (Somers. Rec. Soc. ix) 350.
[288] Ibid. (Somers. Rec. Soc. x) 526.   [289] Ibid. 750.
[290] *Drokensford's Reg.* (Somers. Rec. Soc. x) 749.
[291] Kirkby, *Wykeham's Reg.* (Hants Rec. Soc.) ii, 291.
[292] *Wykeham's Reg.* as above, ii, p. clxvi.
[293] *Bowett's Reg.* (Somers. Rec. Soc. xiii) 66.
[294] Ibid. 72.
[295] Harl. MSS. 6966, fol. 30.
[296] Summoned to Council of Ferrara in April. Wells Epis. Reg. Stafford, fol. 145. Cf. also *Cal. Pat.* 1436–41, p. 205.
[297] Wells Epis. Reg. Beckington, fol. 88.
[298] Winton Epis. Reg. Waynflete, ii, fol. 37–9; cf. Wells Epis. Reg. Beckington, unnumbered folios at end.
[299] *Fox's Reg.* (ed. Batten) 165.
[300] Winton Epis. Reg. Fox, iii, fol. 30.
[301] Wells Epis. Reg. Hadrian de Castello, unnumbered folios.
[302] Ibid. fol. 47.   [303] See above.
[304] *Cat. of Seals B.M.* 4142. D.C., E. 49.

the Virgin and St. Thomas the Martyr of Canterbury.

The house was founded in or about 1210 by William de Courteney, a grandson of Reginald Fitz Urse of Williton, one of the knights who murdered Archbishop Becket. No foundation charter exists. Our information comes from the confirmation of the endowment by Edward II in 1325,[305] and a copy of a letter of William de Courteney to Jocelin, Bishop of Bath, which records the founder's object. The house was in some way connected with the larger house of Austin Canons at Bristol, but the exact nature of this connexion is not clear.

The letter of William de Courteney[306] to Bishop Jocelin is not dated, but as the bishop is called the Bishop of Bath, it is clear that it was written after 1219 and before 1242. He says that he had and he still has in his mind a desire to found a convent at Worspring in his domain, where he had built a chapel in honour of the blessed martyr St. Thomas. The convent was to be for canons of the Order of St. Augustine of Bristol, and he purposed to endow the priory with land at Worspring and with a church at Worle.

The Bath Cartulary[307] gives us an *inspeximus* by Walter the prior of a charter of William Button I, Bishop of Bath and Wells 1262, confirming a charter of Jocelin, Bishop of Bath, to 'the canons of Dodlinch' in the year 1230, which itself is a confirmation of an earlier charter granted by him to the same canons in 1217, by which he confirmed to them the gifts of Sir William de Courteney of the church of Worle and of Master Geoffrey Gibwinne of the church at Locking. The original foundation was at 'Dodlinch,' a place which has never been identified but probably was in the immediate neighbourhood of Worspring, and the site of the first chapel of St. Thomas of Canterbury.

In 1226[308] we find the Prior of Worspring appearing as plaintiff against William de Cantlow concerning the advowson of the church of Bulwick in Northants. The prior did not gain his case, but the incident proves that the transference from Dodlinch to Worspring must have taken place before this date.

In 1243,[309] during the vacancy of the see, the dean and chapter confirmed the appointment of Canon Richard of Keynsham as Prior of Worspring in succession to the late Prior Reginald, and it is recorded that twenty-six canons were present at that election.

On 16 August 1266[310] John the prior ' of the order of St. Victor,' in return for gifts received

from the late William de Wethamstede, provost of Combe, and Alexander de Bamfield, canon of Wells, their benefactors, for 100 marks provided by the executors of William and Alexander, bound himself and the priory to provide 53s. 4d. towards the maintenance of a chaplain in the cathedral church of Wells to celebrate for the souls of the said canons, and also to perform a similar service in their own house on the morrow of St. Vincent with *Placebo* and *Dirige* in the choir for ever, and also provide pittances to the value of 4s. to be divided among themselves and the poor.

On 4 July 1277[311] we find the same John, the prior of Worspring, and the convent on account of the benefactions granted to them by William de Button II, Bishop of Bath and Wells, and for 210 marks paid to them by his executors as a legacy from him, agreeing to pay 10 marks a year towards the obit of the bishop, and the maintenance of a chaplain who should say mass for his soul. This pledge was also confirmed in 1279.[312] The prior says that the bishop's legacy came to them at a time of great need, and had enabled them to pay off an annual payment of £10 due to Sir John de Engayne and his heirs upon the manor of Worle.

In 1298[313] Lucy Lundreys of Wells bequeathed in her will a silver spoon to her brother John, canon of Worspring, and in 1310[314] Sir John de Engayne endowed the priory with rents to the value of 20s.

In 1325[315] we have in the *inspeximus* and confirmation of the charters of the priory by Edward II information concerning the earlier endowments of the priory. The canons owned all the land of Worspring that belonged to William de Courteney and Robert de Newton. Half of the manor of Worle was granted them by Henry Engayne, and the homage and dues of his tenants at Worle, Worspring, Kewstoke, Milton, Ebdon and Locking.

In 1331[316] Henry Cary, vicar of Locking, obtained a licence to alienate to the priory his lands in Sandford Marsh.

In 1410[317] licence was granted to Robert Pobelowe and John Venables to alienate 174 acres in Worle, Winscombe, Rolstone and Poke Rolstone to the priory. In the Valor of 1535[318] the value of the property was assessed at £98.

Bishop Ralph of Shrewsbury visited Worspring

[305] Pat. 18 Edw. II, pt. ii, m. 33.

[306] Cotton MSS. quoted Dugdale, *Monasticon*, vi, 415.

[307] *Somers. Rec. Soc. Publ.* vii (2), 58, 260 n.

[308] *Cal Pat.* 1225-32, pp. 63, 84.

[309] *Cal. Wells D. and C. MSS.* (Hist. MSS. Com.) i, 98.   [310] Ibid. 153.

[311] *Cal. Wells D. and C. MSS.* (Hist. MSS. Com.) i, 70.

[312] Ibid. 71.   [313] Ibid. 166.

[314] *Cal. Pat.* 1307-13, p. 265.

[315] Ibid. 1324-7, pp. 86, 89, 295.

[316] *Cal. Pat.* 1330-4, p. 154 ; *Somers. Rec. Soc. Publ.* ix, 154.

[317] Pat. 11 Hen. IV, pt. ii, m. 21.

[318] *Valor Eccl.* (Rec. Com.) i, 188.

in August 1333,[319] but nothing is recorded as the result of his visitation. The house seems to have been uniformly well-kept. The only trouble it seems to have got into was in 1419,[320] when the prior and canons were summoned for placing obstructions on a public path or causeway called Worall. Richard Spryng, prior from 1491 to 1525, concerning whom a papal letter enlarging and describing his powers is preserved in Bishop Fox's Register,[321] was appointed on 11 July 1505 vicar of Berrow, and licence was given to him to hold Berrow and Worle with the priorship of Worspring.

On 21 August 1534[322] the prior and seven canons signed the acknowledgement of the king's supremacy.

It would appear from a letter[323] written by Richard Byschoppe, the sub-prior of Bruton, to Lady Lisle, that there was some rumour that Prior Tormynton would not sign the Act of Supremacy, and would therefore be expelled from Worspring.

A letter from Humphry Stafford about February 1536 shows that the house was regarded as desirable for a private residence[324] :—

So if it pleasith it yo[r] m[r]ship . . . my naturall ffather willed me to write to yo[r] m[r]ship and to none othere for to be good m[r] unto me for a house of chanons yn somersett their called worspryng where my seyd ffather is ffounder therof and as I do subpose of like value or thereaboutes. And if it wold please yo[r] m[r]ship to be as god m[r] unto me as to helpe me to worspryng Priorie I were and wylbe wylst I leve y[r] bedman and alweys redy to yo[r] m[r]ship suche poore service and pleasure as shalbe come me to doo whillest I do leve god wylling who ever have yo[r] m[r]ship yn his provysshion ffrom Bletherwere this present palme Sonday.

PRIORS OF WORSPRING

Reginald, died 1243 [325]
Richard, elected 1243 [326]
John, occurs 1266, 1276 [327]
Reginald, occurs 1317 [328]
Henry, occurs 1325 [329]
Thomas, occurs 1383,[330] died 1414
Peter Lobiare or Loviare, elected 1414 [331]
William Lusshe or Lustre, died 1458 [332]
John Gurman, elected 1458 [333]
Richard Spryng or Sprynt, elected 1491,[334] resigned 1525 [335]
Peter Tormynton, elected 1525,[336] surrendered 1536 [337]

The early 13th-century seal of the Austin and Victorine canons of Worspring[338] is a vesica, about $1\frac{7}{8}$ in. by $1\frac{1}{8}$ in., having a conventional representation of the house. Below is the martyrdom of St. Thomas of Canterbury, one of the patron saints, before an altar on which stands a chalice. Of the broken legend there remains :—

... GILL SANCTI THOME DE ... PRING.

HOUSE OF KNIGHTS TEMPLARS

19. THE PRECEPTORY OF TEMPLE-COMBE

The vill of Combe was shared at the time of the Domesday 1086[1] by the Benedictine Nunnery of Shaftesbury and Odo, Bishop of Bayeux, half-brother of the Conqueror. The sub-tenant of the bishop's share of the district was Samson the chaplain. In 1185 this manor was held by Serlo Fitz Odo, and he granted it in that year to the Knights Templars. The two manors thus became known as Combe Abbatissa and Combe Templariorum. The parish church which served the tenants of both was in the manor of the Templars. Nothing is known of the history of the Templars here, but their house ranked as a Preceptory or Commandery and was the only one in the county of Somerset.

In 1241[2] the Templars of 'Westcumbeland' were put at the mercy of the Court for receiving William son of Adam Crestred who was suspected of larceny and had been outlawed.

[319] Somers. Rec. Soc. Publ. ix, 153.
[320] Assize R. 5. Hen. V.
[321] Cf. Batten, Fox's Reg. 48.
[322] Dep. Keeper's Rep. vii, App. ii, no. 9.
[323] L. and P. Hen. VIII, vi, 126.
[324] Cotton MSS. Cleop. E. iv, April 9 1536.
[1] V.C.H. Somers. i, 445, 470.

[325] Cal. Wells D. and C. MSS. (Hist. MSS. Com.) i, 98.
[326] Ibid.
[327] Somers. Rec. Soc. Publ. vi, 240; Cal. Wells D. and C. MSS. (Hist. MSS. Com.) i, 153.
[328] Abbrev. Rot. Orig. (Rec. Com.) 178b; and Collinson, Hist. of Somers.
[329] Cal. Pat., 1324–7, p. 86.
[330] Cal. Wells D. and C. MSS. (Hist MSS. Com.) i, 413.
[331] Wells Epis. Reg. Bubwith, fol. 93.
[332] Ibid. Beckington, unnumbered folio.
[333] Six canons joined in the election. Wells Epis. Reg. Beckington, unnumbered folio at end.
[334] Fox's Reg. (ed. Batten) 48. Vicar of Berrow and Worle and Prior of Worspring. Wells Epis. Reg. Hadrian, fol. 16.
[335] Cal. Inq. p.m. Hen. VII, 88.
[336] Five canons took part in the election.
[337] L. and P. Hen. VIII, xiii (1), p. 576.
[338] Cat. of Seals B.M. 4371, lxxi, 78.
[2] Somers. Pleas (Somers. Rec. Soc. xi), 320.

In 1256[3] a case of unlawful disseisin came before Sir Henry de Bracton sitting in assize. It was brought by the master of the Knights Templars against William de Stures of Worle. The Templars declared that William de Stures had given all his lands and tenements at Worle to the Master of the Knights of the Temple of Solomon in England. In defence Stures said that whilst he was staying at a certain manor of the said master and brethren at Combe, the Templars forced his seal from him and made what charter they wished while he was helpless to resist them. The jury however refused to believe his petition and gave a verdict for the master and the Templars.

In 1258[4] Nigel de Kingescot brought an action against brother Amblard, Master of the Knights Templars of England, for the manor of Combe, but allowed the master's right to it on receipt of 30 marks.

In 1307 Pope Clement IV, under the influence of Philip IV of France, issued a mandate to the Kings of England and France, calling on them to arrest on a given day all the members of this order who happened to be in their kingdoms. In England there was great unwillingness to accept as true the charges that were made against the Templars, but on 8 January 1309 all the Templars were suddenly arrested, and by the autumn they had been collected in London. The examination began on 21 October 1309[5] and the first of the prisoners examined was William Raven of the preceptory of Templecombe. He said he had been a Templar for fifteen years and had been received by William de la More, and his witnesses and sponsors were John de Walpole and William de Erynge, and he stated also that on his admission there were a hundred lay people present to witness the ceremony. The official interrogations referred to most abominable acts, apostasy and even to a charge of worshipping a cat. Raven denied any secret or abominable crimes and said that on admission he was sworn to observe the rules of obedience, poverty and chastity, and that he would not lay hands on any man except in self-defence or in war against the Saracens. The trial lasted for two years, and in 1312 the Order was everywhere suppressed and the property of the Templars was handed over, 28 November 1313,[6] to the Knights Hospitallers. William de Burton the preceptor of Combe, John de Aley and Walter de Rokele knights at Combe, were committed to the Tower,[7] and generally those Templars who survived were assigned to various monastic houses to spend in confinement there the rest of their days. In Bishop Drokensford's Register in 1315[8] we have an entry of payments made through him by the sheriff to the Abbots of Glastonbury and Muchelney and the Priors of Taunton and Montacute for the maintenance there of four Templars, William de Warwyk, William de Grandcombe, Richard Engayne and Richard de Colingham. The payment was for their keep for the last sixty-nine days.

HOUSES OF KNIGHTS HOSPITALLERS

20. THE COMMANDERY OF TEMPLE-COMBE

Upon the suppression of the Templars in 1309 their lands were granted to the Hospitallers, who accordingly entered into possession of the manors of Templecombe and Westcombe.

In 1338 the estates of the preceptory were valued at £106 13s., including 'a small church' at Bristol. Robert de Nafford, knight, was preceptor, and there were two brethren under him besides a staff of seven servants.[1]

In the Valor of 1535[2] Edmund Husee was preceptor of the commandery of Hospitallers and the endowments consisted of the manors of Templecombe and Westcombland and estates at Templeton Chudleigh and Clayhanger in Devonshire, Williton, Long Load and Lopen in Somerset and Temple fee in the town of Bristol, and a number of small fees, rents and dues described as Culetts. The gross total income came to £120 10s. 3¼d., from which permanent charges payable to the Abbess of Minchin Buckland and for the payment of a chaplain in the free chapel at Templecombe amounting to £12 13s. 4d. had to be deducted, and the net yearly value was £107 16s. 11½d.

The Hospitallers could not be described as belonging to a monastic order and so Templecombe escaped in 1536 the suppression of the smaller monastic houses and was not dissolved until 1540, when an Act of Parliament[3] placed the possessions of the Hospitallers in the hands of the Crown as of an Order more loyal to the pope than to the king and existing for the promotion of superstitious ceremonies.

---

[3] *Somers. Pleas* (Somers. Rec. Soc. xi), 400.
[4] *Somers. Feet of F.* (Somers Rec. Soc. vi) 202.
[5] Wilkins, *Conc.* ii, 334.
[1] *Knights Hospit. in Engl.* (Camden Soc.) 183.
[2] *Valor Eccl.* (Rec. Com.) i, 203.

[6] *Cal. Pat.* 1313–17, p. 52.
[7] Wilkins, *Conc.* ii, 347.
[8] *Drokensford's Reg.* (Somers. Rec. Soc. i) 98.
[3] *Acts of Parl.* i, 855 (1540 Cap. xxiv).

21. THE PRECEPTORY OF MINCHIN BUCKLAND

In 1166 William de Erlegh, lord of the manor of Durston, founded at Buckland in the parish of Durston a small house of Austin Canons, and endowed it with his lands at Durston, and also gave it the church of North Petherton with the appendant churches or chapels of Chedzoy, Pawlett, Huntworth, Earl's Newton, Thurloxton, Shurton, King's Newton, and the churches of Beckington and Kilmersdon.[4] The only prior of this house whose name is known is Master Walter, prior of Buckland, who witnessed the grant by Alan de Fornellis of the church of Cudworth to St. Andrew's, Wells,[5] and also witnessed a grant to Stowey Church.[6]

John Stillingflete, one of the brothers of the preceptory, in 1434 wrote a chronicle[7] of the early history of the house. He says that sentence of outlawry was passed on the house because of the murder of the steward, and the building and the possessions of the foundation being forfeited to the Crown, Henry II granted it to Garner the Prior of the hospital of St. John of Jerusalem in England. This grant, which was confirmed by King John, 30 August 1199,[8] was made in or about 1186 for the purpose of founding a preceptory and a house for the sisters of the Order.[9] For some time the matter was delayed, the canons with their deposed prior Walter continuing to reside on the spot.[10] But at last, with the judicious assistance of William de Erlegh, the change was made and Garner the prior removed three of the canons to the hospital at Clerkenwell where they took the habit of the order, two others went to Taunton, one to Barlynch and one to the priory of St. Bartholomew at Smithfield.[11]

Soon after the sisters of this order that were scattered in several commanderies in England were gathered together in one house at Buckland, so there was attached to the preceptory the only priory in England of Sisters of the Order of St. John. In later times, because they adopted the rule of the Austin Canonesses for their daily life, these sisters have sometimes been referred to as sisters of that order. The sisterhood began with eight members. Milsant was transferred from the commandery at Standon in Hertfordshire; Johanna also from Standon; Basilia from Carbrooke in Norfolk; Amabilia and Amica de Malketon from Shingay in Cambridgeshire; Christina de Hogshaw from Hogshaw in Bucks; Petronilla from Gosford, and Agnes from Clanfield in Oxfordshire.[12] These were now gathered at Buckland. The house however was not independent. It was a preceptory with preceptors in charge, and a priory of sisters dependent on it, but governed by a prioress.

The priory generally consisted of fifty sisters who wore the habit of the Hospital, a black mantle with a white cross in front.[13]

The earliest endowment for the sisters, as distinct from the hospital of Buckland, was granted by Matilda Countess of Clare, who in 1192[14] gave an annual pension to the sisters of 13s. 4d. from the church of St. Peter at Carbrooke. Other early grants of which the dates are not quite certain are those of Ralph, the son of William de Briwere, who gave the sisters the church of Tolland (c. 1180); Alan Russell gave them the church of Donington in the diocese of Lincoln; Robert Arundell the church of Halse; and Muriel de Bohun land in Sherborne and Primesley.

In 1198[15] Gilbert de Vere, the prior of the Hospitallers, gave to the sisters an annual pension of 100s. out of the manor of Rainham in Essex, and about 1240 Prior Terri de Nussa ordained a yearly payment of 38 marks (12s. 8d.) to be made by the Preceptor of Buckland for the support of the sisters.[16]

On 16 July 1227[17] Loretta Countess of Leicester granted land at Nottiston and elsewhere to God and to St. Mary and St. John the Baptist and to the blessed poor of the hospital of St. John of Jerusalem at Buckland for the upkeep of the sisters of Buckland and to find a proper chaplain for that house, who should say daily mass in honour of the Blessed Virgin 'in majori ecclesia' for her soul and for Robert the late Earl of Leicester.

In the Valor of 1535,[18] the property of the priory is valued at £223 7s. 4¼d., Katherine Bowghshere being prioress at the time.

The *spiritualia* consisted of the rectory of Buckland and the chapel of St. Michael Church, the rectories of Kilmersdon and North Petherton; tithes of Broomfield, and payments in lieu of tithes in Horsey Mead, Bridgwater and 'Stondenhay.' In Lincolnshire Kirton and Donington; in Essex payments from the preceptory of Rainham; in Somerset from the preceptory of Templecombe; in Kent from the preceptory of Swinfield; in Norfolk from the preceptory of Carbrooke. The alms of the king, payable by the sheriff of Herefordshire, were valued at £6 13s. 4d., and in Somerset there were pensions from the churches of Pawlett, North Petherton, Tolland and Beckington.

About 1267 Roger de Vere, the prior of the

---

4 *A Cartulary of Buckland Priory* (Somers. Rec. Soc.), 1–3.
5 *Cal. Wells D. and C. MSS.* i, 42.   6 Ibid. 432.
7 Cotton MSS. Tib. E. ix, fol. 23.
8 Charter R. 1 John, pt. i, m. 17.
9 *Cartul.* 5.   10 Ibid. 3.   11 Ibid. 4.
12 Cf. MSS. in College of Arm. L. 17, fol. 153.

13 *Hospitallers in England* (Camden Soc.).
14 MSS. in College of Arm. L. 17, fol. 148.
15 Cotton MSS. Nero E. vi. fol. 467.
16 *Cartul.* 14.
17 *Cal. Charter R.* 1226–57, p. 52.
18 *Valor Eccl.* (Rec. Com.) i, 210

Hospitallers in England, visited Buckland, and found discord prevailing between the knights and the ladies. He ordered that the sisters should henceforth have their own steward, with a groom and a riding horse. If he proved unfaithful or incompetent the prioress might suspend him, but she could not remove him from office without the consent of the prior. The sisters were also to have a chaplain to celebrate for the souls of benefactors and of Fina, the first prioress. Their steward and chaplain had rooms and board in the preceptory.[19] The larger church belonged to the sisters, and was dedicated to the honour of the blessed Virgin Mary and of St. Nicholas[20]; the smaller church belonged to the Hospitallers.

In 1228[21] Henry III granted to the prioress and sisters $2\frac{1}{2}d$. daily to be paid by the sheriff of Hereford and 2d. daily which Margaret, the nurse of Isabella, the king's sister, was wont to receive, for the support of three girls in the priory. Next year[22] the sisters were granted a weekly cart-load of dead wood from the park of Newton, and also three cart-loads of faggots. This grant of wood was confirmed in 1387,[23] but in 1408 the question of the legal position of these sisters was raised.[24] It was argued that the sisters, as such, were incapable of accepting such a grant since they were only obedientiaries under the prior of Clerkenwell. Bracton[25] quotes them as an instance of legal inability on the part of women to act as distinct from the prior and head of their order. On 14 November 1408[26] Henry IV conveyed the gift afresh to the prior of Clerkenwell, Walter Grendon, for the use of the sisters of Buckland, defining the wood to be taken as thorn, alder, maple and hazel. The importance of a supply of fuel was recognized in 1382, when the prior of the Hospital granted the sisters 15 acres at Buckland, where furze (*firresyn*) grew, for fuel.[27] In the previous century the needs of the brethren of the preceptory had been considered by Henry de Erlegh, who granted them 30 wagon-loads of brushwood yearly from his moors of North Petherton.[28]

In 1232[29] we find William Earl of Arundel granting 40s. a year from his land for the support of his daughter Agnes as a sister at Buckland, and after his death Henry III ordered the continuance of the payments for the rest of her lifetime. In 1234[30] the treasurer and chamber-

lain were ordered by the king to see that each sister received yearly a tunic and a pair of slippers.

In 1234,[31] the house was partially burnt down, and the sisters received a grant from the Crown of thirty oak trees from the park at Newton for its repair, and a further forty oaks were given them in 1236.[32]

In 1311[33] Thomas de Berkelee gave £4 a year rent from lands at Ham for the maintenance of his daughter Isabel, during her life as a sister of the priory.

In the accounts of the Hospital for 1338,[34] the management of the estates of the preceptory seems to have been very careless. All the buildings called for a very great outlay of money in order thoroughly to repair them. The court or manor-house required a new roof, the bakehouse was ruinous, and the manor-house at Halse seemed to be almost destroyed. The estate consisted of 268 acres of arable land, and 42 acres of meadow, three of the latter being held by the sisters, and the brethren had one small church and two mills. The property at Halse consisted of $318\frac{1}{2}$ acres. The 'confraria,' or amounts collected in the district assigned to the preceptory, barely amounted to eighty marks. Special days were assigned for the annual collections at the different villages. Thus they collected at Camley on the Friday after Easter, and at Selworthy on St. John the Evangelist's Day.[35]

The preceptory consisted of the preceptor, John Diluwe, three chaplains, and two sergeants-at-arms, one of them being the steward of the sisters, and John le Port holding a corrody by deed of the chapter.

The sisters then were said usually to number fifty, and the preceptor and his colleagues complained that they had no help but rather a burden attached to them by the presence of the sisters on the estate, for by a fixed ordinance their steward and the three chaplains to serve their church were to be at the expense of the preceptory. But for some time longer the dual arrangement continued, special injunctions being given by the Grand Master of the Order in 1398 for the exercise of care in selecting a preceptor whose age and character should prevent any scandal arising from his association with the nuns.[36] And when the separation was at last made it was the preceptory that fell and the priory that continued.

On 20 January 1500[37] at a grand chapter of the order at Clerkenwell, it was decided to close the preceptory at Buckland and let it out to

---

[19] *Cartul.* 15.   [20] Ibid. 7.
[21] *Cal. Close,* 1227–31, p. 65; *Cal. Pat.* 1225–32, p. 266.
[22] *Cal. Close,* 1227–31, pp. 166, 211, 214.
[23] *Cartul.* 32.   [24] Ibid. 33.
[25] Bracton, *De Legibus* v, 5, 18.
[26] Pat. 10 Hen. IV, pt. i, m. 19.
[27] *Cartul.* 111.   [28] Ibid. 23.
[29] *Cal. Close,* 1231–4, p. 165.
[30] Ibid. p. 405.

[31] *Cal. Close,* 1231–4, p. 402.
[32] *Cartul.* Introd. p. xxiii.
[33] *Cal. Pat.* 1307–13, p. 385.
[34] Larking, *The Hospitallers in England* (Camden Soc.).
[35] *Cartul.* 57–63.   [36] Ibid. 17–20.
[37] Lansd. MS. 200, fol. 84, App. no. xxi.

farm, and a lease was granted to John Vernay of Fairfield at a yearly rent of £93 6s. 8d. Vernay was to provide honest hospitality and to keep five chaplains on the estates of the house, one of whom was to serve the chapel of the sisters, and another the chapel of the preceptory.

Again, on 10 March 1508 another lease was granted (presumably on the death of Vernay) to Edmund Myl of Wells and Anne, his wife. Edmund however must have died very soon, for his wife in 1514 married Lionel Norres, and surrendered the lease, receiving an annuity of £10 a year.

In 1516 the estate was again leased for forty years to Henry Thornton, at a rental of £103 6s. 8d. or the old rent with the annuity added to it. Nominally the preceptory had continued, but the chaplain was only in name the preceptor. The brethren had already departed.

On 10 February 1539 [38] the sisters appeared in their chapter-house and formally surrendered their house and its endowments to the king at the hands of John Tregonwell and William Petre. The Popham family had obtained a large amount of their property on lease, and the action of the prioress accounts probably for the favourable arrangements which were made for her and the sisters. The prioress received a pension of £50 a year, and pensions were granted to thirteen sisters as well as to Sir William Mawdesley, confessor to the house. [39] The prioress also received a gift of £25 [40] by way of gratuity.

In Cardinal Pole's pension list, 1556, there are payments entered to seven sisters still alive and drawing their pensions.

PRECEPTORS OF BUCKLAND [41]
Hugh de Binford, occurs 1185, 1187
Gregory, c. 1220
Richard de Rotundo Fugereto c. 1240
Geoffrey de Cheyne
Ralph de Dames
Richard de Morton, occurs 1253
Richard de Brampford, occurs 1267–81
Nicholas de Chilbanton, c. 1285
John de Messingham, occurs 1308, 1317
John de Wherewell, occurs 1321
John Denglond, occurs 1329
John Diluwe, occurs 1338
Daniel de Carreto, resigned 1364
Hildebrand Inge, occurs 1377, 1394
Robert Normanton, occurs 1402 [42]
Hildebrand Wotton, occurs 1404
William Hullys, occurs 1420
Henry Cromhale, occurs 1432 [43]

PRIORESSES OF BUCKLAND [44]
Fina, c. 1180–1240
Eleanor de Actune, c. 1280
Isabel la Louwe, occurs 1292, 1301
Isabel de Berkeley, occurs 1330–7
Katherine de Erlegh, occurs 1337
Mary, occurs 1371
Alice, occurs 1405
Alice Crok, occurs 1430
Elizabeth, occurs 1492
Joan Coffyn, occurs 1506 [45]
Katherine Bourchier, occurs 1526, surrendered 1539

FRIARIES

22. THE DOMINICANS AT ILCHESTER

Nothing is known of this house of Black Friars at Ilchester beyond the fact of its existence. Of this there is ample evidence from the 13th century downwards.

In 1263 [1] an arrangement was entered into between Thomas Trevet of Ilchester and Walter and Matilda Lune so that through the acknowledgement of Walter and Matilda Lune, Thomas Trivet might grant a messuage in the suburb of Ilchester to Brother Robert de Kilwardby prior provincial of the Order of Preachers in England and the friars preachers of the convent of Ilchester.

The convent soon outgrew this house, for in 1271 [2] we find the friars purchasing from William de Aubeny and Clemencia his wife another messuage in Ilchester. In 1283 [3] licence was granted for the friars preachers of Ilchester to appropriate and inclose 2½ acres of land given to them by John Whytbred adjoining a lane which ran between his land and their wall.

Bishop Ralph of Shrewsbury made great use of the Dominicans in the diocese as penitentiaries and on 14 October 1333 [4] admitted John of Ilchester, reader of the house of preaching friars at Ilchester, presented to him by Symon the prior of that house, as a penitentiary under the constitution *super cathedram*. The register

[38] Lansd. MS. 97, fol. 3, 6.
[39] L. and P. Hen. VIII, xiv (1), 270.
[40] Misc. Bks. Aug. Off. 245, fol. 128.
[1] Feet of F. (Somers. Rec. Soc. vi), 204.
[2] Ibid. 231.

[41] Cartul. Introd. p. xxix.
[42] Bowet's Reg. (Somers. Rec. Soc.) 46.
[43] Wells Epis. Reg. Bubwith, fol. 179.
[44] Cartul. Introd. p. xxvii.
[45] Witness to will of John Verney, esq., whose daughter Joan was a nun at Buckland : Somers. Rec. Soc. Publ. xix, 105.
[3] Cal. Pat. 1281–92, pp. 91, 111.
[4] R. of Shrewsbury's Reg. (Somers. Rec. Soc. ix) 155.

mentions in 1337 [5] an Adam Demercy of the order of Friars Minor of Ilchester, but this must be a mistake for the friars preachers.

On 28 January 1350 [6] licence was granted to Henry Power and Richard Sherewynd vicar of East Chinnock to give to the prior and friars preachers of Ilchester an acre and a half of land for the enlargement of their dwelling place. During the 15th century they shared with the Franciscans the gratitude of the laity of Somerset. They were in constant receipt of legacies which proved how they were valued. In 1411 [7] Sir John Wadham left them 20s. and to the prisoners of Ilchester 40d. So in 1441 [8] did William Wenard with a request that they would pray for him. William Balsham the elder of Ilchester in 1444 [9] desired to be buried in their chapel and left legacies, for every friar priest 1s. and for every friar not a priest 6d., and in 1457 [10] his widow Alice made a similar bequest and left them a pall of cloth of gold. The reference to the preaching friars in close connexion with the prisoners at Ilchester which occurs in several wills seems to show the reason why the Dominicans settled thus close to the county gaol, and the sphere of their daily labour.

The priory is not mentioned in the Valor of 1535, but Robert Sandwich is said to have been in 1536 [11] the prior of the community.

23. THE FRANCISCANS AT BRIDG-WATER

The Minorites were established here soon after 1230 through the generosity of William Briwere, the son of that William who had founded in the town the hospital of St. John the Baptist. Leland in his Itinerary 1540 [12] gives the tradition concerning the foundation as it was preserved in Bridgwater in the time of Henry VIII. 'A goodly howse wher sumtyme a college was of Gray Freres. Wylliam Bruer, sunne of Wylliam Bruer the first, buildid this house. One of the Lordes Botreaux and his wife were especial benefactors to this house. Thereupon his hert and hys wife's body were buryed there.'

As early as 1246 [13] Henry III ratified the gift by the burghers of Bridgwater of a place in their town where the Friars Minor might build for themselves a church and necessary buildings.

For the rest of the century the work of building seems to have been going on, for on 28 December 1284 [14] Edward I sent an order to Richard de Plescy the keeper of the king's forest to allow the friars six oaks fit for timber, and they had already received a similar gift from the Petherton Forest in 1278. [15]

Under the constitution *Super Cathedram* Bishop Drokensford licensed six Minorites on 4 May 1318 [16] to preach in the diocese and to hear confessions, and on 23 June of the same year he issued an official list of the Minorites he had thus licensed. [17] They were of course in priest's orders and they came to work at such times and in such places as might suit the parish priests, and he strictly forbade them to interfere with the parish priest and prohibited any not so licensed doing such work.

On 24 February 1332 [18] Bishop Ralph of Shrewsbury licensed Maurice de la More, a Franciscan of Bridgwater, as Diocesan Penitentiary, and on 8 October 1333 [19] he gave a similar licence to William de Anne the warden of the Franciscan house at Bridgwater, and in March 1353 [20] he gave a similar authority to another Bridgwater Franciscan, Richard Aunger.

In the 14th century certainly the labours of the Minorites were under episcopal sanction and regulation. Bishop Drokensford [21] ordered that his list of names should be everywhere published in the Consistories and in all the chapters of the clergy and in the parish churches. During the 15th century their increasing influence is shown by the increasing stream of legacies which they received. [22] The old restraints concerning property had been put aside and the Franciscans, whose spiritual work was doubtless very much valued, were trusted and enriched by the laity. The right to be buried in their chapel and to have the benefit of their prayers was prized and purchased by the noble families in the neighbourhood.

Among the Minorites of Bridgwater three [23] appear to have attained some fame. Leland records of Brother Henry Cross that he was famous in his age not only for erudition but also for piety. He wrote several books which testify his good affection towards sacred literature. He was made doctor of divinity at Oxford and was the thirteenth reader in the house of the Friars Minor there. He died at Bridgwater and

---

[5] *R. of Shrewsbury's Reg.* (Somers. Rec. Soc. ix) 322.
[6] *Cal. Pat.* 1348–50, p. 468.
[7] Weaver, *Somerset Wills,* 54.
[8] Ibid. 147.   [9] Ibid. 155.
[10] Ibid. 173.
[11] *The Reliquary,* xxv, 77.
[12] Leland, *Itin.* (ed. Hearne) ii, 96.
[13] *Cal. Pat.* 1232–47, p. 470.

[14] *Cal. Close,* 1279–88, p. 309.
[15] Ibid. 1272–9, p. 451.
[16] *Drokensford's Reg.* (Somers. Rec. Soc. i) 11.
[17] Ibid. 16.
[18] *R. of Shrewsbury's Reg.* (Somers. Rec. Soc. ix) 139.
[19] Ibid. 155.
[20] Ibid. (Somers. Rec. Soc. x) 737.
[21] *Drokensford's Reg.* (Somers. Rec. Soc. i) 11.
[22] Cf. *Somers. Wills* (Somers. Rec. Soc. xvi) *seriatim.*
There are twenty-eight entries of legacies.
[23] Dugdale, *Monasticon,* vi (3) 1527.

was there buried among the brethren of his order.

Another was Brother John Sumner [24] of whom Leland says there was scarce his equal at that time in England, but none exceeded him. As a mathematician his works on astronomy were highly commended, and about 1390 his works on Canons of the Stars and Corrections of the Calendar had made him very noted. The third, William Auger, [25] was from Oxford, but he went and settled in Bridgwater as the warden of the house. He took most delight in reading and meditating on the Holy Gospels and wrote a commentary on St. Luke's Gospel. He died in Bridgwater 1404.

William de Worcestre [26] who lived in the middle of the 15th century (1415–90) gives us in his Itinerary some notes of the chapel of the Minorites at Bridgwater. 'Longitudo ecclesiae Fratrum minorum de Bruggewater est 120 steppys et ejus latitudo 30 steppys et latitudo navis ecclesiae 14 steppys. Guardianus ecclesiae monasterii Bruggewater vocatur frater Blackborow et frater Pollard est legista fratrum, Stevyn Byrkcombe discipulus fratris Johannis.' William also says that in the martyrology of the Friary he saw that prayers were asked for the soul of 'domini Willelmi de Cantelupe fundatoris hujus ecclesiae ordinis Sancti Francisci.' This last statement however was certainly incorrect.

The house was surrendered to the commissioners of Henry VIII on 13 September 1538 by John Herys the warden, and his six brethren. [27]

24. THE CARMELITES AT TAUNTON

A house of Carmelites or White Friars is said to have been founded at Taunton by Walter de Meriet, lord of the manor of Combe Florey. The local tradition asserts the site of their house to have been a short distance west of the castle in a place called Paul's field. This seems to warrant us in thinking that at least a beginning of such a house was made, but certainly it never got beyond its initial stage. The official history is as follows :—In 1341 [28] a licence was issued by the Crown for alienation in mortmain by Walter de Meriet to the prior provincial of the Carmelite Friars and the friars of that order of 9 acres of meadow in Taunton to build thereon a church in honour of the blessed Virgin and a house for the habitation of a prior and some friars of the order. Two years after, on 10 August 1343 [29] a grant was issued in mortmain to the Carmelite Friars of 9 acres of meadow called 'Cokkesmede' in Taunton which Walter de Meriet, clerk, had lately granted to the king for a church and dwelling house to be built thereon.

Then on 25 November [30] it is stated that a grant was made for certain causes which cannot take effect for this time and at the request of Henry de Lancaster, Earl of Derby the king has regranted the same to the said Walter.

Walter de Meriet died 18 May 1345. [31]

It is clear therefore that whatever had been done between the years 1341 and 1343, the work was not continued and no house of Carmelites ever existed in Taunton.

HOSPITALS

25 THE HOSPITAL OF ST. JOHN THE BAPTIST, BATH

The hospital was founded in 1180 by Bishop Reginald of Bath (1174–91) for the sick and poor of the city in order that they might have the benefit of the waters. It was endowed with lands and tenements in Bath and with a tithe of hay from the bishop's demesne lands, and in 1331 [1] Bishop Ralph of Shrewsbury granted to the warden and brethren a rent-charge of 100s. in lieu of the sheaves which they were wont to receive from the bishop.

There is a ratification by the Dean and Chapter of Wells [2] of a confirmation by Bishop William Button given at Dogmersfield 15 July 1260 of

the act of the warden, Master Adam, and the brothers and sisters of St. John the Baptist's Hospital establishing a special service for their benefactor Canon William de Wethampsted, provost of Combe, to take place in the chapel of the hospital.

Hugh of Wells who died Bishop of Lincoln in 1235 left the hospital 7½ marks. [3]

On 9 June 1336 [4] Bishop Ralph granted an indulgence to all, otherwise qualified, who should aid the hospital of St. John the Baptist.

In 1417 Canon Richard Benton of Wells left 2s. 6d. to each brother being a priest of the hospital of St. John at Bath. In 1496 Thomas Chaunceler, citizen of Bath, left 'one torche' to the hospital of St. John in Bath. [5]

[24] Steven, *Addn. to Dugdale* (1722), i, 101.
[25] Ibid. 102.
[26] Will. de Worecestre, *Itin.* 136.
[27] *L. and P. Hen. VIII*, xiii (2), 341.
[1] *R. of Shrewsbury's Reg.* (Somers. Rec. Soc.) 87.
[2] *Cal. Wells D. and C. MSS.* i, 144.

[28] *Cal. Pat.* 1340–3, p. 227.
[29] Ibid. 1343–5, p. 102.   [30] Ibid. p. 142.
[31] *Somers. Arch. Soc. Proc.* ix, 40.
[3] *Cal. Wells D. and C. MSS.* i, 432.
[4] *R. of Shrewsbury's Reg.* (Somers. Rec. Soc.) 286.
[5] *Somers. Med. Wills* (Somers. Rec. Soc.), xvi, 89, 342.

In the Valor of 1535 the hospital of St. John the Baptist, with the chapel of St. Michael attached, was valued at £22 16s. 9d. John Symonds was the warden or master.[6] The hospital escaped the dissolution of monastic foundations, and in 1578 Queen Elizabeth gave the advowson of it to the Mayor and commonalty of Bath.

Leland says 'There is a Hospital of St. John hard by the Crosse Bathe of the foundation of Reginalde, bishop of Bathe.'[7]

In the Inventories of Chantries 1546,[8] the contents of the chapel of the hospital of St. John the Baptist, Bath, were valued on 17 March. 'John Symons, incumbent of St. John's chapel in the hospital of Bath.

'First a mass book valued at 8d. Item a pair of vestments valued at 8s. Item two bells valued at 6s. 8d. Total 15s. 4d.'

In the Survey of 1548 [9] the following account of the hospital is recorded.

'There is a hospital called St. John's Hospital within the said parish (i.e. St. Michael's), having lands, tenements, etc. thereunto belonging of the clear yearly value of £25 13s. 8d.

'The hospital was erected as it is said for the relief of six poor men, and one priest or master to serve them, having their continual living upon the same. This hospital is annexed to the parish church of St. Michael aforesaid, and the parson of the said church is master of the said hospital. The residue of the profits are employed and received by the said master.

'The ornaments of the hospital are esteemed worth 15s. 2d. No foundation deeds were shown, neither would the master appear.'

The hospital survived the Reformation, and some account of its later history may be found in the *Report of Commissioners for enquiring into Charities*, v, 283–92.

MASTERS OF THE HOSPITAL OF ST. JOHN THE BAPTIST, BATH

Adam, occurs 1260[10]
Thomas Gosmale, appointed 1343[11]
John Ashmeek, died 1398[12]
John Shaftesbury, resigned 1428[13]
Peter Byryman, appointed 1438,[14] resigned 1457 [15]
John Vobe, appointed 1460[16]
Thomas Cornish, appointed 1483[17]
John Symonds, occurs 1535[18]

[6] *Valor Eccl.* (Rec. Com.) i, 178.   [7] *Itin.* ii, 61.
[8] Exch. K.R. Church Goods, $\frac{8}{2\overline{3}\overline{6}}$.
[9] Green, *Chantries* (Somers. Rec. Soc.), 148.
[10] *Cal. Wells D. and C. MSS.* i, 144.
[11] *R. of Shrewsbury's Reg.* (Somers. Rec. Soc.) 493.
[12] Collinson, *Somers.* i, 125.
[13] Hunt, *Two Chartul.* (Somers. Rec. Soc.) ii, 61.
[14] Wells Epis. Reg. Stafford, fol. 155.
[15] Ibid. Beckington, fol. 221.   [16] Ibid. fol. 261.
[17] Ibid. Stillington, fol. 113.
[18] *Valor Eccl.* (Rec. Com.) i, 178.

26. THE HOSPITAL OF ST. MARY MAGDALEN, BATH.

The hospital of St. Mary Magdalen of Holloway near Bath appears to have been founded before 1212, in which year Hugh, Bishop of Lincoln, made a bequest to the lepers outside Bath. Nicholas, master of this hospital, occurs in 1263 and an undated deed in the *Bath Cartulary* [19] records a grant of land by John Wyssy to the master, brethren and sisters on condition that their chaplains should celebrate in his private chapel at Bath. Bishop Ralph in 1332 [20] granted an indulgence to those who supported the hospital of Holy Cross and St. Mary Magdalen at Bath, and it occurs from time to time as the recipient of legacies, Margery Brokworth in 1407[21] desiring to be buried within its chapel.

The hospital survived the Reformation, but gradually became a sinecure, its endowments being diverted from their original purpose.[22]

27. THE HOSPITAL OF ST. KATHERINE, BEDMINSTER

This hospital was founded by Robert de Berkeley, who died in 1219, for a master and several brethren who should tend the sick and infirm and the needy traveller. It stood on the west side of the street near the bridge called Brightlow Bridge, and nothing remains of the buildings except a portion of the east wall of the chapel where there is a blocked-up Gothic window. William de Worcester in his travels measured the chapel as 49 ft. long and 21 ft. broad, and the chancel as 27 ft. by 16 ft.[23]

On 5 October 1331 [24] the master of the hospital was pardoned for obtaining from Alexander de Alneto lands at Ashton without licence.

On the institution of John Worthy, priest, as warden, 21 April 1414[25] it was stated that the hospital was not a religious foundation, and that the warden had with him at times four, three or two priests as companions, who wore the garments of secular priests with the badge of a St. Catherine wheel on the left breast. The rents then did not exceed £24 yearly, and there was a pension due from them to the rector of Bedminster of 6s. 8d., and two wax lights had to be offered yearly on the Feast of St. John the Baptist.

In the Valor of 1535 the revenues are valued at £21 15s. 8d. and Richard Walgrave is entered

[19] *Cal. Wells D. and C. MSS.* i, 432; *Feet of F.* (Somers. Rec. Soc.) vi, 197, no. 345.
[20] *Somers. Rec. Soc. Publ.* ix, 95.
[21] Ibid. xvii, 32.
[22] *Bath Munic. Rec.* 68.   [23] *Itin.* 294.
[24] *Cal. Pat.* 1330–4, p. 196.
[25] Wells Epis. Reg. Bubwith.

as the warden and master.[26] The hospital escaped the dissolution of the monasteries.

In the Survey of 1548[27] the net rental was estimated at £21 10s., there was a silver chalice weighing 8½ oz., there was 100 lb. of bell metal, and the ornaments were valued at 4s. 6d. William Clerke is stated to be the master on the king's patent, but the commissioners had not then seen the patent. No poor people were maintained or relieved except that Mr. Clerke assigned them cottages belonging to the hospital for poor men to dwell in, and 'other relief they have none but as God sendeth.' No foundation deeds were shown, but the priest was bound to say mass thrice a week.

In the rentals of the hospital we find that Richard Hall held the site and demesne lands, Alice Sparrow 2 acres at Lukemoor, John Coke 1 acre at Wademore, 1 in Boenmede and 1 at Rodmede. Divers persons held lands and tenements at Bedminster, Ashton, and Berkeley, and a certain tenement in the city of Bristol. There were three cottages called almshouses, which brought in no rent because they were occupied by paupers.

MASTERS OF BEDMINSTER HOSPITAL

John de Babcary, appointed 1325[28]
Richard de Borefordescote, appointed 1327[29]
Richard atte Pondfolke, exchanged 1332[30]
John Randolph of Coleshill, appointed 1332[31]
John de Malmesbury, appointed 1338[32]
John de Eggworth, appointed December 1348[33]
William de Foston, appointed April 1349[34]
Walter de Estham, appointed 29 April 1349[35] deprived 1353[36]
John de Kymersden, or Kynemerton, appointed 1353[37]
John Disford, appointed temp. Edw. III,[38] occurs 1390[39]
John Worthy, appointed April 1414[40]
John Dyer, appointed November, 1414[41]
John Coriscomb, 1420[42]

Thomas or John Fulford, D.D.[43]
James Blakden, occurs 1432,[44] died 1464 [45]
Henry Abendon, appointed 1464 [46]
Thomas Collyer or Cosin, appointed 1497 [47]
John Lloyd or Floyd, appointed 1513 [48]
Richard Walgrave, appointed 1523 [49]
William Clerke, appointed 1543 [50]
John Aungel [51]
James Bond, B.D., appointed 1568 [52]
John Bridgwater, appointed 1570 [53]
Edward Mowcroft, 1572 [54]
Francis Nevill, appointed 1573 [55]

The Hospital of St. Katherine had a vesica-shaped seal,[56] 2¼ in. by 1½ in., with a representation of the patron saint crowned and standing in a niche, holding the sword and the wheel of her martyrdom. The legend is:—
SIGILL' HOSPITALIS SCE KATHERINE VILLE BRISTO...

28. THE HOSPITAL OF ST. JOHN THE BAPTIST, BRIDGWATER

The founder of this hospital is said[57] to have been William Bruer or Briwere, one of the guardians of the kingdom when King Richard was absent on the crusade, and the builder of the second castle at Bridgwater. Its foundation was probably before 1213, and was for a master or prior and some brethren who should maintain thirteen infirm persons besides pilgrims and religious who in their journey should pass through the town.[58] Bishop Jocelin of Bath confirmed the foundation in 1219,[59] and confirmed also to the hospital William Briwere's gift of the church of Isle (Brewers). Robert de Boyton obtained licence 9 July 1283[60] to give to the hospital the church of Lanteglos (Cornw.), William Testard on 13 September 1284[61] gave the church and some land at Wembdon and William de Monckton 12 June 1285[62] the church at Moorwinstow (Cornwall). As early as 1213 the

[43] Wells Epis. Reg. Stafford, fol. 12. A Dominican.
[44] Ibid. fol. 168. He became Bishop of Bangor in 1453.
[45] Ibid.
[46] Ibid. Beckington, unnumbered folios at end.
[47] Ibid. King, fol. 10.
[48] Ibid. Hadrian, fol. 107.
[49] Ibid. Clark, fol. 3. A layman.
[50] Ibid. Knight, fol. 14.   [51] Ibid. Barlow.
[52] Ibid. Berkeley, fol. 25.
[53] Ibid. fol. 31. Canon residentiary of Wells.
[54] Collinson, Somers. ii, 283.
[55] Ibid. fol. 38.
[56] Cat. of Seals B.M. 2726, lxvi, 65*.
[57] The foundation of the house is recorded in Bishop Beckington's Register, 6.
[58] Hemingford, Chron. (ed. Hearne) 597.
[59] Lincoln's Inn Bath Reg. no. 105.
[60] Cal. Pat. 1281–92, p. 69.
[61] Ibid. p. 132.   [62] Ibid. p. 176.

[26] Valor Eccl. (Rec. Com.) i, 183.
[27] Green, Somers. Chantries (Somers. Rec. Soc.), 90, 272.
[28] Drokensford's Reg. (Somers. Rec. Soc.) 239, 244. His predecessor, unnamed, was removed for incompetence.
[29] Ibid. 275.
[30] R. of Shrewsbury's Reg. (Somers. Rec. Soc. ix) 90.
[31] Ibid.   [32] Ibid. 328.
[33] Ibid. 560. Probably died of the Black Death in 1349.
[34] Ibid. 590.   [35] Ibid. 607.
[36] Ibid. 727.   [37] Ibid. 728.
[38] Wells Epis. Reg. Bubwith, fol. 83.
[39] Cal. Pat. 1388–92, p. 257.
[40] Wells Epis. Reg. Bubwith, fol. 83.
[41] Ibid. fol. 87.
[42] Collinson, Somers. ii, 283.

hospital is entered as in possession of 5 acres at Bridgwater, and in 1214 as possessing the church of St. Mary, Bridgwater.[63] It had also lands at Toller Porcorum and at Bridport in the county of Dorset. On 10 May 1286 the master and brethren received licence to cut a channel through one of the bends of the River Parret to cleanse the privies of the hospital.[64] Pope Nicholas IV in 1291[65] granted relaxation of enjoined penance to those visiting and making offerings in the chapel of the hospital on the festival of St. John the Baptist or within its octave.

Bishop Robert Burnell of Bath and Wells (1275–92) seems to have attempted to form a school out of a portion of this benefaction, for a bond was given in 1298[66] to Bishop William of March, the immediate successor of Bishop Burnell, by the master of the hospital, promising to maintain six chaplains to celebrate daily in the hospital, the six to make a complement of thirteen besides the master, wearing the religious habit, i.e. a secular priest's dress with a cross on the breast : the corporate funds also were to maintain thirteen poor scholars living within the walls 'habiles ad informandum in grammatica,' who should be excused the full ritual that they might keep school daily in the town. The rector of the schools was to send seven of his mendicant scholars for daily pittances from the kitchen. These new objects, however, were not to abate the original duty of the house, which was for the sick and the stranger. The arrangement is stated to be in consequence of the appropriation of Wembdon, Lanteglos and Moorwinstow Churches.

This new venture was apparently unpopular, for in February 1325[67] Bishop Drokensford appointed a commission to inquire into the truth of the prevalent rumours charging the hospital with wronging the wayfarers of the hospitality due to them. The commissioners were to examine the charters and ascertain the facts.

On 23 March 1327[68] the master and brethren were pardoned for having obtained from Richard de Wiggebere without licence lands in Chilton Trinity and the advowson of that church. This pardon was repeated in 1344,[69] licence having been granted to the hospital to hold this property, 8 July 1336.[70]

In Bishop Ralph of Shrewsbury's register[71]

there is a deed of the master and brethren of the hospital June 1333, setting out the gift by Richard de Wiggebere of land and the churches and chapels of Chilton, Idstock, and Huntstile, for the foundation of a chantry in Wembdon Church for the founder's family, to be served by a priest paid by the master and brethren. They however were not to be compelled to keep the chantry chapel in repair.

In 1337[72] the bishop assigned a sufficient portion for the vicar of Northover, the hospital having had the rectory appropriated to them.

On 10 July 1336[73] the hospital was discharged for the future on account of its poverty from the payment of tenths, etc., and in February[74] 1338 it received licence to acquire land in mortmain to the value of 10 marks yearly. On 4 November 1343[75] the hospital had licence to acquire land from John de Walesyngham, viz., 37 acres in Isle Brewers and a house ; and two messuages and lands of Thomas Fole and Philip Godhale in Northover.

In July 1350[76] Bishop Ralph of Shrewsbury offered an indulgence to all who should contribute to the rebuilding of the hospital 'in quo pauperes Christi debiles et infirmi undique confluentes recipiuntur et recreantur.'

On 6 February 1380 and again on 14 July 1380[77] a commission was issued of *oyer* and *terminer* to hear a charge against certain people who had attacked the master and brethren, broken in the door of their church and held them prisoners and refused permission to the master and brethren to enter either the church or the hospital. The trouble seems to have arisen from an effort on the part of the master and brethren to absorb the vicarage of Bridgwater as well as the rectory. The prior is called in both commissions the master and parson, and on 14 April 1380[78] William Camel the master and the brethren of the hospital obtained a special protection touching the controversy between Thomas Cadecote the late master and the commonalty of Bridgwater which was not yet settled. Cadecote had only resigned in the previous year.[79]

On 15 February 1382[80] Nicholas Frampton, a chaplain in Bridgwater, was pardoned his outlawry which he had drawn upon himself by fleeing from justice in that he had surrendered to the Marshalsea prison, and on 28 March 1383 a much more notorious popular leader of discontent, Thomas Engilby, was also pardoned.[81] He had broken into the Hospital and had seized

[63] Cartae Antiquae, 15 John, no. 11 ; 16 John, no. 23.
[64] Cal. Pat. 1281–92, p. 244.
[65] Cal. Papal Letters, i, 539.
[66] Cf. Drokensford's Reg. (Somers. Rec. Soc.) 268.
[67] Ibid. 240.
[68] Cal. Pat. 1327–30, p. 33.
[69] Ibid. 1343–5, p. 310.
[70] Ibid. 1334–8, p. 303.
[71] R. of Shrewsbury's Reg. (Somers. Rec. Soc.) 321.

[72] R. of Shrewsbury's Reg. (Somers. Rec. Soc.) 341.
[73] Cal. Pat. 1334–8, p. 280.
[74] Ibid. 1338–40, p. 6.
[75] Ibid. 1343–5, p. 131.
[76] R. of Shrewsbury's Reg. (Somers. Rec. Soc. x) 635.
[77] Cal. Pat. 1377–81, pp. 466, 567, 570.
[78] Ibid. p. 458.   [79] Ibid. p. 316.
[80] Ibid. 1381–5, p. 96.   [81] Ibid. p. 270.

William Camel the master and compelled him to deliver up certain bonds of the men of Bridgwater which he held and to release all his rights and profits to Nicholas Frampton and pay 200 marks for the safety of himself and his convent. Engilby had also been into other houses in Bridgwater and burnt writings and court rolls, tearing off the seals, and had beheaded Walter Baron and had gone to the gaol at Ilchester and taken out Hugh Lavenham and had him beheaded and had placed his head on a spear and carried it to Bridgwater and there fixed it with that of Walter Baron on the bridge.

These three entries suggest a forced resignation of Cadecote, and a contested election for the mastership between Frampton and Camel.

In 1423 [82] royal licence was granted to Walter Eston the president of the Augustinian Hospital of St. John the Baptist, Bridgwater, and to the brethren there to select a master in room of the late John Wemedon deceased. The hospital was declared to be of the foundation of the Earl of March and of the Lord de la Zouche, who was then a minor and a royal ward.

In 1463 Bishop Beckington issued orders for the better organization of the hospital.[83]

In the Valor of 1535 [84] the possessions of the priory are valued at £120 19s. 1d.

The hospital was surrendered by Robert Walshe the master, 5 February 1539.[85] There were then seven brethren in the hospital and all received pensions, Robert Walshe £33 6s. 8d., and Thomas Coggyn, Richard Kymrydge, John Colde, John Wyll and Robert Fyssher £4 each, and John Wood and John Mors £2 each. The names of Kymrydge, Wyll, Fyssher, Wood and Mors occur in Cardinal Pole's pension list, 1556.

Priors of Bridgwater Hospital

Geoffrey de Mark, 1297 [86]
Henry de Stanford, appointed 1315.[87]
John de Walsham, appointed 1334 [88]
Thomas de Cadecote, 1349–79 [89]
William Camel, occurs 1380 [90]
John or William Pathul, died 1416 [91]
Thomas Pulton, appointed 1416 [92]
John Wembdon, died 1423 [93]
Roger Cory, appointed 1449,[94] resigned 1456 [95]

John Holford, appointed 1457 [96]
Thomas Spenser, 1498 [97] died 1524 [98]
Robert Walshe, elected 1525,[99] surrendered 1539

The 13th-century seal of the Priory of St. John Baptist at Bridgwater [100] is a vesica, 2⅝ in. by 1¾ in., showing Our Lady with the Child on the parapet of a four-arched bridge over a river. St. John Baptist holding *Agnus Dei* on a roundel stands on the left, and St. Paul with sword and book on the right. The whole design is enclosed in a niche with triple canopy, and what remains of the legend runs:—s' COMUNE HOSPITALIS SANCTI [IOHANNI]S BAPTISTE DE . . . . . ALTERA.

29. THE HOSPITAL OF BRUTON

Nothing appears to be known of this hospital beyond the fact of its existence. In 1417 [101] Richard Bruton, canon of Wells, left 6s. 8d. to the 'spytelhouse' at Bruton, and a similar sum was bequeathed to the hospital of Bruton by Richard Grene in 1496.[102] It further benefited to the extent of 3s. 4d. under the will of John Brent in 1524.[103]

30. THE HOSPITAL OF ILCHESTER

A house of lepers was established outside Ilchester some time before 1212, in which year Hugh, Bishop of Lincoln, made a bequest of 3 marks to them.[104] The brethren received royal protection in 1235, their house being then called St. Margaret's Hospital.[105]

31. THE HOSPITAL OR PRIORY AT WHITE HALL, ILCHESTER

Between the years 1217 and 1220 William Dennis (*Dacus*) of Sock Dennis [106] gave his house of Whitehall in Ilchester, with lands, for the purpose of founding a hospital to the honour of the Blessed Trinity for the reception and entertainment of poor travellers and pilgrims.

In addition to the house called Whitehall he gave two houses close by and both mills which he possessed in Ilchester, with the arable land belonging to those mills, and various other

[82] *Cal. Pat.* 1422–9, p. 23.
[83] Wells Epis. Reg. Beckington, fol. 287; cf. fol. 215.
[84] *Valor Eccl.* (Rec. Com.) i, 207–9.
[85] Aug. Off. Misc. Bks. no. 245, fol. 214.
[86] *Cal. Pat.* 1292–1301, p. 264.
[87] *Drokensford's Reg.* (Somers. Rec. Soc.) 151.
[88] *R. of Shrewsbury's Reg.* (Somers. Rec. Soc.) 167.
[89] Ibid. 646; *Cal. Pat.* 1377–81, p. 316.
[90] *Cal. Pat.* 1377–81, p. 458.
[91] Ibid. 1413–16, p. 397.
[92] Ibid.
[93] Ibid. 1422–9, p. 22.
[94] Wells Epis. Reg. Beckington, unnumbered folio at end. [95] Ibid.

[96] Nine brethren present at the election and two absent. Unnumbered folios at end of Beckington's Reg.
[97] Wells Epis. Reg. King, fol. 15.
[98] Ibid. fol. 24.
[99] Weaver *Somers. Wills*, 197. Rector of St. Andrew's, Northover, 1506.
[100] *Cat. of Seals B.M.* 2709, lxxi, 56.
[101] *Somers. Rec. Soc. Publ.* xvii, 91.
[102] Ibid. 349.   [103] Ibid. xix, 229.
[104] *Cal. Wells D. and C. MSS.* i, 432.
[105] *Cal. Pat.* 1232–47, p. 115.
[106] *Somers. Rec. Soc. Publ.* i, 68; *Somers. Arch. Soc. Proc.* xiii, 21–118.

tenements in the neighbourhood, together with lands near the house of the lepers at Ilchester.

The reason of his foundation was for the good of the soul of Richard Toclive, Bishop of Winchester, who was born at Sock Dennis, and for Adam of Ilchester, Dean of Salisbury, and others. He reserved to himself and his heirs the right to present the warden of the hospital to the Bishop of Bath, in whose protection the hospital was.

The names of witnesses attached to his deed, among which are Stephen Langton, Archbishop of Canterbury, and St. Hugh, Bishop of Lincoln, show that it was made between the years 1217 and 1220.

About 1237,[107] William, Abbot of Cerne, gave the advowson of the church of St. Mary the Less in Ilchester to this hospital, and Bishop Jocelin in 1241 sanctioned its appropriation to the hospital in order that the inmates might have close at hand a chapel for divine service instead of being compelled, as previously, to go through the streets on their way to the parish church. Bishop Jocelin in his appropriation speaks of the brethren and the sisters of the hospital, who, leaving the world for the service of God and the poor under the habit of poverty have taken there the habit of monachism and religion.

The foundation therefore was at first a hospital in charge of the brethren and sisters.

In 1281 [108] we find it described as a priory, and the inmates as the prioress and nuns of 'la Blanchesale' of Ilchester.

On 13 December 1313[109] Bishop Drokensford issued a commission of inquiry as to the length of the vacancy in the office of prioress, and as to the fitness of the lady proposed for that post.

Alice Atteyerd seems to have been appointed prioress, but in the following year we find her deprived for incompetence and unfitness, but appealing to the archbishop against the bishop's action.[110]

Alice Clithorne or Chilthorne, probably one of the sisters of the house, seems to have been appointed prioress by the bishop and the patron, but sympathy with the expelled prioress had induced the sisters at Whitehall publicly to beg alms for their late head to the great reproach of their house as Bishop Drokensford thought, and he therefore wrote to the Archbishop of Canterbury asking him to make some provision for the sisters. The prioress was charged with extreme severity towards her sisters, ejecting them from the house and compelling them to beg for their daily bread.[111]

The prioress seems not alone to be blamed. John de Draycote and Walter de Wouburn,

who had been wardens of the house, had greatly neglected their duty, and the property of the hospital had been wasted to such an extent as called for the interference of the Crown, so that in the previous year the bishop had appointed William de Modiford, rector of Tintinhull, and William de l'Isle, rector of St. Mary Magdalene, Ilchester, to administer the affairs of the hospital.[112]

The appointment of Alice Clithorne, or Chilthorne, was objected to by the escheator of the Crown, because, as it was asserted, the patron, Sir Nicholas de Boleville, had accepted her as prioress before he was of legal age to do so. This difficulty was ended by judgement of the Crown (28 June 1316).[113] The prioress appointed, however, seems to have been quite unfitted for her post, and on 18 September 1323 Henry de Birlaunde, rector of Stoke, and John de Herminal were appointed to take charge of the house and its revenues, for the prioress was charged with incontinence and immorality with John de Passelawe the chaplain, and with wasting and alienating the goods of the house, so that the sisters again lacked maintenance and were compelled to beg.[114]

On 29 January 1324[115] the bishop issued a commission to his official, and to the rectors of Stoke and Tintinhull, to inquire carefully into these charges, made against the prioress, and gave them power to act. Discord certainly existed there, and the prioress appears to have defied the bishop and the patron. On 28 March 1324[116] the chapel of the hospital had to be reconciled since it had been polluted by effusion of blood. Meanwhile the prioress was resisting the action of the commission and refused to be turned out. An appeal 26 June, 1324[117] was made to the Crown against the conduct of the commissioners and the patron of the house who apparently had endeavoured to take possession of it and expel her by force.

The next year, 1325,[118] Bishop Drokensford notified to the patron, Sir Richard de Boleville, that this prioress, Alice, was deprived. Cecilia de Draycote was chosen as prioress, but on 1 September 1334[119] we find Bishop Ralph of Shrewsbury writing to the rectors of Limington and St. John's, Ilchester, informing them that he had sequestrated the possessions of the church and commanding them to take charge of them, supplying the sisters and servants with necessary maintenance only until they should receive further instructions. The prioress was clearly incompetent, and he commissioned Agnes Champflour and Agnes de Wynterbourn, sisters

---

[107] *Somers. Rec. Soc. Publ.* i, 68.
[108] Exch. Rolls, 9 Edw. I, no 79 Appendix iv.
[109] *Somers. Rec. Soc. Publ.* i, 68.
[110] Ibid. 115.   [111] Ibid.

[112] *Somers. Rec. Soc. Publ.* i, 93.
[113] *Cal. Pat.* 1313–17, p. 505.   [114] Ibid. 115.
[115] Ibid. 228.   [116] Ibid. 232.
[117] *Cal. Pat.* 1321–4, p. 455.
[118] *Somers. Rec. Soc. Publ.* i, 245.
[119] Ibid. ix, 177, 240.

of the house, to act with her in the administration of affairs, forbidding the prioress to do anything without the advice and consent of these other two sisters.

We hear of this prioress, Cecilia, again in an action concerning a corrody which she is said to have granted to Simonis the wife of Gilbert Passeware.[120] The terms of the corrody were that she was to have a place 30 ft. by 15 ft. in which she was to build, at her own expense, a room for her living, that she was to sit daily at the table of the prioress, and be attended on by the servants of the house, and wear the habit and veil of the sisters for the term of her life.

In 1370 [121] we hear of Mary, the prioress of 'the Nywe Halle,' a change in name which possibly may have been caused through a rebuilding of the house.

In the clerical subsidy of 1377,[122] Matilda the prioress of Whitehall is mentioned with one sister, and in 1423 we again have mention of the house as consisting of the prioress, Cristina, and one nun and co-sister, Joan Whyttock. What happened afterwards does not appear, but on 3 September 1463 we find in the list of chaplains and their cures in the archdeaconry of Wells the name of John Bonez of Ilchester, chaplain. Between these two dates the priory of nuns seems to have been changed into a free chapel with residence for a permanent chaplain, and in 1485 [123] a successor is described as following the late John Boney or Banys chaplain of Whitehall, Ilchester; and on 30 August 1519,[124] John Moyne was admitted as chaplain of the perpetual and free chapel of Whitehall.

Again in the Valor of 1535 [125] mention is made of Walter Cokkes or Cocks as chaplain of the free chapel of Whitehall, and the endowments were at Ilchester, Taunton, and Sock, i.e. the endowments of the former nunnery, and were worth £18 13s. 8d.

PRIORESSES OF WHITEHALL, ILCHESTER

Alice Atteyerde, 1315[126]
Alice de Chilthorne, 1316[127]
Cecilia de Draycote, 1325[128]
Mary, 1370[129]
Matilda, occurs 1377[130]
Margaret, 'Marjory,' 1377[131]
Christina, occurs 1423[132]

32. THE HOSPITAL OF LANGPORT

In January 1311 Bishop Drokensford [133] ordered that the proctors of the lepers of St. Mary Magdalen of Langport should be allowed access to the churches of the diocese on festivals to collect alms, and a similar expression of good-will was made on their behalf by Bishop Ralph of Shrewsbury in 1337.[134] John Mucheldever in 1403 left 18d. to the hospital by Westover in Langport; [135] the lazar-house of Langport was remembered in the will of Elizabeth Speke, 1537,[136] and as late as 1549 in that of John Walton.[137] The almshouse of Langport West-over continued in use down to the time of the Civil War.[138]

33. THE HOSPITAL OF TAUNTON

The master and leprous brethren of Taunton received royal protection in 1236,[139] which was also granted to 'the brethren of St. Margaret's without Taunton' in 1278 [140] and again under the title of the hospital of the Holy Ghost and St. Margaret, in 1334.[141] Canon Richard Bruton in 1417 [142] left 20s. to the 'spytelhouse' of Taunton, which is called a lazar-house in the will of Elizabeth Speke in 1537.[143] It survived the changes at the Reformation, as in 1552 [144] Thomas Brocke left 6s. 8d. 'to the poor in the spittell house at Taunton,' and it has continued to the present time as an almshouse.

34. THE HOSPITAL OF ST. JOHN THE BAPTIST, WELLS

This hospital was founded by Hugh de Wells, Archdeacon of Wells from 1204 to 1209 and Bishop of Lincoln from 1209 to 1235. He was greatly assisted in his project by his brother Jocelin de Wells, Bishop of Bath (1206–42), and in his charter by which he confirmed his brother's gift Bishop Jocelin gave the hospital a chantry and the right to have and ring bells and a cemetery for the brethren ' qui signati sunt et sub signo viventes ibidem conversati.' [145] The original endowment is not quite evident. In the draft of his will made in 1212 [146] Bishop Hugh gave his brother 500 marks for that purpose, but in his final will he granted to ' my lord the

120 Somers. Arch. Soc. Proc. xiii, 115 ; xxxviii, 17, 18 ; Assize R. 1502, m. 82, 91.
121 Ilchester Almshouse Deeds, no. 26.
122 Cler. Subs. bdle. 4, no. 1, m. 6.
123 Wells Epis. Reg. Stillington, fol. 30.
124 Ibid. Wolsey, fol. 7.
125 Valor Eccl. (Rec. Com.) 199.
126 Somers. Rec. Soc. Publ. i, 93.
127 Ibid. 115.   128 Ibid. 245.
129 Ilchester Almsh. D. no. 26, App. no. 9.
130 Cler. Subs. bdle. 4, no. 1, m. 6.
131 Cal. Pat. 1405–8, p. 306.
132 Ilchester Almsh. D. no. 11–98, App. xii.

133 Somers. Rec. Soc. Publ. i, 37.
134 Ibid. xi, 301.   135 Ibid. xvii, 63
136 Ibid. xxi, 39.   137 Ibid. 108.
138 Ibid. xxiii, 336.
139 Cal. Pat. 1232–47, p. 151.
140 Ibid. 1272–81, p. 262.
141 Ibid. 1334–8, p. 3.
142 Somers. Rec. Soc. Publ. xvii, 91.
143 Ibid. xxi, 39.   144 Ibid. 146.
145 Cal. Wells D. and C. MSS. (Hist. MSS. Com.) i, 49.
146 Ibid. 431.

Bishop of Bath my brother'[147] the wardship of Tunring, to the use and repair of the hospital at Wells, and 200 marks for the work of the hospital and wardship of the land and heirs of Crombwell to apply the profits to the work of the hospital at Wells. It is probable that lands at Keinton Mandeville and Babcary formed either a portion of this bequest or were granted to the hospital in the earlier part of this century, as in the early years of Edward I the prior is entered as possessed of lands there.[148] Jocelin himself had given the church of Evercreech with the chapel of Chesterblade to the house, and the gift was confirmed by Thomas Prior of Bath in 1213.[149]

Prior William bound the hospital to Richard de Button the precentor of Wells[150] to perform services annually at the altar of St. John in their house for the soul of the said Richard, of Bishop William de Button and of his ancestors. In April 1314[151] Bishop Drokensford formally ordained the foundation of a chantry in the chapel of the hospital by John de Wyk, Canon of Crediton, who had given his rectory of West Down, Devon, for that purpose. The hospital however was ill-endowed, and in 1323 [152] the brethren appealed to Bishop Drokensford to grant them the *congé d'élire* without payment of the usual fees. The bishop did so, and confirmed the selection of Philip de Eston as prior or master.[153] Three years afterwards, 1326, the bishop by *inspeximus* ratified the foundation by Philip, the prior, of a chantry of St. Nicholas in the chapel of the hospital for the benefit of the soul of William de la Wythy late burgess of Wells.[154] Wythy had enriched the hospital by giving the brethren five houses and parcels of land in the borough and 8 acres elsewhere in the town.

In January 1331 [155] Bishop Ralph wrote to the prior to admit William Bisshop, clerk 'ad gerendum habitum religionis illius.'

In April 1350[156] the bishop ordained the foundation of a chantry in the hospital chapel, and assigned for its endowment the rents, lands, etc., which he had received as a gift from William de Luttleton, canon and precentor of Wells, and William de Bourwardsleye. A chaplain was to pray for his soul and for the soul of John de Somerton, formerly Abbot of Muchelney, at the altar of St. Martin in the cathedral church of Wells, and the hospital was to provide a chaplain to pray for the bishop and for the soul of William formerly Abbot of Shrewsbury in the chapel

of the hospital, and the number of brethren in the house should be increased to a prior and ten brethren, and if the funds of the hospital could not support this chaplain and so many brethren, then the hospital was to enjoin one of their number so to pray for the soul of Bishop Ralph.

In 1362 Walter de Compton bequeathed 20s. for the repair of the hospital, and other small bequests were made from time to time.[157]

In 1475 through the appeal of William Drew, one of the brethren, Pope Sixtus IV granted certain privileges and protection against hasty interdicts to the brethren of the hospital.[158]

In the *Valor Ecclesiasticus* of 1535[159] John Pynnock is entered as prior, and the endowments of the hospital are valued at £40 0s. 2d. arising from rents of lands and houses in the city of Wells, a mill at Wookey and rents at Wookey, Dinder, Pynckmore, Keinton Mandeville, and the rectories of West Down near Ilfracombe, North Devon, and Evercreech.

The hospital was surrendered to the king on 3 February 1539, and the lands and buildings were given to Bishop Clerk in exchange for the manor of Dogmersfield in Hants.

PRIORS OF ST. JOHN'S HOSPITAL

Peter, 1228, occurs 1251[160]
John, occurs 1292[161]
Walter, occurs 1314,[162] died 1323[163]
Philip de Eston, appointed 1323[164]
Henry de Exton, collated 1348[165]
John Type or Typpe, died 1409[166]
John Bartlett, appointed 13 July 1410[167]
Nicholas Cousin, collated 1439,[168] resigned 1445[169]
Thomas Yle, collated 1445,[170] resigned 1462[171]
John, appointed 1462[172]

[157] *Somers. Med. Wills* (Somers. Rec. Soc.), *passim.*
[158] Batten, *Fox's Reg.* 40.
[159] *Valor. Eccl.* (Rec. Com.) i, 140.
[160] *Cal. Wells D. and C. MSS.* i, 139.
[161] Foundation deed of Canon Lechlade's Chantry in Exeter Cathedral.
[162] *Drokensford's Reg.* (Somers. Rec. Soc.) 223.
[163] Ibid.   [164] Ibid. 228.
[165] *R. of Shrewsbury's Reg.* (Somers. Rec. Soc.) 581.
[166] Wells Epis. Reg. Bubwith, fol. 37.
[167] Ibid. folios at end.
[168] Collated by the bishop through lapse as there were only two brethren who had a right to vote for the master or prior. Wells Epis. Reg. Stafford, fol. 156.
[169] Ibid. Beckington, fol. 40.
[170] Again a collation by the bishop as there were only two brethren in the hospital. He was a brother of the hospital at Bridgwater. Ibid. fol. 41.
[171] Wells Epis. Reg. Beckington, unnumbered folio at end.
[172] Ibid. Five brethren in the hospital. He was a Canon Regular of St. Austin and Vicar of Devizes. Suffragan of Wells 1459-79, as 'episcopus Tinensis,'

[147] Lincoln Lib. Cantarium. fol. 155-6.
[148] *Cal. Wells D. and C. MSS.* i, 68.
[149] Ibid. i, 531.
[150] *Cal. Wells. D. and C. MSS.* i, 531.
[151] *Drokensford's Reg.* (Somers. Rec. Soc.) 71.
[152] Ibid. 223.   [153] Ibid. 228.   [154] Ibid. 265.
[155] *R. of Shrewsbury's Reg.* (Somers. Rec. Soc.) 66.
[156] Ibid. 633.

Thomas Cornish, 1483,[173] resigned 1497 [174]

Reginald ap David, appointed 1487 [175]

John Marler or Morler, appointed 1500,[176] resigned 1510 [177]

Richard Smith, died 1524 [178]

John Bartram, appointed 1524 [179]

John Pynnock, occurs 1535 [180]

Richard Clarkson, surrendered 1539 [181]

The 13th-century seal of the Hospital of St. John Baptist at Wells [182] is a vesica, 2¼ in. by 1½ in., with a figure of the patron saint holding a roundel with *Agnus Dei* upon it, and standing between two croziers which refer to Hugh of Wells, Bishop of Lincoln, the founder, and Jocelin, Bishop of Bath, benefactor of the hospital. The legend is :—

SIGILL' HOSPITAL' SCI IOHANNIS D' WELLES.

35. THE HOSPITAL OF ST. JOHN THE BAPTIST, REDCLIFFE

This hospital, of which one John Farcey or Farceyn was traditionally regarded as the founder,[183] was apparently established about the beginning of the 13th century, as a deed of the time of King John granting a well to the church of St. Mary Redcliffe stipulated that the hospital should have its water supplied therefrom by a pipe.[184] As a result of this stipulation we find that in 1320 the workmen of St. John's were allowed to enter the chapel yard of St Mary's to mend a broken pipe.[185] Several deeds of the first half of the 13th century refer to the ' brethren and sisters ' of the hospital,[186] but the deed by which the chapel of the Holy Spirit in the cemetery of St. Mary Redcliffe was made over to the hospital speaks only of brethren,[187] and the same is the case with the grant of a portion of the rectory of Backwell made by Bishop Walter de Hasleshaw in 1306.[188] The sisters, however, reappear in 1322,[189] and

in 1317 Bishop Drokensford requested the master of St. John's to receive as a secular sister Alice, niece of Edmund de Wyntereshall.[190] On admission the inmates were required to take an oath to follow the rule of St. Augustine as observed in the hospital.[191]

In 1286 Stephen, Master of the hospital of St. John, was fined 20s. for obstructing a public road by erecting a gate.[192] John Monington, Master or Prior of St. John's, resigned in 1348, retaining a room in the hospital and enjoying for life the manor of Bishopsworth.[193] Later in this century, in 1383, the chapel of the Holy Spirit was made over to the fraternity of the Holy Spirit,[194] and it would seem that the hospital was dwindling into insignificance, as in 1442 there was only one brother resident.[195]

In 1534 the Mayor and corporation of Bristol granted the next presentation to the hospital of St. John the Baptist in Redcliffe Pitt, at the request of Queen Anne Boleyn, to Sir Edward Beynton and Dr. Nicholas Shaxton, of the Queen's household, and David Hutton, grocer of Bristol.[196] Their nominee was probably Richard Bromefield who surrendered the hospital in March 1544.[197]

MASTERS OF ST. JOHN'S, REDCLIFFE [198]

Thomas, 1261

Stephen, 1286 [199]

Edmund le Thyelare, 1292

John de Monington,[200] occurs 1344, resigned 1348

Lawrence Cocele [201]

William Topesleye, 1383

John Seympoule, occurs 1394,[202] 1403 [203]

Nicholas Sterr, 1430

John Hall, appointed 1442

William Prowse, appointed 1467

Richard Collins, S.T.P., appointed 1504

Richard Bromefield, surrendered 1544

The early 13th-century seal of the Hospital of St. John Baptist at Redcliffe [204] is a vesica, 3 in. by 2⅛ in., and has a representation of the baptism of Our Lord. The legend is :—

✠ SIGILL' HOSPITAL' SCI IOHIS BAPTISTE DE REDECLIVIA.

[173] Wells Epis. Reg. Stillington, fol. 113. Provost of Oriel College, Oxford, 1493. Suffragan of Wells 1486–1513, as 'episcopus Tinensis.'

[174] Wells Epis. Reg. King, fol. 6. Buried in Wells Cathedral.

[175] Ibid.   [176] Ibid. fol. 139.

[177] Hadrian, fol. 80.

[178] Wells Epis. Reg. Clerk, fol. 9.

[179] Ibid.

[180] *Valor Eccl.* (Rec. Com.) i, 140.

[181] He got a pension of £12 ; and at the same time three other brethren i.e. apparently the whole convent, received pensions, William Markes £4, John Dyte £2 13s. 4d. and John Carnyicke £3 6s. 8d. Aug. Off. Misc. Bks. vol. 245, fol. 111.

[182] *Cat. of Seals B.M.* 4289, lvi, 64.

[183] *Red Book of Bristol*, i.

[184] *Trans. Bristol and Glouc. Arch. Soc.* xxiv, 173.

[185] *Bp. Drokensford's Reg.* (Somers. Rec. Soc.) 145.

[186] *Trans. Bristol and Glouc. Arch Soc.* xxiv, 173.

[187] Ibid. 174.   [188] Ibid.   [189] Ibid. 175.

[190] *Bp. Drokensford's Reg.* (Somers. Rec. Soc.) 9.

[191] Barrett, *Antiq. of Bristol*, 594.

[192] *Trans. Bristol and Glouc. Arch. Soc.* xxii, 174.

[193] *R. of Shrewsbury's Reg.* (Somers. Rec. Soc.) 551.

[194] Barrett, op. cit. 595.   [195] Ibid. 596.

[196] *Red Bk. of Bristol*, ii, 241.

[197] *Trans. Bristol and Glouc. Arch. Soc.* xxiv, 176.

[198] Barrett, op. cit. 595.

[199] *Trans. Bristol and Glouc. Arch. Soc.* xxii, 174.

[200] Richard de Moniton, brother of the hospital of St. John, was promoted from acolyte to subdeacon in 1336 : *R. of Shrewsbury's Reg.* (Somers. Rec. Soc.) 275.

[201] *Buckland Cartul.* (Somer. Rec. Soc.) 74.

[202] Ibid. 77.

[203] *Trans. Bristol and Glouc. Arch. Soc.* xxiv, 175.

[204] *Cat. of Seals B.M.* 3890. Add. Chart. 15204.

The seal of Roger the Procurator, used as a counterseal to the above, is a vesica, 1½ in. by 1 in., with a three-quarters' length figure of the Baptist holding a scroll inscribed : ECCE AGNUS DEI. On the left is the Lamb. The legend is :— ✠ SIGILL' PROCURATORIS HOSPITAL SCĪ IOHĪS DE RADECLIVIA.

36. ALMSHOUSE OF YEOVIL

An almshouse or hospital was founded by royal licence at Yeovil in 1477 by John Woburn and Richard Huett as executors of William Woburn, minor canon of St. Paul's. The deed of foundation sets forth that it was to be for the support of six poor men and six poor women under the control of a master and two wardens, who were to be elected annually from seven or five honest men of Yeovil nominated by the outgoing master and wardens. The poor inmates were required to wear on their breasts a red cross in honour of St. George, who was joint patron with St. Christopher of the almshouse, and were to say daily one psalter of the Blessed Virgin, kneeling if their health would permit ; on festivals they were to say the same psalter two or three times in succession, either standing, sitting or kneeling. Other prayers were ordered on special occasions for the souls of the founders and other persons, and the master and wardens were desired to form a fraternity of the parishioners of Yeovil and other persons willing to contribute to the support of the almshouse.[205] This institution, which was often remembered in the wills of local testators, survived the Reformation and still supports the original number of poor men and women.

COLLEGES

37. THE COLLEGE OF NORTH CADBURY

In 1423 royal licence was granted for Elizabeth, Lady de Botreaux and Sir William de Botreaux to convert the parish church of North Cadbury into a college of seven chaplains and four clerks, one of the chaplains being in charge as rector of the college of St. Michael. The chaplains were allowed to acquire property to the value of 100 marks, including the advowson of the church, and land whereon to build a manse.[1]

In 1454 Bishop Beckington instituted an inquiry into the constitution of this collegiate church and admitted a new rector.[2]

How far Lady Elizabeth's intentions were carried out is not clear, but in 1548 the benefice of North Cadbury was 'commonly callyd a college and hathe ben tyme out of mynde,' while one witness said that ' yt is written in the churche bookes the Obitus Willmi. Botrax fundatoris hujus collegii.'[3]

38. COLLEGE OF STOKE-UNDER-HAMDON

In 1303 Sir John Beauchamp obtained the royal licence to convert his free chapel of St. Nicholas at Stoke into a collegiate church of five priests, of whom one should be warden or provost. The priests were to wear the dress of secular canons, to live together, under the control of the provost. Rules were laid down for the celebration of the five daily masses, certain endowments were specified, including half the tithes from the demesnes of Shepton Beauchamp, and a clause was inserted in the foundation deed forbidding Sir John and his heirs to send horses, hawks or hounds to be looked after by the canons. Reginald de Moncketon was appointed first provost, and arrangements were made by which the rectory of Stoke should be appropriated to the college upon the cession of the then rector, Robert Beauchamp.[4] Papal confirmation was obtained in 1309.[5]

Bishop Drokensford[6] issued a commission for the visitation of the college of Stoke in December 1320, but the proceedings were not recorded. In 1331 the warden of Stoke was licensed to hear the confessions of his brethren and of the family of Sir John Beauchamp.[7] A corrody was granted to the rector of Stocklinch on his resignation, by Laurence provost of Stoke and his ' sodales ' in 1335.[8] Towards the end of this century the college was suffering from poverty and disputes with the vicars of Stoke over tithes ; accordingly Bishop John Harewell granted in 1375 that upon the cession of the then vicar the vicarage should be united to the rectory and the church served either by a resident secular chaplain or by one of the canons.[9]

The college gradually dwindled and at the time of its suppression in 1549 was farmed to

[205] For the statutes see *Rep. of Com. of Endowed Charities*, v, 575.

[4] *Cal. Pat.* 1301–7, p. 161. Chantry ordained Oct. 4, 1304, *Drokensford's Reg.* (Somers. Rec. Soc.) 194; quoted in full by Collinson, *Hist of Somers.* iii, 316–18.

[5] *Cal. Papal Letters*, ii, 63.

[6] *Drokensford's Reg.* (Somers. Rec. Soc.) 185.

[7] *R. of Shrewsbury's Reg.* (Somers. Rec. Soc.) 86.

[8] Ibid. 173. Laurence le Young had been appointed on the death of Provost Nettlecomb in 1328; *Drokensford's Reg.* (Somers. Rec. Soc.) 291.

[9] *Cal. Wells D. and C. MSS.* i, 278.

[1] *Cal. Pat.* 1422–9, p. 190.
[2] Wells Epis. Reg. Beckington, fol. 203.
[3] *Somers. Chantries* (Somers. Rec. Soc.), 130.

A HISTORY OF SOMERSET

one John Kyte, the value of its endowments being £44 12s., from which £8 was paid to the one priest who then served the chapel.[10]

39. THE CATHEDRAL OF WELLS

When in 909[11] Edward the Elder founded the bishopric of Wells, the Glastonbury monk Athelm who became the first bishop found at Wells a church already in existence and a house in which to live. That the bishop had some clergy to live with him we can well believe, but we know nothing of them, nor do we know whether the church of St. Andrew was rebuilt when it was raised to cathedral rank. Our first definite information concerning the clergy of this church comes to us in Bishop Giso's relation of his work in Wells. He came from the town of St. Trudo in Lorraine and was consecrated Bishop of Wells by Pope Nicholas II at Rome on Easter Day 1061.[12] On his arrival at Wells he says 'he made a survey of his cathedral church and the four or five clerks who served it and who had no common refectory or cloister.' He determined at once to organize these priests and to build for the clergy of his cathedral in Wells a cloister, refectory and dormitory and the community life was established. They were now canons of the cathedral church, under the rule or canon of St. Chrodegang.[13] They were also to have a head or leader of their own. Of course as bishop, Giso was their head, but he made them elect from among themselves one to preside over them, and they chose as their first president Isaac, a priest whom by age and learning they considered well qualified for the post.

This constitution however was not to last for long. Bishop Giso's successor, John de Villula of Tours, obtained from King William II a grant of the abbey church of Bath and permission, which Pope Urban II also endorsed, to make the abbey church of Bath the cathedral church of the diocese. Bishop John pulled down the conventual buildings in Wells which his predecessor had erected, the refectory, dormitory, store room and other necessary offices and the private chambers of the canons and turned the canons out to find lodgings for themselves among the people of the town. Provost Isaac apparently was dead and in his place Bishop John, and not the canons, appointed his own brother Hildebert. The provost or steward does not seem to have had any duties but those of managing the estates for the best advantage of the canons. We hear of Benthelius the archdeacon and afterwards of John, son of Hildebert, the archdeacon, who

seems to have directed the services in the cathedral church.

The destruction of the conventual house naturally demanded that each canon, since he lived alone, should have a fixed income paid to him from the funds of the body. Bishop John therefore granted to Hildebert the whole of the church estates, making him liable for a payment of £30 to the canons;[14] and as each canon received £3 a year we may assume that during Bishop Giso's episcopate the number of canons had increased from four or five to ten. On the death of Hildebert his son John, the archdeacon, succeeded to the estates as by hereditary right, and in his last illness bequeathed them to his brother Reginald with a request however that he would restore them to the bishop; and this he did to Bishop Robert (1136–66). Coming to Bath, where Bishop Robert was, he delivered up the lands of the cathedral church of Wells and was made by the bishop precentor of St. Andrew's Church and given a life-interest in the large estate of Combe St. Nicholas which belonged to the see, and which Bishop Robert designed for the further enrichment of the church of Wells.[15] Then the bishop was able to grant £5 a year to each canon instead of the £3 they had received since 1090.

Bishop Robert was certainly the founder of the Wells chapter on lines such as had been adopted at Salisbury and Lincoln, a system which in England became general for chapters of secular canons. His care for Wells began with his episcopate in 1135. The canons had been engaged ever since the departure of Bishop John in 1088 for Bath in a vigorous attempt to recover their lost position. They had never ceased to regard their church as of cathedral rank and though Bishop Robert obtained from Rome the right to call himself 'Episcopus Bathoniensis' they made much of the fact that the popes had always called the bishop 'episcopus Fontanensis.'[16] Bishop Robert undertook the rebuilding of the church of St. Andrew,[17] and the new Romanesque church was dedicated early in 1148[18] by himself in the presence of Jocelin Bishop of Salisbury, Simon Bishop of Worcester and Robert Bishop of Hereford. But it is as the creator of the cathedral constitution at Wells that Bishop Robert is best remembered. During the episcopate of his successor Bishop Reginald[19] (1174–91) we find a good deal in the development of the chapter already in existence, which had clearly arisen under the hand of Bishop Robert. As bishop of the diocese he held large estates in Somerset which were not for his own per-

---

[10] Collinson, loc. cit.
[11] Cf. Wharton, *Angl. Sac.* i, 556.
[12] Cf. *The Historiola of Wells* (Camden Soc. 1840), 16, 19.
[13] See above, 'Eccl. Hist.' p. 8.

[14] *Historiola de Wells* (Camden Soc. 1840), 22.
[15] Ibid. 24.
[16] Cf. *Historiola de Wells* (Camden Soc. 1840), 25.
[17] Cf. Church, *Early Hist. of Wells*, 24.
[18] *Historiola de Wells* (Camden Soc. 1840), 25.
[19] Church, *Hist. of Wells*, App. 352, 353.

RELIGIOUS HOUSES

sonal expenditure but also for the needs of the Church in the diocese. Some of these he now designed to allocate permanently to the church of St. Andrew. He divided therefore the revenues into two funds. One was for the common expenses of the church, and the other for division among the canons. They were to have a distinct endowment in which they had an absolute life-interest. Moreover they were to have a president over them who was no longer to be the archdeacon or the secular steward, but one of themselves, and further Bishop Robert instituted a series of officers with special endowments over and above the payment which they would get as ordinary canons. We only have documentary evidence of the institution of the deanery, but it is certain that he founded also the offices of precentor, chancellor and treasurer and perhaps of the sub-dean.

He assigned the church and manor of Wedmore with Mudgley and Mark and the rectory of Wookey to the office of the dean and also the manor of Litton and ordained that these estates managed by the dean for the time being should provide an income for the dean and for four canons. That there might always be a certain fund for the maintenance and repair of the fabric the manor of Biddisham was assigned to St. Andrew himself. Then Dulcote and Chilcott formed another prebend, and Wormstre, Wanstrow, and Bromfield or Bromley in the Quantocks three more. The manor of Winsham was sufficient for the endowment of five canons, and the manor of Combe St. Nicholas, which had been granted to Reginald for his lifetime, was assigned for five more canons. Whitchurch also, a tithing of Binegar, was the prebend of another canon.[20] To them the bishop added two more prebends from Yatton and Huish in Brent Marsh with the church of Compton Bishop, and King Stephen gave him for another two canons the manors of North Curry and Petherton.[21]

Thus at the very beginning Bishop Robert organized and endowed a dean and twenty-three canons, and Ivo he appointed in 1140 as the first dean. In 1157[22] Dean Ivo and his fellow canons obtained from Pope Adrian IV a confirmation of their possessions, and again in 1176[23] this was confirmed once more by Pope Alexander III.

Bishop Robert however did not forget the common fund which was to be equally enjoyed by those canons who resided in Wells. He gave to it the church of St. Cuthbert in Wells[24] and confirmed also an endowment from lands in North Wootton which had been made in the

time of Bishop Giso to the chapel of the blessed Virgin in the cathedral church.

Another institution, of the origin of which we have no documentary proof, was that of the canons' vicars which it is almost certain Bishop Robert instituted.[25] Any canon who was absent from Wells was bound at his own expense to provide a vicar who should take his place and perform his duties in the church.

As at Bath there was a confraternity of prayer so in Wells there was a fellowship of praise, the work in all probability of Bishop Robert. The Psalter was divided out to all the canons so that bishop and dean and all the officers and canons as members of one great body at Wells should among themselves daily recite the Psalter.[26] This division of the Psalter among the canons appears among the 'Antiqua Statuta' and must be assigned to the founder of the constitution of the church.

The work which Bishop Robert had begun was carried on by his successor Bishop Reginald (1174–91) and during his episcopate there flowed a steady stream of gifts for the needs of the church and a large increase of canons. King Richard confirmed to Bishop Reginald the endowments granted to him.[27] William de Camvilla had given the church of Henstridge[28] for a prebend, Oliver de Dinham the church of Buckland Dinham, near Frome,[29] William Fitz John the church of East Harptree,[30] William Fitz William the church of Haselbergh or Haslebury,[31] Hamon of Blackford the church of 'Scanderford,' or Shalford,[32] James of Mountsorel the church of White Lackington near Ilminster,[33] Ralph son of Bernard the church of Holcombe Rogus on the Devonshire border,[34] the three sisters with the consent of their husbands, Alicia, Christina and Sara the church of Timberscombe,[35] Alan de Fornellis the church of Cudworth with the chapel of Knowle,[36] and Ralph Fitz William the church of St. Dionysius at Warminster.[37] Then ten more prebends were founded and in addition prebends were founded which did not long survive. Gerbert de Perci gave the church of Chilcompton and Matilda Arundel the church of Broomfield,[38] Jocelin de Treminet the church of Awliscombe[39] in Devonshire and Robert de Bolevill the church of East Lydford,[40] four prebends which only lasted for a time.

The story of the formation of prebends to

20 *Cal. Wells D. and C. MSS.* (Hist. MSS. Com.) i, 33.
21 *Historiola de Wells* (Camden Soc. 1840), 25.
22 *Cal. Wells. D. and C. MSS.* i, 440.
23 Ibid. 438.   24 Ibid. 33.

25 Cf. Church, *Hist. of Wells*, 21.
26 Ibid. 20, cf. Reynolds, *Wells*, 69.
27 *Cal. Wells D. and C. MSS.* (Hist. MSS. Com.) i, 24-5.
28 Ibid. 20, 22.   29 Ibid. 69.
30 Ibid. 68.   31 Ibid. 493.   32 Ibid. 56.
33 Ibid. 44.   34 Ibid. 19.   35 Ibid. 46.
36 Ibid. 42.   37 Ibid. 58.
38 *Cal. Wells D. and C. MSS.* i, 27, 43.
39 Ibid. 55.   40 Ibid. 24.

be held by the Abbots of Glastonbury, Athelney and Muchelney and by the alien abbot of Bec has been already told.[41]

On the death of Bishop Savaric Jocelin Troteman, a native and canon of Wells, was elected his successor and was consecrated at Reading 12 May 1206. In a double sense he finished the work which his predecessors had begun.[42] He developed into completion the constitution which Bishop Robert had foreshadowed and he finished the church which Bishop Reginald had largely built. The instrument of his election shows that the organization was almost complete. It is signed by fifty-five priests [43] including the dean, precentor, chancellor, treasurer, sub-dean, succentor and the three archdeacons of Wells, Bath and Taunton. The archdeacons also have already taken up that position in the chapter which their successors to-day enjoy. As the representative of the original personal officer of the bishop and of him whom Bishop John de Villula had given charge over the church which he had himself forsaken the archdeacon of Wells takes the third place, following the dean and precentor and preceding the chancellor. To the other two archdeacons the honourable position is assigned immediately after the five dignitaries of the cathedral church, who became members of this chapter not as archdeacons but as holding prebends of the church.

The completion of the fabric could not have been entered on much before the year 1220. It was finished [44] and the church was dedicated on St. Romanus day, 1239, when in honour of St. Andrew Jocelin assigned the manor and church of Winscombe which he had received from Glastonbury in 1219 to the increase of the common fund of the cathedral.

During his episcopate there was a considerable increase of the number of canons. The church of Wiveliscombe [45] which Bishop Savaric had given to the common fund, Bishop Jocelin now made the prebend for another canon. Then Robert de Meisi gave to the bishop the church of Barton St. David and a moiety of the church of Nunney and this went to form a second prebend.[46] George Desfuble gave him the church of Easton in Gordano which became the prebend of a third canon.[47] In 1226 William Briwere gave the church of Milverton [48] and in 1241 [49] this was made the endowment of two prebends of which the former was definitely attached to the office of archdeacon of Taunton, as the prebend of Huish and Brent had been attached to the archdeaconry of Wells. In 1214 the monks of Bath were induced to surrender the church of Dogmersfield [50] to Bishop Jocelin and in 1215 he made of it another canonical prebend for the church of Wells. In the last year of his episcopate however Bishop Jocelin re-arranged the endowments for the dean; [51] Dogmersfield was added to the Wedmore and Mark estate and a fifth Wedmore canonry was created, the title of Dogmersfield disappearing. There was a considerable rearrangement also of the Combe St. Nicholas prebend. It had formed the endowment for five canons under Bishop Robert's arrangement and now in 1217 [52] it was wealthy enough to form the prebend of ten canons, and with the consent of the chapter Bishop Jocelin so decreed. The estate however was very large and since it was not part of the common fund its management devolved on the canons who enjoyed the revenues. Close by was the large manor of Winsham which had also been assigned for five canons in Bishop Robert's plan. So in 1234 [53] Bishop Jocelin united these two estates, making them the endowment of fifteen canons, and giving the prebend of one as the income of a provost who should manage these estates for his fourteen colleagues. The provost was to be a canon but was to be free from the service at Wells demanded from the others, and so in the 14th century [54] there arose a considerable controversy whether the provost of Combe was a canon and could claim as such entry into the chapter. This union makes us lose sight of Winsham, and the title Combe with its divisional number was given to all of the fifteen canons.

The greatest number of canons forming the chapter at Wells at any time was fifty-three, and we have still to record the creation of the canonries of Ashill, Taunton, Ilton and Dinder. Ashill was given to Bishop Jocelin by Alice Vaux,[55] and the advowson of Ilton was given to him by Robert Abbot of Athelney, and while the latter was made a canon's prebend in 1260 we find Ashill also a prebendal church as early as 1320.[56] Dinder Chapel was made prebendal in 1268 by decree of Bishop William Button II,[57] and Taunton was the title of a prebendal stall as early as 1360.[58]

The increase of the number of canons belonging to the chapter of Wells would have created some embarrassment had they all with their

---

[41] See above, 'Eccl. Hist.' pp. 16–18.

[42] *Cal. Wells D. and C. MSS.* i, 63.

[43] Cf. Wells D. and C. charters 39, 40, 41. The Abbots of Bec and Muchelney probably signed by their proxies.

[44] *Cal. Wells D. and C. MSS.* (Hist. MSS. Com.) i, 59.

[45] Ibid. 67.   [46] Ibid. 70.   [47] Ibid. 486.

[48] Ibid. 489.   [49] Ibid. 469.

[50] *Cal. Wells D. and C. MSS.* (Hist. MSS. Com.) i, 54.

[51] Ibid. 60.   [52] Ibid. 58.   [53] Ibid. 243.

[54] Cf. *R. of Shrewsbury's Reg.* (Somers. Rec. Soc. ix) p. lix.

[55] *Cal. Wells D. and C. MSS.* (Hist MSS. Com.) i, 42.

[56] Ibid. 43, 44.   [57] Ibid. 105.   [58] Ibid. 263.

vicars come to Wells to reside. We find Bishop Jocelin providing for this in the creation of a liberty or area of ground to the north of the cathedral church on which houses for the canons could be built ' free of secular demands.' In this matter Nicholas de Wells and Hugh de Wells were the chief benefactors [59] who through the bishop gave ground and houses for the residences of the canons ' before the great gate of the canons,' i.e. opposite to the north porch of the church.

In 1209 Bishop Jocelin made a decree [60] by which the income of the dean was to be made fitting to his increased responsibility. For this purpose he caused an exchange between the dean and sub-dean and assigned to the dean the church of Wedmore and its chapels and the church of Wookey to the sub-dean. The document seems to suggest that he had done much also for the other dignitaries, the precentor, chancellor, treasurer and succentor, by increasing their endowment in order to insist on their residence. We may clearly identify this work of Jocelin with the row of houses on the north of the cathedral green which originally were the houses of the treasurer, precentor, dean, chancellor and archdeacon of Wells. Soon after, in 1213,[61] he assigned to the dean and chapter the fruit of vacant canonries in the diocese and of vacant benefices as a fabric fund for the cathedral church while he reserved to himself the issues from the vacant dignitaries.[62]

In 1216 there is entered on the chapter register [63] an account of the method which Jocelin decreed for the election of a dean, who since the times of Ivo seems always to have been elected by the canons themselves, the canons and the dignitaries being chosen by the bishop.

In the last year of his episcopate Jocelin strove yet further to increase the common fund of the church and he laid down an increased scale of quotidians or daily allowances. The allowance for the bishop comes as the first on the list. The dean, precentor, archdeacon, chancellor and treasurer are referred to as the five parsons and they have quotidians alike. The other canons enjoyed half of such allowance. At the end of the year any surplus revenue was to be distributed among the five parsons and other resident canons, but only if the parsons had resided for two-thirds of the year and the other canons for a half year.

The vicars choral also now received daily quotidians and also a fixed money payment, but they were still apparently lodged where best they could find room. They were not however to lodge alone but were to live as much as possible together.

The duties of the chancellor included that of the training of the younger clergy and the preparation of youths who aspired to holy orders. There were two schools in Wells. The elementary school for instruction in plainsong was essential. The musical services of the church could not be carried on without it. There was also a school for grammar and ultimately for instruction in theology, and this latter was under the direct care of the chancellor. In 1235 [64] we find Roger, a canon of Wells, assigning his houses with the whole curtilage to the cathedral church for the use of the school provided that the chancellor for the time being shall confer the same on the schoolmaster.

Meanwhile the independence of the chapter was steadily growing. Edward de la Knoll like Jocelin Troteman was a native of Wells. He was Dean of Wells from 1256 to 1284. In 1259 [65] we have the first of a series of constitutional enactments made by the dean and canons towards their better self-government. In the preamble of this decree it is expressly stated that they were passed by the will and with the consent of William Button the bishop. But the chapter was taking the initiative. The time was passing away when everything had to wait for and depend on the leisure and will of the bishop. Again in 1273 [66] yet further statutes were passed concerning the vicars choral, and the four chief quarterly chapter meetings were fixed as audit days and the ordinal of the services was corrected of errors. Dean Knoll's successor Thomas de Bytton followed his example, and in 1286 [67] called together as large a chapter as possible to consider the restoration of the fabric and the completion of the new work of the chapter-house and the upper stages of the central tower. From that time onwards chapter meetings were summoned without reference to the bishop, and important building operations carried out on the initiative of the canons themselves. In the copy of the ancient statutes of the church [68] which was sent to Archbishop Laud at his request in 1634 by Dean Warburton and the then Chapter, reference is made to the Statutes drawn up in 1241 by Bishop Jocelin and afterwards to those drawn up by Dean Knoll in 1273 and Dean Haselshaw in 1295.[69] Self-government such as this was a clear proof of practical independence.

In the next century the chapter measured its strength with the bishop himself. Since the time of Reginald the issues of the vacant

---

[59] *Cal. Wells D. and C. MSS.* (Hist. MSS. Com.) i, 35.

[60] Ibid. 66.   [61] Ibid.

[62] Ibid. 530.   [63] Ibid. 65.

[64] *Cal. Wells D. and C. MSS.* (Hist. MSS. Com.) i, 35.

[65] Ibid. 141.   [66] Ibid. 530.

[67] Ibid. 237.

[68] Cf. Reynolds, *Wells Cathedral*, 57.

[69] *Cal. Wells D. and C. MSS.* i, 253–5. For these statutes, see Reynolds, *Wells Cath.* 57–68.

benefices in the diocese had been assigned to the fabric fund of the cathedral church. This special favour had been confirmed by several subsequent bishops, and Bishop Drokensford in 1321 [70] was made to realize that he had not power to withdraw it. His differences with the chapter referred not only to this financial question but also to the right of visitation. The dean claimed to exercise archidiaconal powers over the church of St. Cuthbert in Wells and over the churches that belonged to the common fund of the chapter. The prebendal churches were the peculiars of the canons holding the prebends formed out of their rectorial endowments, and Bishop Drokensford after some years of controversy yielded to the dean and chapter that the fruits of the vacant benefices in the diocese were to go to the fabric fund of the cathedral church and that he would not visit the churches of the canons except through the dean.

During the episcopate of Bishop Ralph of Shrewsbury (1329–63) the procedure of the episcopal visitation of the cathedral church began to take definite shape. The visitation was now distinctly formal. It must observe the rules and limitations which had been agreed on and it had to be done in person. This latter regulation was obviously desirable seeing that most of the bishop's officials were members of the chapter and as such pledged to obey the dean and chapter. On 13 September 1333 [71] Bishop Ralph met the canons, Dean Richard de Bury being absent, at the manor-house at Wookey. The canons seem to have resented some of his acts when on 31 July he had visited them and he promised them that he would recall any acts which seemed to have infringed their rights and in future would only visit the canons through the dean.[72]

During 1337 [73] there was a general visitation of the diocese and on 22 November 1337 the bishop sent notice to Dean Walter de London of his intention to visit the cathedral church. On the next day the bishop met the dean and canons in the chapter-house and the bishop began to make inquiry concerning the titles of the canons to their prebends. The canons, however refused to make any answer but claimed that they could only be visited through the dean and that he would answer for them. So they all then retired leaving the bishop in the chapter-house with Dean London and such canons as John de Carleton and others who were officials and familiars of the bishop. Dean London then consented [74] that the canons should

be made to show their titles and produced his own. To the bishop's questions concerning the appropriation of the church of Burnham [75] and to questions of defective books, vestments and ornaments he also replied and the bishop took note of what he had said.

On 15 December 1337 [76] the bishop collated Canon Simon de Bristol to the chancellorship of the cathedral church, laying down very definitely his duty to give or cause to be given lectures in theology or *in decretis* at the usual times that lectures were given in the University of Oxford. A fortnight afterwards Chancellor Bristol [77] refused to swear allegiance to the dean and chapter and asserted that as the bishop's officer he could not be compelled to obey.

Then on 5 September 1338 [78] Canon Carleton at a chapter meeting cited the dean and canons to appear before the bishop. On 30 October there was an informal gathering in the bishop's hall of the palace [79] where the bishop met the dean and chapter to discuss the points concerning which the chapter had appealed. The bishop promised to go to the chapter-house on the following Friday [80] and correct what was found amiss in his late visitation and to do nothing else. Then he went to the chapter-house and laid before the dean his injunctions. The church of Burnham had been appropriated for the fabric and must be so applied.[81] The books, vestments and ornaments were to be repaired by next Michaelmas. Dean Godelegh's statutes had been referred to and these were to be produced and of those the bishop would sanction such of which he approved. Canons and vicars were receiving the daily distribution though they were not present at Divine Offices. The canons were to be admonished to attend and the vicars to be punished for their absence. The statutes of Dean Godelegh had been drawn up by the dean and chapter in 1331 [82] and apparently had been quoted in the bishop's presence as authoritative without having been submitted to him for confirmation. However in 1339 Dean Walter de London went to Wookey where the bishop was and exhibited to him these statutes and the bishop does not seem to have greatly objected to them.

The claim of the dean and chapter seems to have been chiefly that the bishop should visit in person. It was insulting to them to be visited by one of their own canons acting as the bishop's commissary, and regardless of Bishop Drokensford's pledge Bishop Ralph seems to have used his officials in a way which annoyed the dean and chapter. Yet throughout in the correction of moral offences, as far as such duty

[70] *Drokensford's Reg.* (Somers. Rec. Soc. i), 191.

[71] *Cal. Wells D. and C. MSS.* i, 546.

[72] Cf. *R. of Shrewsbury's Reg.* (Somers. Rec. Soc. ix), 152.

[73] *Cal. Wells D. and C. MSS.* i, 539.

[74] Ibid. 541.

[75] *Cal. Wells D. and C. MSS.* i, 540.

[76] Ibid. 545.　[77] Ibid. 546.　[78] Ibid. 535.

[79] Ibid. 543.　[80] Ibid.　[81] Ibid. 540.

[82] Ibid. 532.

belonged peculiarly to his office, the bishop never seems to have hesitated to act through his commissary. It was his duty as bishop, which could not be restrained by any conditions of the dean and chapter, and when in 1342 [83] he punished certain altarists for various excesses and delinquencies he assured Dean London that the dean's jurisdiction in the church should remain unimpaired.

Two important steps were taken by Bishop Ralph and his successors Bishops John Harewell and Ralph Erghum to organize and place under stricter discipline the numerous priests in Wells who were serving as vicars of the canons or as chaplains attached to chapels in the cathedral church.

For the use of the vicars of the canons, who were now called the vicars choral to distinguish them from the other assistant priests in the cathedral, Bishop Ralph of Shrewsbury about 1354 [84] began to build a series of small houses to the north of the church. These houses with the refectory at the southern end, and the chapel which Bishop Bubwith built for them at the northern end, formed a long narrow quadrangle and in it fifty vicars were able to find houses. The executors of Bishop Beckington repaired many of these houses [85] and built over the chapel a chamber to form a library. Bishop Beckington himself in 1457 built the chain gateway and the passage over it leading by a series of steps from the cathedral to the refectory of the vicars. The vicars were thus able to go from their lodgings to the church without being able to wander into the town. They were now placed under the care of two senior priests and the college of vicars was effectually brought under discipline.

For the chantry priests and other chaplains Bishop John Harewell began a similar effort. About 1384 [86] he purchased a house in the market-place known as 'Cristesham ynn' in which he placed as many as there was room for. A few years later Bishop Erghum (1388–1400) and the dean and chapter began a larger building to the north of the Liberty to which the name of the New College was given and here the chantry priests were lodged.

The history of the cathedral and deanery of Wells during the troubled period of the Reformation has already been dealt with. [87]

On the final establishment of the Reformed Church under Elizabeth a question arose as to the relationship of the new dean to the old chapter. The dean and chapter for several centuries had formed an ecclesiastical corporation. Did the new dean and the old chapter constitute the old corporation ? The Private Act of 1547 had created a dean who should preside in the chapter. There were doubts however and the chapter was compelled to apply to the Crown for a settlement of this question. The College of Vicars Choral had been reorganized and had obtained a charter confirming to the vicars the rights which their predecessors had enjoyed. The vicars were giving trouble to the dean and chapter and it was mooted that the dean and chapter had no legal power to compel obedience, as they did not form the old corporation of earlier days. On 25 November 1591 [88] therefore at the petition of the Dean and canons of Wells Queen Elizabeth granted a charter of official interpretation. The new dean and the old chapter continued the old corporation. The deanery was now in the patronage of the Crown, but the affairs of the chapter and of the cathedral church were to be regulated by the dean and chapter or the major part of them. So it had ever been and so it was to continue to be. What the Crown had done was merely to deprive the canons of Wells of their right to elect their dean. In all other respects he was as his predecessors.

The charter of Queen Elizabeth however created a new governing body. The affairs of the church were placed in the hands of a new body consisting of the dean and eight residentiary canons. To this body were committed all the estates of the church as well as complete authority over its affairs. The voice of the non-resident canon was silenced except for the election of a bishop. Vacancies in this body, which naturally called itself the dean and chapter, were to be filled by co-option from the body of non-resident canons. If the duties of the dignitaries such as those of the precentor, chancellor and treasurer might remain to them, because the endowments were still theirs, yet the authority which alone could make the performance of those duties effective was now withdrawn. It rested only with the new corporation known as that of the dean and chapter. The number of residentiary canons which at first was fixed at eight, was in the 18th century reduced to six and after 1837 yet further reduced to four, and that is the number which at present exists.

The charter of 1591 has nothing to say of the bishop and his authority in his cathedral church. To him belonged the patronage of all the non-residentiary canons and of the dignitaries, but the residentiaries were co-opted solely by this new corporation. It was possible therefore that the chapter might not contain a single dignitary except the dean. The bishop had always used these dignitaries in the work of the diocese to hold commissions of inquiry or as his vicars general and commissaries and

---

[83] *Cal. Wells D. and C. MSS.* (Hist. MSS. Com.) i, 537.
[84] *Cal. Wells D. and C. MSS.* i, 379.
[85] Ibid. 502. [86] Ibid. 442.
[87] See above, 'Eccl. Hist.' pp. 36, 37.
[88] Reynolds, *Wells Cathedral*, 243.

therefore it was to his interest that at least most of them should reside in Wells. During the 17th century there were often disagreements between the bishop and the dean and chapter in reference to this co-option. The bishop contended that because a man was a dignitary the dean and chapter should prefer him first of all if a vacancy in their body existed, and the dean and chapter contended that if such was the case then their co-option would be a mere form since the bishop had already marked out the man they should choose. The bitter ill-feeling between Bishop Kidder and the chapter in 1695 [89] arose in reference to the vacancy which Dr. Busby's death had caused, the chapter wishing to show their feeling towards the supplanter of Dr. Ken by choosing one whom Bishop Kidder had not made a dignitary.

The question of the visitation of the cathedral by the bishop also entered on a new phase. Bishop Barlow in 1550 had incurred the penalties of Præmunire because he had visited the dean and chapter, the dean being now the nominee of the Crown. However the church was visited in 1592 by Archbishop Whitgift and on 17 June 1594 [90] the dean and chapter decreed—'quod dominus episcopus si in persona sua propria præsens fuerit comperta in visitatione sua vocet et audiat in domo capitulari.'

On 14 July 1692 [91] Bishop Kidder held his primary visitation of the dean and chapter in the chapter-house. He exhibited to them his articles of inquiry and on 23 August the dean and chapter returned answers to them. During the 18th century the bishops rarely visited the cathedral church and in the 19th century never. It cannot be said that there is any longer need for such visitations as the former bishops had held, since all appropriations of benefices had ceased and the estates of their endowment are managed by the Ecclesiastical Commissioners. The co-option ceased in 1879; and the bishop now collates to the prebendal stalls except that of the Dean and also to the right to come into residence. The *jus episcopale* has never been questioned, and any controversy of to-day can only refer to the right of the bishop of the diocese to assume the position which he has not claimed for centuries, of being himself the head of the chapter of his cathedral church. Such a claim is certainly barred by the Elizabethan charter.

DEANS OF WELLS

Ivo, 1159 [92]
Richard de Spakeston, 1160–74 [93]

Alexander, 1180–1204 [94]
Leonius, 1213 [95]
Ralph de Lechlade, 1217 [96]
Peter de Cicester, 1220 [97]
William de Merton, 1237 [98]
John Saracenus, 1250 [99]
Giles de Bridport, 1256 [100]
Edward de la Knoll, 1264, 1284 [101]
Thomas de Bytton, 1284–92 [102]
William Burnell, 1292 [103]
Walter de Haselshaw, 1295 [104]
Henry Husee, 1302 [105]
John de Godelegh, 1305 [106]
Richard de Bury, 1332 [107]
Wibert de Lyttleton, 1334 [108]
Walter de London, 1335–50 [109]
John de Carleton, 1351–60 [110]
Stephen de Pempel, 1361–79 [111]
John Fordham, 1379–81 [112]
Thomas Sudbury, 1381–89 [113]
Nicholas Slake, 1398 [114]
Thomas Tuttebury, 1400 [115]
Thomas Stanley, 1401–10 [116]
Richard Courtenay, 1410–13 [117]
Walter Medford, 1414 [118]
John Stafford, 1423–5 [119]
John Forrest, 1425–46 [120]
Nicholas Carent, 1446–67 [121]
William Witham, 1469–72 [122]
John Gunthorp, 1472–98 [123]
William Cousyn, 1498–1525 [124]
Thomas Winter, 1526 [125]
Richard Woolman, 1529–37 [126]
Thomas Cromwell, 1537–40 [127]
William Fitz James or Fitz William, 1540–8 [128]
John Goodman, 1548–50, 1553–7 [129]
William Turner, 1550–3, 1560–8 [130]
Robert Weston, 1570–3 [131]
Valentine Dale, 1574–89 [132]

[89] Cf. MS. Biography of Bishop Kidder, *penes* D. and C.
[90] Chapter Act Book.
[91] MS. Biography of Bishop Kidder, *penes* D. and C. cap. 12.
[92] *Cal. Wells. D. and C. MSS.* i, 27.
[93] Ibid. 19.

[94] *Cal. Wells D. and C. MSS.* i, 90–110.
[95] Ibid. 53, 54.
[96] Ibid. 491.
[97] Ibid. 29, 37.
[98] Ibid. 28, 35.
[99] Ibid. 60.
[100] Ibid. 135, 138.
[101] Ibid. 99, 106.
[102] Ibid. 151.
[103] Ibid. 149.
[104] Ibid. 220.
[105] Ibid. 170.
[106] Ibid. 176.
[107] Ibid. 232, 235.
[108] Ibid. 235, 236.
[109] Ibid. 238, 246.
[110] Ibid. 263, 411.
[111] Ibid. 270.
[112] Ibid. 282–4.
[113] Ibid. 302–4.
[114] Ibid. 356.
[115] *Bowet's Reg.* (Som. Rec. Soc. xiii), 16.
[116] *Cal. Wells D. and C. MSS.* 446, 469.
[117] Ibid. 441.
[118] Wells Epis. Reg. Bulwith.
[119] *Cal. Wells D. and C. MSS.* i, 470.
[120] Ibid. 329, 468.
[121] Ibid. 464–66.
[122] Ibid. 407, 502.
[123] Ibid. 464, 481
[124] *Hist. MSS. Com. Rep.* x, App. iii, 146.
[125] Wells Epis. Reg. Clerk & Chap. Min. Bks.
[126] *Hist. MSS. Com. Rep.* x, App. iii, 224.
[127] Ibid. 224, 225.
[128] Ibid. 228.
[129] Ibid. 271.
[130] Ibid. 240.
[131] *Athenæ Oxonienses.*
[132] Chapter Minute Books.

John Herbert, 1589–1602 [133]
Benjamin Heydon, 1602–6 [134]
Richard Meredith, 1607–21 [135]
Ralph Barlow, 1621–31 [136]
George Warburton, 1631–41 [137]
Walter Raleigh, 1641–6 [138]
Robert Creyghton, 1660–70 [139]
Ralph Bathurst, 1670–1704 [140]
William Graham, 1704–12 [141]
Matthew Brailsford, 1713–33 [142]
Isaac Maddox, 1733–6 [143]

John Harris, 1736–8 [144]
Samuel Creswick, 1739–66 [145]
Francis Seymour, 1766 [146]
George William Lukin, 1799–1812 [147]
Henry Ryder, 1812–31 [148]
Edmund Goodenough, 1831–45 [149]
Richard Jenkins, 1845–54 [150]
George Henry Sacheverell Johnson, 1854–81 [151]
Edward Hayes Plumptre, 1881–91 [152]
Thomas William Jex-Blake, 1891– [153]

ALIEN HOUSE

40. THE PRIORY OF STOGURSEY

The priory of Stogursey, or, as it should more correctly be called, Stoke Courcy, was an alien priory, an offshoot of the Benedictine Abbey of Lonlay in Normandy. It never became denizen and after the great war with France it was suppressed and its estates used for the endowment of the College of St. Mary of Eton. It arose out of a grant[1] made in the time of Henry I by William de Falaise and Geva his wife of the church of St. Andrew of Stoke to the church of St. Mary of Lonlay, 4 miles north-west of Domfront in Normandy.

This grant of William de Falaise was confirmed by Bishop Robert of Bath and must therefore be anterior to 1160. It included the tithes of the parish of Stoke,[2] two parts of the tithes of Williton, two parts of those of Lilstock, the whole tithes of 'Tientons' a church in Wales and the tithes of Tregnu there. This last gift however is said to have been made by Robert, son of William de Falaise. We also find Anketill the son of Herbert and Bencellina his wife[3] giving certain lands at Monkton and Honibere in Stoke parish to the monks of St. Andrew of Stoke and to their chapel of St. John the Evangelist adjoining the said parish of St. Andrew.

In 1204 Innocent III[4] confirmed to the prior and monks of St. Andrew, Stoke, the churches of Wootton, Lilstock, Holford and 'Kichestoh,' or Idstock, two parts of the tithes of Corniton,

the whole of one inclosure at Combe, two parts of the tithes at Williton, two parts of the tithes at Lilstock, the right they possessed in the chapelry of the Castle at Stoke, the land of Tinelands, land at Breche with a new mill,[5] the patronage of the church of "Traiyn" in Wales, in Ireland all the churches and benefices of the lordship of John de Curci in Ulster except the castle of Maincove, ten carucates of land in Ardes, that is in the land of Maccolochan; in Dalboing in Hailo, that is the town and church of Arderashac and ten carucates of land and in Kinelmolan three carucates of land.

In the *Taxatio* of 1291, the priory is entered as an alien priory and in possession of the churches of Stogursey and Lilstock worth £30 yearly, a portion of the church at Wootton in the deanery of Dunster, a pension in the church of East Quantoxhead in the deanery of Bridgwater and *temporalia* in Stogursey and Charlton worth £4 2s. 6d.

In 1270 Bishop William Button II of Bath and Wells[7] cited Robert Abbot of Lonlay and late prior of Stoke Courcy to appear and answer a charge of maladministration of the property of the priory, sending various sums of money across the sea and burdening the foundation at Stoke with corrodies. For the sake of economy the bishop sent off to Lonlay three of the monks of Stoke to stay in the Norman abbey until an improvement in the condition of the priory estates allowed of their return. These corrodies were a constant source of trouble in all monasteries.

In 1309 Peter Abbot of Lonlay recalled

[133] Chapter Minute Books. In charter Eliz. 1592 the name appears as Harbert.
[134] Ibid. [135] Camden, *Annales.*
[136] Chapter Minute Books.
[137] Bishop's Certificate.
[138] Walker, *Sufferings of the Clergy,* 71.
[139] Bishop's Certificate. [140] Ibid.
[141] Church Book, Home Office. [142] Ibid.
[143] Bishop's Certificate.
[1] Stoke Cartulary, Eton College MSS.
[2] Ibid. [3] Ibid.
[4] *Cal. Papal Letters,* i. 17.

[144] Bishop's Certificate. [145] Ibid. [146] Ibid.
[147] Chapter Minute Books.
[148] Bishop's Certificate.
[149] Chapter Minute Books. [150] Ibid.
[151] Ibid. [152] Ibid. [153] Ibid.
[5] The mill is that at Norham called Mervine's mill and was given by William de Curci. Stoke Cartul. Eton Coll. MSS. charter 6.
[6] *Pope Nich. Tax* (Rec. Com.), 198, 200.
[7] Stoke Cartul. Eton Coll. MSS.

Prior Vincent Tybout and presented to Bishop Drokensford [8] Peter de Grana for institution as prior. The bishop's official however reported that the recall of Prior Tybout without the consent of the diocesan was irregular. Ultimately we find that Grana was received and confirmed as prior.

Seven years afterwards Prior Peter [9] died and the abbey of Lonlay presented Giles Roussee a Frenchman. Bishop Drokensford thereupon ordered a commission of inquiry which returned that Roussee was properly presented and that the priory of Stoke was endowed with the churches of Stoke Courcy, Lilstock and the sinecure chapel of Durborough and that Roussee was a priest, forty years of age and of good conversation. So Giles Roussee became prior in July 1316. The appointment however was unfortunate. The new prior had no idea of economy and Bishop Drokensford, on application from Sir Robert Fitz Payne lord of the burgh of Stoke Courcy, sent down a commissioner to examine into the affairs of the house. The result of this commission was that the bishop in 1326[10] was obliged to write to the Abbot of Lonlay to say that he found the priory impoverished, the prior and one monk, with some servants and useless folk, alone residing there and other monks living lecherously abroad. He also decreed that the sinning monks were to be sent back to Lonlay and no others were to be sent in their room until, by the bishop's and the patron's assistance, the affairs of Stoke were improved. In 1328[11] Roussee was recalled as a wasteful administrator and Godfrey de Duc was sent as his successor. Bishop Drokensford on instituting him insisted on an oath to keep perpetual residence, and the three monks of the house swore obedience to their new prior.

The Crown however had already for some years past been active in limiting the power of these alien priories and stopping the impoverishment of English estates for the benefit of French abbeys, and in consequence Bishop Ralph of Shrewsbury was obliged to look carefully after the alien priory of Stoke. In 1334[12] he proceeded against Prior Godfrey for dilapidation of the goods of the priory and summoned him to appear before him and answer to this charge. Godfrey in reply appealed to Canterbury and the pope and the archbishop appointed the Abbot of Athelney and the rural dean of Taunton to inhibit the bishop from proceeding until the appeal had been heard. But the pope at that time was helpless to protect a French priory and the appeal to Canterbury failed, so Bishop Ralph [13] was able to take the necessary steps to

protect the goods of the priory and place the buildings in fitting repair.

On 6 December 1341 [14] the prior was summoned before the Council and in March of the next year [15] we find Thomas Provost mentioned as the prior and to him was then committed the farm of the priory for £30 a year to be paid to the Crown and he was relieved of all share in the tenths and fifteenths that might be exacted so long as the priory lands were in the king's hands.

There seems to have been some reason for the frequent change of priors in the 14th century and perhaps it was an attempt on the part of the French abbey to gain profit by the new creations. In 1350[16] William Hodierne a monk of Lonlay was sent in place of Thomas Provost, and two years later Hodierne had been recalled and John Gallardi had been sent.

In 1402 Bishop Bowett [17] appointed Richard Amys prior of Stoke as curate and custos of the parish church of Stoke Courcy on account of the age and infirmity of William Horton the perpetual vicar of Stoke.

Amys had been prior for some years, for in 1388 [18] as such he had produced a terrier of the possessions of the priory. This seems to have been a step towards the dissolution of the house. As early as 1347 Edward III had acted as patron of the churches [19] belonging to the priory, appointing to them as vacancies occurred and the monastic property was let on a yearly rent to the prior for the time being.

In 1399 [20] Richard Amys was recognized as prior when the temporalities were provisionally restored and in 1403 [21] an entry exists of the lease of the priory lands to Robert Vise, *monachus*, and Walter Sergeant for £25 6s. 8d. ' pro custodia prioratus de Stoke Curcy aliagenæ.'

The process of dissolution had now begun. On 18 February 1438 [22] John Chinall, king's esquire, received from the Crown a grant of £20 a year out of the issues of the alien priory of Stoke and in 1439 [23] there is a record of £25 a year paid from the same source to Humphrey, Duke of Gloucester. On 11 October of the next year, 1440, we have a statement of the endowments of the new college of St. Mary at Eton. The estates and the advowsons of the priory of Stoke

[8] *Drokensford's Reg.* (Somers. Rec. Soc. i), 27.
[9] Ibid. 8, 9.   [10] Ibid. 261.
[11] Ibid. 287.
[12] *R. of Shrewsbury's Reg.* (Somers. Rec. Soc. ix), 174.
[13] Ibid. 182.

[14] *Cal. Close*, 1341–3, p. 358.
[15] Ibid. p. 488.
[16] *Somers. Rec. Soc. Publ.* x, 616.
[17] *Bowet's Reg.* (Somers. Rec. Soc. xiii), 30.
[18] Esch. Rolls, 49 Edw. III. p. 2 n. 4, pt. ii.
[19] *R. of Shrewsbury's Reg.* (Somers. Rec. Soc. x), 548.
[20] Rymer, *Fœdera*, viii, 104 ; *Cal. Pat.* 1399–1401, p. 71.
[21] Recorda de Termino St. Mich. 6 Hen. IV.
[22] *Cal. Pat.* 1436–41, p. 140.
[23] Ibid. p. 304.

Courcy are among the grants.[24] The house had clearly ceased to exist.

Robert Vise however still remained and in 1442 [25] he is mentioned as prior and as rector or custos of the parish church of Stoke Courcy cited John Vernay of Fairfield, a layman of the diocese of Bath and Wells, before the Archbishop of Canterbury to answer a complaint that at the time of High Mass in the parish church of Stoke after the vicar's sermon, he (John Vernay) had preached to the people in English using opprobrious terms and calling on the people to obey him rather than the prior or the vicar.

PRIORS OF STOKE COURCY.

Geoffrey [26]
Gerin d'Alençon, occurs 1175 [27]

G., occurs 1219 [28]
Vincent, occurs 1260 [29]
Robert, occurs 1270 [30]
Vincent Tybout, recalled 1309 [31]
Peter de Grana, appointed 1309,[32] died 1316
Giles Roussee, appointed 1316, recalled 1328 [33]
Godfrey de Duc, 1328 [34]
Thomas Provost, occurs 1342 [35]
William Hodierne, appointed 1350 [36]
John Gallardi, appointed 1352 [37]
Richard Amys, occurs 1376 (?) 1402 [38]
Robert Vise, occurs 1405–42 [39]

[24] Pat. 19 Hen. VI. pt viii, m. 20. The details of the sequestration are given in Bishop Beckington's Register, fol. 12.
[25] *Hist. MSS. Com. Rep.* ix, App. i, 355a.
[26] Stoke Courcy Cartul. Eton College MSS.
[27] Ibid.

[28] *Cal. Wells D. and C. MSS.* (Hist. MSS. Com.) i, 367.
[29] Stoke Courcy Cartul. Eton College MSS, last entry but one.   [30] Ibid.
[31] *Somers. Rec. Soc. Publ.* i, 27.
[32] Ibid.   [33] Ibid. 8, 9.   [34] Ibid. 287.
[35] *Cal. Close*, 1341–3, p. 488.
[36] *R. of Shrewsbury's Reg.* (Somers. Rec. Soc. x), 616.
[37] Ibid.
[38] *Bowet's Reg.* (Somers. Rec. Soc. xiii), 30; *Cal. Pat.* 1399–1401, p. 71.
[39] Court R. 6 Hen. III; Stoke Courcy Cartul. Eton College MSS; Wells Epis. Reg. Beckington. fol. 12.

POLITICAL HISTORY

THE political history of Somerset, like that of every county, has been largely influenced by its geographical position and peculiarities, and this in two special ways.

In the first place, Somerset, along with the North and the rest of the West of England, has always been among the most backward to acknowledge changes or to leave the paths of its forefathers. Not only did the waves of invasion sweeping over Britain from the east gradually drive those who were previously in possession into the west, but the waves of thought coming in their turn from London and the eastern counties penetrated but slowly to the west. Risings in the west in support of causes overthrown in the east have proved how deeply such feelings are rooted there.

In the second place, the geographical peculiarities of Somerset have told largely on its history. From this point of view it has no homogeneity. The country around Bath, rising irregularly from the basin of the Avon to the Mendip Hills, is by its natural features correlated with Gloucestershire, and as a result has often shared in the fortunes of that county. To the south-west of the Mendips stretched the marsh and bog through which flow the Yeo, the Axe, the Brue, the Parrett and the Tone. Once made fit for human habitation by drainage this district, owing to the water power it supplied, became the home of a population largely composed of small manufacturers, whose political faith generally coincided with that of the eastern shires : discord of opinion was thus added to natural diversities. Beyond this tract rise the heathy uplands which cover the western corner of the county, in close relation to the neighbouring county of Devon.

Very little is known of the early formation of the county boundaries, and those which were in existence at the time of the Domesday Survey remained unchanged until 1844. Dr. Guest thought that the earliest boundary was the line between Longleat and Stourhead, but he founded his opinion on the identification of 'Mons Badonicus' with Badbury Rings : it cuts right through the parishes of Maiden Bradley and Mere,[1] but it is not safe to assume that it is therefore older than the parochial divisions. There is also evidence that in 676 Bath was not included in the county, as in that year Osric king of the Hwiccas founded Bath Nunnery and endowed it with 100 hides.[2] It is impossible to deduce from this however the amount of the modern county then outside Wessex, as when Domesday Book was compiled Bath Abbey held only 47 hides in Bath Hundred.[3] The dependence of the abbey was

---

[1] *Somerset and Dorset Notes and Queries* i, 3.   [2] Kemble. *Cod. Dipl.* i, no. 12.

[3] *Dom. Bk.* fol. 89 D. Eyton, *Dom. Bk. Studies, Somerset* i, 103. Professor Maitland thought that Osric most probably ' gave away the " hundred " of Bath : he gave Bath itself and a territory which in the eleventh century was the site of a dozen villages.' *Dom. Bk. and Beyond* 229, 501.

transferred in 781 from the see of Worcester to the see of Sherborne,[4] so that Bath was presumably included in Somerset not later than that year.

Of the history of the boundary between Somerset and Dorset we know practically nothing. For a mile west of Chard it follows an ancient road: from Yeovil towards Crewkerne it looks like a defensive line, and from Calebridge towards Yeovil, for about thirteen miles as the crow flies, it is identical with the boundary of the possessions of the see of Sherborne, created in 705.[5]

The changes in the 19th century deducted upwards of 5,000 acres from the county. On 20 October, 1844, the parish of Holwell, including Buckshaw tithing, was taken into Dorset.[6] On 31 March, 1896, the boundary was again altered so as to include in Dorset Goathill,[7] Poyntington,[8] Sandford Orcas,[9] Seaborough,[10] and Trent.[11] On the other hand Dorset transferred to Somerset the parish of Wambrook.[12] Finally, in 1897, Kilmington was transferred to Wilts, and Churchstanton taken from Dorset. Since then the boundary has remained unchanged.

In spite of its remote position every recurrent wave of invasion which swept over Britain reached Somerset. The aboriginal inhabitants first suffered at the hands of the Goidels, who in turn were followed by the Brythons. Of these branches of the Celtic race the latter left a far stronger mark on the peninsula than the former, for the Celtic spoken there was Brythonic. The Belgae probably penetrated only into the north-east corner of the county and colonized the country around Bath, but of all these early invaders hardly anything is known: we reach firmer ground with the Roman occupation: this has been fully dealt with elsewhere, and we can pass on at once to the Teutonic invasion.

We may shortly say that the West-Saxon conquest consisted in a series of advances followed by checks and periods of settlement; the Saxon Chronicle, on which all other accounts are based, provides a very slender foundation on which to build; its earlier chronology is admittedly artificial, and it is very doubtful whether the leaders whose doings it relates during the early period ever existed.[13] Of other early authorities Ethelweard had reliable sources of information due to his position as ealdorman of Wessex. Henry of Huntingdon occasionally seems to have other trustworthy sources of information and tradition, and William of Malmesbury had authorities for Athelstan's reign not open to others, but the bulk of their information was derived from the Chronicle and lies under the same suspicion.

According to the authorities the first advance of the Gewissae was begun in 495 and lasted until 519; the second, begun in 527, ended with

---

[4] Kemble, op. cit. i, no. 143.   Somerset was included in the see of Sherborne until 909.

[5] *Somers. and Dors. N. and Q.* i, 6.   At the request of William of Wykeham the boundary between Taunton and Cheristaunton in Devon was defined in Feb. 1386. *Cal. of Pat.* 1385–9, pp. 107, 108.

[6] Under 2 and 3 Will. IV, cap. 64 and 7 and 8 Vict. cap. 61.   It contained 2,423 acres, 92 houses and 388 population.

[7] 298 acres, 10 houses, 51 population.   [8] 1,020 acres, 25 houses, 125 population.

[9] 1,104 acres, 50 houses, 202 population.   [10] 585 acres, 13 houses, 59 population.

[11] 1,618 acres, 88 houses, 354 population.   [12] 1,867 acres, 44 houses, 201 population.

These transfers were under 58 and 59 Vict. cap. 91.

[13] Cf. H. Howorth, 'The Beginnings of Wessex,' *Engl. Hist. Rev.* 1898; W. H. Stevenson, ibid. 1899.

the battles of Old Sarum (552) and Beranburh [14] (556), and was followed by the colonization of Salisbury Plain. If the exploits of Arthur, whose name is generally associated with Somerset, have some foundation in the history of Wessex, the resistance which the Gewissae had to overcome between 500 and 516, and which culminated in their defeat at 'Mons Badon,' was due probably to a Romano-British commander, such as he appears to have been. [15]

The energies of the West-Saxons were for a time deflected to conquests along the Thames and northwards to Bedford, but in 577 they wheeled south-west again and 'slew three kings, Conmail, and Condidan, and Farinmail, at the place which is called Deorham,' [16] taking from them Gloucester, Cirencester and Bath. [17] It has been conjectured that the district thus conquered included only that part of modern Somerset which lies north of the Axe. This theory however rests on the idea that the Forest of Selwood formed an insuperable barrier to the West-Saxon advance; but since it was traversed by a Roman road, there seems no reason to think that the Saxons were as materially hindered by it as this theory implies, or that they would allow a long strip of land running right into the heart of their settlement to remain in the hands of the Britons. The southern boundary has been still more illogically fixed at the Axe on the theory that they would insist on obtaining possession of the lead mines on the Mendips, but the mines seem to have been at that time deserted. [18] Whatever the extent of their new conquest in Somerset may have been, it seems to have been colonized by the main stock of the West-Saxons, while the territory in Gloucestershire and Worcestershire was settled by an offshoot, the Hwiccas. [19]

The battle of Deorham has been generally fixed on as marking an epoch in the conquest. It is important because the separation between the Celts of Wales and of Dyvnaint which it effected made the conquest of the south-west peninsula merely a matter of time, since co-operation between them was no longer possible. Further, 'an age of settlement' is supposed to follow 'a war of extermination,' and when advances are again made the conquerors are content to settle down among the conquered without slaughtering or driving them off. How far the previous advances had been wars of extermination is doubtful, but in the case of Somerset there seems very fair evidence in support of the theory that the Saxons became more and more content to leave the Britons on the soil. The greater proportion of Britons west of the Parrett may be testified to by the pronunciation of Saxon words with a British accent, especially of the initial W as OO; e.g. Ools for Wells. [20] Corroborative evidence is also found in the hidation of the

---

[14] Identified as Banbury, or as Barbury Camp between Marlborough and Swindon : both are doubtful.

[15] Cf. Nennius, who says he fought with the kings of the Britons against the Saxons, but was himself 'Dux Bellorum.'

[16] Identified as Dyrham between Gloucester and Bath.

[17] *Angl.-Sax. Chron.* (Rolls Ser.) ann. cit.

[18] Stevenson, loc. cit.

[19] Ramsay, *Foundations of England* i, 127. Cf. Freeman *Old Engl. Hist.* 36. Cf. *The Primaeval British Metropolis*, pp. 45–7 for the theory that Somerset was entered by the line now taken by the London and South Western Railway, the Britons being defeated at Poyntington and driven along the valley of the Camel and Yeo as far as Langport.

[20] *Somers. Arch. Soc. Proc.* xviii. Introduction to a Somerset Glossary. Mr. Elworthy however (*Dialect of West Somers.* [Engl. Dialect Soc.], 6) does not think this peculiarity is connected with the termination of the Saxon advance.

county. This has been worked out by Mr. Baring, who found that the scale of rating changes as we cross the county: he divided Somerset into five groups, the first representing the advance as far as the upper Parrett, the second up to 682, the third to 710, and the two last still later conquests. In each successive conquest the hides are fewer in proportion to the team-lands; in the eastern division there are 1,241 hides and 1,327 teamlands; in the most western 137 hides and 510 team-lands.[21]

The next West-Saxon advance in Somerset did not take place for nearly two hundred years, the tribe being engaged in hostilities elsewhere.

The first battle in the new forward movement is said by the Chronicle to have taken place at Bradford[22] in 652; this was followed six years after by the battle of Penn,[23] which drove the Britons across the Parrett; from this time forward Wessex is supposed to have included all modern Somerset up to that river, but most of the newly won territory was low-lying marsh land, which for long can hardly have been a valuable acquisition.[24]

During the period which followed Wessex touched the nadir of her fortunes, being subdivided among petty kings. Centwine indeed drove the Brito-Welsh 'as far as the sea' (682), but it was not until Ceadwalla became supreme (*circa* 685) that unity once more brought strength. His successor Ine was one of the strongest West-Saxon kings, who after extending his conquest eastwards as far as Thanet, successfully waged war against Geraint, king of the Welsh. This victory added both prestige and territory to the West-Saxons. Geraint in Teutonic ages was a person of great importance and power,[25] and the victory not only gave Ine enlarged boundaries but provided an admirable site on which to erect a fortress, Taunton, which both defended his possessions from the Britons and was an excellent base for fresh attack when the time should come for renewed aggressions. His original fortress did not however last long, for in the civil war at the end of his reign one of the rebel Ethelings, Ealdbehrt, having seized it, Ine's queen Ethelburh took it and destroyed it, forcing Ealdbehrt to fly to Sussex.[26] With Ine's victory the last section of what is now Somerset passed into West-Saxon hands, and was no doubt quickly colonized by the tribe. It has indeed been suggested that in certain provisions of Ine's laws[27] we read of something like 'a plantation of some parts of Somerset effected by means of allotments made to the king's gesiths who undertake to put tillers on the soil,' and that this may have been a new arrangement since 'the settlement of a heathen folk loosely banded together under a war-lord was one thing; the conquest of a new province by a Christian king who . . . had already been taught that he had land to book would be another.'[28]

---

[21] 'The Hidation of some Southern Counties,' *Engl. Hist. Rev.* 1899. Cf. Maitland, *Dom. Bk. and Beyond*, 436–43.

[22] Identification uncertain.

[23] Kerslake identifies Penn with Poyntington: Earle, Freeman and Ramsay with Penselwood; the latter adds, perhaps one of the Mendips; *Somers. Arch. and Nat. Hist. Proc.* L (2), 64.

[24] Cf. Henry of Huntingdon, *Hist. Angl.* (Rolls Ser.), 60 '. . . et fugati sunt a Pennum usque ad Pedredan; et facta est super progeniem Bruti plaga insanabilis in die illa.'

[25] Cf. Haddan and Stubbs, *Councils*, iii, 268 '. . . domino gloriosissimo occidentalis regni sceptra gubernanti.'

[26] *Angl.-Sax. Chron.* (Rolls Ser.) i, 72; Flor. Wigorn. *Chron.* (Engl. Hist. Soc.); Hen. Hunt. *Hist. Angl.* (Rolls Ser.), 112.

[27] Thorpe, op. cit. nos. 63–8.　　　　　　　　　[28] Maitland, *Dom. Bk. and Beyond*, 367.

Hardly had one set of invaders thus consolidated their power than England became a prey to a fresh series of descents on her shores, at the hands of the Danes and Norwegians. Their first invasion took place in Beorhtric's days.[29] Somerset was not attacked until 845, when the Chronicle tells us that ' Aldorman Eanulf with the men of Somerset, and Bishop Ealhstan and the Aldorman Osric with the men of Dorset, fought at the mouth of the Parret against the Danish army and there made great slaughter, and gained the victory.' The struggles with the Danes continued, but Somerset lay outside the seat of war until 879. At the end of the previous year Alfred had gone into winter quarters at Chippenham, but the Danes made a sudden dash from Exeter where they were encamped, and defeated and dispersed the English forces. All submitted according to the Chronicle, but Alfred, who retired to the ' woods and moor-fastnesses ' : the next place where he is definitely heard of is Athelney.[30]

From the time of this defeat until Easter (which in this year fell on 23 March) his fortunes were at their lowest ebb ; he retreated from Chippenham on the upper waters of the Avon in Gloucestershire to Athelney, where two acres of ground rising from the fens made, according to William of Malmesbury, an inaccessible island.

It was probably because his consistent successes had given him so high a reputation that this retreat made such an impression on his contemporaries. The author of the Saxon life seems to voice nothing short of panic when he says that Alfred ' for fear took to flight and forsook all his warriors and his captains and all his people, and crept by hedge and lane through wood and field till he came to Athelney.' This is undoubtedly the language of exaggeration, but if we remember how small his following was,[31] and how wild and difficult the country through which he withdrew, we may well believe that at times he had none of the necessaries of life except those which he obtained by forage,[32] and that his whereabouts might be uncertain even to his followers.[33] Without subscribing to the stories, e.g. of the cakes, we need not be too sceptical where the results of the crushing blow at Chippenham are concerned.

Alfred seems to have retreated steadily until the defeat of the Danes in Devonshire ; encouraged by that event he fortified Athelney and resumed operations.[34] At first he had the support only of his own followers and ' the men of Somerset that was nearest,'[35] and seems to have led them in a series of raids. But in the seventh week after Easter he felt himself strong enough to take the offensive more seriously, and riding to ' Ecgbryght's stone,' on the east of Selwood, gathered a force composed of all the Wiltshire and Somerset men, and those of part of Hampshire.[36] So successful were the

---

[29] Wm. Malmes. *Gesta Regum* (Rolls Ser.) i, 107. He puts their arrival just after the exile of Egbert, who returned in 802.

[30] *Angl.-Sax. Chron.* (Rolls Ser.) i, 146; Ethelweard, *Chron. sub anno*; Asser, *Life of Alfred* (ed. Stevenson), 41; Flor. Wigorn. *Chron. sub anno*; Hen. Hunt. *Hist. Angl.* (Rolls Ser.), 146.

[31] Ethelweard mentions a Duke of Somerset, Ethelnoth, who had a narrow retinue and seems to have retreated with him. Asser. followed by Florence of Worcester, says he had a few of his nobles, soldiers and vassals. Wm. of Malmesbury makes Hampshire, Wiltshire and Somerset faithful at this time. It should be noticed that the more nearly contemporary the authority the greater the panic.

[32] Asser. op. cit.   [33] Ibid.

[34] Hen. Hunt. op. cit. 147 ; Flor. Wigorn. *Chron.* ann. cit.

[35] *Angl.-Sax. Chron.* (Rolls Ser.) i, 148 ; Ethelweard, Flor. Wigorn. loc. cit.

[36] *Angl.-Sax. Chron.* loc. cit. Wm. Malmes. *Gesta Regum* (Rolls Ser.) i, 125.

operations [37] which followed, that in the same year he was able to conclude the Peace of Wedmore, by which Somerset with the rest of England south and west of Watling Street remained in his hands. The West continued exempt from hostilities until 894, when the Danes sent a fleet to besiege Exeter and some place unnamed on the north coast of Devon. At Exeter Alfred compelled them to re-embark, but their combined force made a dash along the Thames and up the Severn, to meet which Alfred and three aldormen, one of whom was Ethelnoth of Somerset, gathered a force 'from every town east of the Parret, as well as east of Selwood, as also north of the Thames and west of the Severn, and also some part of the North Welsh race,' [38] and besieged them at Buttington, and forced them to return to Essex. The actual hostilities were outside Somerset, but Somerset men must have formed a large part of the force which saved the west of England. [39]

For nearly a century after this the west seems to have enjoyed peace, but with the reign of Ethelred II a fresh cycle of Danish invasions begins. In 988 Watchet was ravaged, and the incursion seems to have been a considerable one since the men of Devon evidently lent aid. [40] Nine years later the whole coast from Land's End to the mouth of the Severn was again harried ; Watchet was once more attacked, 'great evil in burning and man-slaying being wrought.' [41] The Danes then drew off, but in 1001 returned and attacked Devon, and though Somerset joined to oppose them they were completely victorious at Penhoe.

In 1013 the whole of Wessex (following the example of the north of England) submitted to the Danes ; nevertheless two years afterwards Somerset with Dorset and Wilts was again harried. In 1016 however Ethelred died, and a double election to the throne followed, London choosing his son Edmund, while a rival assembly chose Cnut. [42] Edmund, losing no time, made a dash for the west, raised the forces of Somerset and Devon, and prepared to march his west-countrymen to the relief of London : he was met however at Penn, in Somerset (on the borders of Dorset and Wilts) by Cnut : the result of this battle and of another which followed it at Sherston is not given, but he was able to raise the siege of London : the tide of war rolled away from Somerset, and his great campaigns were fought out in the east.

On Edmund's death and Cnut's accession to the whole of England (1017) the latter divided the kingdom into four provinces, retaining Wessex for himself and putting a viceroy into each of the others. The whole question of the political administration of Somerset in early days until the creation of the earldom of Wessex is exceedingly obscure. From the time of Cenwealh we seem able to trace the existence of one supreme king of

[37] The battle of 'Ethandune' was clearly fought at Edington in Wilts (Stevenson's edition of Asser, p. 273), not, as sometimes said, at Edington in Somerset.

[38] *Angl.-Sax. Chron.* i, 169.

[39] The authorities are very obscure on this campaign. We have followed Plummer, as his explanation seems to give the sense of the Chronicle and Ethelweard combined, and is supported by Flor. Wigorn.

[40] Goda 'satrapa Domnaniae' was killed. Flor. Wigorn. *Chron.* ann. cit. Ramsay attributes this attack to the island chief Guthfrith, son of Harold, who had plundered Anglesey in 987, and this year was raiding from Cardigan to Glamorgan. Cf. *Ann. Camb.* (Rolls Ser.), 20.

[41] *Angl.-Sax. Chron.* i, 246.

[42] Flor. Wigorn. *Chron.* ann. cit. Cnut had already been elected by the Danish army on the death of Swegen at Gainsborough.

Wessex with a number of sub-reguli under him, administering what from the beginning of the 8th century appear to have been territorial units, which we have no reason to doubt corresponded with the modern shires.[43]

Somerset was finally consolidated as a West-Saxon conquest by Ine, and in his laws we find shires each placed under a separate ealdorman.[44] In charters of his reign we find the signatures of Baldred and Ethelheard, both with the title of sub-regulus,[45] and both apparently owning land in Somerset, and it has been conjectured that Baldred may have been the first ealdorman of the shire.[46] Ethelweard tells us that at the battle of Ellendun one Hun 'dux provinciae Sumersaetan' was killed;[47] but the name occurs among the witnesses to charters until 826.[48] The Chronicle in 845 mentions an ealdorman Eanulf, who led the men of Somerset, and under Alfred we hear of an ealdorman called Ethelnoth,[49] but these are the only names for this period that have come down to us. In Edgar's reign the charters point to the administration of the South by two ealdormen only. Of these there is some evidence that Ælfheah was ealdorman of Hampshire.[50] Since we have evidence for a later period of the grouping together for administrative purposes of the four most westerly shires,[51] it appears probable that his contemporaries Edmund and Ordgar[52] governed Somerset, for Edmund is called by Florence 'dux Domnoniae,' and Ordgar's successor Ethelweard figures in a charter as 'Occidentalium Provinciarum dux';[53] as he witnessed charters until the year 1015,[54] it seems likely that he remained ealdorman until the creation of the earldom of Wessex. Cnut, however, did not long retain the administration of Wessex in his own hands, but created the dignity of Earl of the West Saxons in favour of Godwin, now rising to power. Godwin's description as 'Dux' occurs first in the year 1020,[55] but Freeman suggests that at first he was earl of a part of Wessex only, and on the return of Cnut to England in 1020 was given the whole. His position would be that of a lieutenant representing the king in a province which he retained in his own hands; its importance is illustrated by the title 'Bajulus' used by Edward's biographer in speaking of him.[56] Somerset did not however remain with the rest of Wessex in Godwin's hands: his son Swegen appears to have held it with Berkshire under the earl, as well as his three Mercian shires, from an unknown date until their outlawry in 1051:[57] Devon, Cornwall, Dorset and Somerset were then formed into an earldom and given to Odda, a relation of the king.[58] But in the following year Harold and Leofwine crossed from Ireland to the mouth of the Severn, landed at Porlock,[59] and ravaged

[43] Cf. Chadwick, *Studies in Angl.-Sax. Inst.* 282 sqq.

[44] Lansd. Chart. 3, 8, 36, 39.   [45] Birch, *Cart. Sax.* nos. 121, 142, 147.

[46] Chadwick, loc. cit. For the question whether Somerset was strictly a shire, see *Somers. Arch. Proc.* xlix (2), 1.   [47] Ethelweard *Chron.* ann. 823.

[48] Birch, op. cit. nos. 377, 390–3, 398.   [49] Ann. 894.

[50] Flor. Wigorn. and a doubtful charter. He is called 'Suthamtunensium dux,' and a successor of his is 'Wentaniensium Provinciarium dux.' Kemble, op. cit. 698. His will shows that he was connected with Hampshire. Birch, op. cit. no. 1,174.

[51] Odda was Earl of Somerset, Devon, Dorset and Cornwall. *Angl.-Sax. Chron.* Ann. 1048.

[52] Edmund's signature to charters ends in 963 (Birch, op. cit. no. 1,121) and Ordgar's begins in 964 (Ibid. no. 1,135); it therefore seems reasonable to conclude that Ordgar was Edmund's successor in office.

[53] Kemble, op. cit. no. 698.   [54] Ibid. no. 1,310. Cf. also nos. 1,309 and 1,307.

[55] Ibid. no. 1,316.   [56] *Lives of Edward the Confessor* (Rolls Ser.), 392.

[57] Flor. Wigorn. *Chron.* ann. cit.   [58] *Angl.-Sax. Chron.* (Rolls Ser.) i, 317.

[59] Hen. Hunt., op. cit. 194. *Angl.-Sax. Chron.* says (Rolls Ser. i, 316), 'near to the boundaries of Somerset and Devon.'

there unchecked until the forces of Somerset and Devon attempted to drive them off.[60] Harold, who seems to have been in command,[61] inflicted a heavy defeat, slaying over thirty thegns, and then sailed away to join his father. Godwin, on his subsequent return to favour, was reinstated as Earl of Wessex,[62] and in the following year, when he died, Harold succeeded him, Somerset being included in his province,[63] but on Edward's death and Harold's succession no Earl of Wessex was appointed.

The Conquest once again involved Somerset in hostilities : William's operations against Exeter did not affect it directly, but in the same year (1067) one or more of Harold's sons crossed from Ireland to the mouth of the Avon and harried all that part until defeated at Bristol : they then sailed down to Somerset and landed : Eadnoth, 'the stallere,' collected the local forces, and an indecisive battle was fought, in which he was killed ; the invaders then withdrew to Ireland.[64] In the following year, encouraged by the revolt raised by Swegen in Northumbria, Wessex rose, and the forces of Devon, Somerset and Dorset together besieged Exeter and Montacute : the siege of the latter was, however, raised by Bishop Geoffrey of Coutances, whose vast possessions in these parts were threatened by a movement having for its aim the semi-independence of the west.

The Somerset Domesday has been fully treated elsewhere : all that has to be noticed here is the extent to which English holders of land were dispossessed and Normans introduced. At the time of the Survey the land still in the hands of Englishmen as tenants-in-chief was computed by the commissioners as equal only to $78\frac{1}{2}$ ploughs, and had paid geld T.R.E. for 67 hides, 3 virgates and $1\frac{1}{4}$ ferlings : the rest of the shire, except that portion of ecclesiastical property which had not been confiscated, had either been retained by the king or granted to Norman tenants or churches.[65] The chief English holder was Harding,[66] son of Eadnoth, but his lands are insignificant compared with those of the more important Normans. William himself retained not only the ancient demesne, consisting of twelve manors, but the forfeited possessions of the house of Godwin, the estates of the Queen Edith which escheated to the Crown at her death in 1074, and a few of the manors formerly held by Wulfward the White, who appears to have been one of her thegns. The possessions of the Church occupy nearly four times as much space in Domesday as the 'Terra Regis,' the largest grants being made to the Bishop of Coutances[67] and Walkelin, the Norman Bishop of Winchester. Of the lay tenants-in-chief, infinitely the most important was the Count of Mortain, William's

[60] The *Peterborough Chronicle* says that Harold did not ravage until he found the country hostile. This view of course meets with Freeman's approval, but the weight of evidence is against it. Cf. *Angl.-Sax. Chron.* and Flor. Wigorn. Hen. Hunt. makes the attack part of a general harrying by the Godwin family from the Severn to Sheppey (op. cit. 194).

[61] The *Angl.-Sax. Chron.* does not mention Leofwine.

[62] Odda died in 1056 (*Chronicle*). Thorpe says he was then Earl of Devon : Green suggests of Worcester and Gloucester as compensation for the loss of Wessex.

[63] Kemble, op. cit. 834–9.

[64] Flor. Wigorn. *Chronicle*, ann. cit.

[65] St. Peter's at Rome received a grant of one manor.

[66] Mr. Freeman has identified him with the founder of the second line of lords of Berkeley. *Norman Conq.* iv, App. N.

[67] This great fief, which comprised nearly one-tenth of the county, was treated as a lay barony, and so dealt with at the Bishop's death.

half-brother. He, like the Bishop of Coutances, held nearly one-tenth of the county, and his great castle of Montacute, which, perched on a high peak, overawed all the surrounding county, was in itself a symbol of the Norman domination. Later when his fief was broken up it became the head of a great honour which comprised his estates in Somerset and Devon. Other important tenants-in-chief were Roger de Courcelle, who held also largely as an under-tenant, Roger Arundel, Walter de Douai and William de Mohun.[68]

The distribution of the most important of these estates is well worth noticing. The ' Terra Regis ' was scattered all over the country, but Mortain's fief was almost entirely situated in the south-east corner ; while the possessions of the Church form a ring around the Count's manors with one extension due north, and another up the strip of land between the Brue and the Cary.

The power which the possession of extensive estates conferred on the great feudatories was quickly shown. When the rebellion of 1087 broke out the Bishop of Coutances and his nephew Robert Mowbray,[69] as well as the Count of Mortain,[70] all joined with Robert of Normandy against William. Robert marched from Bristol on Bath, which he burnt ; then having ravaged West Wiltshire, made a circuit on the uplands and returned to Ilchester, but was repulsed there, a defeat which ended the hostilities in Somerset. Bath and Ilchester were probably singled out for wrath as they were both king's towns, and Ilchester especially as being so near Montacute.[71] In 1093, at the bishop's death, Mowbray succeeded to the 280 manors he had held, but after the failure of the rising in 1095, in which he joined, he was deprived of all his possessions.[72]

With the earlier troubles of Stephen's reign Somerset was intimately concerned. The insurrection in the west from which the beginning of continuous civil war dates appears to have started with the defection of Geoffrey Talbot, who revolted and held his castle at Hereford against Stephen.[73] Stephen however took the castle after blockading it for a month, but Geoffrey escaped to Weobley, and was afterwards taken prisoner by the Bishop of Bath's men after leading an unsuccessful assault against that city : his friends at Bristol obtained possession of the bishop by fraud, and threatened to hang him if Talbot was not given up, but on Geoffrey's being set free they refused to liberate the bishop.[74] Bristol had up to now been a centre of marauding raids conducted by the chief rebels under Robert of Gloucester,[75] the principal Somerset barons who co-operated with him being Lovel of Castle Cary and Mohun of Dunster.[76] Stephen himself then marched on Bath as if to attack Bristol, but abandoning the siege of Bristol directed expeditions against Castle Cary, Harptree and the smaller castles of the rebels. Harptree and Castle Cary having fallen, he marched

---

[68] This name is spelt in many ways, but this is the best known, although it was not so spelt generally until the middle of the 13th century.

[69] Between 1080 and 1082 he had been made Earl of Northumberland. The *Chron. Peterborough* and Flor. Wigorn. *Chron.* (ann. cit.) say he sided with Robert, but Orderic Vitalis (*Hist. Eccl.* iii, 273) says he was faithful to William.

[70] Flor. Wigorn. *Chron.* ann. cit.   [71] Freeman, *Reign of Wm. Rufus*, i, 43.

[72] Flor. Wigorn. *Chron.* ann. cit., Hen. Hunt. op. cit. 218.

[73] Hen. Hunt. op. cit. 261.   [74] *Gest. Steph.* (Rolls Ser.) 36–41.

[75] Hen. Hunt. op. cit. 261.   [76] Ibid.

against Dunster, from whence Mohun had been harrying the country far and near ;[77] but Stephen, believing the castle to be impregnable by assault, and not willing to spare time to blockade it himself, left operations there to Henry de Tracy, one of his most active supporters,[78] and hurried away to scenes where his personal supervision was more necessary. Tracy succeeded in reducing Mohun to order for the time being, but the latter remained an ardent partisan of Matilda, and was rewarded for his exertions by being created one of her earls. His earldom appears to have consisted of Somerset and Dorset,[79] but the date of its creation cannot be fixed more nearly than between April and June 1141 :[80] he was, however, the first and last holder of the title.[81] During the anarchy Somerset suffered comparatively little when once Mohun had been reduced to order ; and this in spite of the fact that hostilities raged on her borders. Gloucestershire and Wiltshire were ravaged incessantly. Dorset was also concerned, and Somerset cannot have been wholly immune; but the chroniclers are silent on the subject : the only references to Somerset after the reduction of Dunster are to the ineffectual parley at Bath between Robert of Gloucester, representing the empress, and the legate, archbishop and queen, representing Stephen,[82] and to the rout of Henry de Tracy by William of Gloucester (who had succeeded his father) during his building operations near Castle Cary.[83]

The Norman period is that with which we usually associate the building of castles, but two of the most important in Somerset were of far remoter origin. The Saxon Chronicle assigns the foundation of Taunton 'burh' to Ine and gives the date 722 for its destruction. Ine's successor Ethelheard gave the manor of Taunton to the see of Winchester, but the site of the castle appears to have remained untouched until the bishopric of William Giffard, who began rebuilding it early in the 12th century.[84] The castle occupied a very strong site on the river, and its importance as a military position lasted until the end of the 17th century.

Dunster, like Taunton, may be of Saxon origin. Built at the end of a ridge of hills, from which it was separated by a natural depression, it may have served in early days as a frontier fortress against the Celts and the piratical invasions of the Northmen. The 'tor' on which it stands covers some ten acres of ground, of which a quarter of an acre constitutes the table top of the hill. The whole area of the castle is about two acres, the hill being made inaccessible by the artificial scarping of the upper 80 or 100 feet. We have seen its importance in the Norman period, but it is doubtful whether

---

[77] *Gest. Steph.* 51.   [78] Ibid. 52, 97, 135, 1,147.

[79] In his foundation charter to Bruton he styles himself 'Comes Somersetensis'; the author of *Gest. Steph.* (80) says that at the siege of Winchester Mohun 'quem comitem ibi statuit Dorsetiae' was among Maud's allies. These two counties were then under one sheriff, so may have been formed into one earldom.

[80] He attested a charter to Glastonbury probably soon after the election of the Empress on 8 April without the title (cf. *Journ. Brit. Assoc.* xxxi, 389), and Maud's first charter to Geoffrey de Mandeville in June as 'Comite.' For the whole subject see J. H. Round, *Geoffrey de Mandeville*, 277, seqq.

[81] Osmond, Count of Seez, nephew of William II, is said by some to have been created Earl of Somerset and Dorset about 1070, but died unmarried 1099 when his honours became extinct (G.E.C. *Complete Peerage*); Reginald de Mohun who died 1258 is sometimes styled Earl of Somerset (see Maxwell-Lyte, *Hist. of Dunster*, 22–6).

[82] Wm. Malmes. *Hist. Novella* (Rolls Ser.) 564.   [83] *Gest. Steph.* 134.

[84] Collinson, *History of Somerset*, iii, 231. G. T. Clark in *Med. Mil. Archit.* says Giffard built the keep and walls, but J. A. Rutter, *Notes and Queries*, 9 June 1900, says 'the building called a keep was pretty certainly nothing of the sort.'

it even then consisted of more than fortifications of timber and earthworks, as the masonry now remaining is not of earlier date than the reign of Henry III.[85]

Of the Norman castles, one of the most important was Castle Cary. Excavations have shown that the keep measured 78 feet square, and that it was probably an early Norman building : the quantities of burnt stone show that it must have been largely destroyed by fire.[86] Of the origin of Montacute we know less. There is no evidence for a Saxon fortification, and the site was obtained by an exchange with Athelney Abbey made by Robert of Mortain.[87] Robert of Mortain's son gave it to a priory of Cluniac monks founded by him at Montacute.[88] Harptree, situated in the defiles of the Mendips, was a Norman castle which was entirely demolished only in the reign of Henry VIII.[89] Stoke Courcy,[90] Ilchester and Nether Stowey were other early castles soon destroyed : Bridgwater was built by Baldwin of Exeter,[91] but Donyatt and Nunney belong to a later period, when the lords were striving with or without leave to fortify their manor houses. The Patent Rolls record the crenellation of Donyatt by William of Montacute without licence, and his subsequent pardon and licence.[92]

Not one of the castles in the county was in the hands of the Crown, and the powers of the barons therefore were correspondingly strengthened by the absence of any considerable centre of royal power : during Richard's reign indeed Somerset was included in John's appanage and became part of what was practically a compact principality in the west with outlyers in the Midlands : in the four western shires the royal power was actually reduced to a shadow by the grant to John of the administration of government and the right to appoint his own justiciar.[93] This anomaly came, of course, to an end with Richard's death, and during his own reign John seems to have visited the west chiefly for sporting purposes : he made however three tours through the county,[94] which included visits to many of the castles.[95]

The seat of the chief hostilities during the Barons' war did not include Somerset, but on the Sunday before the battle of Evesham a large force of Welshmen led by William de Berkeley, a knight of noble birth but infamous character, landed at Minehead with the intention of ravaging the county. Adam Gurdon, however, the warden of Dunster Castle, slew many of them, and put the others to flight, causing many, among whom was Berkeley, to be drowned.[96] Of the landholders of the county we know that Plugenet was loyal to the king.[97]

Turning to the share borne by Somerset in the development of Parliamentary institutions, we find that when Edward summoned the

[85] Clark, op. cit. ii, 24–8. Mrs. Armitage, 'Early Norman Castles of England,' *Engl. Hist. Review* (1904), 229; Maxwell-Lyte, *Hist. of Dunster.*

[86] J. A. Rutter, *Notes and Queries,* 9 June 1900; *Som. Arch. and Nat. Hist. Soc. Proc.* xxxvi, 23.

[87] *Dom. Bk.* i, 93a, 1.

[88] Mrs. Armitage, loc. cit.; Leland, *Itin.* ii, 92. [89] Collinson, op. cit. iii, 589; Clark, op. cit. i, 74.

[90] Clark, op. cit. i, 73. [91] Ibid. [92] *Cal. of Pat.* 1327–30, p. 437.

[93] Benedict of Peterborough, *Gesta Reg. Hen. II* (Rolls Ser.) ii, 73, 99. Cf. R. de Diceto, *Op. Hist.* (Rolls Ser.), 664. Matt. Paris, *Chron. Maj.* (Rolls Ser.), Stubbs, *Introd. to Rolls Ser.* (ed. A. Hassall), 205, 206, 447.

[94] In 1204, 1205, 1207. [95] *Cal. Rot. Pat.* (Rec. Com. 1835), 'Itin. of John.'

[96] Rishanger, *Chron.* (Rolls Ser.) 41. [97] Dugdale, *Baronage, sub* Plugenet.

'Model Parliament' in 1295 writs for the election of representatives from boroughs and cities were sent to Axbridge, Bridgwater, Wells and Bath only. For the Parliament of 1298 Ilchester and Milborne Port were added, but Axbridge dropped out. In the following year Bridgwater, Milborne Port and Ilchester only were represented, and in the second convention of 1300 only Bath, Bridgwater and Milborne Port. In 1302 the latter town received no writ, but Bath, Bridgwater, Ilchester and Wells, and for the first and last time Watchet, were summoned to send representatives. For the Parliament of 1305 writs were sent to Bath, Bridgwater, Ilchester and Wells, which from henceforth were regularly represented, except in 1306, when Wells was unrepresented at the first assembly, and in 1320, when Bath, Ilchester and Wells were omitted ; to Langport and Milborne Port, which sent members to the two assemblies of 1306 and then ceased ; to Montacute, which sent to the first assembly of 1306 and no more ; and to Weare, which was represented twice in 1306 and then ended its career as a parliamentary borough. In 1307 Axbridge again sent members, and Taunton for the first time was represented[98] ; in 1313 Chard was added to the tale of boroughs, which was thus composed of Axbridge, Bath, Bridgwater, Chard, Ilchester, Taunton and Wells.[99]

These continued to send until the reign of Edward III, when fresh changes took place : Chard sent up members for the last time to the 2nd Parliament of Edward III, and Axbridge to his 7th Parliament. Glastonbury received its only writ for his 12th Parliament ; but ' *Ballivi nullum responsum dederunt* ' ; Dunster and Stoke Courcy began and ended their careers by sending members to his 34th Parliament. Ilchester dropped out after the Parliament of 1361, sent up members in 12 Edward IV, and not again until 18 James I, after which it received writs regularly until the Reform Bill. Milborne Port was again added to the boroughs having parliamentary representation in 15 Charles I, and Minehead was enfranchised in the first year of Elizabeth's reign. We thus reach the list of towns sending members until the Reform Bill : Bath, Bridgwater, Wells, Taunton, Minehead, Ilchester, and Milborne Port.[100]

Of the early members of Parliament nothing has come down to us but the names : membership was unpopular, and Somerset was too remote for a journey to Carlisle,[101] York,[102] Lincoln,[103] Northampton,[104] or even Westminster, to be anything but a very serious undertaking. The towns in fact sometimes abstained from sending members. In the reign of Edward II no return was made by Axbridge to seven of the writs sent,[105] by Chard to four,[106] by Ilchester to two,[107] and by Taunton once.[108] Sometimes no answer was made to the sheriff although the writ had been returned to the bailiff ;[109] and in 1307 Bath responded to the writ by declaring that

---

[98] Brown-Willis says Taunton sent in 23 Edw. I (*Notitia Parliamentaria*, 44), but the first entry in Parliamentary writs is 1307. Toulmin says it sent *ab origine* as far as the matter can be traced. *History of Taunton* (ed. Jas. Savage), 295.

[99] For this paragraph see *Parl. Writs* i and ii, Div. 2.

[100] For this paragraph see Brown-Willis, op. cit.   [101] 1306.

[102] 1298, 1300, 1314, 1318, 1322.   [103] 1300, 1316.   [104] 1282, 1307.

[105] For Parliaments held in 1307, 1313, 1314, 1315, 1318, 1319 and 1327.

[106] 1314, 1318, 1319, 1327.   [107] 1318, 1327.   [108] 1327.

[109] 1307 Bath and Wells, 1311 Ilchester, 1319 Taunton and Wells.

the bailiffs had not cared to make any execution of it. In no case however did the county fail to send up its two knights.[110]

In the Welsh wars of Edward I Somerset landowners saw military service. In the previous reign for the expedition of 1257 Mohun had been among the barons summoned to attend the king at Bristol well fitted with horse and arms,[111] and Columbers had fought in Wales in 1223.[112] In December 1276 writs were issued for a muster of all tenants-in-chief at Worcester in the following July,[113] and in reply to the writ we find twenty knights from Somerset, besides representatives from $5\frac{1}{4}$ fees of which the lands were partly in this and partly in other counties. The Abbot of Glastonbury,[114] John de Mohun[115] and Henry de l'Orti[116] appear to have held the largest number of fees in the county, each owing service for three in demesne. Of the Somerset contingent eleven knights and four serjeants were ordered to serve with the king's brother Edmund in west Wales for forty days,[117] and afterwards for as long as he should require.[118]

On the renewal of the struggle in 1282 writs were again issued in May to all sheriffs for a muster of tenants-in-chief at Rhuddlan on 2 August,[119] but the Somerset proffers of service were smaller than on the previous occasion. Eight knights were sent from Somerset, two from Somerset and Dorset, and three from Somerset and Wiltshire; while composition was made for four.[120] In the following November however writs were sent to the sheriffs of Somerset, Dorset, Devon and Wiltshire for the election by each county of ten of their ablest and best knights to appear at or send some of their men to the muster at Carmarthen.[121] After the settlement of Wales by the Shrewsbury Parliament only one revolt serious enough for the use of any considerable force took place (1294), and writs were then sent to the sheriffs of a few counties for a muster of knights at Cardiff, twenty-eight being demanded from Somerset.[122]

The Somerset levies were however not only employed so near home. In May 1294 writs were issued to all tenants[123] of £20 or more to be in London on 7 July with horses and arms in readiness to cross the seas to Gascony.[124] Somerset and Dorset together owed service from 133 such tenants as well as from 28 heads of religious houses and women.[125]

Scotland, not France, was however to be the centre of military interest. Somerset levies appear to have had no share in the first conquest of 1296, but when the revolt led by Wallace broke out a large force was needed; in the spring of 1298 the Somerset contingent was among those ordered to meet the king at York in June.[126]

The victory of Falkirk which followed was only the beginning of troubles: in January 1300 commissions were issued for a muster at Carlisle of all holders of land worth £40 or more, which brought 103 from Somerset and Dorset;[127] a year later fresh writs demanded a contingent of 44 from the two counties for a muster at Berwick on 24 June.[128]

---

[110] *Parl. Writs* vol. ii, Div. 2.   [111] Dugdale, op. cit.   [112] Ibid.
[113] *Parl. Writs* i, 196.   [114] Ibid. 197.   [115] Ibid. 202.
[116] Ibid. 206.   [117] Ibid. 211–13.   [118] Ibid. 213.
[119] Ibid. 224. Some of the tenants were afterwards ordered to repair to Carmarthen, 227.
[120] Ibid. 235–43.   [121] Ibid. 244.   [122] Ibid. 265.
[123] Either *in capite* or of any other lord.   [124] *Parl. Writs*, i, 281.   [125] Ibid. 292–3.
[126] Ibid. 316.   [127] Ibid. 330, 335–7.   [128] Ibid. 347.

From this time forward the demand for contingents was steady. Writs were sent to the tenants-in-chief for a muster at Berwick in May 1303,[129] at Carlisle in July 1306,[130] at Carlisle in August 1308,[131] at Newcastle for the autumn of 1309,[132] at Berwick in September 1310[133] : the proffers of service for this muster are interesting, for they show the landowners sending representatives instead of going themselves : in almost every case from Somerset two *servientes* were sent for every knight's fee, the county contributing one knight and thirty *servientes* for 16½ fees.[134] Again, in the summer of 1311, Edward purposed to 'make a raid' against Bruce, and sent out writs for a muster at Berwick in July[135] ; between that date and the conclusion of a thirteen years' truce in 1323 six issues of writs were made.[136] Ecclesiastics, female tenants-in-chief, and those unfit for service were obliged to compound or send substitutes.[137]

Somerset contained many tenants-in-chief of whom there is direct evidence that they either went to the wars or sent service : Philip de Columbers, Hugh de Courteneye, Nicholas de Moels, William de Zouche, Nicholas Braunche, Ralph Fitz Pain, Alan Plugenet, Richard Lovel, and William Grandison are among the most prominent who received writs of exoneration in 1314 for past services in 28, 31 and 34 Edward I[138] : many other well-known names recur continually in the lists of recipients of writs such as John de Mohun, John de Beauchamp, Simon de Montagu,[139] Nicolas[140] and William de St. Maur, John de Meriet,[141] Hugh and Nicholas Pointz,[142] Henry de l'Orti,[143] Thomas and Maurice de Berkele[144] and others.[145]

The first date when the writs furnish an example for Somerset of a levy other than that of the feudal tenants is in July 1310, when they were issued for raising bodies of foot-soldiers.[146] For his raid in 1311 Edward required, besides the ordinary feudal force, that every township in each county should furnish him with one strong and steady foot-soldier properly armed, his wages paid for seven weeks by the township to which he belonged. Electors to choose them and leaders to conduct them to the muster at Roxburgh were named in the writs : in Somerset John de Beauchamp, Nicholas de Langelond, Ralph de Gorges and Nicholas de Poinz or two or three of them were the electors, and Gorges and Poinz the leaders.

This commission was revoked in July for all but seven counties, but preparatory writs were sent out in case a similar force should be needed in the following year[147] ; and in 1316[148] and 1322[149] like schemes were actually put in operation ; in the latter year a contingent of 2,000 was demanded from Somerset, and letters were also written to the mayors and *communitates* of various towns 'affectionately requesting' them to provide a grant

---

[129] *Parl. Writs*, i, 366.   [130] Ibid. 377.   [131] Ibid. ii, Div. 2, 373–4. Postponed, 377.
[132] Ibid. 381–3. Postponed, 386.   [133] Ibid. 394–6.
[134] Ibid. 401–6. This is not absolutely accurate, as fractions of estates in Essex, Gloucestershire, Bucks and Dorset were included.
[135] Ibid. 415.   [136] Ibid. 421–2, 466–7, 487–8, 490–2, 494–6, 501–3, 504–5, 558, 568–9, 626–7.
[137] Ibid. i, 367, 371 and elsewhere.
[138] *Parl. Writs*, ii, Div. 2, 437–9, 442, 443, 447–9, 452, 453   [139] Ibid. June 1308, 373–4.
[140] Ibid. May 1316, 466–7.   [141] Ibid. July 1309, 381–3.   [142] Ibid. June 1310, 394–6.
[143] Ibid. July 1309, 381–3.   [144] Ibid. May 1316, 466–7.
[145] See also Dugdale, op. cit. for many of these and for Ferrers, who had married the heiress of Mucegros of Charlton.
[146] *Parl. Writs*, ii, Div. 2, 398. The number is not specified.   [147] Ibid. 418.
[148] Ibid. 157, 464–6.   [149] Ibid. 559–60, 575–6.

of foot-soldiers or any other aid[150]; assistance which was apparently not provided, as commissions were issued to compel them to do so. Wells was required to provide three men, Ilchester one, Chard one, Taunton three, and Axbridge one.[151] All bannerets, knights, esquires and other horsemen-at-arms not retainers of others were also required to serve.[152] Commissions of array were issued for a muster at York in 1323,[153] but were superseded on the conclusion of the thirteen years' truce.[154] The relief to the county must have been great, for the strain on its resources both of men and money was considerable, for besides men Somerset had had to contribute both money and provisions. In 1311 Somerset and Dorset were required to send 2,000 quarters of wheat to be paid for out of the fifteenth collected in the county,[155] and when loans were raised from religious houses Glastonbury was requested to produce 300 marks in 1313,[156] 500 marks in 1315,[157] and a further contribution in 1319, the Bishop of Bath and Wells and the Dean of Wells also receiving writs in 1319.[158] In this year also writs for the loan were sent to the bailiffs and *probi homines* of various cities including Bath and Wells,[159] but we have no record of the sums sent.

The system of arrays which had been developed during the Scotch wars proved very useful to Edward in his struggle with the Barons which broke out in 1321. In November of that year he issued a commission to John Beauchamp and John Meriet for raising the horse and foot of Somerset and Devon,[160] while writs issued in the following February for a feudal force include half a dozen other prominent Somerset landholders.[161] After the struggle had been ended at Boroughbridge the process began of making all possible profit out of those who had opposed the king.[162] The memorandum of those who submitted to fines to save their lives and redeem their property contains the following Somerset names and amounts: Walter de Pavely, 200 marks;[163] Matthew de Clyvedon, 400 marks; Simon de Rale, £40; John de Countevill, £20;[164] Andrew de Craucombe, £2;[165] Richard de Pederton, £10;[166] John Ralegh of Nettelcombe, £100, and £100 as surety for good behaviour;[167] and William Baret £20 fine and £100 surety.[168] Commissions were sent for the arrest of Clyvedon,[169] and we also learn that Maurice de Berkeley was one of the rebels.[170]

The possibility of war with France in 1324 produced a fresh crop of writs for commissions of array. In June Somerset was ordered to send 200 bowmen to Plymouth.[171] Commissions were issued to the *custodes* of the maritime counties, including Somerset, for the defence of the ports and harbours against an expected invasion by France;[172] in August writs were issued to the tenants-in-chief, a first contingent of 880 foot soldiers was required from Somerset,[173] and writs were sent to the *bones gens* of various towns and cities for foot soldiers, 16 being requisitioned from Bath, 6 from Somerton, and 20 from Wells.[174] In the following November an attempt

---

[150] *Parl. Writs*, ii, Div. 2, 563.
[151] Ibid. 581–2.
[152] Ibid. 586–95.
[153] Ibid. 623–6.
[154] Ibid. 624–6.
[155] Ibid. i, 400–4.
[156] Ibid. ii, Div. 2, 65, 66.
[157] Ibid. App. 87.
[158] Ibid. 140–1.
[159] Ibid. 141–2.
[160] Ibid. ii, Div. 2, 541.
[161] Ibid. 542, 549.
[162] Ibid. 181.
[163] Ibid. 203.
[164] Ibid. 205.
[165] Ibid. 206.
[166] Ibid. 208.
[167] Ibid. 212.
[168] Ibid. 213.
[169] Ibid. 215.
[170] Ibid. 178.
[171] Ibid. 658.
[172] Ibid. 660, 664–6.
[173] Ibid. 669.
[174] Ibid. 677–80.

was made to get together a force of knights, esquires, and men-at-arms by inquest ; 20 were to be chosen in Somerset and Dorset to be arrayed by the commissioners, and were to be supplemented by a further force of 300 bowmen.[175] A feudal muster was again ordered for March 1325 at Portsmouth,[176] but was put off by successive prorogations until August :[177] a considerable force, including twenty-one landowners from Somerset and Dorset with their followers, was, however, ordered to start in March.[178] Great difficulty seems to have been experienced in keeping the musters together ; writs to sheriffs to arrest deserters seem to have been of little avail even though backed up by orders for imprisonment.[179] In the following December a fresh effort was made : commissions were issued to array the men-at-arms in constabularies and the foot soldiers in scores and hundreds ; beacons were to be erected, and landholders assessed for contributions.[180] In Somerset John de Mohun and afterwards Philip de Columbers were appointed as commissioners under the Earl of Winchester.[181] The men however never started, and on the outbreak of civil war the arrayers were ordered to march their forces to the assistance of the king : all the able-bodied men-at-arms and hobelers, and a force of 3,000 horsemen being demanded from Somerset and Dorset.[182]

The events of the reign of Edward III are reflected in a similar way in the various writs and commissions requisitioning troops, money or provisions from the county. A writ of aid to Richard Lovel appointing him to array knights and others capable of bearing arms who had been assembled by proclamation to resist the rebels [183] suggests the share of the county in the events preceding Mortimer's fall. The chronic rebellion in Ireland was the cause of a levy of archers for Michaelmas 1332, 140 being demanded from Somerset and Dorset by William of Montacute's advice,[184] and some half-dozen Somerset landholders were among those who received the summons to attend the king thither.[185] On the renewal of the war with Scotland however Somerset as usual received writs of purveyance,[186] and at least 100 hobelers went from the county to the Scotch war.[187]

But while war with Scotland was becoming a habit, the far more serious struggle with France, which is the outstanding political fact of the reign, was just beginning. Hostilities began in earnest in the summer of 1338, and accordingly we find commissions of array for defence against invasion[188] nd the appointment of overseers, in Somerset [189] Hugh de Courtney and Philip de Columbers, who were given powers to arrest and imprison recalcitrants.[190] Difficulties arose from the dishonesty of arrayers, who levied money contrary to orders, sent a miserable detachment, and appropriated the funds they had extorted.[191] Purveyance we find again levied,[192] and three years later the holder of a fee worth £5 was to come as or send a mounted archer ; a fee worth £10, a hobeler ; a fee worth £20, a man-at-arms ; a fee worth £50, at least two men-at-arms, and so proportionately at the rate of a man-at-arms for every £25.[193]

[175] *Parl. Writs,* ii, Div. 2, 687.   [176] Ibid. 683-4.   [177] Ibid. 696, 714.
[178] Ibid. 701.   [179] Ibid. 727, 729-30.   [180] Ibid. 735.
[181] Ibid. 744.   [182] Ibid. 292-3.   [183] *Cal. of Pat.* 1327-30, p. 571.
[184] *Cal. of Close,* 1330-3, p. 488.   [185] Ibid. p. 586.   [186] Ibid. 1333-7, p. 26.   [187] Ibid. p. 530.
[188] *Cal. of Pat.* 1338-40, p. 134.   [189] Ibid. p. 135.   [190] Ibid. p. 141.
[191] *Cal. of Close,* 1341-3, p. 370.   [192] Ibid. 1340-3, p. 272.   [193] Ibid. 1343-5, p. 428.

A few years after another force of archers was raised from Somerset and Dorset only for the defence of the Channel Islands, the expenses of which were to be defrayed by the islands.[194]

Amongst Somerset landowners we find Ferrers of Chartley, who served in Brittany in 1341, in Flanders[195] and France,[196] and was present at Cressy, while his son served in Gascony in 1350 and his great-grandson under Henry V in France: Mohun who served in France[197] and Flanders[198]: William of Montacute, Earl of Salisbury, one of the most distinguished soldiers of the war: Sir William St. Maur[199]: Sir William Zouche of Harringworth, who fought in Flanders in 1338, and in 1342 and 1343 was commanded to provide 20 men-at-arms and 20 archers: his grandson and heir who also took a large part in the war[200] being retained by indenture in 1372 to serve with 40 men-at-arms, 15 knights, 34 esquires, and 60 archers: Hugh, Earl of Devon, who led a force of one banneret, 12 knights, and 36 esquires and 60 archers in Brittany in 1342: Sir James Audley (who had inherited estates in Somerset from his uncle Sir William Martin) who was commanded in 1342 to serve with 20 men-at-arms and 20 archers, fought also in many other campaigns,[201] and distinguished himself at Poitiers, his son following his example:[202] John Lovel[203] and his son, another John:[204] John Beauchamp of Hatch,[205] and after his death his son.[206]

The French war dragged on throughout Edward's reign, and its results were among the heritage received by his son. In the year of Richard's accession, from June to September the French ravaged the south coast, and Somerset received orders for a commission of array for men-at-arms and archers to be kept ever ready to resist invasion: beacons were to be set up,[207] and the county was placed among those for whose safety and defence Salisbury was made responsible.[208] In 1380 another order was issued for the array of all men between 16 and 60 as men-at-arms, hobelers or archers to resist a French attack.[209]

Soon after this however the disturbances connected with Tyler's insurrection took place: although in Devonshire it assumed considerable proportions Somerset does not seem to have had any great share in it. The chroniclers never mention the county. Mandates were however sent to the mayor and sheriffs of London, and the sheriffs of Middlesex and Somerset to arrest and imprison Nicholas Frompton, John Blake, and Thomas Ingleby indicted in the county of Somerset for divers treasons, felonies, and insurrections,[210] which looks as if missionaries of disorder may have been sent down from London.

In the following March commissioners were appointed to keep the peace with power to arrest and punish, to suppress meetings, and when necessary to lead the *posse comitatus* against the rebels, nineteen being appointed for Somerset;[211] a very similar commission was issued in the following winter.[212]

---

194 *Cal. of Close*, 1348–50, p. 165.
195 12–14 Edw. III. 196 16, 19 and 23 Edw. III. 197 19, 21, 22, 29, 33, 43 Edw. III.
198 47 Edw. III. 199 21 and 33 Edw. III. 200 33, 43, 44, 46 Edw. III.
201 18, 19, 21, 30, 33 Edw. III and following years. 202 33, 46 Edw. III.
203 10, 18–21 Edw. III. 204 42, 45, 47–48 Edw. III. 205 12, 13, 14, 16 Edw. III.
206 33 Edw. III. For this paragraph see Dugdale, *Baronage*, and G.E.C. *Peerage* under names cited.
207 *Cal. of Pat.* 1377–81, p. 39. 208 Ibid. p. 14. 209 Ibid. p. 473.
210 Ibid. 1381–5, p. 74. 211 Ibid. p. 140. 212 Ibid. p. 248.

The French war meanwhile continued languidly, involving also attacks on Scotland, the ally of France. In 1386, when an invasion was feared, Somerset was ordered to send 200 archers to the muster at London,[213] and in 1392 commissions of array were issued to resist invasion in case of war after the expiration of the truce.[214]

During the troubles at the close of his reign, Richard found as little support in Somerset as elsewhere : the Earl of Salisbury was an adherent of his, but was captured and beheaded by the mob without trial at Cirencester in January 1400, and afterwards attainted : his son however obtained restitution of a portion of his estates. John Lovel, having sided with Gloucester and the Archbishop of York against Richard, afterwards returned to his allegiance and supported the king.[215]

Nor was the county much concerned in the commotions under Henry IV. In the spring of 1402 seven commissioners were appointed to inquire the names of, and arrest and imprison all who wished to subvert the laws, customs and good government of the realm, preaching that the king had not kept his coronation promises ; they were also to bring to the notice of the lieges that it was the king's intention that the commonwealth laws and customs should be observed.[216] Commissions of array against the Welsh[217] were also issued.

The financial difficulties of the Lancastrians are faintly reflected in Somerset. With the ordinary sources of supply we are not concerned, but we find two Somerset landholders, Humphrey Stafford and John Frome, requested to contribute to the benevolence of 1402,[218] and a request for 500 marks from the county when a loan was raised in 1410.[219]

In the contingents for the French wars of Henry V and Henry VI there are many of the same names as in those of Edward III. Lord Ferrers fought under Henry V, being retained by indenture to serve with 20 men-at-arms and 60 archers[220] ; he was present at Agincourt.[221] Salisbury went with Henry V on his first expedition with 40 men-at-arms, 3 knights, 36 esquires, and 80 horse archers,[222] and fought under him until his death from a wound at the siege of Orleans. Lord St. Maur,[223] Sir William la Zouche who led 2 knights, 17 esquires, 20 men-at-arms, and 40 archers on Henry's first voyage,[224] Hugh Earl of Devon who served in the fleet,[225] and his son Thomas, who in 8 Henry VI covenanted to serve with 6 men-at-arms, and 21 archers, and fought for many years in France, are bearers of familiar names in this connexion. New ones are Lord Bonville of Chewton, who was retained by indenture to serve with 20 men-at-arms and 600 archers :[226] John Lord Harington : Tiptoft, who in 1415 led a force of 1 knight, 27 esquires, 30 men-at-arms, 60 mounted and 30 unmounted archers,[227] and in three subsequent campaigns was retained to serve with somewhat similar forces : Audley, who distinguished himself in the early years of Henry V :[228] and last, but most important, the Somersets, father and sons. The father (created successively Earl of Somerset[229] and Marquess of Dorset,[230] but afterwards

---

[213] *Cal. of Pat.* 1385–9, p. 217.
[214] Ibid. 1391–6, p. 93.
[215] Dugdale, *Baronage*, under names cited.
[216] *Cal. of Pat.* 1401–5, p. 126. [217] Ibid. pp. 138, 288, 290, 439.
[218] Nicolas, *Proc. of P. C.* ii, 72–3.
[219] Ibid. i, 343.
[220] 3 and 4 Hen. V.
[221] Nicolas, *Agincourt Roll.*
[222] Ibid.
[223] In 3 Hen. IV.
[224] Nicolas, op. cit.
[225] In 6 and 7 Hen. V.
[226] 21ᵛ Hen. VI for one year.
[227] Nicolas, op. cit.
[228] In 7–9 Hen. V.
[229] Feb. 1396–7.
[230] 29 Sept. 1397.

degraded from the marquessate) held the position of Captain of Calais. His second son John (the eldest died eight years after his father without heirs), created Duke of Somerset,[231] fought constantly, being retained at one time to serve the king with 4 knights, 90 men-at-arms, and 1,400 archers,[232] at another with 4 barons, 8 bannerets, 30 knights, 758 men-at-arms and 1,400 archers ;[233] he held the offices of Lieutenant and Captain-General of Acquitaine and of the whole realm of France. His brother who succeeded him also commanded in France, holding high office until internal dissensions in England made the continued prosecution of the war impossible.[234] For more than a century and a half the political history of Somerset had consisted almost entirely, as we have seen, in the tale of contingents sent to the wars in Wales, Ireland, Scotland and France : such lists are naturally dry reading, but it is only by their cumulative evidence that the importance of the foreign policy of the country as a whole for each county, and of the resources of each county for the country became evident.

With the Wars of the Roses we reach a period when those resources were used not in the service of all, but for party purposes only. During the preliminary period Somerset had been the scene of a miniature civil war for their own purposes between the Earl of Devon, an adherent of York, and Bonville, then a Lancastrian, which culminated in the siege of Taunton by the earl in 1451.[235] Bonville was then induced to accept the mediation of York, and the quarrel smouldered unseen for a time.[236] The sessions in the same year at Exeter before the Duke of Somerset, when the king was making a general progress, may have been held to punish some of the rebels, as 'certeine men' were then 'condemned to die for treason, and had iudjement to be executed to death.' If this had been Somerset's intention it failed, for the bishops and clergy complained that their sanctuary had been violated, and prevailed upon the king to annul the proceedings: Henry thereupon 'released a couple of arrant traitors and reversed all the former lawful proceedings.'[237]

After hostilities were over the Earl of Devon left the West Country, for he joined York in his march on London in February 1452 :[238] his enemy Bonville however remained in Somerset, and in the following year was reported to be enlisting as many men in the county as could be got at 6d. a day, in company with Wiltshire. In 1454 York endeavoured to reconcile them, but in October of the following year the feud again broke out, and Bonville was defeated in a pitched battle on Clist Heath near Exeter.[239] In the meantime York had won the first battle of St. Albans, at which Somerset was killed, and began his second Protectorate, but the peace which followed the reconciliation of the two parties in February 1456 lasted only till the autumn of 1459. Throughout that summer Margaret was busy collecting troops in the north, and the Earl of Devon and the young Duke of Somerset having raised a large force in Wessex marched through Bath, Cirencester and Evesham to join the northern lords.[240]

[231] In 1443.   [232] In 21 Hen. VI.   [233] In 21 Hen. VI.
[234] For this paragraph see Dugdale, *Baronage*, and G.E.C. *Peerage*, under names cited.
[235] Will. Worc. *Ann. Rev. Angl.* (Rolls Ser.) 475.   [236] Cf. Ramsay, *Lancaster and York*, i, 146.
[237] R. Holinshed, *Chron.* (ed. 1586), iii 637.   [238] *Engl. Chron.* (ed. Davies, Camd. Soc.) 69.
[239] *Three 15th-Century Chronicles* (Camd. Soc.) 70.
[240] Will. Worc. op. cit. 184; *Engl. Chron.* (ed. Davies, Camd. Soc.) 106; Gregory, *Chron.* (Camd. Soc.) 209, 210; Hall, *Chron.* (ed. Ellis) 250.

From this date until the year 1471 the varying fortunes of either party were not fought out in Somerset, but some of the more prominent land-holders in the county were among the killed. At Bloreheath Lord Audley, who had raised 10,000 men for Henry, was defeated and slain, a heavy loss, for his son who succeeded him, after being made prisoner at Calais in 1460, joined the Yorkists, with whom he was in great esteem.[241] At Wakefield, where York himself was killed, Salisbury was made prisoner, and having been taken to Pontefract was beheaded there. The manors he owned in Somerset were a very small part of his vast possessions, but they represented a connexion which had lasted for centuries. Somerset lost at Wakefield William Bonville, son of Lord Bonville (who was present at the battle), and his son William, Lord Harington. Lord Bonville, who was an eyewitness of the deaths of his son and grandson, did not survive them long. He joined Warwick, now leader of the Yorkist party, and marched with him to St. Albans, where, during the battle, he was stationed in the rear and given the charge of Henry. On the defeat of the Yorkists and the recovery of Henry by the queen, Bonville was taken prisoner, and though Henry had pledged his oath that no harm should come to him, he was beheaded at Margaret's command in circumstances of great cruelty.[242]

Efforts however were evidently made by the Lancastrians to recruit their forces and stir up the county against Edward. The year after his accession a commission was issued for the arrest and imprisonment of certain evil disposed persons, adherents of the late Duke of Somerset, the late Earl of Wiltshire, Robert late Lord Hungerford, and the elder Lady Hungerford who were making divers suspicious congregations in Somerset, Dorset and Wiltshire.[243] Commissions of array were also issued by the Crown until the overthrow of the Lancastrians at Tewkesbury secured Edward's hold upon the county.[244]

Before that date however Somerset had become the scene of important events. In the spring of 1471 Edward had been driven out, and Henry released from the Tower, but at the battle of Barnet the Neville faction, then supporting Henry, had been destroyed and Edward again restored. Margaret had remained in France during her husband's brief prosperity, but landed at Weymouth with her son, Lord Wenlock, Lang-strother the treasurer, and a few Lancastrians at the head of a body of Frenchmen on the very day, 14 April, of Warwick's death at Barnet. On the day after her arrival she marched to Cerne Abbey, where she was met by Somerset, Devon, Lord John Beaufort and other lords who 'sent alabout in Somarsetshere, Dorsetshere and parte of Wiltshere for to arrady and arays the people by a certayne day,' having before 'greatly laboryd to that extent, preparynge the country by all meanes to them possible.'[245] They then turned westwards and marched to Exeter,[246] and soon collected so large

---

[241] Dugdale, *Baronage*; G.E.C. *Peerage*, under Audley.

[242] *Engl. Chron.* (ed. Davies) 107. 'Natheless notwithstanding that seurte [Henry's promise] at instaunce of the quene, the duk of Exetre, and therle of Devonshyre, by iugement of him that was called the Prince, a chylde, he was beheded.' Gregory, op. cit. 211–14; Whethamstede, *Reg.* (Rolls Ser.) i, 368, seq.; Will. Worc. op. cit. 486; *Three Engl. Chron.* 76.

[243] *Cal. of Pat.* 1461–7, p. 101.   [244] Ibid. p. 529; 1467–77; pp. 195, 219, 284, 350.

[245] 'Arrivall' in *Chron. of White Rose* 22–3. Warwick also had before 'laboured' the county on Henry's behalf, so that it was 'the more lightly enducyd' now. Ibid. 23.

[246] Holinshed, *Chron.* (ed. 1586) iii, 686.

a force from Devon and Cornwall that they were able to move eastwards again. 'Leaving Exeter they sent first their fore riders streight to Shaftes-burie, and after to Salisburie, and then they took the streight waie to Taunton, Glastenburie, and after to Wels, where hovering about the countie they sent another time their foreriders to a town called Yuell, and to Bruton.'[247] 'As they went,' the 'Arrivall' tells us, 'they gathered the hable men of all thos partes.' Two courses had been open to Margaret : either to march on London and attack Edward at once, or to turn northwards and unite with the Tudor levies in Wales. The line of march she was now taking would answer either purpose until she reached the neighbourhood of Gloucester, while as a precaution she was protecting the main body of her troops by the fore-riders who were advancing in a parallel line on their right, the side on which they were exposed to attack. Edward's policy was of course to attack her before she could gather strength, and he therefore set out immediately. Both parties were now racing for Gloucester, which was reached first by Margaret, but the town would not admit her.[248] She then made a forced march to Tewkesbury where next day Edward gained a complete victory, and the death during the battle of Margaret's son Edward, and in the same month of Henry, in the Tower, put an end to hostilities.

Somerset then enjoyed a respite from military operations until Perkin Warbeck's pretensions produced trouble in the west. The necessity for defensive measures against the Scotch, who had espoused his cause, led to a demand for a heavy subsidy, and in Cornwall the people rose to resist the collection of the tax under the leadership of Thomas Flammock, 'a gentle-man learned in the laws of the realme,' and Michael Joseph, a smith, 'men of stout stomachs and high courages.'

The provost of Penrhyn, the receiver in Cornwall of the tax, took refuge in Taunton. The insurgents however followed him thither, where they 'slewe hym pytuously, in such wise that he was dismembered and kutte in many and sundry peces,'[249] and from thence proceeded to Wells, intending to march to London. At Wells they were joined by Lord Audley, who 'took upon him as their cheefe capteine to lead them against their naturall lord and king.' Their march to London was followed by their defeat at Blackheath where many were killed. Some fled, and the rest were taken prisoners, including Audley, Flammock and Joseph, who were executed.[250] One Somerset landholder, Thomas Trowe of Playnesfeld, suffered with them.[251]

Nothing daunted, however, the Cornish and Devon gentlemen and yeomen 'contynuying in their moost malicious and traiterouse purpose—moved and sterred [Warbeck and his friends] by dyvers Messages and Writinges to him sent to enter and invade this the king's Realme, and to levie Warre agaynst his moost noble persone.'[252] Warbeck accordingly sailed from Ireland, landed in Cornwall at Whitesand Bay, and 'with faire words and large promises' collected a force of 3,000 men. He then marched on Exeter, but the town withstood him : he therefore went on to Taunton,

[247] Holinshed (ed. 1586), iii, 686.
[248] Ibid.; Polydore Vergil, *Angl. Hist.* 671 ; J. Warkworth, *Chron.* (Camd. Soc.) 18.
[249] *Chronicles of London* (ed. Kingsford) 217.
[250] Ibid. 213–14 ; Holinshed, *Chron.* (ed. 1586) iii, 781–2.   [251] *Rot. Parl.* (Rec. Com.) vi, 544.
[252] Ibid. 545.

where he mustered his men on 20 September as though ready to give battle. His force at its best could never have been formidable : it now numbered about 8,000 men, ' harnessed,' says Hall, ' on the right arme and naked all the body, and never exercised in war nor marciall feates, but only with the spade and shouell.' [253] They had followed him in the hope that no small number of the nobility would join him, but when they saw that nothing of the sort happened, they began to desert secretly. At the same time the king with the Duke of Buckingham and a strong force was marching on them, preceded by a smaller body under Lord Daubeny, charged to raise the country against Warbeck : Lord Willoughby de Broke was also sent to secure the seaports in case he attempted to take refuge on the continent.[254]

Warbeck's behaviour now showed how signally Margaret had failed to instil even the rudiments of honour into ' her dere darling Perkin,' and gave the lie direct to his claim to be a Plantagenet. Holinshed tells us that ' as soon as Perkin was informed that his enimies were readie to give him battell, he that nothing lesse minded than to fight in open field with the king's puissance, dissembled all the daie time [255] with his companie, as though nothing could make him afraid, and about midnight, accompanied with three score horssemen he departed from Taunton in post to a sanctuarie toune besides Southampton, called Beaudlie, and there he and John Heron, with other registered themselves as persons priveleged.' [256] From this and other authorities [257] it is plain that not only did he desert his force at Taunton, but also the horsemen who fled with him. Many of these were taken by Daubeny, who was sent after him to Beaulieu with 500,[258] and who persuaded him to make an unconditional surrender to Henry.

In the meantime the king himself had been dealing with the rebels at Taunton. ' At first,' we hear, their ' hartes and courages were so encreased and inflamed by deadly desperacion that they earnestly determined and were stedfastly bent either to winne victory and overcome their enemies or else not one of them all to lyve any deye or houre lenger. . . . But when thei were asserteined of [Warbeck's] most shamefull flight, every person, oppressed with this common mischiefe, common fear, and common perell, casting away their armure, submitted themselves to the kyng . . . to whom the kynge not only graunted perdon but receaued theim to his favoure.' [259]

The West Country had still however a heavy penalty to pay. Henry was minded that those who had aided Warbeck with men or money ' for example sake should tast some part of due punishments for their crimes, according to the qualitie thereof. And therefore he appointed Thomas Lord Darcie, Amise Paulet knight, and Robert Sherborne deane of Poules . . . to be commissioners for assessing of their fines that were found culpable. These commissioners so bestirred themselves, in tossing the coffers and substance of all the inhabitants of both those shires, that there was not one person imbrued or spotted with the filth of that abhominable crime, that escaped the paine which he had deserued : but to such as offended rather by

253 Hall, op. cit. 484.   ' Pore and naked ' when at Taunton, and ' rascayll a most parte naked ' at Bodmin according to Vitellius A xvi.

254 Ellis, *Original Letters* (1st Ser.), i, 32.

255 Wednesday 20 Sept.

256 Holinshed *Chron.* (ed. 1586) iii, 784.

257 *Chron. Lond.* 216–17.

258 Ellis, *Original Letters* (1st Ser.) i, 32.   *Chron. Lond.* gives 200, p. 217.

259 Hall, op. cit. 485.

constreint than of malice they were gentle and favourable, so that equitie therein was verie well and iustlie executed.' [260]

The sums tossed from the coffers of Somerset amounted in the aggregate to £7,677 13s. 4d. Of this the Abbot of Muchelney paid £60 and Sir John Speke of White Lackington £200. Fifty-one inhabitants of Taunton paid altogether £441 6s. 8d., six in Bridgwater £166, and forty in Wells £313 13s. 4d. The rest was made up by assessments on the hundreds varying from £4 (Coker) to £683 13s. 4d. (Whitley). [261]

It seems probable that it was not economic causes, but the visitation of religious houses begun in October 1535, and the suppression of the lesser monasteries in the following spring which led to disturbances in the county in 1536, since it was thought advisable that, if Henry went north after the suppression of the Pilgrimage of Grace, special measures should be taken to guard against 'members of this sedition,' particular consideration being had for Somerset. [262] Taunton and Bridgwater appear to have been concerned, but whatever 'the business' was it seems to have been adequately dealt with by Lord Fitzwarren and Lord Houston. [263] Executions followed, [264] but one of Cromwell's 'Remembrances' for May was 'to remember . . . the poor men of Somersetshire for their pardon,' [265] and the list of pardons of those condemned for high treason for unlawful assemblies in the county contained 140 names. [266] After this explosion there is evidence that the inhabitants of the county accepted the ecclesiastical and religious changes quite peaceably. In September 1536 Dr. Tregonwell wrote to Cromwell that he found every one ready to obey the king's injunctions and orders, and the county as quiet and true to the king as any shire in the realm, [267] and when Lord Russell came down in 1549 to restore order during the religious rising in Devon and Cornwall they were ready to assist him with money. [268] In the spring of 1549 there was a rising against inclosures which seems to have been a small affair : the parks of Sir William Herbert and Lord Houston were thrown open, but Herbert assembled a force by royal commission sufficient to quell the insurgents, of whom he slew or executed many. [269] Holinshed states categorically that the commotions in Somerset in 1549 were in resistance to inclosures, while in Devon they were in resistance to religious changes. [270]

During the rising in Cornwall and Devon Taunton seems to have been used as a base for the royal forces. In June Sir Peter and Sir Gawen Carew fled there from the victorious insurgents to meet Lord Russell, who had been commissioned to repress the rising, and had arrived with a small force. [271] Vigorous measures were taken by the Council : the Welsh levies were marched across Somerset to Exeter, and the rebels were finally defeated at Sampford Courtenay. Many of them escaped and crossed the border into Somerset, but Sir Peter Carew and Sir Hugh Paulet were sent after them

---

[260] Holinshed *Chron.* (ed. 1586) iii, 785. So also Hall, op. cit. 486.
[261] *Letters and Papers illustrative of the reigns of Ric. III and Hen. VII* (Rolls Ser.) ii, App. B.
[262] *L. and P. Hen. VIII*, xi, 1410. The county was called on for men to assist in suppressing the Pilgrimage of Grace. There are two lists extant, one giving 740, and the other 440 men.
[263] Ibid. x, 702, 1015 (26). [264] Ibid. xi, 381a. [265] Ibid. x, 929 (ii).
[266] Ibid. x, 1015 (26). [267] Ibid. xi, 405.
[268] Holinshed, *Chron.* (ed. 1586) iii, 1025. This refers to Taunton, which apparently already showed its strong Protestant tendencies.
[269] Ibid. 1002. Cf. S. P. Dom. Edw. VI, vii, 12. [270] Op. cit. 1002, 1014.
[271] Ibid. 1003. See also *Acts of the P. C.* (ed. Dasent) 20 June 1549.

with a large force and caught them up at Kingweston, where they over-threw them and took prisoner their leader, Coffin of Devonshire.[272]

Apart from these risings the political history of Somerset had become once again largely a matter of musters and levies, until the question of ship-money agitated the county. During this period levies were made chiefly for four causes : continental struggles, and especially preparations to resist the Armada ; the intermittent hostilities in Ireland ; the defence of the Channel Islands, and the effort to suppress the pirates who had their head-quarters in the Scilly Islands.

In the summer of 1512 commissions of array for the defence of the coast against the French were issued,[273] and in the following spring Lord Fitzwarren and Lord Daubeny were ordered to hold all men of the county between 16 and 60 in readiness to resist an invasion.[274] This would have provided no inconsiderable force, as in 1524 the number of able men in the county was returned as 3,020 archers and 6,900 billmen.[275] In 1539 fresh commissions for the defence of the coast were issued,[276] and in 1544 when Henry invaded France in person the county was called upon for carriages, horses[277] and wheat,[278] as well as men. Of the gentlemen of England who were called on to furnish men forty-three were Somerset landholders,[279] and 7,825 men were levied from the county.[280]

The Irish campaigns drained the county more severely. In the spring of 1547 the musters were warned to be 'in aredynes,'[281] but there is no evidence that they sailed. In 1561 the lieutenants of the county were ordered to send a small detachment as secretly as possible 'that Ireland be not informed,' and the inducement of grants of land to would-be settlers was held out.[282] The rising in 1566 called however for a levy,[283] and a fresh detachment was raised in 1569.[284] The county had also to furnish money for their equipment,[285] and all ships and mariners in Bristol and Somerset were stayed for their transport.[286] In 1577 the county, although complain-ing bitterly, arrayed 300 men,[287] and two years later 400 were levied,[288] presumably to aid in suppressing Stukeley's invasion. In 1580 the county sent a further force of 200.[289] Purveyors were also constantly at work levy-ing victuals to support the garrisons in Limerick,[290] Galway,[291] and elsewhere in Ireland,[292] as well as for the fleet and garrisons at home.[293] For the garrison of Scilly Somerset was called on to provide men, wages and victuals, but the numbers were small ;[294] a force of 400 men was also levied in the county for the defence of the Isle of Wight and Portsmouth.[295]

In the wars, rumours of wars, and preparations which preceded the coming of the Armada the county bore its share. Immediately after Elizabeth's accession musters were ordered in every county, and the returns

---

[272] Holinshed, op. cit. 1026; S. P. Dom. Edw. VI, viii, 54.

[273] L. and P. Hen. VIII, i, 3393.   [274] Ibid. i, 3688, 3723.   [275] Ibid. Musters for 1524.

[276] Ibid. xiv (i), 398.   [277] Ibid. xix (1), 272 (8).   [278] Ibid. 272 (11).

[279] Ibid. 273.   [280] Ibid. 273 (4)   [281] Acts of the P. C. 26 May 1547

[282] S. P. Dom. Eliz. Addenda xi, 4.   [283] Ibid. xl, 22.

[284] Ibid. liv, 3.   [285] Ibid. lxvii, 90–2.   [286] Ibid. lxxi, 74.

[287] Ibid. cxiv, 14.   [288] Acts of P. C. 28 July ; 8, 11, 12 Aug. ; 14 Sept. 1579.

[289] Ibid. 16 July ; 21, 26 Sept. ; 3, 4, 9 Oct. 1580.   [290] Ibid. 17 Mar. 1573–4.

[291] Ibid. 14 Mar. 1577–8.   [292] Ibid. 25 Nov. 1577 ; 6 Oct. 1580 ; 16 Feb. ; 8 Mar. 1580–1.

[293] Ibid. 13. Nov. ; 30 Dec. 1573 ; 9 Dec. 1578 ; 12 Nov. 1580.

[294] Ibid. 30 Mar. ; 13, 15 June 1554 ; 6 July 1557.   [295] Ibid. 25 Jan. 1557–8.

for Somerset give a total of 4,326 able men; [296] 300 men were also levied in the county for the navy.[297] Another muster in 1560 showed that the able men had increased to 5,330,[298] and the returns show a continual increase.[299] Orders were also issued for providing horses,[300] and directions for improving the quality of the levies,[301] but as the burden on the county was very heavy, in 1584 orders were given for the training of a smaller number.[302] For the campaigns in the Low Countries a levy of 150 volunteers was made in 1586,[303] and of 150 footmen in 1587.[304] Rumours of invasions were also current : in the winter of 1585 it was reported that a raid on Somerset was planned by Arundel, Don Bernardino the Nuncio and Westmorland with some 600 or 700 men ; they were to sail from St. Malo in three or four ships of war and carry off 'some gentlemen of account' to ransom if possible.[305]

The result of such continual expectation was that by 1586 the county was in a very complete state of defence. The coast was defended by towers with cannon at Porlock, Hurlstone and Uphill, while two more defended the shore between Uphill and the mouth of the Yeo. There were also guns at Minehead and Combwich near Bridgwater.[306] The chief gentlemen of the county each commanded a band of equipped soldiers ;[307] arms and ammunition were provided,[308] watches were set and beacons prepared ;[309] and suspected persons or spreaders of seditious rumours were sought out, and ordered by the Council to receive condign punishment.[310] Captains were appointed to inspect all preparations under the superintendence of the deputy lieutenants,[311] and the report to the Council in 1587 declared that the officer had found the county 'beyonnde myne expectacon and vnto my greate comforte . . . so excellentlie furnished with all sorts of armor and weapons, and that verie good in such pfecte rediness, the men so well sorted and chosen,' through the care of the justices of the shire, 'that I do assure Yo Lordshippes yt doth exceede anie countrey that ever I came in.'[312] The same officer reported a year later that the trained forces were brave and well supplied with arms : 'it is a most gallant county for men, armour and readiness.'[313]

In the summer of 1587 there was a false alarm of the Armada ; 220 ships were sighted off Scilly, and the lords lieutenant of the southern counties were ordered to have their men in readiness at an hour's warning.[314] Of the force to be held ready for the defence of the country 3,350 were to be drawn from Somerset, and if Plymouth and Falmouth were attacked 3,000 Somerset men were to advance there at once ;[315] as late as November the

---

[296] S. P. Dom. Eliz. vi, 61.   [297] Ibid. xii, 52.   [298] Ibid. xii, 63.

[299] Ibid. xci, 56, 63; xcvi, 354; cxxxix, 49.   [300] Ibid. lv; xxxvi, 88-9; clxxxvii, 37.

[301] Ibid. xliv, 60; lxxx, 63; clxx, 62, 63, 65; clxvii, 14; clxviii, 26; clxx, 85; clxxii, 42; clxxx, 61.

[302] Ibid. clxx, 85.   [303] Acts of P. C. 13, 15 May 1586.

[304] Ibid. 7 June 1587.   [305] S. P. Dom. Eliz. Add. xxix, 55.

[306] Cf. map in Cotton MSS. 1 Aug. vol. i, reproduced in E. Green, *Preparations in Somerset against the Spanish Armada*, frontispiece. See also 'Cert. of Musters, 1569,' in *Somers Rec. Soc.* vol. xx.

[307] S. P. Dom. Eliz. cxciv, 5, 26, 27, 28.   [308] Ibid. clxxx, vii, 36, 37, 68.

[309] Ibid. cxciv, 53.   [310] Acts of P. C. Mar. 1586-7.

[311] S. P. Dom. Eliz. cxciv, 53; *Acts of P. C.* 26 Dec. 1587.

[312] S. P. Dom. Eliz. cxcvii, 50.   [313] Ibid. ccix, 38. Cf. also cxcvii, 50.

[314] *Acts of P. C.* 9 Aug.; 9 Oct. 1587. Of the 12,000 men certified in Somerset 4,000 were now returned as trained. S. P. Dom. Eliz. ccix, 43.

[315] S. P. Dom. Eliz. ccxi, 74.

Somerset levy of 4,000 for the defence of Poole was held in readiness.[316] When at last the Armada was sighted levies were ordered to proceed to London. Somerset's contingent consisted of 4,000 foot, 50 lances and 100 light horse,[317] but the foot and horsemen were almost immediately disbanded,[318] letters of thanks being sent to the deputy lieutenants and justices for their forwardness and goodwill in the matter. Defensive measures seem to have been continued even after the danger was over, as the county had to petition the Council that the number of horses and soldiers to be kept in readiness might be abated.[319]

Ireland had all along been recognized as Spain's back door into England. In the spring of 1587 a force towards which Somerset was to contribute 200 was commanded to be ready to sail on three days' warning.[320] As late as 15 September 1588 a levy for Ireland was ordered in the county,[321] and in the following year when preparations were made to resist a Spanish invasion 300 men were raised in Somerset and transported from Bristol.[322] In October 1590 the Irish levies were disbanded and sent home,[323] but five years later another demand was made ; the Somerset contingent then numbered only 94 men.[324] The revolt of 1598 however called for more serious measures : in July a force of 150 foot,[325] in October 400 well-equipped troops,[326] and in the following February 100 more men[327] were called for from the county ; in June 1600 100 men[328] and a levy of light horse[329] were demanded, and in November[330] and the following April[331] reinforcements of 40 and 50 men respectively for Lough Foyle. Money[332] and victuals[333] were also raised in the county, but there seems to have been difficulty in collecting both the men and the corn.[334] The sums of money contributed by the county for apparel and arms for the soldiers sent to Ireland amounted for the years 1601 and 1602 to £1,275.[335]

In expeditions abroad or preparations for defence at home Somerset again had to bear a part. A levy was ordered for the expedition planned to attack Spain early in 1589 ;[336] in the following year when an attack was expected on Milford Haven, 1,000 men were ordered to be held in readiness,[337] and in 1591, when Elizabeth was helping Henry IV against the League, 300 men were ordered for service in the Low Countries[338] and 150 for Brittany.[339] The levy for the Low Countries seems to have been very unsatisfactory : half of them had to be left behind, for they were so poor and weak that they could not endure the crossing.[340] In 1592 another batch of 150 men was sent to Brittany.[341] For the expedition against Cadiz the county had to provide both men[342] and victuals,[343] and to supply 4,000

---

316 *Acts of P. C.* 12 Nov. 1587.
317 Ibid. 23 July 1588.
318 Ibid. 3 Aug. 1588.
319 S. P. Dom. Eliz. ccxxiii, 111.
320 Ibid. cxcviii, 60, 61 ; cxcix, 39.
321 Ibid. ccxvi, 26.
322 *Acts of P. C.* 25 Sept. 1589 ; 2 Jan. 1589–90.
323 Ibid. 18 Oct. 1590.
324 Ibid. 5 Nov. 1595 ; 4 Mar. 1595–6.
325 Ibid. 19 July 1598.
326 Ibid. 28 Oct. 1598.
327 Ibid. 18 Feb. 1598–9.
328 Ibid. 26 June 1600.
329 Ibid. 29 June 1600.
330 Ibid. 30 Nov. 1600.
331 Ibid. 28 Apr. 1601.
332 Ibid. 31 Aug. 1598 ; 11 May, 27 June 1600.
333 Ibid. 26 Jan. 1599–1600 ; 18 June, 30 Nov. 1600.
334 Ibid. 23 Aug. 1598 ; 18 June 1600.
335 S. P. Dom. Eliz. cclxxxv, 20.
336 *Acts of P. C.* 14 Jan. 1588–9.
337 Ibid. 29 June 1590.
338 Ibid. 17 Mar. 1590–1 ; S. P. Dom. Eliz. ccxxxviii, 40.
339 *Acts of P. C.* 21 Feb., 17 Mar. 1590–1 ; S. P. Dom. Eliz. ccxxxix, 5.
340 S. P. Dom. Eliz. ccxxxviii, 18.
341 Ibid. ccxli, 24 ; *Acts of P. C.* 1, 20, 25 Oct. 1592.
342 *Acts of P. C.* 7, 18 Mar. 1595–6.
343 Ibid. 14 Dec. 1595 ; 18 Jan. 1595–6.

men for coast defence in case of invasion.[344] In 1596, when Henry was again receiving help, 150 men were levied,[345] and since a reprisal from Spain was expected, 4,000 men were again ordered to be in readiness to resist invasion,[346] and a little later a smaller force of 450,[347] afterwards reduced to 300, who were sent abroad when the scare was over.[348] In the spring of 1598 4,000 troops were once more arrayed to repel invasion.[349]

Somerset was one of the counties which sent bitter complaints to the Council of the disorders attending these musters : ' the losse and deficiencie of armes . . . the releasing or exchaunging of the soldiers either for bribes or for any other partial respects . . . the loose dispersinge and runninge awaie of the men that after their employment should have bin re-tourned to their former state and condicion for their orderly livinge and labouring, each man in his service and trade.'[350] The peace, however, con-cluded in 1598 between France and Spain set a term to these disturbances, since it freed Elizabeth from the necessity of helping her neighbour to resist Spanish aggression, and from the fear of attacks at home.

During the last five years the Channel Islands had been especially liable to attack, and from its position Somerset was a suitable field for the supply of men to defend them. In the spring of 1593 300 men were dispatched,[351] and 300 were again levied in 1597 ;[352] these were called back and a fresh detachment of 100 sent in the following year ;[353] and again in 1599 the governor begged for more men from Dorset and Somerset if the islands were not to be lost.[354]

Mansfield's disastrous expedition appears to have been the next occasion for levies of men in Somerset : 150 men with £76 7s. coat and conduct money were pressed in the end of 1624,[355] in 1625 500 foot were raised,[356] and in 1627 125 men were sent to Plymouth for embarkation for the expe-dition to Rhé.[357] A large number of the men collected were however not needed, and it became a difficult question what to do with them. The commissioners thought that they should be disposed of in petty garrisons along the coast in Somerset and the south-western counties ;[358] but as the plague was raging in Dorset, that county asked that the contingent of 1,000 they should have entertained might be sent to Somerset ;[359] 6,000 men remaining in Devon and Cornwall were billeted on Somerset and five other counties, who were to allow those billeted 3s. 6d. a week and those march-ing through 8d. a day.[360] Besides the disorders consequent on the movements of such bodies of men the counties were thus heavily mulcted : between 20 November 1627 and 20 July 1628 the western division of Somerset spent £1,834 8s. 11d. on billeting soldiers,[361] and the eastern division £1,536 0s. 5d.[362]

Before the question of ship-money agitated Somerset, the county had had, under both Tudors and Stuarts, to contribute to unparliamentary

---

[344] *Acts of P. C.* 7, 12 Nov. 1595; 21 Mar. 1595-6.
[346] Ibid. 31 Oct., 6 Nov. 1596. [347] Ibid. 9 May 1597.
[349] Ibid. 12 Feb. 1597-8. [350] Ibid. 4 June 1596.
[351] S. P. Dom. Eliz. ccxlv, 5. *Acts of P. C.* 14 May 1593.
[352] S. P. Dom. Eliz. cclxii, 114. *Acts of P. C.* 10, 24 Apr. 1597.
[353] Ibid. 21 May 1598. [354] S. P. Dom. Eliz. cclxxii, 103.
[355] S. P. Dom. Jas. I, clxxvi, 36, 50.
[357] Ibid. lxv, 76. [358] Ibid. xii, 79-80.
[360] Ibid. lxxxv, 69. [361] Ibid. cx, 47.

[345] Ibid. 23 Sept. 1596.
[348] Ibid. 30 May 1597.

[356] S. P. Dom. Chas. I, vi, 50.
[359] Ibid. xxxv, 7.
[362] Ibid. cxiv, 77.

grants, the loan of 1542, when £10 from lands and £6 13s. 4d. from goods on the hundred was fixed as the minimum to be levied,[363] the loans of 1589,[364] 1590[365] and 1597,[366] and the Benevolence of 1614. Against the latter Somerset (with Nottinghamshire and Warwickshire) appealed to the statute of Richard III,[367] but the justices of the peace were summoned before the Council and overwhelmed with arguments and precedents.[368] The forced loan, or 'free gift' of 1626 met with less resistance in Somerset; those responsible proceeded 'temperately and discreetly,' and the loan 'passed smoothly; not three men have refused, and no man of any quality.'[369]

We first hear of ship-money in Somerset in the spring of 1588; on 1 April letters were sent to maritime towns for ships above 60 tons to be ready by the 25th; Bridgwater was called on for one ship and one pinnace, and Chard for two ships and one pinnace. Devon, Dorset, Somerset and Cornwall were allowed to compound.[370] In the following summer Bridgwater was required to provide a barque furnished in warlike manner, but composition was allowed at £447 15s. 6d.,[371] afterwards reduced to £333. Great difficulties were however found in raising it, for though the western part of the county was willing to contribute, the eastern refused.[372]

Again in the spring of 1596 Somerset was asked for a similar contribution. Money was required to fit out three ships at Bristol for the expedition to Cadiz, and the county was called on for £600 to be imposed on ' the generall inhabitants of good hability of the whole county ' towards the total cost of £946 13s. 4d.[373] Great difficulty was found in levying the money.[374] In the autumn a letter was sent to the deputy lieutenants of the county stating that Bristol had been obliged to run into debt, for the ships had returned, and the wages of the mariners and the cost of provisions could not be left unpaid. They were ordered to collect the money from the wealthier sort of the inhabitants, 'wherein' run the letters, 'we doubt not but . . . you will shewe that forwardnes in contributing towardes this publicke charge which in other services you have alwaies shewed.'[375] Polite speeches were however of no avail, and a few weeks later much more peremptory letters were sent : '. . . havinge written so many letters unto you (as we have doone) concerning the contribucion of . . . Somerset . . . yt cannot but seeme straunge unto us that neither our letters nor the regard to be had of her Majesty's service hath taken anye better effect. . . . The excuses that have bin alledged by your letters we cannot holde sufficient, for if there have bin any money alredie collected and otherwise employde (as is alleaged) in her Majesty's service, there was no such direccion given from us, and as for the greevaunces of the dearth and scarcetie of corne and victuals and losse of cattell . . . the same difficulties are comon to you with other counties, which nevertheles have not refused in like sort to contribute. . . .'

That the dearth was no exaggerated excuse is plain from a letter of the Council to the Lord Mayor of London ordering him to allow 200 quarters of wheat to be sent to Somerset since the people there were 'like to perishe

---

[363] L. and P. Hen. VIII, xvii, 194 (2).

[364] S. P. Dom. Eliz. ccxxiv, 107.

[365] Acts of P. C. 31 Dec. 1590.

[366] Ibid. 9 Feb. 1596-7; 26 Aug. 1597.

[367] 1 Ric. III, cap. 2.

[368] P. C. Reg. 17 Sept., 12, 14, 16, 30 Nov. 1614.

[369] S. P. Dom. Chas. I, xxxvi, 46; liii, 88.

[370] Acts of P. C. 8 May 1588.

[371] Ibid. 1 Sept. 1588.

[372] Ibid. 17 Mar. 1588-9.

[373] Ibid. 16 Feb. 1595-6.

[374] Ibid. 21 Mar,

[375] Ibid. 7 Sept. 1596.

if they be not in some sorte relieved out of other places.'[376] In the following June the Lords of the Privy Council desired the Lord Chief Justice 'to deale by way of perswacion' with those in the county from whom the money should be raised, for 'wee have written so many letters unto the Deputy Lieutenants and to the Justices of Peace . . . touching the contribucion . . . and do find so little regard taken, or at least wise so little effect proceeded of our letters, as, if it were not in respect of the wants and somme disabilitie of that county . . . we should take it in very ill part, and enquire further after those that are the cause of it as a matter of contempt.'[377] As late as May 1601,[378] however, the Council was still unable to extract the money from Somerset.

In the spring of 1635 the real trouble, foreshadowed by the previous difficulties, began. On 6 November 1634 writs had been issued for ships ; in the case of Somerset to Bridgwater, Minehead and all maritime towns and places between Gloucester and Minehead, to the sheriffs of Gloucester and Somerset, and to the cities of Bristol and Gloucester for a ship of 800 tons for 26 weeks, manned by 260 men and fully equipped.[379] By an Order in Council in the following spring the king lent ships of his own to those maritime counties and ports which could not find them, the *James* being lent to Somerset, Bristol and Gloucester.[380] For this of course payment was to be made.

Opposition was immediately offered by Sir Robert Phelips, at whose instigation the hundred of Tintinhull refused to pay the £20 at which it was rated ; and he was seconded in his obstruction by Napper the constable of the hundred.[381] Ilchester petitioned the Council for relief from Napper's rating, for Hodges the sheriff had rated Tintinhull as a whole, the subpartitioning of the rate being left to the constable, who assessed Ilchester with Northover at £15. This on petition was rectified by Hodges, but Napper 'giving scandalous words to the sheriff' persisted, supported by Phelips, who ordered the constable of Ilchester to refuse to collect the money.[382] Phelips had eventually to give way, and the rate was collected as levied by Hodges, £9 9s. 6d. on Ilchester and Northover together, and £10 10s. 6d. on the rest of the hundred. The parishes of St. Decuman and Old Cleeve in the hundred of Williton and Freemanors also petitioned, Hodges' assessment having thrown the whole rate for the hundred on them alone.[383] But in spite of such difficulties the levy was collected by 5 September, 1635, the total sum paid by the county being apparently £6,735.[384]

On 4 August of this year another writ had been issued to all counties, inland and maritime alike. The Council decided what proportion of the total sum levied on any county each corporate town should pay, and the rest of the sum was divided among the hundreds by the sheriff. A few sheriffs acted instantly and promptly, and Hodges appears to have been one of these, but his very rough-and-ready method of assessment led both himself and his successors in office into endless difficulties ; he had not the strength or influence to force it on the county.[385]

[376] *Acts of P. C.* 4, 14 Apr. 1597.
[377] Ibid. 14 June 1597.
[378] Ibid. 21 May 1601. Cf. also 30 Nov. 1600.
[379] S. P. Dom. Chas. I, cclxxvii, 15.
[380] Ibid. cclxxxiv, 15.
[381] Ibid. ccxc, 75, 77.
[382] Ibid. ccxci, 56, 57.
[383] Ibid. ccxci, 103.
[384] Ibid. ccxcvi, 7, 56-8.
[385] Ibid cccxlvi, 65 ; cccxlvii, 23 ; cccl, 39 ; ccccxii, 13, 14 and elsewhere.

The original assessment appears to have been, Taunton, £100; Bridgwater and Bath, £70 each; Minehead and Wells, £60 each; Axbridge, Ilchester and Yeovil, £30 each; Langport Eastover, £20, and the rest of the county £7,520, making a total of £8,990.[386] A second assessment rated Taunton, Bridgwater, Bath, Wells, Ilchester and Yeovil as before, and charged £58 19s. on Minehead, £56 on Glastonbury, £53 6s. 8d. on Crewkerne, £49 on Frome, and £47 13s. 4d. on Bedminster. The total for the county is here given as £8,000, so presumably the balance of £7,375 1s. was assessed on the hundreds.[387] This assessment immediately met with opposition. Taunton petitioned to be rated at £30 instead of £100, as this was the rate they had always paid.[388] The justices of assize were ordered to inquire into the matter and direct such a course as they should approve for their relief,[389] and the Bishop of Bath and Wells was charged to settle this among many other difficulties.[390] Catsash, Horethorn, Bruton and Norton Ferris complained that they were overcharged to the extent of £80, and were reassessed at the bishop's direction by Hodges.[391] He appears however to have re-rated them at £320 each, £106 6s. 8d. more than they thought they should pay,[392] but the bishop on being appealed to again,[393] confirmed Hodges' decision.[394] The hundred of Tintinhull on this occasion paid up apparently without petitioning,[395] but Bridgwater, with the tithings of Dunwear, Bower, Horsey, Chilton and Hamp (part of the hundred of North Petherton), petitioned the Council successfully against an over-rate of £3 6s. 8d.[396] Complaints from Wellow, Chewton, Milverton and Norton St. Philip were referred to the bishop, who however gave them no relief.[397] Abdick and Bulstone declared that £40 charged to them should be paid by Milverton, but their complaint was not allowed for this time,[398] although a reassessment was ordered.[399] Bath Forum similarly wished to shift part of its rate on to Wellow, but after investigation by Finch the rate was ordered to stand.[400] Bempstone, Kilmersdon, Langport Eastover and Frome Selwood were also dissatisfied and referred to the bishop.[401]

In some cases opposition was met with from individuals. Phelips was again to the fore in the matter of the assessment of Northover;[402] and in retaliation for a re-rate which he considered too high, he ordered his son to deny payment for his demesnes in Sock.[403] Phelips' objection was to the principle: William Strode of Street and Barrington, a merchant, refused because he considered the whole tithing in which he lived unfairly rated, and his case was referred by the Council to the bishop,[404] who declared his assessment just;[405] Strode thereupon submitted.[406] At Batcombe another merchant, Aish, who was reported as worth £15,000, refused to pay his rate of £5, but apparently was forced to submit.[407] Even the royal wards made an effort to be excused.[408] All over the county great difficulty was

---

386 S. P. Dom. Chas. I, ccii, 44.
387 Ibid. ccli, 88.
388 Ibid. ccii, 129; ccli, 60, 61.
389 Ibid. cccxlviii, 48.
390 Ibid. ccclvii, 151.
391 Ibid. cccxxx, 15.
392 Ibid. ccclviii, 47.
393 Ibid. ccclvii, 5.
394 Ibid. ccclxv, 4; ccclxvii, 27.
395 Ibid. cccliv, 69.
396 Ibid. ccclv, 137.
397 Ibid. ccclxv, 1–3; ccclxvii, 23–6; ccclxxvi, 118; ccclxxviii, 53.
398 Ibid. ccclxxxix, 26, 71.
399 Ibid. cccxc, 63.
400 Ibid. ccclvii, 151; ccclxxxix, 73; ccccvii, 51.
401 Ibid. ccclvii, 151, 137; ccclxvii, 11.
402 Ibid. ccii, 44; cccxxvii, 106.
403 Ibid. ccclvi, 8.
404 Ibid. cccxxxvi, 29, 80; cccxliii, 17; cccxlv, 33, 34.
405 Ibid. ccclv, 54.
406 Ibid. ccclxv, 8. Strode, who was a born obstructionist, refused also to pay in Hampshire.
407 Ibid. ccclvi, 103; ccclxi, 10.
408 Ibid. ccclii, 52.

found in collecting the money, even where no petition or complaints were preferred. Strode, who in this matter seems to have been both moderate and truthful, declared that the liberty used by the raters had been the cause of the disorders, and that he himself had paid more than his share of ten subsidies when men of five times his estate had not paid as much as he.[409] When it was decided to re-assess the whole county[410] he foresaw the difficulties which would ensue. 'The business is worse out of order than ever,' he wrote. 'We conceive the ground of rates to be either law or custom, which alterations will utterly destroy, and those that endeavour them will find it will disorder and hinder his Majesty's service.'[411] It was pointed out to the Council by Portman, the then sheriff, that the fact that a new rate was to be assessed was in itself enough to cause refusals, since every one would hope to be eased,[412] and Hampden's refusal and the anticipation of his trial caused fresh difficulties; 'no one will pay on the rumour of the judge's opinion.'[413]

The only method in the sheriff's power for enforcing payment was distraint, generally of cattle, and this had to be resorted to constantly;[414] but in the low feeding country the people turned most of the land into meadow instead of pasture, apparently[415] keeping hardly any stock; beasts were allowed to starve in the pounds, and violence was offered to bailiffs.[416] Constables also refused to bring in the money they had collected.[417]

In December 1636 Somerset was more than £404 behind with instalments due; only Dorset, Essex and Northamptonshire being as much in arrears,[418] and at the end of October 1637 the total arrears were £1,425 8s. 0d.[419] Retiring sheriffs were responsible to their successors for arrears, and Hodges considered himself overcharged by £50 2s. 6d., which he refused to pay,[420] but the matter was referred to the bishop, and he had to submit.[421]

In June 1638 the sheriff reported that the arrears were only £229 7s. 9½d.,[422] but a fresh writ was issued in this summer; the rate however was much reduced, Somerset being charged only with £2,800.[423] Great difficulties were again experienced in collecting it: violence was threatened to constables and bailiffs: when distrained cattle were offered for sale bids of a few pence only were made,[424] and by September 1640 only £300 had been collected.[425] The sheriff again pointed out the difficulties caused by arbitrary alterations of the rates: 'there is no such artifice to make this service intricate and impossible, and to raise disturbance among the vulgar, as by admitting the alteration of ancient hundred rates, except they are generally reformed through the whole county.'[426]

Other matters however now arose to distract attention from the ship-money question. A levy of 1,200 men, horse and foot, was ordered for the Scotch campaign,[427] and the gentlemen of the county were solicited for contributions towards the expenses of the expedition.[428] The men were raised

[409] S. P. Dom. Chas. I, cccxlv, 34.
[410] Ibid. cccxlvi, 65; cccxlvii, 23.
[411] Ibid. ccclxv, 8.
[412] Ibid. ccclxxxi, 2.
[413] Ibid. ccclxxxviii, 124.
[414] Ibid. cccl, 39.
[415] Ibid. ccclxi, 19.
[416] Ibid. ccclxxxviii, 124.
[417] Ibid. ccclxix, 86.
[418] Ibid. cccxxxvii, 52.
[419] Ibid. ccclxx, 73, 74.
[420] Ibid. cccxxxvi, 29.
[421] Ibid. cccliv, 86; ccclvi, 79.
[422] Ibid. cccxcii, 1.
[423] Ibid. cccci, 45.
[424] Ibid. cccclxiv, 23.
[425] Ibid. cccclxvii, 125.
[426] Ibid. ccclviii, 57.
[427] Ibid. ccccxiii, 111.
[428] Ibid. ccccxviii, 56, 99.

without difficulty,[429] but by an unfortunate mistake they were collected at the rendezvous at Bruton and Wincanton sooner than was necessary, and great disorders ensued:[430] many of them deserted, and the officers were placed in great difficulties owing to want of money to pay for the extra time, while to add to the confusion the plague broke out.

The command of one regiment was given to Colonel Lunsford, who reported on it in extraordinary terms. 'I find my regiment in the greatest disorder, divers of them in troops returned home ; all are forward to disband . . . hues and cries are of no effect, . . . we are daily assaulted by sometimes 500 of them together, have hurt and killed some in our own defence, and are driven to keep together on our guard. Notwithstanding we still march forward with as many as we can. . . . The officers have approved themselves careful and discreet, and their lives have been in danger every hour since their march.'[431] That this was no exaggeration was shown only too soon by the mutiny of one company of the regiment at Wellington, where they murdered a Roman Catholic officer, and then all deserted, the bailiffs and constables refusing to interfere.[432] After their departure however the county was reported in good order.[433]

The division of parties in Somerset during the struggle between Charles and Parliament, and after the outbreak of the Civil War, followed natural lines. The landowners and country gentlemen were almost all for the king, but the traders and clothiers, of whom the county contained so many, were for Parliament. There were very few of this party outside the eastern division of the county except some small freeholders and some lesser traders in the towns. The lower classes appear from what evidence exists on the subject to have favoured the Established Church. In 1629 the deputy-lieutenants, after reviewing the trained forces, reported that they were all well affected in religion ;[434] and the country people were indignant at attempts made by ' Humourists ' and Puritans to stop the feasts of the dedication of churches : throughout the county also the old customs of church-ales, clerk-ales, and bid-ales were kept up.[435] That apart from the commercial element the general feeling of the county was Royalist appears from a petition for the maintenance of the *status quo* from the knights, esquires, gentry, freeholders and inhabitants of Somerset to the House of Commons dated 15 June 1642.[436]

During the war Somerset from its position became the scene of important events. Gardiner has explained that, after the failure at Turnham Green to crush the rebels at the outset, ' recourse was had . . . to a scheme in accordance with which combat was to be refused in the centre, while the two wings in Yorkshire and Cornwall pushed on to smother the weaker enemy between them. After this scheme had been tried in vain . . . the very opposite plan was tried,' that of acting from the centre upon the circumference.[437] The campaigns in Somerset and the west are at once comprehensible when this is understood. The battles of Lansdown and

[429] S. P. Dom Chas. I, ccccliv, 64.
[430] Ibid. cccclv, 6 ; cccclix, 7. Much blame is due to Strode who had been chosen treasurer, but ' neglected and slighted the service.' Ibid. cccclv, 6 ; cccclvii, 50.
[431] Ibid. cccclvii, 91.   [432] Ibid. cccclx, 5.   [433] Ibid. cccclxvii, 138.
[434] Ibid. cxlix, 20.   [435] Ibid. xcvi, 7 ; ccxlvii, 24 ; ccl, 20.
[436] Bodl. Shelf Mark, Ashm. H23 (162).   [437] *Hist. of Gt. Civil War*, ii, 63.

Roundway Down mark the close, as far as Somerset was concerned, of the operations from the circumference to the centre, for after Lansdown the royal forces pushed on away from the peninsula. The period beginning with Charles' march from Evesham to the west was that when the operations from the centre were tried. Strategy is impossible however without men with which to carry it out, and the use of local levies involved the King's generals in a considerable difficulty. Local feeling was so strong that it was very difficult to persuade west countrymen to march into the midlands so long as the enemy threatened any important town in the west. As long as Plymouth was in danger Hopton's levies from Devon and Cornwall could not be persuaded to advance, and while Taunton was held by Parliament Goring and Grenville could not hope to bring up the western levies which were so badly needed in the midlands.

The first hostilities took place in Somerset in 1642. The Parliamentary Ordinance for the militia was executed in the county by Colonel Popham, Colonel Pyne, Sir Thomas Wroth, Sir John Horner, Mr. Cole, Mr. Ash, Mr. Hippesly, Mr. Sandford, Mr. Harbyn, Mr. Strode, and others of the county gentry.[438] To check their proceedings Charles sent Lord Hertford[439] to Bath to execute the Commission of Array for mustering the trained bands, imposing arms on all able to find them, and seizing ammunition : with a force thus collected Charles hoped he would be able to relieve Portsmouth which was then besieged. The trained bands were ordered to repair to Wells, ' so that the affections of the people might be wrought upon and their understandings well informed.' Hertford was here joined by Colonel Lunsford and the officers of his old regiment ; three troops of horse under Mr. John Digby, Sir Francis Hawly, and Sir Ralph Hopton ;[440] Lord Powlett ; and Sir John Stowell and his sons.[441] From Wells Hopton made an expedition with three troops of horse, one troop of dragoons, 100 foot, and about 28 county gentlemen with their servants and retinues to Shepton Mallet, where he seized what arms and ammunition he could find. The Parliamentarians in the meanwhile gathered a force at Chewton of over 1,000 men and were reinforced by Mr. Popham's regiment, 300 horse from Wiltshire, 300 ' lusty stout men ' from Bristol, 250 or 300 foot from Gloucestershire and supplies of ammunition. They were also provided with more victuals than they could consume by the whole countryside.[442] Clarendon regrets that Hertford did not at once attack them, for he thinks that they could then have been dispersed, since 80 horse and 14 dragoons under Sir John Stowell, which had been sent to Boroughbridge to secure the passage of the western trained bands to Wells, had charged and routed a greater body of horse and above 600 foot, inflicting considerable loss on them.[443] Besides the supplies from Shepton Mallet, Hertford was reinforced by 20 dragoons, 40 horse, and a wagon full of arms from the western division, but his position was rapidly rendered untenable by reinforcements to the rebels which brought their numbers up

---

[438] Oldmixon, *Hist. of Engl. during the Reigns of the Royal House of Stuart*, 208.

[439] He had been appointed lord lieutenant of the county on 23 March 1638–9, and commissioner of array and lieutenant-governor for the western counties on 2 Aug. 1642. Clar. MSS. 1738 (1).

[440] The latter raised this at his own cost.   [441] Clar. MSS. 1738 (1).   [442] Ibid.

[443] Ash in his letter to the Commons says the rebels were only 120 or 140. *Lds'. Journ.* vi, 278–9. The Clarendon MSS. does not mention the dragoons, and gives the rebels only 600 foot.

to 12,000, and some of his trained bands having deserted he was obliged to retire via Somerton to Sherborne.[444]

The grand jury of the county[445] and the constables of the hundreds[446] petitioned against the Commission, and the grand inquest at the assizes asked that it might be suspended, and that until an act was made for the settlement of the militia question, the militia might be in the hands of the resident justices of the peace.[447] Parliament ordered Hertford to be apprehended for enforcing the execution of the Commission,[448] but although defeated in a sortie against the rebels at Yeovil he remained secure in Sherborne until the news of the capitulation of Portsmouth reached him. His immediate errand was therefore impossible, and as the strong places in the county (Taunton, Wellington and Dunster) were declaring for Parliament he could hope for no reinforcements. He therefore made his way to Minehead, and after being refused entrance to Dunster Castle,[449] crossed to Wales, taking with him the volunteers, foot, baggage and cannon.[450] Meanwhile Taunton had been seized by a parliamentary force under Sir William Portman, Mr. Coles and Mr. Pyne, who collected arms for 1,800 men, 150 saddles, 25 horses, and at least £10,000 in Taunton, Bridgwater, Glastonbury, Ilchester, Ilminster and Bath.[451]

The royal prospects however soon brightened : Hopton, who had retreated into Cornwall when he parted company from Hertford, with the horse and dragoons, had found that county practically solid for the king. Having collected a small but excellent force which defeated Stamford at Stratton, he advanced through Devon and Dorset, and on 4 June 1643 joined Hertford and Prince Maurice at Chard.[452] Since Hertford's departure Somerset had been in the hands of Parliament, for Prince Rupert's attack on Bristol in March had failed. Now however the Royalists had a good chance of recovering the county since Prince Maurice and Hertford had 1,500 horse, 1,000 foot and 10 or 11 field pieces,[453] and Hopton 3,000 foot, 500 horse, 300 dragoons and 4 or 5 guns. They marched on the following day on Taunton, which surrendered at once, the garrison flying to Bridgwater, whither Hertford proceeded on the 6th, only to find that they had not waited for him to come up, but had again fled. On the 7th Dunster surrendered without a blow. This was a very welcome piece of news, for the castle was considered impregnable, and Hertford had been bitterly disappointed at his failure to occupy it the year before, blaming 'the evill dispositions and cowardly behaviour' of Hopton's men. Since then it had been unsuccessfully attacked (in January) by a party of Welsh royalists. The surrender now appears to have been due to the opinion generally held in the west at this time that the king's success was inevitable and resistance useless.

Parliament in the meantime sent Sir William Waller to oppose the Royalists,[454] while Popham and Strode rallied the flying garrison of Taunton

---

[444] Clarendon op. cit. vi, 2–7 ; Lds'. Journ. vi, 278–9 ; Clar. MSS. 1738 (1).
[445] S. P. Dom. Chas I, ccccxci, 88.   [446] Ibid. ccccxci, 118.   [447] Ibid. ccccxci, 117.
[448] Ibid. ccccxci, 104.   [449] Maxwell-Lyte, Hist. of Dunster, 86.
[450] Clarendon, op. cit. vi, 33.   [451] Oldmixon, op. cit. 208 ; Vicars, Jehovah Jireh, 135.
[452] Merc. Aulicus, 303. Clarendon says 'about the middle of June,' op. cit. vii, 96.
[453] Clar. MSS. 1738 (4). Clarendon in Hist. Civil War says 1,600 or 1,700 horse and 7 or 8 field pieces; vii, 96.
[454] Waller was appointed Sergeant-Major-General of the West, with authority to raise five regiments of horse and five of foot, and power of martial law. Lds'. Journ. v, 602, 617.

and the remnant of Stratton's force which had come up. At Glastonbury they were met by Hertford, who had marched to Somerton, and were easily driven off. Hertford did not wish to follow them too far, owing to Waller's position at Bath,[455] but Prince Maurice, who commanded the pursuing force, chased them until he found himself face to face with Waller at Chewton. Here an engagement took place in which the Royalists successfully routed Waller, but the latter was probably content to withdraw to Bath as he was not yet ready for hostilities. After this encounter Hertford marched to Wells, where he stayed for ten or twelve days; he felt himself strong enough to send a detachment under Sir John Berkeley to assist in the blockade of Exeter, but in the meantime Waller was reinforced by Hazelrigg and his 'Lobsters.' When the Royalists again moved, they made a circuit by Frome and crossed the Avon at Bradford, with the object of getting between Waller and London, while threatening an advance on Bath by the Avon valley. This movement was followed by counter-movements on the part of Waller, 'the best shifter and chooser of ground when his side was not Master of the field that I ever saw,'[456] who effectually prevented any advance from this side on the town. Hertford now gave up the attempt to enter the town from the east, and marched to Marshfield on the north, apparently hoping to gain possession of the Lansdown ridge, after which he would have comparatively little difficulty in getting into the town. He quartered in Marshfield on 4 July, and on the 5th marched to Tog Hill, so that a deep valley now lay between him and Lansdown. Waller had however prepared for this move: 'he stood upon a piece of ground almost inaccessible. In the brow of the hill hee had raisd brestworkes, in wch his Cannon and greate store of small shott was placed: on either Flanke hee was strengthned with a thicke wood wch stood vpon the Declining of the hill, in wch hee had putt store of muskeiteires, on his reare hee had a faire plaine, where stood rang'd his reserues of horse and ffoote, some bodye of horse with muskeiteeres hee bestow'd vpon some other places of the hill, where hee thought there was any accesse; thus fortyfied stood the foxe gazing att vs.'[457] Skirmishing followed, but Waller refused to be drawn into fighting, and Hertford accordingly began to retire on Marshfield; Waller thereupon sent a body of cavalry to charge their rear, but the Royalists drove them off, although with difficulty, and took up their former position on Tog Hill. Clarendon bitterly regrets that Hertford allowed himself to be engaged,[458] but the Cornish foot were not to be restrained, and began the assault of Lansdown, followed by Sir Beville Grenville, who sent the musketeers up through the woods on either side of the road, and himself charged up the middle: the wings did their business so well that they were on the hill as soon as the cavalry.[459] A bend in the road to the right gave Grenville the advantage of the shelter of a stone wall, which protected him from the enemy's cannon,[460] but on reaching the top the Royalists had no shelter for their final assault. In spite of this and of five charges by Waller's cavalry,[461]

[455] Bath was then a fortified town.
[456] Clar. MSS. 1738 (3). For details of the manœuvring see Ibid. (4) Hopton's *Relation* (*Somers. Rec. Soc.*).
[457] Clar. MSS. 1738 (4).   [458] Op. cit. vii, 105.
[459] Clar. MSS. 1738 (2).   [460] Cf. Gardiner op. cit. ii. 71.
[461] So Hopton's *Relation*; the account in (4) says three. Clar MSS. 1738.

they carried the breastworks, but with the loss of Grenville himself and of 1,400 out of 2,000 cavalry.

Considerable slaughter took place on the top of the hill, 'cannon on both sides playing without ceasing until it was darke, Legs and Armes flying apace,'[462] but during the night Waller, after a final volley of musketry about eleven o'clock, withdrew into Bath, leaving the Royalists 'seated like a heavy stone vpon the very brow of the hill, w^{eh} with one lustye charge might well have bin rowl'd to the bottome.'[463] In the morning they took possession of a great store of arms and ammunition left behind by Waller, a very welcome find, but their heavy loss in officers was increased by the explosion of an ammunition wagon, by which Major Sheltone was killed and Hopton dangerously wounded. Being unable, through want of ammunition, to follow up their advantage, they withdrew to Marshfield, and two days after by Chippenham to Devizes, where, having been reinforced from Oxford, they practically annihilated Waller's army which had pursued them. Waller, with the remnant of his force, retreated into Bristol, leaving Bath free to the king's army. They were there joined by Rupert, and marched with him to the siege of Bristol, which surrendered on 26 July. Hopton being still invalided from his wounds was left in charge of the garrison; Prince Rupert marched to the siege of Gloucester, and Prince Maurice, with what remained of the western army, marched across Somerset, and having reduced Dorchester and Weymouth, laid siege to Exeter, which surrendered on 4 September.[464] From this date the western counties, with the exception of Lyme, Dartmouth, Plymouth and Wardour Castle, were held by the king.

In the summer of 1644 however Essex, in spite of the opposition of Parliament, insisted upon making an attempt to reconquer the west. At the best it was a hazardous attempt, without much chance of success, and after the collapse of Waller's army in the southern midlands it became a foolhardy adventure, since he was leaving an unconquered enemy behind him.[465]

The moment seemed opportune for an effort to crush him, and Charles accordingly set out himself,[466] and quitting Evesham, reached Bath on 15 July, whence he reached Ilchester via Wells and Bruton on the 20th. His object in stopping at Ilchester was to reinforce his troops with recruits from Bristol and the *posse comitatus* of Somerset. The country people however had no wish to fight : 'they saluted his Majesty with general Shouts and Acclamations, and followed him in Troops from place to place : I cannot say whether with more Admiration or Affection . . . but this added nothing to our Force.' Only about 1,000 men who had formerly fought under Sir Edward Rodney, Sir Henry Berkeley and Colonel Bysse joined the king; 'all the rest, not knowing, or desirous to know the Nature of a *Posse Comitatus* . . . having seen their Sight, went home again.'[467] Charles could rouse no popular enthusiasm ; on 24 July he left Ilchester, stayed that night at Chard, and the following day passed on to Exeter, where he met Prince

---

[462] Clar. MSS. 1738 (2). A short account by a Parliamentarian says that Waller lost only one sergeant-major of dragoons, two cornets and not twenty common soldiers. Tanner MSS. 62 (1)164.
[463] Clar. MSS. loc. cit. [464] Ibid. Hopton's *Relation.*
[465] Gardiner, op. cit. ii, 7 ; Clarendon, op. cit. viii, 52.
[466] Walker, *Historical Discourses,* 37. [467] Walker, op. cit. 40.

Maurice.[468]   The campaign proved successful, and at Fowey Essex deserted his force ; the infantry surrendered to Charles, but the cavalry broke through and escaped to Taunton.[469]

Charles, having attained his object, turned eastwards again.   Leaving Sir Richard Grenville to block up Plymouth, which he had failed to take,[470] he marched to Chard, where he remained for a week collecting supplies ; his army was now considerably reduced, as two detachments had been sent to block up Lyme and Taunton,[471] the latter having been retaken for Parliament in July 1644 by Colonel Blake and Sir Robert Pye.[472]   Essex reported that it was so well provided for that nothing but the 'panic fears' of the garrison could have made the Roundheads masters of the town, but one Lawrence Chislett afterwards claimed to have admitted them without a shot being fired.[473]

Since Charles' object was to relieve the garrisons of Basing House and Banbury, Waller, with a force of cavalry, was stationed at Shaftesbury, but the dissensions among the Parliamentary commanders left him unsupported, and when Charles, leaving Chard, marched through South Perrott, where he was joined by Prince Rupert, to Sherborne, Waller retreated, and so both armies left the west.

Although Somerset had seen little of this campaign but the marches of both armies, the county had suffered so severely from the requisitions of money, provisions and clothes, that they petitioned the king for leave to petition Parliament to end the struggle, promising that if they failed they should hold their lives best spent in assisting Charles ' to compass that by the sword, which by any other fair and just way could not be effected ' : to which end they desired liberty to put themselves in arms on his behalf, should their petition fail.   To this Charles returned a gracious answer, and the 'Gentry, Clergy, Freeholders and others his Majesty's Protestant Subjects' of the county accordingly sent up their petition to Parliament, asking that both houses would lay by ' the too tender Sense of those imaginary Evils which you only fear,' and join hands with them ' in a happy Treaty for the removal of those real Evils which we so sensibly suffer.' [474]

The petition, needless to say, was ineffectual, and in the following month the county declared at a public meeting in Wells that ' the summe of our resolution is, to follow his Majesty towards *London* as one man, either to propose to them (i.e. Parliament) or receive from them, such Propositions as may restore this Kingdome to all the Comforts and Blessings of Peace. . . . And whosoever in this County shall refuse to accompany us, we shall look upon him as an Enemy to Peace, and shall proceed against him accordingly.'   This resolution, they declared, was taken because Charles' ' gracious Messages have found either such cold reception, or such unsatisfying Answers, that they have beene hitherto fruitlesse and ineffectual.' [475]

---

[468] Walker, op. cit. 43–5.   [469] Ibid. 81.   [470] Ibid. 85.
[471] Ibid. 87, 88.   [472] *Cal. S. P. Dom.* 1644, p. 335.
[473] S. P. Dom. Commonwealth, clvi, 72.
[474] Walker op. cit. 99–103 ; Rushworth, *Hist. Coll.* pt. iii, vol. ii, 77–8.   The petitioners appear to have been heard by the Committee of Both Kingdoms on the afternoon of 17 September.   *Cal. S. P. Dom.* 1644, p. 511.
[475] *Declaration of the County of Somerset at a publicke meeting at Wells the* 14 of October 1644.   Bodl. Shelf Mark 4⁰ M. 10, Art. B. 5.

A scheme for a Western Association, comprising Somerset, Dorset, Devon and Cornwall, to counterbalance the Eastern Association, had also been originated before this date. Articles of Association, Agreement and Protestation were drawn up by which the four counties agreed to 'make themselves as one entire body,' the formation of the association dating from 1 May, 1644. They were to raise a force of 30,000 men : Devon supplying 13,500, Cornwall 1,500, Somerset 9,000, and Dorset 3,000 ; of these 8,000 foot, 1,500 horse and 500 dragoons were to be raised immediately, and their payment for three months was to be made by the associated counties in the same proportion : 1,000 barrels of powder and 10,000 fire-arms were also to be provided, and provision was made for the formation and discipline of the force, and for the collection of the money. In conclusion, a protestation in defence of the true reformed Protestant religion established by law, his Majesty's person and rights, and the laws, liberties and privileges of Parliament was drawn up for circulation and signature.[476]

The scheme however hung fire, the Committee for Somerset performing none of their promises for the supplies of either men or money : 'flatness, peremptoriness and inactivity' are the qualities attributed to them by Clarendon, who says that the plan for the Association 'served to cross and oppose all other attempts whatsoever, those who had no mind to do anything satisfying themselves with the visible impossibility of that design, and yet the others who had first proposed it thinking themselves engaged to consent to no alteration.[477]

More paralyzing by far to the royal cause in the west were the disputes between Goring and the Prince's council. One of the most important matters for Charles was the reduction of Taunton, which the blocking force had failed to take. The fact that it had held out so long was an extreme tribute to the courage and resource of Blake and his garrison, for there were no sort of defences round the town : palings and hedges had to serve for earthworks and fortifications, and ammunition and provisions were very short.[478] Parliament had realized its importance both as an outpost and as a means of keeping a considerable body of Royalists occupied who would otherwise be free for the approaching campaign in the midlands. In November Waller had been ordered to send a detachment to relieve the town,[479] but could not spare the forces until December, when Major-General Holborn[480] marching across Dorset reached Taunton, defeated the blockading force and revictualled the town.[481]

Colonel Blake remained in command of the town, and when on 11 March Goring appeared, he sent away Holborn and his forces, since with them his supplies would have been inadequate. When, however, by the advice of Rupert, who had come to Bristol, Goring was asked to leave his infantry and artillery with Sir Richard Grenville, who was advancing to the siege, and to cover the besieging force by occupying the Wiltshire downs with his cavalry, he objected violently, and retiring to Bath allowed

[476] Bodl. Shelf Mark 22856 E 10 (8). A very similar set of Articles *mutatis mutandis* had been drawn up for Cornwall and Devon in Jan. 1643. Bodl. Shelf Mark, 4° M. 10, Art. B. 5.

[477] S. P. Dom. Commonwealth, ix, 16.

[478] Cf. Oldmixon, op. cit. 278 ; Christie, *Life of Shaftesbury*, i, 72.

[479] *Cal. S. P. Dom.* 1644–5, pp. 102, 124, 164.

[480] Ibid. p. 114. Cf. p. 83.   [481] Ibid. p. 196.

his infantry to join Grenville.[482]   To prevent 'mistakes and contests about command' Lords Capell and Culpepper were sent by the Prince to Taunton to settle the disputes, a fortunate arrangement, for on the day that they arrived Grenville was severely wounded, and the besieging force would probably have drawn off if they had not persuaded Sir John Berkeley, who had just arrived,[483] to take over the command : he accordingly held it until the return of Goring in May with greatly increased powers.[484]

Goring arrived just too late to prevent the relief of the town.   Fairfax with his whole army had in the first instance been sent to its succour,[485] but at Blandford he received instructions to return, only detaching a small force under Colonel Weldon and Colonel Graves,[486] which he sent on to relieve the town.   This division was unknown to the Royalists around Taunton, who believed the brigade of 4,000 or 5,000 foot and 1,800 or 2,000 horse to be the advance guard of the whole of Fairfax's army.[487]   When the brigade was within ten miles of Taunton the men discharged ten pieces of their artillery, a signal pre-arranged by spies to give notice that they were ten miles off.   The besieging force had previously divided into two parties, and skirmished outside the town (with blank ammunition) to simulate an attempt by Fairfax and failure on his part to relieve it, hoping that the garrison would come out to help the relieving force and so expose themselves to an ambuscade.   The stratagem was unsuccessful, and was followed by an attempt to storm the town 8 May.   They scaled the wall, but found a second line of defence before them ; they then set fire to some houses,[488] but the wind blew the flames towards them, and they had to retreat ; the day following they renewed the effort and started a fire which burnt down a third of the town, but Blake still held out, although his ammunition was almost exhausted.[489]   On 11 May Colonel Weldon's horse came up, and the Royalists, still believing that they had the whole of Fairfax's force to contend with, retreated to Pitminster, nearly two miles away ; on their march they were harassed by the garrison which sallied out and fell on their rear, but they cut off the pursuit by blocking up the road with tree trunks.   Had they had correct information they would probably have stood their ground, for they had according to their own estimate double the strength required to have defeated Weldon and continued the blockade.   Weldon on the following day entered the town, but owing to lack of provisions and the retreat of the Royalists withdrew in a few days to Chard.[490]

So important was the relief of Taunton considered by the Commons that they appointed a day of public thanksgiving ; letters of thanks were sent to Fairfax, Weldon and the other officers, and grants were voted of £500 to Blake and £2,000 to the garrison.[491]   Rejoicings in the town however were short, for Goring, who had returned with practically the

---

[482] Clarendon op. cit. ix, 154.

[483] He brought with him 1,000 foot, and 500 horse. Clar. MSS. 1834. The whole besieging force amounted to 6,200. S. P. Dom. Chas. I, dvii, 58.   [484] Clarendon, op. cit. ix, 32.

[485] *Cal. S. P. Dom.* 1644–5, pp. 433, 438, 444.   [486] Ibid. pp. 459, 461 ; Oldmixon, op. cit. 278.

[487] Sprigge, *England's Recovery*, 17.   Sir John Digby, writing to his brother, Lord Digby, gives the numbers of the relieving party as 'not above 2,500.' S. P. Dom. Chas. i, dvii, 70.

[488] It had been agreed between Culpepper and Goring that Taunton should be burnt. Clar. MSS. 1852–3 and 1856.   [489] S. P. Dom. Chas. I, dvii, 70.

[490] Sprigge, op. cit. 18–20 ; Toulmin, *Hist. of Taunton*, 421 ; Oldmixon, op. cit. 278.

[491] *Cal S. P. Dom.* 1644–5, p. 491.

supreme command, in conjunction with Grenville, Hopton and Berkeley at the head of about 10,000 men,[492] drove Weldon's brigade back into the town and re-invested it. Skirmishes took place in which Goring had distinctly the worst of it, but he attributed the failure to no fault of his own but to 'the most fantastical accident that has happened since the war began,' that is, one body of the royal army fell upon another and skirmished almost two hours before they knew one another.[493] The Parliamentary troops meanwhile suffered considerably, and Blake applied to Parliament for help in pressing terms : 'if relief came not speedily to them, they should be put into great straits for provisions and ammunition ; . . . they never accepted a parley from the enemy but scorned it, and they had some ammunition left, and were resolved to feed upon their horses ; they requested the house to take into consideration their condition ; and left all to the Almighty, Who, they doubted not, would relieve them.' Parliament replied 'that relief should speedily come to them.'[494] Blake, having been sent a small supply of powder, made a sally and drove back Goring, forcing him to enlarge his quarters to a circle of some five or six miles. Of the officers of the garrison Colonel Lloyd and Colonel Richbel were killed, of Goring's force Major Norwood and Captain Richardson, while Sir John Digby was mortally wounded.[495] Massey was appointed by the Committee of Both Kingdoms to march to Taunton with 3,000 horse and foot, and keep the country to the west of the town open.[496] He was however only strong enough to keep reinforcements from joining Goring, and had to wait for Fairfax, who having fought at Naseby and stormed Leicester, was ready to proceed to the west.[497]

His army was in an enfeebled condition, but he pressed on, having heard that Colonel Massey had been forced to retreat beyond Blandford, as he had few men and Goring was trying forcing tactics ;[498] Massey also believed that Rupert was on his way with reinforcements.[499] The combined Parliamentary forces having met at Blandford, advanced through Dorchester and Beaminster to Crewkerne. Goring meanwhile tried to induce the garrison at Taunton to make another sally, but failing to draw them, took up his quarters at Somerton, and so raised the siege which had lasted five weeks.[500] Fairfax next marched to Yeovil, where his troops and Blake's fraternized and exchanged news, the garrison rejoicing in having been saved from 'another Cornish Hugg' ;[501] on the following day (9 July) he divided

[492] According to S. P. Dom. Chas. I, dvii, 70, 11,000 men.

[493] S. P. Dom. Chas. I, dvii, 74. Goring's story was flatly contradicted, and it is safe to conclude was untrue. Cf. Gardiner, op. cit, ii, 229.

[494] Toulmin, op. cit. 424–5 ; Oldmixon, op. cit. 283,–4.

[495] Oldmixon, op. cit. 284. He gives the losses at above 400 of Goring's men, and 100 of the besieged. Cf. Whitelocke, op. cit. i, 451.

[496] Cal. S. P. Dom. 1644–5, p. 584. Cf. also pp. 587, 595, 617.

[497] The Committee of Both Kingdoms had allowed him to choose his own course, and he decided that the royal army in the west was more dangerous to the Parliamentary cause than that of Charles. He was influenced in this opinion by a packet from Goring to Charles which had been intercepted, in which Goring gave the king hopes of such success at Taunton that he would soon be able to march to his assistance at Leicester. Com. Journ. iv, 182. Proceedings of the Army under the command of Sir Thomas Fairfax, etc., Bodl. Shelf Mark, Wood 378(8) 3–4. Cf. Gardiner, op. cit. ii, 262.

[498] Lds'. Journ. vii, 463. Fairfax to Parliament.

[499] The Letters and Speeches of Oliver Cromwell (Ed. Carlyle), Letter xxiv.

[500] Proceedings of the Army under the command of Sir Thomas Fairfax from the first of July to the sixth, 7–8. Bodl. Shelf Mark, Wood 378 (8) ; Oldmixon, op. cit. 284.

[501] An exact and perfect Relation of the Proceedings of the Army under Sir Thomas Fairfax from the sixth of this instant July to the eleventh of the same, 3. Bodl. Shelf Mark, Wood 378 (10).

his forces, sending a detachment under Massey across the river 'to amuse the Enemy.' Goring at this time held a very strong position on the north banks of the Parrett and Yeo : he had thus a free line of communication with Charles, while, if he were forced to retire, the fortifications of Langport and Boroughbridge would protect him in a retreat on Bridgwater, where the fortifications were very strong. At the same time he was protected from an attack from the south by holding the bridges over the Yeo between Ilchester and Langport, for the river being a mere channel through the bog was unfordable. It was the necessity of manœuvring him out of this strong position which made Fairfax divide his forces, a highly successful move, for Goring at once gave up his position, evacuated Long Sutton and Ilchester, where two of the bridges were, and made a dash to get into Taunton. Fairfax sent Massey after him, and his forces (surprised while bathing) were routed. With those which he could rally he hastily retired to Langport. Here he drew up his army on a hill, in a position which could be attacked only by a lane which led across a ford and was defended by hedges lined with musketeers. He seems however to have had little hope of victory, since he sent his baggage and all his artillery except two guns to Bridg-water. Fairfax, who had marched round by Ilchester, where he crossed the Yeo, to Long Sutton, had no choice but to attack him, for Goring was deter-mined not to advance until he had been reinforced by Grenville and Prince Charles.[502] Fairfax with his now superior artillery first silenced Goring's guns, and then having cleared the hedges followed up his advantage by a cavalry charge. In spite of Goring's strong position and overwhelming preponderance in cavalry, two small bodies of 350 men, the first under Bethell, the second under Desborough, supported by the Parliamentarian musketeers, were completely successful in routing the royal army ; if ever a victory was due to discipline, spirit and audacity at the right moment, opposed to irresolution, faint-heartedness and the depression which comes of preparation for defeat, it was this. Once the rout had begun Cromwell started with the rearguard in pursuit, slaughtered or took prisoners most of the royal horse in Langport, and forced the foot to surrender among the ditches of the moor.'[503]

Few of the Royalist foot were killed, 'thanks to hedges and heels,' but the two cannon and about thirty of their colours were taken ; several officers and about 1,200 common soldiers were made prisoners, while of the Parliamentary army no officers and only about 20 common soldiers were lost.[504] 'To see this, is it not to see the face of God ? ' wrote Cromwell.

The victory at Langport could be of very little use to Fairfax as long as Bridgwater remained in the hands of the Royalists, since it commanded the line of the Yeo and Parrett : he accordingly marched to Middlezoy on the road to Bridgwater on the evening of the same day. Here he was met by the Somerset Clubmen who feared that Goring's troops being dis-persed over the country would repeat their former cruelties, and had

---

[502] *Good News out of the West*, Bodl. Shelf Mark, Wood 78 (9).

[503] Cf. Gardiner, op. cit. ii, 268 seq.

[504] According to Cromwell about 2,000 Royalists were killed or taken. *Good News*, &c., Oldmixon says 300 killed, 1,400 prisoners ; also 100 inferior officers, 40 standards and colours, 4,000 arms and 1,200 horses. Op. cit. 285. Fairfax in his letter to the Speaker of the House of Lords says few were slain but 2,000 were taken prisoners. *Lds'. Journ.* vii, 496.

presented Fairfax with a threatening petition before the battle, but he was able to satisfy them after a conference, at which he assured them that 'he came to protect them from the violence of war, and to further peace by scattering the enemies of it.' [505]

The existence of this third party had already involved Fairfax in difficulties. It had been formed by the farmers and yeomen of Wiltshire, Dorset and Somerset to prevent plunder and the pressing of men into service, and to agitate for peace. The Wiltshire and Dorset Clubmen had met Fairfax at Blandford and at Dorchester, where they requested leave to pass, that they might present their petition to king and Parliament for peace ; [506] Fairfax found their design 'desparately evill against the Parliament,' but held 'it was a point of prudence to be faire in demeanour towards them for a while,' fearing that if he were defeated by Goring after having offended the Clubmen, they would be more cruel even than the Royalists. [507] Such diplomacy was the more necessary as they were very strong in Somerset, and the rebels looked on them as very serious opponents. Oldmixon declares that they were 'spirited up by some Laudaean Priests,' who 'did not counsel them to declare openly for the King, but for a *Neutrality*, and under that Pretext to fall upon those who offer'd to disturb them, meaning the Parliament's Forces only ; ' [508] Sprigge feared that if the movement 'had not been crushed in the Egge, it had on an instant run all over the Kingdome, and might have been destructive to the Parliament.' [509] He says however that they were '*countenanced* by a *neutrall* party within ourselves.' Goring during the siege of Taunton had conciliated them in order to induce them to enlist under him, promising that if they paid their contributions there should be no plundering : until the news of Naseby arrived he had hoped that they would declare for Charles, and had taken their part against Mackworth, the governor of Langport, when they attacked the garrison there, [510] but at the same time he both took their money and permitted excessive plundering, a course which alienated them beyond recall. The Prince of Wales had received a petition from them while he was at Wells (2 June) asking for the redress of their grievances ; to this he returned a sympathetic answer. He took the opportunity however of pointing out that the grievances they complained of would the sooner have no existence if they would 'speedily . . . hasten the levyes agreed vpon, and cheerfully . . . vnite themselves to his Ma[tes] Army and supply it with the Provisions without which it cannot subsiste.' [511] The Clubmen however resolved (30 June) to offer protection to deserters who had been pressed, and to inflict punishment themselves on plunderers. [512] After Langport Goring feared that they would attach themselves to Fairfax, since they had stopped provisions from the royal army and killed some of his

---

[505] Sprigge, *Anglia Rediviva*, 67 ; *A Continuation of the Proceedings of the Army*, &c. 12–22. Bodl. Shelf Mark, Wood 378 (11).

[506] *Proceedings* &c. 5 ; *A Continuation* &c. 7–11.   [507] Sprigge, op. cit. 56–7.
[508] Oldmixon, op. cit. 284.

[509] Sprigge, op. cit. 57. Mr. Bowles, Fairfax's chaplain, in no way concealed his feelings when he wrote of them as 'Club Ambassadours (I leave it to other men to call them Knaves of Clubs, for I will not use myself to ill language).' *Proceedings of the Army* &c. 7.

[510] Clar. MSS. 1907.   [511] Clar. MSS. 1894.
[512] *Perfect Occurrences*. Bodl. Shelf Mark E. 262, 20.

men ;[513] they had also kept a pass over the Mendips, and so prevented his men from marching to Bristol.[514] Fairfax however was concerned to press on against Bridgwater, through which Goring had fled with about 3,000 horse and 400 foot,[515] and wasted no more time upon them.

The garrison at Bridgwater had been settled by Hopton, who had appointed Sir Francis Mackworth to command it. Mackworth had fortified it well, but Goring had taken the contributions for its support to supply his own army, and had forbidden Mackworth to levy the rates which the prince himself assigned to him, with the result that when Fairfax came up the garrison had not two days' provisions.[516] The attack on the town was simplified for Fairfax by his agreement with the Clubmen and by the capture of Boroughbridge with 150 prisoners on the 13th.[517]

At a council of war on the 16th it was decided to storm the town, although the danger of the attempt was recognized. There were 40 guns mounted on the walls of the castle, which were in most places 15 ft. thick : the fortifications were regular and strong and surrounded by a deep moat some 30 ft. wide which was filled to the brim every high tide : there was also a high fortification at the east end supported by mounts.[518] The garrison numbered about 1,800.[519] The chief difficulty for the besiegers consisted in the flatness of the ground, 'there being not a clod which could afford any advantage,'[520] so that there was no shelter for the advancing force.

The town however was divided into two sections by the Parrett, running north and south ; the western division was the more difficult to attack as it contained the castle,[521] and was defended by a battery on the off-side of the moat.[522] The attack was therefore planned on the east side, but before it began a summons was sent to the governor to surrender. Colonel Edmund Windham (now in command) returned a scornful answer, and accordingly at about 2 a.m. on 21 July the storm began. Portable bridges had been prepared by which the moat was passed ; the fortifications were scaled in spite of determined resistance, and the drawbridge over the moat was captured and let down, so that the Parliamentary horse could enter : resistance here was over, and the garrison of this quarter of the town to the number of 600 surrendered, but the Royalists in the other quarter two hours after began a cannonade of red-hot shell by which all the houses except three or four were burnt to the ground. Fairfax again called on Windham to surrender and was again refused ; before the attack was renewed however the women and children in the town were allowed to leave.[523] As soon as they were gone Fairfax bombarded the western half of the town with red-hot shot, and the wind being high the danger from fire soon became great. The townspeople, realizing apparently that their choice lay between surrender or the complete destruction of all their property, gave Windham no peace until he sent to Fairfax to ask for terms ; and after some parley the town sur-

[513] Warburton, *Memoirs of Prince Rupert and the Cavaliers* iii, 138 ; Clarendon, op. cit. ix, 51 ; *Letter to Lenthall* &c. *by a worthy Gentleman of Sir Thomas Fairfax his army*, Bodl. Shelf Mark, Wood 378 (10).
[514] *A more full Relation* &c. *made in the House of Commons by Lilburne*, 8, Bodl. Shelf Mark, Wood 378 (13).
[515] *A Continuation* &c. 1.   [516] Oldmixon, op. cit. 286 ; Clarendon, op. cit. ix, 49.
[517] *A Continuation* &c. 4.   [518] Oldmixon, op. cit. 280.   [519] Sprigge, op. cit. 68.
[520] Ibid. 67.   [521] At the north-west corner.   [522] Oldmixon, op. cit. 287.
[523] *A brief relation of the taking of Bridgwater*, &c. Bodl. Shelf Mark, Wood 378 (14) ; Oldmixon, op. cit. 288 ; Sprigge, 71-2.

rendered (23 July) upon quarter for life only.[524] An irretrievable blow was thus given to the Royalist cause in the west, the more so as Charles had believed the fortress to be impregnable, and Clarendon held Windham's conduct inexcusable.[525]

Fairfax by this victory took prisoner 1,000 officers and men, besides gentlemen and clergy; he also secured 44 barrels of powder, 1,500 arms, 44 pieces of ordnance, four hundredweight of match, and goods of great value which had been stored in the castle, and which were now sold to provide a reward for the common soldiers who each realized 5s.[526] Of far greater importance was the fact that Fairfax now commanded a chain of fortresses from the northern to the southern shores of the peninsula, Lyme, Langport and Bridgwater, with Taunton as an advanced post. The Royalist troops in Devon and Cornwall were thus cut off from the rest of England.

Sherborne, Bath and Bristol were still in the king's hands, and the Clubmen were also a source of danger. Having quartered in Wells, Fairfax sent a brigade against Sherborne, and another against Bath, where he knew there were great dissensions. Colonel Rich, who commanded the brigade sent against Bath, summoned the town to surrender on Tuesday 29 July, but the governor, Sir Thomas Bridges, refused. In the evening the Parliamentary dragoons crept up over the bridge to the gate, seized the small ends of the enemies' muskets which they put through the loop-holes of the gate, and cried to the garrison to surrender; the Royalists, alarmed, ran to their works which flanked the bridge, but the dragoons instantly fired the gate, and so became masters of the bridge. The following morning the deputy-governor sent for a parley and agreed to surrender the town on condition that the officers were allowed to join the garrison at Bristol, and this having been agreed to the town surrendered, about 140 prisoners (the common soldiers), 6 guns, 400 arms and 12 barrels of powder being taken.[527] Rich was lucky in securing the town so quickly, as Rupert was on his way from Bristol with 1,500 men to relieve it, but on finding that he was too late he retreated. Fairfax himself came the next day with two regiments of foot, which he left there as a garrison; then, having settled matters for the safety of the town, he proceeded to the siege of Sherborne.[528]

In the meantime the Somerset Clubmen had joined those of Wiltshire and Dorset, who being under the influence of the Royalist gentry and clergy, and not having suffered from the depredations of Goring's troops, were opposed to Parliament.[529] Intelligence was received that they had collected at Shaftesbury, so Fleetwood was sent to see if he could surprise them, and being successful in this he took prisoner about 50 of their ringleaders, who after the fall of Sherborne were sent as prisoners to London.[530]

[524] Oldmixon, loc. cit.   [525] Clarendon, op. cit. ix, 68.

[526] Sprigge op. cit. 73. For varying estimates see Oldmixon, op. cit. 288. *A brief relation of the taking of Bridgwater*, ut. sup.

[527] Sprigge, op. cit. 76; Oldmixon, op. cit. 288; *A fuller relation of the taking of Bath*, 4–6, Bodl. Shelf Mark, Wood 378 (17).

[528] Sprigge, op. cit. 77; *Two Letters*, &c. Bodl. Shelf Mark, Ashm. 1071 (21).

[529] Sprigge, op. cit. 77; Gardiner, op. cit. ii, 305.

[530] Sprigge, loc. cit. *Two Letters*, &c. Cromwell to Fairfax. The Somerset leaders, according to a contemporary list, were: 'John Lovell . . . a notable stickler against godly men; Nicholas Bingham of Henstridge: it is a pitie any of that family are Malignants; Francis Abbot, son to Jeremy Abbott of Horsington.' Cf. *King's Answer to Propositions for Peace*, Bodl. Shelf Mark, Ashm. 1071 (22).

A larger body entrenched themselves on Hambledon Hill, and having three times refused offers of peace, were attacked by Cromwell ; a few were killed and the rest either surrendered or fled. With this victory the movement was suppressed ; the Parliamentary lines of communication which they had blocked were cleared, and after the fall of Bristol in September Fairfax could turn to the conquest of the west. The only place now holding out for the king in the county was Dunster Castle, and thither Colonel Blake and Colonel Sydenham were sent early in November. A storm seemed practically impossible, and they therefore invested it so completely that surrender appeared inevitable. But the garrison, though suffering from want of water,[531] held out under Colonel Francis Windham, governor here, although plans for their relief failed twice.[532]

In December Blake determined to storm the castle and pushed on the necessary preparations.[533] The first attempt was made at Fairfax's command on 3 January,[534] but the mines by which it was intended to blow up the castle failed, although by making a breach in the walls they greatly increased the difficulties and labours of the garrison.[535] Hope was still kept alive in the castle by promises of help from Sir Richard Grenville,[536] but Blake was able to prevent the two regiments which were sent for the purpose from achieving their rescue. Colonel Finch, however, succeeded a little later in reaching Dunster at a time when the besieging force was engaged in operations against Goring, and supplied the garrison with four barrels of powder, 30 cows and 50 sheep ; he further destroyed Blake's mines and works before retiring to Barnstaple. The castle was immediately reinvested,[537] and the fall of Exeter set Colonel Lambert's regiment free to join the besiegers.[538] Windham would probably have continued to hold out had not Fairfax's successes in the west made relief impossible, but when he heard that both Exeter and Barnstaple had fallen he surrendered 19 April after a siege which had lasted 160 days and during which he had lost 20 men. The terms of surrender allowed him to keep all his private property and that of his wife ; but all the arms and ammunition except a small amount for the immediate use of the force were to be given up ; the prisoners on both sides were released.[539] Six guns and 200 stands of arms were all Blake's booty, but the fall of the castle was great gain for the Parliamentarians : it consolidated their power in the west and secured them the passage to Ireland.[540]

The surrender of Dunster ended the civil war in Somerset : on the conclusion of the fighting the disbanded levies from Somerset were sent to Ireland, their expenses being charged to the county ;[541] the lower classes seem to have been temporarily converted to the Parliamentary cause by Fairfax's victories,[542] and the Clubmen actually fought under Popham against

---

531 Heavy rains helped them. *Perfect Passages*, no. 56.
532 *Perfect Diurnal*, no. 125 ; *Moderate Intelligencer*, no. 38 ; *Weekly Account* (Dec.).
533 *Perfect Occurrences.* 534 *Perfect Passages*, no. 63.
535 *Moderate Intelligencer*, no. 44. 536 *Weekly Account*, no. 2.
537 *Perfect Passages*, nos. 65, 68 ; *A Diary*, no. 3 ; *Moderate Intelligencer*, no. 49 ; *The Citties Weekly Post*, no. 9.
538 *Moderate Intelligencer*, no. 59.
539 *Merc. Civicus*, no. 152 ; *Four Strong Castles Taken.*
540 *Merc. Civ.* no. 152. Cf. for the whole siege Maxwell-Lyte, *Hist. of Dunster.*
541 *Cal. S. P. Dom.* 1645-7, pp. 360, 535. 542 S. P. Dom. Chas. I, dvii, 119 ; Dx, 84, 109.

Goring and helped Fairfax in the siege of Bristol.[543] Nevertheless in the summer of 1648 plans seem to have been prepared for a rising in Somerset, but these were known to Parliament,[544] and the Committee of Both Houses recommended that a force of 2,000 foot should be quartered in Bridgwater and Dunster.[545] The county was also one of those to which Charles II sent instructions for raising forces in the following year, a commission being sent to Windham as commander-in-chief, and to others as colonels of regiments of horse and foot.[546] But once Parliament had taken the irrevocable step of executing Charles the loyalty of the west became beyond question. 'In all these western parts they disobey all orders and commands of the Parliament, and generally preach and cry up his Majesty's interest, and name themselves the Royal party.'[547] Plans indeed were laid for the mobilization of troops for the king, which were greatly favoured by the weakness of the Parliamentary forces there,[548] but, presumably in view of this, the Council of State ordered two troops of horse and as many dragoons as the Commissioners of Militia should think fit to be kept in Somerset.[549] Owing to the damage done at Dunster, which made very expensive repairs necessary, the Committee for Martial Affairs ordered that it should be so far 'slighted' as to make it untenable by the enemy, and that the garrison should be withdrawn to Taunton.[550] So loyal was Somerset that when a rising in the west was planned in the spring of 1650 the Royalists hoped that Devon, Somerset, Dorset and Hampshire together would provide 4,000 foot and 1,000 horse, but their expectations were never put to the proof;[551] another rising planned for 1653 was crushed before it came to anything;[552] and at the time of Penruddock's rising 3,000 Somerset men were prepared to take the field in defence of the existing Government.

This rising quelled, Somerset was placed along with five others under the newly-appointed major-generals,[553] and must have remained quiet, as no troops or garrisons were kept there.[554] Charles II, when escaping after the battle of Worcester, passed through the county, taking refuge at Abbots Leigh, the residence of a Mr. Norton, at Castle Cary, at Trent, Colonel Windham's house, and leaving it under the guidance of Colonel Phelips of Montacute.[555] When rumours of Booth's insurrections were spreading the militia was assembled,[556] and an order sent that Bath should be searched for suspected persons, arms and horses.[557] A company of 175 foot, and afterwards an infantry regiment of 1,000 men, were raised by Colonel Bovett,[558] but were disbanded in the following March, and the Restoration involved the county in nothing more warlike than the preparation of a congratulatory address to the king.[559]

---

[543] S. P. Dom. Chas. I, dxi, 27.

[544] Cal. S. P. Dom. 1648-9, pp. 251, 259.

[545] Ibid. p. 300.

[546] S. P. Dom. Commonw. iii, 24-7.

[547] Ibid. ix, 9. Colonel Keane's report.

[548] Ibid. ix, 54.

[549] Cal. S. P. Dom. 1650, p. 468.

[550] Ibid. p. 281.

[551] Gardiner, Hist. of the Commonwealth and Protectorate, i, 195; Hist. MSS. Com. Rep. xiii, App. i, 577, 591.

[552] S. P. Dom. Commonw. xxxix, 74 (13).

[553] Thurloe, State Papers, iii, 486. The others were Cornwall, Devon, Dorset, Wilts and Gloucester.

[554] Cal. S. P. Dom. 1659-60, p. 18.

[555] Boscobel Tracts, 63-78; Alan Fea, The Flight of the King, tracts 3 and 4.

[556] Cal. S. P. Dom. 1659-60, p. 16.

[557] Ibid. pp. 50, 68.

[558] Ibid. p. 351.

[559] S. P. Dom. Chas. II, i, 44.

Under Charles II Somerset enjoyed peace, but in 1685 it became the chief scene of Monmouth's rebellion. Monmouth appears to have looked upon the west as the most favourable starting-point for his adventure from the fact that the country-party was very strong there, and that there was there a large number of Nonconformists who would welcome an attempt which would relieve them of their disabilities, and free them from the fear of worse restrictions to come.[560]

Moreover in 1680 when, probably at Shaftesbury's instigation,[561] he made a progress in the west, visiting in Somerset Mr. Speke at White Lackington, Sir John Sydenham at Brimpton, and Mr. William Strode at Barrington Court, he was received with every sign of popularity by both the gentry and the poorer classes, and asserted his royal birth by touching for the king's evil, it was reported, with success.[562]

Rumours of his intended descent seem to have reached the west some time before his arrival.[563] The Dissenters of Taunton, 'the nursery of rebellion,' were suspected of having some wicked design on foot,[564] but the rebellion was expected to break out at Exeter Fair on the third Wednesday in May. At Ilminster a letter was intercepted by Captain William Speke[565] giving notice that Monmouth was about to land; with this he rode post to the king, having advised the Mayor of Taunton to search the letter-bags for that town. The mayor was rewarded for his trouble by finding a letter from London advising a 'friend' in Taunton that 'they have notice here at Court that a Certain person will forthwith appear in the West,' and that it was believed that owing to Argyle's successes 'if they be once up in the West they would suddenly be up in all parts of England, all the Protestants being . . . resolved rather to dye than live slaves and papists.' The letter ended 'Make good use hereof, and impart it to such as you can trust, that you may all be prepared and ready against the appearance of a certain person, which will be forthwith if not already.'[566] Another letter which purported to be written by a friend of the king's spoke of the arrival of 'a certain person.' The mayor at once wrote to warn his brother of Exeter.

Little attention was paid in London to Speke's discovery;[567] but an order was sent down that five suspected persons who had been arrested should be sent up to town.[568] Authorities there were also warned by the Rev. A. Paschall, rector of Chedzoy, of portents and phenomena such as earthquakes, mock-suns, births of Siamese twins not only to human beings but to 'inferior sorts of animals, both the oviparous and the viviparous kinds,' and 'other odd things,' which he believed were fore-runners of troubles.[569]

Monmouth's landing took place at Lyme on June 11, his chief com-

[560] The Protestantism of Somerset at this time is shown in the election addresses of 1681, and those to the king from the deputy lieutenants, justices of the peace, militia officers, Bath, Taunton, and Axbridge. The young men of Taunton also addressed the members elected for the borough with reference to the 'common danger and universal slavery which hell and Rome have been and still are, with joint and unwearied endeavours, attempting to involve these Protestant nations in.' Cf. Emmanuel Green, *The March of William of Orange through Somerset*, 5–14, where they are printed.

[561] Dryden, *Absalom and Achitophel*, pt. i, l. 741.

[562] Roberts, *The Life, Progresses, and Rebellion of James, Duke of Monmouth*, i, 94–9.

[563] Harl. MSS. 6845, fol. 65.   [564] Ibid.

[565] On 30 May. He was apparently the only Royalist member of the family.

[566] Roberts, op. cit. i, 214–15.   [567] Ibid. i, 215.

[568] *Hist. MSS. Com. Rep.* iii, App. 97.   [569] Roberts, op. cit. i, 217–18.

panions being Lord Grey of Wark, Fletcher of Saltoun, and Ferguson, who had already been deeply concerned in the Rye House plot. He immediately issued a declaration, drawn up by Ferguson, claiming a 'legitimate and legal' right to the crown, but promising to leave the matter to a free Parliament.[570] Before leaving Lyme he had the misfortune to lose two of his principal adherents, Fletcher of Saltoun, and Dare, a goldsmith from Taunton, as the result of a quarrel in which Fletcher killed Dare. The goldsmith's personal influence in Taunton was so great that Fletcher was obliged to return to the Continent as his presence would have been odious to all who had known Dare.[571]

With the intention of going to London via Taunton, Bridgwater, Bristol and Gloucester, Monmouth proceeded to Axminster at the head of 3,000 men, and was there saved the danger of encountering Albemarle's superior force by the remarkably rapid and unpremeditated strategic movement to the rear of the Somerset militia.[572] This was ascribed by the Axminster *Book of the Independent Chapel* to terror on the part of some, and sympathy on that of others who 'watched opportunities to leave their colours and old officers, and came and joined with this new company.'[573] The 16th June saw Monmouth at Chard, the 17th at Ilminster, and on the 18th he arrived at Taunton, the remnant of the militia stationed there having been withdrawn to Bridgwater.

In London in the meantime the declaration had been burnt by the common hangman;[574] a clause was added to the bill for the protection of his majesty's person 'declaring it to be treason for any person to assert the legitimacy of James, Duke of Monmouth, or his title or pretence to the crown,'[575] and a bill of attainder was passed quickly through both Lords and Commons. Eight troops of cavalry and five companies of infantry were dispatched under Churchill from Salisbury,[576] and on the 17th reached Axminster, reinforcing Albemarle,[577] who then proceeded to Chard. Churchill was evidently hampered by his co-operation with Albemarle. On 20 June he wrote to Somerset, 'I think you should press the Duke of Albemarle to join you, for he has a good force of men, and is not so well able to attend the Duke of Monmouth's march as I am, by reason of the king's horse which I have with me.[578] The Duke of Somerset was indeed left stranded, for the militia at Wells which he commanded had deserted,[579] but the Duke of Beaufort was keeping Bristol for the king until the arrival of reinforcements, and Kirke had brought up his 'lambs' from Andover to Dorchester. All now depended on speed for

[570] Echard, *Hist. of Engl.* (3rd ed.) 1061.   [571] Oldmixon, op. cit. 701.
[572] *Hist. MSS. Com. Rep.* iii, App. 99. Churchill computed that 'half if not the greatest part' went over to Monmouth. Oldmixon regrets that Monmouth did not pursue Albemarle as he could easily have made himself master of Exeter had he done so. Op. cit. 702.
[573] Roberts, op. cit. i, 289.
[574] *Com. Journ.* ix, 736. The Commons were advised of Monmouth's landing on 13 June. Ibid. 735.
[575] Ibid. 737.
[576] *Hist. MSS. Com. Rep.* iii, App. 97. They consisted of four troops of the Earl of Oxford's horse, four of the king's dragoons, and five companies of the queen dowager's regiment. A few days later five more troops joined the royal dragoons and more were under orders to follow as soon as possible.
[577] Clar. MSS. 128, fol. 17b. Clarendon's computation is that Monmouth had then only 4,000 foot and 500 horse, while Churchill had 1,500 foot of the Dorset militia, four troops of Lord Oxford's regiment, two troops of dragoons, and nine companies of foot of the standing forces. Ibid. fol. 18.
[578] *Hist. MSS. Com. Rep.* iii, App. 97.   [579] Ibid.

Monmouth, since Feversham and the Duke of Grafton left London on 20 June with three battalions of foot guards and 150 of the horse guards. Lord Wolseley considers that had the Duke made a dash for Exeter, where he was certain to obtain money, arms and ammunition, as well as men, and then marched upon Bristol, which he could well have reached before the regular troops, he might have had a chance,[580] but instead delay and dilatoriness were the order of the day. His reception at Taunton might well have made him wish to linger there : ' one would have thought,' says Oldmixon, ' the People's Wits were flown away in the flights of their Joy.'[581] The town was decorated, the roads strewn with flowers, and recruits poured in ; but except for one gentleman, one apothecary and one merchant, weavers, carpenters, smiths, bricklayers, masons, shoemakers and brewers were the staple of the growing force.[582] The ' Taunton maids,' carrying twenty-seven banners, one bearing the initials ' J. R.,' presented him with a sword and Bible, and Monmouth replied to the address of the schoolmistress, ' I come now into the Field with a Design to defend the Truths contained in that Book, and to seal it with my blood, if there is occasion for it.'[583] Here he allowed himself to be proclaimed king,[584] although he had promised Argyle and those of his party who were in favour of a Commonwealth that he would not do so. This proceeding seems to have ended the chances of his support by the country gentry,[585] although it increased his popularity among the lower classes. As king he issued passports, proclamations against pillage and looting, against the Parliament then sitting, and against Albemarle as a rebel, and a declaration concerning the collection of the revenue.[586] Before issuing the proclamation against Albemarle, Monmouth wrote to him a letter signed James R., commanding him to cease ' all hostility, and force and arms,' but it was of course ineffectual.[587]

A slight skirmish with Albemarle's scouts at Ashill, and the fear of being blocked up, led Monmouth to resume his march. Before doing so he called a council of war (his first) to discuss the question whether it would be better to march back and attack Albemarle or march forward to Bridgwater. The latter alternative was decided on[588] and Monmouth marched

[580] *Life of Marlborough*, i, 292, so also Roberts, op. cit. i, 330. Had he done so it was arranged that Feversham should follow him and Lord Bath concentrate all his strength at Exeter with the exception of the two eastern regiments of the Cornish militia who were to march to Saltash. Roberts, loc. cit.
[581] Op. cit. 702.
[582] B. M. Add. MSS. no. 33077. This is corroborated by the trades affixed to the names of rebels in Hotten's lists, where the majority are weavers and combers. J. C. Hotten, *Original Lists of Persons of Quality, emigrants, religious exiles, political rebels*, 317–18.
[583] Oldmixon, op. cit. 702.
[584] Harl. MSS. no. 7006. Wade says the first proposal to do so was made at Chard. *Hardwick State Papers*, ii, 322.
[585] He seems to have thought it would increase his chances of support from them. *Hardwick State Papers*, ii, 323. For a discussion of the subject see Roberts, op. cit. i. 311–18, and for an account of the opposition of some of the townspeople *Hist. MSS. Com. Rep.* ix, App. iii, 5. Echard quotes Ferguson as saying that several Nonconformist ministers actually told Monmouth that unless he took the style of king none who had estates would venture themselves in his quarrel. Op. cit. 1064.
[586] H. Ellis, *Original Letters* (1st ser.) iii, 340. Albemarle sent copies of the declarations to Sunderland ' only for his diversion.'
[587] Ibid. 342. Albemarle replied in a letter addressed to James Scott, late Duke of Monmouth, ' If you think I am in the wrong and you in the right, whenever we meet I do not doubt but the justness of my cause shall sufficiently convince you that you had better have left this Rebellion alone, and not to have put the Nation to so much trouble.'
[588] *Hardwick S. P.* ii, 322, 323.

221

out at the head of some 7,000 men.[589]   He was followed by Churchill and Kirke, who had joined hands at Chard,[590] but were naturally playing a waiting game until reinforcements arrived.   Churchill's plan was to hang on his rear, cut off supplies, prevent recruits from joining him and attack his stragglers whenever it was possible.[591]   'This Lord,' Oldmixon says, 'harrassed the Duke's Army more than all the rest of the King's Forces, which were indeed commanded by very sorry Generals.'[592]   Feversham, who had been appointed commander-in-chief, was marching straight for Chippenham, and had sent a messenger to Somerset, who had rallied a part of the militia from Wells, informing him of his route, requesting him to destroy the bridge at Keynsham, and that at Bath if he was uncertain whether he could defend it in case of attack.[593]   Lord Pembroke was bringing up the Wilts and Hants militia to meet Feversham at Chippenham.[594]   Beaufort was in Bristol with 5,000 'very good men . . . such as he can rely upon,'[595] and had prepared the town to resist an attack.[596]   The city was of great importance, as since his landing it had been Monmouth's objective.   Of the necessity for securing it the Government had been well aware,[597] and two ships were stationed in the Severn to prevent the rebels from obtaining help by that channel.[598]

On leaving Taunton Monmouth marched to Bridgwater, where the mayor and corporation read the proclamation of their own accord ; he was here joined by about 700 foot and 160 horse[599] before continuing his advance to Wells.   Wells could not provide for all his troops, so some were quartered in Glastonbury.   The duke, who slept at Glastonbury, heard there that the Clubmen had again risen to prevent plundering.   A Quaker who had attended their meeting at Polden Hill rode over with the information that the country was rising, to ask Monmouth for a commission, and obtained a letter justifying and allowing the proceedings of the Clubmen, and commissioning them 'to disarm, seize, take, prosecute and kill and with force and arms subdue all manner of person and persons that shall appear in arms for James Duke of York the usurper.'[600]   His object, which was to engage the Clubmen in the cause of the duke, was defeated by their refusal to take up arms, their aim being merely to secure their property, and they broke up for the time being.[601]

From Glastonbury Monmouth marched to Shepton Mallet,[602] and from thence due north, intending by Wade's advice to attack Bristol from the

---

[589] On arriving at Taunton he had only 3,000 men, 4 guns and 10 wagons : on leaving he had according to some 7,000, but according to Oldmixon only ' near 6,000 tolerably well armed, the greatest number that ever were for him together.'   Op. cit. 702.   In London it was reported that he had 12,000 foot, and near 1,500 horse.   J. Reresby, *Memoirs* (ed. 1875), 338.

[590] *Hist. MSS. Com. Rep.* iii, App. 98.

[591] Ibid.   'I will follow him as close as ever I can.'   Churchill to Somerset.

[592] Op. cit. 702.   [593] *Hist. MSS. Com. Rep.* iii, App. 98.

[594] Ibid. ix, App. iii, 2.   Feversham and Pembroke met at Chippenham on the night of 22 June and marched into Bristol on 23 June.   Clar. MSS. 128, fol. 23.

[595] Ibid. fol. 23 ; *Hist MSS. Com. Rep.* ix, App. iii, 3.   [596] Clar. MSS. 128, fol. 23.

[597] 'The king thinks much of the importance of Bristol.'   Roberts, op. cit. i, 331, quoting State Papers, ii, 236, 21 June 1685.

[598] Roberts, op. cit. i, 331, quoting Inland Letters ii, 238.   [599] *Hardwick S. P.* ii, 323.

[600] S. Heywood, *Vindication of C. T. Fox's History of James II.*   App.

[601] Cf. Roberts, op. cit. ii, 4–8.

[602] It was reported by Phelips to be a factious town where Monmouth might hope to increase his numbers. *Somers. and Dors. N. and Q.* 1891, p. 97.

Gloucestershire side. To do so it was necessary to repair Keynsham bridge, which was successfully done.[603] Monmouth then crossed the bridge, but recrossed it as a ruse, and encamped at Pensford on the southern side of the river for the night (25 June).[604] While Keynsham was full of rebel troops it was entered by a division of the royal horse under Major Oglethorpe who mistook Monmouth's men for friends. These the duke's horse 'unadvisedly engaged,' for they lost fourteen men and took only three prisoners.[605] From them he learnt that Feversham's forces were at hand, news which caused him to alter his decision to attack Bristol. Delay in fact had had its inevitable result. Had he stayed even two, instead of four, days in Taunton he would have reached Bristol in time to occupy the town before Feversham's arrival, but now his dilatoriness and the prompt action of the government had had their inevitable result. The capture of Bristol, on which his plans hinged, was given up,[606] and another council of war was held to decide on the best alternative : whether to march forward to Gloucester, and so into Shropshire and Cheshire,[607] or to Wiltshire where he was assured of 500 more horse. The less heroic plan of marching into Wiltshire was adopted, Pensford and Keynsham were evacuated, and the next morning saw Monmouth before Bath.[608]

Bath was summoned ' only in bravado, for we had no expectation of its surrender,'[609] and replied by shooting the herald through the head; the rebels then marched south to Norton St. Philip, where they went into quarters for the night. Feversham in the meantime marched along the north bank of the Avon to Bath, where he was met by Churchill and Grafton,[610] and by further reinforcements from London and Portsmouth.[611] He was now strong enough to assume the offensive, and sent Grafton forward with a mixed force with orders to attack Monmouth, whose troops having rested were able to give a good account of themselves : 27 June was spent in a skirmish at Norton St. Philip in which the rebels had rather the better of the fight, which was ended by Feversham's withdrawal of his men. The latter by his own account lost 20 men and some horses,[612] and Wade owns to 'about eighteen.'[613] Needless to say each side believed the enemy to have lost many more. Wade puts Feversham's losses at 80. Feversham thought that the rebels lost more than twenty. At Norton St. Philip the depression which had attacked Monmouth at Taunton became acute : he even contemplated deserting his army and flying with his officers to some port whence he could escape, but he was persuaded to give up a project born perhaps of the knowledge that with such men as he commanded and without money[614]

[603] Apparently in a very temporary way. Cf. *Reg. of Proc. at Somerset Sessions*, 1 July 1685, Bridgwater: Decision to rebuild and repair the bridge, headed ' Keynsham Bridge pulled down *furore Belli*,' App. *Hist. MSS. Com. Rep.* vii, App. 699. [604] Clar. MSS. 128, Col. 32.

[605] *Hardwick S. P.* ii, 325. *Hist. MSS. Com. Rep.* ix, App. iii, 3. The Duke of Somerset reported that eighty of Monmouth's men were killed and the rest fled. Clar. MSS. 128, fol. 35.

[606] ' This disappointment and allarum broke all their measures and prevented them from attacking Bristol and Gloucester.' *Hist. MSS. Com. Rep.* ix, App. iii, 3.

[607] The persecution of Dissenters had been very severe in these counties, so that he was sure of many recruits in them.

[608] *Hardwick S. P.* ii, 325. It was defended by four companies of militia. *Hist. MSS. Com. Rep.* iii, App. 98. [609] Ibid. [610] *Hist. MSS. Com. Rep.* ix, App. iii, 3.

[611] Ibid. ii, App. 99, 5 companies of foot and 8 pieces of cannon and ammunition came from Portsmouth.

[612] Ibid,   [613] *Hardwick S. P.* ii, 327.   [614] Clar. MSS. 128, fol. 47.

success was impossible. The concentration of the royal forces,[615] desertions from his army, the non-appearance of the horse from Wiltshire, the dispersion by Pembroke of the force which had gathered at Frome, and which would have formed a very sensible addition to his troops had it not been completely routed ; the price of £5,000 set on his head, and the fact that he was not safe from treachery among his own followers (he had been thrice shot at),[616] combined to show him how small his chances were, and how great the probability was of ultimate failure.

The engagement at Norton St. Philip having been ended by Feversham's retreat to Bradford-on-Avon, Monmouth wished to advance to Warminster, apparently in the hope of getting to London, but Feversham marched early in the morning to Westbury, probably to prevent such a step,[617] and this news, combined with the tidings that the Clubmen were up again about Axminster 10,000 strong, decided Monmouth to march back and try to enlist them in his cause. He therefore made a night march to Frome, where he was proclaimed king (and heard of Argyle's defeat), to Shepton Mallet where he spent the night of the 29th, to Wells and to Bridgwater, where he was met by the Clubmen, whose numbers proved to be only 160. On this march his best efforts were unable to restrain his men from looting.[618] Feversham in the meanwhile followed him, marching from Westbury via Frome, Shepton Mallet and Glastonbury to Somerton.[619] From Somerton Feversham sent out spies, who reported that Monmouth and his troops were in Bridgwater, that they had barricaded the bridge, and had planted five cannon at different points. Wade says this was done 'only to secure our quarters and amuse the world, intending nothing less than to stay there,'[620] but the Royalists believed that he intended to fortify it seriously.[621] Two days after his arrival (Sunday 5 July) Monmouth heard that Feversham had left Somerton and was encamped near Weston within 3 miles of Bridgwater.[622] Fearful once more of being blocked up he decided to march to Axbridge, and from thence passing Keynsham bridge to Gloucester, and so over the Severn to Shropshire and Cheshire.[623] His return had been very unpopular, and had spread great discouragement among his friends,[624] so that active measures were necessary to keep his adherents together. He had actually loaded his carriages for the purpose when about 3 p.m. he received news that Feversham had encamped his foot on Sedgemoor, sent his horse into quarters in the villages, and drawn up his cannon to command the road into Bridgwater. As it was still possible for him to march out by another way and so avoid them, he called a council of war to decide whether they should advance or should fight if a night surprise were possible. The council agreed that a surprise should

---

[615] Further reinforcements were also on their way to Feversham. Three Scotch regiments, 'excellent men and well-disciplined' had been recalled from the Continent and were on their way, and troops were under orders from Ireland. Clar. MSS. 128, fol. 53; *Hist. MSS. Com. Rep.* ii, App. 217.

[616] A. Fea, *King Monmouth*, App. C.

[617] Pembroke was also at Trowbridge with the Wilts militia. Clar. MSS. 128, fol. 38.

[618] Clar. MSS. 128, fol. 48–50. At Wells they did damage in the cathedral, stabling their horses there, and 'almost utterly' destroying the organ. *Hist. MSS. Com. Rep.* x, App. iii, 264.

[619] *Hardwick S. P.* ii, 328; *Hist. MSS. Com. Rep.* ix, App. iii, 3. Cf. Clar. MSS. 128, fol. 47, 53.

[620] *Hardwick S. P.* ii, 328.   [621] *Hist. MSS. Com. Rep.* ix, App. iii, 4.

[622] Ibid.   [623] *Hardwick S. P.* ii, 305.

[624] S. Heywood, op. cit. Barillon's account.

be attempted if the foot had not entrenched, and the spy who had brought the news was sent back to see whether they had done so. He returned with the information that they had not ; and their position having been examined from the church tower the attack was decided on. Godfrey the spy, being a farmer of the neighbourhood, could not have been ignorant of the great ditch, the Bussex Rhine, running from Weston into the moor, behind which Feversham was encamped, and his failure to mention it, which had such fatal consequences for Monmouth, can have been due only to his ignorance of its importance from a military point of view,[625] for his devotion to Monmouth's cause was unquestioned.[626]

Before setting out the troops were harangued in a sermon by Ferguson, who, whatever excuses have been made for him, must be accounted Monmouth's evil genius throughout the enterprise ; and their hopes were probably raised by the descriptions of the bad discipline in the royal army. ' No more,' Monmouth was told, ' was to be done, than to lock up the stable door, and to seize the troopers in their beds.' [627]

The rebel army now consisted of 3,620 men.[628] Unfortunately the two best troops of horse had been sent to fetch cannon from Minehead,[629] and the cavalry therefore numbered only 640, all of them being commanded by Lord Grey except a small bodyguard of about 140. The infantry, apart from a company of 80 men from Lyme Regis, was divided into five regiments, and to each battalion was attached about 100 scythemen. There were also the four small cannon. Of this force a certain number lost their way in the dark and took no part in the battle. Against Monmouth's force Feversham had, besides 1,500 militia who were not engaged, since from their sympathy with Monmouth they could not be trusted,[630] 700 horse and dragoons, about 2,100 foot and 16 guns, each served by two men. He had set guards on the roads running from Weston to Bridgwater, and sent out a troop of Life Guards under Colonel Oglethorpe to watch Monmouth. This he failed to do,[631] for Monmouth, leaving Bridgwater by the Bristol road, marched straight along it until the turn by Bradley Lane on to the moor, halted there to allow his horse which had been in the rear to precede the infantry on to the moor,[632] parked his forty-two baggage-wagons at Peasy Farm, made a wide easterly circuit to avoid Feversham's outpost at Chedzoy, and drew very near to Feversham's position all unperceived. By one o'clock in the morning he had passed two of the ditches which lay on his path, the Black Ditch and the Langmoor Rhine ; but in crossing the latter he had lost a good many horses who were bogged and men who missed their way. This happened because Godfrey who was guiding them had missed the ford in the fog which covered everything and added to the weirdness of the silent night march over the flat desolate

---

[625] *Hardwick S. P.* ii, 306.

[626] Oldmixon, op. cit. 703. ' He loved the Duke of Monmouth as well as it was possible for a man to love him.'

[627] Toulmin, op. cit. 473.

[628] Echard, op. cit. 1065. Wolseley, op. cit. i, 318. Many contemporary accounts are very untrustworthy, e.g. Feversham's, who puts the number of Monmouth's men at 7,000, and Oglethorpe's, who estimated it at 6,000 foot and 1,500 horse. *Hist. MSS. Com. Rep.* iii, App. 99 ; *Rep.* xii, App. pt. v, 90.

[629] *Hardwick S. P.* ii, 330.

[630] They were brought up when the fight was practically over, and were then quite steady.

[631] *Hardwick S. P.* ii, 307.   [632] Ibid. 329.

moor.[633] Fortunately Monmouth had time to re-form his troops after crossing Langmoor Rhine before his whereabouts were discovered by a vedette of the Life Guards, who fired his pistol to give the alarm and galloped back to camp to arouse the royal troops.[634] Grey was therefore ordered by Monmouth to advance as quickly as possible into Weston and fire it in the hope that the advantage of a surprise might still be secured. Had this succeeded, and the royal infantry been attacked both in front and rear, all might still have turned out well, for Feversham's troops which were sleeping were thrown into the greatest confusion and their commander had to be roused from his bed. Churchill however was afoot at once and reducing chaos to order, and Dumbarton's regiment (the best of the royal infantry) was falling into rank. Grey however on advancing to Weston found himself confronted by the Bussex Rhine and made the irreparable blunder of turning west instead of east : had he turned to his left he would have turned Feversham's flank and avoided a frontal attack, but by turning to his right he brought his troops directly opposite Dumbarton's regiment, who were now drawn up, and who poured a volley into Grey's horse as soon as they realized with whom they had to do. At this the green horses off the marshes, on which the rebels were mounted, taking fright broke madly away, Grey making no apparent effort to check them, and their rout was completed by a charge from the guard at Chedzoy under Sir Francis Compton which had come up.[635] Under the influence of this panic Monmouth's infantry, already in some confusion from the fast pace at which he had led them,[636] lost their nerve ; many fled, and the drivers left at Peasy Farm made for their homes with all speed. Monmouth, seeing that he could no longer carry out his original plan, changed his tactics with commendable promptitude and decided on an immediate frontal attack on the camp with his foot only, by which there was still a chance of demoralizing Feversham's forces and carrying off a hard-earned victory. Unfortunately however his troops opened fire before attempting to cross the ditch,[637] and quickly exhausted their ammunition, while at the same time aiming so high that they did the royal forces no harm. But as the wagon-drivers had fled there was no one to bring them a fresh supply when they cried 'Ammunition ! for God's sake, ammunition !' The only damage to Feversham's troops was that done by Monmouth's guns, three of which had been brought into action on his left.[638] In reply Churchill advanced his guns, and led a troop of dragoons across the ditch, which put Monmouth's out of action.[639] Oglethorpe and Sarsfield also charged but were repulsed, and it was not until dawn had fully come that Feversham allowed more troops to cross, and by a determined attack bring the struggle to an end. Monmouth's men fought

---

[633] To ensure silence Monmouth ordered any man who made a noise to be knocked on the head. *Hist. MSS. Com. Rep.* xii, App. v, 90.

[634] Ibid. Another version says that the alarm was given by Captain Hucker of Lord Grey's Horse, who asserted his treachery during his trial by Jeffreys, but the balance of evidence and probability is against it. Cf. *Hist. MSS. Com. Rep.* ix, App. iii, 6.

[635] *Hardwick S. P.* ii, 329; *Hist. MSS. Com. Rep.* ix, App. iii, 4.

[636] *Hardwick S. P.* ii, 330.

[637] Wade says he did not intend his men to fire, but when Colonel Mathew's men came up and began firing his men did likewise, and after that he could not get them to advance. *Hardwick S. P.* ii, 330.

[638] The fourth had been unaccountably left behind at Peasy Farm.

[639] *Hist. MSS. Com. Rep.* ix, App. iii, 4.

with the desperation of religious partisans who know that their cause is lost, although deserted both by the duke and Grey,[640] who fled together once victory was plainly impossible. Wade stuck to his men and brought off some 150 who took refuge in Bridgwater,[641] but a large number of the rebels were killed in the pursuit which followed. Accounts vary as to the losses on both sides. A news-letter gives 400 rebels killed on the field and 2,000 in pursuit,[642] which seems the most probable estimate. Oldmixon says that 300 rebels and 400 of the royal army were killed in battle,[643] but Clarendon gives Feversham's losses as not more than 100 killed and very few wounded, and another account as 200 killed.[644] On this point Oldmixon is probably more reliable, as he visited the scene on the next day. Monmouth and Grey fled together over Polden Hills and were eventually taken at Ringwood afoot and disguised in countrymen's clothes. Grey's cowardice is rightly considered one of the chief causes of the failure of the rebellion. Before the battle Monmouth was begged by Colonel Mathew to divide the cavalry, so that one part might be under the charge of some person of courage,[645] and after the fight the duke is said to have threatened to save James a labour and hang Grey because he had proved a coward to him twice.[646] Monmouth's own conduct during the fight had been admirable ; ' all agree that hee acted the part of a great generall, and charged afoot in the head of his army.'[647]

As a result of the battle the rebels who remained had been so completely scattered that not ten could be found anywhere together.[648] When Wade got into Bridgwater he found there two or three full troops of cavalry which had fled without striking a blow, drawn up in good order, but they all dispersed after consultation.[649] Of the prisoners taken, 500 were brought into Weston Church, of whom five died of their wounds and nineteen were hanged on the following day, the first to suffer being Captain Adlam, who was actually in a dying state when taken to the gallows.[650] Many of the wounded were buried alive with the dead in the great grave made beside the Bussex Rhine, and the bodies of those who were butchered in the cornfields to which they had fled were cared for by the country people,[651] but the local farmers took care to propitiate Feversham's men by large gifts of cider. About twelve hundred rebels in all are said to have surrendered.[652]

As soon as the struggle on the moor was over Churchill marched with 500 cavalry and 500 foot into Bridgwater, which he found completely deserted, and Feversham followed with wounded rebels in carts, and those who could walk chained together in gangs ;[653] when they left Kirke remained in command.[654] The following days were occupied by a ruthless search for the rebel fugitives, who were either killed where they lay hid, or

---

[640] Grey had fled with his horse, but returned about daybreak.

[642] *Hist. MSS. Com. Rep.* xii, App. v, 92.

[644] *Hist. MSS. Com. Rep.* xii, App. v, 90–1.

[646] *Hist. MSS. Com. Rep.* xii, App. v, 90. Grey had run away at the engagement at Bridport. Oldmixon, op. cit. 701.

[647] *Hist. MSS. Com. Rep.* xii, App. v, 91.

[649] *Hardwick S. P.* ii, 330.

[650] Roberts, op. cit. ii, 87–8. On this subject he gives a transcript of the entry in the register of Weston zoyland.

[651] *Dummer's Journal.* Pepys Library.

[653] Clar. MS. 128, fol. 56. *Hist. MSS. Com. Rep.* xii, App. v, 92.

[654] *Hist. MSS. Com. Rep.* ix, App. iii, 5.

[641] *Hardwick S. P.* ii, 330.

[643] Op. cit. 704.

[645] Echardt, op. cit. 1065.

[648] Clar. MS. 128, fol. 56.

[652] Fea, op. cit. 297.

hanged without any pretence of trial, a long line of gallows decorating the road from Weston to Bridgwater, besides those in the town and village.[655]

Feversham himself set an example of inhuman brutality until warned by Bishop Mews or Bishop Ken[656] that he might be called to account for murder, but was surpassed in brutality by Kirke, whose stay at Tangier seemed to have deprived him of all sense of pity. At Taunton, which he occupied from 9 July to 1 September, so brutal was he that a story is told of him and his company, that, 'observing the shaking of the legs of those whom they had hang'd, it was said among them that they were dancing, and upon that Musick was call'd for.'[657] Oldmixon asserts that his avarice led him to sell many pardons for £20, £30 or £40,[658] for which he was reprimanded severely.[659]

As a result of the military executions the county was now a scene of horrors. Besides the corpses left hanging on their gibbets, the quarters of many of the rebels after execution were boiled in pitch and hung up at the crossways and public parts of the town and neighbourhood;[660] the gaols were crowded with prisoners living during the summer heat under the most appalling conditions, which bred fever and every sort of disease. To try them Jeffreys was sent as president of a commission of oyer and terminer and gaol delivery for the West,[661] accompanied by Sir William Montague, the Lord chief baron; Sir Creswell Levinz, justice of the King's Bench; Sir Francis Wythens, justice of the Common Pleas; and Sir Robert Wright, baron of the Exchequer,[662] and attended by Kirke and a company of troops which must have given them an air of special importance, increased by the fact that Jeffreys, as General commanding the Western Division, was in command of the soldiers.[663] From Winchester, Dorchester and Exeter[664] his reputation preceded him to Taunton, where he arrived to find 526 rebels[665] awaiting trial,[666] while at Wells there were 527. His method of conducting trials was at once simple and expeditious. By letting it be understood that those would fare best who pleaded guilty and by the instant execution of twenty-three prisoners who pleaded not guilty and were convicted, he induced almost all to plead guilty, and then denied them the mercy he had led them to expect.

There is some difficulty in ascertaining the exact number of those who were hanged. Toulmin gives a list of 211 who suffered in different parts of Somerset,[667] but as it appears to be taken from Locke's *Western*

---

[655] Oldmixon says that 'after the defeat everybody expected military Execution, except such as were of the Popish and Tory factions.' Op. cit. 704.

[656] Cf. Fea, op. cit. 381; Roberts, op. cit. ii, 173.   [657] Oldmixon, op. cit. 705.

[658] Op. cit. 705.   [659] State Paper Entry Book, lvi, 268.   [660] Roberts, op. cit. ii, 180.

[661] It was the ordinary summer assize, but a special commission in that it consisted of five instead of two justices.

[662] Of these Montague and Levinz were known as upright judges: Wythens seems to have been a contemptible character, and Wright is justly described by Roberts (op. cit. ii, 189) as a 'true butcher bird': but they played an altogether subordinate part. With them as Judge Advocate came Pollexfen, a known Presbyterian and member of the country party whose appointment had been accounted to James for righteousness. Cf. *Dict. Nat. Biog.*

[663] F. A. Inderwick, *Side Lights on the Stuarts*, 373.

[664] At Salisbury there were no convictions.   [665] According to Inderwick, 513, op. cit. 389.

[666] Before his coming three had escaped by filing the window bars and descending by a rope, not a surprising result of leaving the care of the prison to the gaoler's wife and a maid. *Hist. MSS. Com. Rep.* ix, App. iii, 2.

[667] Op. cit. 506.

Rebellion, collated with that in the *New Martyrology*, it cannot be considered reliable. The gaol books evidently cannot be cited as authorities, as at Taunton they record only four (of which one was reprieved), and none at Wells. The best authority is the Treasury minute books at the Record Office,[668] which give the number of those 'to be executed' at Taunton as 139, besides which there were fifteen not included in the warrant, and at Wells as ninety-six, not including five persons accidentally omitted in the warrant.[669]

The county now received a further decoration of heads and quarters 'boyled and tarred'; churches and houses were 'covered as close with heads as at other times . . . with crows or ravens . . . the trees were loaden almost as thick with quarters as with leaves';[670] and Roberts quotes Lord Lonsdale as writing 'that the stench was so great that the ways were not to be travelled whilst the horror of so many quarters of men, and the offensive stench of them lasted.' No wonder that the Puritan Oldmixon wrote 'England is now an Aceldama . . . Every soul was sunk in Anguish and Terror, sighing by day and by night for Deliverance, but shut out of all Hope by Despair.'[671]

There were several prominent sufferers in Somerset. At Taunton the execution of the brothers Hewling, two young men of excellent character and prominent Nonconformist connexions, was lamented even by the soldiers; Major Perrott; Captain Annesley, who suffered because he refused to impeach others; William Jenkins, who was brought for execution from Dorchester; and Captain Hucher, who was believed by some to have given the alarm at Sedgemoor, were among the best known victims.[672] At Wells, Mr. Charles Speke, the youngest son of the Spekes of White Lackington, was condemned and executed apparently on the grounds of having shaken hands with Monmouth at Ilminster, although it was known that he had taken no part in the rebellion.[673]

Besides those executed many were fined, whipped, or imprisoned: at Taunton also there were twenty pardoned, twenty-three proposed for pardon, two bailed and thirty-three remaining in gaol until further orders. Those who suffered the extreme penalty may in many cases be counted more lucky than those who were sentenced to transportation, of whom there were 282 at Taunton and 383 at Wells.[674] These men were given either to the queen or to favourites at court, where there was angry competition for such grants. Of those thus sentenced in Somerset, the queen had ninety-eight,[675] Sir William Booth 100, Jerome Nipho thirty-three, Sir Christopher Musgrave eighty-four, Sir William Stapleton 100, Sir Philip Howard 200, and William Bridgeman fifty. Of these we have evidence that one ship-load of 100 went to Jamaica,[676] and that Dr. Nipho's and Sir William Booth's were sent

[668] 'An account of the proceedings against the rebells and other prisoners in the severall counties of Southton, Wilts, Dorset, Devon and Somerset, etc.'
[669] Cf. Inderwick, op. cit. 389 sqq. A. L. Humphreys, 'Some Sources of History for the Monmouth Rebellion and the Bloody Assizes.' *Somers. Arch. and Nat. Hist. Soc. Proc.* 1892, xxxviii (2), 313.
[670] Cf. Roberts, op. cit. ii, 223; and ibid. 224, and Fea, op. cit. 396, 391 for transcripts of warrants and other papers: also *Hist. MSS. Com. Rep.* v, App. 373 for a parallel account for Devonshire.
[671] Op. cit. 707.
[672] Toulmin, op. cit. 512–27. [673] Roberts, op. cit. ii, 222.
[674] Treasury Minute. [675] She asked for 100 more.
[676] J. C. Hotten, *Original Lists of Persons of Quality, Emigrants, Religious Exiles, Political Rebels*, etc., 316.

to Barbadoes, two of the former and ten of the latter dying on the way.[677] These unfortunate men were sold either before leaving England or on their arrival to work as slaves in the plantation for ten years, a system which led their owners to get the most out of them in that period without actually killing them or disabling them before it was over. Many of them were ransomed for large sums by their relations ; those who were less fortunate were in many cases in such a state of health from the indescribable horrors of the voyage that they had to be fattened on their arrival before being sold.[678]

The queen had set an example of greed in this matter : she showed if possible less feeling when she allowed her maids-of-honour to accept the 'Taunton maids' as a Christmas box. £7,000 was the sum they hoped to receive for the ransom of the children, and the Duke of Somerset, acting on their behalf in the matter, put pressure on the relations and friends of the little girls by explaining that unless the money was produced suits for outlawry would be begun. The children were exempted from the general pardon of 10 March, 1686, by which those left in prison were freed, but in the event only £50 to £100 was paid for each child, which amounted to something over £3,000, and they were then pardoned.[679]

With this the rebellion and its immediate consequences may be said to have been concluded ; but the recollection of it, still green in men's minds, made them extend the heartiest of welcomes to William of Orange. Before the revolution, however, the opinion of the county had again been made plain. The large dissenting element had replied to the Declaration of Indulgence with addresses of thanks ; Taunton and Chard each sent one ; two were received from Bath, others from the Presbyterian ministers and others from their congregations in the east of Somerset ; the Dissenting ministers of the Gospel, inhabitants of the western parts of the county ; and the combers, weavers and other labourers in the serge manufacture of Taunton ;[680] but the pains taken by the Government to obtain them detracts considerably from their value as evidence of the state of local feeling. There is, however, nothing equivocal about the evidence afforded by the replies of the gentry to the three questions propounded by James. In the summer of 1687 he wished to revise the commissions of Peace and the Lieutenancy with a view to summoning a subservient Parliament, and accordingly the leading county gentry likely to aspire to seats or to influence the elections were asked whether, if elected, they would favour the abolition of the Tests, whether they would contribute to assist the election of such as would do so, and whether they would support the King's Declaration for Liberty of Conscience by living friendly with those of all persuasions. In Somerset only Sir William Basset, Francis Paulet, William Clark and Henry Walrond consented outright : Lord Fitzharding did so with a proviso for the maintenance of the Church of England ; twenty-seven others hedged in varying degrees, six returned themselves as sick, and four as absent gave no answers. The result was that many were removed and sixteen more Dissenters or Roman Catholics

[677] J. C. Hotten, *Original Lists of Persons of Quality, Emigrants, Religious Exiles, Political Rebels*, etc., 319, 320.
[678] For an account of the treatment received by them, cf. Arber's *Garner*, vii, 333. 'A relation of the great sufferings, etc. of Henry Pitman.'
[679] Roberts, op. cit. ii, 245–9.
[680] E. Green, *The March of William of Orange through Somerset*, 17–24.

were added to the Commissions.[681]   The feeling of the county gentry was also shown by their quarrel with the High Sheriff Edward Strode on the ground that he had packed the grand jury so as to obtain an address to the King.[682]

When the boroughs were remodelled, Bridgwater (perhaps because its corporation had sent no address of thanks for the Declaration) was one of the first to be attacked.   Seven capital burgesses were removed and others more favourable to James's plans put in their place, and the charter was forfeited and surrendered.[683]   James had been at pains to obtain reports of the probable action of the boroughs, and Bridgwater corporation, as also that of Taunton, was reported to be in need of total alteration.   Bath and Milborne Port were supposed to be favourable to his plans, and Wells possibly so.   At Minehead Francis Luttrell, 'who will not comply,' was certain to be elected.[684]

In the following autumn, however, when William's intentions were known to James, the deputy-lieutenants and justices who had been re-moved were reinstated (26 September),[685] and Bridgwater corporation was restored.[686]   Rumours were heard in the West that another rising would be attempted under Monmouth (whom many believed to be alive) ; but when William had actually landed the Somerset gentry were at first slow in joining him.[687]   The Bloody Assize was still too vivid a memory.   Large numbers of them, however, came in at Exeter, including Sir Francis Warre, Sir William Portman, Mr. Speke, Sir Edward and Mr. Thomas Seymour, Colonel Bampfield, Colonel Wyndham and his son, Mr. Stawell, Mr. Mallet and Captain Braddon.[688]   William, on his way to London, traversed only a small part of the county, his march being made from Axminster through Crewkerne[689] to Sherborne, and from thence through Wincanton to Salisbury.   At Wincanton, however, a collision took place between some five and twenty of his men under Lieutenant Campbell, and a detachment of Royalists under Sarsfield.   Campbell would have been annihilated had not a report been spread that a large party was coming to reinforce him, which caused Sarsfield to retreat.   Fifteen men altogether lost their lives, of whom six were Royalists, and the others, including Campbell, Orangemen.[690]   With this little skirmish Somerset saw the last of the horrors of civil war, and for the future had to find its excitements mainly in its military or parliamentary associations.

In a county where almost all the gentry had proved themselves so loyal, the years 1640 to 1660 naturally saw many arbitrary dealings with the parliamentary representatives.   The original county members of the Long Parliament, Sir John Poulett[691] and Sir John Stawell, were both disabled by vote of the Commons in August, 1642, for endeavouring to execute the

---

681 E. Green, *The March of William of Orange through Somerset*, 27–31. Rawlinson MSS. 139a, fol. 1, sqq.
682 Ibid. fol. 5–10b.   683 Green, op. cit. 26–7.
684 Ibid. 31–3.   685 Green, op. cit. 55.
686 *Proclamation*, Bodl. Shelf Mark; Ashm. H. 23, 383.
687 *Reply of William to the address presented at Exeter.* Bodl. Shelf Mark. Pamph. 179.
688 Green, op. cit. 57; *Hist. MSS. Com. Rep.* vii, App. 226, 416.
689 At Crewkerne he was met by Dr. Finch of All Souls, bringing him assurances of support from several of the Oxford Heads of Houses. Oldmixon, op. cit. 758.
690 *Hist. MSS. Com. Rep.* vii, App. 417; Oldmixon, op. cit.
691 Afterwards second Baron Poulett.

Commission of Array. The seats remained vacant until the close of 1645, when John Harrington and George Horner were returned. Their election was declared void on petition, but they were re-elected in the following summer and sat until they were both secluded by the 'Purge.'[692] Many of the original borough members were also ejected for their opinions. Taunton chose Sir William Portman and George Searle in 1640, but in 1644 Portman was disabled for attending the king at Oxford, and one John Palmer took his place, who, like Searle, was a keen Parliament man and a member of the Rump.[693] Both the original members for Wells, Sir Ralph Hopton and Sir Edward Rodney, were disabled; so also was Edward Kyston, an original member for Milborne Port, while two other members for the latter, Thomas Grove and William Carent, who were elected in 1645, were secluded in 1648. Thomas Hunt, member for Ilchester, Thomas Hanham, a member for Minehead, were disabled in 1644, and one member for Bridgwater, Thomas Smyth, was also ejected. From 1643 to 1653 that very energetic Parliamentarian, James Ashe, was one of the representatives for Bath, having probably been elected after the disablement of Sir William Bassett, one of the original members.[694] One of the most prominent Somerset members was Lislebone Long, who was the second speaker of the Parliament of 1659,[695] but in the Parliament of 1660, and in the Long Parliament of the Restoration, members of many well-known county families once more took their seats. In 1660 George Horner, Alexander Popham, Sir Thomas Wroth, Francis and William Windham, and Francis Luttrell all sat, and in 1661 Sir John Stawell, Edward Phelipps, Alexander Popham, Edmund and Francis Windham, Francis Luttrell, Sir William Portman, Sir William Windham, and Sir Maurice Berkeley were among the original members.[696] Election petitions are, however, the chief topic in the parliamentary history of the county. None occurred as far as the representation of the county was concerned, but the varieties of franchise in the boroughs offered opportunities for charges of all sorts of illegalities and malpractices.

In Bath, the first contested election, which took place in 1661, was followed by a petition in which the freemen asserted their right to vote, and objected to the limitation of the franchise to the mayor, aldermen, and common councillors.[697] In 1675 the same question was raised and again left unsettled,[698] but in 1705, when the quarrel was for a third time the cause of a petition, it was resolved by the Committee of Privileges and Elections that the franchise was in the mayor, aldermen and common council only.[699] The first petition on a disputed election at Bridgwater was presented in 1669. The Committee reported that the right of election was in the majority of the corporation, consisting of a mayor, aldermen, and capital burgesses, in number 24, who had all voted: the petitioner, Mr. Peregrine Palmer, declared, however, that some of those who voted were

[692] *Somers. and Dors. N. and Q.* 1890, 41-2.   [693] Ibid. ii, 36, 91.
[694] Ibid. iii, 102; iv, 78; *Accounts and Papers: Members of Parliament,* lxii, pt. i, 492, 493.
[695] Brown-Willis, *Notitia Parliamentaria,* 265, 277, 292.
[696] *Accts. and Papers,* lxii, pt. i, 515, 527.
[697] Thomas Carew, *An Historical Account of the Rights of Elections,* etc., 33; *Accts. and Papers,* lxii. pt. i, 515.
[698] *Com. Journ.* viii, 250; ix, 365; Carew, op. cit. 33.
[699] There were nine aldermen, a recorder, two bailiffs and twenty common council men. Brown-Willis, op. cit. 44. *Com. Journ.* xv, 12, 203, 255.

not qualified to do so, being debarred by the Corporation Act since they held conventicles in their houses, and refused to conform or resort to the service of the Church or receive the sacrament. On hearing the evidence the Committee unseated Sir Francis Rolle, who had been elected, and declared Mr. Palmer to be duly returned.[700] In 1678 Mr. Ralph Stawell petitioned against Rolle's return, and after the election of the following year Rolle petitioned against Stawell, but each was unsuccessful.[701] The evidence taken on a petition in 1692 illuminates some of the methods used to influence electors: one candidate, Mr. Gardner, owed an elector £4 15s. for drink supplied to the voters, but the agent of Mr. Balch, the other candidate, by 'engaging to see him paid,' secured his vote. The same agent was said to have promised a voter to have him struck off the list for the poor rate, and to give him a life interest in his estate if he would promise his vote. A more efficient plan, however, than bribery seems to have been simply to lock recalcitrant voters up.[702] The disputes which followed the election of 1768 led to another definition of the franchise by the Commons. The election of Lord Perceval had been followed by petitions from some of the inhabitants, and from Mr. Anne Poulett, one of the defeated candidates; and on hearing the evidence the House resolved that the franchise for the borough belonged to inhabitants of that division of the parish of Bridgwater commonly called 'the Borough,' paying 'scot and lot.'[703] The contention of Lord Perceval's party had been that only the mayor, aldermen and capital burgesses were entitled to vote, and as a result he was unseated and Mr. Poulett's election confirmed.[704] Poulett continued to represent the borough, although in 1780 some of the inhabitants and one of the defeated candidates, John Acland, petitioned on the grounds of bribery, corruption, and illegal practices, and were successful in turning out Poulett's colleague, Benjamin Allen;[705] and in 1784 Sir Gilbert Elliott, who had been beaten, and some voters petitioned against Poulett and Mr. Alexander Hood for bribery and corruption, alleging that 'Meat, Drink, Reward, Entertainment and Provision' had been offered at their expense; the petition, however, was withdrawn.[706]

Ilchester has a shocking record, if the number of petitions can be taken as any index to the morality of the place. The elections for the Parliaments of 1660, 1678, 1679, 1685, 1688, 1700, 1701, 1715, 1722, 1734, 1774, 1780, 1784, 1802, 1803, 1819, 1826, and 1830 all gave rise to petitions. The gravamen of the charge made in March 1678–9 by William Strode and John Speke was that the common seal of the borough had been forcibly taken from the bailiff and affixed to the indenture by which Mr. Phelipps and Mr. Hunt were returned; and as their statement was substantiated by evidence their election was confirmed by the Committee, and the return of Phelipps and Hunt disallowed.[707] The petition of 1689 turned on the question of the franchise,[708] and that of 1700 on bribery by Mr. Anderton,

---

[700] Carew, op. cit. 89; *Accts. and Papers*, lxii, pt. i, 527; *Com. Journ.* ix, 99, 107, 113, 116, 118, 119.
[701] Carew, op. cit. 89; *Accts. and Papers*, lxii, pt. i, 536, 543; *Com. Journ.* ix. 571, 572, 578.
[702] Carew, op. cit. 92–3.   [703] In 1750 they numbered about 160. Brown-Willis, op. cit. 45.
[704] *Com. Journ.* xxxii, 18, 301, 314; *Accts. and Papers*, lxii, pt. ii, 142.
[705] *Com. Journ.* xxxviii, 15, 50, 53, 241; *Accts. and Papers*, lxii, pt. ii, 167.
[706] *Com. Journ.* xl, 14, 92, 247, 264.
[707] Carew, op. cit. 305; *Com. Journ.* ix, 570, 581.   [708] *Com. Journ.* x, 124.

one of the successful candidates; in the event he was not unseated, but a Mr. Allen, who had also stood, was found guilty of notorious bribery.[709] Another petition was brought against Anderton's election for the next parliament, but it failed, as it was proved that most of the petitioner's votes had been obtained by bribery.[710] The petitions of 1715 and 1734 were also unsuccessful,[711] and that of 1722 was withdrawn.[712] The elections for the Parliament of 1774 seem to have been conducted with an even larger allowance of malpractices than was customary. The elections of Mr. Cust and Mr. Innes were voided on petitions by some of the voters and by the defeated candidates Brown and Jones on the ground of illegal practices and bribery, Cust and Innes in their turn making countercharges of bribery; and in December, 1775, another election to fill the vacancy was held, at which Mr. Webb and Mr. Brereton were elected. Brown and Jones immediately petitioned once more, but this time without success.[713] In 1784 it was proved that large numbers of persons were secretly and fraudulently introduced into the borough to influence the elections, and were allowed to vote although unqualified; consequently Mr. Harcourt had to give up the seat to the petitioner, Mr. George Johnstone.[714] The election of 1802 was voided for bribery,[715] but Sir William Manners, one of the petitioners, on being elected, was himself unseated on the same charge.[716]

Milborne Port can show seventeen petitions for the same period against Ilchester's eighteen. The returning officers here were the two under-bailiffs, each of whom was nominated by one of the capital bailiffs for the year, and the petitions turn constantly on their action. The borough consisted of nine bailiwicks, in part the property of the Medlycotts, in part of the Walters, but so intermixed that in following the established rotation for the election of the capital-bailiffs, in some years one was elected by each landlord, and in some both by one. There was, therefore, opportunity and to spare for disputes.[717] In 1701 Mr. John Henley declared that his opponent, Sir Thomas Travell, who was bailiff at the time, had illegally admitted deputies whom he procured to return him; Henley, however, was unsuccessful.[718] In the second parliament of that year the inhabitants petitioned that although Henley had been elected the bailiffs had returned a Mr. Hunt,[719] and after the election for the Parliament of 1702 Henley and Hunt each petitioned, as each had been returned by one bailiff. The bailiffs had differed on the question of the franchise, and after hearing the evidence the Committee ruled that the franchise was in the capital-bailiffs and their deputies, the commonalty stewards, and the inhabitants paying scot and lot. Mr. Medlycott also petitioned against the return of Sir Thomas Travell, who, he said, had had the naming of both the under-bailiffs, whereby in effect he was returned by himself, and who had also distributed great doles of corn to the electors. The decision of 1702 did not prevent Sir Richard Newman and Mr. Devenish from petitioning

[709] *Com. Journ.* xiii, 350, 408; *Accts. and Papers,* lxii, pt. i, 589.
[710] *Com. Journ.* xiv, 7, 147–8; *Accts. and Papers,* lxii, pt. i, 596.
[711] *Com. Journ.* xviii, 33; xxii, 340; *Accts. and Papers,* lxii, pt. ii, 43, 78.
[712] *Com. Journ.* xx, 16, 62.   [713] *Ibid.* xxxv, 30, 50, 409, 431, 473, 563, 583.
[714] *Ibid.* xl, 562; xli, 152, 217, 245; *Accts. and Papers,* lxii, pt. ii, 180.
[715] *Com. Journ.* lviii, 29, 301.   [716] *Ibid.* 339, 345; lix, 138.   [717] Douglas, op. cit. i, 100.
[718] *Com. Journ.* xiii, 652; *Accts. and Papers,* lxii, pt. i, 589.   [719] *Com. Journ.* xiii, 748.

against the return of Travell and Medlycott in 1705 on the question of the franchise,[720] and on the same grounds one successful candidate was unseated after the election of 1715,[721] and unsuccessful petitions were presented in 1741.[722] A bye-election in 1717 was followed by a successful petition by Colonel Stanhope against Mr. Michael Harvey ; five voters allowed to having received five guineas each from Mr. Harvey for their votes, while a sixth promised to vote for Stanhope but afterwards engaged to vote for Harvey since ' he had lost five guineas the last election by staying for Mr. Medlycott's friend, and was resolved not to lose five more now.' Six, seven, and eight guineas a vote were offered by Stanhope, and of one voter it was sworn that when he said he was pledged to Mr. Harvey (he had accepted five guineas from him) Stanhope's canvasser had replied that ' the esquire would lay down one hundred guineas upon the table and he should take as much as he would of it for his vote.[723]

Petitions on the usual grounds of illegal practices or bribery or both were filed in 1708,[724] 1734,[725] 1768,[726] 1774,[727] 1780,[728] 1796,[729] 1807,[730] and 1819 ;[731] in 1796, the franchise being again defined in the same terms as before, and the number of bailiffs declared to be nine, of their deputies two, and of the commonalty stewards two.[732]

Minehead, from its position, was under the influence of the Luttrells of Dunster, who were patrons of the borough, and their name figures largely in its parliamentary history. The first disputed election occurred in 1698, when Mr. John Sandford petitioned unsuccessfully against the return of Jacob Banks, ' a foreigner,' on the ground of bribes, treating, and other undue means.[733] Banks, however, was one of the most famous members of the borough, which he represented ' for sixteen years, and during this time was a benefactor to it on all occasions.'[734] The elections for the Parliament of 1715–22 were followed by petitions on the part of the unsuccessful candidates, Samuel Edwyn and James Milner, against the return of Sir William Wyndham and Sir John Trevelyan, on the ground of the partiality of the constables, who had declared that the latter should be returned if they had but five votes apiece, and other illegal practices, including bribery. Trevelyan seems to have recognized how good the petitioners' case was, as he wrote to Wyndham, ' As to our success, it is what I never had the least concern for provided we can save our friends.'[735] But after hearing the evidence the Commons voided the whole election, and refused to issue a new warrant that session.[736]

The election which took place after the issue of the writ in 1717 resulted in a double return and cross petitions from Trevelyan and Mr. James Milner, the successful, and Mr. Gage, one of the unsuccessful candidates. The first two petitioned against the action of the sheriff in returning Gage

---

[720] Com. Journ. xv, 23.
[721] Ibid. xviii, 619.
[722] Ibid. xxiv, 55.
[723] Carew, op. cit. 395–6.
[724] Com. Journ. xvi, 12, 18, 195.
[725] Ibid. xxii, 505 ; xxv, 450, 456, 457, 788–90.
[726] Ibid. xxx, 696, 784. Accts. and Papers, lxii, pt. ii, 142.
[727] Com. Journ. xxxv, 10, 15, 110.
[728] Ibid. xxxviii, 21, 43, 447.
[729] Ibid. lii, 17, 44, 191.
[730] Ibid. lxii, 43, 44, 70.
[731] Ibid. lxxiv, 88, 328.
[732] In 1750 the electors numbered about fifty only. Brown-Willis, op. cit. 46.
[733] Carew, op. cit. 397 ; Com. Journ. xii, 365.
[734] Inscription on statue of Queen Anne in Wellington Square, Minehead.
[735] F. Hancock, Hist. of Minehead, 335.
[736] Com. Journ. xviii, 33, 303.

and Edwyn, since the constables were the proper returning officers. Gage accused the constables of illegal practices, and the constable and some voters accused Gage and Edwyn of bribery, treating and other indirect practices. The Commons decided in favour of Milner and Trevelyan, and resolved that the right of election for the borough lay in the parishioners of Minehead and Dunster, being housekeepers in the borough of Minehead, and not receiving alms.[737] Mr. Hancock, in his *History of Minehead*, quotes documents which illustrate the conduct of elections in the borough. For the year 1734 he quotes an account of 272 voters who had taken half-crowns,[738] an unusually low price ; but by 1755 the value of a vote to its owner had risen considerably—to two guineas. After this election a Mr. Stent, a supporter of Mr. Shiffner, Luttrell's candidate, was found guilty of bribery, on which Mr. Luttrell commented : 'No justice is to be expected, at least in this part of the world.'[739] For the election of 1761 Mr. Luttrell again backed Mr. Shiffner, while Lord Egremont, who had great interest in Minehead, supported Lord Thomond. Great entertainments were given by Mr. Luttrell, the menu at one consisting of 'a whole buck, viz. a Haunch and Shoulder roasted, and the side pastied ; a Ham and fowls, and a couple of rabbits ; a rump of beef boiled, greens, roots, Sauses, puddings, etc., at each table, also a Hare and 2 brace of Partridges and tarts at table.' To this some fifty-nine voters sat down, and those who were not invited were entertained in smaller parties at the different public-houses.[740] By 1768 the value of a vote had risen to three guineas in hard cash besides entertainment, but Minehead could count on some thirty 'incorruptibles' who could be tempted neither by money nor by invitation to dine at Dunster Castle. A grand effort, Mr. Hancock says, was made before this election to make the Luttrell interest safe, and at a meeting at the 'Plume and Feathers' his supporters drew up a list of suggestions proposing that he should build more houses with good gardens attached to them ; put his cottages in good order; employ local 'artificers'; erect a market-house; keep one of the bowling-greens in repair for the accommodation of his friends indiscriminately ; obtain more weekly relief for certain poor persons ; receive requests 'for little favours immediately, that no unpleasant complaints meet his ear at unreasonable times,' etc., etc.[741] Exertions were necessary as the opposing candidate was promising 'to give the Poor Fellows ten guineas a man,' and when the election took place in March, 1768, some £1,300 was spent in buying votes, and £221 9s. 5d. for spirituous liquors, besides £108 on meat.[742] The amount of liquors provided can be guessed at from the bill for drinks at one of Mr. Luttrell's dinners to eighty-five voters, which contained the following items :—

	£	s.	d.
5 gallons, 2 quarts, and ½ pint Brandy . . .	4	9	0
6 gallons, 2 quarts, and 1 pint Rum	3	19	6
2½ dozen port ⎱	3	12	0
½ dozen white wine⎰			
Ale (probably 6d. a gallon)	1	5	0
	£13	5	6[743]

[737] *Accts. and Papers*, pt. ii, 43. *Com. Journ.* xviii, 33, 303, 505, 564, 651, 751. In 1750 they numbered about 150 (Brown-Willis, op. cit. 45), and in 1831, 215 (Hancock, op. cit. 363).
[738] Op. cit. 337–8.   [739] Ibid. 338–9.   [740] Ibid. 341–3.
[741] Ibid. 346.   [742] Ibid. 347–8.   [743] Ibid.

The inconveniences of opposing so powerful a man as Luttrell come out plainly. John Hill, a woolcomber, who raised an opposition, held a house in a ruinous condition of the manor, and a survey was made of it, 'for Mr. Luttrell intends making examples of the poor who oppose him as well as the rich';[744] and the entry 'Out with him when the time comes' occurs against the names of some tenants in a list of 1774, who were presumably unamenable.[745] Mr. Hancock also quotes a list of voters of 1775 in which they are divided as follows: '(1) voters who would not accept the £5 5s. (very few in this class!); (2) voters who accepted the guineas; (3) voters who would have been against Mr. Luttrell if they had nothing given to them.' One hundred and thirty-five voters altogether took the £5 5s., while in addition the list records a dinner for 212 people, £15 15s. given to the colourmen, £10 10s. to the ringers, £1 13s. for drinks, and £1 10s. 6d to fiddlers.[746] Four candidates, including Mr. Luttrell and Colonel Luttrell, stood at the election in 1796 and 'wild rumours were afloat that a multitude of electors opposed to Mr. Luttrell were to be arrested,' with a view to 'force them to his views,' and that 'a host of Bailiffs were in waiting in Dunster, but that the opposite party were prepared with thirty Bail Bonds,' and that should the bailiffs appear at Minehead their lives would not be safe. Nothing of the sort however happened, and the votes being almost even, the agents agreed to let Mr. Luttrell and Mr. Laryston be elected, and managed the affair with the assistance of a few threats as to 'improper conduct which some called Bribery' against recalcitrants. Their action was evidently popular, for we hear 'the joy and clamour of the town and country is inconceivable.'[747] For the election of 1806 there are astounding bills for liquor, Mr. Luttrell's agent being moved to remonstrate against the alleged capacity of ten men to consume 118 quarts of ale at a sitting or of six to drink eighty-one.[748]

At Taunton there was no such prevailing interest as that of the Luttrells at Minehead or even of the Medlycotts at Milborne Port. In 1680,[749] 1689,[750] 1695,[751] and 1710[752] petitions were filed, and in 1715 the return of Sir Francis Warre and Mr. Portman was voided on the ground of the franchise. The House resolved after hearing both sides that the right of election was in the inhabitants within the borough being pot-wallers and not receiving alms or charity; it was also agreed that a pot-waller might be a lodger provided he furnished his own diet, and that neither alms nor charity could disqualify an elector unless they had been received within a year of the election.[753] Two petitions were filed in 1722, one of which was withdrawn and the other unsuccessful,[754] and in 1775 the sitting members were unseated on charges of bribery and corruption, many of their voters being disqualified for having received charity or alms within the specified time and for not answering the definition of pot-wallers. At bottom the case was a struggle between the corpora-

---

[744] Hancock, *Hist. of Minehead*, 349.   [745] 352.   [746] Ibid. 353.   [747] Ibid. 355-6.
[748] Ibid. 359. See also Sir H. C. Maxwell-Lyte, *Hist. of Dunster* (1909), ii, 229 seq.
[749] *Com. Journ.* ix, 639, 643, 653, 662, 667, 669, 670, 672; *Accts. and Papers*, lxii, pt. i, 549.
[750] *Com. Journ.* x, 10, 19, 20; *Accts. and Papers*, lxii, pt. i, 561.
[751] *Com. Journ.* xi, 355; *Accts. and Papers*, lxii, pt. i, 575.
[752] Carew, op. cit. 192; *Accts. and Papers*, lxii, pt. ii, 23.
[753] Toulmin, op. cit. 295; *Com. Journ.* xviii, 31, 241, 273; *Accts. and Papers*, lxii, pt. ii, 43; Douglas, op. cit. 369-70. In 1722 there were 727 electors. Brown-Willis, op. cit. 44.
[754] *Com. Journ.* xx, 15, 61, 247; *Accts. and Papers*, lxii, pt. ii, 54.

tion and the rest of the townspeople, and the decision in favour of Mr. Halliday and Mr. Popham, the petitioners, was celebrated with a procession, a triumphal arch, a dinner, a ball, and a general illumination, which must have been anything but gratifying to the mayoral party.[755] Other unsuccessful petitions from Taunton were filed in 1790,[756] 1803, 1807, and 1831.[757] Elections in Taunton were apt to be attended with great disorders ; in that of 1754 several lives had been lost,[758] and in 1802 a vacancy in the mayoralty at the time of the election provided an opportunity for a riot. The election was also followed by a petition disputing the election of Mr. Hammet, who, the petitioners declared, was ineligible since as patent-bailiff of the lord of the manor he was the legal returning officer of the borough in the absence of a mayor. The committee however decided that the returning officers were the bailiffs of the borough appointed at an annual court leet.[759] An unopposed petition was presented in 1819, the success of which was celebrated by a grand public entry by the petitioner, dinners, and the consumption of several hogsheads of strong beer.[760]

Petitions were filed from Wells in 1680,[761] 1685,[762] and 1691,[763] and in 1695 the question of the franchise was raised by Mr. Brydges, who petitioned on that ground against the election of Colonel Berkeley ; and after hearing the evidence the committee resolved that ' the right of electing citizens to serve in Parliament for this city is only in the mayor, masters and burgesses of the said city.' [764] In spite of this decision the election of 1715 was petitioned against on the same grounds, and on hearing all the evidence the committee decided that the right to elect was in the mayor, masters and burgesses, and that by-laws made in 1712 by the governing part of the corporation, by which the mayor was debarred from nominating or making any burgess without the consent of the major part of the corporation, and any burgess from taking the oath, or using, claiming, or challenging any freedom or privilege of a burgess without such consent, were arbitrary and illegal. One of the successful petitioners was, however, unseated immediately after on charges of bribery and indirect and illegal practices.[765] The decision of 1715 had left open the question as to the qualification of the freemen, and on this point it was resolved by the committee, after hearing exhaustive evidence on a petition of 1722, that they were ' such persons as are, by consent of the mayor and common council of the said city, admitted to their freedom in any of the seven companies in the said city, being thereto entitled by birth, servitude or marriage.' [766]

Somerset was naturally one of the counties considerably affected by the Reform Act of 1832 : its total representation was reduced from sixteen to thirteen, the constituencies being greatly altered. The county was split

[755] *Com. Journ.* xxxv, 18, 200 ; *Accts. and Papers*, lxii, pt. ii, 154.
[756] Toulmin, op. cit. 331–7 ; *Com. Journ.* xlvi, 16, 91.
[757] *Com. Journ.* lviii, 36, 382 ; lxii, 43, 239 ; lxxxvi, 43, 357.
[758] Toulmin, op. cit. 329.   [759] Ibid. 341–58.
[760] Ibid. 361–3 ; *Com. Journ.* lxxiv, 88, 420.
[761] *Com. Journ.* ix, 664 ; *Accts. and Papers*, lxii, pt. i, 549.   [762] *Com. Journ.* ix, 718.
[763] *Com. Journ.* x, 354 ; *Accts. and Papers*, lxii, pt. i, 561.
[764] *Com. Journ.* xi, 338, 446, 455 ; *Accts. and Papers*, lxii, pt. i, 575.
[765] *Com. Journ.* xviii, 34, 453, 480 ; *Accts. and Papers*, lxii, pt. ii, 43.
[766] *Com. Journ.* xx, 20, 204–7 ; *Accts. and Papers*, xii, pt. ii, 55. In 1750 they numbered about 500. Brown-Willis, op. cit. 44.

into Eastern and Western Divisions, each of which returned two members;[787] Bath, Bridgwater, Taunton and Wells continued to send up two, Minehead, Ilchester and Milborne Port were completely disfranchised, and Frome was allowed one representative. This was the disposition in the first Bill of 1831, and was never varied.[788] Ten out of the sixteen members from Somerset voted for the second reading of the first Bill, the Conservative six being both members for Minehead, and one member from Bridgwater, Bath, Wells and the shire respectively; and when the second Bill reached the Lords, Lord Anglesey, the patron of Milborne Port, and Lord Cleveland, the patron of Ilchester, both voted in the Lords for it. Mr. Luttrell throughout the struggle made great efforts to save Minehead, urging that the borough should be extended by adding to it four more parishes in order to raise its population to 4,333 souls, but in vain.[789] The Act of 1867 created further changes: both members were taken from Wells, and the county was given six members, two for each of the three divisions of East, Middle and West Somerset.[770] Two years later Bridgwater was disfranchised for bribery and corrupt practices, the commissioners reporting that at the election of November, 1868, and at every preceding election until 1831 inclusive, corrupt practices had prevailed extensively.[771] Fresh alterations were made by the Redistribution of Seats Act of 1885: the county was split into seven divisions,[772] each of which returned one member; Taunton lost one of its representatives, and Frome was disfranchised. Besides the county members, the shire therefore now returns only three from boroughs, i.e. two from Bath and one from Taunton.

The connexion between the Somersetshire (Prince Albert's) Light Infantry and the county dates back to 1782, when the old 13th received its territorial name. But from its creation on 20 June, 1685, it was connected with the southern counties of England, and a bare month after it was raised was employed to guard prisoners taken after Monmouth's defeat at Sedge-moor.[773] Its uniform then consisted of round hats with broad brims turned up at one side, and ornamented with yellow ribbon; long-skirted scarlet coats lined and turned back with yellow, yellow breeches and grey stockings, the officers and pikemen being distinguished by white sashes round their waists, and the grenadiers by tall caps of yellow cloth.[774]

Having declared for William at the Revolution, the regiment was sent to Scotland, and distinguished itself under the command of Colonel Hastings.[775] It was afterwards sent to Ireland, fought at the battle of the Boyne, and took part in the sieges of Cork and Kinsale. In 1692 it was detached from the

[787] The Eastern Division consisted of the hundreds or liberties of Bath Forum, Bempstone, Brent and Wrington, Bruton, Catsash, Chew, Chewton, Norton Ferris, Frome, Glaston twelve hides, Hampton and Claverton, Horethorne, Keynsham, Kilmersdon, Mells and Leigh, Portbury, Wellow, Wells Forum, Whitstone, Winterstoke, Witham Friary, and Hartcliffe with Bedminster, except that part of it included in Bristol City. The rest of the county formed the Western Division. 2 and 3 Will. IV, cap. 64.

[788] *Annual Register*, 1831, 8, 10.   [769] Hancock, op. cit. 363–5.

[770] 30 and 31 Vict. cap. 102. East Somerset comprised the sessional divisions of Long Ashton, Keynsham, Weston, Axbridge and Temple Cloud; West Somerset those of Dunster, Dulverton, Williton, Wiveliscombe, Bishops Lydeard, Wellington, Taunton, Bridgwater and Ilminster; and Mid Somerset those of Crewkerne, Yeovil, Somerton, Shepton Mallet, Wincanton, Wells, Frome and Kilmersdon.

[771] 33 & 34 Vict. cap. 21.

[772] Northern, Wells, Frome, Eastern, Southern, Bridgwater and West or Wellington Divisions.

[773] R. Cannon, *Hist. Rec. of the Brit. Army*, 13th Foot, 2.

[774] Ibid. loc. cit.; J. H. Laurence-Archer, *The British Army*, 187.

[775] Cannon, op. cit. 6–8.

Irish establishment and quartered in England, with the exception of a draft of 150 men sent to Flanders. From 1701 to 1703 it fought in Holland under Marlborough, serving at the sieges of Kaiserwerth, Ruremonde, Huy and Limburg, and at the taking of Venloo.[776] In 1703 it was sent to Portugal, and after narrowly escaping capture by a French fleet was landed at Gibraltar in time to take part in the repulse of the assault of January 27–February 7, which practically ended the siege.[777] It was then sent to Barcelona, and saw service under Peterborough at the siege of Barcelona, and at Tortosa and St. Matheo. After the relief of St. Matheo Peterborough, who badly needed cavalry and had been very well satisfied with the conduct of the regiment, determined to change the character of the corps. He collected six hundred horses, and having reviewed the regiment, complimented them, saying that he wished he had horses and accoutrements to try whether a corps of so good a character would maintain a like reputation upon such a change. The regiment, which was in rags, thought nothing less likely, and were wholly unprepared to find horses and accoutrements ready but hidden behind a neighbouring hill, commissions being already prepared for most of the officers. The command of the regiment of dragoons thus formed was given to Colonel Pearce, under whom they fought in Portugal until they were disbanded in 1713, and the remaining officers were sent home to recruit, £900 levy money being paid for the purpose.[778]

A new 13th having been quickly raised, it fought from 1708 to 1710 in the Peninsula, and from 1710 to 1728 formed part of the garrison of Gibraltar, taking part in the defence of 1727. In 1742 it was again sent abroad ; fought at Dettingen and at Fontenoy, where it distinguished itself; came home for the '45, took part in Culloden, and returned to Flanders, where it was present at several actions. During the Seven Years' War it was quartered at Gibraltar, and from 1769 to 1776 at Minorca, and on returning home was stationed at Wells, where its connexion with the county appears to have begun, although it did not receive the title of 1st Somerset-shire until 1782.[779] Between 1791 and 1801 it served with distinction in the West Indies, as well as in Ireland and in the Mediterranean, and there saw service under Abercromby in Egypt. Its officers for services then received the large gold medals presented by the Grand Seignior, and to the 'Dettingen' on its colours the regiment added the Sphinx with the word 'Egypt.' In 1808 it was again sent to the West Indies, and for its services at the capture of Martinique was granted royal authority to bear the name of the island on its colours. From 1813 to 1815 it fought in the American War, distinguishing itself under Major Handcock on the La Cole River.[780]

In 1822 it was made a Light Infantry Regiment, and almost imme-diately after was sent to India, and served at the capture of Ava and else-where during the Burmese War. Its services there were enumerated 'with sentiments of unfeigned admiration ' by the Governor-General in his reports, and the word 'Ava' was added to those already on its colours.[781] In the Afghanistan War, which began in 1838, it took part in an advance into a

[776] Laurence-Archer, *The British Army*, 187–8.
[777] J. W. Fortescue, *Hist. of the Brit. Army*, i, 449.
[778] Laurence-Archer, loc. cit.; Fortescue, op. cit. i, 480; Cannon, op. cit. 24–5.
[779] Laurence-Archer, op. cit. 188.   [780] R. Cannon, op. cit. 57.   [781] Ibid. 74.

country never before penetrated by a British force : it formed part of the main storming column at Ghazni, and took a leading share in subsequent hostilities and in the defence of Jalalabad, where the troops under Sale held out with the greatest courage and determination for five months against an overpowering force of Afghans. During a successful attack on the enemy's camp, made in the hope of facilitating the advance of the relieving force, the regiment lost Colonel Dennie, and in operations which followed the relief some of its junior officers, amongst whom Lieutenant Mein had especially distinguished himself. For these services it added 'Afghanistan,' 'Ghazni' and 'Jalalabad' to the names on its colours ; and for its services at the latter place it also received its present badge of the 'mural crown' and the title of Prince Albert's Light Infantry. Its facings were at the same time changed to royal blue. For subsequent services in the campaign, and at the occupation of Cabul, it added 'Cabul, 1842,' to the other words already borne on its colours.[782]

During the Crimean War it formed part of the 4th Division, was in reserve at Tchernaya, and during the last assault on the Redan.[783] During the Indian Mutiny it assisted at the relief of Azimghur, and saw service in the Jadespore jungle and the Trans-Gogra district. A second battalion was formed in 1858.[784] Later, when quartered in South Africa, the regiment fought in the Sekukani War in the Transvaal, and in Zululand in 1878–9 ; and in the early eighties formed part of the expeditionary force to Burmah.[785]

During the early part of the South African War the second battalion formed part of the line of communication between Maritzburg and Frere, when General Buller began his advance to Ladysmith ;[786] it was one of the regiments engaged in the struggle for Spion Kop,[787] and later took part in operations on the Tugela heights, being the first regiment to cross the Tugela on 21 February.[788] After the occupation of Ladysmith the regiment was detached from Buller's command, and took part in various operations, including the advance from Vryberg to Johannesburg under General Hunter ; operations against de Wet in the Orange River Colony ; the relief of Colonel Hoare at Eland's River ; operations under General Hart in the Gatsrand, Potchefstroom and Ventersdorp districts, under General Barton in the Klerksdorp districts ; in the Eastern Transvaal, where it took part in the actions at Mooifontein and Elandsberg Nek ; and in the Bethel, Ermelo and Piet Retief districts. It returned to England in 1902, with 'South Africa, 1899–1902,' 'Relief of Ladysmith,' added to the words already on its colours.

The organization of the militia remained as we have seen it under the Tudors and Stuarts until the middle of the 18th century, when considerable changes were made. The powers and supervision of the Crown were considerably increased ; a quota was fixed for each county, that of Somerset being 840 ; the ballot was introduced, and the payment for exemption fixed at £10.[789] These regulations were the result of the continental struggle then beginning, and remained in force until the beginning of

---

[782] Cannon, op. cit. 76–107 ; Lawrence-Archer, op. cit. 189.
[783] Lawrence-Archer, loc. cit. [784] Ibid. 191. [785] Ibid. 190.
[786] 'Times' History of the War, ii, 422. [787] Ibid. iii, 260. [788] Ibid. 497.
[789] 30 Geo. II, cap. 25 ; 31 Geo. II, cap. 26.

the Napoleonic wars called for fresh measures.[790]   In 1796, when the quotas were raised, that of Somerset was increased to 2,960,[791] but in 1802 decreased to 2,556.[792]   In 1803, however, the Act for an additional military force for service at home and in the Channel Islands demanded a contingent from the county of 983, which was irrespective of and additional to the militia.[793] Under these Acts the militia gradually lost its distinctly defensive character, and large drafts of men passed from it into the regular army, most of them being employed in the Peninsula ; and this fact, combined with the necessity for a strictly local defensive force which might be made up of men who did not wish to pass into the line, and could afford time only for periodical training, led to the Act of 1808 for a permanent local militia, which, including volunteers, was not to exceed six times the original quotas under the Act of 1802.   By this Act the men who had volunteered when the danger of invasion was imminent had their patriotism supplemented by the inducement of pay, and a body was thus formed by which the regular militia was reinforced.[794]   The close of the Napoleonic wars, however, was followed by the gradual decay of the militia, but it was revived in 1852,[795] and in 1871 placed on an entirely new footing.   Its control was removed from the Lords-Lieutenant and vested in the Crown : it therefore ceased to exist as a distinct body, and the separate militia regiments became battalions of the territorial regiments, the Somerset militia becoming the 3rd and 4th battalions of the Somerset Light Infantry, both having their head quarters at Taunton.[796]   The county had also two yeomanry regiments, the North Somerset with its head quarters at Bath,[797] the West Somerset with its head quarters at Taunton.[798]   During the disturbed period preceding the first Reform Act a body of horse known as the Mudford Troop of Independent Yeomanry was raised by Captain G. Harbin, which assisted in preserving order in Yeovil and the district.   It was disbanded in 1838.

From the year 1779, when the volunteer organization became an integral part of national defence, to the close of the Napoleonic wars Somerset appears to have contributed large quotas to this service.   A list for the year 1805 gives twenty-four separate bodies : Bath, Bath-Forum, Bridgwater, Polden Hill and Yeovil each supplied a whole battalion ; so also did the Somerset and Langport Regiment and the East Somerset Second Regiment ; the Mendip Legion, the East and West Somerset Cavalry, and the East Somerset First Regiment contained two battalions each ; the Frome and East Mendip Volunteers consisted of three squadrons from Frome, Mells, and Nunney, and three troops from Batcombe and Shepton respectively ; and there were also a large number of smaller units.   The Bath and the Wells Cavalry were each commanded by three officers ; the volunteers from Banwell, Coker, Rodney Stoke, and the Taunton Riflemen by three each ; from Wiveliscombe, Milverton and Dulverton by four each ; from Beckington by five ; the Somerset Riflemen by six, and the volunteers from Crewkerne and Petherton and from Frome Selwood by ten each.[799]

[790] Cf. 26 Geo. III, cap. 107.   [791] 37 Geo. III, cap. 3, cap. 22.   [792] 42 Geo. III, cap. 90.
[793] 43 Geo. III, cap. 82.   The county had had to provide 455 men for the Navy also under 37 Geo. III, cap. 4.   [794] 48 Geo. III, cap. 111.   [795] 15 and 16 Vict. cap. 50.
[796] Hart's *Army List*, 1907, 622.   [797] Ibid. 747.   [798] Ibid. 748.
[799] *A List of the Officers of the Militia, the Gentlemen and Yeomanry, Cavalry and Volunteer Infantry of the United Kingdom.*   War Office, 14 Oct. 1805.

POLITICAL HISTORY

The administration of these forces was provided for by Act of Parliament,[800] and a similar course was followed when the scare of 1859 and the following years led to a recrudescence of volunteering.[801] The movement then found warm supporters in Somerset, twenty-three companies being formed by August, 1860. These small corps were by the Act grouped into administrative battalions, but were afterwards formed into consolidated corps, of which there were two for the county, the 1st Bath and the Taunton Volunteers. Since the formation of the Territorial Army, Somerset has formed the 8th district of the Southern Command. The units administered by the County Association are the North Somerset and West Somerset Yeomanry; the 4th and 5th battalions of the Somerset Light Infantry (formerly the 1st and 2nd Volunteer battalions); the 1st and 2nd Wessex Field Companies (Royal Engineers); the 2nd South-Western Mounted Brigade Field Ambulance (Royal Army Medical Corps); the Somerset Battery R.H.A. and Ammunition Column; and the 2nd South-Western Mounted Brigade Transport and Service Column (Army Service Corps), the last two being new units.[802]

[800] 19 Geo. III, cap. 76; 20 Geo. III, cap. 44; 22 Geo. III, cap. 79; 34 Geo. III, cap. 16; 42 Geo. III, cap. 66; 43 Geo. III, cap. 121; 44 Geo. III, cap. 18, cap 54.

[801] 26 and 27 Vict. cap. 65.

[802] *The Territorial Year Book,* 189 seq.

MARITIME HISTORY

A S an objective of naval invasion Somerset need hardly be dwelt upon. Unless an enemy held Ireland he could strike more surely and quickly on the east and south coasts than on the west; and in sailing-ship days his fleet would have run great risk of destruction in the Bristol Channel. A gulf with sands, islands and reefs, often swept by fierce and sudden north-westerly gales, chequered by furiously running tides and currents setting sometimes directly on to the places a ship should avoid, and a seaway of which the navigation has never been well known to foreign seamen, was hardly likely to tempt a foe who could descend elsewhere. The whole of the south shore of the Bristol Channel is less inviting than that of the north in the matter of shelter and harbourage for a fleet; the coast of Somerset is perhaps the worst on the south, for there is not only no port which can receive anything bigger than a coaster, but there is not even a safe roadstead, with the doubtful exception of King Road, which is comparatively shallow, for ships of any burthen. The estuary of the Parret has always been the best port in Somerset, but a century ago no ship of more than 100 tons could go up to Bridgwater, and nothing could pass at low tide.

Such progress in navigation as had been made by the Britons seems to have been confined to the south coast of England, and even there does not appear to have advanced sufficiently to enable them to transport tin in their own vessels. The inhabitants of Somerset must have been still less practised in maritime affairs even if—which is problematical—they had outgrown the stage of the 'dug-out.' It has been generally stated that a Roman road ran west from Salisbury along the top of Mendip, passed the lead mines of Charterhouse, and ended in a harbour at Uphill. Professor Haverfield has however pointed out [1] that the evidence of this road is at present insufficient, that the remains discovered at Uphill are altogether inadequate to prove a Roman harbour, and that the little which we know of the roads leading to the Mendip lead-mines in Roman times implies an access only from the east or north-east. It is also in itself improbable that Roman vessels would have risked the perilous navigation along the dangerous coasts of Cornwall and North Devon and the currents and shallows of the Severn Sea, in order to fetch lead which could have been transferred much more easily and safely by land to the port of south-eastern Britain. We may therefore dismiss the idea of an early harbour at Uphill from the maritime history of Somerset.

The Saxon conquest of Somerset was won entirely by land; until the Northmen come upon the scene there is no naval history to record. Towards the end of the 8th century the Vikings, moving south by the line of the Orkneys, Hebrides, and West Coast, attacked Ireland, and, from that country, were not long in finding their way to England. The Bristol Channel must have attracted exploration at an early moment, but a very little experience of it would have shown them that safer and more profitable regions for exploitation lay to the southward and eastward. Thus, though there were no doubt minor raids, there was no appearance in force between 845 and 878, when Alfred stood at bay in Somerset. Both these events belong to military history, but it may be remarked that the Danish marches across England to the Valley of the Severn in 877, 894, and 896 have an interesting strategical significance. If, when in the east of England, they were either hard pressed and cut off from their ships and from assistance by way of the North Sea as in 894 and 896, or, like Guthrum in 878, expecting reinforcements from the westward, the Bristol Channel would bring help from, or open the nearest passage of escape to, their kindred in Ireland. As soon as Northumbria and the Danelagh were settled and became a reserve for the invaders there was, even after defeat, no necessity for more than a retreat amongst kinsmen, so that the alternative western line of communication with their base—the sea—became of secondary importance. It was, therefore, not any essential attraction of the county itself, but the fact that it was the road to the Bristol Channel that gave Somerset its occasional importance during the 9th century. Danish ships must have been seen often in the Severn Sea in the 10th century, and Flat Holme is reputed, by still existing tradition, to have been one of their footholds. No doubt they made momentary use

[1] *V.C.H. Somerset*, i, 350.

245

at various times of all the islands of the Bristol Channel, but there was no tactical reason to tempt them to make any one of them a base, and there are good sailor reasons against it.

By the 11th century the Bristol Channel was in common use as a sea road, although it was probably navigated in summer only; that there was ordinary communication with the Welsh ports is shown by the occurrence of Somerset names among the Norman settlers in South Wales. But on the whole there can have been but little over-sea trade to stimulate the growth of shipping; even that with Ireland cannot have developed to any extent until after the English conquest. The commercial importance of Bristol was no doubt a factor, however, in forming a seafaring population in the county of Somerset, for the great port must have attracted many men from the county to help to man its ships.

There was little use for a navy during the greater part of the 12th century; perhaps the first occasion for a levy of Somerset ships on a large scale was the collection of the fleet of 400 vessels with which Henry II crossed to Ireland from Milford Haven in 1171. To form this fleet the resources of the western counties were drawn upon principally. The ordinary requirements of the crown for ships for the transport of troops to and from Normandy, and for the passage of the sovereign himself and his household, were usually satisfied by the towns between Yarmouth and Southampton; if Somerset was called upon (which is unlikely) there is no evidence of it. The inferior position of the county is shown in an order of 1208 to the officials round the coast to send a return of ships and shipowners to London where Somerset is almost the only maritime county omitted. On the other hand, in 1205 it was, with Bristol, Devon and Cornwall, ordered to send up all shipwrights and seamen available for the king's service, which seems to indicate that there were men if not ships.[2] In the same year there is a list of fifty-one royal galleys stationed round the coast, but there is none at any port between Exeter and Bristol. Towards the end of the reign, in 1214, when another return of ships and owners was required, Somerset was included;[3] and as it was to be a return of vessels of 80 tons and upwards, it may be presumed that it was expected that some of that size were to be found in the county. John often raised large fleets, but we lack details of their composition; in 1210 he sailed from Pembroke to Ireland with a fleet, to which Somerset probably contributed a quota. The chief civil officer of such naval administration as existed during this reign was William de Wrotham, Archdeacon of Taunton, whose connexion with the county may have had a certain effect in causing more demands to be made upon its ships and men than would otherwise have been the case.

The naval history as a whole, of the reign of Henry III is not important, so that there would naturally be even less relating to Somerset than to others of the greater maritime counties. What evidence exists is mainly negative. In 1224, war with France being expected, there was a general arrest of shipping, but no place between Dartmouth and Bristol was called upon. In 1226 there was an embargo on ships intended for French ports, and this time there was no writ to any town between Falmouth and Bristol. In 1230 there was a general arrest of ships capable of carrying sixteen horses;[4] the order was addressed to the sheriffs of Somerset as well as to those of the other coast counties, but in 1255, when similar writs were issued, Somerset was omitted. In 1233 a fleet was concentrated at Ilfracombe to carry troops to Ireland, and it no doubt included ships from the adjoining county.[5] The Barons' Wars produced a raid from South Wales which fell upon Minehead, and is only of interest as showing a normal water communication between the two shores of the Bristol Channel.[6] A feature of the naval history of the 13th century is the appointment of one or more persons, sometimes for one county and sometimes for a group of counties, as keepers of the coast, a step towards organization and systematic defence. The duties of the keeper were both judicial and military, but his chief office was to put down piracy, to keep the peace at sea, and summon the county to arms to repel invasion. No appointment, in the usual form, is known for Somerset until much later, and this, with other examples of omission, tends to show the subordinate place of the county among the maritime shires. John Marshal, however, was keeper of the sea ports of Somerset in 1215;[7] if his employment was of the same character as that of the later keepers it is one of the earliest nominations known, but it is more likely that it was a temporary appointment for an especial purpose and with narrower powers. Historically, the keeper of the coast seems to have been the ancestor of the conservators of truces instituted locally by Henry V, and of the later vice-admirals of the coast we find acting from the middle of the 16th century. A part of the system of defence under the care of the keeper was the line of beacons, corresponding to the modern coastguard stations, which encircled the coast; they were usually placed on the hills nearest to the sea, and guarded in war time by a watch from the neighbouring parishes.[8]

[2] Pat. 6 John, m. 2.   [3] Close, 16 John, m. 16.
[4] Ibid. 14 Hen. III, m. 17 d.   [5] Ibid. 17 Hen. III, m. 7 d.
[6] Rishanger, *Chron. et Annales* (Rolls Ser.), 41.   [7] Pat. 17 John, m. 17.
[8] 'Signa consueta vocata beknes per ignem.' See Southey, *Lives of the Admirals*, i, 360 (quoting Froissart), as to the method of constructing them.

The Welsh wars of 1277 and 1282–3, and the Scotch war of 1295, were mainly fought by the feudal armies assisted by squadrons from the Cinque Ports. Some local ships were also employed as victuallers; in 1277 we find the sailors of Bridgwater in pay for the conveyance of provisions for Edward's troops.[9] In 1295 and 1297 there were general arrests of ships of 40 tons and upwards in consequence of war with France, and Bridgwater and Dunster were called upon for help.[10] That Dunster was brought in among the other ports in 1297 may point to its increasing prosperity or may be because the king's nets were sweeping very closely at the moment, as he considered the then political strain 'the greatest and most arduous that he has had to deal with in any times past.' A Wardrobe Account of 1299–1300 shows that Sir Simon de Montacute was the owner of two galleys and a barge which sailed from Bridgwater to join the ships acting on the west coast of England in the latter year.[11] In both 1301 and 1302 Bridgwater only, of the Somerset ports, was assessed at one ship for the fleets;[12] the burgesses neglected the orders of 1301 and sent no ship, so that in the following year two of the king's clerks were sent down with directions to inflict punishment at their discretion.[13] In the case of the 1302 levy security was to be taken from the owners for the appearance of the ships. Probably owners at Bridgwater, as elsewhere, found piracy or privateering more profitable than the king's service, but there was as yet no general disinclination to respond to the demands of the crown. The constant levies of ships and men were not nearly so ruinous to the shipowner as, at first sight, they would appear to be. A trading voyage involved great risk of loss from wreck, piracy, or privateering; the royal service meant certain pay for the fitting and hire of the ship, with 6d. a day for the officers and 3d. for the men, very liberal wages allowing for the different value of money. The incessant embargoes which harassed trade—then much increased—under Edward III were not yet common, and the alacrity with which most of the ports responded to the demands made upon them shows that the services required were not oppressive nor even unwelcome, especially as those who contributed to the sea service were freed from any aid towards that by land. There was no permanent naval organization at this time; the king possessed some ships of his own, and the commanders were usually charged with their maintenance. When a fleet was to be raised from the merchant navy a certain extent of coast was allotted to one of the king's clerks, or to a serjeant-at-arms, who acted with the bailiffs of the port towns in selecting ships and men and seeing them dispatched to the place of meeting. If a ship did not appear, or the men deserted, they or the owner might be required to find security to come before the king, and although there was as yet no statute dealing with the offence[14] they were imprisoned or otherwise punished, as at Bridgwater in 1301, by the authority of the king alone.

The townsmen of the various ports soon found the methods of Edward II to be in disagreeable contrast to those of his father, for they were frequently called upon to supply ships at their own expense. This happened to Bridgwater in 1310;[15] but in 1311, when that town was linked with Ilfracombe and Barnstaple for three ships, it was at the expense of the crown.[16] The plunder of wreck was of course more or less common all round the coast, and although the Somerset men had fewer opportunities than those of some other counties, they do not seem to have neglected such as came in their way. In 1310 the lord of the manor of Stoke Courcy complained that although entitled to all wreck between Lilstock and 'Machespol,' the country people, in defiance of his rights, had recently pillaged a ship lost at 'Laverkesond'[17] from which no one had escaped alive.[18] A year later an owner petitioned that the Dunster men had made off with the cargo of a vessel, belonging to him, wrecked there.[19] In the case of small owners it is very certain that but few of them possessed the necessary time and money required to put in motion the procedure of the crown, and that there were unnumbered instances of illicit plunder of wrecks for every one that comes under notice in the records. Where a lord of a manor acted under a legal grant of the right of wreck the result, in practice, differed little from the open robbery used by labourers and fishermen; in 1380 Joan Moion of Dunster was ordered to deliver to the owners the cargo of a Genoese merchantman, lost in Minehead Bay, which she had seized. Piracy, too, was as prevalent as occasion permitted; in 1311 both the French and the men of Aquitaine—English subjects—protested vehemently about the excesses of the Somerset sailors.[20]

In 1314 Bridgwater was again required to find a ship for the Scotch war, and in 1317 it was

---

[9] Pat. 5 Edw. I, m. 22.

[10] Ibid. 23 Edw. I, m. 7, m. 6; 25 Edw. I, pt. 2, m. 10; Close, 25 Edw. I, m. 17 d.

[11] *Liber Gardrobae* . . . (Lond. 1787), 272, 275, 279.

[12] Pat. 29 Edw. I, m. 20; 30 Edw. I, m. 2.   [13] Ibid. 30 Edw. I, m. 14, m. 10.

[14] The first statute was 2 Ric. II, stat. 1, cap. 4 by which deserters were fined double their wages and sent to prison for a year.

[15] Rot. Scot. 3 Edw. II, m. 13.

[16] Pat. 4 Edw. II, pt. 2, m. 7. The ships were to be provisioned for seven weeks.

[17] The Lark Spit Sand in the River Parret.   [18] Pat. 3 Edw. II, m. 18 d.

[19] Ibid. 4 Edw. II, pt. 1, m. 17 d.   [20] Ibid. pt. 2, m. 20 d.

coupled with Bristol for another for the same service.[21] The vessel of 1317 was to serve one month at the cost of the towns, and then at the king's charges. This was followed in 1319 by a demand for ships to serve for three or four months at the expense of the towns before the king took over the responsibility.[22] Bridgwater, although only of minor rank, was clearly the only port of Somerset which could hold a place with those of other counties. Dunster, if it had little shipping, must have had some commerce, for in 1338 it was the only town in Somerset, besides Bridgwater, in which proclamation was made that Spanish, Italian, and Gascon merchants might come and trade in safety.[23] In 1316, when vessels were taken up at Bristol to convey troops to Ireland, the officials were directed, if the resources of Bristol were insufficient, to seek others, not in Somerset, but in South Wales, the county being evidently supposed to be unable to provide any assistance. A two years' truce with Scotland was made in 1320, but in 1322 the war was renewed, and on 3 April Edward applied to Bridgwater, among other ports, for ships to serve as long as they would at the expense of the town, and afterwards at his payments.[24] Apparently there was no ready response to this proposal, for on 25 April a king's clerk was sent to the western counties to give further explanations and hasten the proceedings. To sweeten the potion the sheriffs were directed not to raise soldiers in those ports which gave naval aid.[25] A thirteen years' truce was concluded with Scotland in 1323, but war with France followed immediately, and a general arrest was proclaimed of ships of 40 tons and upwards to provide transports for the conveyance of an army to Gascony. A series of embargoes and preparations, attended by little result, succeeded until the menacing attitude of Isabella in 1326 caused urgent measures to be taken to meet the imminent invasion from France. On 12 August an embargo was placed on every ship in England; those of under 50 tons belonging to the western ports were to remain in harbour, while all others were to meet at Portsmouth by the 29th. In Somerset this order was directed to Dunster and Bridgwater.[26] It seems that this and other steps dealing with the strategical disposition of the fleets, excellently planned, were taken too late, or that there was treachery among the higher commanders, for when Isabella landed in the Orwell on 26 September she met with no resistance.

A short war with Scotland in 1327–8 hardly affected the south of England, but the threat of French hostilities caused a general levy which touched Dunster and Bridgwater.[27] In 1330 the sheriffs of Somerset and Dorset were ordered to provide pigs, beans and pease to be sent to Bordeaux in ships from various ports (unnamed) of the two counties; the ships were to collect at Bridgwater.[28] A more serious Scotch war broke out in 1332 and for several successive years there were levies of ships, but in each case only Bridgwater was called upon in Somerset. The incessant embargoes, and consequent injury to trade, were now causing some discontent in the port towns; but Edward knew when to rely on persuasion rather than on the prerogative, and in December 1336 sent officials round the coast to explain 'certain things near the king's heart.'[29] At the same time the ports were requested to send representatives to London to discuss matters, and several came from Bridgwater.[30] A catalogue of the orders, which rapidly succeeded each other during this reign, for arrests of ships in the various ports would be barren of interest unless the connexion with general history was shown. In 1338 and 1339, when the French had joined the Scots, the balance of maritime war went against England until the victory of Sluys in 1340 restored our supremacy for many years. Several disasters occurred to towns on the south coast, but Somerset lay quite outside the raiding field and, also, did not promise much booty.

By 1340 the continuous strain was telling upon the English reserve of shipping, so that the sheriffs of the coast counties were instructed to prevent any sales of ships to foreigners 'as the shipping of England has deteriorated for a long time past.'[31] This does not seem to have proved sufficient, so that in 1341 a council was convened at Westminster to advise upon that and other subjects; the more important ports each sent two delegates, the others one, but Bridgwater was not even among the latter. In 1342, 1344 and 1347 similar meetings were convoked at Westminster, but in none of them was any Somerset port represented. In 1342 political difficulties arose in Brittany, owing to the death of the duke without heirs, which led to the dispatch of a large fleet and army under Sir Walter de Mauny; Edward himself crossed later in the year. In one fleet alone there were 357 vessels, but Somerset sent none of them; an undated list, probably relating to another fleet prepared for this expedition, gives a total of 119 vessels, of which Dunster supplied a barge, and Bridgwater and Combwich, together, four ships and a barge.[32] Subsequently there was a long list of ports whose ships either had not appeared at all or had deserted from Brest,

[21] Rot. Scot. 7 Edw. II, m. 6; ibid. 11 Edw. II, m. 17.   [22] Ibid. 12 Edw. II, m. 3.
[23] Close, 12 Edw. III, pt. 1 m. 40 d.   In 1327 it had been treated as a passage port (ibid. 1 Edw. III, m. 15 d).
[24] Close, 15 Edw. II, m. 15 d.   [25] Ibid. m. 11 d.   [26] Ibid. 20 Edw. II, m. 11 d.
[27] Ibid. 2 Edw. III, m. 22 d.   [28] Ibid. 4 Edw. III, m. 33.
[29] Ibid. 10 Edw. III, m. 4 d.   [30] Rot. Scot. 10 Edw. III, m. 3 d.
[31] Rymer, *Foedera*, v, 210.   [32] Chan. Misc. bdle. 2, no. 46.

leaving the king and his troops ' in very great peril,' but there were no delinquents among the Somerset ports. For the campaign of Crecy and the siege of Calais a huge armament was collected, but according to the Calais Roll, of which the copies existing are late 16th-century transcripts of a contemporary Wardrobe Account now lost, the county was only represented by one ship and fifteen men from Bridgwater. From 1350 onwards the maritime strength of England, overtaxed by long years of war, steadily decreased in offensive capacity until at last the coasts were constantly harassed by French incursions or the fear of them, and the sense of helplessness was increased by the losses suffered from privateers and the consequent exhaustion of the shipowning class. An unstable peace, diversified by marauding, existed between 1360 and 1369; the outbreak of war in the latter year caused another council of provincial experts to meet in Westminster, in November, to which Bridgwater sent two delegates.[33]

The renewal of the war was attended by the complete loss of English supremacy in the Channel. Levy followed levy without result; the Commons laid before the king the causes to which they attributed the decay of shipping, and in June 1372, after the defeat of the Earl of Pembroke off Rochelle, the crown was reduced to issuing commissions of array for the maritime counties instead of defending them by action at sea. The ordinary rate of hire was 3s. 4d. a ton for every three months, but now both that and wages were left unpaid, in contrast to the quick and liberal settlement of the crown liabilities which characterized the earlier years of the reign. The year 1375 was marked by a great commercial disaster in the shape of the capture or destruction of thirty-nine merchantmen, ranging from 300 tons downwards, in Bourneuf Bay; among them was the *Saint Marie*, cog, 75 tons, of Dunster, and the *Saint Marie*, cog, 170 tons, of Bridgwater, valued with their cargoes at £275 and £810 respectively.[34] The latter ship was no doubt the one referred to in an order of 1374 directing fifty-four seamen to be impressed at Bridgwater for the *Saint Marie* of that town commanded to join the royal fleet at Plymouth.[35]

Edward III died in June 1377, and in July the French were raiding the southern counties at their will. The English fleet was practically non-existent, therefore in November Parliament decided that the country generally should be required to build ships by the following March. No port in Somerset was assessed, but Bath and Wells, in conjunction, were requested to provide a balinger; as an inducement the subscribers were promised that after its service in the king's fleets was completed the vessel should be returned to be sold or used by the townsmen.[36] Such a ship would naturally be built at Bristol or Bridgwater, therefore the fact that the cost was thrown upon two inland towns is evidence of the poverty of the ports of the county. Although Somerset was not able to send many ships to sea, it does not seem to have been behind other counties in furnishing adventurous men. In 1378 some Bayonnese ships were hired and must have been manned, at least in part, by Englishmen, for when, shortly afterwards, they were defeated a contemporary writer mentions that there were many young Somerset and Devon esquires on board them. There were frequent levies of shipping during these years, but without details of the part taken by the several ports; the county must have experienced more of the expense of war than of its actual terrors, for few of the enemies' ships can have been seen in the Bristol Channel. A Bridgwater ship of 120 tons joined the fleet under the Duke of Lancaster in 1385, when he sailed to obtain possession of his kingdom of Castile.[37] In 1394 there was an arrest of ships in Somerset, Devon, Cornwall and Dorset for the king's passage to Ireland; it is noteworthy that the Cinque Ports service was also ordered to Bristol, as though it was expected that the resources of the western counties would not be sufficient.[38] There is an undated list of this reign of ships taken up for service, which may relate to this voyage; in this four Bridgwater ships, one of them being of 160 tons, are enumerated.[39]

Hostilities with France ceased in 1389, and for some years maritime commerce suffered only its normal afflictions, for although official peace existed private war always continued. No declaration of war came from either side during the reign of Henry IV, but conditions at sea differed nothing from actual belligerency except that there were no royal fleets making war formally. In consequence of this state of things not only the ports, but many of the inland towns as well, were ordered on 11 January 1400-1 to build and equip ships, singly or in combination, at their own cost by the following April. No letter was sent to Bridgwater, but Dunster was grouped with Ilfracombe and Mount's Bay for one of the smaller class of ships—a barge.[40] Parliament met on 20 January and protested against the proceeding; Henry's position was too uncertain to allow him to insist, as he might have done, on the strict legality of his action, and the order was withdrawn. As no new fleet had been built there was a general arrest in May of vessels of 30 tons and upwards, which affected Bridgwater and Dunster.[41] The foreign trade of Bridgwater is indicated by an incident of the

[33] Rymer, *Foedera* (ed. 1816), iii, 880.
[34] Chan. Dipl. Doc. P. 324.
[35] Rymer, *Foedera* (ed. 1816), iii, 999.
[36] Close, 1 Ric. II, m. 22.
[37] Exch. Accts. K.R., bdle. 42, no. 18.
[38] Rymer, *Foedera*, vii, 784, 789.
[39] Exch. Accts. K.R. bdle. 42, no. 22.
[40] Rymer, *Foedera*, viii, 172.
[41] Pat. 2 Hen. IV, pt. 3, m. 16.

same year, when a Spanish merchantman from Bilbao, lying in the Parret, was boarded and plundered by Bristol men, although this seems in reality to have been a case of taking goods under letters of reprisal and therefore no piracy.[42] In 1405 there was a considerable amount of fighting at sea off the Welsh coast, in which Somerset must have taken some part, in connexion with French attempts to aid the Welsh rebels, but few particulars have come down to us.[43]

To crush privateering and piracy Henry V, in 1414, instituted in every port officials called conservators of truces, who, holding their authority from the High Admiral and assisted by two legal assessors, were to have power of inquiry and punishment concerning all guilty of illegal proceedings at sea. They were to keep a register of the ships and seamen belonging to each port and to act as adjudicators in such cases as did not go before the Admiralty Court.[44] They seem, so far as related to civil functions, to have been a stage of development between the earlier keepers of the coast and the vice-admirals of the coast established in the 16th century. That the statute was strictly enforced and helped to keep a little peace at sea is shown by the fact that two years later the king consented to some modification of its stringency by promising to issue letters of marque when equitable. In 1435 it was entirely suspended, being found 'so rigorous and grievous,' said the Commons, taking advantage of a weak rule; in 1451 it was brought into force again for a short time, and once more renewed by Edward IV.

Henry V began his reign with the intention of having a great fleet of his own. The custom of general impressment was now expensive, both for the shipowner and for the crown, besides being slow and inefficient, and the continual complaints of the merchant class as voiced in Parliament were not safely to be neglected. The system could not be, and was not, at once abolished, but it became much less frequent during the 15th century. The great fleet of upwards of 1,400 vessels required for the campaign of Agincourt included a contingent from Somerset; but very many were hired in Holland and Zealand, the resources of the kingdom being insufficient or Henry resolved not to tax them unduly. Another large fleet was collected for the campaign of 1417, but out of 217 vessels of which we have details, 117 belonged to Holland and Zealand. Many of the English ports were unrepresented; some of the most flourishing sent only one or two ships, and it may be surmised that for political reasons the king found it preferable to hire foreign ships as transports rather than to disturb English trade. For this service, however, Bridgwater sent one ship.[45] In August 1419 there was an arrest of every vessel in Somerset and the other western counties to form a fleet to intercept a French expedition intended to proceed to Scotland by way of the west coast.[46] An important branch of English maritime traffic in the 15th century was the transport of pilgrims to enable them to perform their devotions at the shrine of St. James of Compostella. They could only be carried in licensed ships, and nobles and merchants seem to have been equally eager to obtain a share in what must have been a profitable trade. Most of the vessels licensed belonged to the southern ports; Minehead is the only place in Somerset which appears in lists extending over a long series of years.[47]

After the death of Henry V one of the first proceedings of the Regency was to sell off the Royal Navy by auction, but the loss was not at once felt because there was no French force capable of contesting the mastery of the sea. There were arrests of shipping in 1428 and 1430, but there was now a general feeling that, in this method, 'the long coming together of the ships is the destruction of the country.'[48] Vessels were still impressed for the transport of troops, but the military service was handed over to contractors who undertook to keep the sea with a certain number of ships and men for a specified time. There are in existence several lists of ships taken up for the transport of troops in 1439, 1440, 1443, 1447 and 1452.[49] Seeing that they represent only a portion, large or small, of the merchant marine they show that notwithstanding war and weak government, it was still prospering both in number and tonnage, some of the vessels being of 300 and 400 tons. But they also show the maritime inferiority of Somerset compared with many of the counties, for in all these years only two ships from Minehead and one from Bridgwater were employed. The *Katherine*, 80 tons, of Minehead was probably the largest sea-going vessel belonging to the town, and was the one for which the owners obtained a pilgrim licence; the other, the *James*, was of 30 tons. The Bridgwater ship was the *Marie* of 80 tons. The fact, however, that the ancient Bridgwater seal was a one-masted ship of archaic type shows that from an early period the burgesses had considered themselves to belong to a port of some importance, if of lower rank than others which also adopted an especial maritime distinguishing mark.

Somerset was Lancastrian in temper during the Wars of the Roses, but no maritime incident affecting the war occurred in the Bristol Channel. Probably such commerce as existed continued nearly unchecked, and the fisheries remained the staple occupation of the seafarers of the coast.

---

[42] Pat. 2 Hen. IV, pt. 3, m. 6 d.   [43] Walsingham, *Hist. Angl.* (Rolls Ser.) ii, 272.

[44] 2 Hen. V, stat. I, cap. 6.   [45] *Rot. Norman* (ed. Hardy, 1835), pp. 320–9.

[46] Rymer, *Foedera*, ix, 791–2.   [47] Rot. Franc. *pass.*   [48] *Proc. of P.C.* (1st ser.) v, 102.

[49] Exch. Accts. K. R. bdle. 53, nos. 23, 24, 25, 39; bdle. 54, nos. 10, 14.

The Bristol Channel has never been a very fertile fishing ground for more than local supply, so that the presence of Somerset fishermen on the Irish coast in 1427 was no doubt only the continuance of an old custom, although it comes into notice in that year by reason of the capture of some of them and their imprisonment in Scotland.[50] A curious letter of 1475 from the mayor and bailiffs of Youghal to the officials of Bridgwater, lamenting the riots and disturbances which had interrupted the ancient friendship between the two towns, perhaps relates to the conduct of the Somerset fishermen in Irish waters.[51] Breton pirates came up the Severn Sea, attracted by the hunt for Bristol traders, just as, later, French, Dunkirk and Biscayan privateers and Mohammedan pirates cruised there with the same object. If a Bristol ship was not to be found, smaller game was not despised, and the minor ports on both shores suffered; in 1450 Sir Henry Stradling, while crossing the Severn, was taken by a Breton corsair and had to pay a heavy ransom.[52]

A writ of September 1461 ordered a crew to be taken up for the *Trinity* of Minehead, then preparing for sea, to act against Edward's enemies;[53] this probably means that some outlawed Lancastrians were hovering off the coast. Bridgwater and Minehead were the two leading ports. In 1480 there were three Minehead ships trading between La Rochelle and Bristol,[54] and this suggests that at least some of the ships belonging to the county would never have been built but for the commercial needs of Bristol. In 1483 Thomasine Hylle, a widow, conveyed her shares in three Bridgwater ships, being a fourth, a fourth, and an eighth, to a purchaser.[55] In the same year a French vessel, chartered by some Bridgwater merchants for a voyage from Lisbon to their own town, was attacked by an English ship while at anchor at Ilfracombe at the instigation, it was declared, of two inhabitants of the Devon port.[56] In 1475 there were several arrests of ships for the French war; one of them, for ships of 16 tons and upwards, from Newcastle to Bristol, must be almost, if not quite, the last example of a general arrest affecting the whole coast. It has been stated that some of John Cabot's men in the voyage of 1497, when Newfoundland or North America was discovered, were from Bridgwater,[57] but there is not a particle of evidence in support of this assertion.

With the reign of Henry VIII the era of general arrests and impressment of shipping may be said to have terminated. The port towns were sometimes to be called upon to provide ships, but such towns were usually associated in order to lessen the expense, and, eventually, the county as a whole contributed to the cost. Improvements in shipbuilding and armament had now differentiated the man-of-war from the merchantman. The latter was of little use in fleets except, as an Elizabethan seaman said, 'to make a show'; and to have required the ports to furnish real men-of-war would have ruined them. It was one of the purposes of Henry's life to create a national navy, and there was not a year of his reign that did not witness some accretion to its strength. Such merchantmen as he required were hired without the exercise of the prerogative; it is not until the reign of Elizabeth that we find in force the further development of the right of impressment—the demand for fully armed ships at the cost of the ports and counties, the principle upon which the ship-money levies were based. The first war with France, of 1512–13, was fought chiefly by men-of-war, although there were some hired ships in pay, but none came from Somerset, nor can any of the impressed crews be traced to the county. Equally, when shipwrights and caulkers were brought from all parts of England in 1513 to build the *Henry Grace de Dieu* at Woolwich, no Somerset port sent any. If obscurity implied happiness the people of the Somerset seaboard should have been contented during this reign, inasmuch as they seldom appear in official papers. In 1533 some Minehead men were ordered to come to London to answer a charge of depredations done on a Breton ship, from which it would seem that maritime activity, as exercised by individuals, still existed.[58] In 1534 Richard Sare of Minehead was tried for piracy and acquitted, but he was involved in another case in 1535.[59]

About 1539 Henry feared a continental alliance against the kingdom. The new navy, although more powerful than any England had yet possessed, the foundation stone of the future empire, was as yet an untried weapon. The preceding centuries were fraught with the lesson that the defence of England was best maintained on the English seas; but there was a natural inclination, especially in an age which was tending towards formalism in military science, to supplement the sea service by falling back on the orthodox defences of castles, sconces and bulwarks to prevent a landing or to support a defending force. The idea of coast fortifications had been in the air in 1535, when Cromwell noted in his 'Remembrances' that a small tax, formerly paid to Rome, might well be diverted 'towards the defence of the realm to be employed in making fortresses.' At that time, however,

[50] Rymer, *Foedera*, x, 382.
[51] *Hist. MSS. Com. Rep.* iii, App. 313.
[52] Collinson, *Hist. of Somerset*, iii, 335.
[53] Pat. 1 Edw. IV, pt. 3, m. 25 d.
[54] Ibid. 20 Edw. IV, pt. 1, m. 21.
[55] *Hist. MSS. Com. Rep.* iii, App. 313.
[56] Pat. 1 Ric. III, pt. 1, m. 4 d.
[57] Jarman, *Hist. of Bridgwater*, 35; a quotation, but no authority is given.
[58] *L. and P. Hen.* VIII, vi, 1382.
[59] Ibid. vii, 258; viii, 281.

Calais and Dover were the only places upon which money was being spent lavishly, and nothing was done elsewhere until 1539, when the political conditions seemed to render immediate action advisable; then plans were drawn up for fortifications at various places between Yarmouth and Bristol. Early in the year commissioners were appointed to survey and report upon suitable positions; those for Somerset, Dorset, Devon and Cornwall were grouped together, but Sir Hugh Paulet was the only Somerset man of any note among them.[60] A contemporary map shows the defences proposed, and perhaps ordered;[61] but others on the English Channel and North Sea were more urgently required, and no doubt when the opportunity came the circumstances had changed and those for the Bristol Channel were then considered unnecessary. There is no reference in the official papers which would suggest that they were even commenced. There was to be a blockhouse at Woodspring ('Wolspringpill'), at the mouth of the River Yeo, two in Uphill Bay, one at Hurtstone Point and one at Porlock Weir; guns were to be mounted, but only on platforms, at Minehead and at the mouth of the Parret on the left bank. The map also shows breakwaters, in the shape of semicircular pile constructions, in front of Porlock and Watchet; they were probably of the same character as the early type of the Cobb at Lyme, that is, wooden piles inclosing a core of stone.

War with France and Scotland broke out again in 1543, and in consequence returns of shipping were called for and sent to London. That of Somerset is a poor one.[62] At Minehead there was a 70-ton vessel, with four small guns, belonging to William Hill; two, each of 60 tons, belonging to Robert Quyrk and Denys Marrane; and one of 100 tons owned by Lady Luttrell. There were seventy-seven mariners, of whom forty were at sea. The return goes on, 'Item, there is no other ship nor balinger belonging to any port or creek in Somerset but at Comage (Combwich), pertaining to the port of Bridgwater are thirteen mariners.' According to this not a single sea-going ship sailed from Bridgwater, which seems incredible, but may have been momentarily true. As the proposed fortifications existed only on paper, a local squadron was equipped at Bristol for the protection of the coast.[63] There are various lists of merchantmen hired for service during 1543, but none from Somerset can be found among them. A proclamation of 1544[64] licensed all subjects to fit out vessels against the French and Scots; the result was a remarkably successful outburst of privateering, in which the Somerset owners may have shared if the crown left them the use of their ships and men. Devon, Cornwall and Dorset were, we know, denuded of men to serve in the royal fleets, so that it is unlikely that Somerset escaped. If privateering was not possible there was always piracy available. In 1549 Robert Cole of Minehead confessed to having been a pirate for a year with a result of 'divers prizes.' He claimed to have earned his pardon by taking an Irish castle from the Scots at the bidding of the Lord Deputy of Ireland.[65] In none of the wars of Edward VI and Mary is the county known to have been called upon for ships, but no place possessing a seafaring population evaded the demand for men. In 1557 the sheriffs were ordered to assist an Admiralty official pressing along the seaboard, and, as some of the sailors were known to have run away, those who were obstinate were to be committed to prison.[66] A year previously measures had been taken to clear the Bristol and St. George's Channels of pirates by sending out hired ships for the purpose; to sail in a private ship, whether on the side of the law or against it, was much more congenial to the 16th-century sailor than serving in the national fleets. On his own business he showed no lack of enterprise. We find that John Kerry, a Minehead man, was master of the *Lion* of London, one of the three ships which made the second trading voyage to Morocco in 1552; the captain of the *Lion*, and commander of the squadron, was Thomas Windham, of Marshwood Park in Somerset.[67]

Through several centuries the right of wreck had been coveted by manorial lords and corporations, both for profit and, incidentally, as evidence of exemption from the inquisition of the High Admiral. Legally, if man, dog, or cat, escaped alive from a ship it was no wreck; but if the cargo once came into the hands of the dwellers on the coast there was little chance of recovery. Every corporation used what influence it possessed to obtain local jurisdiction in Admiralty matters, not only as a question of dignity and profit, but even more in order to escape the arbitrary and expensive proceedings of the High Admiral's deputies who brought much odium upon their master. But such exemptions were usually confined to the great ports whose maritime aid was valuable to the crown, and whom it was well to reward; therefore we find no privileged port in Somerset. About 1393 Bridgwater joined other western towns in a petition complaining of the encroachments of the Admiral's representatives,[68] but that would refer to trespasses on their chartered liberties in the Parret. Private owners, especially when spiritual or temporal lords, found less difficulty in obtaining rights of wreck. The Hundred Rolls show that in 1275 Roger Mortimer and Eudo

[60] *L. and P. Hen. VIII*, xiv (1), 398.
[62] *L. and P. Hen. VIII*, xviii, 547 (2).
[64] Harl. MSS. 442, fol. 213.
[66] *Acts of P. C.* 1556–8, pp. 141–2.
[66] Prynne, *Brief Animadversions*, 79.

[61] Cott. MSS., Aug. I, i, 8.
[63] Ibid. (1) 265.
[65] Tytler, *Edward VI and Mary*, i, 270.
[67] Hakluyt, *Voyages* (ed. 1888), xi, 70.

La Zouche possessed such rights at Bridgwater ; the Bishop of Bath and Wells, the Abbot of Glastonbury, and others held similar rights elsewhere.[69] The owners of the manor of Dunster had rights along the stretch of coast between Shurton Bars and Countisbury Foreland ; a long series of accounts of the 15th century, preserved among the records of Dunster Castle, proves how profitable wreck on the stormy and dangerous Bristol Channel was to the lords of Dunster.[70] The Luttrells even held an admiralty court of their own,[71] a most exceptional proceeding, and one which there is little doubt would have brought down on them the heavy hand of the High Admiral if a case involving their decision had come before the Admiralty Court in London. Certainly in 1564 the Lord Admiral was exercising his inquisition in Porlock Bay, within the district they claimed as their own ;[72] but on the other hand a committee of inquiry of 1856 recognized the Luttrell privileges as established between the western border of the county of Somerset and the eastern boundary of the parish of Lilstock.[73]

The question of piracy and wrecking became noticeable during Henry's reign, not because the offences were more prevalent—there were probably fewer than during preceding centuries—but because suppression was taken in hand more seriously. The king was as resolved to make himself obeyed in material as in spiritual matters, and was determined that the law should be feared as much at sea as on land. No single life could have been long enough to see complete success, but the steps he took mark a great advance in the organization of repressive measures, and only the application or extension of them was left to his successors. It had been found that the existing system of trial for piracy was nearly useless, the offender having to confess before he could be sentenced, or his guilt having to be proved by disinterested witnesses who, naturally, could seldom be present at sea. By two statutes, 27 Hen. VIII, cap. 4, and 28 Hen. VIII, cap. 15, such crimes were in future to be tried according to the form of the common and not, as hitherto, the civil law. Probably for the better administration of these statutes and for other reasons—namely, the execution of a treaty of 1525 with France concerning maritime depredations, the strict protection of the king's and Lord Admiral's rights in wrecks and other matters, the registration of ships and men available and the levy of seamen, the inspection and certification of ships going to sea touching their armed strength and the peaceful nature of the voyage, the exaction of bonds from captains and owners as security for good conduct, and the safe keeping of prizes and prize goods—it was deemed advisable to have round the coast permanent representatives of the Lord Admiral who should be of higher social standing and armed with greater authority than were the deputies who had hitherto visited each county or district collecting his profits or maintaining his rights. The new officers, the vice-admirals of the counties, were, in their civil functions, the successors historically of the keepers of the coast and the conservators of truces of the 13th, 14th and 15th centuries, and there is not one of the duties of the vice-admirals which cannot be paralleled among those performed by the earlier officials. There are traces of occasional appointments, similar in character to those of the vice-admirals, but less ample in scope, in some of the counties during the 14th and 15th centuries ;[74] but now instead of acting temporarily and only in one or two districts they became a band of crown officials[75] stationed round the whole coast, backed by the power of the Tudor despotism, and continued without any interruption during which their authority might diminish by intermission.[76]

The scheme did not come into operation simultaneously over all England, but developed out of necessity and according to opportunity. The first nomination known by precise date is that for Norfolk and Suffolk ; that for Somerset, although the date of establishment is not known, is of about the same time as Sir Edward Gorges was acting in 1536. The post was usually held by peers, or by members of untitled county families, for whom it was a source of influence and profit ; the chief gains were from the produce of wreck and salvage, usually shared with the Lord Admiral, or from less lawful receipts. Each vice-admiral had a miniature admiralty court of his own ; they had to give bonds to render their accounts half-yearly, but this duty was often ignored ; about 1553 ordinances were drawn up by which they were to regulate their own conduct and that of their subordinate officers. The vice-admiralty of Somerset was often united, in the same person, with that

[69] *Hund. R.* (Rec. Com.) ii, 127, 130–7. See also *ante,* p. 247.
[70] F. Hancock, *Minehead,* 36, 37.
[71] *Trans. Som. Arch. Soc.* xxxv (2), 46; Anct. Corresp. lii, 42. See also *Engl. Hist. Rev.* xxii, 472.
[72] Marsden, *Select Pleas in the Court of Admiralty,* ii, 128.   [73] Hancock, op. cit. 35.
[74] A grant to Alexander Cely of the office of clerk of the admiralty of the king's river of Severn, for life, from 'le Marke' of Scilly to Worcester bridge, may be referred to here. The fees were to be as in the time of Edward III and Richard II (Pat. 1 Edw. IV, pt. 3, m. 11). From the wording this does not appear to be an appointment of the type alluded to in the text, but it is possibly a local variation.
[75] The patents of appointment were from the Lord Admiral, sometimes for life and sometimes during pleasure.
[76] On this subject I am greatly indebted to Mr. R. G. Marsden, to whose learned researches in admiralty law the history of the evolution of the office of vice-admiral is mainly due.

of Bristol ; and the county is rather exceptional in that so many of the vice-admirals were strangers, the post, in most counties, usually being held among families seated in them. Gorges belonged to a Somerset family, and his successor, Sir Hugh Paulet, was also a native, but Thomas Arundel, in 1549, was a Cornishman. During the greater part of the reign of Elizabeth the office was held by the Winters, who were strangers, and not until 1628 is it again found in the possession of a Somerset family, the Rodneys. The same peculiarity is noticeable among the later vice-admirals, of whom the most notorious was Bubb Dodington, nominally of Somerset descent but a Dorset landowner, the 'servile place hunter' of the 18th century, who held the appointment from 1715 until his death in 1762.

One of the primary objects in the installation of the vice-admirals had been, by policing the coast-line, to deny a base of operations to the pirates, but this end was not attained because the conditions became in some respects much more difficult during the second half of the 16th century. The reign of Mary sent many of the outlawed and discontented to the refuge of the sea, and the more or less continuous warfare existing in western Europe during the reign of Elizabeth tempted many such men to continue their vocation. Therefore the plague of piracy, and its near relative, privateering, was virulent during the latter reign, although a number of cases which the sufferers called piracy were really seizures of enemy's goods in neutral ships and were, justly, questions for the judge of the Admiralty Court. The peace of 1564 and the protests of neighbouring powers forced Elizabeth to more energetic action than she had previously taken, and a circular letter to the vice-admirals of the counties called their attention to the suggestive fact that although many pirates had been captured not one had been hanged.[77] At the same time the Bristol Channel was to be cleared by the voluntary efforts of certain citizens of Bristol, to whom commissions from the Admiralty Court had been granted to set out ships for that purpose.[78] The pirate bases for the fraternity working in the Bristol Channel and on the coasts of the south-western counties were at Berehaven and similar Irish ports, and tentative essays at destroying them in their lairs were also made by the queen's ships and merchantmen hired for the service. In November 1565 piracy commissioners with large powers were nominated for each county, and they were to appoint deputies at every creek and landing-place.[79] The Somerset commissioners were Sir Ralph Hopton, Sir George Norton, Humphrey Coles and Henry Portman. As the pirates had friends, agents, partners and informants in nearly every port, the proceedings of the commissioners were not of much avail, especially when the business became further complicated by the Prince of Orange's issues of letters of marque, many of which were taken out by Englishmen, while many Dutch ships had Englishmen on board. The Orange privateers were an element of *la haute politique*, and Elizabeth did not hold it advisable entirely to crush them even if it had been in her power to do so. Subsequently the Spanish Netherlands followed the precedent of the Dutch and sent out privateers, the beginning of the affliction of 'Dunkirkers,' which plagued the coast for more than a century, while English subjects also obtained letters of marque from the Huguenot leaders in France.

In 1577 new commissioners were appointed, and still more stringent methods of repression were adopted.[80] If the number of commissioners is a guide the Somerset men should have been reckless and daring pirates, but there is little evidence to justify such a conclusion. Probably the object of such close supervision was rather to prevent pirates' plunder being run ashore for sale, and the revictualling of their ships, than any expectation that piratical vessels were sailing from the ports of the county. There was need of close scrutiny, for the Bristol Channel was infested by pirates who made Milford Haven their base, a place described at this time as their general refuge where they were sheltered and protected.[81] When, also, we find the deputy vice-admiral of Bristol ordered to appear before the Council, in June 1577, to answer a charge of taking bribes to release captured pirates it can be understood that a strict watch was necessary to keep the coastmen reasonably honest. Some of the vice-admirals were suspiciously slow and unsuccessful in taking action ; in a few cases, notably in that of Cornwall, they were openly friendly with the pirates, dealt with them and helped them. In 1563 the Privy Council referred publicly to accusations of connivance brought against the vice-admirals, but nothing is known involving those of Somerset. It was no doubt the lack of confidence in the ordinary officials which caused the original appointment of especial piracy commissioners. Those of 1577 were now empowered to prosecute and fine the aiders and abettors ashore, and the fines were to go towards recouping the victims ; the takers of pirates were to have a proportion of the goods found on board, and commissions were to be granted to private persons to send out ships pirate hunting.[82] It may be supposed that the Somerset commissioners went to work energetically, but, so far as the results have come down to us, they do not

---

[77] *Acts of P.C.* 1558–70, p. 182.   [78] Ibid. 164.   [79] Ibid. pp. 278–80.

[80] S. P. Dom. Eliz. cxv, 32. For Somerset :—Lord Paulet, Sir Geo. Norton, Sir Maurice Berkeley, Sir Hen. Portman, Thomas and Edward Popham, Sir John Clifton, and four others.   [81] Ibid. cxi, 16.

[82] Add. MSS. 34150, fol. 61, 64. There had been some doubt whether accessories ashore could legally be prosecuted (*Acts of P.C.* 1575–7, p. 339).

seem to have found many criminals. In one list the county shows £2 10s. levied in fines, and in another one person is condemned.[83] The commissioners may have prevented the infection spreading on their particular zone of coast, but they could not deal with the plague spots elsewhere, and the sea was no safer than it had been for years before. In 1579 the commander of a squadron of queen's ships going to Ireland was ordered to detach one to clear the Severn;[84] as late as 1590, when much of the superfluous national energy was expending itself in more patriotic fashion against Spain, there were 'two terrible pirates' who made Milford Haven their home, terrorizing the Bristol Channel.[85] In one instance, at least, the Somerset spirit of adventure displayed itself in a more respectable form than active or passive aid of piracy, for the *Emanuel*, or 'Busse,' of Bridgwater, Captain Newton, master, James Leach, was one of the fifteen vessels which composed Frobisher's squadron in his third voyage of 1578. This vessel had the distinction of having named after her 'The sunken land of Busse,' which her crew supposed themselves to have discovered and that long appeared on old maps. She was nearly wrecked, and an account of the discovery was written by Thomas Wiars, a passenger on board.[86]

The bounty system inaugurated by Henry VII, by which an occasional tonnage allowance was made to the builders of new ships suitable for service in war, had, under Elizabeth, settled into a grant of 5s. a ton on all vessels of 100 tons and upwards. The expansion of trade and the attraction of privateering stimulated shipbuilding generally in first rate, and even in second rate, ports during the Spanish war, but had little effect in Somerset, which was outside the chief lines of sea communication, and whose harbours were worse than second rate. Thus the assistance that the county was able to afford in the way of ships during the Elizabethan war was of a minor character, and, as a necessary corollary, its contribution of seamen was also relatively small. It has been noticed that from at least the reign of John it had been customary to call upon the officials of the ports for returns of the ships and men available; most of the earlier ones are lost, but several, complete or fragmentary, remain for the Elizabethan period. War with France and Scotland existed in 1560, which was the cause of the first Elizabethan list of that year of vessels of 100 tons and upwards; there is none from Somerset, either because the return is lost or because there was no vessel of that size owned in the county. But, judging from the evidence of later lists, the latter explanation is the true one. The next returns, of December 1565, and January 1566, are existing for most of the counties, but Somerset is again missing; as vessels of all sizes are included it cannot be because those of the county were below any particular limit of tonnage. In August 1570 a general embargo was ordered, and at the moment it was found that there were eleven ships and sixty-three men at home in Somerset, including Bristol; of the ships eight appear to have belonged to Bristol.[87] In 1572 Thomas Colshill, surveyor of customs at London, compiled a register of coasting traders belonging to the ports; only three are given for Somerset—Bridgwater with one vessel of 25 tons, and Minehead with one of 30 and one of 10 tons.[88] It is not quite clear what dividing line Colshill had in mind, but he would appear to have excluded ships engaged in oversea trade; even so the total is extraordinarily poor compared with the other counties for which he gives statistics. A return of 1577 shows no 100-ton ship in the county, and the next of 1582 none of 100 tons and none between 80 and 100 tons. Of vessels between 20 and 80 tons Bridgwater possessed eight, and the town was the only one in the county scheduled.[89] Somerset and Bristol are linked together in the return of men, of whom there were 48 masters and 464 seamen. An order of 7 March 1589–90 directed that the names, ages and dwelling-places of all sailors, fishermen and gunners between sixteen and sixty years of age were to be registered, but unfortunately there are no details of the information obtained.

In the spring of 1585, in consequence of a dearth in Spain, Philip II invited the importation of wheat, promising immunity to vessels bringing it over. However, on 29 May he issued an order to seize all such vessels and imprison their crews, the ships, guns and stores being destined to strengthen the fleet preparing under the Marquis of Santa Cruz for the invasion of England. This flagrant breach of faith was answered here by the issue of letters of reprisal; the letters were only to be given to persons who could prove that they had suffered by the seizure, and the event, with Drake's expedition of the same year, marks the commencement of the Spanish war.[90] Bridgwater was damnified to the amount of £700, and letters of reprisal were granted to John Petrie and others to set out one ship,[91] but of course it does not necessarily follow that the loss was suffered in a Bridg-

---

[83] Add. MSS. 12505, fol. 333; S. P. Dom Eliz. cxxxv, fol. 21.

[84] *Acts of P.C.* 1578–80, p. 251.   [85] S. P. Dom. Eliz. ccxxxix, 92.

[86] Hakluyt, *Voyages* (ed. 1888), xii, 98, 172.   [87] S. P. Dom. Eliz. lxxi, 74 (1); lxxiii, 48.

[88] Ibid. Add. xxii.   [89] Ibid. clvi, 45.

[90] Philip's promise of safe-conduct was needful in consequence of the strained relations existing. The issue of letters of reprisal was not, in itself, an act of war; in fact, international jurists held that they were only consistent with a state of peace.

[91] Admir. Ct. Exemp. xiii, nos. 211–13; ibid. Inq. iv, 7 Sept., 1585.

water vessel. Neither in 1585 nor in 1587 is any Somerset ship known to have been with Drake. The near approach of war to their own doors was brought home to the men of the county in December 1587 by the appearance of a soldier, Captain Horde, sent by the Privy Council to inspect the trained men and report on their fitness and the preparations for defence.[92] The experience of 1587 and of later years showed that the brunt of any action had always to be borne by the men-of-war, and that armed merchantmen were at best useful only for secondary operations. But in 1588 this was understood only by a few seamen; therefore in that year the whole of the English coast was called upon to help, not by a general impressment of shipping, but by sending a specified number of vessels to join the royal fleet. On 31 March a general embargo was proclaimed, the object being not so much to retain the vessels as the men. This was followed, the next day, by orders to the port towns to furnish ships at their own expense, all to be more than 60 tons.[93] In Somerset Bridgwater was rated for one ship and a pinnace; Chard and Taunton were to assist Lyme Regis.[94] Bridgwater responded loyally, and when, in July, the burgesses were asked to supply more provisions they replied that they had already arranged the re-victualling before the receipt of the Council's letter, and volunteered an additional two months' store if necessary.[95] Chard and Taunton were less amenable to official desires; perhaps, as inland towns, the inhabitants thought that any demand on them was an unjustifiable exercise of the prerogative.[96] They had made difficulties originally about helping Lyme and now flatly refused any supplementary assistance. The Bridgwater ship was the *William*, and was ordered to join Drake's division at Plymouth; she does not appear in the later lists of the fleet, but may, in those, be the ' bark of Bridgwater ' of 70 tons, Captain John Smyth, which was in the Lord Admiral's division and was then in the queen's pay. Of the pinnace there is no trace.

In many of the counties the ships ordered in April were at sea in time only in virtue of the assistance of some wealthy members of the community who advanced the money necessary. The *William*, it appears, was set out by Robert Bockinge, and in 1592 he was complaining that he was still owed £198 due in Bridgwater and West Somerset.[97] The reference to West Somerset shows that the smaller ports had been assessed to help Bridgwater, although there is no other evidence of the fact. In September 1588 the civic authorities of Bridgwater petitioned that their ship had cost them £447, and asked that a previous promise of the Council that contributions should be obtained from the inhabitants of the county should be carried out.[98] The Privy Council assisted Bockinge by ordering that any who refused to pay should appear before them in London, a journey which, in view of the expense of travelling and the delay in awaiting their pleasure, might obviously be made equivalent to a very heavy fine. The county took no part in the Portugal voyage of 1589, for which ships were hired by Norreys and Drake on their own responsibility and not demanded by the crown. In the summer of 1591 Lord Thomas Howard was cruising off the Azores, intending to intercept a Spanish flota from the West Indies. The government here, having received information that the flota would be more strongly convoyed than had been expected, resolved to reinforce Lord Thomas and called upon some of the ports for ships. The fighting reinforcement consisted of six large London merchantmen; as the other port ships were all to be of about 100 tons, they must have been intended to act as victualling and storeships. Bridgwater was asked for one 100-ton vessel; the townsmen answered that they had suffered heavy losses from the war and that ' our harbour when we were best traded never, or very seldom, yielded any shipping of any such burthen,' and that they possessed nothing of more than 40 or 50 tons.[99] It was no doubt true that such small trading centres as Bridgwater had suffered since the commencement of hostilities, for they had lost their former traffic to the Spanish and French ports, a traffic never very large but important to them, while there had been little privateering or especial war industry to replace it. Minehead considered itself ruined by the war,[100] although, as its chief trade was with Wales, the reason is not so obvious.

The failure of the 1589 expedition had daunted Elizabeth from undertakings on a large scale, so that it was not until 1596 that the attack on Cadiz was ventured. In the interval Thomas Gregory of Taunton, and others, were granted licences authorizing them to trade for ten years on the west coast of Africa,[101] but it is fairly certain that if they took up ships for the purpose it was in Dorset or Devon ports. There was also some ordinary privateering, at least from Bridgwater; between 1590 and 1594 three vessels belonging to the town paid prize-tenths to the Lord Admiral.[102]

---

[92] *Acts of P.C.* 1587-8, p. 310.
[93] Ibid. 1588, p. 9.
[94] Ibid. p. 56.
[95] S. P. Dom. Eliz. ccxii, 43.
[96] Some of the Taunton people were engaged in maritime speculation. In 1588 Robert Pope, Thomas Withcomb and others had fitted out a ship for a voyage to the Guinea coast. *Acts of P.C.* 1588, p. 294. See also *post*, p. 258.
[97] *Acts of P.C.* 1591-2, p. 224.
[98] S. P. Dom. Eliz. ccxvi, 27.
[99] *Cecil MSS.* (Hist. MSS. Com.) iv, 121.
[100] *Hist. MSS. Com. Rep.* x, App. vi, 79, 81.
[101] Hakluyt, *Voyages* (ed. 1888), xi, 341.
[102] Harl. MSS. 598,

The first sign of the inception of the Cadiz expedition was a demand made in December 1595 upon many of the counties for supplies, Somerset being put down for wheat. This was followed by a warning that ships would be wanted to serve with the navy in the following spring ; three ships were required from Bristol to the expenses of which the Somerset ports were to contribute.[103] Bridgwater ultimately paid £50 as its share ;[104] the whole county was assessed at £600, the original intention being to place the burthen on the ports alone, but in view of their poverty a wider basis was found to be necessary, and a levy was made upon the inhabitants generally ' being in manner as much interested herein by loss or benefit as the ports maritime.'[105] Some Somerset people refused to pay, and the usual stimulus was applied of ordering them to appear before the Council.[106] The Bristol creditors were equally dissatisfied, for long afterwards they were asking in vain for the Somerset apportionment, and in 1597 the Council, recognizing that the county was in a poor condition, directed the Lord Chief Justice, then going on circuit there, to use persuasion.[107] In 1600 the expenses of one of the Bristol ships were still owing, because the Somerset contributions remained in arrears ; then the Privy Council appear to have lost patience and directed the Bristol officials to settle the account, promising that Somerset should be compelled to liquidate the liability. Those of Bristol may have doubted the power of the Council for, concerning this Cadiz expedition, several awkward questions were asked, especially from Yorkshire, as to the right of the crown to make these levies. At any rate in 1601 the money was yet unpaid, and the Council in despair turned the matter over to the Lord Chief Justice again to take what steps he might ' think be agreeable to reason ' ; at the same time they pointed out to the corporation of Bristol that the city was answerable to the shipowners and men with whom the contract had been made whether or no Somerset paid.[108] This may have been true in the letter of the law but not in the spirit, for there was an implicit understanding that the authority of the crown guaranteed the advances made to equip assessed ships ; but it is very evident that the Privy Council were afraid to stir into active life the nascent temper of protest and resistance, and preferred to sacrifice Bristol rather than have Somerset questioning the prerogative.[109]

A number of private ships, sent on the chance of finding prizes or of getting a freight from the plunder of Cadiz, accompanied the fleet from nearly all the southern and western ports, and probably Bridgwater was represented. One Somerset seaman, Robert Crosse, obtained his knighthood at Cadiz. Crosse belonged to a Charlinch family and served ashore and afloat, but mostly afloat, from boyhood, finally securing a position among Elizabethan sea commanders of the third rank.[110] After 1596 the government made no more applications to the counties for ships during the remainder of the reign. As piracy died down the scourge of Dunkirk privateering, which was little different, made itself felt. The favourite cruising grounds from the Flemish ports were the east and south coasts, but some came into the Bristol Channel, which, however, was mostly favoured by privateers from the north coast of Spain. In September 1600 there were so many at work that some of the ports, including Bridgwater, refused to send to sea ships belonging to them taken up to convey stores to Ireland because they regarded their capture as certain. The government assured the various town authorities that transit was quite safe—which was not the case—but promised to send men-of-war to sea and threatened to commit to prison those who remained obstinate.[111]

There was a general commission of piracy for all the counties in 1608, and there are occasional references to the presence of the marauders in the Bristol Channel. One notorious pirate, Thomas Salkeld, constituted himself King of Lundy and made preparations for his coronation ; but George Eskott, who belonged to a Bridgwater ship which had been taken, led a revolt of the other prisoners, and Salkeld, dethroned, fled away.[112] Eskott was granted a pension of eighteen pence a day for life.[113] Captain Peter Easton, who was an admiral at the head of a pirate fleet, at one time haunted the Bristol Channel, the islands of which were at this time described as ' pirates' dens.' Besides Christian there were the Mohammedan pirates to fear ; for them the Bristol Channel was so profitable a cruising ground that Algerine ships sailed direct for the Severn.[114] Notwithstanding these drawbacks, and their complaints of losses during the reign of Elizabeth, there was still a certain amount of shipping belonging to the Somerset ports. A list of ships' names occurring in legal and historical

[103] *Acts of P.C.* 1595, pp. 123–4.
[104] *Cecil MSS.* (Hist. MSS. Com.), vi, 278 (22 July 1596).
[105] *Acts of P.C.*, 1595–6, p.124. [106] Ibid. 296–8 ; ibid. 1596–7, p. 143.
[107] Ibid. 14 June, 1597. [108] Ibid. 1600–1, 21 May, 24 June, 7 July, 1601.
[109] Suffolk, also, was giving the same trouble ; Norfolk and other counties were but little more compliant.
[110] For notes on his life see *Naval Tracts of Sir William Monson*, edited by M. Oppenheim (Navy Records Soc.), i, 213. Another well-known Elizabethan seaman was Sir Amyas Preston of Cricket, near Crewkerne.
[111] *Acts of P.C.*, 1599–1600, pp. 717–18.
[112] S. P. Dom. Jas. I, liii, 100. See also *V.C.H. Devon*, 'Maritime History.'
[113] Devon, *Issues of the Exchequer*, 309.
[114] Moule, *Catalogue of Charters, etc., of Weymouth and Melcombe Regis*, 173.

MSS., and in various printed sources, during the reign of James I has been compiled by Mr. R. G. Marsden, in which four of Bridgwater, two of Minehead, and one of Portishead are mentioned.[115] There must have been others, probably the majority, that sailed through an uneventful career without attracting the attention of the law, the admiralty officials, or the officers of customs. There is no indication that the Somerset ports took any share in the Newfoundland fishery, which was not only a source of wealth for Devon, Dorset and Cornwall, but, in the 16th and 17th centuries, was still more valuable as the training school in which was bred the race of seamen who did so much to humble Spain and weaken Holland. A few men may have engaged themselves at Bristol or in the North Devon ports, but it is evident that Minehead and Bridgwater had neither the ships nor the capital necessary to join in the trade.

The war with Spain caused preparations to be made for the Cadiz fleet of 1625, but no armed ships were required from the counties. Transports had to be provided, and for this Somerset and Gloucestershire were put down to bear one-third of the expenses of Bristol.[116] No Somerset vessel appears in the Cadiz fleet list, but the port of origin is not always given. In 1626 Charles, on the brink of war with France, resolved to follow the precedents of Elizabeth's reign, and called upon the maritime shires for fifty-six ships to join the royal fleet. The lowest serviceable tonnage for armed ships was now so much higher than anything owned in Somerset that the county was no longer asked for vessels, but only to help Bristol with money. Bristol was rated for three vessels to be of 200 tons each, and armed, victualled and stored for three months;[117] a general levy was ordered on Somerset to meet one-fourth of the Bristol charges, to which the justices replied that such a levy was without precedent.[118] It is not clear how it differed from the demands of the Elizabethan government in similar circumstances, but the Privy Council seem to have admitted a distinction, for they replied that if it was without precedent it was for 'the public service and common defence.'[119] They told the Somerset justices that the people would have to contribute, but they evidently feared that pressure would evolve organized resistance and eventually the Bristol aid was reduced to one ship. Similar reductions were made elsewhere in consequence of protests and refusals.

A survey of the coast of this date says that 'along Somersetshire there is no coming near the coast with vessels of any burthen except it be for seven or eight miles west from Purshot Point;[120] the rest is all almost flat ground whereon is only two fathoms water even to Porlock a little creek, the march between Somerset and Devon.'[121] There were several large fleets equipped during 1627, 1628 and 1629, but if they contained any Somerset ships it could only have been in the form of small tenders and storeships. In the meanwhile the Bristol Channel was a happy hunting ground for Biscayners, Dunkirkers and French privateers, who found even fewer checks than in the English Channel. The Bristol Channel was supposed to be patrolled from the Irish station, but the squadron there was too small even for its local work, and cruisers from it seldom appeared east of Lundy. In 1628, in view of 'the great power of the Frenchmen and Dunkirkers in the Severn,' it was decided to commission two Bristol ships to go after them, but vessels of 150 tons were considered too weak for the force they would have to deal with.[122] A year later there was 'much crying out' about the numerous privateers sweeping the Bristol Channel;[123] and the Frenchmen, when they took a prize, declared their indifference to the fact that peace had been made.[124] Among the coast towns generally there were very many letters of marque issued during the war; Bridgwater showed no speculative enterprise in that direction, which is perhaps explained by a reference to its decay at this time,[125] but three Minehead ships of 80, 60 and 30 tons sailed with them.[126] One, the *Dove*, of 80 tons, was taken by a Dutch ship while convoying some Bridgwater traders to Ireland; the reason is not very clear, perhaps she had Spanish goods on board, but the injured owners brought their case again and again before the government, and as late as 1651 letters of reprisal were being granted to the then representatives of the owners. Altogether they exacted reparation, it is said, to an amount many thousands of pounds in excess of the damage suffered.

After the conclusion of peace there were still many complaints of the proceedings of the Biscayan and Dunkirk privateers, who continued to plunder in the Bristol Channel under pretence of searching for Dutch cargoes; their presence there, and all round the coasts, was one of the excuses for the ship-money imposts. Charles had intended an issue of ship-money writs in 1628, but alarmed by the feeling aroused he withdrew from the first trial. Forced, at length, to choose between facing

[115] 'English Ships in the Reign of James I,' *Trans. Roy. Hist. Soc.* xix, 311. Mr. Marsden informs me that he has found several references to members of the Blake family of Bridgwater, with the Christian names of Robert and Humphrey, in the Admiralty Court papers as shipowners during the Elizabethan era.

[116] S. P. Dom. Chas. I, xxxiii, 107.
[117] Ibid. xxx, 81.
[118] Ibid. xxxvi, 18.
[119] Ibid. 94.
[120] Possett, or Portishead, Point.
[121] S. P. Dom. Chas. I, cxxvi, 43.
[122] Ibid. cix, 6.
[123] Ibid. cxix. 69.
[124] Ibid. cxliv, 54.
[125] Ibid. cxlviii, 72.
[126] Ibid. cxv,

a Parliament or raising money by this method, the writs of 20 October 1634 were sent out, addressed to the port towns and maritime parts of the shires. The coast of Somerset was joined with Bristol and part of Gloucestershire for a vessel of 800 tons victualled, armed, and stored for twenty-six weeks' service.[127] As the ships required were larger than those possessed by any port except London, an equivalent in money might be paid to the Treasury to be applied to the preparation of a king's ship; therefore the grouped counties here were given the option of paying £6,735. Probably few, even of the seamen, of the three districts had ever seen an 800-ton ship. In the beginning most of the counties submitted in a more or less sullen silence, but Somerset gave trouble from the first. Bridgwater at once protested against the rate of assessment;[128] the people of the hundred of Tintinhull complained that they were rated as maritime although there were no ports in the hundred, but that they had submitted and allowed the sheriff to charge the parishes 'which he was pleased to interpret to be maritime.'[129] They also brought accusations of favouritism and unfairness against the sheriff, Henry Hodges.

The second writ, of 4 August 1635, was general to the inland counties as well as to the coast; Somerset, by itself, now stood as responsible for the production of an 800-ton ship or £8,000.[130] The spirit of resistance was rising, as is shown by the fact that in October 1637 the county was still £1,056 in arrear on this writ.[131] As Hampden's case did not come up for argument in court until December of that year it shows also that the growing revolt was independent of any central leadership. The third writ, of 9 October 1636, was again for an 800-ton ship, and the note of opposition became still more marked. The then sheriff, William Bassett, knew what to expect, and thought he knew how to deal with the difficulty; he wrote to the secretary of the Council that when complaints were referred to the justices it should be to three or five of them, 'the odd voice being sure quickly to make an end of it.'[132] Minehead had been assessed at £58 19s., Bridgwater £70, Taunton £100, Wells £60, and Bath £70.[133] In January 1637 William Strode refused to pay,[134] and many others must have followed his example, for in March Bassett wrote to the Council that most people were forcing him to issue distress warrants, without which no money could be obtained, that the constables were threatened with legal proceedings, and that the farmers were clearing their ground so that there should be nothing to levy upon.[135] In July the same story of distraint was being continued, and the constables were 'disheartened by threats and more than menaces';[136] in October there was the further trouble that several of these men had disappeared with the money they had collected.[137] In the meanwhile the sheriff was called before the Privy Council in the beginning of September to be censured for the delay; it must have been in order to escape that he promised payment in full by the end of the month, for he, of all men, knew the impossibility of keeping his word. The fact that in July 1636 an Algerine pirate had, notwithstanding the pretentious ship-money fleets, landed men within twelve miles of Bristol and carried off into slavery some living on the coast, could not have assisted to reconcile people to the tax as the news spread through the country side.[138] In the same year the Privy Council received information at one moment from Plymouth that there were then five 'Saleemen' in the Bristol Channel making many captures.[139]

There was no writ in 1638, but the officials had sufficient vexation in collecting the money due on those of the previous years. In May the sheriff reported that when cattle were seized the owners injured them or permitted them to starve in the pound, and that at least one collector had been repulsed with a pike wound.[140] The fourth writ was issued in 1639, and the assessments were reduced, but by now it was destined to make no difference in the result whether they were large or small. The constables were no longer to be relied upon, and in January 1640 Samuel Foy, high constable of the hundred of Horethorne, was in custody for negligence in collecting; this no doubt means either that he was on the popular side or was physically intimidated by the fierce hostility Charles had succeeded in arousing.[141] Then, in March, there were difficulties in the hundred of Catsash; the sheriff wrote to the Lord Keeper, 'I find so much delay and unwillingness . . . that it seems impossible . . . to get in half of that which is laid upon this county.'[142] Even this estimate proved unduly optimistic, for in August not more than £300 was raised of the £6,000 laid upon the county;[143] no one would buy distrained property, only a few pence were offered, ironically, for an ox worth £8, and actions against the constables and bailiffs were being threatened on all sides. In November the Long Parliament met and there was no longer any necessity for individual opposition.

Most of the port towns, the worst sufferers from Charles's political and naval maladministration, stood by the Parliament, and those of Somerset formed no exception. The military history

---

[127] S. P. Dom. Chas. I, cclxxvi, 64. [128] Ibid. cccvi, 56. [129] Ibid. dxxxv, 69.
[130] Ibid. ccxcvi, 69. [131] Ibid. ccclxx, 73. [132] Ibid. cccxlvii, 23. [133] Ibid. ccccli, 88.
[134] Ibid. cccxlv, 33. [135] Ibid. cccl, 39. [136] Ibid. ccclxiii, 11. [137] Ibid. ccclxix, 86.
[138] Hist. MSS. Com. Rep. iv, App. 291. The precise spot is not stated. [139] Ibid. v, App. 582.
[140] S. P. Dom. Chas. I, ccclxxxix, 124. [141] Ibid. ccccxliii, 82.
[142] Ibid. ccccxlviii, 78. [143] Ibid. cccclxiv, 23.

of the county during the Civil War does not concern us here, and its naval history was of but little importance. Both king and Parliament struggled for the command of the Bristol Channel, but the strategic centre was Bristol and the Welsh coast; from the latter Charles desired to send troops, while in its ports he tried to receive supplies. The battle of Langport, in 1645, is said to have been fought to enable the Royalists to pass reinforcements across to Watchet and Minehead, but as Goring lost the battle that scheme failed. The Parliamentary navy, as a whole, was far too small for the amount of work thrown upon it; only forty-nine vessels were intended for commission during the summer of 1645, and of these seven were destined for the Severn and the blockade of Bristol. A six-gun fort at Portishead, probably built at the beginning of the Civil War,[144] was taken on 28 August 1645 by the Parliamentary troops, and a few days afterwards Vice-Admiral Moulton occupied King Road with his squadron.[145] The fall of Bristol and the subjection of South Wales rendered the Parliamentary cause supreme in the neighbouring sea.

The first Dutch war only affected Somerset by the drain of money and men, and in the losses caused by the enemies' privateers, for of course no fleet operations occurred near it. One of the first indications of approaching war was a demand, in March 1652, from the Council of State to the officers of the various ports, for a report of the number of merchantmen available to act as tenders or auxiliary fighting ships, but no town between Barnstaple and Bristol was addressed. The war was a national one in the sense that the seamen on both sides hated each other and had many real or fancied scores, accumulated through two generations, to settle, therefore there was little difficulty at first in obtaining men. Later, when the early enthusiasm wore off, and the fleets grew larger in size, the pressgang had to be used rigorously. Thomas Hewitt and John Pene were the pressmasters for the district in 1653; and in May they complained that the Bristol traders set their men ashore on the coast of Somerset, before entering the Avon, thus disappointing them.[146] A few days afterwards Hewitt and Pene wrote to the Navy Commissioners that they thought that armed force could procure 400 men in Bristol Bay, 50 in Minehead, Watchet and Porlock, and 20 in Bridgwater; inferentially they confessed themselves powerless.[147] Besides the evasive habits of the seamen they had to contend with more or less active and passive opposition from private persons and the officials who were supposed to help them. Not only was the new spirit, in virtue of which the Commonwealth itself existed, adverse to impressment, but the commercial interests of the most influential shipowners and merchants in the seaports were injured when their towns were swept bare of men. It was of more importance to them, when a certain stage of scarcity was reached, to have crews for their own ships than that the men-of-war should be manned, and when that point was touched every obstacle was thrown in the way of the impress authorities everywhere. Thus a complaint from Hewitt and Pene, in June 1653, that ten persons, named, had assaulted them and enabled pressed men to escape is probably only one of many of their experiences;[148] as the letter was written from Minehead that place was no doubt the scene of their trouble.

The Navy Commissioners during the first Dutch war were one of the ablest bodies of men who have ever constituted an English administrative department. It was owing to their energy, foresight and ability that the admirals were kept supplied with the necessary *matériel* to enable them to conquer at sea. Perhaps the foremost of them was Major Nehemiah Bourne, soldier, sailor and administrator, who, like Sir Robert Crosse, belonged to a family seated in the parish of Charlinch.

There was no reason for the appearance of Dutch men-of-war in the Bristol Channel, but their place was sufficiently taken by privateers, both those flying the Dutch flag and those sailing under a commission from Charles II. In April 1653 Thomas Skelton of Minehead took William Balthazar, ' a notorious pirate,' which in all probability means that he was sailing with a commission from Charles.[149] After the Dutch war came that with Spain, and then the Dutch made room for Biscayners and Dunkirkers. In 1656 the people of Minehead joined with those of Bideford, Barnstaple and Ilfracombe in petitioning for cruisers to protect their Irish trade from Spanish and Royalist privateers;[150] in 1657 we have a reference to an Irishman who had taken seven prizes in the Bristol Channel, so that there was clearly good reason for the request for protection.[151]

The second and third Dutch wars only brought upon Somerset the minor distresses which attend a state of hostilities. A memorandum of December 1664, just before the commencement of the war, notes that 150 seamen were available in the county, comparing with 200 in Cornwall,

---

[144] Sprigge (*Anglia Rediviva*, xii) does not positively say, but implies, that the fort had been built recently by Charles.

[145] Phelps (*Hist. of Somerset*, i, 98) says that King Road was named from the fact that William III landed there in 1690, but the name occurs on a map temp. Henry VIII.

[146] S. P. Dom. Interreg. xxxvi, 41.

[147] Ibid. 67. By ' Bristol Bay ' they probably meant part of Gloucestershire and South Wales, as well as Somerset.

[148] Ibid. xxxvii, 146.   [149] Ibid. xxxv, 109.

[150] Ibid. cxxxi. 71. There are fifteen Minehead signatures.   [151] Ibid. clvi, 1.

700 in Devon, and 300 in Dorset.[152] No doubt these figures do not represent the total number of men in the counties, but they probably indicate the relative strength. There are several references to Dutch privateers in the Bristol Channel, especially after the attack in the Medway of 1667 ; subsequently to that Ruiter sailed down to the Scillies and may have detached a few ships to sweep the Severn. However, there could have been few losses, for shortly afterwards the Minehead owners were boasting that they had not lost a single merchantman during the war.[153] As there is evidence of their trade at this time to France and Lisbon as well as to Ireland they must have been very fortunate. Somerset people, who had forgotten the experiences of their fathers, must have been startled to hear, in 1668, that there was then a ' Turkish ' pirate with two English prizes in the Bristol Channel, and that a Dutch trader had been twice forced to take refuge in an English port to escape him.[154] In 1671 Sir William Wyndham recommended Bridgwater to the Navy Commissioners as a suitable place for building war ships ; [155] Sir William was anxious to bring government work into the county, but it was peace time and there were many more convenient towns eager for the notice of the Navy Board. As a fact no man-of-war has ever been built in Somerset, unless those launched at Bristol are to be associated with it. Bridgwater could only have built men-of-war of the smallest class, and all timber and other materials especially required for them would have had to be brought there at heavy extra expense. The third Dutch war brought the usual complaints of the presence of the enemy's privateers in the Bristol Channel, but probably not many prizes were taken ; [156] the navy papers show that the *Dartmouth*, a fifth rate, was often on the station.

The heavy excise and customs necessitated by the wars of expansion which began with the Commonwealth were the cause of smuggling—which in early times had been chiefly confined to the illicit export of wool—in its modern form. Somerset was not worse behaved than most of the other counties, and certainly not as bad as some of them, but a report on it of 1682 by two surveyors of customs, William Culliford and Arnold Browne, shows that distance from the capital and loose organization gave opportunity for many irregularities or worse.[157] The subordinate officials hastened to turn king's evidences as soon as inquiry was made ; but it is evident that several of them had personal reasons for bearing witness against their superiors, and of course it was the object of Culliford and Browne to show that their zeal in investigation was justified. For whatever it may be worth, however, the report is damning enough. At Bridgwater two officers immediately gave particulars ' of several notorious frauds committed by themselves and others, the officers of this port.' They confessed to a knowledge of 101 tuns of wine and brandy and 2,357 packages of Irish linen smuggled there within three years. They took Culliford for an excursion to the mouth of the river and showed him several places where merchants were wont to run goods. The town was searched, and much wine, brandy and linen seized ; the collector was drunken and dishonest, the surveyor ' seldom or never sober,' and the average bribe was from one to five guineas. At Watchet it was found that several small vessels had no other business but that of running goods, and that the collector of customs there usually sat drinking with the masters of the ships while gangs of men were unloading them. The rate of bribe at Watchet is not stated, but when the collector, Robert Dashwood, heard that Culliford was coming he coached his subordinate, William Perry, to say that he ' was a very devil ' for strictness. Perry did tell that to Culliford, and many other things as well ; in reward he was promoted to Dashwood's post, and ' has begotten himself a general hatred ' in Watchet. Culliford noticed that the result of the free trade there was that ' from being beggars within this ten years the whole town has grown exceeding rich.' At Minehead two of the tidesmen confessed at once ; but one of them, who also kept an alehouse, afterwards denied his confession and his guilt upon an assurance from Colonel Luttrell that he should be maintained in his post. Luttrell's interference is suggestive of one of the difficulties with which the Customs' Commissioners had to contend, where influential local magnates were either interested in smuggling themselves or, for other reasons, supported incompetent or dishonest officials. At Porlock one of the two officers stationed there was suspended, so that there was no custom house in Somerset which passed the test of inquiry.

The revenue organization became more effective as time passed on, but so did the methods of the smugglers, and, as is well known, no government was able to cope successfully with the evil. By an act of 7 and 8 William III the Admiralty were ordered to maintain preventive sloops round the coast, but there was only one between Bideford and Bristol.[158] About 1698 there were twelve riding officers and a surveyor ashore watching the Bristol and Somerset seaboard ; as this compared with thirty-six officers for Kent, it is a measure of the relative innocence of the district. Of course smuggling continued during the whole of the 18th century, and there are references in local historians to evidence of its existence, but in Somerset it was never carried on to anything like

---

152 Add. MSS. 9316, fol. 79.   153 S. P. Dom. Chas. II, clxxvi, 93.
154 Ibid. ccxlvii, 206.   155 Ibid. ccc, 47.   156 Ibid. cccxxv, 88.
157 Treas. Misc. Var. 52.   158 Treas. Papers, lvi, 12.

the extent common on the east and south coasts. The demand was less, and the sources of supply were farther afield. The county is seldom mentioned in official papers during the 18th century; and when such references do occur they are connected with the acceptance by the Customs' Commissioners of a sum of money in composition from some person detected. Thus in 1729 Caleb King of Crewkerne, discovered in running brandy, paid £50 13s. 4d. in settlement. The usual result was that the compounder still made a handsome profit, but the revenue obtained something; many of these compositions were made in compliance with applications from voters, 'who cannot be refused,' in view of election possibilities. Violence and bloodshed were not infrequent in most of the counties, but little of the kind appears in Somerset. In 1770 there is a reference to the Minehead custom house having been broken into, and some seized spirits having been carried off, no doubt by the smugglers from whom they had been taken; [159] but this is a solitary instance, while lawless outbreaks occurred much more often elsewhere.

A Parliamentary Committee of 1783 reported that there were upwards of 300 English vessels continuously engaged in smuggling, besides foreign smacks, post-office packets, East Indiamen, ordinary trading ships, and fishing boats which did an occasional business. How many of either class belonged to Somerset, or how much of the 2,000,000 lb. of tea and 13,000,000 gallons of brandy supposed to be smuggled between 1780 and 1783 entered the county there is, of course, no means of ascertaining. To this date there had been only one revenue sloop in the Bristol Channel, but then the number was increased to two; the Admiralty cutters, helping the customs, employed nearly 4,500 officers and men, but the Admiralty themselves confessed that the seizures made were inconsiderable. Besides smuggling, wrecking in the Bristol Channel must have proved a steady and profitable industry; in 1752 thirty-eight vessels were known to have been lost between the Land's End and Bristol in one September gale, and minor calamities were always to be expected year by year.

The period of the Great War is that of the familiar stories of smugglers' hiding-places associated with old Somerset houses, and also of storage in churches, a legend common to many counties. Important as was the revenue question, the strain and anxieties of a world-wide war prevented the government giving to it more than a relatively perfunctory attention, but the fall of Napoleon and return of peace saw the beginning of the end of smuggling. After 1815 there were many navy men available who were not open to the intimidation, or were less amenable to the bribery, that had coerced or persuaded their civilian predecessors. The institution of the 'coast blockade' in Kent and Sussex, forming a chain of posts within hail of one another, a system which, in a modified form, was soon extended to the remaining counties, proved eventually too strong for the smugglers. Through several stages the coast blockade has developed into the present coastguard, although that is now far more a naval than a revenue force.

The wars of William III and Anne were only marked by occasional complaints about the depredations of privateers in the Bristol Channel; in 1693 Roger Hoar of Bridgwater and his partners had lost four ships there in eighteen months.[160] Somerset shipping suffered because, while not nearly rich enough in itself to tempt privateers to come into the Bristol Channel after it, it lay in the track of the Bristol trade and was of course harassed incidentally. By 1693 Bristol had lost 120 merchantmen, which is good evidence of the extent of its commerce. An Order in Council of December 1696 for the levy of 8,100 men placed 700 on Bristol and Somerset, compared with 1,300 from Devon and 350 from Cornwall, but probably nearly five-sixths of the 700 men were expected to come from Bristol. In 1698 a tour round the coast was made by the Surveyor of the Navy and others with a view to the choice of some harbour in which to establish an additional dockyard, then much needed; but Somerset offered no suitable port nor any prospect of a convenient supply of naval necessaries. The Surveyor in question was Edmund Dummer, one of the ablest among the civilian naval officials of that age, and he came of a family originally a Somerset stock.

Seeing the extent and value of the Bristol trade, it is rather surprising that no lighthouse was placed in the Bristol Channel until 1737. It is possible that in the mediaeval period lights were shown from some of the religious houses established on the islands and on both shores of the Channel, but there is no application known to have been made to the crown for a licence during the 17th century, although such licences were being freely applied for in relation to the other parts of the English coast. At the request of the Bristol merchants the Trinity House Corporation obtained a patent, dated 2 June 1737,[161] authorizing them to erect a lighthouse, to be lit with a coal fire, on Flat Holme because the navigation of the Bristol Channel was exposed to 'extreme danger by the Nass sand, the Culver, the Two Fathom sand (which is daily rising), and the two small islands called the Flat and Steep Holms, together with the Wolves, Monkstones, Welsh Hook and English Grounds, and also a new sand arising between the two Holms.' The patent says that many ships and crews had been lost for want of a lighthouse. The original powers of the Trinity House

---

[159] Home Office Papers, 27 Mar. 1770.   [160] S. P. Dom. Will. and Mary, v, 90.
[161] Pat. 10 Geo. II, pt. 1, no. 42.

permitted them to put up seamarks, beacons and lighthouses, but gave them no right to levy tolls for their support; hence the necessity for a patent when, as here, rates were to be charged. With the consent of the Bristol applicants, vessels 'going foreign' were to pay 1½d a ton, both outwards and inwards, and ships owned by aliens paid double; those trading to Ireland were charged 1d. a ton each way, and coasters 1s. for the whole voyage. Fishing boats were free.

The Trinity House Corporation immediately sub-let the light on a long lease, from September 1737, to Mr. W. Crispe at a rental of £10 a year, and perhaps the payment of a sum of money as a fine. Crispe afterwards took a Mr. Lund into partnership; the partners became bankrupt and the property passed through Caleb Dickinson into the ownership of William Dickinson, M.P., and others. In 1822 twelve years of the lease had yet to run, and by that date Parliament was giving close attention to the private lights, for which the owners received large payments as commerce had increased but still rendered very indifferent service in return. The committee of 1822 recommended the re-purchase of Flat Holme, and in March 1823 the remainder of the term was bought from Mr. Dickinson and Admiral Nichols for £16,057; the tolls were at once reduced by a half.[162] The lighthouse of stone was built by the original lessee, but even allowing for the money thus sunk the amount paid for the few years remaining of the lease is some indication of the enormous net profit made on the £10 rental and cost of maintenance. It was lit with oil from 7 September 1820.[163]

The early history of the Burnham light is a legendary one. It began as a lamp shown in the window of a fisherman's cottage, placed there by an anxious wife to guide her husband to his anchorage.[164] This must have been towards the end of the 18th century, and when the fisherman and his wife were both dead the light, poor as it was, had been found so useful that it was succeeded by a more efficient one for which some kind of licence, which cannot now be traced, must have been obtained. This was built either by John Goulden, vicar of Burnham from 1764, or by Walter Harris, who followed him in 1799. As the volume of maritime trade grew with years, the light, which was sufficient originally, did not satisfy more exacting needs, and eventually an application was made to the Trinity House to undertake the responsibility. The corporation obtained a patent of 20 May 1815 [165] which recites that 'a light which hath been for some years exhibited at Burnham opposite to the narrow channel left at half ebb between the Gore sand and the main,' was of great utility, but that the owners and masters of Bridgwater and Bristol had represented to the Trinity House that the approaches to Bridgwater were very dangerous, and had promised to pay tolls for a light. The patent does not say why they were dissatisfied with the existing conditions, and for the Trinity House it was an opportunity to get another lighthouse under their control. Only vessels going to and from Bridgwater and Bristol were to be charged; every ship from an oversea voyage going into the former port was to pay 5s. if English owned and 10s. if a foreigner; coasters paid 3s. Bristol ships trading to Ireland paid 1s. a voyage and coasters 6d.; a graduated rate, according to tonnage, was charged for vessels 'going foreign,' and in all cases it was double if they were owned abroad.

The Trinity House at once gave a ninety-nine years' lease at a rental of £1 a year, and their conduct in doing so was stigmatized by a parliamentary committee later as 'most injudicious.' As in the case of Flat Holme, the committee of 1822 recommended the re-purchase of the light, and the remaining term of eighty-five years was bought in 1829 from the holder, the Rev. David Davies, for £13,681.[166] The one thus bought was the high light; in 1832 this was rebuilt and the low light established in addition.[167] In consequence of the extra expense the tolls were not reduced as was usual when the private lighthouses came into the hands of the corporation, although such reductions were due to the close parliamentary supervision to which they were now subjected, and not to any desire to lessen their own profits.

The English and Welsh Grounds lightship was first lit on 18 July 1838; Watchet west breakwater 1862, east breakwater 1903, west groyne 1892; Blacknore Point 1894; Weston-super-Mare pier 1903; Clevedon pier 1869. The Minehead tidal light probably dates from about 1701.[168]

The earliest sea marks were hills visible from the sea, clumps of trees and church towers; the second were considered so important that any owner who cut down trees which were an accustomed sea mark was liable to a heavy fine, and of the first there are so many in Somerset that they have perhaps obviated the necessity for artificial beacons. There is none in the county belonging to the Trinity House, and, except local river marks, but one other, at Weston, put up in 1885 to show the shore end of the Commercial Telegraph Company's cable. Brent Knoll, Burnham church tower, St. Thomas' Head, Quantocks Head, West Quantock Wood, Weston-super-Mare new church, Brean Down Point, Anchor Head, Walton Castle and Uphill Church are still used as leading marks in

[162] *Parl. Papers* (1834), xii, 99.
[164] Hardy, *British Lighthouses*, 205.
[166] *Parl. Papers* (1834), xii, 98.
[168] F. Hancock, *Minehead,* 301.

[163] Ibid. (1861) xxv, 440.
[165] Pat. 55 Geo. III, pt. 7, no. 11.
[167] Ibid. 334, 348.

navigation. It is said that before the Burnham lighthouse was working the spire of East Brent Church was kept whitewashed to serve as a sea mark.

Somerset has no naval history during the wars of the middle of the 18th century and that with the American colonies. Its ports invited attack so little that no guns were mounted in them for defence against an occasional privateer, as was done with most of the others round the coast; but for casual and rare references the county might almost be supposed to have no connexion with the sea. One such reference shows that, besides supplying men for the navy, it also helped to man privateers during the war which ended in 1784. An advertisement for seamen, for the *Tartar*, captain, Aaron Floyd, a Bristol privateer, refers to the fact that the ship and captain were well known at Minehead and in the neighbourhood,[169] no doubt in consequence of previous successful voyages. The proximity of Bristol, with its great maritime trade and the attractions it offered, may have had the effect, by drawing men and capital to itself, of preventing maritime enterprise in places near at hand. The most famous of Somerset seamen, George Brydges Rodney, gained his place high in the roll of British admirals during the American war, but his story belongs to national rather than to local history.

When the Revolutionary War broke out the great need was for men. Years of ever-widening commerce and of naval victory had their effect eventually in attracting thousands of men to the sea, but at first the supply of sailors was altogether insufficient to man the royal and merchant navies. Therefore, besides the impress system, always working, and a suspension of certain sections of the Navigation Acts, Parliament sanctioned in 1795 and 1796 an experiment analogous to the ship-money project of Charles I by requiring the counties each to provide a certain number of men for the navy who were to be tempted by a bounty to be raised by an assessment charged in every parish like other local rates. In 1795 the county was called upon for 351, and in 1796 for 455 men,[170] comparing with 142 and 184 for Dorset and 192 and 252 for Cornwall. The men were not necessarily all to be seamen, but the comparative numbers show that Somerset must have been considered a prosperous county and able to pay liberal bounties. The ports also were required to procure men, an embargo being placed upon all British shipping until they were obtained; these, of course, were to be seamen. Bridgwater was assessed at twenty-six men and Minehead at eighteen; no other coast town in the county was rated.

In 1798 the need of men was greater than ever; Ireland was in revolt, the discontent which had flamed into the mutinies of 1797 was still smouldering in the fleets, the French armies were terrorizing the continent, and the battle of the Nile was not won until August. In view of the ever-present fear of invasion and the lack of men all protections from the press, for fishermen and others, were suspended in May 1798, and by an order in Council of the 14th of that month a new force, the Sea Fencibles, was created. It was raised with the intention of meeting an invading flotilla by another of the same character and for the purpose of manning the coast batteries; it was to be composed of fishermen and boatmen as well as the semi-seafaring dwellers of the shore who were not liable to impressment. The order applied to the whole of Great Britain and Ireland, but there was little or no prospect of a raid, much less of invasion, in the Bristol Channel. Even privateering had become exceptional there since the Royal Navy had increased in strength and ubiquity and, on the other hand, the Revolution had destroyed the French royal and merchant marine, thus restricting the scope and limiting the enterprise of private adventurers. The men of the Sea Fencibles were to be volunteers, and the principal inducement offered was that, while enrolled, the seafaring members were freed from the liability to be impressed; they were under the command of naval officers, and were paid 1s. a day when on service. From Hartland to King Road formed one district, and, as might be anticipated, it was one of the weakest in the kingdom, being manned by a captain, four lieutenants, and 144 men. This points to a scanty maritime population along that stretch of coast, for the South Wales and Severn districts formed much stronger sections.

We know now that not one of the French schemes of invasion had Somerset for its objective, and only one, the galley slave raid of 1797 which ended ignominiously at Fishguard, was intended for Bristol. The French accounts of the expedition note that it sighted Porlock before the Bristol idea was relinquished and it stood over to the Welsh coast. The Sea Fencibles of the British Channel were never called upon to face an enemy, nor did they impress professional observers anywhere by their efficiency. When the war was renewed in 1803 the force was reconstituted in deference to popular fears, but among Service men it was regarded with contempt as a refuge for skulkers in the lower grades and for officers with sufficient influence to obtain an easy berth ashore. The outer ring of fleets, with a great volunteer army at home, were relied upon for security until Trafalgar extinguished the possibility of invasion. That Somerset was held to be out of the zone of probable operations is shown by the fact that it was one of the few coast counties in which signal

---

[169] *Bristol Journal* (3 March 1784). [170] Exclusive of Bristol.

stations were not established during either war.   The only fortifications erected were batteries at Portishead and King Road to protect the anchorage ; these batteries date from 1799 and 1800.[171] In consequence of the report of a parliamentary committee of 1860 it was resolved to defend the Severn by a chain of forts extending across the Channel, the southernmost one being on Brean Down, two others on Steep Holme and Flat Holme, and a fourth on the Welsh coast.   These forts were commenced in 1867, and were heavily armed with the ordnance of that day ; that on Brean Down was blown up in July 1900, it is supposed by a gunner stationed there, and the batteries of Steep Holme were demolished by H.M.S. *Arrogant* in 1899 [172]

It has been noticed that no men-of-war were built in Somerset, and as, after the introduction of the gun-brig class towards the end of the 18th century, no private builder whose yard was adapted for the work need have lacked government contracts, the absence of the county builders from the construction lists is indicative of their small importance.   In 1804 there was one builder, Bailey, at Burnham ; two, Williams and another, at Bridgwater ; and one, Radford, at Minehead ; of these Williams had the largest business and employed eleven shipwrights with subsidiary workmen.

[171] W. O. Ordn. Min. Bks. 2726 ; Estimates, 30.
[172] Knight, *Seaboard of The Mendips*, 324.

SOCIAL AND ECONOMIC HISTORY

THE county of Somerset, distinguished in the old ballad as 'the flower of all the west countree,' is well watered by the Parrett, the Avon, the Brue, and the Tone, and its mild climate, rich soil, and abundant rainfall, made it from the beginning what it is now—a typically agricultural county.[1] The wide-spreading plains of the county, with their mile upon mile of rich meadow-land, are divided by hills. The vale of Taunton Deane, lying south of the Quantocks, is separated by hills from the great central plain which touches the foot of the Mendips, and north of the latter are undulating lands spreading up to Bath, and divided from the bleak uplands of Wiltshire by a forest tract. South and west of the vale of Taunton is another hilly district with Blackdown and beacon-crowned Exmoor as ramparts on the Devon border. This geographical division of the county into the three districts of mid-Somerset, the north-east, and the south-west, does not, however, coincide with the historical division into two parts, in which the River Parrett is the boundary line. Differences in the place-names, the type of settlement, and to some extent in the speech of the inhabitants of the eastern and western halves of the county, still reflect this division.

The Saxon period is marked by a deepening of the cleavage between east and west Somerset, the Parrett being the Saxon frontier for more than fifty years.[2] The type of Saxon settlement prevalent on the seashore, on the rivers, and on the frontiers of the county was a group of warriors, who in most cases did the work of agriculture personally. In these settlements the military leader was in a position of authority, and from the first there was no equality. Another type of settlement, common in the west of the county, was that of a hamlet of conquered British, who formed a dependent cultivating class; while a third form of settlement, in which the military element was less powerful and in which the Germanic tradition of equality lingered longest, was found in the plains and the defensible parts of the county.[2a]

The communities of these various types, at first isolated and independent, were forced into cohesion by the danger from the Welsh, by the attacks of

---

[1] 'The Air is nowhere sharp as in many other Counties but is everywhere so gentle and mild at all times that some have thought the County takes Name from the Summerliness of the Air . . . . an ingenious Derivation drawn from long Experience of the Softness and Pleasantness of the Air.' Camden, *Magna Brit.*

[2] A difference in physique may still be noticed, east of the Parrett the Saxon, and west of it the Celtic, type predominating. *V.C.H. Somers.* i, 376.

[2a] The manors in which there were no serfs were probably isolated survivals of the normal status of early times in the county.

the Irish Norsemen, and, later, of the Danes upon the undefended coast, and by the growth of trade. From the Burghal Hidage, which represents a scheme of West Saxon defence, five townships appear in Somerset as the military centres of the districts surrounding them, these being Watchet, Axbridge, Lyng, Langport, and Bath.[3]

The existence in Somerset before the Conquest of a system of taxation based on the five-hide unit, which had originally been responsible for sending one man to the host, explains the prevalence of the five-hide unit in the east of the county at the time of the Domesday Survey.[4] The rights of the West Saxon king included military service, fiscal and judicial rights, and in the conveyance of lands to churches or to his followers he probably conveyed part of these rights. Rent in kind was probably a commutation of the king's right of living at his subjects' expense,[5] and this developed into the 'farm of one night,' which survived in the Survey in a commuted form on the twelve manors which made up the ancient demesne.[6] Professor Maitland interprets some of Ine's laws as a reference to a settlement or plantation of some part of Somerset by large allotments to the king's gesiths, who undertook to put tillers on the soil.[7] It is clear that before the Conquest the county had a flourishing trade; references to grants of markets and fairs are frequent,[8] and there was a general diffusion of coinage, mints being already in existence at Taunton, Bruton, Ilchester, and Langport.[9] The general type of settlement was that of the manor, the actual tillers of the soil being connected with the king through a chain of intermediaries.

The physical characteristics of the Somerset mirrored in the Domesday Survey[10] were different in many respects from what they are at present. Of the five great forests of the Survey but little remains; the rich lowlands that now occupy the centre of the county were water-covered wastes, studded with scattered island settlements,[11] or reed-bearing peaty marshes. In the Survey, for instance, the produce of two plough-lands, pasture for six pigs and thirty she-goats, and a tribute of 6,000 eels from two fisheries, was all that could be returned as of value in the Abbot of Muchelney's three islands of Muchelney, Middleney, and Thorney, the swamps then surrounding them being now some of the finest meadow-land in the county.[12] In most cases the moorlands were entirely omitted as valueless, the *morae* at Wedmore, for instance, being described as of no value in the Exeter Book, are consequently

---

[3] The hidage assessed against these five is 4,813 as compared with the 2,951 of the Domesday Book. This great reduction may be explained as a necessary correction of exaggerated estimates by ascertained fact, with the addition of some equitable consideration for the declining wealth of this among other western counties owing to the ravages of the Danes and Irish pirates.

[4] J. H. Round, *Domesday Studies*, i, 120; *Feudal England*, 44; *Somers. Arch. Soc. Proc.* xlv. (2) 51; *V.C.H. Somers.* i, 386–8.

[5] The curious variety of commodities enumerated in one of the early laws suggests an attempt to avoid fluctuations of value when money was scarce. Cunningham, *Growth of Engl. Ind. and Commerce*, i, 117.

[6] Maitland, *Dom. Bk. and Beyond*, i, 238–9.   [7] Ibid.

[8] Thorpe, *Angl.-Sax. Laws;* Laws of Athelstan, no. 13, of Edward the Elder, no. 1, of Alfred, no 25. [*Anct. Laws and Inst.* (Rec. Com.), 37, 69, 88]. These early laws contain references to the slave trade centred at Bristol.

[9] Many Saxon coins have been unearthed, some of which are deposited in the museum at Taunton. Athelstan passed laws regulating mints. Laws of Athelstan, no. 14 [*Anct. Laws and Inst.* (Rec. Com.), 88].

[10] For Somerset the Survey is supplemented by the Geld Inquest of 1084 and by the Exon Domesday, which gives more details of stock. For a full discussion of the Survey, see *V.C.H. Somers.* i, 383–432.

[11] Muchelney, Athelney, Edgarley, &c., for instance, show their origin in their terminations, while Meare and Pamborough are also described as islands in the Survey.   [12] *V.C.H. Somers.* i, 468a.

ignored in the Exchequer Domesday.[13]   In the few cases where moors are mentioned the land was probably partially reclaimed.[14]   The vineyards mentioned in the Survey must have been of some value,[15] and references to them appear constantly until the 16th century.[16]

The population of Somerset in 1086 as given in the Exeter Survey was 13,307, and in the Exchequer Book was 13,764, and from this it has been calculated that there was only one person mentioned for every 79 acres,[17] but this apparent desolation compares favourably with most of the other counties of England.   Only six counties were more densely populated, while its neighbours Devon and Dorset were more sparsely inhabited with 80 and 95 acres respectively to each inhabitant recorded in Domesday.[18]

As regards comparative wealth Somerset occupied the twelfth place, a typical team-land being approximately worth 15s. 9d. annually, while a Dorset and a Devon team-land were worth respectively £1 6s. 8d. and 5s. 3d., the most valuable land in England, in the county of Kent, being worth £1 14s. 11d.[19]   It has further been calculated that the average value of the recorded hide in Somerset was £0·85, as compared with an average value of £1 over the whole of England,[20] but this apparent under-rating of Somerset was equitable, since the western part of the kingdom was much poorer than the eastern.[21]

Beneficial hidation had begun to appear in Somerset, and royal favour or justice assigned to holdings of very unequal size the payment due from one hide of land.[22]   There was great variation in the value assigned to a hide of land, the range being from 10s. at Thorn Falcon to £8 at Huntspill.[22a]   From the few cases where the acreage is named and comparative certainty is possible, it appears that arable land was worth about 2d. per acre yearly.[23]   Large amounts of pasture are often wholly neglected, but occasionally very small amounts are set down and valued.[24]   On the whole the value of land had gone up, the most striking example being that of the manor of Taunton, which had increased in value from £50 to £154 1s. 1d.[25]

The typical Somerset estate of Domesday was the manor, but the variation in size throughout the county was immense.   A Somerset manor

---

[13] *V.C.H. Somers.* i, 458a.   [14] R. W. Eyton, *Somers. Domesday*, i, 40 ; *V.C.H. Somers.* i, 455b, 458a, &c.

[15] Ibid. i, 460b, 468a.   Earlier references to vineyards are found in 956 and 962.   Birch, *Cart. Sax.* iii, 89, 324.

[16] *Bath Chartul.* (Somers. Rec. Soc.), ii, 74.   The place-names ' Vineyards ' and ' Winevats ' at Glastonbury and Bath still recall the ancient vineyards, and as late as 1701 £28 was paid for four hogsheads of wine 'of the vineyards of Claverton.'   Canon Ellacombe, ' Vineyards of Somers. and Glouc.' *Bath Field Club Proc.* (1890).

[17] Maitland, op. cit. 400–4.   The acreage upon which the calculation is based is that of the modern county.

[18] Twelve counties had more than 100 acres to each inhabitant, and the county of Stafford had 235. Ibid. 400–4.   [19] Ibid. 402–3, 412.   [20] Ibid. 463, 465.

[21] Even in 1341 this comparative poverty was still clearly marked, equal sums being paid by 1,020 acres in Wilts, 1740 in Somerset, 3,215 in Devon, and 3,550 in Cornwall.   Thorold Rogers, *Hist. of Agric. and Prices*, i, 110.

[22] e.g. the lands of Queen Edith at Milverton.   *V.C.H. Somers.* i, 440.   In the assessments of Somerset the contrast between the east and west of the county appears again ; in the former the five-hide unit is the basis of assessment, in the latter it is much less obvious, and, in fact, nearly disappears, the system being akin to that of Devon.   Ibid. 386–8.   There are many cases of increased assessment after the Conquest, which point to a general economic recovery ; *e.g.* Martock, Chewton Mendip.   Ibid. 440, 439.

[22a] Ibid. 477b, 500a.

[23] Forty-five acres of arable land at Weacombe in West Quantoxhead were worth 7s. 6d., exactly 2d. per acre, and a plough-land at Bedminster was worth 20s.   Ibid. 489a, 436b.

[24] Ibid. 486b.   [25] Ibid. 442b.

in fact varied from the little kingdom of the Bishop of Winchester at Taunton, ' the classical example of colossal manors,'[26] where many almost royal rights were in the hands of a subject, to the extremely small holdings, very sparsely populated, found in the west of the county.[27] One villein alone is mentioned on William de Mohun's manor of Exford, no stock being mentioned, while one bordar, with half a plough, is the solitary figure on another Exford estate.[28] The existence of a manor, therefore, did not presuppose the holding of a manor court or the presence of free tenants. In the later history of many places in West Somerset there is no trace of a manor court being held; in fact, such a suggestion would be grotesque in the case of many of the small vills in the west of the county, and disputes were probably settled in the courts of the hundred.[29]

Unfortunately the 13th-century Hundred Rolls for Somerset do not contain the details that are available for some other counties, and it is therefore impossible to obtain from them any figures which, compared with those of Domesday, might illustrate the spread of freedom. This comparison, however, can be made in the case of the individual manors belonging to the abbey of Glastonbury, the figures being taken from a survey of 1189.[30] On the whole the tendency was towards the spread of freedom. On the manor of East Pennard, for instance, where at the time of the Domesday Survey there had been 4 serfs, 17 villeins, 9 bordars, and 10 cottars, there were in 1189 3 free tenants, 57 villein tenants, and no *servi*,[31] and this evidence is borne out all over the Glastonbury estates.[32]

The difference between the 12th century and the 13th was too slight to warrant separate treatment. The one difference which lends itself to generalization is that commutation of military service for a money payment was much rarer in the 12th century than in the 13th.[33] There had been a great tendency towards the subdivision of fiefs, and holdings of one-fifth, one-fifteenth, or even one-twentieth of a knight's fee were common;[34] but on the other hand there were many large fiefs, which owed the service of $32\frac{1}{2}$, or of $40\frac{1}{2}$ knights.[35] Some free tenants holding by military service owed in addition other personal services or rents, such as being constable ' when the lord wills,' or paying 50 ploughshares annually.[36]

Tenure by serjeanty, of which there are a few examples in the Survey, was fairly common later. The various serjeanties include carrying a towel before the queen at Easter, Whitsuntide, Christmas, and the king's coronation,[37] performing the same service for the king on Whit Sunday,[38] keeping the

---

[26] Maitland, op. cit. 276.

[27] The west is ' the land of small hamlets, the old Celtic influences have not been overlaid by the Germanic tendency to nucleated villages.' Maitland, op. cit. 15.

[28] Maitland, op. cit. 116–20 ; *V.C.H. Somers.* i, 490, 503.

[29] Maitland, op. cit. 19–21. The average vill in the hundred of Carhampton had about half a dozen villeins and no freemen. In that district the village community cannot have been a very highly organized entity, and elaborate regulation of the business of agriculture by manorial courts was neither necessary nor possible when the lord and one villein were the only holders of the land.

[30] *Glaston. Inq.* 1189 (Roxburghe Club).

[31] *V.C.H. Somers.* i, 464 ; *Glaston. Inq.* 40.

[32] e.g. Batcombe, *V.C.H.* i, 465 ; *Glaston. Inq.* 34.

[33] *Glaston. Inq. passim ; Custumaria of Glaston.* (Somers. Rec. Soc.), 23.

[34] *Cal. Inq. p.m. Edw. I,* 174–8.   [35] *Testa de Nevill* (Rec. Com.), 161*b*, 162.

[36] *Glaston. Inq.* 5, 6.   [37] *Testa de Nevill* (Rec. Com.), 162*b*.

[38] *Hund. R.* (Rec. Com.), 121*b*, 140*b*.

king's hawks,[39] making the bread of the king within the hundred,[40] buying what is necessary for the king's kitchen,[41] weighing money at the king's exchequer,[42] filling the offices of chamberlain-in-chief,[43] of sergeant of the king's kitchen, of baker, of doorkeeper, and of usher of the great hall.[44] Many of the serjeanties were held by personal services of a military character, such as finding a man and horse with a sack and a battle-axe at the summons of the king for his army in Wales, or finding one knight for fifteen days in England,[45] the service due being sometimes very vague, land being held by following the king in the army [46] or by service 'with his body.' [47] Most curious of all were the conditions attached to land in Holnicote, which was held of the king by the service of hanging on a certain forked tree-trunk the bodies of the stags dying of murrain in Exmoor Forest, and of entertaining the poor, aged, and infirm for the benefit of the souls of King Edward's ancestors.[48]

A tenure which seems to have approximated closely to serjeanty—that is, holding by royal service—is frequently found in Somerset, and the term denoted some well-ascertained obligation. Thus the manor of Norton was held by the royal service due from 2 hides of land.[49]

Somerset furnishes many examples of tenure in frankalmoign, sometimes accompanied by a money rent, as in the case of the hundred and barton of Bath held by the prior in free alms and by the rent of £20 yearly.[50] The Abbot of Athelney held all his lands ' by his prayers for the king.' [51] But the grant of land in free alms was occasionally coupled with burdensome obligations. Certain land was granted to Bath Priory in free alms, but the prior was bound to pay a yearly rent of 3s. 6d., to maintain the lights in Bath Church, to widen one of the city gates, make a road through a close to the priory mill, and build a new parish church of St. James in place of the old one, which had been appropriated by the bishop as a private chapel.[52]

Tenure by barony was common in cases where a number of manors were held by one man ; the manor of Stowey, for instance, the head of the barony of that name, was held in this way, rendering the service of two knights, ' when the king goes forth with the army.' [53] The Bishop of Winchester held his great Taunton estates by barony, and his almost royal authority there included the return of writs, the assize of bread and ale, view of frankpledge, and the power of erecting a gallows. All these rights he held *per antiquam tenuram*, and as belonging to his barony from time immemorial.[54] The great franchise of the Bishop of Bath, also held by barony, was warranted by royal charter.[55]

Many Somerset estates were held by honorary tenures, rents of pepper [56] or cummin [57] being the most common ; while other rents frequently found

[39] *Testa de Nevill* (Rec. Com.), 161*b*.　　　[40] Ibid. 166.　　　[41] Ibid.

[42] Ibid. 171.　　　[43] Ibid. 164.

[44] Ibid. 162*b*, 164, 171 ; and *Cal. Inq. p.m. Edw. I*, 436 ; Chan. Inq. p.m. incert. temp. Hen. III, no. 123.　　　[45] *Testa de Nevill* (Rec. Com.), 162, 161*b*.　　　[46] *Cal. Inq. p.m. Edw. I*, 95.

[47] *Testa de Nevill* (Rec. Com.), 161*b*.　　　[48] Chan. Inq. p.m. 35 Edw. I, no. 1.

[49] *Hund. R.* (Rec. Com.), ii, 119*b*.　　Other instances of this tenure are found as follows :—*Testa de Nevill* (Rec. Com.), 161*b* ; *Cal. Inq. p.m. Edw. I*, 98 ; *Glaston. Inq.* 64, 107.

[50] *Testa de Nevill* (Rec. Com.), 161*b*.　　　[51] Ibid. 163.　　　[52] *Cal. Chart. R.* 1257–1300, p. 219.

[53] *Cal. Inq. p.m. Hen. III*, 145 ; Chan. Inq. p.m. 47 Hen. III, no. 11.

[54] *Testa de Nevill* (Rec. Com.), 162 *seq.* ; *Hund. R.* (Rec. Com.), ii, 125*b*.　　　[55] Ibid. 119*b*.

[56] *Bath Chartul.* (Somers. Rec. Soc.), ii, 5.

[57] *Cal. Inq. p.m. Hen. III*, 54 ; *Muchelney and Athelney Chartul.* (Somers. Rec. Soc.), 85.

are gilded spurs,[58] a sparrow hawk,[59] a pair of gloves,[60] a peppercorn,[61] and an orphray.[62] Another honorary tenure was that of laying a garland of roses on the altar of the church at midsummer.[63]

A form of tenure which was becoming increasingly common was the holding of land by the payment of rent alone. The average rent of a virgate varied between 2s. and 5s., the rent of a hide was about 20s.[64]

Rents in kind were frequently found. Honey and salmon rents were common; one hide for instance was held by the rent of thirty salmon and two sesters of honey payable at the abbot's kitchen at Glastonbury on the feast of the Assumption B.V.M.[65] Land in the marshes round Langport returned the appropriate rent of twenty stick of eels (price 4s.) and Stone Easton rendered to the king a sextary of spiced wine (*vini galioferrati*).[66] Many manors paid rents in grain. Cathanger owed one quarter each of wheat, barley, and beans, and two quarters of oats.[67] The monks of Montacute held land by a rent of one monk's gown and one pair of monk's boots yearly.[68] Other rents were 10 horse-loads of salt, 1 pound of incense, a buck and a fawn, and rents of wax and oil, of iron for the lord's plough, shoes for his plough-horses or oxen, and finished ploughshares were common.[69]

The rent due from a manor usually included two distinct payments, *gabulum* and *donum*. The latter, originally a free gift, had become as compulsory as rent itself;[70] the *donum assisum* being a certain sum due from the whole manor and levied from individuals in proportion to their holdings, e.g. 'Omnes simul dant de dono xl solidos secundum terras quas tenent.'[71]

Rents in money or kind were by no means the only contributions made by free tenants. They owed labour services as well, but the amount due from them was fixed and certain. One free tenant of Glastonbury, for instance, had to carry hay and corn once and owed one ploughing of wheat, one of barley, and one of fallow land; another held by the service of going with the monks on horseback (apparently as a riding knight or guard),[72] while a third held a hide of land with two daily allowances of food (one a monk's portion and the other a servant's portion) by finding a worker in gold (*aurifabrum*) for the abbey.[73] Certain rights and privileges or obligations were attached by custom to some of the free holdings. One tenant who held five knights' fees had the privilege of bringing in the first dish to the

---

[58] *Feud. Aids*, iv, 290–1; *Muchelney and Athelney Chartul.* (Somers. Rec. Soc.), 174.
[59] *Cal. Inq. p.m. Hen. III*, 54, 78. The sparrow hawk is valued at 4s. [60] Ibid. 54.
[61] Rev. W. Buckler, *Ilchester Almshouse D.* 1200–1625, p. 45.
[62] *Bruton and Montacute Chartul.* (Somers. Rec. Soc. viii), 43. Other common rents were roses, carnations, and white wands.
[63] *MSS. of D. and C. of Wells* (Hist. MSS. Com.), i, 410.
[64] *Glaston. Inq.* 1, 5, 6. Rent was occasionally reckoned in bezants, which were worth about 2s. *Bath Chartul.* ii, 4.
[65] *Glaston. Inq.* 3. According to Adam de Domerham a 12th-century abbot arranged the salmon rents to improve the monks' diet, and to enable them to keep high festivals with greater hospitality and cheerfulness. Ibid. 2, 145.
[66] *Hund. R.* (Rec. Com.), ii, 122.; *Cal. Inq. p.m. Hen. III*, 293. [67] Ibid. i, 54.
[68] *Bruton and Montacute Chartul.* (Somers. Rec. Soc.), 180, 181.
[69] *MSS. of D. and C. of Wells* (Hist. MSS. Com.), i, 335; *Bath Chartul.* ii, 1, 2, 3, 7; *Muchelney and Athelney Chartul.* 73.
[70] 'Debet dare de dono' is the phrase that appears in the *Glaston. Inq.* 5.
[71] Ibid. 115; see also pp. 29, 33, 39.
[72] The agreement was that if the monks travelled outside the county they should bear the cost; in other cases he paid his own expenses. [73] *Glaston. Inq.* 3, 4, 5.

Abbot of Glastonbury on Christmas Day, remaining to dine with him if invited, and if not, going dinnerless away.

The free tenants, of course, owed suit at the courts of the lord of the manor, the hundred courts and the county court, in addition to homage and reliefs, while their lords had the wardship and marriage of their heirs.

The tenants in socage, usually found on the manors which formed part of the ancient royal demesne or on Church lands,[74] form a link between freeholders and villeins. They drew near to the unfree status in their payment of hidage, tallage, and heriots, and fines for the marriage of their children, but they are invariably classed as freemen,[75] and the services due from them, though similar in nature to the services due from villeins, differed from them in being fixed and certain.

The Domesday classes of *villani, bordarii, cotarii, coliberti,* and *servi* had undergone a change to which attention is directed by the difference in nomenclature. Nothing more is heard of the *bordarii* and *coliberti,* and the name *villani* is used as a generic term to cover all the unfree cultivators, that is the great class of customary tenants, which included some who were almost free and some who were almost slaves. In Somerset those who held in villeinage are usually classified as virgaters, who cultivated 30 acres; half virgaters, with 15 acres; ferdellers, who held a ferdel or furlong; and cottars, with about 5 acres of land.[76] The terms *nativi, servi, rustici* seem to have been applied indiscriminately to all the unfree class.[77] The nomenclature varied in different parts of the county, but the underlying theory, which drew a deep line between the free and the unfree—however closely the actual conditions of their lives approached each other—is never lost sight of.[78]

A special class of 'privileged villeins' is found on the ancient royal demesne, which was interpreted as the land vested in the Crown at the time of the Conquest, and which therefore included land that since had passed into private hands by royal grant. They were liable to the ordinary villein services, but the amount of them was certain, and their privileges included comparative fixity of tenure, exemption from attendance at the shire and hundred courts, from the payment of danegeld, amercements, and murder fines, from tolls at markets and fairs, from the payment of tallage when demanded from the rest of the county, from the sheriffs' jurisdiction, and from certain county burdens, such as the liability to contribute for the maintenance of roads and bridges, &c.[79]

The actual conditions of life on a Somerset manor in the 13th century depended to a large extent upon the lord's interpretation of the nature of the flexible bond that bound the little community together. The rank of the

[74] *Cal. Inq. p.m. Hen. III,* 82 ; *Edw. I,* 70, 238 ; *MSS. of D. and C. of Wells* (Hist. MSS. Com.), i, 332.
[75] The usual expression is 'holding in free socage,' and they did homage like freemen for their lands ; *Cal. Inq. p.m. Hen. III,* 82 ; *Edw. I,* 168.
[76] The land measures used on the Glastonbury manors varied from this common type, and were as follows :—10 acres = 1 furlong or ferdel ; 40 acres or 4 furlongs = 1 virgate ; 4 virgates or 160 acres = 1 hide ; 4 hides or 640 acres = 1 knight's fee. *Glaston. Inq.* (Roxburghe Club), 145. At Dunster and Minehead the half virgate comprised 24 acres and the ferling 12 acres. Maxwell-Lyte, *Hist. of Dunster,* 314.
[77] Legal theory recognized no distinction of status among the serfs, *servus, villanus,* and *nativus* being equivalent terms, but the latter term was most frequently applied to those who were born in a servile state. Vinogradoff, *Villainage in Engl.* 45.
[78] The form of conveyance reflected the distinction, and the villein swore fealty in a different form from that prescribed for the freeman. *Glaston. Inq.* 143.
[79] Maitland, *Bracton's Note Bk.* iii, 209 ; Vinogradoff, *Villainage in Engl.* 88.

lord, varied from that of the Bishop of Winchester or the Abbot of Glastonbury, who ruled many of their manors as absentee landlords through their stewards, down to the small landowner who owned only one estate and personally attended to its business; but the same system of management was almost universal throughout the county.

The Somerset manor-house was usually placed in the centre of the village, which itself stood in the midst of the common fields. It was generally built round a quadrangle, and before the 15th century usually consisted of a hall occupying most of the ground floor, with a bower or parlour opening from it. A long dormitory occupied the floor above, the wings of the building contained the various offices, kitchen, buttery, porter's lodge, cellar, &c., while the bartons and rickyards, barns, granaries and stables, cattle sheds and dovecotes, were quite near.[80] The chapel was a feature of the larger manor-houses, and the chartularies of Bath, Montacute, Bruton, Athelney and Muchelney contain many notices of licences for lords of manors to have their private chapels, a proviso being added as to the duty of occasionally attending the parish church.

The furniture of the manor-house was rude. Early inventories include trestle tables, stools, a few chairs and chests, and the necessary kitchen and household utensils, while the floors were strewn with rushes. Round the manor-house lay a few closes of choice meadow-land,[81] while beyond were the houses of the tenantry, which were merely wattle and mud huts, lacking even appliances for baking, a fact which explains the frequency of references to the common oven of the manor. All round the village lay the open arable fields, usually three in number, which were divided into strips in the usual manner.[82] Though the two-field system was still prevalent in some parts of the county it was rapidly giving place to the three-field system,[83] but the system of division seems to have been the same in both cases. The holdings of the lord and of the individual tenants were scattered up and down the common fields and intermingled in a manner which made the description of land in deeds of gift and the like a tedious affair.[84]

In many manors a few closes of pasture for the milch cattle lay on the outskirts of the arable land. The valuable meadow-land was sometimes owned by the lord and his tenants jointly, according to the strip system that

[80] Chan. Inq. p.m. 30 Hen. III, no. 33; 33 Hen. III, no. 41; 38 Hen. III, no. 43; 50 Hen. III. no. 30; 1 Edw. I, no. 16; 7 Edw. I, no. 13; 30 Edw. I, no. 33; 4 Edw. III, no. 28. *Pipe R. of Bishopric of Winton.* (ed. Hall), xxviii, xxix. Comparatively few of these 13th and 14th-century manor-houses remain, but the old hall can be identified at Sutton Court, and parts of 14th-century manor-houses may be seen at Meare, Martock, Compton Dundon, Clevedon, Doulting, Clapton-in-Gordano, and Cannington. At Muchelney, Bratton, Dunster, Glastonbury, Lytes Cary, and Wells there are remains of domestic architecture of this period.
[81] Eight acres of meadow within the close made around the new grange are mentioned. *Muchelney and Athelney Chartul.* 80.
[82] *Custumaria of Glaston.* (Somers. Rec. Soc.), 40; *Bath Chartul.* ii, 63–4. For a description of the strip system see Cunningham, op. cit.; *Journ. Brit. Arch. Assoc.* xiii, 147. Examples of the land measures in use and of the varying nomenclature in different parts of the county may be found as follows: *Glaston. Inq.* 2, 21, 37, 66; *Custumaria of Glaston.* (Somers. Rec. Soc.), 29, 40, 55, 68, 71; *Muchelney and Athelney Chartul.* 63, 68, 71; *Bruton and Montacute Chartul.* ii, 45; Rev. W. Buckler, op. cit. i.
[83] *Bruton and Montacute Chartul.* 52, 53; *Muchelney and Athelney Chartul.* 71. The two-field system survived at Charlton Adam, which belonged to Bruton Priory. *Bruton and Montacute Chartul.* 44–5.
[84] *Bruton and Montacute Chartul.* 91; *Bath Chartul.* ii, 100; *Muchelney and Athelney Chartul.* 68. A grant of land in the Bruton Chartulary takes up 2½ pages of print, the separate strips being identified by their position between those of neighbours—e.g. a certain acre lying between the land of Michael Berd and the land of Roger le Blake; while in another grant 31 pieces of land, the largest of which is 2½ acres, had to be elaborately described.

governed the division of the arable, but in other cases the lord's demesne meadows lay apart and were inclosed in his park.[85]   In any case a small piece of meadow-land usually accompanied every holding of arable.   On the outskirts of the manor were the common pasture, waste, and woodland, over which the lord and his tenants, both free and villein, had grazing rights in proportion to the size of their holdings.   Separate grants of pasture for a stated number of beasts, or of pannage in the woods for a limited number of pigs, were frequent during the 12th and 13th centuries.[86]   Bruton Priory, for instance, obtained in the 13th century a grant of a virgate of land, with pasture for six oxen, one plough-beast, six cows with their calves of two years, ten hogs quit of pannage, and 100 sheep with their lambs of one year.[87] The tenants also had the right to pasture their cattle on the stubble in the arable fields after the harvest, and on the common meadows after the hay was carried, the phrase 'common of pasture' being used to describe all these rights.[88]   Common pasture rights for limited periods were sometimes the subject of grants ; for instance, the Priory of Bruton had a grant of this kind one week out of every three.   Disputes as to pasture rights were a frequent cause of litigation in this early period.[89]   The sheriff, on behalf of the king, is found making an unsuccessful attempt to restrict the rights of the Abbot of Athelney and his men in Kingsmoor.[90]   Common of pasture included, besides grazing rights on the woodland and waste, the privilege of cutting underwood and brushwood and a certain amount of timber, the terms *husbote, heybote, wainbote*, &c., being used to determine the exact character of the right.   The right of taking larger timber, such as a log of wood at Christmas, or so many oaks, usually formed the subject of a special grant. Over the whole waste and woodland the lord had hunting rights, and there were many charters of free warren granted to knights and churchmen, great nobles and small landowners in Somerset.[91]

Almost every Somerset manor had its mill, water-mills being those most commonly found, and the profits of the mill came from the tolls paid by the tenants for grinding their corn there, as they were bound to do. Later, the mill was usually farmed by the miller at a yearly rent, the grinding of the lord's corn being done without payment.[92]   Any weirs or fisheries on the manor were the property of the lord.   The most common in Somerset were eel fisheries on the great undrained moors, though the frequency of salmon rents points to river fisheries.[93]   The valuable fishery of the

[85] *Muchelney and Athelney Chartul.* 108 ; Chan. Inq. p.m. 35 Hen. III, no. 40 ; 13 Edw. I, no. 20 ; 27 Edw. I, no. 71 ; 34 Edw. I, no. 54 ; e.g. 10 acres of land and one-third of 2 acres of meadow ; *Bath Chartul.* ii, 39 ; 2 virgates of land and 2 acres of meadow ; *Muchelney and Athelney Chartul.* 153 ; and *passim*. Leases of meadow-land appear early ; *Bath Chartul.* ii, 99.

[86] e.g. pasture for 100 pigs every year in Selwood Forest. *Bruton and Montacute Chartul.* 2 ; *Bath Chartul.* i, 64.   [87] *Bruton and Montacute Chartul.* 72.

[88] Ibid. 52–3.   At Babcary, for instance, it was decided by the verdict of a jury that common of pasture in Babcary included the right of feeding the cattle on 80 acres of arable land which lay fallow all through the year, on the remaining 160 acres from harvest to seed time, on 16 acres of meadow after the hay was carried, and on 10 acres of pasture all the year round.

[89] *Somers. Pleas* (Somers. Rec. Soc.), *passim*.

[90] *Muchelney and Athelney Chartul.* 128–9, 191.

[91] *Cal. of Chart. R.* 1226–57 ; 1257–1300, *passim* ; MSS. *of D. and C. of Wells* (Hist. MSS. Com.), 185, 247, 272 ; Inq. p.m. 37 Hen. III, no. 12.   See also article on 'Forestry,' below.

[92] *Muchelney and Athelney Chartul.* 88 ; *Bruton and Montacute Chartul.* 176.   In the latter it is recorded that the monks had the right to break or weaken the mill pool if the miller failed to pay his rent.

[93] Fisheries of 6,000 eels, worth 20s., are mentioned in 1180. *Muchelney and Athelney Chartul.* 165.

Abbot of Glastonbury in Meare is mentioned down to the date of the Dissolution.[94]

The lord of a manor and his men were bound together by a complicated network of rights and obligations. Of all these rights and duties of the villein the liability to agricultural service was the most important. The cultivation of the lord's demesne depended almost entirely upon the labour services due from the various classes of tenants. These services included almost every kind of agricultural labour, of which ploughing, harrowing, reaping, mowing and carrying were the most important, while the variety of minor labour works due was almost endless.

The passage of time brought a greater definition of services. In 1189, for instance, the labour services of a virgater in Street were apportioned in the four quarters of the year. Between Michaelmas and Christmas he had to plough and harrow 1 acre every day, and do three 'precariae,' 'with what cattle he had in the plough.' He had to carry loads to Glastonbury every week as often as necessary, and to do one handwork every week. In the second and third quarters of the year he owed the ploughing of half an acre every week, and two handworks every week with one boon day in each quarter at the lord's request. Finally, from the Feast of St. John to Michaelmas, he had to work every week-day except Saturday, plough 3 acres 'ad bederipe,' and load at any time.[95]

About fifty years later the daily work due, in the last quarter of the year, for instance, is defined as mowing until dinner-time every day, except Saturdays and feast days, until all the lord's meadow has been cut, and after dinner carrying hay from the meadow.[96] His services at harvest are fixed as reaping 3 acres when requested, and carrying half the corn from them to the abbot's grange. It is also provided that when he is neither reaping, carrying, nor stacking, he owes a day's handwork every day. In the first quarter of the year, whenever the weather was too bad for ploughing, the virgater was to do three extra handworks instead, and when ploughing all his cattle must be joined to the lord's plough. It is significant that the phrase 'carrying loads to Glastonbury whenever necessary'—a vague burden which might lead to much exaction—had become 'carrying loads in his turn' in the later record. The latter also provides for holidays at feast days and in Whit-week, and gives elaborate details of allowances of food and drink, which are wanting in the 1189 account.[97]

Next in order came the class of half-virgaters, who owed about half the rent and half the services, and below them the ferdellers, usually five-acre men, and cottars owing rent and services in proportion.[98] The small holdings and comparatively light services of the latter cannot have taken up all their time, and from them was obtained the extra labour required almost from the first on the demesne lands of the lord. They usually owed services on a certain day of the week, and were later known as Mondaymen. The class of cotsetlers found on some manors owed very light services, as, for instance, folding sheep.[99]

[94] Glaston. Inq.; Custumaria of Glaston. (Somers. Rec. Soc.) ; Adam de Domerham, Hist. Glaston. ii, 333–51.
[95] Glaston. Inq. 62.
[96] The comparison is valuable, the same holding being in the hands of the son of the earlier tenant.
[97] Custumaria of Glaston. 12–15.
[98] Ibid.; Glaston. Inq. 61–3, 77, &c.
[99] The term 'cotsetle' connoted a known amount of land. Glaston. Inq. iii, 114, 137.

SOCIAL AND ECONOMIC HISTORY

Among the other labour services owed by the villein tenant were threshing and winnowing specified amounts of corn—for instance, one-tenth of a heaped quarter of wheat before Christmas and 4 bushels of oats after Christmas[100]—being present to superintend the mowing of the common meadow in white gloves and with a white rod in his hand, and making hurdles for the sheepfold from stakes and saplings. Other services were fencing, trenching, carrying brushwood, covering the rick, making a water leat, scouring pools and ditches.[101]

One man held a few acres by the service of 'providing a boat which was to carry eight men, and being steersman of this boat to carry the lord abbot wherever he wills on the water at Meare, Brent, Butleigh, Andersea, Godneye, and la Bowe, with his men and kitchen, and huntsmen with their dogs.' The same man had to carry the writs of the abbot, guard his vineyards, summon the tithings to the abbot's court, collect fines, help the bailiffs of the court, follow the cellarer of Glastonbury 'when he goes fishing at Meare,' oversee fishing and arrest fishermen, oversee all the abbot's boats, fish every day in Lent and take what he caught to the abbot's kitchen, guard the bodies of those found drowned until viewed by the coroners, and help to carry 'the offering of St. Dunstan' to Wells—to perform all of which services he must have required considerable versatility.[102]

Allowances of food at harvest time were general. At the boon ploughing for the winter wheat two meals a day were allowed, a breakfast of beer, bread, and cheese, and a dinner of the same with a dish of fish or meat added.[103]

Custom assigned to the labourers, especially at harvest and haymaking, small rewards in kind, known as the *averoc* or *haveroc*.[104] The reapers at North Curry had as their averoc one sheaf 'made with a band long enough to go twice round the reeve's head,' and a haymaker had as much grass as he could lift from the ground with his scythe. The man who made hurdles could take thirty cut saplings, and the hayward received a '*medkniche*,' that is as much hay as he could raise to his mid knee.[105]

On a great many Somerset manors, especially on church lands, the lord gave a *gestum* or feast in his hall on Christmas Day, followed by a *medale* on the following day.[106] All his tenants, free and villein, had the right of being present, and their allowances of food, and even their seats in the hall, were minutely defined by custom. The *hundredarius* of North Curry, who received and executed the king's writs, had a sumptuous *gestum*. He could take two men with him to share two white loaves of wheat and a cheese, with as much good beer as they liked to drink as long as daylight lasted, a good dish of beef with mustard, another of *broweti de gallinis* (apparently the mediaeval form of fricassee of chicken), fuel to cook his allowance and that of the other tenants, candles, and firing, with liberty 'to sit if they pleased

---

[100] *MSS. of D. and C. of Wells* (Hist. MSS. Com.), i, 336.

[101] Ibid. i, 327, 331–6, 342, 346–51 ; *Glaston. Inq.* and *Custumaria of Glaston. passim.*

[102] *Custumaria of Glaston.* 177.

[103] *MSS. of D. and C. of Wells* (Hist. MSS. Com.), i, 342. Harrowing 'ad preces' was known as 'bedhurch.'

[104] The name comes possibly from 'overhook'—as much as will cover the hook. *Glaston. Inq. passim.* An 'averocacra' is mentioned at Ilchester. Rev. W. Buckler, *Ilchester Almshouse D.* 67.

[105] *MSS. of D. and C. of Wells* (Hist. MSS. Com.), i, 327–42.

[106] Ibid. 329–34 ; *Custumaria of Glaston.*

and drink as long as two candles burning one after another shall last.' Another tenant of the same manor had to bring his own cloth, cup, and trencher to the *gestum*, taking away in his cloth anything that was left. Apparently games were played after the *gestum*, one being mentioned as ' the ancient Christmas game played with a wastel.' [107]

In addition to rent and labour services the lord could demand from his tenants a great number of payments. On the death of the tenant a heriot was due, which was the best living beast, or, in default of that, the crop from the best acre of land.[108] Merchet, a fine paid on the marriage of a daughter, which was apparently proportionate to the financial position of the tenant, was a typically servile burden, as was also the fine for having a son ordained.[109] Reliefs, usually a year's rent of the tenement, were payable when a free tenant took up the estate of his ancestor ; [110] and fines were paid on alienation of the holdings.[111] Chevage or *capitagium*, apparently a poll-tax, was sometimes paid in kind ; on Bicknoller Manor, for instance, it took the form of a ' slabbe of iron ' from each tenant.[112] *Auxilium*, a yearly tax on the villeins laid primarily on the whole township,[113] tallage and hidage, and a great many other payments were also due. Among these were Peter's penny, or hearthpenny, and *churset*. The latter, a payment usually made in hens, occasionally in corn, and in one case by half a day's work, was due from nearly every householder, and was said to be of British origin ; [114] it was paid into the lord's court and was not devoted to ecclesiastical uses.[115] Other payments were *lardarium*, *lardersilver* or lard money,[116] *faldicium*, a due for the maintenance of the lord's sheepfold, *hurtpenny*, *wodegable*, *wardpenny*, *lesesilver*, *grasshurthe* (a payment in lieu of ploughing grass-land), *taberna*, a fee paid in kind at each brewing of ale, *multura*, payment for grinding at the lord's mill, and payments for pannage and *morright*.[117] Custom also regulated the payment of certain offerings on festivals ; for instance, a bushel of wheat at Easter, a cheese on Ascension Day, ' one penny towards a sheep ' at Hockday, and a great variety of other payments on the same day. Offerings known as Martin's wheat were rendered on the feast of St. Martin.[118]

[107] *MSS. of D. and C. of Wells*, i, 332, 335. See also *Pipe R. of Bishopric of Winchester* (ed. Hall), 72–3, for description of yearly feast at Rimpton.

[108] Ibid. 334. The heriot was probably of Saxon origin, the arms and horse of the warrior being surrendered to be passed on to his successor.

[109] *Bath Chartul.* ii, 166–7. In the case of certain tenants in villeinage on the manor of North Curry we are told that they might marry their daughters, and have their sons ordained without licence of their lord, while some might do the latter only. *MSS. of D. and C. of Wells* (Hist. MSS. Com.), i, 333–5.

[110] *Glaston. Inq.* 6. Sometimes two years' rent was payable, and in one case half an ounce of gold was the relief due. *MSS. of D. and C. of Wells* (Hist. MSS. Com.), i, 327 ; *Bath Chartul.* i, 64.

[111] *Glaston. Inq. ; Glaston. Rentals and Surv.*

[112] *MSS. of D. and C. of Wells* (Hist. MSS. Com.), i, 346.

[113] Vinogradoff, *Villainage in Engl.* 293.

[114] *Glaston. Inq.* 40, 65, 74, 77. In one case a woman sowed half an acre for churset. Ibid. 23 ; *MSS. of D. and C. of Wells* (Hist. MSS. Com.), i, 330 ; *Cal. Inq. p.m. Edw. I,* 233 ; *Custumaria of Glaston.* 12. The whole manor of Pilton was liable for 100 hens as churset.

[115] There is in the Glastonbury Rentals a note that the churset due from a married man was 2 bushels of wheat, one bushel being due from a widower. *Custumaria of Glaston.* 12–15.

[116] *MSS. of D. and C. of Wells* (Hist. MSS. Com.), i, 347 ; *Custumaria of Glaston.* 12–15.

[117] *Custumaria of Glaston.* 35, 109, 212, &c. ; *Glaston. Inq.* 77, &c. ; *MSS. of D. and C. of Wells* (Hist. MSS. Com.), i, 327–30. A payment of ½d. for each pig killed is also found ; ibid. 330. *Stanegrist*, for which a sum of 12d. was paid, is found only once, and it has been suggested that it was a fee paid for the right of plying a grindstone for hire. *Custumaria of Glaston.* 224, 256.

[118] *Hist. MSS. Com. Rep.* x, App. iii, 158 ; *Glaston. Inq.* 65, 70, 77, 133 ; *Cal. Inq. p.m. Edw. I,* 18, 233 ; *Testa de Nevill* (Rec. Com.), 174b.

Another form of service was the liability of the villein to serve as one of the manor officials if chosen by his fellows. These officials were the steward, the bailiff, the reeve, the *berebrittus*, and the hayward,[119] the last three being elected by their fellow villeins in the manor court.[120] The reeve was responsible for the cultivation of the arable land, especially the direction of the reaping, and his remuneration consisted of exemption from the payment of rent during his year of office, the assignment of certain pieces of arable land and of pasture rights, and special allowances of food and fodder.[121] Among the other privileges of the reeve was that of having meat and drink from the lord from August 'until all the corn and hay is in the grange,' with pasture for his draught horse in the summer, and hay in the winter. The bailiff had very similar duties to the reeve, but, though usually one of the villein tenants,[122] he was appointed by the lord to act on his behalf as a check on the reeve.[123] His exemptions and allowances were like those of the reeve.[124] The duties of the *berebrittus* are not very clearly defined, but he had some authority over the threshers. His allowances were similar to, though smaller than, those of the reeve, while he had no provision for his horse.[125] The hayward had special duties at hay-making as overseer of the work done by the customary tenants. He was also responsible for the maintenance of fences and hedges and for the impounding of strays.[126]

Almost from the first the skilled labour required on the manor was provided by certain tenants, who in return for work of this specialized character were exempted wholly or in part from ordinary services and from the payment of rent, while food allowances and special pieces of land were assigned to them. Such were the ploughmen, plough-drivers, carters, swineherds, millers, cowmen, woodwards, moorwards, parkers, foresters, shepherds, huntsmen, smiths, gardeners, and carpenters. The *catchpollus, hundredarius,* and *brevitor,* are also mentioned.[127]

At Glastonbury there was a special manor official in charge of the bridges, known as the *pontarius*,[128] and the abbey also gave permanent employment to a gold-worker, who held a virgate of land by rent and by doing goldsmith's work in the church of Glastonbury, and by mending the clock,[129] to the *vannator* who was also a master-brewer, to four gardeners, a hoopmaker, a charcoal burner, the master of the vineyards, and a washerwoman.[130]

---

[119] The word 'messor' is usually thus translated.

[120] *MSS. of D. and C. of Wells* (Hist. MSS. Com.), i, 333–4.

[121] To one reeve, for instance, was assigned the best acre of the lord's wheat he could find except the 'compostum' and 'faldicium,' and one 'stallum' of hay up to his loins. The land allotted to the reeve was known as 'reveland.' *Custumaria of Glaston.* 6, 18, 64, 106, 140.

[122] *MSS. of D. and C. of Wells.* (Hist. MSS. Com.), i, 347.

[123] He saw that the villeins did the proper amount of ploughing and that they did not unyoke their oxen until the day was over.

[124] Ibid. 343. An appointment of a bailiff dated 1333 contained the provision that the bailiff was to make good any damage to wood or meadow caused by his negligence. *Bath Chartul.* ii, 114, 141.

[125] *MSS. of D. and C. of Wells* (Hist. MSS. Com.), i, 334 ; *Custumaria of Glaston.* 118 ; Maxwell-Lyte, *Hist. of Dunster,* 323.

[126] His allotted land was known as 'bedelmede,' and at the reaping he had a sheat from every *corrigia*. *Custumaria of Glaston.* 108.

[127] *MSS. of D. and C. of Wells* (Hist. MSS. Com.), *passim ; Glaston. Inq. ; Custumaria of Glaston.* The 'carucarius' on the Glastonbury Abbey manors was allowed the use of the lord's plough every other Saturday throughout the year, the gardener was allowed the apples off one apple tree and two gallons of cider. *Custumaria of Glaston.* 118 ; *Glaston. Inq.* 142.

[128] *Custumaria of Glaston.* 34.   [129] *Glaston. Inq.* 191.   [130] Ibid.

The 13th century was marked by the gradual development of a money standard in terms of which these customary services were translated. The end of the 12th century saw tentative efforts in this direction on some of the Somerset manors.[131] It was, however, recognized by both parties that it was in the power of the lord to decide whether he would accept labour services or a money rent in lieu of them. At Glastonbury, jurors were directed to inquire into the extent of the change, and in their reports, when the money rent received from a holding was very small, the words 'utilius esset in manu domini,' or 'utilius esset ad opera' followed.[132] The variations in the rent paid even on the same manor for holdings of one size make it almost impossible to fix upon any sum as the average rent of a given quantity of land. But it is clear that as soon as the services due from the villeins began to be valued in terms of money, the total rent paid by them was much heavier than that paid by freemen for holdings of the same size. On the manor of Winscombe, for instance, a free tenant held a virgate for the rent of 12s., while a villein paid for a virgate a rent of 3s. and services valued at 14s.[133] Further, there was a marked tendency to group the villeins on a manor into three or four classes. Thus the virgater owed a rent of 3s. and services valued at 14s., the half-virgater a rent of 18d. and services valued at 8s. 9d., the ferlinger a rent of 12d. and services valued at 6s. 1½d., and so on, the rent and money value of the services corresponding in each group with the size of the holding. Towards the end of the 13th century the money value of the separate labour services is usually set down, and the following schedule is found at the beginning of two custumals drawn up in 1290.[134]

One day's ploughing	2½d.
Ploughing 1 acre	4d.
Harrowing 1 acre	1d.
Haulage	2s.
One day's mowing	1d.
One day's carriage	4d.
One day's reaping	1½d.
One daywork	½d.

Although such schedules are wanting on a great number of manors, incidental valuations of services prove that the standard was almost uniform throughout the county.[135] Reaping, binding, and stacking half an acre of wheat was valued at 2d.; threshing and winnowing one bushel of seed corn at ¼d., while the same value was set on tossing the hay behind the mowers.[136]

Yearly wages were already being paid to domestic servants. At Glastonbury the cook and baker received a mark, the undercook 3s., the scullion of the hall 6d., the hostiller and the *pincerna gristae* half a mark each yearly, paid at Easter and Michaelmas. Most of these servants received also allowances of food and drink, fodder for their horses, garments, fuel, houses and land rent-free, gifts at Christmas out of the offerings, exemption from certain tolls, and special perquisites.[136a]

[131] *Cal. Inq. p.m. Edw. I*, 265, 321.
[132] *Glaston. Inq.* 21, 63.
[133] *MSS. of D. and C. of Wells* (Hist. MSS. Com.), i, 336.
[134] Ibid 336, 342.
[135] North Curry Manor. *MSS. of D. and C. of Wells* (Hist. MSS. Com.), i, 332, 334, 344–6.
[136] Ibid. 334–5, 342–6.
[136a] *Custumaria of Glaston.* i, *seq.* The 'scutellarius' who saw to the table furniture could claim the giblets and feathers of all geese killed (the abbot taking the down) and the trimmings of all meat except venison, while the porker had the tails of all pigs killed. The latter, in return for providing the rennet for the dairies, received a cheese from each. *Glaston. Inq.* 13, 16, 17 ; see also *Pipe R. of Winton.* 65–8.

The food of the Somerset labourer at this date seems to have consisted of bread, 'pottage' (apparently a kind of porridge made with oatmeal), and cheese, with the addition of fish, which abounded in the county, and of meat and poultry occasionally, beef, mutton, and pork being mentioned. Butter and milk seem to have been but little used. Beer was the usual drink of the people, cider and mead made from honey being only rarely mentioned at this date. A loaf of bread of the weight of sixty shillings is mentioned as a daily allowance. The allowance of the vicar of Muchelney consisted, in addition to bread, of two gallons of the best conventual ale, a dish of flesh meat twice a week, and a dish of eggs or fish on the other days.[137]

One thing that made for the comfort of the peasants was the abundance of fuel that could be gathered from waste and woodland. The provision of Yule logs for the lord's hall is frequently mentioned.[138] Wax candles were in use in the large manor-houses.[139] Salt was of considerable value, being evaporated in salt-pans and brought long distances.[140] Pepper, cummin, and mustard are the only spices dealt with in these early records. As to the dress of the people, linen and woollen stuffs are mentioned ; we hear of ' a good robe of burnet ' with a hood trimmed with squirrel, of leather boots and gloves.[141]

The influence of the great monasteries upon social conditions must not be forgotten in the picture of the 13th century. At that date religious houses like those of Glastonbury, Bath, Athelney, and Bruton attracted and employed local talent, and were the only places in the county where men could hope to develop the arts of writing, painting, and music in leisured security, while in gardening and the practice of estate management [141a] the monks set an example which was later imitated by their neighbours. They focussed the intelligence of the county, and had practically a monopoly of all knowledge of science and literature. The magnificent state maintained by a great Somerset magnate is reflected in the record of the number of officials and servants depending on the Abbot of Glastonbury, and their allowances give some idea of the standard of living on the great Somerset manors of the Church. The higher officials included the chamberlain, the cellarer, the *granatarius* (with an underling who received half a mark yearly), the precentor (with his ' writer '), the hospitaller, the refectorar (*refectorarius*), the *medarius*,[141b] the *infirmarius* and the almoner, the steward, the *dispensator*, and the provost of the market, who paid a barrel of herrings yearly for his office, which he held for life. The offices of master-cook, baker, and butler were hereditary, the first in 1189 being in the hands of five cooks, who divided the office, the last having passed to a woman, the daughter of Adam the Butler, who exercised her craft by deputy.[142]

A great deal of travelling was done in the 13th century. We hear much of pilgrims and friars, palmers, minstrels, vagrants, rogues, and vagabonds.[143] The great households were continually on tour from one manor to

---

[137] *Muchelney Chartul.* 108–9. See also *Glaston. Inq.* and *Custumaria of Glaston.*

[138] *Bruton and Montacute Chartul.* 19, 20.

[139] The Prior of Glastonbury was allowed 10 lb. of wax and 10 lb. of candles yearly. *Glaston. Inq.* 8.

[140] *Bruton and Montacute Chartul.* 160.

[141] *Hund. R.* (Rec. Com.), ii, 126 ; *Bruton and Montacute Chartul.* 83.

[141a] Church lands were usually carefully managed, and the arrangements in force on lands which were the property of corporations sole foreshadow the stock and land-lease system of later times. *Glaston Inq.* 3, 4.

[141b] The officer in charge of the medary, who received the rents paid in money, making and storing the mead. *Custumaria Glaston.* 253.   [142] *Glaston. Inq.* 1–17.

[143] *Somers. Pleas* (Somers. Rec. Soc.), Introd. xix, no. 203, 213, 388, 604, 624, 784.

another, and the lord aimed at staying long enough to consume the produce without leaving the manor in debt.[144] This accounts, too, for the meanness of the typical 13th-century manor-house; it was a temporary rather than a permanent dwelling.[145] All necessaries the manor could itself provide, luxuries were purchased at Bristol or elsewhere—wine, wax, silk, and fine cloth, in fact any clothing more elaborate than that provided by the manor sheep. The money required for these purchases, and for the wages of the regular labourers and artisans, like carpenters, tailors, and smiths, seems on the typical Somerset manor to have been raised by the sale of corn, cattle, and sheep, and later of wool. From many Somerset estates large sums were sent to the lord in the years when he did not visit the estate.[146] At the same time the system of keeping accounts developed, and inventories were made of household furniture, farm produce, and stock.[147]

The prosperity of Somerset is shown clearly in the appearance of an inclosure movement during the 13th century, the greatest activity being displayed on the manors belonging to the Church.[148] This took the form of the partition and distribution of a portion of the common waste and woodland which was added to the meadow, or in some cases to the plough-land of the village. The land thus redeemed was usually held at a fixed rent, and in this way the number of rent-paying tenements on the manor increased. Part of Saltmoor, for instance, was imparked for meadows by the Dean and Chapter of Wells in 1233, the other part being similarly dealt with by the lord of a neighbouring manor.[149] On the partition of Thealmoor in 1327 between the Dean and Chapter of Wells and the Abbot of Glastonbury, special reservation was made of the free and villein tenants' rights of turbary, of building piggeries, of watering their cattle, and of crossing the river between sunrise and sunset.[150] In many cases the meadow land thus inclosed was thrown open for common pasture after the hay was carried.[151] About the same time it became the custom for the rights of husbote and heybote in the common woods to be surrendered in return for a definite number of loads of brushwood yearly.[152] In many places land hitherto uncultivated was being brought under the plough. Occasionally hunting rights over these assarts were preserved, as in the case of the grant of 25 acres on the outskirts of Selwood Forest.[153]

From incidental notices only can any idea of 13th-century prices be obtained, and the wide fluctuations prove that a standard of value was only beginning to emerge. The price of an ox, for instance, varied from 5s. to

[144] Walter of Henley, *Husbandry* (ed. Lamond), 127, 145. At Michaelmas an estimate of the available supplies was made. The Bishop of Bath and Wells had sixteen houses kept in readiness for residence, and moved constantly from one to another. *Reg. Bp. Drokensford* (Somers. Rec. Soc.), Introd. xvii, App. 313.

[145] Cunningham, *Growth of Engl. Ind. and Commerce*, i, 241-3.

[146] Special messengers were sent from Farleigh Hungerford to London to carry the money in silver to the lord. Mins. Accts. bdle. 970, no. 13.

[147] Cunningham, op. cit. i, 432-4; *Glaston. Inq.*; *Custumaria of Glaston*. The 'accopa' or great tally and the 'anticopa' or counter tally were used for the deliverer and receiver respectively in the accounts. Chadwyck Healey, *Hist. of West Somers*. App. i, 494. *The Pipe Roll of the Bishopric of Winchester*, 1205-9 (ed. H. Hall), is a fine example of 13th-century account keeping. A series of Computus Rolls of the stewards of the Glastonbury manors exists (among the MSS. of the Marquess of Bath at Longleat) covering the whole period from 1242 to 1540.

[148] *MSS. of D. and C. of Wells* (Hist. MSS. Com.), i, 8, 11, 28, 145, 184, 219, 220.

[149] Ibid. 11. These agreements between neighbouring lords are common. Ibid. 145.

[150] Ibid. 8, 227.

[151] Ibid. 11.

[152] Ibid. 71-2, 184.

[153] *Bruton and Montacute Chartul.* 19, 20.

4 marks.[154]   A cart-horse was valued at 6*s*.,[155] a cow at 3*s*. and 5*s*.,[156] a calf at 10*d*. 'Muttons' were 8*d*., 9*d*., and 12*d*. each, ewe sheep 8*d*. and 9*d*.,[157] lambs 2½*d*. and 4*d*. each.   The price of a quarter of wheat was 3*s*. and 4*s*., barley and beans were 2*s*., and oats 10*d*. a quarter.[158]   Cummin was 2*d*. and pepper 6*d*. a pound,[159] a sparrowhawk was worth 4*s*.,[160] and 20*s*. was the price of 6,000 eels.[161]   We hear of a gown worth 14*s*., a robe of 9 ells with a border worth half a mark, a leather jacket worth 12*s*., a hauberk 10*s*., a russet robe 40*s*. 4*d*. A sword was valued at 4*d*., and two Turkish coifs (*coifas turcosias*) were worth 2*s*.[162]

Justice was administered in Somerset by the shire court, the hundred courts and the manor courts, and by the courts of the itinerant justices. The shire court met first at Somerton and later at Ilchester.   Its jurisdiction in criminal cases, and in cases concerned with the land, was already ceasing to be of much importance in the 13th century, as it was being gradually superseded by the justices in eyre and the royal courts.[163]   The sheriff presided, and theoretically all the freeholders of the county, with the reeve and four men from every vill, were the suitors, but there are many cases of manors, or even whole liberties, being relieved of the burden by charter or prescription.   There is one case of an individual being exempted for life by royal charter.[164]   The duty of attendance might be discharged by attorney or deputy,[165] but the first example of this given in the Assize Rolls can hardly have popularized it, as the bailiff appointed by a woman to sue for her in the county court unjustly dispossessed her of her property.[166]   At the assizes of 1242–3 fifteen persons in the county were hanged, forty-five took sanctuary or abjured the realm, while 100 were outlawed.[167]

The hundred courts met every three weeks, and twice a year for view of frankpledge.   In those that remained in the king's hands the sheriff presided, in those in private hands the lord's steward presided, judgements in both cases being made by the suitors of the court.[168]   The townships were responsible for raising the hue and cry, for the behaviour of strangers and guests, and for the due presentation of all offences, omission even of trifling details being punishable,[169] and as might have been expected, they were continually incurring fines for the neglect of some of their many responsibilities.[169a] The hundred courts, then, were usually occupied with a general super-

[154] *Hist. MSS. Com. Rep.* iii, App. 311 ; Adam de Domerham, *Hist. Glaston.* (ed. Hearne), 214, 225. Other prices found are 5*s*. 4*d*., 6*s*. 8*d*., 8*s*., 13*s*. 4*d*., while four calves were sold for 3*s*.   *Muchelney and Athelney Chartul.* 54 ; *Hund. R.* (Rec. Com.), ii, 128 ; *Cal. Inq. p.m. Edw. I*, 436. See also *Pipe R. of Winton.* 63–73.

[155] Adam de Domerham, op. cit. 225.

[156] Ibid. ; *Hist. MSS. Com. Rep.* iii, App. 311.

[157] Adam de Domerham, op. cit. 214, 225.

[158] *Muchelney and Athelney Chartul.* 54.

[159] Ibid. 55, 88.

[160] *Cal. Inq. p.m.* Hen. III, 78.

[161] *Muchelney and Athelney Chartul.* 165.

[162] *Somers. Pleas* (Somers. Rec. Soc.), no. 1001.

[163] Ibid. Introd. xxxii.

[164] Ibid. Introd. xxxi, no. 1511.

[165] Ibid. no. 440, 515, 677, &c.

[166] Ibid. no. 1280.

[167] Ibid. Introd. xxxiii.   The position of the outlaw as a lawless and friendless man has been thus described : ' Of every proprietory, possessory, and contractual right he is deprived, he forfeits his chattels to the king, who is entitled to lay waste his land, which then escheats to his lord.' Pollock and Maitland, *Hist. of Engl. Law*, i, 460–1.

[168] Ct. R. portf. 200, no. 56, Whitley Hund.

[169] *Somers. Pleas*, no. 880, 1042, 1148, 1154.   A case is even found of a township being in mercy for not presenting that the cause of a boy falling into a leaden vessel full of hot water was ' that he wished to strike a certain dog.'   Ibid. no. 935.

[169a] Ibid. no. 189, 207, 770, 771, 923, 942, 1094, 1138, 1148, 1153, &c.   Amercements for harbouring evildoers, for allowing prisoners to escape, and for neglecting the pursuit of offenders are often found.

intendence of the police system of the county, and dealt with assaults, thefts, &c., and with suits concerning land, which seem to have been carried on in a very dilatory fashion.[170] Some of the cases that came before the hundred courts were very trifling. Matilda Chynne came all the way from Middlezoy to Whitley Hundred Court to complain that a certain William had struck a cock belonging to her, 'ob quod fregit crus eius et alia enormia ei intulit ad dampnum vid.' The condition of the roads also received some attention from the hundred courts.[171]

The manor courts brought justice to the door of the peasant. In the 13th century there was, as yet, only one court for free and villein tenants, and the suitors, who were the judges (the lord's steward acting as president only), were probably both the free and unfree. The scope of the manor courts varied widely. In their humblest form their jurisdiction was purely civil as far as the free tenants were concerned, actions for debt and damages below the value of 40s. coming within their scope, but they had certain police jurisdiction over the villeins. In the case of most of the large manors the lord had the right to hold view of frankpledge. This excluded the sheriff from the manor, and gave the lord the profit of the police jurisdiction. Further rights, not usually granted to any but the lords of honours or baronies, were those of *infangenethef* and *utfangenethef* (by which the lord obtained powers of life and death in cases of theft), the assize of bread and beer, and the right to have gallows, tumbril, and cuckingstool for the punishment of offenders.[172] Rarer still were the grants of the higher franchises,[173] the right of the lord to have the return of writs within his lands (by which he was empowered to hang an offender on his private gallows after he had been sentenced by the judges), to have the chattels of felons and fugitives, and to take amercements, even if inflicted in the royal courts. The king's coroners did not enter the Bishop of Winchester's hundred of Taunton,[174] but the Abbot of Athelney's attempt to exclude them without warrant was punished by the confiscation of his franchise.[175] The Abbot of Glastonbury even claimed to exclude the justices in eyre from the 12 hides of the Isle of Avalon.[176] Most crimes of violence were brought before the justices, the manor court dealing only with petty assaults between villeins.[177] Its time was chiefly occupied with actions for debt, damages and trespass, and with land actions and alienations, cases being decided by juries of villeins or by compurgation, the latter method surviving much longer here than in the royal courts.[178] An increasing freedom in dealing with land may be noticed, holdings being granted out subject to curious services, or being surrendered in return for an annuity or allowance in kind.[179] The most general and

---

[170] On the Court Rolls many entries are repeated time after time, the hearing of the matter being continually postponed for lack of the presence of essential witnesses or even of the parties to the suit.

[171] Ct. R. loc. cit.

[172] Occasionally the lord raised his gallows without warrant. *Somers. Pleas,* no. 870, 871.

[173] The Bishops of Bath and Winchester enjoyed the most complete franchises in the county. *Hund. R.* (Rec. Com.), ii, 130 (1256).

[174] *Somers. Pleas,* no. 1076.   [175] Ibid. no. 164.

[176] Ibid. p. 134. The liberties of the abbey are set out at length in a charter of Henry III, printed in *Hemingi Chart.* (ed. Hearne), ii, App. 603 ; *MSS. of D. and C. of Wells* (Hist. MSS. Com.), i, 438.

[177] Ct. R. portf. 199, no. 3.

[178] Ibid. portf. 198, no. 27, 28 ; Court R. Lambeth Pal. (Congresbury and Yalton, 1277).

[179] *Muchelney and Athelney Chartul.* 81.

constant business of the manor court was the management in due order of the lord's estate. The man who put too many beasts on the common pasture, who encroached on the high road, who neglected to repair his tenement or the causeway outside his house, who allowed his beasts to stray, or who broke into the lord's park and drove off his cattle, appeared to answer for his misdeeds in the lord's court.[180] The punishment almost invariably took the form of a fine, the offender in most cases being 'in mercy,' which involved an arbitrary amercement at the will of the lord. Cases of alleged slander occupied much of the time of the courts. For the breach of the assize of bread and ale the usual fine was 6*d*.,[181] but deceiving the tithing by a fraudulent measure was punished much more severely.[182] Other matters dealt with were surrenders and admittances to tenements, the payment of heriots and fines for admittance, and of merchet and *capitagium*, and the election of manorial officials.[183] The manor court probably already issued general rural regulations or by-laws, though few of this date have survived.[184]

At the assizes held before the king's justices the most important cases in the county came on for decision. The growing popularity of the assizes of novel disseisin, mort d'ancestor, darrein presentment and utrum, and the Grand Assize swelled the civil cause list of the justices,[185] the first two being the most constantly used, especially for the settlement of the endless disputes over pasture rights.[186] The criminal offences which as pleas of the Crown came before the justices were murder, felonious assault, larceny, burglary, breach of the assize of wine or of cloth,[187] tampering with the coinage, and arson, the last two being recent additions to the pleas of the Crown.[188] The murderer was punished by death, if caught, but by outlawry if he fled. Theft, the commonest of all offences, was punished in the same way, though cases of petty theft were not usually presented as pleas of the Crown.[189] The practice in these matters was very elastic, and there seems to have been no definition of the point where the line was to be drawn.[190] Imprisonment was the rarest of all punishments, the county gaol at Ilchester and the local prisons of the lords being designed only for temporary detention before trial, and this function they fulfilled most ineffectually. Cases of breaking prison abound ;[191] the fugitive either took sanctuary or fled the country, leaving the punishment for his escape to fall upon his tithing or town-

---

[180] Ct. R. portf. 200, no. 56.

[181] A 13th-century document in the *Muchelney Chartul.* (p. 73) limits the fine for the breach of the assize of bread and ale to 4*d*.

[182] Ct. R. portf. 200, no. 56, Whitley Hund.

[183] Ibid.   [184] Ct. R. portf. 200, no. 23–5, Shepton Montague.

[185] In the Assize R. published by the Somers. Rec. Soc. there are 151 cases of the use of the assize of novel desseisin, 62 of the mort d'ancestor, 6 of darrein presentment, and only one of the assize utrum.

[186] *MSS. of D. and C. of Wells*, i, 181 and *passim*. ; *Somers. Pleas*, no. 322, 1272, 1501, and many others.

[187] Ibid. no. 790, 806, 828, 1058. The rolls of gaol deliveries in Somerset begin in the reign of Edward I. Gaol Delivery R. no. 59.

[188] A man who was proved guilty of clipping the coins was hanged. *Somers. Pleas*, no. 1105.

[189] The offence of the man who stole ' two fish called hake ' was, however, presented before the justices, and the offender abjured the realm. Ibid. no. 797.

[190] Owing to the severity of the punishments and the horrible frequency of the death penalty, men accused even of trifling offences fled from justice. They were declared outlaws and their goods and chattels were forfeited. A similar fate overtook false coiners or those accused of arson. *Pipe R. 9, 12, 14, 15 Hen. II* (Pipe R. Soc.), vi, 27, ix, 99, xii, 153, xiii, 6 ; *Somers. Pleas*, no. 994, 1074.

[191] *Somers. Pleas*, no. 122, 147, 148, 168, 177, 185, 240, 250, 258, 276, 284, 839, 1094, &c. *Cal. Pat.* 1301–7, 39. Even the she-thief ('latrona'), as Mr. Chadwyck Healey points out, was able to make good her escape. Ibid. no. 1254.

ship.[192] The commonest of all punishments was a fine. Extremely heavy fines were inflicted for *murdrum* (when the vill where a dead man was found could not prove his Englishry),[193] and the fines were not only heavy but arbitrary, varying in one year from 1 mark to 5 marks, the fine for a concealed murder being enormous.[194] Fines, again, punished neglect to raise the hue and cry, raising it on insufficient grounds, or raising it unsuccessfully.

Another source of profit arising from the administration of justice was the system of deodands. Examples of these in Somerset are the surrender to the Crown of the beam in Taunton Church (valued at 6*d*.) from which a man fell, the boats from which men were drowned, the trees from which they fell, the mill wheels that crushed them to death, and the boar that killed a boy who fell into his sty.[195]

The growth of sub-infeudation had made the incidence of the burden of suit and service very complicated. An estate of less than 400 acres which owed services to eight different lords, and suit of court at White Lackington, Ashill, Ford, Muchelney, and at the hundred court of Abdick may be quoted as typical rather than exceptional.[196] This burden was very unpopular, and in many cases was wholly or partially compounded for, or limited by agreement to four suits annually at the hundred court or the like.[197] The great magnates of the county escaped these irksome burdens by withdrawing themselves and their men from the service due, and there was no power strong enough to force them to perform the services they had repudiated. Great leniency too, was shown in allowing *essoins*, or excuses for the non-appearance of jurors, witnesses, or even the plaintiff and defendant in civil suits, and cases dragged on from term to term, or even from year to year, being put off from time to time owing to the non-appearance of the necessary parties.[198] The most usual excuses pleaded were absence on the king's service, bodily sickness, or being overtaken by illness en route for the court, absence on a pilgrimage or beyond the seas.[199]

The judicial system in Somerset as elsewhere was going through a period of transition. The most striking changes were the disappearance of trial by ordeal, and the growing unpopularity of the judicial duel, both being superseded by the development of the jury system. Ordeal by water decided cases of burglary, assault, and homicide in the 12th century,[200] but there is no record of its use later than 1201. In the same way the judicial duel was becoming obsolete, and the transitional character of the period

---

[192] When a criminal took sanctuary, the church was surrounded by the coroner and his men, and he was penned in until he swore to abjure the realm, when he was allowed free passage to the nearest port, being outlawed if he dared return. *Somers. Pleas*, no. 185, 1255. Occasionally, however, the fugitive escaped the cordon of watchers and made good his escape from sanctuary. Ibid. no. 785, 1119, 1253.

[193] *Pipe R. 6, 8 Hen. II* (Pipe R. Soc.), 58, 22. A fine of 1 mark represented, according to the average value of commodities at this date, an ox and a half or 64 days' labour as a mason. *Somers. Pleas*, Introd. lxxii.

[194] *Pipe R. 14, 15 Hen. II* (Pipe R. Soc.), xii, 151, xiii, 6.

[195] *Somers. Pleas*, no. 1076, 802, 876, 1031, 1041, 1039. See also no. 803 (caldron of lead) and no. 1005 (mare from which a man fell).

[196] *Cal. Inq. p.m. Edw. I*, 326.

[197] *Bruton and Montacute Chartul.* 9, 36, 187. Here there is the record of a provision that if at any time there is no freeman within the manor, suit shall be exacted from the land which freemen formerly held.

[198] *Somers. Pleas*, and Ct. R. *passim*.

[199] *Somers. Pleas*, no. 23, 32, 382, 1309–16, 1337, 1344, 1347, 1376, 1385, 1391, 1395, 1459.

[200] *Pipe R. 6, 8, 12 Hen. II* (Pipe R. Soc. ii, v–ix), 58, 21, 99.

is illustrated by a case where the judicial duel was tried, being followed, on its failure, by an inquest by jury.[201]

At the same time there was a growing tendency to extend the use of the jury system to other than judicial matters, custumals of manors being drawn up and pasture rights defined after inquest by jury.[202]

Another point to be noticed is the definition of the villein status by means of legal theory. On the one hand there are records of lords recovering their fugitive villeins,[203] but the villein had an opportunity of proving himself a freeman, either by the charter of a former lord or by descent from free parents.[204]

Towards the end of the 13th century there are signs that in Somerset, as elsewhere, during the turmoils of the Barons' War, the weakness of the central government had led to the unwarranted usurpation of quasi-royal privileges by the Church and the great nobles, and the Hundred Rolls record the efforts of a strong king to recover his rights.

There were many cases of refusal to contribute to the sheriff's aid, the battle of Lewes in one case being given as the date of the last payment.[205] The royal officers were disobeyed and insulted, and the king's bailiffs were refused entry into many manors when they appeared to claim debts due to him.[206] It was the golden age of the feudal nobility; and all over the county, from Dunster to Bristol, their great castles rose to overawe the surrounding country. In these strongholds they ruled as despots, levied private war on their neighbours, and defied the power of the Crown. Alienations of the royal territory had become very serious. North Curry had been handed over by Richard I to the Bishop of Bath in return for the advance of money for his ransom,[207] and John 'in the time of his trouble' had enriched Bath Priory by the grant of lands worth £50 yearly to be held at a rent of £20.[208] The encroachments on royal territory[209] varied in importance from the thefts of the bailiff of Cheddar, who stole 12 oaks from the king's forest and 'did his will with all the underwood,'[210] to encroachments on royal woods and high roads, the building of walls to obstruct the latter,[211] and the appropriation of royal manors,[212] while the walls of the royal city of Bath became a quarry for the neighbourhood.[213] Elsewhere the nobles who coveted further powers had set up gallows and tumbrils,[214] taken wreck of the sea,[215] held assizes of bread and ale,[216] and unauthorized markets and fairs, and withdrawn the suit due to the hundred courts that were in royal hands.[217]

The king's officers, too, were frequently overbearing and corrupt. Sheriffs took bribes, imprisoned men without cause, exacting fines for

---

[201] *Somers. Pleas,* no. 820 ; ibid. no. 88, 91, 95, 100 ; *Hund. R.* (Rec. Com.), ii, 121*b*, 126*b*.

[202] *Hist. MSS. Com. Rep.* x, App. iii, 73, 85.

[203] *Somers. Pleas,* no. 535 ; *MSS. of D. and C. of Wells,* i, 411. The villein with his 'sequela' and his land was frequently sold by one lord to another. *Muchelney and Athelney Chartul.* 136 ; *Bruton and Montacute Chartul.* 28.   [204] *Somers. Pleas,* no. 535, 729: Vinogradoff, *Villainage in Engl.* 74, 75.

[205] *Hund. R.* (Rec. Com.), ii, 118*b*, 119.

[206] At Downhead a drawbridge was raised to prevent the bailiff of the hundred from entering. *Somers. Pleas,* no. 1017 ; *Hund. R.* (Rec. Com.), ii, 118*b*.

[207] *Hund. R.* (Rec. Com.), ii, 122*b*. When in prison Richard made several other grants of Crown lands in Somerset to the bishop, who was a relative of the Emperor. Ibid. 119.

[208] Ibid. 119, 121, 123*b*.   [209] Ibid. 130*b*.   [210] Ibid. 126*b*.

[211] Ibid. 119*b*, 131, 131*b*.   [212] Ibid. 121*b*.   [213] Ibid. 123*b*.

[214] Ibid. 122, 138 ; *Somers. Pleas,* no. 570, 571.   [215] *Hund. R.* (Rec. Com.), ii, 119.

[216] Ibid. 122, 125.   [217] Ibid. 118, 119, 119*b*, 120, 128*b*, 132*b*, 139*b*.

their release, and even fined men who refused them hospitality ;[218] the bailiff of West Perrott (who seems to have been a specially insubordinate person) took a man accused of murdering his brother out of Williton prison 'by means and warrant unknown'; and then, going to the other extreme, threw an unfortunate lady into the same prison, without accusation or warrant, exacting a fine of 16s. for her release.[219] A coroner refused to view dead bodies until given a bribe of 2s.,[220] and the stewards of several lords were in the habit of imposing extortionate amercements for slight offences.[221] Crimes of violence abounded, one of the commonest presentments being of men found killed, 'by the roadside,' 'on the common high road,' and 'outside the vill,' as well as 'in the forest.'[222]

The necessities of Richard I and King John gave an impetus to the growth of chartered boroughs, and by 1275, besides the cities of Bath and Wells, there were boroughs at Taunton, Ilchester, Axbridge, Chard, Nether Stowey, Weare, Dunster, Stogursey, Milborne Port, Langport, Bridgwater, and Glastonbury.[223] Many of these boroughs owed their growth to their trade in wool or wine, and their population consisted in part of merchants, tradesmen, and artificers,[224] but they still preserved their rural character, and numbered among their officials haywards and pinders.[225] A gild merchant was established in Bath in 1189, and in Bridgwater in the reign of Edward I,[226] and for the latter borough there is a very early collection of by-laws. One of these imposes a fine of 12d. on any burgess who accused another of theft, murder, forgery, 'neifty,' &c. ; while another, to prevent regrating, forbids the sale of flesh or fried fish before 9 a.m.[227]

The 13th century was the 'zenith of mediaeval progress.' The boroughs were prospering, the gilds merchant being so far protective rather than restrictive, the rural districts were quietly moving along the path of progress, while the relations between the lord and his man were beginning to be modified by the introduction of a money link. The growth of wealth in the form of movable property is proved by the reliance of public finance upon the tenths and fifteenths,[228] while the sculptured west front of Wells Cathedral shows a local appreciation of the development of art. The prosperity of the county, however, compared with that of the rest of England was only moderate, its wealth being slightly below the average. For the wool tax of 1341 it contributed 600 sacks, that is at the rate of about one sack to 1,740 acres. Of its neighbours, Dorset and Gloucestershire were richer, contributing one sack for 1,310 and 1,365 acres respectively, while Devon was poorer, 3,215 acres furnishing one sack.[229]

---

[218] *Hund. R.* (Rec. Com.), ii, 127, 128.   [219] Ibid. 125.   [220] Ibid. 127, 128.   [221] Ibid. 127b.

[222] *Somers. Pleas*, no. 988, 1178, 1201, 1205, 1212. The eastern part of the county was much more settled than the west. Ibid. Introd. lxxiii.

[223] *Hund. R.* (Rec. Com.), ii, 118, 120b, 121, 123, 126b, 128b, 139b.

[224] The following members of the industrial population are mentioned in the *Somers. Pleas:*—bakers, carpenters, cobblers, cordwainers, drapers, goldsmiths, hornmakers, mercers, smiths, tailors, tanners, vintners, and weavers.

[225] At Axbridge, for instance, a piece of common pasture called a 'moorhay' was appurtenant to each burgage ; *Hist. MSS. Com. Rep.* iii, App. 305, 306.

[226] C. Gross, *Gild Merchant*, ii, 23, 351. Subsequent references to the stewards of the Bridgwater gild appear in the 14th and 15th centuries, e.g. *Hist. MSS. Com. Rep.* iii, App. 311, 314, 315.

[227] *Hist. MSS. Com. Rep.* iii, App. 316.   [228] Cunnnigham, op. cit. i, 293.

[229] Thorold Rogers, *Hist. of Agric. and Prices*, i, 110, 111 ; *Parl. R.* ii, 131 (1348). An ordinance of 1343 fixed the minimum price for the sale of English wool at 11 marks, which proves that the wool must have been of excellent quality (Rymer, *Foedera*, ii), since 9 marks was a fair price. Cunningham, op. cit.

Early in the 14th century there was foreshadowed the movement that was to replace the service-owing villein by either the rent-paying tenant who held a lease of the lord's demesne or the paid labourer who cultivated it. The villein was beginning to shake off his burdens, and to join the ranks of the free tenants. He could acquire his freedom in several ways—by express grant of his lord (the churchmen leading the way in this respect),[230] by purchase,[231] or by a covenant with his lord by which the latter agreed to receive a payment in lieu of personal service; or he might gain practical freedom by obtaining a licence to dwell outside the manor in return for a small yearly tax.[232] He then took up elsewhere, free from base obligations, one of the small freehold tenements, which were multiplying everywhere owing to the cultivation of assarts.[233] There were many constructive manumissions. If the lord received homage from a villein, gave him a grant of land, allowed him to be on a jury or to enter religion, the law pronounced him free. If he fled from his manor, a year and a day's residence on the ancient demesne or in a chartered borough cleared him of the villein taint. Even in the absence of such residence the process of recovering a villein by action in a court of law was tedious and unprofitable. Again, the villein tenement thus made vacant by flight could be, and constantly was, taken up by a freeman without loss of status.[234] Another way in which the villein obtained relief from the burdens attached to his tenure was by the commutation of services for money. Once the amount of money due for these services was well known, the lords seem in many cases to have gladly availed themselves of this plan of being rid of the troublesome and wasteful method of cultivation by the enforced labour services of the tenants.[234a] On many manors at this time the sums received for rent and for the sale of customary services was almost equal, and on a few the rent was considerably larger. The prices at which labour services could be commuted rose steadily after the beginning of the 14th century. Ploughing, harrowing, and mowing were valued at 4d. per acre each; boon ploughing at 2½d., in addition to the 1½d. which the labourer took by custom for this work.[234b] The labour lost by the sale of works was made up, to some extent, by an increase in the number of hired farm labourers, while at the same time the amount of demesne land to be cultivated by the lord was diminished by the practice of granting out portions of the demesne on lease.[234c]

The rapidity with which this movement spread may be seen by comparing the manor of Porlock in 1319 and 1345. At the earlier date

---

[230] *Bath Chartul.* (Somers. Rec. Soc.), ii, 103, 107, 110, 115, 123. In 1316 a villein of the Prior of Bath was manumitted 'so that he serve the Priory all his life in the office of plumber or glazier'. Ibid. 164. One case of manumission was accompanied by the proviso that a penalty of 40s. should be payable at any attempt to recede from the emancipation. *Bruton and Montacute Chartul.* 154–5; *Athelney Chartul.* 130; MSS. *of D. and C. of Wells* (Hist. MSS. Com.), i, 71. [231] Ibid. i, 62, 80.

[232] Ibid. i, 346–51. Ten men paid 3s. 11d. and half a pound of wax yearly for chevage.

[233] This 'terra assisa' as it was called, though quite distinct from ordinary bondage land—being held at a fixed rent—was at first distinguished from freehold land also, though ultimately the gulf was bridged, and it was regarded as free.

[234] P. Vinogradoff, *Villainage in Engl.* 80–1, 88.

[234a] Ct. R. portf. 198, no. 49; MSS. *of D. and C. of Wells*, i, 382–4, 336, 342–51.

[234b] Ibid. 346–351.

[234c] *Bath Chartul.* ii, 135; *Bruton and Montacute Chartul.* 62. The usual method of alienation—by copy of court roll—was on many manors held insufficient for a lease of demesne land (e.g. Templecombe Manor, 1346). De Banco R. 344, m. 140.

the rents from free tenants amounted to 35s. 1d., while the rent of the villeins was 60s. yearly, their works and those of the cottars being valued at 40s. and 24s. 6d. In 1345 the rents of free and villein tenants together came to £8, while the value of their works only amounted to 10s. yearly. Again, while in 1319 the demesne lands included 120 acres of arable land, 17 of meadow, and 50 of wood, by 1345 they had been reduced by leases to 100 acres of arable land, 6 acres of meadow, and 40 acres of wood, while 100 acres of waste mentioned in the earlier survey had entirely disappeared. This diminished demesne, however, was worth almost as much as the original amount, the value of the arable land having risen from 3d. to 4d. per acre and the meadow from 10d. to 20d. per acre.[235]

But it was clearly recognized that commutation was a matter for the discretion of the lord,[236] and the number of works sold fluctuated from year to year according to his convenience. There are instances of freed land being 'reduced into due servitude,' not without great trouble and expense.[237] Conservative landlords were still giving away their villeins with their *sequela*, and the contrast with the position of the rent-paying villein, who could soon make enough to buy his freedom, was sufficiently galling to make for discontent and for the ultimate triumph of the new methods.

This development, however, was to be influenced in an unforeseen way by a great catastrophe. The Black Death reached Somerset in the winter of 1348, and if the mortality was at all commensurate with that of the rest of England, one-third of the inhabitants must have perished. The sources of evidence vary. In November 1348 the Bishop of Bath and Wells filled nine vacant livings, in the first month of the plague the number rose to thirty-two, while during the month when it was raging with the greatest violence forty-seven presentations were made, the number dropping to seven again in June.[238] Again, the number of monks in Bath Priory fell to one half of the number living there in 1344, and the earlier figure was never again reached,[239] while one cell of Bruton Priory received fifty oxen and cattle as heriots and mortuaries.[240] An eloquent silence in most of the local records during the year of the plague shows the extent of the visitation. Some evidence, however, may be obtained from the court rolls as to the ruinous state of the countryside. Presentations of deaths increase alarmingly, there are notes of heriots due but not paid, 'because there is nothing living there'; many holdings were in the lord's hands for lack of tenants; everywhere the empty houses of the tenants were fast falling into ruins. The villeins who remained took advantage of the general confusion and the scarcity of labour to exact better terms for themselves.[241]

The Black Death set in motion a strong reaction against the emancipation of the labourer from compulsory service. The lords of manors found that the Black Death had both reduced the labour available, and, also,

[235] Chadwyck Healey, *Hist. of Part of West Somers.* 50–8, quoting Chan. Inq. p.m. 13 Edw. II, no. 27 ; 19 Edw. III (1st nos.), no. 26.
[236] *Athelney Chartul.* 166.   [237] Adam de Domerham, op. cit. (ed. Hearne), ii, 533.
[238] Chadwyck Healey, op. cit. 19 ; Weaver, *Somers. Incumbents, passim.*
[239] *Bath Chartul.* Introd. xxi ; ii, 180 ; Clerical Subs. R. bdle. 4, no. 2, 21 Edw. III. Grants of vacant lodgings were frequent after the plague had thus diminished the number of inmates.
[240] *Bruton and Montacute Chartul.* 94.
[241] Çt. R. portf. 200, no. 3, 23–5 (Odcombe and Shepton Montague).

by raising wages, had made the commutation of services unprofitable. The result was an attempt to exact the old services and stop the practice of commutation. On many manors the reaction towards the old system was fairly complete, the rolls being filled with notices of admissions to tenements to be held in bondage 'according to the custom of the manor,' of the strict exaction of merchet and poll tax, and of all the labour services due, while the number of 'works' sold showed a sudden decline.[242] Many villeins were presented for withdrawing themselves from their service. One man declared that he 'would not be a bondman,' his protest, however, ending in his being handed over to the homage in custody, while another offered to the lord 2s. in lieu of the service due from him.[243] At the same time hints are not wanting that a way was being found out of these difficulties in the entries that record leases of *terra servilis* at fixed rents by copy of court roll. The Ministers' Accounts for the manor of Wellow in 1346–7, 1349–50, and 1350–1 bring out very clearly the havoc wrought by the plague, and the rapid and almost complete recovery of the manor.[244] Of the total receipts of £54 12s. 7½d., £38 9s. 4d., and £56 11s. 7½d. the following are the chief items :—

YEAR ENDING MICHAELMAS

	1346–7 £	s.	d.	1349–50 £	s.	d.	1350–1 £	s.	d.
Arrears	9	7	4½	25	7	5¼	7	16	1
Rents	7	16	1½	2	6	8½	7	5	1
Rent of fishery	0	2	0	0	0	6	0	1	6
					(tenant dead)				
Issues of the manor.	1	17	4½	0	4	10	0	9	2¼
Received from dairy	1	2	0		—		0	18	9
Sale of works.	1	11	7½	0	6	4	1	1	4¼
Sale of corn	18	7	9	0	2	10¾	6	0	10
Sale of stock	3	12	10	0	4	3¼	1	15	11
Profits of manor courts. . . .	7	6	8	4	11	8	24	18	2
Profits of hundred courts . . .	1	11	0	2	12	8	5	4	2

The recovery in 1350–1 is shown by the great increase in the profits of the lord's courts, through the fines received for taking up new holdings.

A comparison of the chief items of expenditure on this manor for the same years brings out the same points :—

	1346–7 £	s.	d.	1349–50 £	s.	d.	1350–1 £	s.	d.
Quit-rents and defects of rent .	0	5	8½	0	2	7	0	13	7¾
Cost of the plough	0	9	9½	0	0	6	0	10	10
,, ,, wagon	0	1	0	0	0	1	0	2	6
,, ,, sheep	1	4	7	0	3	10	0	16	6
Corn bought		—		0	16	7½		—	
Stock bought	2	7	10	1	19	3	0	2	6
Threshing and winnowing . .	0	14	0	0	1	3	1	1	3½
Hoeing and mowing . . .	0	0	2		—		0	1	6
	(all the rest done by the customary tenants)								
Autumn expenses (threshing, carrying, &c.).	0	6	4		—		4	10	4
Wages	1	1	0		—		1	9	0

[242] Ct. R. portf. 200, no. 3, 23–5 (Odcomb and Shepton Montague).
[243] Ibid. no. 3 (Odcomb). [244] Mins. Accts. bdle. 974, no. 20–5 (Wellow).

The most important features, of course, are the items of corn bought in the year 1349–50, the great increase in the amount of paid labour required, and the larger amount paid for wages to the regular farm servants under a new agreement made by the reeve, *causa pestilationis*. Their allowances had also been increased 'sub nova convencione per ordinacione senescalli per defectum servientium propter magnam mortaliam gentium.' The recovery of the estate continued, the total receipts of the manor advancing to £49 in 1352–3, £78 in 1364–5, and £68 in 1376–7.[245] Much of this was due to the great increase in the rents received[246] for leased demesne lands. In these accounts, notices of tenements once held in bondage being granted out for money rents are usually followed by a note that the grant was made only until such time as the steward should find a tenant to hold it at the old services, but, though the lord thus kept on record his intention to restore the old conditions, the pressure of circumstances was too strong for him.

Toward the end of the reign of Edward III the receipts of the same manor were usually between £60 and £70 annually, though there were considerable fluctuations from year to year. The most obvious features of these later accounts are the steady increase of receipts from rents (which by 1377 amounted to more than half the total incomings), and the large sums received for the sale of wool and skins, which suggests that the demesne land retained in the lord's hands was already being used for sheep-farming.[247]

Even though the material effect of the Black Death was comparatively evanescent,[247a] it left a legacy of increased discontent among the mass of the villeins; for although the bulk of the serfs were no worse off than they had been before the plague, the increased advantages of emancipation made their lot seem much harder by contrast.

The attempt of the Statutes of Labourers[248] to solve the labour problem by fixing prices and settling a maximum rate of wages (the year 1347 being taken as the standard) seems to have failed almost completely, for from all parts of the county there are records of much higher wages being paid than the rates fixed by law.[249] Its failure was really due to the changes in the coinage, which prevented prices from falling back to their old level as had been expected, when the country began to recover from the Black Death.[250] The inadequacy of the legal rate of wages, therefore, was another factor that made for the discontent, which culminated in the Peasants' Revolt of 1381.[251]

[245] Mins. Accts. bdle. 974, no. 23, 24 ; bdle. 975, no. 4.

[246] The rents received at the above dates were £13 12s. 4d., £17 0s. 9½d., and £17 9s. 0½d., while under the heading 'new rents' 4s., £1 7s. 6d., and £5 11s. 11d. was received in these three years, the last account showing a further item of £12 13s. 4d. for demesne lands rented out.

[247] Mins. Accts. bdle. 974, no. 23, 24. After this time there is less change in the expenditure and receipts, and the rolls are of less value owing to the omission of the detailed items that make up the whole account. Ibid. bdle. 975, no. 5, 10. See also ibid. bdle. 970, no. 13, 14 (Farleigh Hungerford).

[247a] Charters releasing bondsmen from all servitude and 'neifty' had again become common. Rec. of Borough of Axbridge (*Hist. MSS. Com. Rep.* iii, App. 305–6).

[248] Stat. 23 Edw. III, cap. 3, 6, 8 ; 25 Edw. III, cap. 1 ; 31 Edw. III, cap. 6 ; 12 Ric. II, cap. 4.

[249] See below.

[250] Cunningham, op. cit. i, 325.

[251] The discontent is reflected in the Court Rolls of the period, which are filled with notices of villeins fleeing from manors, and being caught and brought back, of tolls and dues being withheld and services refused, of rents in arrears, and of a general state of disorganization which led to many assaults and scenes of violence. Ct. R. portf. 199, no. 2–6 ; ibid. 200, no. 5 (Milverton and Odcomb). The wholesale destruction of manorial records and court rolls proved that the villeins appreciated the necessity of destroying the records of their servitude. G. M. Trevelyan, *Peasants' Revolt.*

SOCIAL AND ECONOMIC HISTORY

The share of Somerset in the rising does not appear to have been considerable, but the detailed story of the rebellion of the bondmen of the Bishop of Bath and Wells at Wellington has been preserved. Being ordered to carry hay to Wiveliscombe they refused to obey, and on the following day, armed with swords and staves, assembled 'in magnis conventiculis cum magna potencia' to resist the bishop. Another band of rioters, led by Thomas Ingleby, broke into the Hospital of St. John the Baptist at Bridgwater, and detained the master until he surrendered 'certain bonds between him and the men of the town' and paid a heavy ransom. They then attacked the neighbouring manor-houses, burning and destroying the court rolls, and finally broke open Ilchester gaol.[251a] The county was still in a very disturbed state in February 1382, when a commission was issued for the arrest of all homicides, robbers and insurgents then more than usually present in Somerset, Dorset, Devon, and Cornwall, and for their delivery to the gaol of the county in which their offence was committed, as it appeared that they escaped from one county into another.[252] In March a similar commission was appointed, and another followed in December,[253] after which order was apparently restored in the county.

The direct effect of the revolt, after the temporary concessions wrung by panic from the reluctant lords had been revoked, seems to have been but slight. It is probable, however, that it indirectly hastened the emancipation of the villeins, and gave an impetus to the tendency to farm out the demesne lands. Stock and land leases were not unknown before the Black Death,[254] but they did not become a noticeable feature in the county until the shortage of labour became a serious difficulty. An example of such a lease on the Bath Abbey lands contains the following clause :—

> We have granted, lett, indented and confirmed all our wether flokke of Combe aforesayde, containing 360 wethers, with all issues, profits, and revenues coming from the said flokke, with all pastures, closes, meadows, hills or downs, on which the said flokke usually pastured for £6 yearly.

A bond of £161 was given for the redelivery of the flock 'hoole, sounde and stronge, not rotten, banyd nor otherwise diseased.'[254a] The system spread rapidly in Somerset, and fostered the growth of a yeoman class, since the tenant was often able to save enough to buy his own stock and ultimately the land itself. The proportion of demesne land kept in hand to that let out on lease shows a progressive diminution. On the manor of Glastonbury, for instance, at the Dissolution, the annual value of the demesne lands was only about one-sixth of that of the leased property.[255]

Some idea of 14th-century farming in Somerset may be obtained from the Ministers' Accounts of the period. The wages of the regular servants, which seem small compared with the earnings of carpenters, tilers, and others, were supplemented by allowances of wheat, the usual amount given being one quarter of wheat every twelve weeks. Allowances of mixed grain

---

[251a] Assize R. 774, no. 7 ; *Cal. Pat.* 1381–5, p. 270.
[252] *Cal. Pat.* 1381–5, p. 136.   [253] Ibid. 140, 248.
[254] Early examples are to be found on the Glastonbury manors. *Glaston. Rentals and Surv.* 39.
[254a] Harl. MS. 3970, fol. 20, 29–30 (printed in Cunningham, *Engl. Ind. and Commerce*, App. 587).
[255] *Chron. of Peter Langtoft* (ed. Hearne), ii, 343 ; other examples may be quoted ; *Rentals and Surv.* Rolls 562, 570, and portf. 14, no. 28, 35, 38, 39 ; portf. 16, no. 34 ; portf. 32, no. 35. At Blagdon, for instance, in 1422, the demesne lands were worth £9 7s. 10d., and those rented out £32 12s. 0½d.

for brewing ale were given in the same way, and twenty-four ploughmen ploughing one boon day at Wellow were allowed bread (at the cost of 19½d.), ten pennyworth of cheese, and twenty-two pennyworth of ale.[256] Most of the farms were given over to corn raising, and stock was reared for the plough-teams and the use of the household only. A great many beasts were killed in the autumn, and salted for the use of the household during the winter months, but in spite of this hay and straw had to be bought for the winter keep of the plough-cattle.[257] On farms where there were a considerable number of sheep the ewes were milked, and the labour question was shelved by letting them out at 1½d. a head, while cows were let out at from 1s. 3d. to 4s. The fluctuations in the price of corn must have caused great distress among the peasants, which the regular farm servants escaped through the system of allowances.

A very considerable amount of travelling was done. Both the neighbouring markets and those at a great distance were attended for the purchase of stock, and some was brought from Salisbury and Bristol.[258] It cost a horseman 20s. to go from Farleigh Hungerford to London and back, while the five days' journey of the man who was sent to carry £27 in silver to the lord cost 5s. The accounts were made up and audited yearly by an auditor who presided over the exchequer of accounts, and who received £3 6s. 8d. as his salary for a year and a half.[259]

At the end of the 14th century prices of all commodities except labour were only slightly above the level from which they had been forced by the Black Death. Arable land in the open fields varied from 3d. to 6d. an acre ; two notices of arable land worth 1s. 3d. and 2s. 8d. an acre must refer to small pieces of choice inclosed land. Various acres of meadow-land were valued at 10d., 1s., 1s. 3d., 1s. 8d., and 2s. 6d., and pasture-land in the park at ½d. and 1d. an acre. A rush bed was worth 5s.; pasture for five sheep was worth 1d. yearly, and for one ox 5s. yearly.[260] Wheat, sold at 6s. 8d. per quarter in 1317, rose in 1346–7 to 9s. 4d. and 10s. 8d., while in the year following the plague it was sold at 4s. 4d. to 6s. 8d., rising in 1350–1 to 8s. 8d. The following years showed considerable fluctuations, prices ranging from 4s. 8d. in 1353–4 to 10s. 4d. in 1376.[261] The price of barley and oats varied in much the same way, the lowest prices of the century being 1s. 10d. and 1s. in 1349–50, and the highest 7s. and 3s. 4d. in 1346–7.[262] 'Vesc' was sold at from 7½d. per bushel to 10½d.; drage varied from 1s. 4d. to 4s. per quarter, while four loads of hay were sold for 11s.[263] Oxen, sold at 13s. 4d. in 1334, had fallen to 10s. and 11s. 6d. in 1341, were sold at 13s. 4d. to 16s. 8d. in 1346–7, and rising to 20s. in 1350–1, fell again to 13s. 6d. in

[256] Mins. Accts. bdle. 974, no. 20 ; Wellow, 14–15 Edw. III.
[257] Ibid.
[258] Mins. Accts. bdle. 970, no. 13 ; Farleigh Hungerford.
[259] Ibid. no. 13–21.
[260] Chan. Inq. p.m. 34 Edw. I, no. 31 ; *MSS. of D. and C. of Wells* (Hist. MSS. Com.), i, 346, 362 ; Chan. Inq. p.m. 13 Edw. II, no. 27 ; ibid. 19 Edw. III (1st nos.), no. 26 ; *Mins. Accts.* bdle. 974, no. 20, 14–15 Edw. II.
[261] (1317) Adam de Domerham, *Hist. Glaston.* (ed. Hearne), 215 ; (1321) Mins. Accts. bdle. 974, no. 20 ; (1346–7) ibid. no. 21, and bdle. 970, no. 12 ; (1349–50) bdle. 974, no. 22, and bdle. 970, no. 13 ; (1350–1) bdle. 974, no. 23 ; (1353–4) ibid. no. 14, 15 ; (1376) bdle. 975, no. 4 ; Hubert Hall, *Pipe R. of Bishopric of Winchester.*
[262] Mins. Accts.. bdle. 970, no. 12, 13–15 ; bdle. 974, no. 12, 23.　　　　[263] Ibid.

1353-4.[264] Hogs were sold at 1s. in 1340, the price rising to 2s. 6d. and 3s. 4d. in 1349-50 ; boar pigs were sold at 3s. and 3s. 4d., and sows at 2s. The price of ewe sheep varied from 9d. to 1s., except immediately after the plague, when they fetched from 14d. to 16d. Wethers and lambs, which averaged 8d. and 14d., rose to 14d. and 16d. The price of bulls varied from 12s. to 13s. 4d., and a plough horse was sold at 10s. Geese were sold at 4d. each, capons at 2d., and young doves at 3d. per dozen.[265]

The rise in the rates of wages due to the Black Death is very clearly marked. The yearly wages of drivers, shepherds, and ploughmen were 3s. in 1346-7, but rose to 4s. in 1349-50 and to 5s. in 1350-1. At the same time the wages of a dairyman rose from 2s. to 3s. Carpenters, paid 3d. daily in 1346-7, received 3½d. and 4d. in 1349-50,[266] and 2s. weekly in 1353-4. Some other wages, which cannot be compared at different periods, may be mentioned. A carter received 5s., a plough-driver 8s., a cowman 2s. 6d., and a bailiff 10s. yearly.

Reaping, usually paid at 3d. an acre, cost 6½d. an acre in 1349-50. Ploughing was paid at 5d. per acre, harrowing at 1d. an acre, stacking at 2d. a day, and carrying hay at 1d. a day. Piece work appears occasionally. 'Tiling the lords chamber' was paid at 8s., carrying rye from Exeter to Porlock, and from Dunster to Porlock, was paid at 3d. and 1d., and, by agreement with the steward, a tiler undertook to do all the necessary repairs to the manor-house for one year for 8s.[267]

Among the miscellaneous articles the price of which is recorded, tar was sold at from 5d. to 8d. a gallon, rising, however, to 10d. the year after the plague, and lime was 8d. per quarter. Apples cost 4d. to 8d. a quarter, salt varied from 4½d. to 9d. per bushel, pepper from 1s. 2d. to 1s. 8d. per lb. Cummin was 1½d. per pound, candles 2d., wax 8d. Half a stone of cheese was 4d., milk cost ¾d. per gallon, ale ¼d. per gallon, and twenty-four eggs were sold for 1d. A pipe of wine cost 2s. A 'fur robe and a double cloak' together cost £1 6s. 8d., while the high prices fetched by the skins of dead oxen (1s. 8d., 2s. 6d., and 2s. 8d.) account for the dearness of leather. A hay-cart cost 4s. 6d., a ploughshare 12d., and a yoke for oxen ½d. A 'slabbe' of iron cost 2½d., a thousand lath nails 4d., while paint varied from 10d. to 1s. a gallon.[268]

There is a great divergence of opinion about social conditions in the 15th century. Some have regarded it as a time of great prosperity, while it has been painted in the darkest colours by others. Support can be found for both views in Somerset.

---

[264] (1334) *MSS. of D. and C. of Wells* (Hist. MSS. Com.), i, 235 ; (1340-1) Mins. Accts. bdle. 974, no. 20; (1346-7) bdle. 970, no. 12, bdle. 974, no. 21; (1349-50) bdle. 974, no. 22, bdle. 970, no. 13 ; (1350-1) bdle. 974, no. 23 ; (1352-3) bdle. 970, no. 14 ; (1353-4) bdle. 970, no. 15 ; Hall, op. cit. 63-73 ; the average price for the whole of England was 9s. in 1350, rising to 14s. 8d. in 1358, and to 15s. 8¾d. by the end of the century. Thorold Rogers, *Hist. of Agric. and Prices*, i, 315-19.

[265] (1340-1) Mins. Accts. bdle. 974, no. 20; (1346-7) bdle. 970, no. 12, bdle. 974, no. 21; (1349-50) bdle. 974, no. 22, bdle. 970, no. 13 ; (1350-1) bdle. 974, no. 23 ; (1352-3) bdle. 970, no. 14 ; (1353-4) bdle. 970, no. 15.

[266] At this date 4½d. was the average carpenter's daily wage throughout England. By 1400 it had dropped slightly, to 4d. Thorold Rogers, loc. cit.

[267] (1340-1) Mins. Accts. bdle. 974, no. 20 ; (1346-7) bdle. 970, no. 12, bdle. 974, no. 21; (1349-50) bdle. 974, no. 22, bdle. 970, no. 13 ; (1350-1) bdle. 974, no. 23 ; (1352-3) bdle. 970, no. 14 ; (1353-4) bdle. 970, no. 15.

[268] Ibid. and *MSS. of D. and C. of Wells* (Hist. MSS. Com.).

Disturbed by the Wars of the Roses, and discouraged by the difficulty of obtaining labour,[269] many of the owners of land neglected the cultivation of their estates and the repair of roads and watercourses;[270] discontent and misery were rife among the peasants, while bands of soldiers—ruffling adherents of the red or the white rose—and of able-bodied vagrants (who came into prominence as a social danger about this time) roamed about the countryside. The weakness of the Crown left the seaboard counties exposed to attack from the 'king's enemies' and from pirates, the Somerset headlands flamed with beacons in vain, and the Government even failed to protect its merchant shipping in English waters. It was 'daily robbed by the King's Enemies upon the Sea, and the King's poor subjects dwelling by the Sea Coasts nigh . . . are taken and carried by the said Enemies where it please them,' and the growing boldness of the pirates made it 'a perilous dwelling by the sea coast.'[271] The decay of the central authority appears in complaints of escapes of felons from prison, of smuggling and piracy, of subsidies being withheld, of the king's lands wasted, and of debts and chattels concealed.[272] The petition of Roger Twynho against thirty-four 'rioutouse and misgoverned persons,' acting under the authority of George, Duke of Clarence, 'of his subtile and confected ymaginations', who forcibly seized a Somerset lady and carried her off to prison at Warwick on a charge of having given to Isabel, Clarence's wife, 'a venymouse drynke of ale myxt with poyson, of whych drynk she sekenyd and dyed' is typical of the disturbed state of the county.[273]

Many of the famous religious houses of the county were in great straits. They never really recovered from the shock of the Black Death; the burden of the great wars, the barrenness of the land, and a too lavish hospitality were all given as reasons for their decline.[274]

The bright side of the picture in Somerset may be seen in the growth of the flourishing boroughs, where considerable progress was being made, for which the growth of the cloth trade was mainly responsible.[275] The condition of Bristol, Bridgwater, Bath, Taunton, and many other towns contrasts vividly with that of much of the rest of Somerset. They had replaced the great local fairs as the centres of trade, which was organized within the towns by the Craft Gilds, the most important in Somerset being that of the clothiers. Under the rule of these gilds the towns were beginning to develop a more complex social organization, in which the modern division of capital and labour was foreshadowed, the burgesses being divided into masters, journeymen, and apprentices, all bound together by a common calling and accepting mutual responsibilities like the modern Friendly Society. The wealth acquired by the development of the wine and wool trades was in the hands of native capitalist merchants, who had replaced the Jews, and who were beginning to turn their attention to improvements in domestic architecture, beautifying their native towns with buildings like the house of William

---

[269] The population did not recover from the Black Death until nearly the end of the 15th century.

[270] The Court Rolls abound with cases of this kind, and with complaints of the high roads being flooded, owing to the neglect of ditches and sluices. e.g. Ct. R. portf. 200, no. 31.

[271] Stat. 20 Hen. VI, cap. 1 (preamble); *Paston Lett.* (ed. Gairdner), i, 114; *Cal. Pat.* 1467–77, p. 56.

[272] Ibid. p. 464.   [273] *Parl. R.* vi, 173–4.

[274] *Bruton and Montacute Chartul.* (Somers. Rec. Soc. viii), 201–4.

[275] References to the Somerset cloth trade were frequent in contemporary legislation. Stat. 47 Edw. III; 13 Ric. II; 4 Edw. IV, cap. 52; 4 Hen. VII, cap. 11; *Cal. Pat.* 1381–5, p. 384; 1467–77, p. 238.

Canynge at Bristol.[276] Their growing wealth appears in the list of sums contributed by them as loans to the king in 1382, 1386, and 1397. Bristol contributed £800, being second only to London, while Wells contributed £53 6s. 8d., and Bath £20.[277] Some of the boroughs were already occupied with the question of water supply. The arrangements made at Wells in 1451 are a curious mixture of mediaeval and modern methods. The water was to be obtained from St. Andrew's Well, and the description of conduits, engines, and reservoirs, above and below ground, of trenches, lead cisterns, and lead pipes 12 in. in circumference, has a very modern sound ; but the burgesses paid the bishop in a mediaeval manner for permission to use his water, promising to visit yearly his burial place in the cathedral to pray for his soul.[278]

The borough courts were very active, and many of the by-laws and ordinances drawn up by them about this time have been preserved, while the other records and accounts give a vivid picture of the social life of the little Somerset towns.[279]

At the same time the profitable business of wool production made it possible for magnificent Perpendicular churches to be built in the heart of rural Somerset, buildings which cannot be ignored as evidence of prosperity. The ill-feeling aroused by the conflicting interests of the lord and his men was beginning to die down with the spread of new methods. New life was springing from the decay, ' mediaeval groups were breaking up and modern distinctions were beginning to appear . . . the lines of cleavage had become horizontal and not perpendicular,' as the money link between employer and labourer, landlord and tenant, replaced the old personal tie between lord and man.[280]

The manorial system, however, still had a firm hold on the county. New land was still granted out to be held in villeinage—heriots and merchets were still exacted, runaway villeins reclaimed, and tenants fined for neglecting their services.[281] The manor courts passed ordinances dealing with a great variety of subjects, the most common being rules for the use of the common pasture, and for the method of cultivation of the arable fields.[282] Others relate to the enforcement of sanitary measures, the prohibition of keeping pigs in the market-place, and the removal of nuisances from highways and ditches.[283] Appeals were made to earlier court rolls in cases where the conditions under which a tenement was held were in dispute. In addition to the election of officials, which was carried on as before, the courts still exercised their diminishing police jurisdiction, and inflicted fines for the breach of the assize of bread or ale, which came to a considerable amount in the aggregate, though 3d. was the usual fine inflicted. Fines also were the

---

[276] Cunningham, op. cit. i, 360.   [277] Ibid. 385.

[278] MSS. of D. and C. of Wells (Hist. MSS. Com.), i, 433.

[279] e.g. Bridgwater Bailiffs' and Water Bailiffs' Accts.; Rolls of the Debt Court; Wells Chamberlain's Accts. ; Hist. MSS. Com. Rep. i, App. 99, 107. The customs of the borough of Taunton are recorded in a series of by-laws of the late 14th century. Mary Bateson, Borough Customs (Selden Soc.), i, Introd. 51, 52.

[280] Cunningham, op. cit.

[281] Ct. R. portf. 200, no. 23–5 (Shepton Montague, 27 Edw. III to 6 Hen. IV) ; ibid. portf. 200, no. 31 (Somerton, 1394). In this roll the custom as to the marriage of daughters and ordaining of sons of villeins is set out at length.

[282] Ct. R. portf. 200, no. 31–32. Tenants, for instance, were frequently forbidden to feed geese, pigs, or goats on the common pasture. Carrying arms ' within the lordship,' shooting with arrows, and playing games after eight o'clock, were forbidden. Hancock, Hist. of Minehead, 157.

[283] Ct. R. portf. 198, no. 14 (Bridgwater, 45 Edw. III).

punishment of a number of minor offences,[283a] poaching game or fish, or cutting timber. Scolding women were fined 1d. Many examples are still found of customary payments or rents in kind. The cathedral church of Wells received its yearly payment of two loaves, two pigs, and two bottles of mead from Glastonbury Abbey ;[284] land was held by the rent of 20 marks and two cartloads of hay,[285] while a rent of strawberries had been recently commuted for 2s. in 1438.[286] It is significant, however, that, in the great majority of cases, the service due from land to its overlord had been forgotten. In the reign of Henry VII, for instance, the phrase 'by what service held unknown' meets the eye everywhere.[287] The few cases in which the obligation to a customary or honorary payment is set down, such as rendering a rose or a pair of spurs, are interesting survivals rather than common incidents.

Besides the development of sheep-farming, another proof of prosperity in 15th-century Somerset is the revival of inclosing, though as yet only for the purpose of cultivating land hitherto waste, or for the division of the common pasture lands. Examples of both movements are found in the Ministers' Accounts of the manor of Porlock,[288] which also show a great increase in the amount of hired labour required to do work hitherto done by customary tenants, such as repairing walls, driving beasts, reaping sedges and reed, in addition to greatly increased expenditure for labour at haymaking and harvest. The process of inclosing was already going on at Porlock. Men were hired at 3d. per day to inclose the lord's park and the 'Broadfield' (which occupied them for 198 days), and in the following year sixty-seven days' labour was spent in digging after the plough in the park, and removing thorns and briers there.[289] Examples of the survival of customary methods are found ; allowances of corn were continued,[290] the customary tenants received grants at the sheep-shearing, and tolls of the mill were still paid in kind, a man receiving 3d. yearly 'for keeping the chest to receive the lady's tolls.' On this manor sheep-farming was already more important than corn-growing ; in 1421 only 21 acres of corn were sown, while 21 stone of wool was the product of 504 fleeces.[291]

As the years went on, in spite of a decrease of revenue, there was an increase in profits, the expenses of labour in ploughing and harvest being diminished.[292] Towards the end of the period corn was bought, the amount raised being insufficient for the needs of the manor. The tendency to let out the demesne land seems to have been checked to some extent by the profits derived from sheep-farming. In 1424 land hitherto farmed out was taken back into the hands of the lady of the manor, a first sign of the land-hunger that appeared in the following century. The prevalent uncertainty of employment is reflected in these accounts, men being hired for very short periods to do work usually done by regular farm labourers.[292a]

[283a] Ct. R. portf. 200, no. 32, 42.   [284] *Hist. MSS. Com. Rep.* i, App. 93.   [285] Ibid. iii, App. 363.
[286] Ibid. 364.   [287] *Cal. Inq. p.m. Hen. VII*, no. 18, 22, 38, 41, 87, 118, 156, 257.
[288] Mins. Accts. bdle. 973, no. 24, 25.   [289] Ibid. no. 25.
[290] The usual allowance at Porlock was 2 bushels for every three weeks.   Ibid.
[291] Domestic spinning and weaving were important, 7 stone of this wool being taken over by the lady of the manor for cloth-making.
[292] The increase in profits was in spite of a murrain among the cattle and sheep. In 1419–20 one ram, 6 wethers, 13 ewes, and 18 lambs died of murrain, and in 1422 the mortality was even greater. The live stock on the estate included, besides sheep, a fair number of oxen and pigs, but only one cow. The poultry included 6 peacocks and peahens.   [292a] Mins. Accts. bdle. 973, no. 25.

At another manor it may be noted how greatly the expenses of the up-keep of the manor-house, mill, and farm buildings varied from year to year, the cost of repairs to the manor-house ranging from 8s. 11½d. to £5 12s. 1½d. This latter expense was incurred when the hall was retiled and repaired 'against the coming of the lady,' whose advent also accounts for money spent for 'cutting rushes for the hall and chamber' and for 'straw to make the lady's bed.' This manor was a corn-growing and cattle-raising estate ; sheep-farming was on a very modest scale, one ram, one wether, one ewe, and one lamb being the whole flock, while there were 150 head of cattle, including the large number of 55 cows.[292b]

An account of the household expenses at Porlock about fifty years later[293] throws light on the social conditions on a large Somerset estate in the 15th century. The household expenses for the year amounted to £844 13s. 4d. It is obvious that the produce of the Porlock estate alone could not have supported such a large establishment, and there is evidence that corn, cattle, and poultry were brought in from the other estates.[294] The household consumed 76½ quarters of wheat (2½ quarters being used for pastry), 5 bullocks, 6 oxen, 7 cows, 10 calves, and 16 other cattle, 128 wethers, 1 boar, 10 hogs, 8 pigs, 148 geese, 60 ducks, 251 capons, 59 cocks, 48 hens, 15 pullets, 234 chickens, and 4½ bushels and 1 peck of green peas. About 34 dozen of fish of all kinds, including fresh and dried congers, mullets, and ling (all bought at Exeter), and dried pollock, were disposed of.[295] The household probably consisted of about eighteen persons, since there is an entry, 'Travelling of the lord from London to Porlock with eighteen persons, with food by the way, £3 11s. 5½d.,' while the expenses of the household of the lord at London for nine days are set down at £4 4s. 2d. The provisions in the larder on the eve of Whit Sunday included 1 carcase of beef, 4 sheep, 1 calf, 1 hog, 4 lambs, 1 swan, 2 dozen partridges, 1 dozen plovers, 1 quail, 3 salmon, 1 conger, shell fish, fresh eels, salt fish, and 'hard' fish, 60 loaves, 10 gallons of wine and 60 of ale.[295a]

No great change had taken place in farming, and though improved methods involving a four-course rotation had been introduced in some parts, three-course or even two-course rotation of crops was the rule.[296] The customary methods in force were very complicated, and rights over the same piece of land were curiously intricate. In a moorland pasture of 34 acres in Knowle, which belonged to the tenants in common, the lady of the manor had a separate close of 8 acres, which was hers for haymaking alone, that is, from the Feast of the Purification until 1 August. After this latter date the Abbot of Athelney held the 8 acres until Michaelmas, taking the profits (which must have been very small), and then the lady of the manor came in again and held till the Purification.[296a]

[292b] Mins. Accts. bdle. 826, no. 21.

[293] These accounts were found by Mr. Chadwyck Healey among the records of the Corporation of Rye and have been printed by him. (*Hist. of part of W. Somers.* App. 494–6.)

[294] The older plan of an itinerant household making a tour of the various estates was becoming obsolete.

[295] There is no notice of the use of any bread except wheaten bread. 3 qrs. 2 bus. of barley malt and 81 qrs. 2 bus. of oat malt were used for brewing strong and small ale, and 3 qrs. of 'roscorn' for household ale.

[295a] Chadwyck Healey, op. cit. App. 494–8. The household accounts of Sir Hugh Luttrell of Dunster contain similar information. Maxwell-Lyte, *Hist. of Dunster*, 79–108.

[296] *Muchelney and Athelney Chartul.* 162, 194 ; *Bruton and Montacute Chartul.* 20.

[296a] *Muchelney and Athelney Chartul.* 130, 131.

The problem of poverty first became acute in the 15th century. Hitherto local organizations—the religious houses, the landowners, and the Craft Gilds—had been equal to their responsibilities. The monasteries had taken the chief part. They gave hospitality to travellers and doles of food to beggars,[297] were the hospitals of the sick[298] and the homes of the dying, and relieved those 'who for shame would blush to beg,' by granting corrodies or daily allowances of food and clothing.[299] It was no uncommon thing for the lord of a manor to pension poor and infirm dependants, and anniversaries of deaths were celebrated by giving feasts to the poor.[299a] The wills of the period contain many bequests to the poor of food, clothing, and fuel, and of money to maintain them in almshouses or hospitals.[300] The sick, infirm, lame, and blind were also the object of many bequests, as were the prisoners in Ilchester gaol.[301] Charity of this kind, however, proved quite insufficient to deal with the poverty produced by foreign and civil wars, plagues and famines, and by the social and economic changes of the 14th century. National legislation superseded local effort, and the Act of 1388 for the punishment of able-bodied beggars and the maintenance of the impotent poor has been called the first English poor law.[302]

It is curious to notice that no instance of direct almsgiving appears in the 15th-century Churchwardens' Accounts. Many gifts to the church are recorded, but the funds thus obtained seem to have been used for the maintenance of or addition to the fabric and not for almsgiving.[303] The necessities of the poor must have been provided for by private generosity or by gild fellowships; the parish as such was not concerned with the relief of the poor until the reign of Henry VIII.[304] Gifts of live stock to the churches were so numerous that at Pilton special wardens had to be appointed to keep the parish cows, known as key or kye wardens. The flock of sheep belonging to St. Michael's, Bath, was farmed out, as were the Yatton cows.[305]

[297] On 19 days in the year the monks of Bath fed 100 poor persons. *Bath Chartul.* Introd. xv, and ii, 33,152.
[298] In 1328 Master John the physician gave a bond to give his attendance upon the infirmary of Bath with medicine, &c., being given a chamber within the gate of the priory and a corrody. Ibid. ii, 121.
[299] The allowances given by Glastonbury Abbey, for instance, to widows or the crippled consisted of an allowance of bread and ale and a small sum of money—usually 1d.—weekly. *Glaston. Inq.* 17. A corrody of a loaf of bread and a pot of ale daily was the provision of Maud the anchorite (*inclusa*) of Stapleton. *Bath Chartul.* ii, 30 ; see also p. 140. The king's superannuated servants were often maintained in the Somerset religious houses, and the right of nomination to corrodies of this kind was jealously watched ; e.g. *Bath Chartul.* ii, 113, 137–9, 181. *Muchelney and Athelney Chartul.* Introd. xii. Many grants of land to monasteries were made on the condition that the grantor should nominate a servant to a corrody (*Bath Chartul.* ii, 162) or in trust for the distribution of food or money to the poor (*Muchelney and Athelney Chartul.* 55) or *ad susceptionem hospitum. Muchelney and Athelney Chartul.* 154–5 ; *Cal. Pat.* 1381–5, p. 221.
[299a] Mins. Accts. bdle. 973, no. 23, 25 (the lord's obit at Porlock) ; *Bruton and Montacute Chartul.* 59, 60, 136 ; *Bath Chartul.* 152–160. Many chantries provided for similar charities ; e.g. *MSS. of D. and C. of Wells* (Hist. MSS. Com.), i, 458.
[300] Among those mentioned are the hospitals of St. John at Wells and Bridgwater, of St. Cuthbert at Wells, of St. John the Baptist at Bath, of St. Bartholomew at Bristol, and others at Taunton, Langport and Glastonbury, and almshouses at Stogursey and Yeovil. *Somers. Medieval Wills* (Somers. Rec. Soc.), 63, 164, 168, 291, 364, &c. *Churchwardens' Accts.* (Somers. Rec. Soc. iv), 248–9.
[301] *Somers. Medieval Wills,* 1401, 1407, 1417, 1447, 1457, 1458, 1487 (pp. 8, 25, 91, 92, 157, 176, 183, 270, &c.). References to Ilchester gaol appear on pp. 54, 158, 244, &c.
[302] Stat. 12 Ric. II, cap. 7. In the following year the first law of another long series was passed, a Game Law enacting 'that none should hunt but they that have a sufficient living.' 13 Ric. II, s. i, cap. 13.
[303] *Churchwardens' Accts.* (Somers. Rec. Soc. iv), 53, 65, 125, 213, 215, 229.
[304] Ibid. Introd. xiii, 458 ; ibid. 69, 225.
[305] Ibid. 69, 225. 2s. was received in 1437–8 for the hire of a church cow (p. 178) ; a flock of ewe sheep was let out for seven years at 2s. yearly with the proviso that 'if they die or mynish' 16d. apiece was to be returned. (Yatton, 1524–5, p. 37).

The hard lot of the peasant in the 15th century, with his long hours of labour, irregular employment, poor food and poorer housing, had some compensations. The great feasts of the Church were holidays for the labourers, and were enlivened by sports and shooting at the butts, while Hockday was especially a time of revelry.[306] Evidence has been found of the existence of gilds in the majority of the parishes;[306a] at Croscombe, for instance, there were seven—those of the Webbers (weavers), the Tuckers and Fullers, the Archers, the Hogglers, the Young Men, the Maidens and the Wives, each with their yearly revel.[307] The surplus funds of these gilds were usually handed over for the service of the church. The Churchwardens' Accounts also contain notices of the performance of religious plays. At Tintinhull there were usually three plays yearly; the proceeds of the Christmas play in 1451 amounted to 6s. 8d. and were given to the new rood loft.[308] The 'play kings' or 'mock kings' presented secular subjects, in the summer and autumn and at Christmas—while a play called the 'Coming in of Robin Hood' was performed nearly every year at Croscombe.[309] All these plays brought in substantial sums which were applied to church purposes by the wardens. The monotony of rural life was also relieved by the church ales, which were very popular as social gatherings and were a source of income to the parish.[310] Occasionally two parishes combined to hold an ale—Yatton is found visiting Congresbury and *vice versa*—or some benefactor would give the parish an ale.[311] Lesser gatherings known as 'clerks' ales' for the maintenance of the parish clerks, or 'bid-ales'—arranged (as the mediaeval form of the 'benefit performance' or 'charity matinée') to obtain funds for some special person or cause—were also frequently held. The whole system reached its greatest development at the end of the 16th century, but abuses began to creep in.[311a] There were many complaints of disorders at the church ales. At Yeovil in 1607 it was alleged that they led to 'minstrelsye and dauncinge on Sunday' and 'carrying men upon a cavele stafe,'[312] and the result was their suppression, the judges at the assizes of 1631 ordering that no church ales, clerk ales, bid-ales, woodward ales, bull-baitings or bear-baitings should be held henceforth in the county.[313]

The growth of the church house as the centre of the social life of the parish is a feature of 15th-century Somerset. At Tintinhull, for instance, it began as a bakehouse and brewhouse occasionally let out for hire to private

---

[306] It is interesting to notice the custom of 'crying the neck' after harvest, which survived until recently, the expenses of 'le necke' in 1522 being set down at 14d., while 18d. was paid for victuals at 'le necke' in 1425. Mins. Accts. bdle. 973, no. 24-5.

[306a] F. W. Weaver, *Wells Wills.*

[307] *Churchwardens' Accts.* pp. xiii, 7, 69, 225. The annual 'club walking' of the male and female Friendly Societies, which includes a procession through the village, a church service, dinner and dancing, is the modern counterpart of the gild feasts.

[308] *Churchwardens' Accts.* (Somers. Rec. Soc.), pp. xiv, 153, 184, 209.

[309] Ibid. 30, 31. In 1510 this play brought in £3 6s. 8d. There was a similar show at Wells. *Hist. MSS. Com. Rep.* i, App. 107.

[310] 'Our taverne ale at Wysontide' brought in £5 1s. 8d. at Yatton, and three other Yatton ales yielded £14. In 1446 two men had to be hired at a cost of 10d. to help brew. *Churchwardens' Accts.* 139, 140, 142.

[311] Ibid. 94. In 1505 there is an entry of 12d. paid for scot at a neighbouring ale.

[311a] A bid-ale was arranged in 1592, 'in the name of some poor men,' to provide funds for the defence of men who had poached red deer in the forest of Exmoor. *Somers. Arch. Soc. Proc.* 1883, p. 55.

[312] *Quarter Sess. R. Somers.* ii, no. 61 (Somers. Rec. Soc. xxiii), 5.

[313] Ibid.; *Hist. MSS. Com. Rep.* iii, App. 286; *Churchwardens' Accts.* 245-7.

persons ; [314] but by the reign of Henry VII it had become the scene of village feasts and church ales, with a resident cook. The church-house continued all through the reigns of Elizabeth and James I to be the chief source of income for the parish, but the suppression of church ales in the reign of Charles I was followed by the decline of the church-houses, many of them being afterwards used as poor houses.[315]

There was certainly a great improvement in the standard of comfort in the 15th century,[315a] and domestic architecture was beginning to show signs of the development characteristic of the century that followed. The wills of the period [316] contain bequests of elaborate beds of arras, cloth of gold tapestry or ‘ Saracen work,’ described as ‘ powdered with figures ’ or ‘ embroidered with Griffonys ’ ; hangings in the hall, parlour, and chamber are mentioned, and the other household furniture included chests, coffers, hall tables, stools, wardrobes, cushions, and a great variety of household utensils. Musical instruments mentioned in these wills are the ‘ cittern,’ harp, and lute. The plate was both beautiful and elaborate. Mention is made of silver basins and bowls ‘ pounced with knots of sykols,’ silver ewers, cups ‘ with arms engraven ’ or ‘ with a stag on the cover,’ dishes, goblets, horns, jugs, powder-boxes, saltcellars, and spoons. A large proportion of Sir Hugh Luttrell’s plate in 1421, including fifteen cups, was of silver-gilt. The wearing apparel mentioned is occasionally gorgeous—gowns of silk, satin, velvet, cloth of gold or damask (the colours mentioned being scarlet, tawny, russet, green, red, violet, or ‘starling colour’), kirtles and kerchiefs, shoes, tippets and tunics, girdles of silk, silver, or velvet ‘ with pearls and mordaunt ’ ; the materials less frequently met with include ‘ cloth of Lankeshire make,’ ‘ bord Alexander,’ ‘ garnesye,’ ‘ lawnde,’ and ‘ tyssu.’ Furs of beaver, fox, marten, miniver, and lambskin are often mentioned. The jewellery mentioned includes rings, brooches, chains, crosses, and seals, while sapphires and ‘ the stone called Diamunde ’ also appear. Bequests of books were not uncommon. Most of them were theological, but among the others mentioned are Cicero, Pliny, and Livy, ‘ the earthly law of courts of Chancery,’ and works on ethics and politics, medicine and physic.[317]

Craftsmen were sent for from considerable distances to beautify the churches. £6 was paid at Yatton to an embroiderer from Bristol ; [318] a freemason came from Exeter to build St. George’s Chapel, Croscombe, 30s. being his payment for setting up an image of St. George ; [319] and a Bristol glazier was hired for the windows at Yatton.[320] In 1499 a processional cross for the same church cost £18, while in 1534 £30 was spent on vestments.[321]

[314] The parish in 1446–7 received 7d. for hire of brewhouse, and 16s. 6d. from the rents of the bakehouse in 1437–8. *Churchwardens’ Accts.* 182, 178, 196, 201, &c.

[315] The late 19th century has seen a revival of the idea of the church-house in the building of church-rooms in many Somerset parishes, which are used for social as well as church purposes.

[315a] An account of a dinner given at Wells in 1424 shows that cookery had become very elaborate. Vegetables were little used, but the dishes included venison, heron, swan, pheasant, peacock, curlew, woodcock, snipe, plover, and lark, with fresh and salt fish, puff pastry, and custards. Each course was concluded by a ‘ soltelte,’ an ambitious design in sugar and paste, e.g. ‘ the Trinity sitting in a sun of gold.’ *Downside Rev.* xiv.

[316] *Somers. Medieval Wills* (Somers. Rec. Soc.) ; Smith, *Somers. Wills* ; F. W. Weaver, *Wells Wills.*

[317] *Somers. Medieval Wills,* 51, 117, 153, 170, 179, 203, 210, 224, 253, 263, 301, 323, 370, &c. ; Maxwell-Lyte, op. cit. 93, 94.

[318] *Churchwardens’ Accts.* 149.   [319] Ibid. 30.   [320] Ibid. 168, 190.

[321] Ibid. 79. In 1548 a Bristol painter came to Yatton to cover up the sacred pictures, receiving 11s. and 43s. for his work, and three years later a gilder from the same city received 13s. 8d. for gilding the king’s arms, the latter entry being significant of the new doctrine of the royal headship of the church.

There was little change in prices and wages from 1400 to 1540, before the debasement of the coinage had lowered the standard of value.[322] The average price of wheat for the whole of England in this period was about 6s. per quarter, and a list of the prices of grain in Somerset between 1420 and 1473 proves that prices were steadying, the widest range in the price of wheat being from 4s. 8d. to 8s., the average being 6s. 8d. Barley varied from 2s. 6d. to 6s. 2d., oats from 1s. 8d. to 2s. 8d., rye from 4s. to 6s. 8d., beans from 2s. to 4s., and green peas from 2s. 8d. to 4s.[323] Farm horses were valued at about 10s. on the average, though much lower prices are found,[324] oxen at from 9s. to 13s. 6d., cows at 5s. 10d. to 9s. 6d., though a cow and a calf fetched 18s. 6d. in 1451.[325] Ewe sheep fetched 5d., wethers 9d., a pig 2s., while a goat was sold for 3d.

The wages of a tiler varied from 2½d. to 3d. a day if food was provided, and were 4d. or 5d. if without food, his man receiving 2d. with food or 3d. without; the carpenter received from 5d. a day to 6s. 6d. a week, the latter, however, including his man; the stone mason 4d. or 2s. 4d. weekly; the ordinary labourer from 2s. to 2s. 6d. weekly;[326] the ploughman received 12s. yearly, the shepherd 10s., the plough-driver 10s. yearly or 1½d. daily. The bailiff's wages were 20s. yearly, with an allowance of 12d. weekly ' when not at the table of the lady.' 'John the Cook with his livery for the year' received £1 14s. 8d., a laundress was paid 4s. for the year, and a bookbinder 3s. 4d. for a week.[327] Harrowing was paid at 2d. a day, hay-carrying at 3½d., cleaning the mill-leat at 4d. Mowing was paid at 6d. per acre, and mowing and carrying together at 1s. 3d.[328]

Some prices of miscellaneous articles may be mentioned. Lime was 8d. to 9d. a quarter, tar 4d. a quart, plaster 2s. a quarter; one cartload of stone cost 8d. to 1s., twelve seams of Welsh boards cost 8s. (while the freight came to 1s. 7d.), one load of timber was 3s., and an oak tree fit for timber cost 2s., lead was 5s. a hundredweight, 200 tiles cost 10d.,[329] 1,000 lath-nails 18d. and 20d., and 100 hatch nails 5d. Wool was 2s. 6d. to 2s. 8d. a stone. One doeskin for bookbinding cost 7d., three sheep-skins cost 8d., and four goat-skins 3s. 4d. Wax was 6d. per lb., candles 1d. per pound; two gallon jars of beer cost 4d., and one gallon of wine 10d. A mill-wheel cost 11s., a mill-brake 2s. 6d., a new pair of stocks 12d., a ladder 5d., a rake 1d., a wheelbarrow 10d., a waggon rope 20d., two harrows 13d., and one pair of traces 4d. Fourteen yards of Irish cloth were bought for 18d., nine ells of canvas for sacks for 3s., four ells of woollen cloth for 7d., while twelve ells of linen cloth were bought for 7s. 7d. and 9 yds. of buckram for 3s.[330] A

[322] Thorold Rogers, *Agric. and Prices*, iv, 718.
[323] Ibid. iii, 21, 30, 41, 42, 47, 58, 68, 45–66, 152. Most of these prices have been taken from the quotations at the markets at Yeovil, Taunton, and Bath. The dearest years were 1430 and 1444, and the cheapest 1459. See also Mins. Accts. bdle. 973, no. 24–7 (Porlock 1419–26).
[324] Mins. Accts. as above.
[325] Ibid.; Thorold Rogers, op. cit. iii, 152.
[326] *Hist. MSS. Com. Rep.* x, App. iii, 289, 291; Mins. Accts. bdle. 973, no. 24–7; *Churchwardens' Accts.* 13, 82, 87, 153, 179, 198.
[327] *Hist. MSS. Com. Rep.* iii, App. 365.
[328] Thorold Rogers, op. cit. iii, 611–13.
[329] Elsewhere in the county 1,000 were bought for 14d.
[330] Mins. Accts. bdle. 973; *Churchwardens' Accts.* 13, 82, 87, 153, 161, 179, 187, 198; *Chron. Peter Langtoft* (ed. Hearne), ii, 343; *Hist. MSS. Com. Rep.* iii, App. 365; x, App. iii, 289; Thorold Rogers, op. cit. iii, 373.

Bible, ' of the largest volume,' cost 11*s.*, and a ' Paraphrasus of Erasmus ' 11*s.* 4*d.*

The manorial system in Somerset, which had never quite recovered from the strain of the Black Death and the shock of the Peasants' Revolt, received its death-blow from the inclosure movement of the early 16th century, which replaced the hunger for labour by a hunger for land as the motive force affecting the relations between master and man. The central period of the movement was between 1490 and 1510, and its most conspicuous form in Somerset was the inclosure of arable lands and their conversion into pasture for sheep-farming. The inclosure movement involved a great displacement of population. Comparatively few men were required on a sheep-farm which as arable land had employed dozens, and the result was a bitter outcry about the depopulated countryside and the empty and ruined cottages. The fact that it was no longer necessary for the landowner to migrate from one manor to another to consume the produce, since wool could be readily turned into money, led to many manor-houses being shut up, and explains the constant complaints of the decay of good and substantial houses.

Another form of the inclosure movement showed itself in the division of the open arable fields and the consolidation of the scattered strips into small fields. These were fenced round, and the method of cultivation was settled by the will of the owner instead of by the decision of the court of the manor.[330a] Comparatively little, however, is heard of this form of inclosure in the county in the 16th century, and still less of the inclosure of commons and wastes, which were at this time usually added to the parks of the great lords. Such encroachments, though extremely unpopular, were relatively unimportant.[331]

This 16th-century inclosure movement was almost entirely confined to the western half of the county. When Leland visited Somerset in 1537 or 1538 the western part could be described as ' al in Hegge rowes of Enclosures,' while the land he describes as ' champaine ' was in East Somerset.[332] This limitation of inclosures, which recalls an early distinction in character between the two halves of the county,[332a] was partly due to the survival of Celtic methods in the West Somerset villages, by which the annual re-allotment of the strips in the open fields was continued probably up to the date when co-aration ceased to be practised, and when individual cultivation was about to be adopted. Since there had been no appropriation of particular strips it was natural for the peasants when they dissolved plough partnership to divide the land in blocks instead of scattered strips.[333] In villages of this type, therefore, inclosure whether for continued tillage or for conversion to pasture, being to the obvious

---

[330a] This change was economically a great gain. On Porlock Manor, for instance, inclosed arable land was worth 2*s.* per acre and uninclosed arable only 12*d.* Aug. Off. Misc. Bks. vol. 385, fol. 97 (printed Chadwyck Healey, op. cit. 412–22).

[331] Chan. Misc. bdle. 7, no. 2 (4). Some of the largest deer parks were those of the Abbot of Glastonbury. Northwood Park, where there were ' 160 dere of auntler and 540 dere of Rascall,' was 4 miles in circuit, while the neighbouring common of Glastonbury Moor was 16 miles round. *Chron. Peter Langtoft* (ed. Hearne), ii, 344, 345.

[332] Leland, *Itin.* ii ; Leland's description is borne out by the fact that when the later Parliamentary inclosure movements of the 18th and 19th centuries followed, most of the west of the county was not involved because already inclosed. G. Slater, *Engl. Peasantry and Enclosure of Common Fields*, 161, 246.

[332a] See above, p. 267.   [333] Slater, op. cit. 175.

advantage of everyone, came early and without outside interference. The comparatively small number of freeholders in these West Somerset manors, and the great power of the lords, led to a very large number of inclosures for sheep-farming, for which the comparatively poor soil of that part of the county was specially adapted. West Somerset was thus very early inclosed, and was almost untouched by the inclosures by Act of Parliament which came two centuries later.[334]

The movement was not allowed to go on without opposition. It was suspected and unpopular, labourers began to find it difficult to get work, and the 'unemployed problem' leapt to a prominent position. There were pamphlets directed against the 'inhuman practices of the madded and irreligious depopulators, these despoilers of towns, ruiners of commonwealths, occasioners of beggary, cruel inclosiers,' and the central government made every effort to check the process by legislation, the Act of 1488 being followed by a proclamation in 1514, and by further Acts of Parliament in 1515 and 1516.[334a] The comparative failure of legislation [334b] led to the appointment in 1517 of a royal commission of the principal noblemen and gentlemen of the shire.[335] Unfortunately the returns for Somerset have not been preserved, but it is clear that West Somerset at all events had been inclosed to a considerable extent in the 16th century.[336] The movement made much less progress in the eastern part of the county, where inclosure was the exception rather than the rule.[337]

One of the results of the inclosure movement appears in the further weakening of the manorial system. The rendering of customary services was becoming comparatively unimportant. On the great manor of Old Cleeve, for instance, out of a total revenue of £102 12s. 6½d., the value of the customary services was represented by 10s. 6d. only,[338] and similar evidence can be found for all parts of the county.[339] Although the phrase 'to be held by all due and accustomed service' appears in most 16th-century grants of land, it became an empty form when once the lord had lost the desire for his man's labour, and the average manor court of the period was increasingly concerned with the formal business of land conveyance.[340]

In the great strongholds of conservatism, however, the broad lands of the monasteries, many examples may be found of the vitality of the old methods. Land was still let out on lease to be held by a rent paid partly in money and partly in kind. The tenant of land held from Bath Abbey on a lease for three lives paid a rent of 26 quarters of wheat to be threshed and winnowed and carried into the prior's granary at the tenant's expense. This wheat was to be delivered weekly between Michaelmas and Whitsuntide

---

[334] Slater, op. cit. 161.   [334a] Stat. 4 Hen. VII, cap. 9 ; 6 Hen. VIII, cap. 5 ; 7 Hen. VIII, cap. 1.

[334b] Evasion of the law was as easy as it was profitable, and a single furrow drawn across a wide expanse of pasture brought it within the definition of land under the plough.

[335] Several cases of each kind of inclosure may be found in Chan. Misc. bdle. 7, no. 2 (4). See also L. and P. Hen. VIII, ii, 3927 ; Pat. 9 Hen. VIII, pt. ii, m. 6 d.

[336] The extreme narrowness of many of the West Somerset lanes points to inclosure before carts were in general use.

[337] Adam de Domerham, Hist. Glaston. (ed. Hearne) ; B.M. Add. R. no. 28241, 28242 ; Aug. Off. Misc. Bks. vol. 385, fol. 97. Part of some of the Glastonbury manors had been inclosed, and the value of the land was much enhanced, inclosed pasture being worth 1s. 6d. an acre and arable 1s. an acre.

[338] Rentals and Surv. portf. 14, no. 34.

[339] Ibid. R. 562, 570 ; ibid. portf. 14, no. 35–9.

[340] Ct. R. portf. 198, no. 16, 20, 24, 45, 52, 61 ; portf. 200, no. 1, 14, 17–20.

according to demand, a burdensome arrangement which involved carting in the winter months. The rent also included 22 quarters of best barley to be similarly delivered, and four wainloads of wood to be cut down before May, and carried and piled within the monastery or manor-house as directed. The tenant was also bound to feed and fatten in his stall yearly one ox for his landlord, and to do suit at the hallmote court of Lyncombe and the hundred court of Barton, and he was to act without fee as collector of the priory rents, making quarterly payments and handing in an account.[341] A 16th-century terrier of Glastonbury sets out the manor customs 'as appears in the ancient custumary.' The reeve still held land in virtue of his office without payment of rent, the amount allotted to him being 11 acres 1 perch of meadow and pasture for twelve oxen. The customary works due from the tenants called 'Mondeymen' are set out at length; each was to work for forty days (the days being fixed by the reeve 'at the will of the lord and not at the will of the tenant'), working six full hours every day, and taking each day ½d. They also owed eight autumn works, for each of which they were paid 1d. for six hours' work. Other regulations follow, more characteristic of the 14th than of the 16th century, and it is specially recorded that the commutation of these works for 2s. 4d. yearly is 'at the lord's pleasure.'[341a]

There are also examples of land being newly granted out in the 16th century to be held under mediaeval conditions; a lessee, for instance, under Cleeve Abbey was bound to find dinner and supper once a year at the grange for the abbot and twenty of his men, 'secular and regular,' in attendance on him.[341b] Though in most cases it may be said that the grants of manumission which are found at this date were only important as setting the stamp of legality on freedom already acquired in practice, the survival of old obligations on some estates must have made the grants more than a nominal boon. The *nativi* were still paying *capitagium*, and merchet was being paid for the marriage of *nativae* on the Glastonbury manors, where the number of bondmen 'whose bodies and goods are always at the lord's pleasure' is enumerated at the date of the Dissolution.[342]

After that date the rapid decay of the manorial system all over the county became obvious, owing to the replacement of the monks by new men whose anxiety to make the most of their property showed them the futility of insisting upon the old services; manorialism in Somerset was inevitably giving way to the modern methods of land tenure.[343]

The inclosure movement, followed by the displacement of labour, the higher rents and harder terms imposed by the new landlords who had replaced the easy-going religious houses, the rise of prices following the debasement of the coinage,[344] and the inadequate wages fixed by the court of quarter sessions, all together produced a time of scarcity and distress which was intensified by bad harvests into almost a famine. The result was the revolt

---

[341] (29 & 30 Hen. VIII), Harl MS. 3970, fol. 20, printed Cunningham, op. cit. i, App. 587.

[341a] Terrier of Glaston. (8 Hen. VIII). John of Glaston. *Chron.* (ed. Hearne), 306–51.

[341b] Anct. D. (P.R.O.) A, 13069.

[342] *Chron. of Peter Langtoft* (ed. Hearne), ii, 343 ; *Hist. MSS. Com. Rep.* x, App. iii, 223.

[343] The tenacity of the old system and the inherent conservatism of the land-owning class appears in the interesting survivals of manorialism in the 18th century, which will be noticed later.

[344] Between 1541 and 1582 the average price of wheat was 13s. 10½d. per quarter—that is, rather more than twice as dear as the average price for the previous 140 years. Thorold Rogers, op. cit, iv, 718.

of 1548–9, in which the county of Somerset took some part. The bitterness of the social discontent was increased by religious difficulties, and the 'reformed religion' was a convenient scapegoat. The rioters threw down the inclosures of Sir William Herbert and Lord Stourton, but were easily suppressed.[345] An inquiry into the causes of distress was followed by an attempt to fix prices at a reasonable rate, the first of a long series of similarly well-meant but futile attempts. In 1550 the sheriff of the county was ordered to proclaim the highest prices at which corn and stock might be sold. The price of best wheat was fixed at 13s. 4d. a quarter, poor wheat must be sold at 8s.; the highest prices of barley were to be from 7s. to 9s., of rye from 6s. to 7s., beans 3s. 8d. to 5s., oats 4s., while the maximum prices for oxen were to be 27s. to 45s. in the summer, 39s. 8d. to 46s. 8d. in the autumn, and 41s. 4d. to 48s. 4d. in the winter. Sheep were to be sold at 2s. 4d. to 4s. 4d., and butter at ½d. per lb. The justices of the peace were meanwhile ordered to search all 'barns, stacks, garners, cellars, sollers, loftes, wikes, dairies, grenades, and other houses,' to decide how much corn the owner could spare, and order it to be taken to the market and sold at the proclaimed price.[346] No result followed this action. Thereupon the searching justices of the peace were replaced by commissions, 'with the force of the shire if necessary'—again without result, and the attempt was abandoned for the time, prices being left to the influences of supply and demand. Two years later there was another dearth with a sharp rise in prices, followed in 1565 by another rise, caused by panic at the secret buying of Government agents for export to the army in Flanders, though the amount purchased in Somerset was only 300 quarters of beans.[347] By 1572 prices had reached a still higher level, wheat varying according to quality from 17s. 4d. to 28s. per quarter, while rye was 16s., barley 8s. 8d., oats 5s. 4d., and peas 5s. The justices of the peace accompanied this return of prices by the statement that the county could not spare any corn for export, 'our county being populos, and Devonshire adjoinynge unto us being barreyne of wheat and ayded thereof by us.'[348] A little later another commission was appointed to try to force the farmers to send their corn to the markets, licences being granted to informers, who were to be rewarded with 75 per cent. of the fines. This constant meddling bred suspicion and panic, and made the farmers conceal their corn still more carefully.[349]

There was great scarcity in Somerset in 1585 and 1586; butter rose to 6d. a pound and cheese to 3d., and the hungry people attacked the farmers' barns and granaries, threshing out the corn 'whether the farmer would or no,' while the poor 'made uproars' and many hanged themselves from want.[350] The policy of the Government varied from year to year. In 1573, in spite of the likelihood of a scarcity, licences were given for the exportation of wheat from Somerset to Ireland, while in the following year a commission

---

[345] Harl. MS. 6021.

[346] E. Green, 'Attempts to Fix the Price of Corn in Somers.' *Bath Nat. Hist. and Antiq. Field Club. Proc.* iv (1881), quoting S.P. Dom. Edw. VI, ix, 55; x, 30, 40, 43.

[347] S.P. Dom. Eliz. xxxviii, 38; xxxix, 15.

[348] Ibid. xc, 36. There were great variations in price in neighbouring counties, the prices in Dorset at this date being much lower, wheat selling at 13s. 4d. to 16s., rye at 10s., and other grain in proportion.

[349] Ibid. xcii, 41, quoted by E. Green, loc. cit.

[350] Ashmolean MSS. (Bodleian), quoted by E. Green, op. cit.

was appointed to restrain exportation.[351] In 1608 a scarcity led to the order that neither peas nor beans were to be used for feeding sheep, 'because the same may serve the poorer sort to make bread,' and that no corn was to be used for feeding dogs, or in making 'the stuff called starch.' The fluctuations of prices were enormous. In 1621 wheat was sold at 16s. the bushel, and the poor were 'searching the markets for the finest wheats'; next year, with corn at 53s. 4d., the poor in Somerset were rioting and taking corn from the farmers on their way to markets.[352] In 1628 wheat was sold at 23s., next year at 32s.; in 1630 it rose to 37s. 11d., and in 1631 to 64s. The 'badgers of corn' and engrossers were regarded about this time as mainly responsible for the high prices, and in 1623, following an earlier precedent, returns were ordered from the various hundreds of Somerset as to the amount of corn in the hundred and the number of badgers settled there.[353] Most of the hundreds declared that they had no badgers, but six were admitted in Hartcliffe and Bedminster, their presence being defended as necessary for the provision of Bristol. Frome Hundred was already losing its rural character, a 'great neglect of tillage upon many great farms' and an increase in the number of people engaged in cloth-making being reported, while the chief supply of corn came from Wiltshire, Frome Hundred 'being forest or woodland and the rest very barren for corn.'[354] In 1631, when the period of scarcity was over, wheat selling at 5s., Frome Hundred was again in want of corn, it being reported that, while the hundred contained 6,506 inhabitants, 'mostly clothiers, weavers, and spinners,' much arable land had been converted into pasture, and that there were only in store 250 quarters of wheat and rye, 'barely enough for a fortnight.' These reports of 1630–1 are very elaborate, the justices of the peace being directed to take account of prices, of how much corn every grower had in his barn, how many acres there were to be sown, and how many buyers the hundred contained.[355] Exportation to Ireland was thought to be one of the chief causes of scarcity, and a case was quoted of a man conveying $24\frac{1}{2}$ bushels of peas 'secretly into a bark at Watchett,' concealing the cargo with great stones from a man who attempted to search, and then sailing under cover of night. The high price of oatmeal, 'with which the poor are wont at an easy rate to relieve themselves,' was set down to its use by the clothiers, who were therefore watched like the badgers, bakers, and millers.[356] Already observers were beginning to realize the futility of this constant regulation, and a report from Williton and Freemanors, and Carhampton aptly remarks 'that the constant viewing and searching for corn caused an imminent dearth,' thereby producing the scarcity it was designed to prevent. This view began to spread, the attempts to regulate the price of corn were abandoned, and the badgers were left to equalize the prices of corn by carrying it to the dearest markets.[357]

[351] *Acts of P.C.* 1573–4, pp. 141, 174, 210; 1574–5, pp. 66, 264.

[352] S.P. Dom. Jas. I, cxxx, 99.

[353] Catsash Hundred returned as follows:—Wheat, 1,991 bushels; meslin, 964 bushels; barley, 456 bushels; beans, 759 bushels; peas, 138 bushels; oats, 100 bushels; rye, 74 bushels. It is curious to notice that the growth of beans was even then characteristic of the Martock district, which had 3,857 bushels of wheat and 1,731 of beans; S.P. Dom. Jas. I, cxliv, 24.   [354] Ibid.

[355] Ibid. Chas. I, clxxvi, 29–40; clxxxv, 40; cciv, 112.

[356] Ibid. clxxvi, 29.

[357] Licences to be a common lader, badger, kidder, buyer, and transporter of corn, butter, and cheese were frequently issued later. *Sessions R.* bk. ii, pt. i (Somers Rec. Soc. xxiii and xxiv *passim*).

SOCIAL AND ECONOMIC HISTORY

The marked upward tendency of the prices of corn and stock after 1540, owing to many causes, of which the debasement of the coinage was the most important,[358] was repeated in the case of most other commodities. Nearly every necessary of life was doubled in price,[358a] but wages rose much more slowly, the average rise being 1·6.[359]

The problem of poverty had reached an acute stage. Voluntary contributions were quite inadequate, and it is curious to notice that the amount of money contributed voluntarily in any parish diminished in a most striking way after the Reformation.[360] In 1552 poor-boxes were set up, and the churchwardens were ordered to gather and distribute the people's alms. A compulsory poor-rate was instituted in 1572,[361] and, under the famous Elizabethan Poor Law of 1601, the whole question was dealt with in a statesman-like manner, on the principle of providing work for the able-bodied and relief for the impotent, the justices and the overseers being jointly responsible for the condition of the poor.[362] The latter administered the funds of the parish, whether arising from rates, fines,[363] or charitable bequests. The poor were fed, lodged, and clothed by the parish, their clothing bearing some distinctive mark to show that they were paupers. They were usually lodged in a poor-house belonging to the parish (often the building formerly used as a church-house).[364] The overseers also provided for the care of the poor in sickness,[365] and for the expenses of their burial, the latter being arranged in the most economical manner possible. In 1696 a pauper was shrouded and buried, the burial tax of 4s. paid, and the bell rung—all for 19s. 6d.—while a pauper woman's funeral cost 11s. 6d.[366]

On the whole the problem of poverty was adequately dealt with by these parish officials, under the supervision of the justices,[366a] and during the 17th century the central government was content to control rather than to interfere. Under the settlement clauses of later Poor Law Acts, however, the parishes were involved in great trouble and expense in removing the paupers to the parishes where they were chargeable, or in legal expenses owing to litigation between parishes about disputed liability. At Luccombe, for instance, in 1692 the parish had to spend £3 19s. 6d. in removing a Welsh child to Cardiff.[367]

[358] In 1532 an item in the churchwardens' accounts is a striking comment on the condition of the currency—13s. being allowed for broken money, Irish groats, and 'dandyprats' (*Churchwardens' Accts.* 155); while in 1541 £3 6s. 4d. had to be allowed 'for the fall in the money,' out of a total of £7 6s. 4d. (ibid. 162).

[358a] A bull was worth 30s., a steer £1, and oxen £1 6s. 8d. Star Chamber Proc. Hen. VIII, viii, 152.

[359] Thorold Rogers, op. cit. iv, 718, 719.

[360] *Churchwardens' Accts.* 163.

[361] 14 Eliz. cap. 5, stat. 16. This was followed by further measures in 1576 and 1597. 18 Eliz. cap. 3, stat. 4 ; 39 Eliz. cap. 3.

[362] 43 Eliz. cap. 2.

[363] The overseers collected fines for petty offences (such as selling beer without a licence, or stealing 'a duck out of a pond'), the proceeds of which were distributed among the poor. Chadwyck Healey, op. cit. 132.

[364] Clothing for Joan Sheer in 1630–1 cost 20s., and badges for the paupers cost 1s. 4d. in 1704. Luccombe Overseers' Accts. ; Chadwyck Healey, op. cit. 180–2.

[365] 1732. Paid Dr. Ellice 7 guineas for curing Thomas Clatworth's child. Ibid. 180.

[366] The poor were buried without coffins until the latter part of the 18th century.

[366a] Examples of the activity of the justices in matters of poor-relief may be found in the State Papers, e.g. S.P. Dom. Eliz. cclxxxviii, 43, 76, 85, 57 ; cclxxxix, 20, 29, 30, 57. See also *Sess. R.* (Somers. Rec. Soc. xxiii, xxiv). [367] Chadwyck Healey, op. cit. 180.

The State also undertook the supervision of charity by issuing licences to ask alms, known as 'briefs' or protections, an early one being that issued in 1591 to Sir Richard Pepyn, 'guider of the poorhouse of Langport West-over,' to 'gather' in the counties of Somerset and Wiltshire.[368] Occasionally licences were given to the poor of one parish to seek alms in another, if it appeared that there was an unusual amount of poverty in the former, and these formed a rough-and-ready way of equalizing the burden of poor relief in the different parishes of the county.[369]

The funds subscribed for the hospitals of the eastern and western divisions of the shire were managed in the 17th century by separate treasurers, and from them grants were made to the needy by order of the justices.[370]

The 16th and 17th centuries were a time of great prosperity for the landowning classes. They had money to spare for the building of the magnificent Tudor mansions, which add so much to the charm of the county at the present day, being constructed of the Ham Hill stone eulogized by Gerard, 'which for beautie, largenesse, lastinge and antiquitie . . . gives place to none and indures fire, water and all things else.'[371] This activity in building possibly accounts for the scarcity of 14th-century manor-houses in the county. Thus the Elizabethan manor-house of Barrington probably stood on the same site as the 14th-century structure,[372] while at Sutton Court the older work is dwarfed by the later building added to it. This too was the period when the yeomen became important in the history of the county, owing to the development of sheep-farming, and the dispersal of many of the great estates of the Church, and examples of their substantial homes may still be seen in nearly every Somerset village.

The development of the powers and functions of the justices who inherited the active social supervision of the old manor courts continued all through the 17th century. In addition to their responsibility for poor-law administration, which, with their work in regulating prices, has already been noticed, and their ordinary judicial functions,[373] they exercised a general superintendence over social conditions. In a commission of 1630, for instance, the Somerset justices were ordered to inquire into gifts for charitable uses, the training of youth in trades, the reform of disorderly persons,[374] the repair of highways, 'keeping watch and ward for the punishment of rogues and vagabonds,' and the relief of the poor and setting them to work.[375] One of their most constant functions during the 17th century may be illustrated from the records of 1631, when they ordered the constables of every tithing to publish the wages rates as settled.[376]

[368] S.P. Dom. Eliz. ccxl, 128. Licences were also issued to beg for alms, owing to losses by fire, &c.
[369] Sess. R. bk. i, pt. 1 (Dunster, 1597) ; bk. iii, 108 (Somerton) and passim (Somers. Rec. Soc. xxiii).
[370] Sess. R. passim. There was also a treasurer for the maimed soldiers.
[371] Gerard, Partic. Descrip. of Somers. 102.
[372] Bruton and Montacute Chartul. (Somers. Rec. Soc.), 35.
[373] The Privy Council kept a close watch on the judicial action of the justices. They were ordered, for instance, to be more diligent in inquiry into a 'foule murder committed in Somerset.'
[374] Orders were frequently given to the justices 'to examine the behaviour and quallety of men accused of being of a very evil disposition,' &c. ; Winsford, 1607 ; Sess. R. ii, 45.
[375] S.P. Dom. Chas. I, clxxxii, 80 ; clxxvii, 32.
[376] Ibid. cxcii, 50. The authority for this action by the justices was the Act of 1563. Compare attempts to regulate wages in 1666. Cunningham, op. cit. ('Modern Times'), pt. ii, App. A.

The following are the maximum rates of wages fixed by the county magistrates in 1685 :—[377]

	£	s.	d.	
Men servants	4	10	0	per annum
Women servants	2	10	0	,,
Mowers, per diem	0	1	2	(finding themselves)
,, ,, ...	0	0	7	(at meat and drink)
Haymakers ,, ...	0	0	7	(finding themselves)
,, ,, ...	0	0	4	(at meat and drink)
Reaping corn, per diem	0	1	2	(finding themselves)
,, ,, ...	0	0	8	(at meat and drink)

Masons, carpenters, tilers, thatchers—

	£	s.	d.	
15 March to 15 September, per diem .	0	1	2	} (finding
15 September to 15 March ,, ,, .	0	1	0	} themselves)
,, ,, ,, ,, .	0	0	7	(at meat and drink)

Threshers and dekkers, per diem—

	£	s.	d.	
15 March to 15 September . . .	0	1	0	(finding themselves)
,, ,, ,, . . .	0	0	5	(at meat and drink)
15 September to 15 March . . .	0	0	8	(finding themselves)
,, ,, ,, . . .	0	0	4	(at meat and drink)

PIECE WORK

		s.	d.
Men mowing 1 acre of grass	}	1	2
,, making 1 acre of grass to hay . . .	}	1	6
,, mowing 1 acre of barley	finding	1	1
,, reaping and binding 1 acre of wheat . .	themselves	3	0
,, cutting and binding 1 acre of beans and hooking	}	2	0
,, drawing 1 acre of hemp	}	4	6

SPINNERS

Pinions	3d. per lb.
Spanish wool	10d. per lb.
County wool	10d. per lb.
Worsted wool	10d. per lb.

The magistrates also issued regulations as to the price of bread, varying in accordance with the price of wheat. On 19 August 1776 the mayor and justices of Bath drew up the following Assize of Bread, to be in force for fourteen days :—

	If Wheaten lb. oz. dwt.			If Standard lb. oz. dwt.			If Household lb. oz. dwt.		
1d. loaf to weigh	0	11	0	0	12	10	—		
2d. ,, ,, ...	1	6	1	1	9	4	—		
3d. ,, ,, ...	2	1	1	2	5	14	2	12	13
6d. ,, ,, ...	4	2	3	4	11	13	5	8	7
12d. ,, ,, ...	8	4	6	9	7	11	10	0	15
18d. ,, ,, ...	12	6	10	14	3	8	16	9	6

The wheaten loaf was to be marked with a large W, the household loaf with a large H, neglect so to mark them being punishable with fines of from 5s. to 20s., and any deficiency in weight was punishable by a fine of 1s. per oz.[378]

From Wells, in 1631, comes a report of an inquiry by the justices into the town charities, when it was found that the 'masters of the city' were misemploying a loan fund in their hands, weak excuses being urged to justify

[377] *Hist. MSS. Com. Rep.* vii, App. 698–9.
[378] *The Bath Journ.* 19 Aug. 1776. Another example from the *Bath Chron.* 1 Jan. 1784 shows the rise in the price of bread. The penny wheaten loaf was to weigh 9 oz. 4 dwt., the 2d. loaf 1 lb. 2 oz. 8 dwt., the 3d. loaf 1 lb. 11 oz. 12 dwt., and the other sizes in proportion.

the money being spent 'in superfluous feasts or privately eloyned.'[379] The county justices also tried to deal with the ever-present problem of vagrancy,[380] punishing vagabonds so severely that in the Yeovil and Martock districts it was reported that 'few passed that way, except Irish only, who abundantly pestered that part, causing great expense in sending them back to Ireland.' The report suggested, as a delightfully simple solution of the problem, that an order should be sent into Ireland to prevent them coming forth thence.[381] The county magistrates were also employed, in the maintenance of the Game Laws, to preserve venison, hares, and pheasants.[382] They granted licences to and regulated tippling and ale-houses,[383] supervised the maintenance of highways, sea walls, and bridges,[384] dealt with the numerous cases of illegitimacy,[385] overlooked the building of new cottages,[386] ordered the maintenance of butts,[387] and busied themselves in general with the most minute details of county administration.[388]

The vigilance of the justices, however, was insufficient to maintain order in the county. In one year (1596) it was stated that '40 persons within the county were executed for robbery, theft, and other felonies, 37 were burnt in the hand, 37 were whipped, 183 were discharged, yet the fifth part of the felonies in the county were not brought to trial, and the rapines committed by the infinite number of wicked, wandering people were intolerable to the poor countrymen, and obliged them to keep a perpetual watch of their sheepfolds, pastures, woods, and cornfields.'[389] Heinous murders were of frequent occurrence,[390] piracy and smuggling were rife in the seaport towns,[391] and wrecking was common on the coast.[392] There were houses of correction for different parts of the county at Taunton and Ilchester, and in 1624 another, for the eastern part, was built at Shepton Mallet at a cost of £220.[393]

The central government found in the churchwarden, as in the justice of the peace, a convenient instrument for county business. Already, in the reign of Henry VIII, they had organized the military business of the parish, seen to the keeping of the parish 'harness,' and provided for maimed soldiers.[394] Their accounts contain many entries of 'coat and conduct money' for soldiers

---

[379] S.P. Dom. Chas. I, cxciv, 19. For other examples of action of this kind see the *Sess. R.* (e.g. bk. iii, no. 26).

[380] *Sess. R.* bk. iii, no. 18, 19 ; and 1621, no. 4.

[381] In 1621–2 the parish of Porlock spent 48*s.* 4*d.* restoring poor people to Ireland. *Sess. R.* 1622, no. 14.

[382] *Hist. MSS. Com. Rep.* iii, App. 238.

[383] *Sess. R.* iv, no. 81 ; vii, no. 95 ; bk. iii, no. 34 ; bk. vi, no. 3.

[384] In 1621 a county rate was imposed for the repairs of Hele bridge (*Sess. R.* Sept. 1621, no. 8). See also (Markbridge) Jan. 1621–2, no. 14 ; (Borough bridge) May 1621–2, no. 4 ; bk. iii, no. 107. Hitherto roads and bridges had been maintained by semi-private efforts, being the object of many bequests by will in the 14th and 15th centuries.

[385] *Sess. R. passim.*

[386] Ibid. bk. vi, no. 3. The object was that the new cottages might not give a settlement to strangers who might become chargeable. At Yeovil, in 1622–3, it was complained that 'strangers settled there do break and tear and spoil other men's hedges.' *Sess. R.* July 1622–3, no. 6.

[387] Ibid. 1621, no. 16.

[388] Such, for instance, as issuing licences to shoot with a hand-gun ; Min. Bk. *Sess. R.* 1616–24.

[389] Strype, *Annals*, iv, 290.

[390] A Somerset murderer who would not confess was to be brought to the Tower and 'offered the torture of the rack there.' *Acts of P.C.* 1558–70, p. 367.

[391] Ibid. 1565, p. 283.   [392] Ibid. 1575–7, p. 113.

[393] *Sess. R.* 1620, no. 7 ; April 1624, no. 5.

[394] *Churchw. Accts.* (Somers. Rec. Soc. iv), Introd. xiv, xv (1537). 'Paid for setting forth the soldiers, 30*s.* 9½*d.*' (p. 159). In 1560 an agreement to pay the harness scourer 12*s.* 7*d.* is mentioned (p. 172).

(the provision of which by the localities was a new feature of the Tudor period) and of payments for their uniform.[395]

This activity continued, provision for ' hurted soulgers ' and ' maimed seamen,' as well as for ' poor passengers,' being constant items on the 17th and 18th-century accounts.[396] Notes are found of doles of 1*s.* 3*d.* to ' 8 poor passengers from France,' 6*d.* to ' one man and one woman that come out of Ireland,' 3*d.* to ' one souldier that had lost his arme.' As the manor courts became less active, the churchwardens gradually took over many matters with which the former were once occupied. At Yatton, for instance, in 1548–9 they had been busy ' making good a sluice against the rage of the salt water,' the silver cross of the church being sold to raise the necessary money,[397] and, later, money was paid by the churchwardens for ditching in the Yeo, and mowing its bank, both being services due from the men of Yatton Manor.[398] The churchwardens are later found undertaking the repair of the village stocks and whipping-post, the maintenance of the village pound, the repair of parish roads and bridges, and the destruction of vermin.[399] The average Somerset parish, apparently, was infested with polecats, kites, stoats, rats, and many other noxious beasts and birds, payment for the destruction of all of which was made according to a well-known tariff.[400]

The churchwardens further showed their interest in agriculture by investing in technical books at the expense of the parish, the Luccombe wardens in 1745 paying 4*s.* 6*d.* for three books on ' the distemper in horned cattle.' They also employed an official known as the dog-whipper, who received 2*s.* in 1660, but whose salary had increased to 5*s.* in 1666.[401]

The cloth trade in Somerset reached its highest development during the 17th century,[402] stimulated by the immigration of weavers from the Netherlands.[403] Frome, Ilminster, Taunton,[404] and Bridgwater and many other boroughs shared in the trade, which was of the domestic type, the wool being carded, woven, and spun by the workmen in their own homes. The prosperity of this industry probably accounts for the wealth of Somerset about this time. In the ship-money assessment of 1636 Somerset paid £8,000,

[395] *Acts of P.C.* 1547–50, pp. 95–501 ; 1596, *Bath Chamberlain's Accts.* xxxvi.

[396] West Luccombe, Churchw. Accts. quoted Chadwyck Healey, op. cit. 178. In 1638 at Cheddar a man was appointed for life ' to keep the armour of Cheddar with buckels, nails, and leather,' at a yearly salary of 8*s.* *Hist. MSS. Com. Rep.* iii, App. 329, 330 ; A. L. Humphreys, *Mater. for Hist. of Wellington*, 123–30.

[397] *Churchw. Accts.* (Somers. Rec. Soc.), iv, 160.

[398] Ibid. 157. They also paid 16*d.* for making a bill of the subsidy.

[399] A. L. Humphreys, *Mater. for Hist. of Wellington*, 123–6 ; *Hist. MSS. Com. Rep.* iii, App. 329 ; Chadwyck Healey, op. cit. 178.

[400] At Luccombe, in 1749, a man was actually appointed to keep the parish clear of foxes for 10*s.* a year. At Porlock in 1757 Thomas Smith, the fox-catcher, was paid 15*s.*, and the sparrow-catcher at Cheddar in 1613 received 12*d.* Chadwyck Healey, op. cit. 177–80, 385–7 ; A. L. Humphreys, op. cit. 128 ; *Hist. MSS. Com. Rep.* iii, App. 329, 331.

[401] Humphreys, op. cit. 177 ; Chadwyck Healey, op. cit. 178.

[402] The following Acts of Parliament dealt with the Somerset cloth trade : 5 & 6 Edw. VI, cap. 6 ; 2 & 3 Phil. and Mary, cap. 12 ; 4 & 5 Phil. and Mary, cap. 5 ; there were other Acts in 1593 and 1607. See also Cunningham, op. cit. (' Modern Times '), i, 32, 375 ; S.P. Dom. Jas. I, cxxviii, 73–7 ; *Hist. MSS. Com. Rep.* iii, App. 63.

[403] *Acts of P.C.* 1550–2, p. 510 ; *The Flemish Weavers at Glaston.* 1551 (Somers. Arch. Soc. Proc. 1881), xxvi.

[404] In 1633, according to Gerard, Taunton equalled if not surpassed any town in the county ' for frequencie of trading which moste consists in woollen clothes and stuffe,' and was constantly served by 140 butchers. Gerard, *Partic. Descr. of Somers.* 1633 (Somers. Rec. Soc. xv), 55. Somerset cloths known as ' Dunsters ' and ' Bridgwaters ' were famous.

an amount equal to that contributed by Suffolk, Lincoln, and Kent.[405] Only two counties paid more. In 1641 it came eighth in order, being assessed at 58·75 acres to £1, and falling to the thirteenth place in 1649, rose again in 1660 to the tenth, and in 1672 to the ninth place. In 1690 there was one house to every 22·81 acres, and in only six other counties was the proportion higher. In a calculation of the number of hearths to each house, which is evidence of the spread of comfort, Somerset occupies the fourth place.[406]

The social life of the county was deeply affected by the period of Puritan supremacy, and although the gloom lifted a little at the Restoration, the sports and pastimes of the county never recovered their former position. In the struggle for mere existence which occupied the people at the close of the 18th century, all prospect of the revival of the characteristic amusements of the county faded. Many curious pamphlets published by Somerset authors during the Commonwealth show the strength of the Puritan spirit in the county.[407] Attempts were made to put down many of the rural sports and pastimes. May-day games, the Whitsuntide morris-dancing, bull-baiting, cudgel-playing, and shove-groat were discouraged, and the Puritans showed great hostility to the strolling players. The punishment of such 'as did prophanely swear' was a fine which varied from 1d. to 5s., paid to the use of the poor, while women were set in the stocks 'for their cursinge,' and the use of expressions like 'rogue' and 'foule toad' brought a man before the bench.[408] Drunkenness was severely punished, the offenders remaining in the stocks all night, and there were many fines for playing unlawful games.[409] The triumph of the fanatic spirit appears in the great number of convictions for neglect of Sunday observance—tippling, absence from church, travelling, or even mirth on Sunday being severely punished.[410] The governing bodies of the towns were much occupied during the 17th century in drawing up observances minutely regulating social life. They fixed the price of bread and other provisions, drew up sumptuary regulations limiting the 'abundance and superfluity' of the mayor's feasts, regulated apprenticeship, punished immorality, and made rules as to the conduct of inn-keepers and against bad language.[411] The fines inflicted at Bath included 5s. for selling ale without a licence, 3s. 4d. for 'ingrossinge upp Butter and Cheese,' 2s. 6d. for brewing without a licence, 3s. 4d. 'for a bluddshed.'[412] In matters political these corporations seem to have been little less than tyrannical, pursuing their opponents, whether Dissenters or Jacobites, with elaborate malice. In an

[405] Thorold Rogers, op. cit. v, 707.

[406] Ibid. 80, 118, 119, 120–2.

[407] The titles of these pamphlets are very quaint ; e.g. 'One groan more from under the Altar,' 'Against Babylon and her merchants,' 'One blow at Babel,' &c. The titles of other old Somerset chap-books may be seen in Somers. and Dors. N. and Q. iv, 13.

[408] Hist. MSS. Com. Rep. iii, App. 362 ; G. Roberts, Social Hist. of the Southern Counties, 156, 243–4.

[409] Ibid. One man was fined for playing cards from ten in the morning till four in the afternoon. In 1633 'wakes' or feasts of dedication were suppressed. Hist. MSS. Com. Rep. iii, App. 286.

[410] 10s. was the fine paid for tippling on the Sabbath, and even children were fined for playing on Sunday. Ibid. Alehouses were minutely regulated, e.g. Regulations of 1645 (Somers. and Dors. N. and Q. i, 45). We hear of 'the Lord's day being greatly prophaned' at West Chinnock in 1653 (Hist. MSS. Com. Rep. vii, App. i, 694), and of an objection being made to the appointment of a baker and innkeeper as constable because both his professions 'are very subject to abuses and he not soe fitt an instrument for punishing others who in all probabilitie will be guilty himselfe' (ibid. 695).

[411] Ibid. 303. 'No bourgess shall mysfame or name or calle other as knave, thyffe, or lober or anye other fyltie like wordes in geste or in anywise.' Ibid. Rep. iii, App. 302, 350 ; Rep. x, App. iii, 248.

[412] A. J. King and B. H. Watts, Munic. Rec. of Bath, xxxvi.

affidavit drawn up on behalf of an accused Jacobite in 1718 it was stated that the accused usually said his responses to the prayers for the royal family loud enough to be heard by anyone near him (if not asleep), but that the informer 'doth usually sleep, or lye in a sleeping posture, upon his seat in the time of service,' adding, as a proof of loyalty, that he did blot the name of Queen Anne out of his prayerbook, writing that of King George above.[413] Political feeling must have run very high when watch was kept to see whether a man duly knelt in church 'except when troubled with gout,' or whether the tunes played by request in an inn included 'The king shall enjoy his own again,' or not, and when the town of Bridgwater was disturbed by the attacks of the country folk upon the meeting-house, or by people going up and down the streets in a riotous and seditious manner crying 'Ormonde for ever!' 'He is come!'[414] The borough officials were also concerned with sanitary regulations. The streets of the small Somerset towns were narrow and foul, with noisome gutters and refuse heaps ; pigs and cattle were allowed to wander about, while at the gates the limbs of the executed traitors hung in chains. There is little wonder that epidemics were frequent in the 17th century. When the plague had actually appeared, the measures taken to prevent its spread were stringent enough. The sick were locked up and, if necessary, whipped to keep order.[415] The streets of even a great city like Bath were in such a deplorable state that in 1602 a rumour that the queen meant to visit the city caused a desperate hurry to get paviours from Sodbury, Cirencester, Bristol, Frome, Warminster, and Chippenham.[416] The arrival of distinguished visitors [417] was celebrated by processions with music and pageants, by banquets and the presentation of gifts.[418] Dinners were given to the sheriffs and justices, who also received gifts.[419] Itinerant mountebanks, who combined the professions of jester, acrobat, musician, and quack doctor, frequently visited the towns. A typical scene is the procession at Bath to celebrate the coronation of Charles II, which is minutely described in Collinson's history.[420] The town spit, with its attendant turnspit dogs, was to be found in most towns, and the importance of the latter, before the invention of a mechanical roasting jack, appears from the description of the consternation in the city of Wells when it was discovered that all the turnspit dogs were missing, an enterprising midshipman having taken the whole pack

[413] *Hist. MSS. Com. Rep.* iii, App. 301–4, 310–19.

[414] Ibid. 319.

[415] Accounts of Chamberlain of Wells ; *Hist. MSS. Com. Rep.* i, App. 107. In 1649, when the plague was raging at Yeovil, a contract was made by which the dead were to be buried, the men receiving 14*d.* daily. The contract was continued for eleven weeks ; *Hist. MSS. Com. Rep.* viii, App. 694. Between June and September 1645 seventy persons died of plague in the parish of East Coker. *Somers. and Dors. N. and Q.* iii, 35 ; v, 91. For the great visitation of 1625, see *Sess. R.* (Somers. Rec. Soc. xxiv), p. xxi.

[416] King and Watts, op. cit. 49.

[417] A list of the famous people who visited Bath between 1569 and 1602 is printed by King and Watts, op. cit. 56.

[418] Lady Russell, for instance, received two dozen chickens and four couples ot rabbits. Sugar and wine were usual gifts. Thus we find gifts of a pottle of sack, a pottle of claret, and Canary, Gascony, Malaga, and Rhenish are also mentioned. Another gift was a 'box of marmylade.' Ibid. 32, 33, 35, 41.

[419] The expenditure at Bath in 1601 includes 8*s.* for a 'bancetinge Dishe,' 14*d.* for 2 lb. of raisins, 20*d.* for a pound of 'shuger,' 2*s.* 8*d.* for a gallon of claret wine, and 20*d.* for a 'potle of sacke' (ibid. 33). Presents were also given to 'the players of the Earl of Sussex and the Earl of Leicester,' to the 'tumblers of the Earl of Warwick,' and to the 'waytes of Bristowe against my lord of Pembroke's coming,' and to the 'Drum players before the mystery.' Ibid. 49–56 ; *Hist. MSS. Com. Rep.* i, App. 107.

[420] Collinson, *Somers.* i, 29, 30. See also extract from Wells Corporation Rec. (*Arch. Soc.* xvi).

for exercise on the Mendip Hills.[421] The stocks, the cage, and the pillory were still in constant use.[422]

Many famous Somerset charities were founded during the 16th and 17th centuries, especially after the dissolution of the monasteries.[422a] Almshouses were founded all through the county, usually under a deed providing for the maintenance of a fixed number of paupers, qualifications as to age and sex being added, with, occasionally, a further provision that the inmates should be unmarried, or should be widows, or that they should not be in receipt of parish relief.[423] Thus, a bequest to the poor of Nether Stowey was limited to those 'who were known to have lived an honest, civil, and laborious life, and to have constantly resorted to the parish church to hear divine service,' while the testator 'earnestly desired and required and solemnly charged the trustees to take special care that the bread which is ordained for the relief of the children of God be not cast unto dogs and the limbs of the devil.'[424] Frequently a school was attached to the pauper hospital, children being educated and apprenticed to trades according to the terms of the foundation.[425] Other charities took the form of weekly or yearly doles of loaves of bread to the poor, or of money for their 'convenient clothing.' Occasionally the market rents or tolls were distributed among the poor,[426] and there are cases of money being left to be lent without interest.[427] The bequest of money to provide sermons in the parish church was common in the 17th century,[428] but a very curious form of charity was the bequest, in 1689, to the parish of Portbury, of a copy of a mathematical treatise in folio, entitled 'The Marinors' or Artises Magazen,' which was to be kept chained and locked in a desk in the church, and to be consulted only after security had been given for £3 sterling, that the reader would not in any way damage the precious volume.[429]

The manor courts were no longer the arbiters of all village disputes and the authority for regulating social matters, but their activity in their rather limited sphere continued long. Their most important business was the conveyance of land,[430] granting and renewing leases, and receiving fines and heriots. Leasehold tenure, holding for lives or terms of years, was becoming more common in Somerset,[431] but copyhold tenure was still widespread. As the

[421] Roberts, op. cit. 30.

[422] The borough records of the period contain some very curious records. Osborne from Bath was paid 14d. 'for carrying a hue and cry to Bristol of a fained report that London was a-fire,' and £4 3s. 4d. was the exorbitant interest paid for the use of £100 for three months, King and Watts, op. cit. 36.

[422a] The Grammar School at Bath was the first of a long series of similar foundations. See p. 443 below.

[423] Collinson, Somers. i, 35, 259; ii, 496; iii, 484, 554. Very elaborate regulations drawn up for Yeovil almshouse, twenty-two in number, are printed, iii, 211. The almshouse founded at Staple Fitzpaine was for six poor persons, each to have 2d. a week, one black gown every two years, 'which they are obliged, if well, to wear at Church every Sunday or forfeit 6d. to the Clerk.' Ibid. i, 61.

[424] Ibid. iii, 554.   [425] e.g., at Bruton and Wellington. Ibid. i, 212; ii, 483.

[426] Ibid. iii, 520.

[427] Thus, a Wiveliscombe charity consisted of £40 to be lent to eight honest laborious men two years gratis 'towards keeping them on work or from becoming chargeable.' Ibid. iii, 491.

[428] Ibid. i, 259; iii, 151.   [429] Ibid. iii, 151.

[430] Copyhold tenants could alienate their holdings by surrender into the lord's hand by a verge, pen, or mote to the use of the alienee.

[431] There was a tendency, especially on the part of corporate bodies and churchmen, to change twenty-one-year leases into leases for three lives, taking a larger fine for the renewal. Charles I ordered that this practice should be discontinued, as it tended to enrich the present members of the corporation at the expense of their successors. *Hist. MSS. Com. Rep.* x, App. iii, 257.

rents of the copyhold tenements were fixed by custom, there was a tendency for the fines on renewal to become heavier, the landlords following in this way the general rise of prices. Thus at Bossington, in 1655, 24 acres of land were held for life at a rent of £1 13s. 8d., the rendering of a heriot being commuted for £3, but the fine for this grant was £190. Nearly 100 years later the same rent was payable and the amount of the fine had not changed, but £5 was paid in lieu of the heriot.[431a] Land newly taken up and cultivated was not subject to the usual customary services, and was known as 'overland,' as distinguished from 'bondland.'[432] On the manor of Taunton and Taunton Deane, the lord's officials, who included the constable and bailiff of the castle, the porter or keeper of the gate, the clerk of the castle, the receiver, the woodward and the overseer of the waterworks, still received their wages partly in kind, while in addition certain fields were assigned to the holders of each office (known as the Porter's Mead, &c.), and various perquisites were their due.[433]

On the same manor, every customary tenant was bound to attend the two law-days, the two 'fulfilling' courts, one 'choice' court, one 'offeringe' court, and one 'pannage' court, paying in default a fine of 3d.; but for 8d. per annum he could be discharged of attendance at all the three-weekly courts.[434] At Bossington the tenant was bound to grind his corn at the lord's mill, and to provide a labourer, with a shovel, every Whit Monday to labour twelve hours cleaning the mill pool.[434a] Some of the conditions under which land was held were not relics of manorialism, but were obviously of recent growth. In 1716 there is the record of a bottle of Nantes brandy being paid yearly in addition to the rent. In 1748 one piece of gold of the value of £1 16s., and in 1750 one guinea of gold had to be rendered.[435] The manor courts still exacted fines for defaults in suits of court, for neglect to keep in repair holdings, watercourses, fences, and walls. There are notices of the homage measuring the arable land, viewing the land to settle disputes as to boundaries, electing haywards, tithing-men, ale tasters, bread searchers, searchers and sealers of leather, and scavengers.[436] Waifs and strays were still a source of profit, and notices of 'one score and three stray sheep, and one redde cowe, pinned by the pyndere,' were read out in West Luccombe Church in 1653.[437] The jurisdiction of the courts was confined in most cases to petty offences like leaving pigs unringed, stealing walnuts from the lord's waste (which was punished by a fine of £5 !), inclosing potato-ground on the common lands (the fine for which was 6d. only), or 'cuttinge downe Great Limms from Apple Trees,' contrary to good husbandry.[438] In a few places

[431a] Chadwyck Healey, op. cit. 11–13. See also Add. Chart. (B.M.), 40088; Exch. Dep. Mich. 18 Chas. II.

[432] This recalls the ancient distinction between overland and land of 'old aster'. Hist. MSS. Com. Rep. x, App. iii, 199; Richard Locke, Customs of Manor of Taunton.

[433] The woodward could claim the tops and rinds of all trees felled for repairing the castle mills, with windfalls, starved trees, and herbage of the woods. Ibid.

[434] Ibid.

[434a] Chadwyck Healey, op. cit. 12, 13, 140–1.

[435] Ibid. 13.

[436] Aller Court R. 1632 (B.M. Add. R. no. 28279); Porlock, 1757 (Chadwyck Healey, op. cit. 301–7); Wellington, 1662 (A. L. Humphreys, op. cit.).

[437] Chadwyck Healey, op. cit. 182.

[438] Aller Court R. 1632 ut sup.; Porlock, 1752, 1776 (Chadwyck Healey, op. cit.); Wellington, 1692 (Humphreys, op. cit. 32).

the lord of the manor had succeeded in retaining a supervision over trade, and his rights in the matter had survived even in a place so considerable as Porlock. Tolls were paid to him on a great variety of articles—wine, salt, iron, horses and bullocks from Wales, and pigs and sheep from the same, herrings, coal, hops, leather, oysters, oranges, lemons, tobacco, and timber, while the court leet busied itself with by-laws for the preservation of the quay and harbour, and against strange fishing-boats, and the water-bailiff was responsible for the payment of dues to the lord of the manor.[439] These survivals of manorial activity, however, became rarer as time went on, since by the spread of leasehold tenure the copy of court-roll became of less importance, and by the inclosure of the arable fields the agrarian supervision of the courts became obsolete.

The rise in prices which had marked the 16th century continued until about 1650, when they had reached the level maintained with little variation until about 1775. Before 1650 the effects of the influx of gold and silver, together with a series of bad harvests, showed themselves in a steady rise, but by that date the force of the movement was spent.[440] Wheat, which had been 53s. 4d. in 1617, rose to 96s. during bad harvests, but had fallen to 37s. 4d. in 1691, and was 32s. 6d. in 1750 and 30s. to 34s. in 1756.[441]

In 1691 barley was 20s. per quarter, malt 20s., oats 8s. to 12s., rye 16s., beans 11s. to 20s., grey peas 18s. 8d. to 24s., and white peas the same price. In 1756, while wheat was slightly lower, other kinds of grain were a little higher, selling at 28s., 38s. 6d., 14s. 6d., 20s. 6d., respectively.[442] A load of hay was 20s., cheese was 24s. per cwt. and tallow 25s. 4d.[443] In 1617 chickens were sold at Bath at from 4s. 10d. to 6s. a dozen, capons at 30s., ducks at 6s., pigeons at 3s. 4d., snipe at 3s. 6½d., and turkeys at 30s. Roasting pigs were 2s. 6d. each, butter was sold at 3s. 8d. for 12 lb., and pepper at 2s. 9d. per lb. Mutton sheep were 18s. to 20s. each, and lambs 8s. 6d. to 10s.[444] In 1750 cheese was 3d. to 3½d. a pound, bacon 4d. to 5d. beef and mutton 3d. to 3½d., butter 5d. to 6d. Wool was 18s. 8d. to 21s. per tod, sugar was 3d. a pound.[445]

The end of the 18th century produced two movements which deeply affected the life of the county—the agrarian and the industrial revolution. The former was the more important in Somerset. Much of the county still lay uninclosed, the eastern half being almost untouched by the 16th-century movement. The increase of population in the manufacturing districts created a great demand for corn, which was intensified during the wars of the period, by the limitation of the supply to the amount produced in England. Grain rose to famine prices, and a prospect of high profits to the farmers appeared. When it became clear that the new and very profitable

---

[439] Chadwyck Healey, op. cit. 471–3.

[440] There were dearths in 1630–7, 1646–51, 1658–61, 1693–9. Thorold Rogers, v, 779–84. In 1673, wheat being at 96s. the quarter, 'the Charitable Farmer of Somersetshire sold out his store at 72s., being derided by his neighbour, but rewarded in the following year by a miraculous crop of wheat, with from seven to thirteen ears on one blade.' E. Green, *Bibliotheca Somersetensis*, iii, 391.

[441] Thorold Rogers, op. cit. v, 20, 102–7, 221, 326, 339; David Davies, *Case of Labour in Husbandry*, 64, 65. Intermediate prices of wheat were 37s. 4d. in 1691, 44s. in 1692, 40s. in 1700, 56s. in 1728–9; Thorold Rogers, op. cit. vi, 102–5, 106–7; Sir F. M. Eden, *State of the Poor*, iii, pp. lxxi to lxxviii.

[442] Ibid.   [443] Ibid.

[444] Thorold Rogers, op. cit. v, 269, 270, 315, 326, 339, 434.

[445] Ibid. op. cit. v, 350.

methods of farming, the improved rotation of crops, by which more corn could be raised, were barred to the open-field farmer until the advantages of change had convinced the thickest-headed among his neighbours, a new inclosure movement sprang up.[446] The price of corn made it possible to bring under the plough land hitherto beyond the margin of profitable cultivation, and the growing demand of the towns for meat led to the inclosure for stock-raising of land hitherto open. Under the combined pressure, the open arable fields and the waste and common lands of the villages began to disappear.[447]

An account of Somerset, written by Mr. Billingsley at the height of the inclosure movement, seems to prove that inclosures, though unpopular, were economically to the advantage of the county generally,[448] but the social changes produced were not equally advantageous, as will be seen below.

The first instance of the inclosure of the open fields is found in the parish of Tintinhull in 1794, and in the following years other parishes were similarly inclosed. The bounty on exported corn gave a new stimulus to the process. Before 1801 there had been fifteen Acts of Parliament dealing with 18,869 acres in Somerset, and between 1801–18 there were twenty-seven Acts which affected 18,148 acres.[449] Large holdings became the rule, the smaller men, lacking the capital required for inclosing and higher farming, sold their land and joined the crowded ranks of the underpaid labourers, and the social gap between farmer and labourer became almost impassable.[450]

The inclosure of commons and wastes seems to have been less prejudicial to the interests of the poor than has been generally supposed, fairly adequate compensation being given by the commissioners. The value of the stocking rights were small owing to general overstocking ; the beasts were often half-starved, leaving the common in poorer condition than when first put out, and owing to the frequency of floods on the undrained moors, had to be withdrawn for several months of the year. It was impossible, therefore, in many parts of Somerset for the cottager to make much use of his rights, unless he had wherewithal to keep his beasts when off the moors in the winter. The stocking rights of one tenement on Wedmore could usually be bought for 10s. to 12s. a year, but after the inclosure the land could be let at 30s. to 60s. per acre, three times the former amount of stock being kept.[451]

Much of the common land of the county lay in the great undrained moors like Sedgemoor, Wedmore, and Brent Marsh, and in these cases the

[446] 'The famine prices of 1796, doomed to recur again in 1800–1, 1812, and 1817, were acting as a powerful solvent to all old agricultural customs.' Slater, *The Engl. Peasantry and Enclosure of Common Fields*, 90.

[447] Many references to the then recent inclosures are found in Collinson's *Somerset*, e.g. i, 52, ; i, 84 ; i, 146.

[448] Billingsley, *Gen. View of Agric. in Somers.* 1795 (2nd ed. 1797). In 1797, in one session, fifteen inclosure bills for Somerset were brought forward. An account of the new rotations of crops is given, pp. 107, 108, 279.

[449] Slater, op. cit. 145. There was renewed activity after 1847 in pursuance of the second report of the Inclosure Commissioners.

[450] Slater, op. cit. 131. One of the chief drawbacks to the arable field inclosure as it affected the small holders was that it meant the loss of common pasture over the fields in the autumn. One of the very few examples where improved farming was introduced without ruining the small holders comes from Weston-zoyland, where the open fields were divided and allotted (the scattered strips being consolidated), but were not inclosed. Common pasture over the whole 500 acres after harvest is still allowed. Ibid. 61, 62.

[451] Billingsley, op. cit. 51–3. This optimistic view, however, is not universal. Many are still of the opinion that the loss of common pasture rights was the greatest possible loss to the peasant, who often took a larger piece of arable land in lieu of it, which he could not cultivate profitably owing to lack of the manure from his stock. See Slater, op. cit. 115.

inclosure movement carried with it the draining of the land by ditching, and was probably an unmixed benefit. Already, even in the 17th century, observers had been alive to the profit obtainable by draining. Gerard, writing in 1633, said 'The commons of Sedgmoor, if severall, would yield a vast revenue, as in Winter theis Moores are soe covered with water that you would rather deeme them Sea than land.'[452] At the end of the 18th century, 10,000 acres of Sedgemoor had been inclosed at a cost of £209,624, but the result was an improvement in the yearly value of the land from 10s. per acre to 35s., and an addition of 10s. yearly to the value of the adjacent land, the total profit being £365,376.[453] On the drained and inclosed land sheep-rot became much less common, and the health of the district improved, ague being less prevalent.[454]

At this time the farmers of Somerset were enjoying a period of great prosperity, and were showing an interest in new methods which promised well for the future of the county.[455] Most of the farms were of moderate size, the rents varying from £50 to £500, a very considerable proportion being held in fee by the occupiers, who formed a prosperous yeoman class. Owing to the fact that the rise in the price of labour, meat, butter, and cheese had for a time outstripped the rise in the price of grain, a certain amount of the newly-inclosed arable land was laid down to pasture. Small grass farms of 50 or 60 acres, managed by a farmer and his wife and family, were becoming common,[456] and a very fair profit could be obtained.[457] The dairies of larger farms were usually managed by dairymen employed by the farmer, the latter providing hay in the winter and receiving a rent of £7 or £8 per cow. Mr. Billingsley frankly expresses his opinion of this change. 'It is due,' he says, 'to pride or indolence on the part of the farmer's household, and the practice should be checked by the landlord.'[458] Grazing farms for fattening stock were also becoming common in the county, and much fat stock was exported to Bristol and London.[459] The breeds of sheep had been improved

---

[452] Gerard, op. cit. 220. The moors round Somerton, he says, 'presented in winter but a watery spectacle yet it is a great commoditie to the fowlers who furnish not only this town, but many other places with such traffique.' Ibid. 231.

[453] Billingsley, op. cit. 196.   [454] Ibid. 55, 206, 207, 230.

[455] A great deal of literature dealing with agricultural subjects appeared about this time, and in 1777 the Bath and West of England Society was founded.

[456] Billingsley, op. cit. 152–8, and Arthur Young, *Eastern Tour*, iii, 413–83.

[457] Mr. Billingsley, op. cit. 250–1, gives the following budget for 60 acres of grass land :—

EXPENDITURE.	£	s.	d.	RECEIPTS.	£	s.	d.
Rent of 60 acres at 30s. per acre	90	0	0	70 cwt. of cheese at £2 10s.	175	0	0
Tithe and taxes	20	0	0	Butter	20	0	0
Haymaking 20 acres	10	0	0	Calves	20	0	0
Labour of family, cattle (at 30s. per cow), utensils, &c.	30	0	0	Hogs	20	0	0
Manure	10	0	0		235	0	0
Repair of fences	2	0	0	Total Expenditure	172	0	0
Accidents with cattle	10	0	0				
				Profit	63	0	0

He mentions another case of an annual profit of £117 10s. being made from a dairy of twenty cows.

[458] Ibid. 200, 206. This is one example of the general rise in the standard of life among the farmers. In addition it was becoming less customary for the farm labourers to live in the farm-house, and the wives and daughters of the farmer were giving up spinning the wool of the sheep on the farm into yarn.

[459] Lean cattle bought at £7 to £13 were sold at £13 to £18, the profit on 200 acres of grass land rented at 40s. an acre being £277 10s.; ibid. 240.

by the introduction of the Spanish ram, the flocks of Lansdown were famous, also the small breed fed on the Mendips and on Exmoor.[460]

Unfortunately, while farming was profitable, the lot of the labourers was growing steadily worse. Until the last twenty-five years of the 18th century there had been no great advance in prices, as the growth of population had been checked to some extent by the great plagues of the 17th century, and the area of land under corn had been extended owing to the bounties on exported corn.[461] After 1775 there was a great change. It was a time of great wars and heavy taxation.[461a] Population had increased more rapidly than the means of subsistence, and the closing of foreign sources of supply during the wars drove up the price of corn.[462]

Wheat, which in 1776 had sold at 33s. to 38s. a quarter, rose in 1784 to 47s., in 1790 to 45s. 6d., in 1791–2 to 60s. 6d., and in 1795 to 81s. 6d., and in the years that followed the price was often 112s. Barley rose in the same way from 25s. in 1776 to 40s. in 1795 ; oats from 16s. to 28s. 8d. ; malt from 36s. 6d. to 48s. and 50s. ; flour from 3s. 4d. to 8s. 4d. a bushel. The price of cheese advanced from 24s. per cwt. to 40s. in 1791, and 56s. in 1797, and from 3d. a pound to 7½d. in 1797. Bacon rose from 4d. and 5d. in 1756 to 9d. in 1797, and beef and mutton from 3d. to 6d. Butter in 1750 was 5d. or 6d. a pound, but in 1797 was 11d. or 1s., and sugar rose from 3d. to 8d.[463] But while the price of the necessaries of life was nearly doubled, the payment of labour had only advanced one-sixth or one-seventh. The average wages of the Somerset agricultural labourer in 1771 were 1s. a day all the year round, with an allowance of beer or cider and of food at hay-making and harvest. Reaping and binding an acre of wheat was paid at 4s. 6d. with drink, or at 5s. without ; the payment for mowing and binding an acre of barley was 1s. 4d. to 1s. 6d. Twenty years later, when prices were much higher, wages had risen very slightly, if at all.[463a] The average labourer's wage varied from 6s. to 8s. weekly, with an allowance as before, and it was quite impossible for a family to live without help from the parish, even if the possibility of sickness and lack of employment were left out of account. In the case of four families in the parish of Stogursey, whose circumstances were inquired into by Sir F. M. Eden in 1795, there was a yearly deficit in the case of all four, varying from £1 3s. 6d. for the family of four persons, to £16 17s. 6d. for the family of seven persons, the expenditure of the latter being 13s. 1d. weekly, while their earnings came to 8s. 10d. only. In this weekly budget payments for rent, fuel, clothes, and sickness were not entered, and this, with the weekly deficit, made up the annual

[460] The most common breed was the Dorset. The flocks were usually small, and folding was not practised. Arthur Young, *Eastern Tour*, iii, 431–83.

[461] Thorold Rogers, op. cit. v, 784.

[461a] The revenue, which had been £5,561,944 in 1703 and £6,690,000 in 1753, had risen in 1786 to £14,408,702.

[462] Contemporary observers suggested some subsidiary causes of the general advance in prices, among which were the more general consumption of butchers' meat, the use of corn to feed the extra stock kept on the converted arable land, the use of land once ploughed for canals, roads, parks, and pleasure grounds, and the great number of horses kept, ' each of which costs as much to keep as a labouring man's family.' David Davies, *Case of the Labourer in Husbandry*, 44–6.

[463] Thorold Rogers, op. cit. vi, 42–4, 102–5, 106–7, 326, 339 ; Eden, *State of the Poor*, iii, pp. lxxi-lxxviii ; ii, 463 ; David Davies, op. cit. 64–5 ; *Bath Journ.* 19 Aug. 1776 ; *Bath Chron.* Jan. 1784; Billingsley, op. cit. 152–8.

[463a] Davies, loc. cit. ; Young, *Eastern Tour*, iii, 419.

shortage.[464] In the case of large families of small children the labourer's earnings were utterly inadequate.[465] The standard of living was necessarily extremely low.[465a] Their clothing was of the poorest character ; 'they can spare little and waste their time patching rags' it was said. With the people thus in the depths of poverty, some very absurd reasons were given to account for their distress. They were accused of extravagance in using wheaten bread, of being over nice in the use of potatoes, of luxurious excess in drinking tea,[466] all rather extraordinary indictments.

Of the subsidiary causes of the distress, the inclosure movement was the most important. Inclosures deprived the labourers of fuel from the wastes and commons,[467] and increased their numbers, and consequently their absolute dependence on the farmers, by reducing a great number of small holders to the condition of landless labourers ; and the result of the disappearance of the small holders was that the labourer lost all hope of rising out of his miserable condition.[468]

The industrial revolution of the 18th century, and the introduction of machinery, had no bad effect upon Somerset, until the replacement of water by steam power drove the weaving industry from the streams of Somerset to the coalfields of the north. Even before the effects of the revolution were felt the cloth trade in Somerset was declining, and efforts were being made to bolster it up by prohibiting the export of wool from the country.[469] The industry in Somerset was one of the first to be organized capitalistically, and much ill-feeling was the result. In 1715 'unlawful clubs formed by wool combers and weavers' were declared to be dangerous to the public peace in Somerset, and to be the cause of many riots and outrages.[470] The industrial revolution completed the ruin of the industry in the county.[471] Many towns, once centres of the cloth trade, entered upon a period of decline from which they have never recovered. Bath, Bruton (in Leland's time 'much occupied with the making of cloth'), Buckland Denham, and Milverton came into this class.[472] Ilchester had lost its thread lace industry, and, even in 1633, was but the 'Carkasse of an auncient Citty.'[473] Frome was still famous for the manufacture of woollen cloth, 'but of late,' writes Collinson in 1791, 'it has been rather declining than increasing.'[474] The woollen trade still flourished in Wiveliscombe, Shepton Mallet, Dulverton, and Mil-

---

[464] Eden, *State of the Poor*, 1797, iii, App. cccl. [465] David Davies, op. cit. 26–30.

[465a] See the weekly accounts given by Eden, op. cit. One family of eight persons lived on 6s. 8d. per week.

[466] It was even asserted that the money spent by the poor on tea and sugar would keep four millions of men in bread (David Davies, op. cit. 37–9); but, as the writer pointed out, tea-drinking was not the cause, but the consequence of the distresses of the poor. He was, however, opposed to it on the ground that it was 'the occasion of much idle gossipping among the women, and absorbed money which might go a little way towards providing the family with beer' (ibid. 39).

[467] Between 1761 and 1801 there were 521 Acts for inclosing wastes and common pastures in England. Slater, op. cit. 92, 267.

[468] Ibid. 131.

[469] Acts of 1688 and 1692 13 Geo. I, cap. 23 ; 15 Geo. II, cap. 27 ; 26 Geo. II, cap. 11 ; see also 'Applications and petitions to Parliament on behalf of the Somerset wool trade, to prevent further exportation, and observations on the necessity of introducing improved machinery,' George Clerk, 'Case of decay of wool growing and wool manufacture' ; and Defoe, *Tours*, ii, 19, 20, 22, 25, 38, 39.

[470] Cunningham, op. cit. (Mod. Times), i, 508.

[471] The last attempt to give an artificial prosperity to the trade by the prohibition of the export of wool occurred in 1800, but by that time it had become comparatively unimportant in Somerset. Cunningham, op. cit. ii, 646.

[472] Collinson, *Somers.* i, 29 ; ii, 213, 451 ; iii, 13, 300.

[473] Gerard, op. cit. 203. [474] Collinson, op. cit. ii, 187.

borne Port in 1791, but at South Petherton it had been replaced by the manufacture of dowlas ticking, at Yeovil by gloving, and at Taunton by silk manufacture.[475] The decay of the domestic industry of spinning[475a] removed a subsidiary source of employment, and still further intensified the prevailing distress. One great reason for the very low wages and great misery in the west of England was the difficulty of communication with other parts of the country where the labour market was not overstocked. Even the wealthy found travelling costly, difficult, and frequently dangerous. The local newspapers are filled with accounts of accidents to coaches, and of coaches being delayed owing to the state of the roads.[476] In 1784 it took two days to get from London to Bath, outside passengers paying £1 6s., and inside passengers 15s. each.[477] Further, the labourer who left home in the hope of getting better paid work had to battle with the law of settlement.[478] 'Labour does not flow, it crawls' it has been said, and if that is true to-day, it is rather an under statement of the case a hundred years ago.

The misery of the people led to a series of attempts to lessen the rigour of the poor law, attempts which, though designed in a philanthropic spirit, sapped the self-reliance of the people. The best-known of these experiments was Gilbert's Act of 1782, which included provisions forbidding the admission of the able-bodied poor into the workhouse, and increasing the power of the justices to afford relief, suggested the provision of work for the poor by the parish near their own homes, and supplemented wages from the rates. The last provision set a mischievous example, copied by the Berkshire justices in 1795, and by other county magistrates subsequently. By the poor law thus modified English labour was pauperized in a wholesale manner. The poor rate rose steadily, and by 1795 was double what it had been fifty years before. In 1740 the rate at Minehead produced £178 6s. 1d., in 1794 it was £359 6s. At Frome it rose from £1,971 13s. 6d. in 1793 to £3,125 14s. 9d. in 1795, and these examples taken from opposite ends of the county could be multiplied indefinitely.[479] The misery of the people led to riots and rick burnings, vagrancy and poaching ;[480] and 'to be a clever poacher was deemed a reputable accomplishment in the county.'[481] Dearness of food was at the bottom of most of the rioting of the early 19th century, the price of corn being kept at an artificially high level by legislation. In 1800–1 corn was 116s. 8d. per quarter ; the average from 1802–8 was 73s. 6d., and in 1812 it was 155s.[482]

---

[475] Collinson, op. cit. iii, 106, 204, 352, 459, 520. The migration of the silk weavers to Taunton was possibly due to the attempt of the manufacturers to evade the Spitalfields Act (13 Geo. III, cap. 68); Cunningham, op. cit. ii, 519 n.

[475a] Proof of the former prevalence of domestic spinning may be found in 16th and 17th-century wills. In a few places it lingered at the end of the 18th century. Ibid. iii, 80.

[476] 'The London machine overturned and the coachman killed' is an example of a not uncommon entry. *Bath Chron.* 1784.

[477] Highway robberies were frequent, and the *Bath Chron.* of 1784 contains an advertisement of 'The Mail Diligence. Persons and Property Protected By Government Authority with a Guard. Leaves Bristol 4 p.m. Reaches London 8 a.m.'

[478] 43 Eliz. cap. 2 ; 13 & 14 Chas. II, cap. 12 ; 3 & 4 Will. and Mary, cap. 11, &c.

[479] David Davies, op. cit. 44 ; Eden. op. cit. ii, 643, 647, 648. For the later development of the system in Somerset, see p. 327.

[480] Even the comparatively low prices of 1753 led to a riot at Shepton Mallet, where 500 colliers invaded the market and sold corn at a price fixed by themselves. Letters of Lord Poulett to the Secretary-at-War, B.M. Add. MS. n. 32731. [481] David Davies, op. cit. 59.

[482] Townsend Warner, *Landmarks in Engl. Industrial Hist.* 302.

The local newspapers show that the contrast between the conditions of life among the different classes of society was more striking than ever before or since.[483] Bath had become a fashionable resort, and side by side with accounts of distress and riots, advertisements for runaway apprentices (many of whom were described as 'marked with the small pox'), reports of deaths from exposure and starvation,[484] and of a malignant fever in Ilchester Gaol carrying off thirty people in a few weeks, we find accounts of concerts and assemblies, news of fashionable arrivals, theatrical intelligence, accounts of duels, reports from the card-rooms, advertisements of lottery tickets and tontines,[485] and descriptions of the Bath races on Claverton Downs, and of air balloon exhibitions.[486]

There is evidence, however, of the efforts of the charitable to meet the distress. In February 1784 the Mayor of Bath collected £600, which was distributed in food, &c., to 4,532 poor persons, and subscriptions were constantly being raised for the prisoners in Ilchester Gaol, and for Bath Hospital, which had been opened in 1742. Sunday schools and schools of industry had been established in the city, and 150 children of Bath, Widcombe, and Walcot, taken in rotation from the Sunday schools, were instructed in weaving and spinning.[487] A pauper charity for medical attendance on the poor had been founded in 1742.

The country gentleman imitated his fashionable neighbours at Bath in his amusements. Racing, hunting, drinking, gambling, duelling, and cock-fighting were 'Squire Western's' occupations, enlivened by an annual visit to town. The brightness of his intellect may be gauged from the popularity of literature dealing with witchcraft, horrors, and miracles, or giving accounts of 'crying murthers,' of the last moments of murderers and their 'awful confessions,' and of the exploits of the 'Somerset dœmon.'[488] The labourer had no share in the amusements of his social superiors. The village revels were dying out, a few only being mentioned by Collinson as surviving in 1791.[489] Except in the comparatively few places where charity schools had been founded, the villagers were absolutely ignorant and illiterate. The first signs of the coming change, however, appeared in 1789, when a village school was started by Hannah More at Wrington.[490] The Christmas feast, however, was still kept up on the manor of North Curry, the average tenant receiving two 5-pound loaves of good white flour, 8 pennyworth of beef, and twopence in money, and, just as two centuries before, he had the right to sit drinking ale after dinner until

---

[483] The press was first established in Somerset at Taunton in 1718, the *Taunton Journal*, the first local newspaper, being issued in 1725. In 1729 and 1747 printing began at Bath and Yeovil. See E. Green, *Bibliotheca Somersetensis*, i, xvii, for the newspapers of the county.

[484] In the *Bath Chron.* of 8 Apr. 1784 five deaths in the snow are reported in the county.

[485] This was at the height of the fashionable craze for lotteries, and the Bath papers advertise lotteries for money prizes, lace, 'fashionable coaches,' houses, and freehold estates.

[486] *Bath Journ.* 1776, *Bath Chron.* 1784 and 1789. A possible connexion with the last may be surmised from the notice 'Ladies are humbly informed that the new-fashioned hats called Balloon hats as they are contrary to the established rules of Bath will not be admitted to the Rooms on any evening.'

[487] *Bath Chron.* 1789.

[488] There were a great number of pamphlets of this kind published in the county, beginning in 1584, with one called 'The discourse of a woman possessed with the devill, who, in the likenesse of a headlesse beare, fetched her out of her bed at Ditcheat.'

[489] Collinson, op. cit. i, 31, 35, 39, 53, 44, 64, 158.

[490] Green, *Bibliotheca Somersetensis*, iii, 63–100.

two candles each 1 lb. in weight had burned out, the toast being 'To the Mortal Memory of King John,' whose effigy figured in paste on a mince pie.[491] This, however, was an exceptional survival ; in most places feasts as well as revels were things of the past.

Punishments were excessively severe. There were nine capital convictions at the Bath Assizes in 1784 ; one man was hanged at Taunton for stealing a silver watch, and three men for being concerned in one burglary. A man was transported for seven years for stealing a shirt, while other punishments were public whippings, standing in the pillory, branding in the hand and on the forehead. In 1801 nine men were hanged on the stone gallows in Wellington for stealing bread.[492] Sheep-stealing was a very common offence, though the penalty of detection was death. Highwaymen and footpads were numerous in the county, and held up the London coaches on Claverton Down, and elsewhere, the road between Nunney and Lamyatt being a favourite haunt. On 15 April 1784 there is an account of the execution of a highwayman, who had terrorized Freshford and the seven adjoining parishes, each of which had offered a reward of two guineas for his capture.[493] Owing to the great number of import duties, smuggling was a very profitable employment, and many of the county magnates were mixed up in it.[494] It had already begun in the 17th century, especially in the west of the county, where in 1682 there are accounts of the smuggling of wine, brandy, and cloth under cover of innocent cargoes of salt. Sir William Wyndham patronized the smugglers, the port of Watchet, his town, being used to escape the custom house at Minehead, and growing exceedingly rich from that cause. Colonel Luttrell, who owned Minehead, was similarly indisposed to help the preventive officers.[495] A century later the trade had reached formidable proportions, when there was much smuggling from Ireland, Lisbon, and the West Indies, and one hundred horses were sometimes waiting for the arrival of the cargoes, temporary hiding-places for the goods being found under the floors of barns, in the thickness of farm-house walls, and in caves and holes along the coast.[496] The exploits of the Doones of Bagworthy related in *Lorna Doone* were drawn from local traditions of a robber band who long flourished unchecked in the parish of Oare, and the existence of a 'desperate clan of banditti' in Selwood is recorded by Collinson.[496a]

The shameful state of the county gaols was beginning to arouse attention. John Howard, writing in 1788, describes the condition of the Somerset prisons as most unsatisfactory. There was no classification of prisoners, felons and debtors being herded together, while the prisons themselves were dirty and neglected. The chapel of Taunton Bridewell was used for the confinement of the dirtiest prisoners. 'I found it,' he writes, 'as bad as a pigstye.' There was no employment for the prisoners. Discipline

---

[491] *Hist. MSS. Com. Rep.* x, App. iii, 313. This customary feast was abolished in 1860, the money so saved being vested in the Charity Commissioners.

[492] *Somers. and Dors. N. and Q.* iv, 309.

[493] *Taunton Courier*, 29 July 1829 ; *Bath Journ.* 1776 ; *Bath Chron.* 1784–9.

[494] The local papers are full of references to it. In 1784, for instance, 58 gals. of rum, 46 of brandy, 52 of gin, and 5 bags of tea were seized at Farleigh. *Bath Chron.* 1784.

[495] Treas. Papers, 1682. Culliforde's Rep. (pp. 67–84), quoted by Mr. Chadwyck Healey, op. cit. 33–8.

[496] *Hist. MSS. Com. Rep.* xv, App. i, 177, 215.

[496a] Collinson, op. cit. ii, 194.

seems to have been much neglected ; at Shepton Mallet many prisoners were found 'smoking and heated with liquor in the keeper's room,' and for the payment of 2s. weekly the privilege of living in the keeper's house could be obtained. Bridgwater Town Gaol was in a still worse condition. Bath City Gaol was an exception to the general rule of scandalous mismanagement. The prison was clean and quiet, there was a separate room for debtors and a workshop for the employment of prisoners.[497] The old county gaol at Ilchester had long been notorious for epidemics of gaol fever. In the spring of 1784 a 'malignant fever' had carried off thirty prisoners in a few weeks,[498] but a new gaol had just been completed in 1789.[499] Each new cell contained four iron staples with rings attached for chaining down the prisoners. This provision was part of the cruel discipline that prevailed in gaols of the period, the practices at Ilchester being exposed some thirty years later by Henry Hunt. The situation of the gaol was unhealthy, some parts being below the bed of the river, and it was much too small for the number of prisoners.[499a] Classification had not been extended to the female prisoners, the water supply was insufficient and polluted with sewage, and there was no hospital, sick ward, or resident surgeon, though epidemics of typhus were terribly common. Each debtor received the county allowance of 1d. a day and half a pound of bread every other day. The gaoler's revenue was estimated at £1,500, and his house was the scene of gambling and drinking parties, at which favoured prisoners were present. Worst of all, the punishments for prison offences were unspeakably cruel, and Mr. Hunt's book is a miserable recital of horrors and brutalities, the solitary cell, flogging, and loading with irons being frequent punishments.[500] The position of the debtors was hopeless. One man, imprisoned in 1807 for a debt of £34 17s. 10½d., had already been in gaol for fifteen years when Hunt wrote. He was then seventy-four years of age, and his only hope of release was death.[501]

Some improvement had been effected by 1840, but Ilchester still retained an evil reputation for unhealthiness. The food of the prisoners consisted of bread, oatmeal gruel, and potatoes ; once a week only (on Sundays) they had an allowance of half a pound of meat each. At Taunton and Shepton Mallet prisoners sentenced to hard labour were employed on the tread-mill, breaking stones, or pumping water, or in workshops as tailors, carpenters, and shoemakers. The female prisoners were employed in the wash-houses and laundry. The prisoners' labour produced £274 18s. 8d. at Taunton and £152 9s. 7¾d. at Shepton Mallet in 1839. Prisoners were still housed in wards containing from eight to ten persons, and the Shepton Mallet Gaol was specially overcrowded, owing to its being under a contract with the Bath magistrates to take their prisoners. Twenty-six debtors were accommodated in Ilchester Gaol, the greatest number of prisoners there at one time being 103. Prison punishments still included loading with irons and solitary confinement for long periods, and, as to the latter, the report on

---

[497] John Howard, *Acct. of Prisons and Houses of Correction in the Western Circuit*, 1789, pp. 38–40.
[498] *Bath Chron.* 1 Apr. 1784.
[499] John Howard, op. cit. 37.
[499a] The gaol contained an average number of 200 prisoners.
[500] One man was kept in irons nine days and nine nights with his head touching his feet, till the iron rings sank into his flesh.
[501] Henry Hunt, *A Peep into Prison, or the Inside of Ilchester Bastile*, 1821.

Shepton Mallet Gaol states, with grim humour, that 'those prisoners who had been put into solitary confinement under the reduced allowance of one pound of bread per day, with water, began to exhibit more penitence than when they received the full county allowance.'

The prisons contained a number of young offenders. At Taunton there were eighteen males and four females under the age of seventeen, and Ilchester Gaol also housed an insane prisoner who had been committed for stealing bread and bacon, and who was reported as 'still insane.' In 1839 three men were executed in Somerset, one of them for burglary, while of eleven who were transported for life, seven were guilty of theft only. These reports throw some light on the level of education in the county. Of the offenders committed for trial in Somerset this year, 136 were under twelve years of age, 281 could neither read nor write, 375 could read imperfectly but not write, and only 118 could read and write well ; while the one person of whom it was stated that he was of 'superior instruction' was found guilty of embezzlement.[502] In 1843 the county gaol at Ilchester was taken down, the inmates being transferred to the prisons at Shepton Mallet and Taunton, and five years later the county asylum for insane paupers was opened at Wells.[502a]

The end of the 18th and beginning of the 19th century was in Somerset, as elsewhere, a time of great distress, which was intensified rather than alleviated by the efforts of legislation. Chief among these was the interpretation of the Poor Law known as the 'Speenhamland Act.' The example of the Berkshire magistrates was speedily copied in Somerset, with fatal results.

The system adopted varied in different parishes, but it always took the form of relief in aid of wages given to those in private employment, varying according to the size of the family of the labourer, and in some places given on a scale laid down by the magistrates, which varied with the price of wheat. In Bishop's Hull parish an allowance of 1s. 6d. weekly was given for every child, beginning with the third, with the result that the poor-rate was more than doubled in thirty years, the rate per head of the population being 6s. 9d. in 1801 and 13s. 6d. in 1831.[503] In an average year eighteen able-bodied labourers were in receipt of this allowance. Elsewhere, as in the Brompton Regis district (which included twenty-two parishes), the allowance was granted in accordance with the price of wheat, a bushel of wheat being regarded as the amount required for the support of a labourer, his wife, and three children. In Bruton allowances were given in accordance with the price of the standard wheaten loaf, and the same system prevailed throughout the county.[504] The relief was given without any inquiry as to the character or claims of the people relieved, and at Bedminster it was stated that 'three out of every four relieved are in some way or another impostors.' The people came to regard the allowance as a right, and soon lost any sense of shame in receiving it. To the farmers it was a source of profit, saving them from the expense of raising the wages of their labourers to a point where it would

[502] *Parl. Papers*, 1840, xxxviii, 138–46.
[502a] This is now supplemented by another asylum at Cotford near Taunton. Shepton Mallet gaol is now the only county prison. [503] *Poor Law Com. Rep.* 1835 (44), xxx.
[504] Details are available for the parishes of Bedminster, Bruton, North Cadbury, Crowcombe, North Curry, Curry Rivel, Huish Episcopi, Pitney, Spaxton, Stogumber, Stoke St. Gregory, Taunton, Weston, Whatley, Yeovil, and the districts around these parishes. Ibid. 1834 (44), xxxi.

be possible for them to live. The result was that the poor-rate grew by leaps and bounds, the expenditure per head of the population rising in the Stoke St. Gregory district to the huge amount of £1 6s. 10d. In Stogumber it was stated that the system was a 'crying evil,' nearly all the work done being partly paid for by the parish, while in Taunton Vale 'all the farm labourers during the whole or part of the year receive a portion of their wages out of the poor-rates.'[505] In the parish of Weston, where there was no allowance system, the expenditure never went above 10s. 4d. per head, and by 1831 had fallen to 3s. 5d., while relatively small poor-rates were also found in Huish and Pitney, where the allowance system was not in vogue. Attempts had been made to give up the allowance system in some other places, but without success. At Chilton Cantelo, where the experiment was tried, the paupers, thinking they had a vested interest in the poor-rate, claimed that the overseers must provide work or maintenance. The relief frequently took the form of exempting the poor from the payment of rates, of house rent, or of both.[506] In many places it was actually given in the form of weekly payments of 1s. 6d. or 2s., a system favoured by the parish officers, as it was much cheaper than maintaining the paupers in a workhouse, but aptly described as a bounty on idleness and crime, able-bodied paupers being sometimes assembled in a gravel-pit or old quarry to sit still doing nothing.

The Roundsmen system, by which the parish paid private individuals to employ the poor at a rate of wages fixed by the parish, was very prevalent in some counties, but the only cases of it that have been found in Somerset occur in Bruton and the neighbouring parishes. In this district, too, are found instances of the somewhat similar system, under which the ratepayers agreed each to employ a certain number of labourers, according to some scale, corresponding with the rental, the rates, or the acreage of the holding occupied. Instances are also found in the parishes of Batcombe and Drayton.[506a]

The only form of relief for the able-bodied poor that had legislative authority, that of parish employment, was the most unusual of all. In most cases where it was the custom, the work required was very trifling, and the wages were higher than in ordinary employment, the paupers regarding short hours and light work as their right.[507]

The only parishes in Somerset which had workhouses were Taunton, Yeovil, Stoke St. Gregory, North Curry, Frome, and Bruton, while about half the whole number had poorhouses for the infirm paupers. The number in receipt of out-door relief was enormous. In one week seventy-two families received out-relief in Batcombe, thirty-five in Bishop's Hull, seventy-six in Brompton Regis, 276 in Bruton, eighty in North Cadbury, 131 in North Curry, and 178 in Yeovil. Attempts were made with some success in Frome Selwood workhouse to provide profitable work for the inmates, and by their labour in making serge and bedding and knitting stockings £118 6s. 4½d. was realized in 1831–2, which brought down the expense to 2s. 2¼d. a head weekly. At Taunton, where the only work provided was a little for children in the silk factories and for a few men breaking stones, the

---

[505] *Poor Law Com. Rep.* 1835 (44), xxx.

[506] The parishes of Pitney and Thorne Coffin, which gave neither form of relief, were the exception to this general rule. Ibid. xxxi.

[506a] Ibid. 1834, xxv, xxvii.

[507] Road-mending seems to have been a favourite form of parish employment.

cost per head was 4*s*. 2*d*. At Shepton Mallet the poor were farmed out to a person who received 3*s*. weekly for adults and 2*s*. for children. It was a method that saved the parish money and trouble at the expense of the unfortunate paupers, the farmer making his profit by half starving them.[508]

One result of these well-meant but misdirected efforts was the alarming increase of pauperism, the poor-rates rising to an astonishing extent, as the following table shows :—

Poor Rate	1803 £	1813 £	1821 £	1831 £
Batcombe	229	579	535	568
Bedminster	991	2,188	2,921	3,498
North Curry	475	990	982	1,102
Drayton	182	406	351	200
Whatley	185	281	241	401
Yeovil	936	1,399	2,084	1,851 [509]

Another result was the prevalence of very low wages, which were in most cases inadequate for the support of the average labourer's family. In the Taunton Vale district the labourer earned 7*s*. a week, supplemented by an allowance of cider supposed to be worth 1*s*. 6*d*. to 2*s*. a week, with the doubtful privilege of buying 'tailing' wheat from the employer at a reduced price. At Batcombe the wages were from 6*s*. to 8*s*. a week, with beer or cider all the year round, and with food at harvest time. The average throughout the county was about the same, except in the few districts where piece-work could be obtained, and where much higher wages were the rule. Thus, in Huish Episcopi and Nether Stowey 18*s*. a week could be earned in the summer, and 8*s*. a week in the winter. The report, on the whole, showed that it was only possible for a family to be maintained on the average wages if they lived on the cheapest food (bread and potatoes with a little bacon very occasionally), and then only provided that they were excellent managers and escaped sickness.[510] There seems to have been but little possibility in Somerset at this date of supplementing the family income by the earnings of women and children. Women and boys were employed at harvest time, earning from 4*s*. to 6*s*. and from 2*s*. to 3*s*. a week respectively, but except for this brief period employment of women was the exception. Employment in the silk mills at Bishop's Hull could be obtained for women at 9*d*. a day, and for children under sixteen at 6*d*. a day, but the number of women and children employed by the silk throwsters at Bruton had fallen off through the decline of trade.[511] At Whatley weeding could be obtained for four months in the year at 4*s*. a week. The gloving trade, which has since given so much employment to women, was beginning to be important in Yeovil, but it was complained that ' it spoiled the women for domestic or husbandry employment.' In many places children from the age of nine were bound out as parish apprentices—hard work, poor food, and ill-treatment being too often their lot.

It was quite exceptional in Somerset for the labourer to own the cottage he lived in, or to be in a position to rent a piece of land. The parishes in which a

---

[508] *Poor Law Com. Rep.* 1834 (44), xxxi. [509] Ibid. xxxv.
[510] Ibid. xxxi.
[511] The earnings of the former were from 2*s*. 6*d*. to 4*s*. weekly, and of the latter from 6*d*. to 2*s*. 6*d*.

fair number of labourers had these advantages were Bedminster, North Curry, Pitney, Stoke St. Gregory, and Yeovil, while in the parish of Stogumber they were in a very fortunate position—the rule on the lands of Sir John Trevelyan being 'reasonable rent, most ample gardens, and land let to cottagers at half its value, to their great comfort and contentment.' [512] At North Cadbury, Drayton, Nether Stowey, and Yeovil, potato ground was let out by the farmers at the high rent of £8 to £10 per acre, the ploughing and manuring of the ground being done by the farmers. Allotments, however, had been tried very successfully at Wells, where the bishop had let out 50 acres to 203 persons in small lots at the rent of 12s. 6d. per quarter of an acre, 2s. 6d. a year being allowed as a rebate if the land was kept well fenced and in good condition. The system was begun in 1826, with the result that many formerly in receipt of relief had been enabled to do without it, and that there was very good feeling in the parish, 'the Bishop's pheasants were safe, and during the riots the labourers offered to come and protect the Bishop's palace.' [512a] The reports of the Poor Law Commissioners also deal with the question as to whether the available agricultural capital was increasing or diminishing. In the majority of Somerset parishes it was reported that there had been a great diminution of capital, the pressure of the poor-rate and maladministration of the Poor Law being the cause most frequently assigned. Very depressing accounts were given of the decline in the industry and character of the labouring class ; it was noticed that deterioration speedily followed on the receipt of relief. Great complaints were made of the bad effect of the recently established beershops. At North Curry it was stated that owing to the establishment of these 'the labouring drunkard can waste his time and money without being observed. Idleness and vice are more prevalent, and the worst of crimes are often planned in these houses with impunity.' [513] Very various views were held as to the causes of the instability of service, the general opinion in Somerset being that movement was more frequent than formerly, and among the different reasons suggested are reliance on parish relief, the poor character of the labourer which made frequent discharges necessary, the discharge of labourers to prevent them obtaining a settlement, and the discontinuance of the practice of the labourer living in the house of his employer, [514] while the only hopeful suggestion—that the instability of service might be due to the increasing knowledge and active spirit of the people—comes from Weston. [515]

The misery of the people came to a head in the winter of 1830–1. In Somerset, as elsewhere, the farmers received letters signed 'Swing,' threatening rioting, which almost immediately followed, with rick-burnings, destruction of threshing-machines, and other outrages. About half the parishes in the county were concerned, panic spread everywhere, and very far-fetched reasons were given for the outbreak, in addition to the obvious one of general privation and misery. At Weston there was the curious suggestion that the

[512] *Poor Law Com. Rep.* 1835, xxxi. The land was let at 18s. per acre.
[512a] Similar experiments at Frome and Shepton Mallet were, however, discontinued as failures.
[513] *Poor Law Com. Rep.* 1835, xxxii.
[514] The discontinuance of this practice dated from the second period of inclosures, and had very far-reaching effects. Among other things it encouraged early and improvident marriages, and certainly weakened the bond between employer and employed. Slater, op. cit.
[515] *Poor Law Com. Rep.* 1835, xxxiii.

rioters were under the impression 'that their proceedings were sanctioned and encouraged by authority.'[516]

The great increase of vagrancy in Somerset in the early years of the 19th century was aptly described in a report drawn up in 1833:—

> Men of all trades wander for employment, the failure of manufacturers and destruction of machinery send many hundreds on the tramp. Soldiers' wives and children are scrambling in all directions after regiments ordered to new stations, sailors ramble from port to port, the settlement law compels the infirm to wander from the place where a temporary ailment suspends their employment to some very distant parish ; wives are hunting for runaway husbands (rarely the reverse) and children for runaway parents, and the excitement induced by political agitators has produced a general spirit of restlessness.

In addition, there was a considerable class of tramps who made a trade of wandering in the summer and returning to their own parishes in the winter, the latter (probably to be rid of them) starting them off with a small sum in the spring. The vagrant was usually committed to prison for a month, at a weekly expense to the county of 5s. 10½d. Seven-eighths of the vagrants were said to be 'vicious and idle, not unavoidably in want, and the treadwheels had little effect on the old offenders.'

Bath had tried the experiment of setting up a Vagrant Office, which helped poor travellers by gifts of soup, bread, and small sums of money ; but in 1833, after the society had existed for twenty-eight years, the mayor reported that it had a decided tendency to increase vagrancy and the poor-rates, and it was therefore discontinued.[517] Among the many suggestions made for reform was that all parish relief should be given by way of loan under the Act of George III ;[518] that the parish should in lieu of giving allowances look after the labourer's family, taking charge of, feeding, and employing the children during the day, and that the procedure of granting relief should be modified by removing the right of appeal from the vestry to the magistrates. The suggestion that the parishes should tax themselves to provide an emigration fund met with a very mixed reception in Somerset. The report from Bishop's Hull was that it would be an 'effectual remedy,' while at Bedminster it was thought that it would bring 'inevitable ruin.'

Many of these suggestions were embodied in the Poor Law Amendment Act of 1834,[518a] which immediately produced a fall in the poor-rate and in the percentage of paupers to the population.

The 19th century saw a great improvement in the means of communication by means of roads, canals, and railways.[519] Of Porlock it could be written in 1791 'the roads are so steep that no carriages of any kind can be found, and all the crops are carried in with crooks on horses,' and the roads in Stoke Pero were so 'steep, narrow, and encumbered with large loose stones, that it is dangerous even for horses.'[519a] Some progress, however, had been

---

[516] *Poor Law Com. Rep.* 1835, xxxiv. Reports from Bedminster, Bishop's Hull, Brompton Regis, Chilton Cantelo, North Cadbury, Crowcombe, North Curry, Curry Rivel, Drayton, Dulverton, Huish, Northover, Pitney, Spaxton, Stogumber, Stoke St. Gregory, Vale of Taunton, Thorne Coffin, Weston, Whatley, and Yeovil.

[517] Ibid. xxxviii, App. E.   [518] 59 Geo. III, stat. 29, cap. 12.   [518a] 4–5 Will. IV, cap. 76.

[519] The highways and bridges of the county during the early periods owed much to private benevolence, and were often the object of legacies in wills ; e.g. 'to the fabric of the highway between the hamlets of Budleigh and Wotton 4 marks' ; will of John Campbell, 1487, *Somers. Medieval Wills* (Somers. Rec. Soc. xvi) ; see also pp. 19, 115, 214, 313, 344, 349, 355, &c.

[519a] Collinson, op. cit. ii, 35, 43 ; iii, 542.

made ; the roads leading to Bristol, Bath, and Bridgwater had been repaired and improved before 1750,[520] and the process of making new roads and improving the old was continued, until the county was well opened up.[521]   At the same time most of the bridges of the county were being repaired or rebuilt.[522]   Communication by water was also improved.   An Act of 1711 for making the Avon navigable was followed in 1749 by another dealing with the navigation of the Avon and Frome.[523]   The first canal scheme appeared in 1794,[524] when a canal to connect the Somerset collieries with the proposed Kennet and Avon canal was projected, and this was rapidly followed by others. A canal-making mania seized upon the county, many schemes (like that of the Grand Canal from Seaton in South Devon to Bridgwater Bay) were mooted and abandoned, and many of the canals constructed at this date have gone out of use since the making of railways.[525]

Side by side with the canal schemes, and in many cases dependent upon them, the work of reclaiming, draining, and dividing the great moors of the county was carried on.   From very early times efforts of this kind had been made.[526]   The Abbots of Glastonbury, for instance, had drained and cultivated the district round Meare, but after the Dissolution the tenants failed to perform their customary services of keeping the ditches clear, the district was again submerged, and the timber-covered lands of the abbey became again a reed-covered marsh.   Before 1812, however, drainage had begun again, and after the cutting of the Glastonbury Canal, Brent Marsh was completely reclaimed. Many schemes for draining the whole of Sedgemoor, the earliest of which dated from the reign of James I, had proved abortive, but the moor was ultimately drained under an Act of 1791,[527] and turnpike roads were driven across a hitherto impassable swamp.[528]   Allermoor and Westmoor were still almost untouched in 1835, but a movement was then set on foot which resulted in the reclamation of what is now some of the finest pasture land in the county, while the health of the surrounding districts has been much improved by the drainage of the marshy land, and by the extension, during the last fifty years of the 19th century, of the practice of planting thousands of acres of Westmoor and Sedgemoor with osiers.[529]

With the reform of the Poor Law some of the worst evils of the old system of dealing with poverty were swept away.   Unfortunately the inauguration of the system of union workhouses in Somerset was followed almost immediately by revelations of grave mismanagement at the Bridgwater Union

---

[520] Stat. 13 Geo. I, cap. 7 ; 3 Geo. II, cap. 34.

[521] The first macadamized road in England was made between Bath and Bristol in 1816.

[522] Stat. 34 Geo. III, cap. 105 ; 49 Geo. III, cap. 84.

[523] Stat. 22 Geo. II, cap. 90.   [524] Stat. 34 Geo. III, cap. 86.

[525] A curious instance of the replacement of canal by railway schemes is to be found in 1846, when an Act was passed to enable the Chard Canal Company to convert into a railway a portion of their canal, while in the following year they obtained permission to stop up their canal and extend their railway. 9 & 10 Vic. cap. 215, and 10 & 11 Vic. cap. 175.   Recently, the question of the utilization of many now disused canals has been discussed, owing to the development of the motor-boat industry, since by means of motor barges heavy goods of all kinds could be carried at very cheap rates.

[526] The first Commission on Sewers for the county was appointed in 1304. R. W. Phelps, *Marshes and Turbaries of Somers.*

[527] 31 Geo. III, cap. 91.

[528] Stat. 59 Geo. III, cap. 76.

[529] The Land Drainage Act of 1861, under which many parishes were reclaimed, was followed by the constitution of a Drainage Board under an Act of 1877 (28 & 29 Vic. cap. 23 ; 40 & 41 Vic. cap. 36). Parts of Westmoor and Sedgemoor, however, are still subject to autumn floods.

Workhouse, brought forward by John Bower in 1839, under the title 'Is Killing in an Union Workhouse criminal if sanctioned by the Poor Law Commissioners ?' He proved that an outbreak of dysentery, which resulted in ninety-four deaths among the children and aged poor, was due to the substitution of oatmeal gruel for milk in the dietary, the change being continued in spite of the unfavourable report of the surgeon. The disease spread rapidly owing to the overcrowded state of the workhouse, six children sleeping in one bed, and 50 in a dormitory 27 ft. by 15 ft. Thirty-eight deaths occurred in eight months ; the visiting guardians did not visit the workhouse for forty weeks, and the number of deaths enabled the chairman to congratulate the Board on a saving of £4,843 ! This epidemic was followed later by an outbreak of typhus, which caused six deaths in twenty days. The evidence given on an inquiry instituted by the House of Lords supported the statement that while the deaths among the convicts were 3 per cent the deaths in the Bridgwater Union had reached 41 per cent.[530]

A great deal still remained to be done to improve the condition of the agricultural labourer. Overcrowding was one of the most crying evils. The usual type of cottage had but one bedroom, and as many as twenty-nine people lived in one Somerset cottage.[531] There was no attempt at drainage, pigstyes were often found on a higher level than the cottages, and frequent outbreaks of typhus were the result. Women were less employed in agricultural work in Somerset than in the neighbouring county of Dorset, and in the former it was rare to find women employed out of doors in the winter. Their work usually took the form of attending to threshing-machines, winnowing and dairy work, with employment at haymaking and harvest, and their earnings varied from 3s. to 5s. a week. In the towns where gloving had been introduced, however, women could earn much more. Boys were employed for very long hours, the work expected from them, like bird-scaring and driving cattle, being tedious rather than severe. Men's wages were still lamentably low, the average in Somerset in 1842-3 being about 9s. 6d. weekly, with an allowance of three pints of cider daily, valued at 1s. 3d. a week. The food of the labourer was still wretched, the usual breakfast being 'kettle broth' (a mixture of flour and butter with hot water) and dinner a few potatoes and a little bacon. The allotment system had not yet spread in Somerset to the same extent as in Dorset, Wilts, and Devon.[532]

Ten years later the labourer was in even worse distress. The repeal of the Corn Laws had led to great agricultural depression, the ruin of the farmers had involved that of the labourers depending upon them, and the conversion of arable farms to pasture meant a falling demand for labour. The average wages in the south and west of England were 37 per cent. lower than in the coalfields and the Midlands.[533] In fact, while wages in Lancashire had almost doubled, in the south they had been practically stationary since 1750, while meat was 80 per cent. dearer, and wool and butter were doubled in price. Drunkenness was very prevalent, the statute or hiring fairs

---

[530] John Bower, *New Poor Law ; The Bridgwater Case*, 1839.
[531] F. G. Heath, *Peasant Life in the West of England*, 30–7.
[532] Ibid.
[533] James Caird, *English Agriculture*.

occasioned disgraceful scenes, and the state of morality was very low.[534] The system of binding out children as parish apprentices, however, had nearly died out. Even twenty years later, in 1872, the conditions were very bad. The average wages in Somerset were not more than 7s. to 8s. a week. Cottage rents were very high, £7 being often paid for a cottage or £9 for a cottage and garden, and even of these highly-rented cottages there was a very serious deficiency.[535] On the other hand, while these conditions were causing many of the labourers to seek better fortune in the towns, to migrate to Wales, to the North, and to America, signs of improvement were visible in some parts of the county, particularly in districts where glove-making employed the wives of the labourers at very fair wages. The flourishing condition of the parish schools at Burrington, where the children of farmers and labourers were educated together with excellent results, and the admirable allotment system, which gave the peasants an opportunity of improving their diet by rearing pigs and poultry and growing vegetables, may be quoted as hopeful signs.[536]

The opening up of the county by means of railways had a good effect upon the position of the labourer. The first railway to affect the county was the Great Western, opened to Bristol in 1839.[537] The Bristol and Exeter (absorbed by the Great Western Railway in 1876) was opened in 1844 ; and at different dates branches have been made from the main line to Frome, Portishead, Clevedon, Weston-super-Mare, Wells, Yeovil, Chard, Minehead, and Barnstaple. The Great Western Railway extension from Chippenham to Weymouth by way of Frome and Yeovil, with a branch to Wells, was opened in 1857. To avoid the detour through Bristol, a new line was made in 1906 from Castle Cary to Langport, and by this route trains run from Taunton to London (144 miles) in two-and-a-half hours. The London and South Western extension from Salisbury, skirting the southern edge of the county, was opened in 1860, when a joint station was opened at Yeovil. There are short branches from Yeovil Junction to Yeovil, and from Chard Road to Chard.

The Somerset Central Railway from Highbridge to Glastonbury was opened in 1854. It was subsequently extended at either end to Burnham (1858) and Wells [538] (1859). In 1862 it was amalgamated with the Somerset and Dorset line, which originally was laid from Wimborne to Glastonbury, and later the main line was extended from Evercreech to Bath over the Mendips, attaining near Maesbury Station an elevation of 800 ft. Since 1876 this line has been the joint property of the Midland and South Western Railways. The West Somerset Mineral Railway from Watchet to Combe Row, at the foot of the Brendon Hills, was abandoned in 1899.

---

[534] Letters of the Hon. and Rev. Sydney Godolphin Osborne to Poor Law Commissioners.

[535] In Athelney and Stoke St. Gregory there were many mud houses, and in the prosperous district of Montacute most of the cottages had earthen floors. With bread at 7d. the quartern, 7s. 6d. a week left a family of seven persons in Cannington without even a sufficiency of bread (Heath, op. cit. 146, 160). Candles were rarely used ; sugar, butter, and milk were rare luxuries.

[536] Wages had already risen in the districts where labour was comparatively scarce, in the north of the county where the competition of Bristol was felt, in the vicinity of the flourishing towns, and in the parishes along the line of the railway.   [537] Stat. 6 & 7 Will. IV, cap. 36.

[538] Owing to the comparatively recent development of motoring there are signs that some of the towns which, like Wells and Ilchester, are on the great high roads, but are isolated by the shifting of traffic from road to rail, will recover some of their vanished prosperity.

This development of the means of communication by making movement from place to place easy tended to equalize wages in all parts of the county,[539] and made the competition of higher rates of wages in the towns and abroad a factor in the problem. A great change in the position of the Somerset labourers took place between 1870 and 1880. Wages made a great advance, 14s. being the average, cottage accommodation was much improved and the standard of living raised. The growth of the gloving trade continued, and in many parts of the county the earnings of the wives of the labourers are very considerable.[540] The friendly society movement developed rapidly,[541] clothing and blanket clubs were formed, and—most important of all —the granting of allotments to labourers at reasonable rates became general.[542] In the districts where there is a subsidiary industry employing women and children great prosperity is the rule. In the parish of Kingsbury Episcopi, for instance, it is quite common for the labourer to invest his savings in the purchase of land and build his own house on it, and there are signs that a new yeoman class may develop in this way from the labourers.[542a]

At the same time the life of the average labourer, in spite of the spread of bicycling and of cheap railway excursions, is monotonous in the extreme. Holidays are very rare, amusements are few. The towns continue to attract an ever-growing stream of emigrants from the villages, and the cry 'back to the land' falls on deaf ears. Further, every year a great number of young emigrants leave the villages for Canada and the United States, and rural depopulation has become the most marked feature of the county as it is to-day.[543]

The great decline in the numbers of the agricultural population has been more than balanced by the growth of the manufacturing towns, the total population of the county in 1901 being nearly double that of 1801.[544] The future of Somerset then lies in the towns, where alone there is progress and movement, but the social and economic life of the small towns of all counties varies little from a common type, and survivals of local peculiarities must be sought in the country districts, which support a diminished but more prosperous population. The picturesque Somerset villages, with their cottages of Ham Hill stone, often dating from the Tudor period and earlier, with their village crosses, or remains of monastic buildings, grouped round a

[539] The western corner of the county still lagged behind. As an isolated and purely rural district, untouched by the railway, it had felt the general agricultural depression to the full. Wages were very low, and the labourer was often mischievously dependent upon private benevolence. Here the so-called privileges of the labourer which had already become obsolete in other parts of the county still lingered (e.g. the cider truck system, the right to buy corn from the farmer at a certain price, &c.).

[540] Willow stripping also gives employment to women and children in the central district of the county.

[541] The Wellington Industrious Man's Friendly Society, established in 1873, was followed by many others. See also *Rep. of Com. appointed to enquire into Friendly Societies*, 1880.

[542] The effect of the possession of an allotment on the comfort of the labourer can hardly be exaggerated. The pig, it is said, has become the local savings bank.

[542a] The Small Holdings Act of 1907 affords facilities for this development.

[543] Many remedies have been suggested to bring the labourer back to the land, varying from reactionary protection to socialistic land confiscation, but few of them seem very hopeful. One suggestion, however, holds out some prospect of success, without being founded, as many are, on a violent revolution in the system of land tenure. A revival of the co-operative method of cultivation—the cultivators combining to buy seeds, stock, and agricultural machinery—might overcome the difficulty of competition with large farmers.

[544] The high-water mark for rural Somerset was 1841. Since then the decline has been marked. Some of the parishes in the hundred of Carhampton, for instance, have lost nearly half their former population. See App. II.

magnificent square-towered church, are obvious links with the past, and shelter the survivals of old-time customs and superstitions.[545] In some of the most backward districts, in the west for instance, and in the once island villages of Sedgemoor, the social life of the peasant is not unlike that of his predecessors a thousand years ago, and other districts still show an interesting variety in dialect and customs which can often be explained historically.[546] Little villages like Montacute, Athelney and Muchelney, looming large in the early history of the county, are rather obvious contrasts perhaps to the comparatively mushroom growths of Bedminster, Radstock, and the like. The future of the latter, which is in the making, will probably not present any typically Somerset characteristics, but much of the local history of the county is still enshrined in its deserted villages.

APPENDIX I

INCLOSURE AWARDS [547]

11 Jan. 1720	.	Baltonsborough
4 June 1722	.	Glastonbury
13 July 1751	.	Claverton Commons
21 Oct. 1771	.	Horsington, Wincanton, and Maperton
21 July 1773	.	Ubley
4 „ 1776	.	Doulting and Stoke Lane
2 May 1778	.	Wedmore
22 June 1779	.	Compton Bishop
23 Sept. 1779	.	Winscombe and Shipham
17 Jan. 1780	.	Brislington Common (in Brislington)
20 Apl. 1780	.	Crowcombe
6 „ 1782	.	Huntspill
8 Jan. 1783	.	Meare
„ „	.	Weston
6 Oct. 1783	.	Glastonbury
28 July 1784	.	Shapwick
22 Sept. 1784	.	Mark
23 Mar. 1785	.	Blackford (in Wedmore)
„ „	.	Wedmore
11 Oct. 1785	.	Shepton Mallet
5 „ 1786	.	Wookey
6 Jan. 1787	.	Blagdon
11 „ 1787	.	West Pennard
21 Aug. 1790	.	West Harptree
5 Mar. 1791	.	Compton Martin
25 June 1791	.	Meare and Wedmore

20 Sept. 1791	.	Westbury
22 „ 1791	.	Bleadon
2 Mar. 1792	.	Road
22 Apl. 1793	.	Dinder and Croscombe
15 June 1793	.	Edington (in Moorlinch)
„ „	.	Moorlinch
23 Sept. 1793	.	Rodney Stoke
25 Mar. 1794	.	East Horsington and Chilcote (in Out parish Wells)
„ „	.	St. Cuthbert, Out parish, Wells
5 Sept. 1794	.	Kewstoke, Milton (in Kewstoke)
22 „ 1795	.	East Brent
28 „ 1795	.	St. Cuthbert, Out parish (Wells)
22 Oct. 1795	.	King's Sedgemoor
21 Jan. 1796	.	North Wootton and Pilton
18 June 1796	.	*Tintinhull
30 „ 1796	.	East Harptree
29 Aug. 1796	.	Weare, Chapel Allerton, and Biddisham
28 Sept. 1796	.	Butleigh, East Brent
4 Jan. 1797	.	Mark (East)
28 Feb. 1797	.	Burnham
21 Sept. 1797	.	Banwell
23 Jan. 1798	.	Queen Camel
21 Mar. 1798	.	Puriton

[545] The folk songs of Somerset have been collected by the Rev. C. L. Marson and Mr. C. J. Sharpe, and set to music by the latter. *The Somerset and Dorset Notes and Queries* have preserved the memory of many quaint local customs, e.g. i, 29, 74, 75, 124 ; iv, 13, &c.

[546] In 1849 the Somerset Archaeological and Natural History Society held its opening meeting. It has a fine museum and library housed in Taunton Castle, and its yearly publications contain much of historical and antiquarian interest. Of even greater value are the publications of the Somerset Record Society, which have made an unrivalled collection of material available for county history. *Bibliotheca Somersetenis* (ed. Green) is an index of the printed sources for parochial and county history, while *Somerset Parishes* (ed. Humphreys) gives references to deeds, manuscripts, wills, and other sources, arranged under the parishes to which they refer.

[547] These awards are in the Shire Hall, Taunton, and were noticed by the Hist. MSS. Com. in 1879 ; *Rep.* vii, App. 699–701. An asterisk (*) signifies that the title of the award mentions the inclosure of common arable fields. See *Ret. of Commons (Inclosure) Awards*, 1903, pp. 142–5.

INCLOSURE AWARDS (continued)

22 June 1798 . Street	18 Sept. 1817 . Milborne Port
12 July 1798 . Ashcott	28 Oct. 1817 . Exmoor
14 „ 1798 . North Petherton	26 Mar. 1818 . Berkley and Standerwick
7 Sept. 1798 . *Aller	30 „ 1818 . Uphill
27 Sept. 1799 . High Ham and Huish Episcopi	11 Sept. 1818 . Drayton
	3 Nov. 1818 . Combe St. Nicholas
28 „ 1799 . Huish Episcopi	20 Apr. 1819 . Dundry
13 Nov. 1799 . Moorlinch	12 May 1819 . Exmoor
13 Dec. 1799 . Holwell	13 Oct. 1819 . Chard
21 June 1800 . North Curry, Stoke St. Gregory, West Hatch	25 Nov. 1819 . Nailsea, Wraxall, and [Flax] Bourton
15 July 1800 . Glastonbury	28 Jan. 1820 . Wellington
29 Sept. 1800 . Moorlinch	10 Mar. 1820 . Ilminster
22 Nov. 1800 . Middlezoy	20 May 1820 . *Long Ashton
18 Dec. 1800 . Chewton	28 „ 1820 . Isle Moor
3 June 1801 . Clevedon	14 „ 1821 . *Rodney Stoke, Cheddar, and Priddy
17 „ 1801 . South Brent and Lympsham	
16 Sept. 1801 . Cheddar	25 Sept. 1821 . Charlton Musgrove, Kilmington, Wincanton, and Penselwood
3 Oct. 1801 . Locking	
21 Jan. 1802 . Bridgwater, Chilton Trinity, Wembdon, Durleigh	
	6 Oct. 1821 . West Monkton
15 Apl. 1803 . Cannington, Huntspill, Stockland, Bristol and Stogursey	29 „ 1822 . West Sedgemoor
	1 Aug. 1823 . Portishead
„ „ . Worle	17 Nov. 1823 . Crewkerne
26 Sept. 1803 . Tickenham	7 Jan. 1825 . West Combland (in Buckland St. Mary)
15 Mar. 1804 . Brompton Regis, Upton and Skilgate	
	4 Aug. 1826 . Congresbury Drainage
3 Oct. 1804 . *North Perrott	14 „ 1826 . *Martock and Muchelney
8 „ 1804 . South Petherton	28 Dec. 1827 . West Lydford
4 Mar. 1806 . Portbury	6 Aug. 1829 . Compton Dundon
21 Aug. 1806 . *Alford	„ „ . Kingsmoor
13 Sept. 1806 . Brue Drainage	8 Apr. 1830 . Wiveliscombe
6 Dec. 1806 . Somerton	30 June 1830 . Week Moor (in Curry Rivel, &c.)
10 July 1807 . Pitney	
23 Oct. 1807 . Cossington	18 Feb. 1831 . Elworthy
9 Aug. 1809 . Weston in Gordano, Portishead, North Weston	10 May 1832 . Chilthorne Domer
	19 July 1833 . Milverton
26 Feb. 1810 . West Bagborough	4 Sept. 1833 . Neroche Forest
11 Apl. 1810 . Kingsdon	28 Apr. 1834 . Middlezoy and Weston-Zoyland
13 „ 1810 . Charlton Adam and Charlton Mackrell	
	23 May 1835 . Kingsbury Episcopi
17 „ 1810 . Keinton Mandeville	19 „ 1837 . Chipstable
19 June 1810 . Ashington, Ilchester, Stoke under Hamdon, Tintinhull, and Limington	4 „ 1838 . Westmoor
	25 June 1838 . *East Lydford
	10 July 1839 . Northover
26 July 1810 . Axe Drainage	27 Mar. 1841 . Middlezoy, Othery, and Weston-Zoyland
28 Sept. 1810 . Martock	
21 Oct. 1811 . *Lilstock	13 June 1842 . Wanstrow
3 July 1812 . Backwell	25 Mar. 1843 . Clapton
30 Dec. 1813 . Kenn, Wrington, and Yatton	24 June 1843 . Barton St. David
30 Sept. 1814 . Long Sutton	1 Aug. 1844 . *Ditcheat
10 Oct. 1814 . Creech St. Michael	13 June 1845 . Brompton Ralph, Huish Champflower, and Clatworthy
27 Jan. 1815 . Yatton and Kenn	
27 Feb. 1815 . Weston Drainage	
17 June 1815 . Weston-super-Mare	19 July 1847 . South Petherton
31 Aug. 1815 . West Buckland	26 Jan. 1848 . Exford, Almsworthy
21 Sept. 1815 . Charlton Horethorne	12 „ 1849 . Shepham Moor (in Creech St. Michael)
14 June 1816 . Congresbury, Wick St. Lawrence, and Puxton	
	„ „ . Ruishton
10 July 1816 . Moorlinch and Edington	5 Feb. 1849 . Hutton

INCLOSURE AWARDS (continued)

4 June 1849	.	Henstridge	30 Mar. 1857 .	Kewstoke
26 Oct. 1849	.	Yeovil, Greemoor in Yeovil	8 Nov. 1858 .	Ashbrittle (Hennington Hill)
10 May 1850	.	Buckland Hill (in Buckland St. Mary)	27 Sept. 1859 .	Hawkridge
			12 Jan. 1863 .	Oare
23 Nov. 1850	.	Stoke Ridge	16 May 1863 .	Blackford (Blackford in Wedmore)
14 Feb. 1851	.	Winsford (Ison Hill and Shaddon Hill)	17 Mar. 1866 .	Dunster Salt Marsh (in Dunster)
14 June 1851	.	Winsford		
2 Aug. 1851	.	Saltford	14 Feb. 1867 .	North Moor and South Moor (in Cannington and Otterhampton)
16 Mar. 1852	.	Trent [548]		
22 Apr. 1852	.	Exford, South Commons		
3 July 1852	.	Dulverton (North Moor, Streamcombe Common)	15 Oct. 1867 .	Porlock Common (in Porlock)
8 Aug. 1853	.	Loxton	9 Sept. 1869 .	Bathford (Warleigh Common)
28 Feb. 1855	.	Halse		
25 Sept. 1856	.	Ditcheat (Wraxall and Kilkenny Greens)	3 Oct. 1872 .	Wootton Courtney
			3 „ 1873 .	Chard
15 Dec. 1856	.	Hutton (Elborough Hill and Hutton Hill)	11 May 1874 .	Chillington Down (in Chillington)

APPENDIX II

TABLE OF POPULATION, 1801 TO 1901

Introductory Notes

AREA

The county taken in this table is that existing subsequently to 7 & 8 Vict., chap. 61 (1844). By this Act detached parts of counties, which had already for parliamentary purposes been amalgamated with the county by which they were surrounded or with which the detached part had the longest common boundary (2 & 3 Will. IV, chap. 64—1832), were annexed to the same county for all purposes ; some exceptions were, however, permitted.

By the same Act (7 & 8 Vict., chap. 61) the detached parts of counties, transferred to other counties, were also annexed to the hundred, ward, wapentake, &c. by which they were wholly or mostly surrounded, or to which they next adjoined, in the counties to which they were transferred. The hundreds, &c., in this table are also given as existing subsequently to this Act.

As is well known, the famous statute of Queen Elizabeth for the relief of the poor took the then-existing ecclesiastical parish as the unit for Poor Law relief. This continued for some centuries with but few modifications ; notably by an Act passed in the thirteenth year of the reign of Charles II which permitted townships and villages to maintain their own poor. This permission was necessary owing to the large size of some of the parishes, especially in the north of England.

In 1801 the parish for rating purposes (now known as the civil parish, i.e. ' an area for which a separate poor rate is or can be made, or for which a separate overseer is or can be appointed ') was in most cases co-extensive with the ecclesiastical parish of the same name ; but already there were numerous townships and villages rated separately for the relief of the poor, and also there were many places scattered up and down the country, known as extra-parochial places, which paid no rates at all. Further, many parishes had detached parts entirely surrounded by another parish or parishes. Parliament first turned its attention to extra-parochial places, and by an Act (20 Vict., chap. 19—1857) it was laid down (a) that all extra-parochial places entered separately in the 1851 census returns are to be deemed civil parishes, (b) that in any other place being, or being reputed to be, extra-parochial, overseers of the poor may be appointed, and (c) that where, however, owners and occupiers of two-thirds in value of the land of any such place desire its annexation to an adjoining civil parish, it may be so added with the consent of the said parish. This Act was not found entirely to fulfil its object, so by a further Act (31 & 32 Vict., chap. 122—1868) it was enacted that every such place remaining on 25 December, 1868, should be added to the parish with which it had the longest common boundary.

The next thing to be dealt with was the question of detached parts of civil parishes, which was done by the Divided Parishes Acts of 1876, 1879, and 1882. The last, which amended the one of 1876, provides that every detached part of an entirely extra-metropolitan parish which is entirely surrounded by another parish becomes transferred to this latter for civil purposes, or if the population exceeds 300 persons it may be made a separate parish. These Acts also gave power to add detached

[548] Transferred to Dorset in 1896.

parts surrounded by more than one parish to one or more of the surrounding parishes, and also to amalgamate entire parishes with one or more parishes. Under the 1879 Act it was not necessary for the area dealt with to be entirely detached. These Acts also declared that every part added to a parish in another county becomes part of that county.

Then came the Local Government Act, 1888, which permits the alteration of civil parish boundaries and the amalgamation of civil parishes by Local Government Board orders. It also created the administrative counties. The Local Government Act of 1894 enacts that where a civil parish is partly in a rural district and partly in an urban district each part shall become a separate civil parish ; and also that where a civil parish is situated in more than one urban district each part shall become a separate civil parish, unless the county council otherwise direct. Meanwhile, the ecclesiastical parishes had been altered and new ones created under entirely different Acts, which cannot be entered into here, as the table treats of the ancient parishes in their civil aspect.

POPULATION

The first census of England was taken in 1801, and was very little more than a counting of the population in each parish (or place), excluding all persons, such as soldiers, sailors, &c., who formed no part of its ordinary population. It was the *de facto* population (i.e. the population actually resident at a particular time) and not the *de jure* (i.e. the population really belonging to any particular place at a particular time). This principle has been sustained throughout the censuses.

The Army at home (including militia), the men of the Royal Navy ashore, and the registered seamen ashore were not included in the population of the places where they happened to be, at the time of the census, until 1841. The men of the Royal Navy and other persons on board vessels (naval or mercantile) in home ports were first included in the population of those places in 1851. Others temporarily present, such as gipsies, persons in barges, &c. were included in 1841 and perhaps earlier.

GENERAL

Up to and including 1831 the returns were mainly made by the overseers of the poor, and more than one day was allowed for the enumeration, but the 1841–1901 returns were made under the superintendence of the registration officers and the enumeration was to be completed in one day. The Householder's Schedule was first used in 1841. The exact dates of the censuses are as follows :—

10 March, 1801	30 May, 1831	8 April, 1861	6 April, 1891
27 May, 1811	7 June, 1841	3 April, 1871	1 April, 1901
28 May, 1821	31 March, 1851	4 April, 1881	

NOTES EXPLANATORY OF THE TABLE

This table gives the population of the ancient county and arranges the parishes, &c. under the hundred or other subdivision to which they belong, but there is no doubt that the constitution of hundreds, parishes, &c. was in some cases doubtful.

In the main the table follows the arrangement in the 1841 census volume.

The table gives the population and area of each parish, &c. as it existed in 1801, as far as possible.

The areas are those supplied by the Ordnance Survey Department, except in the case of those marked ' e,' which were calculated by other authorities. The area includes inland water (if any), but not tidal water or foreshore.

† after the name of a civil parish indicates that the parish was affected by the operation of the Divided Parishes Acts, but the Registrar-General failed to obtain particulars of every such change. The changes which escaped notification were, however, probably small in area and with little, if any, population. Considerable difficulty was experienced both in 1891 and 1901 in tracing the results of changes effected in civil parishes under the provisions of these Acts ; by the Registrar-General's courtesy, however, reference has been permitted to certain records of formerly detached parts of parishes, which has made it possible approximately to ascertain the population in 1901 of parishes as constituted prior to such alterations, though the figures in many instances must be regarded as partly estimates.

* after the name of a parish (or place) indicates that such parish (or place) contains a union workhouse which was in use in (or before) 1851 and was still in use in 1901.

‡ after the name of a parish (or place) indicates that the ecclesiastical parish of the same name at the 1901 census was co-extensive with such parish (or place).

§ after the name of a parish (or place) indicates that the civil parish of the same name at the 1901 census was co-extensive with such parish (or place).

o in the table indicates that there is no population on the area in question.

— in the table indicates that no population can be ascertained.

The word ' chapelry ' seems often to have been used as an equivalent for ' township ' in 1841, which census volume has been adopted as the standard for names and descriptions of areas.

The figures in italics in the table relate to the area and population of such subdivisions of ancient parishes as chapelries, townships, and hamlets.

TABLE OF POPULATION

1801—1901

—	Acre-age	1801	1811	1821	1831	1841	1851	1861	1871	1881	1891	1901
Ancient or Geographical County [1]	1,043,409	273,577	300,520	354,972	402,371	435,599	443,916	444,873	463,339	469,109	484,337	508,256

PARISH	Acre-age	1801	1811	1821	1831	1841	1851	1861	1871	1881	1891	1901
Abdick and Bulstone Hundred												
Ashill † ‡ . . .	1,790°	316	299	378	403	438	464	445	477	469	414	325
Beer Crocombe † ‡	871°	137	148	186	182	179	158	175	146	136	139	129
Bickenhall † . .	1,004°	155	179	215	270	264	215	229	172	155	149	151
Bradon, South † ‡ .	390°	21	31	32	34	41	42	38	40	25	43	26
Broadway † ‡ . .	2,072°	328	376	396	450	570	490	431	493	446	372	401
Buckland St. Mary † ‡	3,494°	418	454	565	646	696	758	715	717	608	586	474
Cricket Malherbie † ‡	540°	64	60	73	28	36	38	21	19	53	46	45
Curland † . . .	777°	157	163	168	167	228	267	247	233	187	184	166
Curry Mallet † . .	1,650°	364	379	461	496	630	584	549	510	483	404	369
Curry Rivel [2] † . .	4,108°	974	1,030	1,192	1,378	1,647	1,687	1,704	1,751	1,573	1,496	1,465
Donyatt ‡ § . . .	1,241	417	465	518	557	525	551	494	506	382	. 355	340
Dowlish, West † . .	586°	40	40	32	38	31	59	52	63	47	59	57
Drayton † ‡ . . .	2,165°	370	426	469	519	469	551	557	547	472	448	407
Earnshill † . . .	375°	20	16	13	12	12	13	17	14	7	9	11
Fivehead † . . .	1,721°	280	307	326	387	412	438	489	481	416	415 .	340
Hatch Beauchamp † ‡	1,120°	196	227	245	324	329	315	324	355	359	382	313
Ilminster † ‡ . .	4,050°	2,045	2,160	2,156	2,957	3,227	3,299	3,241	3,505	3,281	3,135	3,135
Ilton †	1,719°	363	390	460	530	557	528	492	450	425	369	388
Isle Abbots † ‡ .	1,935°	254	330	342	380	413	437	397	381	348	332	356
Isle Brewers † . .	1,243°	181	184	219	254	338	323	314	371	316	279	240
Lackington, White † ‡	1,465°	190	249	242	254	283	256	260	281	284	214	211
Puckington † . .	610°	171	152	220	182	229	231	260	244	229	198	176
Staple Fitzpaine † .	2,864°	279	310	385	415	361	267	264	234	188	196	236
Stocklinch St. Magdalen †	199°	89	85	79	95	92	110	116	95	92	70	42
Stocklinch Ottersey †	299°	119	130	140	120	132	129	69	83	118	113	98
Swell [3] † . . .	891°	120	122	133	87	109	137	116	126	142	110	101
Westmoor Extra Par. [4]	—	—	—	—	—	13	54	31	7	—	—	—

[1] *Ancient County.*—The county as defined by the Act 7 & 8 Vict. cap. 61, wnich affected Somerset to the following extent:—The parish of Holwell was transferred from Somerset to Dorset. Part of the city and county of Bristol (viz. the parishes of St. Mary Redcliffe, St. Thomas, and the Temple) was *anciently* in Somerset, but has always been included in Gloucestershire for Census purposes.

The area is taken from the 1901 Census Volume.

The population is exclusive of (1) in 1811, 2,316 militia; (2) in 1821, 817 militia; and (3), in 1831, 1,424 militia, who could not be assigned to the places to which they belonged (see also notes to Maiden Bradley, Stourton, Lufton, Thorne).

[2] *Curry Rivel.*—The area and population (1881-1901) includes those of Westmoor, which has been added to the parish.

[3] *Swell* includes the area and the population (1841-1901) of the formerly extra parochial place of West Sedgemoor.

[4] *Westmoor.*—The population included with that of *Niden* in 1831. The area and the population (1881-1901) of Westmoor included in those of *Curry Rivel Parish*, to which it has been added.

TABLE OF POPULATION, 1801—1901 *(continued)*

PARISH	Acre-age	1801	1811	1821	1831	1841	1851	1861	1871	1881	1891	1901
Andersfield Hundred												
Broomfield † ‡ . .	4,274°	369	362	489	503	497	472	525	495	420	394	342
Creech St. Michael † ‡	2,304°	628	714	812	1,116	1,296	1,219	1,121	1,073	1,166	1,041	1,054
Durleigh (part of)⁵†	886°	104	124	127	139	134	138	153	158	145	122	111
Enmore † ‡ . . .	1,112°	254	254	287	294	302	343	314	293	285	275	261
Goathurst † ‡ . .	1,438°	296	318	342	349	341	303	304	276	254	238	229
Lyng⁶†	1,409°	253	264	335	363	422	393	390	384	353	337	327
Bath Forum Hundred												
Batheaston⁷† . .	1,863°	1,072	1,298	1,330	1,783	2,191	1,795	1,698	1,645	1,637	1,725	1,648
Bathford⁸‡§ . .	1,819	565	660	688	870	1,099	906	892	964	953	886	891
Bathwick . . .	594	2,720	3,172	4,009	4,033	4,972	5,162	5,266	5,271	5,167	4,714	4,284
Freshford ‡ § . .	594	624	571	587	666	645	622	584	588	615	543	531
Kelston ‡ § . . .	1,114	221	248	248	274	255	259	212	224	185	188	204
Langridge † ‡ . .	655°	86	96	103	109	109	91	102	85	80	82	62
Lyncombe and Widcombe *	1,849	2,790	3,740	5,880	8,704	9,920	9,974	9,900	11,020	12,277	13,770	14,372
Monkton Combe §	686	369	525	855	1,031	1,107	1,270	1,271	1,388	1,495	1,760	1,743
St. Catherine † .	1,040°	79	112	127	154	159	135	84	160	136	112	109
Stoke, North ‡ § .	791	108	113	129	128	173	194	160	158	190	178	145
Stoke, South ‡ § .	867	177	188	258	266	330	337	375	355	389	410	405
Swainswick ‡ § .	835	182	230	381	427	572	604	632	579	633	629	558
Walcot (part of :— viz. Soper's Farm)⁹ †	186	—	—	—	—	10	14	5	25	32	30	13
Weston † . . .	2,650°	1,010	1,291	1,919	2,560	2,899	3,088	3,127	3,570	3,606	4,936	5,968
Woolley § . . .	381	80	93	101	104	89	63	71	64	64	72	70
Bempstone Hundred												
Allerton, Chapel † ‡	1,169°	226	225	335	313	331	294	292	259	249	232	183
Biddisham ‡ § . .	572	88	88	136	158	145	131	147	162	123	119	111
Brean ‡ § . . .	1,194	70	90	86	134	126	132	145	161	148	159	112
Burnham . . .	3,907	653	742	920	1,113	1,469	1,701	2,252	3,257	3,645	4,200	4,922
Mark † ‡ . . .	4,354°	875	991	1,150	1,289	1,308	1,245	1,217	1,169	1,097	1,024	909
Weare † ‡ . . .	2,146°	433	608	800	764	784	715	677	720	650	536	537
Wedmore† . . .	9,986°	2,122	2,480	3,079	3,557	3,995	3,905	3,653	3,434	3,060	2,902	2,741
Brent with Wring- ton Hundred												
Berrow¹⁰ ‡ § . .	2,221	371	480	449	496	578	534	489	510	442	413	476
Brent, East † ‡ .	3,037°	571	672	820	802	849	780	797	772	709	683	648
Brent, South, or Brent Knoll¹⁰ † ‡	3,426°	500	637	764	890	1,074	937	905	863	792	789	698
Burrington † ‡ . .	2,009°	423	462	559	579	531	488	477	467	453	409	417
Lympsham¹⁰ ‡ § .	2,082	334	408	496	521	567	540	496	458	453	420	436
Wrington § . . .	5,913	788	1,109	1,349	1,540	1,589	1,620	1,617	1,500	1,551	1,472	1,552
Bruton Hundred												
Brewham, North †	2,026°	274	310	389	395	392	369	321	319	227	240	197
Brewham, South †	2,671°	396	508	600	573	513	540	519	465	350	329	257
Bruton¹¹ † . . .	3,631°	1,631	1,746	2,076	2,223	2,074	2,109	2,232	1,905	1,849	1,776	1,776

⁵ *Durleigh* is situated in Andersfield Hundred and Bridgwater Borough. The entire area, and the population (1801–1831), are shown in Andersfield Hundred.

⁶ *Lyng.*—The 1841 population included forty labourers on the Bristol and Exeter Railway.

⁷ *Batheaston.*—The 1841 population included 265 labourers (and their families) temporarily employed on the Great Western Railway.

⁸ *Bathford.*—The 1841 population included ninety labourers on the Great Western Railway.

⁹ *Walcot* is situated in Bath Forum Hundred and in the city of Bath. The entire population (1801–1831) is shown in Bath City.

¹⁰ *Berrow, South Brent, and Lympsham.*—The 1841 population of each of these parishes was temporarily increased by the presence of some railway labourers.

¹¹ *Bruton and Pitcombe.*—The 1861 population of these parishes included some excavators engaged in railway construction.

TABLE OF POPULATION, 1801—1901 (continued)

PARISH	Acre-age	1801	1811	1821	1831	1841	1851	1861	1871	1881	1891	1901
Bruton Hundred (cont.)												
Eastrip Extra Par. †	160°	26	20	17	12	13	27	15	26	11	9	9
Four Towers Extra Par.†		—	—	—	—	9	12	6	8	7	6	3
Milton Clevedon‡§	1,243	206	199	189	242	213	207	210	194	171	169	145
Pitcombe [11] †	1,050°	326	310	431	480	394	411	443	389	421	397	317
Upton Noble ‡ §	679	223	200	285	282	241	238	217	185	216	202	178
Yarlington ‡ §	1,204	252	268	301	283	297	234	246	210	228	179	181
Cannington Hundred												
Aisholt †‡	1,252°	136	150	176	228	201	199	181	180	121	127	115
Cannington :—	4,635°	878	1,001	1,228	1,437	1,349	1,548	1,419	1,440	1,392	1,384	1,186
Cannington †	—	850	981	1,215	1,424	1,334	1,531	1,398	1,423	1,369	1,363	1,168
Edstock and Beer Hamlet †	—	28	20	13	13	15	17	21	17	23	21	18
Charlinch †‡	1,432°	183	198	251	199	215	236	241	229	199	197	158
Fiddington †‡	825°	147	172	185	210	220	260	213	241	187	194	156
Otterhampton †	1,017°	176	209	221	240	222	210	235	218	239	206	211
Spaxton †‡	3,387°	662	737	816	963	1,002	1,080	1,057	985	918	874	797
Stockland Bristol †‡	1,150°	144	173	199	202	193	181	142	138	188	161	140
Stogursey (or Stoke Courcy) †‡	5,853°	1,168	1,208	1,362	1,496	1,467	1,472	1,455	1,489	1,262	1,116	1,034
Stowey, Over †‡	3,647°	468	461	587	592	568	561	613	582	512	433	441
Stringston †	1,193°	121	130	131	128	143	159	144	140	114	121	97
Carhampton Hundred												
Carhampton †‡	5,199°	601	532	587	658	682	672	706	724	645	612	547
Culbone, or Kitnor ‡ §	1,337	56	44	45	62	34	40	41	33	37	31	34
Cutcombe †	7,231°	594	602	664	709	843	860	793	689	564	442	431
Dunster †‡	2,870°	772	868	895	983	1,078	1,184	1,112	1,156	1,126	1,114	1,182
Exford ‡ §	5,956	375	316	373	447	473	580	546	465	456	430	394
Luccombe (or Luckham) †‡	4,126°	457	417	481	546	580	512	474	430	371	349	398
Luxborough †	3,740°	332	344	387	381	485	512	521	535	417	346	316
Minehead †‡	3,991°	1,168	1,037	1,239	1,481	1,489	1,542	1,582	1,605	1,774	2,073	2,782
Oare ‡ §	4,017	64	57	66	70	59	57	60	60	61	80	77
Porlock †‡	5,664°	600	633	769	830	892	854	835	777	765	814	751
Selworthy †‡	2,219°	418	458	483	558	505	489	437	407	410	403	363
Stoke Pero ‡ §	3,508	63	61	81	61	84	68	51	63	49	55	38
Timberscombe †‡	1,902°	356	388	409	453	476	442	434	378	357	307	265
Treborough ‡ §	1,829	132	111	113	105	138	142	183	195	150	126	120
Withycombe †‡	1,787°	283	283	319	332	318	329	349	337	279	233	223
Wootton Court-ney †‡	3,145°	345	372	411	426	418	411	378	392	329	297	264
Catsash Hundred												
Alford †	722°	99	96	136	137	90	94	109	125	95	95	101
Ansford, or Almsford †‡	844°	237	244	300	304	293	269	306	298	296	309	306
Babcary ‡ §	2,412	337	330	422	453	465	425	426	407	322	336	277
Barrow, North §	770	101	113	142	150	140	115	114	111	118	100	115
Barrow, South §	764	122	128	155	139	140	126	140	117	122	115	108
Barton St. David ‡§	989	288	358	368	410	455	442	404	379	338	308	277
Cadbury, North †‡	2,810°	810	908	1,003	1,109	1,075	1,052	997	980	896	850	718
Cadbury, South ‡ §	695	214	236	257	231	254	256	287	236	187	159	148
Camel, Queen †‡	2,498°	584	656	712	664	739	772	734	651	542	502	417
Castle Cary ‡ §	2,629	1,281	1,406	1,627	1,794	1,942	1,860	2,060	2,021	2,034	2,096	1,902
Compton Paunce-foot §	673	207	211	228	228	256	229	253	223	185	172	175
Keinton Mande-ville ‡ §	685	206	261	349	459	586	584	538	523	537	506	508

[11] See note 11, ante.

TABLE OF POPULATION, 1801—1901 (*continued*)

Parish	Acreage	1801	1811	1821	1831	1841	1851	1861	1871	1881	1891	1901
Catsash Hundred (cont.)												
Kingweston † ‡. .	1,166*	90	111	111	122	128	149	172	143	148	121	112
Lovington ‡ § . .	828	174	195	206	214	239	230	239	233	203	179	155
Lydford, West † ‡.	1,900*	313	402	437	357	368	385	320	290	267	255	237
Maperton † ‡ .	1,534*	171	178	165	187	214	210	207	221	203	201	188
Sparkford ‡ § . .	1,026	239	228	273	257	286	280	305	261	253	287	224
Sutton Montis, or Sutton Montague ‡ §	514	147	158	165	178	191	179	155	154	115	118	109
Weston Bampfylde ‡ §	636	140	142	119	123	133	119	146	143	104	106	77
Chew Hundred												
Chew Magna † .	5,006*	1,345	1,527	1,884	2,048	2,096	2,141	1,855	1,838	1,643	1,511	1,526
Chew Stoke ‡ § .	2,162	517	524	681	693	825	819	758	693	696	653	635
Clutton * ‡ § . .	1,698	935	998	1,206	1,287	1,434	1,480	1,149	1,101	1,019	1,095	1,265
Dundry † ‡ . . .	2,799*	355	417	454	583	536	592	556	550	565	534	531
Norton Hawkfield, or Norton Hautville (Vill) † . .	620*	36	43	40	32	35	42	34	37	48	24	
Norton Malreward ‡	1,073	114	141	118	110	98	113	108	98	142	114	132
Stowey †	814*	170	195	208	234	188	187	181	151	127	153	143
Timsbury ‡ § . .	1,161	714	841	1,090	1,367	1,666	1,639	1,551	1,462	1,425	1,390	1,515
Chewton Hundred												
Brockley † ‡ . .	692*	111	109	173	171	171	128	93	98	109	107	88
Camely ‡ § . . .	1,648	454	498	604	658	643	594	526	497	522	465	403
Chewton Mendip:—	6,650*	1,155	1,225	1,327	1,315	1,216	1,139	976	938	824	749	683
Chewton Mendip [12] †	5,939*	1,015	—	1,159	1,155	1,071	1,039	875	837	760	688	644
Widcombe, North, Tything §	711	140	—	168	160	145	100	101	101	64	61	39
Chilcompton † .	1,233*	348	402	474	487	618	694	730	667	642	624	608
Compton Martin † ‡	2,314*	404	498	534	572	601	577	558	534	415	325	375
Emborough † . .	2,039*	241	220	250	207	210	197	178	188	178	161	188
Farrington Gurney §	928	344	359	526	568	605	518	482	538	535	562	630
Harptree, West § .	3,046	379	463	528	536	571	616	539	471	399	347	326
Hinton Blewett ‡ §	1,130	255	252	264	325	336	322	302	301	218	176	170
Kingston Seymour ‡ §	2,667	267	290	320	368	375	373	336	352	293	252	209
Littleton, High ‡ §	1,303	811	804	864	911	1,116	951	860	740	775	798	812
Midsomer Norton †	3,922*	1,552	1,717	2,326	2,942	3,509	3,799	3,836	4,010	4,422	5,053	5,800
Paulton † ‡ . . .	1,056*	1,019	1,160	1,380	1,784	2,009	2,104	1,958	1,998	2,122	2,313	2,372
Ston Easton † . .	1,374*	389	364	419	386	430	471	431	367	357	373	302
Ubley ‡ § . . .	1,821	316	342	393	340	369	294	307	338	285	250	332
Crewkerne Hundred												
Crewkerne † ‡ . .	5,331*	2,576	3,021	3,434	3,789	4,414	4,497	4,705	4,872	4,986	5,093	5,172
Hinton St. George ‡ §	1,572	575	611	737	850	832	728	761	733	681	649	477
Merriott ‡ § . .	1,750	1,017	1,058	1,212	1,405	1,467	1,439	1,413	1,452	1,376	1,349	1,305
Misterton ‡ § . .	1,361	368	345	362	460	475	564	588	556	670	677	681
Seaborough ‡ § .	585	82	100	92	124	84	104	123	93	105	71	59
Wayford † ‡ . .	1,618*	162	185	224	219	223	238	191	212	224	220	185

[12] *Chewton Mendip Township* includes the area, and the population (1841–1901), of Green Oar Farm, which was formerly extra parochial. The population of Green Oar Farm was in 1831 included in that of *Witham Friary Parish.*

TABLE OF POPULATION, 1801—1901 (*continued*)

Parish	Acre-age	1801	1811	1821	1831	1841	1851	1861	1871	1881	1891	1901
Curry, North, Hundred												
Curry, North [13] † ‡	5,556°	1,193	1,346	1,645	1,833	2,028	1,856	1,839	1,699	1,600	1,604	1,525
Hatch, West † ‡ .	1,681°	249	297	367	396	465	453	432	450	415	378	359
Stoke St. Gregory †	3,790°	907	1,031	1,369	1,507	1,499	1,477	1,617	1,593	1,418	1,340	1,326
Thorn Falcon † ‡ .	814°	157	187	221	273	266	229	196	182	179	173	152
Thurlbear § . .	982	151	202	215	202	194	212	192	165	133	151	172
Frome Hundred												
Beckington † . .	1,830°	1,469	1,551	1,645	1,340	1,190	1,173	1,036	1,005	924	809	742
Berkley [14] † ‡ . .	1,927°	598	577	550	531	496	495	386	395	322	336	343
Cloford ‡ § . . .	2,261	257	303	312	302	253	242	218	193	197	160	173
Cranmore, East §	1,059	53	47	68	64	66	68	70	69	131	112	126
Elm :—	893°	331	368	449	427	421	408	377	347	353	357	208
Elm, Great † ‡ .	893°	—	—	—	—	349	318	323	279	288	289	180
Elm, Little, Hamlet [15] †	—	—	—	—	—	72	90	54	68	65	68	28
Frome Selwood * †	7,092°	8,748	9,493	12,411	12,240	11,849	11,916	11,200	11,495	11,181	11,219	11,828
Laverton † . .	1,034°	134	133	189	196	199	181	164	143	123	119	116
Lullington § . . .	703	157	178	224	145	139	118	137	156	134	119	103
Marston Bigot † ‡	2,207	366	301	471	485	534	449	379	430	357	440	340
Nunney ‡ § . . .	2,505	919	1,124	1,120	1,204	1,185	1,115	1,088	1,123	1,018	914	840
Orchardleigh § . .	730	32	32	27	27	44	32	34	38	41	47	38
Road †	928°	927	957	1,217	954	861	790	663	619	570	484	464
Rodden † ‡ . . .	990°	200	230	272	295	270	268	234	228	175	211	185
Standerwick [16] †	303°	—	—	86	97	89	78	60	62	78	59	71
Wanstrow ‡ § . .	2,099	325	365	397	410	438	471	454	396	330	321	303
Whatley [17] † . .	1,391	304	247	354	386	440	361	423	406	433	336	305
Witham Friary [18] §	5,456	485	533	589	574	581	556	576	547	482	413	395
Woolverton † . .	} 736° {	169	159	184	207	153	170	171	157	129	130	92
Chatley Hill Extra Par.		—	—	—	—	5	4	4	4	2	4	2
Glaston Twelve Hides Hundred												
Baltonsborough † ‡	2,472°	547	644	671	675	718	760	763	743	703	718	617
Bradley, West † .	625°	116	117	114	132	116	131	136	176	132	134	103
Glastonbury † . .	7,083°	2,035	2,337	2,630	2,984	3,314	3,125	3,593	3,802	3,828	4,215	4,141
Meare †	8,269°	753	972	1,151	1,296	1,522	1,605	1,640	1,631	1,409	1,398	1,308
Nyland with Batcombe †	590°	—	—	38	52	44	38	40	38	43	51	44
Pennard, West † ‡	3,063°	727	831	890	920	819	874	836	794	749	762	662
Wootton, North † .	1,536°	224	148	278	307	375	335	322	289	279	257	255
Hampton and Claverton Hundred (or Liberty)												
Bathampton ‡ § .	933	157	227	243	314	354	356	382	387	410	402	460
Charlcombe [19] † ‡ .	571°	75	100	124	107	84	91	378	577	622	597	730
Claverton ‡ § . .	1,245	123	123	137	166	177	155	213	165	251	362	496
Hartcliffe with Bedminster Hundred												
Ashton, Long * .	4,239	895	1,073	1,168	1,423	1,926	1,921	2,000	2,013	2,335	2,361	2,103
Backwell [20] § .	2,929	604	593	863	1,038	1,161	1,074	926	974	960	956	936

[13] *North Curry* includes Newport, an ancient borough. By the year 1841 the borough had become merely a name and was said to contain five houses and twenty-four people.
[14] The population of *Berkley* in 1801 and 1811 included that of *Standerwick*.
[15] The area of *Little Elm Hamlet* is included in that of *Whatley Parish*.
[16] See note 14, *ante.*   [17] See note 15, *ante.*   [18] See note 12, *ante.*
[19] *Charlcombe.*—The 1861 increase in population was mainly due to the erection and occupation, since 1851, of the Kingswood School for the sons of Wesleyan Ministers.
[20] *Backwell.*—The 1841 population included a large number of railway labourers engaged in the formation of the Bristol and Exeter Railway.

TABLE OF POPULATION, 1801—1901 (*continued*)

Parish	Acreage	1801	1811	1821	1831	1841	1851	1861	1871	1881	1891	1901
Hartcliffe with Bedminster Hundred (cont.)												
Barrow Gurney [21] ‡ §	2,064	203	231	285	279	303	405	321	361	302	338	358
Bedminster . . .	4,167	3,278	4,577	7,979	13,130	17,862	19,424	22,346	32,488	44,759	54,194	70,107
Butcombe † ‡ . .	983°	133	146	213	242	256	269	223	225	189	189	186
Chelvey † ‡ . . .	1,077°	43	62	62	70	54	55	54	53	42	45	48
Winford [21] † . . .	2,991°	641	751	849	865	852	1,022	934	911	947	1,011	928
Horethorne Hundred												
Abbas Combe and Temple Combe ‡ §	1,910	425	416	458	448	461	486	487	561	590	632	678
Charlton Horethorne † ‡	2,363°	512	526	489	485	569	544	506	527	478	456	434
Cheriton, North† ‡	1,088°	233	232	216	246	290	296	302	315	228	219	186
Corton Denham‡ §	1,392	377	422	469	494	480	428	413	403	339	303	255
Goathill ‡ § . . .	298	24	17	20	35	37	43	57	57	45	54	51
Henstridge † ‡ . .	4,252°	827	875	911	1,074	1,146	1,136	1,173	1,273	1,298	1,263	1,165
Horsington † ‡ .	3,591°	833	880	925	968	915	834	869	870	734	751	643
Marston Magna† ‡	1,068°	303	303	324	346	357	387	379	383	305	272	271
Milborne Port † ‡ .	3,277°	953	1,000	1,440	2,072	1,740	1,746	1,814	2,033	1,877	1,951	1,685
Poyntington ‡ § .	1,020	157	172	162	165	192	183	174	168	116	135	125
Sandford Orcas ‡ §	1,104	269	290	332	353	370	340	318	319	255	223	202
Stowell † ‡ . . .	902°	88	97	102	123	117	103	133	116	110	94	97
Trent ‡ §	1,618	320	442	479	449	505	530	512	530	468	419	354
Houndsborough, Barwick, and Coker Hundred												
Barwick ‡ § . . .	785	339	352	400	415	446	451	458	497	534	454	443
Chilton Cantelo § .	634	129	138	140	127	134	115	112	118	123	116	93
Chinnock, East ‡ §	1,360	505	519	581	673	735	685	552	570	580	513	412
Chinnock, Middle † ‡	471°	129	124	173	216	222	230	238	191	150	126	116
Chinnock, West † .	642°	327	388	477	523	561	594	553	497	418	385	289
Chiselborough [22] § .	797	298	355	434	483	540	480	419	421	361	285	258
Closworth ‡ § . .	1,083	195	188	187	195	164	169	184	150	121	112	99
Coker, East ‡ §. .	2,185	859	1,007	1,103	1,330	1,334	1,340	1,186	1,224	1,029	863	798
Coker, West ‡ § .	1,419	758	782	928	1,013	1,046	1,052	1,012	1,054	957	892	818
Hardington Mandeville ‡ §	2,677	489	532	537	603	760	719	668	676	633	459	399
Haslebury Plucknett ‡ §	2,083	677	664	768	826	809	856	834	756	592	537	470
Norton-under-Hamdon † ‡	642°	334	417	482	513	527	504	467	496	539	515	468
Odcomb † ‡ . . .	1,276°	428	477	540	616	666	713	652	663	624	554	519
Pendomer ‡ § . .	1,115	95	78	70	98	81	78	96	91	69	72	54
Perrott, North ‡ § .	1,281	426	394	387	454	431	399	374	387	322	291	275
Sutton Bingham‡§	556	65	72	78	78	66	75	67	64	52	56	54
Huntspill and Puriton Hundred												
Huntspill [23] † . .	5,944°	1,012	1,256	1,337	1,503	1,634	1,594	1,695	1,740	1,920	2,004	1,898
Puriton ‡ § . . .	1,570	332	332	350	509	452	451	604	723	753	744	636

[21] *Barrow Gurney, and Winford.*—A number of labourers employed by the Bristol Waterworks Co. temporarily present in 1851 in each of these parishes.

[22] *Chiselborough.*—In 1851 cretinism was said to be very prevalent among the children; some families migrated in consequence.

[23] *Huntspill.*—A number of railway labourers on the Bristol and Exeter Railway temporarily present in 1841.

TABLE OF POPULATION, 1801—1901 (*continued*)

Parish	Acreage	1801	1811	1821	1831	1841	1851	1861	1871	1881	1891	1901
Keynsham Hundred												
Brislington [24] ‡	2,309	776	1,052	1,216	1,294	1,338	1,260	1,489	1,561	1,767	1,771	5,300
Burnett ‡ §	619	64	70	75	82	100	95	98	105	69	68	71
Charlton, Queen ‡ §	970	143	149	147	168	190	177	141	118	115	110	87
Chelwood ‡ §	1,118	192	205	222	246	260	238	180	185	145	131	155
Compton Dando ‡ §	1,979	330	346	344	382	359	384	347	340	328	324	284
Farmborough ‡ §	1,508	532	621	752	924	1,149	1,055	965	915	845	895	948
Keynsham * † ‡	4,171°	1,591	1,748	1,761	2,142	2,307	2,318	2,190	2,245	2,482	2,811	3,152
Marksbury ‡ §	1,293	283	306	354	371	328	310	307	271	230	234	203
Nempnett Thrubwell † ‡	1,772°	253	225	264	225	289	284	259	261	216	235	223
Pensford St. Thomas [25] †	—	306	296	319	355	360	316	312	323	262	211	232
Priston ‡ §	1,865	314	318	286	308	322	308	292	276	253	213	171
Publow [26] ‡ §	1,375	786	820	836	839	841	810	643	670	536	492	429
Saltford ‡ §	890	223	249	327	380	427	417	373	375	459	479	480
Stanton Drew [27] †	2,075°	660	682	622	731	704	592	523	553	437	405	500
Stanton Prior ‡ §	832	131	144	158	159	148	149	136	126	96	95	81
Whitchurch, or Felton [28] † ‡	2,194°	362	310	403	423	416	428	394	417	505	495	544
Kilmersdon Hundred												
Ashwick	1,530	776	710	829	995	945	848	778	819	755	814	774
Babington † ‡	607°	215	176	156	206	163	117	129	154	194	199	157
Buckland Denham ‡ §	1,432	429	403	440	532	516	531	459	483	444	428	373
Hardington §	860	30	26	31	28	21	19	22	26	38	47	31
Hemington §	3,133	357	339	323	384	483	444	459	504	581	630	658
Holcombe † ‡	780°	581	509	527	538	468	464	388	403	531	509	503
Kilmersdon †	3,460°	1,737	1,780	1,991	2,129	2,143	2,196	2,194	2,531	2,323	2,424	1,990
Radstock ‡ §	1,014	509	567	902	1,165	1,447	1,792	2,227	2,651	3,074	3,438	3,355
Stratton-on-the-Fosse † ‡	1,148°	267	269	317	407	464	413	335	345	277	294	336
Writhlington ‡ §	784	108	167	216	245	301	292	367	401	409	390	496
Kingsbury Hundred—East Division												
Chard *	5,716	2,784	2,932	3,106	5,141	5,788	5,297	5,316	5,636	5,682	6,075	6,318
Combe St. Nicholas ‡ §	4,343	870	941	1,046	1,202	1,293	1,312	1,228	1,215	1,131	1,069	989
Huish Episcopi † ‡	2,314°	367	437	472	574	713	760	679	688	661	637	706
Kingsbury Episcopi † ‡	3,646°	1,134	1,181	1,470	1,695	1,779	1,856	1,838	1,707	1,514	1,440	1,286
Winsham †	2,953°	864	844	878	932	999	1,062	1,033	991	859	776	721
Kingsbury Hundred—West Division												
Ash Priors † ‡	635°	155	150	201	210	226	237	207	212	191	140	121
Buckland, West §	3,697	676	689	750	793	887	1,001	901	897	899	785	721
Fitzhead ‡ §	1,247	336	304	300	311	339	356	309	311	264	250	241
Lydeard, Bishop's [29] † ‡	4,686°	1,068	1,053	1,016	1,295	1,295	1,366	1,459	1,344	1,196	1,093	1,622
Wellington * §	5,295	4,033	3,874	4,170	4,762	5,595	6,415	6,006	6,286	6,360	6,808	7,283
Wiveliscombe [30] ‡	6,105	2,571	2,550	2,791	3,047	2,984	2,861	2,735	3,172	2,612	2,246	2,214

[24] *Brislington.*—The occupation of a new lunatic asylum appears to be the main cause of the increased population in 1821.

[25] *Pensford St. Thomas.*—The 1871 population included forty-five strangers engaged in railway construction. The area is included in that of *Stanton Drew.*

[26] *Publow.*—The 1871 population included sixty-two strangers engaged in railway construction.

[27] See note 25, *ante.*

[28] *Whitchurch.*—The 1871 population included fifty-one strangers engaged in railway construction.

[29] *Bishop's Lydeard.*—The 1861 population included a number of labourers engaged in railway construction. A County Lunatic Asylum was opened and occupied between 1891 and 1901.

[30] *Wiveliscombe, and Milverton.*—The increased population in 1871 was principally attributed to the temporary presence of labourers engaged in railway construction.

TABLE OF POPULATION, 1801—1901 (*continued*)

PARISH	Acreage	1801	1811	1821	1831	1841	1851	1861	1871	1881	1891	1901
Martock Hundred												
Martock † . . .	7,302°	2,102	2,356	2,560	2,841	3,025	3,154	3,155	3,091	3,005	2,848	2,571
Mells and Leigh Liberty												
Leigh-upon-Mendip ‡ §	1,437	534	562	666	640	619	581	534	512	461	480	387
Mells [81] †	3,611°	1,113	1,061	1,147	1,259	1,261	1,186	972	1,039	972	953	799
Milverton Hundred												
Ashbrittle † ‡ . .	2,489°	595	508	579	625	540	552	525	466	380	308	325
Bathealton ‡ § . .	946	123	138	105	98	135	118	135	147	126	123	107
Kittisford ‡ § . .	966	143	143	175	171	152	155	133	138	113	103	91
Langford Budville † ‡	1,853°	524	503	564	608	608	577	457	435	363	340	371
Milverton [32] † ‡ .	5,475°	1,667	1,637	1,930	2,233	2,154	2,146	1,895	2,018	1,735	1,600	1,452
Runnington † ‡ . .	323°	82	94	90	127	107	93	100	94	73	63	66
Sampford Arundel ‡ §	1,216	319	303	376	427	448	415	425	355	364	336	339
Stawley † ‡ . . .	830°	138	170	195	180	222	187	188	178	153	163	121
Thorne St. Margaret ‡ §	824	143	155	145	165	136	143	144	134	118	115	102
Norton Ferris Hundred												
Bratton Seymour † ‡	1,093°	62	79	80	59	103	106	80	87	87	111	86
Charlton Musgrove † ‡	2,153°	383	385	366	415	409	428	418	484	409	385	314
Cucklington § . .	1,795	358	297	320	280	339	356	280	273	269	290	239
Kilmington ‡ § . .	2,876	504	528	556	580	635	640	587	601	477	369	327
Maiden Bradley (part of) [33] :—												
Yarnfield Hamlet	1,281	101	—	94	91	91	85	61	55	48	51	24
Penselwood † ‡ . .	1,101°	265	299	332	361	397	431	442	401	420	362	294
Shepton Montague † ‡	2,424°	365	371	367	452	398	412	433	376	326	303	249
Stoke Trister † . .	1,090°	336	382	377	428	436	440	395	415	421	375	345
Stourton (part of) [33]	1,298	343	—	312	303	288	288	295	259	233	172	163
Wincanton * † ‡ .	4,130°	1,772	1,850	2,143	2,123	2,296	2,488	2,450	2,377	2,410	2,176	1,950
Petherton, North, Hundred												
Bawdrip ‡ § . . .	1,898	244	315	372	373	425	458	472	439	393	340	333
Chedzoy †	1,655°	457	402	472	549	507	509	442	384	356	317	330
Chilton Trinity [34] †	1,381°	50	46	49	49	74	52	53	102	169	79	77
Durston [35] † . . .	1,022°	169	167	211	226	267	258	223	211	222	206	182
Pawlett ‡ § . . .	3,108	429	433	529	577	595	536	555	597	531	483	346
Petherton, North †	9,972	2,346	2,615	3,091	3,566	3,759	3,845	3,943	3,985	3,723	3,548	3,534
St. Michael Church ‡ §	46	41	48	50	32	29	30	29	30	31	26	27
Thurloxton § . .	563	136	156	178	229	188	192	207	196	161	210	157
Wembdon (part of) [36] †	2,471°	244	296	293	289	366	812	927	962	1,233	1,238	1,766

[81] *Mells.*—The decreased population in 1861 was attributed to a regulation which prohibited more than one family to a cottage. [32] See note 30, *ante.*

[33] *Maiden Bradley and Stourton Ancient Parishes.*—The remainder of each is in Wiltshire (Mere Hundred). The entire populations of both are shown in Wiltshire in 1811.

[34] *Chilton Trinity.*—Too large an area was taken for Census purposes in 1881 and probably in 1871. The parish includes Chilton Common, which contained no population in 1901.

[35] *Durston.*—The 1841 population included thirty-seven persons temporary employed on the Bristol and Exeter Railway.

[36] *Wembdon* is situated in North Petherton Hundred and in Bridgwater Borough. The entire area, and the population (1801–1831), are shown in North Petherton Hundred.

TABLE OF POPULATION, 1801—1901 (continued)

PARISH	Acreage	1801	1811	1821	1831	1841	1851	1861	1871	1881	1891	1901
Petherton, South, Hundred												
Barrington [87] † . .	1,656*	374	402	453	468	531	511	501	494	418	416	353
Chaffcombe ‡ §. .	1,016	165	195	225	243	288	265	246	280	206	192	228
Chillington § . .	925	216	251	270	311	321	320	298	295	228	195	163
Cricket St. Thomas †	875*	69	74	75	86	78	69	66	110	107	108	97
Cudworth § . . .	1,125	163	140	144	146	155	181	151	162	140	115	86
Dinnington † . .	514*	219	259	208	187	231	218	146	143	162	137	119
Dowlish Wake † .	826*	241	251	319	380	374	322	319	326	345	290	222
Knowle St. Giles†‡	540*	61	62	91	108	99	92	104	118	105	75	90
Lopen ‡ § . . .	502	326	331	425	502	506	477	419	369	354	292	279
Niden, or Knighton Extra Par.[88]	—	—	—	—	—	66	65	50	41	23	—	—	—
Petherton, South‡§	3,494	1,674	1,867	2,090	2,294	2,597	2,606	2,423	2,573	2,424	2,250	1,997
Seavington St. Mary †	988*	269	313	319	366	374	390	330	325	304	264	218
Seavington St. Michael §	286	103	150	212	210	275	265	244	256	229	176	146
Shepton Beauchamp † ‡	836*	439	559	567	648	637	647	658	696	640	670	619
Whitestaunton ‡ §	1,918	259	269	327	318	321	261	250	263	208	205	187
Pitney Hundred												
Langport ‡ § . .	169	754	861	1,004	1,245	1,172	1,117	1,133	1,018	897	890	813
Muchelney ‡ § . .	1,591	283	261	329	310	349	340	308	278	256	240	231
Pitney † ‡ . . .	1,500*	243	279	301	368	465	454	374	373	321	306	263
Portbury Hundred												
Abbots Leigh ‡	2,276	292	341	317	360	366	343	366	355	364	312	327
Bourton, or Flax Bourton ‡ §	630	161	197	192	219	232	228	215	221	175	211	215
Clapton † ‡ . . .	1,066*	123	131	157	167	138	162	173	230	196	137	152
Clevedon § . . .	3,027	334	455	581	1,147	1,748	1,905	2,941	4,039	4,869	5,412	5,900
Easton-in-Gordano [89] †	1,596*	1,668	1,820	2,109	2,255	2,199	1,984	2,028	2,137	2,112	2,077	2,189
Nailsea † . . .	2,771*	1,093	1,313	1,678	2,114	2,550	2,543	2,278	2,237	1,852	1,793	1,718
Portbury † . . .	3,719*	509	552	594	621	647	648	677	766	791	815	700
Portishead † . .	2,122	387	369	506	800	1,079	1,084	1,201	1,987	2,730	2,787	2,938
Tickenham ‡ §. .	1,629	276	336	405	427	423	424	401	390	332	299	289
Walton-in-Gordano ‡ §	1,190	147	151	161	297	217	225	191	345	484	705	731
Weston-in-Gordano ‡ §	708	90	113	111	124	155	203	175	192	177	182	150
Wraxall † ‡ . . .	3,773*	540	731	769	802	986	1,016	912	952	897	887	844
Somerton Hundred												
Aller † ‡	3,651*	389	409	454	490	559	552	518	533	473	429	367
Camel, West ‡ § .	1,993	224	281	304	322	344	376	338	294	281	231	232
Charlton Adam † ‡	3,910*	254	251	377	480	472	550	530	470	416	295	322
Charlton Mackrell † ‡		268	239	309	366	405	381	387	419	290	231	288
Kingsdon † ‡ . .	2,064*	455	545	536	610	553	523	472	431	353	294	252
Lydford, East † ‡ .	706*	143	139	137	166	194	214	178	193	162	168	130
Somerton † ‡ . .	6,925*	1,145	1,478	1,643	1,786	1,981	2,140	2,206	2,302	1,917	1,962	1,797
Sutton, Long † ‡ .	3,955*	735	725	856	957	979	1,050	958	963	876	802	716
Yeovilton ‡ § . .	1,779	200	236	255	275	294	329	342	307	240	217	164

[87] See next note.

[88] *Niden* inclosed between 1831 and 1841. The area, and the population (1881–1901), are included in those of *Barrington Parish*, to which it has been added. And see note 4, *ante*.

[89] *Easton-in-Gordano.*—The 1871 increase in population was attributed to the presence of labourers engaged in constructing a dock.

TABLE OF POPULATION, 1801—1901 (*continued*)

PARISH	Acre-age	1801	1811	1821	1831	1841	1851	1861	1871	1881	1891	1901
Stone Hundred												
Ashington † . .	554°	62	71	81	74	71	80	57	67	58	32	31
Brympton † . . .	465°	133	124	125	100	123	111	135	129	109	102	72
Chilthorne Domer ‡ §	1,398	167	213	234	236	291	269	242	246	204	208	176
Limington † ‡ . .	1,602°	242	243	268	313	342	344	341	320	296	266	204
Lufton [40] ‡ § . .	297	26	26	21	20	21	24	31	25	51	35	41
Mudford † ‡ . . .	2,035°	352	315	375	422	436	429	421	401	382	355	311
Preston Plucknett †	790°	260	284	317	347	379	329	363	305	266	301	358
Yeovil * † . . .	4,056°	2,774	3,118	4,655	5,921	7,043	7,744	8,486	9,368	9,507	10,943	11,704
Taunton and Taunton Dean Hundred												
Angersleigh † ‡ .	403°	62	54	64	54	42	41	30	40	36	27	25
Bagborough, West ‡ §	2,006	352	376	421	453	449	450	495	461	475	400	353
Bishop's Hull [41] † .	1,341°	683	844	928	1,155	1,263	1,677	1,614	1,487	1,530	1,565	1,478
Bradford † ‡ . .	1,782°	447	436	525	525	550	569	552	479	462	444	422
Cheddon Fitzpaine ‡ §	971	268	255	272	325	357	337	338	305	295	275	271
Combe Florey ‡ § .	1,382	249	289	306	316	304	380	383	343	317	260	255
Corfe † ‡ . . .	1,127°	194	188	232	271	279	396	381	395	386	335	313
Cothelstone † ‡ .	906°	103	118	108	120	104	115	107	111	133	135	118
Heathfield ‡ § . .	696	120	122	131	136	146	135	124	111	102	111	68
Hillfarrance † ‡ .	920°	438	425	483	579	564	616	582	490	422	396	392
Kingston † ‡ . .	3,477°	834	847	954	902	921	948	892	843	942	943	925
Lydeard St. Lawrence ‡ §	2,748	604	575	618	654	641	711	664	594	525	508	390
Norton Fitzwarren ‡ §	1,358	371	442	475	545	606	639	634	585	642	530	602
Nynehead † ‡ . .	1,448°	353	324	308	311	349	357	321	327	318	314	289
Oake † ‡ . . .	865°	172	182	189	147	174	168	155	127	108	90	113
Orchard Portman †	635°	131	100	100	112	114	49	66	81	57	46	43
Otterford ‡ § . .	2,446	239	286	366	406	491	461	476	457	405	391	328
Pitminster ‡ § .	5,355	1,070	1,206	1,416	1,426	1,512	1,607	1,572	1,592	1,382	1,262	1,118
Rimpton ‡ § . .	1,010	193	201	219	208	223	298	282	288	260	257	208
Ruishton ‡ § . .	1,027	262	267	329	400	482	453	506	452	467	483	456
Staplegrove [42] † ‡ .	1,059°	319	350	403	457	471	513	469	608	571	778	822
Stoke St. Mary † .	923°	190	210	248	275	315	275	266	254	229	231	211
Tolland † ‡ . . .	824°	105	117	113	121	124	147	138	116	129	102	113
Trull † ‡ . . .	2,233°	407	499	528	506	547	716	779	861	960	866	914
Wilton † ‡ . . .	700°	374	473	579	795	799	949	1,030	1,197	1,201	933	974
Withiel Florey † ‡	2,485°	83	86	86	89	113	104	164	219	262	114	107
Tintinhull Hundred												
Ilchester [43] † . . .	653°	942	745	994	1,095	1,068	889	781	743	683	564	433
Kingstone † ‡ . .	1,000°	197	227	264	292	301	298	276	246	228	199	231
Montacute † ‡ . .	1,485°	827	857	973	1,028	1,047	1,042	992	954	859	853	758
Northover ‡ § . .	435	56	73	121	138	114	89	122	90	91	79	46
Sock Dennis and Sock Wyndham Extra Par. †	880°	—	—	10	13	11	17	26	28	28	33	22
Stoke-under-Hamdon † ‡	1,330°	766	868	1,072	1,365	1,367	1,404	1,395	1,391	1,516	1,726	1,614
Thorne [44] §	413	94	94	97	101	87	102	99	97	110	100	92
Tintinhull † ‡ . .	1,828°	333	388	383	460	553	529	437	432	403	426	437
Wellow Hundred												
Camerton † . . .	1,748°	594	786	1,004	1,326	1,647	1,543	1,368	1,268	1,361	1,386	1,326
Combe Hay ‡ § .	1,054	232	278	237	260	239	272	245	172	184	190	163

[40] *Lufton.*—The 1801 population is an estimate.

[41] The Independent Collegiate School (containing about 150 persons in 1871) removed from *Bishop's Hull Parish* to *Staplegrove Parish* between 1861 and 1871.

[42] See note 41, *ante.*

[43] *Ilchester.*—The gaol ceased to be used between 1841 and 1851.

[44] *Thorne.*—The 1801 population is an estimate.

TABLE OF POPULATION, 1801—1901 (*continued*)

PARISH	Acre-age	1801	1811	1821	1831	1841	1851	1861	1871	1881	1891	1901
Wellow Hundred (cont.)												
Corston [45] ‡ §	1,217	268	278	368	433	604	531	472	445	385	369	373
Dunkerton †	1,233°	238	305	365	718	825	1,111	1,060	1,048	1,019	953	885
English Combe † ‡	1,852°	226	249	311	388	486	500	559	533	524	426	386
Farleigh Hungerford † ‡	904°	167	149	174	168	154	166	127	146	184	147	140
Foxcote, or Forscote ‡ §	610	100	129	115	102	84	54	46	64	61	62	68
Hinton Charterhouse ‡ §	2,483	619	677	640	735	797	719	615	566	548	622	519
Newton St. Loe [45] ‡ §	1,593	371	384	431	477	527	440	401	417	352	392	363
Norton St. Philip ‡ §	1,547	557	593	669	767	775	788	672	565	551	536	455
Tellisford † ‡	757°	153	125	167	162	150	124	119	102	85	62	59
Twerton † ‡	971°	764	1,111	1,500	2,478	3,342	2,958	3,012	3,634	4,833	7,657	11,057
Wellow §	5,387	770	728	817	960	1,018	1,142	1,087	1,117	1,383	1,430	1,485
Wells Forum Hundred												
Binegar † ‡	1,216°	324	321	363	376	338	358	302	314	267	316	242
Cranmore, West §	1,858	229	268	270	298	319	306	292	285	284	287	295
Dinder ‡ §	1,080	185	215	175	210	248	270	244	187	207	240	218
Evercreech ‡ §	4,110	918	1,105	1,253	1,490	1,449	1,376	1,321	1,195	1,126	1,120	1,188
Litton † ‡	1,171°	366	347	378	414	430	421	313	285	217	214	154
Priddy §	1,375	119	109	141	202	313	254	251	249	226	199	188
Wells St. Andrew Liberty Extra Par. §	52	268	329	298	381	313	346	326	386	420	358	361
Wells St. Cuthbert :—	14,866°	4,237	4,827	5,590	6,268	6,737	7,055	7,120	7,307	7,678	7,955	7,929
St. Cuthbert In*†	—	2,229	2,594	3,024	3,430	3,563	3,635	3,546	3,300	3,338	3,634	3,702
St. Cuthbert Out†	—	2,008	2,233	2,566	2,838	3,174	3,420	3,574	4,007	4,340	4,321	4,227
Westbury §	2,997	429	493	622	681	647	625	664	617	594	605	578
Wookey †	3,420°	740	859	1,040	1,100	1,187	1,158	1,129	1,139	1,017	954	972
Whitley Hundred												
Ashcott †	2,272°	358	463	712	834	843	859	817	839	718	656	598
Blackford †	578°	159	140	154	192	178	175	164	148	140	118	118
Butleigh † ‡	4,467°	694	710	809	952	872	1,035	1,038	954	771	782	698
Compton Dundon † ‡	2,571°	446	476	544	623	679	725	662	625	574	504	474
Cossington ‡ §	1,442	237	254	268	280	248	236	252	247	227	218	209
Greinton † ‡	845°	128	155	237	219	213	193	161	127	133	108	90
Ham, High *† ‡	4,229°	713	783	953	1,027	1,281	1,303	1,283	1,256	1,116	989	898
Holford †	796°	125	180	240	188	185	181	170	145	157	169	125
Holton † ‡	491°	179	201	235	209	224	237	208	186	169	207	161
Middlezoy †	2,520°	494	536	605	679	700	737	725	681	565	574	593
Monkton, West † ‡	3,079°	794	903	1,004	1,155	1,164	1,146	1,153	1,067	1,027	964	917
Moorlinch :—	9,358	1,514	1,563	1,887	2,192	2,281	2,439	2,329	2,273	1,922	1,939	1,751
Moorlinch §	1,125	234	220	251	350	331	378	334	326	250	249	261
Catcott Chap.‡ §	2,302	391	445	579	651	750	772	740	699	550	559	500
Chilton-upon-Polden Chap.§	1,880	310	302	352	423	425	544	511	494	397	363	360
Edington Chap.§	2,191	284	284	341	401	428	378	432	459	435	482	383
Stawell Chap. §	977	144	168	200	214	221	211	173	173	177	167	126
Sutton Mallet Chap. §	883	151	144	164	153	126	156	139	122	113	119	121
Othery †	1,820°	384	433	509	581	704	681	698	638	578	531	439
Podimore Milton‡§	1,005	154	158	176	175	149	136	131	136	89	103	74
Shapwick †	3,781°	399	418	414	452	411	416	407	423	436	352	358
Street † ‡	2,913°	540	634	791	899	1,219	1,647	1,898	2,157	2,514	3,535	3,997
Walton † ‡	2,502°	397	479	635	732	782	768	731	680	535	494	411
Westonzoyland †	2,729°	677	724	807	937	1,000	1,007	894	802	663	654	592
Wheathill ‡ §	325	45	39	47	56	28	36	38	43	37	30	17
Woolavington † ‡	1,725°	294	325	381	412	448	405	415	419	336	314	336

[45] *Corston, and Newton St. Loe.*—A number of workmen temporarily present in 1841 in these parishes engaged in railway construction.

TABLE OF POPULATION, 1801—1901 (continued)

PARISH	Acreage	1801	1811	1821	1831	1841	1851	1861	1871	1881	1891	1901
Whitstone Hundred												
Batcombe ‡ §	3,238	677	719	792	839	780	750	713	691	619	588	461
Croscombe 46 47 † ‡	1,432°	705	668	742	803	804	673	729	625	576	586	530
Ditcheat 47 †	4,511°	1,010	1,236	1,223	1,238	1,244	1,197	1,218	1,065	955	821	771
Doulting †	3,600°	539	524	633	630	666	657	667	697	604	667	688
Downhead §	1,573	225	172	208	221	207	250	249	213	178	156	143
Hornblotton †	1,082	96	88	111	118	104	92	93	110	113	113	92
Lamyatt ‡ §	1,028	206	220	243	204	255	209	240	265	250	180	198
Pennard, East †	2,829°	644	629	755	726	657	675	631	622	608	548	497
Pilton 47 † ‡	5,593°	780	1,158	1,100	1,118	1,116	1,159	1,202	1,140	1,113	1,008	996
Pylle † ‡	1,055°	150	182	176	205	216	184	207	213	267	244	200
Shepton Mallet 47*†	3,572°	5,104	4,638	5,021	5,330	5,265	5,116	5,347	5,149	5,322	5,493	5,446
Stoke Lane, or Stoke St. Michael §	2,081	860	861	1,000	980	1,056	921	734	733	677	667	648
Williton and Freemanors Hundred												
Bicknoller † ‡	1,390°	246	204	251	285	345	351	345	372	327	270	211
Brompton Ralph †‡	2,690°	406	396	449	424	492	530	436	425	424	365	322
Brompton Regis † ‡	8,810°	702	682	771	802	875	968	929	916	756	688	626
Brushford ‡ §	2,848	303	291	311	351	340	335	328	328	326	370	371
Chipstable 48 † ‡	2,252°	301	288	337	343	389	395	361	420	327	304	265
Clatworthy ‡ §	2,964	197	238	280	246	309	323	313	259	225	190	146
Cleeve, Old †	4,973°	1,040	1,074	1,251	1,347	1,351	1,550	1,529	1,689	1,670	1,400	1,307
Crowcombe ‡ §	3,271	575	611	600	691	673	614	573	594	440	418	374
Dodington †	543°	71	75	113	93	114	102	98	65	91	72	73
Dulverton 49 † ‡	8,337°	1,049	1,035	1,127	1,285	1,422	1,497	1,552	1,376	1,373	1,259	1,364
Elworthy † ‡	1,635°	150	196	187	210	210	216	197	185	155	162	110
Exmoor Forest (part of) Extra Par. 50	20,344	—	—	113	52	163	275	323	339	313	269	268
Exton ‡ §	4,230	251	225	301	347	380	381	410	396	405	334	286
Halse † ‡	1,301°	383	425	447	444	421	412	453	449	404	352	345
Hawkridge †	3,725°	72	75	50	67	79	69	110	95	90	102	95
Huish Champflower † ‡	2,909°	321	317	317	345	454	445	444	384	368	303	226
Kilton †	1,551°	114	126	149	141	161	181	174	136	141	100	85
Kilve §	1,775	176	218	263	233	240	256	226	260	222	186	149
Lilstock †	710°	56	91	71	64	48	62	71	74	94	72	58
Monksilver † ‡	1,005°	260	233	306	322	308	311	304	287	264	191	143
Nettlecombe † ‡	2,800°	329	328	372	325	338	353	327	344	295	259	250
Quantoxhead, East ‡ §	2,338	262	261	276	277	282	281	339	268	238	199	149
Quantoxhead, West ‡ §	1,467	192	187	225	222	232	250	223	244	278	248	195
Raddington ‡ §	1,519	105	101	101	105	126	120	121	104	98	86	89
St. Decumans 51 *†‡	3,761°	1,602	1,659	1,865	2,120	2,660	2,783	3,196	3,244	3,233	3,127	3,302
Sampford Brett † ‡	932°	180	185	194	197	238	246	280	257	217	185	158
Skilgate ‡ §	2,135	226	201	226	227	271	266	214	235	219	177	161
Stogumber † ‡	5,777°	1,285	1,214	1,281	1,294	1,384	1,456	1,398	1,330	1,242	1,028	898
Stowey, Nether † ‡	1,215°	586	620	773	778	787	833	876	856	779	641	581
Upton ‡ §	3,845	232	241	297	344	358	344	314	348	278	247	190
Winsford ‡ §	8,740	503	486	518	524	581	604	574	545	485	418	358
Withypool †	3,630°	144	146	204	212	251	259	307	259	253	197	146
Winterstoke Hundred												
Axbridge ‡	528	819	835	988	998	1,045	939	799	830	718	732	713
Badgworth † ‡	1,815°	260	305	319	352	321	343	279	333	281	263	238

46 *Croscombe.*—A silk factory in this parish was destroyed between 1841 and 1851.

47 *Ditcheat, Pilton, Shepton Mallet, and Croscombe.*—Railway construction going on in (or near) these parishes in 1861, which temporarily increased their population.

48 *Chipstable.*—The increased population in 1871 was principally attributed to the temporary presence of labourers engaged in railway construction.

49 *Dulverton.*—A Union Workhouse erected and occupied between 1851 and 1861.

50 *Exmoor Forest.*—The remainder is in Devonshire. The Forest became a parish in 1857 under the provisions of the Exmoor Forest Act (55 Geo. III, cap. 138).

51 *St. Decumans.*—Several hundred navvies employed in 1861 on harbour and railway works at Watchet in this parish.

TABLE OF POPULATION, 1801—1901 (continued)

PARISH	Acre-age	1801	1811	1821	1831	1841	1851	1861	1871	1881	1891	1901
Winterstoke Hundred (cont.)												
Banwell § . . .	4,974	1,082	1,166	1,430	1,623	1,819	1,878	1,853	1,748	1,717	1,584	1,413
Blagdon † ‡ . .	3,535*	797	818	1,068	1,109	1,178	1,128	1,083	975	911	939	1,131
Bleadon [52] ‡ § .	2,962	381	441	518	599	778	587	623	615	616	563	607
Charterhouse-on-Mendip (Vill) Extra Par. †	2,410*	76	74	115	105	99	107	82	87	79	73	64
Cheddar † . . .	6,998*	1,150	1,276	1,797	1,980	2,325	2,185	2,032	2,200	2,366	2,248	2,394
Christon ‡ § . .	574	69	57	55	83	91	86	81	68	57	62	56
Churchill ‡ § . .	2,444	599	740	824	985	970	870	810	786	733	728	744
Compton Bishop*‡	2,536	391	484	513	554	802	795	663	655	551	496	523
Congresbury † . .	4,443*	827	913	1,202	1,327	1,380	1,258	1,190	1,243	1,185	1,204	1,222
Harptree, East § .	2,595	467	502	627	695	772	722	657	675	655	604	595
Hutton ‡ § . . .	1,877	244	243	325	381	462	395	359	362	344	304	303
Kenn † ‡ . . .	1,018*	160	195	276	274	322	323	282	245	289	259	227
Kewstoke † . . .	2,428*	349	379	429	467	545	560	550	645	740	809	1,173
Locking ‡ § . . .	1,030	137	168	198	212	166	156	152	140	122	127	125
Loxton ‡ § . . .	1,199	97	165	165	148	168	209	154	145	134	154	136
Puxton † . . .	613*	131	122	137	145	162	151	147	157	125	166	132
Rodney Stoke † .	2,345*	186	257	272	333	356	315	323	360	323	369	289
Rowberrow † ‡ .	954*	249	263	334	392	369	318	241	228	168	110	105
Shipham ‡ § . .	772	493	539	635	691	707	610	520	477	408	390	382
SteepHolme Island Extra Par.	47	—	—	—	—	—	—	—	6	5	9	5
Uphill ‡	1,128	144	209	270	306	400	422	447	477	645	835	1,299
Weston-super-Mare †	1,590*	138	163	738	1,310	2,103	4,034	8,038	10,568	12,884	15,524	18,275
WickSt.Lawrence†	1,530*	221	246	267	281	347	300	270	240	224	218	181
Winscombe ‡ § .	4,158	922	1,113	1,428	1,526	1,436	1,439	1,326	1,335	1,259	1,379	1,328
Worle † ‡ . . .	1,810*	422	467	673	770	885	960	980	906	965	1,000	1,284
Yatton †	5,374*	1,006	1,215	1,516	1,865	1,978	2,061	1,851	1,832	1,825	1,879	1,995
Bath, City of												
St. James . . .	53	3,962	5,253	6,278	5,848	6,194	5,861	5,788	5,678	5,043	4,758	4,314
St. Michael ‡ . .	26	3,700	2,916	3,462	3,526	3,336	3,022	2,951	2,679	2,322	2,035	1,625
St. Peter and St. Paul ‡	19	2,465	2,767	3,025	2,666	2,574	2,764	2,347	2,155	2,070	1,668	1,202
Walcot (part of)[53]†	739*	17,559	20,560	24,046	26,023	26,200	27,457	26,276	25,754	24,948	24,918	24,074
Bridgwater Borough												
Bridgwater [54] * †:—	3,539	3,634	4,911	6,155	7,807	10,450	10,965	12,120	12,636	12,704	13,246	14,900
Part in Borough	—	—	—	—	—	9,899	10,303	11,308	11,906	11,878	12,319	13,639
Part outside Borough	—	—	—	—	—	551	662	812	730	826	927	1,261
Durleigh (part of) [55]	—	—	—	—	—	9	7	5	8	63	36	70
Wembdon (part of) [56]	—	—	—	—	—	4	7	7	145	66	81	76
Taunton Borough												
St. James † . . .	1,455*	1,614	1,856	2,248	3,120	4,047	4,595	5,239	5,804	7,067	8,953	11,269
St. Mary Magdalen * †	1,300*	4,180	5,141	6,286	8,019	8,019	8,524	8,481	8,564	8,553	8,532	8,266

GENERAL NOTE

The following Municipal Boroughs and Urban Districts were co-extensive at the Census of 1901 with one or more places mentioned in the Table :—

Municipal Borough or Urban District	Place
Clevedon U.D.	Clevedon Parish (Portbury Hundred).
Radstock U.D.	Radstock Parish (Kilmersdon Hundred).
Wellington U.D.	Wellington Parish (Kingsbury Hundred—West Division).

[52] *Bleadon.*—The 1841 population included eighty-four labourers employed on the railway
[53] See note 9, *ante.*
[54] *Bridgwater Ancient Parish*—The 1841 population included 311 labourers temporarily present and 92 persons in vessels.   [55] See note 5, *ante.*   [56] See note 36, *ante.*

INDUSTRIES

INTRODUCTION

FROM an industrial point of view Somerset has many resources. Moryson truly describes the county as: 'Large and rich, happy in the fruitful soil, rich pastures, multitude of inhabitants, and commodity of havens.'' [1] Further than this the abundant water-power available in the county favoured the early establishment and rapid local extension of its staple textile industry. For many centuries Somerset fruit and cider, dairy produce and cheese have been famous far and wide, while the mines and quarries of the county are the industrial expression of its diversified geological structure.

The long history of Somerset lead-mining, although less important economically than that of Derbyshire, merits nevertheless the close attention of both the mining expert and the student of customary law, on account of the probable continuity of the industry from the Roman period, and the curious customs peculiar to its conduct. Lead-mining and the working of calamine, an ore of zinc, will accordingly be dealt with in separate sections. In spite of the fact that the coal of Somerset has never competed for household purposes with that of the better known and more widely extended coalfields of the North, many of the seams, notably those of Radstock and Farrington, are of a good and useful description; and are well adapted for steam and loco-motive purposes, for the manufacture of gas, and for smiths' coal and iron-smelting. [2] Some account of the earlier history of the coal-mines of Somerset will also be found in a separate section.

Brief notices of other minerals found in the county will appear later on; amongst the rarest may be mentioned the appearances of amethysts near Bristol and Cheddar, [3] and of agates at Sandford near Banwell, Worle and Cleve-don. [4]

Clay.—Although the potters' kilns found at Shepton Mallet, Huntspill, Norton Fitzwarren, Chilton Polden, Bathampton and elsewhere clearly demonstrate the ancient existence of their craft, one branch at least of the economic uses of clay was notably absent from the early records of the building trade, the prevalence of excellent building-stone accounting, as in the case of Gloucestershire, [5] for the scanty discoveries of mediaeval bricks and tiles. [6] An extensive and prosperous brick trade is however carried on in modern times at and in the neighbourhood of Bridgwater, the output being largely exported to Ireland and abroad. [7] A product peculiar to this town is the manufacture of Bath bricks, the material used in their composition being the mud, or sandy mould, obtained from the bed of the River Parrett, or from reservoirs into which the river overflows, leaving a deposit. This mud has been described as having a blackish, slimy appearance, with a certain degree of tenacity, which allows of its being shaped with little or no trouble into the form of bricks, employed for scouring, polishing, knife-cleaning, and other uses. They derive their name from their original manufacturer, a Mr. Bath. [8] In 1856 the output was at the rate of 8,000,000 a year, representing a value of £12,000 to £13,000. [9] The bricks are made by hand, except for the grinding and preparation of the clay. Young boys are employed in carrying off, etc., and women in dressing the bricks when finished. [10] Bricks and tiles are made from the fuller's earth clay at Crewkerne. At High Cross Hill, East Chinnock, red and mottled or yellowish tiles and coarse earthenware are produced. [11] The clay raised in the county in 1907 according to the official

---

[1] Moryson, *Itin.* 137.

[2] Prestwich, *Rep. Coal Supply*, 1871, p. 39. Large quantities of Somerset coals were being sent to Birmingham and Reading for use at the ironworks in 1870. Middling smiths' coal of the Smith coal seam at Bishop Sutton was largely employed for lead smelting on the Mendips. Ibid. 60.

[3] *Geol. Mag.* ix, 129.

[4] Buckland, *Trans. Geol. Soc.* (Ser. 2), ii, 421.

[5] *V.C.H. Glouc.* ii, 189.

[6] *Somers. Arch. Soc. Proc.* xxiv, 5; xxix, 42.

[7] *Ann. Rep. Factories and Workshops*, 1888, p. 80.

[8] Woodward, *Geol. Engl. and Wales*, 525.

[9] Murray, *Handbook*, 1856, p. 166.

[10] *Ann. Rep. Factories and Workshops*, 1888, p. 80.

[11] Woodward, *Jurassic Rocks*, iv, 492.

returns amounted to 114,972 tons.[12] Included in these figures are 135 tons of fireclay from the coal measures.[13]

Fuller's Earth.—Fuller's earth, so indispensable to the cloth-making industry, is chiefly found in the neighbourhood of Bath, at Combe Hay,[14] English Combe, Old Down, South Stoke, Midford, Widcombe, and Wellow.[15] Both the blue and yellow varieties are obtainable. Fuller's earth, according to Professor Woodward, is ' a bluish or greenish-grey clay, which weathers to a brown or yellowish-brown colour.' In texture, adds the same authority, it is ' soft, dull, earthy, and greasy to the touch.'[16] The yellow earth, which is found near the surface, is sometimes esteemed the best, but the blue variety is frequently as good, especially for coarse cloths. The veins vary from 18 in. to 5 ft. in thickness. At Combe Hay and elsewhere they are worked by shafts sunk to a depth of from 20 to 30 ft., sometimes from levels driven into the outer-penetrating earth, in galleries 4 ft. to 6 ft. in height. The following is the method of preparation for the market :—

The raw earth is conveyed in trucks to a pug-mill, where it is ground up with about three times its bulk in water. The ' slurry ' thus produced is turned into little tanks or catch-pits, where the fine fuller's earth remains in a state of suspension, the coarse sinking to the bottom. It is then run into long earthenware drains underground to the works, in some cases half a mile distant. The turbid water flows into a long shallow trough or ' maggie,' where the coarser particles subside, and are caught by a series of little wooden steps placed across the bottom of the trough. The purified ' slurry ' next runs into large tanks where the suspended earth gradually settles down, the surface water, which drains off, being pure, soft and drinkable. The settling down process usually occupies about thirty days. At the end of this time the damp, clayey mass in the tank is removed to a large drying-shed, where it is dried by means of a furnace and hot air flues, and is then ready for the market.[17]

In the year 1908, 3,757 tons of fuller's earth were raised in the county, according to the Government Returns.[18]

Stone.—Monastic and manorial houses throughout the county furnish the best evidence of the excellence and durability of the material drawn from the quarries of locally-distinguished oolitic limestones, which have been exploited, as reference to the section devoted to their history will show, from the earliest times.[19]

Ochre.—The raising of ochre, umber and red oxide of iron which in 1906 yielded 962 tons from mines and 8,639 tons from quarries, the total valued at £8,784,[20] was formerly a considerable industry in various parts of the county. The ruddle-pits of Winford were largely worked at Heath Hill, the mineral being a highly ferruginous red ochre, specially used for marking sheep and for pigments.[21] Ashwick yielded a yellow variety, also found at Harptree.[22] The pits were sunk at convenient distances about 18 yds. deep, connected underground, and wrought by pickaxe in the broadway only. Mining was only carried on in dry seasons, the pits being usually flooded in winter.[23] Other topographers record the presence of this mineral at Hutton Hill,[24] and at Bishop's Chew or Chew Magna.[25]

Gypsum.—Gypsum, which is found at Watchet, Somerton, and High Ham, occurs in veins, nodules, and isolated masses.[26] The mineral is one of considerable commercial importance, as the source of plaster of Paris, massive gypsum of fine grain being known as alabaster.[27] Defoe writes of the cliffs of Watchet as being ' stored with alabaster,'[28] whilst another topographer alluded to ' little grots along the Watchet cliffs, entirely walled with alabaster.'[29] The economic uses of gypsum formerly created a considerable traffic at Watchet, whence the mineral, which was collected along the coast, was exported to Bristol, Swansea, and other places,[30] the white

---

[12] Martin, *Rep. Mines and Quarries South Dist. for* 1907, pp. 88, 6, 28, 38.

[13] Ibid.

[14] The fuller's earth of Combe Hay is said to have been ' much inquired for by foreign chemists ' in 1822. Sutcliffe, *Geol. of the Avon*, 25.

[15] The Rev. John Skinner writes in his Journal of the soil at Wellow being constantly turned up by the clothiers in search of the earth. Add. MS. 33688, fol. 29.

[16] Woodward, *Jurassic Rocks*, iv, 489.

[17] Ibid.

[18] *Gen. Rep. and Statistics Mines and Quarries for* 1908 (publ. 1909), 172.

[19] See section on Building Stone.

[20] *Mines and Quarries*, 1906, pt. iii, 231. The figures for 1908 show 1,296 tons from mines and 7,615 from quarries. The companies now working this red oxide of iron are the Winford Iron Ore and Redding Company and the Regil Mining Company.

[21] Woodward, *Geol. East Somerset*, 167 ; Sutcliffe, *Geol. of the Avon*, 25.

[22] Collinson (*Hist. Somers.* i, 16) names the following varieties of Somerset ochre :—' the hard, heavy, pale yellow ' ochre of Ashwick, ' the light, friable, gold-coloured kind which is found hanging to the sides of old mines,' the ' heavy, friable, ordinary, yellow sort,' and the well-known ' ruddle of Somerset,' found at Chew and Winford. A ' peculiar kind,' found on Winford Hill, was ' bright and smoother, not soluble in water.'

[23] *Geol. Soc. Trans.* (Ser. 2), i, 368

[24] Tymms, *Family Topographer*, ii, 215 ; Rutter, *Delineations of Somers.* 101.

[25] *Compleat Hist. Somerset*, 55.

[26] *Somers. Arch. Soc. Proc.* vi, 144. See *V.C.H. Somers.* i, ' Geology.'

[27] Miers, *Mineralogy*, 526.

[28] Defoe, *Tour*, ii, 18.

[29] Maton, *Western Counties*, ii, 108.

[30] *Geol. Assoc. Proc.* i, 384, 435.

gypsum having been, apparently, most in demand.[31] There was also a pink variety dug at Blue Anchor.[32] That found in the marls of the New Red Sandstone at High Ham is conveyed to Bridgwater for the purpose of manufacturing cement.[33] According to the latest returns, 2,395 tons were obtained from the quarries of Somerset in 1906, the value of this amount being £599.[34]

Copper.—'The copper adventures of the county,' according to De la Bèche, 'appear never to have been of much value.'[35] The chief workings were at Dodington, on the north-east of the Quantocks, the ores being principally carbonates. Shafts were also formerly sunk, but without any profitable return, at Grabbist Hill, near Minehead, and elsewhere, the industry having altogether ceased by 1839.[36] Copper is mentioned as having been found at Broomfield, near Wookey Hole,[37] in Ham Wood, near Croscombe, and in the conglomerate quarry behind Alcombe, near Minehead,[38] whilst Maton writes of a vein of copper at Over Stowey.[39]

Manganese.—The native places of manganese in the county, according to Professor Woodward, are Wookey Hole and East Harptree.[40] Mining for this mineral has also been carried on at Croscombe;[41] whilst in 1822 it was being dug in thin veins at Leigh and Mendip. The ore was said to be 'compact, hard, and heavy,' whilst its economic use at this period would appear to have been to give 'a beautiful light brown tint to earthenware, and to form other enamel colours by combination, chiefly a purple-blue and a mulberry.'[42] Within the last twenty-five years manganese has been mined at various points about Banwell.[43] Manganese also occurs as hereafter stated together with carbonate of iron in the well-known lodes of the Brendon Hills, theoretically containing from 13 to 14 per cent. of protoxide of manganese.[44]

In the middle of the last century, heavy spar or baryta was dug in pits near Hill End, to the north of the Tower at Banwell.[45]

Peat.—Peat[46] is very largely dug in the moorlands of the county between Glastonbury and Highbridge. Some of the beds have been worked for fuel, says Professor Woodward, from the Roman period, some still earlier.[47] In some places the peat is 14 ft. or 15 ft. thick.[48] Young, on his Northern Tour, speaks of ' a vast moor called the turfery, near Glastonbury, in which they dig turf for burning.'[49] The Eclipse Peat Manufacturing Company manufacture moss litter at Shapwick, Bridgwater, and Great Plain, Meare, Glastonbury. The peat is cut up, dipped into combustible matter, and converted into firelights, the refuse being compressed, and done up into packages for horse bedding. The industry has suffered much from German competition.[50]

Salt.—Salt was formerly made in considerable quantities at East Chinnock, a spot being marked on the Ordnance Map as the Salt House.[51]

Means of Communication.—Before passing on to consider certain transitory as well as permanent industries of minor importance, it will be of interest to glance briefly at that problem of the roads, which, here as elsewhere, has played so important a part in the economy of this wool and cloth producing district. Early Somerset roads doubtless owed much of their maintenance to the monks, the suppression of the monasteries bringing decay upon more than one highway in the county.[52] Mediaeval benefactors were not unmindful of the pressing necessities of 'feble weyes and brigges'; we find Sir Richard Choke bequeathing £20 in 1483 for 'the amending' of the same in his neighbourhood.[53] Similar generosity on the part of John Cammell of Glastonbury in 1487 was somewhat discounted by the proviso that the parishioners of Budleigh and Wootton, to repair whose highway he left 4 marks in his will, should carry the material for doing so ' to the said way.'[54] Isabel Horte

[31] *Geol. Assoc. Proc.* i, 384, 435.

[32] Ibid. Gerard, writing of Minehead, which he possibly confused with Watchet, in 1633, says, 'At this place in our tyme a Duch man hath found out mynes of excellent alabaster, which they use much for tombs and chimney pieces. It's somewhat harder than yᵉ Darbeshire alabaster, but for variety of mixtures and colours it passeth any I dare say of this kingdom if not others, for here shall you have some pure white, others white spotted with redd, white spotted with black, redd spotted with white, and a perfect black spotted with white.' Gerard, *Particular Description of Somerset* (Somers. Rec. Soc. xv), 12.

[33] *Somers. Arch. Soc. Proc.* xi, 20.

[34] *Mines and Quarries*, pt. ii, 195. In 1908 the output fell to 1,597 tons. *Gen. Rep. and Statistics Mines and Quarries for* 1908 (published 1909), 209. Alabaster from Hurcot sold in 1791 at 2s. 6d. per cwt. at the quarries. Young, *Annals of Agric.* xvi, 295.

[25] De la Bèche, *Geol. West Somerset*, 609.

[36] Ibid.

[37] *Geol. Mag.* ix, 129.

[38] Ibid. x, 166.

[39] Maton, *Western Counties*, ii, 110.

[40] *Geol. Mag.* ix, 129.

[41] *Quart. Journ. Geol. Soc.* xxiii, 457.

[42] Sutcliffe, *Geol. of the Avon*, 17.

[43] Knight, *Seaboard of Mendip*, 453.

[44] Phillips and Louis, *Ore Deposits*, 241.

[45] Knight, op. cit. 43.

[46] See Phelps, *Marshes and Turbaries of Somerset.*

[47] Woodward, *Geol. Engl. and Wales*, 330, 358.

[48] Ibid.

[49] Young, *Northern Tour*, iv, 17.

[50] *Ann. Rep. Factories and Workshops*, 1888, p. 80.

[51] *Compleat Hist. Somers.* 126; *Somers. Arch. Soc. Proc.* xxxvii, 69.

[52] Archbold, *Somerset Religious Houses*, 295.

[53] Weaver, *Somerset Wills* (Ser. I), 242.

[54] Ibid. 27.

of Yatton left 13s. 4d. for the repair of the king's highway between Weare and Axbridge in 1534.[55]

'With the history of the roads of the kingdom,' at a later date, 'Somerset,' says Mr. Emmanuel Green, 'has a special connexion, the first macadamized road having been constructed between Bath and Bristol,'[56] whilst, according to another authority, Taunton was the first town in the West of England to apply to Parliament for a turnpike Act.[57] In 1752, when a bill for road repairs in the neighbourhood of Wellington was introduced into Parliament, Mr. Thomas Prowse declared that it would cost less to make these highways *navigable* than to mend them.[58] By the close of the century, few counties could boast of better roads, says Billingsley, than were to be found almost throughout Somerset.[59] The growth of the stone industry provided abundance of road-metal,[60] whilst great attention was paid to stone-breaking.[61]

The railway traffic of the county at the present day is mainly carried on by the Great Western, the London and South Western, and the Midland Companies. One section of the Great Western enters Somerset at Bathampton on the north-east and runs viâ Bath and Bristol, Weston-super-Mare, Bridgwater and Taunton, quitting the county for Exeter near Sampford Arundel. From Norton Fitzwarren branches run to Minehead on the north coast and along the southern skirts of Exmoor to Barnstaple. The Bath and Bristol section of the Great Western main line was opened 31 August 1840, and by 1 January 1845 the original main line of the Great Western and the Bristol and Exeter Railway Companies from London to Exeter, as well as the branch to Weston-super-Mare, was in working order.[62] Another impor-

tant section of this system enters the county at Frome and passes south-west to Weymouth by Witham, Castle Cary, and Yeovil; thence a branch runs north-west by way of Martock and Langport to the main line at Durston, near Taunton. By the opening of the new main line between Castle Cary and Langport in 1906 Taunton was brought within 2½ hours of Paddington. From Witham a branch line runs to Clevedon by Shepton Mallet, Wells, Cheddar and Axbridge. There is also a direct line from Frome to Bristol by way of Radstock, while a branch railway passing through Ilminster connects Taunton and Chard. A short line also joins Bedminster and Portishead, to which also the Weston-super-Mare and Clevedon light railway was extended in 1907. The West Somerset Mineral Line was finally closed in 1899.

The main line of the London and South Western runs along the southern border of the county, this section between Templecombe and Yeovil having been opened in 1860 by the Salisbury and Yeovil Company, which in 1878 was amalgamated with the London and South Western. Just before leaving the county the London and South Western sends a branch northward to Chard. From Templecombe it has a joint line with the Midland Company through Evercreech to Bath. From Evercreech Junction a branch also runs to Highbridge and Burnham, and there are connexions provided on this section of the line with Bridgwater and Wells. The conjoint enterprise of the Midland and London and South Western originated in two local lines, the Somerset Central Railway, then a broad-gauge system, incorporated 1852, and the Dorset Railway Company, a narrow-gauge line dating from 1856, which were in time amalgamated as the Somerset and Dorset Company with 66 miles of road. The directors of the amalgamated company determined to effect a junction with the Midland Railway at Bath, and a connexion 26 miles in length from Evercreech Junction to the Midland Station at Bath was opened for traffic in July 1874. Finally in the November following the Somerset and Dorset line was leased for a period of 999 years jointly to the London and South Western and the Midland Railway Companies, and the Midland Railway thus secured a through route from Carlisle to Bournemouth.[63] Besides these main lines and their branches the Wrington Vale Light Railway, which joins Congresbury and Blagdon, may also be mentioned.

The rivers in part navigable are the Avon, the Parrett from Thorney Mill to Bridgwater Bay, the Brue below Highbridge, the Tone from Ham Mill (near Creech St. Michael) to Borough Bridge, and the Yeo from Long Load[64] to

---

[55] Brown, *Somerset Wills* (Ser. 1), 301.
[56] Green, *Bibl. Somers.* pref. p. xxvi.
[57] Toulmin, *Hist. Taunton,* 176.   [58] Ibid.
[59] Billingsley, *Agric. Somers.* 260.
[60] The white flints or popple-stones of the district around Wiveliscombe, for instance, described as 'clean and bright,' are largely utilized for road repairs, (Jeboult, *Hist. West Somers.* 162). These stones are yielded from the conglomerates or pebble-beds of the Triassic formation (Woodward, *Geol. Engl. and Wales,* 136). Limestone, 'an excellent material where judiciously applied,' was being employed with good results, especially on the roads around Bridgwater at the close of the 18th and the opening of the 19th century. (*Rep. Highways and Turnpike Roads,* 1810, App. C. p. 28.)
[61] Small sledges were usually employed, the charge in 1798 being 6d. per ton (Billingsley, op. cit.). Maton saw labourers breaking stone in this county with a one-handled hammer. (*Hist. Western Counties,* ii, 33.)
[62] Sekon, *Hist. of Gt. Western Railway,* 59 et seq. In 1876 the Great Western Railway and the Bristol and Exeter Railway were amalgamated, and in 1892 the broad gauge was finally removed.

[63] Stretton, *Hist. Midland Company,* 228.
[64] De Salis, *Bradshaw's Canals and Navigable Rivers,* 360.

Langport. About the beginning of the 18th century attempts were made to improve the navigation of the Tone and Parrett, and these works were followed later by the inauguration of a canal-system designed largely with a view to the cheaper conveyance of corn, as well as coal and stone from the quarries and mines near Bath. The original idea of the Kennet and Avon Canal, for instance, was to supply the town of Abingdon with coal from the Radstock and Paulton mines. The competition of the Great Western Railway, which now owns the canal, has however diverted a large portion of its traffic both in stone and coal. Traffic from Bristol through the Kennet and Avon Canal is conducted in boats or barges of 30 tons and under, some 68 ft. long and 7 ft. broad, and when fully laded drawing 3 ft. 9 in. of water. In dry summer weather indeed partial loads only can be taken. The western portion towards Bristol is most neglected and sorely needs dredging.[65] The Somerset Coal Canal dating from 1794, which connected the Kennet and Avon with the Timsbury and Camerton collieries, is now disused. In 1902 it was reported as practically derelict, although four years previously the traffic for the twelve months of 1898 had been estimated at 30,887 tons, and the site was accordingly vested in the Great Western Company,[66] who have used it for the construction of a light railway. The Bridgwater and Taunton Canal is about 14¼ miles in length and formerly carried large quantities of coal; at the present time there is still a little traffic in coal as well as in deals, salt and bricks. The Creech St. Michael to Chard, Grand Western (Taunton to Exeter), Langport to Westport and Highbridge to Glastonbury Canals have been long disused.

Fisheries.—The decline of the fishing industry, for which the capricious migration of the herring must be held largely responsible, leaves the county in possession, nevertheless, of records,[67] preserved for the most part in the mediaeval accounts of great households, such as those of Dunster Castle, which acquaint us with the ancient methods of the fisherman's calling at Minehead, Porlock, and Watchet.

Textiles.—The textile industry, at one time of the first importance, will be considered at length elsewhere in this article, together with the wool traffic which was indispensable to its conduct. In this place, however, it will be sufficient briefly to glance at one or two of the subsidiary industries which grew up around the clothworker's craft. Such, for instance, was that of the cardmakers of Frome,[68] the now extinct but once thriving culture of woad,[69]

and the scarcely less prosperous growth of the teasels which were so indispensable to the mediaeval and even to the more modern clothmaker.[70]

Paper and Printing.—The paper and printing industry has from time to time given employment to scattered groups of the population. At a paper-mill at Banwell, afterwards converted to a brewhouse, paper was made for Bank of England notes in the 18th century.[71] A Mr. Snelgrove owned a paper-mill at Cheddar in 1825;[72] the same, doubtless, where 'paper,' we are told, was 'reduced to pulp in five minutes' in 1856; the mill had by that time passed into the possession of Messrs. Tanner Brothers.[73] Martha Wood had a paper-making establishment at Bishop's Hull, Taunton, in 1830.[74] At the same date, the manufacture was being carried on at Watchet by Robert Pole of Egrove Mill, and by William Wood & Son.[75] Parchment was formerly made at Castle Cary by John Lewis, who died in 1707, leaving 12s. per annum to be expended on bread for the poor.[76] Leather board, very thick paper used in the process of manufacture, has long been a specialty of Glastonbury.[77] The following firms are now engaged in the paper trade in the county :—At Bathford, the Bath Co.; at Street, the Avalon Co. (chiefly millboards); at Creech St. Michael, Taunton, R. Sommerville & Co. (writings, fine printings, envelope, tobacco, art, chromo, and enamelled papers); at Wells, Messrs. Hodgkinson & Co., and Pirie; at Watchet, the Wansbrough Paper Works of St. Decuman's produce rope and other browns, glazed and unglazed, and grocery papers.[78]

Although 'first place typographically, against all other counties,' is claimed for Somerset by Mr. Green, with a work by Douglas, a monk of Glastonbury, printed by Caxton in 1480, and next

[70] Teasels were chiefly grown at Wrington (Smith, *Mem. of Wool*, ii, 477), also at Blagdon, Ubley, Compton Martin, and Harptree (Billingsley, *Agric. of Somers.* 110). Those of West Hatch and Hatch Beauchamp are still sent to the North of England for cloth-dressing (Jeboult, *Hist. West Somerset*, 129). At Winscombe tithes were paid on the plants in the early part of the 18th century (Exch. Dep. by Com. Trin. 13 Will. III, no. 19). Teasels sold in packs of about 20,000 at £6 per pack. 3,000 were consumed on a piece of cloth 40 yds. in length (Bischoff, *Hist. Wool and Worsted*, 398). 'The tame teasel,' says Lyte, 'is sown of fullers and clothworkers to serve their purposes' (*Herball*, 521).

[71] Knight, *Seaboard of Mendip*, 406.

[72] Add. MS. 33683, fol. 27.

[73] Murray, *Handbook*, 1856, p. 198.

[74] Pigot, *Dir.* 727.   [75] Ibid. 728.

[76] Grafton, *Hist. Castle Cary*, 21. Serlo the parchment-maker was a frequent witness to documents relating to the priory of Bath in mediaeval times. *Bath Chartulary*, Linc. Inn. MSS. fol. 2 et seq.

[77] *Paper Mills Dir.* 1907, p. 81.

[78] Ibid. 17.

[65] *Royal Com. Canals and Waterways* (1906), Evidence, 252, 311 et seq.

[66] Ibid. 4.   [67] *Vide infra.*

[68] See 'Card-making,' *infra.*

[69] See 'Dyeing,' *infra.*

by the *Joseph of Armathy* of Wynken de Worde in 1502,[79] the local art of printing seems actually to have taken its rise at Bath in 1645, when a pamphlet entitled *Newes from the King's Bath* was produced there by R. P. of Bath.[80] Hotten gives 1649 as the date when George Treagle was printing and selling books at Taunton.[81] The earliest Bath book was Jardine's *Discourses* in 1702. In 1736, Mary Chandler's *Poems* were printed by J. Leake, and T. Boddeley was printing in 1746.[82] In 1708 Henry Chalklin was printing at Taunton,[83] whilst R. Goadly & Co. were printers in 1748 at Yeovil,[84] where the industry is now chiefly represented by the *Western Gazette* Co., Ltd. B. Lyon, near the North Gate, Bath, printed *A Family Piece*, by Captain Goulding, in 1729, also Robert Spurrell's *Elements of Chronology*. Leading 18th-century printers at Bath were the Farleys, members of the family supplying early work at Bristol, Exeter and Salisbury. In 1733 Felix Farley was established at the Shakespeare's Head, without West Gate. In 1741, S. & E. Farley had succeeded to the business. From their press issued Wood's *Origin of Building*. Clement Cruttwell was a printer of repute in 1785.[85] The first newspaper press in the county was at Taunton in 1718, at Bath in 1729, and at Yeovil in 1747.

In 1797 we hear of a printer named W. Crockford working at Frome, and it is possible that from his small business was developed the present well-known modern firm of Butler & Tanner at the Selwood Printing Works. In 1852 Langford and Butler were chemists and printers there, and in the following year Mr. Butler started for himself on the site of the present factory, being joined in 1863 by Mr. Joseph Tanner. A few years later Mr. Butler retired, and in 1895 Mr. Joseph Tanner also left the firm, being succeeded by his two sons, Messrs. Russell R. Tanner and Lanfear R. Tanner. The business has been greatly enlarged since its establishment, and quite recently a new additional factory was begun. This will eventually occupy about 11 acres and be equipped with the latest machinery for the printing and binding of high class books. At present some 500 hands are employed at the Selwood Works. At Taunton Messrs. Barnicott & Pearce of the Wessex Press occupy a prominent position as printers and publishers and have worthily produced many works on local topography, while the well-known publishing firm of

Sir Isaac Pitman & Sons carries on an extensive industry at Bath and Twerton.[86]

Various Small Manufactures.—The manufacture of stockings existed in former times at various towns, the knit hose of Shepton Mallet being especially noted.[87] The industry was also carried on at Wells, [88] at Glastonbury,[89] Axbridge,[90] Bruton [91] and as a village industry at Wrington in 1810, when the waste wool from the brambles and furze was collected by the women and children and made into stockings.[92]

The manufacture of collars is a modern industry at Taunton, Ilminster, Chard and elsewhere, but the industry, like that of glove-making, is at the mercy of every caprice of fashion. Thus in 1901 trade we learn was dull, owing to the vogue of soft neck-wear for ladies. The profit on men's collars was also reduced, owing to the fancy for high turn-over collars.[93] Shirt-making gives employment to 915 women and 148 men.[94]

Felt hats, also those known as Carolinas, were formerly made in large quantities at Wiveliscombe.[95] These hats are spoken of in a trade treatise of 1702 as 'a slight, coarse, mean commodity,' (the fur of hares and rabbits was used in the manufacture) introduced by the French, but soon made ten times better by the English, who received orders for them from abroad.[96]

At Chard Mr. James Gillingham is one of the best known surgical instrument makers in the country.

Rugs.—The manufacture of rugs has been carried on for more than half a century at

[86] Green, op. cit. 37.
[87] In 1831 the town was still carrying on 'its ancient manufacture of fine knit hose.' Pigot, *Dir.* 1831–2, p. 719.
[88] Phelps, *Hist. Somerset*, ii, 17.
[89] Lewis, *Topog. Dict.* ii, 226. From the evidence of trade tokens of the county issued 1651–71, the following were engaged in the industry at that date in this town : William Allwood, George Carey, Henry Mabson, and Christopher Summer. *Somers. Arch. Soc. Proc.* xxxii, 131. In 1830, Richard Chapman of Benedict Street was the only stocking-maker in the town. Pigot, *Dir.* 1830, p. 710. The stockings made in Wells, Shepton Mallet and Glastonbury supplied the Spanish trade, according to Defoe. *Tour through Great Brit.* ii, 27.
[90] Hannah More's scholars at Cheddar spun worsted for the stocking-makers at Axbridge in 1795. *Mendip Annals*, 24.
[91] Cooke, *Modern Brit. Traveller*, xvi, 164 ; Maton, *Nat. Hist. Western Counties*, ii, 182.
[92] *Somers. Arch. Soc. Proc.* xxxiii, 8.
[93] *Ann. Rep. Factories and Workshops*, 1901, p. 3. At Ilminster in 1908 the four shirt and collar works employed 300 hands at least, for the most part women and girls. (*Ex informatione* Rev. Prebendary Street.)
[94] *Rep. Cost of Living*, 1908, p. 465.
[95] *Somers. N. and Q.* 1856, p. 83.
[96] *A Brief Hist. of Trade*, 124.

[79] Green, *Bibl. Somers.* ii, 9.
[80] Cotton, *Typog. Gaz.* (Ser. 2), 17.
[81] Hotten, *Topog. Engl. and Wales*, 207.
[82] Green, op. cit.
[83] Cotton, op. cit. 222.
[84] Green, op. cit. 36.
[85] Ibid. At this printing office, in St. James Street South, were printed Collinson's *History of Somerset* in 1791, and Warner's *History of Bath* in 1801. Green, *Eighteenth-Century Architecture in Bath*, 17.

Glastonbury, where in 1825 Cyrus Clark of Street began utilizing the sheep-skins from the surrounding farms for this purpose. As the business developed he took into partnership a younger brother, James, who turned those skins with very short hair which would otherwise have been wasted to account by making them into fur slippers. Eventually the two businesses were separately conducted, the boot and slipper manufacture, which was the outcome of James Clark's inventive genius, being now carried on by Messrs. C. & J. Clark, whilst the rug factory, about a mile distant, is under the management of Messrs. Clark, Son & Morland. The method of manufacture is interesting enough to merit a brief description. The factory occupies two sides of a quadrangle, the interior being an open space in which are frames of wood, on which skins are stretched for drying. These are in almost all cases those of sheep, goat-skins and others being however occasionally utilized. Some are English skins, though the Scandinavian variety are said to be of excellent quality, whilst for close, flat rugs, the Chinese skins are found to be most suitable. On arrival at the factory the skins are subjected to a variety of processes, including washing, rinsing, squeezing through a machine resembling a mangle, combing, drying and stretching. The instrument used is a large wooden frame, consisting of four strong pieces of wood, and is rather longer than broad, whilst along the sides stout wooden pegs are inserted. The skin is then taken in hand by a workman who ties stout cords to convenient points in the edges with strong knots, and by means of these cords the skin is stretched very tightly on the frame and left to dry. Weather permitting, the process of drying goes on in the sun, but in case this is not possible, in a large heated chamber. When thoroughly stretched, the skin is dyed, as many as forty different shades being available, the skin being again stretched after dyeing, and again dried. The shaping, mounting and joining of the skins completes the process, these being all done by hand, the cutting being performed with ordinary shears, the patching, joining and mounting by expert needlewomen. Special skill is required for the matching and selection of skins.[97]

Tanning.—The industry of the tanner was in early activity in the county. The Carthusians of Hinton Charterhouse had a tannery in the reign of Edward III. Some of their neighbours complained that the religious paid too high a rate of wages, and apparently did not keep up prices. In retaliation these complainants, who were probably trading rivals, frightened away some of the Charterhouse workmen by actions under the Statute of Labourers. The Carthusians petitioned the king for redress, who granted to the prior and his brethren that they or their lay-brothers (*conversi*) or other servants might buy and sell hides for their tannery at their own prices, and that the brethren might pay their servants according to any agreement they made with them, without regard to the Statute of Labourers.[98] Allusions to the tanner's craft are frequent in Somerset wills, as for example to the Tanhouse at Pensford in 1536,[99] to John Davy, tanner, of Bridgwater, in 1461,[100] to John Melowes, engaged in the same calling in 1531,[101] John Gardiner of Haslebury bequeathing three tan-vats in 1558 to his son William.[102] Montacute formerly was famed for its leather market.[103]

At Street the industry of boot-making, under the management of Messrs C. & J. Clark, gives employment to 1,500 hands. With the exception of tanning the leather every part of the business is done at the factory, including the making and repairing of machinery and the making of boxes. Every variety of leather and skins is utilized, calf, kid, horse-skin and lizard-skin, sealskins, leopard-skins and lamb-skin being used for ornamental slippers. The business was originally started by Cyrus Clark and his brother James, whose sons succeeded him until the conversion of the industry into a limited company. The first department is the 'clicking-room,' where the uppers are cut out, either by presses which stamp them out with dies, or by hand with a sharp knife. In the machine-room women are exclusively employed. In the making-room the soles, which have been previously cut from oak tanned butts or bends of ox hide, are allotted to the uppers, various machines being in use for making up and heeling. After heeling, the rough shoes traverse a whole series of machinery until they are perfected, ready to be put on trees, polished up, and slipped into cardboard boxes for packing. In a special department girls are engaged in making up nursery shoes and children's sandals.[104]

Brushmaking.—This industry is carried on at Wells. The trade is divided into the following branches :—

1. Household, trade, and machinery.
2. Fancy (toilet, hair, nail and shaving).
3. Bone (tooth and nail).
4. Painters' and whitewashers'.
5. Artists'.

These are further divided into 'simple' and 'compound,' and again into 'round' and 'flat,'

[97] Communicated by the courtesy of the *Western Gazette* Company, Limited, Yeovil.

[98] Vexatious suits were apparently brought by neighbouring laymen on more than one occasion. See Pat 29 Edw. III, 5 October and 32 Edw. III, 14 April, recited Charter R.1 Ric. II.

[99] Weaver, *Somerset Wills* (Ser. 3), 31.

[100] Ibid. (Ser. 1), 194. [101] Ibid. (Ser. 3), 11.

[102] Ibid. 218.

[103] Pulman, *Local Nomenclature*, 165.

[104] We are indebted to the courtesy of the *Western Gazette* Company, Limited, for the above information.

and 'set' and 'draw.' The processes of manufacture are concerned (1) with the wood, and (2) with the brush. With regard to the first, the processes are those of sawing, shaping, boring, and drilling; in the second case, those of hair, bristle, or fibre dressing, drawing by hand or machine, pan work, trimming, finishing, and polishing. Women are largely employed in this industry, chiefly in lathe-boring and sandpapering. The materials used in the brush manufacture are of three kinds :—

1. Vegetable :—Bass, pasiava, palm fibre, Mexican aloe and cocoanut.
2. Animal :—English and foreign horsehair, bristle (Chinese, Indian, English and American), cow, badger and squirrel hair and whalebone.
3 Mineral :—Steel wire.

In the case of bristles, these are received at the factories in bundles, those imported from abroad being packed in casks or in boxes.[105]

Engineering Works.—The manufacture of oil engines gives employment in Yeovil to nearly 200 men, the engines produced being largely for agricultural purposes, grinding corn, cutting chaff, and sawing timber, as well as for pumping, generating electricity, for electric lighting, etc. The industry was started in Yeovil by Messrs. Petter in 1896, consequent upon the discovery by them of a new method of vaporizing the ordinary paraffin or lamp oil which supplies the motive power. Some twenty finished engines, of sizes varying from 1½ to 35 horse-power, are dispatched every week from the works in Reckleford. The 'Petter' engines have been supplied to most of the Government Departments, to fog-signal and lighthouse stations in Ireland, and for wireless telegraphy stations both at home and abroad. The works comprise a drawing office, where the designs are worked out and drawn on paper, from which sun prints are made and mounted on boards for use in the shops; the pattern shops, where wood parts are made to be copied in cast metal; three machine shops, to which is attached a tool room; erecting and paint shops. The works' power station contains two 100 h.p. gas engines and gas generators, the whole being lighted by electricity from dynamos placed in the power house, the current being also utilized for power purposes.[106] Besides this enterprise, there are in most of the towns of Somerset admirably equipped foundries and engineering works, as for example at Taunton the firms of Messrs. C. Allen & Son at Bridge Street, and Easton & Bessemer, Ltd., of the Whitehall Iron Works; at Martock, Sibley & Son of the Parrett Iron Works, and Mr. William

Sparrow at The Somerset Wheel and Wagon Works; at Bridgwater, Messrs. J. Culverwell & Co. and W. & F. Wills, Ltd.; and at Wellington, Messrs. Bishop Bros., North Street, and Ford Bros. & Co. of Chamford Lane. Other firms of good local repute, which limitation of space forbids us to mention particularly, exist at Bath, Chard, Frome, Highbridge, Watchet and Bruton.

Metal-working.—The art of working in precious metals had at least one notable and early exponent in Somerset in the person of Dunstan, Abbot of Glastonbury. And there is good reason for believing on the evidence of the 12th and 13th century rentals and custumals of this religious house that a goldsmith was a permanent member of the staff of skilled craftsmen attached to the abbey. For instance in the Inquisitions of Henry de Soliaco we read that Andrew the goldsmith held the *misterium aurifabrise* [107] which Henry Bishop of Winchester granted to Thurstan his brother with a virgate of land and a corrody for his service and other privileges. Again Hugh [108] the goldsmith (*aurifaber*) held one ferdell of land in Chalewe about the middle of the 13th century and a little later we hear of William the goldsmith [109] who holds a virgate for which he pays 3s., does repairs in the church and mends the cups (*cyphos*) and clock (*clipsadram*) in the 'freytur' at the expense of the monks. Again in the lay subsidy [110] of 1327 Richard 'le Goldsmythe' of Glastonbury is assessed at 3s. At Yeovil again in the same roll Thomas Goldsmythe's [111] name is down for 15d., while goldsmiths are found [112] at the same date at Taunton and Langport. 'Le Goldsmith' figures amongst early Parliamentary representatives of Bath,[113] whilst it has been suggested that the curiously-named Bridgwater street of Penel Orlieu probably owes its name to the fact of its having possibly been a goldsmiths' quarter. In a deed of 1398, it has been pointed out, we find mention of a street called 'The Orfaire,' and again in the Churchwardens' Accounts in the reign of Edward IV we have 'Orlew Strete,' the 'Gold Place,' or 'Goldsmithery.' [114]

It is not however until the 17th century that the art seems to emerge definitely from obscurity in the county. There were then several workers in silver and gold in Somerset.

[105] *Ann. Rep. Factories and Workshops*, 1902, App. D, 207–9.
[106] From information courteously supplied by the *Western Gazette* Company, Limited, Yeovil.

[107] Op. cit. (Roxburghe Club), 13.
[108] Add MS. 17450, fol. 56 d.
[109] Ibid. fol. 90 d.
[110] *Kirby's Quest*, etc. (Somers. Rec. Soc.), 205.
[111] Ibid. 215.
[112] Ibid. 274, 276.
[113] *Bath Nat. Hist. and Field Club Proc.* iii, 75. Reiner the goldsmith witnessed the signing of various documents for the Prior of Bath in mediaeval times. Bath Chartulary, Linc. Inn MSS. fol. 2.
[114] *Hist. MSS. Com. Rep.* i, 99.

Spencer Ryves was a goldsmith of Crew-kerne at this date. We learn that one of his apprentices, William Mantle, was discharged from his apprenticeship 'upon many reasons and good causes,' at the General Sessions held at Ilchester 14–16 April 1618.[115] John Freke was another who practised his art at the same place in this century. A specimen of his work is preserved among the church plate of Crew-kerne, the cover of the oldest cup bearing the inscription dotted in, 'This cupp was new made by Mr. John Freke, of Croochorne the 4th of Mrche, 1607.'[116] Thomas Dare was a gold-smith of Taunton, who seems to have been at work from 1673 to 1691, but the examples of his mark (T. D.) are few.[117] A cup at Woolavington is of great interest as bearing these initials, and also the Taunton mark proper, namely, a tun lying across a T, the whole inclosed in a circle, the initials surmounting a fleur de lis in a shaped punch.[118]

A single mark, a monogram of the initials T. H., found on saucers at Chilton Trinity, Durston, and Puriton, is assigned by Mr. Bates to a Bridgwater silversmith.[119] The modern metal-working industry in the county is repre-sented by Messrs. Singer & Sons of Frome.

The art of engraving seals seems to have flourished at Bath about the middle of the 18th century, when the famous local architect, Wood, was consulted by John Wicksted, who introduced the art, with regard to building a house for his workers, Wood suggesting the name of 'Sigil-larium' for the building in question. The project however fell through.[120] The same authority mentions the manufacture of 'Bath rings' as part of the trade of the city.[121] In 1797, from 200 to 300 hands were employed at Bridgwater in the production of urns, tea-waiters, and other japanned articles, 'the paintings and ornaments thereon' being 'equal,' we are told, 'in every respect to the Birmingham ware of the same kind.'[122]

The manufacture of edge-tools has been largely identified, throughout its history, with the town and neighbourhood of Mells, where fifty-six men were employed in this industry in 1831.[123] The scythes made in this town were said to owe their temper to the water of the locality, which was impregnated with lime from the limestone formation.[124] Mr. Fussell owned an edge-tool mill at Nunney in 1856.[125]

Biscuits.—A famous industry of Bath is the manufacture of the Bath Oliver Biscuit, invented in 1735 by Dr. William Oliver, sometime physician to the Bath Mineral Water Hospital. On his death in 1764 the secret of the manufacture passed to the doctor's coachman, together with 'a sum of one hundred pounds and ten sacks of flour,' with which he set up business in a small shop in Green Street. In the course of the 160 years which have elapsed since then, many different methods of manufacture have been adopted, some of the processes being curious enough to merit a brief allusion. The staff brake was the earliest of these methods. 'This was,' we learn, 'an appliance of the simplest description: merely a staff of wood attached at one end to the side of a table or board, on which the dough was placed in such a manner as to allow of its being freely pressed. The dough was first thoroughly kneaded with the staff in this way, then each biscuit was weighed and moulded by hand, and lastly, separately rolled with rolling pins.' To this somewhat slow and cumbersome method succeeded the steel roller, the principle being that of the ordinary mangle, this in turn being replaced by modern machinery. The present maker and proprietor is Mr. James Fortt, 13, Green Street.[126]

A Somerset dainty of the time of Defoe were the elver cakes of Keynsham, which were made from little eels, 'no bigger than goose quils,' which were caught on the river at that place.[127]

Oare.—The collection of the oare weed found on the foreshores of the manors of Dunster, Minehead, Carhampton, Old Cleeve, East Quantoxhead, Kilve, and Kilton, is a very an-cient industry. On 24 May 1597 George Luttrell let to Robert Batten of Watchet 'all the oare now being or growing or that hereafter shall come to be within the ebbing and flowing of the sea in and upon the soil and inheritance of the said George Luttrell from the full sea mark unto the low water mark extending from the bridge called Mouth Bridge unto the Warren House of the said George Luttrell commonly called or known by the name of the Whithouse.' from Midsummer next for twenty-one years at a rent of 26s. 8d. There is a covenant that Batten 'shall not burn any oare upon any contrary winds, that is to say upon any easterly, north,

[115] *Quarter Sess. Rec. Jas. I* (Som. Rec. Soc. xxiii).

[116] Bates, 'Inventory of Church Plate,' *Somers. Arch. Soc. Proc.* xliv (2), 184. Ed. Sweet of Crewkerne, gold-smith; xlv (2), 140, John Arding of Crewkerne, gold-smith (*Ancestor*, vol. x). This man was shot dead by Ferguson when the Duke of Monmouth landed at Lyme.

[117] Bates, op. cit. xlvi (2), 150, 161.

[118] Ibid. xlvii (2), 173.   [119] Bates, op. cit.

[120] Wood, *Essay on Bath*, ii, 423.

[121] Ibid. 419. These rings, which were made of copper, were fixed at the side of the wall in the King's Bath so that cripples could hang on to them, by patients who had been restored to health through the virtue of the waters. Some of these rings date from the 15th century, and many still remain. Com-municated by the courtesy of Mr. T. Sturge Cotterell.

[122] Add. MS. 33635, fol. 7.

[123] *Pop. Ret.* 558–9.

[124] Murray, *Handbook*, 173.   [125] Ibid.

[126] From information kindly supplied by Mr. Fortt.

[127] Defoe, *Complete Engl. Tradesman*, 235.

or north-easterly wind, whereby the smoke and noisome savour and smell of the said oare so burning may or shall be driven or carried towards the castle and house of the said George Luttrell, at Dunster aforesaid, or towards any of the lands of the said George Luttrell at Carhampton and Dunster aforesaid.' [128]

On 1 May, 1582, Alice Wether was admitted to a cottage and garden and 4 acres of land and one part of le ore (*unam parcellam le ore*) between Minehead Quay and Horestone, which premises had been in the tenure of her father, to hold according to the custom of the manor. Horestone is situate a little to the west of Burgundy Chapel. [129]

William Besley, one of the tenants of the fishery from Minehead Quay to Bradley Gate, and who is now over sixty years of age, can recollect, when he was a little boy, the oare weed being collected on the Old Cleeve foreshore for the purpose of being burnt, and made into kelp, which was sent to Bristol, where it realized from £7 10s. to £10 per ton, and was used in the manufacture of bottles. In recent times, the trade has ceased, and the oare weed has only been taken by the lord of the manor's tenants, with his permission, for manuring their land. [130]

The export of kelp constituted almost the entire trade of Watchet in 1797, [131] laver being also exported from the same coast as pickle in earthen pots. [132]

' A very profitable industry' in 1791 was that of ' pulling the feathers of the myriads of geese' raised on Sedgemoor, the process being repeated several times during the summer months. The birds were kept on the ' Moor' all the winter, and only specially fed if the frost set in for any length of time, and then chiefly on beans. [133]

Other miscellaneous and minor industries were those of spar-cutting and thatching, mentioned by Mr. Green as industries which have ' declined at Castle Cary; [134] shoe-binding, which was formerly largely carried on as a separate industry, though accessory to the shoemaking trade, at and around the village of Street; [135] and basket-making, which is carried on in various localities, the extent of the industry being largely determined by agricultural demand, and by the neighbourhood of the ' withy' culture, as for example at Stoke St. Gregory and Ruishton. [136]

In conclusion a short account may be given of the merchant tailors of Bath. Their industry was one of ancient standing, the gild having received its charter from Richard I. An apprenticeship of seven years was required, members being admitted ' having done all their duty.' [137] Widows of freemen might keep one apprentice and one journeyman, to assist them in carrying on their late husbands' business. [138] Stringen regulations were in force respecting the conduct of the gild; the production of misfitting garments, for instance, being punished by the loss of civil rights. [139] No freeman could open a shop until he had taken the oath, under penalty of 6s. 8d. [140] Nor was any freeman allowed to open his shop window, nor to do any work on Sundays or holy days, except market and fair days, infringement of this rule being punished by a fine of 3s. 4d. [141] Before commencing work, even when an employer had been found, a journeyman was obliged to obtain the consent of the master of the Company, and within tea days pay 3d. for free sewing, and 2d. for quarterage, as long as he continued to reside in the city. [142] Threepence per man was paid for piece sewing from 1695 to 1721, when this payment ceased. [143]

LEAD MINING

Of the various forms of mining practised within the county of Somerset the working of lead most insistently appeals to the archaeologist. Its origin is indeed lost in prehistoric mists and shadows, but the Romans found the industry in being, [1] with their practical genius organized and developed it, and carried the product of the Mendip mines beyond the bounds of Britain. However, we are not here concerned with the vigorous youth of Somerset lead-mining; our task is to piece together the rare references of the Middle Age and sketch in summary fashion the activities of the 16th and following centuries

[128] Luttrell Deeds, B. 21, no. 17. Mouth Bridge is now called Pill Bridge, and the White House is now the Warren House, near Warren Point (see Ordnance Survey). The shore described in the lease is the whole of the foreshore of the Manors of Carhampton and Dunster.

[129] Luttrell Deeds, B. 29, no. 3.

[130] Ex. inform. Mr. J. H. Davis. ' Kelp,' says Colwall, ' is made of a seaweed, called tangle, such as comes to London on oysters. Being dried, it will burn and run like pitch; when cold and hard, it is beaten to ashes, steeped in water, and the lees drawn off to two pounds weight or thereabouts.' *Philos. Trans.* xii, 1054.

[131] Maton, *Western Counties*, ii, 109.

[132] Ibid.

[133] Marshall, *Rural Econ. of West of Engl.* 182.

[134] Green, *Rural Industries of Engl.* 108.

[135] Ibid. 117.

[136] Jeboult, *Hist. West Somers.* 123–4.

[137] *Bath Nat. Hist. and Field Club Proc.* ix, 251.

[138] Ibid. 275.   [139] Ibid. 250.   [140] Ibid. 235.

[141] Ibid. 252.   [142] Ibid. 255.   [143] Ibid. 255.

[1] *V.C.H. Somerset*, i, 198. For an account of the Roman lead-mines see ibid., 334 et seq.

till their exhaustion in the almost complete quiescence of our own time.[2]

The lead ore of Somerset is far from being confined to the Mendips, but there alone in the county, as it seems, the Romans worked it, and there also in later times a code of mining law grew up similar in many respects to the customary regulations of the ancient fields of Derbyshire, Alston Moor and the Forest of Dean.

For the Saxon period and century following the Norman Conquest we have no details as to lead-mining in the Mendips or elsewhere in Somerset; it is highly improbable that it was entirely discontinued, but no issues from the Somerset lead-mines are even alluded to by the compilers of the Domesday Survey.[3]

In the year 1189 Richard I granted to Reginald Bishop of Bath all the lead ore[4] on his lands in Somerset without condition or hindrance and also permission to make a borough (burgum) in his land of Radeclive (Rackley) with a market. A question arises as to the exact force of this grant. Did it convey fresh privileges or confirm an already existing practice and right? Rackley where the Cheddar water runs into the Axe had probably from the Roman period at least been the port where barges loaded lead from the Mendip mines to be carried seaward and transhipped into larger craft.[5] It is again practically certain that the Bishops of Bath were already working or leasing the mines within their manors at the time when this charter passed. Richard was also as we know in urgent need of money, and Bishop Reginald may have thought it worth his while to purchase a grant which would shelter his miners from fines for purprestures on the royal forest and meet any demand of the Crown for an account of the silver extracted from the lead—since it is possible that the precious metal was already being claimed as an exclusive royal perquisite. That the activities of the miners had brought them into conflict with the forest officials is shown by an entry on the first Pipe Roll of Richard I that the Bishop of Bath is liable for £100 for the purprestures of his miners and for keeping dogs contrary to the assize.[6]

During the earlier portion of the 13th century little evidence is available for estimating the condition of the industry. But there is no reason to suppose an entire cessation at this time. Indeed in the year 1235 the king granted a licence to the Bishop of Bath to mine for both lead and iron within the royal forest of Mendip, while 40 acres of wood at Cheddar were allotted for the smelting of the ore.[7]

During the latter years of the reign of Edward I and in the time of his successors there is slight but sufficient evidence that lead was being produced to some extent in the minery of Bath and Wells and elsewhere in this district. From 25 October 1292 till 19 March 1293 the temporalities of the see[8] were in the hands of the king owing to the death of Robert Burnell, and the royal accountant John of Hardyngton returns a sum of 27s. partly derived from the sale of lot-lead from Mendip (de decimo pede plumbi inventi in fundo episcopi super Menydep) and partly from the lease of a stone quarry, doubtless at Dundry. This short entry is of great value and interest since it furnishes unimpeachable evidence not only that as early as the 13th century the lot-lead raised from the bishop's fee was paid to him, for this was likely from other considerations, but also that the exact proportion, a tithe, was already fixed.

More intimate details of the Mendip mining industry at this time may however be obtained from a letter[9] unfortunately undated but apparently addressed to a Bishop of Bath in the closing days of his episcopate. It may well belong either to the late 13th or early 14th century. Freely rendered it runs as follows:—

I have to inform you, my lord, that your workmen have discovered very good ore (mineram) on Mendip near Priddy towards the east, and that, without any further labour beyond opening the surface soil to the depth of five or six feet. As workmen of this kind are frequently thieves, and in the process of separating the silver from the lead by their craft (artificialiter) in smelting, secretly appropriate the silver and after they have got together a great quantity desert their business (a frequent occurrence on Mendip [ibidem] in times past according to the tale of ancient men) your bailiffs take care that the said ore shall be carried down to your court at Wookey (ad curiam vestram de Woky). There at a furnace built in the midst of it your workmen smelt the ores (illa mineralia) under the superintendence (sub visu) of certain

---

[2] The small amount of lead now obtained is derived mainly from the slags and slimes of the old mines.

[3] It may be suggested that at this early period, as certainly two centuries later, mining royalties in the shape of lot-lead went to the chief lords of the soil.

[4] Wells MSS. R. I. fol. 15; R. III, fol. 343, printed N. and Q. Somerset and Dorset, vi, 152. 'Quod habeat mineram de plumbo ubicunque eam invenire potuit in terra sua de Somerset . . . absque ulla conditione vel impedimento.'

[5] N. and Q. Somers. and Dors. vi, 152.

[6] Gt. Roll of the Pipe, 1 Ric. I (Rec. Com.), 151.

[7] This licence was first granted on 4 May 1235 and authorized a search for iron ore and every other kind of mineral 'apud Hidun in foresta regis de Munedep' (Close, 19 Hen. III, m. 12). A fortnight after an amended licence was issued which authorized the bishop 'quod . . . perfodi faciat apud Hydon et alibi super montem de Munedep in terris quorumcunque licentiam optinere poterit ad querendum mineram ferri et plumbi' (Close, 19 Hen. III, m. 11). Evidently the miners of the bishop could not enter lands outside the episcopal fee unless they obtained permission from the holders.

[8] Pipe R. 22 Edw. I, m. 5.

[9] Anct. Corres. Exch. vol. 48, no. 177.

persons[10] appointed by your seneschal for the purpose. Both the seneschal and bailiff as well as the workmen consider that this lead is highly argentiferous on account of its whiteness and sonority. They ask you to be so kind as to have sent to them some good and loyal workman whom they can thoroughly trust as soon as you can provide one. I myself have seen the first pig (*peciam*) of lead smelted there of great weight and size which as often as it is struck almost rings (*resonat*) like silver. For this reason I and others think that if the refining (*artificium*) were loyally carried out it would yield immense benefit to you and the whole neighbourhood. Also if a workman (*artifex*) were obtained who could be depended on (*fidelis*), I believe it would be desirable to smelt the ore at the mine (*ubi minera effoditur*) owing to the labour of carrying the heavy mineral to distant localities. The ore is found in the form of sand or small gravel (*Et se habet illa minera sicut sabulo sive arena minuta*).

So luminous is this letter that little comment is needed. Owing to the necessities of the royal exchequer in the reign of Edward I every effort was made to open up fresh supplies of silver, the chief medium of exchange, and this in England implied the working of argentiferous galena. Ultimately the rich mines of Birland or Beer Alston and Combe Martin were found especially profitable, and during the reign of Edward I and his successor we have no definite knowledge that any substantial amount of silver was obtained from the Mendips. Successive writs directed a constant supply of labour to the mines of Devon, and this labour was mainly recruited in Derbyshire. It is doubtful whether the mine referred to in our letter ever reached a paying stage in respect of the precious metal, but the testimony of the 'ancient' men referred to shows that the extraction of silver from the lead ore had been commonly practised at one time on the Mendips.

One other point only in this letter may be noticed; it would seem that smelting had within the memory of the 'ancient' men been practised on the hills themselves and there can be no question that the recommendation at the end of the letter of a return to this practice was sooner or later carried into effect. But as to the length of time the furnace or hearth was at work at Wookey we know nothing. We are also without any technical details of the processes employed.

Of lead-mining during the reign of Edward I on other fees than that of the Bishop of Bath little evidence exists; we may reasonably suspect that it was proceeding, to some slight extent at least, in the lordship of Glastonbury, as well as at Chewton and East Harptree, but at present no notices are available. We know however that the Prior and convent of Witham acquired a grant[11] in 1283 to work whatever lead-

mines they found in their several soil and take the issues thereof without hindrance. This was possibly a confirmation of an existing practice and would be of use to defeat the claims or exactions of forest officers or the neighbouring lords, ecclesiastical and lay.

Other occasional notices[12] of profits derived from the Mendip mines occur in the accounts of the receivers of the issues of the temporalities to the see of Bath and Wells during the next two reigns, but since we know nothing as to the amount of lot-lead employed in the episcopal manors, and have no particulars of the mining industry outside the bishop's jurisdiction, it would be profitless to hazard a guess at the annual output of lead from the district at this period.

While Derbyshire was constantly called upon to furnish skilled men for the mines royal, especially in Devon, Somerset, probably on account of the few miners available, seems to have escaped more easily, though a general order[13] was sent to the county authorities of Somerset, as well as to officials in other mining centres, to supply a very few men in 1295, and later instances[14] occur. In 1319 the sheriff was called upon to furnish twelve lead-miners to Hugh le Despenser the younger, lord of Glamorgan, for his mines, while in 1358 four Somerset metal founders and 'four miners, of the best in that county' were sought for the mines royal in Devon. They were offered adequate wages, and these were to be promptly paid.

As early as the year 1314 mining had been going on beyond the limits of the forest of Mendip at Brushford near Dulverton,[15] for we hear of a quarrel about money between the miners employed, in consequence of which one of them found himself in Newgate. It is possible from the facts that this silver-mine which the adventurers Simon le Armurer, Merlin de Sene, Hermann de Alemannia, Geoffrey de Shapelegh, John de la Mine and Henry de Shapelegh worked for their own and the king's profit had not fulfilled sanguine anticipations. The chief interest of the episode to us is that though most of these miners were Devonshire men, one was undoubtedly a German adventurer.

---

[10] Possibly an early reference to the lead-reeves.
[11] Pat. 11 Edw. I, m. 11.

[12] During the vacancy of twenty-two weeks one day following the decease of Walter Hasleshaw, 18s. was received from this source. Mins. Accts. bdle. 1131, no. 4. In the enrolment of this account 28s. is mentioned as coming from the lease of Dundry quarry and the Mendip lead-mines. Pipe R. 3 Edw. III, pt. ii, m. 6. Again during the short spring and summer vacancy after the death of John de Drokensford we hear of 2s. 4d. 'de una pecia plumbi perveniente de exitu minerarum.' Mins. Accts. bdle 1131, no. 1.
[13] Close, 24 Edw. I, m. 11d.
[14] Close, 12 Edw. II, m. 13d.; 32 Edw. III, m. 2.
[15] It was somewhere on the lands of the Prior of Taunton. Cf. Close, 7 Edw. II, m. 6.

Teutonic mining enterprise in England has a long history.

Returning to the Mendips we hear [16] in 1339 of another reputed silver mine 'in a certain place at Wells.' The Sheriff of Somerset was ordered to take gentlemen of the county and experts to examine the mine [17] and forthwith report to the royal chancery. In default he was threatened with a visit from 'certain faithful men' from the king's council. As nothing is heard subsequently of any issues of value, we may be allowed to infer that this enterprise proved one of the multitudinous blanks in the lottery of mining adventure.

So fragmentary are the accessible records remaining to us which bear on the history of mediaeval mining in the county of Somerset that all attempts to trace its ebb and flow must be to a great extent provisional and tentative. With this *caveat* a suggestion may be hazarded that the reigns of Richard II and his successor saw little fresh activity and possibly some retrogression in the Mendip lead-mining. However this may be, on 3 February 5 Hen. V, a royal mining licence [18] was granted to John Bays of Priddy and William Milward the younger to remain in force for the space of one year. Unless it refers to some lordship temporarily in the king's hands it must have been issued in virtue of the forest rights of the Crown. The mine, whatever its exact situation, lay within the forest of Mendip and according to the letters patent had not been worked (*non extitit occupata*) for 200 years past. The lessees were to pay to the Crown the usual Mendip lot-lead, 'every tenth hundredweight' and in return had the enjoyment during their lease of 'all kinds of easements within the aforesaid forest which were reasonably necessary for their work (*occupatione*) as long as they committed no waste,[19] with the proviso always that if the aforesaid John and William should make a mine of this kind in a stranger's soil (*in fundo alieno*) then they should give proper satisfaction to the lord or lords of that same soil.' As a result of the year's working some 1,900 lb. of lead were obtained and a tithe of this, 1 cwt. 3 quarters and 17 lb. was sold for 10s. for the king's benefit at the rate of 5s. 3d. the cwt. The price obtained for this lead was much higher than the rates ruling some thirty-five years later, for at the very beginning of the reign of Edward IV, during the reparation or rebuilding at the bishop's manor house of Wookey,[20] a large amount of lead was purchased in part from Mendip at 3s. 6d. the cwt. the remainder, rather more than a half, being Peak lead brought from Bristol at 4s. 2d. the cwt. This incident is worth noting for another reason, since it shows us Peak lead competing with the product of the Mendip Hills in its own place of origin. Indeed during the 13th and the two following centuries, whatever the case earlier or later, the output of Mendip lead was probably less than that of Derbyshire. As to the popular estimation of the two kinds, it may be remarked that in the 16th century at all events Peak lead was considered the best in England,[21] ranking before Mendip lead, which however took precedence of the lead of Yorkshire.

Leaving on one side for the present the story of the dispute as to the Mendip pastures between the Prior of Green Ore and the lord and tenants of Chewton which is referred to the reign of Edward IV, we may gather from indications in local accounts which are still extant that the mining industry on Mendip was fairly active in the second half of the 15th century, though probably in no way an equal rival of the pastoral interest. As to the lands of the see of Bath and Wells the industry was apparently confined to the rural manor of Wells and especially Priddy. In an account [22] for the year 1515–16 we hear of 13s. 4d., which would have been received from the sale of 4 hundreds (400 lb.) of lead at 3s. 4d. a hundred, coming from the issues of the manor at Priddy, if it had not been assigned to the lord's own use. Also of 2s. 6d. 'de lede owre' the produce of the lord's mine (*mynere domini*) there according to the Michaelmas Court, and of 3s. 4d. similarly according to the Candlemas Court, as well as 20d. paid at the Hockday Court. Mining may also have been going on at or near Burrington [23] within the jurisdiction of the Abbot of Glastonbury, for in February 1489 the churchwardens of Yatton bought there a 'tonne of lyde' for £4 13s. 8d. And the men of Chewton as well were doubtless at work.[24]

---

[16] Close, 13 Edw. III, pt. i, m. 9.

[17] 'Terram in loco illo fodere et minam hujusmodi ibidem perscrutari facias.'

[18] By letters patent of which a copy is annexed to Accts. Exch. K. R. bdle. 265, no. 6. Cf. also Foreign Accts. 155 (9 Hen. V) D.

[19] These reasonably necessary easements would certainly include wood for timbering their pits and perhaps 'white coal' (dried wood) and charcoal for the smelting.

[20] Lambeth Mins. Accts. (1–2 Edw. IV), no. 1133.

[21] Lansd. MS. 31, fol. 164.

[22] Mins. Accts. 6–7 Hen. VII, 584. On the dorse of this account of Wells Manor is what appears to be a [lead] reeve's account for the year 7 Hen. VII which may be summarized here as supplementary to the details in the text.

No arrears, as all the lead remaining from the previous year had been sold. But he answers for amounts of 300 lb., 400 lb., 100 lb. and 400 lb. delivered at the Michaelmas, Candlemas, Hockday and Midsummer halmotes, 'que liberantur. . . infra palacium ibidem.'

[23] *Churchwardens' Accts. of Croscombe, etc.* (Somers. Rec. Soc. iv), 116.

[24] The lead got by the churchwardens of Pilton was probably obtained from the mines in Chewton Manor, even if in part bought at Shepton Mallet.

At this point in our survey it may be convenient to consider very briefly the more ancient customs and laws which regulated the mining industry on Mendip. The earliest detailed copies of these apparently belong to the 16th century. One written or revised in the reign of Elizabeth or far more probably her predecessor will be found among the State Papers Domestic,[25] but several other copies of the 16th and 17th centuries exist, some inscribed on certain old manorial maps of Mendip forest, together with a popular report of an important case concerning commoners' rights of pasture on Mendip purporting to belong to the reign of Edward IV, while others are found entered in books of later mining orders, such as Browne's Book now preserved at the Wells Diocesan Registry. The frequent juxtaposition of the report of the Green Ore case and the Miners' Customs has not unnaturally provoked the inference that they formed one whole and that in fact these customs received some sort of ratification and embodiment when the Green Ore case came before Sir John Choke. Until however the official enrolment of Sir John Choke's award is found, it is perhaps undesirable to assert definitely that the customs of the miners were at that time embodied and formally approved. For however probable this conclusion may be, there are certain difficulties in accepting it. If the version printed by Mr. J. McMurtrie in his most valuable account of the laws of Chewton minery is considered, it will be noticed that the report of the Green Ore case is said to be 'enrolled in the King's Highnesse Exchequer by the time of Edward IV,' while the miners' customs are headed ' Irrot. in Scaccario Domine Regine.' This divergence may suggest that we have here documents derived from two different sources. And again the semi-official [26] copy—if we may so style it—of the Miners' Customs among the Elizabethan State Papers Domestic is found by itself and apart from the report of the Green Ore case. As the manorial maps of Mendip would be in special request in questions of common rights as well as in mining disputes it was natural that both these important documents, the award and the early customs, should be recorded on them. It is also rather curious that if an authoritative embodiment of the Mendip mining customs had been made with the approval of the king in the 15th century the Chewton mineral court in 1554 should have denied the existence of any ' ancient writing ' relating thereto.[27] What, however,

can be asserted with confidence from the actual nature of the customs themselves is that they date in part at least from a period much earlier than even the 15th century, and we have actual evidence that one of them dealing with the question of lot-lead was well recognized under Edward I. We can then well believe that the miners' customs may have been referred to when the Charterhouse brethren were at strife with the men of Chewton and were perhaps later enrolled in the Exchequer in connexion with some Mendip suit in the reign of Mary or of Elizabeth.

Before we pass to the detailed consideration of the customs a few words may be devoted to the case of the ' great debate that was in the county of Somerset between the lord [28] Bonvills tenants of Chewton and the Prior of Green Oare.' The main matter of dispute was evidently in connexion with the great pastoral industry of Mendip, and by the Prior of Green Ore or Greneworth is possibly meant the Prior of Hinton Charterhouse of which Green Ore was merely a grange. This religious house was accustomed to keep 1,000 sheep by the long hundred or 1,200 by the common reckoning on the pastures or ' sleights ' of Greneworth or Green Ore, namely 800 on Fursehill and 400 upon Stockhill and Cokesclyffe. An old servant of the Charterhouse, Richard Davis *alias* Trehearne, who had known Prior Taylor, *alias* John Chamberlayne,[29] in his youth has left us an account of these ' sleights ' or ' slaits,' since he deposed [30] when already well over ninety years of age that ' Furshill sleight doth extend in length from the hiewaye going from Greneworth to Prydy unto a stone standing upon the est parte of the hie waye betwene Wels and Brystoll, [and] in bredth from a lane end leading from Enborar highway and so to go to Hartrey, there standing a stone betwene the lordship of Hartrey and the sleight of Furshill.' And further that ' the sleight of Stockhill and Cocesclyves extend in length from the same Prydye waye end to

this time have claimed customes to and for their occupation in and upon the said disaforested ground and amongst themselves to be observed and kept, having *no ancient writing*, or prescription of antiquity to be showed for the same, so that for lack thereof their said customes were altered, changed and used amongst them divers and sundry ways, etc.' See *Trans. Fed. Inst. Mining Engineers*, xx, 538.

[28] If the minute accuracy of this title is insisted upon—which is perhaps unnecessary—it would force us to put the dispute before the accession of Edward IV, as Lord Bonvill was beheaded after the Lancastrian victory at St. Albans in February (1460–1) and his heir was his great-granddaughter the lady Cecilie, a minor.

[29] ' So called that he was borne in Chamberlayne Streate in Wells.'

[30] On 15 January 19 Eliz. Cf. Dep. Hil. 19 Eliz. no. 3, Somerset.

[25] S. P. Dom. Eliz. cclxxxvii, 97.

[26] Ibid.

[27] In the preamble to the edition of the laws of Chewton miners approved by the lord in 1554 occur the significant words ' For as much as the said miners and workmen upon the said mineries there before

Horewall corner; and in bredth from the west, the highe waie comyng from the west corner of Whitnell going up by the lane that goeth from Furshill to Hartrey.'

It would seem that the lord of Chewton was not unwilling [31] to abet his tenants in trespassing on the lands of the Charterhouse at Greneworth and that the prior in self-defence may have claimed to hound or pound strange cattle found on his sleights. Possibly, too, the prospecting miner may have without proper licence from the prior entered on the land of the Carthusians. However this may be we are told that the prior complained to the king 'of great injuries an wrongs that hee had upon Meyndeepe being the king's forest.' According to the popular English account of the business, of which, as we have said, many copies [32] exist, 'The said King Edward commanded my Lord Chocke being Cheife Justice of England to goe downe into the Countrey of Meyndeepe and sett a concord and peace in the countrey upon Meyndeepe upon paine of his high displeasure. The said Lord Chocke sate upon a place of my Lord of Bathes called the fordge upon Meyndeepe where hee comanded all the comoners to appeare there and in especiall the foure Lords [33] Royall of Meyndeepe that is to say my Lord the Bishop of Bath and Wells, my lord of Glastonbury, my lord Bonvile, lord of Chuton and my lord of Richmond with all the appearance to the number of tenn thousand people. A proclamacion was made to inquire of all the said companie how they would be ordered; then, they all with one assent made answer and said that they would be ordered and tried by the foure Lords Royal. Then the foure Lords Royall were agreed that all the comoners of Meyndeepe dwelling in theire Tenements being within the bounds of Meyndeepe should turne out theire cattle att theire outletts as much the summer as they bee able to keepe the winter without hounding or pounding upon whose ground soever they went to take their course or recourse. To this the said foure lords put theire seales, and alsoe were agreed that whosoever should breake any of these bounds should forfeite

[31] But as Davis deposed in 1579 'He never knewe any duties or tythes paide to the farmers or lordes of Chewton saving a cheiffe rent for the watering at the pole without the gate which he thinketh to be under 12d.'

[32] See *Trans. Fed. Inst. Mining Engineers*, **xx**, 528 et seq. and *Somers. Arch. Soc. Proc.* **xv** (2), i; **xli** (2), no. 62 et seq.

[33] Leland tells us in his *Itinerary* (vii, 82) 'Ther were of ancient tyme four comptyd as chefe lords of Mendepe. First the kynge and his parte came to the Bysshope of Bathe as by a Fee Ferme. Glastenbyre had a nothar parte. Bonvill Lord of Bonvile, and now Graye Lord Marques of Dorset was the third owner. The fourthe was Gurney, now Caradoc, *alias* Newton.'

to the king one thousand markes and all the comoners theire bodyes and goods att the king's pleasure that doth either hound or pound.'

We may now consider the Miners' Customs, the version here followed being that found among the State Papers Domestic.[34]

The oulde auncyent custum of the occupasyon of the mynerys in and uppon the Quyns maiestes forest of Mendip wythyn hyr gracys countye of Somerset beyng one of the iiij stapulls of Ynglon whyche hath bene exersysd and contynuyd thrugh the seyd forest frome the tyme wherof man hath noo memory as here after doth pertyculerly doth (sic) apere.

Fyrst of all yeff any man what soever he be that doth intend to venture hys lyfe and to be a workman of the occupasyon he must fyrst of all requere lycence of the lord of the soyll where he doth purpose to work or in hys absence hys offyser cauly[d] the lede-reve or bayliff, whereupon the lord nothyr hys offysers cannot by the ould custm of the occupasyon deny hym that doth so aske lycence.

Item after that fyrst lycense so askyd never to aske lycence no more agayn but to be at hys fre wyll to pyche wythyn the seyd forest of Mendyp and to brecke the ground where and yn what place he or they shaull thynk best hymself for hys oune byhouff and proffyt yowsyng hymself justly and trewly accordyng to the occupacyon.

Item that every man when he doth begyn hys pyt other wysse caulyd a grouff shaull have hys haks throw ij weys after the rake so that he do stand to the gyrdyl or wast in the gruff, that then no man shaull macke nother mell wythyn that ground by the custum of the occupasyon.

Item that when any workman hath landyd any wore he maye carre hyt to weshyng and blowyng to what myndry he semyth best for hys proffyt and commodyte so that he doe paye the tenth of that in lede or wore to the lorde of the soyll where hyt was dyged.

Item that yeff any lorde or lordes of the myndrys or hys offysers have or hereafter doo once gyve lycence to buyld or set up any herth or herthes, howse or howsys to weshe and blowe there wore yn, the tenants once so havyng licence maye kepe hyt, sell hyt or gyve hyt for ever to whom yt shaull plese hym wythout any let or contradcyon so that he do yowse hym self justly and trewly and paye the lote lede the whyche ys the tenth of the flyght and proffytt of that herth and all so to kepe yt tenauntabull accordyng to the lawe and custum of the occupacyon.

Item and yff any man of that occupacyon do peke or stell any lede or lede wore to the valew of 13½d. the lord or hys offyser maye arest and sese apon all hys lede and lede wore, herth and howss, grouff and goods and to kepe hyt as a forfet to hys one yowss and byhouffe and shaull tacke the persson that so hath offendyd and bryng hym where hys howss or wore hys, hys work and towlls with all instruments belongyng to that occupacyon and then put hym yn hys howss or workyng place and set fyer yn all together abowt hym and banyshe hym from that occupacyon for ever by fore the face of all the myners there.

Item and yeff that seydd persson do ever offend

[34] S. P. Dom. Eliz. cclxxxvii, 97. It is undated but may probably belong to the reign of Queen Mary.

any more in that occupasyon by pekyng or stelyng then he shaul be comyttyt to the Quyns geyle for the occupacyon hath no more to do with hym.

Item the lord or lordes of every soyll upon Mendyp ought to kepe a court ij tymes every yere and to caull the myners togyther and to chowse xij of the onestys[t] men so to swere them for the redress of all mysdemeners as concernyng that occupasyon.

Item the lord of every soyll or hys offyser maye mack ther maner of [a]rests as concernyng to that occupasyon, the fyrst ys for stryff bytwyne man and man for there worke under the yerth, the second ys for hys oun dewty of lede and wore wher so ever he or hys offyser do fynd hyt wythyn the seyd forest and the thyrd ys fellons goods as consernyng that occupasyon wheresoever the lord or hys offyser do fynd hyt wythyn the sayd forest.

Item and if there be any man by thys doutfull and dangerous occupasyon tack hys deth and ys slayne by faulyng of the yerth upon hym, by drownyng, by styfflyng with fyer or wother wyse as in tymes past meny hath ben so murthryd the coroner [35] nother no offyser of the Quyns majestys hath not to do with the boddy nother with hys or there goods but the myners of that occupasyon shaulle fetche up that ded boddy, out of the yerth at their oune proper costs and chargs and also to burye hym in Chrystyn buryall allthough he do tacke hys deth lx faddum dyp [36] under the yerth as hereby sore meny a man so hath ben lost.

This copy of the more ancient customs of Mendip may represent as old a text as exists although such a phrase as the 'Quyns maiestes forest' suggests that it was either put into writing or brought up to date in the reign of Queen Mary or of Queen Elizabeth, and more probably at the earlier rather than the later date. In fact it may have been sent up to London when Chewton Mendip, by the attainder of Henry Grey Marquess of Dorset, came into the hands of Queen Mary in 1554. But even as it stands it is not exhaustive of the ancient customs already well-established in the 16th century, or claimed by the miners. Perhaps one of the most striking of these here omitted was the making lawful of any pitch by means of wooden 'stows' or 'styllyngs.' As Charles Dudley said in his deposition [37] with respect to the custom of the 'hill at Lambden upon Mendip' in 1580 'the first pytcher in any grounde muste make yt perfecte wyth a caddel of tymber and a payre of styllyngs within fowre and twentie howers next after the pyching. Yf he doo not so than any other may take the same and woorke yt notwithstanding suche a

firste pytche.' Although both in the depositions of witnesses and in orders of the minery courts stress is laid upon the work being done within twenty-four hours, probably a certain serious amount may have been required and not the absolute completion of the wooden framework which if it were to be of practical value probably necessitated more than one day's work. [38] At least William Bynny of Wookey declared that 'the custom upon Mendip thirty years past was that every first pitcher should set up a cadell of timber within fowre and twentye hours and then within a monthe after a payre of styllyngs, and that was sufficient for a year and a day.' But there may have been some variation in details in different manors. That this custom as well as the various regulations as to the size of claims and their manner of working was of great antiquity there can be no doubt, [39] but they do not seem to have been rigorously formulated in recorded orders of the minery courts until the 16th century. It may indeed be said with some confidence that while the recorded orders of the minery courts were often of the nature of legislation to meet new needs, they sometimes re-stated old customs long before in force, but with suitable adaptation or extension as the circumstances required.

While these ancient customs represented the rights claimed by the miners they could only have been enforced in their entirety when the mining interest was particularly strong. For instance, although the customs lay down very clearly that a miner need be licensed only once and can then dig where he will, the instructions issued by the surveyors [40] of Henry Duke of Suffolk for Chewton Manor insist that 'no manner man begin anie woorck within the said mannor without license and shurties to be brought in to observe the customes belonging to the myndereye' and also 'that no manner tenaunt or other mane begyn anie grove in anie ceverall ground within this mannor but by

---

[35] This very ancient specific repudiation of the coroner's interference is not found in the copy inscribed on the Waldegrave map. See J. McMurtrie, F.G.S., 'Notes on the Forest of Mendip' in *Trans. Fed. Inst. of Mining Engineers*, xx, 534.

[36] This, as Mr. McMurtrie has observed, 'was no doubt an extreme depth in the days to which it refers, possibly a depth rarely if ever reached.'

[37] Memo. R. (L.T.R.) Hil. 22 Eliz.

[38] Silvester Dudley uses the terms 'a lawfull payr of stowes and a lawful cadill of tymber.' Memo. R. (L.T.R.) Hil. 22 Eliz. m. 1. et seq. Again an old and experienced miner early in the reign of James I deposed 'that there was an auncient custom used as well within the libertie of the said Mr. Walgrave (i.e. Chewton) as in other parts of the said forest, that if any person beinge a workeman allowed, did make any pitch within any the said liberties as especially within the liberties of the said Mr. Walgrave and did sett in one course of tymber, with speeks and stoppings and a pair of stillings, yt was and should be lawful for the owners of the said pitche to have and enjoy all such pitch and pitches by the space of one yeare and a daie . . . against any other which shall make claime to the same sol as the same be lawfully kept.' Exch. Dep. by Com. Mich. 9 James I, no. 15.

[39] For similar regulations in Derbyshire see *V.C.H. Derby*. ii, 323, et seq.

[40] S.P. Dom. Add. Mary vii, 42.

specyall lycense from the lord.' The more powerful lords royal used every effort to ensure that lead ore raised on their own lands should be smelted at the furnaces of the lordship. The surveyors already quoted ordered 'that no man sholde have anye hearth in the sayde mannor to smelt leade but the lorde onelie like as the same order is taken in other mynderies to the same adjoyning, also that none shoolde smelt but at the lordes hearthes without license of the officer.'[41] For the particulars of the revision of the ancient customs, agreed upon in 1554 at Chewton Mendip and the later orders of the minery courts of this manor the reader must be referred to the exhaustive account of Mr. J. McMurtrie already referred to. Whether any formulated codes of early orders for the Harptree and Glastonbury mineries still exist does not appear, but under the names of the mineries of Richmond and Charterhouse Hidon mineral grand juries still met and did business in the 17th century.

One copy of the revised customary laws and later orders of the minery of Bath and Wells is contained in a 17th-century MS. known as Browne's Book at the Bishop's Registry, and as this has not yet been printed in full, some account of its chief features may be given here. The particular codification contained in this book was approved in 1612 by a grand jury of a mineral court for the liberty of Bishop Montagu, but it largely represents the usages prevalent in this minery during the reign of Elizabeth and so may be considered in this place. Appropriately enough as befits an episcopal jurisdiction the code opens with an order that none 'shall woorke watche or keepe possession in or all anie grooffe or woorke uppon the hill of Mendippe or all the mineries on anie Sabboath daie or holiedaie uppon paine of £5.' Later, after the year 1638, with the growth of Puritanism this order as to holidays was modified but the prohibition as to Sundays remained. There were also penalties for removing or stealing of goods left on the hill during holidays or Sabbath days. The third order forbade the maintenance of a banished man on pain of the forfeiture of lead ore, hearths and goods. Lead-ore carriers again or other workmen were warned not to have with them ' anie dogge to thannoyance or huntinge of anie manes cattell or sheepe ' on pain of half a mark to the lord and making good the damage. Relations between graziers and lead-miners were often strained enough without such gratuitous provocation. The fifth order denied the right of any man in mineral causes to sue at common law without the licence of the grand jury. Mining cases should be tried by ' the lawe of this hill.' The penalty of such disloyal abandonment of the minery courts was that the

offender should for the first offence lose all his goods within the liberty, one half to the lord and the other half to the party sued. A repeated offence entailed perpetual banishment from the hill of Mendip. But a suit at common law was permitted for ' debt, dutie or agreement by writinge.' Order 6 deals with the making lawful of the mine—

We order that yf anie person shall pitche anie gribbe or pitch within this libertie hee shall within fower and twentie houres after make the same lawful with a paire of sufficient stillinges, beames and forkes and then shall work the same according to the custome, provided alwayes that yf anie pitche grib or grooffe lye unlawfull by the space of eight and twentie daies and the lead-reeve cause proclamacion either at the hill or mineries to be made in a waiedaie in the hearinge of twelve workmen att the leaste and recordinge the names of the saide woorkmen to witnesse the same in his booke, then it shall be lawfull for the said lead-reeve after fowereteene daies after the saide proclamacion made, yf tholde partneres shall not worke the same in the meane season according to the custome to give the saide grib pitche or grooffe freelie and without rewarde or other promises to anie workeman that shall worke the same accordinge to this order.

And provisions were added against corrupt practices or favouritism on the part of the lead-reeve or other officer concerned.

Apparently in the past much harsh dealing had taken place under colour of ' arrests ' and order was taken that henceforth the lead-reeve only was to make arrest on any man's goods ' for anie controversie between partie and partie,' and it was further provided under penalties sharp and severe that none should carry away goods arrested by the lead-reeve, his deputy or servant ' before sufficient suerties be putte in to the lead-reeve or triall thereupon or agreement with the party.'

The rules for the throwing of the hacke [42] are very curious, and certain details seem to be recorded in the Priddy minery customs alone :

Whosoever throweth the hacke in anie grooffe or gribbe shalbe one of the then eldeste parteners of the same grooffe or gribbe and that without fraude or deceipt. That is not meant eldest in age onlesse hee be the then elder partener and noe man shall have the benefitte of the hackes throwe but twoe waies viz. after the rake according to the custome and the hacke to be in waighte three poundes fowreteene ounces as the more aunciente hacke is.

The younger pitcher shall compell thelder pitcher and his partners to throwe the hacke when they have theire chine, rake or course, within 14 daies after the saide hacke is proffered unto them by the lords officer or else the offender to loose the benefittes of the saide hackes throwe unto the partie grevied and hee that throweth shal be the partie in the order aforesaid.

---

41 S.P. Dom. Add. Mary vii, 42.

42 Cf. the fixing of distances between pits in the Forest of Dean by the miner standing and casting ' ridding and stones soe farr from him with a bale as the manner is ' (V.C.H. Glouc. ii, 222).

It was also ordered that whoever possessed a lawful 'grooffe within this libertie shall have eighteene foote of grounde on everie side of his pitche as he is or shal be thelder pitcher and it shalbe lawfull for him to enjoye the saide grounde in lengthe and breadth accordinglie how manie courses or chines soever hee findeth within the plumme of the aforesaid grounde so as hee findeth the said chines or courses lawfullie within the 18 foote of his firste pitche.'

Disputes about encroachments were frequent, although it was ordered that none should work out of his own ground or pitch within the ground of another ; indeed the grand jury of 1612 affirmed that stealing underground should be from henceforth felony and the culprit or culprits ' shall lose all his or their goodes in as ample manner ' as if they had committed felony above ground. If any miner suspected that he was being robbed or wronged by his neighbour workman underneath the earth ' whiles he is bringinge downe his grooffe after the pins and bounds of his grooffe and grounde beinge knowen above the earthe ' he might complain to the steward or his sworn deputy or to the grand jury, when it should be lawful for the 'steward, deputie or jurie to swear and appointe twoe or more honeste discreete and skilfull men at the charges of the plaintiff to examine and plumme the said groundes and groofes ' and report thereupon in order that measures might be ' taken for reformacion and securing of the wronged partie when he shall bring downe his groofe.' It is evident from additional rules and penalties that the ' plummers ' were sometimes resisted [43] or found the ' grooffes to be walled, dammed or filled' in order to hinder their survey, that occasionally dishonest groviers took advantage of Sundays and holidays to spy out the secrets of their neighbours' works or even broke down stillings to make a ' lawful groof or pitch' unlawful. Assaults and riots were not unfrequent, but a malicious blow entailed a fine of half a mark and another half mark if blood were drawn, or if a weapon were used 20s. A lad under twenty-one years of age was forbidden to work ' at his owne hande '; he must either have a master or work with his father.

All who had ' anie dealinges in mineral matters uppon this foreste ' were bound to serve on the minery juries when warned by the lead-reeve or his deputy under pain of a fine of £1 to the lord and ' further yf anie man ympannelled shall make defaulte to meete and theire to doe his service att theire meetings with his fellowes he shall loose for everie such offence 5s. to be levied forthwith by the lead-reeve towards the diett of the rest of the jurie.' If an empanelled man left the meeting before the verdict was given he was liable to a fine of £10. It was the duty of the lead-reeves or one of them ' to give their attendance to doe such service as shal be required by the Grand Juries att theire meetinges ' and in the case of the petty jury it was the rule that the ' lead-reeve that made the arrest and received the warrante and ffee shall give attendance.'

All ' pawnes, pledges or mortgages ' on ' partes grooves, leadore or goods ' must be recorded in the lead-reeve's book or be utterly void. The fee for such entry should be 2d. and no more and the ' leidger book ' was to lie at the minery storehouse where it was allowed that '·everie persone maie search for such recordinge' freely without fee but for a copy of the entry the lead-reeve was entitled to charge 1d. If the absence of a record was due to the lead-reeve's fault, he must forfeit £5, and the mortgage or pledge should stand good notwithstanding his negligence. Trial after an arrest was not to be long delayed, the extreme limit being twenty-eight days, and wilful perjury was punished by forfeiture of goods to the lord and banishment from the occupation.

The interests of the working miner were well guarded by the twenty-sixth order of the Wells code, which enacted that :

If anie workeman shal be sette on worke by anie man and shal be behinde of his wages for the space of eighte days and prove the same due by his owne oathe and one honeste witnes more to anie of the lordes leadreeves and that he wroughte six howres in winter and eighte howres in sommer each daye then presentlie after suche oathe taken the said officer shall sell soe much goods of such partie or parties as shoulde paie the saide wages. But yf hee cannott finde so much goods within this libertie of the said parties as shall satisfie the said parties of this saide wages, then the officer shall warne the partie or parties yf hee maie speake with them or him to paie the saide wages within twoe daies after, or else, yf he cannot convenientlie speake with him shall make proclamacion att the grooffe or place where the saide wages was earned in the audience or hearinge of three or fower to bring in and paie the same within seaven daies then nexte followinge or else to lose 11s. or theire part or partes in the grooffe, worke or pitch soe wroughte to the saide workeman or to anie other that shall paye or laie oute the same att choise of the woorkeman.

Such a procedure evidently furnished a summary and cheap process for the recovery of wages from a dishonest or shifty employer. It is evident from these and later regulations that the harmony and order of the mining community on Mendip would be largely affected by the honesty and tact of the lead-reeves and we find stringent orders against bribery, maintenance and other abuses.

Order 30 is of importance as defining to some

[43] The Chewton code contains one order of a much later date, insisting on the proper ' timbering' of grooves to ensure the safety of the official inspectors.

extent the distinction between the petty and grand juries:

If anie verdicte by anie petite jurie parse, yf itt be withoute exceptions, itt shall stande for ever excepte itt be reversed by the nexte or ensewinge grand jurie of the courte followinge and that shal be onlie saide a grand jurie whearein are above twelve persons in the saide jurie.

Apparently the normal twenty-four of the grand jury was not always reached. It fell to the duty of the lead-reeves to summon the petty juries, but ' if it be a waightie cause, that then yf the plaintiff will it shal be tried before the steward ' at the Guildhall at Wells. It is worth note that order 53 forbade the corrupt packing of a jury. No convicted perjurer could be received to testify, but all other witnesses summoned were bound to give evidence if the parties calling them paid 8*d.* a day to each witness for his attendance. Adverse decisions were not always received with silent resignation, but opprobrious words against any officer, grand jury or juryman were punishable by a fine of 20*s.*, a moiety to go to the person or persons vilified and the other moiety to the lord. The scale of fees payable was on the whole moderate, when the expeditious process and speedy relief obtainable are taken into account.

To steward for his warrant for a jury	4*d.*
Copy of the order of presentment	4*d.*
To the swearer of the jury at the Hill	6*d.*
To the steward for swearing the jury at the Hall	6*d.*
To lead-reeves for an arrest	4*d.*
To lead-reeves for summoning a jury	4*d.*
To the crier for the petty jury	6*d.*
For trial of any cause by the grand jury to be paid by him for whom the verdict shall pass	4*d.*
To the jury at the Hill	6*s.*
To the jury at the Hall	8*s.*
For the steward's warrant for execution	4*d.*
To the lead-reeves for serving the execution	4*d.*
And for a proclamation and recording of the same	2*d.*

As to the keeping of records it was provided in and possibly before 1612 that:

All verdicts and presentments of any grand juries or petite juries hereafter to be made shal be within two moneths recorded in the parchment leidger booke alreadie provided for that purpose upon paine of £5 for recordinge of which severall presentments of petite juries and grand juries the steward shall have 1*d.* onlie and noe more, to be paid by him before the record shall passe, and such other consideracion as itt shall please the Lorde Bushoppe for the time beinge to allowe.

Several regulations dealt with shares or ' partes to the share ' in pitches or grooves, their proper working and the rights of the ' freeman ' or his assigns in certain contingencies, but they simply affirm the principles of equitable dealing and must be passed over here for lack of space.

One very important proviso was, however, that in case of dispute about any groof claimants must see that arrests be made ' before the said grooffe or pitche be wroughte or sunke down five fadome.'

Many orders relate to the buddling and smelting of the ore, as no. 43, which enacts that no man shall let out the water of the minery ponds ' otherwise then it hath beene there used continuallie beyond the memorie of man ' while by no. 45:

Whosoever beinge a woorkeman in the minerie uppon lawfull warninge given vnto him by a leadreeve for the castinge [44] repairinge and amendinge of the common sowe [45] shall helpe bestowe his beste labour or yeald charges accordinge as in times paste hath beene used and whosoever shall refuse to perfourme this order shall forfeite for everie such offence to the lorde of this libertie twoe shillinges to be levied of his oare, lead and goodes.

Owing to its insufficiency this order was supplemented a little later by the decree that:

Henceforth every hearth within this liberty shall pay to the casting of the common sowe 1*s.* 6*d.*, every workinge howse shall pay 12*d.*, every broad buddle that taketh his water out of the common sowe or turneth his water into the same shall pay 6*d.* and every other buddle shall paye 3*d.*

With a jealous pastoral interest ever at hand to resent interference with a very limited water-supply, a situation made especially acute in a lead-mining district owing to the poisonous character of the refuse, orders as to buddling abuses were frequent. In the code of 1612 no. 47 decrees that:

Whosoever hath more broad buddells then one that belongeth to a howse shall pull it upp under the paine of 40*s.* and that noe man laie anie more broade buddells from hencefoorthe to one howse without license of the grand jurie or leadreeve under the like paine of 40*s.*

And another order adds:

That all buddles that are att Whorewalles(?) that are within howses and without, the owners theareof, shall surcease theire workinge or cause the same to be surceased yearlie hereafter att or before the thirde daie of Maye nexte unto the firste of November nexte uppon paine of everie man so offending £5. . . . And when there is anie working theare that then the watercourse shall be sufficiently kepte and scowred to the swallet *for safetie of the cattell* under the payne of £5.

Soon after the settling or confirmation of this order it was decreed that ' whereas there hath been heretofore in Priddy mynery many abuses committed by workemen by castinge of holes for old stuffe and by layinge of buddles whereby the highway that leadeth through the said mynery is much annoyed and the water pound and the bankes thereof much spoiled and decayed '

[44] i.e. digging.　　[45] i.e. drain or water-course.

these encroachments must cease and the workmen fill up their holes and take up their buddles. Constant orders and verdicts dealt with buddling at Pen Pools, and were as constantly being revised or revoked. One of the latest in Browne's Book, a verdict of a grand jury after 1651 apparently, orders :

That every person or persons that now hath or hereafter shall have any buddle or buddles in Priddy minery shall make a sufficient pitt to take the *solime* in within fourty foote of his buddle and shall keep the sayd pitt soficiently scowred and from thence shall make a streame to carry the water in the common sowe.

It was further ordered that no person should turn the water out of the ancient water-courses called the common sowe into any swallet 'before the sayd water run to Crowmbridge.'

In respect to the hearths in use it was enacted by no. 44 of the code of 1612 :

That no slagge hearthe [46] shalbe sette on worke to beate anie oare hearthe beinge att worke uppon paine of fortie shillings uppon everie one offending theerin for everie offence.

Of the penalty one-half to go to the lord and one-half to the party aggrieved. This may refer to competition between slag-hearths with an artificial blast and the older development of the bole sometimes known as the turn-hearth. The matter is complicated by the fact that Schutz and his partner Humfrey had between 1560 and 1570 erected improved furnaces with bellows either sheltered in a building or in some way covered at Beauchief in Derbyshire, and these modifications may have possibly spread elsewhere. But some contemporary accounts of the Mendip hearths will be noticed later in the article.

It was also ordered, as might be expected, that no ore was to be carried from the bishop's mineries to be blown or smelted elsewhere except by the licence of the lead-reeve, and this would not apparently be granted unless the home hearths were insufficient. There were again strict regulations at Priddy minery as to the weighing and stamping of the metal smelted. The usual weigh-days were Tuesdays and Fridays between 8 a.m. and 4 p.m. unless they happened to be holidays, when the weighing took place on the eves. It was also ordered that no man should sell or receive any 'dagon' or piece of lead or 'potterne ore' [47] unweighed, while each 'dagon' or piece must be stamped with the minery mark. Either seller or buyer violating this rule was liable to severe penalties, for the first offence a fine of 20*s.* which should go half to the lord and half to the informer, and for the second a penalty of £10 or in default banishment from the occupation.

The last order of the code of 1612 deals with the case, by no means infrequent, when a workman by his workmanship should strike the groof or workmanship of another. Both miners were then to cease working, and the grand jury if sitting, or otherwise the steward, should cause three or four sufficient workmen to plumb or examine the workings and report to a jury which would decide the controversy.

After the codification of the customs of the bishop's minery in 1612 all earlier orders not confirmed were to be void. The members of the grand jury who at this time signed the code of customs were fifteen in number and of these nine made their mark. The list includes several well-known mining names, as for example John Sage, Thomas Browne, Thomas Kingeman, John Horler, John Mattocke and Richard Shephard.

Some of the later orders of Priddy minery have already been referred to, but one other may be mentioned here as bearing on a technical matter of importance in the working of the mines or grooves. Not long after 1612 it was ordered that :

None shall lay any ffyer in their grooffe or grooves in their chyne, rake or course after itt is knowne that the smoake thereof may hurte or offend their neighbour grovyers by reason of any leare underneath the earth or by means of workemanshipp or by another means whatsoever butt on the Satturday at afternone or on holiday eves at afternoone.

And further no fires were to be kindled until their neighbours had received sufficient warning. Gunpowder does not seem to have been employed until towards the end of the 17th century.

Some light is thrown on allusions in these customs to the smelting processes employed on Mendip by certain documents we owe to some legal proceedings in 1582 and the following years, relating to patents originally granted to Humfrey an assayer at the mint and his German partner Schutz, which had already been infringed or were alleged to have been infringed before Humfrey's death, as well as afterwards during the lifetime of his widow. The 'Relation [48] of the Order and manner of gettinge, cleansinge and meltinge of Lead Ewer at Mendip' here quoted was made by Cornelius Avenant and apparently represents the depositions of miners and other expert witnesses before Mr. Baron Clynche in the Court of Exchequer.

---

[46] In order 46 also there is a reference to the presentment of 'all newe and younge hearthes of the mineries within this libertie whensoever anie of them shall annoye and hurte anie of the elder hearthes.'

[47] By 'potterne ore' it is probable that manganese may be intended. See Dr. Merrett's observations on chap. 13 of Antonio Neri's *Art of Glass* (1662), 289.

[48] Lansd. MS. 40, fol. 159 d. et seq.

First they get up their ewer myngled with earth, calke and sparr forth of the growffes or rakes and after they carry the same downe by waynes to a place where water is, called the mynery, provided for the washinge clensinge and meltinge thereof where they have erected certen washinge trowhes of one ell a pece in length, and one yard a pece in breadth through which their is turned a litle small streame of water runinge through them. Into which troughes they put the said ewer by certain quantityes accordinge to the contentes of the said trowghes, and puddele it there to and fro with a puddling spade or shovell. After suche puddelinge they cast the said ewer into an other trowgh in a howse where they washe it agayne. After such puddelinge and washinge they cast up the said ewer and laye it upon a great stone which they call a bynge-stone or knock-stone, whereupon they beate it with yron hammers (which they call bucker [s]) unto the smallnes of bay salt. Then they riddle or syfte the same beaten ewer with a riddle or sive muche like of the wydenes of a pease riddell.

Then they clense the same syfted ewer agayne in the trowghes aforenamed with such puddelinge shoveles aforesaid till they have made it perfect and clene ewer and then they cast it uppon a binge or heape. After all this they melt the same ewer at a turne-harthe made without howse for gruff or great ewer only. And for that by and after suche workmanshipp in the premisses there is allweyes left some quantitie of smetham or small ewer called forsleddes which the water from tyme to tyme beareth downe to the neather ende of the trowghes. Therefor nowe of late within the space of x yeares last past they have founde meanes to part and devide the same smetham with syves (which they call northern sives) muche like unto the sive nowe used in Darbie and brought in by Humfries, for the better view and tryall whereof one of the same sives used in Darbie was brought to Mendip 14 April 1584 and sene and compared together by the workemen and witnesses of these presentes hereunder namely expressed.

Avenant goes on to relate that the northern sieves had been introduced into Somerset by Dennis Pynner of Wedmore, 'a workeman or wassher of ewer at Mendip' who had worked at the Beauchief works in Derbyshire, and 'for some reward gyven subtilye and secretly' obtained one of Humfrey's sieves which he had delivered to his partner Powell, who had first used it in Mendip. This is an *ex parte* statement and was rebutted apparently by other evidence which the author of this relation unkindly terms the 'perjury of William Furnace and others'; at least according to Coke it was decided that there had in the case of this sieve been prior user at Mendip.[49]

The writer of our relation then declares :

that by and throughe suche syves they (the Mendip workmen) devide in fattes or tubbes of water the said small smetham. But they cannot melt the said smetham or ewer, so gotten by the syve, at their turneharthes aforesaid, but by another harth called a slageharthe, much like the ould slagharth used in Derbie before Humfryes invencion of his newe harth. Note allso

[49] *Law Quarterly Rev.* xii, 148.

the nature and propertie of the ewer uppon Mendip is suche, that they cannot melt it till they have beaten it as small as bay salt, for if it be molten bigger, then the ewer will sparcle and flye away to their great losse, for which cause they have had allweyes a longe tyme little riddels some of wood, some of heare, some of yron and some of brasse or pewter made basonwise, full of holes like a cullinder, therewith all to part and devide the great ewer from the small that the great ewer maie be carryed to the byngestone, and the small ewer to the slage harth aforesaid.

Also in summing up the relation the author, Cornelius Avenant, again alludes to the 'meltynge the same gruff ewer at their *turneharthes* without howse and not usuall for all weathers and the smetham or small ewer at their *slagharth*' and contrasts :

the great difference thereof from the clensinge and meltinge of their ewer in Derbie after Humfryes newe invention there, where they onely bringe fattes or tubbes of water as well to the mynes syde as to the ould rackes and so with no more adoe they clense the gruff ewer even as the small ewer in the same fattes with the newe syve of Humfreyes invention and presently melt the same both sortes of ewer all at one manner of harthe[50] made there, with a howse usuall at all weathers, by that excellent, speedye and most profitable invention of Humfreyes.

Now it is quite clear from the above, as well as from the orders of Priddy minery, that two types of hearth were at this time in use at Mendip, the turn-hearth or ore-hearth and the slag-hearth. And it would seem not unlikely, judging from analogy elsewhere, that the turn-hearth was a development of a primitive bole or wind-hearth with machinery for adjusting it to any prevailing wind, while the slag-hearth from its very name suggests a furnace supplied with an artificial blast where charcoal was used for smelting black work or slag and also apparently ore otherwise intractable. But some difficulty is raised with respect to the turn-hearth by a certificate[51] relating thereto of the year 24 Elizabeth.

Item we fynde the hearthes that are now used at Mendip aforesayde for the meltynge of rawe leade owre the lyke have byn ther contynuallie used to be turned about as the wynde doth change and none others by the space of fortie yeare and upwards by the testimonye of one Robert Saige of Predye of his knowleidge by the space of fiftie yeare, and of one John Wylmott of Predye aforesayde of his knowleidge by the lyke space and we verified by dyvers others ; but before that tyme we fynde by examynation that they were made first upon the grounde and not to be turned and then as the wynde did turne they were enforced *to remove ther bellowes to other hearthes*. Also we fynde the firestone of everye hearthe, whiche com-

[50] Humfrey's hearth seems to have been an improvement on the older slag-hearth and may have resembled one of those furnaces figured in Agricola's *De Re Metallica*.

[51] Exch. Spec. Com. 24 Eliz. no. 1955.

monlie within a wyke ys burnt out and must be newe made, are altered and made broder or lesser, hier or lower as the owre doth differ if nature for some will have a greater [heate ?] and some a lesser.

Now if ' bellows ' in the above extract must be interpreted as referring to fixed bellows for the production of an artificial blast it is difficult to see how the old hearth from which the turn-hearth was developed differed in essence from the slaghearth. It is unfortunate that we have here a certificate rendered by three gentleman commissioners and not apparently the very words of the depositions of the expert witnesses at Wells.[52]

During the 16th and early 17th centuries mining on Mendip was as active as at any time in the history of this field, the local groviers constantly opening up fresh shafts, for the most part of no great depth, within the chief minery districts of Priddy, Chewton, Richmond and Charterhouse Hidon as well as at Winscombe, where the Dean and chapter of Wells were lords royal, and elsewhere. Speculators and adventurers were ready to advance capital in return for ' parts ' or shares and mortgages. Bristol merchants, neighbouring gentlemen, local publicans [53] all took a hand in the game. Disputes were naturally frequent, with all the conflicting interests involved, and now and again carried from the minery tribunals into the king's courts by some wealthy litigant unpopular with the local groviers. In the 16th century at least much lead was exported from Bristol, and a portion of this—possibly the largest portion—was from the Mendips. Spain was a ready customer and in spite of the feverish activities of the council doubtless many an ounce of Mendip lead found its billet in Englishman or Netherlander.[55] During the most prosperous time of the Mendip lead-mining the revenue from lot-lead received by the lords of liberties was enormous. In Priddy minery as Strachey wrote [54] in the 18th century ' Bishop Still is

said to have had the harvest, Bishop Montague the gleanings, and Bishop Lake the stubble; and yet the profit of lead to this last was very considerable, as it hath also been to some of his successors.'

The technical methods employed by the smaller men were little different in the 16th century from what they had been three or four centuries previous; most groviers avoided deep-level mining with its attendant expense for keeping water under, although they appreciated drainage works done by others and were quite ready to strike in and take advantage of the profit without paying any share of the costs. The nearness of the pitches and shafts led to constant clashes underground, and a vivid idea of the conditions prevailing may be obtained from the Elizabethan depositions, though it is at times difficult to rescue truth from the bottom of the well to which she has been consigned by the sworn deponent. Richard James of Kilmersdon,[56] belonging to a family who did well both by coal and lead, testified that after any man ' hathe fownde a rake or a chyne he may not pas over nor through any clyff to follow an issue or a sparre by the custom of the hill into another man's rake for he sayeth the cliffe is alwayes a barre and therefore the hole in the harde gruffe may not geve any advantage to passe into the rake on the other syde of the cliffe. And for example he sayth that a woorke in Grene Owre one William Bynnye and his partner were putt backe in Pykeringes rake in such a case.' Charles Dudley at the same time confirms James' account and declares ' that Roger Tyllye of Chuton and his partners were in lyke maner putt back for enteringe by an issue or sparr in through a clyffe to a woorke of William Plumley and his partners at Greene Owre.' Again Richard Fyler of Ubley had been a workman from childhood on Lambden and was at the time of his evidence aged fifty-five. He and his partners ' were the fyrste pytchers at a place called Haresdowne and folowing an yssue through a cliffe cam into another mans woorke named Henry Radford whereuppon a jurye was called and they gave verdict that the said examinate and his partners had no right so to doo and so they were putt back.' William Bynny of Wookey above-mentioned not only remembered cases of similar encroachment and ' putting back ' in Green Ore, but also deposed that he was ' partner in a gruff called Broad Rake in Rowepytts and there found a chappe of wore and then one Thomas Terry and his partners came following an issue owte of theire owne ground through a cliffe and entered upon the woorke of this examinate

[52] It is practically certain that at an early period the wind-hearth or bole was in use in Somerset as in Derbyshire, Durham and Devon. At or near the Devon mines in the early 14th century some kind of ' versatile ingenium ' was used for a time in connexion with a furnace employed largely for dealing with slag from the boles. Note payments in January 1304, ' Waltero Smalhyghe mundanti conductum aque et removenti terram a puteo fornelli versatilis per tres dies et dimidiam. . . . Item Willelmo le Wowere fornellario fundenti nigrum opus et facienti fornellum super *ingenium versatile.*' Accts. Exch. K. R. bdle. 260, no 22. But it may be argued that this refers merely to a bellows worked by water-power. The subject requires further investigation.

[53] Cf. Court of Req. bdle, 49, no. 43.

[54] *Compleat Hist. of Somerset*, 128a.

[55] Constant allusions to illegal export of lead will be found in the various collections of State Papers.

Cf. Lansd. MS. 64, fol. 71 and *Cecil MSS.* (Hist. MSS. Com.) iv, 176.

[56] The illustrations here given are in part from Mem. R. (L.T.R.) Hil. 22 Eliz. m. 1 et seq.

and his partners, and upon complaynt made the offycers took order that the sayd Terry and his partners did recompense to the sayd examinate with 16 hundred of leade, and so they didd and were also put back again.' Such encounters were indeed frequent and their consideration and settlement formed a large part of the work of the juries of the mineral courts.

Besides the usual ventures of the smaller men, occasionally a capitalist of influence and position attempted to deal with the deeper and as he hoped richer deposits of ore, and to that end embarked on extensive drainage schemes, employing the latest machinery, doubtless introduced from Germany or at least copied from German models. Bevis Bulmer is the best known example of a wealthy and scientific mining adventurer who worked during the 16th century on the Mendips. The scene of his operations was at Rowpits within the jurisdiction of the Chewton mineral courts. About the middle of the 17th century there were ancient miners still living who remembered [57] that 'the forebreast of Sir Bevis Bulmer's work was nine foot wide in ore,' and it was probably this Broad Rake that first attracted his attention. Bevis Bulmer, at this time 'gentleman' and not yet 'knight,' was soon in controversy with such 'claymers and pitchers' as had pitched and taken up the ground from him upon or near Broad Rake where he was then working or within 100 feet on either side. The pitchers evidently desired to profit by the 'engines and instruments for the drawing of water from the same workes' of Bulmer but had neglected to take their share of the very heavy charges expended. The ringleader was one Edward Morse 'a verie troublesome person and at this tyme banyshed by the lawes and orders for the mineryes within the manour of Chewton from working within the said manour, notwithstanding [which] he doth molest and troble the workes of the said Bulmer.' Ultimately Bulmer seems to have abandoned his works which soon became waterlogged, and a few years later is found exploiting the old silver-lead mines of Combe Martin where he was no longer hampered by ancient customs or jealous groviers.

Late in the time of the Commonwealth [58] Bevis Bulmer's abandoned work was again taken in hand by Mr. Thomas Bushell, a mining speculator of original views and great repute who was never weary of proclaiming his discipleship to Lord Chancellor Bacon. For the philosopher of the New Atlantis had not only instructed his pupil in mineral secrets but on

several occasions paid his debts. In April 1657 Bushell wrote to certain representative Mendip miners that he had been informed by their fellows that 'millions of wealth lie in Rowpits near Chewton minery which yet cannot be recovered from the inundation of water by the greatest artists of former ages.' He however having considered the matter and viewed the place proposed to place at their disposal 'the experience of practical endeavour.' The miners closed with the offer. 'Manna from heaven was not more welcome to the pilgrims of Israel than the good news your letter brought to us.' 'For a month or two of a droughty summer,' they continue, 'we behold the appearance of much treasure lying in the veins of those metal lodes and so soon as we are preparing for harvest to reap a mite of its mineral profit, the inundation of water takes away our present position and leaves us exposed to a sad condition having no other profession for our livelihood.' In short they begged him to drain 'the rake called the Broad Rake of Sir Bevis Bulmer's works in Rowpits near Chewton minery, which is known to be the lowest level and sole of those works.' Further the miners declared :

We do herein engage ourselves under our hands and seals and on the behalf of all others that shall hereafter work in the said rake that you and your assigns shall have the moiety of the whole paying half the charge ; and likewise procure the lord of the soil to do the like, if you please to proceed with speed for the perfecting of the same ; and in token of our affection to serve you we have presumed not only to petition his Highness in your behalf for the better encouragement, but also oblige ourselves to tender you the first refusal of all our parts and shares of ore, paying ready money and giving us from time to time the same rate as other merchants shall conceive it to be worth.'

This letter was signed by twenty-nine miners or mineral men of Chewton Mendip and other mineries, while petitions were soon after addressed to the Lord Protector by the 'mineral-bounders within the county of Somerset' signed by thirty-eight members of the grand jury of Richmond liberty and by twenty-five members of the grand jury of the liberty of Charterhouse Hidon.

But in spite of all this enthusiasm Bushell, though favoured by the central authorities, found himself face to face with all the difficulties experienced by his Elizabethan predecessor. The native groviers, or some of them, feared that Bushell intended to make the works a mine royal to the prejudice of their ancient customs and liberties, and resented as well the employment of 'foreign workmen.' Indeed his manager Christopher Wright made affidavit on 3 December, 1658 :

that by some malicious persons there was a great lake of muddy water turned about the hour of midnight,

---

[57] Bushell's *Abridgement*. Cf. *Acts P.C.* (New Ser.) xiv, 353, under date 'The last of Feb. 1586.'

[58] This account is mainly based on the documents printed in Bushell's *Abridgement*, on notices in the S.P. Dom. and the Orders of the Mineral Grand Jury of Chewton.

and upon a great flood, into the swallow, on purpose as is conceived to choke it, and so consequently to drown his men that came from foreign parts and were then working 20 fathom deep, which this deponent doth aver were forced to save their lives by running up their grooves at the same time, the swallow being not able to receive the torrent of its water. And this deponent doth likewise depose that about 10 Oct. last there was some other such envious person who pulled down so much of the under timber of his shaft that the whole groove of earth fell into Mr. Bushell's drift, when his men were at work underneath, and it was supposed by divers never to be recovered. But thanks be to God the danger is past and Mr. Bushell's drift goeth on towards the rich works known to lie 150 fathom before him; for this deponent was one of the workmen that landed £100 per week out of one shaft this last summer and saw £200 per week out of another; but the charge of drawing water though in the drought of summer stood (as is reported) in £80 per week apiece, which Mr. Bushell's drift will prevent, and likewise to 1,000 more of the like nature as are supposed to be within the verge of Rowpits.

Besides these specific offences we know from a sympathetic preamble of an order of the Chewton grand jury certain groviers had stolen Bushell's tools from his works, depraved his person with scandalous language and made new pitches in Rowpits before him ' so soon as they saw the forefield of Mr. Bushell's drift from his swallow had but a vein of ground ore 4 foot wide and 3 fathom high to cherish his undertakings,' uncivil actions, as they said, contrary to all equity and good conscience. In fact the better sort of local mining-men were fain to urge the Protector not only to confirm the banishment from the occupation decreed by the grand juries against evildoers but also to transport these to the 'mines' of Jamaica. Precisely how long Bushell continued his efforts at Rowpits is a matter of uncertainty, but there is little reason to suppose that his enterprise was a financial success. Soon after the Restoration, we know that this veteran royalist was being hounded by his creditors and at his wits' end to escape them.[59] He seems however to have been assisted in these Somerset schemes by Sir Edmund Windham, whose name is associated with his in the efforts made to drain the mines at Rowpits.

The depositions [60] taken in a suit of law in the reign of Charles II contain much information of various interest relating to the mining industry of Mendip. We there learn that in Chewton Manor the tenants of certain customary holdings known as 'Neate Places' had always severally paid 3d. a ton yearly for the carriage to Bristol or other ports of the lot that is the tenth of the lead digged and made within the manor under the name of 'loading money,' while the holders of other tenements called 'Fardell Places' have paid 2d. a ton and the holders of the 'Landlesse Places' 1d. a ton in similar fashion unless a composition had been made. The full 3d. was not however always paid without some deduction, for Richard Plaister declared that he never knew the loading money refused except that since thirty years they have paid for only seventeen out of twenty tons lot-lead at 3d. as aforesaid. In the case of the 'Fardell' and 'Landlesse' tenements twenty tons had been paid for as seventeen tons, ' which answered the lord's demand after the rate of 5s. per ton loading money.' He remembered that in 1653 when he was lead-reeve some of the 'Neateplace tenants did pay him as collector the full 3d. the ton and some did deduct part of it.' A much later witness called for the defendants may perhaps have been right when he expressed a belief that the loading money due was 5s. but that the regular rates if paid furnished an overplus. This the 'lead-reeves did convert to their own use which when the tenants came to understand . . . made them not to pay the full sums of 3d., 2d. and 1d.' Probably the carrying service for which the loading money was a commutation had its origin in remote antiquity,[61] though the defendants whose refusal to pay had brought about the suit considered the carriage of the lord's lead had been a 'voluntary and free act of kindness.'

As to the election of the lead-reeves evidence was given ' that the lords of Chewton did about Michaelmas yearly keep a manor-court, and customary tenants were there chosen and presented by the homage to be lead-reeves for the year ensuing and were then at the mineral court following their election sworn by the steward for the time being. John Purnell declared that:

this was usually done for many years together, and so it continued till of late years and that the said lead-reeves so chosen do each of them receive a certain salary of 6s. 8d. for their service of the lord of the said manor, and further saith that the said lead-reeves are sworn to give a just account of what lead or money or ore they shall receive to the lord's use at Our Lady Day next after their being sworn and at Michaelmas ensuing they are to pay the money so accompted for at Our Lady Day before, and at the same Michaelmas they are to account for the other half year and to pay in the money at our Lady Day then next.'

The same witness also declared that for eight, nine or ten years past no manor court had been kept by the complainants John Buckland, esq. and John Bendish, gentleman, lords of the manor of Chewton, to choose lead-reeves and other

[59] S.P. Dom. Chas. II, lxx, 47. For a rather later silver-mining venture by Prince Rupert, see *Hist. MSS. Com. Rep.* ix, App. iii, 6a. His right-hand man was the notorious Captain Hucker of Athelney Farm.
[60] Dep. by Com. Mich. 27 Chas. II, no. 9, Somerset.

[61] Certainly the carriage of lead formed part of the service of certain customary tenants at Chewton in the early 16th century. Aug. Off. Misc. Bks. 385, fol. 33 et seq.

officers as formerly the lords of the manor had been accustomed to do. James Yorke and John Buckland late deceased had for the time mentioned been in the said office and since Lady Day last one Joseph Halstone 'was elected by the homage and with the said Mr. Yorke sworn to serve in the office of lead-reeve for the said manor.' James Francke alias Yorke himself admitted that about forty years he was lead-reeve at Chewton for three or four years, and twelve years ago he was again elected lead-reeve and had been in office ever since. He was also store-bailiff and 'is to continue the same office of store bayly for his life, and formerly was steward for the mineral and hundred court within the said manor which office of stewardship he now enjoyeth.' This is a notable instance of divers functions lodged in one holder, doubtless in the lord's interest. Like many other possessors of lucrative billets Yorke did not magnify his office of lead-reeve. ' It was very troublesome and prejudicial.' During the first tenure of it in his own right 'he verily believes he lost the better part of £100.' Several persons, for example Henry Tucker, John Stanford, Richard Adams, John Cole and others had been very great losers in executing the office and he knew three of them who did sell their estates as he believes to make up the lord's account. In fact the fees were so small and the trouble so great that in his opinion any one who undertook the office must lose thereby. However, this was not by any means the opinion of all, for Richard Plaister 'was hired by one John Beach to execute the said office and had 10s. for his pains and a promise to give a day's work with his plough, though this deponent should have been willing to have executed the said office *gratis* and would have gladly continued in the said office for the profit of the same.' The opportunity of turning over the lord's money in the half-yearly interval between the rendering of the account and the actual payment must have proved profitable among a reckless mining community who spent as readily as they gained and were ever ready to borrow. This is not obscurely hinted in the depositions before us, which also prove clearly that by the reign of Charles II—and probably long before—although the homage may have normally elected, the lord exercised a right to approve or disapprove and in fact could effectually bar whom he would, while substitutes were allowed. Thus James Francke *alias* Yorke declared that :

he knoweth there was a great dealer one Mr. John Curtis who was chosen lead-reeve by the homage, who did buy great quantities of lead ore within the said manor and melted the same into lead but saith that the surveyor and steward belonging to the lords of the said manor did refuse to accept of him for that by means of the said office he might have opportunity to deceive the lord of his tenth part being

both debtor and accomptant. And the deponent further saith that the homage of the said manor do only present lead-reeves, and the lord by his steward or agent doth approve or disapprove of their choice as he or they think fit.

Particularly he remembered that one Jacob Hoskins and divers others had been refused, and he had heard that the lord of the manor or his agents 'did pay to one James Phelps the sum of £4 for executing the said office of lead-reeve in the stead of the said Jacob Hoskins.'

Two other points may be noticed in these depositions. It is stated that the four lords royal of the Forest of Mendip then existing were the lord or lords of Chewton, the Bishop of Bath and Wells, Sir Thomas Gore and Sir John Newton, and secondly some statistics are given as to the lot-lead paid in Chewton Mendip during a short series of years from which we may gain some idea of the total lead production within that manor for the same period. To get the results shown here the lot-lead has been multiplied by ten.

1667	. . . .	530 tons	
1668	. . . .	620 „	
1669	. . . .	880 „	' due or received.'
1670	. . . .	640 „	
1671	. . . .	370 „	
1672	. . . .	300 „	
1673	. . . .	260 „	
1674	. . . .	250 „	

A considerable margin must be allowed for fraud in each minery and perhaps we may conjecture—for conjecture alone is possible—that the annual production of lead on Mendip between 1665 and 1675 fluctuated between 1,500 and 2,000 tons, and may have even reached a much higher figure. And this estimate does not include lead smelted from ore dug at Broadfield Down, Brockley or other outlying localities. There can however be little doubt that in 1675 the output of lead from the Somerset mines was less, and probably considerably less, than three-quarters of a century before.

Little technical advance seems to have been made in the Mendip lead-mines during the 17th century, but towards its close ' a new way [62] of cleaving rocks with gunpowder ' was introduced. The ' gun ' used for this purpose was 6 in. long and 1¼ in. in diameter and had a hole drilled through it to receive the priming powder. A hole was made in the rock somewhat deeper than the length of the gun to receive the blasting-powder, in amount some 2 or 3 oz., over which the miners placed a thin paper. On this paper they placed the ' gun ' which they fixed into the hole by driving in against the flat side of the upper part of it a little iron wedge 4 in. in length, by the miners called a ' quinnet.' The

[62] See *Philos. Trans. Abridged* (ed. Lowthorp), ii, 368.

operator then passed down a wire through the hole drilled in the gun, pierced the paper which covered the powder and finally primed the gun and laid a train for firing, when all the workmen had got to a safe distance. The new method of blasting saved a great deal of time, since work could be proceeded with almost immediately, while if the old practice were followed and fire laid in a shaft, at least twenty-four hours' interval was necessary before the rocks had cooled sufficiently to permit the resumption of work. It may be worth notice [63] that in the summer of 1679 two slight explosions of fire-damp are mentioned as occurring in the Mendip lead-mines and remarked upon as a novelty, though in the Mendip coal-pits at the same time they were only too common. Mr. John Beaumont, to whose scientific curiosity we owe the particulars just recited, has a further title to fame as the early and intrepid explorer of the great caverns on Lamb Hill, south-west of East Harptree village. [64]

During the second [65] half at least of the 17th century some lead-mining was pursued in the neighbourhood of Dulverton. Mr. Andrew Paschal after the Restoration sent to John Aubrey a sample of 'beat and washed' Dulverton ore. The friend who had procured it for him described the ore from that district as hard and barren, producing lead harder than Mendip lead, since the Dulverton ore was nothing like so rich and full of metal as the other. 'There is silver in it [the Dulverton ore] but scarce exceeding the worth of the lead: if any one could extract it, and save the lead, it might be worth while, otherwise not.'

With the beginning of the 18th century we must conclude the story in detail of the Somerset lead-mining. A very short summary only can be given of its later progress, or rather decline, for its further course, in spite of occasional outbursts of activity, was that of a dying industry. During the 18th century a large amount of lead was still raised, though the calamine sent to Bristol was probably more sought for at this time. Strachey in mentioning [66] the lead dug at 'Broadwell Down and other parts thereabouts' states his opinion that it is 'not so soft, pliant, and equally fusile as that in Derbyshire and so is not so proper for sheeting, because when it is melted it runs into knots, and therefore not being used by London plumbers, they know little or nothing of it; for being of a harder nature it is generally transported beyond sea and used for bullets and shots, for which purpose it is excellent.' In 1774 we hear of further projects for draining

the Row Pits and Small Pits and the names of certain Bristol capitalists, Moses Underwood, Jacob Riddle and a Mr. Shapland are mentioned. [67] Billingsley again, writing in 1795, suggested the cutting of a level or audit through the base of the Mendips from Compton Martin to Wookey Hole to explore the undiscovered riches of the mountains. [68]

In the early part of the last century that indefatigable antiquary the Rev. John Skinner on more than one occasion encountered miners searching the ancient refuse heaps or smelting surface ore and ancient slags. [69] By 1824 the lead-mining still carried on in the county was mainly the occupation of men with little or no capital, prosecuted in a nerveless manner, while the workings were almost invariably shallow. [70] Hunt's *Mineral Statistics* in 1855 show no returns from the county, which however need not necessarily imply an absolute cessation of work. In 1860 from 800 tons of Mendip lead ore and slimes 357 tons of lead were got and 850 ozs. of silver. In 1864 three surface deposits of lead slag and débris were being worked on the Mendips. The Mendip Hills Mining Company had one furnace in blast, another was in blast at the Waldegrave Works while at St. Cuthbert's Lead Works in Priddy minery 3 miles north of Wells one furnace was in blast and five in process of erection. [71] In the following year [72] Charterhouse minery returned 326 tons 10 cwts. of lead and 1,300 ozs. of silver, while Chewton, Tar Hole and Priddy together furnished 300. In 1870 [73] the returns of the estimated ore washings were 1,333 tons, divided pretty equally between the Charterhouse, Waldegrave and East Harptree works, the lead returns being 523 tons and the silver *nil*.

During the 'seventies' and 'eighties' of the last century the three or four lead-smelting enterprises working on the Mendips struggled against a complication of adverse circumstances, [74] extravagant and yet inefficient plants, difficulties in ore-treatment and in the later eighties the declining price of lead. One by one they gave

---

[63] See *Philos. Trans. Abridged* (ed. Lowthorp), ii, 382.

[64] Ibid. 369 et seq.

[65] *Miscellanies on Several Curious Subjects* (1714), Letter 55.

[66] *Compleat Hist. Somerset*, 128a.

[67] See Order of Chewton Mineral Court, 18 August 1774, printed by Mr. J. McMurtrie, F.G.S. op. cit. 581.

[68] *View of Agric. of Somers.* 20.

[69] Cf. Add. MSS. 33648, fol. 17; 33653, fol. 91; 33656, fol. 3, 4; 33668, fol. 93.

[70] *Geol. Soc. Proc.* (1824) 233. Lead-reeves were occasionally elected as late as the first quarter of the 19th century, but the old activity of the mineral courts was a thing of the past.

[71] *Mining and Smelting Mag.* (December 1864), vi, 321.

[72] Hunt, *Min. Statistics*, 38.

[73] Ibid. (1870), 34.

[74] A little earlier in the century the old difficulty of water pollution had led to a suit in the Queen's Bench. See H. C. Salmon, *Mining and Smelting Mag.* vi, 323, and cf. J. A. Clark, *Bath and W. of Engl. Agric. Journ.* ii, 127.

up the contest and by 1890 all operations had for the time ceased.

In 1900 the St. Cuthbert's lead-works, where a concentrating and smelting-plant of the latest and most improved type [75] had been erected, were alone active on the Mendip Hills [76] and the St. Cuthbert's Lead Company were not only treating the ancient tailings and slimes close to the works but also dealing with ancient débris on Chewton Warren.

According to the official returns [77] of the Somerset output of lead ore and lead, the dressed ore in 1906 reached 350 tons and the amount of lead obtained by smelting was 155 tons, while the ore at the quarries was valued at £1,963. The ore also contained an unascertained amount of gold and silver. Last year (1907) however the dressed lead ore obtained in Somerset amounted to 936 tons, a welcome increase on the figures of the previous year.[78] The New Chaffers Extended Mining Company were then at work on the Mendips.

COAL

The Somerset coalfield, though small in size and at present in no way comparable in respect of its output with the northern and midland districts, yet possesses many features of interest, in its geological formation [1] already elsewhere considered,[2] its past history and its possible future development.

Solinus,[3] an industrious compiler of the 2nd or 3rd century of the Christian era, refers, though not by name, to the hot springs of Bath, where in the temple of the tutelary goddess undying fires never whitened to ash, but as they faded turned to balls of rock. This passage has long been interpreted and with reasonable probability as an allusion to mineral coal easily obtainable from the outcrops of the strata near the city and more apt than wood for feeding a perpetual fire.

No indication has survived of any coal-mining in Somerset during the Saxon period, but after the Conquest we know that coal was dug at least as early as the 13th century on its borders in Kingswood Forest. Indeed, although for domestic use and for smelting of both lead and iron ore wood, either dried or charred, was employed till a quite modern period, it is not improbable if we consider the collateral evidence derivable from the history of such fields as those of Durham, Gloucestershire and Derbyshire, that small amounts of surface coal were dug both in Northern Somerset and within the ancient and wider limits of Mendip Forest as early as the 13th century for use at limekilns or smithies. But no definite and specific reference to the existence of mineral coal within the county has yet been produced of as early a date as this. In fact the earliest mediaeval notice which has been adduced as referring to Somerset coal is unfortunately ambiguous and may possibly be taken as an allusion to charcoal. This reference occurs in an Inquisition after the death [4] of Elias de Albiniaco, who held amongst other property the manor of Kilmersdon. There the 'proficium carbonum' is said to have been 2s. 4d. With regard to the interpretation of this phrase it may be remarked that the item in question immediately follows a reference to the woodland of the manor, and that in the first half of the 14th century mineral coal is usually but not invariably distinguished from charcoal [5] by the addition of some qualifying epithet as sea-coal or less commonly earth-coal. Mineral coal may indeed be meant, but it seems impossible to come to any absolutely certain conclusion. Yet in the neighbouring parish of Stratton-on-the-Fosse the raising of coal seems to have been a well-established industry by the 15th century,[6] and as in these brief historical notes some selection is necessary Stratton may be noticed here as an early and highly important centre of the Mendip coal-trade.

During a period of nearly eight months following the death of Sir John Typtoft, which occurred 30 January 1443 (21 Hen. VI), the accountant in charge of the manor answers for a sum of £2 16s. 1d. which had been received for coal sold on the lord's behalf.[7] It is worth notice that the coal

---

[75] Wilfley tables, for instance, had been substituted for the old-fashioned round buddles.

[76] T. Morgan's 'Notes on the Lead Industry of the Mendip Hills' in *Trans. Fed. Inst. of Mining Engineers*, xx, 478 et seq. where an excellent account is given of the various smelting processes employed from 1864 onwards.

[77] *Gen. Rep. and Statistics of Mines and Quarries for 1906* (published 1907), 221.

[1] Its undulating and faulty character is especially noticeable.   [2] *V.C.H. Somerset*, i, 12 et seq.

[3] *Collectanea Rerum Memorabilium* (ed. Mommsen), 115. Cf. *V.C.H. Somerset*, i, 221.

[78] Martin, *Rep. Mines and Quarries South. Dist. for 1907* (publ. 1908), 38. The Government returns for 1908 now available show a decreasing output of 576 tons of dressed lead ore. *Gen. Rep. and Statistics Mines and Quarries for 1908* (publ. 1909), 234. C. Pass & Son of Bristol still carry on business as leadsmelters in the county.

[4] Chan. Inq. p.m. 33 Edw. I, no. 81.

[5] Old iron-pits and slag have been found near by at Holcombe and charcoal would have been essential for the working of a mediaeval bloomery.

[6] Indeed quite possibly long before, but we have seen no Ministers' Accounts for the 14th century.

[7] Mins. Accts. bdle. 1123, no. 1. The accountant writes 'Stratton super le Vosse,' following the local pronunciation.

is here termed 'carbonum terrestrium,' a description much rarer in most districts than 'carbo maris.' A decade and a half later [8] we hear that the 'coal-mine of the lord' of Stratton had been leased to John Wolley or Welley and his partners, who were paying a yearly rent of £1 6s. 8d. In 1477 this coal-mine was being worked by the same firm.[9] But in addition the accountant of the manor answers for £1 6s. 8d. of 'new rent of a new coal-work (operis carbonarii) close to the place of the ancient works there' which had been 'leased to John Wene, Richard Warre, Thomas Frampton, John Benet, Richard Robyns, and Julian Frampton to dig in that new work until it shall be wrought out and so in all other works within the same metes and bounds as often as they think expedient, according to the custom of the manor as set forth in the court-roll of the foregoing year.' It is probable that these pits were of no great depth and no soughs or adits were yet required.

Besides these direct notices of activity in the parishes bordering on the Mendips we find from casual references in the accounts of Somerset churchwardens that coal was being bought during the 15th century for lime-burning and other purposes. In 1458 [10] for instance 13 weys (pisis) of coal (carbonis terrestris) were purchased for £4 3s. 11d. by the wardens of St. John's, Glastonbury.

Early [11] in the reign of Henry VIII both the old and new coalworks at Stratton were still in active operation and a yearly rent of £1 6s. 8d. was still being paid in both cases.

In November [12] 1530 a lease of the demesne lands of the manor of Stratton, together with the coal-mines late in the tenure of John Welley, parcel of the earldom of Huntingdon, was granted to John Hide engrosser of the Great Roll of the Exchequer. But this grant was vacated on surrender 30 June 1544 in order that another patent might be granted to the famous John Horner.[13] And again in 1545 in a grant to Robert Long, mercer of London, we hear both of coal-mines, late in the tenure of John Welby (?Welley), in addition to two coal-mines in tenure of John Horner and Walter James, lying within the parish of Stratton-on-the-Fosse.[14]

Among the most vigorous mining adventurers in Stratton and its vicinity during the early 17th century were various members of the Long and Salmon families, especially William Long and John Salmon the elder, better known locally as 'Gentleman Salmon,' a son of Henry Salmon.[15] Of their activities and those of their sometime partner Hercules Horler many stories were told.

Either late in the reign of James I or early in that of his successor W. Long and Hercules Horler took a lease of the coal-mines on the Barow at Stratton and after a time admitted John Salmon and possibly others of that family into partnership. When their lease expired in 1641 or 1642 the council of the Duchy of Cornwall were unpleasantly impressed by the state of the pits surrendered and the too evident results of active but unscrupulous exploitation. One clause in the original lease enjoined that two pits only were to be worked at a time, but Richard Wilcock of Kilmersdon, one of the working miners, deposed that the said Mr. Long and Hercules Horler or their servants have landed cole at 3 pitts at a tyme in one day and did keep another pitt there going att the same tyme for to find out more cole. And this deponent further saith that if the said Mr. Long and Hercules Horler had kept but two pitts for landing of cole att one tyme, the said ground called the Barrow might have bene of a greater value to the king's majestie and the present lessee to the some of £100 at least or thereabouts.

This evidence was fully confirmed, and the three pits worked together at the close of the lease were named the 'Naish,' the 'Topp of the Hill' and the 'Wall.'

The Duchy officers seem also to have been aggrieved that two pits were not handed over in working order, and one expert witness declared that 'the two pitts which William Longe, esq. and Hercules Horler should leave to the Prince His Highness or his lessee were quite wrought out and the pillers rubbed out before such time as Mr. Wykes his Highnes lessee did enter on the same.' Hercules Horler, it is true, denied that the pillars had been rubbed out, but much confirmatory evidence was given as to the dangerous state of the pits and the expense necessary for putting them in order. James Huish, for example, an old and experienced miner, declared that 'at his going into one of the cole pitts in the Barrowe lying in the side of the Hill he found the same to be ruinous and annoyed by the water therein and the cutt pitt belonging thereunto fallen together.' There were other issues involved which cannot be considered here, but it would certainly seem that the mining adventurers had, as one witness, at least, put it, 'overwrought' the pits to the disadvantage of the duchy.

We also hear that Horler and 'Gentleman' Salmon on one occasion, possibly but not certainly, in connexion with the lease already mentioned, under a licence from the lord of the manor

[8] Mins. Accts. (35–6 Hen. VI), bdle. 1095, no. 7.
[9] Mins. Accts. (16–17 Edw. IV), bdle. 1123, no. 3.
[10] N. and Q. Somerset and Dorset, iv, 284.
[11] Mins. Accts. (6–7 Hen. VIII), bdle. 3030 Somerset.
[12] L. and P. Hen. VIII, iv (3), g. 6751 (11).
[13] Ibid. xix (1), g. 1035 (42).
[14] Ibid. xx (2), g. 496 (57).

[15] Exch. Dep. Mich. 30 Chas. II, no. 11, Somerset. Much of the matter here summarized is derived from these depositions or from Misc. Bk. L.R. 207.

did beginn to colework in the common belonging to the manor of Stratton and in theire workeing and prosecuting the drift of the cole they were lighted on, drove the same into a sideling ground next adjoyning the said common belonging unto Perthill in the possession of Toby Salmon tenaunt thereof and there wrought the same.

Toby tried to prevent this trespass on his close, but Hercules Horler, whose utterance was as heroic as his name, declared 'There is never a Salmon of them all that shall governe me and I will not be put by of the right I have.' Apparently the matter was settled by certain payments, and the mention of this case may excuse a few words as to the conditions under which coal was worked during the early 17th century in Stratton-on-the-Fosse and the neighbouring parishes.

A local witness deposed [16] late in the reign of Charles II that ' the forest of Mendipp where colepittes are or have been wrought doe extend in length between fowre and ffive miles and about one mile in breadth, and the mannours of Ashweeke, Kilmersdon, Holcombe, Mells, Babington, Luckington and Stratton are manours bordering upon and adjoyneing to the forest of Mendipp '—that is, as another witness put it, the part of the forest where coals were worked extended ' from Mells or near to Binegar.' Even as late as 1679 Stratton parish in part at least, as for example Perthill and Plummer's Close, was reckoned and reputed parcel of the forest of Mendip. Again coal raised in the parishes above-mentioned was known as ' Mendip coles,' and it was a common expression of the dealers ' they goe to Mendip for coles.' As far as Stratton is concerned the coal-pits were at first situated in the common divided by bounds into two parts, the Holmes and the Barrow. And it is probable that no inclosed ground was broken for this purpose until after the beginning of the 17th century. Directly however the mining adventurers, acting on a grant or licence from the lords of the manor, began to enter copyhold and leasehold properties and started working therein serious disputes arose. There is no doubt that in these parishes bordering on Mendip the miners, after having once obtained licence from the lord of the manor to prospect for coal and dig within it, sometimes entered copyhold and leasehold lands and began work against the will of the tenants. In several manors there seems to have been an old custom that if this happened treble damages were due to the tenant. As to Stratton, one witness deposed in the reign of Charles II ' that if any tenant or occupier of any inclosed ground within the said manor did refuse to permit and suffer any grantee or lessee of the colemynes to work the same there that then it hath bene taken and reputed to be the custome of the said

manour that such grantee or lesee might notwithstanding beginn and proceed in the said worke ' and then pay damages by view of one man appointed by the miner and one appointed by the tenants or by view of two appointed by the miner if the tenant refuse to name his man. Usually, when miners and tenants were on reasonable terms, an agreement as to compensation seems to have been made before work was started, and sometimes the amount obtainable from the miner was of much greater worth than any treble damages. In the reign of James I Charity Plummer was the copyhold possessor of Plummer's Close, and Austin Vagg her son was copyholder in reversion. ' Gentleman Salmon ' agreed with them that if he were allowed to work for coals in their close he would give the occupant one-eighth and the copyholder in reversion one-sixteenth of the coal raised as well as pay an allowance for trespass and loss of herbage and when the pit was worked out carry away the ' warke' and cleanse the ground. Henry Vagg, Charity Plummer's grandson, believed that the pit in question was the first that ever was digged within the inclosed ground of Stratton Manor.

Occasionally the leaseholder or copyholder stood out stoutly against the mining invasion and denied the right of the adventurers to enter. Some time before the Civil War William Long, Hercules Horler and ' Gentleman ' Salmon, partners in a coal-work on Stratton common, followed their drift into the inclosed land of one Nicholas Everett and begged his leave to sink a new pit in his land. He however refused them although they offered treble damages [17] and the adventurers ' did utterly relinquish theire sayd worke dueringe his (Everett's) lifetyme.' But when Everett died ' Hercules Horler, one of the said partners, did marry the daughter of the said Everett. And thereupon the sayd partners came to an agreement with the said Everett's widowe in whose possession the sayd inclosed lands then were concerninge the sayd coleworkers.' The adventurers undertook to pay £3 10s. to the widow for breaking the ground, also to clear the ' warke,' that is the earth raised from the pit off her land and fill up the coal-pit when left and ' cover it two foote deepe with good earth.' Some of the ' warke ' was carried off but some left ; this latter breach of contract was however ' made upp upon the marriage of Hercules Horler.'

When however the lord of the manor was adventuring for coal on his own account the unfortunate copyholder stood a poor chance. For instance Thomas Pacy, lord of Babington, was resisted by two of his copyholders, Edmund Cornish and John Atkins, but ' Mr. Pacy would not be hindered by them but did goe on and

---

[16] Exch. Dep. Mich. 30 Chas. II, no. 11, Somerset.

[17] See Deposition of John Cleare.

pursue his worke and continued the same soe long as he had any incouragement thereunto by the coles there. And thereupon there was a suite or suites commenced betweene the said Mr. Pacey and the said Cornish and a tryall thereuppon had, and the said Mr. Pacy had the best of itt.'

If a substantial copyholder was unable to keep out miners backed by the lord the small cottier was in worse case still. The experiences of John Gleare, or Cleare, of Holcombe, near Kilmersdon, though rather late in date—between 1670 and 1680—are instructive. His cottage holding was small, a house and 3 acres of land, held of Mr. Edmund Trowbridge of Kilmersdon. Apparently about the year 1673 Mr. Trowbridge granted licence to William Salmon, Samuel Salmon and Thomas Perkins to work coal-mines in his lands at Holcombe. Thereupon they entered Gleare's land without his privity and consent and after two or three days the cottier demanded satisfaction for the trespass committed and an agreement as to future working. The adventurers refused this ' until they found and landed coles.' When coal was found Gleare again approached his unbidden guests and repeated the demand, suggesting 8d. a week as a proper payment to him while the work continued. The miners offered him half, which he refused. However, Mr. Trowbridge, who was interested in the miners' venture since by the terms of the licence he was to receive a ' free share,' that is one-eighth of the coals landed without deductions for expenses, informed Gleare that if he would not take 6d. a week he should get nothing, and the cottier yielded and so agreed. The adventurers worked the mine for a year and gave over. A year after they had left Thomas Perkins returned, but with two fresh partners, William Blanning and John Lane, and under licence from the lord began another work without Gleare's consent. The cottier opposed them and threatened to attach the horses which came for the coal, but the miners let him know that Mr. Trowbridge would bear them out. Gleare on ' seeing his landlord interesting himself therein ' ceased opposition and again accepted 6d. a week. This second partnership worked their mine for a year and then lighted on a ' veine of cole ' which led them out of Gleare's ground into that of a near neighbour and there against his will, for he also was a tenant of Mr. Trowbridge, worked their drift or vein; but with all this they still kept ' their cabbin ' and timber in Gleare's ground. The unfortunate subject of their new enterprise got no compensation for six months. But Gleare was by no means rid of the miners, as Henry and Thomas Chivers with James James next worked in his land and from them he received 6d. a week. About eighteen months after their departure James

James returned with fresh partners but after working for a few weeks found that the most profitable coal was practically wrought out and so relinquished the work without paying Gleare anything at all.

When disputes arose there was often considerable conflict of testimony as to the amount of damage done; some said the land was improved owing to the number of horses which waited there for coals, others magnified the damage done by the passage of wains and the ' haunt of custom.' The most optimistic adventurer could hardly maintain that the ' warke ' enriched the soil, but Henry Aishman of Kilmersdon ' cole myner ' deposed in the reign of Charles II that ' he doth verily believe that there is generally a greater improvement occasioned by tyeing and serving of horses in such grounds as doe more than countervail the damage done there by the casting upp and the lyeing of the *warke*.' As to the value of the coals to those who actually got them, one witness deposed ' that he doth believe that coles raised out of one acre of land may be worth more than the inheritance thereof.'

Some account having now been given of the history of the Mendip coal-mines [18] down to the Restoration, it is necessary to return and add a few notes as to coal working on the more northerly manors.

At Timsbury coal was certainly raised in the 16th century and probably long before, since there was a great market for the output of this district in the neighbouring city of Bath. As to the working of the coal-pits in the neighbouring parish of Clutton we have [19] some interesting details in a report of the year 1610. The surveyor there tells us :—

There be now three pits near widow Blackers house the highest about 4 fathoms, the middle six fathoms, the lowest 8 fathoms deep. At these depths they cut out their lanes about 4 feet high and broad. They need no great store of timber-work for support. The lane we crept through was a good quoits cast in length, wherein we found but two cross lanes, whereby it may appear that the mine is yet but newly entered into. They now work in two pits at once, and have below two or three men and four or five boys, and also three men to wind up the coals. At the end of every lane a man worketh, and there maketh his bench, as they call it, and according to the vent they make more or fewer benches. The wages allowed to the men is to him that hath most 4s. the week, and to the boys, 1s. 6d. Adding for candles, increase of wages for work by night, ropes, sharpening of tools, baskets, &c, the whole week's charge may arise to £3. Reckoning 100 horse loads a day at 3d. the receipt coming to £7 10s. the week, and the net gain

---

[18] It may be noted that when the manor of Stratton was sequestrated as part of the royal property in 1651 the coal-pits and coal-mines or ' drifts of coal ' commonly called the Barrow were estimated at a yearly value of £2. Parl. Surveys, Somers. no. 39.

[19] *Hist. MSS. Com. Rep.* xii, App. i, 71.

is £4 10s. of which one-fourth for the tenant, and the rest remaineth for the lord. It is said that the works at Timbury are near worn out, and all smiths use the coal of Clutton and none of Timbury.

Some notion may be derived from this description as to the depth of the pits and their manner of working at Clutton. Already the contemporary Mendip coal-leases show that water had to be reckoned with, and at Stratton [20] in 1617 William Long and his sons were granted leave to dig in 'Les Holmes' not only 'pro inventu carbonum, Anglice for fyndinge of cole,' but also 'pro deductione aquarum,' and probably the necessity of dealing with the drainage of the mines had found expression in Somerset leases even before this time.

Indeed in a survey of the manor of Stratton of the reign of James I we hear of the difficulty experienced in working coal on the commons, especially on the Barrow, 'by reason that the springes are soe superfluente.' 'As for the Holmes,' proceeds the surveyor, 'they have latelie found meanes with more facillitie to exhaust the water though with great charge namelie with pumpes whose wheeles are moved by the fall of a streame conducted to the same which cannot be brought to the service of the Barrowe so far surmounting the level.' At the time of this survey the mines on the Holmes were held as copyhold, the tenants having paid a fine of £300 to 'Mr. W. Longe, the late supposed lord of the manor' while they were also liable for a yearly rent of 18s. 2½d.

Coal had not only been worked in the Gloucestershire portion of the old forest of Kingswood from an early period, but also probably in its Somerset half, Fillwood Chase and its neighbourhood. Norden in his report on Fillwood mentions the coal-pits of Brislington and probably a search among 16th-century surveys might furnish fuller details as to the working of coal at this place.

After the Restoration notices of coal-mining in Somerset are so abundant that only very cursory attention can be given them here. One indication of the increasing though still relatively moderate depth of the Mendip coal-mines may perhaps be derived from reference to explosions of fire-damp. In the reign of Charles II Mr. John Beaumont informed [21] the Royal Society

that about 2 miles on the South-East of Stony Easton at a place nearly bordering to Mendip Hills begins a running of coal consisting of several veins which extends itself towards the East about 4 miles. There is much working in this running and firedamps continually there happen, so that many men of late years have been killed, many others maimed and a multitude burnt. Some have been blown up at the work's mouth and the turn beam (which hangs over the shaft) has been thrown off its frame by the force

of it. . . . The middle and more easterly parts of this running are so very subject to these fiery damps, that scarce a pit fails of them. Notwithstanding which our colliers still pursue their work, but to prevent mischief they keep their air very quick and use no candles in their works but of a single wick, and those of 60 or 70 to the lb. which nevertheless give as great a light there as others of 10 or 12 to the lb. in other places; and they always place them behind them, and never present them to the breast of the work.

The miners declared that the damps were worst in the winter and chiefly in a black frost 'when the air runs best.' Beaumont mentions as a novelty that in the summer of 1679 two explosions of fire-damps occurred in the neighbouring lead-mines, but so slight were they that no one was hurt.

In 1719 Mr. John Strachey in a letter [22] communicated to the Royal Society described the strata observed in the coal-mines of Somerset. Speaking of the practice of the mines near Farrington Gurney he mentions how in prospecting the miners search for the Crop, a very weak and friable coal which sometimes 'appears to the day as they term it; or else for the Cliff which is dark or blackish rock and always keeps its regular course as the coal does lying obliquely over it.' He then points out that all 'coal lies shelving like the tyle of a house' unless it be broken by a ridge of clay, stone or rubble. The obliquity or pitch was generally in the mines near Farrington and Bishop Sutton about 22 inches in a fathom, and when it rises to the land is called the crop, but in the north basseting.

Speaking of the various coal-seams at Sutton Strachey declares that the first or uppermost vein was called the Stinking Vein, 'a hard coal for mechanick uses but of a sulphurous smell.' From 5 to 7½ fathoms under this lay the Cathead Vein, so-called from the lumps of stone in it, and below this at much the same distance again the Three Coal Vein, so named because it was divided into three different coals, between the first and second of which was a stone band from 1 ft. to 2 ft. thick. These three upper veins were sometimes worked in the same pit, but the Peaw Vein [23] which lay from 5½ ft. to 7 ft. below the Three Coal Vein was usually worked in a separate pit. Mr. Strachey assigns as the reason for this that the cliff between it and the vein above is hard and subject to water. Under the Peaw Vein at about five or six fathoms lay the Smith's Coal Vein some 3 ft. thick, and near the same depth under that again the Shelly Vein, and under that a vein 10 in. thick which being little valued has not been wrought to any purpose. He also points out some variations

---

[20] Ct. R. (14 James I) bdle. 200, no. 40. Cf. P.R.O. Misc. Bk. L.R. 207, fol. 9d.

[21] Lowthorp, Philos. Trans. Abridged, ii, 381.

[22] Philos. Trans. xxx, 968 et seq.

[23] 'So denominated because the coal is figured with eyes resembling a peacock's tail, which bird in this country dialect is called a peaw' according to Mr. Strachey.

of the position of the strata in neighbouring manors. At High Littleton for instance their undermost and deepest vein, which at Farrington was so small, proved to be the best coal.

At Burnett, Queen Charlton and Brislington four veins were worked. These *pitched* to the north nearly, and consequently the *drift* lay almost east and west. The surface was usually red land to the depth of 4 or 5 fathoms. At Brislington the top vein was from 3 ft. to 6 ft. thick, but less at Burnett and Charlton. Six fathoms below the uppermost vein was Pot Vein 18 in. thick and all hard coal. The third vein averaged from 2½ ft. to 3 ft. of solid coal and was known as the Trench Vein. It lay 7 fathoms below the Pot Vein. The fourth vein or Rock Vein, though reckoned to lie 7 fathom below the Trench Vein, is never worked in the same pit with it, but 'about 200 yds. more to the south or to land as they term it,' since the Rock Vein is distinguished by a covering of Pennant stone, sometimes 20 ft. or more in thickness. It is probable, as Mr. Galloway [24] points out, that the working of these seams was by some species of longwall. With the thinner seams it could hardly have been otherwise and this may be legitimately deduced from statements of Mr. Strachey printed elsewhere. [25]

By 1719, if not before, gunpowder was in use for piercing the hard beds of rock occasionally encountered in sinking the coal-pits. [26] At the Mendip lead-mines it had been used as early as 1683.

The middle of the 18th century witnessed a considerable development in the southern part of the Somerset coalfield. At this time coal had long been mined in the Vobster, Nettlebridge and Morewood valleys and probably at Paulton and Grayfield, where there are traces of early opencast works. But even experienced miners in the early part of the century disbelieved in the existence of coal in the manor of Radstock, and an old collier used to say that 'if ever coal was found in Radstock he would get on the top of Norton tower and *flee* down.' Coal however was ultimately found at Radstock by the sinking of the Old Pit about 1763, a landmark in the history of this field.

In 1750 the methods of coal-mining in use showed little advance on those employed in the pits a century before. For raising the coal horse drums or gins were usually employed worked by two horses at a time with two boys to drive them. The shafts as a rule were 4½ ft. in diameter, but they were widened at 'meetings' to allow the ascending and descending corves to pass one another. The coal was brought from the interior of the mine to the bottom of the shaft in 'puts,' whence it was unloaded into a 'wreath cart' and then raised to the surface. The procedure is thus described by Mr. J. McMurtrie [27] :—

Originally the put consisted of a sledge frame, with iron pins fixed at regular distances in its upper edge, hazel rods being *wreathed* between as in the corves of the North of England. When the coal reached the bottom of the shaft, it was transferred to what was termed a 'wreath cart.' This was of a circular shape, its dimensions being about 2 ft. deep by 2 ft. diameter; it had a strong circular wooden bottom, with iron pins bolted at regular distances through the rim; these pins were *wreathed* with hazel rods, and riveted to an iron rim which went on the top of the wreathing, a strong iron hoop passing over the top, by means of which it was attached to the rope. When the load reached the surface, the loaded cart was unhitched and an empty one attached, and the horses, having in the meantime been turned about, were trotted round in a contrary direction.

By this means about 400 bushels or 20 tons per pit on an average could be raised in a working day, but during the summer months work was usually slack. This primitive method remained the principal means of raising coal in the Radstock district till about 1804. Occasionally water wheels were employed, as at the Middle Pit, Radstock, and as late, as 1795 at Welton, [28] where a natural supply of water was available, a water-gin was in use for drawing up the coal, 'the use of horses as in the old way being entirely superseded; and the consumption of fuel as in the new way by the steam-engine altogether saved. [29] A steam-engine for pumping purposes had been erected at the Paulton Engine Pit about the year 1750, and others followed in the course of the next half-century. At Radstock also Jonathan Hornblower set up the first of his compound steam-engines in 1782, but Watt, who declared this engine a direct infringement of his patent, asserted also that 'it was obliged to stand still once every ten minutes to snore and snort.'

In 1795, according to Billingsley, the seams of the northern collieries dipped 9 in. per yard, and were nineteen in number, from 10 in. to 3 ft. thick, the workable depth being seldom under 15 in. The coal was generally worked from 400 to 500 ft., occasionally deeper, while the recent introduction of machinery was about to facilitate working at a much greater depth. In the northern district the coalworks were twenty-six in number and from 1,500 to 2,000 tons were being raised weekly, the average price of coal being 5d. per bushel at the pit by the nine gallons measure. In the southern district coal-working at this time was on a more limited scale. The seams, twenty-five in number, dipped 18 in. to 30 in. in the yard and in some

---

[24] *Annals of Coal Mining*, i, 341.
[25] *Philos. Trans.* xxxiii, 396.
[26] Galloway, op. cit. 227. Cf. Strachey, *Observations on Strata* (1727), 9.

[27] G. C. Greenwell and J. McMurtrie, *The Radstock Portion of the Somersetshire Coal Field* (1864), 6.
[28] Billingsley, op. cit. (ed. 2) 2, 7 n.
[29] Muirhead, *Life of Watt*, 388.

cases were even perpendicular. Billingsley reports that they varied in section from 6 in. to 7 ft., but under 18 in. were seldom worked. The depth of the pits ranged between 200 and 350 ft. but it was hoped to attain a much greater depth by the steam engines which were being then introduced. The quantity of coal raised weekly was from 800 to 1,000 tons. Thus for the whole Somerset field, as Mr. Galloway suggests, the annual average production would have been about 138,000 tons, but this may be an under-estimate. By this date the southern collieries had ceased to be known as the ' Mendip collieries.' [30] A large part of the coal raised at this time in the southern district was regarded as less valuable than that of North Somerset and the average selling price was 3¾d. the bushel.[31]

. In 1795 Welsh coal was selling at Watchet at 8d. per bushel. The poor, however, burned wood, or tanners' old bark, made into square pieces and called tan turfs, as well as turfs cut from the surface of the Quantocks.[32]

In 1797 240 bushels were landed daily from the pits at Clapton, the best coal selling at 3½d. per bushel, the smallest being shipped at Portishead for Wales, where it was used for lime-burning.[33] At Nailsea at the same date 2,500 bushels were landed in a day; the best coal being priced at 3½d. per bushel, the middle at 3d., and the smallest at 2d. per bushel. One of the coal-works was under contract to serve the glass-houses at 1¼d. per bushel, 2,000 bushels being consumed every week.[34] In the opinion of the glassworkers themselves, this coal was ' very sulphurous.' [35] White's seam was that most worked at Nailsea.[36]

In 1808, ' the valuable collieries at Radstock ' were spoken of as ' at present resorted to by the Wiltshire people, as far as the neighbourhood of Warminster; and notwithstanding the Canal is now connected with the pits, I should imagine,' adds the writer, ' it will yet continue to supply the chief markets for land carriage conveyance in those parts.' [37] The output there had lately increased owing to the introduction of engines for hauling coals. One erected at the Old Pit, Radstock, by an engineer named Jeffreys about 1804 was not long in use, but another set up at Middle Pit continued at

work for many years. By its means the daily output was increased from 20 to 50 tons.[38] An entry in a diary for 1819 describes the road in the neighbourhood of Priddy as ' rendered bad by the farmers' carts going to Paulton from this part of the country for coal.' [39] The same observant writer saw colliers in Deepcombe on the way to Burrington engaged in 1820 in boring for coal. The boring rods, he says, were screwed together at different lengths, the ends furnished with a sharp chisel to cut the stone met with in the progress of the work.[40]

In 1824 Professor Buckland [41] and the Rev. W. D. Conybeare communicated to the Geological Society an excellent account of the ' South-Western Coal District of England,' and in the course of their observations remarked that while the number of collieries formerly at work in Somerset was probably greater than in their own time, yet that ' the enlarged scale and spirit with which those mines are worked that are now in activity much more than compensate for the diminution in numbers.' At this time the whole line of collieries at Brislington, Queen's Charlton and Burnett had been for many years abandoned and also most of the pits in Pensford and between Pensford and Marksbury. They also drew attention to the extraordinary thinness of many of the seams worked.

The aggregate thickness of the seams worked in any single coalpit scarcely exceeds that of one of the ordinary seams in the principal districts; and the total of all the beds in the mining-field would be little more than double of the largest main of Staffordshire. That seams so thin should be sought for through Lias and Oolite at the enormous depth of 200 fathoms, as on Clandown, must excite surprise in those acquainted only with other coal districts; and that, under these circumstances, the seams should be worked with profit must be attributed chiefly to the highly improved machinery introduced into this district, the result of which is, that the quantity of coal delivered at the mouth of one of these pits in a single day averages at from 60 to 100 tons.

It is also interesting to notice that these expert observers thought the continuance of the coal measures beneath the valley of Wrington between the Mendips and Broadfield Down to be highly probable, and while recognizing that no coal had as yet been found south of the Mendips suggested that—

Since the mountain limestone dips beneath the marshes in that direction, and re-emerges in Cannington Park to the north of the Quantock range, it seems probable that there exists an intermediate basin beneath the red marl, which forms the uppermost substratum in this alluvial tract.

Hallatrow coal-mines had just ' begun to be profitable ' in 1825, according to the Diary of

[30] Billingsley, op. cit. (ed. 2) 26 et seq.; Galloway, op. cit. 342.

[31] Young, Northern Tour, i, 150.

[32] Young, Annals of Agric. xxiv, 209.

[33] Billingsley, op. cit. 29. In 1789 prices were 5d. per bushel (9 gallons, weight about 90 lb.) for the best, 4d. the next, and 3d. furnace coal; 2d. lime coal. Young, Annals of Agric. xi, 342.

[34] Ibid. 30. In 1870 the glass-works consumed 15,500 tons. Rep. Coal Supply (1871), iii, 127. Large coal sold at 10s. to 12s. 6d. per ton; small at 4s. 6d.

[35] Sutcliffe, Geol. of the Avon, 13.

[36] Anstie, Geol. Somerset, 53.

[37] Add. MS. 33625, fol. 1–2.

[38] Greenwell and McMurtrie, op. cit. 8.

[39] Add. MS. 33653, fol. 97.

[40] Add. MS. 33656, p. 45.

[41] Geol. Soc. Trans. (Ser. 2), i, 210 et seq.

the Rev. John Skinner. The mineral was being found, he states, in Gravel's Field, at a depth of 26 fathoms.[42]

In 1836 Clandown represented the maximum depth attained by the Somerset coalfield, namely, 1,210 ft.,[43] in 1841 seams 12 in. thick were being worked.[44] Children of six or seven years old were employed at the pits at this date. Amongst 100 hands at the Coal Barton and Vobster collieries in 1842 there were several.[45] The youngest were generally employed in opening and shutting doors for ventilation, others acted as pushers, whose work it was to pull along the carriages of coal, or help to turn the gug-wheel.[46] In 1844 the maximum depth reached in the coalfield was 1,488 ft.[47] The coal of Twerton was being largely utilized in 1856 for coking, and exported long distances for malt-kilns.[48] In 1858 the industry was giving employment to 5,274 men and fifteen women.[49]

In the first half of the 19th century several minor improvements were made in working the mines of the Radstock district. Iron hudges were substituted for the old wreath carts. Cages and guides were then introduced, so that the same puts and carriages used for hauling coal underground could be raised up the pit and run out to the stack or carts. From 1854 to 1864 more rapid progress still was made in this district. Mr. J. McMurtrie wrote[50] in 1864 :—

At the Countess of Waldegrave's Radstock and Tyning Pits, wide shafts with two cages have been substituted for the 'pump wells' and single cages formerly in use there ; powerful direct acting high-pressure engines have taken the place of the old second motion condensing engines originally used ; tubs holding 11 cwts. have been introduced in several instances to take the place of the 'puts' ; an engine bank has been constructed, by means of which the coal is hauled from the deep for a considerable distance underground by steam instead of horse power ; and whereas the inconsiderable feeder of water used to occupy six pumping engines and about a mile of pumps, it is now raised in a few hours by means of water tanks.

Similar improvements were gradually carried out at several other collieries, and the output largely increased throughout the field.

In 1869, there were thirty-four collieries at work in the county, situated and named as follows :—

Nettlebridge.
Nettlebridge, Newbury, New Rock, Vobster, Edford and Mells.

Radstock.
Braysdown, Clandown, Foxcote, Huish, Old Welton, Radstock Works, Welton Hill, Writhlington (Upper and Lower) and Wellsway.

Paulton.
Bishop Sutton, Conygre Lower (Timsbury), Conygre Upper, Camerton New Pit, Farrington, Fry's Bottom, Grayfield, Old Grove Timsbury, Old Mills, Paulton Engine, Withy Mill (Timsbury).

Twerton.
Twerton.

Bedminster Coal Field.
Ashton Vale, Bedminster Dean Lane, Starveale, Malago.

Nailsea Coal Field.
Nailsea Heath.[51]

In 1870, the Great Western Railway brought 64 tons of Somerset coal to London.[52] According to Prestwich there were at this date 109 parishes in the coalfield, eighty-three collieries, and sixty-five seams.[53] Prices ranged as follows per ton at the pit's mouth :—

Radstock.
Clandown, 8s. 6d. per ton ; Old Welton, 9s. 6d. and 10s. per ton ; Welton Hill, 7s. 3d. per ton.

Paulton.
Conygre, 10s. per ton ; Camerton, 10s. per ton ; screened, 8s. per ton ; unscreened, slack, 3s. per ton. Farrington, 7s. 1d. per ton ; Withy Mill, 8s. per ton.

Bedminster.
Ashton Vale, 4s., 8s., 10s., 11s., per ton.[54]

From 1870 to 1879, the output of the Somerset coalfield was 6,515,755 tons ; from 1880 to 1889, 8,469,177 tons, and from 1890 to 1900, the amount raised was 8,651, 651 tons.[55] This total of 27,537,126 tons attests the growing prosperity of the industry throughout the period in question. In 1901 the output was 1,341,393 tons from about sixty collieries.[56] The manager of the Braysdown Colliery, Bath, examined before a Parliamentary Commission, in 1903, gave the amount of coal landed in thirty-eight years from that colliery as about 1,500,000 tons, from very thin seams, the maximum not exceeding 24 in., the minimum being 10 in.[57] The thickness of the seams in the Radstock coalfield is 107 ft. 5 in., in 8,318 ft. of strata.[58] The increase of brick-burning in this district accounts, it is said, for the proportionate increase in the sale of small coal.[59] A royalty is paid to the landlord of one-twelfth the selling price, irrespective of the cost of mining.[60]

An account of the geology of the Somerset coalfield has already been given in the first

---

[42] Add. MS. 33656, fol. 29.
[43] *Min. Journ.* iii, 135.
[44] *Child. Empl. Com.* App. ii, 31.
[45] Ibid. xv, 22.   [46] Ibid. 105.
[47] *Newcastle Chron.* 19 October, 1844.
[48] Murray, *Handbook*, 1856, p. 147.
[49] *Bath and W. of Engl. Agric. Journ.* vi, 131.
[50] *The Radstock Portion of the Somersetshire Coal Field*, 10.

[51] *Rep. Coal Supply.* (1871), iii, 125.
[52] Ibid. 109.   [53] Ibid. 65.   [54] Ibid. App. 213.
[55] *Rep. Coal Supply* (1905), xvi, 13.
[56] Hull, *Coalfields of Great Britain*, 78.
[57] *Rep. Coal Supply* (1903), 60.
[58] Ibid. 195.   [59] Ibid. 64.   [60] Ibid. 63.

volume of this history, but it may be of use to add here a general section of the Somerset coal measures within the Radstock district, together with the overlying formations, which cover four-fifths of the entire area, and form a distinguishing feature of the district.[61]

[61] This table was supplied to the Coal Commissioners in 1903 by Mr. J. McMurtrie, F.G.S., who has done so much to increase our knowledge of the Somerset mining field.

	Number		Coal	Total Coal	Total Thickness of Strata
			Ft. In.	Ft. In.	Feet.
Overlying formations as at Braysdown.	—	Inferior oolite			26
	—	Lias			116
	—	New red sandstone.			176
		Total			318
Upper or Radstock Series.	1	Withy Mills Seam (generally absent) . . .	1 4		
	2	Great Vein	2 0		
	3	Top Little Vein	1 4		
	4	Middle Vein	2 0		1250
	5	Slyving Vein	2 3		
	6	Under Little Vein	1 2		
	7	Bull Vein (absent at several collieries) . . .	2 2		
	8	Nine Inch Vein, 9 in. to 1 ft. (seldom workable)	1 0		
				13 3	
	Unproductive Strata, 550 to 750 ft. (say)				640
Second or Farrington Series.	1	Cathead Seam	2 4		
	2	Top Seam	1 9		
	3	Peacock Seam	1 2		
	4	Middle Seam	2 4		310
	5	Church Close Seam (or New Vein)	1 8		
	6	Seventeen Inch Seam	1 5		
		N.B.—Two or more seams in this group are generally unworkable.		10 8	
	Unproductive Strata, including the Pennant Rock (here of great thickness) and two or three thin seams of coal generally unworkable to profit . .				3000
		Lower Division.			
New Rock Series.	1	Globe Vein	3 0		
	2	Small Coal Vein	3 0		
	3	Two Coal Vein	2 0		
	4	Walkey Course Vein	5 0		
	5	Garden Course Vein	3 6		
	6	Strap Vein	2 6		
	7	Great Course Vein.	4 0		
	8	Firestone Vein	3 0		
	9	Little Course Vein.	1 6		
	10	Dunny Drift Vein, 2 ft. to 5 ft.	3 6		
	11	Hard Coal Vein	3 0		
	12	Perkins Course Vein	2 0		
	13	Foot Coal	2 0		
	14	Branch Vein.	4 0		
	15	Golden Candlestick Vein	2 6		2800
	16	North Shoots Vein.	4 0		
	17	South Shoots Vein.	3 0		
	18	Standing Coal	4 0		
				55 6	
Vobster Series.	19	Fern Rag Vein	2 0		
	20	Stone Rag Vein, 2½ ft. to 6 ft.	4 0		
	21	Main Coal	8 0		
	22	Strap Vein	3 0		
	23	Perrink Vein	3 6		
	24	White Axen Vein	3 0		
	25	Red Axen Vein.	3 0		
	26	Wilmots Vein	1 6		
		(Some of these veins are generally thin and unworkable.)		28 0	
		Total		107 5	8,318

Underlying Strata.—Millstone Grit and Mountain Limestone.

The long-wall system is that invariably adopted at the present time in this coalfield. In the Nailsea district, however, pillar and stall was also worked, but the pits there are now idle. The amount of water and dead ground met with, and the large proportion of small coal produced, led to the closing down of the Nailsea collieries.[62] One attempt was made in the Radstock district to open out a seam by driving a pair of narrow headings with pillars of coal between, on the lines of the system in use in the North of England, but the experiment has never been repeated.[63]

Near Bristol fire-damp is met with in the Bedminster and Ashton seams. Candles can generally be used in the Radstock, Farrington and New Rock series, which are not fiery. The serious explosion which took place at the Norton Hill Colliery, Midsomer Norton, about 10 o'clock on 9 April 1908, and resulted in the death of several miners, was due to coal dust. In the Vobster series however gas is met with and at the Vobster, Edford and Newbury collieries safety lamps are used. As early as the 17th century, as we have already noticed, fatal explosions of fire-damp occurred in the pits of the southern district.

A somewhat primitive method of haulage is still employed to some extent in working the thin seams of the Somerset coalfield, where the coal is 14 in. to 16 in. thick, since 'roads from 4 ft. to 5 ft. high are carried up to the face at distances of about 40 yds. apart, and along these tubs are brought. In the face the coal is loaded on to an ordinary plank, about 12 in. broad and 6 ft. long, one end of which is fastened to a piece of chain having a hook at the end farthest from the plank. The chain is passed between a boy's legs and the hook connected to a ring on a leather belt fastened round his waist. The plank is dragged to the way-end, and its load placed in the tub waiting there.'[64] At the New

Rock Colliery, for instance, where the Small Coal and Garden Course seams are worked, and at the Edford where the seams worked are the Standing Coal, Main Coal and Perrink, with sections measuring fully 4 ft., no ponies are used underground. In the neighbouring Newbury collieries however horses take the coal to the pit bottom from the stages or from the gug-bottoms.[65]

Haulage by steam-power and to a less degree by compressed air has also of late years been more widely extended in both the Radstock and Bristol districts. There are many recorded attempts to find coal south of the Mendips, as for example at Hutton,[66] Badgworth,[67] Brewham near Bruton,[68] in the bituminous beds of the Lower Lias at Chard,[69] when a sum of £3,000 was uselessly expended, at Compton Dundon in 1815,[70] at Ebbor in 1871 in the Lower Limestone shales, between Easton and Priddy, at High Ham near Langport, and at Witham Hole near Frome.[71]

Regarding the future of this coalfield, Sir William Lewis writes as follows : 'Assuming an average colliery consumption of 5 per cent., the estimated quantity down to a depth of 4,000 ft. (4,198,301,099 tons) would yield a marketable quantity of 3,988,386,041 tons; which on the basis of the output of the year 1903 (1,395,287 tons) would endure for 2,858 years.'[72]

Among the chief collieries now at work in Somerset may be mentioned the Bishop Sutton and New Rock, the Braysdown, Bromley, Camerton, Clandown, Conygre, Dunkerton, Edford, Farrington, Greyfield, Kilmersdon, Newbury, Norton Hill, Old Mills, Radstock, South Liberty and Writhlington.

According to the latest returns, 6,199 persons are engaged in the industry,[73] the amount of coal raised in the county in 1908 being 1,136,506 tons, a slight decrease on the output of the previous year.

ZINC

No definite record of the mining of any of the ores of zinc in Somerset before the second half of the 16th century has yet been brought to light. Elizabeth however had not been many years on the throne before a revival of interest in mining and metal-working was

fostered and encouraged by the Government. One of the chief English movers was William Humfrey, chief assayer of the Mint, who was ably seconded by skilled metallurgists from Germany and especially his associate and partner, Christopher Shutz, ' a jewel not to be lost,' as

[62] 'Methods of working the Thin Coal-Seams of the Bristol and Somerset Coal-field,' by Mr. G. E. J. McMurtrie, Assoc. M. Inst. C.E. in *Trans. Fed. Inst. Mining Engineers*, xx, 348.   [63] Ibid. 194.

[64] Hughes, *Text-Book of Coal-Mining*, 224. For a fuller account of the various systems of haulage employed in the Somerset collieries see 'Methods of Working the Thin Coal-Seams of the Bristol and Somerset Coalfield' by Mr. G. E. J. McMurtrie, Assoc. M. Inst. C.E., in *Trans. Fed. Inst. Mining Engineers*, xx, 340 et seq.

[65] *Trans. Fed. Inst. Mining Engineers*, xx, 340 *ut supra.*

[66] Phelps, *Hist. Somerset*, i, 30.

[67] Woodward, *Geol. E. Somerset*, 47.

[68] Woodward, *Geol. Engl. and Wales*, 195.

[69] De la Beche, *Geol. Devon*, etc., 515.

[70] *Quart. Journ. Geol. Soc.* xxiii, 457.

[71] Woodward, *Geol. E. Somerset*, 48.

[72] *Rep. Coal Supply* (1903), i, 13.

[73] *Gen. Rep. and Statistics Mines and Quarries for 1908* (publ. 1909), 179.

Humfrey told Cecil. Amongst other projects considered was a factory for making latten. For this copper could be got easily, but some difficulty was at first encountered in finding the necessary calamine [1] in England, though its occurrence here seems to have been suspected by or even known to certain expert metallurgists. The following letter of Humfrey, dated 27 November 1565,[2] speaks for itself :—

As touching the callamyn stone whereof I have dyvers presumptions, one of them allready fayleing in the late travayle of Christopher Shutz, notwithstanding yf all the rest shold fayle (which God defend) yet is not the grownde of my travayle so sclender as that preveledge which the Quenes Majesty hath graunted for battery sholde thereby be of smalle force ; may it therefore pleas your honor to understand that my principall grounde for callamyn is from the mynes of Akon wher it is to be had in great aboundance for the said myne lieth open to all people that will buy therof withowte restraynte, and that which is to be brought into this realme for 7s. the hundred waight cannot be recovered to Nurhenburgh for 14s. the hundredwaight by reason of land carriage and allso when yt is made into battery thear that which serveth Fraunce Flanders England, Skotland and other places is allso brought by land carriage to Handwarp which is very chargeable, the which cuntryes lieth all open by sea to England, and as any place of the northe est parte of this reallme cann recover the said stone from Akon better cheap then that citie of Norhenburgh by reason of carriage so may this reallme serve yt sellf of all manner battery or anything made of latten and allso serve many other countryes better cheap then Germany can doo having the principall matter within this reallme therto belonging (which is copper) for callamyn will not comyx with any mettall to becum mettall but with copper only. And as yt hathe pleased God to dyscover aboundance of copper so doo I believe that when it shall pleas God to remove the tokens of his dyspleasure from me to fynde or have dyscovered within this realme the Callamyn stone allso, and as one Ewstace Rogo, a straunger, sumthing skyllfull in drye mynerealls and drawing oyles from them dyd use conference with me in dyssolving and comyxing mettales so did I speak of the straunge nature of the callamyn which will neyther becum metalle of himselfe by any arte neyther with the helpe of any other mettall but with copper only, which stranger ys nowe with my lorde Mengy, and most like have spoken to my lorde of the said stone who after he had lerned to know yt dyd make serch for the same and hath founde yt as my lorde himself have said unto me. There is also gyven me twoo other tokens one frome the Bathe, thother from the Isle of Wight. And Danyell Howghstetter did tell me that he did knowe that here was callamyn in England, but he wold not tell me whear he had founde yt, for he is very secret and so is Hance Louer.

In no long time after the writing of this letter Humfrey was able to announce [3] that calamine had been definitely located by his agents, and that he hoped that Shutz, then lying ill in London, would very shortly be ready

to travayll westward abowte such busines as we have determyned for a tyme to kepe seacret from all menn saving my Lorde of Lecester and your honor because no brute shold be made thereof untyll all things comodious may be effectually wrought. The matter is that sithence February last a straunger and an Englyshman have rangyd by dyrection to the most likely places for the fynding of the callamyn and now thanks be gyven to The Creator of all things, it is founde and yet unknowne to the fynders for they have brought it by resemble of such descriptions as have bene gevin them.

He goes on to speak of its superior quality as shown by the assay when compared with samples brought from Germany, and declares distinctly that it 'is founde in Somersetshire in mo places than one.' These however are not named, but one was almost certainly Worle.[4] The matter is however of little importance as very soon calamine was also reported to have been found in the neighbourhood of the Mendips and within the common and waste grounds of Wrington. At the time when his agents made this discovery Humfrey was preparing to set up works at Wandsworth, but in consequence this attempt was stayed and a site was sought in Somerset but without success. Finally Tintern was selected, but with the vicissitudes of the Mineral and Battery Works Company and its undertakings we cannot here deal.

From this time forward for at least two and a half centuries the county of Somerset produced the largest amount of the best quality of calamine raised in England. Late in the reign of Elizabeth the ore was being obtained largely at Wrington on the commons and waste grounds of Sir Arthur Capell, as we learn from depositions [5] taken in a lawsuit in the summer of 1599. A wain load of calamine stone was then stated to consist of 20 cwt. Unburnt and unpicked ore was worth 7s. or at the very most 8s. a ton, according to report, while from 3 tons of the unburnt or raw stone, 2 tons of the prepared ore might be obtained. Edward Jenynges, a London grocer, declared he had often bought and sold calamine. Sometimes he paid 40s. the cwt., sometimes 20s. 8d., and on one occasion only he bought 4 or 5 cwt. of the stone at 16s. the hundred, but at no time under that price. The prices at which he had sold were 56s., 40s. and 37s. 4d. the cwt., but never under that price. With these prices may be compared the experience of another London grocer, Edward Collyns, who at various times had bought calamine at 40s., 26s. 8d. and 20s. the hundred and on one occasion only at 16s. His selling prices had ranged from a maximum of 56s. the cwt. to as low as 30s. and even 28s. William Oldaway, a London gold-

---

[1] That is carbonate of zinc.
[2] S.P. Dom. Eliz. xxxvii, 73.
[3] Ibid. xl, 17, 30 June 1566.

[4] See Lansd. MS. 81, fol. 1. A lease was acquired at Worle Hill from Sir Henry Wallop.
[5] Exch. Dep. by Com. Trin. 41 Eliz. 8, Somerset.

smith, a man of middle age, deposed that he knew 'the callamine stone for he hath wrought with it thes seaven yeares and it is used to be commixed with copper and thereof is made a mettall called lattyn and this deponent knoweth the same by his owne experience for that he hath wrought more thereof, than any man in Ingland as he thincketh' but he had never bought any though he had wrought much.

Another London goldsmith who knew and used calamine was one Francis Leake, aged thirty years or thereabouts, who stated that 'an hundred weight of the like callamine stone, which was shewed unto this deponent . . . is well worth fiftene shillings the hundred weight as he taketh it for that he this deponent in working thereof hath made as much of an hundred weight of the like, above all chardges.'

Of the processes employed by Mendip and Wrington calamine 'groovers' we have a detailed account in 1684 when Giles Pooley described [6] what he had seen in Wrington and the neighbourhood for the benefit of the Royal Society. The miners informed him that there existed no certainty at all in finding out the calamine but that it was a mere lottery. Pooley however shrewdly observed that they always dug for it upon and near the hills.

The method they take for finding out a vein is by digging a trench as deep as till they come to the rocks where they expect it lies, across the place where they hope for a course; which trench they generally dig from north to south or near upon that point, the courses usually lying from east to west, or at 6 o'clock as they term it. Though this is not constant neither for sometimes the courses, seams or rakes as they call them lie at nine o'clock and sometimes are perpendicular, which they call the high time of the day or 12 o'clock and these courses they esteem the best. These seams or courses run between the rocks generally wider than those of lead ore unless they are inclosed in very hard cliffs and then they are as narrow as the veins of lead. The colour of the earth where calamine lies is generally a yellow grit but sometimes black; for all countries as they term their underground works are not alike.

The calamine ore was found of various colours, but the best was blackish. It was sometimes intermixed with lead. Generally, as Pooley pointed out, 'it riseth in small particles, some more, some less, and some about the bigness of a nut and this they call a small calamine.' He mentions however as exceptional 'one entire piece of 8 or 10 tuns which by reason of its bigness was forced to be broken in the groove before it could be landed.' When ancient works were re-opened and worked, 'damps and staunches sometimes arise,' but trouble from this cause could be got rid of by means of air-shafts.

[6] Letter to Sir Robert Southwell, P.R.S. in *Philos. Trans.* xvii, 672 et seq.

The ore dug was landed by 'winding it up in buckets from their works' and then carried away to be buddled. For this purpose

they enclose a small piece of ground with boards or turfs through which a clean stream of water runs; within this enclosure they shovel their calamine with the rest of the impure and earthy parts; and these impure and earthy parts the running water . . . carries away, and leaves the lead and the calamine and the other heavier, stony and sparry parts behind; and for the better cleansing or buddling the calamine . . . they often turn it, that so the water passing through may wash it the better. When they have thus washed it with this running stream as clean as they can, having raked up the bigger parts both of the lead and the calamine, they afterwards put the smaller parts that they may lose none of their ore into sieves made of strong wire at the bottom, and these sieves with the calamine, lead and the remainder of the earthy, sparry and stony parts which the water could not wash away they often dip and shake up and down in a great tub of water, by which the parts of the lead . . . sink to the bottom of the sieves as being heaviest, the parts of the calamine in the middle and the other sparry, stony and trashy parts rise up to the top, which as they rise they skim off, and then take off the calamine and after that the lead.

The calamine was then spread upon a board and any stone or trash that remained carefully picked out by hand. The processes just described were necessarily followed in the preparation of the smaller calamine. Some ore however was got big enough out of the works 'to be cleansed and pickt fit for the calcining oven without all this charge and pains.' Pooley had himself seen several loads of this great calamine.

His description of the calcining-oven [7] in use at this time is somewhat minute:—

The oven, at least that which I saw, is much bigger than any bakers oven and made much in the same fashion, only this way of heating, burning or baking the calamine is different; for it is not done as bread is, for they cast in their coals into a hearth made on one side of the oven which is divided from the oven itself by a hem or partition made open at the top, whereby the flame of the fire passeth over and so heats and bakes the calamine. They let it lie in the oven for the space of four or five hours, the fire burning all the while, according to the strength of the calamine, some being much stronger than others and so requiring longer time; and while it continues in the oven they turn it several times with long iron cole-rakes. When it is sufficiently burnt, baked and dried, they beat it

[7] Dr. Merrett writing rather earlier than this in 1662 explains that the calamine stone 'must be first calcined in a furnace like the *calcar* with a small hole on one side to put fire in, which may be either of coal or wood, but wood is best, because it maketh the greatest flame, and consequently the best *reverberation*. . . . Almost half of the *calamie* (as the workmen call it) is wasted and flies away in flour, which sticks to the mouth of the furnace, of divers colours of little use with them.' Neri, *The Art of Glass*, 300

to a powder with long iron hammers like mallets upon a thick plank, picking out what stones they find amongst it.

A large portion of the calamine thus prepared was exported from England, for the most part to Holland as ballast, but during the 18th century at least the brass-works of Bristol and after 1743 its newly-introduced zinc-smelting took a considerable portion of the output of the Somerset mines.[8] Keynsham also took a portion of the output and later Birmingham and perhaps other places at some distance. In the second half of this century as Watson[9] tells us Somerset calamine fetched from 65s. to 70s. a ton before dressing, while the Derbyshire variety could be obtained at 40s. He was also of opinion that by calcination the picked ore lost between a third and a fourth of its weight. Even as late as 1791, the date of Collinson's work, the mining of calamine was still in a very flourishing condition in and around the Mendips. Nearly all of the men of Shipham[10] were miners 'constantly employed in raising the *lapis calaminaris*.' There were then according to his account 'upwards of one hundred of these mines working, many of which are in the street, in the yards, and some in the very houses. The usual depth of the shafts was from 6 to 12 fathoms.' An industrious miner could at this place earn as much as a guinea a day. At Rowberrow the industry was almost equally active and at that time very little wood throve near the village owing to the destructive fumes arising from the calcination of the ore. Several mines were working on Broadfield Down at Wrington. Indeed the aggregate annual production of calamine in Somerset between 1780 and 1790 must have been very considerable. Collinson's account is corroborated by Billingsley[11] in his *General View of the Agriculture of Somerset*. He states that valuable mines of *lapis calaminaris* existed in the parishes of Rowberrow, Shipham and Winscombe, while in the parishes of Compton Martin and East Harptree were others affording constant employment to a number of men. The use of the divining-rod, vulgarly called 'josing,' was still in request for the location of new seams of ore. 'So confident,' he declares, 'are the common minds of its efficacy, that they scarce ever sink a shaft but by its direction; and those who are dexterous in the use of it, will mark on the surface the course and breadth of the vein; and after that with the assistance of the rod, will follow the same course twenty times following blindfolded.' A gentleman added a note to Billingsley's remarks in the 1798 or second edition of his *View* that:

[8] Black Jack or blende as well as calamine was used at the Bristol brass-works.
[9] *Chemical Essays* (1786) iv, 9.
[10] *Hist. of Somerset*, iii, 600.
[11] Op. cit (ed. 2), 21 et seq.

At Merchant's Hill in the parish of Binegar, several tons were raised some years ago. It was of very good quality, and more would have been landed, had not the influx of the water put a stop to the works. At the same time a large quantity was raised at Mells, remarkably pure, free from heterogeneous mixture, and of excellent quality. It did not there descend, in regular courses, between the limestone rocks, but was found in large masses or hulks, lying horizontally, at about 4 or 5 ft. from the surface, on a thin scale of freestone which covered the rock.

Disputes seem to have arisen during the 18th century as to whether miners of calamine and ochre were bound to pay the tenth or lot-ore as in the case of lead, and the matter was considered by the mineral grand jury of Chewton. Mr. J. MacMurtrie[12] has brought to light an order of this court, dated 25 November 1773, and confirmed on 15 December following, which after reciting the circumstances necessitating its promulgation enacted:

that all and every person and persons whosoever adventuring, digging, mining and trying for and after Lapis Calaminaris otherwise Calamy or Calamine, Magnes Oker or yellow earth shall be henceforth subject and conformable to all the Mineral Laws and orders of the said forest of Mendip relating to Lead and Lead Ore in as full and ample a manner, and to all intents and purposes whatsoever, as if the said Minerals or Fossils were of the same species, kind or quality, whether they adventure, work, digg, mine or try in or upon the said forest of Mendip or in, upon or within any of the said inclosed lands lying and being within the royalty and liberty aforesaid: provided that all such person and persons so mining working and adventuring in the said inclosed lands, have no lease or grant for mining and working such inclosed lands from and under the hand and seal of the lord or lords of the fee.

This of course involved, as the order afterwards exposed in detail, that the 'full tenth part and customary lott or share' must be paid to the lord under pain of forfeiture of the 'goods landed' and that all disputes about the ownership or working of pitches where these minerals were being dug must be decided by the mineral grand jury of Chewton.

With the 19th century, if not before, began a decline in the mining of the ores of zinc in Somerset, which ended at last in the utter extinction of the local industry. Changes in the methods of brass-making had no doubt something to do with its rather rapid descent. In 1839 Sir H. G. De La Beche tells[13] us that at Worle Hill and the Bleadon Hills the working of calamine had been discontinued for some time but that one or two mines were still at work elsewhere in the county. At the present time no calamine is raised in Somerset, nor has there been any appreciable amount worked for at least half a century.

[12] *Trans. Fed. Inst. Mining Engineers*, xx, 579.
[13] *Report on Geology of Cornwall, Devon and West Somerset* (1839), 88, 320, 616.

IRON

Iron ore is widely distributed in the county of Somerset, but though there are clear indications that in several quarters it was mined and smelted at an early period,[1] documentary evidence is slight. According to tradition the spathose ores of the Brendon Hills were worked by the Romans. There is some probability in this, although the tools found at Luxborough[2] may quite possibly belong to miners of a later time. Yet even if the existing refuse heaps and scoriae are mainly of the Middle Age, the iron-slag discovered at Whitestaunton Villa seems to imply the existence of iron-smelting in the neighbourhood during the Romano-British period, while the very early occurrence of the name Sindercombe reminds us of the parallel use of Cinderford in the Forest of Dean and suggests an obvious explanation.

At Glastonbury[3] eight smiths are mentioned in the Domesday Survey, but the iron there used may quite possibly have been procured from the manor of Pucklechurch in Gloucestershire which then belonged to the monks. Whether the blooms of iron rendered by several manors in 1086 were produced within the county must be regarded as an open question, but the iron-pits and slag found in certain places as at Holcombe point to the existence of small local bloomeries.[4] Even in the Middle Lias round Ilminster, as modern analysis shows, the marlstone often contains a proportion of carbonate of iron reaching as high as 36 per cent. and may have been worth working when ways were bad and there was little competition from outside. On the Mendips iron was certainly worked in the 13th century,[5] and three hundred years later Harrison speaks of the ore existing there. By the 15th century the smiths of Bristol and Long Ashton can hardly have been ignorant of the haematite and argillaceous iron which lay close at hand, especially as coal had been certainly worked in Kingswood at least as early as the 13th century and possibly in northern Somerset also.

One cause of the slight development of any local iron industry in Somerset may be found in the flourishing iron trade of the Forest of Dean. We know that in the 13th century the citizens of Bristol were accustomed to resort thither to purchase the metal.[6] Two hundred years later the quantity of Spanish iron brought into Bristol had reached enormous proportions. During the month of May[7] 1475 the value of foreign iron declared at the customs[8] was between £800 and £900, besides such manufactured goods as '4 gonnez worth 20s.' and 30,000 'bourdeneylls' worth £3 12s. 6d. Probably this was an exceptional month which witnessed the arrival of several ships of Spain sailing together for mutual protection. Without however attaching too much importance to particular figures, we may reasonably conclude that the combined competition of Gloucester and Spanish iron was too powerful to permit the rise of a robust industry in Somerset iron during the later Middle Age.

In the reign of Elizabeth certain iron-mills existed in the county, notably one named Horner Mill situated in the parish of Luccombe and set up by George Hensley of Selworthy and his brothers William and Robert. Some at least of the iron was bought from 'one Jeremy Waters.' Whether this was Somerset iron is not quite clear. It is possible that it was obtained outside the county.[9] Later again in the 18th century we hear of two iron forges at work in Wadbury or Modbury Vale, near Mells, and a considerable manufacture of implements of husbandry which found a ready market in the West of England, and even occasionally in America.[10]

In modern times iron-mining in the county has been intermittent but in the aggregate a considerable amount of the ore has been raised. At Ashton Vale in 1871 an extensive iron trade was being carried on, a great variety of ores being reduced, including the Clay-band ores from the neighbouring colliery, the Red Haematites also from the county, the Brown Ores of Northampton, and a small amount from Barrow-in-Furness. Good ironstones have been found in the measures of the Nettlebridge Valley, the most important being the Red Haematite. The ironstone was wrought in several geological positions; in the Carboniferous Limestone of the Mendips and Leigh Down, it lay in pockets, the quality being good, though the mode of occurrence rendered the return uncertain. At Priddy successful workings have been carried on, in spite of the long distance to which the

---

[1] Iron seems to have been worked in the county even before the Roman occupation. See *V.C.H. Somerset*, i, 198.

[2] Now in Taunton Museum, figured *Somerset Arch. Soc. Proc.* viii, 18, pl. ii.

[3] *V.C.H. Somerset*, i, 460.

[4] *Somers. Arch. Soc. Proc.* xxx, 81. Cf. for Carhampton parish, Collinson, op. cit. ii, 21. It may be worth notice that in a few Somerset and Hampshire manors chevage was at an early period paid in iron bars (*esperducae*) or 'sclabbes.' At Chedzoy this practice lasted as late as the early years of Edward III (B.M. Add. R.R. 16117 et seq.).

[5] Close, 19 Hen. III, m. 11, 12.

[6] For. Proc. Tr. of Rec. no. 29, m. 5 d.

[7] K.R. Customs Accts. bdle. 19, no. 11.

[8] It must be remembered, however, that Bristol included besides the port of that name several creeks.

[9] See Chadwyck-Healey, *Hist. of Part of West Somerset*, 102, et seq.

[10] Collinson, op. cit. ii, 461.

ironstone required to be carried by cart over hilly roads.[11] Nodules of iron ore were burnt and ground at Chew Magna for ruddle, a red powder used for common paint and for marking sheep.[12]

Since 1852 the spathose ore of the Brendon Hills has been largely worked by the Ebbw Vale Company, who constructed a railway to Watchet for the purposes of their industry. Carbonate of iron has near the surface been converted into brown hæmatite.[13] The ore, containing from 13 to 14 per cent. of the protoxide of manganese, was largely utilized for the manufacture of spiegeleisen. From 1873 to 1878 the average annual production of these mines exceeded 40,000 tons, in 1882 it was 36,000 tons. After this the output greatly decreased. In 1895 the iron ore raised in Somerset from open works or quarries was 4,313 tons, in 1900 6,139 tons, but in 1906 and 1907 no returns were made.[14]

Since then however the Somerset Mineral Syndicate have again started to mine the rich ores of the Brendon Hills. The syndicate has obtained exclusive mining rights over about 9½ miles of country, covering the district between Ison, near Withypool, on the one hand, and Elworthy on the other.[15] In 1908 2,550 tons of ore were raised, showing an average 55 percentage of iron and valued at the mines at £1,800.[16]

BUILDING STONE

Few counties are richer in excellent building stone than Somerset, and among its quarries those of Ham Hill, Doulting and Bath have won pre-eminent repute.

The buff iron-tinctured stone of Ham Hill on the uplands north-west of Yeovil was quarried as early[1] as any, for there may be seen in the museum of Dorchester a Roman coffin evidently wrought from the stone of a well-opened quarry on the slopes of Hamdon.[2] From the Norman period right down through the later Middle Age Ham Hill stone not only was used locally,[3] as at Montacute and Sherborne, but also made its way southward to Cerne, Ford and Lyme Regis, north-westward to Bridgwater and Taunton. In Somerset it was sometimes employed together with the freestone of Doulting and rougher material from local quarries, as for example in the walls, now levelled, of Castle Cary.[4]

Some of the finest ecclesiastical work[5] in Ham Hill stone which still remains was done in the 15th century, which seems to have witnessed a special activity at the quarries. About 1455 we hear[6] of ten quarries 'super Hampdon' belonging to the manor of Stoke which were leased to John Dore and his partners, the yearly rent payable to the lord being 4d. each in the case of nine of these and 1s. in the case of the tenth, until they were utterly worked out, 'according to the custom of the quarries there.' By 1478 these workings were apparently exhausted,[7] but a rent of 4s. 8d. had been received for several fresh quarries let to divers tenants, including among others the Abbot of Ford, Thomas Vestmentmaker, William Cole, Robert Solley, Thomas Trevelian and Richard Bray,[8] at the rate of 4d. a year for each quarry as before.[9] In another quarry mentioned the size is specified as 24 ft. square (*in longitudine 24 pedes et in latitudine tantum*). The annual rent was the usual 4d., but 6s. 8d. had also been paid as a fine. It was leased for life to Alnold Craftman. Early in the reign of Henry VIII there seems to have been slightly less activity and the issues of divers quarries within the manor in 1516 amounted to the sum of a quarter of a mark.[10]

Other important quarries belonged to the parish of Norton. From a 16th-century terrier[11] it appears that the ancient quarries here were 20 ft. square by measure and that when this survey was drawn up there were fourteen of them occupied and worked. The lessee on receiving the quarry from the bailiff paid a fine of 40s. ' of certainty of old time used ' as well as a yearly rent of 12d. And according to the accustomed order of this manor, ' Every such taker of any

---

[11] South-west of Frome also iron has been worked intermittently, as for example by the Furzeham Iron Ore Company at Nunney in 1873.

[12] Wood, *Hist. Chew Magna*, 2.

[13] Phillips and Louis, *Ore Deposits*, 241.

[1] For mill-stones and whetstones, however, the famous Pen Pits were excavated first in pre-historic times and may be of equal antiquity with the oldest quarries on Hamdon.

[2] Trask, *Norton-sub-Hamdon*, 215.

[3] As Leland says, ' The notable quarre of stone ys even therby at Hamden out of the which hath beene taken many a day stones for al the goodly buildinges thereabout in al quarters.' *Itin.* ii, 64.

[4] *Somerset Arch. Soc. Proc.* xxxvi, 171.

[5] e.g. the quire of Sherborne.

[6] P.R.O. Mins. Accts. bdle. 1095, no. 7.

[14] Ibid.; *Mineral Reports and Statistics.*

[15] *Western Morning News*, 27 May 1907.

[16] *Gen. Rep. and Statistics Mines and Quarries*, 215.

[7] Another quarry worked out is described as a ' hoterell quarrera petrarum super Hampdoun vocata Iopesboure sic nuper dimissa Willelmo Power.'

[8] Mins. Accts. bdle. 1123, no. 3 (16–17 Edw. IV).

[9] There was doubtless also a substantial fine on entry.

[10] Mins. Accts. 6–7 Hen. VIII, Somerset.

[11] Cited by Mr. Trask in his *History of Norton-sub-Hamdon.*

quarry, his executors and assigns shall hold and enjoy his quarry as long as he will work and occupy the same and pay the said rent. And if he cease working upon the said quarry for the space of one whole year together then his interest in the same quarry shall be forfeited to the lords.'

It is evident that the old workings were comparatively shallow and above the workable building stone the heading was formed of rubble and thin layers of hard stone, which provided the tiles so often employed in ancient buildings of the better sort. A tile-pick[12] was formerly used in working these upper layers to an even thickness, but owing to changed fashions in roofing as well as the depth of the modern quarries, the ancient craft of tile-making is no longer practised at Hamdon Hill.

The free-working limestone of Doulting, light brown in hue, consistent in texture and thoroughly durable, is most nobly used in the existing fabric of the cathedral church of Wells. The abbey of Glastonbury, once her rival, lies dismembered and in ruin. St. Cuthbert's, Wells, with numerous other parish churches and several secular buildings of account happily still remains. The disused St. Andrew's quarry at Doulting is pointed out as that whence the greater portion of the stone used in the building of Wells Cathedral was taken, and the remaining records of the secular canons of Wells and the monks of Glastonbury, fragmentary though they be, contain numerous references to the Doulting quarries.[13] These were indeed for many centuries a source of considerable profit to the abbey.

In the thirteenth year of his rule Abbot Walter de Monyngton granted[14] twenty wain loads of stone from Doulting quarry to William de Cammel, canon of Wells, and in the following year at the instance of the Dean and chapter of Wells allowed fifty wain-loads of freestone to be taken for the repair of the great bell-tower of the cathedral church.[15] When leave was given to strangers to obtain stone from the abbey quarries at Doulting instructions[16] were issued to the bailiff and reeve as well as the keeper of the stone quarry with reference to the conditions under which the grantees were to work. Nine years after the last warrant mentioned Walter de Monyngton at the request of the Bishop of Bath gave permission for the taking of freestone 'signanter de petra in petram' as it lay 'in the place where the workmen of Whatelegh last

left off, southward to that place where the workmen of the said church [of Wells] have dug at other times.' The officers of the abbey were to keep the tale of the loads of stone removed and give account thereof to their lord. They were also 'thrice in the week at least' to inspect the Wells quarrymen and take care that they did no damage to the abbot's quarry but dug lawfully (pure) and within their proper bounds. If, however, in spite of precautions any damage was done the stranger workmen must pay for it (sufficienter emendent) before they left.

Rather later in the same century, in the year 1381, Henry Parker vicar of Doulting,[17] with the consent of Abbot John of Glastonbury, granted 1 acre called Estheyforlang, a parcel of his glebe measuring in length on the south side 15 perches 8 ft., on the north 16 perches, at the east head 9 perches 6 ft. and at the west head 8 perches 4 ft., to the Dean and chapter of Wells to provide a quarry for the use of the fabric of the cathedral church. For this a yearly rent of 18d. was to be paid at Easter.

The remaining fabric-rolls[18] of Wells, unfortunately for the most part late in time and in some cases imperfect, contain numerous references to the Doulting quarries, their working, the provision of tools and wheel-barrows and the carriage of the stone to Wells. In 1457 for instance we hear that 12d. a wain load was the rate of carriage from the quarries to the cathedral church. John Parsons was paid for 'ridding' 16 ft. sq. of the quarry 4s. for twelve days' work or at the rate of 4d. a day. Thomas Nabbe received 13d. for providing elm-boards for a wheel-barrow. 6d. was paid for making it and for iron 14d. For two 'vangis ferreis' for the quarry weighing 19 lb. Thomas the Smith was paid 19d. at 1d. the lb. and we hear of other crowbars and quarrying tools purchased for use at Doulting.

The wardens' accounts of St. John's Church, Glastonbury, contain several allusions to the Doulting quarries, especially in reference to the existing 15th-century fabric. About[19] 1428 we hear of expenditure 'in liberis petris tractandis et frangendis apud Doulting,' and for their carriage to Glastonbury. 'Walston' however was procured at Street[20] at the same time, while £4 was paid to John Gryme the mason for making anew the church porch and covering it with freestone and 'walston' by piecework. Later,[21] but probably before 1458, we hear

---

[12] Trask, *Norton-sub-Hamdon*, 217.

[13] As may be imagined several surnames were derived from the chief industry of Doulting. In the Vicesima Roll for the first year of Edward III occur Walter atte Quarere, 6d.; William atte Quarere, 12d.; Robert atte Quarere, 3s. Lay Subs. Somerset, bdle. 169, no. 5.

[14] B.M. MS. Arundel 2, fol. 18 d.

[15] Ibid. fol. 27.   [16] Ibid. fol. 79 d.

[17] Liber Albus fol. 281 d; *Cal. D. and C. of Wells MSS.* (Hist. MSS. Com.) i, 290, 291.

[18] Cited in *Hist. MSS. Com. Rep.* x, App. iii, 285 et seq.

[19] *N. and Q. Somerset and Dorset*, iv, 143.

[20] Occasionally also ordinary building stone was brought from Overleigh.

[21] *N. and Q. Somers. and Dorset*, v, 285.

of no less than 152 wain loads of freestone being obtained from Doulting and of the purchase of saws, wedges and other iron tools, while on one occasion Robert Prusshe the quarrier was propitiated with a gratuity (*in rewardo*) of 20*d.* presumably beyond his wages.

The abbey of Glastonbury was still deriving considerable profit [22] from their quarries at Doulting right up to the time of the dissolution of the house, for in the account of this manor for 26–27 Henry VIII the eleventh year of the last abbot martyred on Glastonbury Tor, we read of £2 5*s.* 5½*d.* from the issues of the freestone quarry there beyond the expenses incurred 'in extraccione earundarum liberarum petrarum.'

While much Bath oolite was certainly raised in Somerset for local use during the Middle Age,[23] the most famous quarries of this stone then worked apparently lay within the county of Wiltshire and the main exploitation of the Combe Down stone seems to have been undertaken after the 16th century. Of other quarries beyond those briefly noticed here much might be gathered from fragmentary local records if our limited space allowed. One of these however, the quarry of Dundry, cannot be entirely passed over since it so often figures on the early accounts of the see of Bath. This quarry was usually let on lease by the Bishop of Bath and Wells, and we hear of 2*s.* 6*d.* rent being paid at the Midsummer term during the vacancy of the see [24] following the death of William of March in 1302 (12 June 30 Edw. I) while during the vacancy caused by Walter Hasleshaw's death a few years after [25] the stone quarry 'super Dundray' was linked by the accountant with the lead-mines of Mendip, and the joint receipts for about five months amounted to 28*s.* Dundry stone was employed to a considerable extent in mediaeval Bristol and in the manors adjacent. At Yatton for instance in 1491 much stone was brought from Dundry for use at the parish church.[26] Not only has the inferior oolite been quarried at Dundry Hill but also at Felton and Broadfield. The hardbed of the Felton quarries supplied stone for Bristol Bridge as well as for the noble churches of Wrington, Yatton, Backwell, Congresbury and many other places in the North Marsh.[27]

The development of the Combe Down quarries at Bath in the 18th century was owing

to the enterprise of Ralph Allen,[28] who, on the completion of the Avon navigation in 1727, set about the extension of the Bath freestone trade. As a preliminary he constructed a road from the summit of the hill to the riverside, thereby reducing the cost of transporting stone to the waterside from 10*s.* to 7*s.* 6*d.* per ton. He next proceeded to build houses for the workmen engaged at the quarries, locating the quarrymen on Combe Down, and the banker masons at Widcombe. Some of these houses, says Mr. Green in his *Eighteenth-Century Architecture in Bath*, may still be seen at Old Widcombe, where they continue to be known as Allen's Cottages, characteristic features of their construction being their roofs of worked stone tabling, as in the lodges on Carriage Drive.[29] A modern architectural authority claims for this roofing that a more artistic covering can hardly be conceived.[30]

About 1730, Allen began to develop the Hampton Down quarries, now closed. Nearly all the stone from these quarries was hewn in the open, dressed with much care, and laid by for seasoning. In order to convey the stone from the hill-side, a series of short trams were laid on to a centre, where a large drum was constructed, worked by some kind of machinery the secret of which is unknown. On these lines the stone was carried down the slope to the stoneyard or basin at the quays below. The Hampton Down quarries were worked for a short time in 1810 by the Kennet & Avon Canal Company for constructing docks, &c., but it was found that all the best stone had been exhausted, only the inferior kind being left.[31]

The Combe Down tram-road was constructed in 1731. It consisted of two narrow lines, the frame and machinery being fixed on the Down. The lines were so adjusted that the descending tram drew up the empty one at the same time, starting, stopping, and speed being regulated by it. The stone was conveyed on small square wagons, very strong, mounted on small wheels running on low platforms. In the case of contract, the blocks were dressed on the down, having been long seasoned by exposure in the rough. In ordinary cases, the blocks were brought down in the rough. At the bottom of

---

[22] Mins. Accts. 26–27 Hen. VIII.

[23] Leland for instance after leaving the stone bridge over the Midford Brook describes the road to Bath as ' 2 good miles al by mountayne ground and quarre and litle wood in syte ' (*Itin.* ii, 33). The quarries by Holloway were certainly of great antiquity.

[24] Pipe R. 23 Edw. I, m. 32.

[25] Pipe R. 3 Edw. II, pt. ii, m. 6.

[26] *Churchwardens' Accts. Yatton* (Somers. Rec. Soc. iv), 118.

[27] Rutter, *Delineation* (1829), 281 n.

[28] This remarkable man, who from a humble position in the post-office of St. Columb, Cornwall, rose to be Mayor of Bath, amassed a considerable fortune by obtaining from the Government at a cost of £6,000 per annum the lease of the cross posts which he was instrumental in establishing throughout the country. Allen built Prior Park as a practical demonstration of the excellence of the stone with which his name is so closely associated. Green, *Eighteenth-Century Architecture in Bath*, 84.

[29] Wood, *Essay on Bath*, ii, 424; Green, op. cit.

[30] Green, op. cit. 147.

[31] Peach, *Life of Allen*, 76.

the slope, the wagons were placed on a sledge invented by Richard Jones, and transferred to the boats at the quays.[32]

In 1738 the price of block freestone delivered at the Avon side from Ralph Allen's quarries on Combe Down was 7s. 6d. per ton of 20 cubic feet. The price at the present day would be nearly three times as much. Sixteen cubic feet are now reckoned to the ton, and the stone is priced according to the cubic foot, not according to weight.[33]

The Bath stone was not only utilized for building, but a considerable industry was carried on in the city in the production of ornaments in stone, such, we are told, as crests, vases, and fruits. A notable establishment was that of Thomas Greenway, who had several apprentices. Here were manufactured chimney-pieces, door cases, window cases, pedestals, piers, obelisks and balustrades.[34] The house known as The Garrick's Head was built, it is said, by Greenway to display the elaborate Bath stone ornamentation.[35]

Wood's opinion of his native freestone is as follows : ' Our freestone,' he writes, ' is beyond dispute a most excellent building material, as being durable, beautiful and cheap. It has been generally worked in the quarries upon the hills round about the city by men who style themselves Freemasons, that is, men whose province it is to work freestone, and from thence carried ready wrought to the several places where it was to be used in building, by which means the sharp edges and corners of the stone are generally broken. In this condition, the freestone work is usually set up by other men who call themselves Rough Masons, that is, masons whose province it is to work the refuse of the freestone, or the common wall stones. And thus, by dividing the mason's trade into two branches, the works in Bath lose that neatness in the joints between the stones, and that sharpness in the edges of the mouldings which they ought to have, and which people accustomed to good work in other places first look for here.'[36]

According to the Parliamentary Report of 1839 on the building stones of the kingdom, six quarries were then at work, the blocks varying from 12 to 96 ft. cube, the average price being 6d. per cubic foot.[37]

Difficulty is sometimes experienced in determining the bed to which the Bath stone belongs, as it is essential for good building that the stone should be laid in building as it originally lay in the quarry.[38]

Winwood divides the Great Oolite or Bath stone into 20 to 35 ft. of Upper Rags, comprising coarse, shelly limestones, more or less fine oolites, and tough brown argillaceous limestone ; 10 to 30 ft. of fine freestone, and 10 to 40 ft. of Lower Rags, made up of coarse, shelly limestone.[39]

Mr. Randall divides the Bath Oolite into

1. The Upper Ragstones, containing no beds of workable value.

2. The Fine Freestones of building beds.

3. The Lower Ragstones, the chief economic value of which is for local purposes.[40]

The Great Oolite series in the neighbourhood of Bath was thus divided, according to Professor Woodward, by Lonsdale :—

	feet
Upper Rags, coarse, shelly limestones, tolerably fine oolites, tough, brown, argillaceous limestone	20–55
Fine Freestones	10–30
Lower Rags, coarse, shelly limestones . .	10–40 [41]

There are but two quarries now worked in Somerset by the Bath Stone Firms, Limited, that on Combe Down, where the operations are both surface and underground, and Stoke Ground, where the quarrying is entirely underground. At the Shaft or Lodge Style quarry on Combe Down, the stone was taken for building portions of Buckingham Palace and Windsor Castle.[42] These quarries are worked by tunnelling, the stones being produced in blocks up to 5 or 6 ft. in depth, and sometimes 10 to 12 tons in weight. The Combe Down stone, being a good weather stone, is quarried and brought to the surface during the winter as well as the summer.

The following method of winning the Bath stone prevails throughout the quarries, the system being an exact inversion of the mode of working coal. The quarryman commences his operations at the roof of the stone. This picking operation is effected by means of adze-shaped picks on the heads of which longer handles are inserted as the work proceeds, and the men thus make their driving a distance of 6 to 7 ft. back into the rock. The width or span of these stalls must of course depend upon the soundness of the rock. For cutting the rock into blocks of the required dimensions, a one-handled saw is used. These saws are worked in lengths of 4, 5, 6, 7 ft., and are made broad deep at the head or extreme point, so as to ensure the saw sinking to its work at that point. The saw is worked in first horizontally, dropping a little as the cut goes on, and after the rock is thus opened down to the next natural parting, and the block thus separated laterally from the parent rock, levers are introduced into the bed or parting at the bottom of the block, and these levers are weighted and shaken till the block is

---

[32] Peach, *Life of Allen*, 81.

[33] Green, *Eighteenth-Century Architecture* in Bath, 64. [34] Wood, *Essay on Bath*, ii, 424.

[35] Peach, *Life of Allen*, 99.

[36] Wood, *Essay on Bath*, ii, 338–9.

[37] *Rep. Building Stone*, 1839, pp. 7–8.

[38] *Bath Nat. Hist. and Field Club Proc.* viii, 270.

[39] Winwood, *Geol. Bath Dist.* 22.

[40] *Rep. Brit. Assoc.* 1864, p. 152, 4.

[41] Woodward, *Geol. Engl. and Wales*, 187.

[42] T. Sturge Cotterell, *Bath Stone*, 8, 9.

forcibly detached at the back. It is then drawn down by crane power, and the broken end and the bed dressed with the axe, so as to make the block shapely; it is then placed on a trolley, and allowed to run to the loading platform. After the first block is removed, the workmen have access to the back of the bank of stone, and they avail themselves of this to work the saw transversely, the first block of each face being the only stone broken from the rock. To each face a 10-ton crane is erected so as to command the whole heading of work. These cranes are now constructed telescopically, which enables them to be adjusted with less trouble and loss of time to slight variations in the headings, and also to the periodical shifts from old worked-out localities to fresh centres of operation. After a block of stone has been loosened, a lewis bolt is let into the face of it, and the block is drawn out by means of the chain attached to the crane. By the removal of the first stratum, the workmen are able to enter under the roof, vertical cuts are again carried through the next bed to the parting below, and transverse cuts readily made. Meanwhile the cutting is continued in the picking bed, the upper layer removed as before, and everything below this point quarried away, with all the sides of the block sawn, except the bed on which it has rested, and those abutting on the natural joints. Hence each block comes out ready to pass into the hands of the mason and builder. The character assigned to the Bath stone by a modern lithological expert is that of 'one of the best known and most extensively used building stones in the kingdom,' [43] being particularly valuable for moulding and carved work. [44]

The latter part of the 19th century, according to Mr. Trask, witnessed a great development in the Ham Hill quarries, notably with regard to the deep quarries, situated partly in Norton, partly in Montacute, which have only been worked for the last sixty years. [45] The quarrying of the stone, says Mr. Trask, preparatory to its removal, is done much as it was 500 years ago. It is cut in grooves with a pick, where necessary (the 'joints' [vertical fissures] being of great assistance in saving this part of the work), then lifted from its natural bed by wedges, driven under by sledge hammers. Heavy iron bars are used as levers, and when the stone is raised a few inches, a chain is put under the block, which is hoisted to the surface by steam cranes, whence it is transferred to tramways. [46] The workable stone is capped by the beds of sand called ochre, and by inferior hard stone, about 40 ft. thick, both of which have to be cut through to reach the Ham stone. The principal quarries

are 90 ft. deep from the surface to the basement bed, or 'clout,' as it is termed by the quarrymen. [47]

About 200 men are employed at 6d. per hour, or 30s. per week, the best workmen formerly earning only 13s. per week. [48] Various customs of long standing were in vogue among the quarrymen, with whom the industry seems to have been an hereditary one, followed by successive generations of one family. Payments of a shilling were exacted from each apprentice on different occasions, as for instance when he entered on his apprenticeship, when he was half through his term, when he married, etc. Fines were inflicted for allowing the stone to fall off a 'banker' when at work, also for working an undercut straight through a quoin, which was called 'cutting its throat.' [49] As in the case of the Purbeck Marblers, Shrove Tuesday was regarded as a traditional festival, the apprentices claiming a half-holiday. [50]

To its Carboniferous Limestone formation, it may be noted in passing, Somerset is indebted, as Professor Woodward has pointed out, not only for the presence of its ores of lead and zinc, but for the picturesque beauty of many of its cliffs and combes. [51] The limestones of Street, [52] Kingweston, and Keinton Mandeville furnish good paviours' slabs, 12 ft. square. This stone has also been experimentally utilized for lithographic purposes, as well as for kerbstones, building blocks, troughs, steps, and garden fences. [53] Fourteen beds were formerly worked at Keinton Mandeville, the stone being from 2 to 4 ft. below the surface, in layers 3 to 12 in. thick. It is fine-grained, and takes a good polish, chimney pieces and headstones having been made from it. [54]

Varieties of this stone are quarried near Taunton under the name of the Thurlbear Lias and Knapp stones. [55] The total amount of limestone from the mines in 1906 was 1,446 tons, from the quarries, 561,297 tons; the total value being £64,948. [56]

[43] Notes on Building Construction, pt. iii, 59.
[44] Ibid.
[45] Trask, Norton-sub-Hamdon, 218–19.
[46] Ibid. 230.

[47] Trask, Norton-sub-Hamdon, 219.
[48] Ibid. 218.   [49] Ibid. 221.   [50] Ibid.
[51] Woodward, Geol. Engl. and Wales, 86.
[52] 'A typical Liassic settlement,' according to Professor Woodward, so largely has the Blue Lias of the district been employed for building. Geol. Assoc. Proc. ii, cciv.
[53] Woodward, Jurassic Rocks, iv, 484.
[54] Phelps, Hist. Somerset, i, 472. In 1831, 49 persons were engaged at the quarries at Keinton Mandeville. Population Returns, 1831, p. 531. The chief limestone quarries of Somerset are at Shepton Mallet, Yeovil, Keinton (Somerton), Load Bridge, Rimpton, and Langport. Notes on Building Construction, pt. ii, 69.
[55] Woodward, Geol. Engl. and Wales, 156.
[56] Gen. Rep. and Statistics Mines and Quarries, 1906, p. 227. For 1908 the Government Returns show a Somerset output of 78,877 tons of sandstone, 509,940 tons of limestone, 2,000 tons of flint and

Slates,[57] which were dug to the amount of 1,894 tons in 1906 valued at £3,055,[58] are found in Somerset at the Tracebridge quarry, Wellington, the Treborough quarry, Treborough, and the Okehampton quarry, Wiveliscombe.[59] The stone slates of Treborough were early in request, for in 1426 Sir Hugh Luttrell paid 20d. for 2,000 tile-stones or slates (petris tegulinis) and 3s. 4d. for the carriage of them from Treborough to Dunster Castle.[60] The slate quarries of Charlwood, in the parish of Box, 5 miles from Bath, are no longer worked.[61] The Okehampton slates are of two sorts, the blue variety, which is most sought after, and the purple, which is more durable, the lowest quarry yielding the finest slates, which are found 300 ft. from the surface.[62] They are used for mantelpieces, flooring, window-sills, hearth-stones, water and beer cisterns.[63]

The marbles of Somerset comprise that known as Marston Magna or 'Yeovil' marble,[64] Draycott stone,[65] the two varieties, grey and green, found in the Quantocks,[66] the 'bluish-black limestone' of Street already alluded to,[67] the brown marble or 'landscape stone,' of Bristol,[68] and the black marble of Cheddar.[69] Marshall writes in 1798 of the marble quarries on either side of the road from Somerton to Shepton Mallet. The marble was raised in large slabs, 6 to 8 in. thick, and several feet in dimension. The slabs lay horizontally, and near the surface. The traveller saw men engaged in polishing them. Marble stiles, he adds, were common along the road. The dolomitic conglomerate has furnished some fine pillars in Wells Cathedral, which have the appearance of brecciated marble.

The beautiful breccia known as 'wonder-stone' is found both in the neighbourhood of Wells and at Bleadon. It may be described as a dark red dolomite sown with transparent yellow crystals of carbonate of lime.

The chief quarries in Somerset are in the proprietorship of the following owners: The Bath Stone Firms, Limited, whose operations extend into the adjoining county of Wilts., have their head quarters at the city which gives its name to this famous building material. Other firms in this district engaged in the quarrying industry are those of Messrs. Edward Hancock, Claverton Down; the Hard Stone Firms, Limited, North Parade, Bath; Messrs. Love & Son, Combe Down and Odd Down; Messrs. Shelland & Son, Union and Beehive Quarries, and the Vobster Limestone Quarries.

At Keinton Mandeville Messrs. Oliver Chalker & Sons, Brooks Bros., Combe Hill Quarry, and Mr. James Cox are leading owners.

The Doulting Quarrying Company are at Chesterblade, Evercreech, whilst the Ham Hill and Doulting Stone Company, Limited, have branches at Norton-sub-Hamdon, Stoke-under-Ham, at Doulting, Shepton Mallet, and West Hendford, Yeovil.

At West Cranmore are the Mendip Mountain Granite Quarries and Stone and Marble Asphalte Works, owned by the Mendip Granite and Asphalte Company, Limited.

Messrs. John Wainwright & Company, Limited, are proprietors of the Downside and Hamwood Granite Quarries, tar-paving and asphalte works at Shepton Mallet, Stoke St. Michael, Wells and Cheddar.

SEA FISHERIES

The sea fisheries of Somerset, which are so unimportant at the present time that the Board of Agriculture and Fisheries has no collector of

Fishery Statistics on the coast,[1] are not without interest as an ancient industry.

The first mention of Minehead as a port, according to Prebendary Hancock, is in 1380, when Ralph Cooke and others were forbidden to sell fish outside the harbour;[2] whilst early records of the manor go to prove that, in the fishing, as in the textile and woollen industry, the connexion between Ireland and the port in question was already firmly established by the 15th century. In a paper compiled from such sources, we have an interesting account of a lawsuit in mediaeval times touching the lease, by one William Kyste of Swansea, to Robert Bassher of Minehead, of a fishing boat called a pykard in 1497, Kyste to have one-seventh of the fishing, and one quarter of the freight. Ample evidence abounds in these

chert. Gen. Rep. and Statistics Mines and Quarries, 170, 241, 254.

[57] See Quart. Journ. Geol. Soc. liii, 438. (Dr. Hicks on the 'Morte Slates in North Devon and West Somerset.')

[58] Gen. Rep. and Statistics Mines and Quarries, 1906, p. 243. For 1908 however only 789 tons of slate are returned in the Government Returns as the Somerset output.

[59] Notes on Building Construction, pt. iii, 32.

[60] Maxwell Lyte, History of Dunster, 357.

[61] Woodward, Nat. Hist. Foss. Engl. ii, 101.

[62] Jeboult, Hist. West Somers. 157.   [63] Ibid.

[64] Woodward, Jurassic Rocks, iii, 297.

[65] Lee, Marble and Marble Workers, 25.

[66] Ibid. 26.   [67] Ibid.

[68] De Luc, Geol. Travels, ii, 415. This writer also saw the white marble of the same place placed as seats before the houses in the village.

[69] Marshall, Rur. Econ. of West of Engl. ii, 199–201.

[1] From information courteously supplied by Mr. R. F. Martyr.

[2] Hancock, Hist. of Minehead, 37.

documents of the frequent expeditions made by Somerset fishermen at this date to the coasts of Ireland.[3]

Some details relative to the fishing industry of Minehead in the 15th century may also be gleaned from the Household Accounts of Dunster Castle at that date. In the accounts of John Bacwell, steward to the household, dated June 1405 to June 1406, there are numerous entries relating to the fish supply. On 28 June 1405 twelve congers of the custom of the manor of Minehead were bought for 4s., this fish being still frequently caught in the bay; two ray fish were bought for 6d., and twelve milwells, a coarse green fish, were a further item. In 1417 various fishermen of Minehead were paid 42s. for fish and the carriage of the same to Gillingham. In 1419 13½ dozen ling and milwell were bought at 3s. a dozen. On one occasion we find an entry of 4s. for 'carrying the fish of the lord from Minehead to Dunster.' In 1430, Ryvers, receiver for Sir John Luttrell, paid 3s. 10d. for a barrel of herrings. Sprats seem to have been plentiful; sturgeon figures occasionally in the accounts. In one year 678 milwell and ling and fifty-three congers were purchased, the greater part probably for salting.[4]

In the manor of Dunster the fishery over the foreshore is a several fishery belonging to the lord. There is a continuous chain of evidence by inquisitions, bailiffs' accounts, court rolls, leases, and agreements, to show that the foreshore was fished by means of fishing weirs regularly and continuously, and that the sites of the weirs were let by copy of Court Roll by lease and otherwise, and the rents paid to the lord of the manor. Anciently these weirs were constructed by building a rough wall of low stones on the shore, into which were fixed upright stakes laced with freething or wattles, in the form of a hedge. There are remains of these weirs along the whole coast with hardly a vacant space. They are in the form of the letter V, the angle being towards the sea. They were originally constructed in two lines, one for spring tides, and the other for neap tides, all having

particular names; one being known as 'Knaplock Weir,' another, nearly a mile long, as 'Warren Weir,' 'Parlour Weir' being situated near Warren House. The modern practice, however, has been to drive large stakes into the foreshore at intervals, in the shape of a crescent or triangle, the apex of which extends to or near to the low-water mark. On these stakes nets are hung in which the fish are taken by stranding on the reflux of the tide. There are thousands of stakes on the foreshore, the stakes being four or five yards apart, in rows about 500 yds. long, called 'Hangs.' There are now about forty 'hangs' on the shore between Minehead Pier and Bradley Gate. These structures are similar to, but more substantial in character than, the kiddles in use on other parts of the English coast.[5]

In the time of the Conqueror, William de Mohun gave two fishing-places (duo piscatoria), one in Dunster and one in Carhampton, to the priory of Dunster, the grant being confirmed by William II and Edward III.[6] Rents for fishing weirs within this manor are returned in the bailiffs' accounts of the manor from the time of Edward I. The rents are included in the gross total of rents received by the accountant.[7] An extent of the manor of Dunster taken on the death of the lord in 4 Edward III (1330–1) shows that there were belonging to and parcel of the manor divers weirs super mare worth 10s. yearly.[8] In 49–50 Edward III (1375–6) the quarterly rents of the manor are returned as '£7 11s. 8d. of the rent of St. Martin's with the weirs in the sea.'[9] In 4–5 Henry IV (1403–4) the bailiff answers for '6d. of new rent of John Pynke for a fishery in the sea next Le Mouthe to hold for six years as appears by the Court Roll.'[10]

On the Court Roll of the manor of 6 Henry IV (1405–6) there is a suit in the manor court by one tenant against another for fishing his weirs in the sea and taking his fish.[11]

In 2–3 Henry V (1414–15) the bailiff is allowed for the rent of 'duo loca gurgitum pro piscibus capiendis juxta mare.'[12]

In the following year the bailiff accounts for

---

[3] Batten, 'Admiralty Court of Minehead,' *Somers. Arch. Soc. Proc.* xxv, 46 et seq.

[4] Dunster Castle Accounts. In several of the entries of admission to 'stakes ad litus maris le traynes and staches ad litus maris,' in the reign of Elizabeth, there is a reservation that, if any 'head fish,' i.e. porpoise or salmon, are taken in them, they are to be conveyed to Dunster Castle for the use of the lord, on pain of voiding the grant.

Task-works of fishing were among the services rendered by tenants in this manor. Chan. Inq. p.m. 6 Hen. VI, no. 32; 14 Hen. VI, no. 30.

For the references to the Bailiffs' Accounts, etc. contained in this article, the writer is indebted to the courtesy of the late Mr. George Fownes Luttrell of Dunster Castle, and the kind assistance of Mr. J. H. Davis.

[5] 'Attorney-General v. Emerson,' *Law. Rep. App. Cas.* 1891, p. 655.

[6] Dugdale, *Monasticon*, iv, 200.

[7] Allowance was made to the accountant under the head of 'default of rent,' in which the rents of several weirs are specified as holden by particular tenants. Under one such heading 'William the Fisherman holds one weir, rendering at the feast of St. Martin four horse-shoes. Henry White holds a weir rendering one axe of iron. John White and John Scherpe each hold one in the same manner.' B. 4, no. 3a.

[8] Inq. p.m. 4 Edw. III (1st nos.), no. 35.

[9] Bailiffs' Accts. Dunster Castle, 9, no. 2.

[10] Ibid. 10, no. 1.

[11] Bailiffs' Accts. Dunster Castle, 9, no. 3.

[12] Ibid. 10, no. 1.

13s. 4d. for new rent of a certain weir (which Alice Carter late held) the item occurring in subsequent accounts; [13] and these references might be indefinitely extended.

Early in the reign of Richard II we hear of the small ponds with fisheries in the sea called 'le Weres' in Watchet and its neighbourhood. They had come to the king's hands owing to a trespass committed by the Earl of Devon, who had acquired them without the king's licence. They were apparently farmed out at 4s. 4d. a year. [14]

In 1403–4, the bailiffs' accounts [15] of the manor of East Quantoxhead under the title of 'Issues of the Manor,' account for '12d. for the fishery of the water of Rygge,' which later entries (24–26) show to be a 'ridge' or 'rigg' in the sea. In 4 James I (1606) John Corche paid 3s. a quarter 'pro were at sea.' [16] From 1853 to 1865 a Mr. Strickland regularly paid acknowledgements for permission to fish on this shore, with stakes and nets. There are two weirs on the East Quantoxhead foreshore which are visible at low water.

The rents of the weirs in the manor of Carhampton are accounted for by the bailiffs in their accounts (which are similar to those of Dunster) under the general head of 'Rents of Assize,' but we find occasional entries of new tenants when a letting of a weir takes place. [17]

In the time of Elizabeth we find that the weirs were frequently let by copy in conjunction with other tenements and cottages. On 27 September 24 Elizabeth (1582) Joan Blake 'who held of the lord of the manor a tenement and cottage and two acres of woodland and three 'stachis' and one 'le weytre,' surrendered them to George Waller and William Waller, who were admitted tenants. [18]

On 27 July 1596, George Luttrell, the lord of the manor, brought an action against Robert Ragland for fishing in his several fishery at Carhampton and taking fish, viz. flounders, soles, shrimps, salmon, etc. The defendant pleaded not guilty, but there was a verdict for the plaintiff with damages and costs. It appears from the proceedings that there were at this time seventeen weirs in Carhampton belonging to Mr. Luttrell. [19]

On 21 May 1616, George Luttrell let by lease to Nicholas Engram 'one weir at sea called or commonly known by the name of Geaes Weir, late in the tenure of Robert Ragland'; also another named 'Gellyo's Weir, now in the tenure of Robert Ragland,' for twenty-one years from Lady Day 1615 at a rent of 25s. [20] Similar items occur in the bailiffs' accounts in successive Stuart reigns. In 1633 Thomas Luttrell let to Joan Goole a house and land with 'two fishing weirs with burrowes at sea in Carhampton formerly in the tenure of Hugh Goole, her grandfather.' [21]

At the beginning of the 17th century, Somerset was included with Devon and Cornwall in an Act for the better preservation of fishing in these counties, and for the relief of balkers, conders, [22] and fishermen against malicious suits. [23] Herrings, pilchards, and 'sea fish' are particularly specified in the Act as affording a 'very great and profitable' industry to the West-country fisherman. [24]

From the evidence of a bill in Chancery filed by Richard Popham of Porlock in 1624, it would appear that a certain yeoman named John Frase kept a guest or lodging-house for persons who came to buy herrings at that port. [25]

William Culliford, Surveyor-General of Customs in the reign of Charles II (1682) made the following report 13 June, 1682, of his visit to Porlock, 'where there is a very deep bay and a good harbour for small vessels, to which place there are several that belong, which trade oversea. The officer, Richard Davies, is an active young fellow; hath hitherto been paid £5 per annum by incidents; he very well deserves £10 per annum and be established it being a place of trade, and where great quantities of herrings are taken and cured.' [26]

In an 18th-century survey of the manor of Minehead the names of Francis Bastowe and John Alloway appear as occupiers of 'red herring houses.' [27] According to a schedule of harbour dues of the manor of Porlock every barrel of herrings paid 1d. or, in the case of a stranger, 2d. 'For every maise [28] of herrings brought by a Jouder (sic) or any other person

---

[13] Bailiffs' Accts. Dunster Castle, III, no. 1.

[14] Foreign Accts. 8 Ric. II, C.

[15] Bailiffs' Accts. at Dunster Castle, 22, no. 5.

[16] Ibid. no. 38.

[17] In 6–7 Henry V (1418–19) the bailiff accounts for '13s. 4d. new rent for a fishing weir by the sea which Alice Carter late held.' In 23–4 Henry VIII (1531–2) the bailiff returns an increase of rent of 3s. 6d. for one 'weir' in the tenure of Thomas Jay. Ibid. no. 9.

[18] Luttrell Deeds, B. 20, no. 14.

[19] Common Roll, Fine R. 38 Eliz. rot. 355d.

[20] Bailiffs' Accts. 20, no. 30.

[21] Pits dug in the foreshore to catch eels. 'Head Burrowes' and 'Clad Burrowes' were let to Andrew Poor in 1635. Ibid. 21, no. 8.

[22] Balkers—persons who stand on high places near the sea coast, at the time of the herring fishery, to make signs to the fishermen which way the shoals pass. Halliwell, Dict. Archaic Words, 126. Conders—the same. Ibid. 267.

[23] Stat. 2 Jas. I, cap. 23.

[24] Ibid.

[25] Chan. B and A Jas. I, bdle. 21, no. 52.

[26] Hancock, Hist. Minehead.

[27] Ibid. 218.

[28] A mace of herrings, 500. Welsh, mwys, mesh? used by the fishermen of Cardigan. Bye-gones, 16 February, 1898, p. 298.

or persons either fresh, salt, and not put into barrell, 1*d*.' Every fishing boat was required to pay 1*d*. per 'maise.' Any master omitting to see that this was paid was fined 5*s*. Boats paid keelage by the year, 4*s*. Strange boats in the season paid 4*s*.[29] Towards the close of the 18th century Billingsley mentions the salmon and especially the herring fishery of Porlock, Minehead and Watchet as considerable in extent. He also expressed a hope that it could be further promoted and encouraged since it would then be a means of furnishing employ during the winter for those sailors who are engaged in the limestone and culm trade during the summer months.[30] These men owing to their thorough knowledge of the Bristol Channel were excellent pilots and would form, as Billingsley pointed out, a valuable recruiting ground for the Royal Navy if necessity arose. In 1816 the Rev. Skinner records in his journal the purchase from a Berrow fisherman of a dish of soles for 3*s*., salmon being at the same time 13*d*. per lb.[31]

By the middle of the 19th century the sprat had become the most valuable fishery on the Somerset coast. The method of catching this fish was by stake-nets, the season lasting from October to Christmas. As much as a ton was known to have been carried in one day to Taunton market, the value of the fishing being £10,000 in a season.[32] Lines of sprats, sus-

pended from the kitchen ceiling, could be seen in the cottages for months after the season was over.[33]

In 1851 the herring was being taken along the whole coast westward from the mouth of the Parret with drift and stake-nets,[34] from September to January. Small cod was taken at Stolford by hooks from floated lines.[35]

The sprat and herring fishery of Weston-super-Mare supported numbers of the poor in the time of its greatest activity.[36] The island of Birnbeck was used by the fishermen of this town for a drying place for their nets. Rutter describes the hut used by the fishermen as 'low, thatched, and kept in repair by a fund raised amongst themselves.'[37] Two men called 'gull yellers' were employed to keep off the gulls from the nets as the tide went down. Leases of the fishing stalls were granted by the lord of the manor of Weston, to whom the first basket of fish and the first salmon were due.

There were until recent times productive oyster beds near Knaplock Weir which were rented of Mr. Luttrell by James Smith. Indeed oysters are still found here at low water in spring tides.[38]

A fishery by 'glatting' sticks has been carried on from time immemorial on the coast of the manor of Kilve and Kilton for conger eels, and the same method is adopted in spring tides for green eels at Dunster and Carhampton.

BREWING

In the Middle Ages the brewer's craft was practised throughout the county, though not without certain interesting local features. Thus, at Wells, in mediaeval times, a custom called *tolcestre* was paid to the bishop on every brewing.[1] Early in the 15th century, according to the Dunster Household Accounts, beer cost 1½*d*. per gallon from Midsummer to Michaelmas, 1¼*d*. from Michaelmas to Christmas, and 1*d*. from Christmas to Midsummer. One year's beer bill was £34 1*s*. 2¼*d*.[2] Church-ales[3]

[29] Healey, *Hist. West Somers.* App. E, 471. 'The lords of the manor of Porlock,' says Gerard, 'enjoyed great royalties for fishing.' *Description of Somerset*, 10.

[30] Billingsley, op. cit. 296.

[31] Add. MS. 33648, fol. 157.

[32] *Somers. Arch. Soc. Proc.* ii, 106.

[1] *Cal. D. and C. of Wells MSS.* (Hist. MSS. Com.), i, 260. This 'tolcestre' or 'tolsester' was doubtless one *sextary* of beer from each brewhouse. Compare a parallel case at Marlborough. *Cal. Charter R.* 1226–57, p. 168.

[2] Maxwell-Lyte, *History of Dunster*, 97.

[3] These rural festivals, which included Bid-ales and Clerk-ales, in addition to the above, were of frequent occurrence and importance in the parochial life of the county. 'Throughout Somerset,' we

[33] *Somers. Arch. Soc. Proc.* ii, 107.

[34] Ibid. 140.

[35] Ibid. 107. Superior anchovy have been caught at the mouth of the Parret. Day, *Zoologist*, 1879, p. 758.   [36] Pigot, *Dir.* 733.

[37] Add. MS. 33692, fol. 733. Cod-lines have been in use for over 150 years. Day, *Zoologist*, 1879, p. 757.

[38] *Ex informacione* Mr. J. H. Davies. In a Court Roll of 4 Henry V (1416–17) we find the admission of John Hull to a weir called 'Knapoley' to hold according to the custom of the manor by the rents and services accustomed. Bailiffs' Accts. 18, no. 1.

learn from the State Papers of 1633, these sales of ale for specific purposes were common. 'By Church-ales,' runs one local report, 'many poor parishes have cast their bells, repaired their towers, beautified their churches, and raised stocks for the poor.' Clerk-ales, according to the same authority, were for the maintenance of the parish-clerk; their 'putting down' causing a fear at this date among the country clergy that it would shortly be impossible to find any applicant for the office in question. Bid-ales were held 'when honest men decayed in estate' were thus 'set up again by benevolent friends who celebrated the occasion by a feast.' *Cal. S. P. Dom.* 1633–4, p. 276. Cf. *Quarter Sess. Papers Jas. I* (Somers. Rec. Soc. xxiii).

furnished a considerable part of the revenues of Stogursey Church in early times, the usual price of the ale sold at Whitsun being 5d. per quart. In 1516 these revenues amounted to £6 13s. 4d. and in 1525 to £7 1s. 8d.[4] There was a public brewhouse at Banwell in 1530, when the parish records state that 1s. 2d. was 'received of Rychard Scheppard for the Brewing-house.'[5] Bequests of brewing vessels, &c. figure in Somerset wills. John Stourton of Preston Plucknett in 1438 bequeathed all such vessels and 'all in his brewing house.'[6] Brewing kettles, 'lede' vats, trendells and 'trye' (tray) are to be found in other wills.

Offences against the assize of ale are constant incidents of courts legal in mediaeval times. In 1380 for instance we find Robert Lyddon and Thomas Dobell presented by the Alcombe tithing-man at Minehead for this offence and fined 1s. 6d. On the same occasion Thomas Truman, presented by the Staunton tithing-man, and Meleward John were fined 6d. Several persons who sold ale without a sign were fined 17d. Lucy Lyddon sold ale against the assize and was fined 3d., three barrels of ale being at the same time forfeited to the use of the lady of the manor. A Minehead brewer named John Baker was fined 6d. 8d. was paid for licence to brew and sell in this manor.[7] Joan Russell and Joan Hoper were presented in 1507 for selling beer in unmarked measures.[8] The ale-taster was duly protected by law against insult or slander in the conduct of his office. Fines of 6d. were inflicted at Minehead on certain persons for saying that he did not 'behave well in the execution of his office.'[9]

At certain 'auntient innes' in Wells in 1606 the landlords were presented for selling ale against the assize, that is 'of 1 quart of the best for 1d. and 2 quarts of the smallest for 1d.' Others were presented for selling smaller quantities of ale than 1 quart and charging for it 1d., the assize price of 1 quart of the best.[10] Not only the beer brewed on such premises but the diversions of the alehouse were also strictly overlooked. Edward Hort, 'brewer and tippler' in the city of Wells, was presented in 1608 'for that he did keep and maintain in his house aforesaid unlawfully a common shuffleboard whereupon divers persons resorted to play.'[11] Here as elsewhere throughout the country superfluous alehouses were summarily dealt with. At Wells in 1613 'all alehouses upon Mendip were ordered to be suppressed.' In 1615, a

similar order was made with regard to Wedmore, where there were held to be 'too many tipplers.'[12] In 1613 the justices of the peace were directed within their several limits to call before them all the tipplers and appoint them to sell according to the standard of Winchester.[13]

At the General Sessions held at Ilchester, 18–20 April 1615, among the fees claimed by the clerk of the market was the sum of 1d. for recording every victualler's name and dwelling-place, and for viewing and examination of every particular ale and beer measures, be they never so many, and for entering the same.[14]

At Ilchester Sessions, 19 April 1616, a petition was presented from 'the chiefest of the inhabitants of Chard, that there are many tipplers who do all brew their own beer, by reason whereof they doubt that wood and other fuel will in short time become very scarce and dear, and whereas there is such strong drink brewed that drunkenness and much other inconveniences doth thereby ensue, so that God is much dishonoured by reason thereof: Ordered that one Richard Munday of Chard shall from henceforth be licensed as a common brewer, and that he only and none else shall brew beer and ale to be sold in the said town according to the statute.'[15]

At a General Sessions held at Wells 13–16 January 1617–18, all alehouses and tippling houses in Croscombe were ordered to be suppressed, only Thomas Delton being permitted to tipple there.[16]

At the General Sessions held at Taunton 11–14 July 1615, it was ordered by the court that no innkeeper or alehouse-keeper should brew any beer or ale to sell again, but that they take the same from the common brewers, viz. Mr. Robert Hill, John Thompson, Tristram Gardner, and Michael Smalls, being allowed this Sessions, who are to make good and wholesome beer at 3d. the gallon to be spent now or to be kept stale as the innkeeper or tippler will bespeak it. The said brewers not exceeding the rate of 3d. the gallon, and that every barrel or vessel shall be kept sweet and wholesome, and to be marked on their heads how much they do contain. If any beer be brewed unwholesomely or otherwise defective, and not in the default of the drawer, that thereupon complaint might be made to the authorities, in whose discretion the brewer should receive the same back again, and supply good and wholesome beer in its stead.[17]

The right to grind malt at a private quern was called in question at Mells in 1661, when it was stated that the five querns erected had damaged the manor mill, and had, moreover, deceived the people, 'in regard that the malt

4 *Somers. Arch. Soc. Proc.*, xxiii, 77.
5 Knight, *Seaboard of Mendip*, 451.
6 Weaver, *Somerset Wills* (Somers. Rec. Soc. xvi), 143.
7 Luttrell Deeds, B. 26, no. 4.
8 Ibid. B. 26, no. 16.   9 Ibid.
10 *Hist. MSS. Com. Rep.* iii, App. 350.
11 Ibid.

12 *Quarter Sessions Rec.* (Som. Rec. Soc. xxiii).
13 Ibid.   14 Ibid.   15 Ibid.
16 Ibid.   17 Ibid.

made less beer, for that the corns are broken, not ground.'[18]

At the present day several towns in the county possess excellent local breweries and the ales of Taunton, Bath and Frome still retain their ancient repute. At Shepton Mallet indeed brewing is one of the chief industries of the town, since at its centre the Anglo-Bavarian Brewery stands in the Commercial Road, while another large brewery is situated at Charlton.

CIDER AND WINE

Monastic and manorial accounts, as well as other ancient documents, furnish sufficient evidence of the early activity of the cider industry in the county. One of the earliest of these references is to be found in a grant in frankalmoign to Jocelin Bishop of Bath, in 1230, whereby it was specified that, in the event of his death whilst in occupation of his see, his executors should have the fruits of his lands up to the Michaelmas following and also the use of the courts, granges, and cider presses, to store produce therein until they were required for the crops of the following year.[1] Cider (*cisera*) and apples also appear in 1242–3 as sources of profit on the account of the same bishopric when in the king's hand from 27 November 1242 to 10 May in the following year.[2] When Glastonbury was in the king's hand in 1290 (28 September to 26 October, 19 Edw. I) fifteen casks of cider (*doleis cisere*) were sold.[3] This was just before the election as abbot of John of Kent. At Portbury, on the land of a rebel in 1323–4, the following is accounted for under the head of *vendicio operum* : ' Et de 3*s*. 3*d*. de consuetudine diversorum customariorum ibidem pro sisera facta.'[4] Bequests of cider figure in Somerset wills, as for example in that of William Garland of Dinnington in 1557,[5] the amount of the legacy being one hogshead.

In Evelyn's time, ' a generous cider, strong, and sufficiently heady,' was being made in the county ' of promiscuous kernels or ungraffed trees.'[6] This author, in the preparation of his *Pomona*, owed, he tells us, ' infinite obligations ' to the ' most excellently learned Mr. Beale of Yeovil,'[7] one of the early fellows of the Royal Society. As a native of Hereford, associated later in life with Somerset, Evelyn's informant was doubly qualified to express sound opinions[8] on fruit-growing and the manufacture of cider and perry. Mr. Speke, he tells us, had shown him ' in his park some store of crab-trees of such huge bulk, that in this fertile year[9] he offered a wager that they would yield one or two hogsheads of liquor each of them ; yet were they small dry crabs.' Beale was all in favour of the apples being well ground —' rather too much than too little '—and mentions ' a mill in Somersetshire which grinds half a hogshead at a grist, and so much the better ground for the frequent rolling.' Again in speaking of bottling he mentions the practice of placing two or three raisins in every bottle and adds that in Somerset he had seen ' as much as a walnut of sugar, not without cause, used for this country cider.'

Celia Fiennes relates in her sprightly Diary that the natives of Somerset were ' careless when they made cider.' Very large presses were in use at this date, and a ' cheese '[10] yielded as much as two hogsheads.[11] The diarist describes the method of cider-making in her day as follows : ' They pound their apples, then lay fresh straw on the press, and on that lay a good amount of the pulp of the apples, then they turn in the ends of the straw, cover it all round, and lay fresh straw, then more apples up to the top.'[12]

Young, passing through Somerset on his Northern Tour, gives the average yield of an

---

[18] Exch. Dep. by Com. Hil. 13 & 14 Chas. II, no. 11.

[1] *Cal. Chart. R.* 1226–57, p. 137.
[2] Pipe R. 31 Hen. III, m. 14.
[3] Pipe R. 19 Edw. I, m. 27.
[4] Mins. Accts. bdle. 1148, no. 8.
[5] *Somers. Arch. Soc. Proc.* xxi, 211.
[6] Evelyn, *Pomona* (1664), 6.   [7] Ibid.
[8] Beale, ' Aphorisms concerning cider,' printed in Evelyn's *Pomona*, 21 et seq.

[9] Probably 1661 when Mr. Speke was high sheriff of Somerset.
[10] The quantity or charge of ground apples put in the press at one time. The grinding of the apples and piling the pomace on the press with layers of straw (' reed ') is called ' putting up a cheese.' The pile of apples and straw, after being pressed down very tightly for about twenty-four hours, is then sliced down on all sides, and the cuttings piled on the top of the central mass, which is again pared down and the process repeated till the pile, originally 5 ft. square, is a solid cake a quarter of that size. (Elworthy, *Somers. Word Book.*) Thin cloth called ' Netting Shading ' is now used instead of straw. (Lloyd, *Bath and West Journ.* xiv, 99. The chief feature of the American cider-mill which has lately been introduced at the Long Ashton Fruit and Cider Institute is a revolving bed, so arranged that when one portion of the pomace is under the mill and having the cheeses built up, the other is under the press having the juice extracted from it. (*Ann. Rep. Board of Agric.* 1904–5, pp. 74–5.) Richard Westcombe of Dodington invented the Westcombe cider-press. (*Somers. and Dors. N. and Q.* x, 255.)
[11] Fiennes, *Through Engl. on a Side-saddle*, 8.
[12] Ibid.

orchard as ten hogsheads per acre, a hogshead fetching from 20s. to 25s., twenty-four bushels of apples going to a hogshead. Some sorts of cider in his time fetched as much as from £3 3s. to £5 5s. a hogshead. The sort of apples most in esteem, he adds, ' are the White Sours, Cackagee, Royal Wildings, Redstreak,[13] and Golden Bushels.' [14]

At the close of the 18th century Billingsley records [15] that

there were many gentlemen in the neighbourhood of Taunton who sold their best cider at £5 or £6 per hogshead. And it is supposed that they possess an art peculiar to themselves of conducting the fermentation and thereby preserving a rich and delicious flavour. The best fruit delights in a strong clayey soil and it is common to mix a quantity of bitter apples which add much to its quality for keeping; but unless great attention be observed in making the labour is in vain, for cider requires much greater nicety of management than malt liquors. The apples are suffered to fall off the trees or when thoroughly ripe are picked with great care. They are then put in heaps to ferment, and remain in that state for three or four weeks; after they are ground, and the liquor is expressed, it is suffered to remain in tubs from thirty to forty hours when a scum or froth will rise on the top. This they narrowly watch, and when it breaks, they rack for the first time into vessels; after which unremitting attention is necessary to prevent excessive fermentation, by early and frequent rackings.

The north-eastern district of Somerset Billingsley found [16] full of orchards, and reported that ' the fruit produced at the northern base of Mendip Hills, as at Langford, Burrington, Rickford, Blagdon, Ubley, Compton Martin and Harptree afforded a cider strong, palatable and highly esteemed as a wholesome table liquor.' The favourite apple in that district both as a table and cider fruit was the Court of Wick Pippin. Mr. Good, who occupied a large farm in Hutton, employed a special method of making cider which Billingsley describes as follows :

The apples are ground by a horse-mill. The pummice is then wrung in hair bags; after which it is put into a tub and chopped. It is then ground

over again, and made into a cheese, which stands in the press all night. In the morning the press is strained as tight as it will bear by a level or cap-staff; by these means the cheese is made so dry, that it is cut into narrow strips, tied up in faggots, and burnt. He can make one hogshead upon eight more than by the common method. Two men make and tun five hogsheads in a day, and the horse will grind the apples in three hours.

Practical cider-makers however seem to have been rather afraid that the quality of the cider showed deterioration when this method was employed.

Cider fruit is generally grown on one of the two systems known respectively as those of Hereford and Somerset. The characteristic of the latter system consists in grafting a strong grower on a seedling stock, and then head grafting them.[17] In 1830 the following cider apples were chiefly used in the Vale of Taunton : Kingston Black, Court of Wick Pippin, Fry's Pippin, Monday Apple, Jersey, Buckland, and Redstreak.[18] The following summary gives a list of the various apples now grown in the county, and the different ciders made therefrom.

Ciders made from single varieties of apples comprise the ' sweet, sharp, full cider, flavour clean and pleasant, made from *Cap of Liberty* ; the sweet, slightly sharp, full cider of a pleasant and fruity flavour, yielded by the *Kingston Black* ; the somewhat similar cider of the *Yeovil Sour* ; sweet varieties including ciders from the *Farmer's Glory*, bitter-sweets the *Ashton Early Red Jersey*, the *Ashton White*, the *Chisel Jersey*, the *Dabinet*, *Horners*, *Red Jersey*, *White Jersey*. At the Long Ashton Cider Institute, the following ciders were made on a small scale from the following varieties : *Neverblight* and *Rouge de Trèves* (sharp) ; *Ansell*, *Brown Jersey*, and *Douce Amers* (sweet) ; *Masters Jersey*, *Medaille d'Or*, *Royal Jersey*, *Silver Cup*, *Special Silver Cup*, and *Yarlington Mill* (bitter-sweet).[19]

Different counties have their own known particular varieties of cider apple, two standing out particularly, the Kingston Black of Somerset, and the Fox-Whelp of Herefordshire,[20] although it is estimated that there are over 800 varieties of vintage or cider apples, not an eighth part of which are named.

The orchard acreage of Somerset is 25,265 acres.[21]

With the establishment of the National Fruit and Cider Institute at Long Ashton near Bristol, which is the only experimental station in the kingdom, this ancient and important West-

---

[13] This famous apple, the beau-ideal of the cider-maker, is characterized by Worlidge (*Vinetum Britannicum*, 24) as imparting to the cider made from it the following qualities, ' racy, poignant, oily, spicy.' ' Above all cider fruit, the Redstreak hath obtained the preference.' Ibid. 209. The true Redstreak, according to evidence before a Paliamentary Commission on Agriculture in 1896, has disappeared. Billingsley declares that ' a sour yellow apple, streaked with red on the sun side, be its name what it may, is undoubtedly a good cider fruit.' (*Agric. Somers.* 221.)

[14] Young, *Northern Tour*, iii, 244.

[15] Billingsley, *Gen. View of Agric. Somers.* 282 et seq.

[16] Ibid. 124 et seq.

[17] *Rep. on Fruit Culture*, 1906, p. 34.

[18] Savage, *Hist. of Carhampton*, 11.

[19] Communicated by the courtesy of Mr. B. T. P. Barker, M.A., Director of the Cider Institute, Long Ashton.

[20] *Bath and Southern Counties Journ.* xiii, 63.

[21] *Rep. on Fruit Culture*, 1906, p. 2.

country industry has received a fresh impetus, to which the investigations of Mr. Lloyd, as recorded in the publications of the Bath and West Society and of the Board of Agriculture, have contributed in no small degree. For his work in this direction it is interesting to learn that he has been awarded by the Société Nationale d'Agriculture de France their Diplomé de Médaille d'Or. At the Institute advice, assistance, and instruction may be obtained by all who are desirous of extending its usefulness; whilst the numerous leaflets issued from the laboratory will be found invaluable to those who are engaged in the work. Satisfactory and important results have also rewarded the scientific research of the resident director, Mr. Barker, as regards fermentation droppings of bright and sick ciders. In the nurseries, numbers of vintage and other apples are being propagated to found subsidiary experimental orchards in the contributing counties of Gloucester, Devon, Worcester, Hereford and Wilts.

The farmers of the county have also started a movement for ensuring the purity of cider, great harm having been done to the trade by spurious liquors being sold as cider. As the result of a deputation to the Board of Agriculture, prosecutions were ordered against two firms who sold as cider liquor that did not contain apple juice. Penalties of £5 and £20 costs were inflicted, and cider was thus defined as the fermented juice of the apple.

A large cask trade was formerly done in cider, but the modern demand appears to be for bottled cider, which sells at from 10s. to 15s. per dozen reputed champagne quarts. Prices however tend to increase, owing to the disproportion between production and demand. As it is estimated that an apple tree takes fully fifteen years to yield a profitable return, this fact further tends to keep up the price. The cider consumption of the agricultural labourer seems to be less than in former times, when one man has been known to dispose of two gallons per day during hay-making.

Vine culture, if only on a limited scale, would seem to have been an ancient industry of the county. The earliest notice of vineyards occurs, according to Canon Ellacombe,[22] in a confirmation of a grant by King Edwy to Glastonbury Abbey in the 10th century. Domesday assigns to the church at Glastonbury 3 arpents, with 2 arpents at Mere (Meare) and 3 arpents at Padanebene (Panborough). A ruined wall and the field-name of the Vineyards still marks the site of the Meare vine-industry. According to an inquisition [23] made by Abbot Henry de Soliaco in 1189, several tenants of the abbey of Glastonbury were bound to assist in the vineyard either at digging, pruning or gathering in the vintage, one tenant, 'Elwinus Custos Vinel,' apparently having chief charge. Similar references to labour-services in the vineyard are also noted in the 13th-century rental of this religious house.[24] At the time of the Dissolution, reference is made to lands called 'Wineyats,' whilst on the southern slope of Wirrall Hill is a site named as at Meare.[25] There were also vineyards at Dunster and Minehead, belonging to the Mohuns; the former ceased to be cultivated in the reign of Henry IV and was added to the Park.[26] A vineyard at Timberscombe was granted by the Prior of Bath to Richard le Tort in 1245.[27] At Bath, a 'close of pasture called the vineyards' is mentioned in the reign of Elizabeth.[28] As late as 1805, there were vineyards at Claverton, £28 having been paid by Richard Holder, who bought the Vineyards Farm in 1701, for four hogsheads of wine from the same.[29]

TEXTILES

Wool.—It would seem at first sight that Somerset was largely dependent for the supply of wool for its cloth manufactories upon neighbouring wool-producing districts. Although no fewer than 180 religious houses [1] in England supplied the Flemish and Florentine markets with wool in the 14th century, none from Somerset figures in the list. Even at Bath, where the cloth trade, we are told, flourished under the patronage of the monks, and where grants of cloth were frequent,[2] we find Prior Thomas purchasing wool to the amount of 900 sacks in 1334 [3] from a dealer of Marlborough, and Prior Walter from a dealer of Devizes.[4] A

[22] *Bath. Nat. Hist. and Field Club Proc.* i, 35.

[23] *Liber Henrici de Soliaco* (Roxburghe Club), 22 et seq.

[24] Add. MS. 17450, fol. 56 et seq.

[25] *Bath Nat. Hist. and Field Club Proc.* i, 35.

[26] The issue in 1279 was worth 18s. per annum. Chan. Inq. p.m. 7 Edw. I. no. 18. Maxwell-Lyte, *History of Dunster*, 324, 325.

[27] *Bath Chartulary, Linc. Inn MSS.* (Somers. Rec. Soc.), 55.

'One furlong at the vineyard which we and our monks of Dunster have of the house of Henry of the vineyard in the manor of Timberscombe.'

[28] *Bath Nat. Hist. and Field Club Proc.* i, 36.

[29] Ibid. 41.

[3] *Bath Chartulary* (Som. Rec. Soc. vii), 143.

[4] Ibid. 84.

[1] Cunningham, *Engl. Industry and Commerce*, App. 628. The list in question first appeared in Pegolotti's book entitled *La Practica della Mercatura*, compiled by a foreign merchant, probably from Flemish sources.

[2] *Bath Chartulary* (Som. Rec. Soc. vii).

reason for the scarcity of wool in the county may be that houses of Cistercian monks, the great sheep grazers, were few, the majority of the monks in the county being Benedictines, who were agriculturists.[5] A closer inspection of early records however points to an extensive mediaeval wool trade, which has hitherto scarcely received the attention it merits.

In 1314–15, the burgesses of Melcombe complained that they had lost the cocket on wool from Somerset. Some of the wool of Somerset had formerly been brought to that town.[6] In 1337, the price of wool in Somerset was 9 marks per sack, in Wilts. and Rutland 7½ marks, and Dorset 7 marks. Hereford wool was 12 marks per sack, while in the four northern counties it averaged 5 marks the sack. In this year, 30,000 sacks having to be bought for the king's use, 1,000 sacks were assigned to Wilts., Dorset, and Somerset, while 4,500 were assigned to Lincoln and Rutland.[7] In 1339 the Abbot of Glastonbury accounted for 5 sacks and 22 cloves of wool, valued at £27 2s. 2d. (at 100s. per sack), and in the same year Richard Polrouan of Taunton made an acknowledgement of £65 10s. 10½d. due for 10½ sacks and 2 cloves of wool, at 9 marks the sack.[8] Again, in the same year, orders were issued to the collectors of customs in the port of Bristol to deliver to the firms of the Bardi and Peruzzi or their attorneys 219 sacks, 17 cloves, of the king's wool of the county of Somerset, out of 322 sacks, 7½ cloves, due from the same county in part payment of 5,000 sacks which the king granted to them.[9] In 1341 John de Hetheye was appointed to 'hasten the forwarding of wool in Somerset, 300 sacks to be sent to the port of Southampton,'[10] which thus appears to have been an export town for this commodity at that date. The amount contributed by Somerset to the wool tax which was paid by the various counties to the king in this year was 601 sacks, 2 stone, 3½ lb. Yorkshire, Lincolnshire, Kent, and Norfolk, were the largest wool-producers at this date, but Bucks., Bedfordshire, Rutland, Derbyshire, Herts., Herefordshire, and Salop each produced less than Somerset, whilst the amounts assigned to Wilts. and Dorset respectively were 845 sacks, 4 stone, ½ lb. and 480 sacks, 3 quarters, 2 stone and 2¾ lb.[11] In 1343, when the price of wool was fixed throughout the kingdom, that of Somerset compared favourably with other counties. The best wool at this date was that of Lincolnshire, priced at 14 marks the sack, and of Hereford, which

was 12 marks; Somerset wool ranked next at 11 marks, that of Dorset being 8 marks, and Rutland 10 marks.[12]

In Professor Thorold Rogers' schedule of wool values in 1454, Somerset wool is rated at 80s. per sack,[13] the weight in use at Cheddar at this date being the pond, i.e. 21 lb.[14] Wool was forbidden to be bought unshorn in the county in 1464,[15] a prohibition which was re-enacted in 1467.[16] Wool at Wiveliscombe was valued in 1477 at 10s. 8d. the tod.[17]

This commodity was a favourite form of bequest in Somerset mediaeval wills. Forty lb. of wool 'of a blue colour,' that is, probably, ready woaded for conversion into cloth, were bequeathed in 1412 by John Lyndenyssch of Woodland Abbatis, to Edith Homan.[18] In 1414 Robert Passewater, rector of Sampford Orcas, bequeathed a stone of wool, or a noble, to his sister Emmota.[19] John Northmore of Taunton gave a stone of wool to Alice Hych by his will dated 1415.[20] In 1421 John Smert of Bishop's Lydeard left 'a fleece of sheep's wool to each godson of mine.'[21] Joan Atwell of Glastonbury left 'all the wool and cloth in her house at the time of her death' to Joan Austen in 1485.[22] In 1490 Henry Burnell of Poyntington left 'a good weight of wool' to his daughter Jane.[23]

Throughout the cloth-making era of the county's industrial activities, we find that of the wool production keeping pace with the demand. Towards the close of the 18th century prices were as follows: In 1785, horn fleece wool was selling at 9½d. per lb., the fleeces averaging from 3 lb. to 4 lb. each. Knot[24] fleeces, weighing from 5 lb. to 8 lb., sold at 7½d. per lb. In the next year, the two kinds of wool averaged respectively 9d. and 8d. per lb. In 1787 horn fleece was 10d., and knots, 8d. per lb. Some small fleeces, weighing from 2 lb. to 2½ lb., sold at 1s. per lb.[25] In 1789 the price of wool was rising, the common, coarser kind selling at 8d. per lb.

In 1828 the sale of wool in Somerset was reported to be 'very difficult,' some growers having three years' wool by them, owing to the excessive quantity of foreign wool in the market. A remunerative price at this date was considered to be 1s. per lb. The wool of the county was described at this date as 'a Dorset, not a combing wool,' which was generally used

---

[5] Archbold, *Somerset Religious Houses*, 294.
[6] *Parl. R.* i, 317b.
[7] Close, 11 Edw. III, pt. i, m. 3d; pt. ii, m. 20d.
[8] *Cal. Pat.* 1338–40, p. 294.
[9] Close, 13 Edw. III, pt. i, m. 8.
[10] *Cal. Pat.* 1340–3, p. 274.
[11] *Parl. R.* ii, 131b.

[12] *Parl. R.* ii, 138b.
[13] Rogers, *Hist. of Agric. and Prices*, iii, 704.
[14] Ibid. iv, 309.
[15] Stat. 4 Edw. IV, cap. 52.
[16] Ibid. 7 & 8 Edw. IV, cap. 36.
[17] Rogers, op. cit. iv, 321.
[18] Weaver, *Somerset Wills* (Som. Rec. Soc. xvi), 56.
[19] Ibid. xix, 316.   [20] Ibid. xvi, 71.
[21] Ibid. 107.   [22] Ibid. 255.   [23] Ibid. 291.
[24] A provincialism, used to distinguish between the horned and hornless varieties of sheep. Young, *Annals of Agric.* xxiii, 414.
[25] Ibid. ix, 307.

in the manufacture of seconds, or livery cloths.[26] A great deal of Somerset wool was being sent to the North of England at this date, the local manufacturers meanwhile purchasing largely in the adjacent counties. Wool, we are told, was bought at Cirencester by the combers and wool-carders of Wilts. and Gloucestershire, who supplied the clothiers of Frome and Taunton.[27]

Spinning.—In a county where the raw material lay ready to the worker's hand the industry of the spinner has invariably been of almost equal importance with that of the cloth-maker. On a Subsidy Roll of 1379 the names of eleven *filators* are recorded. These were mostly women, probably yarn spinners.[28] The cost of spinning wool was 2s. a stone in 1586; in 1595 the price was 2s. 4d., in 1599 the same, and in 1616 2s.[29] The spinning wheel and the weaver's frame were common all over England, says Professor Thorold Rogers,[30] in the 17th and 18th centuries, linen, hempen, and woollen yarn being spun in every household.[31] The two occupations were, however, distinct.[32] The wool was bought in the market by the spinner, who returned it a week later in the form of yarn, which was bought by the weaver, who in turn supplied the clothier with the web at so much per yard.[33]

The market spinners of the west country come before us most prominently in the 17th century, when their industry seems to have been threatened with legislative interference, owing, it was alleged, to their being accused of making false yarn.[34] In 1634–5 we find the justices of the peace in Somerset reporting to the Council that, in accordance with the directions received by them, they had 'inquired concerning market spinners and their abuses.' The result of the inquiry seems to have been that 'there were divers of them in those parts, not suspected of using any such abuses, and that the maintenance of the poor spinners of wool much relied upon the trading of the market spinners and of many clothiers.' The spinners in short, adds the report, 'may be considered very necessary members of the commonwealth.'[35] Their popularity, it would appear, was largely owing to their being credited with paying better wages than the clothiers.[36]

A famous commodity of the 18th century was the yarn of Porlock, which was much sought after, we are told, by the cloth factors.[37] This 'excellent yarn' was largely sold in Dunster Yarn Market, which was erected by George Luttrell about 1600.[38] Clothiers again came from all the neighbouring villages to buy the yarn spun by the women of Carhampton.[39] The industry was largely a home one, every farm household spinning yarn, not only for their own use, but for that of the clothiers, tuckers, and weavers as well. At the close of this century spinners were paid at the rate of 7½d. per lb.[40]

The modern industry in the county is chiefly represented by Messrs. Hutchings, Shepherd & Co., who are hemp-spinners at Ilminster.[41]

Cloth-making.—Long prior to the Flemish settlement claimed for Taunton in 1336,[42] there can be no manner of doubt that the industry of cloth-making was already actively established in the county. Adam the dyer, Walter the webber, William the fuller, Alice the webber and Christina the webber are mentioned in an extent of the manor of Dunster as early as 1266.[43] The occurrence of the surname Webbe points, it has been suggested, to a flourishing cloth trade at Axbridge in mediaeval times,[44] whilst names such as those of Richard le Deyare, Henry le Webbere, Thomas le Touker, Ralph le Taylour, Walter le Lindraper, and Nicholas le Chaloner, on a Bath poll tax of 1340,[45] together with the appearance of dyers, fullers, webbers, *filators*, &c., on a Subsidy Roll of the same city in 1379, lead to a similar conclusion.[46] Entries in the bailiffs' accounts for the manor of Porlock in 1425–6 relative to purchases of textile fabrics, indicate a home manufacture.[47]

The gilds of Webbers (weavers) and Tuckers (fullers) were by no means confined to the great

ing, market spinning being the common form. (Cunningham, op. cit. 510. See also S. P. Dom. Chas. I, cclxxxii, 81.) John Etherington and Henry Stracey were appointed to overlook the conduct of the industry, with special directions to enforce the stipulated length of the reel-staff and the spinners' charges.

[37] Lewis, *Topog. Dict.* iii, 556.
[38] *Somers. Arch. Soc. Proc.* xxxv, 238. The Yarn-Market is still a picturesque feature of Dunster, 'with its eight small dormer windows and its quaint octagonal shape.' *The Lady*, 25 June 1908.
[39] Savage, *Hist. Carhampton*, 86.
[40] Young, *Annals of Agric.* ix, 308.
[41] Kelly, *Dir.* 1906, p. 722.
[42] Toulmin, *Hist. Taunton*, 286.
[43] Maxwell-Lyte, *History of Dunster*, 297.
[44] *Hist. MSS. Com. Rep.* iii, App. 305a.
[45] *Bath Nat. Hist. and Field Club Proc.* vi, 295.
[46] Ibid. 313.
[47] Nine ells of linen cloth (canvas) were bought for sacks at 3s. and four ells of woollen cloth for Philip Barron, the lady's driver. Mins. Accts. bdle. 973, no. 27.

[26] *Rep. Wool Trade*, 1828, p. 114.
[27] Ibid. p. 116.
[28] *Bath Nat. Hist. and Field Club Proc.* vi, 313.
[29] Rogers, *Agric. and Prices*, v, 660.
[30] Ibid. 587. Fitzherbert recommends the distaff to be always ready, for a pastime to keep women from idleness. *Book of Husbandry*, 176.
[31] Rogers, op. cit. v, 551.   [32] Ibid.
[33] Cunningham, *Engl. Industry and Commerce*, pt. i, p. 499; Westcote, *View of Devon*, 61.
[34] Cunningham, op. cit. (ed. 4), 510–11.
[35] *Cal. S. P. Dom.* 1634–5, p. 472.
[36] S. P. Dom. Chas. I, ccxlii, 23. There was an attempt at regulating the industry in 1636, which shows, says Professor Cunningham, that the trade was expand-

towns; we find them taking their part also in the life of the village. Thus, at Croscombe in the 15th century, when the cloth trade was the chief support of the parish, we see these members of the industrial community 'presenting at the audit' of the parochial accounts according to their status.[48] Tithes were taken by the vicar of Mudford of websters as well as of brewsters, and of other craftsmen.[49] Numerous allusions to apprenticeships to weaving occur in early Chancery proceedings. William Teypp of Taunton, weaver, for instance, appeared as defendant in a suit of this character, the plaintiffs being John and Robert, sons of Walter Schute, who complained of the defendant's refusal to make indentures of apprenticeships for the complainants, for which he had been paid. An interesting sidelight on the commercial connexion between Somerset and Brittany at this date is afforded by the mention of 'instruction in the language of Brittany' as part of the agreement entered into by the said Teypp.[50]

Apprentices to whom their masters failed to give proper instruction were released from their apprenticeships. We find an instance of this was brought before the justices of the peace at Bridgwater general sessions in September 1615, when Thomas Ilverton, weaver, of Taunton, was charged with ill-usage of his apprentice, Nicholas Hamer, who had moreover 'received small knowledge in his trade,' and had been forced to return to his parents. Hamer was discharged of his apprenticeship, and ordered to be placed with some other 'who might better instruct him.'[51] At Ilchester in the following year, Stephen Ottes was similarly released with regard to William Dryer, weaver, of Taunton, 'in respect that he hath not been taught his trade, but kept at other work.'[52]

From Plantagenet and throughout Tudor times legislative notices of the cloth trade of Somerset are numerous, the most famous being contained in the undermentioned statutes. In 1389 it was enacted that the cloths of Somerset, Dorset, Bristol, and Gloucester, tacked and folded, should not be put to sale before they be opened. Of which cloths, it was declared, 'a great part be broken, bruised, and not agreeing in colour, neither be according in breadth, nor to the part of the same cloth showed outwards, but be falsely wrought with divers wools, so that the merchants who carry them out of the realm be many times in danger to be slain, imprisoned, and put to fine, and ransom, and their cloths burnt or forfeited, because of the

great deceits found in the same when they be untacked and opened.'[53] An Act of 1489 was concerned with ' the maintenance of the drapery and the making of cloth in Somerset.'[54] The famous Cloth Act of 5 and 6 Edward VI dealt with 'the whites, reds, broad plunkets, azures and blues' of the county. All of the first two varieties of cloth were to contain in length, being wet through, between 26 and 28 yds., and to be seven quarters of a yard in breadth within the lists at least, listed according to ancient custom, well scoured, thicked, milled, and fully dried, the weight of every piece to be 64 lb. In the case of coloured cloths, the weight was to be 60 lb. All broad plunkets, azures, blues, and other coloured cloths were to be from 25 to 27 yds. in length, seven quarters within the lists, and 68 lb. in weight.[55] By an Act passed 4 & 5 Philip and Mary, white cloths made in Somerset were to weigh 61 lb.[56] By the same statute, cloth was forbidden to be made in a town or borough.[57] It was no doubt industrial evasions of the statutory regulations touching the viewing and sealing of cloths that led to the special enactments of 1555 with regard to the application of the ordinances in question to the 'cloths commonly called Bridgwaters,' made at Taunton and Chard as well.[58] The passing of this Act resulted, according to Cunningham, in a large migration from the towns into the villages of weavers anxious to escape from legislative interference.[59] The breadth of woollen cloth was again fixed by statute in 1585 and 1593.[60]

The cloth manufactured in Somerset, as in other counties, was brought to Blackwell Hall, the appointed mart in London, which had passed from the possession of a family named Basing into that of the Crown, and had been sold by Richard II to the city of London. The Hall was subdivided into the Devonshire, Gloucester, Worcester, Kentish, Medley, Spanish and Blanket Halls, denoting the various kinds of cloth dealt with. A fee of 1d. was paid on each cloth (pitching-penny), warehouse room (resting) being charged for at the rate of $\frac{1}{2}d$. per week. These fees, which amounted, it was said, to £1,100 per annum, were paid to Christ's Hospital, the governors of which had the sole management of the halls. The sealers and searchers attended on Thursday, Friday, and part of Saturday, the chief market-day however being Thursday, when the wagoners and carriers

---

[48] *Churchwardens' Accts. of Croscombe, etc.* (Somers. Rec. Soc. iv), 21.
[49] *Cal. Wells D. & C. MSS.* (Hist. MSS. Com.) i, 323.
[50] Early Chan. Proc. bdle. 108, no. 42.
[51] *Quarter Sessions Records* (Somers. Rec. Soc. xxiii).
[52] Ibid.

[53] 13 Ric. II, stat. 1, cap. 11.
[54] 4 Hen. VII, cap. 11.
[55] 5–6 Edw. VI, cap. 11.
[56] 4 & 5 Phil. and Mary, cap. 5.
[57] Ibid.
[58] Ibid.; Noorthouck, *Hist. Lond.* 550.
[59] Cunningham, *Engl. Industry and Commerce* (ed. iv), 519.
[60] 27 Eliz. cap. 17 and 35 Eliz. cap. 7.

came in from the country. The hours of attendance were from 8 to 11 and from 2 to 4 o'clock.[61]

The length and weight of cloths having been strictly determined by legislative enactment, certain of the Somerset clothiers petitioned that, if the said cloths fall out to be but of $6\frac{1}{2}$ quarters, they may be tolerated, as it was impossible to guarantee what weight would always produce the same length.[62]

In this, as in every other cloth-making centre, the alnager, whose fee was fixed by statute,[63] was a person of importance, all cloths put to sale before his seal had been affixed to them being forfeited. A curious bequest in this connexion in mediaeval times was that of John Clevelod, clothman, of Beckington, who left to his daughter Mary, besides his fulling-mill, 'sigillum panno-rum, voc' le oynage.'[64] Appointments of deputy-alnagers were frequent. In Somerset, Robert Blake and Robert Pope of Salisbury were thus appointed in 1386, and in 1388 we hear of the office being conferred on John Luwell and Roger Breghnok.[65] The duties of the office were no doubt often unjustly performed, and as a consequence resented by the cloth-makers. In 1401, for instance, when Thomas Neuton, esq. collector of alnage in the county of Somerset, came to Norton St. Philip and wished to proclaim the king's letters patent and other things touching his office at the fair which was being held in that town, he and his servants were set upon by 'certain evildoers,' one of the said servants being killed, and no fewer than 100 mortal wounds being inflicted on the same Thomas, scarcely any of the company being allowed to escape alive from the fair.[66] In 1439 Thomas Bateman was granted £31 14s. per annum out of the subsidy and alnage of cloth exposed for sale in Somerset, and out of a moiety of forfeitures of such cloth.[67] Owing to complaints received in 1591 from the West of England clothiers, as to unjust exactions on the part of the London alnagers, the Privy Council ordered an investigation to be made into the cause of complaint. From the result of the inquiry, several interesting facts are brought to light. The staple cloth manufacture at that time would appear to have been white broadcloths, certain of which were reported by the alnager and his deputy 'not to be just and true.' Cloths

informed against were compelled to be made up again 'not faulty.' Cloths were being made of an unreasonable length, some 40 yds., some more, further frauds causing the cloths to appear shorter than they were, thus defrauding her Majesty's customs of her due. In addition to the seal afterwards to be affixed to each cloth by the alnager, the clothiers, it would seem, were in the habit of attaching to every cloth made by them a seal certifying the length of each piece. The Council ordered 'proper marks and tokens' to be woven into every white broadcloth. Some clothiers however being in the habit of 'beautifying the finer kinds of cloth by working into them with a needle threaded with gold or copper-gilt thread, any device they pleased,' this practice was permitted to be continued in the case of the higher-priced cloths, but to all other kinds a seal of lead, as prescribed by statute, was to be affixed, with the just and true length in plain figures.[68]

The office of alnager was occasionally combined with that of clerk of the market, as at Ilchester, when this official, probably acting in the former capacity, received a fee of 2d. for 'trying and examining cloth,' a further 2d. being exacted for 'new sealing every ell or yard at both ends.'[69]

The office of the 'sealer and searcher' of cloths continued throughout the cloth-making era. In 1803 Mr. Thomas Joyce, clothier, of Freshford, giving evidence before a Parliamentary Committee appointed to consider the wool clothiers' petition in that year, stated that the duties of inspectors of cloth, as the alnagers were then styled, were to attend the mills, to measure the length and breadth of cloths, and to attend the tenters for straining the cloths and setting the lengths. The searcher at Freshford was a shoemaker by trade. The fee for his attendance was 2d. per cloth, and the times of his visits averaged twice a year.[70]

Leland's allusions to the cloth trade of this county are numerous. He writes of Bath, and of its three famous clothiers, Style, Kent and Chapman,[71] of Pensford, 'occupied with clothing,' and furnished with a stream 'that serveth to drive divers tucking mills,'[72] of 'the pretty townlet of Mells,'[73] and the city of Wells, similarly employed,[74] whilst on the road from Frome to Bath the observant topographer saw

---

[61] Broad Tauntons and Bridgwaters were required by law to be from 12 to 13 yds. long, and 7 quarters broad. Every narrow cloth was to be from 23 to 25 yds. long, and 1 yd. wide, both to be 34 lb. in weight.
[62] *Cal. S. P. Dom.* 1580–1625, p. 347.
[63] 25 Edw. III. cap. 1 and cap 4.
[64] Weaver, *Somerset Wills* (Somers. Rec. Soc. xxi), 36.
[65] *Cal. Pat.* 1385–9, pp. 109, 408.
[66] Ibid. 1399–1401, p. 516.
[67] Ibid. 1436–41, p. 364.

[68] *Acts of P.C.* 1591, pp. 97–9.
[69] *Quarter Sess. Rec.* (Somers. Rec. Soc. xxiii).
[70] *Rep. Wool Clothiers' Pet.* 1803, p. 18.
[71] Leland, *Itin.* ii, 67. These names appear in an indenture of 30 November 1523, when the three clothiers in question were appointed commissioners to oversee the levy of a poll tax at that date. *Bath Nat. Hist. and Field Club Proc.* vi, 386. See ibid. 410.
[72] Leland, op. cit. vii, 97.
[73] Ibid. 99.
[74] Ibid. ii, 6.

'certain good clothiers having fair houses and tucking mills.'[75]

Bequests of cloth are frequent in Somerset mediaeval wills,[76] showing how considerable the trade had become and early Chancery proceedings contain frequent reference to the cloths of the county.

In 1547 we find the cloth trade flourishing, as it was to do for many centuries, at Wellington, where William Pyers rented a church house called 'the clothe house,' for a dwelling-house no doubt, as well as for business purposes.[77]

Here, as elsewhere in the history of the textile industries of the kingdom, the element of romance which seems inseparable from the immigration of the 'Strangers' finds expression, the episode of the Flemish colony at Glastonbury in the 16th century being among the most picturesque of Somerset records.'[78] Some time in 1549 there settled at Glastonbury some thirteen 'Strangers' under one Wolfe, who in that year seem to have been in a destitute condition.[79] What became of these people is not known, but a further settlement was made in 1551, when the Protector Somerset agreed with one Vallerand Poullan, 'a man of great worth, both for learning and writing,' to form a settlement of Flemish weavers, 'outlandish, learned, and godly men,' on his estate at Glastonbury, with one Henry Cornish, keeper of the duke's house in Wirrall Park, to 'overlook and assist them.'

Letters of denization were granted, 31 December 1551, to the number of seventy, amongst others to James de Cheri, John de Walle, Francis du Boys, Nicholas Dureau, Nicasius du Puys, Gabriel, Paschasie Fontaine, Stephen le Prevost, and Stephen Lestoulle, invariably designated as 'weavers settled at Glastonbury under Valerandus Pollan.'[80] A loan of £484 14s. was advanced to the new colony, to whom land was allotted in the proportion of 4 acres to each family, enough for 'two kine,' the land in question having apparently been taken over from the earlier strangers, for we find orders emanating from

the Privy Council 14 November 1551, to Henry Cornish, directing him to agree with the latter 'for divers leases that they have within the lands of Glastonbury to the end that they being removed from the same, the strangers brought thither for the use of worsted making may be placed in their stead, as was devised by the Duke of Somerset.'[81] The attainder of their patron brought disaster upon the foreign colony. Threatened with the same fate that had overtaken their predecessors, we find Pollan praying the Council on their behalf that 'the promises and articles entered into with them by the Duke of Somerset might be carried into effect.'[82] Further petitions requested a grant of £13 10s. 9d. to 'pay the Strangers' debts in England.'[83] The king, we are told, 'took up the case,' and commissioned Sir John Paulet, Sir John St. Loo, Sir Thomas Dyer, and Alexander Popham to examine into the matter and take steps for the proper completion of the settlement, to 'supply the foreigners with fit habitations,' money being advanced at the same time for the purchase of wool.[84] The commissioners reported the Strangers to be 'very godly, honest, poor folk, of quiet and sober conversation, willing and ready to instruct the youth of Glastonbury in their crafts.' Many of their pupils, it was added, 'could soon spin as well as their teachers.' The settlement in short was held to be 'likely to bring great commodity to the commonweal of these parts.' Robert Hiet of Street, Pollan, and Sir Ralph Hopton were appointed to forward the building. Two dye-houses were appointed 'for dyeing and calendering[85] their worsteds'; timber and stone being supplied for setting the looms, cauldrons, etc. in the houses assigned them at the king's charge.[86] The colony was made up, it would appear, of weavers, dyers, spinners, combers, collectively engaged in the manufacture of 'worsteds and such like.' Strype 'conjectures' the products of the Glastonbury looms to have been 'kersies, and cloth of that nature.'[87] William Crouche, receiver of the Duke of Somerset's revenues, was directed to advance certain sums to the Strangers, in the first instance £300, and later £700, for wool, 'oade,' madder, copperas, brassell, alum, and other things for their colours, £200 for the loom-makers. Various requests with regard to the conduct of their industry were now forwarded to the Council, amongst others, for a hall for sealing their sayes and worsteds, for permission to choose yearly five of their number as warden and overseers, for

---

[75] Leland, op. cit. vii, 99.

[76] See Weaver, *Somerset Mediaeval Wills* (Somers. Rec. Soc. xvi, xix, xxi).

[77] Green, *Somerset Chantries*, 167.

[78] The episode in question may be studied at length in vol. xxvi. of *Somers. Arch. Soc. Proc.*, to which Mr. E. Green contributed his interesting account of 'Some Flemish Weavers settled at Glastonbury, 1551.' See also W. Page, *Denizations and Naturalizations* (Hug. Soc. Publ. viii), pref. p. xxix.

[79] Subsidy R. 3 Edw. VI, 170–250. 'Peter Mede, alyen, in goods 40s. to 2s. Strangers being there wythe one Mr. Wolfe, beyng more in dett than they be worth, and chargeable for their heddes by the statut of Relyef, in number xij, after viij the pece in rel,' viijs.'

[80] Pat. 5 Edw. VI, pt. iv, m. 38.

[81] Green, op. cit.

[82] *Cal. S. P. Dom.* 1547–80, p. 36.

[83] Ibid. 37.   [84] Ibid.

[85] To smooth, trim, or give gloss to woollen cloths. *N. and Q.* xi, 421.

[86] Green, op. cit.

[87] Strype, *Mem. Cranmer*, i, 346.

free import of all materials necessary to their trade, and for freedom to buy wool with all the rights of denizens.[88]

Although after the fall of Somerset Cecil seems to have extended his patronage to the Strangers,[89] failure seems to have persistently attended their industrial efforts ; or it may be that, influenced as they had been in their coming by religious motives, the accession of Mary gave them good cause to withdraw from their English exile.[90] On 5 September 1553 the Privy Council addressed a letter to Sir John Sydnam and John Wadham, whom they directed to go to Glastonbury, and 'seeing the chauldornes and other the Queen's stuff there in safety,' to permit the foreign settlers to depart, 'delivering to them their passports.'[91] An almsdish of latten or rolled brass still remains in the church of St. John at Glastonbury as sole memorial of their presence there.

A letter from the Privy Council in 1577 directed inquiry to be made into the alleged decay of the cloth manufacture in Somerset,[92] and appointed Sir John Clifton, Sir George Rogers, Sir John Stowell, and Sir Henry Portman to look into the matter.[93] What was the result of the inquiry we do not know, but the reports from Blackwell Hall in 1586 continued to be depressing. To remedy the 'lack of sales of Somerset cloth,' it was ordered by the Privy Council that the merchants of the staple should be at liberty to buy at other than the stated hours, that is to say, from Friday after 12, and on Saturday.[94] The lack of sales in question had, as might have been anticipated, a serious result upon the spinning and carding community. 'On the complaint of the poorer sort of people inhabiting about Bath and other towns in Somerset, wont to live by spinning, carding, and winding of wool, the clothiers were commanded to assemble and take immediate steps for setting the poor to work.'[95]

The vigilance of the legislative authorities with regard to the cloth manufacture was at all times loyally supported by the honest makers themselves. In 1592 we find John Godsell of Taunton, clothier, complaining of John Cole and 'other badd persons,' who were making cloth of flocks and thrums, dyeing in false colours, and counterfeiting the lawful marks thereon, to the great discredit of the trade.[96]

The following extracts from the Book of Customs within Lyme Regis since the Feast

of St. Michael the Archangel 1586 unto the Feast of the Nativity of Christ next ensuing seem to point to the Dorset port as one of those from which the wool and cloth traffic of Somerset was largely carried on in Elizabethan times :—

The xxijth of September.
The fforesighte of Lyme burthen of xxx tons, Nicholas Harte master for the Ilandes.
William Goudbere of Taunton Englishe marchaunte for three pakys contt. 34 peces. taunton reedes makinge 17 clothes shorte.
More the same for two ballotes contayninge 24 pieces coarse hamshire redinges makinge 8 clothes shorte compounded for according to lawe.
Edward Mondaie of Charde Englishe marchaunte for 3 ballotes contayninge 36 peeces redinges and makinge 12 clothes shorte.
Same for two packes contayninge 8 broadcloths coarse compounded for according to lawe.
Robarte Tucker of Charde for 3 ballotes contayninge 8 broadcloths and 13 pieces redinge makinge 4 clothes and one third part compounded for.
Henry Mondaie of Charde merchaunte for 4 ballotes contayninge 48 peeces coarse redinge makinge 16 clothes shorte, compounded for according to lawe.
John Cogane of Charde merchaunte for one pake contt. 12 peeces of baies.
Same for 2 ballotes contt. 24 peeces redinges makinge 8 clothes shorte compounded for according to lawe.[97]

In 1621 the Somerset clothiers were purchasing wools from Pembrokeshire and Carmarthenshire, which were conveyed home, we learn, down the Severn, the trade being of such value to the Welsh that an order from the customer of Milford staying the export of this merchandise caused, we are told, 'great distress' in the principality.[98]

The following year was one of grave anxiety in cloth-making communities throughout the kingdom. The drapers of England alleged the cause of the decay which had set in in the trade to be owing to its practice by inexperienced persons. As a remedy, it was suggested that clothiers, dyers, weavers, tuckers and cloth-workers should be 'restricted to their proper trades,' and the laws with regard to the sealing and searching of cloths, prior to their being put on sale, rigidly enforced.[99] The following 'abstract of causes preventing the sale of cloth' in the kingdom was put forward at the same time : deceits in the making, paucity of buyers, the great impositions laid thereon, foreign causes being wars in Germany, the growth of the manufacture abroad, want of fit marts for merchants, and the export of Scotch and Irish wools.[100]

Multitudes of poor spinners and weavers were out of work in Somerset ; there was great

[88] Green, op. cit.
[89] Strype, op. cit.
[90] Cunningham, *Alien Immigrants,* 145.
[91] Green, op. cit. ; Strype, op. cit. 532.
[92] *Acts of P. C.* 1577–8, p. 28.
[93] Ibid. p. 29.
[94] Ibid. 1586–7, p. 272 et seq.
[95] Ibid. p. 93.
[96] Ibid. 1591–2, p. 406.

[97] K. R. Customs Accts. 23–4, 1586.
[98] *Cal. S. P. Dom.* 1619–23, p. 290.
[99] Ibid. 1619–27, p. 400.
[100] Ibid. 1619–23, p. 452.

want of money in the county, wools and cloth were in consequence 'grown almost valueless,' and the people were desperate for want of work.[101] Bath had so far fallen from its former prosperity, 'clothing' being 'much decayed,' that it was described by its citizens as 'a verie little poore cittie.'[102] On 26 March 1622, John Mackreth, keeper of Somerset Hall, Blackwell Hall, reported that there were 433 pieces of Somerset cloth unsold on his hands.[103]

The Council, having had many complaints of distress in Somerset, among other cloth-making counties, owing to the weavers and spinners being out of work, thereupon ordered the merchants to buy up as much cloth as possible and required them to deal with their clothiers to renew their works, it being unfitting that they should at their pleasure dismiss their work-people, who are thus deprived of livelihood, and disturb the Government. Wool dealers were ordered not to store up wools, to enhance the price, but to sell the same on moderate terms; 'those who had gained in profitable times,' it being argued, 'must now be content to lose for the public good, till the decay of trade be remedied.'[104]

The serious rivalry of Spanish cloth, which owed its excellence, it was said, to the colour being dyed in the wool, caused the appearance on the English market in the 17th century of certain counterfeit cloths, white cloths, we are told, being 'dyed in the say,' that is, before thicking, whilst coloured lists and marks were also sewn on the finished fabric, as in the case of the true Spanish cloths.[105] The whole of this counterfeit cloth, according to one writer, was manufactured, under the name of 'medlies,' in the two counties of Somerset and Wilts.[106]

Frome, for all 'the treasure of its wool,'[107] and the antiquity of its cloth trade,[108] was reported in 1631 to be 'very poor,' its 6,506 inhabitants being mostly clothiers, weavers, and spinners.[109] Ten years later, we find the clothiers of the county complaining that they could not sell their goods for ready money, as heretofore, nor procure payment of any of their debts, the merchants callously declaring in reply to their protests that 'this was no time

to pay money.' The 'deadness of trading,' which was not confined to Somerset, was attributed by the clothiers to 'the tediousness of putting justice into execution.'[110]

Closely interwoven with the fortunes of the clothiers of the 17th century in Somerset were the political events of their times, and Monmouth's rebellion was not without its disastrous effects upon the industrial communities of the West country, for in Mr. Rose's list of sixty-eight servants shipped into slavery in the West Indies on board the *Jamaica*, merchant ship, the names of woolcombers, serge-weavers, and clothiers are of frequent occurrence.[111] Something like disaster again was the result at this date of the long and close commercial connexion which had existed from the earliest times between Ireland and the port of Minehead, which we find noticed by various writers.[112] A small colony of Irish refugees had apparently established themselves in the Somerset town, then engaged in the production of serges. In this manufacture, the immigrants, having 'gained such experience as before they had never understood,' owing to their being employed therein 'in charity,' proceeded, on their return to Ireland, to undersell their former benefactors.[113] 'The Irish,' as a contemporary pamphleteer quaintly puts it, 'encouraged by the merchants, and having plenty of wool, fell into the making part.'[114] Cloth-makers from Somerset, either native or returning refugees, were undoubtedly amongst those 'artisans from the West of England' who set up a manufactory of cloths and stuff at Clonmel in 1675, under the auspices of a London company, similar establishments being founded at Dublin, Cork, and Kinsale, in 1664–75.[115] By 1697, we find the growth of the Irish woollen industry becoming seriously hostile to that of Somerset. The demand for cloth from Ireland was increasing in the Dutch markets, and also in those of New England, large numbers of English workmen in consequence being attracted to the Irish looms. The importation of Irish yarn, moreover, was being extensively carried on in the county, worsted yarn from Ireland being $5\frac{1}{2}d.$ and combed wool $1d.$ per lb. cheaper than the same commodity in England.[116] The attempted prohibition of the import, however, drew forth a strong protest from the clothiers, stuff-makers, dyers, tuckers, and spoolers, engaged in the cloth manufacture in several Somerset parishes, who declared that the mixture of Irish wool with English yarn

[101] *Cal. S. P. Dom.* 1619–23, pp. 392–3.
[102] Ibid. p. 391.   [103] Ibid. p. 363.
[104] Ibid. p. 343.   [105] Ibid. 1634–5, p. 24.
[106] *Treatise of Wool,* 22.
Defoe places the seat of manufacture of the fine Spanish medley cloths of his day at the following towns in Somerset: Frome, Norton St. Philip, Wincanton, Meare, Bruton, Shepton Mallet and Castle Cary. *Tour,* ii, 41 and 28.
[107] Europe, it was said, could not produce a wool equal to that used in the production of the broadcloth of Frome. *A Brief Deduction,* 45.
[108] Matthew Grace was making cloth at Frome in 1475. *Cal. Pat.* 1467–77, p. 503.
[109] S. P. Dom. Chas. I, clxxxv, 40.

[110] Cf. *Hist. MSS. Com. Rep.* iii, 63 and 191.
[111] Hotten, *Original Lists,* 317.
[112] Minehead was 'full of Irishmen' in Leland's time. *Itin.* ii, 100.
[113] *Commons' Journ.* 1691, p. 611.
[114] *A Brief Deduction,* 31.
[115] Bischoff, *Hist. Woollen and Worsted,* i, 80.
[116] *Commons' Journ.* 1697, p. 37.

was necessary for their competition with the foreign manufacturers. The gentlemen and freeholders of the county, on the contrary, declared themselves to be in favour of the exclusion of Irish yarn, which, they alleged, spoilt the market hitherto open to their home-grown wool.[117]

The methods and mode of the Somerset cloth manufacture has been recorded for us in a quaint 17th-century poem on the trade of Shepton Mallet,[118] in 1641, which may well be taken as typical of the same process throughout the county. After declaring that ‘ the glory of our own town remains In making cloth,’ some of English, some of Spanish wool, the varieties being ‘ fine, thick, full, and thin,’ whilst the tending of the sheep that supplied the raw material gave employment to ‘ threescore thousand of the poor of Shepton and Batcombe and other villages,’ the poet enumerates the various craftsmen necessary to the conversion of the wool into the finished cloth :—

As first, the Parter, that doth neatly cull
The finer from the coarser sort of wool.
The Dyer then in order next doth stand,
With sweating brow, and a laborious hand.
With oil they then asperge it, which, being done,
The careful hand of Mixers round it run.
The Stockcarder his arms doth hard employ,
(Remembering Friday is our market-day :)
Then the Knee-carder doth (without control)
Quickly convert it to a lesser roll.
Which done, the Spinster doth in hand it take,
And of two hundred rolls one thread doth make.
The Weaver next doth warp and weave the chain . . .
. . . and cries, come, boy, with quills.
Being filled, the Brayer doth it mundify,
From oil and dirt that in the same doth lie.
The Burler then (yea, thousands in this place),
The thick-set weed with nimble hand doth chase . . .
The Fuller then close by his stock doth stand,
And will not once shake Morpheus by the hand.
The Rower next his arms lifts up on high,
And near him sings the Shearman merrily.
The Drawer last, that many faults doth hide,
(Whom Merchant nor the Weaver can abide),
Yet he is one in most cloths stops more holes
Than there be stairs to the top of Paul’s.’[119]

The cloth and wool traffic of the county was carried on by packhorse, and at a later date by wagons. ‘ The packhorses travelled in lines, with the bales or panniers strapped across their backs. The foremost horse bore a bell or collar of bells, and was hence called the ‘ bell-horse.’ He was selected because of his sagacity, and by the tinklings of his bells the movements of his followers were regulated.’[120] Packhorses to

the number of forty or fifty, in single file, were frequently to be met with in country cloth-making districts, laden with the products of the busy loom.[121] ‘ The trusty steed with his tinkling bell,’ says Mr. Humphreys, ‘ was for long a familiar spectacle over the boggy roads in this neighbourhood ’ (Wellington).[122] Seven wagons at a time, we are told, would leave Frome in the days of its greatest cloth-making activity at the close of the 18th century, for London, laden with bales. The clothiers of Mells and other adjacent villages brought their goods to this centre, whence they were dispatched to town. Each wagon carried 140 pieces of cloth each valued at £14.[123] Messrs. Whitmarsh and Brice of Taunton were paid as much as £6,000 per annum for the carriage of penistones from Wiveliscombe to London.[124]

Famous clothiers of Somerset, at different times in the history of the cloth trade, have been the ancient family of Cogan of Chard who were admitted as entitled to bear arms at the Heralds’ College,[125] the Sharlands of Mells, where they were known as ‘ London merchants,’[126] Richard Maudelyn of Croscombe, whose name comes down to us through the medium of early Chancery proceedings,[127] the North, Chorley, and Featherstone families of Wiveliscombe, many of whose descendants are still to be found in the vicinity,[128] whilst ‘ a certain great clothier in Wellington ’ is claimed by the poet Southey as his ancestor.[129] Leland records for us the names of those three famous clothiers of Bath, Style, Kent, and Chapman, ‘ by whom,’ he states, ‘ that town flourished,’ the trade in which they were concerned, he adds, ‘ somewhat decaying ’ after their deaths.[130] The names of these three early cloth merchants of Bath appear in an indenture of 30 November 1523, as commissioners appointed to oversee the levy of a poll tax at that date.[131] Maudelyn, and afterwards a son of his,’ were ‘ great clothiers of Wells,’ according to Leland.[132]

[117] *Commons’ Journ.* 1697, p. 521.
[118] A modern writer records his impressions of the picturesque old houses in the Longbridge district of Shepton Mallet, formerly occupied by the clothiers. Barrett, *Highways and Byways in Somerset*, 69.
[119] Watts, *The Young Man’s Looking Glasse*, 42–4.
[120] Smiles, *Lives of the Engineers*, i, 179.

[121] *Handbook of Wrington*, 1861.
[122] Humphreys, *Hist. Wellington*, 213. See Dyer, *The Fleece*, bidding the clothier ‘ pile the pack on the long tinkling train of slow-pac’d steeds.’ William Roberts was fined 20s. at Taunton in 1634 for travelling with his pack on a Sunday. *Cal. S. P. Dom.* 1634–6, p. 445. ‘ The yard at Tonedale, Wellington,’ we are told, ‘ might be seen any day filled with a whole array of packhorses and wagons just starting from or returning to the yard.’ Humphreys, *Hist. Wellington*, 213.
[123] *Univ. Brit. Dir.* (1793), iii, 133.
[124] *Somers. Arch. Soc. Proc.* xxix, 34.
[125] Ibid. xxviii, 24.   [126] Ibid. xxxix, 22.
[127] Early Chan. Proc. bdle. 215, no. 20.
[128] *Somers. Arch. Soc. Proc.* xxix, 23.
[129] Humphreys, *Hist. Wellington*, 82.
[130] Leland, *Itin.* ii, 67.
[131] *Bath Nat. Hist. and Field Club Proc.* vi, 386. See ibid. 410.   [132] Leland, op. cit. 69.

Implements of the clothworkers' craft are of frequent occurrence on 17th-century tokens of Somerset. Such for instance are a wool-comb, croppers' shears, and woolpack; whilst a Milverton token bears a teasel-brush, and one issued at Taunton a hand holding a wool-card.[133] Shop-signs of a similar character may be found in the county.[134] The bequest of looms figures occasionally in Somerset wills. In 1550 John Swetyng of Stogumber bequeathed his two pair of looms to his son John, adding that if there were six sleys in the house at the time of the testator's death, the legatee was to have three and his mother the same number.[135] A similar bequest was made in 1577 by Thomas Spoore of Norton-sub-Hamdon to his son.[136]

The clothing industry necessarily gave rise to many subsidiary ones. Such for example was that of quill-making, the quill, now replaced by the bobbin, being used for winding the yarn from the hank or skein. Mary Curtis was quill-maker to the weavers at Wellington at the end of the 18th century.[137]

The mere brief enumeration of all the 'long, countless host of woollen webs,'[138] once fashioned on these flying looms, suffices to call up a whole treasury of textile nomenclature, recorded for us in mediaeval wills, and in the statute-books of the realm. Such are the 'blue cloths called plunkets or azures;'[139] the 'handywarps and broad-listed whites and reds,' the latter peculiar to East Somerset, 'the narrow Somersets;'[140] the Tauntons and Bridgwaters; the coarse cottons of Chard; the ratteens[141] of Bridgwater; the kerseymeres[142] of Dunster; the cloths called 'vesses, rayes, sailing-cloths, park cloths, and sorting-cloths,' which, we learn from the draft of an Act of 1592, were manufactured in Somerset, Wilts., and Gloucestershire.[143] 'Bath Beaver' was no doubt the fabric which Chaucer had in his mind when he wrote of the 'good Wif' of that city;[144] whilst Crewkerne has at all times been

the centre of the sail-cloth manufacture, and Wincanton and Yeovil of the dowlas,[145] ticking, and kindred industries. The textile output of Wiveliscombe in the past comprised blanketings, knap[146] coatings, kerseys, shrouds, ermine, baize and penistones.

Penistones, which derived their name from Peniston, near Sheffield, the place of their origin,[147] had, according to one authority, 'a bad chance in rainy weather,'[148] as the cloth was apt to shrink when wet. Wiveliscombe, however, carried on an extensive trade in this fabric with the West Indies, where it was largely utilized for the clothing of the slave population.[149] Prior to the Emancipation, which gave the industry its death-blow, bringing a loss upon the industrial community of at least £400 to £500 per week,[150] oaken racks might be seen, we are told, in every field, for the purpose of stretching the cloth,[151] whilst the carriage of these goods alone to London was a source of considerable revenue to the carriers of Taunton.[152]

Wiveliscombe was for many years a rival of Wellington in the woollen manufacture. Mr. Fox relates that an old man, still residing there, recollects the time (about 1820), when there were six manufacturers in the town of a sort of stuff called 'Pennystones,' which was a thick blue kersey, rubbed into little knots like an Irish frieze, which was effected by the friction of two circular stones like millstones, worked by a horse. This was a separate business, and was carried on by an old man called from his craft 'Napper' Yandle. The last representatives of the woollen industry of Wiveliscombe were Mr. Featherstone, Mr. Clatworthy, Mr. T. North, Mr. Clement Chorley, Mr. S. Dunn, and Mr. R. Dunn.

'A considerable woollen manufacture has been for more than two centuries,' writes Collinson[153] in 1791, 'been carried on in the town, and still flourishes. The goods made are blanketings, knap-coatings, kerseys, coarse cloths—stroud, ermine, and baize. Many of these are sent to London, Bristol, and Exeter, for home consumption, and for exportation to Spain and Germany.

Kerseys, which, as we have seen, were made at Glastonbury by the Flemish weaving colony,

---

[133] *Somers. Arch. Soc. Proc.* xxxii, 121 et seq. Note also the 15th cent. weavers' panel in Spaxton Church. Ibid. viii, 8. [134] Williamson, *Trade Tokens*, ii, 970.

[135] Weaver, *Somerset Wills*, 121. Sley—a weaver's reed. Worcester, *Dict.* Thomas Chaunceler of Bath bequeathed a weaving loom with its apparel to his parish church in 1496, also two looms to the altar of St. Catherine, Bath Priory. Weaver, op. cit. 343.

[136] Trask, *Norton-sub-Hamdon*, 210.

[137] Humphreys, *Hist. of Wellington*, 228.

[138] Dyer, *The Fleece*, 109.

[139] *Cal. S.P. Dom.* 1580–1625, p. 347.

[140] Rogers, *Agric. and Prices*, iv, 95.

[141] A coarse woollen. Beck, *Drapers' Dict.* 272.

[142] Fairholt, *Costume in Engl.* ii, 265.

[143] *Hist. MSS. Com. Rep.* iii, 7.

[144] 'A good Wyf was ther of bisyde Bathe,
    But she was somdel deef, and that was scathe
    Of clooth-making she hadde swich an haunt,
    Sche passed hem of Ypris and of Gaunt.'
        —Chaucer, *Canterbury Tales*, Prol. 96.

[145] *Somers. Arch. Soc. Proc.*

[146] Henry Yandle, cloth napper, resided in Fore Street, Wiveliscombe, in 1830. Pigot, *Dir.* 736.

[147] Rogers, *Hist. of Agric. and Prices*, v, 572.

[148] *Somers. Arch. Soc. Proc.* xxix, 34.

[149] Negro clothing was distributed annually at Christmas, at which season the ships arrived from England. It consisted of strong blue woollen cloth called 'Pennistowns,' of which the slaves received every year 6 yds. 1½ yd. wide. Carmichael, *Domestic Manners in the West Indies*, 142.

[150] *Somers. Arch. Soc. Proc.* loc. cit.

[151] Ibid.   [152] Ibid.

[153] *Hist. Somerset*, ii, 487.

were those coarse, narrow, woollen cloths, 'early naturalized,' as Professor Thorold Rogers points out, in the West of England.[154] 'Restrained' by Elizabethan legislation to the length of 18 yds.,[155] they were permitted in the following reign to be made 24 yds. long, the weight however remaining, as before, 28½ lb.[156]

A very ancient Somerset manufacture was that of Cary cloth. It was of a coarse quality, and had some popularity amongst country people.[157] This cloth, Mr. Grafton points out, is alluded to in the fifth part of the *Vision of Piers Plowman*, written about 1362. Of the deadly sin of envy, personified in human form, the poet writes, 'He was pale as a pelet, in the palsy he seemed, and clothed in a carimaury.' Skeat's glossary defines carimaury as the name of some coarse material, and adds that of the ploughman in the 'Ploughman's Creed' (1394) it is said that 'his cote was of a clout that was cary y-called.' Colour is lent, in Mr. Grafton's opinion, to the fact of the existence of a cloth manufacture in the neighbourhood at an early date by the occurrence of the name of Laurentia le Touker (fuller) in a list of tax-payers in 1327, her contribution being 18d.[158]

Chard formerly carried on an extensive trade, both in the 'cloths commonly called Bridgwaters and Tauntons,'[159] and also in coarse cottons, which were largely exported in the 17th century to Brittany, Bordeaux, and Rochelle.[160] So important was this industry to the trading community, that in 1609 we find the Mayor of Chard writing to London on behalf of the townspeople, who were seriously threatened by the proposed formation of a French company in opposition to their long-established similar enterprise.[161] In 1613, we find a warrant being issued under the royal sign-manual directing the customer of Lyme to enter as Taunton cottons certain coarse cotton made there and at Chard, and to charge a duty thereon of 16d., instead of a previously existing duty on baize.[162]

Sagathees and duroys, which were largely used in the time of Defoe for gentlemen's suits, as we learn from an advertisement of the period setting forth that such suits were to be had at the 'Two Golden Bells,' Southampton Street, Covent Garden,[163] were chiefly made at Taunton where 1,100 looms were going in 1727 for their weaving, together with other 'such kind of stuffs,' not one wanting work.[164]

A feature of the cloth industry of Frome, which was 'wholly clothing,' all of which, we learn from Defoe, was sent to London,[165] was the manufacture of 'livery cloths.' Mr. Thomas Sheppard, a Blackwell Hall factor, stated before a Parliamentary Committee on the Wool Trade in 1828 that he sold such cloths largely to the American market in 1822–4. Frome was the only place in England, according to this witness, where they could be had of English wool unmixed with Spanish or other varieties.[166] Chard and Ilminster[167] were also engaged in a similar industry about this date.

Crewkerne, in addition to its sailcloth manufacture, supplied its serges to the East India Company, in the early 19th century.[168]

Linsey woolseys were formerly made at Milborne Port,[169] and blankets at Dulverton, but by 1830 this was spoken of as 'a lost trade.[170]

Serge, it is said, owes its popularity as a staple of the woollen manufacture of the west country to the suitability of such a fabric to the long and rather coarse wool characteristic of the breed of sheep peculiar to Devon and Somerset. The treatment of this wool in the earlier processes of manufacture is as follows : The longest fibre from the back and shoulders of the fleece must be combed out to straighten it, and this we find has been done ever since the time of the Flemings. The combed wool is then spun into the strong elastic yarn called 'worsted,' which from this west-country staple is nearly as strong as whipcord. This worsted in a serge is used for the warp (the continuous longitudinal thread), while the weft, with which it was crossed, was prepared in a different manner. For this all the rest of the fleece was used—all the soft lambs' wool, and the short wool scraped off the skins by the butcher, as well as the refuse of the combings of the longer staple. All this was mixed and worked by means of what must have been not unlike flat hair brushes, being set with teasels or thistles, these being

---

[154] Rogers, *Agric. and Prices*, v, 576.
[155] 14 Eliz. cap. 10.   [156] 3 Jas. I, cap. 16.
[157] Grafton, *Castle Cary*, 8.   [158] Ibid. 9.
[159] Act 2 & 3 Phil. and Mary, cap. 12. For sealing and viewing of cloths commonly called Bridgwaters made at Taunton and Chard. No cloth of this kind was to be made before viewing, searching, and sealing of the same. By a later statute however (18 Eliz. cap. 16) persons dwelling out of corporate towns, to which the making had been restricted by the previous Act, were relieved of the embargo.
[160] *Somers. Arch. Soc. Proc.* xxviii, 56 et seq.
[161] Ibid.   [162] Ibid. 57.

[163] *County Journ.* 2 July, 1737.
[164] Defoe, *Tour*, ii, 16.
In the opinion of a contemporary, the replacing of the manufacture of broadcloth, 'the ancient glory of England,' by that of 'sagathies and duroys, a thin and light sort of stuff,' at Taunton and parts adjoining did incalculable harm to the cloth trade. (*A Brief Deduction*, 139.) Sagathee—according to Beck—'a slight woollen stuff, a kind of ratteen or serge, mixed with a little silk.' (*Drapers' Dict.* 285.)
[165] Defoe, *Tour*, ii, 42.
[166] *Rep. Wool Trade*, 1828, p. 293.
[167] Pigot, *Dir.* 438.
[168] *Rep. Wool Trade*, 1828, p. 114.
[169] Pigot, *Dir.* 703   [170] Ibid. 705.

called 'cards,' and the process 'carding.' The form of 'hand card' and hand comb may be seen on several of the trade tokens of Somerset in the 17th century. Towards the end of the 19th century an artificial card, or imitation teasel, was made by passing wire through cloth, and rollers covered by these wire brushes were combined into what is called a 'carding engine.' As late as 1820 however spinning was done by hand. Celia Fiennes,[171] visiting Taunton in the reign of William and Mary, writes of the countrywomen whom she saw 'wrapped up in mantles called west-country rockets, a large mantle doubled together of a sort of serge, some being linsey-woolsey,' with a deep fringe at the end, and reaching to the waist, or, in some instances, to the feet. These distinctive cloaks, which the writer observed were always in the fashion with their wearers, were made of white serge in the summer and red in the winter.

Previous to 1856 combing was done by sets of men (generally four), who worked in their own or in each other's houses, wherever it was practicable to set up the 'pot,' which was a charcoal stove in which their combs were kept constantly heated, which was a necessity of the process.

In remote country places, before the introduction of railways, the processes of spinning and carding were carried on in their cottage homes by women, with a simple loom, the pattern of which, says Mr. Fox, was hardly changed in any single particular from the model of ancient Egypt. On this loom warp and weft were woven into serge or kersey, the diagonal rib or pattern running across the cloth, which was characteristic of both materials, being given by the use of four treadles, by which the threads of the warp were raised in regular succession of four.[172]

In Somerset, as in other clothworking centres, the festival of St. Blaize, patron of woolcombers, was observed every year on 3 February. At Wellington the festival in question was kept until about the middle of the last century. The bishop was chosen from among the woolcombers, of whom there were ten in 1795–1810. The last celebration was held at the house of Joseph Neath in Mantle Street, the bishop being personified by William Eveleigh. The following verse was sung in procession by those in attendance upon the chief personage of the day :—

> Behold our Bishop Blaize,
> Who first invented combing,
> Some say he has been dead long time,
> But now we're come to show him.[173]

Economic disaster threatened the cloth trade at the close of the 17th century, from within as well as from without, the growing import of Spanish wool [174] and the untrustworthiness of the Blackwell Hall factors forcing the clothiers to complain vehemently of the condition of their industry.[175] Trade with Africa, again, which had been largely carried on from Taunton, was menaced by an African Company, against whose monopoly of their trade we find the merchants, clothiers, fullers, dyers, and serge-makers of that town uniting in a petition to Parliament in 1698.[176] The cloth-makers of the county were at variance in 1691 with the wool broggers, as well as with their factors, both being declared 'notorious enemies' to the trade.[177]

At the opening of the 18th century 8,500 persons were making cloth in Taunton,[178] whilst the frequent occurrence in parish registers throughout the county of this date of such occupations as 'serg maker,' 'wofer,' 'comer,' &c.[179] point to an ubiquitous activity in the trade.

Some members of the industrial Dutch colony, planted at Bradford by Sir Anthony Methuen, in the latter part of the 17th century, apparently migrated to Twerton shortly after, for the parish registers of that place record the burials, between 1722 and 1732, of several persons whose names show their Dutch descent, amongst others, John Jockman, John Brick, Thomas Michner, and John Graft, the church of Twerton also containing a tablet to the memory of Nicholas Graft of Viet.[180]

The author of a pamphlet on the wool trade, published in 1727, was of the opinion that Somerset, 'the most intent' of any English county, with the exception of Devon, on the woollen manufacture, was being 'diverted' from the same by grazing, and digging of lead and coal, 'which employed many thousands of the people.' [181]

In 1725, complaints having been received of the excessive straining of broadcloth, which

---

[171] Fiennes, *Through England on a Side-Saddle*, 205.
[172] Humphreys, *Hist. Wellington*, 212.
[173] Ibid. 229.

[174] At the opening of the 19th century numerous bags of Spanish wool were laid up at Blackwell Hall, where 7s. and 8s. per lb. had been refused for them by speculators. 'In view,' we are told, 'of Bonaparte's designs on Spain,' large quantities had been bought up by the West of England manufacturers at 6s. 9d. per lb. (Young, *Annals of Agric.* xlvi, 39.)
[175] Presentment Grand Jury at Bruton, 1684.
[176] *Commons' Journ.* 1698, p. 575.
[177] Ibid. 1691, p. 611.
[178] Gee, *Trade and Navigation*, 30–1.
[179] Prior to 1655, says Toulmin, the serges made at Taunton were in great demand and reputation, as fashionable wearing, being lighter than cloth, and yet thicker than many other stuffs. (Toulmin, *Hist. Taunton*, 372.) The mixed serges made in Somerset and sold in Taunton were to have been among the specialities benefited by the South Sea Company as 'proper for the trade.'
[180] *Bath Nat. Hist. and Field Club Proc.* ii, 278.
[181] *A Brief Deduction*, 6.

was injurious to the fabric, the justices of the peace were authorized to appoint inspectors to visit all premises where the manufacture was carried on, to guard against this abuse.[182] An Act was passed in the following year 'for preventing ill practices used in excessive straining of medley woollen broadcloths made in Somerset.'[183]

'The poor oppressed weavers of Taunton' petitioned Parliament in this year complaining of the great hardships inflicted on them by their masters, the broad clothiers,[184] who, they alleged, were reducing them to want, necessity, and despair, by lengthening their warping bars, causing them to weave 3½ for 3 yards.

A Mr. Sperin was a noted drugget-maker at Twerton in 1729,[185] whilst at Walcot there were two cloth mills.[186] 'Some clothing' was manufactured at Yeovil at this time;[187] a similar manufacture being 'the most important' of the six trades which gave employment to the mills at Twerton.[188] The industry was largely in the hands of a Mr. Brown, whose successors, his son, Mr. Naish, and, eventually, a Mr. Cooke, gave employment to 300 adults and 80 children in 1808.[189]

In 1776 the introduction of machinery at Shepton Mallet caused a riot amongst the cloth-workers, who destroyed the whole of the machines.[190]

The impressions of a traveller at the close of the 18th century were to the effect that few traces of the cloth manufacture were visible, though the industry was carried on in all parts of the county. The cleanliness and prosperity with which the trade appeared to be conducted seemed to him to be in striking contrast to the conditions prevailing in similar centres in Yorkshire and the North of England.[191]

There were at this date in Frome 220 weavers, earning about 20s. per week, 146 shearmen whose wages varied from 15s. to 20s. weekly, 141 scribblers who were paid about 12s. a week, and 47 clothiers.[192] Women were employed in picking wool, burling or dressing cloth,[193] and in attending to the machines, at 8d.

a day, children, engaged in similar work, earning 2s. 6d. a week. The cloths manufactured at this place were distinguished as 'superfine' (made from Spanish wool), 'super,' and 'best super' (in which English wool alone was employed), and kerseymeres, which were chiefly sent to France, the industry being almost ruined in 1794, we learn, by the political troubles in that country. Broadcloth was in great demand that year.[194]

A characteristic and arresting feature of the history of the cloth trade of the West of England in the 18th century was the beginning of that long struggle for supremacy between the old conditions of hand-labour, and the advent of machinery.

The gig-mill[195] in particular was the object of the most vehement hostility on the part of the weavers at this date, clothiers who employed this method of dressing their cloth being compelled to send the material long distances to be thus treated.[196] The erection of a spinning-jenny at Wellington in 1791 caused, we are told, 'some uneasiness amongst the spinners.'[197] A contemporary writer states that 'circumstances of a local nature were peculiarly adverse to the introduction of machinery into the West of England, where the spinners, before its appearance, had been largely employed by the clothiers. The new departure in the process of manufacture threw numbers of the spinners in consequence out of work, and left them without the means of turning their attention to any new means of livelihood.'[198]

Minehead, which was 'driving an indifferent trade to Ireland' in 1720,[199] part at least of which consisted of the serges which were continuously manufactured in the town until the close of the century, had but two representatives of the industry at that date, Robert Blake, clothier, and Samuel Richards, woolcomber,[200] the former selling blanketing at 1s. 1d. per yard, 'bay' being 9d., and serge 1s. 4d. Thomas Pelman was a serge-weaver in the High Town.[201] Coarse cloth was also woven in the seaport, the population being largely engaged in 1795

[182] Cunningham, *Engl. Industry and Commerce*, pt. i, 510.
[183] Stat. 13 Geo. I, cap. 23.
[184] Henson, *Hist. Framework Knitting*, 131.
[185] *Bath Nat. Hist. and Field Club Proc.* ii, 279.
[186] Ibid. ix, 183.   [187] Defoe, *Tour*, i, 321.
[188] *Bath Nat. Hist. and Field Club Proc.* ii, 279.
[189] Ibid. 263.
[190] Bonwick, *Romance of the Wool Trade*, 355.
[191] Marshall, *Rural Econ. West of Engl.* 218.
[192] Eden, *State of the Poor*, ii, 643.
[193] Burl—to pick out from a piece of cloth knots or hay or thorns which have escaped the carding process. Burling was always done by women, who drew the cloth carefully over a sloping bench in a good light, the operation taking place between those of washing and milling. (Elworthy, *West Somerset Words*, 101.)

[194] Eden, op. cit. 644.
[195] Mills used for the perching (looking through cloth with a strong light on the other side to see if there is any defect) and burling of cloth. (Halliwell, *Dict. Archaic Words*, 399.) Gig-mills, for scribbling or raising the nap on cloth by machinery, were invented in the reign of Henry VI, but prohibited in 1551, Act 5 Edward VI, cap. 22, owing to the outcry against the injury done to cloths thus treated. (Henson, *Hist. Framework Knitting*, 32.)
[196] Mr. Sheppard of Frome sent his cloths 90 miles to a gig-mill. (*Parl. Rep.* 1805, p. 14.)
[197] Young, *Annals of Agric.* xli, 489.
[198] Ibid. xv, 494.
[199] Ogilby, *Britannia Depicta*, 170.
[200] Hancock, *Hist. Minehead*, 428.
[201] Ibid. 221.

in woolcombing, the labourers' wives spinning worsted and yarn.[202]

Eighteenth-century prices of textile fabrics are recorded for us in the parochial accounts of Chew Magna, where the poor were provided with cloth and linen, as well as money. In 1745, having complained of their need of cloth, the officers of the town were ordered to buy kersey at a cost of 1s. 5d. to 1s. 6d. per yard. Flaxen cloth was 10d. per ell, narrow cloth 3s. 1½d. per ell, stuff 2s. 2d. per yard. In 1755 spriggs (flaxen cloth) were 10d. per ell, dowlas 1s. 3d. per ell, serge 8½d., white cloth 1s. 4d. per yard, Russian cloth, 6d., stuff for gowns, 11¾d. per yard. In 1763 canvas sold at 1s. 1d. In 1765 linen was 1s. 1d. per yard, and 8d. per ell, worsted, 8½d. per oz.[203]

In 1790, 4,000 persons were employed in the cloth trade of Shepton Mallet.[204] Six mills were manufacturing broadcloths at Chard.[205]

The cloth trade at Twerton was reported to be in a very flourishing condition at this date. There were three cloth mills in the place, the principal establishment being that of Messrs. Bamford, Cooke, & Co., where kerseymeres and broadcloths were extensively woven by means of 'curious machinery,' consisting of thousands of small wheels worked by one large water-wheel.[206] Superfine broadcloth was produced by Mr. Cotticote.[207] A large export trade was carried on, the cloth being sent abroad as well as into all parts of England.[208]

In 1821 Taunton was busily engaged in following its ancient industry. There were in the town from 10 to 12 looms at work, employing 1,000 weavers, 6 to 8 woolcombers, 100 quillers, 100 winders, whilst 500 persons were engaged at the throwing mills, of which there were several in the town.[209]

The Population Returns of 1831 afford interesting statistics with regard to the cloth manufacture at that date. 730 men were employed at Frome, 59 at Street, 32 at Beckington, 42 at Hinton Charterhouse, 565 at Lyncombe and Widcombe, 32 at Freshford, 258 at Wellington and 200 at Milverton, these towns being almost exclusively occupied with the production of woollen cloth, Street in addition being largely concerned in tanning and dyeing of sheepskins for hearth-rugs and gig-rugs. Crewkerne, East Coker, Merriott, West Hatch, and North Perrott were identified with sailcloth and sacking (girthweb) manufacture. Twenty-one persons were engaged at Ilminster in the silk and lace manufacture, 478 being similarly employed at Chard

and Bruton. Taunton and Shepton Mallet maintained their position as producers of woollen cloth, serge, sailcloth, and silk. Dowlas and ticking were made at Corton Denham, Wincanton, and Stoke Trister. Keynsham, with its busy flax-mills, gave employment to 79 men. The decrease of population noticeable at this date in the parish of Queen Camel was attributed to the cessation of the linen trade.[210]

In 1839 16 mills, giving employment to 755 persons, were producing cotton, worsted, and silk in the county.[211]

In 1840 Frome, Twerton, Ilminster, and Chard, were producing fine, seconds, and livery woollen broadcloths. There were 350 looms in Frome, 220 in one parish. The master weavers were allowed to set up 10 or 12 looms each. Surplus work was put out to weavers owning a single loom, at two-thirds of the owner's wages. Ilminster had 7 looms, on which were woven a small quantity of seconds or livery cloths. There were 23 weavers in Chard; at Road there were 3 factories, 11 families of weavers owning 18 looms, valued at 4s. 9¾d. each. Two men and 24 women and children were weaving haircloth at Castle Cary. Wages averaged from 10s. to 14s.[212]

A great advance on the quality and finish of cloth was made at the Twerton Mills, Bath, by Mr. Charles Wilkins from 1825 to 1845. His immediate predecessor was Mr. Norris. Mr. Wilkins made his West of England cloths from the finest Spanish and German wools, the latter mainly from Moravia and Silesia; his connexion with the woollen mills ceased in 1847. They were then successfully carried on by Messrs. Thomas and William Carr, who obtained a medal at the Great Exhibition in 1851. After the decease of Messrs. T. and W. Carr in 1855 Mr. Isaac Carr (under the firm of Isaac Carr & Co.) became the proprietor of these mills and obtained a wide reputation as a manufacturer of Patent Bearns, Elysians and superior Melton Cloths for hunting.[213]

In 1858 textile statistics were as follows: the silk trade was employing 355 men and 1,696 women; 1,841 men and 1,737 women were at work in the woollen cloth trade; whilst rope and sailcloth making were giving occupation to 813 men and 319 women.[214]

From this date onwards the textile trade of the West country found itself seriously hampered by changes in fashion, higher-priced labour, and above all by the development of the manufacturing centres of the North of England, consequent upon the growth of the auxiliary industries of coal and steam. At the present

[202] Eden, *State of the Poor*, ii, 647.
[203] Wood, *Hist. of Chew Magna*, 262.
[204] Farbrother, *Hist. of Shepton Mallet*, 14.
[205] Lipscomb, *Journey into Cornwall*, 139.
[206] Warner, *Hist. of Bath*, 216.
[207] Ibid.   [208] Ibid. 217.
[209] Toulmin, *Hist. Taunton*, 382.

[210] *Pop. Ret.* 1831.
[211] *Rep. Hand-loom Weavers*, 1839, pp. 134-5.
[212] Ibid. 1840, pp. 408-33.
[213] From information kindly supplied by Mr Frederick Shunn.
[214] *Bath and W. of Engl. Agric. Journ.* vi, 131

time, however, the traditions of Somerset's 'countless hosts of woollen webs' are worthily maintained at various points throughout the county which have been associated with the cloth trade for many centuries. The serges of Wellington are still produced by Messrs. Fox, Butler & Co., who employ 30,000 spindles at their Tonedale Mills, and by Messrs. Elworthy Bros. & Co., Ltd., at Westford Mills, these firms being also manufacturers of flannels, blankets, worsted, and yarn spinners. Egerton Burnett, Limited, and Haddon & Sons are well-known woollen and serge merchants. The old Staplegrove mill, which about half a century ago was a silk-mill, is now used by one of the Messrs. Price for the preparation of flock and other material for bedding.

About thirty years ago the Sheppard family, who had long been the leading cloth manufacturers at or near Frome, gave up their extensive factory at Spring Gardens a mile out of the town; it then contained much antiquated machinery. Two or three smaller firms have stopped more recently. At the present day Messrs. Alfred H. Tucker, Limited, employ about 240 hands at the Wallbridge Mills near the Railway Station. Owing to the development of their business of late years they have erected additional buildings. They manufacture tweeds and woollen coatings. Their predecessors in the early 'sixties' of the last century were Messrs. Magill & Stephens, who carried on the business which had been originally established by Mr. Daniel Trotman. At the other end of the town of Frome Messrs. Henry Houston & Son of Vallis Road employ a hundred or so hands in their business, established about a century ago. They manufacture white and drab Bedford cords and buckskins; white and fancy cassimeres, livery and riding cloths. Also at Welshmill Lane, E. Martin & Son make fancy tweeds, polos and whipcords.

At Twerton the firm of Messrs. Isaac Carr & Co. still continue to manufacture the fine cloths already mentioned, which are largely exported to the United States and the Continent in spite of the heavy adverse duties. At Farleigh Hungerford also Charles Salter & Co. still make cloth, but at Taunton the old manufacture no longer exists, the principal factories being devoted to the production of shirts, collars, gloves and clothing, though the silk trade is still represented by one firm.[215] At Freshford, Monkton Combe and Wrington also, the flock manufacture has taken the place of the old cloth industry.

Fulling.—The industry of the fuller, whose duty was defined by statute,[216] and who was so indispensable to the conduct of the cloth-making craft,[217] finds due expression in the economic scheme of mediaeval textile enterprise. The fuller of the west country was usually known as the tucker or touker, and his place of business as the tucking mill.[218] Early instances of these are at Cheddar, where 16s. 11½d. was paid for the rent of four fulling-mills in 1301 ;[219] at Dunster in 1259,[220] at Chard in 1394,[221] and at Taunton, Walter Danyell being seised of this 'Tokyng Myll.'[222] In the reign of Edward II in the accounts of the temporalities of Bath and Wells when in the king's hands from 11 December 1308 till 15 May 1309, the following are recorded at Wells: 'Et de 18d. de redditu unius Rekke fullatici juxta molendinum extra Burgum de eis terminis (i.e. Christmas and Easter). Et de 26s. 8d. de firma unius molendini fullatici, de predictis duobus terminis. And at Wookey: '53s. 4d. de firma molendini fullatici de Lycchelegh de predictis duobus terminis.'[223] Similar entries occur at Wiveliscombe, 'Et de 8s. de firma unius molendini fullatici de predictis terminis' (i.e. Christmas and Easter).[224] In the reign of Henry VI there are several allusions to fulling mills on townships or manors forming part of the temporalities of the see of Bath and Wells.

At Stoke-sub-Hamdon in 1457 the Duke of Cornwall's receiver-general took £4 17s. 5d. from a mill there called 'Petherton mile,' and also 13s. 4d. 'for the rent of a fulling mill attached to the same mill as let to Robert Axe for this year.'[225]

Many names of mediaeval fullers survive for us in ancient records. Richard le Touker inhabited Fuller's Street, Wells,[226] Mayster (master) John Toker being a member of the flourishing cloth-making community of Croscombe.[227] John Hayn, touker, was a steward

---

[217] Cloth that cometh from the weaving is not comely to wear
 Till it be fulled under fote, or in fulling stocks ;
 Washen well with water, and with teasels cratched,
 Towked and teynted, and under talour's hands.
(Langland, *Vision of Piers Plowman*.)

[218] A local word for fuller's stock or beaters for milling cloth. (Elworthy, *Somerset Word-Book*.) Agnes Singer of Wells had 'certain broadcloth' stolen out of her tucking mill in 1615 by John and Katherine Bradshawe (*Quarter Sessions Records*, Som. Rec. Soc. xxiii).

[219] Mins. Accts. bdle. 1131, no. 3.

[220] Maxwell-Lyte, *History of Dunster*, 297–301.

[221] Inq. p.m. 18 Ric. II, no. 26.

[222] *Early Chan. Proc.* bdle. 131, no. 29.

[223] Mins. Accts. bdle. 1131, no. 4.

[224] Ibid.   [225] Ibid. bdle. 1095, no. 7.

[226] *Cal. Wells D. & C. MSS.* (Hist. MSS. Com.) i, 468.

[227] *Churchwardens' Accts. of Croscombe, etc.* (Somers. Rec. Soc. iv), 4.

---

[215] We are indebted for information as to the present condition of the Somerset cloth trade to Mr. John Coles, Junr., Mr. Frederick Shunn and the Rev. E. H. Bates.

[216] Stat. 4 Edw. IV, cap. 1 which declared the same to be 'fulling, rowing, and teaseling of cloth.'

of the gild of Axbridge in 1461,[228] whilst Vyncent Morrice of Taunton, 'tucker,' figures in a list of aliens to whom letters of denization were granted in the reign of Henry VIII.[229] Richard Flawet of Pensford was a touker at that place in 1472.[230]

At Wells, 10 February 1391, a grant was made by Ralph, Bishop of Bath and Wells, to Henry, Agnes, and Alice Spartegrove, of a piece of land in his water-course at Wells in the Berton, at the end of the garden belonging to the said Henry, to build a fulling mill thereon, and also a piece or land to put up a rack (*rakka*) at a rental of 10*s*. per annum.[231] In this connexion it is interesting to note the survival to this day of numerous field-names which mark the former sites of these racks of oak, or tenters, on which the fullers stretched their cloths to dry. Mr. Humphreys indicates such a survival at Wellington, where one or two places still bear the name of 'Rack-closes,'[232] East Reach, formerly East Stretch, and Turkey Stretch, having the same signification at Taunton.[233]

Bequests of tucker's shears were not unusual in Somerset mediaeval wills. Richard Holmede of Bruton, for example, bequeathed these implements of his craft to his daughter Cristian, in 1520.[234] Shears were occasionally hired, possibly in the case of poor, deserving craftsmen, as for instance Thomas Naunden of Bridgwater, who paid 2*d*. a year to the churchwardens of St. Katherine's for the use of 'a pere of towker's sheres.'[235]

The fuller's art is still recalled at Wellington by the 'Tucking Mill Field,' near the town, whilst the following interesting fact is recorded by Mr. Fox in a paper read by him before the Somerset Archaeological Society :—

'The trees felled in South Street to make room for Mr. Burnett's warehouse were found to be so full of tenter hooks deep embedded that they could hardly be sawn ; for when young saplings they had been used to tenter or hang goods to dry.' Opposite this site are buildings still called the 'Trade-House.' Here all the serges made in the country round were brought to be weighed and examined, and here it was that mechanical spinning was first attempted, the motive power being a four-horse wheel. 'Perching places,' as they were called, were also established however at Culmstock, Hill Farrance, Milverton, and Sampford Peverell, memories still being kept alive of the weekly journeys by

cart to Hill Farrance, for the purpose of carrying the wool to the spinners, and bringing back the woven serges. Fulling mills still exist at Wellington at the Tone Bridge, an old stone in one of the gables bearing the inscription 'Thos. and Ely Were, 1754,' the probable date of the reconstruction of the building. On the Tone, near Water Row, there were seven of these mills, each with two pairs of stocks.[236]

Dyeing.[237]—There can be little doubt that to one of its chief agricultural products in the past Somerset was indebted for the excellence of its ancient 'azures' and 'plunketts.' This product was woad, without which, according to John May, there could be no successful dyeing, for 'the ground of good colour is good woading.'[238] Collinson claims for woad that it was 'once peculiar to Somerset,'[239] whilst from the researches of the Rev. F. W. Weaver in that province of archaeological inquiry which he has made peculiarly his own, namely, that of Somerset Wills,[240] we learn that bequests of woad, as well as of the implements connected with its manufacture, were frequent in the county in mediaeval times. The following may be quoted from this source as interesting examples of this form of legacy. In 1481 Simon Lacy bequeaths his woad-vat,[241] John Attwater making a similar bequest in 1500, with the addition of a furnace.[242] Agnes Petygrewe of Publow, who owned a dyeing-house, left the same, together with 'le fatte and furneyse,' and all things belonging thereto, to John Peryn and Margaret his wife, whilst to the church of St. Thomas at Pensford and to that at Publow the testatrix gave one measure of woad each.[243] William Swalowe of Glastonbury left one quarter of woad to Richard Davy in 1501.[244]

[228] *Hist. MSS. Com. Rep.* iii, App. 301.

[229] Page, *Letters Deniz. Aliens,* 1509–1603 (Huguenot Soc. vii), 73.

[230] *Cal. Pat.* 1467–77, p. 320.

[231] *Cal. Wells D. & C. MSS.* (Hist. MSS. Com.), i, 460.   [232] Humphreys, *Hist. Wellington,* 9.

[233] Ibid. 121.

[234] Weaver, *Somerset Wills* (Somers. Rec. Soc. xix), 207.   [235] *Somers. Arch. Soc. Proc.* vii, 101.

[236] Humphrey, *Hist. Wellington.* Topographical records of this ancient industry survive in the Fuller's Pond at Winscombe (Compton, *A Mendip Valley,* 11), and the Fuller's Panel at Spaxton Church, which shows a man at work on a piece of cloth. (*Somers. Arch. Soc. Proc.* viii, 8.)

[237] The writer is indebted to the kind assistance of Mrs. L. B. Lee for much of the information contained in this article. See also *Journ. Brit. Arch. Soc.* ix, 147–60 ; Plowright, *Journ. Soc. Dyers,* July 1902, p. 179.

[238] May, *Estate of Clothing.* See Adam de Domerham, *Hist.* (ed. Hearne), 87, for directions 'To make wode (of which there was a great quantity belonging to the abbey of Muchelney, as well as to the Abbot of Glastonbury).'

[239] Collinson, *Hist. of Somerset,* ii, 400.

[240] See Somerset Record Society's publications.

[241] Weaver, *Somerset Wills* (Somers. Rec. Soc. xvi), 234.   [242] Ibid. 389.

[243] Ibid. (Somers. Rec. Soc. xxi) 2.

[244] Weaver, op. cit. 23. John Hawker of Ilminster inherited from his father Richard in 1496 a 'furnace (fornacem) and dye-house (domum tinctorium (*sic*). Ibid. 345.

Half a pipe of woad was bequeathed by Agnes Burton of Taunton in 1503 'to making and finishing the Tower of Maudelyn.'[245] In 1504 Thomas Upcot of Dunster left to his daughter Joan four bales 'de la ode.'[246] John Flemyng of Glastonbury gave by his will to his son two quarters, and to his daughter Joan one quarter of the same.[247] Thomas Strete of Mells, clothier, bequeathed a woad-vat.[248] The will of Denys Dwyn, a merchant trading between Bridgwater and Bordeaux in the 16th century, contains numerous bequests of pipes of woad, to the masters of his ships, to monastic legatees, to the towns with which he traded, and to others.[249] In 1548 George George, of Westcombe, Batcombe, left a woad-vat and furnace,[250] and in 1548 Margery Hill of Taunton made a bequest to her three grandchildren of a pipe of 'oode.'[251]

The Dunster Court Rolls of the 15th century contain several references to the pollution of the river there with woad water.[252]

The golden era of the woad industry would seem to have been coincident with the Elizabethan epoch of the cloth trade. Much legislative activity in regard to the culture of woad prevailed towards the close of the 16th century, when, it would appear, French woad was being largely imported.[253]

The publication however in 1586 of 'A briefe discription of the true and perfitt makinge of woade, with a declaration of the apte grounde and soyle for that purposse,'[254] setting forth the indispensability of the plant to those engaged in the production of coloured woollen cloths, was followed in 1587 by the strict regulation of the woad industry. The plant was forbidden to be sown except in moderation, payment being made to the queen of 20s. per annum for the right to do so. Nor was it to be grown within 5 miles of any of the queen's residences, nor of any city, market town, or thoroughfare. No one was to plant more than 20 acres in one year, nor were more than from 40 to 60 acres to be cultivated in one parish. Woad was not to be cultivated in any locality where there was a fear that it might take the poor away from their accustomed work, or of its damaging fruitful ground. Finally, a register was to be kept of all growers of woad in the kingdom.[255] Forty acres, it was calculated, would keep 140 persons at work, the most part being women and children.[256]

Somerset, as one of the most flourishing centres of the cloth trade at this date, not only presented a consequent market to the woad-grower, but was possessed in addition of its own local source of supply, the soil of Keynsham, where large quantities were raised,[257] being peculiarly favourable to the growth of the plant.[258]

Women and children earned very high wages at Keynsham in the 18th century, especially after the establishment of a cotton-mill in the parish.[259] They were chiefly employed in hand-weeding and thinning the plants. The industry was also carried on at this date at Mells, were a well-known character, Harvey the Woadman, owned a horse-mill for grinding and sheds for drying.[260] The culture at this period was mostly in the hands of itinerant 'wadmen,' who, with their families, travelled from place to place, growing the woad on newly broken up pasture land, for which very high rents were paid.[261] These gangs built their huts and wad-mills with the sods from off the land, and were brought up to the industry from their childhood. They seldom stayed more than two or three seasons in the same spot, moving to a fresh location as soon as the soil became exhausted.[262] Woad was valued at the close of the 18th century at from £6 to £30 per ton.[263] In 1750 the price was £7 per ton.[264] The first cutting (virgin woad) was esteemed the best, whilst it was customary for the dyers, before completing a purchase, to test the quality of the samples submitted to them.[265] The clothiers of Frome dealt extensively in this commodity; in a directory of 1784, R. and J. Meares are styled 'Blue and Medley Dyers.'[266] The writer of a *Tour in the West of England* in 1808 alludes to 'all the people at Frome being dyed purple with the manufacture of blue cloths.'[267]

Early hints of the state of the dyeing industry at Wellington may be gleaned, according to Mr. Humphreys, from old title-deeds and books relating to that town. It is recorded that Joseph Alleine preached in a dye-house there in 1660. An old lease of Sowden Farm, dated 1740, contains allusion to 'all these messuages and dye-houses.' Here, it would seem, adds

[245] Weaver, *Somerset Wills* (Somers. Rec. Soc. xxi), 53.

[246] Ibid. 61.   [247] Ibid. 79.   [248] Ibid. 269.

[249] Ibid. 64.   [250] Ibid. 54.   [251] Ibid. 100.

[252] Maxwell-Lyte, *History of Dunster*, 298.

[253] Lansd. MS. no. 121.   [254] Ibid.

[255] *Cal. S. P. Dom.* 1580–1625, pp. 207-8.

[256] Lansd. MS. loc. cit.

[257] Collinson, *Hist. Somers.* ii, 400.

[258] *Bath and West of Engl. Agric. Journ.* iv, 273.

[259] Billingsley, *Agric. of Somers.* 113.

[260] Ibid. 115.

[261] Plowright, op. cit. 123.

[262] Ibid. In Lincolnshire also the industry is still carried on by hereditary workers, who receive high wages, and are employed all the year round.

[263] Trowell, *Treatise of Husbandry*, 37.

[264] Plowright, op. cit. 15.

[265] Trowell, op. cit. 35.

[266] Bailey, *Dir.* 575.

[267] Op. cit. 32.

Mr. Humphreys, the cottage-spinners brought their goods to be dyed at a fixed charge.[268]

The industry has long passed away from the west of England. In 1891 there were only four woad farms and factories in the kingdom, all in Lincolnshire.[269] The only use of woad at the present time is as a setter or mordant for indigo and other vegetable dyes.[270]

Silk.—'If,' says Mr. Green in his account of *Some Flemish Weavers settled at Glastonbury in 1551*, to which allusion will be found in the cloth-making section of this article, 'the *saye* (*soie*) made at Glaston was in any sense of silk, in accordance with the then general meaning of the word, this would be the first silk working in England; [271] and so we get from the coming of these strangers the beginning of another local speciality in manufactures.' [272] However this may be, the silk industry does not seem to have become active in the county until towards the close of the 18th century, when Cunningham considers it 'possible that the migration of silk-weaving to Taunton was due to London employers endeavouring to evade the regulations of the Spitalfields Acts.' [273] The introduction of silk weaving into the town in question dates, according to Toulmin, from 1778, when the industry was begun by Messrs. Forbes and Wasedale. Elsewhere in the county, however, silk-throwing had been practised for some years prior to this date, for in 1773, when, we are told, 'three-fourths of the throwing mills in the kingdom were standing still,' establishments of the kind at Bruton and Wells had 'almost stopped.' [274] Messrs. Vansommer and Paul, silk mercers of Pall Mall, purchased in 1781 from Mr. Noble of Upper High Street, Taunton, a brew-house and premises, together with the right to use the water from a mill belonging to a Mr. Pounsberry, and started the manufacture of thrown silk.

In 1783 the property had passed into the hands of Mr. Wilmot of Sherborne, in partnership with Mr. John Norman of Taunton, who became sole proprietor of the undertaking on the death of Mr. Wilmot in 1787.[275] In 1791 from 300 to 400 young persons were employed at Bruton silk reeling.[276] John Dutch, silk throwster, was carrying on his industry at Glastonbury in 1793.[277] Young, on his Northern Tour, relates that there was 'a little in the silk way' being carried on at Wells, which gave employment to a few children.[278] In 1808, there were 'a few manufactories in the silk and woollen lines' at Kilmersdon.[279] At Taunton, meanwhile, the silk trade continued to flourish. There were 32 looms for weaving at the mill belonging to Mr. Norman. Toulmin describes the machinery as set in motion by a woman treading a large wheel. Sixty persons were engaged at this establishment in making the following fabrics : Barcelona handkerchiefs, tiffanies, Canterbury muslins, modes, florentines, ladies' shawls, and other articles.[280]

The crape manufacture, which afterwards spread to Shepton Mallet, Croscombe, and Dulverton, had been started in Taunton in 1775, under the auspices of Mr. Leney, acting on the advice of Sir Benjamin Hammet. Persians and sarsnets were shortly afterwards added to the production of crape. In 1822 there were 800 looms in the town, with an additional 200 in the neighbourhood.[281]

In 1833 Messrs. Nalder and Hardisty were silk throwsters at Taunton, also weaving crape by power looms, and sarsnet and velvet by hand looms.[282]

Eighty persons were employed at the silk-throwing establishment of Mr. John Hendebrouck at Taunton in the same year, three-fourths of the number being women.[283]

In 1830 Messrs. H. Smith & Co. had a mill for silk and crape goods at Dulverton, worked by the Barle stream,[284] Messrs. Leathes and Knowles being engaged in silk throwing at Ilminster.[285] Similar establishments were at work at Over Stowey, Milverton and elsewhere.[286]

In 1831 there were silk factories at Bruton, Milton Clevedon, and Pitcombe, forty-five women and only one man being employed in the industry at the latter place.[287] In the parish of Kilmington the families of the agricultural labourers were largely employed in silk-winding.[288]

Mr. Lamech Swift, silk throwster of Milverton, where he had been established from 1819, furnished a Parliamentary Commission on the Silk Trade in 1831 with interesting details

[268] Humphreys, *Hist. Wellington*, 107, 174 et seq.
Ancient records preserve the names of John Irishe, a manufacturer of woollen cloths, who had a dyeing-house at Congresbury (Exch. Dep. by Com. Mich. 20 & 21 Eliz. no. 3), and of Austyne Atkyn, whose 'faire tenement' in Hollirod Street, Chard, in 1602, contained, besides a fulling mill, 'divers convenient rooms for dyers. (*Somers. Arch. Soc. Proc.* xxviii (2), 36).
[269] *Ann. Rep. Factories and Workshops*, 1891, p. 31.
[270] Plowright, op. cit.
[271] Silk-women of unknown nationality were however carrying on the trade in London in 1455. Stat. 33 Hen. VI, cap. 5.
[272] Green, *Somers. Arch. Soc. Proc.* xxvi (2), 23.
[273] Cunningham, *Engl. Industry and Commerce*, i, 519; Stat. 13 Geo. III, cap. 68.
[274] *Commons' Journ.* 1773, iii, 240.

[275] Toulmin, *Hist. Taunton*, 381.
[276] Collinson, *Hist. Somers.* i, 212.
[277] *Univ. Brit. Dir.* 1793, p. 153.
[278] Young, *Northern Tour*, iv, 20.
[279] Add. MS. 33635, fol. 2.
[280] Toulmin, op. cit. [281] Ibid.
[282] *Factory Com.* 1883, p. 70. [283] Ibid. 72.
[284] Pigot, *Dir.* 705. [285] Ibid. 713. [286] Ibid.
[287] *Pop. Ret.* 1831, p. 533. [288] Ibid. 544.

relative to his business.[289] The raw silk, which was chiefly Italian,[290] very little Bengal and China silk being employed, was sent to Milverton from London and Coventry to be thrown.[291] Women and children were almost exclusively employed in these mills, no man being engaged except a carpenter and a foreman ; there were also a few small boys. Many of the employees worked at home, the wives and mothers winding and preparing the silk for the mills, where it was carried by the children.[292] At one time Mr. Swift had 300 hands at work, with 5,500 spindles ; in 1831 there were only sixty persons employed, for whom work could scarcely be found on three or four days a week.[293]

The decline in the trade was attributed to the low prices solely obtainable for thrown silk, this in turn being caused by the reduction of the duty on foreign thrown organzine from 5s. to 3s. 6d. and of that on foreign tram from 3s. to 2s., which was effected in 1829. The great influx of foreign silk goods also had an unfavourable effect upon the prosperity of the home manufacture.[294] Marabout, which required a special process of throwing, was largely produced at Milverton from about 1826.[295]

Marabout, which was chiefly used for gauze and gauze ribbons, is described as ' very hard thrown tram.' It was generally thrown in three threads. Unlike common tram, when partly thrown, it was sent to London to be dyed, then sent back to the throwster to receive the remainder of the throwing, and to be finished. The silk employed was the very best white Novi. The intricate and lengthy process of marabout silk throwing necessitated the payment of higher wages to the throwsters engaged in this description of work. The throwing of 1 lb. of marabout was equal to 2 lb. of organzine. Organzine throwsters earned from 7s. to 8s. prior to 1826 ; by 1831 the price had fallen to 3s. 6d. or 4s. Marabout throwsters earned 7s. 6d. Tram throwing had fallen from 5s. to 2s. 6d.[296]

Mr. John Sharrer Ward was employing 230 hands at his silk mill at Bruton in 1831, where his father and himself had carried on the business for over sixty-five years. In 1823 this mill had given employment to over 800 persons There were then 15,700 spindles at work. The numbers had declined by 1831 to 7,000. Here as elsewhere throughout the West of England, fine Italian silk was chiefly used for throwing. Women and children were mostly employed, at an average weekly wage of 2s. 3d. The charges for throwing showed a gradual decline. In 1823 9s. to 10s. per lb. was paid for throwing organzine, for tram, 5s. 6d. per lb. In 1829 prices averaged from 4s. 6d. to 5s. for organzine, and 3s. for tram. In 1831 the charge was 4s. for organzine, and 2s. 6d. for tram.[297] The cost of wagon and van carriage of silk goods in this latter year was 7s. per cwt.[298]

The silk industry was represented at Bruton in 1839 by Messrs. Ward & Saxon. In 1859 there was a small silk-throwing industry at Wincanton, women and children being chiefly employed.[299]

Crape and velvet have been manufactured from time to time in various localities ; the crape trade of Shepton Mallet was spoken of in 1831 as ' considerable.'[300] In 1856 Messrs. Hardesty & Phillipps were engaged in the same industry at Yeovil.[301]

The modern silk industry of the county is represented by Messrs. J. Kemp & Sons, Evercreech, Bath ; Messrs. James Kemp & Son, Darshill, Shepton Mallet, and by Messrs. Thompson & Le Gros, Merchants Barton, Frome ;[302] while at Taunton Messrs. Calway and Drillien are silkthrowsters at the East Street and Tancred Street Mills.

Flax, Hemp and Horsehair. — Early evidences abound of the successful cultivation of flax and hemp in the county. The Abbess and convent of the Holy Saviour, the Virgin Mary, and St. Bridget of Syon, took tithes of flax growing in the yards or gardens of Yeovil. The vicar of Yeovil took tithes of hemp in Yeovil and Preston Plucknett, and of flax not growing in yards or gardens.[303] The Bailiffs' Accounts of Coker in 1309–10 furnish evidence of the early hemp and flax culture at that place.[304] Every farmstead had its ' vlex-pit ' and its ' vlex-shop,'[305] whilst no pains was

[289] *Rep. Silk Trade*, 1831, p. 192.

[290] The varieties used included Fossembrone, Bergamo, and Piedmont. An inferior Genoese silk, in imitation of Novi, which was ' specially esteemed,' was occasionally placed on the market.

[291] *Rep. Silk. Trade*, 1831, p. 193.

[292] Ibid. p. 196.   [293] Ibid. p. 193.   [294] Ibid.

[295] Ibid. p. 197. Messrs. Courtauld and Taylor, of Gutter Lane, London, were the first marabout throwsters in this country. Ibid. 199.

[296] *Rep. Silk Trade*, 1831, p. 197. The silk to prepare organzine was sent to the mills in a raw state ; it was then wound on bobbins, the single thread being then subjected at the mill to the process of having a spin or twist put upon it. It was then doubled into two threads, and twisted again the contrary way. In the case of tram, the silk only underwent one process of twisting, having also arrived at the mill in a raw state, wound, doubled, and being more slightly twisted,

[297] *Rep. Silk Trade*, 1831, p. 203.   [298] Ibid. 195.

[299] Phelps, *Hist. Somerset*, i, 191.

[300] Pigot, *Dir.* 719.   [301] Murray, *Handbook*, 180.

[302] Kelly, *Dir.* 1907.

[303] *Cal. Wells D. & C. MSS.* (Hist. MSS. Com.) i, 323.

[304] Batten, *Notes on South Somerset*, 164.

[305] ' Vlex-pits'—pits on farms where flax was steeped. ' Vlex-shops '—outhouses where flax was hackled or dressed. (Elworthy, *West Somerset Words*, 258.) ' Pitcloses,' ' Pit-leys,' and ' Pit-orchards,' are field-name survivals of this ancient industry. (*Somers. Arch. Soc. Proc.* xxxvii, 277.)

spared in order to bring the cultivation of this commodity, so indispensable to the county's thriving industries of ropemaking, homespun linen, and sailcloth, to perfection. Flax was largely used in and around Norton-sub-Hamdon for homespun linen and sailcloth. The will of John Aysshe, sackweaver, of Stoke-sub-Hamdon, was proved in 1619.[306] Frequent purchases of 'turns, vanes, and cexes' are recorded in the parish accounts of Norton, these articles being supplied by the overseers to poor, deserving women, unable to provide them for themselves. 'Turns' were used for spinning homespun yarn or wool.[307] In 1638 we hear of twenty-four of the leading inhabitants of Glastonbury petitioning the justices of the peace at Ilchester on behalf of one Christopher Cockerell, of Elham, Kent, who, they set forth, 'had been sent for by divers gentlemen into these western parts, and had continued therein for the skill he had attained in sowing, dressing, and ordering of flax and flaxseed.' Cockerell, it would appear, had suffered considerable losses through floods in his neighbourhood, and the desire of the petitioners was that some pecuniary assistance should be given to one who had proved himself so valuable an immigrant.[308] In 1692 Houghton writes [309] that 'great quantities of flax were sown in this year about Yeovil,[310] and a considerable quantity of good flax hath been sown last year for making cloth, ticking, and sewing thread.' Indeed Somerset and Dorset [311] 'made extraordinary good linen in imitation of France' in the reign of William and Mary, the value of the manufacture, which was carried on in a district ten miles square, being estimated at £100,000 per annum. But at the close of the French war the local trade suffered from the competition of fine linens imported from abroad.

The impetus of Parliamentary bounties towards the close of the 18th century caused flax to be largely sown, in spite of the prohibitory clauses which were frequently introduced into farm leases, the culture of flax being popularly supposed to impoverish the land. For his skill in bleaching tow and flax, Joseph Bragge of Ilminster was awarded a prize of £10 by the Society of Arts in 1772 and again in 1774.[312] Somerset was, however, at this time gradually losing its hold upon the linen manufacture which had been so prosperous three-quarters of a century before. Interesting details as to the state of the industry about the middle of

the century may be gathered from the evidence of Mr Harvey, a local manufacturer, before a Parliamentary Committee appointed in 1765 to inquire into the condition of the linen trade throughout the kingdom. Dowlas, sheeting, and bed ticks were the principal products of the Somerset looms, the number of these, however, having greatly fallen off. A corresponding decline in prices was consequently noticeable. Dowlas,[313] for instance, which had formerly cost from 13d. to 16d. per yard, was now selling at from 10d. to 1s. The price of sheeting had declined from 3s. to 2s. 6d., and from 1s. 6d. to 1s. 4d., whilst bed ticks, which had previously fetched from 1s. 4d. to 2s. 6d., had dropped to 2s. 4d. and 1s. 2d. Home yarn, supplied by the flax growers of the county, was largely utilized, though foreign yarn, chiefly from Hamburg, was making its way into favour for sheeting. Spinners' wages had decreased at the rate of 3d. in the shilling. 30,000 persons were engaged in the linen trade in Somerset, Wilts., Hants, and Dorset, five out of every seven being spinners. Coarse linen drabs were being largely imported by the lower classes for coats, waistcoats, and breeches, but the woollen manufacture, rather than that of the linen, seems to have suffered from this alien economic invasion.[314]

Sailcloth was for a long period manufactured at East Coker, and Coker Cloth is still a trade name for some of the best quality made in the neighbourhood of Crewkerne. Thirty-three years ago Messrs. Taylor still manufactured sailcloth at East Coker, but in 1878 the trade was abandoned. In the same factory webbing and twine are now produced by Messrs. Felix Drake & Co. Sack or bag-weaving was an East Coker trade in the reign [315] of George II. The Rev. C. Powell of East Coker remembers seeing, exactly thirty-one years ago, 'the last of the bag-weavers at work in a weaving-shed close to his cottage home placed far back from the road.' He was known as 'Bag' Cox, weaver, small farmer and district registrar. 'He and his man made the last flicker in the ancient industry' of the village.[316]

The reputation of Crewkerne as 'a centre of textile work' [317] is of long standing, flax, hemp, and jute being used for the manufacture of

[306] Brown, *Somerset Wills* (Ser. 1), 14.

[307] Trask, *Norton-sub-Hamdon*, 190.

[308] *Hist. MSS. Com. Rep.* vii, App. i, 694.

[309] Houghton, *Letters for Improvement of Trade*, no. 22.

[310] Billingsley places the flax country 'from Wincanton, through Yeovil, to Crewkerne.' (*Agric. Somers.* 213.)   [311] J. Gee, *Trade and Navigation* (1729), 5.

[312] Dossie, *Mem. Agric.* iii, 457.

[313] Coarse, ordinary linen cloths, made originally in Brittany, but chiefly produced in Somerset at Wincanton, Milborne Port, and Penselwood. (Phelps, *Hist. Somerset*, i, 152.)

[314] 'Rep. Linen Manufacture,' *Commons' Journ.* 1765, p. 105.

[315] On 29 Jan. 8 Geo. II Francis Gyles, aged nine years, was apprenticed by the parish to John Barret, sack-weaver.

[316] From information kindly furnished by the Rev. C. Powell, B.A.

[317] *Ann. Rep. Factories and Workshops*, 1887, p. 26. 'Every gaping cottage door at Crewkerne,' we are told, 'had its loom at work.'

its twines, ropes, nets, canvas, and girth webbing. At the present time [318] two firms at Crewkerne are engaged in the manufacture of canvas and sailcloth for yachts, Messrs Hayward & Sons of the Tail Mill, and Messrs. R. Hayward & Co. of North Street, while girth and other webs are made by Messrs. R. Bird & Co., South Street, and Mr. A. Hart, Viney Bridge. Horse clothing is manufactured by Mr. A. J. Haslock, South Street, and there are two factories for shirts and collars, those of the Somerset and Devon Manufacturing Company, Abbey Street, and Messrs. Southcombe Bros., North Street. At Castle Cary a factory for twine and sailcloth was opened in 1797 by Mr. Charles Donne. The hair-cloth industry of Castle Cary dates from about 1815 and was introduced when the manufacture of ticks, dowlas, and knit hose was failing. In 1828 Mr. Thomas Matthews acquired a building which had been intended for a silk factory, on the site of the present Florida factory, and utilized it for making girth webs and hair-seating. At the present time the firms engaged in the horsehair trade at Castle Cary are Messrs. John Boyd & Co. and Messrs. James White & Co. The business of Messrs. John Boyd &

Co. dates from 1837. Originally hand-looms only were used in making the haircloth, but within the last thirty years the power-loom has been generally substituted, though Messrs. John Boyd & Co. still employ several of the old hand-workers. Besides horsehair cloth for furniture and tailors' use, the Castle Cary trade includes curled hair for furniture, drafts for brushmaking, fishing hair and bleached hair for wigs.[319] The rope and twine industry of the town finds its modern representatives in Messrs. Thomas Salisbury, Donne & Sons, flax-spinners and twine manufacturers. At Greenham, in Wayford Parish, the Greenham Mill Company also carry on the trade of flax and hemp spinners. The Dowlishford Mill at Ilminster, once devoted to the silk-throwster's work, has been for fifty years a tow-factory,[320] where the warp of carpets is produced and yarn spun. It is in the hands of the firm of Hutchings, Shepherd & Co. In 1827 a horsehair factory was started. East and West Chinnock was another sailcloth centre, girth-webs and shoe threads being a speciality of the two villages.[321] Mr. E. King weaves apron lin-seys, cheese cloths, and bandages at his factory at Ditcheat.[322]

CARD MAKING

Around one at least of the implements connected with the ancient cloth-making trade of the county, a separate and somewhat extensive industry at one time grew up, only declining with the decay of the manufacture to which it had long been indispensable, and centring at Frome as one of the most important seats of that manufacture. The industry in question was that of the making of the cards [1] used in cloth-making. These 'cards of labour and profit, not of pleasure and idleness,' as Pettus quaintly styles them in his *Words Metallic*, came somewhat prominently before the Legislature in 1710, when a bill was introduced to prohibit the importation of foreign cards, and to prevent abuses in making the same with old card wire.[2] Whilst the bill was depending in the House the clothiers, 'already labouring,' they declared, 'under great difficulties in trade,' expressed themselves as 'surprised that so inconsiderable a number of people should attempt to lay a further weight on the clothiers,' this weight being the proposed hindrance of the clothiers from selling old cards, and the coarse clothier

from buying a cheap commodity. The situation in short was regarded by the clothiers as 'the heaviest burden they were ever threatened with.' [3] There was, it would appear, a considerable traffic at this time in disused cards, which were made new by putting the old wires into new leather and on old boards for cheapness, the result being that the cards were 'too weak for well carding of wool, whereby the cloth was ill made and the buyer cheated. At 3*d.* per pair, however, these 'deceitful' cards commanded a ready sale, new ones costing 7 groats.[4] Certain clauses in the bill seemed to threaten what had by that date become a very thriving industry, 'the using of good wool cards being of great consequence in making of cloth.' [5] The forbidding of the sale of old cards would, it appeared, to the clothiers, benefit the cardmakers rather than themselves, and their grievances were set

---

[318] We are under obligation to Mr. J. Wheatley for information as to the industries of Crewkerne.

[1] Two little quadrangular pieces of board, three or four times as broad as tall, with a handle to each, and thick set with small crooked wires. (Postlethwayt, *Dict. Trade.*)

[2] *Commons' Journ.* 1710, p. 471.

[319] We are indebted to Mr. J. Macmillan for information relating to the industries of Castle Cary. For an interesting description of the horsehair manufacture the reader is referred to the *Western Gazette Almanac* (1906), p. 149 et seq. Cf. *Castle Cary Visitor* (May 1906).

[320] *Ex informacione* Rev. Prebendary Street.

[321] Pigot, *Dir.* 1842.

[322] Kelly, *Dir.* 1906, p. 238.

[3] *Commons' Journ.* 1710, p. 513.

[4] Ibid.

[5] Ibid.

forth in a Dialogue between Dick Brazenface the cardmaker, and Tim Meanwell the clothier, which, claiming fairly to state the dispute between them, was offered for the consideration of the House.[6]

By the close of the 18th century there were still 20 master card-makers in Frome, employing 400 men, women and children, the latter being seven or eight years of age, their wages averaging 2s.6d. per week.[7] In 1784 there were 5 makers,[8] in 1793, 10,[9] in 1830 there were 6,[10] whilst in 1856

Mr Gregory had a card factory at Frome, with 'highly curious machinery.'[11] In 1866 there were two card-makers in the town, George Hinchcliffe and S. Rawlings & Son, both in Christ Church Street.[12]

Frequent entries occur, according to Prebendary Hancock, in the parish accounts of Selworthy, of payments for 'pairs of cards,' evidently for the use of poor spinners.[13] A 17th-century token issued at Taunton bears a hand holding a wool-card.[14]

LACE, NET AND THREAD

Joan Harvey was making bone-lace[1] at Yeovil in 1620, when we find her petitioning the court at this town for redress. Barbara Gaylard of Montacute having first apprenticed her daughters to the said Joan, for one year, they receiving 2s. 6d. a week for their maintenance, had then taken away the children when the best part of the year was coming on, they then being able to do some service and earn some money by their trade for the said Joan.[2] The same art was an industry of Wells, being mentioned by various topographers.[3] Wood, in his *Descriptive Essay on Bath*, claims a place among the commodities of that city for the so-called 'Bath Lace,' but the fabric in question seems to have been actually the production of 'four large towns in Devon,' the patterns being supplied by designers in Bath, whose work was so greatly sought after that one manufacturer was said to have spent as much as £70 in one year in merely writing for the same. The sale of this lace in the city to which it owed its name appears to have been on an extensive scale; prices ranging from 1s. 6d. for small edgings to 3 guineas a yard for fine, broad varieties.[4] In 1830 there were five lace factories at Chard (where the manufacture has always been that of machine-made lace), employing 1,500 hands, three of these establishments being 'on a very extensive scale.'[5] Lace was being made at Taunton in 1831 by two manufacturers, Messrs. Cox & Winter, and George Rawlinson & Co.[6] In 1837 Messrs. Wheatley & Co. were the principal plain

lace manufacturers in Chard. A fire in their factory in this year led to the introduction into their establishment of 72 new 12 qr. machines under the superintendence of Mr. T. Riste, formerly a workman, then a partner in the firm. The new machinery, it was said, more than recouped the proprietors for the loss of £40,000 which they had sustained by the fire.[7] Mr. Riste himself is said to have stated that 'he had himself received for making a yard of net £1 6s., which at the time he spoke would be paid for by the sum of one farthing.'[8] In 1858 368 men and 417 women were engaged in the machine lace trade in the county.[9] In 1862 there were 360 circular machines making bobbin net at Chard.[10]

The Chard lace-factories[11] at the present time do not make fancy laces but bobbin nets which are sold 'brown' or undressed in Nottingham. They are of silk or cotton and vary from the finest tulle to mosquito curtains. Hairnets are also made. Each factory employs 400 or 500 workpeople besides the lace-menders, who are women living in Chard and the villages around. Their business is to mend the holes caused by the breaking of a thread; they work in their own homes and bring the pieces to the factory to be passed. So extensive is this auxiliary system of homework that it is pleasantly said that all the babies in the neighbourhood are cradled on net.

To become an expert mender a girl must begin quite young and the older women say that girls leave school too late nowadays to learn as they used to do. Unless the art of mending is acquired early the worker can only mend cotton

[6] Green, *Bibl. Somers.* ii, 418.
[7] *Univ. Brit. Dir.* iii, 132.
[8] Bailey, *Dir.* 575.   [9] Ibid.
[10] Pigot, *Dir.* 706.
[1] 'Bone lace from fine thread from Antwerp.' (Fosbroek, *Encycl. Antiq.* 466.) So called, in Fuller's opinion, from the bones (sheep's trotters) used before the introduction of wooden bobbins.
[2] *Quarter Sessions Records* (Som. Rec. Soc. xxiii).
[3] *Rural Elegance Display'd* (1768), 304.
[4] Op. cit. ii, 436.
[5] Pigot, *Dir.* (1830), 702.
[6] Ibid. 723.

[11] Murray, *Handbook*, 173.
[12] Pigot, *Dir.*
[13] Hancock, *Hist. of Selworthy*, 127.
[14] *Somers. Arch. Soc. Proc.* xxxii, 121-8.
[7] Felkin, *Hist. Hosiery and Lace*, 377.
[8] Ibid.
[9] *Bath and W. of Engl. Agric. Journ.* vi, 131.
[10] Felkin, op. cit. 397.
[11] We are indebted to Mrs. Gifford of Chard for valuable notes on the lace industry of the town.

net and not the finer silk, earning in consequence lower wages. At each of the lace factories a machinery shop exists where not only are repairs done but also the machines themselves constructed. The lace factory of Messrs. Gifford Fox & Co. is the Holyrood Mill, built in 1827. It contains among other machinery a steam-engine, still in use, which was made by James Watt in 1797.

As a Somerset extension of the Nottingham-shire firm of Ernest Jardine, a lace factory has been established at Shepton Mallet, while at Ilminster, on the border of the parish, the Chard Lace Company own Rose Mills.

It is interesting to note a modern revival of the famous pillow-lace industry of the west under the auspices of the Taunton School of Art, which started in 1902 the Taunton Honiton Lace Class. Lace executed at this school has gained notable rewards at South Kensington, and specimens were on view at the Lace Exhibition held in London 9–14 March 1908.[12]

The manufacture of thread has been carried on from time to time at various localities in the county. Queen Camel was famous in the reign of William and Mary for the production of a brown thread known as 'nun's thread.'[13] The industry was evidently an outcome of the linen trade in the vicinity, for in 1831 the decrease in the population of this place was attributed to 'the cessation of the linen trade in that locality.'[14] At the close of the 18th century a tourist in the west of England saw 'quantities of thread bleaching in the meadows round West Coker.'[15] Shoe-thread was being manufactured at Penselwood in 1859.[16]

GLOVE MAKING

The glove-making industry of Somerset is one which dates from a period before those Elizabethan times when 'a poor token of gloves'[1] was a frequent offering to great personages. In Yeovil, where this handicraft gives employment at the present time to 3,000 people, exclusive of those engaged in the surrounding districts, a John Glover and a John le Scynner are found in the Lay Subsidy Roll for 1327.[2] Again a deed dated 1565, in the possession of a townsman, contains the name of John Boone, glover, as witness; whilst as probably not altogether without its bearing on the trade, attention may be drawn to the fact of the frequency with which a pair of white gloves figured in Plantagenet times as quit-rent for land, &c.[3] There was a 'Glover's House' at Bridgwater in 1505, when it was bequeathed by John Sawnder to his servant Alice.[4] In 1702 John Spurrier, glover, was occupying 'twenty low chambers and rooms' on Puddle Bridge, Minehead.[5]

Throughout its history glove-making has been mainly a home industry, in which women have always been chiefly employed.[6] In years of great agricultural depression and scarcity, and during the incendiary outbreaks of 1830, the glove-making centres of Worcester and Somerset, says Hull, were comparatively happy and tranquil, owing to the women and children in the villages being employed in the glove trade, and mainly supporting the men.[7] In 1831, 600 persons were engaged in the trade in the county, 300 at Yeovil, 150 at Milborne Port, and 45 at Stoke-sub-Hamdon, Montacute and Martock.[8] In 1832 wages averaged as follows: dressers 4½d. per dozen, cutters 10d., sewers 4s.; needles cost 2d. per week, the carriage of gloves to London being at the rate of 5s. per 100 dozen.[9] In 1834 the trade in imitation 'Limerick' and 'York tan' gloves, which were formerly made in large quantities at Yeovil, was said to be 'decayed.' At this date the leading production was that of men and women's fine kid (really lambskin) gloves, the skins utilized being brought from Italy, Spain, and Germany, and dressed in Yeovil, where the manufacturers were leather dressers and large dealers in wool as well as gloves.[10]

In 1856 Messrs Boyd & Fook, the largest glovers in Yeovil, were paying wages to their

[1] *Cal. S. P. Dom.* 1547–80, p. 221.
[2] *Kirby's Quest*, &c. (Somers. Rec. Soc. iii), 215.
[3] Buckle, *Ilchester Almshouse Deeds*, 13, 16, 17.
[4] Weaver, *Somerset Mediaeval Wills* (Som. Rec. Soc. xix), 98.
[5] Hancock, *Hist. Minehead*, 218.
[6] Hull, *Hist. Glove Trade*, 111.
[7] Ibid.

[12] In designs for lace we welcome again . . . the uniformly good productions of the Taunton School. (*The Studio*, September 1903). The Silver Medal awarded to Lydia C. Hammett, of Taunton School of Art, is given mainly for the reticent, well-balanced, and well drawn design for a veil of Devonshire pillow appliqué lace, in which there is a pleasant variety of interesting forms, such as handwork demands. (*South Kensington Official Rep.* 1904).
[13] Fiennes, *Through Engl. on a Side-Saddle*, 11. Nun's or Sister's thread is mentioned, according to Beck, in the Great Wardrobe Accounts of 34 and 35 Eliz., and was formerly 'a great article of commerce, generally made by the nuns of the Flemish and Italian convents.' (*Drapers' Dict.* 347.)
[14] *Pop. Ret.* 535.
[15] Lipscomb, *Journey into Cornwall*, 133.
[16] Phelps, *Hist. Somerset*, i, 191.
[8] *Pop. Ret.* 1831.
[9] Hull, loc. cit.
[10] Ibid.

employees at the rate of £7,000 per annum.[11] In 1858 1,156 men and 8,050 women were engaged in the industry.[12] Lads were apprenticed in the cutting shop at fourteen, and those who were still younger were employed to use the hand press to put studs in the gloves, to punch pieces for the thumbs, to make up material into packets for the women workers to take home, or to pack the gloves in boxes when finished.[13]

The influence of the Franco-Prussian war on this industry made for a period of marked prosperity. Piece-work cutters earned at this date from 32s. to 40s. per week, dyers, 28s., and sewing machine hands, 12s.[14]

In 1887 Stoke-sub-Hamdon, one of the chief centres of the trade, was paying great attention to the manufacture of fabric gloves—gloves, that is, made of silk, cotton, &c. The trade in certain makes, chiefly white gloves, and the lighter evening kinds of ladies' gloves, had largely gone to Italy, but the industry, largely, as before, a home one (the cutting out only being done at the factories), was on a fairly prosperous footing. Wages averaged from 10s. to 25s. per week, the preparation and dressing of the leather giving employment to numbers of men in the neighbourhood.[15]

In 1891, 1,123 men and 2,957 women were employed in the glove trade throughout the county; in 1901 the numbers were 904 men and 2,387 women.[16]

There are three glove factories at the present time in Martock, silk or fabric gloves being the chief output, leather gloves being also made, but in smaller proportion. In Tintinhull there is one glove factory, making leather gloves only, men and women being employed in about equal proportions, children about half the number of men.[17]

Of the three still existing centres of the glove trade, London and Worcester produce the finest and most delicate work, Yeovil manufacturing the heavier class of goods, such as driving gloves, lined gloves, and astrachan and fur trimmed gloves. The material employed is chiefly sheep and lamb skins, though calf and occasionally kid are also used. The best skins come from Spain and the north of Italy, some from the Cape, from Russia, and a few from the East. Arriving at the factory packed in bales and sprinkled with salt, they are thrown into a pit of water for a day or two to remove the wool. On being taken out, the inside of the skins is painted with an amalgam the principal ingredient of which is arsenic; they are then doubled over and replaced in the water. A day later they are again taken out, placed upon a beam covered with buffalo hide, and carefully scraped with a long double-handled knife. This process is known as 'pulling' the skin. The hair, which leaves the 'pelt' clean, is placed by the worker on one of several little heaps, each consisting of wool of a different quality. This wool was formerly of much value, and is still in considerable demand for making blankets, stuffing furniture, &c. The 'pulling' process is continued even after all the wool has been removed, and frequently repeated, in accordance with the theory that the more the skin is 'pulled' the better it becomes. The pelt is then soaked in lime and water, sometimes in an inclosed room, sometimes in an open yard containing numerous pits 4 ft. or 5 ft. deep, capable of holding as many as seventy dozen skins each. Here the skins are soaked in mixtures of lime and water, varying in strength, the process occupying from eighteen days to a month, when the skins are again 'pulled,' and soaked in a mixture known as 'pure,' consisting of bran, kennel manure and hot water. The old-fashioned method was to have the skins trodden underfoot in the vats by boys, but the work of 'treading up' is now done by machinery. Another washing and 'pulling' now takes place, followed by a second 'treading up' with the yolk of egg.[18] The skin is now ready for dyeing, which is done at this or at a subsequent period, in which case it is left in a 'drying-room' suspended by two corners. The method of dyeing is determined by the quality of the skin, both as regards the class of glove for which it is fitted, and the colour, the best skins being usually reserved for light and delicate tints, a defective skin being generally dyed black. The dyes used are always wood-dyes, and are brought from all parts of the world, Australian bark being used to colour tan gloves. Two methods of dyeing are employed; in one the skins are steeped in the ordinary vat, in the other case an alkaline liquid is applied with a brush. 'Paring' consists in scraping the rough side of the skins with one of two varieties of knife, the skin in each case being held extended with the left hand, while the parer makes a downward thrust with the right hand. The first of these knives is called a 'crutch,' from the shape of its handle, the

[11] Murray, *Handbook*.
[12] *Bath and W. of Engl. Agric. Journ.* vi, 131.
[13] Hull, loc. cit.
[14] *Ann. Rep. Factories and Workshops*, 1871, p. 64.
[15] Ibid. 1887, p. 64.
[16] *Pop. Ret.* 1901, p. viii.
[17] We are indebted to the courtesy of Messrs. Southcombe and Sons, glove manufacturers of Tintinhull and Martock, for the above information.

[18] That this treatment is an ancient one is shown by directions 'for to make cheurel leather of perchemyne' by means of a solution of alum mixed with yolks of eggs and flour, in an old manuscript. (Sloane MS. fol. 211.) In 1860 Mr. Wade of Northampton was curing Smyrna sheepskins with alum for the Yeovil glovers. (*V.C.H. Northants*, ii, 315.)

method of using it being to rest the knife under the armpit, and to guide the blade with the hand on the lower part of the handle. The 'paring-knife' proper is curiously shaped like a quoit, with a piece of wood placed across the inside as a handle. The skin is now ready to be given to the cutter, when the actual glove-making process begins. First making measurements, an oblong piece of leather is cut, serving for a whole glove, with the exception of the thumb, for which a smaller piece is cut in the same way. The leather is then 'opened,' pulled and stretched in every direction to ascertain that it is sufficiently elastic, and if necessary a small strip is cut away. The next process is to prepare the glove for stitching. This is done by cutting out the exact shape, fingers, thumbs, 'forchettes' (pieces to be inserted between the fingers), and marks to guide the stitcher in sewing the 'points,' that is to say, the three lines or marks running down the back of every glove. This is now done by punches, elsewhere referred to. The sewing is almost entirely done by machinery, the sole exception being in the case of 'tambour pointing,' which is done by hand. When gloves are required tambour pointed, that is to say, with broad, apparently woven seams down the back, instead of the ordinary narrow points, the holes for the stitches are made by means of a mallet and punch, the silk being then worked in and out with a kind of crochet-hook. After the pointing is finished, the side pieces are sewn into the fingers, the seams closed and the thumbs inserted. Many varieties of machines are in use. For stitching the seams of the fingers, a 'looper' is employed. This consists of an upright stem or rod, carrying a needle, which is met by another needle descending by its side. This stem can be easily passed inside the finger, turned about in every direction, the two needles consequently making the double seam in an incredibly short space of time. The sewing is done exclusively by women, girls being employed to sew on the welts or little edges, and the pieces cut for fastening behind the buttonholes, to prevent the glove from tearing when it is being buttoned, are put on.

The women work in their own homes, sewing-machines being provided by the manufacturers. The work is brought to them in most cases by the 'bag-woman,' who returns the gloves to the factory when completed. Whole families are often engaged, the father being perhaps a cutter, the mother and daughters sewers. Average wages are from 15s. to 26s. per week. At the factory, buttons are sewn on, clasps are fixed, also eyelets, each being riveted in its place by a small hand-press. Furs are affixed by needle-women. In the finishing room, the gloves are put on a hot last, finished off, ironed, and polished, the gloves being then packed in dozens, fastened with paper bands, and packed in boxes.

An outcome of the gloving industry in Yeovil is the manufacture of the punches used in glove-making. These punches, which are driven by means of a hand-press, and cut out at one stroke two or three pairs of gloves, with the exception of the thumbs—side-pieces and pieces for strengthening the buttonholes being cut at the same time and the buttonholes themselves cut—are required in immense numbers, as a different punch is used for each size of glove made, as well as for various kinds of gloves. The cost of a punch is about £3, and the work of producing and repairing them gives employment to numerous hands.[19]

POTTERY AND GLASS

At an early date local potteries existed within the county, since suitable clays were to be found in several districts and 'potterne'[1] or lead-ore for the glaze was easily procurable from the Mendips. One of these potteries of which we possess distinct documentary evidence[2] was situated at Stowey or Nether Stowey, for early in the reign of Edward I Robert de Puriton the seneschal was charged with exacting fines beyond measure. Especially had he mulcted in 20s. Richard de Porta and others for the right of carrying on their pottery ('pro eo quod facere possint ollas in villa de Staweye'), a business which they had been accustomed lawfully to pursue from ancient times.

From time immemorial, the Rev. J. Skinner tells us in his journals, the coarse kinds of ware, such as pitchers, pipkins and flower-pots, have been manufactured at Wanstrow, the most suitable clay for the purpose being found on Wanstrow Common. While passing through this village in 1826, he visited the only pottery then at work, and observed that 'within these few years there were eleven such potteries.'

'What is singular,' adds the writer, 'the Roman road which runs near Green Ore Farm on Mendip is there styled the Potters' Road, from having been used by persons of this trade coming thither for the lead ore, which was required for glazing the inside of their vessels.' The ore, we learn, needed merely to be pounded small, strained through a sieve, afterwards mixed

---

[1] In the 17th century on the Mendips this term, according to Dr. Merrett, was applied to manganese. See *supra* 'Lead.' Manganese was used for colouring the ware black.

[2] *Hund. R.* ii, 127b.

[19] Communicated by the courtesy of the *Western Gazette* Company, Limited, Yeovil.

with water to the consistency of paint, and laid on the inside of the vessels by a brush; when the clay was baked this became fused, and formed a burnish or lacquer, of a yellow hue.[3] On the manor of Bossington also there was formerly a small pottery of unknown date, as is shown by the fact that lumps of clay, red and white, and bits of ridge tiling have been dug up on the site.[4]

The antiquity of the Crock Street pottery of Somerset, the history of which, says Mr. Bates, has yet to be written, is probably attested by the name of the hamlet from which the ware in question takes its name.[5] Writing of Crock Street in 1791 Collinson says: 'there are three potteries here in which a considerable quantity of coarse earthenware is made.'[6] In colour, the ware is either a light yellowish brown, with galena glaze, black, or mottled green.[7] Specimens preserved in the Taunton Museum comprise a glazed porringer with handle, and a large yellow tyg with 'A.M. 1718' in brown slip; but the chief productions of the Crock Street potteries would appear to have been 'jolly-boys' or fuddling-cups, which were three drinking-cups joined in one, so that they could all three be drunk from at the same time. Chimney ornaments were also made at one time, but rough earthenware pitchers and pans are now the chief products.[8]

A potter from Nuneaton in Warwickshire, named Ireson, carried on a factory of delft ware at Wincanton from 1720 to 1767. Bowls, jugs, and plates were among the chief products of this establishment, which had a high local reputation. The ware was of a body similar to pie-crust, with a good glaze, decorated by stencilling. Favourite designs were Oriental subjects, also rustic scenes, fruit and flowers. The name of Ireson is inscribed upon the ware, also 'Wincanton' or 'Wincanto.' One piece bears the name of G. S. Clewill, who was working for Ireson in 1737.

We are indebted to the courtesy of Mr. George Sweetman for the following account of the 'Ireson Pottery' of Wincanton :—

Ireson Pottery is a delft ware, very difficult, if at all possible, to tell from Bristol and other similar wares. Very many pieces are claimed for Wincanton which I think are not so. There are two or three groups of spoiled plates and cups in the British Museum which show the kind of clay, colour, &c. Other pieces, but not many, are dated, and highly but rudely ornamented. One jug, dated 1748, was kept

in the family of Ireson till 1905, when it was sold to Captain Terry Ripley for 15 guineas. This date was that of the building of the chancel of the church at Wincanton. Ireson was then 62 years of age. He came to Stourton about 1720, and four years later came to reside in Wincanton. The pottery must have been kept open several years; 1737 is the earliest I have seen, 1748 the latest, but I have understood that Ireson sold his interest to two brothers by the name of Lindsay, who failed for want of sufficient clay.[9]

Three decorated delft plates, two ornamented with peacocks, and the other with a cock, made at Ireson's factory, were added to the Taunton Castle Museum in 1906.

A very complete loan exhibition of Ireson's pottery was arranged at the Town Hall, Wincanton, on 10 June 1891, on the occasion of the Annual Meeting of the Wincanton Field Club, the collection including plates, vases, a jug, bowls, and a scent-bottle, fragments of pottery found at Ireson's house being also included.[10]

The modern potter's art in the county is chiefly represented by the Elton Metallic and Lustre Ware, carried on as an unique industry by Sir Edmund Harry Elton, bart., of Clevedon Court. The inventor of this ware, which bears his name, is his own designer, and works regularly as finisher and general hand in the pottery near the house. The manufacture was begun by him in 1880, without any previous knowledge of ceramics, and the present ware is the result of original experiment. The specimens vary greatly in form, colour, decoration, and general art treatment. No specimen is reproduced, and the distinct characteristics of the ware have won for it practical recognition in the world of art by the bestowal upon it of no less than sixteen medals at various exhibitions in all parts of the world, twelve of the number being gold. Sir Edmund's kiln, slip kiln, pottery arrangements, wheel and studio, have been largely constructed from his own designs, and no professional potter is employed on the premises. Since 1902 a new departure has been inaugurated at the Elton works, the chief product of the process being 'Fiery Platinum Crackle,' plain gold and platinum crackles being also made.[11] 'The body of this ware has been mainly composed of alluvial deposit which turns red in firing, but of late both white and yellow clays have been frequently used, more particularly in the new " metallic crackle ware," which was put on the market for the first time as a consignment for the St. Louis Exhibition.'[12]

[3] B. M. Add. MS. 33668 (Rev. J. Skinner's Journal, 93).

[4] Hancock, *Hist. of Minehead*, 320.

[5] *Somers. Arch. Soc. Proc.* xlviii (2), 56.

[6] Collinson, *Hist. Somers.* i, 35. Saxon, *crocc, crocca*, a pot; Danish, *kruik*.

[7] *Somers. Arch. Soc. Proc.* loc. cit.

[8] *Ex informatione* Rev. Prebendary Street.

[9] 'The clay of Wincanton,' according to Phelps, 'furnished good pottery.' (Phelps, *Hist. Somerset*, i, 152.)

[10] *Wincanton Field Club Rep.* ii, 1890–1, p. 7.

[11] *Somers. Arch. Soc. Proc.* lii, 74–5.

[12] *Pottery Gazette*, 1 June, 1904, p. 674. Pottery of artistic shape, suitable for painting on, is also produced in the Bridgwater district.

The manufacture of glass was begun at Nailsea by John Robert Lucas in 1788. Prior to this date he owned a glass-bottle factory in Corn Street, Bristol. George White succeeded Lucas in the proprietorship of the Nailsea establishment, he being in turn followed by Samuel Bowen, who sold the factory to Messrs. Chance Bros. & Co. of Birmingham; the undertaking being closed in December 1873.

The existence of 'crown and sheet glass works on a large scale' is recorded by an old Bristol Directory of 1859 at Nailsea. In 1866 there were 350 persons engaged in the industry,[13] among them many French glass-blowers. Products of the works in 1850 were clear green glass flower-pots and saucers.

Mr. St. George Gray gives the following interesting account of the Nailsea 'glass-house people' in 1792:—

They lived in nineteen cottages in a row—mere hovels—containing in all nearly 200 people, who were known as Nailsea 'savages,' or 'heads,' as they styled themselves. Both sexes and all ages herded together. The wages are stated to have been high when there was work to do, and that the eating and drinking was almost luxurious. The high buildings comprising the factories ranged before the doors of the cottages. The inhabitants welcomed strangers who came to minister to them to 'Botany Bay,' or to 'Lettle Hell,' as they were in the habit of designating their little colony. Through the endeavours of Hannah and Martha More, philanthropists and religious teachers, these so-called 'savages' became

considerably tamed before the close of the 18th century.[14]

In 1865, 200 persons were employed in these glass-houses at the following rate of wages: blowers, £2 to £4 per week, gatherers, 24s. to 40s. Four 'journeys' a week was the average, a 'journey' implying the full number of hours with a full set of hands. There were two sheet-glass houses, also a rolled plate-glass house. Each blower had a gatherer and a boy to carry the pipes to the furnace, spare boys being employed to hold shovels at the furnaces to screen the gatherers from the heat. The work allotted to the 'push-boys' was that of pushing the cylinders into the kilns, where they were flattened out by men.[15]

The Bristol Museum and Art Gallery contains the finest collection in existence of Nailsea glass, comprising dark green jugs flecked with white, and clear glass flasks, beautifully veined or streaked with pale shades of pink, yellow, and green. Taunton Castle Museum contains two jugs of a dark yellowish-green common 'bottle' glass flecked with white, or a milky shade, often bluish in tone, the flecks varying considerably both in size and amount. White enamel appears sometimes on the lip of the jugs, sometimes as a double band below the rim. Some have plain bases, but the larger jugs have stout 'feet.' The height varies from 6 in. to 12 in.[16]

In 1815, there was a glass-house at Stanton Drew.[17]

BELL FOUNDING[1]

Somerset is remarkable not only for its church-towers, but for the large proportion of ancient bells which they contain (mostly coeval with the towers), the total number being about 270, two or three counties in England only having more.

These bells were mostly cast outside the limits of the county, the great majority at Bristol. Here we have founders as early as 1296 (Walter le Belyetar) and 1326, in which year one Johannes Belyettar served as *prepositus* of Bristol. There are bells at Emborough and Thurloxton which may be his work.

Not many Somerset bells can be traced to 14th-century founders, but there is mention of Roger de Taunton, *campanarius*, born at Bristol and working at Bridport in 1280, when he was complained of by Roger Mory and Nicholas Makegoye, burgesses of Dorchester, to whom

he owed 10s. for a brass pot of 40½ lb., presumably for the purposes of his trade.[2]

In the 15th century we hear of John Gosselin, about 1440–52.[3] There is a group of bells, of which about ten are in Somerset, bearing the stamp of a ship, which clearly indicates Bristol as the place of their manufacture; they belong to this century, and may well be Gosselin's work.

One William Warwick, probably a Bristol founder, cast a bell for Hereford Cathedral, and his lettering and stamps appear on a bell

---

[13] Kelly, *Dir.* Bristol, 1866; Blackie, *Imperial Gazetteer*, 1856.

[1] The writer is indebted to the courtesy of Mr. H. B. Walters for most of the information contained in this article.

[14] H. St. G. Gray's 'Notes on Nailsea Glass.' *Somers. Arch. Soc. Proc.* lii (2), 166.

[15] *Child. Employment Com.* 1865, pp. 217–18.

[16] Gray, op. cit.

[17] Add. MS. 33648, fol. 7.

[2] *Hist. MSS. Com. Rep.* vi, App. 489. There was a bell-founder named Philip Crese Erle, who cast a new bell for Bridgwater in the reign of Edward II. Ibid. iii, App. 311.

[3] Wadley, *Bristol Wills*, 133; see also Bickley, *Little Red Book*, i, 188. Mediaeval bequests to bells are not unknown, as for instance that of John Chauncelor in 1489, who left 3s. 4d. to the bells of Keynsham. (Weaver, *Somerset Wills* [Ser. 2], 282.)

at Yatton. From the churchwardens' accounts of that parish, we learn that a bell was cast in 1451 by 'Hew the bellman' of Bristol.[4] Possibly this is the one remaining, and 'Hew' was acting as Warwick's foreman.

In 1485 one of the bells at St. Michael's Church, Bath, was recast by John White, who was certainly a Bristol founder.[5] A 'Gyles bellmaker' is mentioned in 1490 as having a seat in St. Ewen's Church, Bristol.

About 1480–1500 the initials of one R.T. appear on several Somerset bells with Bristol lettering and stamps, this founder being succeeded by one whose initials were T.G. The latter may be certainly identified with Thomas Gefferies, whose will is dated 1546; he was of the parish of St. Philip and St. Jacob. He did some work at Yatton in 1533–4; and a bell at St. Michael's, Bath, cast by Thomas Belleter de Borstellio in 1518 was doubtless his work. He was followed by his son Henry Jefferies, who altered the spelling of the name, his initials appearing on his bells as H. I. John White's name occurs again at Yatton in 1531, and at Tintinhull in 1540–1; he died shortly after the last-named date. His bells have not been identified.

At Chiselborough there is a bell by Stephen Norton of Kent (c. 1380), and other London-cast bells at Batheaston, Charlinch, Angersleigh, West Monkton, &c. The first-named of these was by William Revel of London (1350–60).

In the south and south-west of the county, many bells are from the Exeter and Salisbury foundries, but those in the centre and north almost exclusively from Bristol, the history of which foundry between 1450 and 1550 has now been fairly worked out.

The first local founder of whom we hear is Roger Semson of Ash Priors, who is mentioned in the parish accounts of Woodbury, Devon, for 1559.[6] He seems to have been a follower of the older régime, as his inscriptions are usually mediaeval formulae; but his lettering is of transitional quasi-Roman character. There are several of his bells remaining in Devon and Somerset.

Robert Wiseman of Montacute cast several bells 1592–1619.[7]

The important dynasty of the Purdues, who did most of their work in or on the confines of the county, begins with George Purdue of Taunton, whose earliest bell is at Penselwood (1584), his latest at Cothelstone (1632). He is described as 'of Taunton' in the churchwardens' accounts of Nettlecombe (1624).[8]

His bells are also found in Devon and Dorset. He had a brother or a son Roger, whose bells extend from 1600 at Horsington to 1640 at Chiselborough, and whose foundry was at Bristol. The latter's bells are more numerous and more widely spread than those cast by George. Roger Purdue II was casting at Bristol from 1649 to 1687, William Purdue's dates being 1637–73. These two founders retained the foundry established by the first Roger, though William also worked at Salisbury. Their bells, which are numerous in the south-western counties, are especially so in Somerset. William Purdue died in 1673, and is buried in Limerick Cathedral.[9] Thomas Purdue, the last of the dynasty, was at Closworth from 1663 to 1697. He died there in 1711.[10] His bells are commoner in Dorset, and are difficult to distinguish from those of his contemporary, T. Pennington of Exeter, both using a stamp of a bell with the initials T.P.

The Closworth foundry was kept up by Thomas Knight, 1692–1714, by William Knight, 1721–47, and by Thomas Roskilley, 1752–9. Bells by the Knights are to be found in greater numbers in Dorset than in Somerset. Roskilley cast bells for Blackford and Winsham, also for Cheselbourne, Dorset.

Thomas Wroth was a Wellington bell-founder, who worked from 1691 to 1748; many of his bells are in Devon as well as in Somerset. Examples in the latter county are at Milverton, at Curry Rivel (1742), and in the former at Musbury.[11] He was a pupil of Hodson of Whitechapel.[12]

At Frome, William Cockey (probably two of the name) worked from 1696 to 1751; his bells are common in East Somerset, also in Wilts.

Certain bell-founding transactions of Mr. Wroth's with the parochial authorities of Luccombe are recorded in the churchwardens' accounts of that place for 1734. 'Mem. We agreed with Mr. Wroth to give him 3d. by the pound weight for casting one tenor bell, and 2s. 6d. per 100 for wast of mettle in casting and so in proportion for any odd number of quantity such old bell shall be found to weigh, and also if the new bell chance to be lighter Mr. Wroth is to allow we 1s. per pound, but if heavier we are to give him 1s. 2d. per pound, where you

---

[4] Churchwardens' Accts. of Croscombe, etc. (Somers. Rec. Soc. iv), 92.

[5] Somers. Arch. Soc. Proc. xxiii, 14.

[6] Ellacombe, Church Bells of Devon and Somerset, 357.

[7] Ellacombe, Bells of Devon, 53.

[8] Ellacombe, Bells of the Church, 437.

[9] Ellacombe, Church Bells of Glouc. 200. His epitaph runs as follows :—
Here a Bellfounder honest and true
Until the Resurrection lies Purdue.

[10] Thomas Purdue's epitaph is as follows :—
Here lies the bellfounder honest and true
Till ye Resurrection, named Purdue. (Ellacombe, Bells of Devon, 54.)

[11] Mr. Walters suggests that there were two of the name.

[12] Humphreys, Hist. Wellington, 161.

may see it more at large by the articles in the parish chest. The old bell weighed 1260 lb., the new bell weighed 1109 lb.' The expenses incurred in connexion with the casting included ' a journey in riding to Wellington to talk with Mr. Wroth about the casting of the tenor bell, 7s., for carrying the bell up to Wellington and down again, £2 10s. spent when the bell was taken down out of the tower, 2s. 6d. Paid Mr. Wroth for casting the bell in money and 151 pounds of bell metal, at 1s. per pound, £9 15s. 6d.[13]

Edmund Cockey was at work from 1823 to 1831.

The important foundries of the latter part of the 18th century were those at Chew Stoke and Bridgwater. The former was an offshoot of the prosperous foundry of the Bilbies at Collumpton (1715 to 1810) and was managed by Thomas Bilbie II and William and James Bilbie, from about 1770 to 1800. These founders' bells cast at Chew Stoke are to be found at Abbots Leigh (1751), Badgworth (1791), Berrow (1801), South Brent (1777), Mid Chinnock (1779), Dundry (1796), Frome (1788), Keynsham (1791), and many other places. At Street, a

ring of four was cast in 1777, but the others are nearly all single bells.[14]

The Bilbies cast two bells for Dunkerton Church in 1732. The second of these was apparently a good bell when first cast; when broken by some mischance, it was re-cast by Cockey of Frome, and then sent to the Bilbie foundry at Chew Stoke, whence it emerged with the following record of its adventures :—

BEFORE—I—WAS—A—BROKE—I—WAS — AS — GOOD AS—ANEY—
BUT—WHEN—THAT—COKEY—CASTED—MEE— I—NEAR—WAS—WORTH—A—PENNEY— THOMAS—BILBIE—CAST—ALL—WEE—

On the first bell at Bruton is the following :—

ONCE— I'D— A— NOTE — THAT — NONE — COULD— BEAR—
BUT—BILBIE—MADE—ME—SWEET—AND—CLEAR.[15]

---

[13] Healey, *Hist. West Somerset*, 160.

[14] For further details relative to these founders see Raven, ' Church Bells of Dorset,' *Dors. Field Club Trans.* xxvi ; also Ellacombe's works on bells.

[15] *Bath Nat. Hist. and Field Club Proc.* ii, 472.

The Bridgwater founders were Bayley and Street, 1743–73 ; Thomas Pyke, 1776–81 ; George and Thomas Davis, 1782–99 ; Isaac Kingston, 1801 ; J. Kingston, 1803–1829 ; Thomas Kingston, 1808–32 ; Edmund Kingston, 1831.

SCHOOLS

INTRODUCTION

THE number and antiquity of the schools of Somerset give them an important place in the history of the county. The earliest of which we can give any record is the grammar school of the Cathedral Church of Wells, which has an almost continuous history from the 13th to the 19th century. Dunstan, first Abbot of Glastonbury and afterwards Archbishop of Canterbury, is said to have studied with Irish strangers who had settled near Glastonbury some time before A.D. 940.[1] The monasteries must, however, be left out in our story of education in the county of Somerset. There was educational work carried on in them for their own novices and almonry boys, but little record of it has survived.[2] At other places besides Wells schools existed before the year 1548. At Taunton we have recorded in 1293 the names of two scholars attending the grammar school to the rebuilding of which Bishop Fox of Winchester contributed in 1523. At Bridgwater provision for the board and lodging of scholars attending the grammar school was made in St. John's Hospital in 1298. At Ilminster there is evidence of a boarding school carried on by one of the chantry priests in 1440; at Crewkerne there was the chantry school founded in the year 1499; at Bruton a school existed certainly in 1506, probably in 1417, which was permanently endowed in 1519; at Mells a grammar school was in being in 1524, but the date of its foundation is unknown. At Frome the grammar school existed at least before the Chantries Act of 1548. The school at Bath dates from the reign of Edward VI only, though in that cathedral city one must have existed before that date, while that at Yeovil sprang up during the reign of Queen Elizabeth. Early in the next century Nicholas Wadham of Merifield near Ilminster and Dorothy his wife founded Wadham College, Oxford. The Bishop of Bath and Wells was appointed Visitor, and special opportunities were offered to boys from Somerset. At Martock a grammar school was going on at least before 1625. In the same century schools rose at Shepton Mallet in 1626, at Wells in 1654, at Chard in 1671, and at Langport in 1675. Late in the 18th century Hannah More established schools for elementary instruction, both religious and secular, at Cheddar and several neighbouring parishes. Three of her schools, those at Cheddar, Nailsea, and Shipham, were still flourishing in 1825. In 1874 the trustees of the Huish Almshouses at Taunton employed their increasing revenues in founding a secondary school for boys at Taunton. In 1881 the trustees of the Sexey Foundation at Bruton turned their attention to the educational needs of the county and founded the Trade School at Bruton in 1892 and the dual secondary school at Blackford near Wedmore in 1899, and by a large grant of money enabled the trustees of the Strode School at Shepton Mallet to rebuild and give a fresh start to their school there.

THE CATHEDRAL GRAMMAR SCHOOL, WELLS

Wells Grammar School is the most ancient educational foundation in the county of Somerset. It has had indeed a chequered existence, and in quite recent times was for fourteen years in abeyance. It is the school carried on by, or under the direction of, the chancellor of the cathedral church, and though documents are not forthcoming to prove such existence there is no reason to suppose that it is not coeval in its origin with the church itself. From analogy with other cathedrals we may infer that a school arose in Wells when the first Bishop Athelm in 909 made the church of St. Andrew his cathedral church and the clergy who served it his cathedral canons. When Bishop Giso came to Wells in 1060 he tells us[1] that he found only four or five clerks attached to the church, and they were without cloister or refectory. These he increased in number to ten and allowed them to choose one, Isaac, as their provost, and he built them a cloister, refectory and dormitory and imposed upon them the rule of St. Chrodegang.[2] We need not doubt, therefore, that since there was a schoolmaster among the seven canons at York at the time of the Norman

---

[1] *Memorials of St. Dunstan* (Rolls Ser.), 11 and 75.
[2] Glastonbury was one of the Benedictine houses which sent students to Oxford and Cambridge.

[1] *Historiola Epis. Somers.* (Camd. Soc.), 18.
[2] Ibid.

Conquest, one of the ten canons of Wells was also schoolmaster or, as he was later called, chancellor.

Giso's successor, Bishop John de Villula, in 1088 transferred his throne from Wells to Bath and pulled down the buildings which his predecessor had erected,[3] but it is probable that the school at Wells was still carried on by the chancellor, on behalf of the chapter. In 1136 Robert of Lewes became Bishop of Bath, and his interest in Wells and in the claims of the canons of St. Andrew is shown in the 'Carta[4] de ordinatione prebendarum et institutione communae,' by which he began his scheme not only for the enrichment of the canons but also for the re-establishment of the church as of cathedral rank. In place of the former provost he created the office of the dean and reorganized the chapter.[5]

The cathedral body consisted of some forty-nine or fifty canons presided over by a dean elected by the canons from their own body, and the management of the church was placed in the hands of the dean and the resident canons of higher dignity. The most ancient statutes, adapted from those of Salisbury, and dating in substance probably from the 12th century, give us the duties assigned to each of these dignitaries.

The duty of the precentor[6] was to rule the choir in reference to the singing, and he could raise or lower the chant and through his official should regulate the song school. To him pertained the instruction and discipline of the boys and the regulation as to their admission into the choir and ordering. But the school which the precentor administered, personally or by deputy, was not a grammar school, but the song school, which originally was quite distinct. The management of the grammar school was the duty of the chancellor. The 'archiscola' of the ancient statutes is probably the chancellor himself, and his duty was to hear and determine the lessons (lectiones auscultare et terminare), to carry the chapter seal, to keep the letters of the chapter, to draft charters and letters, to read what had to be read publicly in the Chapter House, to inform the assistants concerning all the lessons which were not definitely stated on the table for the week, and to note down on those tables the names of the rota of readers. Later in the 13th century the actual conduct of the grammar school became the duty of his deputy the schoolmaster.

It is clear from this that the school over which the chancellor presided, and which was later taught by his deputy the schoolmaster, was quite distinct from the song school. It had nothing to do with the teaching of plain-song. That was the duty of the succentor under the direction of the precentor.

In a deed which from its signatures belongs to the period 1174–85,[7] and which records the appointment by Bishop Reginald of Thomas de Tornai as parson of a moiety of the benefice of Nunney, we have among the witnesses Peter of Winchester who is styled schoolmaster of Wells (Magister scolarum.) From the position of his name in the list of witnesses it is almost certain that he was the chancellor himself. This is the more likely as the constitution of the cathedral church was then only in its infancy. This charter is distinct evidence of the existence of the school in the 12th century.

The exact site of the schoolhouse during the 12th and the early years of the 13th century is unknown, but in all probability it was ultimately included in the new cathedral buildings of Bishops Reginald and Jocelin. This may have led to the bequest, about the year 1229, by Roger rector of Chewton[8] and Canon of Wells, of a house to be enjoyed by the schoolmaster for the time being for the use of the school of Wells. In return the master and scholars were bound inter alia to offer up prayers every day for the soul of the benefactor and other Christian souls. In 1281 Archbishop John Peckham[9] at a visitation of the diocese of Bath and Wells confirmed to the dean and chapter 'the house of the same Roger, and before him of Reginald of Waltham to the perpetual use of the school in the city of Wells' ('ad perpetuum usum scolarum in civitate Wellensi'). The position of this house was in the Mounterey or Mountroy.

In his charter of 1136 Bishop Robert of Lewes mentions the manor of Biddisham, which was to form the second prebend of the new constitution. The rents, however, were to go for the fabric of the church. From this estate one virgate of land was especially reserved for a vicar, and clearly this vicar was not on the same footing as the other vicars. Perhaps it was Bishop Robert who made the schoolmaster this vicar. Certainly the schoolmaster soon after his time became the vicar of the prebend of Biddisham, and this is expressly stated in a note at the end of the statutes of Dean Haselshaw, 1298,[10] which gives us the table of psalms assigned to the bishop, and to each of the canons of the chapter, to be said as a bond of perpetual praise by the brethren of the chapter of Wells. No psalms were assigned to the prebend of Biddisham, the rents of this prebend going to the upkeep of the church. The manor seems at first

---

[3] Historiola Epis. Somers. (Camd. Soc.), 22.
[4] Cf. 'Carta' printed in Church, Early Hist. of Wells, 11, 13.
[5] See under 'Religious Houses.'
[6] Reynolds, Wells, 45.

[7] Cal. MSS. D. and C. Wells, i, 492.
[8] Wells Orig. D. no. 30; Cal. MSS. D. and C. Wells (Hist. MSS. Com. 1907), i, 35.
[9] Cal. MSS. D. and C. Wells, ut sup. i, 150.
[10] Reynolds, Wells, 72.

to have been merged in the common fund of the church and afterwards in part into the prebend of the dean. The common fund was charged, however, with the payment to the schoolmaster. In 1327 the Communar's Roll has an entry of £1 10s. 4d. for the *magister scolarum*, and in 1343 it had gone down to £1 6s. 8d.[11] So in 1535 in the *Valor Ecclesiasticus*[12] we find the stipends of the prebendaries are recorded and also the stipends of the vicars choral. The connexion, however, between Biddisham and the schoolmaster had ceased. There had never been a stall with this title. The income of the schoolmaster was a charge on the common fund of the church. Biddisham is entered as augmenting the endowment of the deanery, and to the extent of £12 12s. 5d., as an item in the common income of the cathedral. The Communar's Roll for that year, April 1535–April 1536, has an item among the payments —'in communa magistri scholarum hoc anno £1 10s. 5d.'[13]

The communar's account for 1393[14] tells us the name of one of the schoolmasters and clearly indicates that he had a separate endowment. He has to pay tithes to the common fund of the church either from his half-acre of land in the North Field of Wells or from his virgate at Biddisham. Canon Barrington, the communar for the year, received 5s. 'de W. Westerely nuper magistro scolarum nomine decime.' Meanwhile it becomes abundantly clear that the grammar school had a distinct existence, and was separate from that of the choristers. These are constantly referred to : their maintenance, clothing and lodging are a matter of yearly care to the church.

While the teaching of the boys at the grammar school of Wells had now become the almost exclusive duty of the schoolmaster, as the chancellor's deputy, yet the chancellor was still on occasion required to lecture for the benefit of those of the clergy who found it inconvenient to attend the Universities. Such lectures were probably delivered in some part of the cathedral church itself. For instance, Ralph of Shrewsbury insisted that the chancellors should undertake a course of theological lectures. On 20 November 1337,[15] John de Middleton, having been collated to the chancellorship, is called upon by the bishop to take oath that he will lecture or at his own expense provide a lecturer in theology or in canon law in the cathedral church according to the ancient ordinances which apparently Bishop Ralph had revived in 1335.[16]

John de Middleton resigned the chancellorship within a month of his appointment, and the same obligation to lecture was imposed by oath on his successor Simon of Bristol.[17] Bishop Ralph was clearly providing for the needs of the younger clergy. At the grammar school boys intended for an ecclesiastical career had their first grounding in Latin side by side with their fellows of the laity, according to the excellent English practice. Later they could proceed to the University, or if presented to livings at an early age might perhaps be required to attend on the chancellor at the cathedral for instruction in dogmatic or moral theology and canon law.

Towards the end of the 14th century Bishop Harewell and the dean and chapter were active in providing a home for the annellar chaplains or chantry priests who, unlike the canons' vicars, had not yet been properly housed and organized. The New College where they were ultimately lodged was in Mountroy, and the buildings that were being erected seem to have called for the removal of the grammar school.[18] In 1410 Chancellor Richard Bruton surrendered to the dean and chapter a 'house in Torrelane by the Torregate lately given by the chapter to Chancellor Nicholas Danyel for the use of the master of the grammar school (*magister scolarum grammaticalium*), and his successors in which to hold the school, in exchange for a house at the Mounterye wherein the same used to be held.' Clearly the site of the old schoolhouse was wanted for the New College and the house in Torre Lane was a temporary arrangement until some other house could be found. A second deed explains this former one.[19] The dean and chapter having built their New College now assigned to Chancellor Richard Bruton an outhouse on the messuage of Canon Thomas Frome in the Mounterey, for the use of the schoolmaster for the time being in Wells to hold the grammar school therein. Canon Frome was indemnified for his loss by an annual payment of 6s. 8d., and was relieved from all responsibility for the dilapidations of the outhouse. The schoolmaster was to pay 12d. yearly to the chapel of St. Mary in the cathedral church and not to make or have doors, openings or windows on the south side and on the east of this chamber.

The new school being ready for the scholars Chancellor Bruton naturally gave up to the dean and chapter the house which had been lent to him in Torre Lane. The new school was thus set up on a spot within a few yards of the old site given by Roger of Chewton 200 years before.

Dean Walter Mideford or Metford, in his will dated 15 December 1421,[20] gave to the

---

[11] *Hist. MSS. Com. Rep.* x, App. pt. iii, 273, 274.
[12] *Valor Eccl.* (Rec. Com.) i, 135.
[13] Communar's Acct. in Reynolds, *Wells,* p. lxxxiii.
[14] *Hist. MSS. Com. Rep.* x, App. pt. iii, 275.
[15] *Cal. MSS. D. and C. Wells,* i, 239, 548.
[16] *R. of Shrewsbury's Reg.* (Somers. Rec. Soc.), ix, 341 ; x, 617 ; Wilkins, *Conc.* ii, 571.

[17] *Cal. MSS. D. and C. Wells,* i, 240.
[18] Ibid., i, 441.
[19] Ibid.
[20] Weaver, *Somerset Wills,* 320.

schoolmaster of Wells 6s. 8d., and to the scholars 13s. 4d. on condition that on every day for a month they should devoutly stand and say publicly in the school before they went to supper the psalm *De profundis* with the customary prayers and 'oration for my soul and the souls of the faithful dead.'

In 1457 the Fabric Rolls[21] of the cathedral record expenses at the schoolhouse for 200 stone tiles, 10d., lath nails, 10d., and the tiler for four days' work, 16d., total 3s. Evidently Canon Frome's outhouse was in process of enlargement and repair for the grammar school boys.

In 1498 Canon John Anstell, by his will dated 17 December,[22] left to the schoolmaster of the cathedral school for the use of the school there two printed books : *Catholicon*, i.e. a dictionary, and *Opera Gutrunni*.

The extant Chapter Act Books at Wells begin with the year 1487 and on 1 October 1488[23] Chancellor John Wilson through his proctor nominated James Greenhalgh, whom he had appointed as archiscola to a stall in the choir, viz. in the second row, with all its emoluments, and presented him with the habit of a vicar (*habitum vicarialem*).

On 3 October 1500 the chancellor nominated John Smythe as *magister scolarum*.[24] On 6 May 1503 John Draper, chaplain, was admitted master.[25] On 16 January 1506 Thomas Golderege as proctor for Chancellor Robert Dykar[26] publicly protested that if and in so far as he could be required to do so, in case the presentation of the schoolmaster without any special deputation for that purpose belonged to the chancellor, he wished to assert the right of the aforesaid chancellor without prejudice to the Lord Bishop or the dean and chapter. So he presented Roger Wynwode to the office of schoolmaster (*magister scolarum*), and this was allowed by the dean and chapter, and confirmed by Canon Roger Churche on behalf of the bishop.

On 17 August 1510 William Champernoun appears as schoolmaster.[27] On 30 October 1511 John Goddard, schoolmaster, was excused attendance at matins with some exceptions.[28] On 6 July 1512 Robert Hill, M.A., was appointed schoolmaster.[29]

The volume of the Chapter Acts comes to an end in 1513 and there is a gap in the series until 1571. As we have mentioned above we find in the Communar's Roll for 1536 payment made to the schoolmaster, but he is not there

mentioned by name.[30] His name, however, occurs in the *Valor Ecclesiasticus* in the previous year. From the general fund of the church he received £1 10s. 5d. and his name is John Lyshill. He is described as chaplain and as master of the school. If also we may assume that the variants of his name all refer to the same man in the *Valor* we find him in receipt of 1d. from the manor of Cheddar, £6 16s. 8d. his stipend as a chantry priest paid by the dean and chapter, and £3 6s. 8d. in prompt cash paid also by the dean and chapter to the chaplain of the New College of Mountroy, and also a share with seventeen others of £11 18s. 8d. the yearly value of the endowments of that college.[31]

Thirteen years afterwards the commissioners under the Chantry Act of 1547 reported concerning the cathedral church, its chapels and its chantries that— the 'Dean and Chapter of Wells of their free will keepe and mayntayne a free Grammar Scole there and do pay to the Master of the same scole yerely for his stipend or wages £13 6s. 8d. and to the ussher of the said scole yearly £6 13s. 4d.' The dean and chapter desired to carry on this school and trusted that some portion of the endowment for the chantries and obits would be granted them for this purpose. Although bound to keep up a school there was strictly no legal necessity for them to carry on a school free from fees, and so there was some truth in the statement they had made to the commissioners in 1548, Sir Thomas Speke and Sir Hugh Paulet, that 'of their Free Will they keepe and maynteyne a *free* grammar Scole.'

After the Reformation we find John Heather of Milton in the out parish of St. Cuthbert giving by will, 14 August 1558,[32] 'to the Cathedral Church of Wells 40s., to the grammer schole £5, to Master Wyllyam Good schoolmaster 20s. and to Wyllyam Absolon 40s.' The testator also directed that 'Ede Sorell and Thomas Sorell beinge in mynor adge shall be educated by my executors untyll they come to lawfull adge' presumably at the grammar school. The Royal Commission of 1560[33] appointed a shortened form for an early service in the cathedral at which 'the master, the usher and the scholars are to attend.' The scholars are clearly those of the Cathedral Grammar School. On 20 February 1583 the dean and chapter 'objected to the skolemaster of the gramer skoole of Wells that he did carrye with him the children of the gramer skoole and the choristers of the said cathedral churche unto Axebridge to play in the parish churche theare, the which he confessed. It was ordered that the said Skoole-

[21] *Hist. MSS. Com. Rep.* x, App. pt. iii, 289.
[22] Weaver, *Somerset Wills*, 371.
[23] Reynolds, *Wells*, App. 173.
[24] Reynolds, *Wells*, 200.
[25] Ibid. 208.   [26] Ibid. 220.
[27] Ibid. 233.   [28] Ibid. 235.
[29] Ibid. 236.

[30] See note 13.
[31] *Valor Eccl.* (Rec. Com.), i, 128, 141.
[32] *Somers. Med. Wills* (Somers. Rec. Soc. xxi), 214.
[33] *Cath. Com. Rep.* 1885, Wells App. 2.

master the next chapter daye shall come into the Chapter House before the Deane and Chapter viz. *primo Aprilis proximo* and submit himself to the chapter in that behalf and shall further *nomine poenae pecuniarie* pay unto xxiiij of the poore people of the almshouses 2s. viz. to each of them 1d. before the next chapter day and shal ther certifye the same.'[34]

This entry seems to suggest that at this time choristers received their ordinary education with the other boys of the grammar school, which, as we shall see below, had been removed to the neighbourhood of the cathedral church, and that the schoolmaster had enough authority over them to carry them off to Axbridge for this performance. Of course this did not mean that their musical training was given them as part of the curriculum of the school. That was imparted by the succentor or organist or one of the vicars choral, but the master had now control over the choristers out of school hours and when not engaged in the musical services of the church.

In 1592 the charter of Queen Elizabeth,[35] which was granted to the dean and chapter at their request to confirm them in their legal position as the true successors of the mediaeval dean and chapter, definitely mentions the schoolmaster among the ministers of the church and ordains that the same payments as have been usual during the preceding twenty years shall still be made.

The house which had been given as a part of the original endowment had, as we have shown, been absorbed in the site of the New College for chantry priests, but the dean and chapter had afterwards provided and enlarged an outhouse on the messuage of one of the canons in the North Liberty. At the end of the 15th century provision was made for the grammar school near the western walk of the cloisters on the south-west of the church. Payments appear in the communar's accounts for buildings on the external side of the western cloisters and near to the house known as the Organist's House, and a wall was built round this house.[36] The New College and all the chantry endowments had gone and with them the original site of the grammar school and the greater part of Mr. Lyshill's income, since he was a chantry priest. The school, however, was now maintained by the dean and chapter out of its corporate funds.

From time to time references to the school occur in the Chapter Minutes. On 1 October 1606 the scholars were forbidden to play in the cloisters, a decorous rule which must have seemed severe to the boys, seeing that their school was now the long room over the cloisters. The master was appointed by the chancellor, and his appointments are not always entered in the Chapter Minutes.

Yet during the 17th century the school was carried on, though the chapter estates were sequestrated in 1644 and deans and chapters were abolished in 1649. On 22 February 1653 there is an order of the Trustees for Plundered Ministers and Schoolmasters :—

Whereas the yerely pension of £10 was heretofore issuing and payable out of the rents and proffits of the manor of Congresbury in co : Somerset parcell of the possessions of the late deane and chapter of Wells to the Schoolemaster of the Grammer Schoole in Wells which said pencion is by an Act of Parliament for sale of the mannor and gleabs of rectories transferred and charged upon the said trustees. It is therefore ordered that the saide pencion of £10 a yeare be continued and paid unto Mr. Robert Ash, schoolemaster of the saide schoole for and during such time as he shall continue schoolemaster there or till further order of the saide trustees, the same to be accounted from the 16 day of October 1650.[37]

In 1655 the payment for the school seems to have been mixed up with the payment to the poor of Wells.[38]

'19 April 1655 A particular of several augmentacions and allowances charged upon the revenues of the counties of Somerset and Wilts. within the receipt of Mr. Richard Phelpes Receiver

Wells Poore $\Big\}$ £26 3s. 4d.'
Wells Schoole

and this was derived from receipts issuing as follows :—

'Lovington   -   -   -   £2 10s.
Wells Reeveship   -   -   £20
St. John's Hospital -   -   £3 13s. 4d.'

A later order continues the payments but assigns for them revenues from other estates at Ilminster, Long Sutton, and Compton Dando.

Two years later came the news that the master was dead and his successor a failure.[39] On 10 November 1657 Mr. Burges 'informes that Mr. Ash, schoolemaster in Wells, is dead and one Sampson succeedes him, that hath spoiled the Schoole and is not approved.' A further entry appears a few months later—'4 February 1658. Old bedridden schoolemaster dead. Present schoolemaster very unable, cannot give account of his grammer.'[40]

The Rev. Henry Mills, 1710–17, according to a testimonial given him by the dean and chapter when he was a candidate for the mastership of the Croydon Grammar School,[41] 'had in a few years raised the reputation of this school far above what former masters could effect in many years.'

---

[34] Wells D. and C. Chapter Act Bk. H, fol. 20.
[35] Cf. Charter printed in Reynolds, *Wells*, 263.
[36] Ibid. 236.

[37] Lambeth MS. 969, fol. 216.
[38] Ibid. 952, fol. 55, 146.
[39] Ibid. 1012, fol. 150.
[40] Ibid. fol. 164.
[41] *V.C.H. Surr.* ii, 193.

The chapter accounts from 1720 show an annual payment of £10, and in 1841 this was raised to £20 to the master of the school.[42]

On 22 May 1815 Mr. John Vickery the head master was appointed head master of the endowed school known as the Blue School which was then carried on in the North Liberty, and he took over with him a number of boarders to receive whom the governors of the Blue School had to enlarge the house there.[43]

There is no reference to the grammar school in the report of the Commissioners concerning Endowed Schools in 1820, but in the fuller inquiry of 1833[44] it was reported that the collegiate grammar school had twenty-six boys in it, of whom eight were choristers of the cathedral, and that the master was paid by the dean and chapter a salary of £30 a year with apartments and a schoolroom over the western cloister. The master at this time was the Rev. W. Aldrit, who was also sub-librarian of the Chapter Library.

This is our first notice of the chambers over the cloister as the dwelling-rooms of the master. The old house in the adjacent garden had slowly fallen into ruin; it was pulled down in 1876 except one gable which was allowed to remain to mark the site, and the choir boys were lodged in private houses in the vicars' close and with their parents in town. On 8 August 1847 Canon F. Beadon as chancellor appointed Mr. Harold schoolmaster of the Cathedral Grammar School.

In 1852 the dean and chapter replied to the questions put to them by the Cathedral Commissioners— [45]

(1) There is a grammar or choristers' school.

(2) The master is appointed by the chancellor of the church.

(3) He is paid £25 per annum out of the capitular fund. For this payment he gives instruction to the eight choristers. He is allowed to educate other pupils. The number at present is about thirty. He has chambers at the end of a spacious schoolroom over the west cloister.

In 1876 the numbers in the school had sunk to three and the master was superannuated, receiving a retiring pension from the capitular fund of £40 and the school was suspended during the payment of the pension and until the dean and chapter should be in a position to re-establish it on a satisfactory basis. The choir boys were then sent for their instruction to a private school in Chamberlain Street kept by the late Mr. J. Palmer, who afterwards was ordained and became vicar of West Camel.

In 1879[46] the dean and chapter petitioned the Ecclesiastical Commissioners for funds to enable them to reopen the grammar school. The ancient endowment to which they referred was quite inadequate for the needs of a modern school and it was hoped that from the large revenues which the Commission received from suppressed prebends a grant would be made for this purpose. The appeal of the dean and chapter was also supported by another from the Mayor and commonalty of Wells, but as the Cathedral Commission of 1879 was mainly ecclesiastical no response was given to the appeal. The arrangement with Mr. J. Palmer came to an end in 1884. Then, on a site given by the dean and chapter behind the house which had been for one hundred years the Blue School, Chancellor T. D. Bernard erected at his own cost a convenient and handsome set of buildings to the west of and attached to the old Canons' Barn. The new Cathedral Grammar School was opened and a special service held in it by Lord A. Hervey, the Bishop of Bath and Wells, on 1 May 1884. Mr. Palmer handed over his school in Chamberlain Street to the dean and chapter and the boys were transferred to the North Liberty. The school contains about 50 boys, of whom five or six are boarders. The dean and chapter pay £110 towards the stipend of the head master and send 14 choristers free. The old house of the chancellor in the immediate cathedral precincts is also rented by the dean and chapter and granted free to the head master. The late head master was the Rev. Henry John Green, who was appointed a priest vicar in 1898 and head master in 1904. He was educated at Bradford Grammar School and was a non-collegiate student at Oxford. He had three assistant masters under him.

Mr. Green was succeeded as head master and as priest vicar in May 1910 by the Rev. R. E. Lewis, M.A. of Selwyn College, Cambridge, and lately assistant master and chaplain of Sutton Valence School, Kent.

THE SONG SCHOOL

The Choristers' School or Song School was in its origin entirely distinct from the Chancellor's Grammar School. In the earliest extant copies of the ancient statutes[1] of the cathedral church we read that the precentor ought 'to rule the choir . . . and conduct (*regere*) the song school through his officer (*officialem*) . . . and to him belongs the instruction of the boys (i.e. the choir boys) and their discipline and

[42] Chapter Act Bk.
[43] Minutes of Blue School Governors' Meetings.
[44] *Education Ret.* ii, 827.
[45] *Cath. Commission*, 1879, Wells, 28, *Rep.* 1883, App. 6.
[46] *Cath. Com. Rep.* 1883, Wells App. 5.
[1] These in substance may date from the 12th century.

admission to the choir and ordering.'[2] An early specific mention of the choristers is found in or about 1250, when John of Button, provost of the church, left 25 marks a year to be paid by the priory of Barlynch (*Berliz*) and Archdeacon of Wells on his anniversary, of which 20s. was to go to five choristers to sing an anthem in honour of the Virgin before her image in the nave.[3] In 1347 [4] Bishop Ralph of Shrewsbury reciting that 'whereas there are boys called choristers serving in the divine offices at the day and night hours, for whose food and clothing no rents have been assigned, so that often they must absent themselves to seek a living elsewhere,' gave them ten marks out of Chew vicarage, established when he appropriated the rectory of Chew to his own table. In a sort of history of Wells in the Register [5] he is said also to have built them a new manse, by which we may clearly understand their first separate habitation. Before that date they seem to have been distributed among the canons, who for long had been used to feed them. There is no further mention of the choristers' school or master until a century later under Bishop Beckington, who being an early scholar of Winchester and the prime mover in the foundation of Eton, took a keen interest in education. It may be remembered that it was specially provided in the Eton statutes that the choristers of Eton and of King's College were to have the first claim for scholarships at Eton. At Wells Beckington made an elaborate code of statutes for the choristers 6 February 1459-60,[6] confirmed by the dean and chapter 13 January 1460-1. He puts them forward, however, not as now made by himself for the first time, but as 'rules and ordinances which we found healthfully instituted and diligently and holily observed in his time by the praiseworthy man of worthy memory, Sir Robert Catur, such choristers' preceptor and master.' As Catur's memory is spoken of he was presumably then dead. The first statute provides for the master, who is to be appointed by the precentor, not the chancellor, 'a priest, in all things of approved knowledge and manner of life as well wise as discreet at judging what boys are suitable for choristers, both by the disposition of their voices as by natural disposition,' and he enlarges on the necessity for his chastity and sobriety. 'Let him be also learned in grammar, sufficiently well

taught in plain and organ chant, prudent and sufficiently well seen in temporal goods to manage the choristers' property, and to account yearly before the precentor.' He is always called not schoolmaster but choristers' master. Each chorister was to have a purse provided with his name on it, and all monies payable at funerals, obits, and other services put into the purse, and kept for him, and whenever a chorister 'shall wish to proceed to any English university for study and scholastic advancement (*et profectus scholastici*) with consent of his friends, all the money belonging to him shall be paid wholly to him.' The choristers were to give three terms' notice before retiring. If any retired without notice, or for fault, these monies were to be used to pay for his board, schooling, use of utensils, barber, and laundress, for the whole time he had been there. There was to be a deputy, called undermaster (*submagister*) appointed by the master to supply his place in his absence and teach under him. The master and undermaster were to agree on their method of teaching (*modus docendi*), which was to be plain, not obscure, short and to the point; 'for the prolixity of lecturing begets tedium in the learner and is the chief step-mother which causes oblivion of all scholastic progress.' To services the choristers were to walk two and two in order of seniority, and to wear, as hitherto used, long gowns (*togis talaribus*) long tunics and short boots. Every boy on rising in the morning or getting up at midnight was to make the sign of the cross, say *In nomine Patris*, the Lord's Prayer, Angelic Salutation and Antiphon, versicle and orison (*orationem*). Those who got up at midnight were to say Our Lady's Matins silently in choir (*de St. Maria silenter in choro*). Those who got up in the morning were to say the same two and two; while saying it they were to dress, make their beds (*pressoria parent*), wash their hands, then go to school and await the master. He was 'to teach them plain chant and harmony (*plano cantu et organico*) wisely guiding their voices high and low according to their character.' When the bells rang for second prime, which is called *prima diei*, they were to go to breakfast. After breakfast those on duty in the choir go there, the rest stay in school and repeat their lessons (*lectiones*) till 11 o'clock. Then all go to hall for dinner. After dinner they return to school and till the master's coming diligently employ their time in repeating their lessons, and so remain till it is time for vespers. After vespers they go to supper, and then in summer time amuse themselves after the discretion and arrangement of the master. Then as time will allow the master or undermaster shall hear those who have to read and sing at matins, the antiphon, versicle and responsories, the other boys staying in school as before. Then as the masters think best and at the most con-

[2] This follows the text found in the early 15th-century Harl. MS. 1682 fol. 2. In one of the versions printed by Reynolds (*Wells*, 44, 55), presumably from the Liber Ruber, the last clause appears in the margin. Whether this indicates a later addition or merely accidental omission is doubtful.

[3] Reg. i, fol. 22 d.

[4] Pat. 20 June 23 Edw. III, in *Cal. MSS. D. and C. Wells* (Hist. MSS. Com.), i, 436.

[5] Ibid. 454.

[6] Reynolds, *Wells*, pp. clxxx-v.

venient time let there be some play (*fiat aliqualis recreacio in ludendo*). In hall the boys are to come to table in order of height, the smaller first, and say grace. Then sit down quietly and to behave *honeste*, not leaning over the table, or dirtying their napkins : they should take up their meat like courtiers and gentlemen (*curialiter et honeste*), cut or nicely break their bread, not gnaw it with their teeth or tear it with their nails, drink when their mouths are empty (*ore vacuo in repleto*) eat in a gentlemanly way, restrainedly, and not ravenously (*honeste, moderate non ravide*). They should lift up their mouths when they eat (*os cum cibo elevent*) and not pick their teeth with their knives. They must ask for things in Latin not in English, in a low and not a high voice. Their moderate meal over, they say grace as before. No stranger boys (*pueri extranei*, the words are those used in the Winchester statutes for commoners) were to be admitted to meals with them, beyond two, who were to be *honeste conditionis ;* and at most ten or twelve years old, and to stay only two years. Chambers being instituted for rest after labour, immediately after school, which was ended with *Salve Regina*, without notes, followed by the psalm *De profundis* and prayer, *Absolve quaesumus*, they were to go to their common room and kneel two and two at the foot of their beds and say the psalm, *Miserere Deus* with the versicle 'Dignare domine nocte ista sine peccato nos custodire' and the collect *Illumina quæsumus Domine*. Then their clothes off they were to jump into bed. In each bed were to be three boys ; two small boys with their heads to the head of the bed, one older to the foot, who is to put his feet between the heads [7] of the two small boys. There was to be a lighted lamp (*seu mortuarium*) so that the master can see which way they lie. They were to play entirely apart from others, laymen and strangers (*laicis et extraneis*), on ordinary days for half an hour or at the most an hour, before supper in winter, after supper in summer ; on feast days a little after dinner and supper in summer. The prefect system was in force. There were to be *impositores hebdomadales* or praepostors for a week, as at Eton still ; two *ebdomadarii* to supervise shortcomings, neglects and faults in church, hall, chamber, and two others more experienced in 'chaunting' to look after them in school. Finally forty days' indulgence was promised to anyone giving money or help to the house.

On 26 December 1486 [8] Master Richard Swan, who was Provost of the Cathedral Church of Wells, gave twelve spoons to the choristers'

house to the use of the choristers, to pray for his soul. In the first extant Chapter Act Book we meet with several notices of the choristers' master, but always under that title (*magister* or *informator* or *instructor choristarum*) never as schoolmaster (*magister scolarum*) simply, a title which is always reserved for the grammar schoolmaster. Thus on 2 May 1487 [9] the dean and chapter gave Richard Hygons, instructor of the choristers, for his diligent labour and good service spent and to be spent, £1 6s. 8d. a year from a vacant canonry for life, in augmentation of his annual pension ; the amount of which is unfortunately not stated. He seems to have been the same person who is described as 'Richard Huchons, a vicar choral,' at a contested installation of a provost on 6 June following, and on 28 June 1488 under the same name was assigned as superintendent (*ascultor*) of a new vicar choral. Nearly twenty years later, 23 July 1507, [10] Master Hygons, master of the choristers, with consent of the chapter agreed to pay Richard Bramston, vicar choral, 40s. a year out of his portion and fee, to teach the choristers to sing well and faithfully as Hygons had done in times past. Bramston was also to take care of and play at the organs in the high choir and in the Lady chapel. This was probably an appointment of a deputy, as Hygons was getting old. Next year another deputy was appointed, John Clausay being given on 11 April the office of instructing and teaching the choristers and tablers (*tabellarios*), those who were to serve the table of services of the day, singing and descant and other things pertaining to the office ; and keep all services (*sectas*) in the choir and Lady chapel as Hygons had done in time past. He was also to play the organs in the high (*magno*) choir and Lady chapel behind the altar. For this he was to receive four marks (£2 13s. 4d.) from the clerk of the fabric out of vacant stalls, and 40s. from Hygons' fee and portion, and a house worth £1 6s. 8d. a year.

In 1535 [11] the choristers are said to be thirteen in number and to have an income of £27 16s. 1d. 'by ordinance of John Stafford and others,' of which £20 came from St. Cuthbert's Church, which was appropriated to the cathedral and worth £67 a year, the gift of Richard Harewell, as we saw above.

By the reign of Elizabeth it is possible that the choristers received their general education at the grammar school. The changes of the Reformation much reduced the resources of the dean and chapter, who were certainly less inclined than their predecessors of the old religion to favour elaborate services and an extensive choral establishment.

---

[7] Reynolds gives it as 'feet' but this must be a mistake.
[8] *Somers. Wills*, 201.

[9] Reynolds, *Wells*, 102.
[10] Op. cit. 223, cf. 207.
[11] *Valor Eccl.* (Rec. Com.), i, 127.

SCHOOLS

THE FREE GRAMMAR SCHOOL, BATH

In the absence of documents there is no evidence forthcoming of the existence of a grammar school at Bath before the dissolution of the cathedral priory. But it is impossible that one should not have existed.

The monastery at Bath was dissolved by the surrender of Prior Holeway and his twenty-one monks on 27 January 1539. Thirteen years afterwards the mayor and citizens petitioned Edward VI and obtained a grant of lands belonging to the dissolved monastery in the city and suburbs for the maintenance of a free grammar school.

A warrant [1] was made out in the Court of Augmentations 28 June 1552 setting out the particulars of the lands intended to be granted and directing the necessary letters patent for the grant to be prepared. The 'parcels' were set out as follows : ' all the lands, tenements, cottages, gardens and mills in the city and suburb,' which had belonged to the priory, valued at £54 5s. gross and £42 13s. 10d. net as certified by the auditor of the Court of Augmentations 28 June 6 Edward VI. The warrant of the chancellor of the court ran : ' The Kynges majesties pleasour is that the maior and Citizens of Bathe shall have the landes and tenements above mencyoned of his highnes gifte to theym and their successors for ever, to thentent the said maior [and] cityens shall fynd one able Skolemaster with thissues and profettes thereof, to teache a free grammer scole there to have continewance foreuer and also in further consideracion that they shall with thissues and profettes of the saide premises relieve ten poore folke within the said town of bathe for ever. The tenure is free burgage. Make a boke thereof accordingly. Ryc. Sakevyle.'

A rent of £19 a year to the Crown was to be reserved, reducing the available income for school purposes to £37 13s. 10d. a year.

But as a matter of fact a more extended report of the surveyor [2] showed that the premises were in such a bad state of repair that the repairs reduced the net rent to £25. When the patent came to be prepared and passed under the Great Seal 12 July 1552 this was the value stated of the premises. The patent [3] granted that there should be a school in the said city which should be called the Free Grammar School of King Edward VI for the education, institution and instruction of boys and youths in grammar, and such school of one master to continue for ever the king did thereby erect create ordain and found. The property was granted to the corporation in free socage or burgage subject to the rent of £10 a year. The king willed that out of the issues and profits the corporation should find a fit, able and literate person to serve in the said school meet and well learned at least in the Latin tongue, who should have £10 a year. Statutes were to be made with the consent of the bishop. The corporation was also out of the premises to ' help relieve and comfort ' ten poor persons.

On 6 March following, 1552–3,[4] Nicholas Jobbyn of the parish of St. Mary of Stalls, Bath, gave ' to the maier and commons of Bath for the use of the free gramer Scole certeyne books of gramer and learnyng for the use of the Scolemaster and the Scollers ther at the deliveraunce of the Meyer and his bretheren ' and ' to the meyntening of the tenements belonging to the free scole of Bath all my tymber.'

In the reign of Queen Elizabeth the city found it necessary to procure a patent of confirmation, 4 September 1590, and in this patent the lands are said to have been called Katherine land, Chambre land, School land, Alms land, Hospital land and Church land ; names which go to suggest the pre-existence of a school.

During the early part of the 17th century the school seems to have existed in obscurity, but after the Restoration greater interest was taken in it, and during the educational movement of the reign of Queen Anne the citizens and the Rev. Walter Robinson, the head master, seem to have directed their attention to the school endowments and the way they were mismanaged by the corporation. As they were unable to induce the corporation to carry out the terms of the trust, application was at last made to the Court of Chancery for an inquiry by Commissioners of Charitable Uses. This was granted, and their decree of 10 June 1735 found the corporation guilty of grave breach of trust in not rightly applying the lands given for the school or almspeople, and directed this property to be conveyed to a new body of trustees headed by the Duke of Beaufort. The master was ordered to teach ten boys gratis and he was to be appointed in future on the nomination of twenty of the highest ratepayers of Bath. The corporation, it appears, had so mixed up the various properties which they held in trust that they had not cognizance of the lands and tenements of this particular charity. Though followed by a writ of execution of the Court of Chancery [5] on 12 October 1736, the decree of the Commissioners remained a dead letter. The corporation were left in possession of the property, and continued to manage it and the school as before. In 1734 some rebuilding had been accomplished by the corporation, and in 1752 the present building was begun, the foundation stone having been laid on 29 May by the mayor, Mr. Francis Hales.

[1] Aug. Off. Partic. for Schools, Edw. VI, R. 2.
[2] *Char. Com. Rep.* v, App. 512.
[3] Ibid. v, 271.

[4] *Somers. Wills*, iii, 145.
[5] Proc. of Com. for Char. Uses, 1736.

In the report of the Commission[6] on the Education of the Poor in 1820 a ground plan of the messuages claimed as belonging to the endowment is given. The head master was the Rev. Thomas Wilkins, who was also rector of Charlcombe, the advowson of that benefice having been given by a Mr. Robins to the mayor and corporation for the augmentation of the master's stipend. There were then between 70 and 80 boarders, and the Commissioners[7] in 1822 ordered that ten boys sons of freemen of Bath should be admitted free, and this number was to be increased as the revenues of the charity increased in value. The master's income was fixed at £84 a year, to be paid out of the general funds of the charity together with the £140 a year, the estimated value of the rectory of Charlcombe.

In 1872 a new scheme was made by the Charity Commissioners under the Endowed Schools Acts and approved by Queen Victoria in Council. By it the school was definitely separated from the almshouse, and any increase in the value of the endowments was to go henceforth to the maintenance of the school. There were to be fifteen governors and they were to pay over to the trustees of the municipal charities £280 a year under the title of 'Black Alms' for the almshouses. The rectory of Charlcombe was to be sold as soon as expedient. The school was to consist of two departments, junior and senior, under one head master, and was to be known as King Edward's School, Bath. The head master need not necessarily be in holy orders, but should he so be is not to hold any benefice or other appointment which would interfere with his school duties.

As soon as circumstances would allow of it the governors were to make the endowment subserve the education of girls, and until school premises could be built for them the governors were at liberty to hire a building or offer exhibitions and scholarships among the most promising and meritorious scholars of Bath and the neighbourhood. At present nothing has been done towards the establishment of a girls' school, but the governors offer three scholarships for girls tenable at the Bath Girls' High School. There are at present 195 boys in the school under Mr. E. W. Symons, M.A., and nine assistant masters. The minutes of meetings of the governors of the school only go back twenty years. Earlier information is derived from the city records.

THE FREE GRAMMAR SCHOOL, TAUNTON

The origin of this school has generally been ascribed to Richard Fox, Bishop of Winchester 1501–28, in 1523. But there is little doubt that he did no more than assist in its rebuilding out of the episcopal revenues. The manor and hundred of Taunton were part of the ancient possessions of that see. The bishop would hardly leave an estate and town of such importance without a grammar school. There is evidence of the existence of the school there in the reign of Edward I. At an inquisition[1] taken 'for proof of age' of Hugh de la Tour on 7 March 1309–10, before he could get possession of the lands of his father Thomas, one of the witnesses, John of Kent, gave evidence that Hugh was of age the year before, and this he knew because he had a son at Taunton School with the aforesaid Hugh seventeen years ago 'ad scolas Taunton in societate predicti.' Seventeen years brings us back to 1293. It may, however, be observed that this sends Hugh de la Tour to school at the ripe age of five. But as Quintilian, the great Roman writer on education, following the Greek Chrysippus, wanted children to begin school at three years old, and our modern elementary schools have habitually taken them at that age, we need not think Kent's memory was romantic. No further mention of the school is yet forthcoming before the record of its rebuilding by Bishop Fox. In the Pipe Rolls of the estates of the see of Winchester for 1523 there is an entry under the manor of Taunton of an expenditure of £226 5s. 10d. for the building of the schoolhouse within the castle at Taunton.[2] This building, 60 ft. long by 20 ft. wide and 30 ft. in height[3] with Bishop Fox's crest and initials R. F. and the date 1522 carved in stone over the entrance door and a mitre over the crest, is a good example of the late Perpendicular style. It was used as the school until 1874.

The dormitories were adapted in the 19th century for a school chapel and the roof of the schoolroom was ceiled over for the sake of greater warmth. After remaining void for nearly ten years the buildings were put up to sale in 1886 and purchased by the corporation of Taunton, which at the time gave a pledge to preserve the ancient features of the house.

Attached to the certificate of the Chantry Commissioners[4] in 1548 there is the following note—

The inhabitants of the town of Taunton aforesaid 6 April 1548 make humble request unto the Commissioners in manner and form following—Whereas ther is within the said towne of Taunton being the greateste and beste market town in all that shire, in

[6] Op. cit. 269.
[7] Char. Com. Rep. viii (1822), 567.

[1] The Genealogist, iii, 211. For reference to this proof of the pre-Foxian existence of Taunton School, which he had often hypothetically asserted, the writer is indebted to Mr. J. H. Round.
[2] Records of Eccl. Com. (P.R.O.), bdle. 22.
[3] A picture of Taunton School before alterations in Mrs. Green's illustrated edition of the Short Hist. of Engl. ii, 606, shows it in the late Perpendicular style of the 16th century.
[4] Somers. Chant. (Somers. Rec. Soc. ii), 25.

a very holesome, goode and plentifull soyle a faire, large and goodlye house newe builded erected and made for a scolehouse about xxv yeres now past whereyn was a scolemaster and an usher founde the space of xii or xiii yeres for the vertuous education and teaching of yewthe as well of the said towne of Taunton as of the hole countrie to the nombre of vi or vii score scolars by the devocion of one Roger Hill of the same town, a merchant now deceased. The said scole was a greate relief to the said town of Taunton, and now sythe the death of the saide Roger Hill the saide scolehouse standeth voyde withouten either master, ussher, or scolars to the great prejudice hurte and discommoditie of the common welthe of the said shire. Whereupon the said enhabitauntes make most humble sute unto the King's majestie that it may please his highnes to grant and assigne such land and tenements in perpettuytie as shall be thought mete unto hys grace and most honourable consaile to the maintenance and finding of a maister and ussher to teach in the same scole house which no doubt is the most beautyfull and most necessarie place of all that shire.'

It is probable, therefore, that while the lord of the manor, Bishop Fox of Winchester, built the schoolhouse, Roger Hill during his lifetime provided in some way for the maintenance of the schoolmaster. The free grammar school however became known as Bishop Fox's Grammar School.

In 1554 William Walbye, fellow of Corpus Christi College, Oxford, left by will[5] 'to the establissinge of a stipend for the scolemaster of Taunton 20 marks in land or else so much money as may purchase the said 20 marks after twenty years' purchase.' With this bequest 107 acres at Hawkchurch, Dorset, was purchased from William Pole of Colyford and conveyed by deed, which also granted to the warden of New College, Oxford, the appointment of the schoolmaster. As the then Bishop of Winchester was John White, ex-fellow of New College and head master and warden of Winchester College, we may perhaps trace his influence in this provision.

In the Parliamentary Survey of 1647 of the manor of Taunton Deane, part of the possessions of the dissolved bishopric of Winchester, the Commissioners 'present that the school house standing within the precincts of the Castell, time out of mind hath been enjoyed and kept as a free school, the schoolmaster thereof paying unto the lord of the manor in lieu of his rent per annum 4d.' The master at this time was John Prince, scholar of Winchester and fellow of New College, whence he was ejected by the Parliamentary visitors; he is said to have been a major in the Royalist army. His successor at the Restoration, also a scholar of Winchester and fellow of New College, was William Harrison, B.C.L., afterwards a canon of Lincoln. It is probable, indeed, that all or nearly all the

masters were from the same school and college. The master in 1680 certainly was. He was William Budsey, founder's kin, a descendant, that is, of one of William of Wykeham's sisters, who went to Winchester in 1663 and to New College in 1668.

The Charity Commissioners of 1821 report that there existed lease indentures of 5 June 1718, 20 October 1770, and 24 December 1798. On this last date the Rev. James Bernard was the sole surviving trustee of the earlier indenture, and he released the school property to himself, Sir Charles Warre Malet, bart., Alexander Popham and others.

The Commissioners of Inquiry[6] in 1821 reported that the Rev. James Hurley was the master in 1764, when there were about 20 boys, of whom one was a free scholar, but that was only as a kindness and not as a right. Mr. Hurley was succeeded by the Rev. Nathaniel Hine, which appears to be a mistake for Hinde, or Hynde—at least he appears under that spelling in the Winchester *Scholars' Register and Long Rolls*—being a commoner at that school in 1767 and a scholar from 1768 to 1775. He took no free scholars. Then followed the Rev. John Townshend, fellow of New College, appointed in 1796, who with Mr. Barker, curate of St. Mary's, took boys as private pupils.

In 1820 there were 18 boys in the school,[7] of whom seven or eight were boarders. There were then no free scholars, nor were the inhabitants aware that they had any right to claim free instruction for their children.

The endowment was not indeed adequate for the support of a free school, and payment of fees by day boys and boarders was the only way in which an efficient master could be obtained. In 1831 Robert Crotch, the son of the celebrated organist and musician, a scholar of Winchester in 1811, and afterwards fellow of New College, was appointed head master. His celebrated father, who had come to live with him, died in the master's house in 1847. While he was at the school the lands of the Walbee endowment were granted out on long leases, and the fines then obtained seem not to have been used for the permanent advantage of the school. The income from the estates was consequently very small, and the master had very few pupils.

In 1864 the Rev. William Tuckwell, scholar of Winchester and fellow of New College, was appointed head master, and as the result of his energy and ability the number of pupils greatly increased and the quality of the education was much improved. He gave evidence[8] before the Schools Inquiry Commission, and stated that the endowment at that time amounted to £28 a year, but when the ruinous leases had run out

[5] Weaver, *Wells Wills* (Somers. Rec. Soc. xxi), 157.

[6] *Char. Com. Rep.* v (1821), 484.
[7] *Sch. Inq. Com.* v, (1820) 484.
[8] *Sch. Inq. Rep.* v, 144.

the income would probably amount to £150. On his arrival in August 1864 there were only 22 boys in the school. The building was clearly inadequate to the needs of a modern school, and the necessity for a change of site was becoming pressing. A memorial had been presented by the inhabitants of Taunton to the Governors and Trustees of the School House and Walbee endowment proposing to give the school a new site and buildings by raising money by offering shares in a limited liability company. This plan created serious difficulties in regard to an old endowed school, but it was nevertheless accepted and soon carried out. A company was formed with Lord Taunton as chairman, and the College School, as it began to be called, was erected. The foundation stone was laid in 1867, and the school was formally opened 5 October 1870. This change was greatly to the advantage of the school. The number of pupils rose to 146, many of the boys gained scholarships at Oxford, and high passes were won in the Indian Civil Service Examination. In 1877, however, Mr. Tuckwell retired, his plans for the school not being acceptable to the council of the shareholders, and immediately afterwards the school went down and was ultimately closed.

Other schools had been opened in Taunton, and the Huish Secondary School was offering an excellent education to the boys of the town at a much cheaper rate. King's College, as it had come to be called, was sold in 1880 at a great loss to the shareholders to Canon Wooddard, and under his system of education there is now an excellent economical school there known as the King's College, carried on under the Rev. E. B. Vincent. It has ceased, however, to be a local school. There are 137 boys in attendance, but they are all boarders, and drawn from homes outside Taunton and generally from the south-west of England.

The governors of Bishop Fox's school building and the Walbee Trustees had naturally been superseded when the School Company started the College School. The schoolmaster and the boys transferred themselves to the new buildings and took with them the picture of Bishop Fox, which has not yet been returned. Immediately after the governors began a lower secondary school, offering a good commercial education to the sons of the tradesmen of the town, and from 1870 to 1875 this was carried on in the old buildings. When, however, the Huish Secondary School was opened in 1874 this lower school was no longer needed, and shortly after it ceased to exist. In 1887 the school buildings were sold to the corporation of Taunton, the municipal authorities binding themselves to preserve in its original features the old school hall of 1522. The domestic buildings to the west were of no antiquarian value, and were pulled down to make room for the present municipal offices.

As far as can be ascertained the following were head masters :

John Bond, M.A., 1560 ; John Price, 1647 ; Edward Allenson, 1662 ; William Harrison, 1671–7 ; William Budsey, 1680 ; Rev. Thomas Jenkins, 1694–1717 ; Rev. James Upton, M.A., 1730–49 ; Rev. James Hurly or Hurley, B.A., 1749–83 ; Rev. Nathaniel Hine, 1784 ; Rev. George Townsend, 1784–96 ; Rev. John Townshend, 1796–1820 ; Rev. Alfred Barker, 1820 ; Robert Crotch, B.A., 1831 ; Rev. William Tuckwell, M.A., 1864–70.

THE FREE GRAMMAR SCHOOL, BRIDGWATER

About the year 1213 a hospital dedicated to St. John the Baptist was founded in Bridgwater by William Bruere for a master or prior and brethren who should maintain 13 infirm persons and offer hospitality to pilgrims.[1] A copy of the foundation charter is preserved to us in the register of Bishop Beckington. Bishop Jocelin of Bath in 1219 confirmed this foundation, and also William Briwere or Bruere's gift of the church of Isle Brewers to the endowment of the hospital.[2] In 1283 Bishop Burnell of Bath and Wells impropriated to it the rectory of Wembdon, and obtained in 1290 from the Bishop of Exeter the impropriation of the rectory of Moorwinstow.[3] These gifts were confirmed in an *inspeximus* charter of Edward II on 7 March 1315.[4]

In 1298 Geoffrey the prior of St. John's bound himself to Bishop William of March, the successor of Bishop Burnell, to maintain from the corporate funds of the hospital 13 poor scholars living within the walls and fit for instruction in grammar (*habiles ad informandum in grammatica*). The rector of the school in the town was also to send seven of his poorest scholars for daily pittances from the kitchen of the hospital, and gruel is especially mentioned.

It is possible that this provision of bursaries or exhibitions was not approved by certain of the townsmen, for in 1325 Bishop Drokensford issued a commission to his Official Principal to sift the rumours which charged the hospital with wronging the wayfarers of the hospitality that was due to them.[5] The result of the inquiry is not recorded. But the scholars must have been continued, as the *Valor Ecclesiasticus* of 1535 records that the rectory of Wembdon was charged with the support of six boys, and the rectory of Moorwinstow with that of eight boys.

[1] Cf. Hemingford, *Chron.* (ed. Hearne), 597.
[2] *Two Chartularies of Bath* (Somers. Rec. Soc. vii) ; Lincoln MSS. no. 105, p. 22.
[3] Cf. *Reg. Bp. Drokensford* (Somers. Rec. Soc. i), 268.
[4] *Cal. Pat.* 1313–17, p. 258.
[5] *Reg. Bp. Drokensford* (Somers. Rec. Soc. i), 240.

On 13 February 1548 the Chantry Commissioners mention three chantries, of our Lady, of St. George, and of the Trinity in the parish church, but no school.[6] They say, however, 'Thenhabitauntes make their most humble peticion to have a free grammer scole erected ther.'

In 1561 Queen Elizabeth leased to certain persons specified the small and great tithes of Bridgwater,[7] subject to a rent-charge of £6 13s. 4d. to a pedagogue or schoolmaster to teach boys and youths there and from neighbouring towns coming to it, and to instruct them in good literature ('Uni pedagogo sive ludimagistro ad pueros et juvenes ibidem et oppidis vicinis adjacentibus et ad illam confluentes erudiendum et bonis literis instruendum'). On 17 July 1592 Henry Attwood obtained confirmation of his appointment by the alderman of Bridgwater as schoolmaster (ludimagister oppidi) from the Dean and Chapter of Wells, acting for the bishop (sede vacante[8]). The lease of the tithes, which had been surrendered or expired, was regranted by James I in 1613[9] to Phillip and Morris, who granted it to the corporation on the same condition. In 1633 Richard Castleman by his will gave £100 'to the Free School of the town of Bridgwater where he was born towards the teaching of poor scholars to be laid out in lands and houses.' Apparently the money was never laid out in land.

Bequests of small sums were made in 1699 by George Crane and Mrs. Brent. On 10 June 1706 the tithes were finally conveyed in fee to the mayor and corporation on condition that they paid yearly to the schoolmaster £6 13s. 4d. The master was to be appointed by the Bishop of Bath and Wells for the time being. On 16 June 1723 John Morgan left by will his manor of Holcombe to the mayor and corporation of Bridgwater to keep one judicious master to teach writing, arithmetic, navigation, and mathematics. No lad was to be sent to the school until he could read his Psalter and had learnt the Church Catechism, and could give a tolerable account of it, and all the boys of this charity were to wear a distinguishing badge or dress. The trustees were to be the mayor, alderman, and capital burgesses, the Archdeacon of Taunton, the vicar of Bridgwater, and the ministers or vicars of Goathurst, Chedzoy, North Petherton, and Spaxton. The estate, however, was charged with a mortgage and other life interests, and the corporation did not enter into possession of it until 1744.

On 29 October 1781 Edward Fackerell left by will certain lands for the education of his grandchildren. In 1826 there were thirty grandchildren receiving instruction. Eventually this property went to the augmentation of the funds of the school.

The school was certainly in existence in 1786, and in 1793 the governors objected to the master appointed by the corporation as not answering to the founder's will, who designed it as a classical school. At that time the school seems to have been used largely as an elementary school, and this was not in accordance with the Morgan benefaction. The controversy between the governors and the corporation continued for many years, till in 1813 the trustees of the Morgan foundation presented a petition in Chancery to compel the corporation to reorganize the school as a grammar school. On 9 May 1814 an agreement was arrived at between the trustees and the corporation, that the latter should pay over £977 balance and the interest on proceeds of various sales of timber belonging to the Holcombe estate, and that a piece of ground should be purchased and a master's house erected on it and a school for 300 boys. The corporation was to nominate boys from the town up to the limit of the original endowment and the master was to be allowed to take other boys at 3d. a week up to the full capacity of the school.

Thus the elementary school became definitely separated from the grammar or secondary school. An acre of land was purchased at the northwest of the town, and a master's house and schoolhouse for the boys of the grammar school were built in 1816.

In 1826 there were 30 boys in the school, who wore a grey uniform, and four of them were taught classics, reading, writing, and arithmetic free.[10]

After a Chancery suit, by a scheme approved by the Master of the Rolls 1 May 1857, the Municipal Charity Trustees, consisting of the vicar and 14 other residents, were given control of the endowments, which only amounted to £29 10s. a year gross without any schoolhouse, the appointment and dismissal of the master being reserved to the bishop. When this grammar school was visited by Mr. C. H. Stanton in 1866, for the Schools Inquiry Commission,[11] it had recently been placed under the Rev. O. R. Wintle, who had one assistant master. It was held in a private house hired for the purpose by the master, with a very small playground, and had then 30 boys, all day boys, paying 10 to 12 guineas a year. The school was classical. Meanwhile Morgan's school contained 130 boys, but having, in 1850, lowered its fees from 1s. to 2d. a week to get a grant from the Education Committee of the Privy Council, all the middle class boys, tradesmen's

---

[6] Somers. Chant. (Somers. Rec. Soc. ii), 57.
[7] Char. Com. Rep. xv, 424.
[8] Hist. MSS. Com. Rep., x, App. pt. iii, 246.
[9] Cf. Carlisle, End. Gram. Sch. ii, 400.

[10] Char. Com. Rep. xv, 82.
[11] Sch. Inq. Rep. xiv, 185.

sons and the like, for whom it was evidently intended, had left and had been replaced by children of the working classes. These then paid 4*d*. a week, except the 30 foundationers who paid nothing, and received a purely elementary education.

By a scheme made by the Endowed Schools Commissioners under the Endowed Schools Act, 1869, approved by Queen Victoria in Council, 1871, this school was made what would now be called a secondary school.

Under this scheme of 1871 for Dr. Morgan's school and of 1888 for King James's exhibition and scholarship endowment the school is carried on in connexion with the Board of Education Regulations for secondary schools, and under the supervision of the County Council as the local education authority. The buildings have been rearranged and largely increased for the purpose of the development of instruction in science and manual work, and the cost has been chiefly defrayed by grants from the County Education Committee, which, as well as the Bristol University College, is now adequately represented on the board of governors.

The Rev. William Edgar Catlow is head master. He was educated for an elementary teacher at the Borough Road Training College, and took B.A. and M.A. degrees in London University while a master at Alleyn's School (the lower school), Dulwich. He was appointed to Bridgwater in 1900. There are 100 boys in the school, all, but nine, day boys, paying fees of 4 to 6 guineas a year. The standard aimed at is that of the Oxford Local Examinations.

BRUTON GRAMMAR SCHOOL

The beginning of the free grammar school at Bruton is generally assigned to the year 1519, when an extant deed of endowment was executed. But there are indications of the existence of a school many years before. On 30 October 1417[1] Richard Bruton, Canon of Wells, in his will gave 'To Master Roger, master of Bruton, 20*s*.' It is difficult to see who could be meant by a master of Bruton except a schoolmaster. The bequest is immediately followed by one to the chaplain of the parish; which looks as if the 'master' was a cleric. However that may be, in the will[2] of Simon Greene of Bruton, merchant, 26 March 1506–7, there is clear indication of a school. He bequeathed to each chaplain present on the day of his burial 6*d*. and to each scholar 1*d*. and to each chaplain present at 'exequies' and mass on the 30th day after his death 6*d*. and to each scholar and poor person there present 1*d*. It is to be noticed that one of the two overseers of the will, which was proved

22 October 1509, was John Fitz James, senior, of Redlynch, the father of one of the donors under the deed of 1519. Even more direct evidence of the existence of a school is given by will of William Bailey, otherwise called Rawlyns of Wareham, 8 November 1515. He gave to 'William Chyke, son of Robert Chyke, my godson, to his marriage £20. To Robert Chyke, 26*s*. 8*d*. to helpe paye for the sayd William Chyke is table, and my wyfe to deliver hym home to his father, for at Bruton is a free scole.' It may be that the two references to scholars and the free school in 1507 and 1515 may be explained by the fact that the donors of 1519 were already maintaining the school, which they afterwards endowed, as a voluntary 'benevolence.' The prime donor at Bruton was Richard Fitz James, Canon and Chancellor of Wells, who became Bishop of London in 1506, and may have imitated Wykeham, as he probably inspired his dean, John Colet, to imitate him in re-endowing St. Paul's School. With Bishop Fitz James were joined in the endowment of Bruton School his nephew John Fitz James of Redlynch, presumably the son of the John Fitz James of Redlynch called senior in Greene's will, afterwards Lord Chief Justice of England, and Doctor John Edmundes, a native of Bruton who had been a canon of Wells, and became in 1527 Chancellor of St. Paul's, London.

The endowment deed,[3] still in possession of the governing body of the school, was made 29 September 1519. It is an indenture in four parts made between Richard Bishop of London, John Fitz James, John Edmundes, doctor of divinity, of the first part and Richard (Whiting) Abbot of Glastonbury of the second part, Richard Pers, Prior of Witham Charterhouse, of the third part, and William Gilberd, Abbot of Bruton, of the fourth part. The priory of Augustinian canons of Bruton had only in 1510 been elevated to the rank of an abbey and Gilberd was the first abbot. The three gave in trust to the Abbot of Bruton the manor of Blynfield near Shaftesbury, the lands which John Fitz James had lately purchased in Warminster and a tenement in Bruton, where John Edmundes' father had lately dwelt. The manor of Blynfield was subject to the life interest of Joan, widow of John Crukern, gent., after the decease of whom the abbot was to pay 'yerely for ever to the Scolemaster of Brewton for the time beyng,' £10. It was expressly provided that during the life of any of the donors the abbot and his successors 'ne . . . shall putte out, ne putte in and admytte ne chaunge any scholemaister to the said rowme,' but the donors 'shall hav the whole ordryng of the said Scolemaster and Scoole.' Afterwards the abbot must

---

[1] *Somers. Wills*, i, 87 (39 Marche).
[2] Ibid. ii, 98, from P.C.C. 21 Bennett.

[3] *Somers. and Dorset N. and Q.* iii, 241, where the whole indenture is printed.

make an appointment within eight weeks of a vacancy or pay a fine of 40*s.* ; and the appointment was to pass to the heirs of John Fitz James, whom failing, to the Abbot of Glastonbury and the Prior of Charterhouse in succession. The Abbot of Bruton on his part, in consideration of part of the grant of Dr. Edmundes' tenement, covenanted to build within ten years a schoolhouse and a house for the schoolmaster with all other necessary buildings on the site of the tenement in Bruton called William Carpenter's house, occupied by Davy Howell, and to repair it in future. The abbot was not to 'putte oute any Scolemaster' without the assent of the Abbot of Glastonbury and the Prior of Charterhouse. He was expressly forbidden to put the master 'to any maner busoignez [business]' which should hinder him 'fro teachyng of his scolers or kepyng of the said scoole' except to bear witness for the monastery. The school was to be continually carried on in the said schoolhouse except in the times of imminent and contagious sickness, when the schoolmaster might keep his school in some place 'of clene aier' near to Bruton. The abbot and canons covenanted to take 'unto their religion and prefer to the same, parte of such able scholers in vertue and kunnyng after the discrecion of the same abbot or his successors as shall fro tyme to tyme be brought up in the same scoole.'

The school was to be emphatically a free grammar school, free from tuition fees, and to teach grammar, not elementary subjects.

And the said Scolemaster shall teache his scolers Gramer after the gode newe Fourme used in Magdalene College in Oxford or in the scoole at Pawles in London or after such gode fourme as for the tyme shall be moost used. Also the said maister for the tyme beyng shall frely teche all scolers of men children as to hym shall resorte for lernyng and noon other, indifferently after their capacites as well the poore mannes child as the riche nothyng exigyng of any of them or of the frendes of any of theym for his laboure, but if any reward be freely and liberally offered unto the same scolemaster yt shall be lawful for hym to take the same. And the said maister shall not teche his scolers song nor other petite lernynge, as the Crosse Rowe, redyng of the mateyns or of the psalter, or such other small thyngs, nother redyng of English, but such as shall concerne lernynge of gramer. For the Founders of the saide scole intend with our Lordes mercy oonly to have the grammer of latyn tongue so sufficiently taught that the scolers of the same profityng and provyng shall in tymes to come forever be after their capacities perfight latyn men.

The hours were to be such 'as in other gode scooles is accustomed.' The master was not to give a holiday in any week when there was a holy day, at any person's request. Such power of granting 'lusum, remedium or campos be by the especial licence of the abbot.' The school was opened and closed daily with a special office set out which varied slightly as the master was

'a priest, and if he be no prest but a layman.' On leaving school in the afternoon they were to say *De profundis* and pray for the souls of the benefactors and founders of the school. In the matter of the correction of the boys the master is to be discreet, and he is not to 'stryke any of his scolers, beyng obedient, upon the hedde ne on the face with rodde ne with palmes.'

The placing the school in the guardianship of the abbey, which was meant for its preservation, brought it to a speedy end. The canons surrendered this monastery on 1 April 1539 into the hands of Dr. John Tregonwell, the royal commissioner.[4] According to the rule which prevailed in cases of grammar schools or of almshouses which were under the government of monasteries, though in fact the monasteries were only trustees, the endowments were regarded as part of the possessions of the monasteries, and the institutions as dissolved with them. The rule was applied here, as it is so expressly stated in the subsequent charter of refoundation by Edward VI. But the people of Bruton seem to have thought that the school escaped the fate of the abbey only to become the subject of a corrupt bargain between the then master and the Crown, by which on surrender of the lands the master got a pension from the Crown which enabled him to get quit of his duties and either do nothing or seek employment elsewhere, and in this case the use of the house and garden rent free. The truth is that the income-producing endowment, having been by some later deeds not now forthcoming vested in the abbot of the abbey, was treated as surrendered with the abbey. But the schoolhouse having been granted by the abbot to the master was not so vested and was surrendered by him separately. A remarkable memorandum appended by the Chantry Commissioners of Edward VI to their account of 'Brewton'[5] sets out the inhabitants' case.

Memorandum : Thenhabitaunts of the towne of Brewton aforesaide, the 21st. day of Aprill, anno regno regis Edwardi VIti. 2do. made humble request unto the commyssioners in maner and forme following. Wher ther was within the foresaide towne a faire Scolehouse for a free grammer Scole, newly buylded, erected and made [with] landes and tenementes to the yerely value of £12, for the vertuouse educacion and teaching of the yewthe, as well of the saide towne of Brewton as of the whole contrie, nowe decayed by reason that Heughe Sherwoode, late Scolemaster ther, surrendered the saide landes into the Kinges Majesties handes 6 or 7 yeres nowe past [i.e. *circa* 1541], who, indevoring hymself rather to lyve licentiously at will then to travaile in good educacion of yewthe, according to the godly fundacion of the saide Scole, founde the meanes by his saide surrender to obtayne by Decre out of the Courte of augmentacions of the Revenues of the Kinges Majesties Crowne for terme of his lyffe one Annuytie or pencion of £5, and the

---

[4] *Dep. Keeper's Rep.* viii, App. ii, 12.
[5] Chant. Cert. 42, no. 172.

forsaide Scolehouse, with a gardeyn and a close of lande therunto adjoynyng, contaynyng by estimacion 4 acres, lying in Brewton aforesaide, discharged also thereby of any further free teaching or keeping of Scole ther, to the great Decaye as well of vertuous bringing uppe of yewthe of the saide shire in all good lernyng, as also of thenhabitaunts of the Kinges saide town of Brewton, of great relief that came thereby.

Wherfore the saide inhabitaunts made mooste humble sute unto the Kinges Majestie that yt may please his highness, of his bounteouse liberalitie, to restore the saide Scolehouse, landes and tenementes, to the use, godly purpose and intent of the fundacion of the foresaide Byssop, John FitzJames, and John Edmondes.

The petition or a later one to the same effect was successful. About two years afterwards, by letters patent 1 May 1550, Bruton was re-founded as one of the earliest of the free grammar schools so-called of Edward VI. The patent recites that the two Fitz James and Edmundes 'intending to . . . found a Free Grammar School' had 'caused to be newly built a certain house in Bruton aforesaid . . . commonly called the School House to which on the north there adjoined an acre of land'—apparently bought from the abbot for the purpose—and sets out shortly the endowment deed. It then recites that 'the Grammar School was continued for some years . . . until the dissolution and surrender of the monastery . . . by reason of which . . . the manor and lands *except the said School House and the said acre of land thereto adjoining* came into the hands of' Henry VIII and 'remained and is still in our hands and the said school is now discontinued to the grievous loss of our subjects of the said town . . . and of other neighbouring towns,' so that it never was for Bruton boys only. Upon the petition of the inhabitants and 'of a great many others of our subjects of the whole neighbouring country there to us lately made' the king willed 'newly to found' the said school. The charter therefore directed that there should be a school 'which shall be called the Free Grammar School of King Edward the Sixth' of 'one master or instructor.' Twelve of the more discreet inhabitants of the town and parish of Bruton were incorporated as governors and named in the charter, headed by William Northe and Stephen Cheke. The manor of Blynfield and the lands of the old school, which are described as 'late parcel of the monastery,' were regranted and also the schoolhouse and the acre of land 'between the same house and the rivulet there called the Brewe,' the whole being worth, excluding the house, £11 5s. As if to demonstrate that by calling the school a free grammar school was meant only that it should be free from fees, as expressed in the original foundation, and not free from ecclesiastical jurisdiction, as has been wildly alleged, the power of making

statutes conferred on the governors was to be exercised only 'with the advice of the Bishop of Bath and Wells for the time being.' The charter concluded with licence in mortmain to acquire more lands up to the value of £12 a year. The property granted by the charter, about 160 acres in Shaftesbury and Stour Provost in Dorset, produced in 1818[6] about £250 a year, and the lands in Warminster about £15 a year more. Lands in South Brewham bought in 1727 brought in £100 a year, making the total some £345 a year. Hugh Sherwood still retained his pension of £5 and appears on Cardinal Pole's pension list of 24 February 1555–6.

The governors resorted to the example they had been referred to in the original endowment deed, Magdalen College School, for a new master. This is learnt from the registers of Magdalen College,[7] which record that John Slade, fellow of the college in 1544 and a Somerset boy, then master of the school, on 6 September 1550 received leave of absence from the college 'for half a year' to go and open the grammar school for the boys of Bruton (profecturo ad aperiendum ludum grammaticalem pueris Brutonie). He was probably the same person as John Slade, schoolmaster, executed at Winchester 30 October 1583 for denying the royal supremacy.

The first master on the new foundation in the Bruton records[8] is Griffith Williams, who was paid for the year 1558–9. In 1560 he had been succeeded by William Rawston or Rawson, who took his B.A. degree at Oxford in 1546, and was a fellow of University College in 1551. He held the mastership for twenty-five years, resigning on a pension of four marks (£2 13s. 4d.) and was buried at Bruton 11 October 1603. Another fellow of an Oxford college followed, so we may conclude that the school was one of high status. This was John Langhorne, who matriculated at Queen's College in 1573 and was elected fellow there 11 November 1579. He was master of the boys at Queen's College in 1581–2. He held the mastership for twenty-two years, resigning 27 September 1607, being instituted to the rectory of Corton Denham in February 1607–8, and dying in 1620. In Walter Chard the governors resorted again to Magdalen College, where he took his B.A. degree 28 February 1605–6. After having held office from 1607 to 1613 he seems to have retired, for we find a Mr. Beard in 1613–16, and then [Thomas] Whitehead, who went on to Repton, and W. Chard resumed the place in 1618, and died in office and was buried as 'the scholemaster'

[6] Carlisle, *End. Gram. Sch.* ii, 481.
[7] Bloxam, *Magd. Coll. Reg.* iii, 106, quoted in 'Head Masters of Bruton School,' *Somers. and Dorset N. and Q.* v, 103.
[8] The first account book of the governors begins 17 Nov. 1558.

5 June 1636. Roger Nicholles, 24 June 1636, was of Exeter College, Oxford, B.A. 5 May 1636. He left in 1640, perhaps to join in the Civil War, as after the Restoration one of his name was Canon of Wells, and on 20 December 1660 was made rector of Mapperton.

John Randall of Shepton, Somerset, of Lincoln College, Oxford, matriculated 1631, B.A. 23 April 1635, seems to have held office for forty years. He was in 1668 the minister ' or Incumbent of Bruton,' in which capacity he preached a funeral sermon on Viscount Fitzhardinge, and from 25 September 1673 held the rectory of Yarlington.

One Harding is said to have filled the gap in 1680. In 1681 Mr. ' Joinna '(or Jonah) Webb of St. Alban Hall and Wadham College had £2 3s. 10d. paid for his licence from the bishop to teach, and held office to 1700, when he died. The next master, Samuel Hill of Lincoln College and St. Mary Hall, had held three rectories before his appointment, and in 1705 become Archdeacon of Wells.

Two Goldesboroughs—Nicholas, 1708–38, and his son John, 1738–68—followed. The latter combined the mastership with the benefice of Bruton from 1754. He was buried 31 December 1758. Edward Michell of Exeter College came from Kingsbridge School, Devon, in 1769, and spent thirty years here, combining the school with the living of Witham. William Cosens of St. Mary Hall came 1 October 1799, being already vicar of Ipplepen, which he gave up to become incumbent of Bruton in 1801.

By statutes made in 1809 and approved by the bishop, the master's salary was fixed at £100 a year only, the bulk of the endowment going to establish five exhibitions of £40 a year each at the Universities. The master was by these statutes forbidden to hold any curacy or the mastership of Sexey's hospital. The then master, the Rev. William Cosens, who had been appointed in 1799, was in fact perpetual curate or incumbent of Bruton. He had only 12 boys in the school, 11 free boys and one boarder. He held office till 1826. Half a century later, an interval of comparative success ensued under Mr. J. C. Hoskyns-Abrahall, under whom the numbers rose to 60. But owing to his refusing boarders in his later years the school sank to 10, and a scheme of the Court of Chancery was invoked and sanctioned 30 May 1859 to pension him off with £80 a year.

The Rev. S. Middleton by his energy made the school again successful, so that when visited on behalf of the Endowed Schools Commissioners in 1865 it had 43 boys, of whom 19 were day boys, paying 4 guineas a year, while boarders paid about £50. The first and second classes were said to show a fair knowledge of Greek, Latin, and English ; while French was well attended to, but mathematics weak.

In 1878 the Sexey Almshouses Trustees, out of their surplus funds, and the Somerset Technical Education Committee gave a grant towards the building of a laboratory. There are at present 69 boys in the school, of whom 60 are boarders, under Mr. David Evans Norton, himself an old Bruton boy, and afterwards an exhibitioner at Keble College, Oxford, where he obtained a second class in the Final School in classics. He was an assistant master at Brighton College when appointed, in succession to his father, head master at Bruton in 1890. There are six assistant masters.

The following list of head masters was drawn up by the Rev. F. W. Weaver, M.A., one of the governors of Bruton School :—

1539, Hugh Sherwood ; 1550, John Slade, M.A. ; 1559, Griffith Williams, B.C.L. ; 1560, William Rawston, M.A. ; 1585, John Langhorne, M.A. ; 1607, Walter Chard ; 1613, Mr. Beard ; 1616, Thomas Whitehead ; 1618, Walter Chard, B.A. ; 1636, Roger Nicholles, B.A. ; 1640, John Randall, B.A. ; 1680, Mr. Harding ; 1681, Jonah Webb, M.A. ; 1700, Samuel Hill, M.A. ; 1708, Nicholas Goldesborough ; 1738, John Goldesborough, M.A. ; 1769, Edward Michell, B.A. ; 1799, William Cosens ; 1826, Llewelyn Lewellin, M.A. ; 1826, John Charles James Hoskyns-Abrahall, M.A. ; 1864, Shotto Middleton, M.A. ; 1869, Arthur Daniel Gill, M.A. ; 1873, David Evans Norton, M.A. ; 1890, David Evans Norton, M.A.

THE FREE GRAMMAR SCHOOL, ILMINSTER

The property which forms the endowment of this school was a portion of that of one of the chantries of the parish church. In 1440 Robert Laidamis, rector of St. Martin's, Wareham, writing to his friend William Myllys, a merchant living at Rouen, refers to a school at Ilminster, which was a boarding school.[1] ' Worshypfulle and reverent frend and mayster, Y recommande me to youe wyth alle my herte, desyrynge to here and to knowe of youre wellfare by letter how hyt stondyth wyth youe. Doynge youe to onderstond that ye and Y where scoll-felows sumtyme at Hylmyster, ye beynge at borde atte Mose ys house, the wyche he recomaunde me to youe.' There is another letter to William Myllys from his mother Isabella Milles of Martock, which mentions several brothers and sisters. On the dissolution of the chantries in 1548[2] Henry Kelway of Berry Pomeroy and William Leonard, merchant of Taunton, bought from the Crown (1) one house and the building which Robert Sprete lately chaplain of the fraternity of the Holy Cross

[1] *Wars of Engl. in France* (Rolls Ser.), ii (1), 307.
[2] Minutes of Proceedings of Feoffees of Ilminster School Charity.

and John Rippe had built at their own cost, together with a cottage and a curtilage; (2) a building known as Mody's tenement at Winterhay; and (3) Rippe's Mill at Horton. This was then sold in 1549 to Humphrey Walrond of Sea and Henry Greynfelde of Sea for £126, and the purchasers on 3 June 1549 conveyed this to a body of trustees, the first trustees of the school property, and the Patent Roll which sanctions it confirms the endowment for the purpose of the virtuous education of youth in literature and godly learning. The trustees were 'to provide and get one honest and discreet person of good behaviour, name and fame and conversation who shall freely instruct, teach and bring up as well in all godly knowledge as in other manner of learning all such children and youth as shall be brought to him to the same intent and purpose.' These school trustees, John Balche, John Sydenham and others, were to assign to this schoolmaster one tenement called the Cross house, for his residence. There were to be yearly meetings of the trustees on the first Sunday in October, when a bailiff was to be chosen to look after the estates for the ensuing year. The bailiff out of the revenues of the endowment was to keep in repair the Cross house where the master lived and the adjacent building called Battyn's house, where the school was held, which was close to the church. The schoolhouse has the date 1584 upon it, suggesting some alterations in the school in that year. Mody's tenement and Rippe's Mill were let on lease. From time to time the trustees out of the price received for the renewed leases purchased other freeholds for the increase of the endowment. The proceedings of the trustees have all been recorded in a minute book of which the first heading is 'The account of the lands purchased for the School in Ilminster.'[3] The first master is referred to as Sir Robert in 1558. Now the chantry priest attached to the chantry of the Holy Cross in the parish church of Ilminster was Robert Olyver, and he received a pension of £5 a year on its abolition.[4] In 1548 he was forty years of age and is described as of honest conversation.[5] He had been wont to receive £6 a year and three-fourths towards the repair of his house. It is true that the chaplain who is said to have built the Cross house is called Robert Sprete, but as there is no mention of two chaplains attached to the chantry; and as the commissioners report Robert Olyver as the chaplain, there seems to be little doubt not only that Robert Sprete and Robert Olyver are one and the same man, but also that Sir Robert, the first schoolmaster of the revised school, was the chantry priest who lived on in the Cross house and continued his work of teaching the boys of the town.[6] His stipend

was £7 as schoolmaster. He died probably in 1574, for in that year the school account book records that Mr. Walrond rode to Oxford in search of a new schoolmaster. On 29 September 1600 the trustees purchased the free chapel at Yeovilton and a parcel of land belonging to it known as Bridghampton in Yeovilton. On 1 October 1609 they purchased from the Walronds for 1,000 marks the manor of Sandwich near Swanage in Dorset, and in 1620 we find them acquiring a house in Taunton. During the 17th century the minutes of the trustees' proceedings record one uniform succession of purchases. In 1763 we have a survey of the estates of the charity. This is repeated on 29 December 1802 and given in evidence of the increased value of the foundation. There was, the survey records, a messuage or tenement on the north side of the churchyard called the schoolhouse which was supposed to be the house known formerly as the Cross house. The Rev. J. H. Mules was the master at the time of this later survey. Another house adjacent to this was called Withyman's, and a building had been erected there called the New Room. The estates were described as—

Lands in Ilminster	.	.	.	.	7	acres
„ „ Sandwich	.	.	.	.	318	„
„ „ Stewley in Isle Abbots	.		.		48	„
„ „ Yeovilton	.	.	.	.	53½	„
„ „ Donyatt	.	.	.	.	14½	„
„ „ Winsham	.	.	.	.	168	„
„ „ Ashill	.	.	.	.	29	„
„ „ Cricket Malherbie	.	.	.	50¾	„
„ „ Cudworth	.	.	.	.	18	„

and thus are shown to comprise more than 708 acres. Soon afterwards the house at Taunton and two at Donyatt and 27 acres at Cudworth, Yeovilton, and Donyatt were sold to redeem the land tax on the other estates. In 1826 the value of the charity is entered as £518 a year.

The minutes of the trustees are full of interesting local notices.[7] On the first Sunday in October 1635, when they had their yearly meeting, the feoffees record, 'it is now the Sabbath day and wanting time to finish our account it is agreed by those whose names are underwritten to meet again on Tuesday. G. Speke, George Balche, Richard Webbe.' In 1655 the trustees[8] appointed a writing master, and we find them making grants for what was certainly elementary education, and in 1709 payments were made for the instruction of 40 poor children of Ilminster in reading, writing, and arithmetic. In 1765 a permanent master for this elementary work was appointed, and soon after a dame's school was started at Horton on the road to Broadway Hill. The elementary school was in the Court Barton, and gave way to the

---

[3] Street, *The Mynster on the Ile*, 307.
[4] Pole, Pension List, Q.R. Misc. Bks. no. 32
[5] *Somers. Chant.* (Somers. Rec. Soc. ii), 3.
[6] Feoffees' Minute Bk.

[7] Street, op. cit. 308, 309.
[8] *Somers. Arch. Soc. Proc.* xiii, 40.

SCHOOLS

Ditton Street Board School. In this year, 1765, the signature of a future Prime Minister appears among the trustees as 'North.'

In 1826 the Rev. J. Allen was the head master.[9] He had 9 free boys and 40 private pupils who boarded in his house, and the trustees told the commissioners that the master was always in holy orders in accordance with the terms of the charity which laid down that the boys should be brought up in all godly knowledge. There were twenty trustees at the time, and the boys were eligible to compete for the Owston exhibition at Oxford. During the years 1822 to 1855, in which the Rev. John Allen was the head master, the school attained considerable fame, and among his pupils were Henry Alford, afterwards Dean of Canterbury, and Edward Thring, afterwards head master of Uppingham, who, however, used it as a good many others did, as a preparatory school for Eton.

In 1860 the school became the subject of 'a leading case' on the law of schools, *Baker* v. *Lee*, 8 H.L. 495. A scheme was being preferred in Chancery and the question was raised whether Dissenters were elegible as governors. The Master of the Rolls, Lord Romilly, thought that they should not be excluded, two Lords Justices opposed him, and they were upheld by the House of Lords. This decision was probably one of the contributing causes to the passing of the Endowed Schools Act, 1869. Meanwhile under the scheme, besides the grammar school, a so-called commercial school, which was 'very elementary, not much above that of a National school,' had been set up, contained about 90 free boys, and a few who not being resident in the parish paid 3 guineas a year. In the grammar school were 42 boys, 11 of whom were boarders paying 55 guineas a year, and 26 free boys. The upper boys had advanced as far as Greek grammar and Horace, and two had gone to Oxford in seven years. The Rev. G. T. Gowring was master.

A new scheme was prepared by the Endowed Schools Commissioners in 1873 which soon after became law. It reversed the decision of the House of Lords and removed all religious disabilities in connexion with the governing body. It was proposed to erect a high school for girls in Ilminster, but the cost of the effort seemed too great and the governors decided to erect new and larger buildings on the south side of the church on land belonging to the foundation for the boys, and in 1879 a secondary school for girls was started in the old boys' schoolhouse on the north side of the church.

The head masters of Ilminster School are as follows :—[10]

1629, Rev. Nathaniel Conduit, M.A.; 1633, William Baker; 1645, John Mecham; 1649, Nathaniel Conduit; 1658, James Pytt; 1662, Owen Price; 1665, John Goodenough, B.A.; 1670, John Hunt, M.A.; 1677, William Hunt, M.A.; 1688, Rev. William Pritchard, B.A.; 1688, Edward Gatchell; 1704, Rev. James Upton; 1722, Rev. Sydenham Vere, B.A.; 1744, Rev. Thomas Davis; 1767, Rev. Septimus Collison, rector of West Dowlish and Dowlish Wake; 1780, Rev. R. Stubbs, D.D.;[11] Rev. Charles Toogood; 1791, Rev. John Hawkes Mules, M.A.; 1822, Rev. John Allen, M.A.; 1855, Rev. George Masters Gould; 1859, Rev. George J. Gowring, M.A.; 1874, Rev. William John Woodward, M.A.; 1891, Robert John William Davidson, B.A.

THE FREE SCHOOL, CREWKERNE

The school at Crewkerne seems to have been founded by John Combe, Canon of Exeter.[1] Combe was on 14th March 1472 instituted vicar of the parish church of St. Bartholomew, Crewkerne.[2] In 1486 he was made treasurer of the cathedral church of Exeter, and in 1488 he became precentor.[3] In 1496 he resigned Crewkerne and died some short time before 15 April 1499.[4] By deed of 7 January 1499, which has been missing since 1702, he gave to feoffees certain lands in Merriott and Crewkerne. The earliest deed of enfeoffment is dated 1588, and it states that the endowment was for a free grammar school and one schoolmaster, and that the endowment was to go to the repair of the roads and highways of the town if the trustees failed to carry on the school. The earliest account book is dated 1609.

In 1530 Leland describes the school :[5] 'the church standeth on the hylle, and by it is a gramer scole endowed with lands for an annual stipend.' In 1548 the certificate[6] of the Chantry Commissioners[7] says under 'Crukerne': 'The Free School ther sometyms callyd the Chauntrie of the Trinitie ther, is yerly worth in landes' £9 gross, and 'clere' £8 1s. 3d. The endowment consisted of at least seven cottages, in addition to other tenements and some 60 acres of land at Pilsdon in Dorset, Maiden Newton, Comb St. Reine, and Crewkerne.[8] Sir Hugh Paulet and Mr. Henry Cricke are said to have certain copyhold lands of the manor of

[11] Appointment not entered between 1780 and 1791.
[1] MSS. *penes* Governors of the Crewkerne Grammar School.
[2] Wells Epis. Reg. Stillington, fol. 34.
[3] Ibid. Redman, quoted by Le Neve, *Fasti*, i, 411.
[4] Wells Epis. Reg. King, fol. 1.
[5] Leland, *Itin.* (ed. Hearne), ii, 93.
[6] Chant. Cert. 42.
[7] *Somers. Chant.* (Somers. Rec. Soc. ii), 7.
[8] Ibid. 178.

[9] *Char. Com. Rep.* xv, 331.
[10] Street, *The Mynster on the Ile,* 312.

Crewkerne 'to the use of the Trynite and mayntenaunce of the said scole.' The manor had fallen into the hands of the Crown on the attainder and execution of the Marquess of Exeter in 1538. The lands were worth £2 a year in addition, apparently, to the tenements previously mentioned. The commissioners say the incumbent 'John Byrde, Scole Master ther, a man of honest conversacyon well lerned and of goodly judgement, dothe moche good in the countrie in vertuouse bringing uppe and teaching of children having at this present six or seven score (120 to 140) Scolers, receyved the whole proffect for his wages. And the inhabitaunts ther be most humble suters to have the said ffree scole contynued with augmentacyon of the saide Scole Master his lyving.'

On this certificate a warrant was issued [9] by the commissioners appointed under the Chantries Act for the purpose of the continuance of the school. 'Forasmuche as it apperithe . . that a grammer scole hathe been continuallie kepte in Crukerne with the revenues of the late chauntries of the Trynytie in Crukerne aforesaid and that the scolemaster ther hath had for his stipend and wages yerely £8 6s. 8d. we therefore . . . have assigned and appointed that the said scole in Crukerne aforesaid shall contynue and that John Birde, scolemaster there, shall have and enjoy the rome of scolemaster ther and shall have for his wages yerely, £8 6s. 8d.'

On 20 January 1626 the Rev. William Owsley or Ouseley gave £20 out of his manor of Priston for exhibitions for four scholars at Oxford to be nominated by the rectors of Shepton Beauchamp, Puckington, and Cheddington and the nominee of the family of Owsley.[10]

From time to time various changes have been made in the governing body of the school and apparently on their own determination. In 1699 all the feoffees were to be chosen from those who lived in the town. On 25 February 1703 all the estates were transferred to twenty-three feoffees, and in 1823 these had been reduced to twenty. The earliest enfeoffment deeds possessed by the trustees are 22 January 1577, 24 December 1589, 6 April 1630, 12 April 1667, 25 August 1675, and 12 November 1717.

In 1636 the feoffees were engaged in enlarging the schoolhouse. In 1808, owing probably to the inclosure of some of the common fields, the lands of the chantry consisted of about ninety-three acres.

At this time the Rev. J. Allen was the schoolmaster.[11] He had been appointed in 1802 in place of the Rev. Richard Abraham, who himself

in 1792 had succeeded the Rev. Dr. Hordly Ashe, afterwards vicar of Crewkerne. The school was then described as at the extremity of the churchyard, and consisted of a room capacious enough to hold one hundred boys. The boys of Crewkerne were received free and other boys within the limits of a footwalk round Crewkerne were admitted. The master's house was rebuilt in 1827, under a scheme of the Court of Chancery.

There were about that time 30 boys on the foundation who were taught Latin, Greek and English free and who paid for their instruction in writing and arithmetic, and six boarders. The income of the school from endowments was estimated at £318.

When visited in 1866 by Mr. C. H. Stanton[12] the Rev. Charles Penny, D.D., was head master, the Rev. Douglas Mackenzie usher, and there were two other assistant masters. There were 60 boys, of whom 24 were boarders and 36 day boys, the latter if coming from within 6 miles of Crewkerne paying only £4 a year, others £6 a year, a distinction for which there was no warrant in the foundation; and which was a reduction from £8 a year charged to all by the Chancery scheme.

By a scheme approved by the Queen in Council of 21 July 1876, made under the Endowed Schools Acts, a new governing body of fifteen was created.

In 1876 new buildings were erected at Mount Pleasant at a cost of £10,000.[13] Provision was then made for 70 boarders and 60 day boys, and the new school was opened 18 January 1882. It has never, however, been full. The venture of the governors was not successful, and has seriously crippled the revenues of the school. Their ambition to turn the foundation from a local grammar school into a public school drawing the majority of its pupils from a distance has not been accomplished.

In 1883 [14] the late Major Sparkes purchased the old grammar school and handed it back to the governors as the foundation of the scholarships in Ancient and Modern History, the scholars to be known as the Sparkes' scholars.

The school, owing to the large expenditure of capital on the new buildings, fared badly under the educational development of the last decade of the last century. It has since been greatly assisted by the County Education Authority and has reverted to the original plan of a local school, and the curriculum has been very much altered, science and manual work taking their place among literary subjects. A new scheme was drawn up and approved by the Council of Education in 1899, and the governing body has been made representative of the county and the

[9] Leach, *Engl. Schools at the Reformation*, 142, from P.R.O. Schools Continuance Warrant, 4.

[10] School Records *penes* Governors of the School.

[11] *Char. Com. Rep.* ix, 690.

[12] *Sch. Inq. Com.* xiv, 201.

[13] Min. Bks. of the Governors.

[14] Ibid.

454

neighbourhood of Crewkerne. The income had fallen to £190 a year, and the lands to 74 acres. Good progress has been made, however, under the new conditions, and the maintenance grants of the Local Authority, together with the Government grants to secondary schools, have enabled the governors to make the school once more efficient and successful.

THE GRAMMAR SCHOOL, MELLS

There was a pre-Reformation grammar school at Mells, since in 1524 John Robyns[1] of Mells left to 'the scolemaister of Mells 10s.,' and to ' 10 pour scolers of the gramer scole of Mells 3s. 4d. each.' The date at which this school came to an end is unknown, but as late as 1594–5 we hear of the Church House in Mells as usable or in use as a school, and of the upper room therein as a lodging for the school-master.[2]

THE FREE GRAMMAR SCHOOL, FROME

Nothing is known of the foundation of this school, and little evidence exists besides a yearly sum of £5 13s. 4d. paid by the Treasury and the entries in the vestry book of the parish church for the supply of desks and other furniture for the school.[3] There were three chantry chapels annexed to the parish church, those of our Lady, of St. Nicholas and of St. Andrew, with priests endowed for each. It is possible, therefore, that one of these chantry priests may have spent his leisure time in teaching boys. The Crown grant was in respect of some endowments confiscated in 1548. A report[4] by the Bishop of Bath and Wells, 3 November, 1570, states that £6 had been paid for some years by the receivers of the Crown lands in the county to Hugh Kirk, M.A., partly for serving the cure of souls, partly for diligent teaching of scholars there free, also that he was able and fit and the place suitable, especially as there was no other school near. It was stated before the Commissioners of Inquiry into Charities in 1819 that lands at Rodden and at Trudox Hill were charged with payments to the school, and a tenant at the latter place acknowledged he had made payments to a former master. The commissioners in their report of 1820 ventured to think that payments were charged on different estates for the school, the

owners of which had the right to nominate scholars thereto. In 1798 the school building consisted of one large room and a court which was subsequently covered in to form an ante-room to the school. The Rev. Mr. Pocock had been the master at the end of the 18th century and died in 1803, and the school was started again in 1819 under the Rev. W. M. H. Williams, who is said to have had some 50 boarders. On his retirement he remained in receipt of the Crown payment until 1866. There was no school in 1867. The school to-day is carried on as a private one and cannot be reckoned among the public grammar schools of the county. The infant school of the parish of St. John the Baptist is partly on the site of the original schoolroom, all traces of which have disappeared.

THE GRAMMAR SCHOOL, YEOVIL

In the certificate of the Chantry Commissioners of 1548 we find the following entry concerning Yeovil—' Memorandum [1]—there is a chapell situate within the churche yarde of Yeovill kevered with lead, contayning by estimacyon nighe one fooder, praysed worthe to be solde £4, which the inhabitauntes there desire to have for a scolehouse. The town is a great market towne and a thoroughe faire.' It is probable that the town purchased this chapel for the purpose of a school, for in the Churchwardens' Accounts for 1573, which are no longer extant, it was stated that the schoolhouse was in the churchyard and that the building was formerly a chapel and had been converted into a school-house at a cost of £12 13s. 4d., while in 1577 the same Churchwardens' Accounts contained a payment of 4d. for the key for the schoolhouse. Nothing further seems to be known about the school until 1707, when there was a collection and subscription list started, and a legacy was left by Mr. Will. Philips of Preston Plucknett, and a dwelling-house and a few acres of land, a cottage and a garden in Yeovil Marsh were purchased for the purpose of a school.[2]

On 8 August 1718 John Nowes by will gave all his real estate in the parish of Romsey to find £120 a year for the education of 40 boys. In 1719, on the application of the Attorney-General, Jane Nowes, the widow of John Nowes, decided that 20 of these boys should come from Haslebury Plucknett and Alvington and that they should be taught at Yeovil School. On 6 November 1719 Frances Cheeseman by will left the interest of £150 to be paid to Mr. Hibbard the schoolmaster of Yeovil and to such master after him who should be capable to instruct and make young men fit for the universities of Oxford and Cambridge. On

---

[1] Weaver, *Somers. Med. Wills* (Somers. Rec. Soc. xix), 225.
[2] This mention occurs in a covenant of a deed by which Thomas Horner of Mells grants to 19 feoffees for 99 years the almshouse and the church house. (Lease *penes* Sir John Horner).
[3] *Char. Com. Rep.* iii, 335 (1820).
[4] Exch. Spec. Com. (P.R.O.), 12 Eliz. 3231.

[1] Green, *Chant.* (Somers. Rec. Soc. ii), 141.
[2] *Char. Com. Rep.* iv, 325.

20 March 1730 Thomas Cheeseman left £50 to the charity school at Yeovil; and to the Latin school, if any man should be possessed of it, he left £5 a year for the education and right grounding of boys in the Latin tongue. This appears to have been charged on the Horner estate in Dorset.

In 1754 a Mr. Hodges was appointed master of the school, and in 1803 payment of the interest on the Cheeseman legacy ceased because the trustees found that Mr. Hodges was not giving instruction in Latin. It appeared that he was afflicted with gout and had been paralysed, and was really carrying on the school with the help of an usher who was unable to teach Latin. He himself was well qualified, but physically disabled, and in the next year he died.

On 31 March 1805 the school was reopened under the Rev. Thomas Tomkins, and since he was able to give instruction in Latin, the Cheeseman bequest was paid this year.

On 5 January 1806 an information was lodged in the Court of Chancery to determine whether Mr. Tomkins had been properly appointed and to inquire concerning the estates belonging to the various foundations of the school.

In 1820 there were 16 boys of Yeovil educated in the school and one boy was taught Latin. There had been, however, no meeting of the trustees since 1811. The income of the school consisted of £50 in rents, £4 10s. from a rent-charge, and £9 2s. 10d. from dividends. The suit in Chancery begun in 1806 continued until 1842, and from that time the school has been in abeyance. A scheme is now on foot for the transference of the endowments, which are now in the hands of trustees, to the governors of a new secondary school, known as the Kingston School, lately recreated by local enterprise, the corporation of Yeovil, and the Local Education Authority. The scheme, however, under which these endowments are to be administered is as yet only in process of drafting.

THE FREE SCHOOL, LANGPORT EASTOVER

Thomas Gillett of Langport left by will[1] dated 6 December 1675 money to provide for the payment of a schoolmaster to teach the poor children of Langport, and this has been usually reputed the foundation of the school. But as early as 1668 the Corporation Minute Books[2] refer to the school not only as existing, but as even then of some antiquity. In September of that year it is stated that John Doleman had received

J. Bennett and his wife into his house under colour of their keeping 'schole.' Bennett had been appointed as schoolmaster by Mr. R. Hunt, the executor of Gillett's estate, and hence apparently the jealous opposition of the town authorities. The corporation had, it is recorded, procured a schoolmaster for the town, and to encourage such schoolmaster they had been at great charge 'to repayre the anciente schole.' Doleman was therefore ordered to remove the said Bennett and his wife under a penalty of 40s. The Langport Merchants' Gild or Fraternity[3] was in existence and had existed since 1344, and had their chapel of St. Mary, the hanging chapel over the north-east rampart of the town. It is, therefore, possible that this chaplain or chantry priest may have acted as schoolmaster, and the chapel may have served as a schoolhouse, at all events from the dissolution of the chantry.

Gillett's benefaction became the subject of a suit in Chancery, Mr. R. Hunt as executor claiming the appointment of the master, and the corporation refused to recognize his claims.[4] The suit was prolonged from 1686 to 1698 and ended in a compromise, the Court, 12 March 1704–5, adding to the trustees of Gillett's endowment the recorder, the town clerk, and three principal burgesses as representative of the corporation, and directing the benefaction to be laid out in real estate. It was then ordered by the new body of trustees that the school should be a grammar school for boys and that the ordinances drawn up by Mr. R. Hunt for the regulation of the school should be put in force.[5] The schoolmaster was to be over twenty-three years of age and was not to be *either a curate, vicar, or parson*, nor was he to have any cure of souls other than that of his scholars. If at any time he should be instituted to any parsonage or vicarage or become a practitioner in physic, then in six months his salary as master was to be stopped. He was not to receive any stipend for teaching any of the youths of Langport to read and the principles of the Christian religion, but he might demand payment for teaching 'foreigners' or those living outside the town. The master was to go with the boys to the parish church and to be there before the confession had begun, and those of the boys who were able to do it were to take notes each Sunday of the sermon they should hear. The Chancery Court[6] also in 1704–5 ordered that Gillett's bequest should be laid out in real estate, and a farm of 63 acres of land was therefore purchased in the parish of Isle Abbots. It is probable at this time that the corporation gave to the trustees for use as the school the gild chapel of St. Mary, known as the

---

[1] Langport Corporation Minute Bks. i, now in the hands of trustees of the property of the defunct corporation of Langport.
[2] Ibid.

[3] *Somers. Arch. Soc. Proc.* liii, 148.
[4] Corporation Minutes and Entries.
[5] Ibid and Sch. Trustees Minutes from 1706.
[6] Corporation Minutes.

Hanging Chapel. In the portreeve's accounts, 1706, when Mr. Henry Norman became master, there are entries of payment for reglazing the windows of the chapel and for more work done about the chapel, and in 1716 the chapel was retiled at the cost of the corporation. During the 18th century there are various entries of payments by the schoolmaster of Lord's rent for the chapel or schoolhouse, and it is clear that the chapel was during this century so used.

In 1742 Mr. Henry Norman, the son of the former master, was removed from his post by the corporation on account of his neglect of the rules of the school. The corporation portreeve accounts for 1743[7] contain an entry of expenditure for glass for the chapel, but whether the breaking was on a 'burning out' or similar occasion at the Christmas holidays does not appear. In place of Mr. Henry Norman the corporation appointed in 1743 Mr. William Hart as master, and in 1774, on his resignation, his son Mr. Henry Hart became his successor. Mr. Hart died in 1784, and his monument in Langport Church tells how William Hart 'with Christian resignation calmly acquiesced under excruciating pain in the conscious hope of a happier existence.' In 1789 the inhabitants petitioned the corporation to remove Mr. H. Hart, and the trustees appointed a Mr. W. Moore. The latter, however, seeing that Mr. Hart was not prepared to retire, in 1790 withdrew, and the corporation appointed Mr. W. Quekett,[8] and in November 1790 Mr. Hart came to terms and gave up the Hanging Chapel, Mr. Quekett, however, kept the school in his own house in Bow Street, and in 1796 Colonel Pinney was granted the use of the chapel by the corporation as a place in which to store the arms for the local militia, and it was so used till 1816. In 1824 we find the income of the school stated to be £73 a year. The school was open to all boys of the town who were able to read the Bible, and the average number was 30, of whom several were taught Latin and Greek. The present school in Upstreet, which is to-day called the Hill, was not occupied by the boys until 1850, and in the Corporation Accounts[9] for 1849 is an entry of the payment of £200 towards its erection, a public subscription producing an additional £1,000. Modern Langport has done its best to ignore the antiquity of the school, for it has inserted in the present building a stone with the words inscribed on it 'founded 1675,' and a window has been inserted in the parish church to the memory of Thomas Gillett 'the founder of the School.'

In 1867, under Mr. J. Lanchenick, the school was not prosperous, and there were only 35 boys.

Latin was only taught if required, and then as an extra to 11 boys. There were no boarders.

Since the Technical Education Act of 1892 the school has been completely reorganized. A scheme of 12 May 1896, under the Endowed Schools Acts,[10] created a governing body of eleven, of whom seven are representative and four co-optative members. The buildings of 1850 have been largely altered and added to by subscription and grants from the County Technical Education Committee and the later Local Education Authority. Science and the principles and practice of agriculture with manual instruction are being taught with considerable success. The number of boys on an average is 60. There are three assistant masters to Mr. Day, who is an M.A. of London University.

The following list of head masters has been compiled from the minutes of the school governors :—Henry Norman, 1706; Henry Norman, son, 1730; William Hart, 1743; Henry Hart, son, 1774; William Moore, 1790; William Quekett, 1790; Rev. E. D. Green, 1844; E. F. Smith, 1846; John Lanchenick, 1851; Rev. J. Stubbs, 1875; E. Western, 1883; Rev. E. W. Smith, 1891; Solomon George Day, 1896.

THE FREE GRAMMAR SCHOOL, SHEPTON MALLET

The history of this school is contained in a folio MS. now in the possession of the trustees. The book begins on 1 May 1639. By the foundation deed, 4 May 1626, George Strode, esq., of London and William Strode of Barrington granted to Thomas Strode, William Strode, and ten others the site and soil of the court of the manor of Shepton Mallet to be by them converted into five almshouses for poor widow women, a schoolhouse, and a dwelling-place for the master. The limit of the school and dwelling-house was the chambers upstairs and the court and garden on the south side. These were for the master and scholars. The five almshouses were on the ground floor with the court and garden on the north side. There was also to be a chapel where daily morning and evening common prayer was to be read by the master to the poor women and to the boys. The schoolmaster was to be of the degree of a master of arts and should teach twelve poor scholars from the town and parish of Shepton Mallet, and receive for that £12 a year and 20s. yearly for reading prayers daily. There were other clauses, thirty-three in number, laying down rules for the school and the almshouses, and among others that the Bishop of Bath and Wells was to be the visitor of the school. Then followed copies of new enfeoffments, 25 December 1651 and 31 January

1661. On 16 July 1696 Mr. Edward Strode, as the heir and representative of the family, by a deed poll made certain changes in the management of the charity, stating at the time that there had been a neglect on the part of the trustees, of whom nearly all had then died out, of the conditions specified in the foundation deed.

The next document is the finding of an inquisition, 4 June 1735, returned to the Court of Chancery under a commission of 5 August 1734, directed to John Bishop of Bath and Wells and others. The charity was again reported as badly managed, and apparently this was largely due to the frequent delays in the payment of rent of the parsonage of Meare. When funds were not forthcoming the question arose as to who were to be the first to suffer, the schoolmaster or the widows. The Court decided that one-third of the net rentals was to go to the school and two-thirds for the support of four widows. George Verrier was the schoolmaster at the time, and he was paid £10 and dismissed. Next came a copy of an appointment of new trustees, 2 June 1796.

In 1819 the trustees explained to the Commissioners of Inquiry Concerning Charities that in 1766 the Rev. John Dunkerton came to Shepton Mallet and was appointed schoolmaster. He was also clerk to the trustees and kept all their books and legal documents. Soon after his appointment the almshouse women were not renewed as vacancies occurred through death, and Mr. Dunkerton left the premises very much out of repair. When he died his son usurped the office of schoolmaster, kept the tithes of Meare to his own use, and allowed the school building to get into yet further decay. Since for many years the books had been kept by the elder Dunkerton, the trustees had forgotten what books he had or what were the express provisions for the foundation. They made frequent application for these documents to the younger Dunkerton, but without success. The trustees had for many years held no meetings. At last they took proceedings against the schoolmaster, who was sent to prison, and the trustees took possession of the buildings and estates of the charity. One of the almshouses had been used to enlarge the school, and the chapel had gone to enlarge the schoolmaster's house. The four other almshouses had also been used for the school. Dunkerton had regarded the school as his private property and spent the income on the school and on himself. The schoolroom was large enough for twelve, and if the almshouse chambers were utilized there would be room for twenty.

On the imprisonment of Dunkerton in 1796 the school ceased, and the endowments were allowed to accumulate for the purpose of putting the buildings at Shepton Mallet and Meare into repair. The school was reopened in 1803 and the Rev. Thomas Smith, the then curate at Shepton Mallet, was appointed master. Mr. Smith in 1819 had 50 pupils.

The scheme of the Court of Chancery, 19 November 1829, appointed twelve trustees including the rector *ex officio*. It made also the master necessarily a member of the Church of England, though not so by original trust, and limited the foundationers or free boys to 30.

On 29 January 1835 the trustees expended the funds in litigation concerning Godney Moor, and the school was closed and was not reopened until 1844. In 1867[1] there were 91 boys, of whom 41 were boarders paying £28 a year, under Mr. John Farbrother. Some Latin and science were taught. In 1898 the Sexey School Foundation at Bruton came to the assistance of the Strode Trustees and made a grant of £1,500 towards the purchase of a good field and the erection of new school buildings. These were opened in 1900 and the school has since been carried on in a thoroughly efficient way, receiving grants from the County Local Authority and the Board of Education. There are 70 boys under Mr. W. Aldridge, a certificated teacher, B.A., London, appointed December 1897.

The following list of head masters gives all whose names occur in the School Minute Books:—George Verrier, 1735; Rev. John Dunkerton, 1766; Mr. Dunkerton, 1796; Rev. Thomas Smith, 1803–44; Mr. E. Roberts, 1844–5; Mr. Lanchenick, 1845–51; Mr. J. E. Farbrother, 1851–71; Rev. R. C. Stiles, 1871–81; Mr. W. J. Jervis, 1881–4; Rev. C. P. Morris, 1884–92; Mr. A. C. Bidmead, 1892–7; Mr. W. Aldridge, B.A., 1897.

THE FREE GRAMMAR SCHOOL, MARTOCK

The grammar school at Martock existed before 1625, as Farnaby, who afterwards had the first great private school in London, is recorded to have been master at Martock before he went to London, and Anthony Wood[2] tells us that when in 1646 'Mr. Charles Darby was called to teach the grammar school at Martock he found many of his scholars ingenious men and good grammarians even in their grey hairs.'

The present endowment, however, dates from 1662, when William Strode of Barrington by deed[3] 1 March in that year gave to Edward Strode and John Strode of Lincoln's Inn a rent-charge on his manor of Martock of £12 and part of the land of the Court House for the school courtyard, while part of the Court House was converted into the schoolhouse, i.e. the portion on the first story, and the rest into a schoolmaster's

[1] *Sch. Inq. Rep.* xiv, 282.
[2] Clark, *Wood's Life and Times*, ii, 248.
[3] Indentures, Accts. and Min. *penes* the vicar and churchwardens of Martock, cf. *End. Char. Sch. Rep.* ix (1823), 528.

house with a garden and the use of the forecourt for the schoolmaster with the backside and easement thereunto belonging.

The deed then lays down that the schoolmaster was to be chosen by the heirs of William Strode, a man sound of body, well reputed of, having no pastoral charge and by examination found meet both for his learning, dexterity and delight in teaching scholars, as also by his conversation and his knowledge and zeal for God's true religion and worship as now authorized in the Church of England, 'whereunto he shall stir and breed up his scholars.'

He is to teach boys whose parents live in the parish and hundred of Martock and all boys of the kindred of the founder whose parents shall send them to him for 10s. a year and no more. If he shall ever charge and take more it shall be accounted one of his principal faults. He was to have £10 a year paid quarterly for his wages and his house rent-free.

If he is convicted of being a common gamester, or haunter of taverns or alehouses or otherwise becomes a disgrace or infamy to the school he shall be utterly expelled and removed. The master is not to have more than twelve days' holiday in the year, and the master and scholars are to repair to school each morning at 6 a.m. and to remain until 6 p.m. from Lady Day to Michaelmas and from Michaelmas to Lady Day from 7 a.m. to 5 p.m.

The learned languages were to be taught, including Hebrew and the Holy Scriptures. The master was to teach the Catechism every Saturday from 1 p.m. to 3 p.m. to some parts of the school, i.e. the youngest and lowest boys, taking his lessons from Nowell's or some other Catechism in English. Those of better capacity were to learn Nowell's Catechism in Latin or Bercher's Catechism in Greek. The scholars were always to use the Latin tongue with their fellows as well within as without the school. On every Lord's day they were to assemble with their Bibles in school at 8 a.m. and after due inspection to walk two and two to church.

Over the door of the schoolhouse was inscribed the name of God in Hebrew, Greek, and Latin and underneath 'Schola trilinguis. Triuni Deo Gloria. Martock neglect not thy opportunities. Cave. Deus ipse videt. Fundata anno Domini 1661.'

The school accounts are preserved from the beginning. The first master was Mr. Charles Darby. Within the first year there were 40 boys from Martock and 132 strangers and foreigners. The accounts for the following year inform us that Nathaniel Still and Thomas Budd, two pupils in the school, were awarded prizes of 2d. each.

The school certainly prospered.[3a] In 1665 there were 106 boys, and in 1667 115. In 1734 the number had gone down. Mr. William March was the master, and there were only 35 town boys and seven foreigners.

By a deed[4] of 12 April 1740 Zachary Bailey the lord of the manor gave fee-farm and chief rents on certain lands in the parish amounting to £15 5s. 7d. yearly instead of the general charge of £12 on the manor as a whole. In 1747 we find Mr. Charles Lewis was master and in 1757 Mr. Joseph Good. He was curate of the parish and had a flourishing school consisting largely of boarders. In 1823 it had fallen to the parish clerk, who taught only the three R's. It revived later, but on the resignation of the Rev. W. H. Braund in 1862 the school was closed. The buildings were then very dilapidated and the endowment, nominally only £15 5s. 7¾d., was reduced to £14 3s. 1d. owing to the difficulty of tracing the items of the endowment.[5]

In 1871 the old house was sold for £171. After some opposition and acrimonious discussion in the parish the Charity Commissioners in 1871 drew up a scheme for the future management of the charity. There were to be six governors, of whom one, i.e. the vicar of Martock, was to be an *ex-officio* governor. One governor was to be nominated by a governing body of the endowed school at Yeovil, a school which has not as yet come into existence, and four governors were to be elected by the ratepayers of Martock in vestry assembled.

The income of the charity[6] is to be applied by the governors in the advancement of the education of boys and girls who are or who have been in those public elementary schools of the hundred of Martock as admit a course of religious instruction according to the principles and doctrines of the Church of England. Among the methods suggested by the scheme is the provision of exhibitions to induce their parents to keep children at school longer than they would otherwise remain. The income, however, is still being accumulated as it is too small for any effective uses at present.

THE GRAMMAR SCHOOL, CHARD

The account of this school given by Mr. A. H. Stanton to the Schools Inquiry Commission in 1866[1] is still applicable. A quaint old house with a picturesque gabled front in tolerable repair, with a good kitchen garden and about three-quarters of an acre of meadow, forms the only endowment of this school.

[3a] *End. Char. Sch. Rep.* ix (1823), 528.

[4] Ibid.

[5] Minutes of Inquiry in 1871, now in the hands of the vicar and churchwardens.

[6] Scheme as presented to parishioners at the public inquiry, 1871, *penes* vicar and churchwardens of Martock.

[1] *Sch. Inq. Com. Rep.* xvi, 196.

By deed poll[2] of 4 May 1671, William Symes of Poundisford conveyed to Henry Henley, Nathaniel Pitts, and ten others, as trustees, a burgage at the lower end of the north side of the borough of Chard, and one acre of land belonging to it for the purpose of a schoolhouse and habitation for a schoolmaster for the town of Chard for the education and bringing up of youth in virtue and good learning.

On 28 February 1705 Nathaniel Pitts, the surviving trustee, conveyed this to himself, John Pitts, and others, and on 26 March 1709 these conveyed the premises to the corporation of Chard on a lease for one thousand years. On 13 October 1727 a petition[3] was issued with sanction of the portreeve and burgesses of Chard for a brief to beg for money to rebuild the school. The petition set forth that on 25 August last a fire broke out in the adjacent house of Francis Coleman, and in the space of four hours utterly destroyed the grammar school, being a large pile of buildings belonging to the said borough.

On the rain-water pipe of the present building there is the date 1585, which of course cannot be regarded as having belonged originally to this schoolhouse.[4]

On 28 February 1801[5] the portreeve and burgesses, who had been unaware of the conditions attached to the property, reconveyed the house and curtilage to a new set of trustees in trust for a grammar school and schoolmaster's house.

In 1823 the Charity Commissioners report that in the appointment of the schoolmaster the vicar of Chard had the right of veto, that the schoolhouse was sufficient for about twenty boarders, and that at the time there were 30 boys being taught arithmetic, writing, English grammar and reading.[6] There was no income except from the school fees, and the school was practically carried on as a private venture. At the present time the school is still carried on under the same conditions. A scheme was started to bring the school under the County Education Authority a year or two ago, but it has been since dropped. The trustees are appointed by the corporation, and they appoint the schoolmaster, who enjoys the use of the school and dwelling-house. In every other way the school is a private one.

ST. GREGORY'S, DOWNSIDE

This public school for boys of the Roman Catholic Faith is carried on by the English Congregation of Black Monks of St. Benedict,

and is the direct descendant of the famous Benedictine school of Douay.

Late in the year 1605 the exiled English Benedictines founded a community in the university town of Douay, where Cardinal Allen had already established an English College for the secular clergy. In consequence of the penal laws Englishmen who clung to the old religion were obliged to send their sons abroad to be educated, and soon the Douay Benedictines were receiving pupils from English homes. One of the early references[1] to the school shows what difficulties sometimes beset the passage of the boys between England and the Continent. In a letter probably written in the late summer of 1624, the President-General of the English Benedictines informed his correspondent that lately one of his fathers about to cross with four boys for St. Gregory's, and the same number of girls for a school at Cambray, had been captured on the English coast, and the whole party thrown into prison and heavily fined. At this time the school would seem to have been fairly large, for in 1626 Lewis Owen,[2] a spy of the English Government, stated that the Benedictines of Douay 'have many schollers which are beneficiall unto them, and many gentlemen's sonnes (which are their friends and benefactors in England) doe diet in their cloister, but not in the same part where the monks live, but in the other side of the cloister.'

The boys at St. Gregory's, Douay, between 1608 and 1781 were almost without exception British subjects. The names of many well-known Roman Catholic families are found in the Douay accounts, such as the Tichbornes, Throckmortons, Fitzherberts, and Gascoignes.

In the few years preceding the French Revolution, however, the number of English and Irish boys at St. Gregory's, Douay, seriously decreased, and the work was finally interrupted by the events which followed the Reign of Terror. On 26 February 1795 the Benedictines made their final farewell to Douay, and landed at Dover on 2 March. Sir Edward Smythe, bart., formerly one of their pupils, offered them shelter at his Shropshire seat of Acton Burnell, setting aside a portion of the park and adding a new wing to his house that they might open a school for boys.[3] Here they stayed some twenty years.

On 7 September 1813 Dom Kendal, Prior of St. Gregory's, Acton Burnell, purchased the mansion and estate known as Mount Pleasant in the parish of Chilcompton, about six miles north of Shepton Mallet. On 28 April 1814 the removal took place, a few boys

---

[2] Chard Corporation Minutes and Minutes of Trustees appointed by burgesses of Chard; *Char. Com. Rep.* ix, 505.
[3] County MSS., County Offices, Taunton.
[4] *Somers. Arch. Soc. Proc.* xxviii, 21.
[5] Corporation Minutes.
[6] *Digest of Commissioners*, 1843, p. 82.

[1] Cited by Dom H. Norbert Birt, *Hist. of Downside*, 42 et seq.
[2] *The Running Reg.* 94.
[3] Birt, op. cit. 125.

under the direction of Prior Thomas Austen Lawson and three or four monks, the last of whom, Dom Peter Wilson, died in 1890. The family was housed in the old mansion-house, and within a year there were 15 boys under education. Soon after the English Benedictines of St. Gregory at Douay made over any claim they had in their old house at Douay to the Community of St. Edmund in Paris, and settled down at Downside as their permanent home. At once steps were taken to improve the accommodation both for the monks and the boys, and plans were drawn for a school and schoolhouse for 50 boys. The foundation stone of the new building was laid 11 July 1820, and the chapel for monks and boys was solemnly opened 10 July 1823. The new buildings for the boys cost over £7,000, besides £7,000 which was expended on the purchase of more land, and the improvement of the outbuildings of the house. The growth of Downside received a temporary check in 1830 from the competition of a new school established at Prior Park near Bath by Bishop Baines, the Vicar Apostolic of the Western district. For the next few years the numbers at Downside fell off, but gradually the leeway was regained and further progress made.[4] In 1839 plans were drawn by A. W. Pugin for a much larger monastery, a new monastic church and improved buildings for the boys. The new school buildings were opened in 1853, and the new monastic buildings in 1876, and at the same time the Petre Library was completed. Since then still further extensions have been made. There are now about 150 boys in the school, and the university honours gained by the scholars prove the efficiency of the work.

The following list gives the names of the head masters of the school since it was opened in 1814 :—Augustine Lawson, 1814 ; Bernard Barber, 1818 ; George Turner, 1830 ; Joseph Brown, 1834 ; Peter Wilson, 1840 ; Norbert Sweeney, 1854 ; Cuthbert Smith, 1859 ; Alphonsus Morrall, 1866 ; Ildephonsus Brown, 1868 ; Bernard Murphy, 1870 ; Aidan Gasquet, 1878 ; Edmund Ford, 1885 ; Clement Fowler, 1888 ; Wilfrid New, 1891 ; Aidan Howlett, 1900 ; Leander Ramsay, 1902.

THE UNITED CHARITY SCHOOL,
COMMONLY KNOWN AS THE
BLUE SCHOOL, WELLS

For the last two hundred years this school has been practically a grammar school, receiving scholars from the Free Charity School, and it is now one of the largest of the secondary schools of Somerset.[1]

[4] Birt, op. cit. 204.

[1] Three volumes of Minutes of the meetings of the Trustees of this Charity from 1654 to the present day exist. Every statement has been copied from these records, but the books are not paged or indexed.

On 20 December 1654[2] Mrs. Margaret Barkham gave by indenture the sum of £800 to Thomas Coward, William Wykes, Thomas White, jun., Arthur Mattock, Richard Hicks and Alexander Jett in trust for them to found a school and pay an income of £20 a year to a pious schoolmaster conformable to the Church of England, who should instruct so many poor children of the town of Wells whose parents were not able to breed them up to school by reason of poverty, and the rest of the income was to be spent in placing and tending out the aptest of them to a trade in the proportion of £3 or £4 for each. Margaret Barkham was the widow of Ezekiel Barkham of Wells, who in his will, dated 22 September 1640, stated that he had with his wife's consent sold 30 acres of land, and had meant to endow a school in Wells out of the proceeds. The money furnished by the widow was the sum obtained by this sale, which she had the use of for her life, but which she now gave up that the project of her husband might be fulfilled before she died. The register of the earlier meetings of the trustees is clearly a book provided by Mrs. Barkham herself, and has her name stamped upon it, and it is evident that she entered into all the details of the foundation, leaving at first to the trustees merely the management of the fund. She chose for the first schoolmaster the Rev. Francis Standish, the master of the old Bubwith almshouse, and she decided also that the school was not to exceed the number of 14 pupils. The school was actually started on 29 March 1656 in the chapel of the Bubwith almshouse. The names of the 14 boys who were the first to enter are engrossed in this register, and also the nine rules which Mrs. Barkham had drawn up, and which they were to observe most carefully. At the beginning of this register, but after her death, a copy of her will was entered on 15 September 1679. At the March meeting in 1664, without any reason given for their remissness, the trustees report that Mr. Standish the schoolmaster made it appear that the salary allowed him was in arrear one whole year at Our Lady Day last.

In a deed of 23 November 1701, executed by Edward Fuller and Elizabeth his wife, William Salmon, William Shenton, and Thomas Cannington, it is stated that Adrian Hickes of Wells had by his will of 6 April 1675 given £200 to be laid out at the discretion of these trustees for the poor of the parish of Wells, and for an annual sermon. On 19 March 1715 the Barkham trustees enter in their register that they had received a proposal from the trustees of the Hickes Charity that the proceeds of the estate should be yearly employed as an augmentation to Mrs. Barkham's Charity, and especially in binding boys as apprentices. They proposed also that

[2] Also *Education Returns*, ii, 827, and *Com. on End. Sch. Rep.* iii, 361, 4, x (1820).

there should be a union of trustees. This was then agreed to, and arrangements were made for carrying it into effect, and the union was completed on 2 August 1717. Suitable boys were to be apprenticed from the school, and a premium of £5 was to be given to each.

On 19 February 1713 another educational scheme was effected in Wells. Bishop Hooper, the Dean and Chapter of Wells, and Mr. Philip Hodges and other subscribers started a fund for a charity school for poor boys and girls. There were to be two schools, one for 20 boys and one for 20 girls, and in 1720 this scheme was enriched by a legacy of £100 from Mr. William Westley. The boys and girls were to be clothed in a distinct uniform.

One of these benefactors, Mr. Philip Hodges of Wells, in his will dated 18 June 1723 said: 'I have at my own cost erected and built a schoolhouse on the land of the Dean and Chapter of the Cathedral Church of Wells aforesaid for the teaching of such poor children and rooms over the same for the use of master and scholars.' This school was in the North Liberty, and is now known as St. Andrew's Lodge. It was meant for the accommodation of the children who were supported and educated under this new effort. The will was somewhat complicated, and the estate could not for some time be used for the purpose he had in view. He left 40 acres of land in the parish of St. John Glastonbury, a farm at Lympsham, and some land at East Pennard.

On 2 August 1732 a tripartite agreement was arrived at between the executors and trustees of Mr. Hodges estate, and the trustees of the Barkham and Hickes Educational Charities, under which one body of the trustees should ultimately be formed who should carry on the United Educational Charities of the three foundations. Of the two free schools of 1713, Mr. Gravell became the first master and was alive in 1732, and Miss Byron the first mistress and had been succeeded in 1732 by Miss Tick. The boys were taught in Mr. Hodges' schoolhouse in the North Liberty and the girls in a house in the town rented by the trustees for Miss Byron. The united school was to be known as the Barkham, Hickes, and Hodges' School. It is not clear, however, how the two boys' schools were at first managed. As the result of the Hodges' foundation the school gradually came to be known as the Blue School, and took up the position of a secondary school. The elementary or junior school was known as the free school, and the minutes of the proceedings of the trustees from 1764 onwards record regularly the passing out of boys from the Blue School, apprenticed to some trade or to husbandry, and the transference of boys from the free school to the Blue School. In May 1815 Mr. Maurice Davis, who had been the master for many years,

resigned his post, and in his place Mr. John Vickery was appointed on 22 May 1815. Mr. Vickery had been the head master of the Cathedral Choir School, and the governors of the Blue School agreed to make certain additions to the house in the Liberty to enable him to receive a number of boarders. The canons residentiary and other householders in the Liberty were soon, however, disturbed by the noise caused by this increase of boys, and they began to make urgent complaints to the governors about it. In 1816 the governors therefore decided to withdraw their permission given to Mr. Vickery to take boarders and to recoup him the loss which this change involved. Meanwhile they ordered an inquiry to be made for another suitable house, and having failed in October 1814 to purchase Mr. Spencer's house in the Liberty they finally obtained the house and garden on the south-west end of Chamberlain Street which was known as Soho. In 1825 therefore the boys were transferred there, a schoolroom having been attached to the house. In 1829 some cottages were purchased to the west of Soho, and the girls of the Blue School were transferred from the house in the town. In 1833 there were 34 boys and 20 girls in the school. In 1840 a large schoolhouse was erected in the schoolmaster's garden in Soho and to the north of it. In 1862 the uniform of the boys and girls was changed and made similar to that of the children of the Charity School, Bridgwater, and in 1879 the governors decided to abolish it altogether.

In 1896 the boys' and girls' schools were placed under the regulations of the Science and Art Department of the Board of Education, and with the assistance of the County Technical Education Authority a considerable enlargement of the boys' school was made. In 1903 the girls' school was transferred from the cottage south of the boys' playground to new premises in Portway. The schools are now carried on under a scheme of the Charity Commission and Board of Education, 29 March 1889, modified by schemes of 3 October 1895, 16 August 1898, and 29 August 1902. There are about 100 scholars in each school, and about 20 pupil teachers are being trained in it under the regulations of the Board of Education.

THE BLUE COAT SCHOOL, BATH

The Blue Coat School at Bath was founded in 1711 mainly through the exertions and influence of Mr. Robert Nelson. The buildings were erected from private subscriptions on a site given by the corporation and were completed in 1721 as a dual school for boys and girls. In 1728 new and enlarged buildings were erected by the corporation under the direction of Mr. Killigrew, and the present buildings for the accommodation of 100 boys and girls were erected in 1860 from designs furnished by Mr. Manners.

KINGSWOOD SCHOOL, BATH

In 1748, and mainly through the effort of the Rev. John Wesley, a school was started at Kingswood, Lansdown. In 1739 he wrote in his *Journal*,[1] 'I preached near the house we had a few days before began to build for a school, in the Middle of Kingswood.' In 1741 he refers to it again. The first effort was too great for the funds of the society. It was found needful to retrench the expenses, and the staff at Bristol was reduced to two masters and a mistress, and one master and one mistress at Kingswood.[2] In 1783 the Conference decided that at Kingswood either the school should cease or the rules of it be punctually observed, particularly that the children should never play, and that a master should be always present with them.[3] The buildings were removed to their present site in 1851, and in 1882 were enlarged to accommodate 290 boys.

THE HUISH SECONDARY SCHOOL FOR BOYS

There is in Taunton an almshouse charity founded under the will of Richard Huish who in 1615[4] left certain lands and tenements for the erection of an almshouse and for the support of poor aged men and also for exhibitions to enable poor deserving scholars to proceed to the Universities of Oxford and Cambridge. The incomes from this endowment had so greatly increased that by a scheme, 7 July 1874, made under the Endowed Schools Act, the sum of £350 a year was assigned for the almshouses and £200 a year for the university exhibitions of £50 a year each. Out of the residue of the income £400 a year was to be spent in the erection and maintenance of the secondary schools at Taunton for boys and girls, to be known as the Huish Schools. The pupils were to receive a modern education with one foreign language, either Latin or French. The governors were also at their discretion to provide exhibitions consisting of free education at the school for promising boys and girls from the elementary schools, of which half were to be offered for the schools in Taunton. A Huish Secondary School was therefore built for 100 boys and opened 1 December 1874, and in January of the following year the boys from the secondary school which had been carried on in Bishop Fox's old buildings were brought over into it. The

school for the girls was meanwhile in abeyance. Other steps were being taken which might make it unnecessary.

An amending scheme for Huish's Foundation, 3 October 1895, dropped the proposal for a girls' school, and decided that all the funds available were to go to the support of the new boys' school. This school is therefore carried on under the schemes of 1874, 1890, and 1895. The school buildings have since been enlarged, land having been granted adjacent to the master's house by the governors of the Gray Hospital and financial help by the County Local Education Authority. There are now about 100 boys, most of whom come from the town, and a certain proportion of them hold scholarships from the local elementary schools. The head master is A. Goodliffe, M.A., King's College, Cambridge, and he has five assistant masters under him.

THE BISHOP FOX'S GIRLS' SCHOOL

On the transference of the boys from Bishop Fox's school buildings to the Huish Secondary School in 1874 the trustees of the building and of the Walbee endowment began to entertain the idea of a secondary school for girls. The income, however, was not sufficient to allow them to take immediate steps for its establishment, nor had the sanction for such a change been obtained from the Charity Commissioners. At first a house was obtained in the Crescent; the house which had been built for the Roman Catholic priest, and it contained several large rooms suitable for the purpose. The school was begun under Miss Reeves and afterwards carried on by Miss Macdermott, and this effort was regarded as fulfilling the intentions of the Huish Governors as formulated in their scheme of 1874. When therefore in 1895 the Huish scheme was definitely abandoned, the way was opened for the creation of a Bishop Fox's Girls' School and for the transference to it of the Walbee endowment. This had been approved by the Queen in Council on 8 February 1890, and the link between the new girls' school and the old foundation for boys was preserved by the appointment as *ex-officio* governors of the Warden of New College and the President of Corpus Christi College, Oxford. The endowment consists of a chief rent on 30 acres of land at Hawkchurch and a yearly sum of £100 payable to the school by the trustees of what is known as the Taunton Town Charities. This scheme was yet further enlarged under an amended scheme, 3 October 1895, and by means of large grants from the Local Education Authority for the county and the accumulated funds from the endowment, new buildings were erected in 1898 on a site known as the Laurels Nursery in the parish of Taunton St. James, and in 1907 they were again greatly enlarged to receive the women

[1] *Journ. of Rev. J. Wesley*, i, 175.
[2] Ibid. 293.
[3] Ibid. iv, 248.
[4] Scheme, 7 July, 1874.

pupil teachers and student teachers from the local elementary schools. There are now about 170 girls and young women in the school under Miss Wills and seven assistant mistresses.

QUEEN'S COLLEGE, TAUNTON

In addition to Bishop Fox's Schoolhouse in the precincts of the Castle, a girls' school existed during the 18th century in a house in the inner area of the castle which was known as Castle House. This is now the house of the curator of the Somerset Archaeological Museum in the castle and belongs to the Somerset Archaeological and Natural History Society. It was kept by a Mrs. Symonds, and at the beginning of the 19th century had a great reputation as a school for young ladies. This was afterwards carried on by a Miss Prosser who in 1835, owing to the number of her pupils, was compelled to migrate to Mount House. Castle House then became a private adventure boys' school, and in 1843 it was acquired for the Wesleyans by the Rev. Richard Ray, Mr. W. French, and Mr. James Barnicott. As a denominational school it began with 33 boys, and within ten years the number had increased to 100 and the Wesleyan authorities were compelled to look out for another site. The school was from its origin in 1843 and to the year 1888 under a dual management, a Wesleyan minister acting as governor and chaplain and the head master as disciplinarian and organizer of the education of the boys. It was known as the Taunton Wesleyan Collegiate Institution, and popularly as the Wesleyan College. In 1847 the new school on Haines Hill was completed and the boys migrated there from the castle, and ultimately 24 acres of land surrounding it were purchased and devoted to school purposes. The school in 1888 became known as Queen's College, Taunton, and the head master is A. S. Haslam, M.A. The roll of head masters is as follows :—T. Sully, B.A., 1843-82 ; H. Jefferson, M.A., 1882-5 ; J. J. Findlay, M.A., 1885-8 ; T. Darlington, M.A., 1888-92 ; J. Bramley, M.A., 1892-8 ; A. S. Haslam, M.A., 1898.

TAUNTON SCHOOL, STAPLEGROVE

In 1847 a school was started in the Bishops Hall Road under the title of the West of England Dissenters Proprietary School, and in 1870 it was removed to new and large buildings on the Staplegrove Road and assumed the name then of the Independent College. In 1900 this became known as Taunton School, and is now a flourishing secondary school of that denomination and has C. D. Whittaker, M.A., LL.D., as head master with six assistant masters under him.

THE SEXEY SCHOOL FOUNDATIONS, BRUTON

The Sexey Endowment,[1] given in 1617 by Hugh Sexey, a Bruton boy who had been educated at the grammar school, for the erection of a hospital and for the maintenance of eight old men and ten old women, had so increased in value that in 1877 the trustees of this Sexey Charity founded at Bruton a school for girls where they should receive instruction and be trained in housewifery. Soon after, because of the increasing value of this endowment, the trustees began to plan various educational schemes. They came to the assistance of the old King's School at Bruton by a yearly grant of £300 for scholarships, and they also made a capital grant to it for the erection of new buildings. They designed also the establishment of a technical or trade school at Bruton and also the foundation of a school large enough to accommodate 100 boys, to be known as the Sexey County School. On 15 July 1881 they set apart out of the Sexey Foundation a capital sum of £15,000 and £1,400 a year out of the revenue of the estates to be called the Sexey School Foundation. On 28 November 1889 an amended scheme [2] was sanctioned by the Queen in Council which provided that the Training School for girls at Bruton should be managed by the visitors of the Sexey Almshouse Trust and for the establishment of a technical or trade school for boys, and certain sums were assigned from the school foundation for their maintenance.

The Sexey Trade or Technical School was taken in hand soon after 1889 and opened in 1892 at a total initial cost of £5,000. There are now 140 boys in the school. The head master is Mr. W. A. Knight, B.Sc. London, and under him the school has gained great success ; for several years past the boys have carried off the larger number of the County Scholarships, and its record at the Universities proves its high efficiency. Mr. Knight has seven assistant masters.

This scheme was again amended by an Order in Council, 15 January 1897. An ambitious plan which had been discussed for a large county school was withdrawn by the governors, and instead of it was substituted a smaller scheme for a dual boys' and girls' school at Blackford in the parish of Wedmore, where the larger portion of the estates of the Sexey Charity was situated. The site was given and a large grant was made towards the cost of the erection of the school, and £100 a year was assigned towards its maintenance. It was decided also to assist the old Strode Endowed School at Shepton Mallet, which had become inefficient through lack of funds, and

[1] Minutes of Proceedings of Sexey Trustees.
[2] Char. Com. Scheme no. 867.

a grant of £1,400 was made towards the cost of new buildings.

The Blackford School began work in temporary premises at West Stoughton in Blackford, and in October 1899 moved into their new buildings on the high road from Wedmore to Mark. There are about 70 boys and 40 girls in the school, of whom about one-third are weekly boarders.

THE BLUE OR CHARITY SCHOOL, FROME

During the reign of Edward IV a William Leversedge of Vallis, in the parish of Frome, is believed to have founded an almshouse there.[1] The building consisted of a chapel and hall and twelve rooms for the poor. On 10 May 1644 Robert Leversedge executed a new conveyance of it.

In 1720 there had been a movement in the town in favour of erecting a charity school there. The buildings of the almshouse were very old and dilapidated and a charity school was started by means of local subscriptions and a joint building erected for the almshouses and the school. There were seventeen chambers for old women on the north side and fourteen on the south, and the schoolhouse lay between them. During the 18th century many benefactions were made for

[1] *Char. Com. Rep.* iii (1820), 319 ; and Crocker, *Hist. Acct. of the Charities of Frome* (1815). Minutes have been kept since 1751.

this school, and among them provisions for clothing and placing out the boys as apprentices after their education had been completed. The principal benefactors were James Wickham and Jane Hippie 2 March 1721, John A'Court of Rodden 1721, John Wickham of Sherborne 15 May 1728, and John and Richard Stevens 5 April 1809. The school was opened in 1728. In 1819 when the Commissioners of Inquiry visited the school there were 37 boys in it of whom 12 were reckoned on the Stevens foundation. The Court of Chancery in 1751 had drawn up a scheme for apportioning of these charities between the almshouse and the charity school, since many of the endowments were for the joint benefit of both institutions, and it was on this scheme of 1751 that the charity was administered in 1819. The boys were clothed, educated, and apprenticed, but there was no provision for boarding, all of the boys going home at night. Reading, writing, and arithmetic were taught them, but there was an examination before admission, and the boys were expected to know something, before they entered the school. The income of the school was reported to be £125 from rents and £156 10s. from dividends.

During the 19th century the school has been carried on under the old regulations by a body of twenty trustees. In 1905 a scheme was prepared for the recasting it as a modern secondary school. Local prejudice, however, and an inability to arrive at some common basis of agreement, have hitherto prevented this scheme from becoming law.

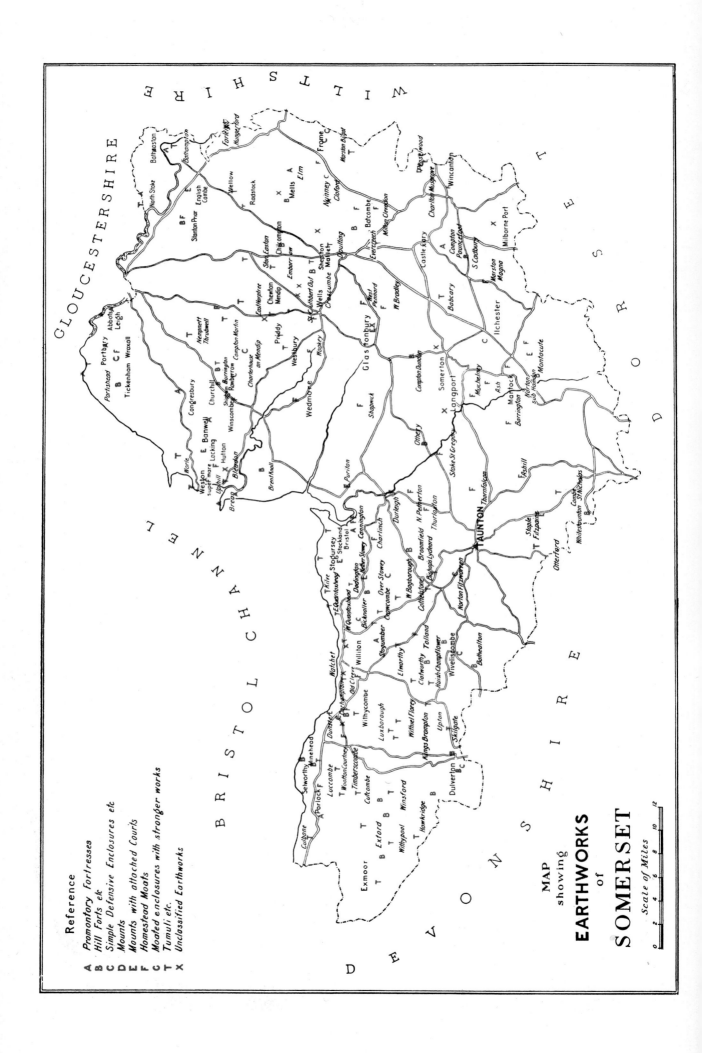

MAP
showing

EARTHWORKS
of
SOMERSET

Scale of Miles

Reference

A Promontory Fortresses
B Hill Forts etc
C Simple Defensive Enclosures etc
D Mounts
E Mounts with attached Courts
F Homestead Moats
G Moated enclosures with stronger works
T Tumuli etc.
X Unclassified Earthworks

ANCIENT EARTHWORKS

SOMERSET contains a relatively large number of ancient earthworks and fortified inclosures, no fewer than eighty-eight being shown on the 25-in. O.S. maps, whilst a few others are not recorded thereon. Many of them are in isolated positions on Exmoor, the Brendon Hills, the Quantocks and other high ground far removed from a railway station or even from a village, and a considerable proportion of them are now surrounded by woods. Few of them have been described previously, and with some notable exceptions the earlier accounts are too vague and lacking in detail to have any substantial value as descriptions of the structures themselves. In the references to early papers given in this article, an endeavour has been made to cite only those of real importance. Papers which contain no descriptions of the earthworks themselves, and general accounts of the works given in the course of some society excursion and containing no new matter, have as a rule been omitted.

The writer has visited and examined almost all the earthworks in the county, the existence of which he was able to ascertain, has verified and where necessary corrected the 25-in. O.S. map on the spot, and whenever practicable has measured typical sections. In very few cases are there any published accounts of systematic investigations by means of the spade, and consequently the works can at present be classified only according to their position and plan. Many of them have been partially destroyed by agricultural operations, afforestation of their sites, quarrying, and building.

The earthworks and fortified inclosures of this county belong to many different types and several of them are of the first rank as regards both size and strength. Somerset stood directly in the path of the westward retreat of the earlier races before the invaders from the east ; was, as regards the northern half at least, an area of long continued Roman occupation ; suffered later from the incursions of the Danes and witnessed some of the severest struggles between them and the Saxons ; was partitioned amongst the Norman conquerors soon after their arrival ; and, much later, saw one of the most notable sieges and several of the sharper minor engagements of the Parliamentary war. It is not surprising that most of these periods of strife have left records in the form of fortifications of the type belonging to the particular time.

For the purpose of provisional classification the scheme recommended

A HISTORY OF SOMERSET

by the Congress of Archaeological Societies has been followed in this article. It is as follows :—

A. Fortresses more or less inaccessible by reason of precipices, steep slopes, or water, and further strengthened by artificial works. They are usually known as 'promontory fortresses.'

B. Fortresses on hill-tops, with artificial defences that follow the natural line of the hill ; or fortresses which, although on high ground, are less dependent than those of class A on natural slopes, etc.

C. Rectangular or other simple inclosures, including forts and towns of the Romano-British period.

D. Forts consisting only of a mount with an encircling ditch or fosse.

E. Fortified mounts, partly or wholly artificial, with remains of one or more attached courts or baileys.

F. Homestead moats, consisting of simple inclosures formed into artificial islands by moats filled with water.

G. Inclosures, generally rectangular, similar to those in Class F but more strongly protected with ramparts and fosses, and in some cases provided with outworks.

H. Ancient village sites protected by walls, ramparts or fosses.

X. Defensive works which cannot be classified under any of these headings.

It is not possible at present to draw any hard and fast lines between some of these divisions. For example, whether some of the Somerset earthworks should be put in class A or class B is largely a matter of opinion. Generally those inclosures have been placed under B which, although owing much to the steepness of their approaches, are nevertheless so well defended by banks and ditches that they would be strong in any situation. Again, it is difficult to decide whether certain circular forts like Elworthy Barrows or the Dunster fort should be placed in class B or C. Some of the earthworks classified under X may have belonged to one of the other classes, but the present remains are too imperfect to enable the original plan to be made out with any certainty.

Reference to the map will show that the works are fairly evenly distributed over the county with the exception of the low-lying central portion and the Mendip plateau and with a distinct tendency to concentration on the elevated lands along the sea-board. Some of the earlier writers made ingenious speculations as to the systematic arrangement of the earthworks over the county (and the adjoining counties) with a view to their occupants being able to communicate with one another by signals. This hypothesis is however scarcely in accord with the fact that many of the camps are not placed on the highest points of the hills, but very frequently are some way down the slope, so that their outlook is limited and they are not themselves visible to a distant observer except from certain points of the compass. This is especially noticeable in the camps in the west of the county. In any case such a concerted strategical arrangement could only apply to camps built by the same or kindred races and therefore of the same type and approximately of the same date.

It is difficult in many cases to explain why a particular hill was selected for a camp in preference to neighbouring heights. An important factor in determining the choice was the nature of the subsoil and the readiness with which it could be worked into banks and ditches ; a hill on which the upper layers of rock were fissile or brittle or had been broken up by weathering was chosen instead of a neighbouring height, the surface rock of which was still hard. Doubtless an equally important consideration was the possibility of inclosing a sufficient area of fairly level ground. One striking feature in connexion with the situation of the camps is that many of them are at a considerable distance from any source of water supply now existing.

What are known in some parts of the county as 'linches' are really natural terraces formed by the outcrops of horizontal beds of rock of different degrees of hardness ; they occur frequently, for example, with the Midford Sand. In some places, as at the base of Ham Hill, such terraces have been scarped and rounded as part of the fortifications, and on the lower slopes of Cadbury and elsewhere their steep escarpments increase the difficulty of ascent. In other places, however, although they have the appearance of artificial terraces and have given rise to a local tradition of a fortification, the structures are purely natural in their origin.

DRY MASONRY.—It is noteworthy that in many of the Somerset earthworks the banks consist mainly of stones, which in most cases were piled up irregularly. In some cases, however, the defences show more or less 'dry masonry,' that is to say the stones, although irregular in shape, were laid with care, but without any mortar, so as to produce a distinct and approximately smooth 'face.' In a few instances where large stones were used there is also distinct 'coursing.'

There seem to be at least five types of dry masonry fortification. (1) An actual wall of stones rising more or less vertically from the natural surface of the ground, as in Cow Castle and parts of Mounsey Castle. (2) The wall was built up in parallel sections with distinct faces running longitudinally through the wall, as at Worlebury. (3) The lower part only of the bank was laid as dry masonry, whilst the upper part was piled irregularly, as in the north rampart of Dolbury. (4) The lower part of the bank was piled irregularly, and on the top of it was built a vertical wall, composed as a rule of larger stones, as at Stokeleigh and Tedbury. (5) The stones were built up against the face of a scarp or bank so as to form a revetment, as on the south side of Dolbury, the west face of Wadbury, and elsewhere.

BIBLIOGRAPHY : Collinson's *History of Somerset* contains only slight references to the earthworks of the county. Rutter's *Delineations of the North-West Division of the County of Somerset and of the Mendip Caverns*, London, 1829, contains references of importance concerning some of the camps in the north of the county. Phelps' *The History and Antiquities of Somersetshire* (1836) contains references, some of them in considerable detail, to the following camps, illustrated by plans, which as a rule give a fair general idea of the fortifications, whilst some of them are especially valuable because the works represented have since disappeared : Banwell, Bathampton, Bathealton, Berwick (Bath), Blacker's Hill, Brean Down, Burwalls, Bury Castle (Selworthy), Cadbury (South Cadbury), Cadbury (Tickenham), Castle Neroche, Clatworthy, Dinghurst, Dolbury, Downend, Dowsborough, Dunster, Elworthy, Glastonbury Tor, Hamdon Hill, Maes Knoll, Maesbury, Merehead, Newbury Hill, Oldbury (Bath), Ponters Ball (called Fonters Ball), Portishead, Portbury, Smalldown (Evercreech,) Solisbury, Stantonbury, Stokeleigh, Tedbury, Trendle Ring, Turks Castle, Wadbury, Worlebury.

The Reverend S. Seyer's *Memoirs Historical and Topographical of Bristol and its Neighbourhood* (1821) contains descriptions of the following camps with plans of several of them : Banwell (camp and earthen cross), Burwalls, Cadbury (Tickenham and Yatton), Dolbury, Failand (two), Maes Knoll, North Stoke, Portbury, Stokeleigh and Worlebury. He also refers to an earthwork near Ashton Court, and to another near Keynsham overlooking Hanham Ferry.

ILLUSTRATIONS : The plans are as a rule reduced to half the scale of the 25-inch O.S. map, that is 1:5000. The sections are to be taken as diagrammatic only, with a vertical scale much greater than the horizontal scale.

PROMONTORY FORTRESSES
[CLASS A]

ABBOTS LEIGH.—BURWALLS, BOROUGH WALLS or BOWER WALLS CAMP occupied the end of the promontory on the side of the valley opposite Stokeleigh Camp, and with it and Clifton Camp across the Avon formed a triangle of fortresses commanding the river. Burwalls Camp has been almost entirely destroyed, but it was triangular in form, two sides being defended naturally by the precipitous fall of hill, whilst the third was defended by three curved ramparts of stone, with the entrance about one-third of the total length from the east end. The area of the inclosure was about 7 acres.[1] The ends of the banks can still be seen where they run out on the edge of the north cliff, and there are some remains in a garden near the west end of the Suspension Bridge.

ABBOTS LEIGH.—STOKELEIGH CAMP, occupying an area of about $7\frac{1}{2}$ acres, stands on the west side of the Avon gorge and is defended on its east front by the precipices of the gorge. On the south the ground slopes steeply and here the defence is a single bank of stones carefully laid, and behind the bank is a natural scarp which increased the difficulty of access.

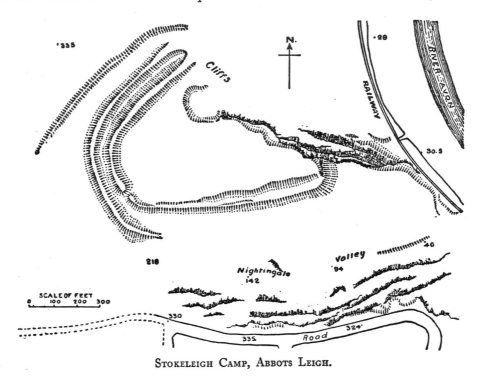

STOKELEIGH CAMP, ABBOTS LEIGH.

Along the west the ground is flat and here the defence is two ramparts of stone, the inner one being in places 30 ft. above the bottom of the ditch. The top of the outer rampart is unusually broad. Both end at the precipice above the gorge. Along the north-west front of the camp there is a third lower ridge starting from the precipice on the north and running north-east and south-west at an increasing distance from the main outer rampart. On

---

[1] Plans are given by Seyer and by Phelps, op. cit. I, 96–7. See also Scarth, *Arch.* xliv, 428–34, and particularly Lloyd Morgan, *Clifton Antiq. Club*, v, 10–15. *Som. Arch. Soc. Proc.* xlvii (2), 217–29.

the top of the inner rampart throughout almost its entire length there can be traced the remains of a vertical wall 4 ft. to 6 ft. across, of dry masonry built of large stones carefully laid.[2]

BANWELL.—BANWELL CAMP is on the top of a hill about half a mile south-south-east of the church and the defence was a bank of earth and stones round the edge of the inclosure with a steep scarp and a ditch below.

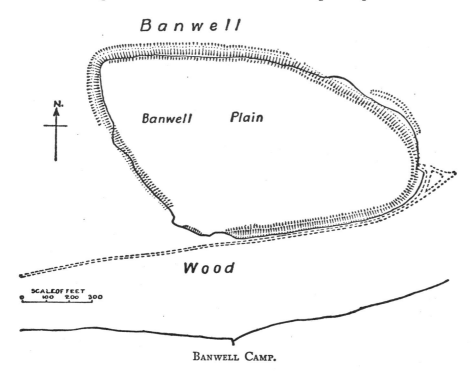

BANWELL CAMP.

Phelps (op. cit. 108–9) describes this camp as having a *vallum* of considerable strength, but the bank is now not more than 4 ft. above the inclosure even at its highest point and in many places it has been almost completely levelled. At the east end there are traces of a second and lower ditch cutting off the lower part of the promontory. The maximum length of the inclosure west-north-west to east-south-east is about 480 yds. and its maximum breadth north to south 260 yds. Arrow-heads and other flints have been found within it.[3] Somewhat more than a quarter of a mile west-south-west is an irregular quadrilateral inclosure, approximately square, formed by a low broad bank with a slight ditch outside. Within the inclosure is a cross of stones and earth about 2 ft. high and 12 ft. broad, the arms being respectively as follows : north, 61 ft. ; east, 56 ft. ; south, 57 ft. ; west, 72 ft. It was probably a boundary mark, not necessarily, nor even probably, of the same date as the camp.[4]

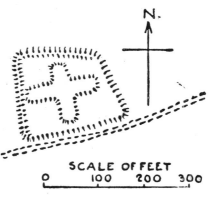

EARTHWORK IN BANWELL WOOD.

[2] Lloyd Morgan, *Clifton Antiq. Club Proc.* v, 19–24.
[3] *Somers. Arch. Soc. Proc.* li (2), 35.
[4] *Clifton Antiq. Club,* iv, 199–208; *Somers. Arch. Soc. Proc.* li (2), 35-40.

BATHAMPTON.—BATHAMPTON DOWN, an extensive plateau forming the summit of a hill which rises to a height of 670 ft. east of Bath and south of Bathampton, was seemingly converted into an inclosure in the same manner as Solisbury Hill, but weathering and quarrying have obliterated the greater part of the original defences. The western and northern faces of the camp were formed by the Wansdyke, which is still distinct on the west but sometimes less distinct on the north. On the west the bank is $4\frac{1}{2}$ ft. to 5 ft. above the present surface of the ditch, which is 3 ft. to 5 ft. across at the bottom with a counterscarp about $1\frac{1}{2}$ ft. high ; on the north the scarp is 7 ft. to $8\frac{1}{2}$ ft. high, but the ditch has been to a large extent obliterated ; on the south the scarp is 8 ft. high with a slight ditch, and bank at its base. At no point is there any bank on the crest of the inclosure. From the north-east corner of the camp the Wansdyke continued across the valley to Wiltshire, and from the south-west corner it continued in a north-easterly and south-westerly direction into Somerset. On the east the natural fall of the ground is very steep and the outcrops of strata form a series of terraces. In the south-west angle of the inclosure there were two tumuli and a third outside on the west, all now destroyed. The surface of the inclosure is crossed by two sets of low parallel banks at right angles to one another. Most probably these are boundary banks representing common cultivation.

BATHEASTON.—SOLISBURY HILL is half a mile west of Batheaston Church and the camp occupied the whole of the extensive plateau which forms its summit. The sides of the hill are a steep natural scarp of rock, aided by artificial scarping in places and especially on the north, but the sides of the hill have been much weathered and quarried into. Along the north side there is a low bank on the crest of the hill, and according to Phelps (op. cit. 102–3) this bank continued round the whole camp. At the north-west angle there is a steep scarp to a broad ledge below, which also terminates in a steep scarp. A road winds over this ledge into the camp and seems to represent the original entrance. The surface of the camp is laid out in long strips separated by slight differences of level and with short thick stones, with one or more initials carved on them, fixed at the angles. These are the relics of common cultivation.

BREAN.—BREAN DOWN is a rocky peninsula about $1\frac{1}{2}$ miles in length and 321 ft. above sea-level at its highest point, running east by south to west by north. It may be said to consist of two hills connected by a lower and narrower neck. There are two distinct sets of earthworks, one fortifying the western hill, whilst the other and stronger fortifies the eastern end against approach from the west. About a quarter of a mile from the eastern extremity at an elevation of about 150 ft. and before the ground begins to rise to the first hill, a bank of stones with a ditch on the western side has been thrown across the ridge. The bank is 4 ft. high on the east and 7 ft. to 8 ft. high on the west ; the ditch 10 ft. broad and the counterscarp 3 ft. to 4 ft. On the north the bank ends on the almost precipitous slope, but the ditch continues, though narrow, down the slope until it reaches the cliffs below. On the south where the slope is more accessible the bank turns at a right angle and runs for about 180 yds. west to east following the contour of the hill, as a bank from 2 ft. to 4 ft. high on the crest of the steep

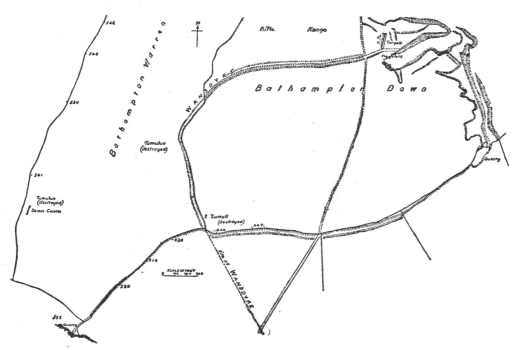

BATHAMPTON CAMP.

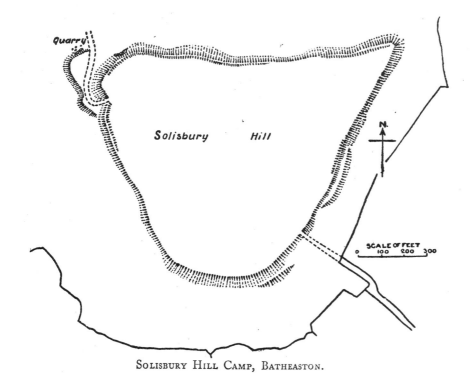

SOLISBURY HILL CAMP, BATHEASTON.

slope. At its east end a roadway which runs up the south face of the hill enters the inclosure and may represent the original entrance, which however may have been over the east end of the hill, now quarried away.

The second set of earthworks is on the west hill and consists of a series of low banks on the eastern slope of the hill. These banks have no ditches and are more like terraces for cultivation than military works, but they may have been defended by stockades. There are five banks facing east, the distances between them being respectively 52, 47, 38 and 47 yds., whilst a sixth bank faces west. The fifth bank facing east is across the highest point of the hill, and projecting westwards from the middle of it is a horseshoe platform of stones 3 ft. to 3 ft. 6 in. high, and 13 yds. east to west and 13 yds. north to south. It may have been a beacon platform, or, if military, a sort of rallying place. All these banks go right across the ridge and end on a natural platform, 2 yds. to 3 yds. wide, which surrounds the upper part of the hill and below which the ground falls very steeply. Running east and west from the middle of the second bank from the east is a low bank

EARTHWORKS ON BREAN DOWN.

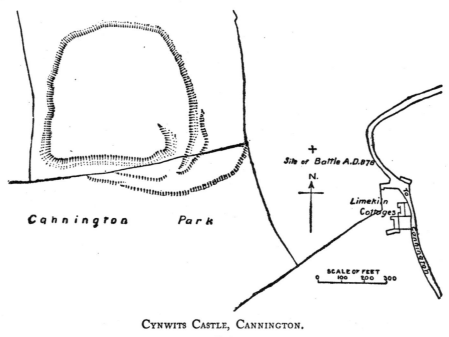

CYNWITS CASTLE, CANNINGTON.

which runs eastwards for 28 yds. and then turns south for 31 yds. forming an oblong inclosure.

Of the hut circles described by Warre[5] there is now no indication and he may have been misled by natural outcroppings of the limestone, the beds of which are here nearly vertical and simulate artificial works at several places.

CANNINGTON.—CYNWITS CASTLE in Cannington Park is a hill one mile north-west of Cannington which has been converted into a camp, probably for temporary occupation only, by scarping the sides some distance from the top. Immediately south-east is the alleged site of a battle with the Danes in 878, and the area of the camp has certainly been used as a place of interment, large numbers of human skeletons having been found there, quite close to the surface. Arrow-heads and other flints have also been found.

CLOFORD. — MEREHEAD CAMP, about half a mile south-west of Leighton and rather more than three-quarters of a mile east of East Cranmore Church, is a triangular camp about 6 acres in area formed

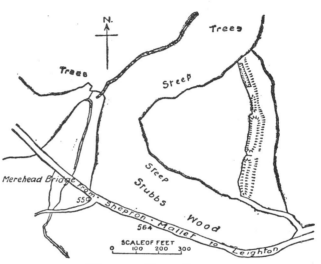

MEREHEAD CAMP, CLOFORD.

by throwing a double bank across the hill, the steep natural slopes being sufficient protection to the other two sides. Phelps' plan shows the two banks with an entrance near the middle of this side. Mr. Gray states (1903) that the bank is not more than 4 ft. high and is so much overgrown that it can only be traced with difficulty.[6]

COMPTON PAUNCEFOOT.—SIGWELLS CAMP is a triangular promontory fortress formed by a ditch 60 ft. wide across the hill from the ravine on one side to the opposite ravine. There are now no remains of any rampart. Flint implements have been found within the inclosure.[7]

CONGRESBURY.—CADBURY HILL CAMP occupies the top of an isolated hill half a mile east-south-east of Yatton and one mile north of Congresbury. The sides of the hill have been much quarried, but for about 110 yds. along the north face there is a

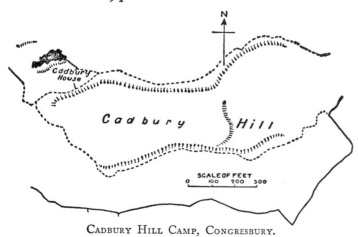

CADBURY HILL CAMP, CONGRESBURY.

[5] *Somers. Arch. Soc. Proc.* xii (1), 65.
[6] Phelps, op. cit. 110; H. St. George Gray, *Somers. Arch. Soc. Proc.* xlix, 173–80.
[7] *Somers. Arch. Soc. Proc.* xxiv (2), 84–8; xlix (2), 173–80.

scarp with a bank of stones at the foot and a ditch below the bank. For about 40 yds. on the north-north-east face there is a scarp with a bank below, but no ditch below the bank. Along the south-east there are indications of the foundations of a bank or thick wall for about 110 yds. from the east end. Approximately in the middle of the camp is an elevated area with a steep bank to the east and a ditch at its base, this bank being rounded at the angles and gradually dying into the general level on the north and south.

GREAT ELM.—TEDBURY CAMP occupies a horseshoe-shaped piece of high ground between Mells stream and Fordbury water, half a mile south-south-west of Great Elm Church. A bank of earth and stones much overgrown, but from 10 ft. to 15 ft. high, runs from one stream to the other in a direction north-west and south-east, and with the high precipitous banks of the two streams forms the defences of the inclosure. Along the top of this

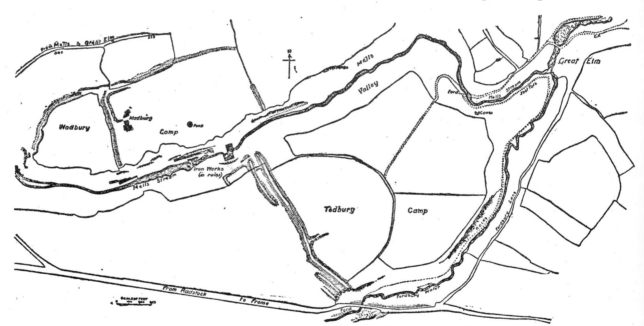

TEDBURY AND WADBURY CAMPS, GREAT ELM AND MELLS PARISHES.

bank for a considerable distance from the south-east end there are remains of the base of a wall 4 ft. to 6 ft. thick of large stones laid as dry masonry. About 170 yds. from the south-east end a bank 11 ft. high from the south-east, 15 ft. broad at the top and sloping gently to the north-west, juts out at right angles from the main bank and runs for some distance into the interior of the camp. In front of the main bank at the south-east end are two others, the middle one being 15 ft. high on the south-west and 13 ft. high on the north-east, whilst the outer one is 7 ft. high on the north-west and 7½ ft. on the south-east. This outermost bank continues for a short distance only, whilst the second bank is now about 100 yds. long. At the north-west end the second bank still exists for about 160 yds. from the steep bank of the Mells stream; it is about 7 ft. high and is from 20 to 25 yds. in front of the inner bank. West of this bank just over the stream is an oblong flanking work possibly protecting an entrance at this corner, but the banks hereabout have been altered by forestry operations.

Phelps (op. cit. 104–5) shows the outer bank complete, and an entrance in the middle of the two banks.

HAWKRIDGE.—BREWERS CASTLE stands on the east end of a narrow but high ridge above the confluence of the Barle and Danes Brook. The steep slope to the east is broken by bands of outcropping strata, which increase the difficulty of ascent. The camp at the top is small in area and irregular in shape. There has been some artificial scarping on the south-west and south ; on the north-east the ground drops very steeply to the River Barle ; on the south-east a steep face of rock makes a natural rampart. At the west end a bank of carefully piled and moderately large stones has been built across the ridge, which is very narrow at this point. The bank is 3 ft. high inside the camp and about 10 ft. above the present surface of the ditch outside, but this ditch is almost completely silted up. This camp may have been occupied in conjunction with Mounsey Castle on the opposite side of the river in order to command the river and valley at this point (see p. 493).

MELLS.—WADBURY CAMP is about half a mile east of Mells Church, just north-west of and on the opposite bank of Mells stream to Tedbury Camp. The defence on the stream side is formed by the high precipitous banks of the stream, whilst on the landward side it is a scarp about 16 ft. high, with a shallow ditch at its base, below the counterscarp of which is a revetment of stones. The ditch and lower scarp cease at some modern buildings, and for the rest of the circuit of the camp the scarp has been affected by planting and other operations of cultivation. On the north-east the line of the defences has been almost completely obliterated, but the end of the camp over the river is shown on the map by the remains of a ditch. The middle bank running north and south and the low bank to north-west of the house are modern.

NORTON MALREWARD.—MAES KNOLL is at the east end of Dundry Hill, an offshoot of the Mendips, and is on the line of the Wansdyke. Across the north-west end, which would otherwise be easily accessible from the top of the hill to the west, a ditch 18 ft. deep and 90 ft. across at the top has been cut and stones and earth piled up on the eastern side forming a bank which is 43 ft. above the present bottom of the ditch and $17\frac{1}{2}$ ft. above the level of the inclosure on the east. At the north end part of the bank has been thrown down and the ditch partly filled up. On the south where the hill-top runs out as a somewhat narrow projection, earth and stones have been piled up to form a steep scarp 18 ft. high across the front of the headland. This scarp has been cut into at the west end to give easier access to the top of the hill. From this point to the bank on the north-west the natural scarp of the hill-side is extremely steep, whilst towards the east the hill-side is naturally steep and is broken by terraces formed by the escarpments of the strata. At the east end the Wansdyke runs up from the south-east and its ditch forms the eastern defence of the camp. On the west of the ditch the scarp rises 17 ft. and there is a slight bank at the top, whilst the counterscarp on the east is 8 ft. to 9 ft. high. Some little distance east of this ditch there are remains of an outer bank running north-west to south-east with a slight ditch in front. From the east the bank is 8 ft. high at its highest point and there is a slight bank when seen from the west. Along the northern side of the camp the natural scarp is

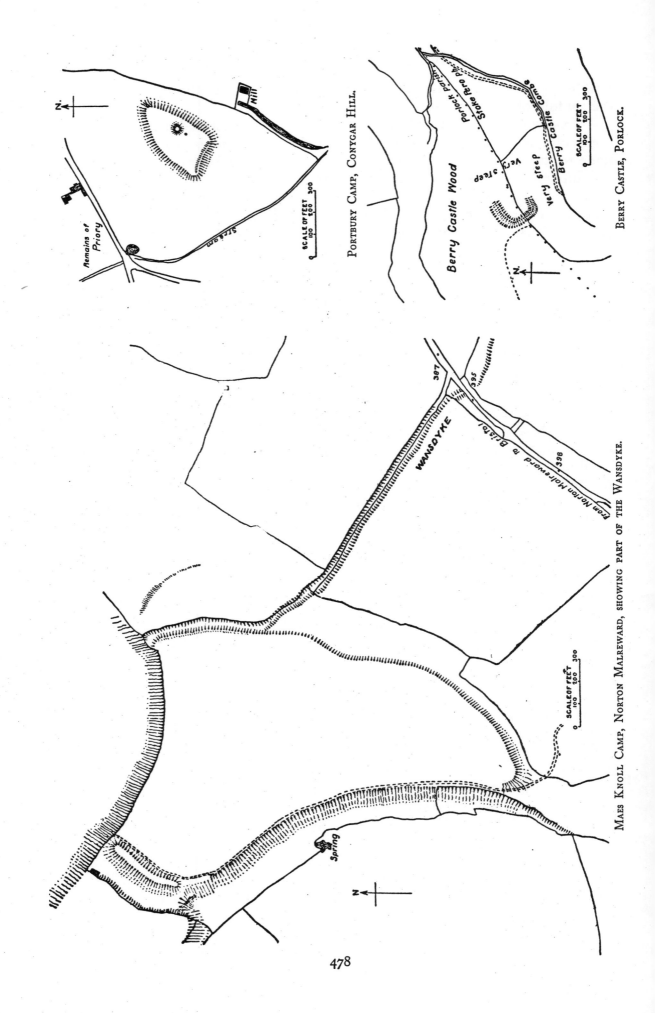

PORTBURY CAMP, CONYGAR HILL.

BERRY CASTLE, PORLOCK.

MAES KNOLL CAMP, NORTON MALREWARD, SHOWING PART OF THE WANSDYKE.

also extremely steep. There is a spring and pond on the west side at the foot of the scarp.

PORLOCK.—BERRY CASTLE, about two miles south-west of Porlock Church, some way down the slope of a very steep and narrow headland at the top of Hornbush Wood, is a rectangular inclosure about 40 yds. square, cut off from the mainland to the south-west by a ditch 8 ft. deep and 28 ft. broad at the top, which is continued at right angles round the sides of the camp. On the south-east side the bank (of stones) is now 12 ft. above the ditch and 1½ ft. above the inclosure ; the counterscarp of the ditch is about 3 ft. high and outside it the ground is almost precipitous. On the north-west the ditch is much silted up and the bank is 7 ft. above its present surface. The boundary wall between the parishes of Porlock and Stoke Pero runs through the middle of this camp, and on the north-west side of it the main ditch is largely silted up, whilst on the south-east side it is still deep. Inside the camp the ground slopes considerably to the north-east, and on this side there is no bank or ditch, the slope of the hill rapidly becoming almost precipitous.

PORTBURY.—A small isolated hill with a flat top, about two miles south-west of the church, has been converted into a triangular fort of 1½ acres by the scarping of the sides near the top and the erection of a bank, now 60 to 70 yds. long and 3 ft. high, along the south-west edge. According to Rutter (op. cit. 255–6) this bank, 3 ft. high, originally encircled the whole camp, and in his day was still visible in many places. There is a small tumulus inside the camp.[8]

PORTISHEAD.—About a mile north of the village a steep and narrow ridge of rock runs east and west, and the east end of it has been fortified by means of a bank and ditch running up the slopes and across the top. The hill is so thickly wooded that the bank is difficult to trace, but it seems to have been at least 10 ft. high and constructed of piled stones. The ditch is almost entirely filled up. The making of roads and erection of houses have almost completely destroyed the bank on the lower slopes of the hill. On the lower

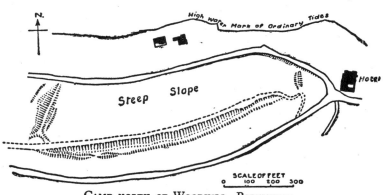

CAMP NORTH OF WOODHILL, PORTISHEAD.

slope of the eastern end there are some remains of a low bank, possibly intended for the defence of a landing place, but this end of the hill also has been altered by the making of a quay and the erection of an hotel.

STOGUMBER.—CURDON CAMP, on the edge of a ridge about one mile north-north-east of Stogumber Church, is not at the highest point, but a little way down the end of the ridge, where it drops steeply to a brook. At the west end, running north and south and turning round at its south end to run east and west, are remains of a bank of stones and

[8] Scarth, *Somers. Arch. Soc. Proc.* xxvii (I), 71.

earth now 8 ft. high, with a ditch in front now almost completely silted up. On the north-west and south, and further down to the east, the rest of the banks' has been quarried away. It seems fairly clear, however, that the eastern defence of the camp was a steep scarp. The ground within the inclosure slopes somewhat rapidly from west to east.

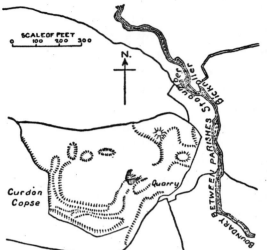

CURDON CAMP, STOGUMBER.

Turk's Castle is the name of a low rounded hill on the opposite side of the valley, but Phelps (op. cit. 115) found no vestiges of an earthwork there. It has since been cut through by the railway.

STOKE, NORTH.—LITTLE DOWN CAMP occupies the end of a westward projection of Lansdown Hill, which rises steeply to the east of the church. The camp is triangular in shape, about 350 yds. across the curved base, and 370 yds. from base to apex, which points west, and it was formed by cutting a ditch 10 ft. deep and 20 ft. to 25 ft. broad across the headland. There is a slight bank on the inner crest of the ditch, now occupied by a wall, and there are irregular mounds of earth some yards from the edge of the ditch on the opposite

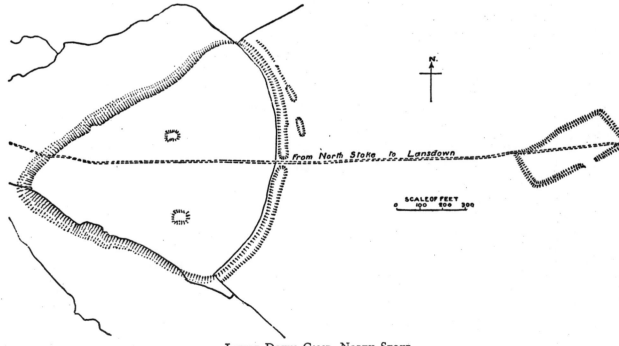

LITTLE DOWN CAMP, NORTH STOKE.

(east) side. There is no bank round the other faces of the camp, but the ground falls almost precipitously. The present entrance is in the middle of the base, and a very low bank runs down the middle of the camp from this entrance nearly to the apex. North and south of this bank there is an oblong tumulus. Three hundred and fifty yds. due east of the base of this camp is an oblong inclosure, 150 yds. in length north-east to south-west, and 60 yds. in breadth south-east to north-west. It is surrounded by an earthen bank with a ditch outside, now almost silted up. On the north side of it are traces of low banks and ditches, probably representing trenches thrown up in connexion with the battle of Lansdown in the Parliamentary war. Collinson[9] states that the entrenchment above North Stoke was formed by the Parliamentary army, but it seems clear that this cannot relate to the triangular fort at the end of the hill, which has all the characteristics of a prehistoric work.

STOKE PERO.—See Porlock.

HILL FORTS
[CLASS B]

BATHEALTON.—THE CASTLES stands on the west end of a high ridge, somewhat less than a quarter of a mile east-south-east from Venn Cross Viaduct, on the Devon and Somerset Branch Railway, and is an ellipse about 230 yds. long and 140 yds. broad. The ground falls steeply to the north, less steeply to the west and south, and is level on the east. At the east end

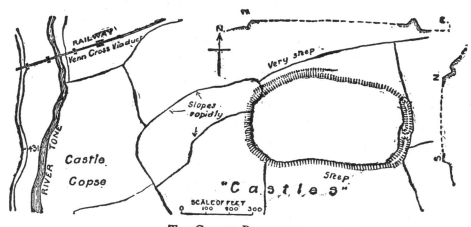

THE CASTLES, BATHEALTON.

is a bank 14 ft. to 15 ft. high on the outside and 6 ft. to 8 ft. high on the inside, and in the middle of this is the entrance, the bank turning inward on either side for 10 yds. to 12 yds. At present there is no indication of any outer ditch. Except at the east end there is no bank along the crest of the inclosure, the defence being a scarp 10 ft. to 15 ft. high, with a gradient rather steeper than one in two. A modern hedge and bank run along the crest of the inclosure on the south-west and inside the bank on the east. The eastern half of the north side has been partly levelled by the plough, and the northern end of the east bank thrown down. Along the western half of the north side there is a ditch 4 ft. to 5 ft. broad with a counterscarp now about 1 ft. high, and this can be traced about half-way round the west front, but then dies out.

9 Collinson, *Hist. of Somers.* i, 134.

BRENT KNOLL.—BRENT KNOLL CAMP occupies the summit of the isolated conical hill on the lower slopes of which the village stands. It is oval, with the major axis running north-east to south-west, and the defences are a bank round the upper edge, with the steeply scarped hill-side below ending in a ditch with a bank on its counterscarp, following the natural line of the hill. On the north-east, where the slope is gentler than on the other sides, there is a second ditch and bank at a lower level. The inside of the camp has been dug out or quarried at various points. Below the main knoll is an extensive plateau separated from the plain below by an inland cliff about 100 ft. high and forming an area adapted to cultivation and cattle rearing by the occupants of the camp. The highest point of this camp is 547 ft. above sea-level.

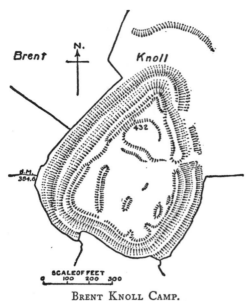

BRENT KNOLL CAMP.

BROMPTON REGIS. — BURY CASTLE stands above the junction of the River Exe with its tributary the Haddeo, at the end of a high ridge running north and south. It is oval in shape, the apex pointing south-west and the base north-east; maximum length about 120 yds., and maximum breadth about 80 yds. The area of the camp is planted, and there is much undergrowth. The ground outside falls steeply on the south-east and north-west, rather less steeply on the south-west, and more gradually on the north-east. The main defence is a bank of earth and flat shale from 16 ft. to 19 ft. high, with a ditch at its base, and a counterscarp, on the north-east, of $5\frac{1}{2}$ ft. On the east - south - east for about 40 yds. this outer ditch is almost entirely silted up. Inside the camp there is a bank along the crest on the north-east and north, but on the east and south-east there is no distinct bank.

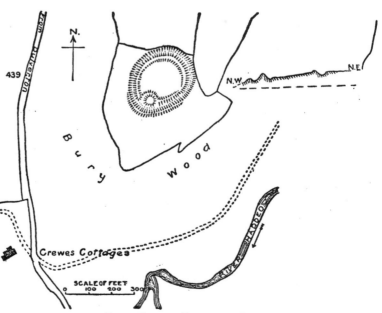

BURY CASTLE, BROMPTON REGIS.

The entrance is at the apex on the south-west and is peculiar in construction. The apex is occupied by a mount with an inclosing ditch; it is 19 ft. above the surface of the ditch on the south, and 12 ft. above the surface of the ditch on the north, its diameter at the base is 88 ft. north to south, and the diameter of its flat top is 15 ft. north to south. South-east of this mount is an outer bank 110 yds. long formed of stones and earth, with a shallow ditch in front of it, the bank on the south being 10 ft. 6 in. above the surface of the ditch. On the north-east side of the mount a shallow ditch separates it from the main area of the camp, its ends running into the outer ditch. The ground within the inclosure falls from north-east to south-west. This camp might be classed with mount and base court forts, but the mount is very small as compared with the area of the inclosure.

BROOMFIELD.—RUBOROUGH CAMP occupies the end of a high ridge one mile north of Broomfield Church. The inclosure is triangular with a truncated apex pointing north-east. The internal length from base to apex is about 230 yds. and the width at the base about 170 yds. The defence is a bank with a ditch below and a bank on the counterscarp of the ditch except where the ground falls very steeply. The bank is 18 ft. and in places more, above the present surface of the ditch, the highest point being at the apex of the triangle. The entrance is near the middle of the base of the triangle. About 100 yds. west-south-west is an outer defence about 220 yds. long consisting of a bank 6 ft. to 10 ft. high with a platform about 8 yds. wide on the western side and a ditch about 7 yds. wide as the outermost western defence.[10]

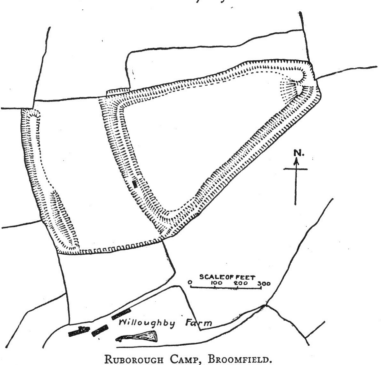

RUBOROUGH CAMP, BROOMFIELD.

BURRINGTON.—BURRINGTON CAMP is on the lower slope of the Mendip about half a mile south of Burrington Church, and on the eastern edge of a steep coomb, down which runs the road from Charterhouse to Burrington. The inclosure is oblong, with rounded corners, its length north by east to south by west being about 120 yds., and west by north to east by south about 80 yds. The defence is a bank of stones 4½ ft. to 8 ft. high with a ditch on the outside and also on the inside, the latter being an uncommon feature. The counterscarp of the outer ditch is 4 ft. to 5 ft. high, and of the inner ditch 2 ft. to 3 ft. high. Another special point is that along the south front, and less distinctly along the east front, the bank seems to have been built to form a rampart walk at a height of about 6 ft., with a breastwork about 3 ft. Along the east the upper part

<hr />

10 *Somers. Arch. Soc. Proc.* xlix (2), 173–80.

of the breastwork has been thrown down. From the south-west corner the bank continues in a straight line almost due west to the edge of the coomb, and from the north-east corner it continues for about 20 yds.

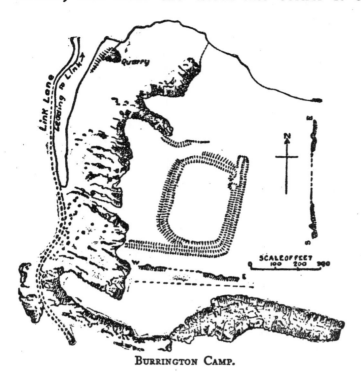

BURRINGTON CAMP.

almost due north, these extensions being clearly of the nature of flanking defences. There is also a short length of bank in front of the north-west angle, just above a quarry, but this is formed by the outcrop of almost vertical beds of limestone. The entrance to the inclosure was at the north-east corner, the banks, of which only the foundations here remain, turning in for about 20 yds.

CADBURY, SOUTH. — CADBURY CAMP occupies with its defences the whole of an isolated hill which rises steeply about 200 ft. immediately south-west of South Cadbury Church. In plan it is a spherical triangle with the angles pointing north, south-east and south-west. The defences are very strong and consist of four concentric steep and high banks with ditches between, which are now best seen on the west. The lowest bank is $42\frac{1}{2}$ ft. high, and the lowest ditch, between it and the second bank, is the deepest, its counterscarp being 15 ft. high, and its scarp 26 ft. The second ditch from the bottom is very shallow and little more than a terrace. At the top the bank is about 10 ft. above the level of the inclosure ; on the north-east and north-west it has been replaced by a modern wall. The sides of the hill are planted, and except along the west the defences are partly obliterated by the silting up of the ditches, but the banks can be traced all the way round. There are two original entrances : one to the east of the northern angle, the uppermost bank turning inwards for a considerable distance to flank the pathway ; and the other, also strongly protected, at the south-west angle. The latter has been somewhat altered by a modern cartway. The entrance in the east side of the camp is modern. Within the inclosure, which comprises about 18 acres, there is towards the west a natural platform with steep sides to the south, west and north-west, and a gentle slope to the east and north-east, and across this a bank has been thrown. There are two springs within the area of the fortifications : one, Arthur's Well, near the foot on the north-west ; and Queen Anne's Well, higher up on the east. Roman coins have been found within the inclosure.[11]

CARHAMPTON.—BATS CASTLE, on the top of the hill about one mile south of Dunster Castle, is an approximately circular inclosure with two

11 Dymond, *Journ. Brit. Arch. Assoc.* 1882, pp. 104–10. *Somers. Arch. Soc. Proc.* xxix (2), 110–16.

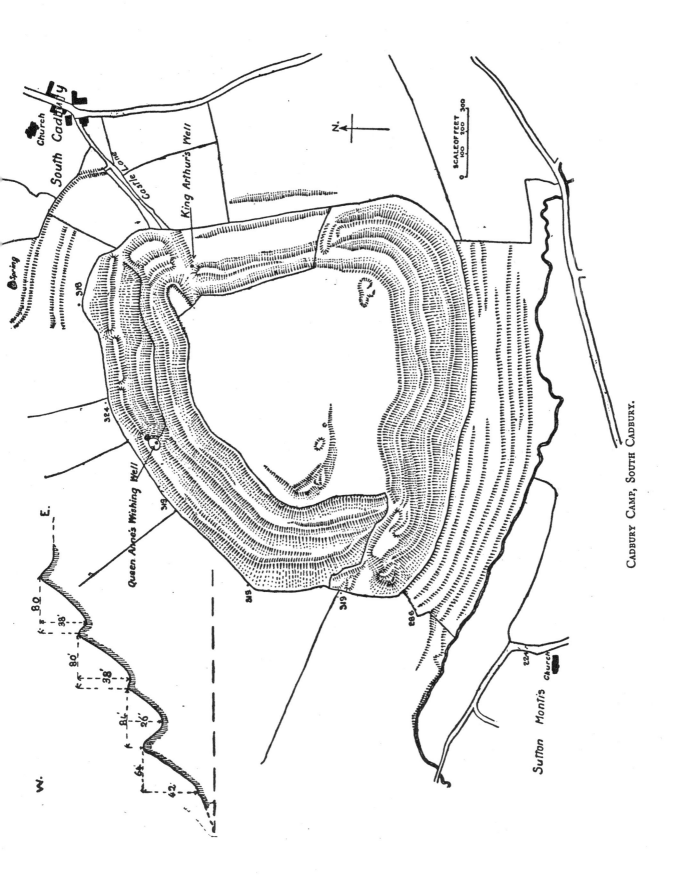

CADBURY CAMP, SOUTH CADBURY.

485

banks of stone and a ditch between, maximum internal diameter 150 yds. On the south the hill drops very steeply to a valley, and on the north it is also steep, whilst on the east and west the hill-top is fairly level. The outer bank is 3 ft. to 8 ft. above the ground-level on the outside, and 6 ft. to 10 ft. above the present surface of the ditch on its inner side. The inner bank is 13 ft. to 16 ft. above the surface of the ditch and 3 ft. to 7 ft. above the level of the inclosure. The outer bank is very slight on the south-west where the ground falls very steeply. In places on the east the outer bank has been destroyed. One entrance is on the west by a pathway 9 ft. broad, the ditch and inner bank being of more than average depth and height respectively, and the bank turns inwards to flank the passage. On either side there are some remains of masonry, but the mortar is modern in

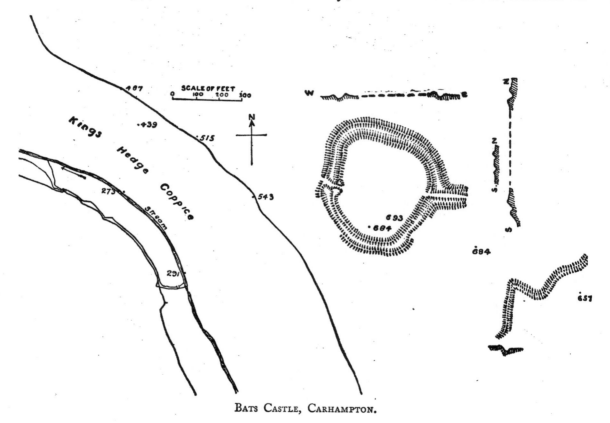

BATS CASTLE, CARHAMPTON.

character, and what is left is probably the remains of gate posts. The opposite entrance is very peculiar; the pathway continues eastwards for about 25 yds. as a raised platform, 8 yds. broad and 2 ft. to 4 ft. high, with a ditch along each side, and a bank 6 ft to 7 ft. high outside the ditch. The east end is a little narrower than the west. On either side of the entrance there are indications that shallow pits, very like rifle pits, have been dug in the outer face of the bank.

About 140 yds. south-east from the camp and lower down the hill is a zigzag bank of stones and earth 15 ft. to 18 ft. high, with a shallow ditch in front. Its total length is about 200 yds., and it commands the ascent of the hill from the valleys on the south-east. It is clearly of much later date than the camp, and is probably one of the outworks thrown up during the siege of Dunster Castle in the Parliamentary war.

ANCIENT EARTHWORKS

CHILCOMPTON.—BLACKER'S HILL CAMP, immediately south-east of Blacker's Hill Farm, occupies a promontory on a high ridge about one mile south-west of Downside Church. On the west the defence is a scarp, below which the ground falls steeply; on the south the natural fall is steep; on the north and east the defence was a double bank of stones and earth with a broad ditch outside; but on the east end of the north face and the north end of the east face the outer bank only now remains.

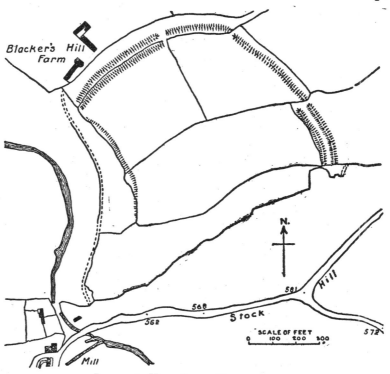

BLACKER'S HILL CAMP, CHILCOMPTON.

CHURCHILL.—DOLBURY CAMP occupies the western end of Dolbury Warren at the north-west corner of the Mendip. It is an oblong with rounded corners, maximum internal length about 525 yds., and maximum internal breadth about 250 yds. The main defence is a great rampart of stones 12 ft. to 22 ft. high from the outside and 8 ft. to 20 ft. high from the inside, which incloses all sides but the south; and outside this is a ditch with a second and lower bank beyond, this bank being about 3 ft. above the bottom of the ditch and $5\frac{1}{2}$ ft. to 11 ft. above the ground outside. This rampart crosses the highest point of the hill at the east end of the camp, but elsewhere follows the general contour of the hill. The ground inside the inclosure slopes somewhat rapidly from east to west, especially at the east end, with the result that at this end the stone rampart is higher from the inside than from the outside. Along the south face the ground falls almost precipitously, and here the rampart is very low with the southern face a steep scarp and a slight bank with a slight fosse between them about 12 ft. below the crest. At the east end the surface of the hill is fairly level for some distance, and not only is the main rampart high and the outer bank substantial, but at a distance of 90 yds. from the outer ditch a shallow and narrow ditch has been cut in the rocky surface across the top of the hill. There is a narrow original entrance near the south end of the east front, close to the precipitous face of the hill, and there is a modern entrance towards the north end of the east front. The principal entrance was on the west, the path (the lower part of which has been quarried away) ascending a steep but shallow coomb formed by a bifurcation of this end of the hill, and being dominated by the southern and higher arm of the fork. Towards the top the path

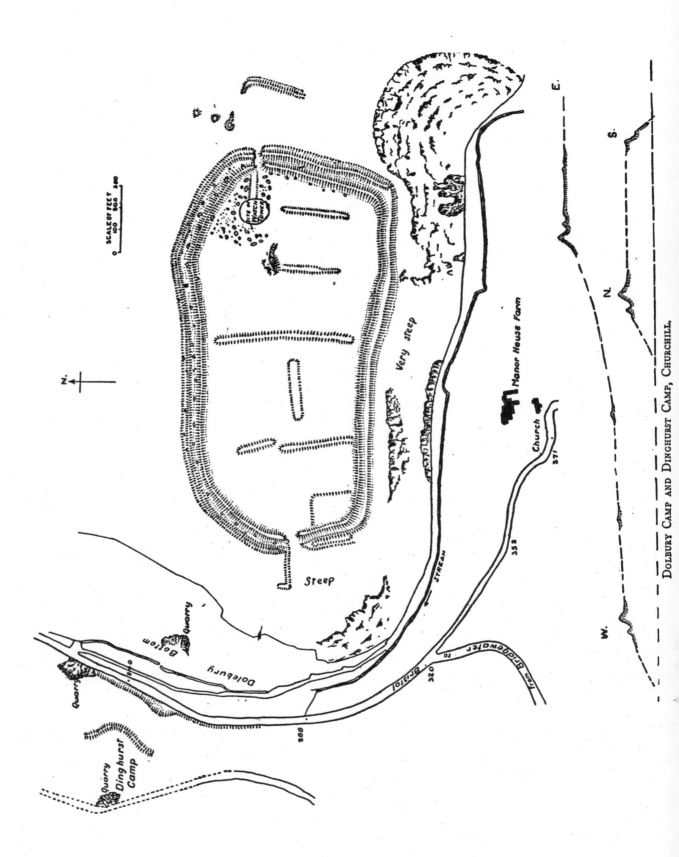

SCALE OF FEET

Steep

Very steep

Manor House Farm

Church

STREAM

Dolebury Bottom

Quarry

Quarry

Dinghurst Camp

Quarry

to BRISTOL

from BRIDGEWATER

DOLBURY CAMP AND DINGHURST CAMP, CHURCHILL.

turned north-west, and was flanked on the one side by the flattish summit of the northern arm of the fork and by the rampart of the camp. An artificial mound defending this path on the north side of the bend has been cut through by a modern cartway which ascends gradually the west face of the hill. At the west end of the camp on either side of the entrance there is a third bank, and from the north side of the pathway a shallow ditch runs west down the face of the hill for about 55 yds., and then turns north for about 10 yds.

A peculiar feature of this camp is that the base of the main rampart, along the north side at least, is formed of dry masonry of large stones of irregular shape piled to form an approximately smooth surface. It would seem that this rose to a height of a few feet, above which the stones were piled loosely. This method is sometimes employed for railway embankments at the present day.

Inside the camp there are remains of an inclosure in the south-west corner about 52 yds. long north to south and about 40 yds. broad east to west. Possibly it was a pond ; possibly it was a sort of amphitheatre, as at Hamdon Hill. Across the inclosure are two banks 12 ft. to 15 ft. broad and $1\frac{1}{2}$ ft. to $2\frac{1}{2}$ ft. high, whilst two similar banks go half-way across from the south side near the east end. In several places, especially just under the inner face of the main rampart, are peculiar X-shaped structures of stones with arms several yards long and a few inches high. They are vermin traps of modern origin. On the highest point of the inclosure are the remains of a war-rener's house and its circular inclosing wall, and here and there are holes caused by digging for minerals. Roman and Saxon coins, iron spear-heads

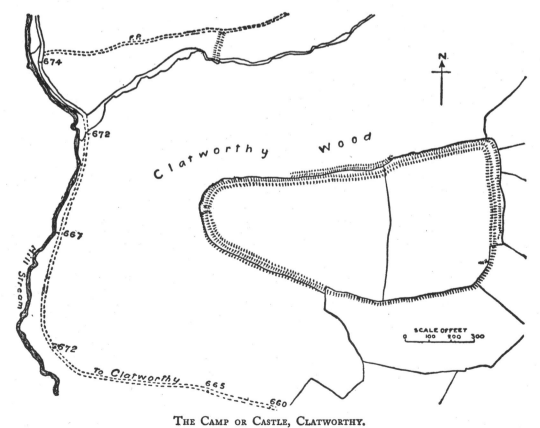

THE CAMP OR CASTLE, CLATWORTHY.

and other weapons, fragments of grey pottery, wheel-made but unglazed, and a few sling stones and flint flakes have been found in the camp.[12]

CLATWORTHY.—CLATWORTHY CAMP, or THE CASTLE, about three-quarters of a mile north-west of Clatworthy Church, occupies the end of a long ridge which here falls steeply to a brook on the north and west sides and more gradually on the south. The inclosure is roughly triangular with a rounded apex at the west end. The base at the east end is practically straight and about 200 yds. long, whilst the distance from base to apex is about 420 yds. The main defence is a bank of earth mixed with some stones, with a ditch below ; the bank is about 15 ft. high and the counter-scarp of the ditch is from 4 ft. to 7 ft. The banks are much overgrown. At the south end of the east face and along the east end of the south face the defence is a scarp with a ditch below and there is no bank along the crest of the inclosure. The entrance seems to have been at the south-east corner, but the bank here has been altered by agricultural operations. On the south-west there is an original entrance which opens on to a triangular platform about 30 ft. across which drops almost precipitously to the stream on the north-west and south-west. For part of the distance on the north there is a double ditch and the scarp above the inner ditch is only about 5 ft., but the ground falls steeply below the outer ditch, which still retains water.

COMPTON DUNDON.—DUNDON HILL CAMP occupies the whole of the top of the hill, which rises steeply more than 250 ft. above

DUNDON HILL CAMP, COMPTON DUNDON.

[12] Dymond, *Somers. Arch. Soc. Proc.* xxix (2), 104–16, and *Journ. Brit. Arch. Soc.* (1882), 104–10.

the surrounding plain. The defence was a bank of stones, 7 ft. high, along the edge of the hill, the outer face of the hill-top being steeply scarped. On the north-west the bank has disappeared and there is only the scarp, but the outcrop of the rock forms two terraces below. At the south end there is a mount with steep sides, known as the 'Beacon,' 12 ft. high above the inclosure and 27 ft. above the slight ditch at its base, and below this is a terrace with a steep scarp. Along the east side about 16 ft. below the top of the bank there is a ledge about 11 yds broad, below which the ground falls very steeply. The entrance was about the middle of this side but has been much altered.

CROSCOMBE.—MAESBURY CAMP is partly in Dinder and partly in Croscombe parish and stands on the western extremity of a long ridge of high ground running west-north-west east-south-east. The ground slopes steeply on the west-south-west and south, less steeply on north and north-east, and gradually on east and south-east. The camp is oval, about 330 yds. long and 260 yds. broad. The defence consisted of two ditches with a

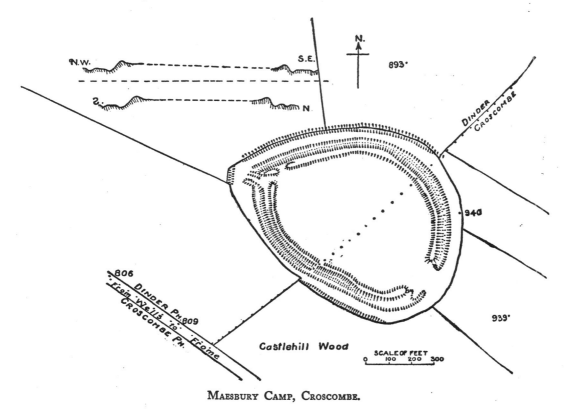

MAESBURY CAMP, CROSCOMBE.

somewhat broad bank between and a steep bank on the inner side of the inner ditch rising about 4 ft. above the level of the inner inclosure. On the south-east the inner bank has been thrown down and the ditch filled up for about 45 yds. In the next field to the south-east there are indications of a triangular or half-moon advance work, probably to protect this, the most easily accessible face of the camp. The banks consist of stones mixed with earth. The intermediate bank is narrow along the north-west and south-west, but broadens out to a sort of platform along the north-east and south-east. Along the north and north-west a modern bank and hedge run down the middle of the outer ditch, and for most of the rest of the circuit the outer ditch is more or less filled up and a bank and hedge occupy its counterscarp. On the north-west face and the northern part of the west face the inner bank has a fairly well marked intermediate terrace which however does not continue along the south front. The entrance was at the west end and was strongly defended. The inner bank on the north continues past the north end of the bank on the west, and the outer ditch on the west turns nearly at a right angle and continues for about 20 yds. alongside the entrance. On the opposite side of the entrance the north ditch turns inwards for about 9 yds. About 30 yds. west of the entrance and directly in front of it is a fragment of an outer bank now about 6 ft. high above the bottom of the ditch at its base.

DODINGTON.—DOWSBOROUGH CAMP (also called Danesborough) two miles west-south-west of Nether Stowey, and one and a half miles south by east of Holford, at the end and highest point of a steep and narrow ridge, is oval in shape with the major axis approximately north-west and south-east, and a maximum length of about 340 yds. and a maximum breadth of 170 yds. The greater part of the camp is covered with oak coppice. The defence is a bank of stones with a ditch and second rampart below, following the natural line of the hill, the bank being 2 ft. to $5\frac{1}{2}$ ft. above the surface of the inclosure and 9 ft. to 17 ft. above the present surface of

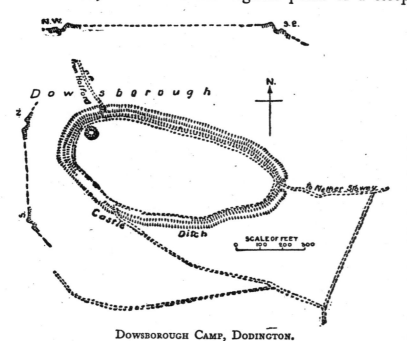

DOWSBOROUGH CAMP, DODINGTON.

the ditch the counterscarp of which is 3 ft. to $7\frac{1}{2}$ ft. high. For a considerable distance along the south face from the west the upper bank has been thrown down. The entrance seems to have been at the apex on the south-east, but here the banks have been altered and the ditch partly filled up. At the north-west end of the camp a few yards inside the rampart is a circular tumulus of stones $7\frac{1}{2}$ yds. north to south and 7 yds. east to west, with a flat top and no surrounding ditch. The ground slopes steeply from the camp on all sides but especially on the south and south-west.

DULVERTON.—MOUNSEY CASTLE stands on a high promontory which projects into a horseshoe bend of the Barle just south of its confluence with Danes Brook. It is an irregular triangle with the curved base running almost due east and west and the apex pointing north-east. At the apex there is a slight bank and ditch across the ridge and behind this a bank of piled stones about 10 ft. high. Further north-east the ridge is very narrow with a steep fall on both sides. At the west end of the north-east bank there was an entrance, the north-west bank turning in to flank it. From this point for a distance of about 200 yds. there is a platform 12 ft. broad below which the slope to the river is almost precipitous, and above rises a bank about 7 ft. high formed partly of natural rock and partly of large stones carefully piled. The top of this bank is level with the surface of the inclosure for about 120 yds., but there is a distinct bank on the inside of the camp for the remaining 80 yards. At the south-west corner is an entrance, the south bank turning inwards for some distance. At this entrance and along the greater part of the south front the bank is formed of large stones carefully piled. In places it seems to have been rebuilt for forestry purposes. Along part of the south front there are distinct indications of a ditch below the bank, which rises 12 ft. to 14 ft. above the present

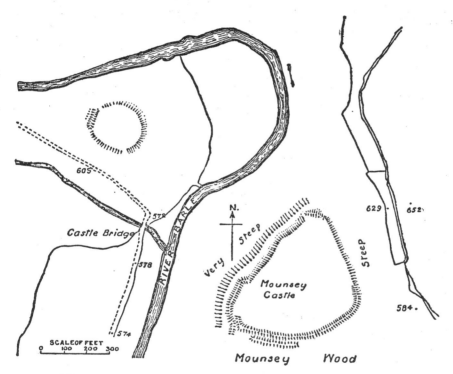

MOUNSEY CASTLE, DULVERTON, AND BREWERS CASTLE, HAWKRIDGE.

surface of the silting. Inside the inclosure the ground rises somewhat steeply from south to north with three different gradients, that to the south being steepest. The ground also falls to east and west from a line running approximately through the middle. On the east as on the north-west, the defence is a slope of piled stones which does not now rise above the surface of the inclosure. Inside and all round it except on the north-east there seems to have been a broad hollow immediately behind the rampart. The whole area of the camp has been planted and the banks and ditches are much obscured by tree roots, undergrowth and silting. The inclosure is about 170 yds. across the base of the triangle and 200 yds. from this base to the apex.

DULVERTON.—OLDBERRY CASTLE, about half a mile north-west of

Dulverton village, on a high promontory with a horseshoe base round which flows the River Barle, was originally an irregular oval about 240 yds. long and 100 yards at its broadest part. At the north-east end over the river there remains a bank of stones 7 ft. to 8 ft. above the present level of the outer ditch, which, however, has been much filled up by forest débris. This bank and ditch continue for 52 yds. round the north-west side and the bank continues in the same direction for about 130 yds., the modern fence being on the top of it and all trace of the ditch having disappeared under agricultural operations. Round the south-east face the bank continues for about 40 yds., but the ditch has been filled up. All along the south-east face the ground falls very steeply and the upper part, though much overgrown, seems to have been artificially scarped, but it is questionable whether there was any ditch along this face. Round the south-west end of the camp all traces of bank and ditch have disappeared and the land is under the plough.

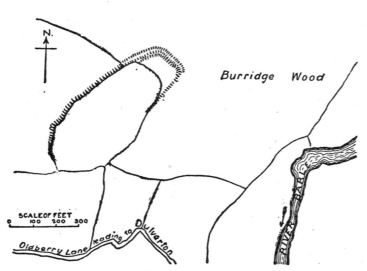

OLDBERRY CASTLE, DULVERTON.

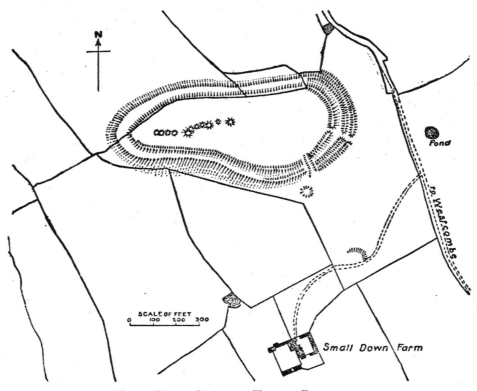

SMALL DOWN CAMP AND TUMULI, EVERCREECH.

ANCIENT EARTHWORKS

EVERCREECH.—SMALL DOWN CAMP occupies the top of a knoll 728 ft. above sea-level one mile north-east of Stoney Stratton and is an oval inclosure of about 6 acres with a maximum external length of 370 yds. and a maximum internal length of 290 yds. and a maximum breadth of 170 yds. The defence was a double bank with a ditch between, following the natural line of the hill. Both defences are now imperfect on the north and north-east and the lower bank and middle ditch are missing on the western half of the south front. On the east where access was easiest there are three banks with intervening ditches, and in the middle of this east end is one entrance 36 ft. wide and another through the south-east corner 30 ft. wide. The outer bank is 2 ft. to 3 ft. above the ground-level, the second bank about 9 ft. above the present surface of the ditch, and the inner bank 17 ft. above the present surface of the second ditch and 4 ft. to 5 ft. above the level of the inclosure. The top of the inner bank is 23 ft. above the bottom of the outer bank. The ditches were originally 5 ft. to 7 ft. deeper than they are now. Along the central and highest part of the camp is a row of eleven tumuli. Excavations by Mr. H. St. George Gray, which yielded flint implements, British pottery, animal remains, cremated interments and human remains, but nothing Roman or post-Roman, show that the entrances are original, and that the camp and tumuli belong to the Bronze Age.[13]

EXMOOR.—COW CASTLE stands on the middle and largest of three conical masses of rock which rise from marshy ground in an amphitheatre formed by the surrounding hills and washed on the west by the River Barle and on the east by the White Water stream. The hill is oval in plan with its apex to the west. A steep dip slope rises from east to west, whilst on the north-west and west the escarpment falls very steeply to the river. The rampart encircles the hill some distance from the top but rises from east to west and consists of a wall 3 ft. to 5 ft. across the top and about 7 ft. high on the outside, formed of carefully piled large stones now covered with earth in many parts. On the inside the wall is now low, but has been much silted up, and whether there was a rampart walk cannot be ascertained without digging. The entrance was on the south-east, the wall rising to about 12 ft. on either side. At the base of the wall was a ditch now very much silted up and no longer continuous, it being visible only along the east face, for a short distance due south, along the west, and on the north-east. The hill within the inclosure is precipitous on the north and very steep on the west. Along these parts there is a flat space about 12 ft. broad between the wall and the steep ground and this space is still swampy. On the north-east there is a modern opening through the rampart.

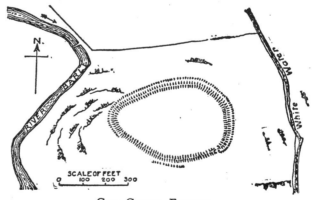

COW CASTLE, EXMOOR.

[13] *Somers. Arch. Soc. Proc.* xlix (2), 183–5 ; l (2), 32–49.

MELLS.—NEWBURY CAMP is on the top of a small hill about one mile north-east of Mells Church, and half a mile north-west of Great Elm Church. The main defence is a bank which follows the line of the hill and is strengthened by a ditch with a slight bank on the counterscarp on the north-west, whilst on the south-west it is still further strengthened by steep scarps along the face of the hill. The inner bank has been destroyed along the eastern half of the south-west front and along the east end.

MINEHEAD.— EAST MYNE CAMP. About three-quarters of a mile east-north-east of East Myne, on a headland above the Bristol Channel, are the remains of an elliptical, almost circular camp, the defence of which was a scarp 6 ft. to 8 ft. high, with a shallow ditch at the base. On the north side the scarp is 8 ft. high, and from inside the inclosure it forms a bank 2 ft. high. On the south the scarp is 6 ft. high, and its top is level with the inclosure.

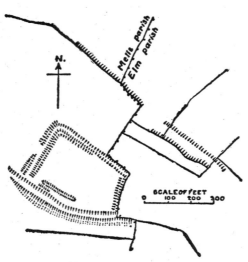

NEWBURY CAMP, MELLS.

The circuit of the camp is practically complete, except at the south-west corner, but the scarp is very low in places. The entrance seems to have been at the north-east corner. Inside the camp the ground slopes considerably from south to north, but is level from east to west. Outside the ground falls steeply on all sides except the west.[14]

NORTON-SUB-HAMDON.—HAMDON HILL is a fortification of unusual extent, north-east of Norton-sub-Hamdon and immediately south of Stoke-sub-Hamdon. It incloses a roughly oblong plateau 400 ft. above sea-level, half a mile across from north to south, and about three-fifths of a mile from east to west. At the north-west angle of this area the hill runs out to the north, forming a fan-tail projection about 600 yds. long, 200 yds. broad at its south end, where it joins the larger area, and 400 yds. broad at the north end. The sides of the hill fall very steeply about 240 ft. to the level land on the east, north and

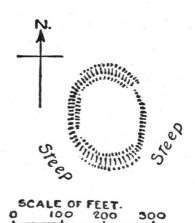

EAST MYNE CAMP, MINEHEAD.

west, and about 200 ft. a little less steeply on the south. The surface of the plateau is either under the plough or has been extensively and deeply quarried, whilst the east and part of the north slopes are thickly wooded, and the west slope has been altered by quarrying operations and the making of roads. The main defence was the same round the whole of the area, a distance of more than three miles. The upper slope of the hill was steeply scarped and a bank thrown up round its edge. A ditch, now

[14] Rev. F. Hancock's *Minehead*, 2.

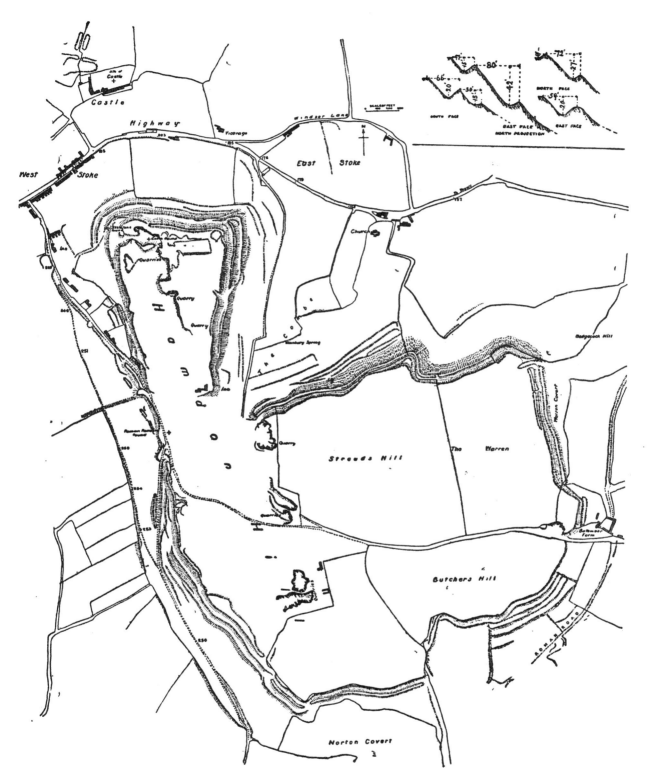

HAMDON HILL, NORTON-SUB-HAMDON.

8 ft. to 12 ft. broad, with a counterscarp which varies in height at different points, was formed some 20 ft. below the natural level of the plateau. Below this again the slope is steeply scarped, and at the south end and along part of the east side, some 20 ft. below the upper ditch, is a second and less important ditch, now almost completely silted up. On the lower slopes of the hill the natural outcrop of the rock forms steep escarpments, which add to the difficulty of the ascent. The bank round the edge of the plateau still exists along the north and east sides of the smaller projecting portion, for 400 yds. along the west side of the larger area, for about 200 yds. at the north end of its east side, and for about 40 yds. on either side of a sharp bend near the middle of the north side of the larger area, but elsewhere it has disappeared. The upper ditch and its bank can be traced all round except at the south-east corner of the main area, along parts of the west side of the projecting portion, where it has been destroyed by the making of a road, and in the north-east angle, where the projecting portion joins the main area.

In the north-east angle of the projecting portion, close under the bank, is an approximately circular amphitheatre 100 ft. in diameter, with an entrance at the south end, whilst immediately south-west of this is an oblong inclosure 100 yds. east and west by 40 yds. north and south, marked on the Ordnance map as 'equestrian camp.'

The principal original entrance now remaining is at the north-east corner of the main area, where a broad path rises steeply through the banks, and the northern bank runs out for about 60 yds. to effectively flank the upper part of it. At this corner of the hill a steep and narrow ridge runs out east-north-east and rises steeply to a cone with an elliptical base known as Hedgecock Hill. The lower bank of the entrenchments continues along this ridge, and dies away some distance from its top. The sides of this hill have been scarped, and not only did the ridge and hill very effectively flank the entrance on this side, but the hill most probably served as a beacon or outlook for the whole fortification.

There is a smaller entrance about the middle of the east side of the projecting part, but this seems to have been intended as a way of retreat from the ditches to the upper part of the camp, or at most was of the nature of a postern. The upper bank turns inwards obliquely so as to flank this entrance at the top.

Whether, as one would expect, there was an entrance in the angle between the projecting part and the larger area, it is now impossible to say, because the area has been much altered by quarrying. There are some indications, by no means conclusive, that the projecting area was cut off from the main part of the hill by a large bank and ditch, so as to form a sort of 'keep,' to which the main hill plateau stood in the relation of a huge bailey. This is a conjecture only, as the ground along the neck of the projection has been much quarried. It is noteworthy however that the banks and ditches of this projecting portion are much more formidable than those of the main area. There are two ditches, and the principal bank rises more than 40 ft. above the present surface of the lower ditch, whilst the upper bank rises 15 ft. above the surface of the upper ditch.

Weapons and other articles of Neolithic, Celtic and Roman work have been found in the camp, and most of them are now in the Taunton Museum. Remains of Roman buildings have also been found.[15]

OTHERY.—BURROWBRIDGE.—KING ALFRED'S FORT is a conical hill (with the ruins of a church on the top), which has the appearance of being terraced, but the terraces are mainly if not entirely due to the outcrop of rocks of different hardness. The escarpments may have been made steeper artificially, but at the present time there is no distinct evidence of human fortifications. There is however a considerable flat area at the top and the place is naturally very strong so that it may well have been utilized in Alfred's struggles with the Danes.

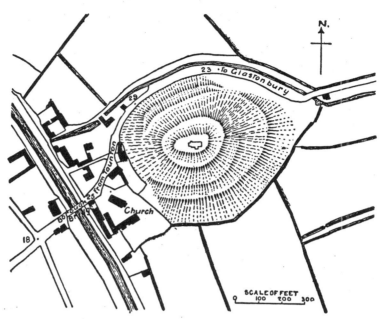

KING ALFRED'S FORT, BURROWBRIDGE, OTHERY.

SELWORTHY.—BURY CASTLE is rather more than a quarter of a mile north of Selworthy Church, on the end of an inland promontory, which is flat on the west, but slopes very steeply on the north and east, and somewhat less steeply on the south. The inclosure is on the brow of the hill somewhat below its highest point, and the ground inside slopes to the east. The camp is approximately square, with slightly convex sides and rounded corners, 70 yds. north-east to south-west, and 50 yds. north-west to south-east. On the east, north-east and south-east the defence is a steep scarp about 12 ft. high with a gradient of 1 in 2, whilst on the north, west and south it is a bank of earth and small stones with a ditch below, the bank being about 6 ft. high inside the camp, and 11 ft. to 12 ft. above the ditch outside, whilst the counterscarp of the ditch is about 6½ ft. The entrance seems to have been on the north-east, the bank projecting beyond the line of the counterscarp of the ditch which here dies out into the main scarp, whilst a path winds up and round the end of the

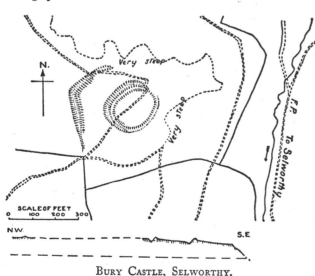

BURY CASTLE, SELWORTHY.

[15] Sir E. Hoare, *Arch.* xxi, 29–42 (plan with hill shading); R. Walter, *Somers. Arch. Soc. Proc.* iv, 78–90 (reproduces Hoare's plan); H. Norris, ibid. xxx, 138–48, and xxxii, 43–50. R. H. Walter, ibid. liii (2), 179–82.

bank. About 30 yds. west of the inclosure a bank and ditch run across the promontory from the north, for a distance of about 100 yds., dying out gradually on the south. The bank is of earth and stones, about 10 ft. high on the east and 11 ft. high on the west. The ditch is 12 ft. to 14 ft. broad, and its counterscarp is very steep and about 5 ft. high. Some 200 yds. further west is a low bank running across the ridge, with a modern boundary bank on the top of it for about half its length.

STANTON PRIOR.—STANTONBURY CAMP is on the line of the Wansdyke which forms its northern boundary. To the east of the camp the Wansdyke has its characteristic structure of a bank with a ditch on its north side, but along the north face of the camp the ditch though distinct is but slight, whilst from the north-west corner of the camp the Wansdyke continues in a north-west direction as a double bank with a ditch between. The camp itself is triangular, with a curved base running north-east to south-west, the

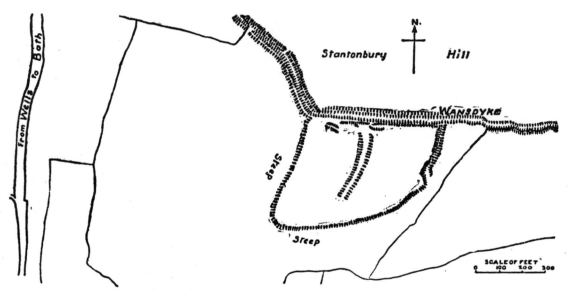

STANTONBURY CAMP, STANTON PRIOR, SHOWING PART OF THE WANSDYKE.

distance in this direction being about 300 yds. ; from east to west 200 yds., and north-north-east to south-south-west 170 yds. On the west face the defence is a scarp much overgrown by shrubs and trees, on the east a scarp with a ditch below, and on the south a scarp and slope which has recently been planted. The camp is divided into two parts by a broad ditch running approximately north and south.

TICKENHAM.—CADBURY CAMP, on the top of the hill three-quarters of a mile north-north-west from Tickenham Church, is roughly circular with a maximum diameter of 300 yds., and is inclosed by double banks of stones mixed with some earth, with a ditch between and a ditch outside. Both outer and inner banks are 10 ft. to 12 ft. above the present surface of the ditches, whilst the outer counterscarp, often formed by the natural rock, is 2 ft. to 4 ft. high. The top of the outer bank is in many places several feet broad, whilst the top of the inner bank is narrow. The banks and ditches are in fairly good preservation all round. The entrance is on the north, and was very strong, the outer and inner banks on the east side being turned respec-

tively outwards and inwards so as to flank the passage. There are modern entrances at the north-west corner and about the middle of the west side, and a pathway cuts through the banks on the south side towards the south-
 .t angle, whilst another pathway cuts partly into the banks on the east side towards the south end. The ground outside the camp falls fairly steeply on all sides except the south, and the view from the camp includes a very wide area. It is probable that whilst the camp was in use the base of the hill was washed by an arm of the sea. About 150 yds. west of the

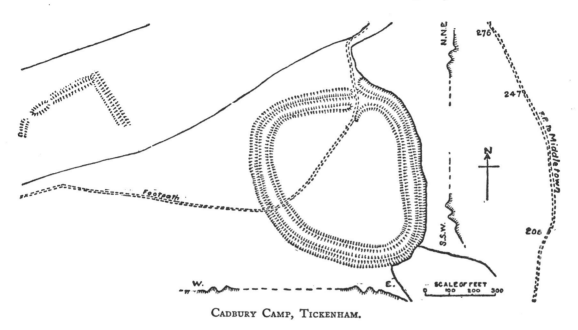

CADBURY CAMP, TICKENHAM.

camp a low bank of stones runs for about 50 yds. down the slope of the hill, and at right angles to its lower termination is a scarp 12 ft. high with a shallow ditch at its base, running east-north-east to west-south-west for about 100 yds., with distinct indications that once it continued further west-south-west and curved round with the curve of the hill-side, protecting the approach from this side. At the top of the scarp, from the inner side, it appears as a bank with a gradual slope. The straight bank running down the hill is about 3 ft. high, and it has a shallow ditch 5 ft. broad on the west-south-west side.

WESTON-SUPER-MARE.—WORLEBURY CAMP occupies the western part of a long, narrow, steep hill, which rises on the north of the town. It occu-pies about $10\frac{1}{4}$ acres, and is an elongated oval, the maximum internal length being about 520 yds. and the maximum internal breadth 140 yds. The main defence consisted of a rampart of stone, not merely piled up, but built in sections of dry walling. At the eastern end, where the approach is easiest, the defence is strongest, and consists of a series of four trenches, now 3 ft. to 4 ft. deep, but originally 6 ft. to 8 ft. deep, cut in the rock across the top of the hill and dying out on the steep hill-side at either end. Behind this is a great curved rampart of stone about 15 ft. high, soon dying out on the steep face of the hill on the north side, but continuing for a greater distance along the south side, and dying out below the main entrance. Behind this again is the main rampart, 15 ft. to 20 ft. high at this point, sloping down to and dying out on the north cliff, but continuing, although lower, all along the south face of the camp to the west end, which is precipitous. Below this rampart, about 20 ft. down the hill-side, was a ditch with a low bank which ran from the main entrance to the west end, but is now filled

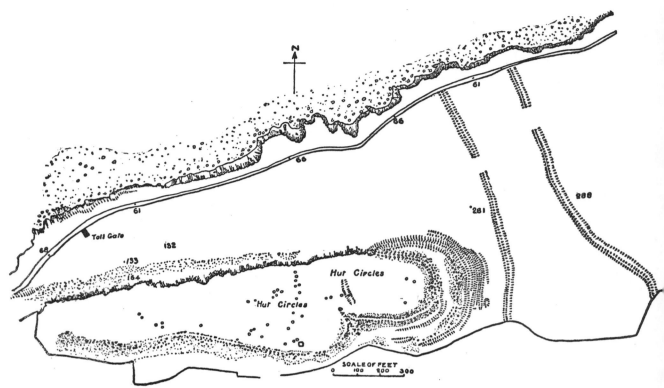

WORLEBURY CAMP, WESTON-SUPER-MARE.

with stones. The stone ramparts were built up in the manner shown in A and B below, each section being built up with a carefully laid face of dry masonry, battering from the ground level. In the great outer rampart at the east end there were five sections, and at the entrance and all along the main rampart there were four sections. At present this structure is visible only at a few points, the rest having been hidden by the throwing down of the upper part of the walling.

There were three entrances : one through both ramparts at the north-east corner, another, very steep and narrow, at the west end, and the main entrance on the south, about one-quarter of the distance from the east end. At this point the main rampart turns in on both sides, forming a re-entrant angle and effectually flanking the passage, now filled up with a mass of loose stones. This entrance was approached by an ancient roadway on the south slope of the hill, now almost entirely destroyed by the erection of villas and the making of gardens. According to the earlier plans, the south slope of the hill had some subsidiary works and a number of triangular patches of stones supposed to be slingers' platforms, but these have been destroyed in the manner stated.

The west end of the hill is precipitous, and the northern side is precipitous in places and drops very steeply to the Bristol Channel. Along these faces there is now no trace of any rampart, and if at any time one existed it must have been but slight.

Rather less than one-quarter of the distance from the east end an inner ditch was cut across the hill-top, converting this end of the inclosure into a sort of 'keep.' The ditch is not quite continuous, but is bridged near the middle by a piece of the undisturbed rock, in which is sunk one of the pits referred to below.

Outside the main inclosure, at a distance of 200 yds. from the outer edge of the outer great rampart, a ditch, now about 3 ft. deep, with a low bank of stones on the west side, was made across the hill-top and continued down the steep sides. On the south it has been curtailed by the erection of houses with gardens, but on the north it continues down to the cliffs over the Channel. One hundred and fifty yds. further west and 50 yds. from the outer great rampart is a similar ditch and bank. It has been conjectured that these outworks formed a cattle inclosure, but they may only have been intended as preliminary obstacles to an approach from this side.

Special features of this camp are the pits, ninety-three in number, and approximately circular in shape, cut in the rock to a depth of 6 ft. to 7 ft.[16]

WHITESTAUNTON. —About one and a half miles south-west of Whitestaunton on the high ground east of the River Yarty is a camp roughly oval in shape, rather less than 300 yds. long by 135 yds. at its broadest part. On the north-east where the approach is easiest the defence is a bank with a ditch in front; along the east, south and south-west there is a bank, but along the west where

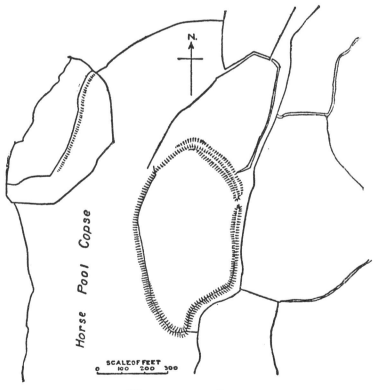

WHITESTAUNTON CAMP.

the hill falls very steeply to the river, the hill-side has simply been scarped. The entrance is on the east side towards the north end.

[16] *V.C.H. Somerset* i, 202. Dymond and Tomkins, *Worlebury* (1st Ed. 1886; 2nd Ed. 1904); F. Warre, *Somers. Arch. Soc. Proc.* ii (2), 64–85; ibid. iii (1), 12–13 and iv (2), 124–7.

WINSFORD.—ROAD CASTLE, on the hill-side above the River Exe, about three-quarters of a mile south-east of Exford, stands some distance below the top of the hill. The defence on the east, south and west was a high bank of stones mixed with earth, with a ditch below, whilst on the north it was a steep scarp with a ditch below, now much silted up, and below this the ground drops steeply to the river. The camp was almost square with the corners truncated and somewhat rounded. On the east the bank has been thrown down and the ditch filled up, a modern bank and hedge occupying its place, and on the west the ditch has been filled up, the adjoining land being under the plough. On the south, which was most easily approached, the bank is 15 ft. above the bottom of the ditch and the counterscarp is 5 ft. high. Inside the camp the bank is

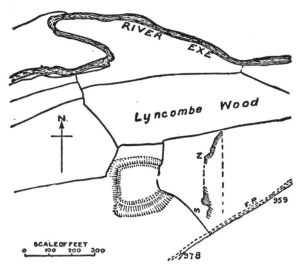

ROAD CASTLE, WINSFORD.

6 ft. high. On the west the bank is 10 ft. above the present surface and on the north the scarp is 13 ft. to 15 ft. above the ditch. The entrance seems to have been in the destroyed side.

WINSFORD.—STADDON HILL CAMP is on the lower slope of the north side of Staddon Hill overlooking the Larcombe Brook and the road from Winsford to Exford, two and a half miles north-west of Winsford and one and a half miles east-south-east of Exford Church. The main inclosure is pseudo-circular, 40 yds. in diameter, but in reality is an irregular octagon with rounded angles, inclosed within a bank of earth and small stones with an external ditch. The circuit is complete, the bank being 1 ft. 6 in. to 5 ft. high on the inside and 6 ft. to 10 ft. 6 in. above the present surface of the ditch. The entrance, 15 ft. broad in the west side, is simple in character. From 21 yds. to 24 yds. south of the inclosure is a bank 5 ft. high with a ditch on the south side running east to west for 33 yds. and then south-east to north-west for 36 yds. A low bank running north-east to south-west connects it with the south-west angle of the inclosure. One hundred and twenty yds. further south is a bank 4 ft. 6 in. high on the north and 6 ft. high on the south with a ditch 5 ft. broad and a counterscarp about 3 ft. high on the south. This bank and ditch run east and west for 90 yds. and if continued further west would end over

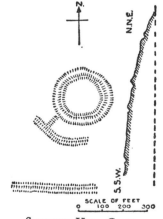

STADDON HILL CAMP,
WINSFORD.

a steep and narrow coomb in which is a spring. The ground inside the main inclosure falls considerably from south to north. Outside on the south it rises gradually, on the east is fairly level, on the north falls steeply and on the west still more steeply.

ANCIENT EARTHWORKS

WIVELISCOMBE.—KING'S CASTLE stands on Castle Hill, an isolated eminence, rather less than a mile east-north-east of the town, but the earthworks have been much destroyed by quarrying on the north and east sides and the erection of a house and formation of grounds on the south and south-west. The northern end has been entirely quarried away. The remains along the west, the northern half of the east side, and the south, indicate that the upper part of the hill was steeply scarped and a bank, now in places 6 ft. high, formed along the crest. At the base of the scarp, which seems to have been generally about 15 ft. high, a ditch and bank were formed, and below this was a second scarp. On the unaltered northern half of the west side the upper scarp is 21 ft. high and there is no ditch at its base but only a steep grass slope. For part of the distance, however, there is a sort of terrace which may represent a ditch, now filled up. There seems to have been a subsidiary entrance of the nature of a postern on the west side along the line of the existing pathway and this entrance was flanked by a scarp on its south-west side. At

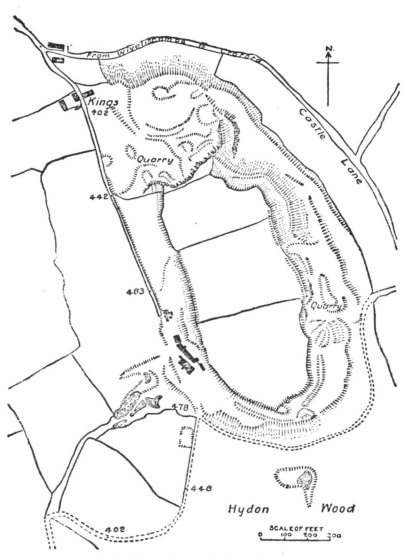

KING'S CASTLE, CASTLE HILL, WIVELISCOMBE.

the south end the approach is easier than on the other sides, and the lower scarp is about 18 ft., the counterscarp of the intermediate ditch being about 4 ft., whilst the upper scarp is about 15 ft. and the bank on the crest is 6 ft. high on the inside. The main entrance was at the south-east corner and crossed the banks diagonally, the total length of the pathway being some 75 yds. Planting and the making of pathways at the base of the hill have made it difficult to say whether there were additional works at the base, but there are indications of an outer bank near the beginning of the entrance. The south faces of the banks have been dug into at several points.

SIMPLE INCLOSED CAMPS
[Class C]

BICKNOLLER.—TRENDLE RING is an irregular quadrilateral with rounded corners inclosed by a bank of stones with an external ditch. On the north-

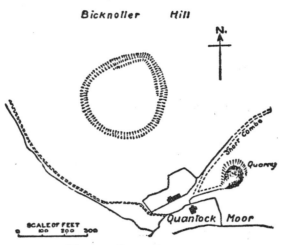

TRENDLE RING, BICKNOLLER.

west the bank has been thrown down and the ditch partly filled up. It stands on the lower slope of the Quantock Hills, half a mile east of Bicknoller Church.

CHARTERHOUSE.—East of Charterhouse a low bank forms an inclosure about 70 yds. square with rounded corners. The western half of the south side, and the south-west angle have been destroyed. Outside the bank was a ditch somewhat broad and shallow and there are indications of a second broad and shallow moat some 25 yds. outside the inner moat.

Amphitheatre.—About three-quarters of a mile north-west of this camp on the hill-side beyond the inclosure marked Town Field on the O.S. map is an elliptical inclosure formed by earthen banks with openings (? entrances) at the east and west ends. Inside the inclosure the ground slopes somewhat from north to south, but the comparatively level surface is approximately 24 yds. north and south and 29 yds. east and

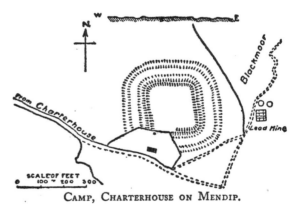

CAMP, CHARTERHOUSE ON MENDIP.

west. The northern bank is about 14 ft. high on the inside and about 3 ft. above the ground-level outside on the north; the southern bank is 7 ft. above the inclosure and 10 ft. above the ground-level outside. The banks are 7 ft. to 8 ft. broad at the top. The crest of the northern bank is unbroken, but in the top of the southern bank there are two shallow depressions, at about one-third of the total length of the bank from each end. The name usually given to this inclosure may well be correct.

DULVERTON.—On the east bank of the Barle about a quarter of a mile north of Dulverton Station and immediately south of the road to Bury there is a small inclosure formed on the bank of the river which at this point is somewhat high and has a fairly steep slope. The inclosure is protected on three sides by a ditch now 8 ft. to 13 ft. broad at the bottom, whilst on the fourth and lowest side the defence is a fairly steep scarp about 11 ft. high with a flat terrace 13 ft. to 14 ft. broad at its face and a scarp about 2 ft. high below its outer edge. This terrace may represent a filled-up ditch, in which case the ditch was originally continuous round the whole inclosure,

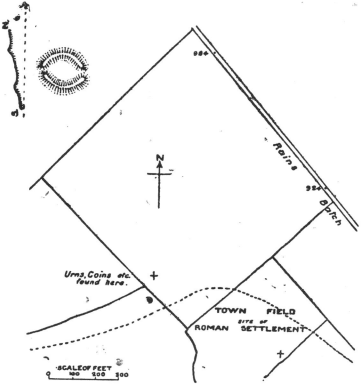

AMPHITHEATRE, NEAR CHARTERHOUSE.

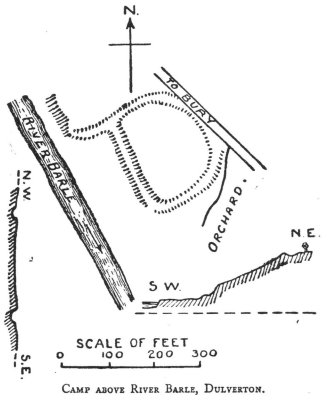

SCALE OF FEET

0   100   200   300

CAMP ABOVE RIVER BARLE, DULVERTON.

The ground inside the inclosure and the side banks slope somewhat steeply. On the north-north-west the bank is 5 ft. high and the counterscarp of the ditch is 3 ft., whilst on the south-south-east the bank is also about 5 ft. and the counterscarp 3 ft. 6 in. On the upper side the bank is low, the ditch being much silted up, and also encroached on by the hedge of an orchard. The north corner has been partly destroyed in making the road. The inclosure measures about 65 yds. along the lower side and is about 50 yds. across. There is a very similar but larger earthwork on the bank of the Usk near Pontypool Road.

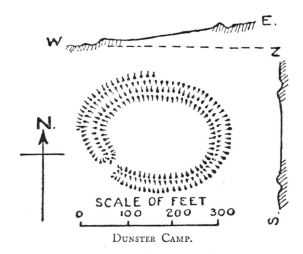

DUNSTER CAMP.

DUNSTER.—About three-quarters of a mile south-south-west of Dunster some little way down the west slope of the hill to the south of the village is a circular camp about 120 yds. in diameter surrounded by a bank of stones and earth, with an outer ditch and also, for about a third of the circumference on the west side, a low bank on the counterscarp of the ditch. The bank is 3 ft. to 5 ft. above the surface of the inclosure and 7 ft. to 15 ft. above the present surface of the ditch, the counterscarp of the latter being about 4 ft. above its surface. The entrance is on the south-west and on the left hand the bank turns inwards and there are indications of the foundations of a circular breastwork or tower about 15 ft. diameter. Inside the camp the ground slopes considerably from east to west. The inner bank is complete though lower at some points than at others.[17]

ELWORTHY.—ELWORTHY BARROWS consists of the fragmentary remains of an approximately circular camp of about 220 yds. diameter which was defended by a bank of earth (containing very few stones) about 13 ft. high with a ditch 7 ft. to 8 ft. broad and a counterscarp now about 4 ft. high. A considerable length of the bank much reduced in height remains on the north, another and higher section on the south-west, whilst the high banks which turned inwards for about 35 yds. and formed the entrance on the south-east still remain. The top of the hill on which the camp stands was clearly once more highly cultivated than it is at present, and the light character of the earth of which the bank consists has made it comparatively easy to level. The camp is on the hill-top two miles north-north-east of Clatworthy and one and a half miles south-west of Elworthy.

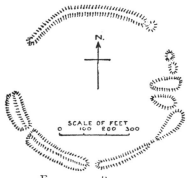

ELWORTHY BARROWS.

FROME.—HALES CASTLE is a circular inclosure 40 yds. in internal diameter defended by an earthen bank with a ditch outside. It is about half a mile east-north-east of Frome Selwood Church.

[17] Page, *Explorations of Exmoor*, 203, states that on the lower south-east slope of Croydon Hill there is a circular inclosure about 27 yds. diameter defended by a bank of stones, but much overgrown.

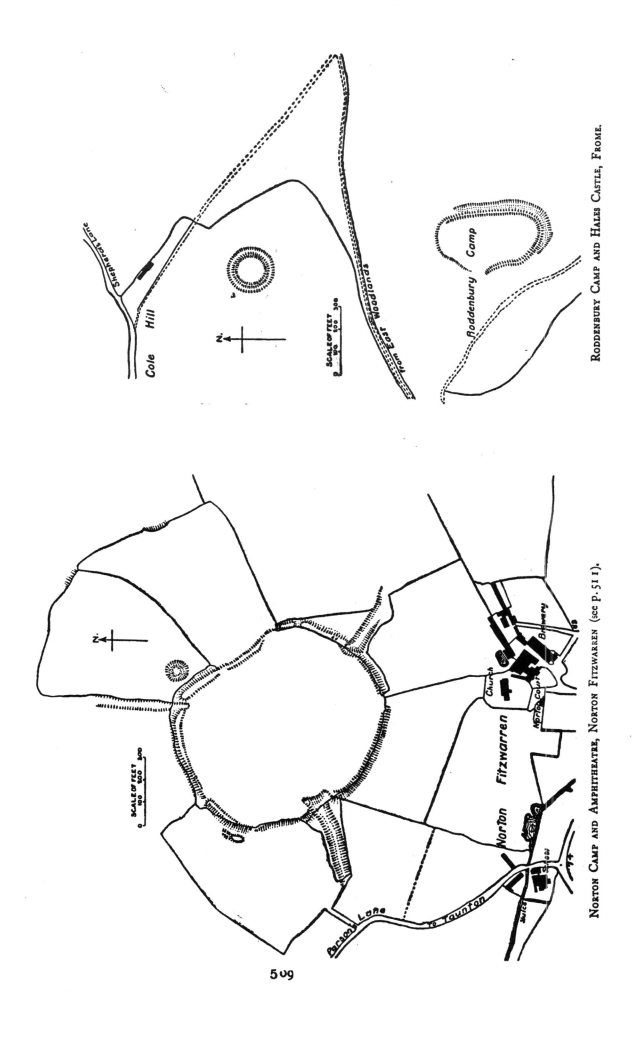

RODDENBURY CAMP AND HALES CASTLE, FROME.

NORTON CAMP AND AMPHITHEATRE, NORTON FITZWARREN (see p. 511).

FROME.—RODDENBURY CAMP, half a mile east of Frome Selwood Church in the north-east corner of Longleat Wood, is an elliptical inclosure 150 yds. long and 75 yds. broad, defended by an earthen bank with a deep and wide ditch below. The ditch has been filled up on the north and west, and on the north there is only a scarp without any bank. The entrance seems to have been on the west.

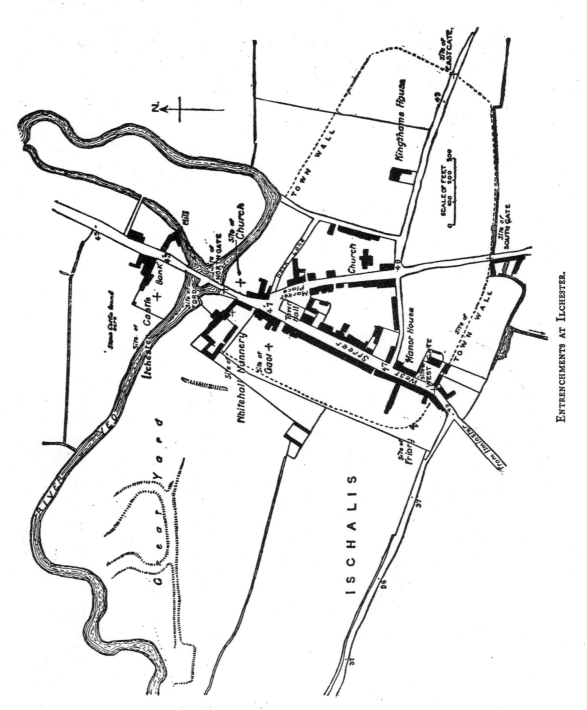

ENTRENCHMENTS AT ILCHESTER.

ILCHESTER.—The existing remains of earthworks are very slight. In the field called 'Great Yard' on the north-west of the town there are the remains of what may have been a moated inclosure, close to the River

Yeo and near the east corner of this field is a slight bank about 70 yds. long.[18]

NORTON FITZWARREN.—NORTON CAMP, approximately circular with a maximum diameter of about 330 yds., occupies the summit of a low hill just north of the church. The interior of the camp is under the plough and the defences have been reduced or thrown down in many places. The main defence was an earthen bank with an external ditch, which remain on the north-west, north-east and south-east. The bank is 4 ft. to 10 ft. above the surface of the inclosure and 7 ft. to 15 ft. above the present surface of the ditch. Along the south-west and south the bank has been largely destroyed and the ditch filled up. The peculiar feature of this camp lies in three deep fosses or 'covered ways,' 130 yds. to 170 yds. long, running out from the inclosure on the north, south-east and south-west respectively. The bottom of these 'ways' is considerably below the level of the ditch encircling the camp, whilst their sides are steep with a sort of terrace or platform mid-way. Presumably they were intended as approaches to the camp, but the arrangement of the entrances is not now at all clear. On the west side of the camp, just outside a modern path through the bank is a low mound, probably a tumulus.[19]

OVER STOWEY.—In PARK PLANTATION on the top of a ridge somewhat thickly wooded is a small camp rhomboidal in shape, about 180 yds. along the longer diagonal which runs nearly north and south and 150 yds. along the shorter diagonal. The bank is made of earth and small stones, with a ditch outside which is now much silted up and has practically disappeared along the north-east side and the greater part of the north-west side. The bank is 1½ ft. to 4 ft. above the surface of the inclosure and 5½ ft. to 15 ft. above the present surface of the ditch, the counterscarp of the latter being 1½ ft. to 5 ft. above its surface. The entrance, of simple character, is at the east angle and is now 12 ft. across. The ground falls steeply on the north-east and north-west, but more gradually on the east and is practically level for some distance on the south, such fall as there is being towards the camp.

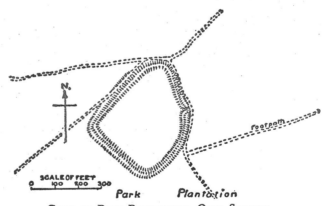

CAMP IN PARK PLANTATION, OVER STOWEY.

PENSELWOOD.—KENWALCH'S CASTLE or Kenny Wilkins Castle. At the north end of the ridge on which Penselwood stands and one and a half miles north-north-west from the church is an inclosure about 240 yds. long and 120 yds. broad through which runs a modern road. It is defended by a bank and ditch below which the ground falls very steeply on the west, somewhat less steeply on the east and gradually on the north, whilst on the south it is flat. The ditch has been a good deal silted up on the east and on the west the contours have been altered still more by the growth of timber.

[18] Phelps (op. cit. 166) gives Stukeley's plan.
[19] W. Bidgood, *Somers. Arch. Soc. Proc.* xliv (2), 198–202.

The bank is much more pronounced on the north and south than on the east and west, where the main defence is a steep scarp with the ditch below and the steep ground below that. On the south the bank is 18 ft. above the ditch and 10 ft. above the interior of the camp; on the north it is 14 ft. above the ditch and 4 ft. above the interior of the camp. Probably the original entrance was destroyed in making the road.

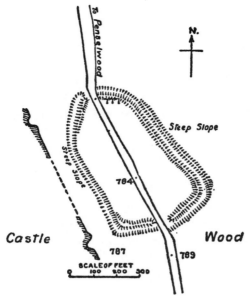

KENWALCH'S CASTLE, PENSELWOOD.

ROWBERROW.—On the south-west corner of Rowberrow Warren some way down the slope of Black Down, a spur of the Mendip, is a simple inclosure, approximately square with rounded corners. It is about 70 yds. across and is traversed by a footpath from Shipham to Charterhouse. The bank is 4 ft. to 7 ft. above the present surface of the ditch on the east, west, and south sides, the counterscarp being 2 ft. to $4\frac{1}{2}$ ft. high. On the north the ditch is silted up to within about 2 ft. of the top of the bank. The interior of the camp slopes considerably from north to south.

SHIPHAM.—In a field just west of Longbottom Farm on the north side of the road from Shipham to Charterhouse on Mendip is a quadrilateral inclosure, in the form of an irregular rhomboid on the lower slope of a west-

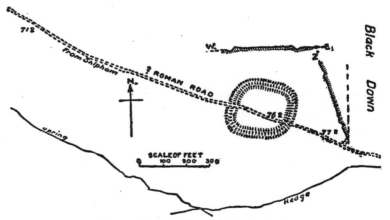

BLACK DOWN CAMP, ROWBERROW.

ern spur of Black Down. Its sides vary in length from 60 yds. to 76 yds. The defence to the south is a scarp about 7 ft. high with a ditch at the foot now largely silted up. On the other sides the defence is a ditch, the bank on the camp side being now only 3 ft. to 4 ft. high, and the counterscarp only $1\frac{1}{2}$ ft. to 2 ft. high. Except at the angles there is no distance bank on the edge of the inclosure itself. The ground inside the inclosure is

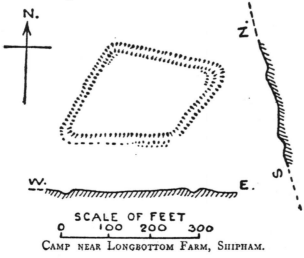

CAMP NEAR LONGBOTTOM FARM, SHIPHAM.

practically level from east to west, but falls considerably from north to south.   The small Rowberrow camp is half a mile east by north.

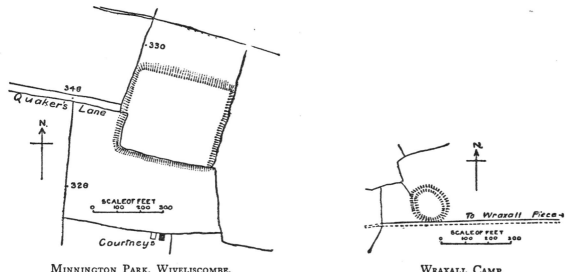

MINNINGTON PARK, WIVELISCOMBE.   WRAXALL CAMP.

WIVELISCOMBE.—MINNINGTON PARK, at the end of Quaker's Lane, half a mile east of the Devon and Somerset Branch Railway, is a simple square inclosure with rounded corners, about 140 yds. across.   The only defence is a simple scarp 5 ft. to 6 ft. high with a gradient for the most part about 1 in 3.   There are now no traces of a ditch at the base of the scarp.   A modern hedge and bank run along the crest of the scarp on the south and the southern half of the west side.   The ground outside the inclosure does not fall steeply on any side.

WRAXALL.—About one and a half miles east of Wraxall Church is a circular inclosure about 50 yds. in diameter surrounded by a bank of stones, without at the present time any ditch.

CASTLE MOUNTS
[Class D]

CHARLTON MUSGROVE.—In COCKROAD WOOD, about one mile east of Charlton Musgrove, is a mount surrounded by a ditch.   The surrounding ground has been much altered by afforesting operations and it is impossible to say with certainty whether this mount had any attached bailey.

CASTLE MOUNTS WITH ATTACHED COURTS
[Class E]

DUNSTER.—DUNSTER CASTLE stands on an isolated hill the upper part of which was scarped to form a mount, whilst the lower slopes were terraced to form a base court and a steep ascent was arranged to wind round the hill, but the original earthworks have been so much altered by building and other operations that it is now impossible to trace their original plan with any certainty.

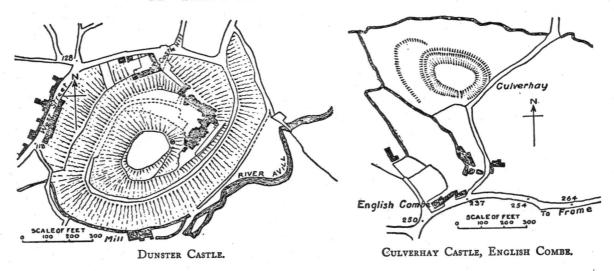

DUNSTER CASTLE.

CULVERHAY CASTLE, ENGLISH COMBE.

ENGLISH COMBE.—CULVERHAY CASTLE, north of English Combe village, consists of an oval mount about 70 yds. long and 40 yds. broad surrounded on all sides by a ditch and on the east, north and west by a bank outside the ditch. The southern end of the east bank has been cut into by a road. On the north, west and south the ground slopes to a stream. On the west there can be traced the remains of a bank of what was most probably a base court, though the inclosed area was comparatively small for so large a mount.

GLASTONBURY.—A short distance south of Glastonbury Station, in a field to the east of the road between Glastonbury and Street, is a mount and base-court fort with some special features. The surroundings have been altered by drainage, the making of the road and the diversion of streams, but it is clear that at the east end of a ridge, which at that time was an island with a considerable depth of water on the east and south, a mount was thrown up and de-fended by a bank and ditch almost completely encircling it. The ditch continues between the mount and the base court and there is a slight bank on the scarp of the ditch on the base court side. The mount is low for its area; at present the flat top of the mount, which is 54 yds. north and south and 36 yds. east and west, is 4 ft.

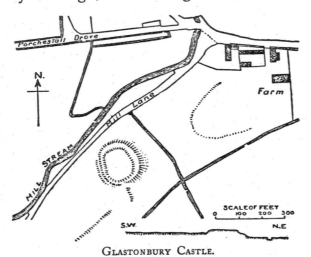

GLASTONBURY CASTLE.

to 5 ft. 6 in. above the top of the ditch, which is almost completely silted up. The base court has no bank or ditch, but before the drainage of the area would be protected by water or marsh on all sides. Somewhat rapid streams now run on the north, south and east of the earthwork, and the water would be deepest immediately to the east of the mount.

LOCKING.—At Lockinghead Farm is a small mount and base-court camp on the edge of an inland cliff. The base court is an irregular quadrangle and the bank along the west and north is 2 ft. 6 in. to 3 ft. high. The mount is only about 4 ft. high and the ditch surrounding it has been largely filled up. In the middle of the mount is the basement of a square building, with a flight of narrow stone steps in one corner. When clearing out this basement in 1903 remains of iron implements and weapons were discovered.[20]

MONTACUTE.—East of the church rises St. Michael's Hill, the former 'Mons acutus,' an isolated conical hill, which has been scarped into a fort of the mount and base court type. The base of the hill, approximately circular, has been steeply scarped, but a sloping path on the south gives access to a plateau which runs round the hill and forms a lower bailey or base court. On the south-east there is an upper bailey several feet above the lower and defended by a steep scarp. The mount itself is oval in plan and has very steep sides. It is reached by a steep and narrow path which winds up the south-east face. At the base of the mount on the west and north is a bank between it and the outer bailey. In general outline this castle distinctly resembles that at Ewyas Harold. The whole of the hill was planted for many years, but it was cleared in 1905 and replanted in 1906–7.

NETHER STOWEY.—STOWEY CASTLE is a mount and base-court fort formed by scarping and otherwise altering a natural hill. The mount, which is some 25 ft. above the ditch which surrounds its base, is mainly natural rock very steeply scarped, and has a flat top about 50 yds. north and south and 45 yds. east and west. On the top are the foundations of a rectangular keep with cross walls at right angles and a small forebuilding. On the edge of the mount are four heaps of débris from digging out the foundations of the keep. There are two base courts. One is to the east of the mount, roughly oval in shape with a bank on its outer edge and a ditch below which runs into the ditch of the mount. The north-east end of this bailey has been quarried away. North of this is a second and smaller bailey at a somewhat higher level with a steep scarp 10 ft. high on its east and north fronts and a further drop of several feet to the lane below. Between the two baileys is a ditch, now shallow, which runs into the ditch of the mount and may have been an entrance. The present entrance on the south from the top of the hill is modern. The counterscarp of the ditch round the mount is 7 ft. high and very steep and on the further side the ground falls very steeply except where the base courts are. On the east there is a very steep natural escarpment above a stream. On the south the hill has been altered by quarrying and building. The original access to the mount was either along the present footpath or by means of a bridge.

PENSELWOOD.—BALLANDS CASTLE, about half a mile south-west of Penselwood Church, is a small mount and base-court fort of an unusual type since it has two small baileys in line, the middle being somewhat lower than the outer. The mount is at the north end and is 28 ft. above the stream on the north, 20 ft. above the ditch on the east and 10 ft. above the bottom of the ditch between it and the inner bailey. On the west there are remains of a shallow ditch 20 ft. below the top, and below this the ground has a rapid natural fall. At the top the mount is oblong, 17 yds. north and south and 11 yds. east and west; no masonry remains. The

[20] *Somers. Arch Soc. Proc.* xlix (2), 186.

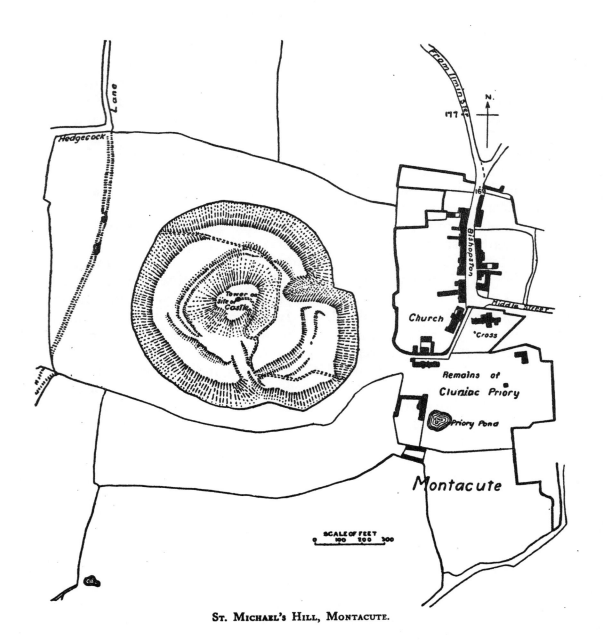

ST. MICHAEL'S HILL, MONTACUTE.

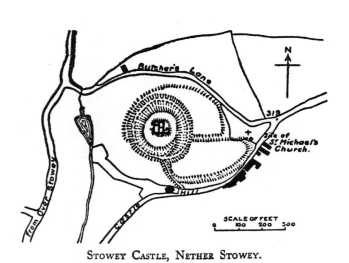

STOWEY CASTLE, NETHER STOWEY.

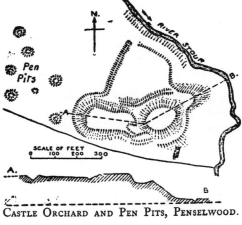

CASTLE ORCHARD AND PEN PITS, PENSELWOOD.

inner bailey is of irregular shape, 23 yds. long by 22 yds. broad at its south end and 14 yds. broad at the north end. On the east there was a ditch now filled by a modern bank and hedge ; on the west the side is steeply scarped and the ground below falls rapidly. On the south a shallow ditch separates it from the outer bailey, which is 53 yds. long and 30 yds. broad. On the east a modern high bank and hedge occupy the place of the original bank and ditch ; on the west the side is scarped and falls about 6 ft. to a shallow

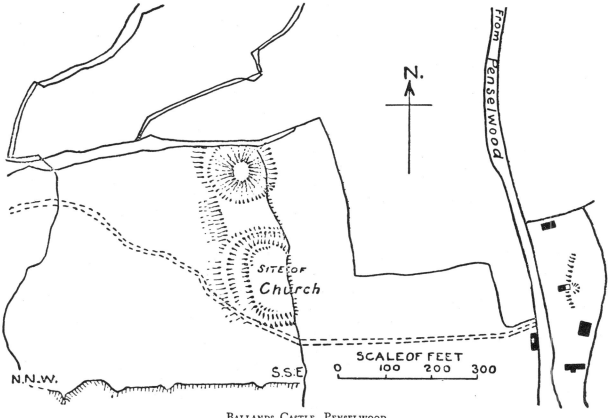

BALLANDS CASTLE, PENSELWOOD.

ditch below which the scarp is continued, the natural slope of the hill being somewhat steep. At the south end there is a ditch about 3 ft. deep, beyond which the ground is level. On the east the ground slopes down to the fort and on the west it slopes steeply away. It seems probable that the southern bailey represents a small rectangular inclosure to which at a later date the inner bailey and mount have been added, but any real strength that the place had must have been mainly due to palisades. The plan on the Ordnance map very imperfectly represents the existing remains.

PENSELWOOD.—CASTLE ORCHARD, about one mile north-east of Penselwood Church and close to the county boundary, is a mount and base-court fort of a peculiar type, the two base courts being at very different levels. Unfortunately it is now so much overgrown that accurate measurements are not practicable. It stands at the end of the long ridge in which occur the great numbers of 'Pen Pits.' The south-east end of this ridge has been cut across by a ditch some 16 ft. deep beyond which the outer bank of the upper base court rises steeply nearly 20 ft. and from the inside has at this end a bank 7 ft. 6 in. high. This bailey is about 70 yds. long by 25 yds.

across, and the ground rises somewhat at the edges without forming any distinct bank. The sides of the bailey are very steeply scarped and drop more than 20 ft. to a shallow ditch running round the hill, below which the fall continues. At the east end of the bailey and separated from it by a shallow ditch is the mount, which rises 11 ft. from this ditch, but 28 ft. above the ditch on the north-west and south-east, this ditch having on the north-west a counterscarp 4 ft. high, whilst the ground outside it falls steeply 11 ft. to the surface of the lower base court to the north-west of the mount. This base court is triangular and is protected on the north-west by a bank 4 ft. high on the inside and 6 ft. high on the outside. It has no outer ditch but the ground outside is still very boggy. On the north-east the ground has been scarped and falls steeply to the stream for about 19 ft. and then precipitously for about 20 ft. more. To the north-east of the mount runs a modern road which rises gradually from the stream level and occupies the place of the main ditch on this side. Beyond the road is a short curved bank rising from 6 ft. to 7 ft., outside of which the ground falls steeply to the stream 60 ft. below. To the south of the castle the ground likewise falls steeply and the ground at the base has evidently been very boggy. An excellent plan of this castle was published by Gen. Pitt Rivers.[21]

PURITON.—At Downend in this parish the northern extremity of the Polden Hills has been converted into a mount and base-court fort by cutting a deep trench across the end of the hill and scarping the cut-off portion so as to form an elliptical mount, about 16 ft. high and 80 ft. maximum length at the top, composed almost entirely of natural rock. From the base of the mount the ground slopes somewhat towards the north, and on this side there is an oblong base court 56 yds. by 19 yds. inclosed by a bank now 3 ft. to 4 ft. high on the east and north sides. If there was any bank on the west it has been to a large extent destroyed. North of this inner bailey is a second area, 36 yds. across, inclosed on the north and east by a curved bank, but now without any bank on the west or any indication that there ever was one on this side. This inclosure is protected on its north face by a low outer bank, highest at the east end where it turns southwards for about 9 yds. and was originally 10 yds. or 12 yds. longer. Outside this second bank and continuing all along the east side of the fortress was a moat 10 ft. to 12 ft. broad, now dry. It has been stated that on the west side there are now no banks to the baileys and it is probable that on this side the ground was so swampy that no other protection was necessary. This swampy ground, now more or less successfully drained, extends round the west and south sides of the mount. The ditch between the mount and the

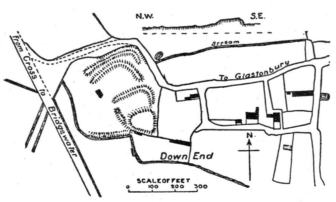

CAMP AT DOWNEND, PURITON.

21 *Somers. Arch. Soc. Proc.* xxv (1), 7–17.

body of the hill has been to a large extent filled up and the south face of the mount has been dug into along the base and a road constructed to some houses on the hill-side just beyond the mount. On the north side the upper part of the mount has been dug into, part of the material having been thrown into the ditch on the east and part of it down the south-west slope of the mount.

STAPLE FITZPAINE.—CASTLE NEROCHE occupies one of the boldest promontories on a line of inland cliffs overlooking the vale of Taunton Dene, and is about one mile due south of Curland Church and five and a

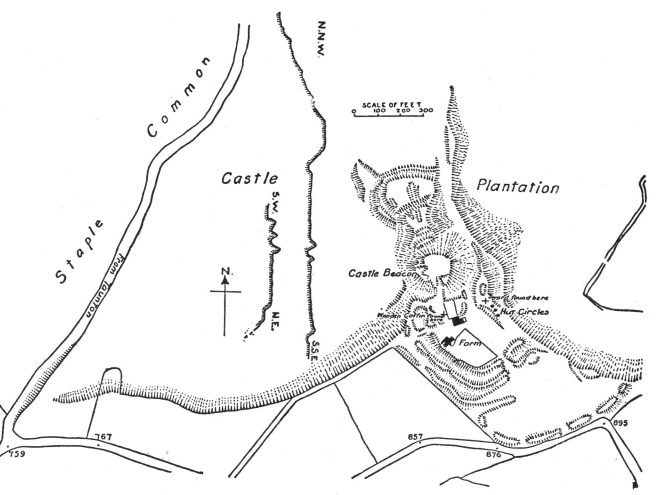

CASTLE NEROCHE, STAPLE FITZPAINE.

half miles north-west of Chard. The end of the promontory is known as the 'beacon,' cut off from the rest of the hill by a deep ditch, and has been formed into a mount, the upper part of which is artificial. The lower slopes of the promontory are defended by scarps and low banks and ditches, now to a large extent overgrown and filled up. There is no well-defined ditch round the mount, and the summit is irregular both in outline and surface. The greater part of the inclosure is on the comparatively level surface of the cliff, and its outer defence is a high bank, 13 ft. to 15 ft. high from the outside and $5\frac{1}{2}$ ft. to 8 ft. from the inside, now cut into at several points, which dies out on the steep face of the cliff at either end,

Outside this bank was a ditch, a large part of which is now occupied by a road. Inside this outer bank and some distance from it is a double bank with a ditch outside and a ditch between, and these again die out on the cliff at the east end and at the west end on the ditch which cuts off the 'beacon' from the mainland. The second bank is 10 ft. to 20 ft. above the present surface of the ditch at its base and the inner bank is 20 ft. above the surface of the ditch between the two. The inner inclosure is now occupied by a farmhouse with its barton and attached buildings, and the original features of the camp have been much altered and destroyed, especially at the point of juncture of the 'beacon' with the main inclosure. If we regard the 'beacon' as a mount or motte, we have an inner bailey defended by a double bank with a ditch between and a ditch outside, and an outer bailey defended by a bank and ditch. Excavations by Mr. H. St. George Gray revealed no implements other than iron, and no pottery that could be regarded as pre-Norman.[22]

STOGURSEY.—STOGURSEY CASTLE is a mount and base-court fortification with a moat, two well-defined base courts, and extensive outer works. The mount is approximately circular, about 50 yds. in diameter and 10 ft. above the flat ground at its base, which was probably at one time at the bottom of the moat, formed by a stream, now restricted to a narrower channel. On the top of the mount is a shell keep.

STOGURSEY CASTLE.

The inner bailey covered the east and south-east of the mount, and along its north front was protected by an extension of the moat, whilst on the east and south-east the bank was steeply scarped to a branch of the stream 21 ft. below. This bailey was banked and sloped artificially along the east and south-east, and part of its inner surface has been dug into. Beyond the stream on the east and at a higher level is the outer bailey, of greater extent, with a steep scarp 25 ft. to 30 ft. high on the west and south, and still higher on the east. Along its crest was a bank of earth 6 ft. to 8 ft. high on the inside, which still remains along the south and east fronts, but has been destroyed on the north to make room for buildings, etc., which obscure the original plan at this end. The stream already referred to runs round the base of this outer bailey on the south and west, whilst along the east runs a modern road, clearly occupying the place of a moat, the counterscarp of which still exists in the field on the east. On the north and east of the mount there are remains of a third bailey of much greater extent, less strongly banked and probably forming a cattle inclosure, protected by a marsh and stream on the north and a bank on the west.

[22] F. Warre, *Somers. Arch. Soc. Proc.* v (2), 29–48, and H. St. George Gray, ibid. xlix (2), 23–53.

ANCIENT EARTHWORKS

HOMESTEAD MOATS
[Class F]

Moated inclosures are not very numerous in proportion to the size of the county, and such as there are are very often imperfect. With the exception of the broad and deep moat still surrounding the Bishop's Palace at Wells, they present nothing remarkable in either size or plan. The following provisional list of thirty-seven has been compiled from the O.S. maps:—

Place.	Name.	Place.	Name.
Ash	Ash Farm	Milton Clevedon	Manor Farm (?)
Ashill	Merryfield (large rectangular, still wet)	Montacute (s. of the castle)	
Barrington	Barrington Court	Muchelney	Abbey Moat
Batcombe	Spargrove Farm	Pennard (West)	The Priory
Bradley, West	Bradley House and Church	Petherton, North	Maunsel House (?)
		Shapwick	Shapwick House
Cannington	Gurney Street Farm and Chilton Trepit Farm	Stanton Prior	Church Moat (?)
		Stoke St. Gregory	Slough Farm
Carhampton	Marshwood Farm	Thorn Falcon	Lower Manor Farm
Charlinch	Currypool Farm	Thurloxton	Chapel Hill, Shearston
Cleeve, Old	Moat of St. Mary's Abbey	Timberscombe	Croydon House
Compton Martin	Bickfield Farm	Tolland	Golden Farm (?)
Durleigh	Rexworthy Farm and West Bower Farm	Wedmore	Blackford
		Wells	The Palace
Hutton	Court Farm	Wincanton	Marsh Court
Luccombe	Sweetworthy (circular)	Winscombe	Rookery Farm and Nye Farm
Marston Bigot			
Marston Magna	The Court (double)	Wookey	The 'Palace'
Martock	Sayes Place	Wraxall	Moat House Farm

MOATED INCLOSURES WITH STRONGER DEFENSIVE WORKS
[Class G]

Nunney.—Nunney Castle is surrounded by an oblong moat probably communicating originally with the stream on the south-east of it. About 70 yds. north-west is a broad bank running north-east to south-west for

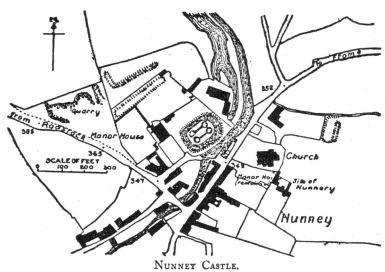

Nunney Castle.

about 90 yds., and 20 yds. further north-east is a narrower bank 65 yds. long which turns at a right angle at its south-west end and runs north-west to south-east for 30 yds.

II 521 66

UNCLASSIFIED EARTHWORKS
[CLASS X]

BATH.—Two camps described by Phelps (op. cit. i, 103–4) have since been destroyed. *Berwick*, one and a half miles from Bath, between the two roads leading to Wells, is said to have been surrounded by a strong *vallum*, and *Oldbury* had a strong entrenchment inclosing about 6 acres.

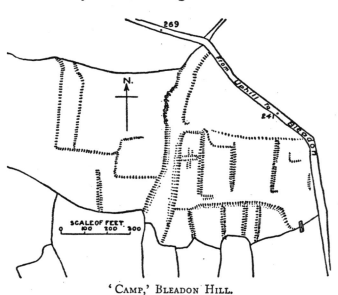

'CAMP,' BLEADON HILL.

BLEADON. — The so-called camp on the slope of the hill to the north of the village contains low banks and ridges, most of which run down the slope of the hill from north to south, but some run east and west. Several of them are due to the outcrops of strata, but others are clearly artificial. They have none of the characters of defensive earthworks, but are remains of cultivation boundaries, possibly ancient but more probably comparatively modern.

CASTLE CARY.—The earthworks now remaining on the site of Cary Castle are fragmentary and consist of two broad banks of earth running

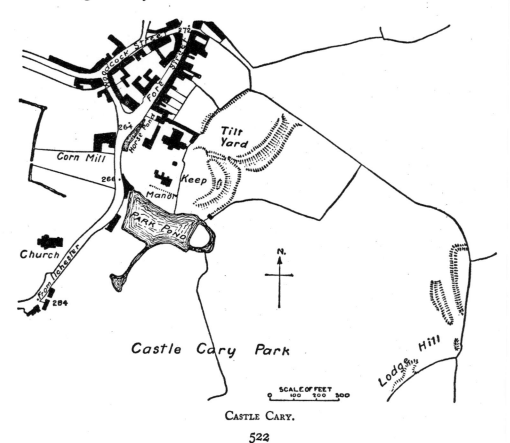

CASTLE CARY.

approximately in line north-east to south-west, each bank being concave to the north-west. On the south-east of each bank there is a ditch, the northern bank being 12 ft. to 20 ft. above the present surface of the ditch and the southern bank 8 ft. to 10 ft. above its ditch. Excavations in 1890 revealed the foundations of a large rectangular Norman keep and showed that the southern bank is probably of later date than the keep, since a concrete platform runs under part of it. No masonry was found on the upper bank.[23]

On the hill to the south-east of these mounts there is a bank 18 ft. to 28 ft. high and about 60 yds. long with a ditch on its west side. To the east of this is a second lower bank about 100 yds. long which turns at right angles for a short distance at its north end. These may be works thrown up during an early siege of the castle, or may be remains of an independent and earlier fortification.

DOULTING.—The O.S. map shows in the extreme north of this parish a circular inclosure about 220 yds. in diameter, containing two tumuli, with a long curved bank running out from its east side in a generally eastwards direction. The tumuli still exist, but there are no recognizable traces of a circular inclosure. There are however extensive remains of surface mining or quarrying. What is shown as a long bank on the map is really an escarpment of rock which follows the line of the hill and seems to be wholly natural.

DUNSTER.—Below the circular fort described in Class C, and so placed as to face the castle and command the coomb running south-west from it, is a line of two shallow trenches about 100 yds. long, cut in the hill-side one 15 ft to 18 ft. above the other. In all probability these are trenches made during the investment of the castle at the time of the Parliamentary War. (See Bats Castle, p. 486.)

A similar shallow trench exists on the east end of Grabbist Hill, which also commands the castle and the road leading westwards from the village. It likewise probably belongs to the time of the siege.

FARLEIGH HUNGERFORD.—FARLEIGH CASTLE stands on the edge of a steep escarpment south-west of the River Frome. The main inclosure stands on a plateau with steeply scarped sides, and on the south side there is a deep ditch. On the hill-side above the castle to the south-west are terraces, partly at least natural in origin, but partly artificially scarped.[24]

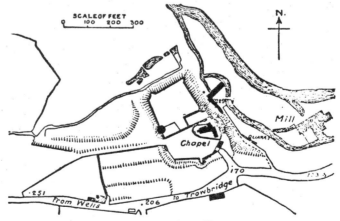

FARLEIGH CASTLE, FARLEIGH HUNGERFORD.

GLASTONBURY. — PONTERS BALL is a bank of earth about 15 ft. high with a ditch on the east side and 10 ft. high on the west, running north-north-east to west-south-west across the high ground between the hamlets

[23] *Somers. Arch. Soc. Proc.* xxxvi (2), 67–174.
[24] *Somers. Arch. Soc. Proc.* iii (2), 114–24.

of Woodland Street and Havyatt, about one mile west of West Pennard. The bank is curved with the concavity westwards and runs across the ridge to the swampy ground on the north and south. Warre regarded it as intended to isolate the peninsula of Avalon.[25]

Warre (op. cit.) also described Glastonbury Tor as a fortified place, but the terrace-like appearance of the sides of this hill is due to the characteristic outcrops of the Midford sand, of which the hill consists. It might have been useful as a beacon or a look-out, but would have been of little value as a camp.

The same writer considered that Wirral Hill in the west of the parish had been converted into a stronghold by scarping both sides of the hill at its narrowest part. There is however no useful camping ground on the top of this ridge, and it would have been useless to construct a difficult entrance whilst the whole of the south slope of the hill remained fairly easily accessible.

HARPTREE, EAST.—To the west of the road from Chew Stoke to Oakhill is a row of three circular inclosures on a line running north-east and south-west. The inclosures are each about 180 yds. in diameter, with about 70 yds. between the consecutive rings, and the boundary is a low bank of earth and stones with a ditch outside. About 400 yds. north is a fourth imperfect ring not quite in the same line, but of the same general character and approximately of the same diameter. This ring has been destroyed on the south-west for about one-fifth of the circumference, and for the rest of its circuit has been almost completely levelled.

LANGPORT is built on the sides of a hill which projects from the south-west face of one of the eastern masses of the Polden Hills. On the south, west and north-west it was protected by the rivers Yeo and Parrett and the marsh through which they ran, but on the east and north it was accessible from high ground. The defences that still exist seem to be comparatively modern and most probably date from the occupation during the Parliamentary war, when Langport was a position of importance because it stands on the main road from Frome to Taunton at its most defensible point.[26] The remains consist of a broad and shallow moat, now dry, running from the marsh at the foot of the hill on the north-east, across the base of the hill in a direction south-east to north-west for 300 yds. and then turning and running west as far as the present road from Bridgwater. At this end it now takes the form of a deep ditch used as a cartway, but this may be a modern alteration. South-west of this moat and almost parallel with it is a scarp, partly natural, partly artificial, about 7 ft. high on the lower slope of the hill, and near the top of the hill facing north-east is a shorter and steeper scarp following the line of the hill. The remainder of the hill has been built over. The watercourse which runs round the base of the hill on the south and eventually joins the Parrett is to a large extent artificial.

MELLS.—KINGSDOWN CAMP is in the north-west corner of the parish of Mells, on rising ground to the north of the Bristol, Radstock and Frome line, half a mile from Mells Road Station. There is a pentagonal central inclosure about 40 yds. across, with one angle pointing north formed by a

[25] *Somers. Arch. Soc. Proc.* ix (2), 144 and xxvi (1), 68.
[26] For an account of the battle of Langport, see *Somers. Arch. Soc. Proc.* xl (2), 123–40.

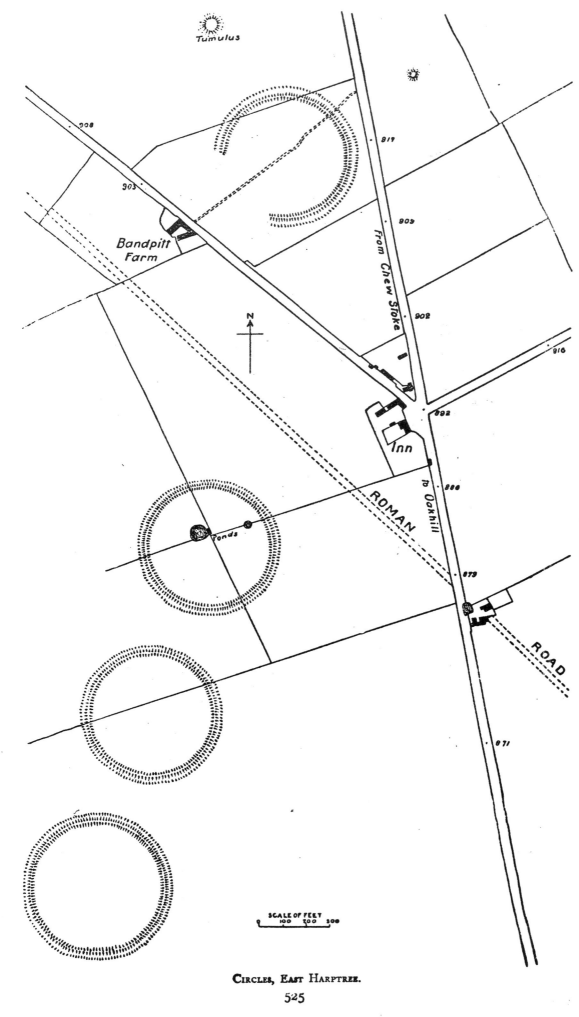

Tumulus

908

903

Bandpitt Farm

N

From Chew Stoke

819

905

902

916

892

Inn

to Oakhill

886

ROMAN

Ponds

879

873

ROAD

871

SCALE OF FEET
100 200 300

CIRCLES, EAST HARPTREE.

525

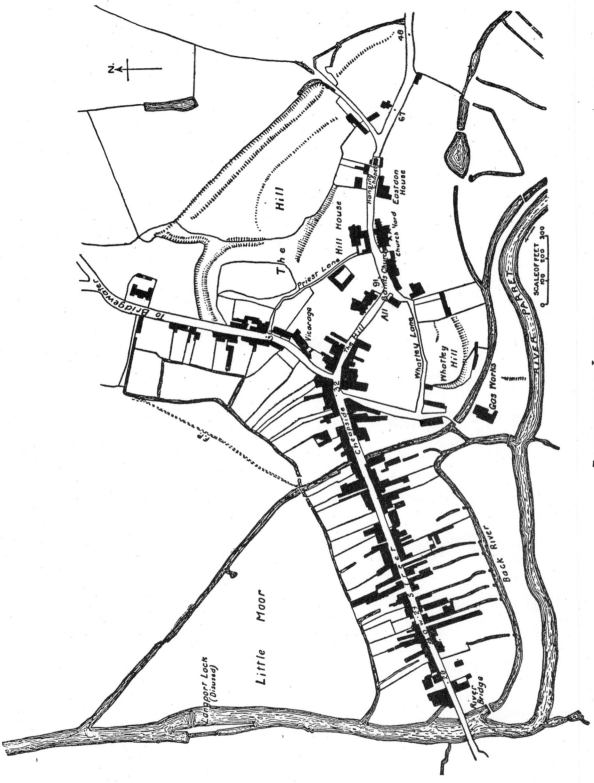

ENTRENCHMENTS AT LANGPORT.

bank of stones and earth 2 ft. to 3 ft. high, with a broad and shallow ditch in front of the north-east, north-west and west faces. The entrance was on the north-east. East of the central in-closure, at a distance of about 70 yds., is a bank which runs north and south for about 120 yds. and then runs north-east and south-west for about 100 yds. From the north of the central inclosure a bank runs east-south-east to west-north-

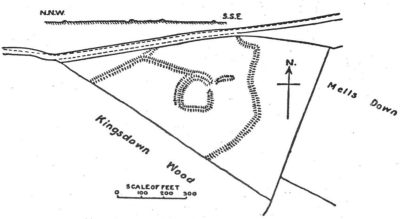

KINGSDOWN CAMP, MELLS.

west for about 70 yds., and then south-west to north-east for about the same distance. The ground falls rapidly on all sides of the camp except the east, where it is fairly level for a considerable distance. The works are com-paratively modern and are probably a small temporary camp of the Parlia-mentary war or possibly of the Monmouth rebellion.

MILBORNE PORT.—At Milborne Wick, just south-west of Milborne Port Station, running south-east to north-west across elevated ground, is a bank of earth varying in height from 15 ft. to 25 ft., with a total length of 300 yds. There is an entrance about 15 ft. broad through the bank at about 120 yds. from the south-east end.[27]

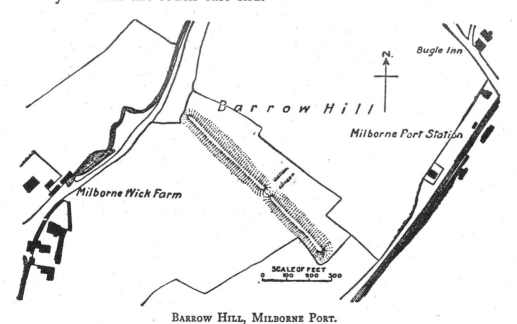

BARROW HILL, MILBORNE PORT.

SOMERTON : HURCOT CAMP.—About one mile north-east of Somerton Church are remains of an inclosure, seemingly oblong, about 130 yds. long and 100 yds. broad, but only the south-east angle remains, with traces of a

[27] F. Warre, *Somers. Arch. Soc. Proc.* vii (2), 60–2.

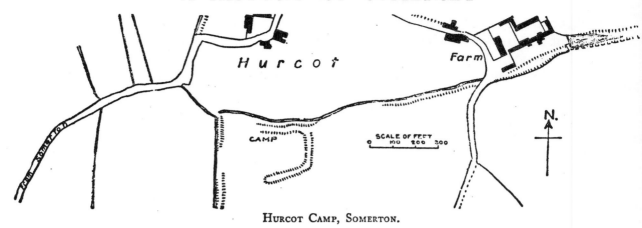

HURCOT CAMP, SOMERTON.

broad and shallow moat on the north and part of the west side which extends southwards considerably beyond the line of the south front. The bank is of earth and the works seem to be comparatively modern. They may belong to the Parliamentary war and represent an outpost commanding the road between Frome and Langport.

STOKE LANE.—See DOULTING.

TAUNTON : TAUNTON CASTLE.—The area occupied by the castle has been so much built over that little of the original earthworks can now be traced. There remains, however, part of a raised platform to the east of the keep, now occupied by a garden.

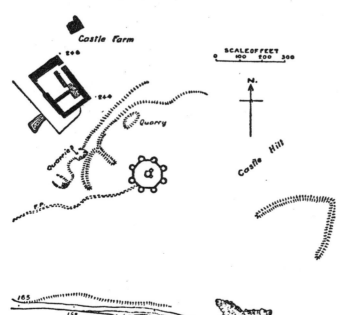

WALTON CASTLE, WALTON IN GORDANO.

WALTON IN GORDANO.—North-west of Clevedon and south-west of Walton, on the Castle Hill, are remains of entrenchments, the original plan of which is uncertain. Some 200 yds. due south of the castle is a bank about 135 yds. long running east and west, and 300 yds. north-east of this is a curved bank of two arms, the junction pointing north-east. The limb running roughly east to west is nearly 170 yds. long and that running north and south is 100 yds. They are of much earlier date than the adjoining 'castle.'

WATCHET.—ST. DECUMAN'S : DAW'S CASTLE. About three-quarters of a mile west of Watchet, between the Watchet and Minehead road and the cliffs over the Bristol Channel are remains of an inclosure which may once have been very extensive, but there have been heavy landslips here from time to time and large masses of the cliff have fallen into the sea. The principal remaining feature is a scarp 5 ft. to 7 ft. and about 200 yds.

long running in a curved line from east to west with its convexity pointing south. At the west end for about 30 yds. there is along the crest of the scarp a bank about 6 ft. broad and 2 ft. high on the inside, composed of earth and some stones, a portion of which has lately been destroyed. The same bank remains at the east end for about 27 yds. Just above the cliff, running east by north and west by south from the west end of the scarp just described, is a low bank which can be traced for about 30 yds. At a distance of 300 yds. to the north-west, just above the cliff, is a short length of bank about 4 ft. high, which has been cut into by the roadway.

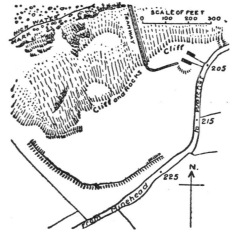

SITE OF DAW'S CASTLE, ST. DECUMAN'S.

WELLS, ST. CUTHBERT OUT.—FENNY CASTLE, 300 yds. south of Fenny Castle House, is an oblong mound with a flat top 80 yds. long and 40 yds. broad, with steep sides. A few yards north-west of it is a similar smaller mound, approximately circular and 30 yds. in diameter at the top. These mounds are natural in origin but the sides may have been artificially scarped.

WELLS, ST. CUTHBERT OUT.—The banks shown on the 25-in. O.S. map to the south of Kings Castle Wood are natural in their origin and no evidence of any artificial works could be found.

WESTON-SUPER-MARE.—Wesley Orchard on the east of the town is an approximately oblong inclosure, some 200 yds. long and 100 yds. broad, which stands a few feet above the level of the surrounding country. It lies at the foot of the south slope of Worle Hill and is mainly natural, consisting of a stiff reddish marl. Even in post-Roman times it must have formed a low island in a marsh or shallow arm of the sea. In its north-west angle there is a circular moated inclosure rather more than 100 ft. from outer bank to outer bank. The ditch varies in width, but is about 12 ft. broad at the bottom for a considerable part of the circuit. The top of the inclosure is from $2\frac{1}{2}$ ft. to 3 ft. above the present surface of the ditch, but little if at all above the level of the surrounding land. From the north-east of the 'island' a sort of causeway of large stones 4 ft. to 6 ft. broad runs across what was then marsh to the foot of the hill. The place recalls the smaller inclosures which are common in Ireland. Excavations have for some length of time been in progress, but they have so far afforded no evidence as to the age of the work.

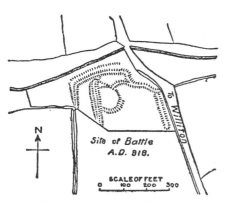

EARTHWORKS NEAR WILLITON.

WILLITON.—Half a mile north-west of Williton in a field called Battle Gore, alleged to be the site of a battle in 918, is a low tumulus, approximately circular, with low banks and ditches round about it. The principal of these is a shallow ditch about 9 ft. wide, which extends for about 100 yds. in a wavy line north of the tumulus, and can be traced for some 50 yds. along the east, and for a shorter distance and less distinctly on the west. There are traces of a very low bank on the south edge of the ditch. Another broad and shallow ditch runs north and south for about 50 yds. on the west of the tumulus, and cuts into part of its west side. A socketed bronze celt was dug up in this field some 40 years ago, and arms of the period of the Parliamentary war have been dug up from time to time in the immediate neighbourhood.

DYKES

WANSDYKE.—This remarkable earthwork consists of a high bank of earth with a broad ditch on its northern side. It runs across Wiltshire on the high ground in the north of that county and enters Somerset on Farleigh Down between Sharp Leaze Wood and Rowbarrow Wood somewhat more than a mile south of Bathford. At Warleigh Lane it turns west and crosses the Avon at the foot of the hill a little below Bathford and then rises to Bathampton Down, forming the north and west boundaries of the large camp thereon, beyond which it runs for about half a mile in a southwesterly direction and then disappears. It is, however, seen again for a short distance in fields behind Prior Park House. Probably it skirted and headed the Midford Valley, but it cannot now be traced in this locality. It is well seen again just beyond the Cross Keys public-house about a quarter of a mile north of South Stoke and from this point runs westwards by Burnt House, crossing the Bath and Wells road and the Fosse Way. For some distance beyond it has been almost destroyed, but it appears again on the east side of Breach Wood on the way to English Combe. The bank is 12 ft. above the present surface of the ditch, the counterscarp being 4 ft. to $4\frac{1}{2}$ ft., whilst on the south side the bank is about 4 ft. high. Immediately west of English Combe Church it is particularly well preserved and runs westwards to Tway Brook. It is not recognizable between this and a point south of Kinery Wood, Newton Park, but from there it runs to Stantonbury Camp and forms its northern boundary, continuing from the camp in a generally south-westerly direction past Wansdyke House to Compton Dando. Beyond the village it has been much defaced, but it is seen between a point about half a mile north of Publow and another point north-west of Cottles Farm ; and further on it runs up the slope, crosses the North Somerset Railway and ascends the hill to Maes Knoll where again it forms the northern boundary of the camp. Beyond Maes Knoll it cannot now be traced. Collinson, however, states (op. cit. iii, 140) that in his time it could be traced across High Ridge Common through Yanley in Long Ashton parish across Ashton Road to Raynes Cross and through Wraxall parish to Portishead, where it terminated. Sir R. C. Hoare[28] could not trace it with certainty beyond Maes Knoll, and Scarth[29] was equally unsuccessful in 1858. Two sections cut through the bank on St. Anne's Hill by Hoare showed that the bank has been increased in height some time after its first construction and is therefore of two different dates and probably the work of two different peoples.

[28] *Antiq. of Wilts.*   [29] *Somers. Arch. Soc. Proc.* vii (2), 9–24.

Excavations at English Combe and on Bathampton Down failed to reveal any such double structure or even the original surface line, and yielded no objects which threw any definite light on the age of the work.[30] Stukeley's supposition that it was the northern boundary of that part of England which was conquered by the Belgae has been generally adopted. Through part of Wiltshire, however, its line is not distinguishable from that of a Roman road which runs on the top of it, and Roman coins, etc., have been found in the camps attached to it. Drayton, in his *Polyolbion*, speaks of Wansdyke as the boundary between the countries of the Mercians and West Saxons. There is no direct evidence as to the age of that part of the dyke which runs through Somerset, and the evidence as to the Roman or post-Roman origin of the Wiltshire part is scarcely conclusive.

TUMULI

Tumuli or barrows are very numerous on the Quantock and Brendon Hills, and on Exmoor. Isolated examples occur in various parts of the county and there are also some remarkable groups on the Mendip. Very few of them have been systematically examined. Some of them have been utilized in defining parish boundaries, and it is possible that a few of them may have been erected for this purpose and are not burial-places. Cutcombe Barrow is at the point where the boundaries of the parishes of King's Brompton, Luxborough and Withiel Florey join, and Alderman Barrow is at the junction of the boundaries of the parishes of Exmoor, Exford, Porlock and Stoke Pero. The following list of 191 is compiled from the O.S. maps, but many of them have been seen by the author.

Babcary.—Wimble Toot.

Bagborough, West.—One about ¼ m. S. of Trescombe; 3 on Wills Neck.

Bathampton.—One W. of Bathampton Camp; one just outside W. end of camp; two inside S.W. angle of camp.[31] All destroyed.

Bicknoller.—One N.E. of Trendle ring, 1 on Weacombe Hill, and 3 on Thorncombe Hill.

Bishop's Lydeard.—One on Lydeard Hill.

Brompton Regis.—Cutcombe Barrow at junction of parishes of King's Brompton, Luxborough and Withiel Florey.

Burrington.—Eight on Black Down, 6 being at the E. end and 2 at the W.

Chewton Mendip.—Two N.E. of Barrow House Farm; Ashen Hill Barrows (8); 3 near road east of Priddy Nine Barrows; 3 on Stock Hill.

Clatworthy.—Tripp Barrow.

Combe St. Nicholas.—One on Coombe Beacon.

Compton Martin.—Three in S.E. corner of Wrights Piece Wood and 3 to S.W. of it; 1 to S. of Lords lot.

Cothelstone.—Two on Cothelstone Hill.

Crowcombe.—Four on Hurley Beacon; 2 on Great Hill, N. of Trescombe; 1 on Fire Beacon.

Culbone.—Quarter Barrow and 2 others on Twitchen plain, Culbone Hill.

Cutcombe.—Rowbarrows (5) along the boundary between Cutcombe and Stoke Pero. Another one on Lype Hill.

Dodington.—One inside Dowsborough camp at the W. end, and 1 to N. of the camp.

Doulting.—Four on Beacon Hill.

Elworthy.—One N.W. of Elworthy Barrows.

Emborough.—One S.W. of the village; 4 in Burnt Wood.

Evercreech.—Eleven in Small Down Camp.

Exford.—Bendels Barrow.

Exmoor.—Alderman Barrow at junction of Exford, Exmoor, Porlock and Stoke Pero parishes; Chain Barrow; one to S.E. in Chain valley; 'Two barrows,' close to the Devon border, with a third, in the same line, just over the border; Roostitchen (1); Little Buscombe (1); Sherdon (1); Letts Barrows (2) are on the county boundary at the W. end of Squattacombe.

Harptree, East.—One to W. of the Ring forts; 1 N. of them.

Hawkridge.—Oldbarrow on Oldbarrow Down.

Huish Champflower.—One in N. of the parish; 2 on Heydon Hill.[32]

---

[30] *Somers. Arch. Soc. Bath Dist. Proc.* 1904 and 1905.

[31] *Somers. Arch. Soc. Bath Dist. Proc.* 1904, 14–15, and 1905, 51–4.

[32] F. Hancock, *Som. Arch. Soc. Proc.* 42 (ii), 22–5.

Kilve.—Four on Black Hill.

Luccombe.—Yonney How, on Luccombe Hill, and another close by on the boundary between Luccombe and Wootton Courtney; Kitbarrow's (2) on Dunkery Hill at junction of Luccombe, Wootton Courtney and Cutcombe parishes.

Luxborough.—Two on Rodhuish Common; one on Monksham Hill, Leatherbarrow at the junction of Luxborough, Treborough and Withiel Florey parishes.

Marston Bigot. One near river S.E. of Marston Moat.

Minehead.—Five small tumuli on Bossington Hill near the western boundary of the parish.

Nempnett Thrubwell.—Fairy Toot, $\frac{1}{4}$ m. E. of Butcombe, now destroyed.[33]

Otterford.—Robin Hood's Butts, 5 long barrows, close to the Chard and Wellington Road: 3 others of the same name on Brown Down.

Portbury.—One inside the camp.

Priddy.—Three near Chancellors Farm, $\frac{1}{2}$ m. N.N.W. of the village.

Quantoxhead, East. Two on Longstone Hill, 2 W. of Alfoxton, 1 W. of East Quantoxhead village, 1 on West Hill.

Quantoxhead, West. One on Beacon Hill.

Radstock.—One in the north of the parish.

Rowberrow.—One, just S. of the church.

Shepton Mallet.—Three on Beacon Hill, N.W. of the Ring fort.

Skilgate.—Three on Haddon Hill, one being near Frogwell Lodge, another E. of it, and the third, with a double ditch, is N. of Haddon Farm.

Stockland Bristol.—One near Steart Drove, N.E. of the village.

Stogursey.—One on North Moor towards the sea coast.[34]

Stoke, North.—Two in Little Down Camp.

Ston Easton.—One in the N. of the parish.

Uphill.—One on a promontory S. of the village. The tumulus shown on the map near the church is a natural mound.

Upton.—One in the extreme N.E. of the parish near the Bampton and Watchet road.

Watchet, St. Decuman's.—One in field called Bloody Plate, S. of Rydon Farm and S.E. of Doniford.

Wellow.—One, chambered, at Stoney Littleton.[35]

Wells, St. Cuthbert Out.—Priddy Nine Barrows in the N. of the parish; 2 to S. of Burnt Wood near the junction with Emborough parish; 1, surrounded by a ring, $\frac{1}{2}$ m. E. of Hunters Lodge Inn.

Westbury.—One on Westbury Beacon.

Weston-super-Mare.—One near Claremont, at the foot of Worlebury, was destroyed years ago.[36]

Williton.—One in the field called Battle Gore, and 1, half destroyed, in the next field.

Winsford.—Three on Winsford Hill.

Withiel Florey.—Wiveliscombe Barrow on the N. border of the parish, N. of Barrow Farm.

Withycombe.—Beacon W. of the village; 1 on Black Hill.

Withypool.—Brightworthy Barrows (3) on Withypool Common; 1 on Green Barrow on the Parish boundary; 1 on Withypool Hill.

Wootton Courtney.—Robin How on Luccombe Hill (see also Luccombe).

Worle.—Castle Batch on hill N.E. of village.[37]

[34] H. St. George Gray, *Excavations at Wick Barrow*, Taunton, 1908.

[35] *Arch.* xix, 43–8.

[36] Dymond, *Worlebury* (ed. 2), p. 117.

[37] See Dymond, *Worlebury* (ed. 2), p. 117.

[33] *Somers. Arch. Soc. Proc.* viii (2), 54–6.

AGRICULTURE

PERHAPS in no other county in the kingdom will there be found such diversity of soil, altitudes, climate and systems of farming as in Somerset. And in many respects these systems of farming have materially altered during the past century.

A glance at the map will show that it is situate in the south-western district of England, bounded on the north by Gloucestershire, and on the west by the Bristol Channel. On the east it is bounded by Wiltshire, on the south-east by Dorset, and on the west and south-west by Devon. All these counties have very distinctive systems of agriculture, and therefore Somerset gleans a little from each, and has at the same time methods all its own. It is the seventh largest on the list of English counties, and comprises an area of 1,630 square miles. It is about 70 miles across and 50 miles north and south; but packed in between these extremes will be found samples of nearly all the soils and formations of which England is made up. Exmoor and Mendip have as their nucleus the Old Red Sandstone. The Mountain Limestone is the backbone of Mendip, with its riches of lead and iron, while coal seams run right up against it. The New Red Sandstone provides ideal tillage lands; the marls and heavy clays are grand wheat lands, while the alluvial flats afford the finest grazing. Away down in the deeper levels there are vast stretches of peat, on which only the willows grow. The Oolite makes Dundry the sweetest and richest hill pasturage in England. Away across to the Wiltshire and Dorset side the Greensand and Chalk are to be found. The hills are Conglomerate, the vales Alluvial. The country being undulating, the physical aspect is picturesque and ever changing. The climate also is most varied. While the strawberry plants are in blossom and the young potatoes being moulded up at Cheddar, the snow drifts may still be lying unthawed on the northern slopes of Mendip; and possibly the cows may be knee deep in rich grass at Glastonbury while the fields in the Vale of Chew have scarcely turned from brown to green. In the sunny corners of the Quantocks flowers are in bloom all the year. The climate is very variable. Mountain fog, a bone-searching, impenetrable mist, known as a cap, may settle on the top of Mendip, while in the autumn the sea fogs penetrate a long way inland. The rainfall is fairly copious, but while every drop that falls on Mendip is absorbed to be again yielded up as deep springs, the hard marl throws it off at once, and thus we have deep-cut water courses with very little water in them. Again, though the moors are highly absorbent, the water is stagnant and therefore undrinkable, thus giving rise to the paradox that where water is most plentiful it is at the same time the scarcest. Such a variety of conditions bring about as a natural result mixed farming. Dairy and arable farming are blended more completely than in any other county, and Somerset may be termed a county of small holders, some being yeomen farming their own acres. The large farmers as known in the eastern counties and Lincolnshire are unknown here.

In the county are 14,046 holdings; of these only 403 are above 300 acres, 4,298 above 50 and not exceeding 300 acres, while 3,362 are above one and under five acres, the whole giving an average holding of 60·8. These small holdings are doubtless accountable for the high rental paid in Somerset, which continues to be one of the highest, if not the highest, in the kingdom, as much as £2 per acre being paid for land of a quality obtainable in other counties at from 10s. to 15s. per acre. At one time exceptional rentals were paid for the rich grazing lands on the levels, particularly the Pawlett Hams, the rich marshes at Kingston Seymour and Wick St. Lawrence, and then right away from Highbridge to Taunton. The grass grown on these lands will fatten a bullock without extraneous help.

The total acreage under crops in 1906 was 854,495 acres; of these 179,526 were arable and 674,969 permanent grass, therefore it must be either a dairying or else a grazing county, and it must have cattle in plenty. The county does not breed all its own, neither does it purchase all the necessary adult stock. Here as in other matters there is much diversity of custom. The rearing districts are principally on the hills, as the land in the moors is much too forward and forcing. Large numbers of young Irish cattle and sheep are purchased in Bristol market. On account of the pre-eminence of the grazing and dairying industry in this county, it may be well to deal first with the live stock.

Cattle.—Above all things, Somerset is a cattle county. In 1906 it had 117,222 cows and heifers in milk or in calf, 45,843 two years old and above, 45,009 one year and under two, and 41,894 under one year, or a total of 249,968. This on an area devoted to permanent grass would give rather over 2¾ acres to each head of cattle. The average rate of increase brings about a renewal of the stock in each sixth year.

Somerset has no breed of cattle particularly its own, except that which is now known as the Somerset-Devon. The true North Devon is a rather small animal, beautifully symmetrical, and furnishing the choicest flavoured sirloin of beef of any breed in existence. But it did not carry sufficient bone for the purpose of working or milk enough for the dairy farmer; in consequence of this, a bigger and coarser breed was evolved on the rich vales around Taunton, and duly became known as the Somerset-Devon. In recent years by means of a judicious blending of the two strains the size of the one has been increased and the coarseness of the other ameliorated. As a result of this the modern showyard decisions denote that this breed is now considered much superior to the original one. A standard of excellence for a bull of this breed is of course registered pedigree: Forehead broad, tapering towards the nose, which should be flesh coloured; nostrils high and open; a broad muzzle; eyes full and yet peaceful; medium sized ears, and fringed with hair; horns growing out at nearly right angles from the head, and then curving upwards; rather stout at base; a full cheek, and a clean throat; good strong neck; fine withers; shoulders flat, sloping, well covered; a deep, broad, somewhat circular chest; ribs should be well sprung, making a rotund middle piece, very level on top and bottom; the ribs should be deep, the hind quarters deep, thick and square, the skin should be moderately thick and mellow, covered with an abundant coat of rich mossy hair of a red colour; a little white in front of the purse is admissible, but it should not extend far forward or appear on the outside of the flanks or any other part of the limbs or body.

Not only is there an increasing home demand for these cattle, as is proved by the growing number of bulls shown and sold at the spring and autumnal sales of the Devon Cattle Breeders' Society, but the average price materially increases on each occasion. The Devons are in great request in South America, especially Uruguay; whilst latterly large shipments have been made to South Africa, where the Devon has been found to do remarkably well even in tick-infested districts. Amongst the best known exhibitors of this breed are the Hon. E. W. B. Portman, Hestercombe, Taunton; Mr. C. L. Hancock, Cothelstone; Mr. R. D. Hancock, Halse; Mr. Sam Kidner, Milverton; Mr. R. Bruford, Taunton; Mr. E. Clatworthy, Cutsey, Wellington; Mr. P. Dibble, Shopnoller, Bagborough; Mr. W. Kidner, Kingston, and Mr. John Kidner, Dodhill; Mr. F. J. Merron, North Petherton, Bridgwater; Mrs. Skinner, Bishop's Lydeard; Mr. Alfred Bowerman, Capton, Williton; Sir Frederick Wills, Dulverton; whilst the late King Edward and her late Majesty Queen Victoria were partial to this breed on the Royal Farms at Windsor.

It is singular that this breed is seldom met with much on the northern side of Taunton, where the majority of the cattle on the rich grazing lands are purchased for fattening. In the dairy districts the majority of the cattle are principally now unregistered Shorthorns; though amongst them may still be seen a few of the old brindles, reminders of the old Longhorn cattle, which were so prominent in some parts of the county. This breed has now gone out, with the exception of the herd kept by Mr. J. E. Coates, Stanton Drew, where they have been kept amongst the druidical remains for a great many years. There are a few herds of Jersey cattle, but these do not make much headway with the general agriculturists. Amongst the few herds known are those of Messrs. J. H. Shore, Frome; C. Tudway, Wells; A. F. Somerville, Dinder; R. P. Wheadon, Ilminster; Lady Smyth, Long Ashton; Mrs. Loader Browns, at Chard. The pure Shorthorn has failed to make headway. Mr. George Taylor established a fine herd at Stanton Prior, but removed with them to Middlesex. Dr. Colthurst and Mr. J. H. Braikenbridge had nice herds at Chew Magna, but these were dispersed on the death of their founders. Mr. A. J. Mullins had a fine herd of dairy Shorthorns at Castle Cary. The most important herds remaining are that established by the late Capt. Whitting at Weston-super-Mare, that being built up by Mr. Barnard J. Bush at Laverton near Frome, as well as those of the late Mr. Sidney Hill at Langford, Mr. G. F. King at Chewton Keynsham, the Rev. Le Gendre Horton at Wellow, Lord Winterstoke at Blagdon, and Mr. A. M. B. Criddle, Locking, Weston-super-Mare. But large numbers of dairy farmers use purebred pedigree Shorthorn bulls.

Horses.—Horse breeding takes a very inferior position, especially so by reason of the absence of high-class studs, which are so favourable to the production of shires in other counties. Practically the only exhibition stud of shires is that of Lord Winterstoke at Blagdon. The brothers Messrs. Bucknell, Holcombe and Bridgwater; and Messrs. Haydon and Paget, Radstock; Major Sherston and Mr. Christopher Moody, Evercreech, have latterly done much to improve the breed of heavy horses in the county. Mainly through the establishment of the Compton stud in the adjacent county of Dorset, though close on the borders of Somerset, the light horse breeding in the southeastern parts of the county has been greatly improved, some very notable hunting horses having been produced by Somerset breeders.

AGRICULTURE

At one time in the western parts of the county were to be seen those sure-footed, strong-backed, light horses known as pack horses, which by many are considered to be the true foundation stock of the hackney. They were very smart, had high action, and yet with that sureness of foot mainly produced by climbing the rough cliffs from the shore with smuggled goods on their backs, and then going inland by the roughest tracks. The writer of this article had one of the last of this breed in his possession.

It would appear that Somerset breeds a large number of horses in proportion to its area of 179,526 acres of arable land, the number being 41,147, or roughly one horse to four acres. But this is in a great measure due to each farmer having to keep one or two horses to work his grasslands; as the work comes on mainly at hay time it is sought to decrease the keep of the mare by breeding a good foal. These are usually sold as suckers at the autumnal fairs and sales, and purchased by the graziers of the middle of Somerset, as these colts will feed and thrive on the snake pipe soils, which are very injurious to cattle. The colts are generally sold at three or four years old, and if bought on the right lines as to quality and soundness they make an excellent return. They are generally bought by upland farmers, who work them a season or two and then pass them on to the towns at high prices.

Sheep.—Somerset is not so favoured with breeds of sheep as its neighbouring county of Devon. In fact, it appears to have had but two indigenous breeds of its own, the old Mendip and the Porlock. Writing of the former, Youatt[1] says :—

> A vast tract of uninclosed hill and moor ground formerly existed stretching from Wells almost to the Bristol Channel, and being part of the great forest of Mendip the sheep which fed on it bore considerable resemblance to the Exmoor sheep and to the Dorsets. They seemed to be an intermediate race between the two. The horns were smaller, and the countenance wilder; the sheep altogether more diminutive, the wool finer, and the flesh more finely flavoured than those of Dorset. They were a hardy breed and would thrive on the poorest soil; these sheep covered the forest in immense numbers, being alternately changed from the moor to the hill and the hill to the moor as the season required. They were likewise said to possess and much more generally a property that has been spoken of as occasionally observed in the Dorset sheep, that of breeding twice in the year. . . . In process of time, however, a considerable portion of this wild tract of country became inclosed. The number of sheep was consequently materially diminished, and the character of the sheep was changed with the changing character of the land. The old and wild Mendips were now out of place, and crosses with the heavier Devons and with the improved Dorsets, with the South Downs, and with the Leicesters were attempted. These experiments were attended with various success, but the result of them was that the genuine Mendip breed became extinct, and that there is at this time no breed of sheep peculiar to this part of the county.

The other indigenous breed which still exists is that known as the Porlock. These are kept on the hills round Minehead; they are very small, with short horns, and are exceptionally wild and endowed with great leaping powers, characteristics which render them difficult to confine when brought down from the hills into the inclosed lands at their foot. Before the trade in frozen lamb from across the seas developed to the present extent young wethers of this breed were often killed and sold as lamb, the small joints readily lending to the deception.

Of the recognized breeds there are those known as the Somerset and Dorset Horn, which to all intents and purposes are now the same breed; but a few years ago the sheep on the Somerset side were larger and lankier and evidently had some of the old Mendip in them, as they bred much more freely, but were not such good mothers. The Dorset Horn is a very useful sheep with white face and legs, and a pink or flesh-coloured nose. The great value of this breed consists in its early lambs, which are dropped from September onwards. Indeed, lambs of this breed frequently come on the table at Christmas, when they realize high values; after this time prices drop rapidly. The ewes generally drop twin lambs and are capable of producing twice a year; but this is not now practised to the extent that it formerly was. Many Somerset farmers purchase the ewes in lamb at the August fairs and first fatten off the lambs, which the ewes soon follow to the butcher, both being gone before dairying commences in the spring. The sheep have a very healthy appetite. The wool is short and good, but it opens more and grows rather longer than in the adjacent county of Dorset. The principal exhibition flocks of these in the county include those of Messrs. John Kidner, Ilchester; Sam. Kidner, Milverton; and F. G. Merson, North Petherton. This breed has a flock book, as has also the Devon long wools, a very popular breed, mostly seen from Taunton going westwards. This is a breed that has evidently a great future before it when once the foreign buyer fully recognizes its merits. Like many of our other breeds of sheep, it was produced by gradual improvements of ancient stock, the Brampton Notts, a breed which in the old days was very much like the Leicester, but rather more evenly made. This breed was first crossed with the

[1] *Sheep* (1837), 255 et seq.

improved Leicester, a dash of Lincoln was added, and a curl to the wool came in with the Cotswold. Here the blending stopped. The Devon long wool has a more pronounced head than the Leicester, since it possesses a longer and larger face with a finer forehead; the nose and ears are also larger. The frame is larger and more readily clothes itself with nice flesh; it fattens very readily, the dock being an infallible indicator. It is an early maturity breed, the wethers never seeing the second season; they are not such heavy eaters as the Dorsets; they average from 80 to 100 lb. carcass weight, and cut from 9 lb. to 11 lb. wool each, but with rams this has been greatly exceeded. The mutton is of good flavour, not over fat. The breed is somewhat variable in appearance by reason of the soil and the altitude at which it is kept. The ewes are good mothers, and drop very hardy lambs. It is anticipated that this breed will be utilized to counteract the excess of Lincoln blood in some flocks in the Argentine, so as to fit the mutton and lamb from thence for the demands of the British market. The best known of the present day flocks of this breed are those of Messrs. F. White, Torweston, Williton; W. Greenaway, Halse, Taunton; C. L. Hancock, Cothelstone, Taunton; and F. S. Merson, Doniford, Watchet; and Mrs. Skinner, Bishop's Lydeard.

In the far western part of the county where the wild red deer loves to roam is another surviving breed of the olden days, known as the Exmoor, for which quite recently a flock book has been established. This breed has existed from time immemorial, and is by some considered to have had ancient relationship with the old Mendip breed. But this can scarcely be so, as in the ancient descriptions of the Exmoors the ram is stated to have been adorned with a beard, somewhat resembling that of a goat, whereas no such description appears in connexion with the old Mendip breed. This breed is often confused by outside writers with that known as the Porlocks; and thus we find them described as having white faces, when these should be yellowish-brown. Their horns are generally spoken of as being light and tapering, whereas the head of a true Exmoor ram is fit to place in a hall, the horns being very large and fine, often with a double circle of curve. The sheep are short, deep and compact, weigh well, and though somewhat long in maturing on the moors, flesh rapidly on the lowlands. The mutton is very nice, and altogether the true Exmoor is a hardy, handsome sheep, particularly the ram. They are most assiduous workers, and will live under most adverse conditions; their wool is close, thick and rain resisting. Amongst the most recent exhibition flocks are those of Messrs. D. J. Tapp and H. Mardon of Dulverton, though there are other flocks which should certainly be better known in the show-ring than they are.

In the north-eastern part of the county about the middle of the 19th century there existed a breed of sheep that were known as Wellow sheep, mainly by reason of the fact that these were purchased at Wellow Fair. To all intents and purposes these sheep were local Oxford Downs and they have now practically disappeared.

Somerset is the county of the crossbred; these do exceedingly well. The climate has a singular influence on the purebred shortwools; no matter how compact the wools may be, in the second generation the fleeces are opened, and the wool is lengthened, and partakes more and more of crossbred characteristics. It would thus seem that semi-long or longwools is the desideratum of the county. In the production of the crossbred the use of the longwool ram has practically gone out. Hampshire Down or Oxford Down is now the principal admixture. The Irish or Roscommon ewe obtained in Bristol market is not now bred from to the extent it formerly was. Lucock assigned to Somerset 500,700 sheep, most of them at that time short woolled. The most recent returns show the number to be 474,096 of all ages.

The Pig.—The pig is very important to the dairy farmer, as it enables him to dispose of his otherwise waste whey and milk in the easiest and most profitable manner. At one time there existed a breed that also extended into Gloucestershire known as the spotted breed. This was a hardy pig, very fertile—indeed, rather too much so, the litters ranging from a dozen to twenty pigs, with a consequent difficulty of rearing. These pigs made alike the best of bacon and pork. Several herds of pigs of this type still exist. At one time an endeavour was made to introduce the white breeds, but the great objection to these was that the sun cracked their ears and the sores were difficult to heal up. More recently the large black breed from Devon and Cornwall has become increasingly popular. The so-called Somerset sheeted breed is obtained by crossing, and is far from being a fixed type. The total number of pigs in Somerset in 1905 was 114,501, but the number kept is decreasing, there being villages where at one time a thousand bacon pigs were fattened annually, which now produce hardly half a dozen fat pigs a year owing to the cheese tub having been abandoned for the milk churn. In the olden days there was a big demand for heavy weight bacon in Bristol, and for heavy porkers in Bath. This enabled the farmers to lay on flesh when it was most profitable to do so.

Modern requirements call for light weight baconers with a small amount of fat in the back; if this is unduly thick the bacon curers make a very considerable dock in the prices, and porkers over 80 lb. are practically unsaleable. The county suffered very much from swine fever regulations, and in later years the selling of milk has had the effect of greatly reducing the number of pigs kept in the county. With this reduction is also going out the practice of each farmer curing his own bacon, and the once familiar picture of a flitch or two of bacon drying in the ingle-nook, beside the fire on the hearth and several more on the bacon rack beneath the kitchen ceiling is now seldom seen. This may be in a great measure due to the dying out of the patriarchal system whereby the farmer fed his labourers in the summer, and often in the winter as well. At the beginning of the 19th century every rural householder kept a pig; now very few do so. The practice has also greatly varied. Formerly it was the custom of small farmers to keep sows and breed from them, and then sell the litter at seven or eight weeks old as 'slips,' or else keep them along running poor for a couple or three months more and then sell them as strong stores to the cheese-makers to consume the sour whey and be converted into bacon. But owing to the swine fever regulations this trade is now very decadent, most of the cheese-makers who feed pigs preferring to breed and feed their own pigs rather than risk an outbreak of swine fever on the premises. Thus in a century pig-keeping has been turned from a considerable source of wealth into a very doubtful source of bare remuneration to the farmer.

Poultry.—As regards poultry, until the latter part of the century the industry was mainly in the hands of the small holders near the large centres of population at the northern end of the county. And this district proved specially suitable to this industry, as the fox was not preserved to the same extent as on the other side of Mendip. The industry remains general rather than specialized, each farmer keeping a mixed stock on his farm; but latterly more attention has been given to poultry rearing and egg production for their own sakes, and egg-collecting depôts have been established in the county. But the humidity in the air renders it difficult to rear some of the breeds that do so well on the higher and drier lands of other counties. The County Council has appointed a poultry expert to instruct the poultry keepers of the county in the most up-to-date methods.

The dairy industry of the county takes precedence of all others, mainly on account of the remarkable verdure of the grass; the average rental of dairy farms may be taken at from 30s. to 40s. per acre. It should be considered that in nearly all instances the arable portion of the farms is made subservient to the dairy lands of which it is a very helpful adjunct, by reason of the growth of straw for thatching and bedding purposes, and the enormous crops of mangold produced for winter feed.

The dairy districts may be said to comprise the whole of the northern portion of the county, with the exception of the grazing lands at Kingston Seymour. This includes the Vales of the Avon, the Yeo and the Chew. Here for a century has been produced some of the finest butter in the world, and all the year round dairying was practised in order to comply with the demands of Bristol. But the winter portion of the trade was the first to fall away by reason of colonial, foreign, and fraudulent competition; and the milk churn has replaced the butter basket. The custom was for these small farmers to churn their butter at home and take it to Bristol by means of the market cart, which also carried fruit, eggs, poultry, and often the carcass of a fatted calf or home-killed porker. It was generally the farmer's wife who went to market and had her recognized round of private custom, these rounds being considered very valuable. The butter was usually made from scald cream, churned in a pump churn, which was ultimately replaced by barrel churns, the work of local coopers, and latterly by more widely recognized makers, the butter so churned being made up in a wooden trendle by means of the hand. In the early years of the 19th century two things were very prominent in a young farmer's courtship, namely, whether the father of his sweetheart made good cider, and the girl herself had a cool hand for butter-making. Many a courtship was made or marred in consequence. The expense of running these small farms was not great apart from high rentals, and rates which were not so oppressive then as now. On the other hand, everything was disposed of to the best advantage. A boy and the farmer did all the winter work; the labour bill was a small one. Most of these farmers reared a few calves, and these grew up to come in and fill the gaps caused by sale or otherwise in the more matured portion of the herd. The first real blow to this system of farming was caused by the advent of 'Danish' butter.

The introduction of foreign butter was not so harmful at first to those farmers near Bristol, as they were enabled to sell their milk at good prices. But the improvement in refrigeration soon enabled milk to be sent from longer distance by rail and the price of road-borne milk went down with a run, until now the prices range from 5d. per imperial gallon for the summer months to 8d. for a few winter months. Indeed, this development of the milk trade has had a remarkable effect on the dairying of the county, and as larger farmers with lower rentals have taken up the trade the lot of the smaller man is becoming an unenviable one. Many of these would again revert to butter making were it not for the impossibility of getting the female section of the household to again undertake the drudgery of the dairy. So they go on leading a hand to mouth existence, few of them even in prosperous seasons increasing their bank account, and in consequence the sons go off to the town and the daughters go out as 'helps.' At one time these farms were handed down like heirlooms from father to son. Now the holdings frequently pass to fresh tenants, and the old names are known no more.

On the eastern side of the county, from a short distance outside of Bath, past Frome on to Castle Cary and Wincanton and Glastonbury, a different type of farmer is met with. Here the manufacture of the world-famed Cheddar cheese and the production of bacon are found as well as dairying. The farms and farmers' capital are larger, as they need to be, though not to the same extent as in days gone by, since the modern cheese-maker sells his drafts more frequently and does not sell his whole season's make at once as he did of yore.

Before, however, we proceed to describe the modern processes of cheese-making, a few notes may be allowed as to the history of this industry within the county. A hint of the value of Somerset cheese in 1086 is given, says Mr. Eyton, by an agricultural rent in kind, 10 bacon-hogs and 100 cheese, paid on the manor of Charlton (Horethorne), the cheeses in question being valued at £17 10s., or 3s. 6d. each.[2] In 1170 Alfred de Lincoln accounted for 40 weighs of cheese made in Somerset at £11, the weigh being 256 lb. Again in 1184 cheese was bought for the use of John the king's son at £10 19s. 4d.,[3] whilst in 1403 Richard Arnold of Glastonbury was supplying cheese to the household at Dunster.[4] This commodity appears to have entered largely not only into the domestic, but also into the Church and parochial life of mediaeval times. In 1495–6, for instance, Harry Mew, keeper of the Croke (processional cross) at Croscombe, was granted the sum of 5s. 6d. to buy cheese, probably, as Bishop Hobhouse suggests, for distribution amongst those who followed him and assisted at the processions.[5] Again, in 1552, 'Cheeses gathered for the Church' figure in the Churchwardens' Accounts for St. Michael's, Bath.[6]

That Cheddar cheese was much esteemed in the 17th century we learn from a correspondence preserved in the State Papers between Lord Conway and Lord Poulett in 1635, the former writing from London to remind his friend of 'a cheese of Cheddar' which he was to send him. Poulett's reply is to the effect that 'he has sent to take up all the cheeses at Cheddar for him.' Finally, however, he has to apologize for being unable to secure more than one, for 'the cheeses of Cheddar,' once 'wont to be common,' had 'grown to be in such esteem at the Court' that they were 'bespoken before they were made.'[7] Pococke records the price of these cheeses on the spot in his day as 6d. per lb.; they were not then 'made larger than common cheeses,' and were 'like Parmesan in flavour.'[8] Defoe gives the following account of the method of manufacture in his day: 'The milk of all the town cows is brought together every day into a common room, where the persons appointed or trusted for the management measure every man's quantity and set it down in a book. When the quantities are adjusted, the milk is all put together, and every man's milk makes one cheese and no more, so that the cheese is bigger or less as the cows yield more or less milk. Those who contributed a small quantity of milk had to wait the longer for payment, none being made, we are told, until each person's share 'came to one whole cheese.'[9] Prices then averaged from 6d. to 8d. per lb.[10]

In 1739 108 lb. of cheese cost 16s. 6d., or 1¾d. per lb. at Selworthy.[11] The writer of *A Sentimental Journey* in 1772 relates that the inhabitants of Cheddar 'usually clubbed together to make a cheese of 100 to 150 lb. in weight,'[12] 'the great and prodigious cheeses of Cheddar,' as they are styled by another topographer,[13] 'requiring more than one man's strength to set them on the table.' Mr. John Billingsley of Ashwick Grove towards the close of the 18th century wrote that the Somerset cheese was much admired, particularly that made in the parishes of Meare and Cheddar. It was then for the most part purchased by jobbers and sent through the medium of Weyhill, Giles's Hill, Reading and other fairs to the London market, where it was sold under the name of Double Gloucester. He prefaced the following description of the process of cheese-making employed in his time by the observation that cleanliness, sweet rennet and attention to breaking the curd, are the principal requisites in this industry.

> When the milk is brought home it is strained into a tub, and about three tablespoonfuls of good rennet put therein (supposing the quantity of milk sufficient to make a cheese of 28 lb.), which remains undisturbed about two hours, then it becomes curd, and is properly broken; when done, three parts

---

[2] Eyton, *Domesday Studies*, i, 47. [3] *Somers. Arch. Soc. Proc.* xxviii, 73.
[4] Hancock, *Hist. Minehead*, 223. [5] *Somers. Rec. Soc. Publ.* iv, 21.
[6] *Somers. Arch. Soc. Proc.* iv, 21. The bulk of the Cheddar cheese made in the county in the middle of the last century was manufactured in a district extending from the village of Cheddar to Wells and Glastonbury on one side, and on the other to Axbridge and Bridgwater (*Bath and West Journ.* v, 171).
[7] *Cal. S.P. Dom.* 1635, pp. 484, 512, 558. [8] Pococke, *Travels*, i, 153.
[9] Defoe, *Tour*, ii, 39. [10] Ibid. 38.
[11] Hancock, *Hist. Selworthy*, 121. Prices in 1850 were 66s. per cwt.; in 1851, 64s.; in 1852, 70s.; and in 1853, 75s. (*Bath and West Journ.* v, 170).
[12] Add. MSS. 30, fol. 287. [13] *Complete Hist. of Somerset*, 115.

of the whey is taken therefrom and warmed, and then put into the tub again, where it remains about twenty minutes; the whey is again put over the fire, made nearly scald hot, and put into the tub to scald the curd about half an hour, and then part of the whey is taken away, and the remainder remains with the curd till it is nearly cold. The whey is then poured off, the curd broken very small, put into the vat and pressed, where it remains nearly an hour; and then is taken out, turned and put in again and pressed till the evening, when it is taken out again, turned and pressed till the next morning. It is then taken out of the vat, salted, put into it again with a clean dry cloth round it, and remains in the press till the next evening, when it is taken out again, salted, put into the vat without a cloth, and pressed till the next morning; and then it finally leaves the press, and it is salted once a day for twelve days.

The great desire of the Cheddar cheese-maker is to have all his cows come into profit in April, to be brought up to full strength for the cheese tub by a number of two and three year old heifers calving in May. The average yield of a cheese-maker's herd may be estimated at 500 gallons per annum. In general practice one gallon of milk will yield 1 lb. of Cheddar cheese curd; the season for making is from April to October, the average make of cheese per cow in that period being 4 cwt., which seldom sells at less than 60s. per cwt. from a good dairy; at one time it reached as high as 80s. Fancy or prize dairies make fancy values. The milk of the cows when the Cheddar season is over is either made into Caerphilly cheese, or in the majority of instances goes to supply the increasing demands of the towns. The pigs are a necessity to consume the whey, but the profit now is a very problematical one with light weights, back fat regulations, and the high prices of foreign maize and barley.

Some notion of the return of a Cheddar cheese farm may be obtained from a consideration of the following facts. A calf is sold worth 30s. when dropped, or else fattened until worth £4; 4 cwt. Cheddar cheese at 60s., £12. The cow becomes dry by autumn, or if she calves in April the sale of the winter milk will return about the same as the calf, as it is worth more at that time than when the calf consumes it in the spring. The return of the pig over an average of seasons is doubtful. Thus it will be seen that the gross return of a Cheddar cheese cow is £16. It will take three acres of Cheddar cheese land to keep a cow all the year round, and a bit of artificial besides. Taking the cost at £2 per acre, on the Inland Revenue calculation of three rents, one for the landlord, the other for rates and labour, it will be seen that the farmer has but £2 10s. per cow as his share. The work of the farmer and his family and occasional casualties amongst his cattle should also be taken into account. Thus a 40-cow dairy will bring in £100 a year, which certainly is not over much on which to live respectably and bring up a family. Therefore the farmer cuts his expenses, and he cannot afford to keep a horse for hunting. Indeed, it is most noticeable that packs of hounds are remarkably scarce in the Cheddar cheese districts of Somerset, as compared with their occurrence in arable counties.

The Cheddar cheese-maker must be a slave to duty. He and his sons must don the milking gown night and morning and go through the other work of the farm at middle day, as whatever lacks the milk pail must hold sway; while his wife and daughters must be in the dairy at early morn to prepare for the milk, and it is often evening again before the cheese is finally put in the press.

It is singular that though Cheddar gave its name to this world-renowned make of cheese there is practically no cheese made there at present. It is noteworthy that the invention of the big Cheddar was due to Somerset and not to that country of big ideas across the Atlantic. At Pennard the produce of 730 cows was made into that big Cheddar cheese weighing 11 cwt., measuring 9 ft. 4 in. in circumference, and 20 in. deep which was presented to Her Majesty Queen Victoria.

In 1856 the Joseph Harding system of cheese-making was made public as the result of a deputation of Scotchmen coming south to investigate the originators of this system. To Mrs. Harding, Marksbury, and her nephew, Joseph Harding, Compton Dando, is due the substitution of a definite procedure for mere rule of thumb; for some twenty years the Harding system was the model, though nearly every maker had his or her variations in detail. The main feature as we view it now was the insistence upon absolute cleanliness. The milkers were not allowed to bring the milk in direct from the farmyard. They had to pour it into a receiver outside the dairy wall, whence by means of a pipe it was conveyed inside to the cheese tub. As this was the opening of the new era of Cheddar making, it may be well to describe how the cheese was then manufactured. The rennet was made in the old-fashioned way of steeping the vells, and not as at present by rennet extract of ascertained strength.

Immediately after the morning milking the evening and morning milk were put together into the tub, the temperature of the whole being brought to 80° by heating a small quantity of the evening milk. The thermometer was regularly used. In spring and towards winter a small quantity of annatto was added (there being annatto factories in Somerset at that period), to improve the colour of the cheese. It was stirred into the milk at the same time as the rennet at about 7 a.m. An hour was allowed for coagulation. At 8 o'clock the curd was partially broken and allowed to subside a few minutes in order that a small quantity of whey might be drawn off and heated. This was done by placing it in a tin heater, and putting the latter in a copper of boiling water. The curd was then most carefully and minutely broken, in order not to beat out the fat, the breaking being done by means of shovel breakers. When this was done the heated whey was put back into the tub until the whole was brought up to 80°; the tub was covered up, and it remained thus for an hour, when more whey was drawn off and brought to a higher temperature than for the first scald. The curd was again broken, and when this was done the heated whey was carefully poured in, the stirring of the curd being continued in order to evenly heat or scald the whole so that no portion of it should become over-heated. The temperature was thus brought up to 100°, and the stirring continued until the curd became somewhat hardened. The curd was then left for half an hour to settle to the bottom of the tub. The whey was then drawn off. The curd was piled up on the convex bottom of the tub. It thus drained itself most thoroughly; it was then cut and turned and piled as before. The effect of this was not only somewhat to dry the curd, but also to ripen it and render it fit for greater pressure. The curd was now broken up by hand, and aerated until it was brought down to 60°. In the summer months this lowering was brought about by placing the curd in a lead cooler. It was then put in vats and subjected to moderate pressure for an hour. The curd was then taken from the vats and the bulk cut in pieces and passed through a curd mill; the ground curd was mixed with salt at the rate of 2 lb. of salt to the cwt. of curd. At about 3 o'clock the same afternoon the whole was put back into the vat and greater pressure was applied; this forced out the remaining whey. Next morning the cheese was turned in the vat and a calico cloth placed on it, the following morning saw the placing of another bandage on the cheese; before it was put on the shelves for ripening it was tightly laced in a canvas fillet. A few years after this Mr. Harding invented his process of slip scalding, the morning's milk being mixed with the evening's at a temperature of about 80°, the rennet was then added, and an hour allowed for the milk to coagulate, when it was broken up. Now comes the variant from the first described process. The scalding whey was added to the curd in its pulpy state before it had time to settle and get hard. This scald was brought up to a temperature of 100° Fahr. At the same time he abandoned the old system of low temperature in the cheese room, or rather a damp cellar, and went in for a heated cheese room kept between 50° and 70°, and thus came about the rapid ripening by which the cheese was ready for cutting in three instead of ten to twelve months under the old plan. Thus was founded the real Cheddar of modern commerce. The name of Harding must go down with it for all time. It will be noticed that he did not use either the acidimeter or sour whey, but he lifted the make out of the old ruts of mere practical chance, and introduced to it the more definite methods of science. Indeed, he must be rightly deemed the first scientific instructor in Cheddar cheese making. The Americans about half a century ago fixed upon the Cheddar as the best cheese for their dairymen to produce; and with their idea of greatness thought farmhouse dairying not sufficient, and so initiated the factory system, which has now run round the world. But Somerset still perseveres with her farmhouse dairies, which can hold their own as regards produce against all comers. A pioneer in this respect was Mr. George Gibbons of Tunly Farm, near Bath, who was intimately related to the Harding family, and who at the International Dairy Show in New York in 1878 won the two chief prizes with six Cheddars made in his dairy. He was also awarded the gold medal for Cheddars at Paris, and seven medals at Amsterdam and Copenhagen. Other systems were afterwards evolved. About 1880 Mrs. Cannon of Milton Clevedon, Evercreech, brought out her fine system, and proved its value by winning all along the line at Frome Cheese Show; success followed her up, so that it was not long before she had won £2,000 in prizes, and a worldwide reputation. In fact, so much was her system appreciated, that it was adopted officially by the Bath and West of England Society when it founded its Cheddar Cheese Schools in 1890, which have now been taken over by the Somerset County Council. The system remains practically the same as when introduced, perhaps with the exception of the inclusion of a more reliable acidimeter, more easily read. The essential characteristic of the Cannon system is high acidity and early ripening.

But still another system was evolved by a member of a Somerset family, who made his home in Dorset, Mr. Theodore C. Candy, a system by many considered equal if not superior to the Cannon system. As a prize-winner, his success has been phenomenal. His system may be best described as being a long maturing one with the certainty of high values. He has discovered the true secret of the keeping qualities of the old Cheddar. We have now mentioned the two systems mostly in use in Somerset at the close of the Victorian era. If more details are needed they can be found in Mr. F. J. Lloyd's *Report of the Results of Investigations into Cheddar Cheese Making*, issued by the Board of Agriculture in 1899.

In Somerset in the last century one name was always associated with Cheddar cheese, that of Archdeacon Denison, a noted connoisseur, who proclaimed its virtues far and wide and kept one piece for forty years.[14] A singular feature in connexion with Cheddar cheese is the manner in which it maintains its value. In the *Farming of Somersetshire*, by Thomas Dyke Acland, junr., and William Sturge, published in 1851, reference is made :—

> The price of the best Cheddar cheese is from 65/- to 70/- per cwt., and varies little from season to season, being a luxury which at all times finds a ready market. The middling and inferior qualities range on the average from 50/- to 56/- per cwt., the fluctuations in price being considerable and depending on the demand in manufacturing districts and on the general state of trade of the country. The farmers have lately complained that the price of these qualities is reduced by competition with American cheese, the manufacture of which is said to be improving so as to be better suited to the English palate than when first imported; but it has not as yet entered into competition with the finest qualities of English cheese.

Half a century later I make another quotation. The fourth draft of the cheese made at the Bath and West Cheese Schools for the Somerset County Council at Glendale Farm, Wedmore, has been sold at 68*s*. per cwt. What other make of English agricultural produce can show such a uniformity of price after half a century?

Cheddar loaf or truckles are small Cheddars. At the close of the Victorian era another make of cheese became very popular. It is mainly made in late autumn and early spring, and is known as Caerphilly. Originally made in Wales, its use was to be cut out in chunks to be eaten by the colliers in the coal mines. Improvement in make brought about a demand that supply can scarcely overtake, and now its merits as a toasting cheese have created a demand for it far away from the miners' homes. It is one of the most profitable cheeses that the farmer can produce, and finds a good and ready market. It is made as follows : Mix the evening's and the morning's milk; see that it gets fairly ripe; no cream must be removed. The acidity should be about the same as for Cheddar. When renneted the milk should be at 90°, and should in 45 minutes be sufficiently coagulated for cutting. This being done the curd should be left for whey to rise 15 or 20 minutes, depending on amount of acidity present. Break rather coarse for half an hour, then test for acidity, which should show ·9 before drawing the whey. It is not easy to draw the whey from the curd, and care has to be taken to keep the latter in a pile in the tub. After having drained for a short time, slice with a curd cutter, spread a cloth over the rack in the cheese cooler; then put the curd into a bowl, and thus put the curd on a cheese rack. This latter facilitates drainage. Tie up lightly, and invert a milk tin over the bundle. Then apply pressure in the form of a half hundredweight ; leave under pressure for 30 minutes for acidity to develop. This should be from ·28 to ·30 ; the latter is considered too high. Open the cloth, turn out the lump of curd, and cut into inch cubes ; put back into the cloth and re-tie and re-apply pressure until the acidity reaches .40, which it usually does in about half an hour. Then put 9 lb. of curd into each vat, the curd during the process being lightly broken by means of the hand. No salt should be added as with Cheddar. Then apply pressure for 45 minutes, take out of vats and turn, being very careful to adjust the cloths smoothly ; return and apply greater pressure. Leave until the morning, then take out and plunge into a saturated brine bath, in which they remain twenty-four hours. They are turned and remain another day, when they are taken out, put on boards to drain and dry. They are fit for sale in a fortnight. Ninety gallons of milk will produce 120 lb. of cheese.

Gerard, writing of Yeovil in the middle of the 17th century, affirms that 'its greatest commodity is cheese.' [15] At this town in modern times Messrs. Aplin & Barrett, Limited, who employ over 200 persons in the manufacture of the St. Ivel products, have revived the ancient industry.

The Somerset County Council supplies a very considerable amount of technical education in dairying matters, mainly by reason of the efforts of that successful dairy farmer, Mr. George Gibbons. There have been migratory butter schools. These produced two notable pupils, Mrs. Walter W. Keel, Stanton Drew, who secured the most coveted gold medal of the butter-making world, that presented by Her Majesty Queen Victoria at the Windsor Royal Show ; another Somerset farmer's daughter, Miss Ada Williams, Regilbury, Winford, was silver medallist at the same show, and several dairymaids were selected from Somerset for service at the Royal farms. The Cheese Schools have already been referred to ; the inception of this dairy instruction was in a great measure due to the Bath and West Society, and Somerset still retains a high position in all dairy competitions. Though there has been a gradual transition by means of improved appliances, still many old and long-tried practices survive in connexion with the dairy industry of the county.

Competition is stimulated by the excellent shows and markets held in the county. At one time Wells was a leading market, often more than 100 tons of cheese being pitched ; among this there was a goodly quantity of prime Cheddars as well as household cheese. These latter were made from skimmed milk, and were known as 'Skim Dicks' or 'Dundry Daps.' Now skim cheese

---

[14] *View of Agric. of Somerset* (1798), 17.　　　[15] *Somers. Rec. Soc.* xv, 172.

making is a lost art, and the market house has been converted into a post office. The dairy industry is much encouraged by the various agricultural societies of the county.

The grazing lands were at one time in great request, and very high rentals were obtained for these lands. The graziers were a most substantial set of men of shrewd judgement, as they had to purchase their lean stock and sell it again fat, since they seldom bred what they grazed either of cattle or sheep. These lands were seldom mown, as this was considered greatly to depreciate their quality. The demand for grazing land is not what it was since the imports of meat have so greatly brought down the prices from 75s. to 80s. per cwt. to 56s. to 60s. The labour bill on these holdings was very small indeed. On some marshlands cattle could not be grazed by reason of a species of cat's tail or snake pipe. At certain periods of the year horses were grazed instead. In mid Somerset is a belt of remarkable land known as the scouring lands. Cattle put on these lands are purged violently, and sometimes die from the effects; but though various investigations have been made, nothing definite has so far resulted. Thus there are two sets of pastures in the county that directly purge cattle, and on some of the best lands.

In Somerset at present only some 84,107 acres are under grain crops, of which 26,140 acres are wheat. At one time Somerset grew a lot of wheat, especially on the clay lands, but the grass has now grown over the plough. In the parish in which the writer resides, comprising some 2,000 acres, formerly two-thirds were under cultivation; last year one and a half acres of wheat only was grown, and that more for the sake of the straw than the grain.

Formerly in close association on the strong lands with the wheat crop was that of the teasel, which when grown produced that ideal tilth that wheat loved, as the strong roots of the teasel penetrated deep down in the subsoil and opened it out. Comfortable fortunes were made when the teasel was an absolute necessity to raise the nap on the old broadcloth so fashionable then, the West of England mills taking large quantities in the middle decades of the Victorian era. These teasels were principally grown on the heavy soils of the north-western portion of the county. In the height of the demand high prices were paid for teasel lands, and the crop was then thought to be such an exhausting one that restrictive clauses as to the area of cropping were often included in farm agreements. But where this was not the case the land was persistently cropped until the soil refused to carry it any longer. The teasel plants, instead of bolting and running up, turned in and formed hearts as does a cabbage. The method of cultivation was as follows : The seed was sown in properly-prepared seed beds, or else it was hacked in drills in the field at the rate of two or three pecks per acre. This was generally done on fresh broken up ley-ground in late March or early April ; from this time onward came the labourer's opportunity with his long-bladed thin spade, the first weeding taking place in May and another following in August. These were rather weedings than workings. In October the real work commenced ; a piece of stubble was ploughed in rather small eight-furrow ridges : this concentrated the surface soil, and at the same time gave room for the labourer to reach the centre of the ridge from each furrow. This ready, the seed bed was gone over and the surplus plants were drawn and planted on the ridges at from 15,000 to 18,000 per acre ; the furrows were not disturbed more than for planting. The original seed bed was then spittled—that is, the soil was cut about two inches deep and turned over. In the early spring the planted out ones were likewise worked, and twice more before August, when the cutting time commenced. A skilled workman was needed for this operation ; he wore gloves of thin horse leather and used a short bladed billed knife ; he first went over the field and selected the kings or the centre teasel on the main stem. These were kept separate, and were not of great value as they were clumsy. The right period of cutting was just as the bloom had set. The cutting of the kings diverted the energies of the plant into the best middlings. This was the largest crop. These had to be cut and graded very evenly ; when a handful had been gathered it was tied ; these handfuls were then put on poles about 8 ft. long, and in dry weather remained in the open to cure, that is to become dry ; if the weather was showery, they were placed in airy sheds. The weather indeed was the greatest difficulty ; if it was damp and wet the teasels rotted as they grew, and the rent and labour of two full years were irretrievably lost within a week. After the best middlings had been cut the field was gone over again and the smaller middlings were cut ; these usually made half the price of the others. The handfuls on the staffs numbered thirty. When the teasels had been dried they were stored in the barns. Then came another source of expense ; the handfuls were undone, the teasels carefully sorted and graded and made up into shorter staffs, the teasel heads being arranged to form a cylinder. These staffs contained thirty handfuls, and thirty 'staffs' made a pack. These varied from nothing up to twelve and even as high as fourteen packs per acre. The prices ranged high, from £5 to £10 or £12 a pack, and it is on record that in times of scarcity they reached as high as £20 a pack, the crop frequently purchasing the field on which it grew. But though in a few instances the gain might be great, the risk was great also. Now the industry has almost died out, only an old farmer or labourer growing a few, and for these he can scarcely obtain £2 a pack or even find a market at this price. The death-blow to teasel growing was the introduction of the wiregig in the cloth mills and the superseding of the old-fashioned broadcloths which needed the hooks on the teasel to bring up the nap, by the looser textured diagonals and serges. Trowbridge used to be the great mart for Somerset-grown teasels, now scarcely any are seen there. The teasel crop was a splendid preparation for the following wheat crop, which was, however, much better where it followed the sown rather than the transplanted teasels; the former by means of their strong penetrating tap root drew their sustenance from the subsoil, and opening it up allowed the finer roots of the wheat to go downwards also. Whereas, when the crop was transplanted the tap root was broken and the fibrous roots ran out into the surface soil, drawing from it much of its sustenance and not aerating the subsoil. This appeared to be the reason why the teasel was such an exhausting crop. Occasionally there were a number of plants that did not bolt; these were known as ' voors,' and were always re-transplanted as they produced the earliest and finest seed. When the teasel crop went an endeavour was made to follow it up by growing beans, but these did not do so well as wheat. Following the wheat came a crop of peas, the result being exceptionally profitable. Teasel growing, however, is now one of the lost industries of the county. But still the stalks or buns are met with in the apex of a few of the old straw thatched sheds that remain in the county.

Another practically departed industry is that of the maincrop of potatoes. At one time these were most extensively cultivated, and it is said that the bouting system of cultivation was first introduced by the inventor of the celebrated Bennet's cord on his farm in Somerset. Indeed, he is said to have obtained his idea from the cord he was making at the time. Before the introduction of the potato disease the potato crop was often met with on the Mendip Hills. There the rough lots were breast ploughed; the parings being burnt, the soil was then ploughed and the potatoes planted; enormous crops were obtained, but very coarse, and they were mainly used for pig feeding. An oat crop followed. On the lighter soils in the vales, however, the crop was grown for market purposes, but after a time owing to the humidity of the atmosphere and the result of ravages of the disease the crop became more and more limited, until now it scarcely suffices for local requirements. It was at one time a common practice for farmers to let potato land to the labourers at £8 per acre, the farmer cultivating the land down to the period of manuring; this was also carted on to the land ready for spreading. The labourer afterwards did all the cultivation, and took the crop. Sometimes the crop was set to 'halves; in this instance the labourer paid no rent but shared the crop with the farmer; but this plan was rarely satisfactory. In only one district has the potato held its own; that is at Axbridge, which lies in a sheltered position under the Mendip Hills. Here large quantities of early potatoes are grown, until recently principally of a variety known as ' Axbridge Jacks,' a very rich mealy potato much resembling the early Jersey. This crop formerly was very remunerative, but latterly has suffered from the competition of early potatoes of the Channel Islands and Cornwall, which come on the market before them. In consequence a considerable portion of the lands formerly under the potato have now been turned over to the strawberry.

Strawberry culture has now assumed the proportions of a very large industry, the berries from this district being famed alike for the firmness of the fruit and the excellence of its flavour. The fruits are packed in 2 lb. and 4 lb. chip baskets, which are tied in sets of five to sticks to facilitate handling. The Great Western Railway puts on special strawberry-trains during the season, the north of England and the south of Scotland constituting the great market for these fruits. Strawberry culture is stated to make a return of £40 per acre, and the industry is fast extending. This district may be considered to constitute the only market garden of Somerset. As the holders of this land are mostly farmers in the district, the great difficulty with the strawberry crop is its clashing with the haymaking season, and the scarcity of suitable pickers; but for this, strawberry culture might have spread over a more extended area in the county than it at present occupies.

The oat acreage of 29,355 is not what it was in the days when Mendip was cultivated; the yield obtained was then enormous, the straw being very short. In those days the autumn and winter skies were lit at night by the glare of the limekilns of Mendip, but now these have become a mass of ruins, mainly due to the enormous increase in the price of small coal. Farmers carted this Mendip lime for many miles for manure, and it was in a great measure due to its use that such excellent crops were grown.

Somerset still continues to produce some of the finest malting barley in the world, but the area contracts and would not be so large as it is were it not for the necessity of changing the root land. At one time various systems of cropping prevailed, but latterly a system of grow-as-you-can has been introduced.

The old-time leases have run out of fourteen, seven or three years with the conditions: Not to convert pasture to tillage, feed or mow pasture alternately; not to burn or pare without leave; not to plant potatoes for sale without leave; not to plant more than a stated acreage with teasels; to spend hay and straw on the holding without acknowledgement; no underletting; to keep buildings in repair, rough timber and wages of thatcher being allowed; not to cut or lop trees, and shooting rights reserved; and the majority of farmers are on yearly tenancies, but landlords do not readily disturb a good tenant. There are very few farms now in hand owing to the difficulty of letting them, as there were after the awful experiences of 1879, and tenants are to be found in plenty. In the peat moor district osier growing constitutes a highly important industry, and any one driving from Athelney to Langport will pass numerous plantations of willows. These are cut yearly, and high rentals are paid for these osier beds. It has latterly been found that the peelings of these willows constitute a very fine manure for potatoes.

The farmers in the richer grazing districts of the county have a system of special drainage provided for their lands by means of main drains or rheens. These are under special commissioners, who levy rates on the various districts for their upkeep.

The homesteads of the county cannot be said to be sufficient; though there is fairly good accommodation for the farmer, still there is an insufficiency for his stock, and a goodly portion of it has to winter out in the open fields. Though the average farmer may be fairly liberal as regards the purchase of artificial feeding stuffs, he is somewhat tight on his purse-strings as regards artificial manures. The Somerset farmer still places great reliance on farmyard manure.

At one time fairs in Somerset were very numerous, but in the majority of instances public auction has replaced private barter, and as fairs decrease or fall into desuetude so auction marts increase.

The county sadly lacks the higher means of agricultural education. There is no college nearer than either Reading or Birmingham where such education can be obtained, and therefore there is not that inducement to apply science to practice which might otherwise be obtained were such means of education nearer to hand.[16] The farmers as a whole are very conservative and much attached to the family roof-tree, and therefore do not wander so far afield as others, but as a rule they are very hard workers.

Of the implements used on the farm there is the usual heterogeneous collection. There is the plough that was, grandfather's old broad wheel wagon, and the most up-to-date chaff cutter driven by a petrol or oil engine, whilst the horse gear lies rusting outside the barn, its period of utility being over, yet the farmer will not part with it. The farms being small it is a happy county for the implement agent, as each farmer prefers his own implement rather than trust to a borrowed one. But this leads to a comparatively large amount of capital being invested for a small amount of work. A binder on a large farm pays for itself in a single season; on a small farm it is out of date before the return is made. The old Somerset farmer has a dread of co-operation; he prefers his own individuality. Just as in the old days he hesitated to shift the slow oxen from the yoke and hitch the more speedy horse to the plough, so he considers that as his fathers never combined there should be no reason for him to do it now. Everything must be brought home to him to try it.

The County Council established an Experimental Farm. It languished and died, because the farmers would not take the trouble to visit it. Itinerant instruction, on the other hand, was immediately successful, because it was taken right home to the villages. Probably the cause of this is that most Somerset farmers being small holders, they have little money in hand, and do the work themselves, and are therefore less dependent on outside help of all kinds, educational and otherwise.

The system of labour has entirely altered. At the beginning of the era the old patriarchal system prevailed, the farmer feeding his labourers and paying very low wages, often not more than 6s. per week. Boys went to live 'in house' at an early age and grew up like trees on the farm, firmly attached to the soil, and the girl only left to become the carter's wife and settle down in a cottage near by. Now this system is changed; it is difficult to obtain either a farmhouse boy or girl, and the labourers are more intent on studying their own than their master's interests as in days gone by. A good man has now no difficulty in obtaining 16s. per week, rising to 20s. during the summer months, with cider; but they have to provide their own food. The difficulty now is to obtain all-round hands, who are more sought after than ever, as work is not so specialized as it was half a century and more ago. The old-time user of the flail, the reed-maker and spar-maker have departed, though endeavours are being made to instruct the rising generation in hedging, ditching, and thatching. There is a general absence of good cottages, but such as there are in the rural districts have a considerable quantity of garden ground attached. There is no general hunger after allotments, except in the neighbourhood of the collieries or other industries. But these works, as well as the attractions of the towns, more than direct emigration abroad, have drained the agricultural districts of their labour. Most of the labourers keep bees and have fruit trees in their gardens. The old-fashioned straw skep is being gradually replaced by the more utilitarian bar-framed hive, and the great value of the bees in pollinating the apple bloom is being more and more appreciated. Nearly all the cottagers have a few head of poultry, but the pig is not kept to

[16] Some of the secondary schools, however, give a course on higher agriculture.

the extent that it was in days gone by. The County Council provides instructors in horticulture, bee-keeping and poultry-keeping. Despite all this, however, nearly every village contains more tumbledown cottages than new ones, and this makes the public health authorities somewhat chary in condemning cottages whose days are only too visibly of the past. Thus, though the old straw thatch is fast disappearing, it is in many instances being covered over with corrugated iron roofing, which renders what were previously sanitary cottages quite unhealthy, as the thatch decays beneath the iron. The rents of cottages have much increased, and are advancing rapidly, as it has become the practice for city families to rent a cottage, come out in relays and reside in it for the summer months, and then shut it up for the rest of the year. Naturally the best cottages are thus snapped up.

It may be interesting to note that in 1881 there were 7,580 farmers in Somerset; in 1901 there were 7,242 or 338 less; farm bailiffs decreased by 10 in the same time, but shepherds increased by 76. As regards agricultural labourers, in 1881 there were 28,141 on the land, but in 1901 only 17,234, a loss of 10,907 in twenty years. Whilst writing of the labourer it will be well to note the improved status of his wife. No more is she with her children seen gleaning their winter bread in the harvest field, nor does she toil in the fields hoeing or at piece work; she seldom goes milking. In fact the absence of cheap female labour is one of the farmer's difficulties. The farm labourer's wife is better fed, better clothed, and vastly improved in every respect. The labourer most truthfully alleges that he can ' avord to kip his missus at hoame,' and he does it. But at the same time it tends to wean her and her children from the land.

Another race of men who have practically gone out of existence during the era has been the renting dairyman. Young men who had not sufficient capital to rent a farm rented a dairy of cattle at from £11 to £12 per head per annum, the owner providing cattle fodder and convenience, the hirer the labour and taking the produce.

Somerset is particularly partial to agricultural societies. The Bath and West of England Society has its permanent head quarters at Bath, though its annual exhibition is migratory. The County Association is very flourishing, and usually opens the outdoor show season. The Frome Show is the most celebrated cheese show in the world, and in connexion with it is held a cheese fair at which from 150 to 200 tons of Cheddar cheese are pitched. The Mid Somerset at Shepton Mallet also holds a grand exhibition of cheese, and is very active in promoting agricultural interests. The North Somerset, the North-East Somerset and the East Somerset each has a goodly exhibition within these respective spheres. The Taunton Farmers' Club is more given to debate than to exhibition. There are numerous Horse Shows and Horticultural Societies. The hand that guides the plough is still encouraged, the Blagdon and Charterhouse and West Mendip Ploughing Society being in a flourishing condition after a half-century's wear and tear, while another of old standing is the Wrington and Burrington. Some societies have come and gone, but the above remain, to the advantage of the local farmers. Most of those mentioned are affiliated with the larger national societies.

In conclusion, what changes have there been wrought in Somerset agriculture in the Victorian era? The grass land has revolted from the plough. The farmer eats a loaf produced from Colonial or foreign flour raised by German yeast, instead of eating his home-grown wheat raised with barm from the brewery near by which purchased his barley. The early maturity steer fed on foreign oil seeds has replaced the stall-fed ox fed on grass and home-grown corn. The farm labourers have to some extent been replaced by labour-saving machinery. No more does skim milk go to the sow. The sale of milk was unknown; now thousands of gallons are sent as far as London, and more milk drunk than made into butter. The sow and her progeny are fed on foreign-grown grain instead of the offals of the farm and the mill beside the stream. The working ox has gone, and motors are running the horses off the roads.

In some respects agriculture has shown retrogression, in others an advance; old customs, old manners have died out and new ones have been introduced and adopted. Seemingly it is only the corn and the labour that have dwindled from the land.

FORESTRY

THOUGH not so profusely wooded as the neighbouring shire of Devon, Somerset as a whole was well supplied with timber in the earlier historic times. The Domesday commissioners made a special point of entering the extent of the woods throughout the kingdom, for not only was timber of great value for building, fencing and fuel purposes, but the acorns and beech mast were invaluable for the fattening of the swine in the autumn pannage season. Hence it came to pass that in not a few counties the Domesday returns estimate the amount of woodland, after a rough and ready fashion, by the number of pigs that it could sustain. In Somerset, however, the more precise plan was followed of giving the size of the woods in lineal measure, namely, by leagues and furlongs, or in some cases by the acre. By the first of the methods it is obvious that only a rough measurement was signified ; thus, if a wood is described as a league long and half a league broad, it is not to be supposed that any precise square measure is indicated. It may however be remembered that the *leuca* or league was in all probability 12 furlongs or a mile and a half.

The woodlands of the 11th century were pretty generally distributed over the county, save in the alluvial, low-lying, and marshy grounds of the centre, and in certain wide-spread moorlands, such as that of Exmoor. Out of the forty or so estates of the king, there were only four in which there is no mention of woods,[1] and of the estates of the church of St. Mary of Glastonbury, about forty in number, there were only five that had no woodland.[2] Glastonbury itself had 20 acres of wood and 300 acres of underwood ; but several of the manors in this alluvial and swampy district had but small plots of either wood or underwood ; thus Westcombe had 10 acres of woodland, Brent 6, North Wootton 4 and Edgarley only 1.

Although the Somerset woods were not estimated by the number of pigs they could sustain, it is quite evident that the swine which fattened on the acorns and which formed the staple food of the poorer classes, were abundant. The mention of swineherds in the wooded districts is a special feature of the Domesday Book of this county. On the king's manor of North Petherton there were actually 20 swineherds who contributed £5 among them, whilst 15 at Kings Brompton paid 35s. At North Cadbury 12 pigs were payable by the swineherd and 10 at East Coker.

The only *parcus* mentioned in the Domesday Survey of Somerset is that of Doniet, Duneheete or Donyatt, near Ilminster, given with other lands to Robert Earl of Mortain, the Conqueror's half-brother and forming part of the great 'Fee of Mortain.' At Donyatt there is still a place called 'Park Farm.' Another Domesday park which may be inferred from its Domesday *parcarius*, though not mentioned by name, is the old *parcus* of North Petherton. Four park farms still exist, one of them called Park House, all forming a separate but easily distinguishable part of that parish.

Somerset abounded in forests, but it would be idle to expect to find their explicit entry in Domesday either in this county or elsewhere, for they were royal wastes and therefore unassessed. Eyton estimates that there are no fewer than 177,970 acres unaccounted for in the Somerset Domesday.[3]

It is also perhaps necessary to reiterate the statement that the use of the term 'forest' as implying a great wood is a comparatively modern rendering which is false to its etymological origin. A forest in early days and down to Tudor times meant in strict legal language a great district, mostly waste, reserved for royal sport and under special forest laws. A certain amount of wood and underwood was necessary as covert for the game, but in several forests such as those of Exmoor, Dartmoor and the High Peak, the woodlands formed an insignificant part of the whole area. The large amount of old royal demesne in this county doubtless served as forest hunting ground for the later Saxon kings ; the area of these 'forests' was considerably enlarged under the Normans.

The old forest lands of Somerset were distributed over a large portion of the county and covered most of the highlands from Frome Selwood on the east to tall Dunkery and Exmoor on the west. At two places, according to the old perambulations, they touched the shores of the Severn Sea ; viz. at Worle and Uphill, where in the neighbourhood of the modern

---

[1] *V.C.H. Somers.* i, 434. [2] Ibid. 460. [3] *Domesday Studies* (Somers.) i, 16.

Weston-super-Mare the outline of the Mendip range gradually descends to the Severn Sea; and at the extreme west of the county, where the Exmoor highlands terminate in a series of tall cliffs and wooded combes from Bossington and Porlock to Culbone and Glenthorne on the borders of North Devon. Here lay the Domesday manor of Aure or Oare. In the Parliamentary Survey of Exmoor (1651) amongst the profits of courts and fines, etc., is mentioned 'Wrecks at Sea' belonging to the king's forest.[4]

In many places such as portions of Selwood Forest near 'Pen-Pits,' 'Ballard's Castle,' or at 'Castle Neroche' on the ridges of the Blackdown Hills, not far south of Taunton, or better still along the deep ferny combes and broad stretches of heath (*bruerae*) of Exmoor itself, the original features of the forest lands remain as they always were, a truly wild region.

Although the highlands of Somerset were, according to the limits of the old perambulations, chiefly forest land, still some of the most famous hunting and fowling preserves, celebrated also for their timber, lay along the levels of the River Parret which with its tributaries the Tone, Cary and Yeo, forms that great central trough or depression which stretches right across the county.

The technical forest lands of Somerset may be considered in the following order: (1) The royal park and warren of Somerton, the ancient capital of the county; (2) North Petherton Park and Forest, in the centre of the county; (3) Selwood Forest on the eastern border, and running into both Dorset and Wilts.; (4) the forest of Mendip, including that of Cheddar; (5) Exmoor Forest in the extreme west, including a small part of Devon; (6) Neroche Forest, in the south; and (7) the forests or chases of Kingswood and Fillwood, near Bristol, sometimes reckoned as pertaining to Gloucestershire.

In conclusion certain space must be given to the brief consideration of ancient private parks, followed by some mention of modern parks, woodlands, and arboriculture. But before proceeding to these details, it will be well to give an account of the forest districts of Somerset considered as a whole, with particular reference to the hereditary chief forestership.

As to the chief forestership of Somerset, Robert de Odburvile, according to Domesday, held Wearne and Low Ham close to Somerton, a mansion called Melcome at North Petherton, the manors of Newton Forester, and Wellisford near Milverton; as well as that of Withypool in the Exmoor district.[5] In the last-named region Robert de Odburvile's predecessors in

the time of the Confessor had been three royal foresters, Dodo, Almar and Godric, who held jointly in right of their office. Dodo the forester had a mansion at Dulverton, whilst Almar held Wootton Courtney in the Exmoor country, part of Stowey on the Quantocks and High Ham, near Somerton. From a careful study of Domesday, it is probable that the Conqueror for the purpose of concentrating authority made a great change in the forest administration of Somerset. The several foresters of the Confessor's days were abolished, and their place and duty were taken by a single official who held his manors and control of the forests by serjeanty of the forest, owing this feudal service direct to the Crown.[6]

The successor of Robert de Odburvile in the reign of Richard I was a certain great forester in fee, William de Wrotham, who held the office *pro feodo j militis de dono Regis Ricardi* as an hereditary possession.[7] The following extract from the Hundred Rolls throws further light upon the tenure of the particular wardenship:

The Jury say that the Warren of Somerton used to belong to the manor of Somerton when of old there used to be no Warrener except by the gift of the King. And afterwards a King whose name they know not gave the custody of the aforesaid warren to a certain William de Wrotham and, afterwards, Richard de Wrotham, *tanquam heres ipsius Wiilielmi* and afterwards, William de Plessy had the custody, who died lately seised of it and now Roger de Clifford, the justice of the Forests south of Trent, has the custody of it and it is worth twenty shillings annually, saving the amercements due to the Lord King arising *de Viridi et Venatione*.

As to the history of this great office it is sufficient to note here that descending from the Wrotham, De Plessy and Pecche families during a period roughly speaking of 150 years, at last, after some transfers, it came by purchase into the hands of the Mortimer family. The fine[8] relating to this event may be quoted here.

At Westminster, in the Octave of St. John the Baptist (1359), between Roger de Mortimer, Earl of March, querent and Roger de Beauchamp and Sibyl, his wife, deforciants. For a messuage, a carucate of land and ten marcs rent in Newton-Plecy and Parkhous and for the bailiwick of the Forests of Menedip, Nerechich and Pederton and the custody of the warren of Somerton and for the third part of the advowson of Hawkridge (on Exmoor) and for the free chapel of Newton-Plecy and for the bailiwick of the Forest of Exmoor . . . Roger and Sibyl acknowledged the right of the Earl and quit-claimed to him from them. The Earl gave them 200 marks of silver.

---

[4] Aug. Off. Somers. No. 18.

[5] Greswell, *Forests and Deerparks of Somers.* 49–50; see the whole chapter 'A Domesday Forest Barony,' 42–55.

[6] Eyton, *Domesday Studies* (Somers.), i, 202 et seq.

[7] *Red Bk. of Exch.* 235.

[8] *Somerset Feet of Fines* (Somers, Rec. Soc.), xvii, 185.

FORESTRY

The succession of the Somerset Chief Forestership in Fee is shown in the following table:

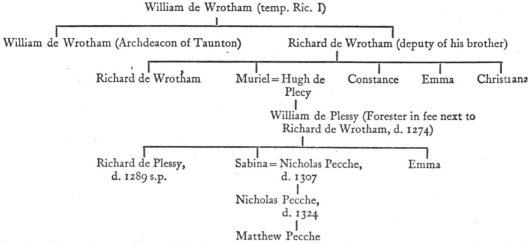

William de Wrotham (temp. Ric. I)

William de Wrotham (Archdeacon of Taunton) — Richard de Wrotham (deputy of his brother)

Richard de Wrotham — Muriel = Hugh de Plecy — Constance — Emma — Christiana

William de Plessy (Forester in fee next to Richard de Wrotham, d. 1274)

Richard de Plessy, d. 1289 s.p. — Sabina = Nicholas Pecche, d. 1307 — Emma

Nicholas Pecche, d. 1324

Matthew Pecche

The hereditary forestership ended in 1337, and the office after one or two purchases finally became the property of Roger Mortimer (d. 1361) Earl of March.

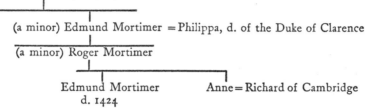

(a minor) Edmund Mortimer = Philippa, d. of the Duke of Clarence

(a minor) Roger Mortimer

Edmund Mortimer d. 1424 — Anne = Richard of Cambridge

This was the beginning of the Mortimer forestership in Somerset which lasted from 1357 to 1424, when the vast possessions of the Mortimer family came into Yorkist hands through Anne Mortimer, who married Richard of Cambridge, and so merged into Crown property. During the Mortimer rule the foresters were generally substitutionary officials acting, however, with considerable powers. Two of these substitutionary foresters were Geoffrey Chaucer, the poet, appointed in 21 Richard II by the Countess of March, and his son Thomas Chaucer appointed in 4 Henry V by Edward Earl of March.[9]

In 6 Edward VI Sir Thomas Wroth petitioned the king to be admitted forester in fee of the king's forests of Exmoor, Neroche, Mendip and Selwood, as being a descendant and representative of William de Wrotham lord of the manor of Newton, forester temp. Richard I, and being the inheritor and possessor of the greater part of the manor.[10] This petition of 1552 was not successful, but an allegation of this petition and right by the guardians of a Sir Thomas Wroth, a descendant, is said to have prevented a person of great eminence from being appointed warden of Exmoor.

There is a peculiarity about this forestership in fee of Somerset that seems to merit passing notice. It appears always to have been held in connexion with the particular hundred of Williton from the earliest date.[11] The various *membra* of the fee, although widely separated, were reckoned part of this hundred.[12] 'Newton-Forester Chapelry' is really a little islanded section lying in the midst of North Petherton Hundred and appears so still in the Land Tax Schedule. It is 15 miles from Williton itself. Nether Ham or Low Ham close to Somerton and more than 30 miles from Williton and part of the old Somerton warren of Saxon days is still described as a tithing in Williton Hundred.[13] As late as 1841 in the census taken during that year the chapelry of Low Ham and the hamlet of Paradise were described as part of Williton Freemanors Hundred.[14] Another place called Cathanger in Fivehead parish and part of the forest bailiwick from time immemorial is a detached portion of Williton Hundred. In 1662 when a benevolence was raised for Charles II in the hundred of Williton Freemanors, Cathanger was still further described as part of Exton Tithing in Williton Hundred. Withypool,

[9] Greswell, *Forests and Deerparks of Somers.* xi, 150–64, 'The Mortimer Foresters in Fee.' It may be noted that the fees etc. sold originally by Richard I to William de Wrotham come back, after a long interval, to the Crown through the Mortimer marriage.

[10] Collinson, *Hist. of Somers.* iii, 62.

[11] Collinson, op. cit.

[12] See a multitude of references in Greswell's *Forests and Deerparks of Somers.* 148–9.

[13] *Great Roll of the Pipe,* 1 *Ric.* I (Rec. Com.), 149.

[14] *Somers. Rec. Soc.* iii, 334.

[15] Ibid.

the Exmoor Forest manor and forest pound, was also reckoned part of Exton Tithing and of Williton Hundred. In writing of Exton on the River Exe Gerard observes in his *Particular Description of Somerset* (c. 1630) 'This with other lands William de Wrotham held by Serjeanty to be King's Forester of Exmore and to keep up his Park at Newton and so gracious was this William with Richard I that he gave unto him the Barony of Ambrevile (or Odburvile) in these parts.'[16]

In the days of Edward the Elder there was a charter of Bishop Denewulf to the king and a counter charter of the king to the bishop, dated in the year A.D. 904,[17] '*pro perpetua libertate illius monasterii quod dicitur Tantune.*' On the other hand the bishop gives certain lands at Stoce (Stoke, near Shalbourne, co. Wilts.) for the privilege, and amongst other customary liabilities due from the monastery are board and lodging to the king for one night : the same for eight dogs and their keeper ; the same for nine nights to the king's falconers : attendance, horses and carts 'when the king was progressing to Curig (North Curry) or Willettun.' This extract is interesting as showing not only the hunting progresses of the Saxon kings but also the importance of Williton as a halting station on the road.

A variety of incidents relative to the forest history of Somerset as a whole, gathered from the Public Records, may now be set forth in chronological order, before proceeding to treat of the special forests.

Occasional royal grants of hunting were made which covered the whole area of the various forests of this great county. Thus Richard I granted by charter to Reginald Bishop of Bath and Wells and his successors the right to hunt with his dogs all beasts throughout Somerset, with the exception of red and fallow deer (*cervum et cervam, damum et damam*). William de Wrotham, Archdeacon of Taunton and forester of the whole of Somerset, was permitted by King John in 1207 to assign to his brother Richard de Wrotham the custody of the forests.[18] In 1218 the custody of Richard de Wrotham the youthful son and heir of Richard de Wrotham, himself the heir of William de Wrotham, was granted to John Marshal ; it is specially stated that this wardenship of the young heir included the custody of the forests of Somerset.[19] A particular selection was made in April 1219 of twelve knights of the county to draw up a true and exact perambulation of the parts of Somerset that had been disafforested in accordance with the recent Forest Charter of 1217 and of the

parts that still remained forest.[20] In July of the same year an inquisition was ordered to be held at Ilchester by the sheriff, verderers, foresters and four special inquisitors as to the assarted or cultivated lands within the forest of Somerset. The order also named the clerk to this commission, who was one Osbert de Stokes.[21]

A great gale that brought much desolation to nearly the whole of England at the close of the year 1222 played such havoc with the forest woods that instructions were sent out in January to all forest officials to draw up careful valuations of the windfall and to account for the sales. A commission of four for this purpose was appointed for the general forest district of Somerset, namely Roger de Reimes, Osbert son of William, Walter de Tilly, and Gilbert de Welinton, with John de Winterburn as clerk. There was also a special commission of two for the forest of Cheddar, namely Walter de Budicomb and William de Bagetrip, with Henry de Hache as clerk.[22] In 1225 Richard de Wrotham came of age, and the king assigned to him the full custody of the forestry (*forestarie*) of Somerset and the park of Newton.[23]

Forest Pleas for the whole county were held at Ilchester in November 1257.[24] There is a long list of defaulters, among whom were many regarders who were fined 4s. or 2s. for not duly making a regard, or for not presenting their rolls on the first day of the eyre. A particular feature of the extant rolls of this eyre is the long list of woodwards together with various references to that office. The woodward, though primarily responsible for the actual timber and undergrowth, as the name implies, was also a forester, that is to say he was at the same time bound to protect the venison. To understand the somewhat complicated position of such an office, it is necessary to remember that all the lands within a king's forest were never entirely royal demesne. Every royal forest had its woods, which were to a limited extent private property. Such woods were not only subject to general forest jurisdiction, such as the free ingress and egress of the king's game, but the owners were not allowed without the royal licence to do anything therein that might be held to disturb the deer, such as clearing for cultivation, erecting buildings, burning charcoal, establishing forges, or even cutting down any timber save for their own immediate use.

---

[16] *Great Roll of the Pipe,* 1 *Ric.* I (Rec. Com.), 149. *Vide supra.*

[17] *Proc. Somers. Arch. Soc.* ix, 22.

[18] Pat. 8 John, m. 3.

[19] Pat. 2 Hen. III, m. 7.

[20] Pat. 3 Hen. III, m. 4. These knights were to be chosen 'de legalioribus et discrecioribus militibus de comitatu Sumersete, qui melius sciant et dicere velint veritatem.'

[21] Ibid. m. 3 d.

[22] Pat. 7 Hen. III, m. 5 d.

[23] Pat. 9 Hen. III, m. 4.

[24] Forest Proc. Tr. of R. 152. Further particulars are given under the respective forests.

To look after their limited rights all such wood owners were expected to have woodwards, who were also required to guard the king's venison within that particular wood, with power to attach and present at the forest courts.[25]

These officials had to be sworn on entering office. From the Ilchester eyre of 1257 it becomes manifest that the presentment of each woodward to the forest justices was at that time obligatory. Thus John Syward, the woodward of the Bishop of Bath and Wells for his wood of Cheddar, had been presented by the bishop's steward to William de Plessy, the hereditary keeper of the whole of the Somerset forests, but not before the forest justice; whereupon the bishop was declared in mercy and the wood taken into the king's hands. Before, however, the closing of this eyre, the bishop's steward appeared, made fine for the wood and presented Syward to the justices. On his taking the necessary oath, the wood was restored to the bishop. Similar proceedings were taken in the case of another of the bishop's woodwards, and also as to a woodward of the Abbot of St. Augustine's, Bristol. At the same pleas, the Abbess of Shaftesbury and two laymen duly presented their respective woodwards to be admitted and sworn.

Forest Pleas for the whole county were again held at Ilchester on the morrow of Ascension Day 1270, before four justices, Henry de Burghulle, Matthew de Columbars, Nicholas de Rumes, and Reginald de Akle.[26] Among the chartered privileges sustained at this eyre was a grant made in 1248 to the Prior and convent of Bruton to gather daily two horse loads of dead wood in the forest of Selwood, and a grant to Jocelin Bishop of Bath and Wells and his successors of the disafforesting of the manor of Congresbury in 1227. An interesting charter, of 1235, relative to episcopal rights in Cheddar woods is cited in the account of Cheddar forest or chase. Amongst many common poachers (*consueti malefactores de venacione*) presented at this eyre by William de Plessy, chief forester for Somerset, and his fellow foresters was Walter who had been parker of ' Stokes.' [27]

The presentments at this eyre included several high-placed secular clergy. Thus Adam canon of Wells, with Henry late treasurer of Wells, William le Cu gatekeeper of the priory of Bruton, and several others were presented for having taken in Selwood Forest without warrant, on Tuesday next after the feast of St. Giles, 1259, a buck and a doe. They made no appearance, therefore the sheriff was ordered to compel their presence from day to day. Subsequently Adam the canon and other delinquents appeared and were detained for a time in prison. Adam was released on payment of half a mark.

Master Alexander, rector of Powick in the bishopric of Worcester, entered Selwood Forest about Whitsuntide 1264, with several others, with bows and arrows and greyhounds for the purpose of hunting, and took a buck. William Spayle, a forester, interrupted them, and took two of the dogs and handed them to Thomas de Bigod. Whereupon came Robert de Vernon who took the said forester and imprisoned him in his dove-cot at Horningsham (Wilts.) until he paid a fine of 2s. 6d. Meanwhile Robert de Vernon took the two greyhounds by force and with them often hunted the forest and took two bucks. None of the delinquents appeared. In the case of Alexander, the Bishop of Worcester or his official was commanded to produce him on the Wednesday before Whitsuntide, and eventually the rector of Powick was fined in the very heavy penalty of 40 marks.

It was customary at the Forest Pleas to have a system of fines graded according to the position and wealth of the offender. Stephen, rector of Godmanstone, Dorset, and many others entered the forest on the Saturday before Christmas 1265 and stretched nets within the precincts (*clausum*) of Witham Charterhouse, taking three roebucks. The Bishop of Salisbury was commanded to produce Stephen, and he was fined 20 marks.

The woodward of the Charterhouse of Witham and other men of that household were, on another occasion (in 1260) convicted of taking two bucks and a hart and carrying the venison into that priory. John the prior was dead; other of the delinquents could not be found and were duly outlawed. Others of the household of this Charterhouse were presented for a night poaching affray in the following year, when they entered the forest with bows and arrows, crossbows, hatchets, nets, and dogs, and took a doe which they carried with them to the priory. The foresters found them and took one of the number, John de Fowel, together with two nets and two dogs and committed him and the dogs to John the tithing-man of Marston, and the nets to Henry de Montfort of Nunney, then one of the verderers. But afterwards all these malefactors came and with force of arms took John out of the custody of the tithing-man together with the dogs, and also forcibly rescued the nets from Nunney. Several other interesting presentments at this eyre are briefly cited under their respective forests.

In 1281 Edward I granted licence for life to Hugh Everard, canon of Wells, to hunt with his own hounds the fox, hare, badger, and cat throughout the forests of Somerset.[28] The

[25] Dr. Cox, *Royal Forests*, 22–3.
[26] Forest Proc. Tr. of R. 153.
[27] Probably Stoke Rodney on the south side of the Mendips.

[28] Pat. 9 Edw. I, m. 26.

Sheriff of Somerset was notified by the king in 1279 that the perambulations of the forests lately made by the Dean of Salisbury and Matthew de Columbars were to be firmly held according to the tenor of the Great Charter of the Forest.[29] In 1289 a commission was issued to Roger de Molis and Richard de Bosco to inquire as to the persons who, during the king's absence beyond the seas, hunted and carried away deer in his forests, chases and parks of the county of Somerset.[30] In May 1315 four justices, namely Richard de Abyngdon, Henry de Cobeham, John Randolf and William de Hardene, were appointed to make a perambulation of the forests of Somerset by their own view, in conjunction with the foresters in fee and the verderers, in order that the Forest Charter might be duly observed.[31]

A very interesting instruction to the Sheriff of Somerset, issued on 14 July of this year, orders him to pay to the King's yeomen, Robert Squier and David de Franketon, whom the king was sending with 2 berners and 24 running dogs, 2 veutrers and 9 greyhounds to take fat venison in the forests of Neroche, Petherton, Mendip, Selwood and Exmoor, their wages of 12d. a day. He was also to pay each berner (the man in charge of running dogs) 2d. a day with ½d. for every dog, and 2d. a day for each veutrer (in charge of greyhounds) with 1½d. for every greyhound. The sheriff was also to deliver salt and barrels for the salting of the venison and to pay the carriage of the same. The respective forest keepers were at the same time instructed to permit the huntsmen to take 20 bucks in each of the forests of Neroche and Petherton, 12 bucks in Selwood, 12 bucks and 12 harts in Mendip, and 20 harts in Exmoor.[32] It hence appears that Exmoor only provided red deer, whilst there were both red and fallow deer in Mendip.

There is a record at the Public Record Office of the sales of wood in various Somerset manors for the king's use in the year 1542.[33]

On the manor of Wrington 12 young ashes were sold for 4s. to one John Catt; the tops of the same trees realized 3s. 4d., an old oak sold to Mr. Leverige, to make a bridge, 6d.; whilst Robert the shoemaker paid 26s. 8d. for 3 ashes. The wood-sales of Blackmore within the parish of Bruton (Beryton) realized 38s. 8d.; the wood sold was chiefly ash, and included 'too hooplages for the Churche of Beryton xxd.' The sales of the king's wood in the manor of Somerton begin with 2s. paid to the churchwarden of Somerton for an ash and an oak. There is a long list of wood-sales of Sharford Park within the

manor of Walton; the total came to £20 4s.; the sales were chiefly of old oaks, 'storben' or 'srubben' oaks and 'blatternes.' The sales of Southmore, within the manor of Glastonbury, realized another considerable sum, which opens with 48s. paid by Sir Thomas Specke, knight, for 6 acres of alders.

SOMERTON PARK AND WARREN

In Domesday Robert de Odburvile is represented as an important forest official. Under the heading *Terra Hunfridi* he is said to hold Warne and its waste. Warne, called variously Wearne, Pitney-Wearne, or Wearne-Plucknett, is close to Somerton, the old capital of Somerset. Pitney Hundred is a small tract of land marked by the Rivers Ivel and Parret, which divide it into two portions. This hundred contains the very ancient borough and appendant market town of Langport, the port of Somerton. The manor of Pitney was of the ancient demesne of the Saxon kings. The term *vasta* as applied to part of Wearne means that it was unoccupied. It is here that it is necessary to look for the 'Warren of Somerton,' the ancient Saxon park, which passed into the hands of William the Conqueror and was given to Robert de Odburvile. Together with Wearne, Robert de Odburvile also held Low or Nether Ham close to Somerton,[34] and in contra-distinction to High Ham the village on the hill. In the *Testa de Nevill*, a later document than Domesday (c. 1300), Low Ham is described as belonging to the manor of Somerton and held *per servicium forestae*. Mr. Eyton notes that the serjeanty of Robert de Odburvile was that of a king's forester, and to foresters of King Edward he succeeded in some estates.[35]

A perambulation of the warren of Somerton (temp. Edward I) exists:[36]

The Warren of Somerton. The bounds of the Warren begin at Carybrigge and go as far as the water of Bathpol—thence along the course of the water of Bathpol to the Fosse: from the Fosse to the bridge of North tone (north town), and thence along the course of the river Ivel to the 'ducellus' (i.e. little stream) which falls into the Yvel between Hywysh (Huish) and Pilbesbury and so along the 'ducellus' as far as Modresford. From Modresford to the willows of William de Burci and thence along the same course to Monkesham: from Monkesham to the Cary as that river descends through the midst of the moor, and from the water of Cary back to Cary bridge, where the Warren began.

The above boundaries are still to be recognized and are very interesting as the boundaries

29 Close, 7 Edw. I, m. 8 d.
30 Pat. 17 Edw. I, m. 6 d.
31 Pat. 8 Edw. II, pt. ii, m. 7.
32 Close, 9 Edw. II, m. 29.
33 Exch. Accts. K.R. bdle. 149, no. 13.

34 See *Great Roll of the Pipe, ut supra*, where 'Homines de Hamme qui pertinent ad forestariam debent xs. vid.'
35 Eyton, *Domesday Studies* (Somers.), i, 68.
36 Forest Proc. Exch. R. no. 154.

of what was probably the oldest known royal Saxon preserve in the county of Somerset, possibly in the kingdom. Somerton was closely linked with King Ine and after the Conquest was still held [37] as *Terra Regis*. Here also the Supreme Court or eyre of the forest was occasionally held.

Somerton is more usually styled a warren than a forest. The word warren was used to denote either the exclusive right of hunting and taking certain wild beasts (*ferae naturae*) in a particular place—as in grants of free warren— or the land over which such right existed. But Somerton was a royal warren, and hence subject to forest law; offences within it were therefore presentable at the forest pleas or eyre.

At the forest pleas held at Ilchester in 1257,[38] various vert (green wood) offenders of the warren of Somerton were presented, nearly all of whom were fined 12*d.*, but a few were excused on the score of poverty. Philip le Chevaler and Robert Seynt Clere, the verderers, presented one Humphrey for killing a buck in 1252; but Humphrey was dead. The proceedings show incidentally that the townships of Somerton, Kingsdon, Pitney, Knowle and Wearne were all held to be within this warren district. A highly remarkable and unique circumstance incidental to Somerton first comes to light at this eyre. Within Somerton warren —and nowhere else so far as is known throughout the kingdom—the king preserved the hare as a beast of the forest.[39] Elsewhere the hare was only considered the principal beast of the warren and did not come within the cognizance of the forest justices. But at Ilchester in 1257 the verderers presented that Richard le Rus and his fellows, on 7 December 1255, killed four hares in this warren. The delinquents did not appear, for they had not been duly attached. The case was adjourned inasmuch as Richard was a clerk of the king's court. The verderers further presented that in Christmas week, 1256, a certain hare was found. An inquisition was therefore made by the four townships nearest to where the hare was found, namely Somerton, Kingsdon, Pitney and Wearne, and the jury found that the hare died of the murrain. To compel the four adjacent townships to hold an inquest on every hare found dead or wounded— in accordance with the laws pertaining to beasts of the forest—through the length and breadth of the vast area then under forest law would have been impossible to execute and absurd to attempt. The custom probably originated

in this small district when some Saxon king, devoted to hare-coursing, used Somerton as a hunting lodge. At the pleas of 1270 the verderers of Somerton warren again presented several delinquents for hare trespass.[40]

The Sheriff of Somerset was directed, in October 1323, to cause a verderer for the forest of Somerton to be elected in the place of Reginald Huse, lately elected, as he could not attend to the office since he had become one of the county coroners.[41]

NORTH PETHERTON PARK AND FOREST

In close connexion with Somerton and lying along the lowlands of the River Parret the forest of North Petherton must be next considered. The whole of the present parish, the largest in the county of Somerset and covering an area of 10,431 acres of land, 53 acres of water, 17 acres of tidal water and 16 acres of foreshore, was, in Saxon days and indeed in Norman days, regarded as forest and contained a royal park within its area. On the south the parish of North Curry covering 5,819 acres of land and 4 acres of water, 11 acres of tidal water and 14 acres of foreshore was a vast, indeterminate area falling within the king's demesne and noted as a favourite hunting ground of King John. On the north side lay the ridges of the Quantock (anciently written Cantok) Hills. Originally this too was a royal hunting forest [42] as we gather from an incidental notice in the Hundred Rolls, where the expression *dum Canntok Foresta fuit* occurs, referring to a certain payment made to the king's curia at Somerton for a *porcheria* at Roborough in Broomfield parish. A *porcheria* was a place where the king's swine were collected and the whole range of the Quantock Hills (the *famosa silva* of *Cantuc-udu* in Kentwine's charter) would appear to have been included under the Ancient Demesne of the Crown.[43] In Andersfeld Hundred, which, together with Cannington, North Petherton and Carhampton Hundreds, was a royal hundred (two of them, i.e. Carhampton and Cannington, being mentioned in King Alfred's will), there were 3,857 acres subject to forest rights of the Crown.[44] Also there was a large quantity of profitless moorland lying in the vicinity of Durleigh and Athelney, the famous abbey founded by King Alfred, which the Domesday Commissioners seem to

---

[37] *V.C.H. Somers.* i, 434.

[38] Forest Proc. Tr. of R. 152.

[39] The four true beasts of the forest were the red, fallow and roe deer and the wild boar. Manwood's statements on this subject are blunders. See Cox, *Royal Forests*, chap. iv.

[40] Forest Proc. Tr. of R. 153; Turner, *Pleas of the Forest.*

[41] Close, 17 Edw. II, m. 35.

[42] Probably as nearly everywhere else in England the limited forest area temp. Will. I was under his successor much extended and under Hen. III and Edw. I again reduced.

[43] Glastonbury Chart, Monkton Chart.

[44] Eyton, *Domesday Studies* (Somers.), i, 100.

have omitted from their estimates. The *vasta* or wastes of Quantock would have come under the definition of Cannington Hundred where, according to Mr. Eyton's [45] somewhat rash estimates, there were about 4,750 acres of the existing parishes of the hundred in the king's forest at the date of Domesday.

There were two 'mansiones' or small manors on the northern slopes of the Quantocks, falling under Whitley Hundred and lying in Holford Parish, which were always regarded as appanages to Petherton Park and Newton-Forester, i.e. Newhall and Corewell or Currill. [46] They are both easily identified and are close to the old residence of Dodo, the Domesday forester. In former days the tenants owed a service to Petherton Park to be paid at fawning season when the woods were swept; this service, commuted into a money payment, still survives as a land tax of 18*s*. paid yearly to the rate collector of North Petherton. A place-name in New-hall, 'Pecche's Oak,' still recalls the name of the Pecche family, foresters in fee in the 14th century, and more than one patch of rough scrub (*scrobetum*), stunted oaks and unreclaimed waste bring back the original features of this ancient forest appurtenance.

There are more entries as to gifts of timber from North Petherton Park and Forest in the Close Rolls than in any other Somerset forest. Here was a deep soil and oaks grew well. In 1221 the king gave Jocelin Bishop of Bath 20 *grossa fusta, tam postes, tam paunas, tam furchias* for a barn. [47] In 1223 William Brewer has a grant of 100 oaks *cum frussura et branchura prostratis*, a perquisite generally of the forester in fee, who had the cablish or windfall. [48]

The nuns of Buckland in North Petherton had a grant in 1229 of three cart-loads weekly *de spinis, alno et arablis*, the latter called also *bois-blanc*, i.e. white wood; it was to be *fyrebote* only and so would not spoil the vert. This grant lasted 300 years, being renewed by Henry VIII, who stipulated that the nuns should pray for the soul of himself and his beloved consort, Queen Katherine of Aragon. In 1228 Richard de Wrotham was instructed to supply the Prioress of Buckland with forty cart-loads of dry wood from the king's park of Petherton for their hearth. [49] The keeper of the Somerset forests was ordered in 1256 to supply ten harts from Petherton Park for royal use. [50]

At the forest pleas held at Ilchester for the whole county in November 1257 it was stated that

Philip de Candover and Richard de Candover, the king's huntsmen, had taken in Petherton Park on warrant ten harts in 1254, ten in 1256 and six in 1257. [51]

In 1261 the king gave the Dominican Friars of Ilchester six oaks out of Petherton Park. [52] Richard de Plessy, keeper of the king's park of Petherton, was ordered in 1276 to supply the Abbot of Glastonbury with twelve timber oaks of the king's gift. [53] Two years later the king's men of Somerton had a gift of three oaks for the repair of their belfry (*clocherii*) out of the same park, and the Franciscan Friars of Bridgwater five oaks for the making of their dormitory. [54] In 1279 the Bishop of Bath and Wells had a grant of six timber oaks from Petherton. [55]

In April 1280 the Sheriff of Somerset was ordered to deliver Philip de Grindeham, imprisoned at Ilchester for forest trespass, in bail to twelve men who were to mainpern to have him before the king in high Parliament at Westminster in three weeks from Easter. At the same eyre a further mandate was served on the sheriff to release from Ilchester gaol Hugh de Bello Joco and six others imprisoned for trespass in Petherton Forest in bail to twelve men who were to have them before the justices of Forest Pleas when they came to those parts. [56] The Franciscan Friars of Bridgwater obtained the royal gift in 1284 of six good timber oaks with all their strippings out of Petherton Forest. [57] In the following year Alan de Plokenet obtained two bucks from Petherton Park. [58]

In 1290 the keeper of Petherton Park was ordered to supply Queen Eleanor with 20 timber oaks. [59] Other timber gifts from this park were 6 oaks for the Earl of Pembroke in 1292; 12 timber oaks for the Dominican Friars of Ilchester in 1293; 2 timber oaks for Simon de Ashton, the king's yeoman, in 1296; 6 oaks to Robert son of Payne in 1297; and 10 timber oaks for Matilda de Mortimer in 1300. [60] Gifts of venison from Petherton Park about this period included 4 bucks to William de Mortimer in 1291; 4 to Master John Lovel in 1294; and 6 in the same year to Alan Plokenet. [61]

At a forest inquisition held at Langport, Friday after Holy Trinity, 1364, before Peter atte Wode, lieutenant of the custodian of the king's forest this side of Trent, by oaths of John Payn, lieutenant of Richard de Acton custodian of Petherton, and the foresters and verderers,

---

[45] Eyton, *Domesday Studies* (Somers.), i, 123. Eyton's estimates of area are sometimes to be regarded with suspicion.

[46] Collinson, *Hist. of Somers.* iii, 451

[47] Close, 5 Hen. III, m. 11.

[48] Close, 7 Hen. III, m. 19.

[49] Close, 12 Hen. III, m. 6.

[50] Close, 40 Hen. III, m. 11.

[51] Forest Proc. Tr. of R. 152, m. 7.

[52] Close, 45 Hen. III, m. 18.

[53] Close, 4 Edw. I, m. 10.

[54] Close, 6 Edw. I, m. 11.

[55] Close, 7 Edw. I, m. 8.

[56] Close, 8 Edw. I, m. 9.

[57] Close, 13 Edw. I, m. 11. [58] Ibid. m. 4.

[59] Close, 18 Edw. I, m. 14.

[60] Close, 20–8 Edw. I.

[61] Ibid. 19–22 Edw. I.

it was presented that the Abbot of Athelney, with dogs, took a sourell (a buck of the third year) at Northmore within the forest.[62] Two years later, at an inquisition held at Somerton before Peter atte Wode, William Parrecombe was presented for having a dog which chased a pricket (a buck of the second year) to the water of Pedret and killed it there. It was also reported that a doe had been killed. Robert Abbot of Athelney was charged with keeping three greyhounds and another dog within the metes of the forest.[63]

At an inquisition held at Somerton in 1376 before John de Foxle, on the oath of John Payn, lieutenant of Edward de Mortimer Earl of March, warden of Petherton Forest, it was stated that John Poterne and two servants slew three does in Petherton Park on 2 November 1374. John Poterne on St. James' day 1371 received 20s. from Thomas Tryvet and Matthew Michel to conceal many trespasses in the park for which they were indicted. It was further stated that John Poterne on Wednesday and Thursday after St. Michael's day, 1372, cut down and carried away 5 oaks value 16s. 8d., also 3 ashes and 5 maples value 7s.; on St. Jerome's day he sold wood value 40s. in the park. Robert Clavill, on the same day and year, cut down and took away 3 oaks value 10s. and 1 maple value 12d.[64]

As to the park within this forest, from evidence on the spot and from a place-name existing still 'Park Wall Clyse' it seems to have been walled, rather than paled. Saxton marks the site in his map. In a forest document allusion is made to the entry of poachers per foram ingentem, i.e. a gateway. Historically, the whole region, from its proximity to Athelney, is interesting, for here it was that the fugitive King Alfred retired, keeping himself and his followers alive on the fish and game of this noted preserve. In an old ballad King Alfred's adventures with Denewulf the swineherd are said to have happened at Newton Court, i.e. the Curia of Newton-Forester close to Athelney in North Petherton Hundred.[65]

From the point of view of forest administration North Petherton Park and Forest figure as the head quarters of forest official life in Somerset for many centuries, dating from the Conquest, if not before. Here can be traced a continuity of forest officials from Saxon thane to Norman baron, and Domesday supplies the evidence. In King Edward the Confessor's time Nordperet (North Petherton), Sudperet (South Petherton) and Churi (North Curry) reddebant firmam unius noctis cum consuetudinibus suis, meaning that they were bound to supply one night's entertainment during a

hunting progress. These manors never paid danegeld, nor was it known how many hides they contained, neither was Somerton nor Cheddar subject to danegeld and they also reddebant firmam unius noctis cum appendicibus suis. But the most important official here, as at Somerton Park and Warren, was Robert de Odburvile who lived at Melcome, known in later times as Melcome-Paulet, which was his caput baronie.

The circuit of Petherton Forest was considerably reduced in 1298. Leland writing about 1540 says of Petherton Park: 'There ys a great number of Dere longyng to this park, yet hath it almost no other enclosure but Dikes to let the cattell of the common to cum yn: The Dere trippe over these Dykes and feede at about the Fennes and resort to the Park agayn. There is a praty Lodge moted yn the parke.'[66] The park had a compass of 4 miles in 1583, but was much decayed. Collinson in 1790 found the whole converted into farms which belonged to Sir Thomas Acland, bart.[67]

SELWOOD FOREST

This forest used to cover the eastern highlands of Somerset, extending also into Wiltshire and Dorset. According to Leland,[68] writing in 1540, 'The Forest of Selwood as it is now is 30 myles in cumpass and streachith one way almost into Warminster and another way unto the quarters of Shaftesburi (Dorset), by estimation a ten myles.' According to another calculation it was 15 miles from north to south, and 6 miles in breadth from east to west. It was a long leafy tract of forest land on the borders of the three counties, Somerset, Wilts and Dorset.

According to Ethelwerd's Chronicle the bishopric of Aldhelm (with Sherborne just outside the borders of Somerset as the episcopal seat) was the provincia quae vulgo Sealuudscire dicitur [69] (c. 709). In the Anglo-Saxon Chronicle, King Alfred (A.D. 878) in his notable Danish campaign 'rode in the seventh week after Easter to Ecgbyrht's Stone (supposed to be Brixton Deverill in Wilts) on the east of Selwood'. Asser, King Alfred's biographer, says that 'the King rode to Aegbryhta's Stone which is in the eastern part of the wood which is called Selwood, which means in Latin Silva Magna, the Great Wood, but in British Coit Mawr.'[70] Simeon the Chronicler called it Mucelwood meaning a large wood.[71] In A.D. 894 King Alfred again fought the Danes and according to

[62] Forest Proc. Tr. of R. 309, m. 3.
[63] Ibid. 6.　[64] Ibid. 7.
[65] Evans, Old Ballads (Ed. 1810), ii, 12.
[66] Itin. ii, 94–5.
[67] Collinson, Hist. of Somers. iii, 53–9; where there is much about this forest and park.
[68] Itin. ut supra.　[69] Ethelwerd, Chron. xi.
[70] Asser, Life of King Alfred (ed. Bohn), 62.
[71] Simeon of Durham, Hist. of the Kings (ed. Stevenson), 47b.

the Anglo-Saxon Chronicle gathered forces from every town east of the Parret, and as well west as east of Selwood.[72] This forest is exceptionally interesting for these pre-Domesday allusions. In Domesday there is no mention of Selwood Forest by name, but we may look for parts of it in the wood 1 league long and as much broad under Frome, held by the king himself as *terra regis*. The manor of Brumeton or Brewton, which was ancient demesne of the Crown and part of Selwood Forest, fell under Bruton Hundred along its south-west borders. Here at Domesday were woods (*silvae*) 5 leagues in length by 1 in breadth and also a swineherd. At an early date Bruton Manor and Hundred [73] were given (1142) to a house of religion at that time of the Benedictine order, but afterwards transferred to Austin Canons.

The monks of Witham Charterhouse formed a kind of 'Liberty' in Selwood Forest, where the usual forest law did not run. 'Prohibeo ne forestarii vel eorum ministri aliquam eis molestiam faciant infra limites suos, nec ingredientibus vel egredientibus per eos' was the royal injunction of the founder King Henry II, when the charter was signed at Marlborough [74] *circa* 1173.

There are numerous references to royal gifts both of venison and timber out of Selwood Forest throughout the 13th century. In 1223 the king permitted Walter de Pavilly to take a buck and 5 live does from the forest of Selwood to place in his park of Broc.[75] In August 1226 the king granted permission to the men of William de Briwere to take four or five bucks in the forest of Selwood.[76] In 1227 Sir Robert de Courteney obtained the grant from the king of five does and a brocket, out of the forest of Selwood, to place in his park of Hemington.[77] Henry III in 1232 ordered the foresters of Selwood to permit the leprous women of Bradley to have free cheminage through that forest for their horses and carts carrying underwood, charcoal or timber for the use of the sisters, brethren or poor of that house, whether the loads were of gift or purchased.[78]

In 1230 Richard de Wrotham was ordered to supply the Bishop of Bath with six does out of the forest of Selwood.[79] In the following year another royal order instructed him to supply Alice the wife of Godfrey de Craucombe with

five does from the same forest, Robert Aguillun with five bucks and Herbert son of Matthew with five bucks.[80] In October 1231 the Bishop of Bath was supplied with five live does and a live buck out of Selwood to help to stock a park of his, and the like number out of Cheddar Forest.[81] Four Selwood bucks were given by the king to Osbert Giffard, and two to Robert de Muscegros in 1232.[82] The king, at the instance of the Prior of Witham Charterhouse, in 1233, pardoned Ralph Cato, the prior's man, who had taken a Selwood deer, and ordered the sheriff to release him from the king's prison at Ilchester.[83] John, Prior of Witham Charterhouse, went to the king at Bordeaux in 1242 complaining that Richard de Wrotham, forester of fee of the forest of Selwood, and the king's other foresters there grieved him and the brethren of his house by entering the bounds (*terminos*) of their house and inflicting other injuries, whereby the quiet of their religion was disturbed. Thereupon the king sent word to the Archbishop of York and William de Cantlow to forbid the foresters to enter the precincts or to distrain the brethren for anything until his return to England.[84]

A grant was made by Henry III in 1252 to the Prior and convent of Bruton that they and their successors for ever may have 25 acres of the lands of the purpresture in their manor of Brewham outside the covert (*coopertum*) of his forest of Selwood, to be cleared and tilled, but subject to the run of the doe and its fawn, and of other wild animals; also that they can have 70 hogs at mast in his demesne wood in Brucombe, quit of pannage for ever; and that they can have one log every year in the same wood for their fuel against Christmas as in times past they were wont to have.[85]

At the pleas of the Somerset forests held at Ilchester in 1257 a very long list of vert offenders in the forest of Selwood was presented to William de Britton and his fellow justices. The fines were chiefly 12*d.*, several 2*s.* and a few 3*s.* In certain cases the fines were remitted in consequence of poverty, and in others an *alibi* was established. Among the venison trespasses in Selwood, the following case presented some unusual features. On St. Mary Magdalen's day 1255 certain grooms (*garciones*) of Master Bernard, rector of Downton, who was since dead, entered the forest in pursuit of game with four greyhounds and they had with them John the rector of Pertwood and Walter of Great Sutton in the county of Wilts.; the offenders did not appear, nor had they

---

[72] As to the extent and position of Selwood Forest, see *V.C.H. Berks.* ii, 2.

[73] *Cartul. of Bruton* (Somers. Rec. Soc.), *passim*.

[74] L. B. Thompson, *Hist. of the Somers. Carthusians.* See also Chart. R. 14 Hen. III, pt. i, m. 9; also Close, 16 Hen. III, m. 11; also Hundred R. 2 Edw. I, 23.

[75] Close, 8 Hen. III. m. 16.

[76] Close, 10 Hen. III. m. 8.

[77] Close, 11 Hen. III. m. 21.

[78] Pat. 16 Hen. III, m. 7.

[79] Close, 15 Hen. III. m. 20.

[80] Close, 15 Hen. III. m. 17, 13, 11.

[81] Ibid. m. 1.

[82] Ibid. 16 Hen. III, m. 9, 5.

[83] Ibid. 17 Hen. III, m. 11.

[84] Pat. 26-7 Hen. III, m. 5.

[85] *Cartul. of Bruton* (Somers. Rec. Soc.), 19.

been attached because they could not be found. Therefore the Sheriff of Wilts. was ordered to cause Walter to appear before the forest justices at Sherborne on the morrow of Ascension Day; and a mandate was issued to the Bishop of Salisbury asking him to see to the appearance of the rector of Pertwood at the same time and place. Subsequently whilst the court was sitting, Walter appeared; he was convicted and detained in prison. But on proof that he was very poor and had nothing, Walter received the king's pardon. Various charter claims of forest privileges in Selwood were made and sustained at this eyre by the leper hospital of Bradley.[86]

At the Forest Pleas held at Ilchester in 1270, the Abbot of Cirencester was presented because of a certain inclosure at Langley in the manor of Frome, within Selwood Forest. The deer often entered this inclosure because the pasturage was good, but they were not able to return save through certain breaches where ofttimes evil doers assembled and captured them to the great loss of the forest. Thereupon the inclosure was assigned to the Crown, and the abbot was summoned to show on what authority he held the inclosure. On the abbot appearing his rights were restored to him on paying a penalty of 10 marks.[87]

Licence was granted in March 1281 to Laurence de St. Maur to hunt with his own hounds, until Midsummer next, the fox and hare throughout the king's forest of Selwood, provided he did not take any great deer, nor course in the warrens of the king or of others.[88] In 1270 Edward I granted two bucks out of this forest to Alan de Plokenet.[89] In April 1280 the Sheriff of Somerset was ordered to release on bail of twelve men from Ilchester gaol Osbert Giffard, Osbert his son, Roger de Kyngeston and Nicholas de Kyngeston, who had been imprisoned for trespass in the forest of Selwood.[90]

At the same time the sheriff received like instructions as to Henry de Montfort, imprisoned at Ilchester for a similar offence; but in this case the twelve mainpernors were to undertake to produce the delinquents before the king in the Parliament at Westminster in three weeks from Easter.[91] In August of this year Master John de Sanford obtained the king's gift of four bucks from Selwood Forest.[92] In 1283 Alan de Plokenet had six Selwood bucks as a royal gift.[93] Blanche, the wife of William de Fenes, obtained the gift in 1285 of twelve leafless oaks (*robora folia non habencia*) out of

Selwood.[94] Laurence de St. Maur, at the instance of Edmund the king's brother, obtained a licence in March 1283, to hunt the hare and fox in the forest of Selwood until three weeks before Midsummer;[95] but in October of the same year the licence was extended for life and included also the badger and the cat.[96] In 1283 William Wulf obtained the grant for life of the bailiwick of the forest of Selwood, in succession to Robert de Ware.[97] Twenty oaks were granted to Queen Eleanor in 1289 out of the forest of Selwood, wherewith to make palings to inclose her park at Camel.[98]

A perambulation of the bounds of this forest was made on 13 March 1298 by two justices appointed by the king and two Somerset knights, having associated with them Peter de Hamme, as lieutenant of Sabina Pecche, forester in fee, and Henry de Careville, Walter Alayne, William Portbref and Nicholas de la Mare, the four verderers of the forest. They returned on oath the following bounds—

Beginning at the bridge of South Brewham, thence by a road to la Barwe, thence by a road as far as the house called Bruke, and thence to the left of that house as far as the gate of the hall of the lord King which stood there when the park of Witham was inclosed; thence by Hayham as far as the water of Frome, and thence by that water keeping it on the right to the bridge of Waledich; thence along the edge of the wood of Selwood, as far as Burtyngburgh above the house called le Noble, and thence, by keeping that house on the right, as far as Wytecoste; thence as far as Radney on the border of the counties of Somerset and Wilts., and thence by a certain streamlet up to the wood of Weremenesyre; from this wood through Trencham mouth along a road called Hunters way as far as Gaer Hill, and thence through the wood of Kilmington, keeping it on the right, to the place called Kingsettle; thence by a road to Penbury, keeping all the wood of Nortun on the right, thence as far as La Penne, and thence by the king's highway to the middle of Bitewood, where the runnel called Stanebrok goes; which comes from the mill of Stavordale; thence by keeping the said mill on the right along a road outside the park of Forshefe towards the east, thence along a high road as far as the church of Brewham, keeping it on the left; and thence up to the bridge of South Brewham, where the first bounds begin. And they say that all on the right within the said bounds is forest.

They also say that all the townships and woods mentioned below, on the left, outside the aforesaid bounds, were afforested after the coronation of Henry II (1155) and ought to be disafforested according to the Forest Charter—namely Kilmington, Penne, part of Bruton, the greater part of North Brewham, a certain part of the townships of Cloford and Postbury, a moiety of Wanstrow, 'Truttokeshall,' Marston

[86] Forest Proc. Tr. of R. 152, m. 2, 11–13.
[87] Ibid. 153.
[88] Pat. 9 Edw. I, m. 23.
[89] Close, 6 Edw. I, m. 5.
[90] Close, 8 Edw. I, m. 9.
[91] Ibid.   [92] Ibid. m. 3.
[93] Close, 11 Edw. I, m. 6.

[94] Close, 13 Edw. I, m. 1.
[95] Pat. 11 Edw. I, m. 21.
[96] Ibid. m. 8.
[97] Pat. 13 Edw. I, m. 3.
[98] Close, 17 Edw. I, m. 9.

Smithwick, Keyford, Feltham, 'Littleford,' Rodden, Yarnfield in Bradley, Norton Ferris, 'Eastrip,' Stony Stoke, Henley Grove and 'Kyngwere.'[99]

Reginald de Kyngeston, to whom Edward I had granted for life the bailiwick that William le Wolf deceased had in his forest of Selwood, rendering for it £10 yearly, was in June 1318 discharged from this payment, as the king understood that the bailiwick was so much reduced by the recent perambulation that it was greatly below that value. The letters patent of Reginald's appointment were ordered to be cancelled, and the king instructed the general keeper of the forests this side Trent to take the bailiwick into his hands.[100] At an inquisition as to the general condition of Selwood Forest, held at Frome in 1367, before Peter atte Wood, four tenants were fined 12d. each for pasturing goats within the forest contrary to the forest assize; one of the delinquents had six goats and the rest three each.[101] In the following year at a like inquisition held at the same place, in addition to several venison trespasses, Robert atte Crouch was presented for selling an acre of alder wood near Penne (Penselwood) within the covert of the forest, and William Gobert was charged with carrying the said wood in his cart.[102] At a third of these special forest inquisitions as to Selwood, held at Frome in 1371, before John de Foxle, warden of the king's forests this side Trent, John Cary attended as the lieutenant of Roger Stourton, then warden of Selwood.[103]

This forest suffered much from gradual encroachments in its later history. It remained under the nominal supervision of the chief forester of Somerset until the early days of Charles I, when a commission was granted to certain lords of the Privy Council for the disafforesting of Selwood. By virtue of this authority the commissioners contracted with the lords and commoners of the various forest manors in the manner following: 'That His Majesty and His successors should have hold and enjoy one third of the several wastes and commonable lands within the said Forest, that one third part should be held and enjoyed by the lords and owners of the soil, and that the other third should be left to the several Commons having right of Common for depasturing their cattle.'[104] The tenants of the manors of Penselwood and Charlton Musgrove were amongst those who had common rights. There were constant disputes between the commoners and lords of the manor, and on one occasion, 13 Charles II, the hedges and boundaries of Marston Bigot manor, 'within the Forest of Frome Sellwood' were thrown down by an unruly mob.[105] The tenants of the manor of Kilmington had common of pasture in Kilmington Heath in the forest of Selwood, containing 500–600 acres. They paid a yearly rent to the king for common on the rest of the wastes of the forest, i.e. 8s. in money and 12s. 1d. in wheat called woodleaze or woodgoale (wood-gavel).[106] In a lawsuit between Amos Isaack, David Chamberleyne and others about the boundaries of lands belonging to Marston Bigot, 'formerly in the Forest of Frome Zelwood', which lands were described as belonging to John Symes, esq., then to John Hippisley, and then to the Earl of Orrery, touching tithes from these lands, it is said, that 'the Forest reached from a water called Old Pound, and from there to a place called Old Dyke and from there to Latchborne water and so foreward.'[107]

Collinson, writing in 1790 of the woodlands in Frome parish, round the new church of that name built in 1712, says they 'are now the only part of the ancient forest of Selwood which bear any resemblance to its former state; and have been, within the memory of man, the notorious asylum of a desperate clan of banditti, whose depredations were a terror to the surrounding parishes. One of their evil practices, and which perhaps was far from being the worst, was that of coining money; but the cutting down large tracts of wood, establishing small farms and building the church have been the means of destroying their haunts, and obliging the possessors to seek subsistence in honest and useful labour.'[108]

THE FOREST OF MENDIP WITH CHEDDAR

There is no mention of Mendip Forest, as such, in Domesday, but the heart of it lay in 'Cedre' or Cheddar Manor, part of the royal demesne. In Saxon days it was a favourite summer hunting resort of their kings. *Interdum aestivabant circa forestam de Mendep* is the tradition recorded in an old Axbridge document of the Saxon kings.[109] An account is given of the celebrated hunt at Cheddar by King Edmund when the stag fell over the Cheddar cliffs and was dashed in pieces. Axbridge was an early

[99] The 1298 perambulations of the different Somerset forests were first printed by Hearne in 1728 in Adam de Domerham's *Hist. of Glastonbury*, ii, 683. They are also given in Collinson's *Somers.* iii, 56 and in an English dress in the appendix to Greswell's *Forests and Deerparks of Somers.*, from which the above rendering is slightly condensed.
[100] Close, 11 Edw. II, m. 3.
[101] Forest Proc. Tr. of R. 309.
[102] Ibid.   [103] Ibid.
[104] Collinson, *Somers.* ii, 195.

[105] Exch. Dep. by Com. Mich. 13 Chas. II, no. 45.
[106] Ibid. 7 Chas. I, no. 20.
[107] Ibid. East. 14 Chas. II, no. 28.
[108] *Hist. of Somers.* ii, 194.
[109] Axbridge documents. *Hist. MSS. Com. Rep.* iii, App. 300.

Saxon borough and the burgesses there claimed to have the somewhat unusual privileges of hunting and fishing in all places, excepting the warrens, from a place called Cotellisasch to the rock which is called Blackstone in the western sea, i.e. the Black Rock still so called at the mouth of the Axe, close to Weston-super-Mare. From the Axbridge documents we gather that the *Villa de Axebrygge cum manerio de Ceddir* was the *proprium dominium regis* at a very remote date.[110] The modern parish has 7001 acres of land and 17 of water; the borough of Axbridge 468 acres. The pre-Domesday notices of the forest are exceptionally interesting. Like Bristol and Bridgwater so Axbridge gives us an instance of a municipal town gradually growing up close to a royal hunting resort, near a tidal river, and gathering some prestige from both these facts of geography. The old forest did not cover much more than the parishes of Axbridge and Cheddar, but the extended forest reached right down to Bleadon and Uphill and the Severn sea and further east, to the manor of Worle, to Sandy Bay and St. Thomas Point. The city of Wells, in the names of its streets, carries with it signs of old forest days. It was divided into four verderies, each of the verderies superintended by the verderers or petty constables, an office said to owe its origin to the *viridarii* of the bishop's part of the forest of Mendip, whose province it was to keep the assize of the forest and to enrol the attachments and presentments of trespasses. The itinerant justices of the forest occasionally held their courts at Wells, as in 1371; but Ilchester or Somerton was more usually selected.

The Close and Patent Rolls of Henry III have various references to Cheddar Forest. Licence was granted in 1221 to Jocelin Bishop of Bath to take four bucks in the forest of Cheddar.[111]

Hugh de Neville was ordered, in 1225, to give William le Marshal ten live does and two bucks out of the forest of Cheddar, which the king had granted him to take to his island of Lundy.[112] In the following year the Prioress of Amesbury obtained a grant of twenty tie-beams, four beams and four *paunas* from the forest of Cheddar, wherever they would be the least missed, for the erection of the chapel of the infirmary.[113] Grant was made to Jocelin Bishop of Bath by the king in 1234 that the 40 acres of wood, which the king had licensed him to assart in one of the bishop's woods of Cheddar, was to be quit of waste and regard and of view of foresters and verderers.[114] In the following year a further licence to assart 20 more acres in Cheddar wood was granted to

the bishop.[115] In 1235, the bishop was granted twenty-five oaks out of Cheddar.[116]

The keeper of Cheddar Forest was ordered, in 1235, to allow Henry de Candover and William Lovel to take all the bucks and does which they could find. The Sheriff of Somerset was to cause all such venison to be salted and kept until further orders.[117]

At the Pleas of the Forests of Somerset held at Ilchester in 1257, there was a long list of presentments for vert trespasses in Mendip. The usual fines imposed on the offenders varied from 2*d*. to 4*s*.; a few were excused on the ground of poverty, whilst others established an *alibi*. At these pleas, however, as was generally the case in forest courts, offenders of position were subjected to heavy penalties; thus Samuel de Melles, a canon of Wells, had to pay 40*s*. Under the venison pleas, mention was made of a hart having been found dead as long ago as the Friday after St. Gregory's day, 1240; it had fallen over the cliffs at Cheddar.[118]

At the Forest Pleas of 1270, it was presented that as James de Thurlebere, forester of Mendip, was passing through the forest on the Saturday after the feast of St. Scolastica 1261, he found Richard le Marshal of Congresbury chasing a buck with three mastiffs. The forester took Richard and the dogs, but afterwards irregularly released him on the warrant or assurance (*per plevinam*) of Roger Harold, Thomas le Fuler, Henry le Macekre, Walter Wymond, Geoffrey Thorgod and Robert Gunsey, all of Cheddar. Richard did not appear and was in mercy, and the sheriff was ordered to produce him; James the forester who illegally released the trespasser was dead, ' and so nothing of him '; of the men of Cheddar who gave irregular bail, one was dead and one was a pauper, but the rest were each fined 1*s*.[119] At the same pleas, John rector of the church of Shipham was presented for having, together with Walter the clerk of the same place, taken a hart in Mendip Forest without a warrant in 1265. A mandate was issued to the Bishop of Bath and Wells to produce him, but it was stated that the rector could not be found, whereupon he was exiled.

Another exceptional and interesting presentment at this eyre was that of Brother William of the Carthusian order and others of the household of Witham Priory who took a hart in 1260, in an inclosure called Bataberm within Mendip Forest, and hunted another hart with mastiffs to the wood of Cheddar. It was also alleged that Brother William was accustomed to sharply point wooden stakes, making the points harder by burning them in the fire and to fix them in

---

[110] *Proc. Somers. Arch. Soc.* xv, 23.
[111] Close, 5 Hen. III, m. 6.
[112] Ibid. 9 Hen. III, m. 4.
[113] Ibid. 10 Hen. III, m. 13.
[114] Pat. 19 Hen. III, m. 18.

[115] Pat. 19 Hen. III, m. 2.
[116] Ibid. m. 15.
[117] Close, 39 Hen. III, m. 1.
[118] Forest Proc. Tr. of R. 152, m. 3, 4.
[119] Ibid. 153, m. 2.

gaps in the aforesaid inclosure where the deer were accustomed to pass and by such engines to secure their capture. The justices ordered the Prior of Witham to cause the attendance of this brother and others of his household to make answer to indictments for trespass in this forest as well as in that of Selwood.

At these same pleas of 1270 a charter granted by Henry III to the Bishop of Bath and Wells was exhibited and allowed. This charter is of interest as showing the confusion that from time to time arose as to respective rights over woods in royal forests and chases. The king had granted twenty-five oaks in the Cheddar woods to one Herbert the son of Matthew believing that the woods were royal demesne. But the bishop approached the king and showed him that there were no royal rights in those woods save in vert (green wood) and venison, and that he (the king) could not fell timber; in proof of which he produced a charter of King John, attested by Richard de Wrotham as keeper of the Somerset forests. Henry, seeing that he had done the bishop an injustice, confirmed to the bishop and his successors the woods of Cheddar as appurtenances of the episcopal manor of Cheddar; and as to the twenty-five felled oaks, Herbert was only to have fifteen, the remaining ten being assigned to the bishop.[120]

The keeper of the forest of Mendip was ordered in 1277 to permit the Bishop of Bath and Wells to assart 60 acres of his woods of Cheddar and Axbridge, to be held by him and his successors when brought into cultivation, provided they are inclosed with a small ditch and a low hedge according to the assize of the forest.[121]

Richard de Plessy, keeper of the forest of Mendip, was ordered in 1279 to assign to Richard du Boys two timber oaks of the king's gift.[122] Roger de Clifford, justice of the forest beyond Trent, was ordered in 1280 to cause Roger de Amary to have five live bucks in the forest of Mendip, in the place of the five bucks that escaped from Roger's park of Ubley.[123]

Licence was granted in 1284 to John Giffard to take five harts in the forest of Mendip and another five in the wood of Petherton.[124]

Thomas de Berkeley obtained a life licence from Edward I in 1283 to hunt with his own dogs the fox, hare, badger and cat in the forest of Mendip and in the chase of Kingswood, on both sides the River Avon, save in the fence month, provided that he took no deer nor coursed in the king's warren.[125]

A formal perambulation of this forest was undertaken,[126] by order of the Crown, on 10 May 1298. It was then declared on oath that

The bounds begin at Stoburghe (Stowbarrow) and thence through the midst of the heath as far as Thurleston, thence through the heath to 'Schynyndecliffe' and up to the gallows of Cheddar Liberty, and leaving the gallows on the right as far as Dunneston; descending thence to Foxweye as far as a stone which is called Sliperstone and thence to the thorn which is called Merthorne; thence as far as the marsh on the right as far as the stone which old Samuel caused to be fixed between the fee of the manor of Cheddar and the fee of the Abbot of Glastonbury; thence to Notepole towards Clyware, leaving on the left the fee of the abbot and through the fee of Philip de Wyky; thence as far as Beremore, along the old watercourse, and thence to Hyndemore on the right in the forest; thence to Scherneham and to la Rede which is of the king's demesne, leaving both places on the right; thence to Morehighes de Axbridge, to Portlakes, to Goreweysmalle, and to the spring which is called Hollewelle; thence through the house of Robert . . . ward, which is within the forest in the town of Axbridge as far as Horneslane; thence ascending to a hill called Calewe, and thence to la Rudynge and through la Rudynge as far as Lynleghspoule; thence ascending along a certain valley and descending as far as Waterscumbe; thence, keeping Waterscumbe on the right, to la Holeweye, to Seweye, to Cheddeford and thence as far as a certain ditch up to Hyndewell; going thence between the fee of the Templars (Temple Hidon) and the fee of the Charterhouse, as far as the Horeclive; and thence in a straight line through the heath as far as Stenebergh and thence to Stoburghe where first the bounds began. And they say that all on the right is forest.

These boundaries of the old forest did not embrace much more than the parishes of Axbridge and Cheddar.

The officials of this perambulation, consisting of the special crown commissioners and the local forest ministers, also stated that all the following townships, with their woods and belongings, outside the bounds on the left, were afforested after the coronation of Henry II (1155) and ought to be disafforested according to the Forest Charter of Henry III, viz. Chewton, Priddy, Stoke Giffard, Compton, Loxton, Uphill, Worle, Christon, Hutton, Banwell, Churchill, Langford, 'Watelegh,' Winscombe, Shipham, Rowberrow, Burrington, Blagdon, Ubley, West Harptree and East Harptree.[127]

Hugh le Despenser, as forest justice, was ordered in 1299 to permit John Giffard to chase and take sixteen harts in the king's forest of Mendip.[128] In 1302 Thomas de Berkeley

---

[120] Forest Proc. Tr. of R. 153, m. 2.
[121] Close, 5 Edw. I, m. 11.
[122] Ibid. 7 Edw. I, m. 5.
[123] Ibid. 8 Edw. I, m. 3.
[124] Ibid. 12 Edw. I, m. 6.
[125] Pat. 11 Edw. I, m. 23.

[126] Collinson, op. cit. iii, 59.
[127] Adapted from an English version in appendix to Greswell's *Forests and Deerparks of Somerset*, cf. *Proc. Somers. Arch. Soc.* xxxvii. (2), 82.
[128] Close, 27 Edw. I, m. 13.

had licence to take two harts in the same forest.[129]

The Sheriff of Somerset was ordered in 1325 to cause a regarder for the forest of Mendip to be elected in place of Richard de Wolfarshull who was insufficiently qualified.[130]

In February 1338 a deed was enrolled testifying that whereas the king granted to Ralph Bishop of Bath and Wells and to his churches of Bath and Wells by charter, that his manor of 'Ceddre, county Somerset, which is within the bounds of the forest of Mendip should be disafforested and remain so for ever, Matthew Pecche forester there has released to the bishop and the church all his right and claim in the forest and custody of forest and forestership in the said manor.'[131] And again in 1346 William de Clynton, Earl of Huntingdon, keeper of Forest *citra Trentam*, or his lieutenant in the forest of Mendip, and Richard Damory, keeper of the forest of Mendip (or his deputy), were ordered to desist from impeding Ralph Bishop of Bath and Wells from holding his manor of Cheddar with other disafforested places and the liberties granted to him by the king, since on 1 September 1337 the king had granted that this manor, anciently royal demesne, should be disafforested.[132]

Leland (1540) has the following note on Mendip—'At such time as Gurney lived the Lord Fitz Warine was master of Mendepe Forest by inheritance and it was well furnished with dere; but, anon, aftar, for riots and trespassys done in huntyngs it was deforestyd and so yet remaineth.'[133] The Gurney family lived at Richmond Castle, East Harptree. This castle was demolished about the time of Henry VIII.[134] Collinson (c. 1790) writes that the forest in ancient times was well stocked with deer, also with wood; but since its disafforestation, it had degenerated into a wild and woodless plain.[135]

In 1770 an act was passed for inclosing that part of Mendip lying between the parishes of East and West Cranmore, which is said to have been the first inclosure made in this forest under such a sanction. An interesting case of Mendip inclosure occurred in 1697 between Edward Strode and the commoners of Mendip. The witnesses elicited that the customary tenants and freeholders of Shepton Mallet had at all times of the year common pasture for sheep, horses and cattle on those parts of that parish which lay within the forest.[136]

THE FOREST OF NEROCHE

The forest of Neroche, Nerachich, Roche or Rache (for there are many ways of spelling it), lies along the slopes and crest of the Blackdown Hills, about 6 or 8 miles to the south of Taunton.[137] In Domesday the chief manor within this forest was Staple (Fitzpaine) forming, together with Ashill, Broadway, Donyatt, Beer (Crocombe) and Bickenhall, part of the great 'Fee of Mortain,' with the Castle at Montacute as the chief place, occupied by King William's half-brother, the Count of Mortain. The *parcus* of Donyatt, the only Somerset park mentioned in Domesday, formed part of Neroche Forest. The historic manor of Barrington, the seat of the D'Albiniaco or Daubeney family, had 1,200 acres of Neroche called the wood of Clayhull as appurtenant to it.[138] Broadway preserves the name of an ancient *via regia* passing through the forest and linking it with Montacute and Ilchester. This forest probably suffered diminution at a very early date. In 8 Charles I (1633) the king's portion (one-third at the date of disafforesting)[139] was said to be 162 acres. Gerard, writing about this time, remarks—'Dirty soil enough it is and something too good for deere which is the cause that very lately it is disafforested.'[140] This small forest seems to have been well stocked with fallow deer about the beginning of the reign of Henry III. In 1221 the king granted to the Earl of Pembroke twenty live does out of his forest of Neroche for restocking his park.[141]

When the Forest Pleas for the county were held at Ilchester in 1257, it was presented that on the morrow of the Circumcision 1250 two greyhounds had killed a doe in the forest of Neroche. The customary inquisition was held by the forest officials and the men of the four nearest townships, namely those of Capland, Ashland, Broadway and Bickenhall; they found that the greyhounds belonged to the rector of Kingston, but that he had no knowledge of the offence. A certain William, son of Gilbert chaplain of Combe, had gone to the rectory at Kingston and had taken the dogs thence to the forest and with their aid had run down a doe and then left them. It was protested to the justices that the said rector was not at that time in the country, nor did he then put in an appearance. Thereupon it was ordered that a mandate should be issued to the Bishop of Bath directing him to cause the rector of Kingston to appear before the justices, with the two dogs, at Sherborne on the morrow of Ascension Day. William did not appear nor could he be found; but it was afterwards testified that he

[129] Close, 30 Edw. I, m. 10.
[130] Ibid. 18 Edw. II, m. 12.
[131] Ibid. 12 Edw. III, pt. i, m. 36d.
[132] Ibid. 19 Edw. III, pt. i, m. 14.
[133] *Itin.*
[134] Collinson, *Hist. of Somers.* iii, 589.
[135] Ibid. iii, 374.
[136] Exch. Dep. of Will. iii, no. 30 Somers.

[137] *Proc. Somers. Arch. Soc.* xlix, (2), 31.
[138] Ibid. xxxvii (2), 41   [139] Exch. Dep.
[140] *Particular Description of Somers.*
[141] Close, 6 Hen. III, m. 16.

had been received at the house of his father Gilbert the chaplain, whereupon the bishop was requested to see that William also appeared on the same day at Sherborne. Of other lesser venison offenders, who entered Neroche Forest with bows and arrows, etc., some were fined and others who did not appear were outlawed.[142]

Among the venison presentments of the forest of Neroche, at the Forest Pleas for the county in 1270, was the case of John, vicar of Martock, who with his brother Henry and two others of his household and four other offenders entered the forest at night on the Sunday next before the feast of St. Peter ad Vincula, 1267, with a great net, 46 toises [143] (276 ft.) in length. With this net they captured a doe, which was carried to the vicar's house, together with the net. The delinquents did not appear, neither had they been attached. The justices sent their mandate to the Bishop of Bath and Wells ordering him to produce the vicar before them. Eventually the vicar was fined in the heavy penalty of 100s. and his brother Henry 20s.[144]

The keeper of the forest was ordered in 1276 to permit Ralph Daubeney to take twelve bucks for the king's use in that forest and in the park of Staple, which belonged to Robert de Brus, deceased, tenant in chief.[145] Two years later Ralph Daubeney had a further grant of two bucks, and the like again in 1279.[146]

On 6 August 1281 the Bishop of Bath and Wells was granted twenty live bucks and does out of Neroche Forest to stock his park of Buckland.[147] On 1 December of the same year the king learnt that the keeper of Neroche Forest had not complied with this order, whereupon the bishop was granted fifteen does and five live bucks out of the park of Dunster to stock his park at Buckland.[148]

In 1285 Alan de Plokenet was granted two bucks, of the king's gift, out of this forest.[149]

In 1291 the sheriff was ordered to cause a verderer to be elected for the forest of Neroche in place of Matthew de Esshe, lately elected, because the king had learnt that Matthew chiefly resided in Herefordshire and could not therefore rightly attend to the duties of the office.[150]

The keeper of this forest was instructed in 1293 to supply William de Mortimer with six bucks of the king's gift.[151]

A formal perambulation of the forest of

Neroche was undertaken on 10 March 1298, by the view of Malcolm de Harleigh and John de Wrottesley, appointed by the king and by Geoffrey de Wroxall and Hugh de Popham, two Somerset knights selected by the two royal commissioners. Among those summoned and present were Sabina Pecche, forester in fee of the said forest, and Reginald de Wytele and Geoffrey de Assland, the verderers. In this case the perambulators did not set forth the old boundaries,[152] but were content to enumerate the large number of extensions of the forest that had been made since 1154, chiefly by the sport-loving King John, who was a constant visitor to the forest districts of Somerset. The perambulators claimed that all the following townships, with their woods, ought to be disafforested according to the tenor of the Forest Charter of Henry III : A certain hill called the castle of Rachich, Capland, a wood in Bickenhall, a moiety of Stewley, the wood of Ottershaw in Isle Abbots, Southwood in Drayton, the wood of Unviet in Ilminster, the wood of Hawksbere in Camel Abbas, Ashill, the wood of Clayhill in South Petherton, Broadway, the hamlet of Staforde in Ilton, a moiety of Horton, a moiety of Donyatt, the hamlet of Sticklepath, Hockey in Combe St. Nicholas, a tenement called Wodehouse, lands and woods at La Grange, the manor of Donyatt, a tenement called Leighe, Isle Brewers and Staplewood and Corylond in Staple Fitzpaine.[153]

At an inquisition as to the state of Neroche Forest, held at Somerton in 1365, the heads of two religious houses were said to be in fault ; Robert Abbot of Athelney was charged with killing a sore (a buck of the fourth year) with dogs, and Ralph Chalfham, Prior of Carswell (a cell of the Cluniac house of Montacute), with killing a doe with his greyhounds.[154]

At another Neroche inquisition held at Somerton in 1365, before Peter atte Wode, fines were imposed on six delinquents for keeping goats ; the goats numbered twelve and the penalty for each goat was 6d. At this inquest it was also stated that William Montagu, Earl of Salisbury, was instructed to take fat venison for the king in this forest in the summer of 1367 ; whereupon a buck escaped from the forest and entered the park of Matthew Gornay, within 3 leagues of the forest bounds, at Curry Mallet. In this park fence were two deer-leaps. William Harecome, a king's forester, entered the park, following the buck to take it for the king, whereupon John Draper, Robert Gurnere, Nicholas Hupe, Robert Tailour, and John Montagu, parson of the church of Curry

---

[142] Forest Proc. Tr. of R. 152.
[143] The *tesia* or toise was a usual measure for nets or ropes ; it was the equivalent of a fathom or 6 ft.
[144] Forest Proc. Tr. of R. 153, m. 7 d.
[145] Close, 4 Edw. I, m. 4.
[146] Close, 6 Edw. I, m. 5 ; 7 Edw. I, m. 5.
[147] Close, 9 Edw. I, m. 4.
[148] Close, 10 Edw. I, m. 8.
[149] Close, 13 Edw. I, m. 4.
[150] Close, 19 Edw. I, m. 1.
[151] Close, 21 Edw. I, m. 5.

[152] A later perambulation taken 28 Edw. I, gives the bounds. [*Somerset and Dorset N. & Q.*, vi. art. 149, quoting Forest Proc. Anct. Chancery no. 102.]
[153] Collinson, *Hist. Somers.* iii, 57.
[154] Forest Proc. Tr. of R. 309.

Mallet, rescued the buck from the forester *vi et armis*, killed it and carried off the venison contrary to the assize of the forest.[155]

At a third inquisition as to this forest, held at Somerton in 1371, before John de Foxle, six more offenders were fined for feeding goats in the forest; the fine of 6*d*. for each goat was again imposed.[156] An Act of 1493 for providing for the queen's jointure assigned to her, *inter alia*, the forests of Neroche and Mendip.[157]

Charles I in 1633-4 procured the disafforesting of Neroche, the usual plan being adopted of assigning a third part to the Crown, a third to the lords of the manors and a third to the commoners. The king's third was ordered to be inclosed and fenced.[158] In 1658 a great number of these fences were pulled down by the commoners and so were those of Sir William Portman and other lords of the soil who had 'bought the king's share,' the objection being on the part of the commoners to the barren nature of the one-third allotted to them. It was mentioned in the ensuing legal proceedings that there were formerly four 'walks' in Neroche, i.e. Bicknill (Bickenhall) Plain, Cage Bush, Grange Wood, Stickell Bare, all furnished with fallow deer of which there were at the time of disafforestation about 1,600, and sixteen years before this 2,000 head. Evidence was also given that some 2,000 persons in the villages and hamlets of Combe St. Nicholas, Donyatt, Drayton, Broadway, Ilton, Ilminster, Ashill, Bickenhall, Curland, Hatch Beauchamp, Beer Crocombe, Barrington, Capland, Staple Fitzpaine, Buckland, Steweley and Curry Rivel claimed commonage in 1658.[159] The result of the Commonwealth disturbances seems to have been a practical reafforesting of much of the district.

As late as the reign of George IV the boundaries of the enlarged forest remained in a technical sense and as a geographical expression, proving that the 1298 scheme had never been accomplished. In 1830 an Act was passed for 'inclosing the Forest of Neroche in the Parishes of Broadway, Bickenhall, Beer Crocombe, Ilton, Barrington, Ashill, Ilminster, Whitelackington, Curland, Donyatt, Isle Abbots, Hatch-Beauchamp and the tithing of Domett in the Parish of Buckland St Mary,' thus showing its extent.[160]

THE FOREST OF EXMOOR

There is no mention of Exmoor Forest in Domesday, but these forest lands and wild heath-covered spaces must be placed amongst the wastes of the hundreds of Williton and Carhampton, which were royal possessions, the latter mentioned in King Alfred's will. Being *terra regis*, neither Cannington, Williton nor Carhampton was subject to the danegeld, nor was the hidage scheduled. The three together in the days of Edward the Confessor *reddebant firmam unius noctis*. King's Brompton, a large parish of 9,003 acres, first the manor of Ghida mother of Harold and then taken over into the Conqueror's own hands, may have been regarded as furnishing part of waste and forest lands in Domesday. It is there described as having woodland 3 leagues long by 1 broad. A portion of Brompton Regis certainly fell within the enlarged forest of Exmoor such as it was in King John's day. The enlarged forest covered the well-known modern parish of Porlock, which at the time of the Conquest was held by Algar, the eldest son of Leofric Earl of Mercia. Here it was said lay in Saxon times an extensive chase with a palace.[161] The abbey of Athelney held the manor of Bossington in Porlock Bay, by gift, probably of King Alfred, and one of the abbots figures in a poaching episode of the forest courts in 1313.[162] According to the census returns Porlock with its manors of Bossington, Porlock Weir, West Porlock and Yearnor covered 7,850 acres. In 1366 Sir Nigel Loring had leave to impark his grounds and woods at Porlock and this park was called 'The High Park.' There was an old decoy in Porlock Bay and 'Whitestones Park' further inland. In the extreme west of Exmoor lay the still wilder manor of Oare. The manor of Oare at the Conquest was held by Ralph de Pomeray who also held Brendon, an adjoining Devon manor, and both of these manors were at one time counted as part of the forest. The parish of Oare is 4,017 acres and lies entirely in Somerset. Together with Exford, Withypool, Hawkridge and Exmoor (formerly an extra-parochial area) the old forest, by a moderate estimate, was 38,000 acres. But if Winsford, Dulverton and Cutcombe were included the area at the time of the Domesday Survey would have been 62,000 acres or more.[163] King John afforested a large area including Culbone, Yearnor, Wilmersham, Stoke Pero, Porlock, Doverhay, Bossington, Holnicote, Luccombe, Withycombe and others which may have brought the area up to more than 80,000 acres lying under forest law in Somerset, omitting the Devon borders. In the perambulation of 1279 the following instructive note occurs, after a description of the ancient forest as reduced by the jury:—

Moreover, all other woods which were afforested

---

[155] Forest Proc. Tr. of R. 309.   [156] Ibid.
[157] 11 Hen. VII, cap. 5.
[158] Exch. Dep. by Com. Hil. 8 and 9 Chas. I, no. 24.   [159] Ibid. East. 1658, no. 37.
[160] 11 Geo. IV, cap. 2.

[161] Collinson, *Hist. of Somers.* ii, 35.
[162] *Cal. MSS. D. & C. of Wells* (Hist. MSS. Com.), 425.
[163] Rawle, *Annals of Exmoor*, 6. This work, published in 1898, contains a valuable collection of transcripts of original records in the P.R.O.

after the coronation of King Henry (II) grandfather of the Lord King Henry, son of King John, were afforested by King John. And afterwards they were disafforested by King Henry (III), son of King John, when a fifteenth part of the movable goods of all England was given to the Lord King Henry (III) for making the charters of common liberties and the Forest Charter. And afterwards they were afforested by Richard de Wyrtham (Wrotham) against the Forest Charter to the great damage of the whole country when the Lord King has no profit.

King John frequently sojourned in Somerset at Bristol, Wells, Bridgwater and held North Petherton Park and Forest in his own hands. He was also known at Axbridge, especially at North Curry, where his memory was kept alive for centuries by a North Curry feast.[164] An incidental notice of his hunting near Taunton is preserved in contemporary documents. During his reign forest law was at its height in the county of Somerset.[165]

The subsequent applications of extended forest law due to the exactions of Richard de Wrotham are worth noting as showing the power of the Somerset forester-in-fee. The grievances generally of the men of Somerset and especially those of Exmoor are set forth in a document which was drawn up shortly after the perambulation of 1298.[166]

The particular grievances of Exmoor are therein set forth with much exactness. It was complained that the foresters attached the ' good folk ' in their demesne woods and lands amercing them grievously, whilst they attached the ' small folk ' at their houses and in their inclosures and crofts among the towns. Men at work in waste ground (not royal demesne) preparing it for corn sowing were attached by the foresters for making waste and purpresture, whilst from each man the foresters claimed the skin of a lamb or a farthing, stating that it was their fee. A further complaint was directed against the foresters for exacting illegal cheminage toll, demanding it in the midst of the king's highway or actually in the midst of market, levying it even on the transport of timber of an old house moved from one part of the forest to another, or on an old chest without iron or on a pair of wheels for a wagon or cart. ' They pray our Lord the King that all such grievances may be amended seeing that the King from such things has no profit.'

At the forest pleas for the county held at Ilchester on 26 November 1257 there was but a short list of vert offenders from Exmoor, twenty-six in all, although the presentments covered a

space of many years since the last pleas ; this may be taken as a proof of the small extent of woodland within the bounds of Exmoor Forest. The offenders were chiefly fined 1s. or 2s. ; in one case the penalty was 5s. Among the venison trespassers was William Herlewyne, who, with three unknown companions, had killed a hart in Hawkridge Wood and taken it to Bampton, Devonshire. Herlewyne did not appear ; he had not been attached or found, and the Sheriff of Devon was ordered by the justices to produce him at Ilchester on the Tuesday after St. Andrew's day. It was certified that Reginald de Moun had taken four harts and three roebucks on Exmoor by warrant from the king. We have not found any mention of fallow deer on Exmoor either at this or at subsequent pleas or inquisitions.[167]

At the Forest Pleas held at Ilchester in 1270 there were about sixty cases of vert trespass, a small number considering that the presentments were spread over the thirteen years that had elapsed since the last eyre was held. The delinquents were nearly all fined 12d., but a few 2s. The venison presentments as to hunting or taking harts or hinds during this period were fairly numerous. In a recent case the justices evidently thought there was either complicity or gross neglect on the part of the foresters. Richard de Dunesleye of Anstey, William de Ruckebere of ' Cridelaunde,' with many other malefactors whose names were as yet unknown, on the feast of St. Mary Magdalene 1269, had entered the forest with bows and arrows and had continued for three days. The delinquents did not however appear, and it was shown that they had never been attached. The Sheriff of Devonshire was therefore ordered to produce them in the octave of Trinity. Inasmuch as William de Plessy the chief forester of Somerset had neither taken them nor proclaimed them either by himself or his foresters, ' therefore to judgment as to him and his foresters.' At the same eyre when two poachers entered Exmoor Forest on Easter Eve, in the fifty-first year of the king, and hunted and killed a hind, they were sheltered by John chaplain of Hawkridge, who was put in prison. But ' he is pardoned for the sake of the King's soul.' Another case is of some interest as showing the strict rule about those who lived within the forest and the boundaries of Exmoor Forest itself. In the forty-eighth year of King Henry III (1264) two men of Bossington, the little village lying on the east of Porlock Bay, caught a fawn which had strayed outside the forest. They fell under strict forest law, however, because they carried ' it to their houses in Bossington which is within the Forest going through the Forest with the same Fawn.' Exmoor Forest was then at its widest and as it

---

[164] Wells MS.

[165] H. Hall, *Pipe R. of Bp. of Winchester* (1208).

[166] A careful translation of this Norman-French document is supplied by Mr. Turner in his *Select Pleas of the Forest*, 127–8.

[167] Forest Proc. Tr. of R. 152, m. 5, 6.

was left by King John, that inveterate hunter in the West of England.[168]

Laurence de St. Maur obtained a life licence in 1283 to hunt fox, hare, badger and cat in the forest of Exmoor in the counties of Somerset and Devon, except in the close month.[169]

Order was made on the justice of the forest this side Trent, in 1291, to cause to be replevied to Nicholas de Bonevil, until the coming of the king's justices, his wood of Dulverton, which was within the bounds of the forest of Exmoor, and which the justices took into the king's hands because no woodward was found there.'[170]

In 1333 Richard le Webbe and Roger Brown and Richard Skill of Molton committed the offence of coming into Exmoor Forest and burning 1,000 acres of heath ' to the damage of the Lord King and to the injury of his deer.'[171]

At an inquisition at Wells 1363 it was found that John Proctor of North Molton surcharged the forest when he had no common to the extent of 60 sheep.[172] From this we gather how the owners of the adjoining Devon manors made encroachments on Exmoor. At an inquisition of Somerton 1365 James de Andele of North Molton was accused of badly inclosing his forest ' so that the deer could enter therein ' probably by making a deer leap. At this inquisition Robert Hacche Abbot of Athelney, who had the manor of Bossington on the extreme east of the enlarged Exmoor Forest, was accused, in company with his brother, Henry Hacche, of making a ' stabulum,' i.e. a shelter or resting place in a wood called Lefhanger without the forest and in the same place caught a hart calf. He is the same Robert who in 1365 was accused of poaching in North Petherton Forest. At an inquisition as to the condition of Exmoor Forest, held at Wells in May 1367, before Peter atte Wood, it was stated that Sir Robert Cornu, knight, had at the previous Allhallowstide killed a hart in Dulverton parish, when supposed to be engaged in fox hunting. It was also stated that two offenders had taken and killed a young hart calf within the Devonshire Hundred of Witheridge, which was within the regard of Exmoor Forest. An official statement had been made in the previous year that all the forest ministers of Exmoor belonged to the county of Somerset, but that

the regard and hence the bounds of the forest extended into parts of Devon.[173] At a further inquisition as to Exmoor, held at Somerton in 1369, Sir John Sully, knight, was charged with taking a staggard (a hart of the fourth year) and a hind on Wednesday in Easter week.[174]

In November 1377 Richard II granted Baldwin Radyngton, king's esquire, and Matilda his wife, to inclose at pleasure, notwithstanding the assize of the forest, all their demesne lands in Somerset within the metes of the forests of Exmoor and Petherton, which had been wasted and destroyed year by year by the deer, so as to prevent the deer from entering and thus to hold these premises for their lives.[175]

Edward IV in 1462 granted for life to William Bourgchier of Fitzwarren, knight, the master forestership of Exmoor, receiving the usual fees in the same manner as Thomas Courtenay, late Earl of Devon. Six years later the king granted the reversion of the same office for life to Humphrey Stafford, knight, on the death of William Bourgchier. In 1470, John Dynham obtained from the Crown the grant for life of the custody of the king's forests of Exmoor and Neroche, with the herbage and pannage and the courts of swainmote, rendering yearly to the king forty marks.[176]

Henry VII, when he came to the throne in 1485, seems to have put the control of the venison of Exmoor into the hands of his chamberlain, Lord Daubeny.[176a]

On the marriage of Henry VIII with Catherine of Aragon, Exmoor was settled on the queen as part of her jointure.[176b] In 1520 Sir Thomas Boleyn covenanted with the Earl of Devonshire to give up certain forests, offices, etc., which he held of Queen Katherine at a yearly rent of £46 13s. 4d., saving and reserving 100 deer to remain in the forest of Exmoor. The forest was afterwards held by Henry's third wife, Jane Seymour.[177]

Leland, writing about 1540, has the following note on Exmoor: ' From Exford to Simonbath's bridge, a 4 miles al by Forest, Baren and Morisch ground wher ys store and breading of yong Catelle, but little or no Corne or Habitation.'

In 1598 Hugh Pollard was ranger of the forest, and kept a pack of hounds at Simonsbath. James I granted Exmoor Forest to his queen, Anne of Denmark. Charles I, on coming to the throne, granted a lease for 22½ years to the Earl of Pembroke of the ' Forest and Chace of Exmore in the counties of Devon and Somerset and of the manor of Exmore for fourteen years

---

[168] There are several perambulations of Exmoor extant, two in 1279, one in 1298, and the Parliamentary Survey of 1651, which gives a very good account of the forest in Stuart times. (Aug. Off. Somers. no. 18.) The earlier perambulations appear in the Wells MSS. rot. 3, fol. 85 in dorso and fol. 86; they are printed in Collinson's *Hist. of Somers.* iii, 57 and also in Rawle's *Annals of Exmoor.* These four perambulations are compared and discussed in Greswell's *The Forests and Deerparks of Somerset* (1905).

[169] Pat. 11 Edw. I, m. 8.

[170] Close, 19 Edw. I, m. 8.

[171] Forest Proc. Tr. of R. 153, m. 15.

[172] Forest Proc. Tr. of R. 309.

[173] Forest Proc. Tr. of R. 309.   [174] Ibid.

[175] Pat. 1 Ric. II, pt. ii, m. 34.

[176] Pat. 1 Edw. IV, pt. i, m. 13; 8 Edw. IV, pt. i, m. 21; 10 Edw. IV, m. 12.

[176a] Cf. *Trevelyan Papers,* Introd. p. ix.

[176b] Pat. 1 Hen. VIII, pt. i, m. 8.

[177] *L. and P. Hen. VIII,* iii, 834; xii (2), 975.

. . . with a further clause of liberty to him to build a lodge in the forest at his charges and to inclose and lay one hundred acres of land there unto.' [178]

In Stuart times Exmoor Forest was leased out to William Pincombe, gent. in the reign of James I for £46 13s. 4d.[179] There were 53 'sutes' or 'sutors' belonging to the forest who for their service had for every 'suite' '140 sheep to strake and goe at their pleasure in the Forest, being put out of their folds every morning and brought back every evening, five horses, mares and colts and as many cattle as they winter on their tenements.' Amongst their services the 'sutors' had to attend the forester or his officer at his request to drive the usual 'prayes and drifts' of cattle, horses and sheep depasturing in the forest to a pound. Each sutor may be required to make 9 'prayes or drifts' and meet at certain places. There is still a place name 'Prayway' close to Simonsbath. The sutors had no right to fish in the river Barrel (Barle), this belonging to the leaseholders of the forest.

In the old forest there were few trees. In 1622 it appears to have been practically treeless. According to the statement of a certain Walter Dollen of Stoke Pero giving evidence in a lawsuit 'there were no woods in the said Forest except one oak called Kite Oak.' [180] Starkey in his description of England wrote that the deer 'love a lean barren ground,' such indeed as Exmoor provides to the deer. But they do not despise the rich lowlands, as farmers know to their cost in the country of the Devon and Somerset staghounds.

In the Parliamentary Survey of 1651,[181] already alluded to, there is an interesting memorandum by the commissioners describing the 'Chase' of Exmoor, as it is there termed : 'The said Chase is mountainous and cold ground, much beclouded with thick fogges and mists and is used for depasturing of cattle, horses and sheep and is a very sound sheep pasture. But a very great part thereof is overgrown with heath and yielding but a poor kind of turf of little value there.'

In a lawsuit of 1657 [182] the chase of Exmoor is described as having formerly belonged to Sir John Poyntz and Elizabeth his wife : as having then passed to their daughter Lady Thurles, wife of George Matthewes, for her life. She with her said husband conveyed her interest in the forest (29 November 1634) to Sir Lewes Pollard, bart., who conveyed the reversion after his death until that of the above Elizabeth to Sir John Northcott, bart., Sir

John Chichester, kt., Francis Pollard and John Rosier, gent. (30 September 1641). There was an ancient custom that after the ninth day before the feast of St. John Baptist, all sheep found unshorn in the forest were forfeited and taken by the farmer or owner of the forest.[183] A goat was always a 'forfeit beast,' and so were pigs and geese.

Within a few months of his accession Charles II granted a lease of Exmoor with the custody of the same for thirty-one years to James Butler, Marquess of Ormonde.[184]

In 1784 a lease of the forest and chase of Exmoor, with the courts and royalties, was granted to Sir Thomas Dyke Acland, bart. This was the last lease granted by the Crown.[184a]

In 1815 an Act of Parliament was passed for the disafforesting and inclosing of the forest of Exmoor [185] in the counties of Somerset and Devon. The extent of the forest was then found to be only 18,810 acres, which were thus allotted : a little more than half to the king; one-eighth to Sir T. D. Acland in lieu of the tithes of the whole forest which he held; and the remainder to 'owners of certain estates, to which free suits were attached, and to several other persons, in respect of old enclosed tenements lying in various parishes bordering on the forest.' The king's portion was at once offered for sale and his 10,262¼ acres were purchased by Mr. John Knight for £50,000. This part of the forest has since been purchased by the Fortescue family of Castle Hill.

KEYNSHAM, FILLWOOD AND KINGSWOOD

A great part of Keynsham Hundred, in the north-east corner of the county, was originally reckoned as a royal chase. Leland, writing in 1540, makes mention of a park of the king's just outside Keynsham, which was walled with stone.[186] In 1224 Ralph de Wilinton the governor of Bristol Castle was made warden of the forest and chase of Keynsham.[187] In 1328 a petition was presented to Parliament by Joan la Warre, complaining that the manor of Brislington, which then and always was outside the bounds of the king's chase called Kingswood and also that of Fillwood, had been included in the said chases by the wardens.[188]

In 1485 Sir Giles Daubeny, a famous Somerset man who was lord of the manor of South Petherton and other properties in the county, was made 'Master of the Game of the forest of

---

[178] *Cal. S. P. Dom.* 1625–6, p. 67.
[179] Exch. Dep. by Com. Mich. 8 Jas. I, no. 6.
[180] Ibid. Mich. 20 Jas. I, Somers. no. 20.
[181] Aug. Off. Somers. no. 18.
[182] Exch. Rep. by Com. East. 1651, no. 31.

[183] Exch. Rep. by Com. East. 20 Jas. I, Somers. no. 20.
[184] *Cal. S. P. Dom.* 1660–1, pp. 142, 496.
[184a] Collinson, op. cit. ii, 20.
[185] 55 Geo. III, cap 138.
[186] *Itin.* vii, 104.
[187] Collinson, *Hist. of Somers.* ii, 299.   [188] Ibid.

Kyngeswode near Bristol and Filwood in Somerset.[189]

The forest or chase of Kingswood was in Gloucestershire, immediately to the east of Bristol, but with it was usually coupled the Somerset chase of Fillwood. This well-wooded tract extending into both counties, on either side of the River Avon, was for a long period held as appendant to the castle of Bristol.[190]

Norden's MS. Survey of Fillwood,[191] made early in the 17th century, is worth quoting *in extenso*.

TOUCHINGE FILLWOODE CHACE

For wante of the boundarie and perambulation of the same chace I could by noe examination find the extente. But it is proved by other that the deere raunginge out of the forest ouer the riuer of Auon freely and without disturbaunce feed as farr as Dundry hilles neer 4 myles from the forest of Kingswood and in diuers places betweene the said hills and the forest. But time and discontinuaunce of vse have forgotten the names, altered the bounds and lost the lands formerly knowne vsed and inioyed as belonginge vnto his Maᵗⁱˢ Chace of Fillwoode.

Some groundes yet retaine the name and they by diuers depositions are affirmed to be fower, all which by othe are proved to be one and the same intirely to be impalled, converted to a parke and stored with deere by one Mr. Hughe Smythe vncle to Sir Hughe Smythe that nowe is possessor of the same and contayned a parke aboute 6 yeares and then disparked and the pales carried to Ashton the howse of Sir Hughe Smythe.

Theis 4 groundes containe aboute 249 acres.

And the particulars are in nature and supposed yearly value as followeth. A medowe contayninge about 35 acr. worth per acre 20s. in toto per ann. £35. A pasture ground next the meadowe about 66 acr. 18s. per acre £59 8s. A more roughe pasture ground west of the wood 69 acre 15s. per acre, £51 15s. The wood, good land were it stocked 79 acr. 16s. per acre £63 4s.

Soe the yeerely value were
the wood cleered might
amounte vnto . . . £209 12s. per annum.
The wood and timber pre-
sently growinge ther vpon
maye be supposed worth £1,300.
So were it cleere in his
Maᵗⁱˢ disposeng it might
well yeald his Maᵗⁱᵉ . . £5,487.

PROBABILITIES OF A FARTHER EXTENTION OF FILLWOODE GROUNDES.

It appeereth by othe that these fower groundes aboue mentioned were sometimes one and not manie years since diuided in the south parte of which groundes is a spacious pasture now knowne by the name of Leaze Wood containing about 113 acres which peice of land appeareth allso to be all one with the former before the impalling, as appeareth by a quicksett hedge, seemeinge to be of the same antiquitie with the quick settes of the fower closes, or litle elder, the field allso in the tenure of Mr. Hughe Smythe.

Moreouer there is at this presente a wast ground or a reputed Comon knowne allso by the name of Leaze Wood adioyninge to the pasture called Leaze Wood afforesaid and proued by othe to have bene all one and deuided not manye yeares since in the memorie of the deponents and now as the deponents thinke that parte which lyeth comon is vsed as Comon by the tenauntes of Whitchurch and the timber trees and wood growinge vpon the same are claimed and taken by Sir Hughe Smythe.

If this prove parcell of Fillwood groundes as is most probable, the land and wood will yeald his Maᵗⁱᵉ being recouered nere £4,000.

It is allso supposed that ther is a common or wast ground, within the supposed bounds of the same chace called Bristleton Heith, which is supposed to containe about 200 acr. and that ther are or have bene coale mines within the same, which the confining lords have taken and have inclosed much of the same Comon and take the profittes both of the land and mines.

It may be probable that manie other grounds within the perambulation of this chace maye vpon further inquisition be found to appertaine in righte of his Maᵗⁱˢ.

ANCIENT PARKS

It may be well, in addition to the old parks which have been already incidentally mentioned—such as those of Witham and Forshefe in the 1298 perambulation of the forest of Selwood—to give a few particulars relative to ancient inclosures of the county, whether within or without forest jurisdiction.

The Bishop of Bath and Wells obtained licence from King John to inclose a park at Wells.[192] Leland noticed two other parks belonging to the church : 'A mile on this syde Bathe by southe est, I saw two parks enclosed with a ruinus stone waulle, now witheout Dere, one longyd to the Byshope, an other to the Prior of Bathe.'[193] The Bishop of Bath and Wells had also an inclosed park within his manor of Cheddar. The licence to disafforest this manor and to make a park there brought about a riot, which was suppressed in 1338 by Thomas, third Lord Berkeley.[194] Poaching in parks outside forest jurisdiction was punished by the common law of the land. Thus at Montacute in 1314, Aukel the son of John de Bourville and others were presented before the *Custodes Pacis* for breaking the park of Henry Lorty (de Urtiaco) near Stoke Trister and for setting nets and other engines for the taking of venison.[195]

There were seven parks appendant to the abbey of Glastonbury. The largest of these was Northwood which, at the time of the Dissolution, was in splendid condition. 'It contained in circuit four miles, the pales well repaired, the herbage very good and sweet, wherein are 800 deer, whereof there are of deer of antler 160,

---

[189] Greswell, *Forests and Deerparks of Somerset*, 204.
[190] *V.C.H. Glouc.* ii, 264-5.
[191] (P.R.O.) S.P. Dom. Jas. I (1615), lxxxiv, 46.

[192] Pat. 3. John.   [193] *Itin.* vii, 100.
[194] Smyth, *Lives of the Berkeleys*, 130.
[195] Misc. R. Chan. bdle. 16, no. 25.

deer of rascall (does) 640. Within this park there are 172 acres of wood of the age of twenty years and heretofore have always been used to be felled and sold every sixteen years, every acre thereof at this present survey worth 20s.—£172 10s. 6d.' [196] Northwood is thus noticed by Leland, 'Northwood Park a mile by est from Glaston; John Selwood, Abbott, builded a place there.' The total area of this park, which was in two divisions, was 570 acres.[197] Sir Simon de Montagu with others was indicted in 1304 for cutting down 100 trees in an alder-grove of the Abbot of Glastonbury.[198]

Sharpham, a country seat of the abbot, 2 miles from Glastonbury, is described in the survey just quoted as having a park 2 miles in circuit wherein were 160 fallow deer. The park also included 80 acres of wood well set with oak, ash and maple which used to be felled and sold every fourteen years and each acre was worth 6s. 8d. There were also within this park 200 oaks fit for timber, valued at 11s. each.

The same survey names Wyrral Park to the west of Glastonbury, which had a circuit of a mile and a quarter and a hundred deer, as well as Pilton Park to the east of Glastonbury, with a circuit of 3 miles and 350 deer.

In the neighbourhood of the forest of Neroche were several old parks, of which that of Mery-field was the most considerable. The parks of White Lackington near Ilminster and Hinton St. George are both noticed by Leland. The latter attracted the special attention of Cosmo III, Grand Duke of Tuscany in his remarkable travels through England in the year 1669.[199]

There were a few other old parks in the county, such as Ubley in the north-east, licensed to be imparked in 1329 and Ashill in the south, licensed for imparking in 1411 [200]; but one of the most interesting old park districts yet remains for brief notice.

In 1220 Peter de Mauley was commissioned to look after ' nostram Forestam de Dunne-storre,' but what was meant by this is not exactly clear as the phrase does not occur else-where.[201] It probably means the forest lands contiguous to Dunster and belonging to the great barony of the Mohuns, in Minehead, Car-hampton and Cutcombe-Mohun. There was a very ancient ' Deerfald ' at Minehead mentioned in old documents,[202] now utterly bereft of its old

features. In Dunster Park there was the old park still known as ' The Hanger Park.' The mediaeval park of Dunster would seem to have included the sloping ground between the town and the river as well as the northern portion of the level beyond the river, now known as ' The Lawn.' [203] Nearer the sea was a park at Marsh-wood long known by that name, and more im-portant, as long as it was maintained, than the park at Dunster.

The certificate of the musters for the county of Somerset, forwarded to the Privy Council on 30 September 1583, included, according to instructions, a list of the parks and inclosed grounds, which was furnished in connexion with projects for furthering the breeding of horses. The following is a transcript of this interesting list :

Sr George Speake Knight hath twoe parkes and inclosed groundes for deere eache of them of one myle compasse and keapeth iiijor mares according to the Statute.

George Luttrell Esq. hath ij parkes the one at Dunstar the other at Quantock head each of them one myle compas and keepeth iiijor mares according to the statute.

John Coles Esq. hath one parke at Coripole in the right of younge Mallett being one Myle compas and keepeth ij mares according to the statute.

Edward Stradling gent holdeth in Leas from the said George Luttrell one parke at Marshwood of one myle compas and keepeth ij mares according to the Statute.

Sir John Clifton knight hath twoo parkes or in-closed groundes for deere, thone at Staple being twoo myles compas and thother at Barington being one myle compas and keepeth v mares according to the statute.

Sir John Stowell knight hath one grounde inclosed for deere at Cothelston of one myle compas and keapeth twoo mares according to the Statute.

The La: Elizabeth Pawlett widowe hath one parke or inclosed grounde for deere at Georgehenton of twoo myles compas and keapeth iij mares according to the Statute.

Nicholas Wadham Esqr hath one parke at Merifeld and keapeth ij mares according to the Statute, the same parke little above one myle compas.

Edward Popham Esqr hath one grounde inclosed for deere at Huntworth of one myle compas and keapeth two mares according to the Statute.

Thomas Wrothe Esqr and five other of his brethren dwelling about London have one parke at Petherton of iiijor myles compas almost decayed but doe keape no mares in yt.

Christopher Smythe Esq. dothe holde one parke at Sharpham of twoo myles compas and keapeth iij mares according to the Statute.

All theis are furnished bothe of their mares and stallyons of their owne sufficienc except the owners of Petherton Parke.

[196] Dugdale, Mon. i, 10.
[197] Leland, Itin. iii, 120.
[198] Assize R. 764, m. 1.
[199] His travels were published in English 1821.
[200] See Shirley, Deer and Deerparks, 95–9; and more especially the concluding chapter of Greswell's Forests and Deerparks of Somers. 242–62.
[201] See preceding account of Neroche Forest and grant of king to bishop of deer from Dunster, 10 Edw. I (1281).
[202] Bruton Chart.

[203] Sir H. Maxwell-Lyte, History of Dunster, ii, 344. To this work the reader is referred for a fuller account of the parks at Dunster and Marshwood than can be given here.

And for the matter of severall pastures of one myle compas and the comens within this countye with the use thereof to be dealt in according to the direcions for that they are manye and in manie places dispersed, yt could not be dispatched with this expedition according to the direcions, but shal be dealt in accordinge to the same with all expedition.

This certificate is signed by Sir John Stowell, Sir John Clyfton and four other commissioners.[204]

MODERN DEER PARKS AND ARBORI-CULTURE

There are at present eleven deer-parks or paddocks within the county, namely those of: Ashton, Dunster, St. Audries, Ammerdown, Halswell, Pixton, Nettlecombe, Alfoxton, Brockley, Combe Sydenham and Hatch.

Ashton Court, the seat of the Dowager Lady Smyth, near Bristol, stands in a beautifully wooded park of 1,000 acres, stocked with 400 fallow and 200 red deer.[205]

Dunster Castle, the historic seat of Mr. Alexander Fownes Luttrell, has a beautiful and finely-timbered park of which Leland says ' Ther is a praty park joyning to the est part of the Castelle.'[206] The deer park contains about 348 acres; it is now stocked with about 150 head of fallow deer, the number of which has diminished in recent years. The following are the sizes of some of the finest timber, the measurement being taken 3 ft. from the ground :

Elm Pollard	22 ft.	in circumference		
Oak Pollard	20 ft.	in	,,	
Oak	,,	16 ft. 4 in.	,,	
Plane	,,	16 ft. 5 in.	,,	
Ash	,,	14 ft.	,,	
Poplar	,,	21 ft. 6 in.	,,	

There is also in the park a rare black poplar. In 1901 the old woods of this estate comprised 972 acres, and the plantations 660 acres. Since that date 100 additional acres have been planted. Mr. Luttrell has always planted for profit.[207]

At that beautiful point of the West Somerset coast where the Quantock Hills dip into the Bristol Channel there is a noble stretch of parkland near St. Audries, or West Quantockshead, close to the seat of Captain Sir Alexander Fuller-Acland-Hood, bart. The old Luttrell (East Quantockshead) park is mentioned by Leland in the time of Henry VIII :[208] ' St.

Audries; In this paroche, I saw a fair Park and Manor place of the Lutterelles caullid Quantok Hedde.' In 1583, as already stated, it is described as being a mile in compass. The modern St. Audries deer park, consisting of 350 acres, is stocked with 120 fallow deer and twenty-five red deer. About 50 acres on this estate have been planted with ash, elm and sycamore, for commercial purposes, since 1892.[209]

Ammerdown, in Kilmersdon parish, the seat of Lord Hylton, stands within a park about 4 miles in circumference surrounded by a wall, 8 ft. high. The acreage thus inclosed is about 500, but at the present time the deer range over only about 200. The herd is of fallow deer, and they now number about a hundred. This is not an ancient deer park; it was in the first instance formed by Thomas Samuel Jolliffe, an ancestor of Lord Hylton, between the years 1787 and 1790 by throwing together certain fields and down-land. Some additions have been made to its area at a later date. His son, Col. John Twyford Jolliffe, first started the herd of deer about the year 1834, with a few imported from a park in Gloucestershire. The park is beautifully wooded. Beech is the tree which thrives the best; there are some good clumps and groves of this tree which are now 120 years old. There are also a few fine Turkey oaks, which are probably of the same date. The common oak attains no special size. There are also a few ancient elms and ash, which appear to be relics of the original hedgerow timber before the formation of the park. Silver fir grows well on the upper ground and limes on the lower ground of this undulating park. During the last thirty-five years, many small plantations have been made on this estate; but practically all for game or landscape purposes. There are, altogether, some 400 acres of woodland on this estate. The coppice is cut in rotation, every 9 or 10 years, when such timber as has reached its prime is then thinned out. Underwood fetches from 30s. to £2 an acre. There is no demand for faggots, and sheep-wire is largely used in place of hurdles.[210]

Halswell Park, in the parish of Goathurst, the seat of Mr. Charles Kemeys-Tynte, stands within a noble and well-wooded park of 220 acres, which is stocked with 150 fallow deer and sixty red deer. In the thickets above the park is a heronry. The park, which is undoubtedly a

---

[204] S. P. Dom. Eliz. clxii, 44 (2).

[205] These are the figures given by Mr. Whitaker in 1892.

[206] Leland, *Itin.* ii, 98.

[207] From information kindly supplied by Mr. J. H. Davis the estate agent.

[208] Leland, *Itin.* ii, 98. But Leland confuses West Quantockshead, i.e. St. Audries (where the deer park is quite modern) with East Quantockshead, the Luttrell manor which has ' never been bought or sold since the Conquest ' and the site of the old

Elizabethan Park mentioned in ' the Musters ' (*vide supra*).

[209] From information courteously supplied by Sir A. Acland-Hood.

[210] From information courteously communicated by Lord Hylton. His lordship adds, ' There is no encouragement for landowners to plant for other objects than game or landscape, as we are heavily rated on our young plantations, during all those years when they are only an expense and not a profit.'

portion of the old forest of Petherton, contains several very ancient oaks 'which a competent judge of timber considers to be upwards of nine hundred or even a thousand years old.' Sixty acres of this estate have been replanted during the last four years at Kingscliff, and 30 acres adjoining the park, principally of larch, Japanese larch and Douglas fir.[211]

Pixton Park, near Dulverton, a former seat of the Earl of Carnarvon, is beautifully situated in a deer park of about 150 acres which is at present stocked with 118 fallow deer. It is well timbered, with oak, beech, ash and other forest trees.[212]

Nettlecombe Court, the seat of Sir W. J. Trevelyan, bart., stands in a most beautifully wooded park of 97 acres, containing exceptionally fine oaks, chestnuts and other forest trees and stocked with a small herd of fallow deer. The oaks in this park are far famed and used to be in great request for navy purposes. Among the muniments at Nettlecombe Court is the original grant made by King Edward III on 5 July 1359 of free warren in all his domain lands of Nettlecombe and Rowdon. Among the witnesses to this grant are the Earls of Lincoln, Lancaster, Gloucester, Hereford, Essex and Warwick.

Alfoxton is a modern park of about 80 acres, on the northern slopes of the Quantock Hills. It has some fine timber and is stocked with a small herd of fallow deer. The house is celebrated as having been the residence of the poet Wordsworth in 1797 when Coleridge was at Nether Stowey.

At Brockley Court, near Weston-super-Mare, the seat of Mrs. Smyth-Pigott, there is a small deer park of about 27 acres in extent, stocked with a score of fallow deer. It is well timbered with old oak trees and some very fine larch; during the last four years there has been considerable planting of forest trees for landscape purposes. Within the park is an old-established heronry.[213]

At Combe Sydenham Hall, in the parish of Stogumber, the seat of Mr. Marwood Notley, there is a small deer park of 13 acres stocked with about a score of fallow deer and a few red deer.

Hatch Park, in the parish of Hatch Beauchamp,

the seat of Mr. W. H. Lloyd, has a small park of 8½ acres, which is thickly stocked with a herd of about forty fallow deer. The estate is well timbered with elm, oak and ash in hard wood, as well as with Scotch fir and larch.

THE WOODLANDS

A General View of the Agriculture in the County of Somerset was drawn up by John Billingsley in 1794 under the auspices of the Board of Agriculture. The usual plan adopted in the county reports of this date of giving a special section to woods and plantations was not followed with regard to Somerset. There are, however, various remarks as to the woodland and timber interspersed in the accounts of the different districts. Of the north-east division it is remarked that there are many woods, the largest being that of Kingswood which covered 230 acres. The timber was mainly oak, but did not grow to any great size. The underwood was cut 'for wreaths or faggots.' The valleys were richly laden with hedgerow elms; the method practised here of lopping off the side branches, to what is called a besom head, cannot be too much execrated.

In the division of the Mendip Hills, the coppices were frequent and rapid in growth. The more ashes in these coppices the more valuable they were, for the poles were very saleable at the coalpit and instances are cited of an acre producing the large sum of £16 after the expenses of cutting and carriage had been deducted. In the eastern part of this district there were also some large and productive woods such as Mells, Leigh, Edford, Harwich, Compton and Camely. Those near the coal works were very valuable.

As to Selwood, Mr. Billingsley considered that the ancient forest comprised a vale of about 20,000 acres, about 18,000 of which had been 'cleansed and converted into pasture and arable land the remainder being chiefly in a state of coppice wood.' The chief sorts of timber in these coppices were oak and ash of a small growth but good of their kind, the oak selling from 50s. to £3 16s. a ton, and the ash from 45s. to £3. There had been little grubbing of woodland during the past forty years, but much new ground had been planted, particularly on the hills belonging to the Marquess of Bath, Mr. Beckford and Sir Richard Hoare.

In the west district, particularly round Dulverton and Dunster, special attention is drawn to the beech hedges or banks 6 or 7 ft. high and between 4 and 5 ft. wide at the top. The hedge, consisting of three rows of beeches a foot apart, grows rapidly, and becomes 'not only beautiful to the eye and an excellent fence and shelter but also an annual source of profit to the proprietor.'

[211] From information kindly supplied by Mr. Theobald L. Walsh, agent for the Halswell estate.

[212] In 1901 Lord Carnarvon sold the house, park and about 5,000 acres of the surrounding property to the Dowager Countess of Carnarvon. Lord Carnarvon still retains about 6,000 acres in the Dulverton district and during the last six years has planted about 50 acres, chiefly for commercial purposes. From information kindly supplied by Mr. J. D. Scott, the estate agent.

[213] From information kindly supplied by the estate agent.

In 1796 Mr. W. Marshall published two volumes on *The Rural Economy of the West of England*. His remarks on Somerset are far briefer than those on Devon and Dorset. In passing through the vale of Taunton, he noted how the old 'Damnonian Fence,' or high coppice-crowned mound, gave way to a low broad bank, loaded with coppice and interspersed with large hedgerow elms. On the Blackdown Hills, Mr. Marshall passed ' a young plantation of forest trees of different species, put in among dwarf furze ; the first instance of planting observed in this journey of near a hundred miles ! At North Curry there was an instance of a young field orchard ; the plants tall and set out at good distances in the best Herefordshire manner, that is in a state of arable culture. Several of these orchards were noted when journeying from Taunton to Somerton.

The county has long been celebrated for the size and beauty of its trees in the more fertile parts.[214]

Loudon mentions an elm at Nettlecombe, 210 years old, 100 ft. high, with a girth of 17 ft. ; it had its head blown off in 1890.[215] Loudon also tells of an elm at Leigh Court, fourteen years old, which was then 50 ft. high. Mr. Chisholm Batten names a magnificent Turkey oak, having a girth of 15 ft. and a height of 60 ft. ; it is probably the same Turkey oak that is named by Loudon as having been planted in 1754 and which had then a girth of 9 ft.

At Chipley, near Nynehead, there is a magnificent occidental plane, with a height of over 100 ft., and a spread of 120 ft. which was planted in 1760.[216] An oriental plane at the vicarage, Lydeard St. Lawrence, is 80 ft. high, 10 ft. in girth and has a spread of 53 ft.

An oak at Hazlegrove Park (Queen Camel) long known as the ' Old Oak ' and thus mentioned in old papers of the 16th century, has a girth of 35 ft. at 5 ft. from the ground, and there are others almost as large. There are also some singularly fine old oaks at Alford House, as well as an elm, the height of which in 1888 was estimated to be 112 ft. At Mells Park there is a pollard oak which had a girth in 1888 of 23 ft. 6 in. at 5 ft. from the ground. Two oaks at Cucklington have a girth of 19 and 16 ft. with a spread of 90 and 80 ft. respectively.

The common walnut, which originally came to Europe from Persia and Cashmere, was thriving in England as early as Elizabethan days. This tree appears specially to love the soil of Somerset ; it flourishes more particularly in the west of the county in the neighbourhood of Minehead, Porlock and Luccombe, where the roads are often flanked with walnut trees.[217] The Cothelstone walnut at the southern base of the Quantocks, blown down in 1897, was said to have been the finest specimen in England. Loudon in 1836 gave the height as 64 ft., but in 1888 the height had reached to 94 ft. 9 in., whilst the girth was 18 ft. The spread of the branches at the latter date was 27 yds. by 22 yds. The little village of Bossington is sheltered beneath several giant walnut trees. The largest of these, owing to its closeness to the village street and cottages, has had to be cut back in some of its largest limbs on more than one occasion. Its height is about 50 ft., the girth 2 ft. from the ground is 21 ft. 4 in., whilst at 5 ft. from the ground it has a girth of 16 ft. It far surpasses the Cothelstone walnut or indeed any other such tree throughout England in massiveness and picturesque effect.

Somerset is famed for the frequency and size of its churchyard yews. Forty-two receive special mention in the volumes of Collinson's county history. In Mr. Lowe's monograph on this subject eight Somerset yews appear in the schedule of large trees ; the girth measurement is taken 3 ft. from the ground. Dinder, 31 ft. in girth ; Ashill, (*a*) 20 ft., (*b*) 15 ft. ; Allerton, 16 ft. ; Broomfield, 16 ft. ; Buckland St. Mary, 15 ft. 6 in. ; Puckington, 11 ft. and Stogursey, 10 ft. 6 in. (now gone). The Puckington yew is of interest, for it is known from the parish records that it was planted in 1727.[218]

Mr. Lowe has, however, omitted to include in his list several of the most noteworthy of the Somerset yews. There is for instance a grand old trunk in Porlock churchyard, which has a girth of 14 ft., one at Kilve with a girth of 19 ft. at 3 ft. from the ground with a beautifully preserved head. In Wootton Courtney churchyard there is a most noble wide-spreading yew. Its beauty attracted the attention of Collinson at the end of the 18th century. Its present girth at ground level is 18 ft. 2 in. and 4 ft. from ground 14 ft. 10 in. whilst the spread of its branches from north to south is 64 ft. 7 in. and from east to west 59 ft. 2 in.

Nowhere in the whole county has there been so much beautifully marshalled planting throughout the 19th century as on the Somerset estates of the Acland family, in the vale of Porlock on the eastern fringe of Exmoor and also at Winsford. This planting has chiefly taken the form of various conifers in which the Douglas fir largely predominates. The beauty of the Selworthy woods stretching out from that village until they nearly reach Hurtstone Point can scarcely be exaggerated. On the crown of these woods, where they overshadow Allerford

---

[214] There are good papers on ' The Forest Trees of Somerset ' in the *Proc. Somers. Arch. Soc.* xxxvi (2), 175 et seq. and xxxvii (2), 106 et seq. by Mr. Chisholm Batten.

[215] Loudon, *Arbor. Brit.* (1838), iv, 1393.

[216] Selby, *Forest Trees*, 360.

[217] Loudon, op. cit. 1421.

[218] Lowe, *Yew Trees of Gt. Brit. and Ireland* (1897).

and Bossington, the present baronet has erected a plain roughly squared wooden cross, some 30 feet high, in a clearing at the top of the hill, with the simple inscription, In Memoriam T.D.A. 1809–1898. Near the centre of the Selworthy woods is a guide post to the various footpaths, the centre shaft of which bears this inscription— '600 feet Silver Firs, T.D.A. 1809.' This date supplies the year of the beginning of the planting.

The acreage of Somerset woods in 1891 amounted to 42,438, exclusive of plantations; the latter, which included all that had been planted within the last ten years, amounted to 2,100, giving a total of 44,538. There was an increase of about a thousand acres up to 1895, when the full return reached 45,650. During the next ten years there was a further gain of about a like amount, for the last return of England's woodlands, made on 5 June 1905, gives a total for Somerset of 46,788. Of this total 1,557 acres had been planted or replanted within the past ten years; whilst 16,421 acres are entered as 'coppice,' that is woods cut over periodically which reproduce themselves naturally by stool shoots.

SPORT ANCIENT AND MODERN

HUNTING

THERE is hardly a shire in England, save perhaps her sister Devonshire, that offers a greater variety of sport than the fair county of Somerset. On her moors roam at will the wild red deer, her coverts are tenanted by wild foxes, her combes are the haunt of the badger, her downs are the playground of the stoutest of hares, and her rivers and streams hold trout and salmon, and otters too in great abundance. For the shooting man there is nearly every variety of bird that finds a place in the game lists—pheasant, partridge, black game, snipe, woodcock, plover both golden and green, curlew, wild duck, wild geese, and occasionally swans. Surely Somerset has been rightly named the sportsman's paradise. In our county are kennelled the Devon and Somerset (once styled the North Devon) Staghounds at Exford, the Quantock Staghounds at Quantock Lodge near Bridgwater, and Sir John Amory's Staghounds at Hensleigh near Tiverton; Oare was once the home of Mr. Peter Ormrod's Staghounds, while the now disbanded Barnstaple Staghounds occasionally hunted in Somerset by invitation.

STAGHOUNDS

THE DEVON AND SOMERSET AND THE QUANTOCK

The earliest record of the existence of a pack of staghounds in this district is in the year 1598, when Hugh Pollard, ranger to Queen Elizabeth, kept a pack of staghounds at Simonsbath. The succeeding rangers of the forest continued to keep hounds for the purpose of hunting the deer; and about the year 1700 the pack passed into the possession of Mr. Walter of Stevenstone and Lord Oxford, who were foresters of Exmoor under grant from the crown. Mr. Dyke succeeded Lord Oxford, and hunted the country for many years with great success. Then came his kinsman Sir Thomas Dyke-Acland, third baronet, also ranger of the royal forest, who hunted the country till 1770 in princely style. His second son, Thomas, afterwards the fourth baronet, succeeded him, though

from 1775 till 1784 Colonel Basset of Watermouth was in command, the first person not ranger of the forest to be master of the hounds. From 1784 till 1794 Sir Thomas Dyke-Acland was again at the head of affairs, but on his death Colonel Basset once more took the country, which he held till his death in 1801. Hugh, first Earl Fortescue, now came forward for one season, keeping the hounds at Castle Hill; but in 1802 they became a subscription pack under the rule of Mr. Worth of Worth House, Tiverton. He held office for eight years (1802–10), resigning in 1811 in favour of Thomas North, second Lord Graves, of Bishop's Court near Exeter. One season passed, and then Lord Fortescue again became master, holding office till 1818. Once more the pack became a subscription pack, under the guidance of Mr. Stucley Lucas of Barons Down, Dulverton, for six seasons, when the hounds were sold in 1825 to go to Germany. There was now a gap of two seasons; but in 1827 Sir Arthur Chichester, seventh baronet, became master until 1833. There is another gap of four years till 1837, when a committee hunted the pack for a like period of time. The Hon. Newton Fellowes next carried on the hunt till 1847, when Sir Arthur Chichester, the eighth baronet, took command for one season. In 1849 Mr. Theobald, the first master who was not a west-countryman, took office for one season, as did also Captain West; while in 1850 Mr. George Luxton of Winkleigh brought his harriers to hunt the deer. From 1852–5 Mr. T. Carew of Colipriest was master.

It was in 1855 that staghunting, after experiencing many vicissitudes, took a new lease of life. It was Mr. Mordaunt Fenwick Bisset, known as 'The General,' who came from Berkshire to be the tenant of Pixton House, Dulverton, who restored the fallen fortunes of staghunting. For 27 years he reigned, till in 1881 he handed over the reins of office to Hugh, Viscount Ebrington, now fourth Earl Fortescue. Lord Ebrington held office till 1887, when Mr. C. H. Basset of Watermouth became master; only to be succeeded in 1893 by Colonel Hornby, once vice-master of the Royal Buckhounds. In 1895 Mr. R. A. Sanders took command and hunted the country (with Mr. Morland Greig as deputy-master during the latter portion of his term of office) till 1907, when Mr. E. A. V. Stanley from the Quantock Staghounds became master of the parent pack. Such is a brief outline of the history of stag-hunting; it remains to fill in the details of the picture.

There is but little record of the sport shown by the two Aclands except the inscriptions under the antlers kept as valued trophies at Holnicote. In the reign of Sir Thomas his Honour, boundless hospitality was the order of the day, and it was the regular practice of the master to entertain the whole field after hunting.

After the Aclands came another old west-country family, the Bassets. Their successors were the Fortescues, whose second tenure of office in 1812 revived the glories of the Acland dynasty. The best preserves were the North Molton and Porlock countries. Deer were scarce in the Barnstaple and Dulverton districts, for the hunt was unpopular. Between 1812 and 1818 the number of deer in the country was reckoned at ' 200 head in all, perhaps one hundred short of what there was in old Sir Thomas Acland's time, but still quite enough for sport.' The Bray, North Molton and Porlock coverts held the bulk of the deer at that time. It was then the plan to begin tufting at nine o'clock, or at ten o'clock if the meet were a long way from the kennels. If they tufted till one o'clock without finding a stag they would lay hounds on to a hind, but never went home without running one or the other. Lord Graves indeed says: ' We should begin tufting at 8 o'clock instead of 10 or 11 as heretofore; at that late hour we have gener-ally missed our deer. If it can possibly be avoided a young male deer should never be run; such a chase kills the hounds and horses, or ren-ders them unserviceable for a fortnight, without killing the light galloping deer you pursue.' Perhaps he spoke feelingly, for the first stag he ever saw killed was a ' light galloping deer,' which ran from Castle Hill to the borders of Dartmoor in the course of a six or seven hours' chase.

There were some odd payments made in Lord Graves' day; for instance, a guinea to those farmers who rode the chase and were in at the death, half a crown to the farmer who stopped the tufters, and half a guinea to the foot folk who helped to headline the stag at bay. Lord Graves on resigning the country to Lord Fortes-cue was able to say: ' At present we have the undivided support of every great proprietor in the resort of the deer.' It is not surprising, therefore, that his successor enjoyed many good runs, including the longest chase ever remem-bered—from Dunkery to Satterleigh, 26

miles as the crow flies. For reasons which are not chronicled the fortunes of the hunt did not prosper between 1818 and 1824, and the old pack of true staghounds was sold in 1825 never to return. In those early days Sir Thomas Acland (1784-94) accounted for 150 deer (73 stags, 77 hinds); Colonel Basset (1794-1801) took 124 (49 stags, 75 hinds); Mr. Worth (1802-10) totalled 101 deer (42 stags, 59 hinds); Lord Fortescue (1812-18) scored 90 deer (42 stags, 48 hinds). Of the pack the chronicler says: ' A nobler pack of hounds no man ever saw. They had been in the country for years, and had been bred with the utmost care for the express purpose of staghunting.' How these hounds were bred is not known, but the blood-hound and the old southern hound were beyond doubt among the ancestors of the pack, which when sold consisted of some thirty couples. In height the hounds were about twenty-six to twenty-eight inches, in colour generally hare-pied, yellow, yellow and white, or badger-pied, with long ears, deep muzzles, large throats and deep chests. In tongue they were as near per-fection as possible, and when hunting in the water, or on half scent, or baying a deer, they might be heard at an immense distance. Even when running at speed they always gave plenty of tongue, and their great size enabled them to cross the long heather and rough sedgy pasturage of the forest without effort or difficulty.

Thus closes what may be called the first chapter of Somerset staghunting. Its glories have never been revived, for though deer are now more plentiful and there is no lack of the sinews of war, yet hounds, if faster, are less musical, and the invasion of strangers has naturally curtailed the lavish hospitality and good fellow-ship of the old days. Of this period there is no record left by the various masters, save a manuscript at Castle Hill, the seat of the Fortescue family; but one of those sporting parsons for whom the west-country is so famous, the Reverend John Boyse of Hawkridge and Withy-pool, kept a short journal of the sport between 1780 and 1825. He was known as ' Staghunter Boyse,' was a light weight and a good horseman and knew the moor like a book and the run of the deer better than most men. We find his name frequently mentioned as among those in at the finish of some extraordinary run, indeed more than once ' Boyse was the only one with them ' is the entry in the journal. And here we may note that the clergy of those days appeared at the meet in sober black; but each parson carried a white flannel jacket strapped to his saddle, which he exchanged for his black one when the pack was laid on. Thus clad the parsons rode the chase, only to change once more on the way home that they might give offence to no man. Of these divines the most famous was the Reverend John Russell, ' Parson

Jack' as he was affectionately styled, one of the links between the old times and the new in staghunting; for he saw his first stag killed in 1814 when the first Earl Fortescue was master of the staghounds, and his last in 1884 under his great-grandson, the present earl. It was from Russell that the present generation received the oral traditions of the palmy days of staghunting. Thus it may truly be said that these two parsons, John Boyse and John Russell, the one in manuscript, the other in the flesh, alone have preserved the history of the hundred-year period from 1780 to 1880. Another chronicler must be mentioned—Charles Palk Collyns, to wit, surgeon of Dulverton, who was for nearly half a century the most enthusiastic of staghunters. He was the author of *The Chase of the Wild Red Deer*, a standard work, to which the writer is indebted for very much of the information in this article.

We now enter upon a second period in staghunting history. When the old pack was sold in 1825 staghunting was at its lowest ebb, for poachers and deer-stealers harried the herds incessantly and on all sides land was reclaimed, fenced and planted, and the deer were driven to seek 'fresh woods and pastures new.' But after an interregnum of two years another west-country family, the Chichesters, came to the rescue when Aclands and Bassets and Fortescues had all taken their turn at the helm. It was with a pack of foxhounds that Sir Arthur Chichester hunted the country from 1827 to 1833. Then there was trouble again till in 1837 Mr. Palk Collyns organized a pack that failed for want of funds in 1841. The Hon. Newton Fellowes stepped into the breach and hunted the country till 1847, showing good sport, but offending against the canons of the chase by hunting deer out of season. For one season Sir Arthur Chichester ruled and Mr. Theobald succeeded him. A 'foreigner' to the country he was more used to carted deer, and never took a single wild deer on Exmoor during his one season. Mr. George Luxton's harriers from Winkleigh met with little better success till 1851, when another 'calf' hunter, Captain West, took command, and showed good sport. With Mr. Carew's mastership and Captain West's second mastership this second period of staghunting history closes.

With the advent of Mr. Mordaunt Fenwick Bisset in 1855 staghunting entered upon its third and present period, when staghunting became *the* established sport of the west-country, founded on the sure basis of the good will of landlord and tenant alike, of high and low, rich and poor, when 'Prosperity to Staghunting,' the hunt motto, found an echo in every heart in Devon and Somerset. That this should have been brought about by a shooting man and not by a hunting man is all the more remarkable,

for it is a fact that what attracted Mr. Bisset to the west was not the hunting but the shooting. Before he took Pixton he had never in his life heard of a 'forester,' as a wild deer is called. He soon, however, entered with enthusiasm into the sport of staghunting, one more instance of the influence of environment. It was in the spring of 1855 that Mr. Froude Bellew who had inherited from his uncle, the well-known Parson Froude, a yellow-pied pack of harriers with which he hunted fox, purchased the pack of foxhounds belonging to Mr. Horlock, a well-known M.F.H. of that day.[1] He offered to Mr. Bisset a large draft from this pack, as the nucleus of a pack of staghounds. Relying on promises of support, both financial and otherwise, Mr. Bisset agreed to hunt the country, provided he should be at liberty to give the hounds up at once if sufficient subscriptions were not forthcoming.[2] Thus a novice reluctantly took office, and thus were established the Devon and Somerset Staghounds as we know them to-day. The pack consisted of Mr. Bellew's draft, four and a half couple from Captain West and the Reverend John Russell, a couple and a half of old hounds and four couple of puppies purchased from Mr. Pomeroy Gilbert, eighteen couple in all. These were kennelled at Churchtown kennels, with John Babbage as huntsman; while Arthur Heal, who was to make his mark in after years, and is now hale and hearty in retirement at Exford, left hunting the hare to become whip to the new pack of staghounds. Mr. Bisset held his opening meet at Simonsbath 21 August 1855. Deer poaching was at that time rife, and even the villagers of Exford, now the home of the pack and the holy of holies of staghunting, would turn out to rejoice over the carcass of a poached deer. Nothing daunted, Mr. Bisset proceeded on the even tenour of his way, and on 28 September killed his first stag in the Haddon stream by candlelight at 7.50 p.m. Poor sport however marked his first season, only two stags and two hinds being killed and one stag saved in twenty-five days' hunting. Four of these were blank, and weather stopped hunting on two more. Owing to the constant raids of the deer-stealers, the deer had been scattered far and wide. Thus in his first season Mr. Bisset found them in places so far apart as North Molton and Brendon, Dulverton and Horner.

Not the least of the master's difficulties was

---

[1] He was the author, under the *nom de plume* of 'Scrutator,' of *Horse and Hound*, one of the best books on hunting.

[2] It may be of interest to compare the receipts and payments then and now. For the season 1895–6 the master received the sum of £1,200, and the farmers were paid £408 for deer damage. In 1905–6 the total receipts were £3,308, out of which £1,800 were paid to the master, and £994 to the farmers for deer damage.

the want of a harbourer—that most important functionary of the hunt—Jim Blackmore of Haddon being the only dependable harbourer in the country. Sheep-killing also was a vice to which the new pack were prone.[3] Thus ended Mr. Bisset's first season; little support was forthcoming, the landowners held aloof, and only a handful of the original supporters, a few keen farmers, rallied round the master. But Mr. Bisset was not a man to give up in the face of difficulties. He drafted the whole of the pack but six couple, procured twelve couple of Mr. Petre's staghounds from Essex, and with the loan of six couple more from Captain West, he began hindhunting in April 1856. The new pack did better than its predecessor, but with the exception of two fine runs across the Forest sport was indifferent in that year. There were thirty hunting days and seven deer killed, of which two were 'unwarrantable,' that is too young to be killed according to the laws of venerie. Mr. Bisset, unlike some later masters, was much vexed at this and determined to follow closely the old canons of staghunting. With the advent of the season of 1857 the outlook became brighter, and Mr. Bisset in his journal marks it as the 'best on record.' Four stags were killed on four consecutive days—a feat unprecedented in the preceding forty-five years. The average number of hunting days between the years 1812 and 1818 was thirty-three, a fact to be compared with the four days a week of the present time. In 1857 there were only three blank days, and there were many fine runs. The total of deer taken was but eight, of which six were killed and two saved.

The year 1858 opened with a brilliant spring hindhunting season, during which took place what is perhaps the finest run ever known—from Cloutsham to Woody Bay, 22 miles as the crow flies, in 2 hours 20 minutes, without a check from find to finish. Now Mr. Bisset introduced new blood into the herd, the result of which is even now occasionally seen in the curious heads carried by certain stags. From Mr. Legh of Lyme in Cheshire were procured two stags, two male deer, and three hinds. One stag and two hinds were turned out in the Haddon, and the rest into the Horner strongholds. The two hinds from Haddon were killed after good runs in the spring of 1859 and 1860 respectively, and the stag after a poor run in the autumn of the latter year; but the Horner deer ran badly, and met with disaster one after another. One Horner stag was poached soon after his arrival, hounds killed by mischance one

[3] The Exmoor sheep seem to have a scent similar to that of the red deer, and masters of hounds on Exmoor are always having this trouble in a country where hounds are of necessity left to themselves and where the nature of the ground prevents a whipper-in from getting to them in time to check them.

of the male deer, the other died after a poor run in 1865. The hind however gave many good runs, but was spared only to fall a victim to the poachers in 1860. Thus the experiment was hardly a successful one and the master was blamed, as is always the case.

The year 1858 was also a good season. In thirty-five hunting days fourteen deer were taken (four stags and seven hinds being killed). But the poacher's gun still took toll, and hounds once more developed a taste for Exmoor mutton. A day of disaster indeed was the last day of this season. A dead-beat hind saved herself by running to herd, hounds killed a hind-calf, a horse broke Pilgrim's leg, Jack Babbage had a fall and cricked his neck, and the master's horse came down in the road up from Chettisford Water, breaking his rider's collar-bone. The next season, 1859, opened gloomily. Subscriptions were few and far between, while the landowners were apathetic. But Mr. Bisset was persuaded to go on in hopes that matters might improve, and he had the satisfaction of seeing on the opening day a little herd of seven stags and male deer on the Forest. The late Mr. (afterwards Sir Frederick) Knight of Exmoor and Mr. Nicholas Snow of Oare were at the time the deer's best friends on the north side of the country; but the southern side continued to furnish most sport, and it was not till some years later that the well-known woodlands of Horner, which belonged to Sir Thomas Acland, completely eclipsed the glories of Haddon, owned by Lord Carnarvon. However, thirteen deer were taken this year, five stags and six hinds being killed. Funds in 1860 were still at a low ebb, and Mr. Bisset threatened to resign. The spring hindhunting was, however, remarkably successful, five hinds being taken in as many days, while the autumn staghunting also yielded extraordinarily good sport. But there were clouds on the horizon. Six deer were found dead between Dunkery and Badgworthy, and only one calf was to be seen on the whole of the Forest. Mr. Bisset's tenancy of Pixton also came to an end. But Mr. Froude Bellew and the Hon. Mark Rolle saved the situation, the former by lending his house, stables and kennels to Mr. Bisset for three years, the latter by giving £100 a year as his subscription to the hunt. In 1861 hounds were kennelled at Rhyll, and there were only twenty-eight hunting days. Eleven deer were taken (four stags and five hinds being killed); but this year is more notable for the establishment of the herd on the Quantock Hills, thanks to the co-operation of Lord Taunton, the chief owner of land there. Poaching still went on in Horner, while the Luxborough and Bray coverts were tenantless. The season of 1862 was a short but a good one. Ten deer (seven stags, three hinds) were taken, and only six stags killed. This season is noteworthy for the abolition of spring hindhunting, as many hinds heavy in calf fell victims. Neither Mr. Bisset nor Mr. Knight approved of it, and the result of its cessation was a rapid increase in the number of deer.[4]

In 1863 and 1864 staghunting continued to prosper, but two good staghunters, Tom Webber and Dr. Palk Collyns, were taken away. In 1865 Horner had ousted Haddon as the main stronghold of the deer, and for the first time in Mr. Bisset's mastership a stag was roused in the Cutcombe coverts. Meanwhile, however, the growth of Lynton as a summer resort had driven the deer from the Brendon coverts. In the same year Mr. Bisset inaugurated hunting on the Quantocks, killing his first stag there on 29 August, and owing to the complaints of the farmers of deer damage, the Horner coverts were drawn in August instead of in September as in earlier days. Thus originated the opening meet at Cloutsham, which has been a recognized institution ever since, with but one or two exceptions.[5] In 1866 the Horner hinds began to run badly, and not one faced the Forest; but the Dulverton and Forest herds showed they had got into touch with one another by thrice running from the one country to the other. The spring of 1867 found five young deer dead round Oare, killed by the severity of the weather; but the season far surpassed all records up till then. There were thirty-three hunting days and eighteen deer were taken (twelve stags, six hinds). In 1868 another link with the past was broken when Mr. Nicholas Snow of Oare died in his eightieth year. 'He was,' wrote Mr. Bisset, 'a staunch preserver of the deer and an ardent lover of the sport. Up to the very last season he had been a constant attendant on the staghounds on his favourite mare, Norah Creina. Few went harder, and none knew better how to go and where to go than he and the old mare.' It is not too much to say that the deer owe their existence on the north side of the country to the jealous protection of Mr. Snow, who maintained, as does his successor, the large tract of moor known as the Deer Park, as a sanctuary for them. In 1868 the deer in the Horner coverts made their

presence felt, and it was found necessary to start the first of many future Cloutsham campaigns by hunting there on five consecutive days. Indeed before Mr. Bisset resigned, twenty and even thirty consecutive hunting days were devoted to the Horner herd. Hunting days this season numbered forty. The year 1869 calls for little comment; but 1870 eclipsed all previous records. Eight stags were killed in eight hunting days, and the last stag of the season ran from Badgworthy to Ilfracombe. Thirty-six hunting days yielded twenty deer (twelve stags, eight hinds), and all were killed but two hinds. At last the countryside awoke to enthusiasm, and showed their appreciation of the sport shown by Mr. Bisset by presenting him in 1871 with a testimonial to which over four hundred persons contributed.[6] In 1868 Jim Blackmore, the harbourer, had died, and in 1870 Arthur Heal carried the horn in place of Jack Babbage. Hitherto the energies of the master had been devoted to securing the preservation of the deer in sufficient numbers for the sport, but now those same energies had to be employed in keeping the numbers of the various herds in due bounds. For throughout the country the deer were increasing very fast, and returning to their former haunts and coverts. Once more stag and hind drank their fill at 'dimpsey' of the waters of the Bray, so much so that a meet in September 1871 was fixed for North Molton. Even in those days the herds of hinds in Horner began to be troublesome, and many days were devoted to the task of reducing their numbers. Of the year 1871, when there were fifty hunting days and thirty deer taken (twenty-six killed), Mr. Bisset writes, 'Not so bad, but still the cry is legion. On two occasions a brace of hinds were fairly taken in one day, but as usual the hinds in the Horner country were the great difficulty.' What would he have said, one wonders, to the taking of 370 deer in one season by five packs operating in Red Deer Land, or the capture of six deer in one day as has occasionally happened during the past decade?

With a renewed tenancy of Rhyll and a subscription list all but doubled, Mr. Bisset carried on the hunt somewhat against his inclinations. But he set the seal on his fame by purchasing the kennel lands at Exford in 1875; and in the kennels erected there the pack have remained ever since 1876. Hitherto hounds had been obliged to lie out one night at Exford and Larkbarrow and various places for their fixtures on the Forest side. With increased sport came increased crowds to participate in it, so that even in those days the master had to complain of the mob at the opening days at Cloutsham and on the

---

[4] In 1908 in deference to the representations made by Sir Thomas Dyke-Acland, Mr. Luttrell, Mary Countess of Lovelace, and other landowners deprecating the hunting of hinds late in the spring, the master and committee of the Devon and Somerset Staghounds decided that there should be no hindhunting after March 31, and that it should terminate at an earlier date when possible, with due regard to the welfare of the hunt and the interests of the farmers who suffer so much from the great number of deer still in the country.

[5] Notably the death of the late Sir Thomas Dyke-Acland, seventh baronet, in 1898, when the *venue* was changed to Haddon.

[6] A similar testimonial was presented to Mr. R. A. Sanders, on his retirement, in Aug., 1907.

Quantocks. Nor had hounds been able to cope with the increasing herds, and in 1872 there were ten consecutive meets at Cloutsham, for which the pack were kennelled at Sir Thomas Acland's seat at Holnicote. Forty deer were accounted for that season, three hinds being taken in one day. The practice of hunting hinds with relays of hounds which has since prevailed began in this year. In 1873 three deer were killed in one day and in 1874 two stags were for the first time fairly accounted for in one day—a common occurrence of late years. In April 1874 Mr. Bisset took his first Bray stag, and was horrified at the presence of a passing train (over Filleigh Viaduct), as 'a clashing of two distinct ages, indicating but too surely what must be ere long—the ancient occupant of the primeval forest being trampled under by the Juggernaut representative of advancing civilization.' The Bray coverts distinguished themselves in 1875, two deer from there crossing the Forest to the Porlock country. On three days a brace of stags were fairly killed, and during hind-hunting four deer were killed in one day from Cloutsham. Mr. 'Peter' Dene of Barnstaple, one of Mr. Bisset's most valued supporters, to whom was due the re-establishment of the herd in the Bray coverts, died in this year. The hunt also lost the valuable services by death of George Fewings, the whip. The season of 1876 provided but poor sport, although hind-hunting somewhat atoned for it. Twenty consecutive meets were held at Cloutsham, one at Hawkcombe Head, and one at Larkbarrow, in which twenty-three hinds were taken. Four of these were enlarged on the Quantocks, three male deer and a stag were killed by accident and two male deer were taken and saved. In 1877 the season, which had hitherto ended by February, was prolonged into March—sixty-one hunting days yielding sixty deer (four saved). In 1878 rabies, which broke out in the kennel, entailed the formation of a fresh pack. There were now two packs, the 'mad pack' and the 'new pack' hunting on alternate days, and segregated the one from the other.

Three days a week was the order of the day, and the mob at Cloutsham provoked the master into saying, 'Cloutsham opening day is becoming seriously too much of a rabble and fair.' Among the new pack were many sheep-killers, and the mad pack broke out again, and at last all had to be destroyed in the early days of 1879. 'A bitter pill to swallow, but there was no help for it,' says Mr. Bisset. The season was continued into April, and fifty-six deer were killed in seventy-four hunting days.

The staghunting season of 1879 is memorable for the visit of King Edward VII, then Prince of Wales, who stayed with Mr. Luttrell at Dunster Castle. His Royal Highness was in at the death, and stuck the stag himself.[7] Sport was good till the end of November when frost stopped hunting for a month. Then rabies broke out again and nothing could be done before March. The pack were exercised in muzzles, and one day broke away at Hawkcombe Head and killed two hinds at Blackford and Horner, their muzzles not preventing them from drowning their beaten deer. On the same day over a hundred deer were counted between Stoke Pero and Porlock Common. Only sixteen hinds were killed, and they gained an advantage on the Forest side of the country which, said Mr. Bisset, 'It would be difficult indeed to recover.' As a matter of fact, the deer have never since been well in hand. Next year there were ninety-one hunting days, 3 August 1880 to 6 April 1881, and seventy-five deer were killed (fourteen stags, forty-four hinds, seventeen young deer). Herds of forty-four and twenty-three were to be seen that year. Thus closed Mr. Bisset's long reign, for in 1880 Viscount Ebrington, now Earl Fortescue, succeeded him in the mastership. The 'Father of Staghunting,' as he was called, Mr. Bisset died at Bagborough in 1884. His modesty is shown by the fact that the word 'I' never once appears in the thirteen volumes of his hunting journal. He was a giant, over six feet high, and a welter weight to boot, riding twenty stone; but his knowledge of the country, the deer, and their runs enabled him to see the best of the sport. By his will he provided that his small property at Exford, on which he had built kennels, stables and dwellings at a cost of £7,000, might be leased for a term of twenty-one years by the master for the time being and any four members of the committee, so long as staghunting was continued in the same manner as it had been during his mastership and during the time wherein Lord Ebrington had held command since his retirement. The rent required was but £70 a year, practically covered by the 17 acres of grass land round the kennels. To him is due not only the existence of the hunt, but the very existence of the wild red deer of Exmoor.

Thanks to Mr. Bisset, his successor, Lord Ebrington, found himself at the head of an excellent pack of hounds with Arthur Heal, the best of huntsmen, at his service, and with the good will of the owners and occupiers of land in West Somerset and North Devon. But there was one drawback that ever since 1881 has always spoilt the sweets of office for successive masters. There were too many deer. A small herd had taken up its quarters in the Eggesford coverts, and stray deer had even reached Dartmoor and

---

[7] This he did not by cutting the stag's throat, as hitherto done on Exmoor, but in the Scotch fashion, which has ever since obtained.

the Blackmore Vale and the Duke of Somerset's park at Stover, while in the home country deer were literally swarming. The new master hunted regularly from 3 August 1881 till 1 March 1882. In eighty-nine hunting days hounds accounted for eighty-three deer (twenty-six stags, fifty-seven hinds), besides six young male deer and three crippled deer. Nine deer also met their death by misadventure. In this season the grand total of deer taken first passed the century (101). There was much alarm among staghunters, and fears were expressed that the herd would never stand such merciless thinning; but Mr. Bisset was undismayed, and predicted that another season would find the deer as numerous as ever.

The season of 1882 was very wet, and there were ninety-three hunting days, in which eighty-seven deer were killed and six saved. Deer wandered even as far as Crediton,[8] and in this year it became necessary to devote a fortnight to hunting the deer in the Taw and Mole Valleys. In 1883 an extra subscription was guaranteed to enable the master to hunt stags four days a week. Sport was excellent. In this year death removed some well-known staghunters—Mr. Granville Somerset, one of Mr. Bisset's chief supporters, the Reverend John Russell, Jack Babbage, the old huntsman, and Mr. Warren of Dulverton, who had been secretary to the hunt throughout Mr. Bisset's long reign, and had done much to promote its prosperity. With Mr. Bisset's death in 1884 the season opened gloomily, and there was another outbreak of rabies among the young hounds, which had one and all to be destroyed. Fortunately the old hounds escaped the scourge. But misfortunes never come singly, and on the third day of hunting four of the best hounds were killed. Sport, however, was good, though hounds did not get blood as often as they deserved, so that the season's bag was smaller than it had been since 1879.

In January 1883 Mr. Bisset wrote to Lord Ebrington, 'Go on and kill as many deer as you can, never mind what people say,' and gradually the outcry against the so-called slaughter of the deer died out. It was found, indeed, that the herds continued to increase at an alarming rate from the point of view not only of sport, but also of the hill farmer, who so loyally suffers the depredations of the deer. After a six years' tenure of office Lord Ebrington made way for Mr. Charles H. Basset in 1887, who held office for a like period.[9] His wife was the heiress and descendant of that Colonel Basset of Watermouth, who a century before had hunted the country for seventeen years. Mr. Basset was a thorough hound man, and under his *régime* the pack was raised to a higher standard of good looks than they had ever before attained to, nor was their work one whit behind their appearance. It was during Mr. Basset's mastership that Arthur Heal, the huntsman, retired in favour of Antony Huxtable, who had been whip to him for many seasons. It was in the last week but one of the season of 1889 that the remarkable run from Leworthy to Luccombe Rectory took place. Smithapark Wood held the hero of the day, and hounds were laid on by the Friendship Inn at 12.55. By Chapmans Barrows, the Chains and Furzehill they came to Hoar Oak Water, then across Cheriton Ridge to Farley Water. Here was a short check, and the pace had been a cracker all the way for five and forty minutes. The line then lay by Brendon Two Gates to Badgworthy Water, whence the stag bore on across Chalk and Weare Waters to Porlock Common and Lucott Moor till he came to Nutscale and Wilmersham. He gained the Horner woodlands, only to be fresh found under Cloutsham. His bolt was now nearly shot, and he carried on to Luccombe only to die in the Rectory grounds just after 3 o'clock. Distance, 20 miles; time, 2 hours, 10 minutes. He proved to be a seven-year-old stag, with brow tray and three atop, brow bay tray and an upright with two small offers (B.T. 3—B.B.T.).

Cloutsham that season held some straight-necked stags. At least three good runs took place from there over the open, the best from the lay-on at 1.5 on Tarr Ball to Weare Water and the Deer Park and Brendon Two Gates—time, sixty-five minutes. But the end was not yet, for Pinkworthy Pond was passed and Parracombe left behind as the chase swept on to Trentishoe and Heddons Mouth, and the mort sounded at 3.30 over a fine five-year-old stag with brows and trays and two atop one side, two and an offer the other. This run could hardly have been less than twenty-three miles. It was, perhaps, Mr. Basset's fairness to the deer, his rigid adherence to the canons of the chase and laws of venerie, that contributed, together with the very few hinds killed during his successor's two years' tenure of office, to the enormous increase of the various herds of deer from Horner to Haddon in later years. Mr. Basset took the greatest interest in every detail of the establishment from the harbouring to the horses, and at his sale his stud fetched very good prices. Owing to an accident he only had one hand, but he was a hard man to beat across the moor. To him in 1893 succeeded Colonel Hornby, who had acted under Lord Coventry as vice-master of the Royal Buckhounds. He brought down a stud of big blood-horses, who were not so well suited to the moor as horses on shorter legs would have been; but he inaugurated his season with an unusually good run, and in July of all months. The last day

[8] In Feb. 1908 Sir John Amory's pack took a hind in the ponds of Shobrooke Park near Crediton.
[9] Mr. C. H. Basset died in Feb. 1908.

of that season saw the last race for life of a stag known as the Black Stag of Badgworthy, which for several seasons had eluded the best efforts of Arthur and Anthony. Roused in the Deer Park, he made his way to Blackpits and the green morasses of the Chains, but changed his mind and swung round over the North Forest and away to Lucott Moor, thence to Dunkery and down to the Holnicote Vale. Across to North Hill and past Wydon, hounds drove on to Bratton Court where they ran him to a standstill at 4.35. He proved to be a very old and dark-coloured stag, and carried twelve points. Colonel Hornby also had the good fortune to secure the finest head on record on 25 October 1893 from the meet at Bagborough on the Quantocks, Mr. Bisset's former home. The stag carried all his rights and four atop each side, with an offer as well on one of them. The measurements of this head, known as the St. Audrie's head, are as follows: Round outer curve of near horn, 36 in.; width across at the fork, 30¼ in.; from inside to outside, perpendicular height, 29 in.; size round beam at fork, 7½ in.; and same between brow and bay, outer curve of brows, 14 in. But for some reason Colonel Hornby did not take sufficient toll of the long-necked hinds, and they gained such a start in point of numbers that to this day all efforts to keep the herds in due bounds have proved unsuccessful. The master was seriously handicapped by the death of Miles, who had been harbourer for five and twenty years.

In 1895 Mr. R. A. Sanders became master, and his twelve years of office are full of incidents that go to make staghunting history. It was during his mastership that Anthony Huxtable retired and Sidney Tucker became huntsman, with success both in field and kennel quite equal to that of old Arthur Heal at his best. Hounds were improved in condition and smartness, and tufting became a less tedious wait than it had been for years. Four ancillary packs were established to hunt the deer in Devon and Somerset; Fred Goss, the harbourer, proved himself an apt pupil of old Miles; while artificial aids were employed to capture the deer, and the calves were killed in June. Last but not least it was in this mastership that the record number of deer killed was reached, as many as six falling victims on one famous day, while the staghunting season of 1906 will probably never be beaten for the number of good runs, enjoyed for the most part in an east wind under a blazing sun.

Mr. Sanders' first season opened auspiciously with a bye-meet at Hawkridge on 19 July 1895, when a stag of great weight and carrying a splendid head stood up before hounds for three hours despite the heat of the day and the fact of his well-filled paunch. He was a 14-pointer, and yielded no less than 11 score 7 lb. (227 lb.) of clean venison, when paunched, beheaded, and without his slots. This season occurred a good run across the Forest from Popham Wood in the Bray valley to Badgworthy Water, the time from the lay-on at Whitfield being exactly sixty minutes.

The year 1896 is memorable, for in that season was established the first ancillary pack under the name of Sir John Amory's Staghounds. So plentiful were the deer in the home country that the parent pack at Exford were hard pressed to cope with them, and were quite unable to devote enough time to the deer on their borders. Mr. R. A. Sanders therefore suggested that the new pack should be established to hunt the country some thirty miles by twenty miles south of the Taunton and Barnstaple Railway, with various days in the Dulverton country by invitation. Sir John Amory of Knightshayes Court, Tiverton, was to be the master, with Mr. Ian Amory to carry the horn and the Messrs. de las Casas, the well-known polo players, to act as amateur whippers-in. Thus was founded a pack whose runs recall the old chases of the early years of the 19th century. But beyond this it is important to note that for the first time we find an amateur as huntsman. The experiment has proved a great success, and Mr. Ian Amory, being a born huntsman with a knack of getting to his hounds in any country, has shown himself not only quite equal to the best professional in the field, but also a thorough hound man, who has spared no time, trouble or expense to make as smart and efficient a pack of staghounds as could be desired. Mr. Peter Ormrod also was his own huntsman during his one season on Exmoor, as was Captain Patterson of the Barnstaple pack. This latter pack owed its inception to the late Mr. Charles H. Basset of Watermouth Castle, a former master of the Devon and Somerset Staghounds, to whom was lent the country beyond the light railway from Lynton to Barnstaple, which included the Chelfham and Bratton Fleming Valleys, with occasional meets by invitation on the Forest itself, and at such places as Challacombe and Woolhanger. It was in September and October 1900 that Mr. Peter Ormrod brought his pack from Lancashire to hunt this district, and in 1901 Captain Ewing Patterson, D.S.O., and Mr. Arundell Clarke, both of Fremington, undertook the mastership. Miss Chichester of Arlington Court, however, set her face against deerhunting, and a deer fence had to be erected to keep the hunted deer out of her sanctuary. Even this proved ineffectual, and it was found impossible to continue hunting under these conditions. A second Jorrocks, a Barnstaple grocer with sporting proclivities, named W. L. Ashton, held on fitfully for another season or so, but even he was finally extinguished by the opposition of the lady of Arlington Court. There were several good runs to Badgworthy Water and beyond during these few seasons, notably one in the return direction from an invitation meet at Larkbarrow in 1902. Captain Patterson was hunting hounds which ran a stag from Badgworthy Wood to Loxhore in three hours. It should be added that Mr. E. E. Chichester, son of Admiral Sir Edward Chichester, was field-master for Mr. W. L. Ashton in 1903.

With the Devon and Somerset pack a good run took place in 1896, with a 'nott' or hornless stag from Allercombe on the side of Dunkery to Malsmead. In 1897 and 1898 the total of deer taken reached 148.

The second meet of 1898 was at Hawkcombe Head, and a bumper meet it was; for the stag-hunters of the north side of the country do not often undertake the long journey to Haddon, whose great woodlands do not as a rule provide the best of sport. On that day a stag from the Culbone coverts led hounds and horses a terrific gallop of full twenty miles, going by way of the Warren, where he took an unusual line, swinging round to Chibbet and Exford. Thence he made his way to Dunkery and down into Horner, being set up to bay at Luccombe Allers four hours from the lay-on. He carried a good head, with all his rights and two atop (B.B.T. 2—B.B.T. 2). In the season of 1898-9 the total of deer taken was still on the increase, being 176.

The season of 1899 saw the run of half a century placed to the credit of the Exford pack. For four and a half hours a stag led the way from Hawkridge, over the South Forest to Brendon Two Gates and Lynton, till he leapt to death over the cliff at Glenthorne, followed by one brave hound named Guardsman, which shared his fate. The stag had a light head, with eight points only (B.T. 2—B.T. 2).

The season 1901 saw the establishment of the Quantock Staghounds, another landmark in staghunting history. Ever since Mr. Bisset's death the Devon and Somerset Staghounds had visited the Quantock Hills for a week's stag-hunting and a week's hindhunting, in accordance with the provisions of Mr. Bisset's will. But with more than enough work for them to do at home, the parent pack could not spare time to satisfy the demands of the farmers on the Quantocks, who began to be alarmed at the rapidly increasing numbers of the Quantock herd. Thus, with the good will of the owners and occupiers of land, and with the permission of the parent hunt, who reserved the right of hunting as heretofore, claiming all subscriptions and liberty to terminate the arrangement at six months' notice, were established the Quantock Staghounds. The master and huntsman in 1907 succeeded Mr. R. A. Sanders in command of the parent pack, and abandoned the Quantocks once more to the periodical visits of the Devon and Somerset, having in the last six years reduced the herd to due dimensions.

For the first time the deer total passed the double century, for in the season 1901-2 no less than 240 deer were taken by the three packs now hunting Exmoor and its environs. Good sport with all the packs marked the season of 1903, when an extra subscription was guaranteed to Mr. R. A. Sanders to hunt four days a week. The season had been extended, and the number of packs trebled, nevertheless the deer continued to increase. More hunting days per week were required if hounds were to cope with the herds, especially in the home country. It was at about this time that it was decided to kill the calves in June, a practice repugnant to many staghunters and sportsmen, and in one season about forty were thus killed on one landowner's property. Deer traps of wire netting were set up in the Winsford country and beside Horner Mill stream; but they did not prove so successful as was anticipated, and the public raised a somewhat indignant outcry. The use of them was accordingly abandoned after one season's experiment, as was also the calf killing in 1905 or 1906. In 1903-4 the deer total kept increasing, and reached 266. The last day of staghunting produced an extraordinary trophy. A stag from Rowdown Wood, Hawkridge, when killed was found to have a most curious head. He carried all his rights, brow bay tray on either side with a good point on one side and eight small knobs or 'offers' on the other, a good point on top with six similar 'offers,' and the tops were palmated measuring $7\frac{3}{4}$ in. across the fan or palm. The season of 1903 was one of the best for sport and runs. No less than fifty-four stags were killed by the four packs, viz.: Quantock, 10; Amory, 3; Barnstaple, 2; Devon and Somerset, 39.

The season 1904-5 was remarkable in many ways. In spite of fair means and foul the deer had increased at an alarming rate, and the farmers' complaints of their depredations were long and loud. Mr. Peter Ormrod, who was then master of the Exmoor Foxhounds and resident at Oare House, was invited to bring his private pack of staghounds into the district and harry the herds. Cloutsham and Culbone were his principal fixtures, and his operations were restricted to hinds, though he was allowed one stag at the beginning of the season and one at the end. Mr. Ormrod had got together a pack very similar to what that 'old pack' must have been which was sold in 1825 to go to Germany. There was a great deal of old Southern, Welsh and bloodhound blood in Mr. Ormrod's hounds. Their music was a treat to hear, but they rather failed when they came to water hunting. They killed a fair number of deer, including a one-horned stag at Glenthorne, which had on a previous occasion nearly caused the death of Sidney Tucker, the huntsman of the Devon and Somerset, by charging him and his horse on a narrow bridle-path on the cliffs. Mr. Ormrod would undoubtedly have taken more deer than he did if he had not been so anxious to collect his hounds before darkness set in, for he could not bear to leave a hound out for the night. Will Lock, who was first whip and kennel huntsman to the Exmoor Foxhounds, acted in like capacity with the staghound pack, and Dick Aldren, the whipper-in whom Mr. Ormrod had brought from Lancashire, did likewise. After Christmas 1904 Mr. Ormrod also had the services in field and kennel of Mr. Arthur Heinemann of Porlock, who was lucky enough to capture the last stag of the season with 9½ couple of hounds at East Watersfoot from the Cloutsham meet. Thus in 1904-5 the deer total reached the record figure of 370, compiled by no less than five packs.

At the end of this season Fred Barber retired, and was succeeded as whipper-in by Ernest Bawden, a young Hawkridge farmer. It was on 23 March in this year that six deer were first taken in one day by the parent pack, a feat (if feat it can be called, being rather 'a bag') that was repeated in 1907. In 1904 the parent pack took 180 deer. Owing to an outbreak of dysentery among the Exford pack, hounds were moved temporarily to kennels at Rhyll. Stags ran badly and without enterprise, or Tucker was too smart for them, for he killed forty-three stags in forty-one hunting days. Spring staghunting was this year revived, and some good runs took place, one especially from Venniford to Dunkery, Lucott and Robber's Bridge, Oareford, in 2 hours 10 minutes from the lay-on (a three-year-old stag).

In 1905, though there were no runs across the Forest, sport with the stags was on the whole better. Earl Fortescue passed away and was succeeded by Lord Ebrington, a former master of the Devon and Somerset. This year the Barnstaple pack was dispersed, and Mr. Peter Ormrod's staghounds were sold to Prince Max Taxis in Hungary. The Quantock pack accounted for seventy deer (some of them from the home country), and had a good run with a stag from Cloutsham to the Minehead Marshes, and with another from the Quantocks to Culmstock, while a hind from Aisholt led hounds almost to Bridgwater, and another past Taunton town to Durston. The Devon and Somerset took a stag with a splendid head of all his rights and four atop each side (B.B.T. 4—B.B.T. 4). He was roused in Haddon and set up to bay at Bampton. From Dunkery Hill Gate in one day no less than five deer were taken, viz.: three hinds, one stag, one calf, by the parent pack. This was one of the best seasons ever enjoyed by Sir John Amory's staghounds, while the Devon and Somerset

never put a better hindhunting season to their credit.

The brilliant season of 1906 [10] opened badly. There was little luck and less venison at the preliminary bye-meets. After this the run of

[10] DEVON AND SOMERSET RECORD FOR 1906

Date.

Aug.	6.	Found in Lee Plantation; killed under North Hawkwell, B.B.T. 3—B.T. 2.
,,	8.	Found at Cloutsham Ball; killed at Hurlstone Point, B.T. 2—B.T. 2.
,,	10.	Found in Yarnor Plantation; killed at Barkhouse, B.T. 2—B.T. 3.
,,	13.	Found in Corkhill Brake; killed below Torrsteps, B.B.T. 2—B.B.T. 2.
,,	15.	Found in Edgecott Allotment; killed below Wyngate, B.B.T. 3—B.B. 3.
,,	17.	Found in Lillycombe; killed below Cornham Ford, B.T. 3—B.T. 2.
,,	23.	Found in Edbrooke Wood; killed below Exebridge, B.B.T. 3—B.T. 2.
,,	24.	Found in Deer Park; killed in Yarnor Plantation, B.T. 4—B.B.T. 3.
,,	27.	Found in Lambpark Wood; killed at Bishmill, B.T. uprights—B.T. uprights.
,,	29.	Found on Haydown; killed at Hartford, B.B.T. 3—B.B.T. 4.
,,	31.	Found in Aldercombe; killed at Chalk-Water, B.T. uprights—B.T. uprights.
Sept.	3.	Found in Bradley Ham; killed under Batsom, B.B.T. 2—B.B.T. 2.
,,	10.	Found in Storridge; killed at Coupleham, B.T. 2—B.B.T. 3.
,,	12.	Found in Deerpark; killed below Ashton.
,,	14.	Found in Hurdledown; killed at Porlock Weir, B.T. 2—B.T. up.
,,	15.	Found in Yealscombe; killed below Horner, B.B.T. 2—B.T. 3.
,,	17.	Found in Storridge; killed under Hinham.
,,	19.	Found in Yarnor Plantation; killed on Acland's Allotment, B.B.T. 2—B.T. 3.
,,	20.	Found on Trout Hill; killed below Glenthorne, B.B.T. 2—B.B.T. 2.
,,	22.	Found in Lambpark Wood; killed at Porlock, B.T. 2—B.B.T.
,,	24.	Found below Knaplock; killed at Hiscombe, B.T. up—B.T. up.
,,	26.	Found at Hollowcombe; killed at Glenthorne.
Oct.	1.	Found on Rhyll Common; killed under Batsom, B.B.T. 3—B.B.T. 3.
,,	3.	Found in Yarnor Plantation; killed at Porlock Weir, B.B.T. 2—B.B.T. 2.
,,	5.	Found in Haddon Wood; killed below Weir, B.B.T. 3—B.B.T. 2.
,,	6.	Found in Bincombe; killed at Roborough Farm, B.B.T. 4—B.B.T. 3.
,,	8.	Found in the Allotments; killed below Horsen Ford, B.B.T. 2—B.B.T. 2.
,,	10.	Found in Bincombe; killed in Parks Porlock, B.T. 3—B.B.T. 3.
,,	12.	Found in Storridge: killed at Bradley Bottom, B.T. up—B.T. up.
,,	13.	Found in Deer Park; killed at Porlock Ford, B.T. 2—B.B.T. 2.
,,	15.	Found in Aldercombe; killed at West Luccombe, B.B.T. 2—B.B.T. 2.

luck set in, and three times in one week an August field crossed Badgworthy Water and traversed the sedgy swamps of the North Forest in the wake of the Devon and Somerset. September saw the inauguration of a regular hunt-week, the Devon and Somerset putting in four days, Sir John Amory's meeting at Haddon and South Molton station on two, and the Quantock pack a like number at The Heath-Poult and Raleigh's Cross. The deer this year carved out new lines for themselves, or reverted to very ancient ones. Selworthy deer would run to Haddon, and so would the deer from the Luxborough coverts. The Quantock pack this month brought off two good runs, the one from Luxborough to Venn Cross, the other from Cloutsham to Badgworthy, Brendon Two Gates and Driver Cot. Another good run was that of the Devon and Somerset from Weare Wood to Driver, and yet another from Popham Wood to Porlock town. Not for twenty years or more had Cloutsham failed to hold a stag, yet such was the case one day this September—as also one day in spring stag-hunting in April 1907. This has ever been a stronghold and sanctuary for the herd, thanks to Sir Thomas Acland and his sporting steward, Mr. Christopher Birmingham. Constant harrying in winter and summer alike, dread of the deer trap, the killing of the calves or the annual hecatombs of slain, may one and all have contributed to this result. However, a great run from Lady Lovelace's plantations at Culbone retrieved the fortunes of the day. Hounds were laid on at 1.10 on Mill Hill, when they ran to Badgworthy, Chapman Barrows, Longstone, Challacombe, Moles Chamber, Brayford and back to the North Molton coverts, having to be stopped at 6.10 at Higher Fyldon, when horses could go no further. Many horses did not reach their own stables that night, and more than one ended his career that day.

With the advent of October, sport with the stags continued both fast and furious, and the Devon and Somerset ran a stag from the Cut-combe coverts to Cloutsham back to the Chargot coverts over the Brendon Hills, past Withiel Florey to Roborough near Upton. There they pulled him down in the open, full ten miles south of Dunkery Beacon. He carried a grand head of thirteen points (B.B.T. 3—B.B.T. 4). As was only in accordance with the fitness of things, Cloutsham, which witnessed the opening meet of the Devon and Somerset season, was the *venue* on the last day of stag-hunting and again a good run ensued to set the seal on the best staghunting season on record. Hollowcombe held the hero of the day. He set his face for the Chargot coverts but changed his mind and turned back to Poole Bridge, at the head of the great Horner woodlands, which he beat through till his strength failed

him at West Luccombe. This stag was presented by Sir Thomas Acland to Exeter Museum, to complete a group of red deer and to illustrate the fauna of Devon and Somerset. There were a few bye-days after this, on one of which a young stag from Lord Poltimore's covert at Long Wood near North Molton led the chase far south to Alswere and Highridge Moors, where his bolt was shot.

Sir John Amory's pack in November covered an entirely new line of country, for they ran a stag from Tiverton to Mohun's Ottery, four miles north-east of Honiton. Thus ended such a staghunting season as has never been, and probably never will be, surpassed. Run followed run in bewildering succession, and hounds crossed ground never before traversed by their flying feet. Hindhunting in 1906-7, however, was not equal to that of the previous season.

And now staghunting enters on a new era. The too numerous herds are thinned considerably, if not unduly ; the new master, described as ' one of the best amateur huntsmen in the kingdom,' comes fresh from his six years' successful mastership of the Quantock pack [11] with youth and health and means to carry on the sport ; the Exford kennels hold the pick of the two packs, strengthened by this year's entry of the Belvoir draft ; the farmers are to a man upholders of the sport, and the hunt servants are to be magnificently mounted. Sidney Tucker will carry the horn on alternate days with Mr. E. A. V. Stanley, and Fred Goss as harbourer will again display all his knowledge of woodcraft. There will, however, be but two packs hunting the wild red deer, Sir John Amory's being the only pack left out of those four which took the field in 1904-5. Thus the time may not be far distant when the season will be shorter and hunting days fewer, though sport should in no wise deteriorate in consequence.

The writer has only to add that he is *largely* indebted to Dr. Collyns' *Chase of the Wild Red Deer*, to *Stag Hunting on Exmoor* by the Hon. J. Fortescue, and to *Stag Hunting with the Devon and Somerset*, by Mr. P. Evered, for much of the earlier portions of this history of the Devon and Somerset.

HUNTSMEN, WHIPS AND HARBOURERS

No history of the Devon and Somerset Staghounds, however brief, would be complete without a detailed mention of the men who have

[11] QUANTOCK SUMMARY, JULY 3 1901–MAY 1 1907

In Quantock country, 111 stags, 118 hinds, total 229 deer, killed in 257 hunting days. In Devon and Somerset country, 27 stags, 39 hinds, total 66 deer, killed in 98 hunting days. Grand total: 295 deer, killed in 355 hunting days.

been responsible for the actual hunting. It must be borne in mind that it is not enough for a man to be a good man to hounds or with hounds, to win success in hunting the wild red deer. He must also from his youth up have been reared in a knowledge of this particular and peculiar branch of the chase, which requires daily a display of woodcraft, watercraft and moorcraft such as no other form of hunting demands.

James Tout, who carried the horn in the reign of Lord Fortescue (1812–18) heads the list. Times have altered since his day, when after a good stag had been killed the huntsman entered the master's dining-room in full costume and sounded a mort which was the signal for the company to pledge ' Success to Staghunting ' in a bumper of port. Then he would again retire to his own place and rest himself after the labours of the day in company with one or two favourites, whose escape from the kennel had been connived at. Such, so the chronicler of those days tells us, was the regular procedure. ' There,' says he, ' before the ample fire the huntsman dozed away his evening and killed his deer again while

> The staghounds, weary with the chase,
> Lay stretched upon the rushy floor,
> And urged in dreams the forest race
> From Castle Hill to wild Exmoor.'

Joe Faulkner was another huntsman of whom many tales are told. He had a marvellous aptitude for the chase, but his temper was abominable and unrestrained, and his flow of language was both painful and free. He would curse all the gentlemen except Lord Fortescue, and he displayed a great fondness for strong waters, with the consequence that he was for ever being discharged and as often reinstated, for his services were found to be indispensable. Then there was Jack Babbage, who had been huntsman to Mr. Carew, and served under Mr. Froude Bellew. He was a quiet, dapper little man, and carried the horn in the early years of Mr. Bisset's mastership.

It was in his time that Arthur Heal became whip after serving his apprenticeship with harriers. Arthur Heal is still alive at Exford, where he became a farmer on his retirement. He retained his quickness and dash to the very last, though he was sadly crippled with rheumatism and had to be lifted on his horse. A rare knowledge of the run of a deer, combined with infinite patience, helped to make him the great success that he was. He was as quick as lightning in a big woodland and was all wire and whipcord, a feather weight, just as Anthony Huxtable his successor, and both spoke in the dear Devonshire tongue. Anthony Huxtable served the hunt for five and twenty years under five masters. Four years he spent in the hunt stables, nine years as whipper-in to Arthur Heal, and twelve years as huntsman. He also retired to farm at Exford after receiving a handsome testimonial, but did not long survive to enjoy his well-earned ease. He had a splendid voice, and blew a good horn. In his time he played many parts, for he was born in Kentisbury parish of working parents, and was brought as an infant in arms to Driver Cot, where he made his first acquaintance with Exmoor from the pommel of his father's saddle at Larkbarrow, where the latter served as bullock herd to the late Sir Frederick Knight. Anthony was in turn farm boy, milk carrier in Barnstaple, teamster, iron miner, peat cutter and drainer (actually cutting many of those trappy gutters on the North Forest over which in later years he had to ride), quarryman, 'bus driver and billiard-marker—a variegated career truly ! On Anthony's retirement Sidney Tucker, who had ridden second horse for Mr. Basset and was whipper-in to Huxtable, stepped into his shoes. In spite of having to take the field on four days in the week and having to contend with heart-breaking herds of deer, Tucker has proved himself quite the equal of Arthur Heal at his best. ' Tucker and two couple ' has become a proverb in the west. But with Tucker a new era has dawned, and while appreciating his quiet ways as a hunt servant one cannot help missing the broad Devon speech and independent attitude of Arthur Heal and Anthony Huxtable.

Fred Barker, who was whip to Sidney Tucker, was succeeded by Ernest Bawden, son of that sporting farmer of Hawkridge who in September 1871, riding bareback and with only a halter for bridle, was one of the six to see the finish of an extraordinary run of five hours through twelve parishes.

So much, then, for the huntsmen and their whippers-in ; but the man who holds the key to success in a staghunting establishment is the harbourer, whose duties are not learnt in a day —in fact, there are not more than half a dozen men to-day in Red Deer Land who can be depended on to harbour a stag. Blackmore is the first harbourer of whom we can find mention, and he was a master of the game. Then came Andrew Miles, who entered Mr. Bisset's service in 1862 and went to Haddon in 1868 as Lord Carnarvon's gamekeeper. For five and twenty years he acted as harbourer under four masters, and located over five hundred stags. Fred Goss, the present harbourer, was appointed in 1894 by Colonel Hornby. He is also keeper to Lord Carnarvon, and has shown himself an apt pupil of Miles and a capable man. Nor must we omit mention of those gentlemen who have done so much to promote the interests of the hunt as honorary secretaries—Mr. Warren of Dulverton, Mr. James Turner of Porlock, Mr. A. C. E. Locke of Northmoor, Dulverton, a genial sportsman and popular with all; he retired in 1894 to be succeeded by the present secretary, Mr. Philip Evered, an all-round sportsman, who, besides contributing a valuable work on the sport, has graphically told of many a run of recent years in the columns of *The Field* and of the local press.

THE HUNTING OF THE STAG

Of all branches of the chase staghunting is, perhaps, the oldest. As it was in the days of William Rufus, who 'loved the tall red deer as if he were their father,' so is the sport carried on to this day in Somerset by the Devon and Somerset Staghounds and its ancillary packs. To-day are used the proper terms of venerie that have been in use for hundreds of years: to-day the procedure of the hunt is the same as it ever has been since the earliest days. A warrantable stag has been well and truly harboured, and to the meet comes the harbourer, a personage who appears indeed insignificant in his mufti compared with the master and hunt servants gay in all the glory of scarlet coats and silver buttons. Only a field-glass slung round him betokens his office, yet on him depend the fortunes of the day. The pack, having arrived and been duly paraded, is kennelled in some convenient farm-buildings, and the master, huntsman and harbourer hold a council of war. Nor are the 'field' taken into their confidence, though sharp ears and eyes may gather for themselves some indication of the coming scene of operations. Then, list in hand, the huntsman proceeds to draft one, two, three or even six couples of the fastest and staunchest hounds, called 'the tufters,' amid the disappointed baying of their kennelled comrades. Mounting his tufting pony the huntsman clatters away down some stony lane, while the master takes up a coign of vantage on an adjoining hill-top, and the whipper-in gallops off for the point at which the harboured stag is likely to break covert. Occasionally a glimpse is gained of a galloping figure in scarlet silhouetted against the distant skyline; ever and anon the deep challenge of the tufters echoes up from the green depths of some combe or fold in the hills. Perhaps a deer, usually a hind, appears and is greeted with vociferous yells as 'the biggest stag that ever was seen.' Hour after hour passes by, and the uninitiated almost begin to wonder what they have come out for. Suddenly a whistle rings out shrilly across the combe; a white handkerchief flutters, and the huntsman's horn twangs loud and long as he gallops back headlong for the pack. All is now bustle and excitement; half-smoked cigars are thrown aside, girths are tightened and habits adjusted, and the infection spreads to the kennelled hounds, which whine and whimper in their eagerness for release. Quickly the huntsman changes his tufting pony for a stouter nag, the kennel doors are flung wide open, out into the sunshine troops and tumbles the exultant pack. 'Hounds, please, gentlemen! Hounds, please!' and off all scurry in their wake to the scene of the lay-on, where the whipper-in and second horseman with difficulty hold up the straining tufters.

But before all this has come to pass the huntsman and his trusty tufters have had many difficulties to face. True it is that the harbourer has led them to the very couch or harbour of the antlered monarch of the glen selected for the day's chase. At the first deep-mouthed challenge of Didcot or Michael or Slow Boy he has sprung to his feet, head erect, defiance in his eye—and then he has plunged forthwith into the depths of some brake-clad göyle. But the beast that hounds have forced from its covert is not the warrantable stag, but a smaller, younger one, which he has pushed up to be his substitute. Away stream the tufters, perhaps for a couple of miles before the whipper-in can get to their heads. And now the huntsman lays them on to the heel-way of the second stag, which results in a second rousing of number one. Like a pointer he quarters the coverts for fresh deer, putting up hinds and calves and all such 'small stuff.' But Tucker is up to every move in the game and checkmates him at every turn, until at last, forced to fly or die, he boldly faces the open moor and sets his proud head for distant Badgworthy.

Now the tufters are stopped, and the pack fetched to the scene of the lay-on. As hounds strike the line of the fugitive, one after another dashes grimly forward, the bitches throw their tuneful tongues, and in a long-drawn-out file the great hounds stride away through heather and ling, brake and fern and whortleberry, cheered to the echo by their huntsman's voice and horn. Thundering in their wake, a thousand hoofs scatter the heather-pollen in purple clouds as mile after mile is flung behind them. Across combe after combe, splashing through the stream that ever trickles down each fold in the hills, the gallant band of riders press ever onward, down over and up over through wet ground and good going, all cheerfully encountered in the ardour of the chase. Like cloud shadows the flying line of black and white and tan seems to skim over the ground, and soon against the distant skyline appears the dark form of the Forest stretching away far as the eye can see.

But the pace has begun to tell its tale not only on horses, which sob and lather foam-white under an August sun, but also on the staunchest stag that ever crossed the moor. Gleaming and glinting in the sunlight, the tumbling trout pools of Badgworthy Water lie temptingly spread before him. Down stream he plunges, sinking to soil, as it is termed, to cool his heated flanks. A splash on the stones, a slot's imprint on some spit of mud, tells the huntsman's quick eye whether to cast his hounds, now at fault, up or down stream. Past Badgworthy Wood and Malsmead the chase sweeps on. Below Southern Wood there is a loud view holloa from the men of Brendon. Down the bed of the stream splashes the stag, hounds now tight on his haunches, throwing their tongues furiously with all their hackles up, for they know their quarry is all but delivered into their jaws. And so they come to lovely Watersmeet, while the gorge echoes with their cry and the notes of the horn. Against a rock the stag stands to bay and bids defiance to all his foes, who surround him in a respectful if resentful ring.

While louder and louder the challenge resounds,
Till it rings through the combe in a chorus of hounds,
And the music of death with its echo surrounds
The King of the West.

The whipper-in produces a headline and lassoes the stag's horns, the huntsman deftly plunges his knife into the proud throat and so 'Whoo-whoop'! As Kingsley so well has it, 'Who does not remember the blowing of the mort and the last wild halloo, when the horn-note and the voices rang through the autumn woods, and rolled up the smooth flat mountain sides; and Brendon answered Countisbury, and Countisbury sent it on to Lynmouth Hill, till it swept out of the gorge and died away on the Severn Sea?'

HUNTING THE HIND

The less fashionable hindhunting occupies the attention of the various packs from November to April. Exmoor in winter is a cruel stepmother, very unlike the smiling mistress she shows herself to be in the summer and autumn. Driving rain that finds its wet way into the weak points of the galloping horseman's most weatherproof kit, fog, frost and snow, stinging sleet and icy hail, one and all combine to damp the ardour even of the bravest enthusiast. As for the hinds themselves, they usually run with harelike crookedness, not making such bold or straight points as their antlered lords.

It is the fashion to speak of the hind as a guileless beast, but, as a matter of fact, she is full of cunning. Running to herd is her favourite ruse, and the present writer has seen them running doubles like a hare. They will join a herd of bullocks to stain the foil, run along a bank to and fro, jump off it and on again, and so forth. When dead beat a hind will bound into some almost impenetrable thicket, and thus breaking the thread of the chase will lie fast till all danger of discovery has passed away. Her tricks when she comes to water are many and various, and her powers of leaping almost incredible. Should she have a calf running beside her she will butt it aside, when it will lie still while she leads on her pursuers. A good hind will weigh some five score pounds avoirdupois, but on 12 February 1889 an old yeld hind was found to weigh 135 lb. That a hind has some weapons of defence, if not of offence, anybody who has come in contact with the sharp claws of her fore slots, can bear witness. Hinds take very different lines from stags, and thus in hindhunting one finds oneself at the finish of the day at all sorts of out of the way and unknown spots.

For endurance and staying powers a yeld or barren hind can give points to any stag that ever stepped the forest; indeed, some of those long-legged, long-necked, grey-faced matrons of the herd seem to have solved the problem of perpetual motion. One never knows when one's hind is dead beat, nor how much go she may have left in her. She may have made two or three big rings at best pace across heavy going, uphill and down dale, and then have come to water, only apparently to beat down stream and die. And then when hounds at last seem about to reap their reward, away she goes up over again, as fresh as a rose, and makes her point at last for some distant harbour of refuge. There are no horns to take stock of, and there is often but the difference in size and slight variation in colour to guide the huntsman or whip. One hind looks so much like another, especially when a herd has been run; there are several steaming mire-splashed beasts at last scattered in every direction, and it is difficult to prevent hounds changing deer or even to tell when they are on their original quarry.

Thus it comes about that the one-horse man, who is in the majority on Exmoor, finds himself left lagging hopelessly in the rear while the flying hounds steal swiftly over the brown flank of Dunkery or across the rain-washed swathes of the Forest. There is but one thing to do—to hang on patiently at some coign of vantage such as Webbers Post or Hawkcombe Head, until his horse has come again, and the hind has perhaps returned to make her last effort across the Porlock Marshes or down Horner Mill-leat. Possibly the best plan is to take things easily during the morning, then later on when the herds have been well harried and scattered, to let your horse go at last, when there seems a fair prospect of a run in the desired direction, and of a successful issue before the early darkness of the short winter days sets in. There is no tufting in hindhunting, no certain return to kennel to bring forth the pack and duly lay them on. Perhaps eight or nine couple are at once taken and laid on to a herd of perhaps five, perhaps fifteen, deer. Then you must make up your mind either to go on with them, or to watch their operations and excursions from some adjacent hill-top, or to wait till the huntsman returns for a fresh draft of hounds. You must not hesitate to go on with one, two or three couple of hounds; you seldom will see the whole pack settled on to the line of an individual hind. It is the fastest hound that kills his hind, and this same hindhunting tends to make hounds very independent—foxhunters would call them skirters—for each plays his own game. In 1905–6 hinds ran both fast and far, and in a good acorn year this will often be found to be the case.

At length the ruthless laying of the hinds has begun to have its effect, and the enormous herds of hinds that one used to see show no longer on the bleak skyline of Rowberrow or Challacombe Common—desolate and exposed spots which the hinds prefer, when once the leaf is off and their calves are well grown, to the shelter of the combes and coverts.

HARBOURING

One may safely aver that the best efforts of staghounds and huntsman would be of no avail but for the patient work of woodcraft undertaken in the early hours of dawn by the harbourer. The day before the appointed fixture the harbourer makes his round of the coverts and gathers from ocular and oral evidence what information he may of the presence of a ' warrantable ' stag—that is to say, a stag of five years of age or over. To avoid rousing younger stags or hinds, and to guide the huntsman to the ' couch ' of the stag in a chain of woodlands extending perhaps for three hundred acres is a task far easier to write about than to accomplish. Yet often, on his appearance at the meet, the harbourer is able to assert with confidence that he can literally put his hand on a warrantable stag.

Going his rounds, then, the day before hunting the harbourer keeps his eyes wide open, and if he sees the young ash shoots of a newly-laid fence nibbled off short, or turnips uprooted and flung aside with but one bite out of them, or the bark and ivy on some big tree trunk bitten transversely, he will know that here is the mark of a stag ; for a hind feeds greedily, not with the dainty fastidiousness of her lord and master, and will eat a turnip right down to the ground or gnaw the bark and ivy up and down. More reliable tests, however, are the ' gait ' and ' slot.' A stag's slot or hoof leaves an imprint, round, wide at the heel and blunt at the toe, while a hind has pointed toes, narrow heels, and a longer slot. A stag's dew-claws are large and point outward, a hind's, on the contrary, are small, turn inward, and point straight down. In his gait a stag crosses his legs right and left, and moving with the confidence born of centuries

of freedom, has regular paces ; but a hind puts her hind feet in direct line with her forefeet (except at such time as she is heavy in calf) ; she walks timidly and distrustfully, and so has irregular paces. A yeld or barren hind copies the gait of a young stag, but the wise harbourer who knows his business can tell the one from the other, for she always opens or spreads her toes, whereas a young stag keeps the toes of his hind feet closed. Again, there are several signs by which the harbourer may discern an old stag. There is the difference in the size of the fore and of the hind slots, the closeness of the dew-claws to the heel, the trailing of the toes of his hind slot, which he places on the ground well behind the imprint of his fore slot. Miles, a famous harbourer now dead, was wont to declare that unevenness in the length of the claws of the hind slot was an infallible sign of a big stag, and that the biggest stags were those which chose the big isolated pine trees for ' fraying-stocks,' on which to rub their horns clean of the August velvet.

On the day of the meet the harbourer will be up before daylight and will endeavour to get a peep at his stag, if fortune and the wind so favour him. It is a work which will tax all his knowledge of woodcraft, for he has to make sure that the stag has not passed on, but has really made his couch for the day in that quarter of the covert which but now swallowed him up from view. To do this he makes a wide circuit, taking due care and precaution that the stag does not get wind of him, and closely scrutinizing every track and path that may reveal the tell-tale slot-print. Gradually and cautiously the harbourer narrows his circles until he is satisfied that the stag is lying within a certain defined area or ' rap ' of wood ; and thus at last he has him ' well and truly harboured ' against the coming of the pack some six or seven hours later. Once harboured the stag will remain there for the rest of the day, except when, in the rutting season in October he becomes restless, or when his winged tormentors, the horse-flies, are too troublesome. Wort-pickers and nut-pickers sometimes disturb a harboured stag all unwittingly, when there is much wailing and gnashing of teeth on the part of the hunt.

It is only in such favoured localities as Sweet-worthy, or on the plains and prairies of the Forest that the harbourer can watch his stag in. More often he has to depend on the signs of a stag's presence, rather than on a sight of his great bulk. There are days when the harbourer does not come to the meet to report, but stays on his pony watching some restless stag, until the arrival of the tufters themselves on the scene. A stag will often jump into a covert and then out again, doubling on his foil, and it is always well to make a back cast when slotting a stag into covert, for these feigned entries, as the French call them, have been the cause of many a blank day.

In days gone by, Jim Blackmore was a well known expert in harbouring, next came Andrew Miles, who began in 1862 in Mr. Bisset's reign, harbouring some 500 stags during his twenty-five years' service under four masters. He imparted his lore to a fellow-keeper of the Earl of Carnarvon, Fred Goss, the present harbourer. Goss came in 1894 with Colonel Hornby, and has shown himself an apt pupil, his best achievement being perhaps the harbouring of six warrantable stags in six consecutive days of one week in 1900 for the Devon and Somerset and Sir John Amory's Staghounds. And the fee for all this is but a guinea a stag! Other men there are in Red Deer Land who can harbour a stag at a pinch, such as Tom Yandle, John Lang, Leonard Fowler and Charles Wensley, but Goss is the only official harbourer of the Devon and Somerset Staghounds.

FOXHUNTING

Foxhunting is the same in most counties, whether it be Leicestershire or Yorkshire, but in Somerset it presents one or two special features. Thanks to the nature of the ground and the smallness of the 'fields,' you can on Exmoor enjoy the pleasure of watching hounds drag up to their fox, as one terms the hunting of his line to where he lies snugly kennelled in some tuft of rushes or clump of ferns, his sharp black nose tucked away under his brush. Then to attract the autumn crowds of staghunters and to help to fill the coffers of the hunt the Exmoor Foxhounds meet for cub hunting in September at the convenient, if unorthodox, hour of 11 a.m. April is perhaps the best month for foxhunting on Exmoor; and both the West Somerset and the Exmoor usually kill a May fox.[12]

THE EXMOOR

Years ago, before Mr. Nicholas Snow of Oare established the Exmoor Foxhounds, 'the Stars of the West,' as they were then called, so brilliantly did they shine in the foxhunting firmament, the Reverend John Russell used to bring his pack to Porlock to hunt the foxes of the adjacent moors. It was in the spring of 1830 that Russell paid his first visit to Porlock to hunt hare as well as fox. He was accompanied by the Reverend J. Pomeroy Gilbert and the Reverend H. Farr Yeatman—a notable trio of hunting parsons—and also by Mr. George Templer of Stover. Head quarters were, as so often now, at the Ship Inn at Porlock, Southey's favourite haunt, and the manner in which the hostess, Mrs. Smith, wanted to deal with a recalcitrant covert-owner forms

one of the most amusing portions of Russell's biography. That week at Porlock was memorable, to quote Russell's own words [13]:—

'The very day Tamlyn went to Porlock to forbid my hunting, I found a fox in the heath on Lucot Common, his property. Thinking it was a vixen, I rode up to the bush, out of which she jumped, and, behold! curled up in a warm nest were four live cubs. I tied my handkerchief to a bush hard by, and rode after the pack as fast as my horse would carry me.

'But it was a blaze of scent all the way; and in thirty minutes, to my great annoyance, they ran into and killed poor little Vicky. I then returned to her kennel, took up the cubs—all four vixens—and sent them by Bat Anstey to Iddesleigh, fifty miles away. An earth was made for them, under Halsdon, Mr. Furse's residence; and in and around that earth they remained, being ear marked, and thriving well, till the following October, when suddenly they disappeared, and I never had the good luck to find one of them again with hounds.

'Six years afterwards I met the late Mr. Newton of Bridestowe, in Barnstaple, and he asked me if I had ever ear-marked—describing the mark—any foxes and lost sight of them. "Yes," I said; "four cubs, all vixens." "Then," he replied, "I found them last March in some brakes near Broadwoodwidger, twenty-five miles below Halsdon; had good runs with each, and killed all four."'

Next we find Mr. James Stoate of Meyne near Minehead hunting hare and fox, and then Mr. Abraham Phelps with his kennels at Porlock and Johnny Stone, only recently deceased, as his factotum. This brings us to 1869, when Mr. Nicholas Snow hunted fox only from his home kennels at Oare. He held office for twenty years and established the fortunes of the hunt on the firmest of bases. George Barwick was his right-hand man, and carried the horn jointly with the master, who never hunted in pink himself, just as Mr. William Chorley, his contemporary with the Quarme Harriers, never wore a hunting cap or coat. In 1887 the Hon. L. J. Bathurst assumed command and held it till 1894, when he left to become master of the Puckeridge and later of the Cambridgeshire. Sir William Williams took his place and brought the pack to a high standard of efficiency; in fact, they were too fast for their field over the 'wet ground' of the forest. Sir William had previously hunted the Stevenstone country and the country round Barnstaple. Hounds were kennelled at Ashford near Barnstaple during the off season, as the kennels at Oare conduced to kennel lameness. Sir William Williams bred a few hounds himself but relied in the main on Lord Fitzwilliam's draft. In 1903-4 Mr. W. J. Matthews was in command, and in 1904-5 Mr. Peter Ormrod. But the former did not take to Exmoor, and the latter's heart was more with his private pack of stag-

[12] On Jubilee Day, 1887, Mr. Snow met at 5 a.m. at Oareford for cubbing to celebrate the occasion.

[13] Russell, *Memoirs*, 198–9.

hounds, so that the fortunes of foxhunting fell to a low ebb, nor did the coming of Mr. Hubert F. Brunskill from the South Pool Harriers improve matters. Mange was rife and foxes scarce, and but for Mr. Nicholas Snow, the foes of foxhunting, and they were many and in hitherto unsuspected quarters, would have triumphed. But in 1906, backed by Mr. Snow and a local committee, Mr. Michael H. Salaman took office for a term of years with George Barwick once more as huntsman and Mr. H. M. Ross of Lynton as secretary, and at the present time foxhunting on Exmoor appears to have taken a new lease of life.[14]

The Exmoor country, which lies partly in Devon and partly in Somerset, extends some 15 miles from east to west and about the same from north to south. On the north the sea is the boundary, on the west the country is not hunted, on the south is the Dulverton Hunt,[15] on the east the West Somerset, while the Devon and Somerset Staghounds hunt over the whole of the territory of the Exmoor Hounds. Moorland, big woods, grass inclosures and plough form the bulk of the country. Mr. Peter Ormrod bought the pack from Mr. Nicholas Snow, and sold them to Mr. Brunskill, who took them away with him to hunt the Silverton country. Thus Mr. Salaman had to form a new pack, consisting mainly of draft hounds from the Belvoir and Quorn kennels. The pack is the joint property of Messrs. Salaman and Ross (hon. sec.), with kennels at Oare, lent by Mr. Snow. Porlock, Exford and Lynton are the best centres.

THE DULVERTON

The Dulverton Foxhounds, as now established, date from the year 1875, when the fifth Earl of Portsmouth handed over the country he had hunted in spring and autumn to Mr. J. Froude Bellew, the Squire of Anstey. Mr. Froude Bellew was—to quote his own signature to an account of a wonderful run through many parishes—a 'lover of little bitches,' which he sold to the late Lord Guildford on his retirement in 1884. For one year the country remained unhunted, but in 1885 Mr. Connock Marshall took office, and held it till 1889. Mr. Ludovic E. Bligh, afterwards master of the East Kent Foxhounds, and the present master of the Minehead Harriers, succeeded him, only to give place in 1891 to Mr. E. C. Dawkins. In 1899 Mr. Jasper H. Selwyn assumed control till 1905, when he sold his pack and gave the proceeds to be divided between the Hunt Servants' Benefit Society and the Royal Agricultural Benevolent

Society. In 1905-7 no master being forthcoming, neighbouring packs drew the Dulverton country by invitation. This country also lies in Devon and Somerset, and extends some 25 miles north by south, 18 miles east by west. On the north it adjoins the West Somerset Hunt, on the west the Exmoor, on the south the Eggesford, and on the east the Tiverton. It consists chiefly of banking country and open moors, and is a fine country for foxes if well worked. Dulverton and South Molton are the best centres.

THE WEST SOMERSET

The West Somerset with their black velvet collar was originally known as Mr. Luttrell's, being hunted by members of that family from 1824 till 1883. The Hon. R. C. Trollope of Crowcombe then took office for two seasons, to be followed by Mr. C. E. J. Esdaile of Cothelstone for six seasons. Mr. Birt St. Albyn Jenner of Alfoxton comes next on the roll of masters; he handed the country over in 1894 to Captain H. A. Kinglake, who left in 1896 to take command of the Radnor and West Herefordshire Hunt, and later the Taunton Vale Foxhounds. Mr. Wilfred Marshall of Norton Manor near Taunton then took office and did much to promote the welfare of foxhunting in West Somerset. He was exceedingly popular with the farmers and very painstaking and courteous, so that he found himself able to hunt three days a week instead of two. Puppy shows became an annual institution under his *régime*. A bitch called Melody bred him no less than twelve puppies, all of which came in from walk and were duly entered with the pack. Much of his success, as that of other masters, is due to the care in kennel and skill in the field of Will Tame from the Llangibby, who has for so many years carried the horn. In 1904 Mr. Wilfred Marshall passed away, and Mr. (now Lieut-Colonel) Dennis F. Boles stepped into his shoes, undertaking to hunt the country two days a week on a guaranteed subscription of £550. Kennels are at Carhampton near Dunster, and the hon. sec. is Captain Henry T. Daniel of Over Stowey, Bridgwater.

Hill and woodland are the main features of the West Somerset country, with large coverts on the Brendon and Quantock hills. There is a good flying country in the vale round Cannington and Stogursey, and the whole country carries a good scent, especially the old pasture lands on the Brendon Hills. Mr. Holloway's gorse at Coombes Head, King's Brompton, is indeed a wonderful fox covert, one season furnishing eighteen foxes on eighteen consecutive draws, and this despite, or perhaps because of, the presence of numerous badgers there as well. Dunster and Minehead are the best centres.

[14] In 1907 they killed 21½ brace and ran 6½ brace to ground in 75 hunting days; subscriptions have exceeded £400.

[15] For some seasons the Dulverton country remained derelict; but in 1908 Mr. Lockwood of Kirby Moorside resuscitated the hunt.

The Taunton Vale

The Taunton Vale Hunt dates from 1876, and the list of masters to date is as follows :—

Mr. Lionel Patton	1876–1885
Capt. Fitzroy	1885–1888
Mr. Wilfred Marshall	1888–1892
Mr. W. Barrett	1892–1894
Mr. W. Barrett and Mr. R. M. Doddington	1894–1896
Mr. R. M. Doddington	1896–1897
Hon. E. W. B. Portman	1897–1900
Mr. F. C. Swindell	1900–1902
Capt. H. A. Kinglake	1902

The Taunton Vale country lies entirely in Somerset, extending some 25 miles from east to west, and 14 miles from north to south. On the north it adjoins the West Somerset, on the west the West Somerset and the Tiverton, on the south the Cattistock and the Cotley Harriers' country, on the east the Blackmore Vale. It is very varied and contains much pasture land, but it has no large woodlands. The Quantock Staghounds and the Devon and Somerset Staghounds (occasionally) hunt over this country. No subscriber of less than £7 7s. is entitled to the hunt button, and a cap is taken for the poultry fund. Under Captain Kinglake's auspices sport has been excellent; the master carries the horn himself, with W. Daniels and E. Godby to turn hounds to him. The kennels are at Henlade near Taunton. The pack consists of thirty-five couples and hunts two days a week, with occasional bye-days. Taunton is the best centre.

Besides these packs, the Blackmore Vale, the Cattistock and the Tiverton packs hunt portions of the county of Somerset.

HARRIERS

Somerset certainly stands well among hare-hunting counties, for she can put into the field some eleven or twelve packs, which hunt over the great variety of country within her borders.

The Bath and County

The Bath and County are first on the list, hunting the country round Bath, but chiefly to the east of that town, and extending their operations into Gloucester and Wilts. In 1906 they hunted part of the Stanton Drew country as well. Theirs is mostly a grass country with a small portion of plough, and there is very little wire to stop hunting. Mr. Hugh Clutterbuck established the pack in 1892, and hunted it three seasons before he handed it over to Mr. James Baldwin, who bought the hounds and carried on till 1899. Then came Captain D. C. Astley, master from 1899 to 1903, Mr. C. F. Garrard from 1903 to 1904, Mr. Henry Hunter from 1904 to 1906, when the present master, Mr.

A. D. A. Bruce, assumed command. The pack consists of twenty-two couple of stud book harriers, 20–21 in., with their kennels at Claverton Down, Bath. They hunt two and three days a week, and the hon. sec. is Mr. Horace Mann. Four years prior to 1902 Major Yeele with his Avon Vale Harriers hunted the same country.

The Cotley

Next on the list comes The Cotley, a very famous west-country pack, which is kennelled at Broad Oak, Chard, and hunts two days a week. These harriers were established about 1796 by Mr. T. Deane, grandfather of the present master, and were hunted as a private pack till 1886. In that year Mr. T. P. Eames, brother of the present master, Mr. Edward Eames, took over the hounds. They hunt hare and fox, and the master who owns the pack accepts subscriptions but has no guarantee, while a cap is taken for earth-stopping expenses. Mr. N. W. Spicer of Durston, Chard, is the hon. sec. The seventeen and a half couple of 21-in. hounds are a fine old-fashioned pack of pure English harriers. Foxes are more plentiful than hares, and show good runs over the Cotley territory, which extends into Devon and Dorset. There is a lot of rough and stiffly banked country, with a fair proportion of down land, and as there are no foxhounds hunting the district there is no clashing of any sort. Mr. Eames is a past master of the noble science, and his hounds can run as well as hunt over this somewhat rough country. The sport of the 1906–7 season was excellent, hounds having accounted for 35½ brace of hares and 16 brace of foxes.

The Minehead

The Minehead Harriers, formerly styled the Hindon Harriers, for very many years under the late Mr. Joshua Clarke, are kennelled at Minehead, with Mr. Cecil Archer as hon. sec. and the Hon. Ludovic E. Bligh, a former master of the East Kent and Dulverton Foxhounds, as master. The pack consists of fifteen couple of 20-in. pure harriers which take the field twice a week, hunting over pasture, plough, moor and woodland in the eastern portion of the staghunting district. Mr. William Usborne Benfield succeeded Mr. Clarke, bringing down his own pack of old southern hounds from Frittenden in Kent. Then came his brother-in-law, Mr. William Paramore, a well-known staghunting yeoman who farmed at Bratton Court.[16] He was master from 1891 till 1898, when Mr. Algernon Rushont from the Cotswold Foxhounds succeeded him. He only held office one season, returning to the Cotswold country to be master

[16] In the season of 1906–7 sport has been more than average, and hounds have in 58 hunting days accounted for 57½ brace of hares.

of the foxhounds there once more, when the present master took office, and has done much to improve the pack.[17]

THE NETTLECOMBE

The territory of the Nettlecombe Harriers lies entirely in Somerset. They are a private pack, the property of Sir Walter J. Trevelyan of Nettlecombe Court, who established them in 1895. The pack consists of twenty-two couples of harriers bred from the packs of Mr. Vaughan Pryse and Mr. Jones of Bridgnorth. J. Pearce carries the horn with J. Clatworthy to turn hounds to him. The West Somerset Foxhounds hunt over this country, which includes some excellent moorlands for hare hunting on the Brendon Hills.

THE QUARME

The Quarme Harriers, usually styled the Q.H., are well known to every one who has ever hunted on Exmoor. One of the most popular and best known yeomen of Somerset, Mr. William Loveband Chorley of Quarme, purchased the pack in 1860 at the sale of the late Captain John Guy Evered of Stone Lodge, and maintained them till just before his death in 1900 at his own expense. Mr. Morland Greig of Exford, the deputy-master of the Devon and Somerset, purchased the pack, and built new kennels at Edgcott, Exford, for the pack, which consists of sixteen couple of 18½-in. pure harriers (entered in H. and B. Stud Book). Their country is a very large one, much of it open moor and heather in Somerset and Devon, including Exmoor itself. It is a private pack and there is no capping.

THE SEAVINGTON

The Seavington, whose master is Earl Poulett and hon. sec. Mr. C. J. Trask of Broadshard, Norton-sub-Hamdon, are kennelled at Hinton St. George. They hunt two days a week over an area of 27 miles by 17 miles, which extends into Dorset, and is mostly pasture with little plough and very little woodland. Flying fences and wide ditches make it a fine country to ride over. The pack consists of twenty couple of 20-in. harriers and crossbred hounds. There have been many masters since Mr. Tom Naish established the pack in 1863—Major Churchill Langdon, 1871–91; Mr. J. King, 1891–3; Mr. Jefferys Allen-Jefferys, 1893–9, when Mr. Piers Clarke bought his pack of pure 19-in. harriers and hunted them two seasons; Mr. R. Hole, 1901–4; Mr. H. Stuart Menzies, 1904–6, when the present master purchased the pack from the committee.

THE SPARKFORD VALE

The Sparkford Vale, known from 1895 to 1905 as Mr. Holt Needham's, during that gentleman's

[17] Deceased in 1907.

mastership, were started in 1888 by Mr. H. Turner of Cary Fitzpaine, who was succeeded by Captain W. P. St. John Mildmay, 1893–5 The pack consists of seventeen couple 20-in. pure harriers, and hunt a tract in East Somerset some 14 miles square, chiefly pasture. It is a subscription pack, and Mr. Walter J. Savage of Wales House, Queen Camel, Bath, is the present master, with Mr. A. Dickinson of Somerton as hon. sec.

THE STANTON DREW

The Stanton Drew, a pasture country in North Somerset with some moorland country on the Mendip Hills, is, or was, hunted two days a week by a mixed pack of 21½-in. foxhounds and harriers.

THE TAUNTON VALE

The Taunton Vale—eighteen couple of 20-in. harriers—hunt two days a week a nice country, comprising a good proportion of grass and arable land in the Vale. It is a subscription pack, Mr. George Scarlett of North Street, Taunton, being hon. sec., and the kennels are at Blackbrook. In 1904 Mr. John White of Leacroft, Taunton, succeeded Mr. Ben Cleave as master.

THE WELLS SUBSCRIPTION

The Wells Subscription Harriers—eighteen couple of pure harriers and foxhounds, 20–21 in.— are kennelled at Coxley, Wells, and hunt two days a week. Their country extends for a radius of 10 miles round Wells, and consists of some three parts pasture with the rest woodland and plough. On the Mendip Hills the going is good, and the fences consist of stone walls. They hunt fox as well as hare, and are a subscription pack, the property of the master, Mr. L. F. Beauchamp of Norton Hall near Bath, whose hon. sec. is Mr. Reginald A. Hobhouse of Oakhill near Bath. When Colonel Luttrell gave up his foxhounds about 1860 the Wells Subscription Harriers were established and kennelled at Milton. They were subsequently mastered by Captain John Wedgwood Yeeles, and hunted by Mr. John Phelps. Captain Yeeles then took the pack to hunt the Avon Vale country in 1882, when another pack was formed. The following were the masters after him : Captain Hastings G. Hicks, 1882–5; Committee, 1885–7; Mr. Philip H. George and a Committee, 1887; Colonel Perkins, 1887–92; pack in private hands, 1892–3; Mr. B. C. Bird, 1893–4; Mr. H. W. Selby Lowndes, 1894–7; Committee, 1897–8; Mr. Arnold Hall, 1898–9; Major C. D. Sherston, 1899–1900; Mr. R. G. Evered, 1900–2.

THE WESTON

The Weston Harriers hunt a country 30 miles long by 14 wide, entirely in Somerset. No foxhounds hunt this part of the county, which is nearly all grassland, and lies in the neighbourhood of Weston-super-Mare. Mr. E. A. Hardwick, the master, is guaranteed a sum of £400 a year, and S. Louch carries the horn. Occasionally a straggler from the Quantock herd of deer leads these twenty-two couples of 20-in. pure harriers a rare dance over the 'rheen' country.

OTTER HUNTING

Nowadays otter hunting is a sport that one may enjoy practically in every county of the kingdom ; but there was a time when Wales and the western counties shared with the north of England the only packs of otter-hounds in the kingdom. Of these none were more famous than the Culmstock pack in Somerset and the Cheriton pack in Devon. Like all otter-hound packs, they both have had their vicissitudes ; but both to-day are on a sound basis. Mr. William P. Collier of Nicholashayne established the Culmstock pack. Thanks to his good relations with the farmers of the district, he was always in possession of the best of information, and was thus enabled to bring his pack to hunt this river and that directly he had news that an otter had passed up stream. For no less than fifty-three years Mr. William Collier held office, and his voice and his horn were both famous—the former in the church choir as well as in the field. In his early days the spear was freely used, but its use has now for many years been discontinued in connexion with every pack of otter-hounds. In former days hounds were not so good as they are now, less was possibly understood of this branch of the chase, and fields, ruling smaller, gave the huntsman less help, for in otter hunting one has to depend to a great extent on the voluntary assistance of one's field, to guard a ford, line a stickle, or watch the water for the tell-tale bubbles of the otter's 'chain.'

Before 1850 the Culmstock pack used to visit the North Devon rivers periodically, and they have not been unknown at Umberleigh and Hatherleigh. A good story is told of the starting of a rival pack, the Cheriton. Hearing that the Culmstock were coming, Mr. William Cheriton assembled his forces and stood beside the river in full view of the windows of the train by which the Culmstock hound-van was due to arrive, and just as it steamed into the station threw a stuffed otter to his hounds. This was enough for the rival master, who withdrew without unboxing his pack, and thus left Mr. Cheriton in peaceful possession of his home waters. In 1889 Mr. Fred Collier, his nephew, took over the pack because of the serious illness of his uncle, and held office till 1898. The Colliers, like their successor, were always great believers in the working powers of the foxhound in preference to the pure rough otter-hound. Certainly the foxhound entered to otter is a better finder and killer. In 1898 Mr. James H. Wyley, a Staffordshire gentleman, became master. The old pack was sold, part to go to France and the remainder to form the nucleus of the Essex Otter-hounds. Mr. Wyley bought the Pembroke and Carmarthenshire Otter-hounds and had great sport for three seasons, killing close on 100 otters. On his resignation in 1901 the pack was sold to go to Ireland to join the King's (Regiment) Otter-hounds.

Captain Aldham Graham Clarke of Frocester Manor in Gloucestershire then stepped into the breach, leasing Mr. Hastings Clay's pack for the season, and putting on drafts from various kennels, including the Badminton. Mrs. Graham Clarke was a most enthusiastic joint-master, and on one occasion carried the horn herself, hunted hounds and accounted for a brace of otters. John Jackson from Mr. Clay's establishment now took the place of Arthur Lenthall, who had gone to Ireland as whipper-in. Campaigning in South Africa is not the best preparation for otter hunting, and Captain Graham Clarke found his health not proof against the exertions by land and water entailed by otter hunting, and accordingly retired. Mr. Clay now took back his portion of the pack, while the remainder were sold to establish the Crowhurst pack in Sussex.

Thus the Culmstock pack may be said to have sired the two new packs hunting Essex, Kent and Sussex. Mr. Fred Collier now came forward again, backed by the late Mr. Harry Bellew of Wiveliscombe. They purchased the Brookfield pack belonging to Mr. Jennings of co. Cork, and set to work in the Culmstock country. But success did not crown their efforts, for hounds—good trail hunters indeed, but poor finders—were literally not up to the mark. One season was enough for the joint-masters, who sold their pack, some here, some there. Once more Mr. James H. Wyley took office with the Rev. Reginald D. Wade to turn hounds to him. Drafts from the Cheriton and other packs made up his very small, if efficient, lot of eight and a half couples, all smooth hounds, and this season he hunted 100 days and killed about thirty otters. With a full pack he would doubtless have scored more frequently than he did. In 1906 a former secretary, Mr. H. G. Thornton of Warmore House, Dulverton, obtained the loan of the King's (Regiment) Otter-hounds and the services of Arthur Lenthall, and took over the Culmstock country from Mr. Wyley. Otters came somewhat easily to hand, the pack was a smart one, and though the practice of tailing was somewhat freely indulged in, the streams of the Culmstock country are so well stocked that they have successfully stood the great depletion of the stock of otters that has taken place since 1899.

Mr. H. G. Thornton only held office one season, when he was succeeded in 1907 by

Mr. Henry Welch-Thornton of Beaurepaire Park near Basingstoke, who brought his own pack from the Cheriton country. Mr. E. A. Vaughan of Rosemount, Ilminster, now became hon. sec., and new kennels were built at Norton Fitzwarren. Mr. H. G. Thornton had kennelled at Morebath, Mr. Wyley at Ashill, and Messrs. Collier and Bellew, as well as Captain Graham Clarke, at the old kennels at Culmstock.

The Culmstock hunt the Tone, Culm, Barle, Otter, Axe, Yarty, Yeo, the Exe and tributaries (save the Creedy), and all the streams flowing into the Bristol Channel from Lynton on the west to the eastern boundary of Somerset, and all streams and tributaries flowing into the English Channel between Weymouth and Exmouth. The Tone, Otter, Axe and Exe generally afford the best sport, and there are many secluded streams where the otter pursues the even tenour of his way. In 1904 the Cheriton pack were kennelled for the winter at Porlock, and by invitation of the water owners, Mr. Arthur Heinemann drew the streams in the neighbourhood—the Avill, the Horner and the Lyn. These waters, which for many years had not been visited by the Culmstock pack, provided excellent sport. Perhaps the earliest date for an otter hunt was 25 January 1905, when the Cheriton pack killed an otter at Sir Thomas Acland's place at Holnicote. Occasionally Mr. Hastings Clay brings his pack to hunt the waters round Castle Cary and Wells, but for general purposes the county of Somerset is only served by this one pack, the Culmstock.

BADGER DIGGING

Few animals are more maligned than the badger (*meles taxus*), and many are the fallacies about him and his habits. These misconceptions are caused by ignorance of his nocturnal way of life, and fostered by his retiring disposition, which leads him to shun the light of day and take up his abode deep down in the very bowels of the earth in some remote combe, rocky cleft or impenetrable thicket. To the minds of many the very word 'badger' conjures up recollections of what they have read of the long obsolete sport of badger-baiting or badger-drawing, and thoughts of an overpowering stench. Yet there is no more cleanly animal in all his ways than a badger, which only uses his offensive secretion if attacked, and then probably to attract to his aid the other members of his tribe. In West Somerset, where he abounds, every indulgence is shown him, and the badger is treated, when bagged, either to a prompt and merciful dispatch if circumstances require it, or as is more often the case, he is granted a speedy release in a different district. By interesting the country people in Brock and his ways, by proving to them that his chief food consists of slugs, snails, beetles, pig-nuts, wasp-grubs, young rabbits, moles, and such small deer, and by treating him with every consideration when captured, the writer has done much to secure his preservation and freedom from trap and poison. Mr. Charles Glass, late of Ellicombe, Dunster, and Mr. Philip Everard especially have united with him in dealing out fair play to what all naturalists regard as the most ancient and interesting of existing British mammals. So well have one and all learned their lesson that it frequently happens that farmers and even keepers themselves voluntarily plead for the sow badgers to be spared, and trappers often release them from their traps.

Many years of badger digging have led up to this result. As a sport badger digging flourishes in Devon and Somerset, and it is conducted on most humane and sporting lines. A fine day, a sturdy team of diggers, some skill in engineering and a knowledge of the badger's ways, a good team of trained terriers,[18] infinite patience, and last, but not least, the badger himself are necessary to a successful day's digging. Not all shooting tenants and landowners will tolerate the presence of too many badgers on their holdings or estates, for they do a certain amount of damage to grasslands which they nuzzle like pigs, roll about in standing corn, 'play up works', as they say in Somerset, with banks and fences, and, if one believes the shooting tenants, eat eggs, though personally the present writer does not believe that they do. Thus one is often called upon to dig them out and move them to save their lives. Nor is it difficult to find fresh homes for them. Many farmers are only too glad to let them go on their ground to keep down the rabbits, while some landowners protect them; and occasionally there is a demand for them from other parts of the country, such, for instance, as Epping Forest, where there is a desire to establish a badger colony.[19]

Badger digging is a genuinely exciting sport, in which fortune inclines now to the badger or now to his excavators. Trench after trench may be dug only to find that the badger has shifted his quarters farther into the ground. Mine and countermine are then sunk, tunnels driven in perhaps twenty feet or more, until at last the terrier has hunted his quarry from gallery to gallery and set him up to bay in the remotest of his subterranean *cul-de-sacs*. Through all these long hours neither badger nor terrier will have received any punishment from each

[18] The west country has ever been the home of the working terrier, the hunt-terrier as he is called, and from the days of the Reverend John Russell to the present day the breed has been maintained by the writer, among others, solely for its working qualities and with no thought of show bench honours.
[19] The writer has found fresh homes for badgers in Sussex, Lancashire, Essex and even in Scotland.

other, the object being not to use a terrier too hard or game, only to be needlessly punished by his foe, but rather one which will employ all due caution and by constant yapping tell those outside where to dig and also to prevent the badger from escaping by burying himself as he is wont to do when disturbed.

Some seasons ago there was a small pack of basset-hounds kept at Dulverton to hunt the line of a badger, which was dug out and given twenty minutes' law. Away he would go for the nearest earth he knew, and away they would go on his line. Yet these hounds would never close with the badger nor molest him in any way; indeed, badger and basset-hounds have been seen to run down to the Barle, where both drank, and when the badger had slaked his thirst he swam out and went on again, while the hounds took no further heed of him. It was a pleasant afternoon's amusement for all concerned, and quite devoid of cruelty. If the badger got to ground he was left in peace; if hounds set him up to bay he was bagged and released at night-fall.

Owing to the presence of deer in most of the coverts in West Somerset, it has been found impossible to hunt badgers by moonlight with hounds, with the earths all stopped, as is done in East Devon, where the badgers get shorter shrift than they do in Somerset.

Thus it will be seen one only regulates the number of the badgers by digging, taking due toll only of their numbers, while by changing them from place to place the breed has undoubtedly improved in size and general health. Without badger digging one would never know the value of one's terriers, which are thereby trained to go to ground and to stay there till dug out; and as one's object is not to breed a dog that will close with the badger, but only have heart enough to lie up to him for hours, there can be no question of cruelty. Occasionally, but very seldom, there are accidents, when dog or badger or even man gets buried by a fall of earth. We have once known the two former thus succumb,

and the writer had a narrow escape of a similar fate quite recently.

The longest dig that we can recall was at Pendon Hill near Bridgwater (1899), where we dug for two days before securing a fine pair of badgers, the larger 34 lb. On another occasion we dug from noon to midnight in Stowey Quarry, Timberscombe, when the badger beat us. We once got four badgers out of an earth near Challacombe (1907), four out of one near South Molton (1908), and four from one at Trentishoe (1908), five out of one near Porlock (1906), six out of one near Exford (1897), all full-grown badgers. We have been able to prove that badgers lay down their cubs in March, often in February; but the question of their period of gestation still remains an unsolved problem for the naturalists. It has always been our custom not to dig in the fence months (February, March, April) unless circumstances compelled us to do so, when we have reared many of the cubs and made pets of them. Charming pets they are, and would even follow us into the sea or return every morning if let out at night.[20]

In 1894–5 we dug out 23½ brace, of which only 8½ brace were killed, and from 1 August 1906 to 1 May 1907, 19 brace; in 1897 10 brace; in 1898 10½ brace; in 1899 12 brace; in 1900 12½ brace; in 1901 6½ brace; from 1 August 1907 to 1 February 1908 17½ brace.

Of 88 badgers dug out in 4 years, 1894–8, 42 were boars, 42 were sows, and 4 unknown. Boars and sows of 30 lb. are frequently met with in West Somerset; one of 34 lb. taken at Bridgwater in 1897, another of 32½ lb. dug out at Trentishoe in 1907, and a third of 31 lb. captured at Wingate in 1900, being three of the biggest; while we have dug out sow badgers of 32 lb. (Wootton Courtney, 1897), and 4 sows dug out in 1906 weighed respectively 32 lb., 31 lb., 31 lb., 30 lb. Of the 19 brace taken out in 1906–7 only 4½ brace were killed, the rest being released or sent to fresh homes, where they were given their liberty.

COURSING

Somerset is hardly adapted for the pursuit of the hare with greyhounds, or long dogs, as they are termed in local parlance. This sport circles round Cothelestone House near Taunton, the home of Mr. Charles E. J. Esdaile, and in fact very few public meetings were held anywhere else until lately. It was about 1840 that Mr. Edward Jeffries Esdaile began holding coursing meetings at Cothelestone, which extended over two days and were well supported. All the best known west-country coursing men were Mr. Esdaile's guests for these meetings, open house

being the pleasant order of the day. After Mr. Esdaile's death in 1867 these coursing meetings came to an untimely end, as his successor took no interest in the sport. On succeeding to the property in 1881 Mr. Charles Edward Jeffries Esdaile opened the ground to the public once more, and from 1882 till 1899 one-day meetings were again held at Cothelestone. But there were difficulties in securing

[20] Badgers average three in a litter, occasionally four, rarely five.

entries. In 1900 the stakes failed to fill, and in 1901 coursing was again abandoned. Wentworth was judge and Souch slipper during the last era of these meetings.

About a score of years ago a good meeting was started at Pawlett, where the famous pastures, 'The Hams,' provide an excellent arena for the display of the greyhound's powers. Mr. Henry Smith-Spark, agent to Lord de Mauley, was the prime mover in its inception. He and the tenant farmers used to invite some of their friends who kept greyhounds to come informally on a certain day and enjoy some coursing. As years went by the coursing was carried on under a club, and has continued to flourish up to the present day.

RACING

The once famous Bath meeting has fallen from its high estate, and no longer does the two-year-old form there displayed give a clue to the classic winners of the following year. It must indeed be many years since a Derby winner ran at Bath as a two-year-old. Of hunt meetings we may mention the Beaufort Hunt and the Vale of White Horse held in April, and the Taunton Vale Hunt meetings. At Minehead and Bridgwater race meetings were held, but not 'under rules' and were abandoned, among other reasons, for want of adequate support. The Devon and Somerset Staghounds have held two Point to Point Race meetings, and two only; and some interest must attach to these spasmodic efforts to amuse the Exmoor hunting man. Indeed Exmoor, where you can start your field say at Hawkcombe Head and tell them to get to Dunkery Beacon as best they may is an ideal ground for such sport. There it is for all to see, and the man would win whose horse was the best stayer and galloper, while much would depend on the horsemanship of the riders, quite apart from any knowledge of the country.

The first meeting took place Monday 20 September 1897 at Larkbarrow, and aroused great local interest. Unfortunately the course selected being over a very treacherous and almost unfair country, there were two accidents. Mr. J. Yandle's Tiny Tom was killed, and Mr. Morland Greig on Rufus broke his arm. For the Farmers' Race there were eleven entries, and Mr. E. Bawden, now whipper-in to the Devon and Somerset, won it on Reeago by Black and Blue, his father's horse. For the Light Weights' Race there were twenty entries, and Mr. J. C. de Las Casas won it on his horse O.D.V. For the Heavy Weights' Race there were but seven entries, and Mr. J. C. de Las Casas also won this on Mr. C. W. Nelder's Bluestocking. Some years elapsed before the second and last meeting took place, this time over a better course, at Hawkcombe Head.

POLO

Polo has of late years made enormous strides in popular favour; and a county so famous as Somerset for its pony blood, and containing so many hunting men, was not likely to be long without a polo club. In 1904 the West Somerset Polo Club [21] became affiliated to the County Polo Association. The season is from 1 April to 15 October. Games or matches are held each Wednesday and Saturday in May and June; on Monday, Wednesday and Saturday in July; and on every non-staghunting day in August, September, October. Early in September the club goes on an invitation tour. The ground at Newbridge near Porlock on the Minehead Road is 260 yds. by 120 yds., and is boarded. Few prettier or more picturesque spots could have been selected than this meadow beside the babbling Horner Brook, under the shade of the wild coppices of Breakneck Gorge, with North Hill and the Selworthy Woods in the near distance. Many an antlered monarch of the moor has stood to bay here, and many a timid, crafty hind has paid the last penalty beside the polo ground, while more than one otter has been found, hunted and killed in the stream adjoining.

In the Quantock country near Fairfield, Bridgwater, an effort was made in 1907 to start a second polo club in Somerset. Mr. H. M. Crosby of Knaplock and Mr. G. Archer of Alfoxton Park were the prime movers in the matter.

[21] A list of these pioneers of polo in Somerset will be of interest. The president of the club is Sir C. T. D. Acland, bart.; the vice-presidents are Sir Alex. A. Hood, bart., M.P.; Mr. R. A. Saunders, M.S.H.; Mr. E. A. V. Stanley, M.S.H.; Mr. M. H. Salaman, M.F.H.; Mr. D. Boles, M.F.H.; Mr. L. E. Bligh, M.H.; Mr. Morland Greig, M.H. There is a committee of thirteen with Dr. Henry as chairman. Mr. J. P. Goddard is hon. sec., Mr. W. Withycombe, assistant hon. sec., and Mr. G. Richardson, hon. treasurer.

SHOOTING

Few counties save Devon can show such a varied game-bag as Somerset; but as a shooting county it has not the fame of Norfolk, Suffolk and Cambridgeshire. Near Taunton and Bath game-preserving is carried on as elsewhere, but there would be a certain monotony in a mere enumeration of big bags, which are by no means peculiar to the county of Somerset.

Perhaps the chief interest that Somerset possesses for the shooting man is its black game. Grouse have been introduced, but have failed to establish themselves; and of late years the black cock and the grey hen are becoming scarcer and scarcer. Many reasons are advanced to account for this, but probably the stock itself has become effete. Some say the heather is not burned sufficiently, or too late in the year; others that there are too many cocks left to fight one another, and worry the hens. Certainly there is little or no driving, when the cocks are supposed to be the first to fall to the gun, but the pointer and setter in Somerset find employment. No better clue to shooting in Somerset can be had than the lists [22] from the game book of a famous Exmoor estate. On it no birds are reared, and the pheasants killed represent the unaided efforts of the wild stock. But little vermin killing is done on the moor, on some estates none at all, so that it is a question of the survival of the fittest in a land where you may daily see the buzzard hawk wheeling in idle circles or hear the croak of the raven on the Culbone Cliffs.

ANGLING

Somerset possesses many charms for the faithful follower of Izaak Walton, though she just misses her share of the salmon rivers of the west country. Yet even so the upper reaches of the placid Exe and the brawling Barle lie within the borders of the county. Of trout streams and brooks Somerset claims a goodly number, more especially on the west and north and south, while further east her rivers lose their wild moorland character and

[22] GAME BOOK: HOLNICOTE AND WINSFORD.

Date	Black game	Part-ridge	Phea-sant	Land-rail	Wood-cock	Snipe	Hares	Wild-fowl	Plover
1836	102	40	327	—	21	1	65	—	3
1837	54	—	439	—	84	3	83	15	—
1838	53	53	323	—	25	3	75	—	—
1839	31	42	286	1	30	3	63	—	1
1840	19	48	315	1	88	11	100	17	—
1841	1	57	192	—	21	4	112	—	—
1842	66	42	408	2	65	25	117	—	—
1843	27	23	140	2	78	5	113	18	—
1844	51	63	319	—	75	12	101	4	—
1845	43	78	182	2	36	2	32	—	—
1846	45	—	—	—	—	—	—	—	—
1847	59	5	47	—	17	14	28	—	—
1849	55	30	208	1	25	7	51	2	—
1850	51	56	204	2	10	1	35	1	1
1851	75	31	162	—	29	1	60	1	—
1852	61	60	70	—	13	—	39	1	—
1853	65	19	105	—	28	—	43	2	—
1854	58	27	120	2	23	—	48	1	6
1855	57	24	83	1	14	1	28	4	—
1856	69	25	106	—	21	2	53	—	—
1857	109	49	190	4	32	1	84	—	—
1858	133	63	229	2	32	1	48	—	—
1859	115	64	288	1	26	—	60	—	—
1861	75	12	110	—	32	—	48	—	—
1865	100	85	300	—	35	—	181	—	—
1866	96	96	425	—	61	—	275	—	—
1867	1	65	285	—	35	—	136	3	—
1868	77	42	410	—	15	—	185	—	—
1869	27	59	329	—	55	—	189	—	—
1875	34	98	234	—	42	—	108	—	—
1876	62	—	—	—	—	—	—	—	—
1877	71	31	219	—	29	—	132	—	—
1878	71	39	133	—	42	8	150	4	—
1880	33	64	253	—	14	3	151	8	—
1881	84	86	394	—	18	—	89	—	—
1883	53	121	417	1	19	1	55	—	—
1884	96	81	492	1	37	—	78	—	—
1885	47	99	424	1	36	1	133	—	—
1886	63	138	223	1	21	4	—	3	—
1887	163	192	549	2	38	—	124	—	—
1888	64	164	309	—	22	1	67	2	—
1889	113	242	610	—	18	—	34	—	—
1890	78	175	533	1	18	1	37	1	—
1891	42	109	554	—	18	1	24	8	—
1892	85	112	760	—	31	5	39	1	—
1893	93	155	970	—	28	1	23	1	—
1894	121	119	536	—	53	5	27	4	—
1895	104	93	809	—	25	—	20	1	—
1896	208	162	934	3	14	2	34	2	—
1897	61	242	914	—	54	6	46	12	—
1898	78	147	730	—	46	10	53	12	—
1899	86	154	767	—	35	7	46	75	—
1900	90	153	782	—	46	—	23	53	23
1901	57	223	788	—	32	7	8	50	—
1902	57	60	664	—	26	7	16	43	—
1903	49	71	701	—	28	2	26	37	—
1904	114	58	823	—	29	8	18	72	—
1905	153	89	956	—	26	5	9	97	—
1906	115	134	1029	—	24	5	23	37	—

harbour in their sluggish depths fish of a less sporting character.

There is one stream that is well worth the attention of those interested in fisheries, for it presents somewhat of a problem to the un-initiated. We refer to the Horner Water that flows through Sir Thomas Acland's wide domain from Chettisford to Bossington. This stream not only contains an abundance of the ordinary brown trout, but also in its lower reaches a variety of silver-coloured trout with pink flesh, which display the agility of ' rainbows ' when hooked. These fish, locally termed ' peal ' (whether rightly or wrongly the writer is unable to assert), always make their way to the lowest pool of all, as if to get to sea, and are seldom taken above Newbridge, though the writer has caught them under Cloutsham. They rise very freely at times to a fly, but seldom on days when the ordinary trout are taking. In weight they average not more than a quarter of a pound, but they have been taken up to two pounds. Occasionally in winter flood the Horner Water breaks through the pebble ridge by Hurlstone Point and salmon do then come up, as has been proved by their capture. But for most months in the year this stream has no direct outlet to the sea, but percolates through the beach.

There is not a tiny trickle of a stream that rises on or near Exmoor that does not con-tain trout, and though the little fish may be of insignificant size, for sweetness they cannot be beaten. Badgworthy Water, Weare Water, Chalk Water and Horner are among the best known trout streams in West Somerset, and with the exception of Chalk Water, strictly preserved by Mr. Nicholas Snow of Oare, the angler can fish them all by ticket to be obtained at the local hostelries, or of the agents of Lady Lovelace of Ashley Combe, Mr. Robert Blath-wayt of Porlock Manor, and Sir Thomas Acland of Holnicote. The Barle and the Exe may also be fished by ticket, with the exception of certain private waters, and some hotels lease the fishing for the use of their guests. The Aville Brook, which rises on Dunkery and flows through Timberscombe and Dunster to the sea, abounds in goodly trout; it is in the hands of Capt. A. Fownes - Luttrell of Dunster Castle and Sir George Farwell of Knowle, from whom leave to fish may occasionally be obtained by a favoured few. Around Washford and Williton are several good trout brooks, and parts of the famous Upper Axe are within the borders of Somerset. Those who would fish the moorland streams of Exmoor should certainly study Mr. Claude F. Wade's charming book, *Exmoor Streams*. For flies the little blue upright and the pheasant tail are perhaps the most useful; while good bags may on favourable days be secured by dapping with wood-lice or the caddis grub.

CRICKET

Few sides have played more popular and delightful cricket than that which has repre-sented Somerset; it is indeed not too much to say that the attractiveness of the sporting cricket played by the county eleven far outweighs their actual achievements, which show 68 victories to be set against 148 defeats, 61 matches being drawn.

The county only reached the first class in 1891, but between 1878, the starting point of modern cricket, and that year it had enjoyed very varying success. In the earlier years the well-known fast Oxford bowler, Mr. A. H. Evans, was a most effective member of the side. In 1878 he captured 34 wickets for 333 runs. Against Cambridge he actually claimed for his univer-sity 35 wickets for 304 runs, and for Gentlemen against Players 26 for 330. Somerset has always rejoiced in a plentiful supply of first-rate wicket-keepers, eminent among whom was Mr. F. T. Welman. It is interesting to recall that Mr. S. E. Butler, who took all ten Cambridge wickets for 38 runs in the University match of 1871, played for Somerset in the last important match in which he appeared. During the chrysalis period of Somerset cricket, the best batting came from Messrs. E. Sainsbury, Hamilton,

Ross and D. D. Pontifex. In 1880 Mr. W. M. Massey played against Sussex an aggressive 120 not out, which included a six and a seven. Fothergill had the useful analysis of 42 wickets for 8 runs each in the season, and in 1882 replaced Morley for the Players at Lord's.

Cricketers of importance who from time to time lent valuable aid were Messrs. W. N. Roe and J. B. Challen. The former, who had scored 404 in a long vacation match at Cam-bridge, proved a fine bat and an active field whenever he was released from his scholastic duties at Elstree. The latter, wonderfully agile at cover-point, was also a valued run-getter. Mr. R. C. Ramsey, the Australian, who played for Harrow and Cambridge, was an effective slow bowler, though his inclusion in the team of Gentlemen of England that played against the Australians was not justified by his perform-ance in the match. Mr. E. W. Bastard, an Oxford slow bowler educated at Sherborne, failed to fulfil expectation. A name more in-separably associated with Somerset was that of Mr. H. T. Hewett, a superb point and a terri-fically hard left-handed hitter, who, after doing little at Harrow and Oxford, became the captain of the county. Mr. L. D. Hildyard, who made his first appearance for this county, went to Lancashire; while Mr. O. G. Radcliffe, who also graduated in Somerset, preferred to cast in his lot with Gloucestershire. On the other hand, from the neighbouring county came Nichols, who had previously played as an amateur, but now became professional and the bowling mainstay of the side.

A yet greater acquisition was Mr. S. M. J. Woods, a lion-hearted cricketer whom it is difficult to over-praise. A tremendously dangerous fast bowler in his earlier days, always a magnificent field and a formidable bat, who never failed at a pinch and had an absolute contempt for all classes of attack, he has also proved himself an admirable captain, and the most stimulating personality of the modern cricket field. While still a schoolboy at Brighton (where in 1885 and 1886 he captured 128 wickets with an average of 8·50 and made 900 runs with an average of 36), he failed to score in his first match for his county, but took 12 wickets for 57 runs.

Another cricketer who qualified was Major W. C. Hedley, who had been left out of the Kent team on account of objections to his delivery. He was of great service to Somerset, not only with the ball, but as a fine if uncertain bat. In 1888 Tyler, the successful slow bowler, began his county career by taking 74 wickets for 10 runs each. His action was, however, always condemned by some of the best judges. While still schoolboys at Repton, the brothers Palairet obtained their first trial for their county. Mr. R. C. N. Palairet showed himself an excellent bat and a capital fielder in the slips, while Mr. L. C. H. Palairet is unquestionably the most graceful and stylish bat of modern times. In 1890 Somerset achieved the splendid performance of winning every one of the eight fixtures played against minor counties, besides opening their long series of engagements with Middlesex by a victory and a tie. Thenceforth the county became first-class, and has thoroughly deserved the distinction.

It will be interesting to recall the part that Somerset men have played in international cricket. Mr. A. E. Newton went with Mr. G. F. Vernon's team to Australia in 1887 as principal wicket-keeper, and Mr. L. H. Gay put on the gloves for Mr. Stoddart's first team in 1894. Braund went with Mr. MacLaren's combination in 1901 and with the M.C.C. team in 1903 and 1907. Mr. P. R. Johnson was a member of Lord Hawke's New Zealand and Australian eleven in 1902, and of the M.C.C. side in 1906. Mr. S. M. J. Woods played for Australia against England in the three test matches in 1888, while Mr. L. C. H. Palairet played in two, and Braund in all five matches, between England and Australia in 1902, also in all three between England and South Africa in

1907. Messrs. R. C. Ramsey and F. T. Welman have represented the Gentlemen against the Colonials, and Tyler and Braund have appeared for the Players. Messrs. S. M. J. Woods, W. C. Hedley, L. C. H. Palairet, Braund and Cranfield have been chosen for M.C.C. against the same opponents. Somerset has never beaten the Australians, but has four draws to set against two defeats.

The performances of the newly elevated county excited the greatest interest in cricket circles in 1891; indeed it may be said that they formed the salient feature of that summer. The comparative novelty of any western county, save Gloucestershire, taking a prominent place, and the unusually attractive play in which the majority of the side indulged, established the eleven as a prime favourite. Their record was five victories against six defeats, which gave them fifth place. Their least successful effort was at the Oval, when Lohmann and Sharpe sent them back for 37 and 37, after Surrey had compiled 449. A five-wicket success over Kent and a ten-wicket defeat of Gloucestershire were features not so sensational as a seven-wicket victory over Yorkshire, when Mr. S. M. J. Woods, bowling with untiring energy, took 13 wickets for less than 10 runs a piece and scored 50 in 40 minutes after six wickets had fallen for 18 runs. The climax was reached when the promoted county on 15 August was the first to beat Surrey in the championship competition. The metropolitan team were 40 to the bad on first hands. Messrs. L. C. H. Palairet and Hewett put on 97 for the first wicket, and after Mr. J. B. Challen had given a singularly fine display for 89 the innings was declared at 331 for 9. With four hours to play for a draw, Surrey began well, and an hour before the end had five wickets to fall. Disasters followed until, with ten minutes to spare, Sharpe joined Wood, and was bowled on the very stroke of time by Mr. Woods.

Third position was assumed in 1892, and on the Taunton ground Surrey was the only side to beat them. After Tyler's bowling against Notts, 6 for 63 and 9 for 33, the spectators subscribed £44. Against Yorkshire Messrs. Hewett and L. C. H. Palairet created a record by putting on 346 for first wicket in three hours and a half. The captain scored 201, being the first to go, his partner made 146, and Major W. C. Hedley subsequently hit hard for 102, the total of 592 being obtained off only 179 overs. A last wicket stand in the match with Kent for pace has rarely been beaten, Rev. A. P. Wickham and Mr. C. J. Robinson adding 47 in 12 minutes. Mr. H. T. Hewett, who averaged 40 and was the only cricketer in England to score 1,000 runs that season for his county, Mr. L. C. H. Palairet, Major W. C. Hedley and Mr. S. M. J. Woods all represented the Gentlemen during that summer.

A marked retrogression in 1893 proved that high-water mark had been touched. A clever victory by 39 runs over Surrey was notable for the hitting of Mr. Woods, who obtained 62 out of 86 in an hour. Successive single innings victories over Notts and Gloucestershire were materially assisted by Mr. H. T. Hewett, who in two hours with Mr. L. C. H. Palairet scored 120 out of 257 and 112 out of 163. Mr. S. M. J. Woods bowled grandly against the Australians, claiming 6 for 26 and 3 for 31. For the Players at Lord's, Tyler captured 8 for 58. After this year Mr. Hewett retired from all participation in Somerset cricket, though in 1894 he scored 579 with an average of 34 in other first-class matches. At the Oval, Mr. S. M. J. Woods, the new captain, played two superb innings of 80 and 85. With Mr. D. L. Evans in, 100 runs were at one time added in sixty-eight minutes. The victory by one wicket over Sussex might have been lost had a ball been properly thrown in. It was in this summer that Mr. Woods first strained himself, and it was a succession of these accidents that finally ruined his bowling. In the extra match with the South Africans, Somerset made the necessary 238 for the loss of only one wicket.

The remarkable wealth of amateur wicket-keepers enjoyed by Somerset has been already mentioned in connexion with the name of Mr. F. T. Welman. Through a long number of years Mr. A. E. Newton wore the gloves with remarkable efficiency. The Rev. A. P. Wickham kept wicket well, and the season of 1894 was notable for the advent of Mr. L. H. Gay, previously associated with Hampshire. Whenever he played he proved admirable. Later, one superior even to these eminent cricketers was found in Mr. H. Martyn, who, with the possible exception of Mr. Gregor MacGregor in his Cambridge days, proved himself the finest wicket-keeper who ever turned out for the Gentlemen.

If the earlier portion of 1895 was disastrous, August proved triumphant for the Somerset men. Their great achievement was the defeat of Surrey by 53 runs. Tyler was the hero of this match, for he took all 10 wickets for 49 runs, an unique record in the county. After being 59 down at half play in the Yorkshire fixture Somerset amassed 353, Mr. L. C. H. Palairet showing masterly form for 165; and though, when Tunnicliffe and Wainwright had added 140, the Northerners needed only 117 with 8 wickets to fall, the rest could not cope with Tyler whose brilliant bowling helped his side to win by 29 runs. Seldom has slow bowling been more severely punished than in the match between Gloucestershire and Somerset, for Tyler's 13 wickets cost 222 runs, and Mr. C. L. Townsend's 12 cost 225. To a total of 518 by Sussex Somerset responded with 465, Mr. S. M. J.

Woods actually scoring 215 in two hours and a half, with thirty-two fours to his credit. Less happy was the fate of the side in having to field out to 801 compiled by Lancashire, when Mr. A. C. MacLaren obtained the unparalleled individual first-class innings of 424.

In spite of the batting of the redoubtable captain, assisted by the brothers Palairet, the figures of 1896 showed a lamentable falling off, though Robson began his useful career, obtaining 6 for 22 against the Australians. Nor did anything satisfactory illumine 1897, except the double victory over Surrey. At Brighton defeat only came by one wicket. In the home match with Sussex Mr. S. M. J. Woods stood out of a Somerset match for the first time for six years. Mr. F. A. Phillips, a steady bat previously associated with Essex, came into the side, as did Gill and Cranfield. Gill was a fast bowler and hard hitter, who eventually went to Leicestershire; and Cranfield, a slow bowler, took the chief part in the attack at the opening of the twentieth century. Only one success was chronicled in 1898, when Sussex were beaten at Eastbourne ten minutes before time. In this match Mr. S. M. J. Woods, who had made 143 out of 173 scored while he was in, took 3 wickets, all clean bowled, for 10 runs at the crisis. The spasmodic brilliancy of the hard hitting during the season did not atone for the uncertainty of the form. In 1899 matters were infinitesimally better, despite the absence of Mr. L. C. H. Palairet, just because Mr. S. M. J. Woods batted better than ever. The end of the century was signalized by double victories over Surrey and Hampshire, to be set, however, against eleven defeats, six of them with an innings to spare. The sensational feature was the no-balling of Tyler by James Phillips. Braund, a splendid all-round cricketer, who had been insufficiently tried for Surrey, became qualified, and has proved himself to be the finest professional who has yet represented any of the three western counties.

The most memorable thing in the annals of Somerset cricket is the double defeat inflicted on the Yorkshire eleven when that great team was in the full tide of its unprecedented success. The first occasion was in July 1901, at Leeds. The visitors started their second innings in a minority of 238, and yet won by 279 runs. Mr. L. C. H. Palairet and Braund, who had both been bowled without scoring at the first attempt, each made a century, putting up 222 for the first wicket. Subsequently Mr. F. A. Phillips played fine cricket for 130, and the total reached 630. Yorkshire collapsed in shocking fashion before Braund and Cranfield. In the following June at Sheffield, for the second successive season Yorkshire sustained its solitary defeat in county matches at the hands of Somerset. It was a small scoring game, and the bowlers had a rare harvest, Haigh taking his five last wickets without a run being scored off him ; but Braund was the real hero. He scored the highest aggregate, 31 and 34, and bowling with an excellent length, getting on a lot of leg-break and now and then sending down an irresistible fast ball, he claimed 6 for 30 and 9 for 41. Pitted against the same side for M.C.C. and Ground in the Scarborough week, he made top score and took 6 for 77 and 6 for 34.

Somerset enjoyed a better year in 1902, for four victories could be set against seven defeats. They dropped back a little owing to decline in the bowling, but Mr. H. Martyn and Mr. L. C. H. Palairet with Braund were invaluable as run-getters. Cranfield's hard work with the ball was the best feature of 1904, a season memorable also for the superb off-driving of Mr. L. C. H. Palairet when obtaining his 203 at Worcester.

There is no temptation to dwell on the deplorable experiences of the county in 1905 ; but improvement was to be noted in 1906. After being 74 runs behind on the first innings, Somerset defeated Gloucestershire by 212 runs. Mr. P. R. Johnson batted well and Mr. F. A. Phillips also rendered good service. A well-deserved testimonial was organized for Mr. S. M. J. Woods. Mr. L. C. H. Palairet, elected captain for 1907, expressed himself sorely disappointed with the play of the side. A sensational first appearance was made by Mr. B. L. Bisgood, who only just failed to score two centuries at Worcester, but it was felt that in 1908 Mr. J. Daniell would to a large extent have to build up a new eleven.

The following averages, specially compiled, give the principal figures in Somerset first-class cricket ; it will be noticed that Mr. S. M. J. Woods, Major W. C. Hedley, Braund and Robson are in both tables.

BATTING.

	Innings.	Runs.	Average.
L. C. H. Palairet . .	354	12,764	36·20
H. T. Hewett . .	68	2,104	30·64
Braund	195	5,748	29·93
S. M. J. Woods . .	457	11,505	25·80
P. R. Johnson . . .	119	3,015	25·40
Lewis	228	4,854	21·68
R. C. N. Palairet . .	125	2,677	21·52
Robson	329	4,854	20·57
V. T. Hill . . .	164	3,187	19·71
W. C. Hedley . .	116	2,161	18·73

BOWLING.

	Runs.	Wickets.	Average.
W. C. Hedley . .	5,10)	249	20·119
Tyler	17,878	804	22·190
Nichols . . .	6,092	259	23·135
Cranfield . . .	9 930	423	23·201
S. M. J. Woods . .	12 935	523	24·383
Braund	13,319	517	25·494
Gill	6,017	219	27·184
Robson	11,374	406	28·6

GOLF

Somerset has fewer golf links than its long coast-line would lead one to expect. The county has indeed only four courses that can claim to be of seaside quality ; but the eldest of these four, which belongs to the Burnham and Berrow Club, is of the very best, and the club has an additional title to fame as being a nursery of J. H. Taylor. Two clubs have courses which, though within· sight and sound of the sea, can advance no more than their proximity to the salt water as a claim to be regarded as true seaside links. The rest of the golf courses of Somerset are inland, and have the natural limitations that their situations impose.

It will be convenient for purposes of detailed description to enumerate the links of the county under the heads indicated, keeping them at the same time in chronological order of foundation.

It was not until golf had been played for ten years in Somerset that the Burnham and Berrow Golf Club was instituted in September 1890 on the initiative of Mr. T. Holt, who has been one of the honorary secretaries since the founda-

tion of the club. Its magnificent 18-hole course, over 6,000 yards in length, is of a most sporting character. Laid out among the sandhills to the east of the Berrow lighthouse on the shore of the Bristol Channel, the links, with enormous natural bunkers bordering and intersecting the narrow course on which straight and ' pawky ' play is absolutely essential, afford a test of the very best golf. The course is always in good order, although, being for the most part on pure sea sand, it is apt to burn in summer. The par score of 79 is fixed with obvious consideration for the trials that beset the average golfer in that wilderness of sand that has to be crossed on the outward journey ; but the club records of 65 by Ernest Foord, the professional, and 69 by Mr. C. H. Alison indicate that good play meets with its due reward. The club is rich in prizes, and at the meetings held in the spring and autumn the Kennard, the Holt, the Lysaght, the Berrow Manor, the Burnham and County Club, the Tradesmen's Silver Challenge, the Houldsworth and the Captain's Cups are offered for competition, together with the Eldon, the Scott and the Scratch Gold Medals for aggregates.

The Burnham Ladies' Club, founded two years later, has a good little course of 18 holes lying over sandy soil of a less terrifying character between the men's course and the town. Miss F. Walker-Leigh holds the record of 69 for the green. There are two meetings, in the spring and the autumn, and the club prizes include the Bowl, played for in the autumn, and the President's and the Vice-President's prizes.

The links of the Minehead and West Somerset Golf Club, instituted in 1882 by the efforts of Dr. Clark of Dunster, are on the shore of the Bristol Channel on land known as the Warren, situated between Minehead and Dunster. This excellent 18-hole course, laid out by F. Goldsmith, the professional of the club, has a length of about 5,500 yards with a long hole of 500 yards and one very short hole of 90 yards. The soil is sandy pasture with hazards of water and sand bunkers, some of which are artificial. The best months for play are April and May. An easy Bogey of 77 has been defeated in 68. There are meetings in the spring and summer, at which the Silver Open Challenge Cup is offered for competition, and there are several silver challenge cups open to members only. A club for ladies is a branch of this club.

It was not until 1892 that the Weston-super-Mare Golf Club was founded by Dr. Crouch and others with links on a level tract of land about a mile from the town. The course of 18 holes is about three and a half miles round; its longest hole is no less than 520 yards in length. The most interesting part of the links is the stretch along the seashore occupied by the first five holes. There the hazards are natural sand bunkers, the turf is of the true seaside character, and the large greens have that undulating surface which is the joy of seaside links. The holes lying on pasture inland are of more ordinary character. The early summer and autumn months are the best time for play. Bogey's 75 has been beaten by Mr. G. G. Fraser in 68 and by J. Donald, the club professional, in two more strokes. The Bennett Scratch Cup is played for at the spring and autumn meetings.

The Clevedon Golf Club was founded in 1898, when a 9-hole course was opened round the ruins of Walton Castle. Gorse is the principal hazard here.

The links of the Portishead Golf Club, which was instituted in 1906, are on down and light pasture land of a sandy nature at Nore Road, half a mile from the town. Harry Vardon laid out this course of 18 holes, which has a length of a little over 5,000 yards, the longest hole being 515 yards, and the shortest 135. The hazards are for the most part banks and artificial pot bunkers. The going is good all through the

year. Harry Vardon's round of 69 is the record for this course.

What is now the Bath Golf Club was founded in February 1880 under the name of the Kingsdown Club. Three years later it became the Bath and Kingsdown Golf Club, and the name was finally altered to the Bath Golf Club exactly ten years after its original institution. The 18-hole course is on Bathampton Down. It is three miles round, its longest hole being 490 yards, and its shortest 100 yards. Tom Dunn was the architect, and his arrangement, with some alterations introduced by J. H. Taylor, still stands. The soil is a not very deep clay that quickly dries, and the hazards are stone walls, quarries and bushes, with some made bunkers. The best months for play are April and May, October and November. A too liberal par score of 79, which as we write is under revision, has been soundly beaten by Harry Vardon in 66. Meetings are held in the spring and autumn.

The Bruton Golf Club, instituted in 1891 by the efforts of the Rev. C. Leir, has a short 9-hole course under 2,000 yards in length on the downs at Creech Hill, one and a half miles to the north of the town. The hazards are gorse and a quarry; there are no made bunkers. Play is only possible from October to May, the best months being February, March and April.

The Wells Golf Club, founded in the next year, has its 9-hole course at King's Castle Hill.

In 1895 the Frome Golf Club was founded by the initiative of Mr. A. C. Polehampton and other golfers of the town and neighbourhood. The sporting course of 9 holes is on hilly ground at Vallis Leaze, just outside the town. The hazards are stone walls, roads, disused quarries and hedges. Unfortunately the ground is heavy and the grass grows rankly on parts of the course, with the consequence that there is no play in the summer. Bogey for two rounds is 70, a score that takes a good deal of beating. There is a Ladies' Club at Frome, which is a branch of the men's club.

The Lansdown Golf Club was instituted in 1895 by Sir Henry W. Lawrence, bart. It has an 18-hole course of some 4,800 yards in length on downland overlooking the Avon Valley, three miles from Bath, where walls and trees with artificial bunkers are the hazards. The longest hole is 467 yards in length and the shortest 133 yards, and the going is always good. The par score of 78 has been equalled by J. White, and Mr. C. Sommerville has returned a card of only one more stroke.

The Pickeridge Golf Club, founded in 1896 by the Rev. T. Crump and others, has a 9-hole course on common land on Pickeridge Hill in the parish of Corfe, four miles from Taunton. The course, which is on clay subsoil, has a length of 2,650 yards, the longest hole being 450 yards and the shortest 120 yards. There are no artificial hazards, but remains of bygone mining operations give difficult patches of broken ground that serve as natural bunkers. Spring and summer are the best times of year for play on these links.

The Ilminster Golf Club, instituted in October 1897, has its 9-hole course on the outskirts of the town. The hazards here are roads, whins and hedges.

The Ivythorn Golf Club, founded by the Hon. R. Tollemache in 1898, has its 9-hole course on common land at Marshall's Elm near Glastonbury. The course is about a mile and a half round, and the hazards are gorse, hedges and ditches and a quarry. The soil being clayey is apt to burn in the summer and to become heavy in winter, with the consequence that April and May, September and October are the best months for play.

The Bladud Golf Club was started in 1898 by a few inhabitants of Bath, and a 9-hole course 2,420 yards long was laid out by the members on good dry pasture land a mile and a half south of the town. The nature of the soil is such that the going is good all the year round. The hazards are hedges and stone walls, with a few artificial bunkers. Bogey is 76 for a double round. The Fox-Andrews Cup, played for in the autumn, is the principal prize of the club.

In 1900 the Dulverton and Brushford Golf Club was founded by the efforts of Mr. C. W. Nelder. A 9-hole course was laid out by Thomas Braund close to Dulverton on the west bank of the River Barle, on pasture land with a loam and peat soil. The round journey is about a mile and a half, and the hazards comprise banks, rushes and streams.

The 18-hole course of the Saltford Golf Club, founded by the initiative of Mr. Archer Symes and Mr. H. S. Radcliffe in April 1904, is on down and pasture land about midway between Bath and Bristol. Its length is about three miles, the longest hole being 485 yards and the shortest 115 yards. It was laid out by the Green Committee, and has been somewhat altered on the advice of Harry Vardon. Many of the hazards are natural, and there are some artificial bunkers. Summer and autumn are the best times of year for play. Bogey is 74, and the amateur record is held by Mr. H. J. Andrews with 68. The Moseley Challenge Cup is the chief prize of the club.

Of the Limpley Stoke Golf Club we have no further information than that it was founded in 1906.

The Somerset County Ladies' Golf Club, founded in 1902, was the winning county in the south-western division in 1907, and third in the County Final played at Budleigh Salterton in November of that year. County matches are played on the Burnham, Bath, and Weston-super-Mare links.

The Editor desires to express his best thanks to secretaries of clubs who have given him information that has been of much help to him in the compilation of this account of golf in Somerset.

INDEX TO DOMESDAY OF SOMERSET

PERSONAL NAMES[1]

[1] Including those of religious houses holding land.

PLACE NAMES

INDEX TO VOLS. I AND II

(See separate Index for Domesday Survey and Text)

Abbas Combe, ii, 345
Abbot, Fran., ii, 216 *n*
Abbotsbury, ii, 88
Abbots Leigh, ii, 9, 218, 348, 433, 470
Abbott, Jeremy, ii, 216 *n*
Abdick and Bulstone, Hund., ii, 202, 340 ; Court, ii, 286
Abendon, Hen., ii, 154
Abingdon, ii, 357
Abraham, Rev. Rich., ii, 454
Absolon, Will., ii, 438
Abyngdon, John, ii, 82 ; Rich. de, ii, 552
Ace, Barth., ii, 116
Acemannesceaster, *see* Bath
Acland (Dyke Acland), Sir C. T., ii, 577 *n*, 583, 595 *n* ; John, ii, 233 ; Sir Thos. 3rd. bart., 573-4 ; Sir Thos. 4th bart., ii, 573-4 ; Sir Thos. 5th bart., ii, 573 ; Sir Thos. 6th bart., ii, 566 ; Sir Thos. 7th bart., ii, 578 ; fam., ii, 571
A'Court, John, ii, 465
Act of Supremacy, ii, 38
Act of Uniformity, ii, 38
Acton Burnell (Shrops.), ii, 460
Acton, Rich. de, ii, 108, 554
Actune, Eleanor de, ii, 150
Acum, Hen. de, ii, 100
Adam the Butler, ii, 281
Adams, Rich., ii, 377
Ad Axium, road to, i, 349-50 ; supposed Rom. village, i, 368
Adbeer (Trent), ii, 114
Adela of Louvain, ii, 229
Adelard of Bath, ii, 71
Adelburga, w. of Ine, ii, 4
Adelnold, Adelwold, Will., ii, 38, 96
Adlam, Capt., ii, 227
Adrian IV, pope, ii, 73, 79, 163
Adzor, ii, 8, 10
Aedvi, the, i, 217
Aegbryhta's Stone, *see* Ecgbyrht's Stone
Ægelnoth, abbot of Glastonbury, ii, 85, 98
Ælfere, abbot of Bath, ii, 70
Ælfheah, ealdorman, ii, 179
Ælfhere, abbot of Bath, ii, 80
Ælfig, Ælfwig, abbot of Bath, ii, 70, 80
Ælfsige, abbot, ii, 11, 70, 80
Ælfswyda, ii, 70
Ælpheah, *see* Canterbury, archbp. of
Æscwig, abbot of Bath, ii, 70, 80
Æthelbald, king (Mercia), ii, 69
Æthelfleda, the lady, ii, 84
Æthelhard of Bath, *see* Adelard
Æthelmod, ii, 69
Agates, ii, 353
Agrarian revolution, ii, 318
Agricola, Rom. general, i, 203
Agriculture, ii, 313, 320-1, 333, 533-45
Aguillun, Rob., ii, 556
Aish, —, ii, 202

Aishman, Hen., ii, 382
Aisholt, i, 180 ; ii, 342
Aisholt Common, i, 184
Akle, Reg. de, ii, 551
Alan, abbot, ii, 107
Alayne, Walt., ii, 557
Albemarle, dk. of, ii, 220-1
Albin, Harry, ii, 53
Albiniaco, *see* Daubeney
Alcombe, ii, 355
Alderman Barrow, ii, 531
Aldhelm, St., *see* Sherborne, bp. of
Aldren, Dick, ii, 582
Aldridge, W., ii, 458
Aldrit, Rev. W., ii, 440
Alehouses, ii, 330, 402
Alemannia, Hermann de, ii, 364
Alençon, Gerin d', ii, 171
Alewy, Matth., ii, 135
Alexander III, pope, ii, 12-3, 87, 163
Alexander VI, pope, ii, 143
Alexander of Lewes, ii, 125
Aley, John de, ii, 147
Alford, ii, 337, 342 ; House, ii, 571
Alford, Hen., dean of Canterbury, ii, 453
Alfoxton, i, 363 ; ii, 532, 589 ; deer-pk., ii, 569-70
Alfred, King, i, 378 ; ii, 6, 7, 99, 102, 177-9, 245, 553, 555, 563
Alfred Jewel, the, i, 376-80
Alfwold, abbot, ii, 107
Algae, freshwater, i, 53 ; marine, i, 54
Alien priories, ii, 69, 128, 169-71
Alison, C. H., ii, 600
Alleine, Jos., ii, 51-3, 421
Allen, —, ii, 45, 50, 234 ; Benj., ii, 233 ; Card., ii, 460 ; Rev. J., ii, 454 ; John, quaker, ii., 59 ; Rev. John, ii, 453 ; Jos., i, 319-20 ; Jos., divine, *see* Alleine ; Ralph, ii, 395-6 ; Rich., ii, 45, 50, 52 ; Messrs. C., ii, 360
Allen-Jefferys, Jefferys, ii, 591
Aller, ii, 53 *n*, 337, 348 ; 'peculiar,' ii, 67
Allercombe, ii, 581
Allerford, ii, 571
Allermoor, ii, 332
Allerton, famous yew, ii, 571
Allotments, ii, 330, 333-5
Alloway, John, ii, 400
Almar the forester, ii, 548
Almsford, *see* Ansford
Almsworthy, ii, 337
Alncombe, ii, 81
Alneto, Alex. de, ii, 153 ; Sir Alex. de, ii, 79 ; Fulco de, ii, 79
Alno, Alex. de, ii, 79
Alslot, —, ii, 53
Alsop, Will., ii, 53
Alswere Moor, ii, 583
Altarnun (Cornw.), ch., ii, 114
Alured, ii, 8

Alvington, ii, 455
Alvorde, Rich., ii, 138
Amary, Rog. de, ii, 560
Ambresbury, nunnery, ii, 123
Ambresbury, Mich. de, ii, 89, 90
Ambrevile, barony, ii, 550
Ambros, Hen., ii, 102
Amesbury, prioress of, ii, 559
Amethysts, ii, 353
Ammerdown, ii, 569 ; deer-pk., ii, 569
Amory, Ian, ii, 580 ; Sir John, ii, 573, 580-3, 588
Amys, Rich., ii, 170-1
Anchor Head, beacon, ii, 263
Andele, Jas. de, ii, 565
Andersea, ii, 277 ; man., ii, 87
Andersfield Hund., ii, 341, 553
Anderton, —, ii, 233
Andresia, ii, 102
Andrew, John, ii, 66
Andrewes, Will, *see* Wyllyams
Andrews, H. J., ii, 602
Angersleigh, ii, 349, 432 ; adv., ii, 142 ; ch., ii, 142
Anglesey, Ld., ii, 239
Angling, ii, 596-7
Anglo-Saxon remains, i, 373-81 ; weapons, i, 374 ; *see also* Coins ; Ornaments
Annatto factories, ii, 539
Anne, Queen, ii, 60 ; statue, ii, 235 *n*
Anne of Cleves, Queen, ii, 31
Anne of Denmark, Queen, ii, 565
Anne, Will. de, ii, 151
Annesley, Capt., ii, 229
Anno, Walt. de, ii, 74, 80
Ansford, ii, 26, 342
Anstele, John, ii, 438
Anstey, West, ii, 117
Aplin & Barrett, Messrs., ii, 541
Aquae Bormonis (Gaul), i, 220
Aquae Sulis, *see* Bath
Arachnida, i, 124
Arboriculture, ii, 569-72
Arbor Low (Derby), i, 191
Archer, Cecil, ii, 590 ; G., ii, 595
Ardagh, chalice, the, i, 379
Arderashac, ii, 169
Ardes, ii, 169
Ardimur, ii, 98
Arlansart, i, 304 *n*
Armurer, Sim. le, ii, 364
Arnold, John, ii, 131 ; Rich., ii, 538
Arnwood, man., ii, 71
Arthur, King, i, 359 ; ii, 83-4, 91, 96, 175
Arthur, John, ii, 53
Arthur's Well, ii, 484
Arundel, Will., earl of, ii, 149 ; Agnes, dau. of, ii, 149
Arundel, Matilda, ii, 163 ; Rob., ii, 142, 148 ; Rog., ii, 181 ; Thos., ii, 254 ; Sir Thos., ii, 117, 122, 138
Ash, *see* Ash Priors
Ash, —, ii, 205 ; Rob., ii, 439

Pucklechurch (Glouc.), ii, 86,
392 ; ch., ii, 87 ; man., ii,
17, 20, 88–90, 98 ; vicarage,
ii, 138
Puddle Bridge, ii, 427
Puddletown St. Mary (Dors.),
chap., ii, 109
Pugin, A. W., ii, 461
Pulborough Graffham, ii, 135
Pulham, Matilda, ii, 110
Pulton, Thos., ii, 156
Purdue, Geo., ii, 432 ; Rog., ii,
432 ; Thos., ii, 432 ; Will.,
ii, 432
Puritanism, ii, 39, 42–4, 46, 49,
51–4, 204, 314, 369
Puriton, i, 204 ; ii, 22 n, 336,
345, 361, 518 ; ch., ii, 23
Puriton, Rob. de, ii, 429
Purnell, John, ii, 376
Purse Caundle (Dors.), ii, 111,
114 ; man., ii, 102
Purshot Point, ii, 258
Putsham, Rom. rem., i, 363
Puxton, ii, 337, 352 ; man., ii,
10
Pycoteston, Steph. de, ii, 144
Pye, Sir Rob., ii, 209
Pyers, Will., ii, 66, 410
Pylle, ii, 66, 351; see also Cock-
mill
Pynckmore, ii, 159
Pyne, Col., ii, 205–6
Pynke, John, ii, 399
Pynner, Dennis, ii, 373
Pynnock, John, ii, 159–60
Pytt, Jas., ii, 453

Quakers, see Friends, Society of
Quantock Hills, ii, 142, 163, 267,
355, 385, 398, 467, 506, 531,
533, 548, 554, 569–71, 576,
578, 580, 589, 595 ; prehist.
rem., i, 167, 178, 180, 184, 190
Quantocks Head, ii, 263
Quantockshead, Quantoxhead,
East, ii, 351, 532 ; ch., ii, 169;
man., ii, 361, 400 ; pk., ii, 568–9
Quantockshead, Quantoxhead,
West, ii, 269 n, 351, 532 ; ii,
569
Quantock Staghounds, ii, 573–7,
581–3, 590
Quantock Wood, West, ii, 263
Quantoxhead, see Quantockshead
Quarme Harriers, ii, 591
Quarme Hill, i, 185
Quarr, ii, 128
Quarter Barrow, ii, 531
Queen Camel, ii, 22 n, 336, 342,
418, 427 ; ch., ii, 116–7 ;
rectory, ii, 118
Queen('s) Charlton, ii, 346, 384–5
Quekett, Will., ii, 457
Quiller-Couch, A. T., i, 320
Quill-making ind., ii, 414
Quyrk, Rob., ii, 252

Rachich, castle of, ii, 562
Racing, ii, 595
Rackley, ii, 363
Radcliffe, H. S., ii, 602 ; O. G.,
ii, 598
Raddington, ii, 351
Radney, ii, 557
Radstock, ii, 336, 352, 356–7,
385–8, 524, 532, 534 ; ch., i,
316, 366 ; ii, 79 ; man., ii,
384 ; prehist. rem., i, 183 ;
Rom. rem., i, 289, 316, 349,
363, 366, 370
Radyngton, Baldwin, ii, 565 ;
John, see Waskham ; Matilda,
ii, 565

Ragland, Rob., ii, 400
Ragun, Gilb. de, ii, 100
Raigners, Reigners, Avice de, ii,
110–1
Raikes, Rob., ii, 64
Railways, ii, 332, 334–5, 356
Rainham (Essex), man., ii, 148 ;
preceptory, ii, 148
Rains Batch, Lower, i, 335
Rains Batch, Upper, i, 335
Rale, Sim. de, ii, 187
Ralegh, John, ii, 187 ; Will. de,
see Winchester, bp. of
Raleigh, Dean Walt., ii, 47–8,
169
Raleigh's Cross, ii, 583
Ralph, of Shrewsbury, see Bath
and Wells, bp. of
Ramo, John de B., ii, 115
Ramsay, Leander, ii, 461
Ramsbury, see of, ii, 7
Ramsey, R. C., ii, 597–8
Randall, John, ii, 451
Randolf, John, ii, 552
Randolph, John, ii, 154
Rathmoylan (Ireland), adv. and
rectory, ii, 79
Raulun, Steph., ii, 115
Raven, Will., ii, 22, 147
Rawe, Thos., ii, 66
Rawleigh, see Rewleigh
Rawlings & Son, Messrs. S., ii,
426
Rawlinson & Co., Messrs. Geo.,
ii, 426
Rawlyns, Will., see Bailey
Rawston, Will., ii, 450–1
Ray, Rev. Rich., ii, 464
Raynes Cross, ii, 530
Reach, East, ii, 420
Reading, ii, 353 n ; fair, ii, 538
Reckleford, ii, 360
Recusancy, ii, 40–1, 47
Redcliffe, ii, 22 n, 67 ; ch., ii,
160 ; deanery, ii, 67
Redcliffe, Hosp. of St. John, ii,
160–1 ; seals, ii, 160–1
Redlinch Park, i, 351
Redlynch, chap., ii, 136 ; ch.,
ii, 134
Redynges, Phil. de, ii, 100
Reeves, Miss, ii, 463
Reformation, the, ii, 31–2
Regilbury, ii, 541
Reginald of Waltham, ii, 436
Regouefe (France), ch., ii, 134
Reigners, see Raigners
Reigny, Osmund de, ii, 102
Reimes, Rog. de, ii, 550
Religious Houses, ii, 68–171,
195, 281, 300 ; dissolution, ii,
32–3
Rents, ii, 272–3, 278, 280, 282,
289–90, 292, 306, 317, 334, 393,
399, 533, 537
Reptiles and Batrachians, i, 139
Repton, ii, 450
Revel, Will., ii, 432
Revesby, abbey, ii, 115–6
Rewleigh, ii, 123
Rexworthy Farm, ii, 521
Reynolds, Jas., ii, 66
Rhodgate Hill, i, 307
Rhyll, ii, 576–7, 582
Rice, John ap, ii, 137
Rich, Col., ii, 216
Richard I, ii, 13, 17, 73, 88, 154,
163, 287–8, 362–3, 548–50
Richard II, ii, 189–90, 253 n,
365, 400, 408, 549, 565
Richard III, ii, 29
Richard, of Glastonbury, ii, 135,
138 ; of Muchelney, ii, 18 ;
prior of Worspring, ii, 145
Richards, Sam., ii, 417

Richardson, Capt., ii, 212 ; G.;
ii, 595 n ; Ld. Chief Justice, ii,
43–4
Richbel, Col., ii, 212
Richmond, ii, 375 ; minery, ii,
369, 374
Richmond Castle, ii, 561
Richmond, ld. of, ii, 367
Rickford, ii, 404
Ridgehill, ii, 9
Ridge Road, i, 185
Ridgeway, the, i, 182, 315
Ridgeway Lane, i, 184
Ridgeways, i, 181–5 ; see also
Roads
Rimpton, ii, 349, 397 n
Ringwood, ii, 227
Riots, ii, 195, 307, 323, 330, 417,
567
Ripley, Capt. Terry, ii, 430
Rippe, John, ii, 452
Rippe's Mill, ii, 452
Risingdone, Hugh de, ii, 26
Riste, T., ii, 426
River-drift man, i, 168–9, 173–8,
204
Road, ii, 336, 344, 418 ; ch., ii, 9
Road Castle, camp, ii, 504
Roads, ii, 331–2, 355–6 ; pre-
historic, i, 181–5, 190, 201 ;
Rom., i, 182, 203, 215, 219–20,
228, 263–7, 286, 289, 302, 306,
308–9, 318, 325 n, 328, 334,
345–51, 366–9, 371, 375 ; ii,
1, 175, 178, 245, 429, 500, 531
Roadwater, ii, 117
Robber's Bridge, ii, 582
Robert, abbot of Athelney, ii,
164, 555, 562 ; of Bath, ii, 98 ;
archd. of Taunton, ii, 16 ;
of Winchester, ii, 16, 98
Roberts, E., ii, 458
Robin Hood's Butts, i, 182; ii, 532
Robinson, —, ii, 53 ; C. J., ii,
598 ; Hugh, ii, 48 ; Rev.
Walt., ii, 443
Roborough, ii, 553, 583
Robson, —, ii, 599, 600
Robyns, John, ii, 455 ; Rich., ii,
380
Roche, Gerald de, ii, 115
Rochester, bp. of, John, ii, 93
Rodberd, Will., ii, 66
Rodbery Farm, ii, 521
Rodden, ii, 344, 455, 465, 558
Roddenbury Camp, ii, 510
Rodeney, Walt. de, ii, 119
Rodhuish Common, ii, 532
Rodmarten (Glouc.), i, 191, 304 n
Rodmede, ii, 154
Rodney, Sir Edw., ii, 208, 232 ;
Adm. Geo. B., ii, 264 ; Sir
Walt. de, ii, 130 ; fam., ii, 254
Rodney Stoke, ii, 242, 336–7, 352
Rodway, ii, 109
Roe, W. N., ii, 597
Roger of Chewton, ii, 437
Rogers, Sir Geo., ii, 411 ; Sir
John, ii, 33
Rokele, Walt. de, ii, 147
Rolfe, Will., ii, 132
Rolle, Sir Fran., ii, 233 ; Hon.
Mark, ii, 576
Rolleston, —, i, 189
Rolstone, ii, 145
Roman Catholics, ii, 57, 65, 230
Romano-British remains and
settlements, i, 207–371 ; ii, 1,
499 ; implements, i, 307, 318,
325, 337, 352, 367, 369 ; ii,
392, 498 ; weapons and ar-
mour, i, 229, 266, 275, 293,
296, 298, 360 ; see also Burials;
Coins ; Ornaments ; Pave-
ments ; Pottery ; Roads